DATE DUE

MAR 1 3 2002	
MAY 2 5 2002	
JUL 0 1 2002	
JUL 2 3 2002	
SEP 1 2 2002	
GAYLORD	PRINTED IN U.S.A.

THE
UNGOVERNABLE
CITY

John Lindsay
and His Struggle to Save New York

VINCENT J. CANNATO

BASIC
BOOKS
A Member of the Perseus Books Group

Published by Basic Books,
A Member of the Perseus Books Group

Designed by Brent Wilcox

Library of Congress Cataloging-in-Publication Data
Cannato, Vincent, 1967–
The ungovernable city : John Lindsay and his struggle to save New
York / Vincent Cannato.
p.   cm.
Includes bibliographical references (p.) and index.
ISBN 0-465-00843-7
1. Lindsay, John V. (John Vliet)—B   2. Mayors—New York (State)—
New York—Biography.   3. New York (N. Y.)—Politics and govern-
ment—1951–   4. New York (N. Y.)—Social conditions—20th century.
I. Title.

F128.54.L55 C36 2001
974.7'1043'092—dc21
[B}   2001018102

01 02 03 04 / 10 9 8 7 6 5 4 3 2 1

To my parents,
Vincent and Maria Cannato

CONTENTS

INTRODUCTION

The decline of the city and the crisis of liberalism: these two interrelated developments have profoundly shaped the second half of the twentieth century. For a third of a century after World War II, during liberalism's peak, American cities began to falter, precipitating what became popularly known as the "urban crisis." The cumulative effect of such concurrent factors as a declining population, a rising crime rate, and an eroding industrial and manufacturing base devastated many American cities. These changes altered the face of the urban Northeast and Midwest. At the same time, the political coalition assembled by Franklin D. Roosevelt in the 1930s began to fray. Union members, urban Catholics, blacks, middle-class liberals, and white Southerners could no longer be held together under one political tent.[1]

All of the symptoms of the decline in both liberalism and the city are present in the battles of 1960s New York. And no one is a better symbol of this dual crisis of liberalism and the city than John Vliet Lindsay, who served as mayor of New York from 1966 to 1973. The trajectory of Lindsay's political career followed the path of America's descent from the heights of postwar confidence in the 1950s through the traumas of the late 1960s and into the era of Watergate, when recession, oil shortages, and stalemate in Vietnam created a gnawing insecurity and malaise.[2]

All but forgotten is the handsome, energetic young congressman who bucked his party's leadership and refused to endorse Barry Goldwater in 1964. Forgotten is the promise with which Lindsay entered City Hall in 1966. Forgotten is the man's national stature, which led party leaders to consider him a future Republican presidential candidate. Lindsay was a leader of the moderate-to-liberal wing of the Republican party, a vocal opponent of the Vietnam War, the nation's leading spokesman for cities, a strong supporter of civil rights, and the driving force behind the National Advisory Commission on Civil Disorders, better known as the Kerner Commission.

During his 1965 campaign, Lindsay promised to bring a new approach to urban problems. He argued that New York was in crisis and laid the blame at the feet of the three-term retiring mayor, Robert F. Wagner, the Democratic machine, and the city's bureaucracy. Lindsay's campaign slogan was "He is fresh and everyone else is tired." Elected by a plurality of New Yorkers in 1965, Lindsay offered the city not so much new policies as a fresh face and new energy. As a young, idealistic, good-looking, energetic, ambitious family man in the late 1950s and early 1960s, he possessed an almost sure ticket to political stardom. This combination led to the inevitable comparisons with John F. Kennedy and allowed Lindsay to tap in to the allure of the New Frontier. Between JFK's assassination and the turmoil of the late sixties, Americans were still enthralled by the afterglow of a period of idealism that came to be called Camelot. During this brief window of opportunity, John Lindsay's idealism still seemed plausible.

But much is expected of those who promise so much. And John Lindsay foundered on the shoals of his unfulfilled promises. By 1969 Lindsay was admitting that "it was clear that a broad segment of the electorate felt a special ill will toward me." As New York City began to lose its luster, Lindsay's political star began to dim. In 1969, he lost the Republican primary and was forced to run for reelection as a third-party candidate. Reelected by another plurality (thanks to strong support from his liberal base), Lindsay soon found that some of his liberal friends had turned against him. Former *New York Times* reporter John Corry wrote: "The problem was that Lindsay had been a myth to begin with, and when a myth dies, it leaves a huge void. Lindsay critics were like disappointed lovers. They had offered him their hearts, but now they pursed their lips and shook their heads."[3]

Woody Klein, a former *New York World-Telegram and Sun* reporter who became Lindsay's first press secretary, detailed his disillusionment with his former boss in a 1970 book, *Lindsay's Promise: The Dream That Failed*. *Village Voice* columnist Mary Perot Nichols, who had worked in the Lindsay administration for Parks Commissioner Thomas P. F. Hoving, was another apostate. In 1965 she wrote that Lindsay offered New Yorkers "the only chance for a renaissance in city living." By 1971, five years of Mayor Lindsay had Nichols nostalgically asking about the once-hated Robert Wagner, "Where are you now that we need you?"[4]

A similar change of heart overtook Nichols's *Voice* colleague Nat Hentoff. In 1969 Hentoff wrote a book favorable to the mayor entitled *A Political Life: The Education of John V. Lindsay*. Three years later, in a *Voice* article entitled "John V. Compromise," Hentoff admitted the book "was the single biggest error of judgment I have made as a journalist." In Hentoff's opinion, Lindsay "dwindled in moral size through his years as mayor." He added scathingly that Lindsay's tenure had been "a pilgrim's regression which might be poignant if there were any weight to the man any more." Journalists Jack Newfield and Paul Du Brul put it more kindly: "John Lindsay gave good intentions a bad name. . . . He wanted to do good, but he didn't know how."[5]

Though Lindsay's reputation had begun to decline during the late 1960s, two later events permanently sealed his image. In 1971, Lindsay switched to the Democratic Party, and in 1972 he ran for that party's presidential nomination. His poor showing in the Florida primary, so soon after he had switched his political allegiance, dramatically reduced his stature. The second event to tarnish Lindsay's reputation occurred after he left office. The fiscal crisis of 1975 so damaged Lindsay's standing that in January 1978, the *New York Times Magazine* dubbed the ex-mayor "an exile in his own city."[6]

Assessing Lindsay's legacy is not a straightforward exercise. To those who still remember him, Lindsay is a Rorschach test of the political and social changes of the last thirty-five years. Some see a shining white knight who brought back a sense of style to a city badly in need of it during the sixties and seventies. Others see a man who helped destroy New York City with his policies. Some see the man who held together the city in the face of tremendous social changes tearing at New York and the rest of the nation. Still others see a tragic figure who suffered from the inability to translate his lofty promises and idealism into concrete improvements.

A recent survey of American urban historians ranked Lindsay the sixteenth worst big-city mayor between 1820 and 1993. Historian Fred Siegel has called Lindsay the worst New York mayor of the twentieth century. "Lindsay wasn't incompetent or foolish or corrupt, but he was actively destructive," said Siegel. Still others defend Lindsay's record. Former Lindsay aide Robert Laird wrote in 2000: "We Lindsay people did great things and, yes, made great mistakes, all in a time of shattering change." A vice president of the liberal Republican Ripon Society remembers Lindsay as "the great dreamer, the eternal optimist, and to many, the courageous knight, who used the sword of justice, despite the political consequences, to right the many social and racial wrongs in a cold, troubled, complicated world."[7]

Both Lindsay's critics and defenders would admit, though, that New York during the 1960s and 1970s was a city with serious problems.

NEW YORK CITY AND URBAN DECLINE

The urban crisis is linked in the public's mind with the idea of decay: crime in the streets, filthy sidewalks, bombed-out slums, drugs, moral decline, overcrowding, traffic jams, racial tension, pollution, labor unrest, and political corruption. In some respects, the idea of decay is nothing new to New York. Charles Dickens and Henry James both wrote of the less-than ideal conditions of the city in their respective eras. E. B. White, in his famous 1949 essay "Here Is New York," described a city that "should have destroyed itself long ago, from panic or fire or rioting or failure of some vital supply line in its circulatory system or from some deep labyrinthine short circuit. Long ago the city should have experienced an insoluble traffic snarl at some impossible bottleneck. It should have perished of hunger when food lines failed for a few days. It should have been wiped out by a plague starting in its slums or carried by ship's rats."

Writing in 1953, John Steinbeck described New York as "an ugly city, a dirty city. Its climate is a scandal, its politics are used to frighten children, its traffic is madness, its competition is murderous." Lindsay himself rode to office on public anger at the condition of a once-proud city. *Fortune* writer Richard Whalen published a jeremiad in 1965 entitled *A City Destroying Itself: An Angry View of New York*. In 1966, Tom Wolfe observed his fellow New Yorkers scurrying about the overcrowded, hectic city, falling into a "behavioral sink," much as happened to laboratory rats that were subjected to experiments in overcrowding. *U.S. News and World Report* argued that life in New York of 1966 "had tended to become more and more unsettled, uncomfortable and downright dangerous, less and less pleasant."[8]

Yet it was John Lindsay's New York that has come to symbolize a city in chaos within a society in turmoil. During this time, many New Yorkers felt that they were living through a crisis of urban decay and demoralization that was infinitely more debilitating than anything else in recent memory.

One anecdote symbolizes the changes in New York City during the 1960s and early 1970s. When a major blackout paralyzed New York in November 1965, a few weeks after Lindsay's election, the city remained calm. Twelve years later (three and a half years after Lindsay left office), another citywide blackout occurred. This time some New Yorkers used the crisis as an opportunity to loot, riot, and burn. Areas of the South Bronx and Bushwick, Brooklyn, were leveled by fires and to this day have not fully recovered. Something obviously went awry deep inside the social fabric of the city between 1965 and 1977.[9]

A 1971 Ford Foundation report found "a general deterioration of the city environment, visible and palpable in streets, subways, the air and the water around New York." In 1971, Roger Starr, the executive director of the New York Citizens' Housing and Planning Council, wrote that New Yorkers suffered from "a double sense of diminution: first, that the mundane problems of life in their city become daily more difficult; and, second, that the unique element in New York that compensated for its hardships—the pride of cosmopolitan citizenship—is wasting away." Architectural historian Robert A. M. Stern has argued that by 1975, "New York teetered on the brink of collapse. It had lost its economic clout; worse still, many Americans seemed to regard the city, once the nation's standard of quality and sophistication, as the embodiment of all that was wrong with modern life. Even many New Yorkers agreed, and New York's self-esteem was at an all-time low." Political scientist Andrew Hacker admitted in 1975, "Of course New York has problems. By virtually every accepted measure, it is deteriorating."[10]

New York's problems also found expression in some of the novels from this time. Saul Bellow's 1969 novel, *Mr. Sammler's Planet*, is a pessimistic tale of New York, where "you could smell collapse. You could see the suicidal impulses of civilization pushing strongly." From his Upper West Side apartment, the émigré intellectual Arthur Sammler chronicled the daily humiliation of life in a New York slowly descending into crime, filth, sexual license, indifference, and racial hatred. After spotting a pickpocket on a bus, Sammler rushes to call the police from a telephone booth on Riverside Drive but finds the phone broken.

> Most outdoor telephones were smashed, crippled. They were urinals, also. New York was getting worse than Naples or Salonika. It was like an Asian, an African, town, from this standpoint. The opulent sections of the city were not immune. You opened a jeweled door into degradation, from hypercivilized Byzantine luxury straight into the state of nature, the barbarous world of color erupting from beneath.

To Sammler, "New York makes one think about the collapse of civilization, about Sodom and Gomorrah, the end of the world."[11]

Had Sammler ever encountered Alexander Portnoy, he would have been even more convinced of that diagnosis. Vain, narcissistic, sexually obsessed, ungrounded by family or friends, the protagonist of Philip Roth's novel *Portnoy's Complaint* (1967) is an example of the amoral modern man. What makes this novel relevant is Portnoy's occupation: assistant commissioner in the Lindsay administration's (fictional) Commission on Human Opportunity. Roth juxtaposes the public Portnoy—the selfless, liberal, antipoverty bureaucrat worried about the disadvantaged—with the morass of selfishness that is his private life.[12]

How much responsibility Lindsay bears for New York's decline is a matter of some debate. In some ways, Lindsay was a victim of circumstance. Many of the ills plaguing New York—rising crime, reckless fiscal policies, racial tensions, middle-class flight, growing slums—predated his tenure. John Lindsay did not create the urban crisis. In fact, he was elected mayor in 1965 on a platform that promised to halt the city's decline. What he can be blamed for is exacerbating this decline. Furthermore, Lindsay was a victim not only of the raised expectations he had encouraged but also of the increasing radicalism and polarization of American society during the late sixties. During Lindsay's mayoralty, the political ground beneath him shifted dramatically. Student radicalism, the counterculture, racial tensions and riots, growing conservatism, and antiwar protests made Lindsay's brand of earnest, idealistic, good-government liberalism seem quaint and ineffective and helped create an aura of chaos and dissension beyond his control.

Yet Lindsay, as a nationally prominent liberal, must himself take some responsibility for these changes. Increasingly, the actions of the Lindsay administration were based upon the premises of a new liberalism forged during the 1960s from the fading embers of the New Deal coalition. As Mayor, John Lindsay wanted nothing less than the complete overhaul of city government. From education to police to budget policy, Lindsay's reform administration sought to root out inefficiency, bureaucratic plodding, racial inequality, and other urban sins and create a new, progressive city government. From his troubles with municipal unions to his poor fiscal management to his uneasy relationship with the police to his mishandling of the controversy over school decentralization, Lindsay's tenure as Mayor cannot be viewed as a success.

The urban crisis that New York and other big cities suffered helped discredit liberalism in the eyes of many Americans. Not only could Lindsay not stem the tide of urban decay that had begun in the 1950s, he added to the feeling that New York City was both unlivable and ungovernable. The failure to deal adequately with the confusion and tumult of the era weakened liberalism's legitimacy. As the journalist Nora Sayre wrote, Lindsay "unfortunately convinced many that liberalism had to mean chaos."[13]

IF FIORELLO LA GUARDIA'S NEW YORK embodied the politics and policies of the New Deal, then John Lindsay's New York personified the troubles and turmoil of the Great Society and the polarization of the 1960s. By this time, the dual crises of the city and liberalism had become inextricably intertwined.

Speaking about the failures of 1960s liberalism in general, political scientist Aaron Wildavsky could well have been describing the mayoralty of John Lindsay when he outlined this "recipe for violence":

> Promise a lot; deliver a little. Lead people to believe they will be much better off, but let there be no dramatic improvement. Try a variety of small programs, each interesting but marginal in impact and severely underfinanced. Avoid any attempted solution remotely comparable in size to the dimensions of the problem you are trying to solve. Have middle-class civil servants hire upper-class student radicals and lower-class Negroes as a battering ram against the existing local political systems; then complain that people are going around disrupting things and chastise local politicians for not cooperating with those out to do them in.

One of the fairest interpretations of the Lindsay years comes from Nora Sayre, writing in 1973: "No one with his brains intact would hold Lindsay fully responsible for the condition of New York, though few could forget that the disintegration had speeded up under his management." His problems were personal and political. As his former aide Jeff Greenfield noted: "His mistakes were not forgiven easily, his triumphs not applauded easily, because he seemed most of all a stranger to the ordinary experiences of New

York's people." These two quotes summarize the tragedy of John Lindsay—a man who was loved and admired by some, but also despised and vilified by others.[14]

His small successes could not outweigh the disillusionment caused by unfulfilled promises; the soaring rhetoric could not wipe away the dreary reality of the streets; the elevated moralism could not soothe the many feathers it had ruffled. Had Lindsay been elected U.S. senator, where he could have focused on broader issues like foreign policy or civil rights, his idealistic progressivism might have won him the role of statesman. But as Mayor, Lindsay was responsible for hard decisions. The decline of postwar American cities and the crisis of New Deal liberalism, though not of his creation, converged during the troubled mayoralty of John V. Lindsay.[15]

THE DISTRICT'S PRIDE, THE NATION'S HOPE

Lindsay is the product of a phenomenon peculiarly untimely, at least in literature: a white, Protestant, Anglo-Saxon, upwardly-mobile family.

—Roger Starr, "John V. Lindsay: A Political Portrait," 1970

There was little in John Lindsay's background that suggested a political career in New York City. Young men from Yale usually carved out careers for themselves on the upper floors of the city's skyscrapers as lawyers or bankers and raised families in some suburban enclave. When they entered the political arena it was usually to donate money. By contrast, those who ran for office typically came from more modest backgrounds, armed with diplomas from City College or St. John's University in Queens. Mayor Robert Wagner was an exception—he graduated from Yale—but he had the hangdog look that seemed typical of politicians representing the workingmen and women of New York City. Wagner's persona, though belying a shrewd intelligence, put him at home among the city's traditional Democratic clubhouse politicians and helped the average New Yorker to identify with him.[1]

In contrast, everything about Lindsay seemed patrician. Six feet four, he looked rich and acted rich. In fact, though, Lindsay's family came from a humble background, and contrary to popular myths about the city's WASPs, he was not descended from old-stock blue-bloods, nor did he come from the "new" money families of Gilded Age businessmen like the Rockefellers or

1

Vanderbilts. He did not know financial security as defined by New York society. He would have been considered wealthy in Kansas City or Cleveland, but in New York he was, in monetary terms, only middle class.[2]

Lindsay's grandfather was a brick manufacturer named John James Lindsay who emigrated to the United States after his brick kiln on the Isle of Wight failed in 1884. He settled in New York and worked at the National Bank of Commerce, where he never rose above the rank of clerk. His son, George, attended New York University Law School at night while working as a clerk on Wall Street during the day. After earning his law degree, George Lindsay became an investment banker. Along the way he married Florence Eleanor Vliet, the daughter of a successful contractor in Newark, New Jersey. Vliet, descended from an old Dutch family that helped settle colonial New Jersey, had graduated from Wellesley College and gone to New York to attend drama school. She toured with a traveling acting company and even acted once with Edward G. Robinson. Although she gave up her thespian aspirations to marry George Lindsay, she bestowed the love of the theater on her son John.[3]

George and Florence Lindsay began their married life in an apartment on West End Avenue in the Eighties, a thoroughfare nestled between Broadway and Riverside Drive on Manhattan's Upper West Side that was home to many in the city's respectable professional class. Eventually, the Lindsays had four sons and a daughter. The third and fourth children—John Vliet Lindsay and his twin brother, David—were born on November 24, 1921. As George Lindsay prospered in his banking career, the family moved across Central Park to the more fashionable Park Avenue. Later in his career, George Lindsay became president of American Swiss Corporation, an international banking firm affiliated with Credit Suisse in Zurich, and his name was an established entry in the Social Register.

All of the Lindsay children attended the best schools. John went to Buckley in Manhattan before prepping at St. Paul's, in Concord, New Hampshire. He then became a member of the class of 1944 at Yale, where he rowed crew and was elected to Scroll and Key. (David Lindsay also attended Yale; he was selected for the more prestigious Skull and Bones, and was elected to Phi Beta Kappa.) As was the case for many of his generation, Lindsay's education imbued him with a sense of the importance of public service. When World War II dimmed the importance of traditional academic and social pursuits, John Lindsay graduated early, in 1943, and received a commission in the U.S. Navy. Soon, in the summer of 1943, he saw action in the Mediterranean during the invasion of Sicily. As a gunnery officer aboard the destroyer USS *Swanson*, he called in the ship's artillery strikes from the beach. After nine months in the European Theater, the *Swanson* spent the next two years in the Pacific in the fleet that supported the landings on Biak, Hollandia, and the Admiralty Islands. Later, the *Swanson* took part in the invasion of the Philippines. After three years at sea,

Lieutenant Lindsay left the service in March 1946 as executive officer of the *Swanson*.[4]

Like most other combat veterans, Lindsay rarely spoke of his war experiences, but these experiences undoubtedly left their mark. Lindsay later wrote: "The war played a part in my entering politics, as it did with other veterans. . . . Consciously or unconsciously, there is no doubt that three years of active service in the Navy contributed to my decision. Postwar frustrations—the restless strivings to find direction and moorings—led me toward government service." Initially, Lindsay's postwar frustrations led him to spend a few months as a ski bum in the West and two unhappy months in a training program as a bank clerk in Manhattan. The aimlessness ended with his enrollment in Yale Law School in 1946. Graduating in 1948, ahead of schedule, he finished an undistinguished eightieth out of a class of one hundred. In 1949, he married Mary Anne Harrison of Greenwich, Connecticut, whom he met at the wedding of Nancy Bush, the daughter of Connecticut's Senator Prescott Bush. John was an usher and Mary a bridesmaid. A Vassar graduate, Mary counted as distant relations two U.S. presidents, William Henry Harrison and Benjamin Harrison. After a Greenwich wedding, the twenty-seven-year-old John and twenty-two-year-old Mary moved into Stuyvesant Town, a huge, middle-class, partially subsidized apartment complex on the eastern edge of Manhattan between Fourteenth and Twentieth Streets.[5]

Lindsay began his law career at the firm of Webster, Sheffield, Fleischmann, Hitchcock & Chrystie, founded by the venerable Bethuel Webster, a reform-minded Republican who became one of Lindsay's mentors. John's older brother, George, had graduated a year before from Yale Law School and was working for the firm of Debevoise, Plimpton, McLean. His twin brother, David, graduated a year after John and followed his brothers by taking a position at another big firm—Davis, Polk, Wardwell, Sunderland & Kiendl. The youngest brother, Robert, became a successful banker. But politics was more important to John than the law and this set him apart not only from his brothers but from others in his social set. As one family friend said in 1966, John and Mary "could so easily have turned into bloodless Long Island types like everybody else they knew." But they chose not to.[6]

Lindsay's politics were inherited, as was the case for many of his generation and class. Well into the second half of the twentieth century the Republican Party was predominantly the party of white Northern Protestants: penny-pinching New England Yankees, small-town Midwesterners, and urban WASPs who saw themselves on the front lines defending American democracy from immigrant hordes and the urban Democratic machines that represented them. As an adult, Lindsay took a critical look at his political inheritance. "It seemed to me," Lindsay concluded, "that it was important that this was the party of the individual—as I saw it, and as I still see it. It's the party of Lincoln, of civil rights, the protection of the person and his liberties against the majority, even against big business or the federal bureaucracy." As a teenager Lindsay once visited Mayor Fiorello La Guardia at City Hall, where the "Little Flower" impressed upon young Lindsay the anti-Tammany, good-government values of reform Republicanism. Lindsay's parents were Republicans, though George had voted for Al Smith for president in 1928 out of a sense of local pride. It would have been peculiar if John Lindsay had not become a Republican.[7]

As a young lawyer at Webster, Sheffield, he began giving street-corner speeches on behalf of Republican candidates in the 1950 midterm elections. Increasingly immersed in local politics, he and his brother David helped found Youth for Eisenhower in 1951. By that summer, Lindsay was vice president of the New York Young Republicans and went to Paris to urge the popular General Eisenhower to run for president. Lindsay later spent much time volunteering on the 1952 Eisenhower campaign. After the election, he became president of the New York Young Republicans.[8] The pull of politics increasingly outweighed the benefits of his life as an attorney in private practice. According to the journalist Roger Starr, Lindsay entered politics "not because he represented a constituency trying to change American life for its benefit, or to prevent its being changed to its detriment, but because he liked the competition, the feeling that in politics he could sense his movement forward even without compromising his 'deep-rooted beliefs.'" Lindsay was lured into politics not by the desire to control other people's lives or to have access to the numerous perquisites power confers, but because it offered an escape from the dull, if comfortable, life of a Wall Street lawyer and allowed his beliefs and ideals, rather than material acquisitions, to define his life. Certainly, success was almost guaranteed to young Lindsay; but he wanted to make it his own kind of success, on his own terms.[9]

Public service soon beckoned. When Lindsay's friend Charles Metzner left his position as executive assistant to Attorney General Herbert Brownell in the Eisenhower administration, he recommended Lindsay for the job. Starting at the Department of Justice in 1955, Lindsay worked on civil liberties cases and the 1957 Civil Rights Act, and on immigration issues, traveling to Austria and Germany to handle the Hungarian refugees fleeing from the 1956 Soviet invasion. In Brownell, an Establishment Republican stalwart, Lindsay found another mentor. In Lindsay, the young, ambitious attorney, Brownell found not only an able lawyer but also a possible Republican star in the traditional mold of Eastern Republicanism. Brownell suggested that Lindsay return to his practice in New York and run for Congress in 1958. By this time, John and Mary had three daughters, Katherine, Margaret, and Anne. Any decision to run for office would inevitably lead him away from his young family. Urging against such a run was his father, who warned him of the financial dangers of politics and told him he could accomplish more as a respected member of the bar. "If a person wants to go into public life," George Lindsay told his son, "he should first become established and financially successful. Then, if he still feels the urge, he can try to become secretary of State—if he can afford it." The self-made man warned his son of the dangers of patrician dreams.

The Seventeenth Congressional District, on the East Side of Manhattan, provided an ideal opportunity for the thirty-six-year-old Lindsay. Congressman Frederic (Fritz) Coudert was a six-term conservative Republican whose grandfather had founded the respected law firm Coudert Brothers. To win his seat, Coudert had defeated the incumbent, the liberal Republican Joseph Baldwin, in the 1946 primary. Coudert was backed by the New York County Republican club, led by a conservative, Tom Curran. The young liberal John Lindsay had volunteered on Baldwin's campaign while still in law school, having been impressed by a speech the congressman gave to Lindsay's class at St. Paul's on the value of public service.

The Seventeenth District had long been known as the Silk Stocking District, a term popularized by Theodore Roosevelt. The Silk Stocking District used to embody what Michael Barone, the editor of the *Almanac of American Politics*, terms "*Herald Tribune* Republicanism," named for the newspaper once owned by John Hay Whitney and preferred by the residents of the district. Home to the city's upper-class Protestant elite, the Silk Stocking District once stood for a genteel, though partisan, Republican politics that was generally conservative on economic issues and contemptuous of the urban masses and their political machines, but strong on issues of conservation, civil liberties, and civil rights. The district's cosmopolitan nature led to its support for a strong internationalist foreign policy.

During the first half of the twentieth century, the Silk Stocking District was represented by some famous names. Herbert Claiborne Pell Jr., descended from the family that lent its name to Pelham, New York, and the father of the future Rhode Island Senator Claiborne Pell, represented the district as a Democrat from 1918 to 1920. Bruce Barton, the founder of the advertising firm of Batten, Barton, Durstine & Osborne (BBD&O) and the author of the best-selling book *The Man Nobody Knows*, represented the district as a Republican from 1937 to 1940. His opposition to Roosevelt's domestic and foreign policies earned him inclusion in Roosevelt's famous denunciation of the Republican trio of "Martin, Barton, and Fish" (the other two being the Congressmen Joseph Martin and Hamilton Fish.)[10]

The Seventeenth District achieved great fame owing to the wealth and power of its constituents as well as the fact that within its borders lay the institutions that define New York as a world-class international city, from the skyscrapers of Midtown Manhattan to bohemian Greenwich Village. During this time, the district was home to many of the nation's best-known cultural and communications institutions: the United Nations, the Empire State Building, Radio City Hall, Rockefeller Center, St. Patrick's

Cathedral, Madison Avenue, NBC, CBS, the *New York Times*, the *Daily News*, the *Herald Tribune*, Lincoln Center, Times Square, the Garment District, the Theater District, Broadway, New York University, Carnegie Hall, the Metropolitan Museum of Art, the Museum of Modern Art, and the Whitney, Frick, and Guggenheim Museums. In addition, the Silk Stocking's congressman represented New York's rich and powerful living at Park Avenue, Fifth Avenue, and Sutton Place addresses, including politicians such as Governor Nelson Rockefeller; the 1948 Republican presidential candidate, Thomas Dewey; former New York Governor Averill Harriman; state Attorney General Louis Lefkowitz; and Senator Jacob Javits.

A great transformation in the district began in the 1950s. As Coudert observed in the early 1960s, "When you come down Park Avenue through the great mass of office buildings, those were once apartment buildings housing Republican voters. There isn't a voter on Park Avenue now below 61st Street." As Midtown office buildings pushed north into previously residential sections of the East Side, large, modern apartment buildings were being built throughout the Upper East Side, especially east of Lexington Avenue, replacing aging tenements. Into these buildings moved thousands of well-educated, professional, mostly single young men and women. By the early 1960s, the Silk Socking district contained the greatest concentration of single Americans of any district in the nation.[11]

The era of "*Herald Tribune* Republicanism" ended when the *New York Herald Tribune* folded in 1966. The new paper of choice for Silk Stocking residents became the Democratic *New York Times*. As the countercultural revolution swept the nation during the 1960s, liberal politics became fashionable. Insurgent Greenwich Village Democrat Ed Koch, an early opponent of the Vietnam War, became the district's congressman in 1968. Politically, some residents became concerned with symbolic issues like support for the Black Panthers and the boycott of California grapes, or with issues of personal freedom like feminism, abortion, sexual liberation, civil liberties, and gay rights. Tom Wolfe spoofed the combination of *nostalgie de la boue* and traditional upper-class snobbery as "radical chic." His essay of that name was a satirical portrait of a fund-raiser Leonard Bernstein and his wife gave for the Black Panthers in their thirteen-room East Side penthouse duplex in January 1970. According to Barone, the change in the politics and composition of the district from "*Herald Tribune* Republicanism" to "radical chic" represented "a significant revolution in New York City politics—one made even more notable by the counter-revolution that has occurred in the rest of the city. Indeed it can be said that greening here set the stage for the making of the Silent Majority in the middle-class neighborhoods of the outer boroughs."[12]

The early signs of change in the Seventeenth District came during Coudert's reelection campaigns in 1954 and 1956. In the off-year election of

1954, Coudert won by a mere 314 votes against Tony Akers, a young Democratic war hero. Two years later, running on Eisenhower's coattails, Coudert managed to defeat Akers in a rematch by almost 2,500 votes. But Coudert received 20,000 fewer votes in the Silk Stocking District than did Eisenhower. So, inspired by Coudert's apparent weakness, John Lindsay declared his intention in April 1958 to challenge Coudert for the Republican nomination for Congress.

Supporting Lindsay in his congressional bid was his mentor, Herbert Brownell, former Congressman Bruce Barton, Mrs. Wendell Willkie (the widow of the 1940 Republican presidential candidate), and Franklin Roosevelt's lone Republican son, John. When Coudert announced he would not seek reelection, the Republican regulars chose Elliot Goodwin. Like Lindsay, he was an Ivy Leaguer (Harvard), a World War II Navy veteran, and a lawyer. They even attended the same church: St. James' Episcopal on Madison Avenue. Lindsay, displaying a tenacious street campaigning style he would later utilize as mayor, defeated Goodwin in the August primary by a little over 2,000 votes. In the general election, Lindsay bested Akers by nearly 8,000 votes, leading the *Times* to call Lindsay "one of the bright hopes of the Republican Party." In the increasingly Democratic Silk Stocking District, John Lindsay represented a bridge between the old patrician Silk Stocking Republicanism and the new cultural liberalism.

Lindsay's congressional tenure got off to a rocky start. By tradition, freshmen congressmen did not challenge statements made on the House floor by senior members. But John Lindsay quickly signaled to his fellow congressmen he would not play by traditional rules. In late January 1959, Congressman Noah Mason, an eleven-term Republican from downstate Illinois, gave a speech criticizing the activism of Earl Warren's Supreme Court. After several congressmen spoke in agreement with Mason, Lindsay rose to defend the Warren Court as "one of the great courts of our country" and ended by proclaiming his belief in "the theory that the Constitution is a living and growing document."[13]

Lindsay quickly made a name for himself in his first two terms as a staunch defender of civil liberties and as something of a maverick, often casting lone votes against popular measures. In September 1959, the Pennsylvania Democrat Kathryn Granaham introduced a bill that would have extended the power of the postmaster general to impound obscene mail. The bill also would have shifted to the sender of the mail the burden of disproving charges of obscenity. The Justice Department's report of the bill labeled it unconstitutional. When Lindsay read the report, he became angry. In the House debate, Lindsay pointedly asked Granaham why Congress should pass her bill if the Justice Department believed it to be unconstitutional. At this, Speaker Sam Rayburn gaveled Lindsay into silence and took the floor himself in defense of the bill. Speaker after speaker spoke in favor of the bill. On a voice vote, Lindsay was the sole voice opposing the Granaham bill.

Later, the Silk Stocking congressman realized he had broken another unwritten House rule: never ask a critical question of a female member in House debate. Back in his office, an angry Lindsay pounded his desk with both fists as he told his aide, Robert Blum, "We have to stop this thing!" Lindsay ordered Blum to find the Justice Department official who had written a similar bill, but with proper constitutional safeguards. Lindsay convinced Senator Jacob Javits to introduce this version of the bill as a substitute during Senate debate. Eventually, the watered-down bill supported by Lindsay passed.[14]

In 1961, Lindsay and his fellow New York congressman William Fitts Ryan, a reform Democrat from the West Side of Manhattan, were the only votes in opposition to two bills proposed by Francis Walter, a Pennsylvania Democrat and chair of the House Un-American Activities Committee (HUAC). Walter's bills allowed federal interception of mail from Communist countries and barred "subversives" from working on merchant ships or on waterfront docks. During each of his terms in Congress, Lindsay proposed legislation aimed at disbanding HUAC and moving its functions to the House Judiciary Committee, of which Lindsay was a member. Failing to abolish the committee or transfer its power to his committee, Lindsay hoped to curb HUAC's power in other ways.

In 1962, Lindsay found his first victory against Walter's committee when he succeeded in blocking the Industrial Security Bill, supported by the Kennedy administration, which would have extended an Eisenhower executive order screening "security risks" among defense plant workers. Walter tried to pass the legislation on a procedural move. As long as there were fewer than three votes in opposition to the measure in committee, the bill would pass without a floor vote. Lindsay rounded up three other opponents—Ryan, James Roosevelt of California, and Henry Reuss of Wisconsin—and forced a floor vote. By the time the bill reached the floor of the House, Lindsay and his allies had rounded up a sizable number of votes. The vote was 247–132 in favor, but fell short of the two-thirds majority necessary for passage under House rules.

Lindsay's civil liberties positions received good press at home and were only mildly upsetting to the House Republican leadership. But his role in a 1961 procedural vote sealed his marginalization with House Republicans. The function of the House Rules Committee is to decide which legislation will go to the floor. The committee, then headed by Virginia Democrat Howard Smith, had consistently bottled up liberal legislation, especially in the area of civil rights. In response, Speaker Sam Rayburn offered a bill that would have enlarged the Rules Committee from twelve to fifteen members. The new members, chosen by the Speaker, would be more amenable to allowing legislation backed by liberals to make its way to the House floor. The vote on enlarging the Rules Committee pitted Republicans and conservative Southern Democrats, who opposed the idea, against liberal Democrats, who supported it. The swing votes proved to come from a small band of liberal Republicans, mostly from the Northeast, led by John Lindsay.

When the bill passed by a vote of 217–212, twenty-two liberal Republicans, including Lindsay, provided the winning margin. Two years later, a new Congress had to approve the expansion of the Rules Committee. The move passed by a margin of 235 to 196. This time, though, Lindsay had been up for a much-coveted opening on the Foreign Affairs committee. After the New York Republican gave a speech reiterating his support for enlarging the Rules Committee, House Republican Whip Leslie Arends reportedly told him: "John, in all my life, I never saw a man talk himself off the Foreign Affairs Committee so fast." Lindsay, much to his eternal dismay, would never find himself with a seat on the coveted Committee.[15]

In light of these episodes, many of his fellow Republicans felt Lindsay went out of his way to embarrass them. In 1962 Lindsay was the first person to testify in favor of a Kennedy administration bill to create a federal Department of Urban Affairs. It was bad enough that Lindsay supported a Democratic-sponsored bill increasing the size of the federal government, but that he was so vocal about it rankled his fellow Republicans.[16]

Lindsay spent little time garnering federal money for New York City projects. Meanwhile, congressmen from the South and the West were busy focusing on parochial concerns like military and public-works projects for their districts, helping to fuel the boom in the Sun Belt. Lindsay and other northern urban congressmen instead often spent much of their time on larger national issues that affected their constituents only in the abstract. He spent much of his time in Congress concerned with the heady issues of the Judiciary Committee, foreign policy, national urban policy, and reforming House rules. Adherence to parochial issues would have offended the high-minded Lindsay. In many ways New York suffered because many of its representatives, like Lindsay, did not use their powers to bring federal dollars back to the city.[17]

Lindsay spent much time prodding his colleagues to improve their collective ethics, hoping to weed out the petty sins to which congressmen were prone. For Lindsay, "Behind the glittering marble facade of the Capitol, the same old legislative machinery groans, creaks, and sometimes breaks down. . . . It needs more than oil; parts should be replaced and, in some instances, brand-new equipment should be ordered." Lindsay's remedies to fix this creaky machine included reducing congressmen's franking privileges (government-paid postage for mail from congressmen to their constituents), putting in place stricter rules for congressional expense accounts and conflict-of-interest rules, creating a Joint Committee on Ethics to draw up an ethical code for Congress, and reducing a congressman's ability to revise and extend his remarks for the *Congressional Record*. In introducing legislation to create a Joint Committee on Ethics, Lindsay argued the bill was necessary because "the people are entitled to expect from their elected representatives . . . a standard above that of the market place."[18]

Lindsay went to great lengths to make sure his own ethics were above those of the marketplace. In order to avoid the appearance of impropriety, Lindsay sent back a pair of bookends engraved with his name that an old friend had sent him. Speaking about his fellow representatives, Lindsay estimated that "a comfortable majority of the congressmen are very decent people who want to do right, but many have inadequacies of one kind or another. Maybe thirty per cent of the House consists of reasonably conscientious men who generally know what they're doing." When Hentoff remarked that that was a rather low number, Lindsay replied: "Yes, but you've got to remember that Congress is a microcosm of the people it represents."[19]

Like many great urban reformers, John Lindsay brought to office a demeanor and style that perhaps can be best described as "Protestant moralism." According to former Deputy Mayor Richard Aurelio, this moralistic tone gave Lindsay the appearance of "WASPish haughtiness." In the words of the historian Arthur Mann, Lindsay was part of a "long line of men and women in Western civilization who have fixed their eyes on what ought-to-be." Lindsay's senior thesis at Yale was on the English Puritan Oliver Cromwell. He wrote approvingly that Cromwell's "faith and intelligence were completely individualistic, guided by a sense of the immanence of God which made his will, once resolved, an inflexible cutting instrument which was to clean through tradition and opposition with irresistible force." The adult Lindsay admitted to being intrigued with Cromwell's life because "although he gave the appearance of being absolutely convinced he was right, he was always bumping into himself. The experience has not been entirely unfamiliar to me as a congressman and then as mayor." Being influenced by this "inflexible cutting instrument," Lindsay's political career was imbued with the Puritan notions of liberty of conscience and reform. According to the political scientist Edward Banfield, reform was meant to purge society of its sinfulness and make it conform to a pure and idealized notion of the good society. In turn, "Actions taken from good motives count as good even when in fact they do harm." Lindsay's reformist zeal led him to view the world as the setting for a constant struggle between good and evil.[20]

Lindsay won high marks from the press. After Lindsay's first term, *Newsweek* asked fifty Washington reporters to rate the Eighty-sixth Congress. They voted Lindsay the top Republican freshman, and, remarkably, also ranked him ninth overall among all congressmen regardless of tenure. In 1962, the *National Observer* named Lindsay one of a half dozen lawmakers with whom the Kennedy administration would have to deal. The *Village Voice* dubbed him the "Congressman from the Constitution."[21]

The men and women of the Seventeenth District reelected Lindsay to Congress by wider and wider margins. Lindsay defeated William vanden

Heuvel in 1960 by almost 28,000 votes and defeated Martin Dworkis in 1962 by more than two to one. Now occupying a safe seat, Lindsay moved his family from Manhattan to a house in the Cleveland Park section of Washington, D.C. During his first term in Congress (the last two years of the Eisenhower administration), Lindsay stayed true to his former boss and voted with House Republicans over 60 percent of the time. By the 1963–1964 term, however, Lindsay was voting with the House Republicans only one third of the time. From the Eisenhower fifties to Lyndon Johnson's Great Society, Congressman John Lindsay followed not only his conscience and his constituents but also the general liberal trend of the nation.[22]

In his last two terms in Congress, Lindsay found himself gravitating toward the ideas embodied in Johnson's Great Society program. He was an early supporter of federal aid to education and Medicare; argued for the establishment of a federal Department of Urban Affairs; spoke out for a National Foundation for the Arts and Humanities; introduced legislation to provide the District of Columbia with an elected legislative assembly and a nonvoting delegate to Congress; and proposed liberalizing the nation's immigration laws, arguing on behalf of the 1965 Immigration Bill that "the abandonment of the quota system will not open this country to a flood of immigrants." In foreign policy, he supported foreign aid, NATO, and the United Nations while, true to his Eisenhower roots, being critical of the nation's military-industrial complex.

By 1965, Lindsay's political philosophy had become almost indistinguishable from that of Great Society Democrats. In his 1965 State of the Union speech, President Johnson argued that "we're only at the beginning of the road to the Great Society. Ahead now is a summit where freedom from wants of the body can help fulfill the needs of the spirit." Lindsay called the speech "straight Republicanese, a sort of Republican utopia. If we had done these things under Eisenhower, we'd still be in power."[23]

The biggest issue for Lindsay during his congressional career was civil rights. As early as 1960, Lindsay argued for a strong civil-rights plank in the Republican Party's platform. Such a plank would support *Brown v. Board of Education*, oppose the poll tax, recognize the sit-in movement in the South, champion federal anti-lynching and anti-discrimination laws, and endorse the refusal of certification by the National Labor Relations Board of segregated unions. A strong proponent of the failed 1960 civil rights bill, Lindsay played a significant role in the passage of the historic 1964 Civil Rights Act. As a member of the Judiciary Committee, Lindsay and the committee's ranking Republican, Ohio's William McCulloch, not only helped guide the legislation through the committee but also put together a coalition of Republicans and liberal Democrats to pass the bill. In gratitude for his work, President Johnson gave Lindsay a front-row seat at the bill's signing. The following year, Lindsay and four other Republicans joined liberal Democrats in opposing the seating of the all-white congressional delegation from Mississippi.[24]

It is ironic that this pro–civil rights legislator's career was made possible by gerrymandering of the Silk Stocking district.[25] The boundaries of the district had been carefully crafted by lawmakers in Albany to keep the district safely Republican by ensuring that it was nearly 90 percent white. This meant excluding, among others, black and Puerto Rican Democrats who resided directly to the north of the district. Though New York's black and Puerto Rican communities later strongly supported Lindsay for mayor, early in his career there was a good chance that large numbers of Democratic voters would have pushed the district beyond the reach of even the craftiest liberal Republican. Lindsay's exasperated opponent in 1962, Martin Dworkis, claimed the district was gerrymandered on "white supremacy principles." Even a sympathetic Lindsay biographer noted it was "odd that this piece of real estate covering approximately one-fourth of Manhattan is so constituted that all of its zigzagging boundaries stop just short of the masses of minority voters." But it was not only to the north that the district had quirky boundaries; placing the district's southern boundary at Fourteenth Street excluded Jewish and Puerto Rican Democrats who lived on the Lower East Side.[26]

Lindsay's liberal voting record and poor relations with fellow Republicans during his years in Congress led both critics and supporters to ask: What kind of a Republican is he? The Lindsay biographer Daniel Button answered that question as follows: "Intellectually, he is a strong Republican; emotionally, he is fiercely independent; spiritually he is a progressive and in that sense frequently finds common cause with the Democratic liberal group. But much more importantly, he is morally and ethically committed to principles he holds to be paramount in value to all other considerations." Though one can debate the feasibility of being a Republican intellectually while spiritually siding with Democrats, there is little doubt that Lindsay paid a price for his principles. As a liberal Republican in the Democratic-controlled House of Representatives, Lindsay was in the unenviable position of being a minority within a minority. One of Lindsay's colleagues said: "If John were a Democrat, he'd be among the dozen most important members of the House." With a sigh of resignation, Lindsay himself admitted that he was "sufficiently independent to have come close to the edge of being ineffective."[27]

So what made Lindsay a Republican? The basis of his Republicanism lay in both the dynamics of New York City politics and in his plodding, yet earnest, attempts to build a coherent political philosophy. During the late 1950s and early 1960s, New York City Republicanism was still defined by its opposition to Democratic clubhouse politics. Yet these were hard times for "regular" Democrats. In 1959, a group of prominent reform Democrats, led by Eleanor Roosevelt and former New York Governor Herbert Lehman, formed the Committee for Democratic Values (CDV), which pledged to purge "regular" Democrats from positions of power within the party. Under pressure from reform groups like the CDV, Mayor Wagner turned against those who had been his allies in the political clubhouses during his 1961 re-election race. Reform Democrats received a major boost when a little-known lawyer named Jim Lanigan defeated the Tammany Hall boss, Carmine De Sapio, in 1961 for the post of male district leader in Greenwich Village.

The Republican John Lindsay joined this chorus of voices denouncing the Democratic bosses and their political machines. Speaking on WCBS-TV's program *New York Forum* in June 1961, he reiterated his opposition to Democratic machine rule:

> There is no question in my mind but that the city has suffered and suffered badly at the hands of Tammany Hall, men connected with Tammany Hall, men who think like Tammany Hall. Basically, this has led the city down the drain. . . . Government has been abandoned, I think, to boss rule and I feel that until we have a clean sweep of this kind of maladministration, which has infected this city for so many years, it's going to be impossible for New Yorkers to continue their self-respect and their pride in our great city.[28]

The connection between Democratic rule and the decline of New York City was fixed in Lindsay's mind. If New York Democrats were corrupted by their association with machine politics, they were further defiled on the national level by their partnership with anti-civil-rights white Southerners. In many ways, party allegiances in this era were still based on the political battles of the previous century. White Southerners supported the Democratic Party as the party opposing Lincoln, the Union, and Reconstruction. The white urban working class backed the Democratic Party as the defender of unions and the workingman. On the other side, the Republican Party became defined by its defense of the Union, its support for business, and its opposition to urban machines. By the end of the 1960s, the reform attacks on urban machines destroyed inherited party allegiance in the urban North, while the civil-rights movement destroyed it in the white South.

This paved the way for an ideological realignment of American politics. John Lindsay's political career straddled both these worlds of inherited political allegiance and ideological commitment.

As late as 1967, Lindsay was still trying to reconcile Eisenhower Republicanism with the new liberalism by putting the primacy of the individual at the center of his own political philosophy:

> The Republican Party must take on the special task of defining the role of the individual in the midst of our part garrison, part welfare state. . . . The Republican Party must demonstrate that a concentration of power through a government-dominated industrial-military complex may be

just as threatening to steady economic growth and to individual free-doms as are all other excessive power groupings. . . . The Republican Party must understand also that safeguarding of individual worth in-cludes the creation or protection of basic conditions of living that will not permit any person, who cannot help himself, to live below a mini-mum standard of decency in a civilized nation.

Whereas prohibition, immigration reform, Sunday blue laws, antiprosti-tution, antigambling, and antiobscenity campaigns were an integral part of the Protestant political tradition that accompanied progressive social policy in the late-nineteenth and early-twentieth century, modern liberalism no longer sought to regulate behavior. Instead it argued for expanding the realm of personal liberties to include behavior previously thought obscene or im-moral. Less emphasis was put on reforming man because it was deemed that society was sick—with poverty, racism, and inequality. The modern liberal turned his attention toward the ills of society rather than man's vices. Con-sequently, less was expected of citizens. An expanded welfare state promised to pick up the mess left by its free, but profligate, citizens. The historian Fred Siegel calls this development "dependent individualism." Lindsay's troubled career as a House Republican revealed deep tensions within the national Re-publican Party that would be ripped open in 1964, forcing the young Con-gressman to reconsider his basic political values.[29]

The presidential candidacy of Arizona Senator Barry Goldwater was a di-rect attack on liberal Republicanism. Goldwater and his constituents repre-sented emerging Sun Belt communities and shared a dislike for what they called the "Eastern Establishment." As Goldwater wrote many years later: "The double standards and selfishness of the Eastern Establishment ex-cluded most of the nation. These had to go if conservatives were to rebuild the GOP from the grass roots up and broaden our base into mainstream America. That is precisely what I intended to do—remake the party." Iron-ically, liberals like Lindsay also believed the Republican Party needed to broaden itself: "Our party must understand that if it is to be the party of the people, by the people and for the people, it must so approach the affairs of government, at home and abroad, that it constantly makes clear that it offers a government that is truly of *all* the people, not just some of the people."[30]

New York Governor Nelson Rockefeller, the leader of the party's liberal wing, was an early favorite for the 1964 presidential nomination. But the public backlash against his divorce from his first wife and sudden May 1963 marriage to Margaretta (Happy) Murphy—who divorced her first husband and left her small children to marry Rockefeller—damaged his candidacy. After losing the California primary to Goldwater, he dropped out of the race. In response to Rockefeller's collapse, Pennsylvania Governor William Scranton entered the race. Liberal Republicans, in a last-ditch attempt to stop Goldwater from receiving the nomination, flocked to Scranton. The showdown between conservative and liberal Republicans reached an emotional height at the San Francisco convention in mid-July. John Lindsay attended the convention as a member of the New York delegation and pleaded the case of liberal Republicanism before the Platform Committee:

> The Republican Party must take on the special task of defining the role of the individual in the midst of the part-garrison, part-welfare state. It must establish guideposts for unfettered individual betterment, and open avenues for the pursuit of individual excellence. . . . It should reject the anti-individual, antilibertarian forces that stem from every organized power group, whether that power group be the Central Government, the industrial-military complex, the big city machine or the local constabulary.[31]

Specifically, Lindsay argued for greater vigilance in the area of civil liberties; an internationalist foreign policy; federal aid for cities, education, and the arts; and a federal health insurance plan for senior citizens. Most important, Lindsay argued for a plank affirming support for the 1964 Civil Rights Act. To conservatives, however, Lindsay's platform suggestions sounded too much like an echo of Johnson's Great Society liberalism—"A Choice, Not an Echo," they demanded.

Lindsay was swimming against the stream of Goldwater delegates who dominated not only the platform committee but also the whole convention. In this situation, the only hope for Lindsay and other liberals was to force certain platform amendments upon conservatives. These too were consistently voted down. One of Lindsay's tasks at the convention was to present the case for a Scranton-backed civil rights amendment, but it was ultimately defeated by a vote of 897 to 409. In its place was inserted a civil rights plank supported by pro–civil-rights Republicans Everett Dirksen and William McCulloch. That plank pledged Republicans to the "full implementation and faithful execution of the Civil Rights Act of 1964, and all other civil rights statutes, to assure civil rights and opportunities guaranteed by the Constitution to every citizen." Still, liberal Republicans were not satisfied.[32]

Liberal Republicans could only shake their heads and scold their conservative adversaries. On the night of July 14, Rockefeller gave a speech in defense of an amendment against extremism. A thinly veiled attack on the Goldwaterites, the speech included talk of "Nazi methods," and was met with a hailstorm of boos, catcalls, and chants of "We Want Barry." After Rockefeller's speech, John Lindsay was one of the first people to greet the governor "enthusiastically" after he left the podium. The *New York Times* called the Republican Convention a "Bastille Day in Reverse" led by "Cactus Jacobins." The Republicans left San Francisco anything but a unified party. With resignation and frustration, Lindsay wrote that "the trouble with this 1964 Republican national convention is that nothing has made any difference. Nothing Scranton could do made any difference to Goldwater. Nothing the moderates could do made any difference to the conservatives. Nothing the demonstrators outside the Cow Palace could say made any difference to what went on inside." For Lindsay, the Goldwater campaign was the "Never Never Land of this campaign year," a somewhat ridiculous flight of fantasy based on an outmoded ideology.[33]

The convention put Lindsay in a quandary. Goldwater and his supporters were anathema to him, ideologically as well as culturally. Sun Belt conservatives tended to be anti-urban, with a special animus toward New York City. Eastern liberals like Lindsay returned the favor by looking down at their less-cosmopolitan adversaries. Lindsay, having little use for Goldwater or his supporters, admitted his befuddlement to Jimmy Breslin: "I can't understand what this man [Goldwater] has in his mind." Liberal Republicans and conservative Goldwaterites differed most in their approach to the size and scope of the federal government. Lindsay's belief in a Republican party dedicated to civil rights and to "surround[ing] the individual with great protections against" the power of local majorities, big business, and the "weight of federal bureaucracy" almost by definition necessitated an activist government. Goldwater, on the other hand, argued that such a beneficent government would result in the "elimination of any feeling of responsibility for [a citizen's] own welfare and that of his family and neighbors. . . . and transform the individual from a dignified, industrious, self-reliant spiritual being into a dependent animal creature without his knowing it." These contradictory views could not coexist in the same party for long.[34]

Baffled by Goldwater and his beliefs, Lindsay hinted that a nonendorsement of Goldwater was a strong possibility. Immediately after the convention, Lindsay said that he and other Republicans would "search their conscience very deeply" over whether to support Goldwater in the fall. Lindsay said that he was "not going to desert" the principles that he and other liberal Republicans had fought for at the convention and then made it clear that his main concern was civil rights: "I continue to be disappointed by Senator Goldwater's refusal to acknowledge the Republicans' traditional commitment to the nation's responsibility for individual human beings in the field of equal protection of the laws." For Lindsay, principle now trumped party allegiance and challenged the vestigial Republicanism that had been as much a part of his inheritance as the small sum of money his father had left him at his death in 1961.[35]

Within a month of the convention Lindsay decided against supporting Goldwater. Ruling out the possibility that he would endorse President Johnson, Lindsay announced he would run for reelection to Congress as an independent Republican without reference to the national ticket. Because of Goldwater's unpopularity in New York City, the decision was shrewd in the short run, but could have caused Lindsay problems with upstate Republicans if he ran for governor in 1966. At present, Lindsay was being challenged by both a Democrat, Eleanor French Clark, and a candidate from the fledgling Conservative Party, Kieran O'Doherty. Regarding O'Doherty's challenge, Lindsay argued that the "Conservative Party and its early organizers for Senator Goldwater in New York State are bent on a course of destruction in the 17th Congressional District and I have no choice but to fight back." Lindsay mentioned Goldwater's name only twice in his statement and was careful not to attack the senator personally, but he made it clear there was a schism within the Republican Party that could not be bridged with compromise and handshakes.[36]

In response, William F. Buckley's conservative *National Review* lashed out against Lindsay, derisively calling him "Destiny's Tot" and claiming that "Lindsay had done his savage best to cut" Goldwater's political throat since the San Francisco convention. But Lindsay was not the only Republican disavowing the Goldwater campaign: New York Senators Jacob Javits and Kenneth Keating (Keating was himself in a tough reelection fight against Robert Kennedy), Clifford Case of New Jersey and Thomas Kuchel of California, Michigan's Governor George Romney, Idaho's Governor Robert Smylie, and Congressmen Seymour Halpern and Ogden Reid of New York, Stanley Tupper of Maine, and Silvio Conte of Massachusetts all refused to endorse the Republican standard bearer.[37]

Lindsay's reelection slogan—"The District's Pride—The Nation's Hope"—was meant to give the impression that there was a national significance to the race in terms of both his future political plans and the kind of Republicanism he represented. Despite having to defend himself from Clark's attacks that he was too conservative and O'Doherty's attacks that he was too liberal, Lindsay won in a landslide. In the presidential race, Goldwater managed to win only six states, five in the Deep South and his native Arizona. Whereas Goldwater received only 27 percent of the vote in New York City (801,877 votes), Lindsay racked up 71.5 percent of the vote in his congressional race, defeating Clark by nearly 100,000 votes. His was the second widest margin of victory of any Republican congressman that year. (Congressman James Quillen, a Tennessee Republican, won 71.6 percent in his race.) The Conservative Party's O'Doherty was held to under 10,000 votes, less than 5 percent of the vote.

In the ashes of the Goldwater debacle, conservatism appeared a spent force. In a January 1965 interview, Lindsay declared that the Republican Party was "a pile of rubble." Liberal Republicans could point to Lindsay's outstanding victory after repudiating Goldwater as a sign of the direction in which the party needed to move. In a series of articles for the *New York Journal American*, Robert Donovan wrote that the 1964 election showed that that the Republican Party could not play a dominant role in national politics, "much less play it in the White House, until it casts off the extreme right-wing conservatism of Sen. Goldwater and his faction." Liberal Republicans sounded off to the press. "The Goldwater people will be washed out pretty fast," one anonymous Eastern Republican told *Business Week*: "I don't think the party will ever make this mistake again." An anonymous New York Republican went one step further, suggesting: "After this election, the conservatives simply are not entitled to be heard any more." The liberal *New York Post*, which editorially chastised the "right-wing sickness" of the "lunatic fringe, the kooks, and the extreme conservatives," hailed Lindsay as the "GOP's Big Winner." The *New York Times* declared: "Lindsay's Status Enhanced by Vote." The *New York Herald Tribune* listed Lindsay as one of the nine leaders in the Republican Party, along with Nixon, Rockefeller, and Scranton.[38]

Though now possessing a safe congressional seat, Lindsay was in a box regarding his political future. His fellow Republican, Senator Jacob Javits, would not be up for reelection until 1968, and all signs pointed toward his running for reelection. The Senate seat of the newly elected Democrat, Robert Kennedy, was a possibility, but he would not face reelection until 1970. If Nelson Rockefeller declined to run for a third term as governor in 1966, Lindsay would be a top candidate. If Rockefeller bowed out and Javits chose to run for governor, Lindsay would most likely be appointed to Javits's seat. But it appeared that Rocky would stay in Albany to gear up for another bid for the White House. Lindsay's only option to advance his political career was City Hall.

MUGWUMP FOR MAYOR:
THE 1965 CAMPAIGN

That year was the hinge of our postwar history.
The prestige of government, and government's
confidence, not to say hubris, were at apogees.

—George F. Will,
"Looking Back to 1965," 1995[1]

In 1965, few people expected John Lindsay to win the New York City
mayoralty. He was a Republican in a city where Democrats outnumbered Republicans three to one; a white, Anglo-Saxon Protestant in a city
that was largely Catholic and Jewish, Irish and Italian, black and Puerto
Rican. The *Herald Tribune* had Lindsay trailing in all of its polls, though he
gained steadily on his Democratic opponent Abe Beame in the final month
of the campaign. A third mayoral candidate running on the Conservative
Party ticket, the columnist William F. Buckley, was running well behind
Lindsay and Beame. On the day before the election, the *Herald Tribune* poll
had Beame ahead by less than one percentage point. Only the *Daily News*
consistently put Lindsay ahead in its polls, but just barely. The day before the
election, the famous *Daily News* straw poll predicted a "thin Lindsay win."
As late as 10 P.M. on election night, November 2, 1965, the big board had
Beame ahead by 50,000 votes. It looked to most people as though Beame
would be the 103rd mayor of New York City. The mood at Lindsay's headquarters was morose.[2]

Bob Price, the abrasive yet brilliant thirty-two-year-old brains behind
Lindsay's campaign, was cautiously optimistic. All night he had been keeping tabs on thirty key electoral districts, and the news was promising. Late

in the evening, Price whispered to a campaign aide, Jay Kriegel, "It looks all right." Price called his friend Abe Rosenthal, the metropolitan desk editor at the *New York Times*, to talk him out of running a story declaring Beame the victor in the bulldog edition (the early edition, available around 11 P.M. that evening). By 11:45 P.M., Price knew John Lindsay was on his way to City Hall when a yellow piece of paper containing the results from an electoral district in the Riverdale section of the Bronx revealed that middle-class Jewish Democrats—the swing group key to a Lindsay victory—had voted against Beame, a fellow Jew. Lindsay, still in doubt over the outcome, asked Price what he should do. Price told him to comb his hair, wash his face, put on a clean shirt, and get ready to make his acceptance speech.

Shortly before midnight, word reached Lindsay headquarters that Buckley had ended his quixotic campaign. In a somber mood over the death of his father-in-law the previous day, Buckley briefly thanked his supporters, predicted that the Conservative vote would "vastly affect politicians in New York City, in Albany and Washington for years to come," and walked out. Across town, Beame waited until 2 A.M. to concede. The indignity of a Democrat losing the mayoral race in New York City was compounded by the fact that Beame's fellow Democrats, Mario Procaccino and Frank O'Connor, won handily as comptroller and City Council president, respectively. O'Connor, the popular Queens district attorney, outpolled Beame 1,366,260 to 1,030,771 and was already the favorite for the Democratic nomination to challenge Governor Nelson Rockefeller in 1966.

But the night belonged to John Lindsay. Seven thousand people crowded the ballroom at the Roosevelt Hotel at Madison Avenue and Forty-fifth Street. Many were young volunteers who, turned off by the colorless Beame and his clubhouse support and excited by Lindsay's Kennedy-esque idealism and vigor, had been recruited to man the campaign storefronts established in all five boroughs. Some were too young to vote and wore buttons proclaiming: IF I WERE 21 I'D VOTE FOR LINDSAY. After viewing the crowd, one hard-bitten political reporter observed how different this Lindsay crowd was from the crowds normally found at city political affairs: "Never in my long, squalid political life have I seen so many Yalies and Vassar broads under one roof on a New York City Election Night." The crowd had "Princeton and Radcliffe etched in their Scott Fitzgerald faces," wrote Jack Newfield.[3]

Although the crowd had dwindled somewhat by the time Lindsay entered the ballroom at 2:30 A.M., its energy had not. Thunderous cries of "We want Lindsay" greeted the Lindsay family as they walked to the podium following a path made by a phalanx of police. Besides his wife, Mary, and their three daughters, there was John Jr., five years old, carried on the shoulders of a New York policeman, making the V-for-victory sign with his stubby little fingers. As Rockefeller, a fellow Republican and a financial benefactor of the campaign, tried to make his way to the platform, some Lindsay aides physically tried to block the governor from the limelight. Not to be deterred, Rockefeller managed to find Lindsay on the platform, put his arm around the embarrassed mayor-elect, and say, "Well, *we* did it." As Rockefeller later reminisced, "I had a hell of a time getting in there."[4]

In his short acceptance speech, Lindsay warned that "rigorous and exacting struggles" lay ahead for Gotham, but he promised that a united city would "assure the eventual conquest of the pending, recurrent, and unforeseen crisis afflicting our city." John Lindsay, rumpled and exhausted, was no longer fresh. But he was the winner.

GEARING UP FOR CITY HALL

Gracie Mansion seemed an unlikely place for a promising young politician to further his career. (Only three New York City mayors have ever gone on to higher office: the nineteenth-century mayors DeWitt Clinton and John T. Hoffman both later became governor, and Fernando Wood was elected to the U.S. Congress after his days as mayor.) Jimmy Walker and Bill O'Dwyer left office in disgrace, and even the popular Fiorello La Guardia could not move beyond City Hall.

As early as 1963, Lindsay was telling the *Herald Tribune*'s editorial board that he felt a run for City Hall made sense, especially in light of the growing importance of big cities. Lindsay was also getting restless in Washington. "Washington, compared to New York City, is a very shallow place," Lindsay said. "It's got politics, endless white marble, and some very good museums. Beyond that it has very little." After eight years as Mayor, Lindsay looked back on his years in Congress and had few regrets about leaving. "I think if you stay there [Congress] too long everybody tends to become mediators," said Lindsay. "You become a skilled craftsman at the business of legislating, but you tend to become isolated in a curious way. There's too much marble all around." The grit and grime of New York was more alluring to Lindsay than the hallowed halls of Congress.[5]

Lindsay began honing his message and gaining a national reputation as the leading spokesman for cities. In a January 1965 speech before the Executive's Club of Chicago entitled "The Republican Challenge," Lindsay outlined his belief that in order to recover from their devastating presidential defeat two and a half months earlier, Republicans needed to "recapture the center." He stressed the importance of civil rights and the need to protect individuals from the power of big business, big labor, big city machines, and big government. He added that "the Republican Party cannot be in the center if it ignores the cities, where 70 per cent of our population now lives and therefore where 70 per cent of the vote is found. How can Republicans as the best pragmatists of all ignore this area?"[6]

Lindsay's Chicago speech revealed the mind of a man mulling his political future, trying to convince himself of the need to run for office. Arguing for the importance of running for office, Lindsay said, "Those who wish to shape the government will do so by their involvement in local campaigns and with the daily headache that people in office or standing for office have. . . . Involvement is the answer and involvement is the obligation." Other men entered politics for their personal benefit. For men like Lindsay, though, public service was an "obligation." Governing New York City would present Lindsay with a plethora of problems, but the Protestant moralistic fervor that stoked the fires of his ambition gave him little choice but to take on the challenge.[7]

Despite Lindsay's smashing November 1964 victory, something else was needed to make a reform campaign in New York credible: a scandal or crisis to discredit the governing Democrats. New York's two previous reform mayors had been thrust into office in the wake of embarrassments suffered by Democratic administrations. John Purroy Mitchel was elected in 1913 following a wave of police scandals that embarrassed Tammany Hall. La Guardia was elected in 1933 after the Seabury Commission (appointed by Governor Franklin Roosevelt to investigate civic corruption in the city) forced Jimmy Walker to resign. Unfortunately for Lindsay, the ethics and integrity of Mayor Wagner, who had repudiated Tammany Hall during his 1961 reelection campaign, were beyond question.

Lacking a handy scandal, reform forces developed another weapon that would ease their bid for power: a sense that the city was moving in the wrong direction. In 1965, the journalist Richard Whalen published a book entitled *A City Destroying Itself: An Angry View of New York*. In a tone of unrelenting doom, Whalen wrote: "New York shows alarming signs of spiritual malnutrition and death-by-inches. It is frowning, tight-lipped, short-tempered, the most nervous city in America. It is a city without grace."[8]

In anticipation of the 1965 mayoral election, *Look* magazine ran a story called "A Tough Day in New York" portraying the difficulties of life in a city that was acting "dangerously like an underdeveloped country. . . . New York is a city crying for help. It is dirty, thirsty, tired, scared, old, worn, fouled and poor." The issue of urban decay snowballed when the *Herald Tribune* published a daily exposé, beginning on January 25, 1965, and continuing throughout the spring, entitled "New York City in Crisis," that chronicled the myriad failures of the city to provide a decent life for all of its citizens. The first installment of the series was subtitled "New York, Greatest City in the World—And Everything Is Wrong with It." Beating a constant drumbeat of pessimism, the series told of the troubles facing Gotham: narcotics, air pollution, poor education, welfare, ailing hospitals, one-party rule, business exodus, middle-class exodus, black and Puerto Rican poverty, elderly poverty, fear in the streets, and an inefficient city bureaucracy.

> For the poor, the aged, the Negro, the Puerto Rican, and the blue-collar
> worker who is unemployed because of automation and the exodus of

business, New York today is a nightmare—a hopeless city whose administration offers promises and handouts but little in the way of rehabilitation and retraining.

For the young and the middle-class white and Negro, New York has become a terrible place to live because of unsafe streets, poor schools, and inadequate housing. They have been driven out to the suburbs just when the city needs them the most.

And even for the wealthy—those who can afford the best—the air pollution, the traffic-clogged streets, and the violence have come to outweigh the delights afforded by New York's stores, restaurants, and cultural events.

Though this series did not create the "urban crisis," it added another layer to the growing unease with life in New York City.[9]

Lindsay later admitted that the *Herald Tribune* series had provided a "raison d'être" for him to run. The paper was owned by John Hay (Jock) Whitney, one of Lindsay's top financial backers. As early as 1963, Dwight Sargent, the editorial-page editor of the *Herald Tribune*, had written Whitney about the necessity of electing a reform mayor to replace Wagner, and the paper's possible role in such an event. "I think that some old-fashioned, hard-hitting, imaginative journalism could shake the city out of its lethargy," wrote Sargent.[10]

The genesis of the series came out of Whitney's desire to put together an entity in emulation of Philadelphia's Citizen's Council, an organization that sought to move the city in a reform direction. Councils of this type were traditional upper-class good-government vehicles that tried to curb the power of machine-dominated political establishments. In 1964, Whitney and Walter Thayer, publisher at the *Herald Tribune*, brought twenty prominent New Yorkers together for a lunch in the private dining room of the *Herald Tribune*. Although everyone agreed that the city seemed to be heading for a crisis, most of the attendees, led by David Rockefeller, the governor's brother and the head of Chase Manhattan Bank, were against the idea of challenging Wagner publicly. They all felt Wagner would remain in office one more term and there was no reason to jeopardize their relationship with him. Thus, the idea of a Philadelphia-type Citizen's Council never took hold.[11]

Instead, Whitney and Thayer used the power and influence of their paper not to replace Wagner, but to prod him into action. Barry Gottehrer, the editor of the series, later noted that the project "was done as a way in their [Whitney and Thayer] mind to get rid of Wagner without getting rid of Wagner." A team of researchers set out to study the problems of the city for six months. The *Herald Tribune*'s exposé of the decaying city led citizens to report their own complaints about potholes, broken street lights, and garbage-strewn parks. Much of this was gleefully recorded by Gottehrer's staff. According to Gottehrer, "It was the kind of journalism that would drive an incumbent nuts." When a *Herald Tribune* reporter asked for Wagner's response to the series, the mayor's spokesman said, "The mayor says to tell Jock to shove it up his ass."[12]

Whatever the rationale for the series, it soon evolved into an anti-incumbent vehicle. Though a good-government Citizen's Council would not be created, the *Herald Tribune*'s series paved the way for a candidate like Lindsay to discredit the Wagner administration and run a successful, non-partisan reform campaign. Gottehrer believes that without the series, Wagner would have run for another term and Lindsay would have stayed out. The series was needed, according to the paper's editorial page, because "New York has passed the stage at which mediocrity could be tolerated as the normal condition of municipal life. The nation's greatest city cries out for a greatness of civic vision, translated into reality by get-it-done performance. New York has the resources, human and material in greater abundance than any other city. What it needs is to put them to use." In the first article of the series, Lindsay was quoted as saying that "under Mayor Wagner New York has lost its will power, its great energy, and its great leadership. . . . to run this city properly and get it going again, the mayor has to be very tough. . . . If we don't get going again soon, New York will become a second-class city."[13]

Wagner realized the potency of this argument and quickly responded by saying that New York was "full of bright and cheering aspects," with economic indicators showing a "throbbing vitality." But Wagner was fighting an uphill battle. While he was dealing with cold numbers, Lindsay and the *Herald Tribune* series tapped in to a malaise that statistics could never assuage.[14]

Still, Lindsay was ambivalent about running. Although Mayor Wagner was a weak incumbent, Lindsay knew that New York was still a Democratic stronghold. But one person strongly believed the congressman should take the plunge: Bob Price.

Who was Bob Price? More than a decade younger than Lindsay, Price served as Lindsay's political confidant. In contrast to the tall, cool, WASPishness of Lindsay, Price was short and somewhat dumpy with a moon-shaped face perpetually darkened by a five o'clock shadow. Whereas Lindsay was St. Paul's and Yale, Price was Bronx High School of Science and New York University. Former Republican Congressman Theodore Kupferman noted that despite the startling contrast between the two men, they got "along almost like brothers." Woody Klein, a former reporter who later became Lindsay's first press secretary, called Price "a strange, brilliant, restless person, talented but without a trace of grace." Lindsay's appointments secretary, Harvey Rothenberg, called Price "a brilliant tactician, his brilliance was surpassed only by his ruthlessness." In campaign photographs, Price is often pictured with a telephone receiver at each ear. Abrupt, brusque, and rude, Price had a genius for politics and was "fascinated by the manipulative, conspiratorial side of politics."[15]

Price's Jewish immigrant parents had come to the Bronx from Eastern Europe as infants. They owned a grocery store in Washington Heights, where Price worked part time while going to school. Price joined the Republican Party because Boss Charlie Buckley's Bronx Democratic Party "did not seem to me the honest place to be." With his nonideological, antimachine Republicanism, Price became president of the New York University Young Republicans, where he caught the eye of the president of the New York City Young Republicans: John Lindsay. When Lindsay's campaign manager for his first congressional campaign in 1958, Charles Metzner, moved to the staff of Rockefeller's first gubernatorial campaign, Lindsay called on Price, then in his last year in law school, to run his campaign.[16]

Price's stock continued to rise within state party circles. He engineered Rockefeller's Oregon primary win in 1964, the only primary the governor won that year. Price continued to be an adviser to Congressman Lindsay, although he refused to move to Washington. The two men spoke together almost daily by telephone. Price would handle all of the political work for Lindsay, but would never interfere in the congressman's votes. According to Charles Moerdler, a friend of both Price's and Lindsay's from the New York Young Republicans, "Lindsay placed total, total, total credence and authority in Bob Price to handle all of the political details."[17]

In late 1964, Lindsay's political alter ego had a feeling that Wagner would not run for reelection and he began to talk to people like Herbert Brownell, John Lindsay's older brother, George, Bethuel Webster, and Fred Sheffield. They were men who, in Price's words, had "Lindsay's best interest at heart." Price talked about a possible Lindsay candidacy with a widening circle of the congressman's acquaintances. Most thought that running for mayor was a bad idea. Still, Price remained optimistic and told everyone to keep these discussions secret from Lindsay. There were two people Price knew he had to convince: Brownell and Scheffield. The latter called Price and told him that despite his doubts, he would go along with his plan. Next, Price met with Brownell. The former U.S. attorney general said that he could be counted on for support. Price has said, "To me there was no doubt that if I had Brownell or Scheffield with me that eighty-three friends and his whole family could vote no and the ayes would have it."[18]

With Brownell and Scheffield behind him, Price began plastering maps of state assembly districts about his office and scouting the city for locations at which to open up neighborhood campaign storefronts. He believed that Lindsay could win if he blanketed every part of the city in an old-fashioned street-level campaign. As one aide said: "He [Price] knew the city intersection by intersection. He had reviewed the returns from all of the 5,000 election districts through the years and he knew precisely where the key districts were." One of the campaign's Brooklyn coordinators, Robert Blum, remembered that

> for fully a month Price's knowledge of my area far outstripped my own. It was incredible. Somebody would suggest opening a storefront at, say, Bell Boulevard and 132nd Street. Price would think about it and then say, "No good, that's two blocks away from the point of heaviest traffic. There's an empty store next to the movie theater. Try that instead." It was literally a tour de force. He must have put in 150 or more hours just walking and driving all over the city.

When the campaign began, Price recruited young, energetic lawyers to volunteer as campaign coordinators for sections of the city. Some, like Charles Moerdler and Arnold Fraiman, would later take prominent positions in the Lindsay administration. Price rented out half a floor in the Hotel Roosevelt for office space for the fledgling campaign. Meanwhile, the would-be candidate was never told of any of these machinations, despite the fact that Price spoke with the Congressman several times a day.[19]

If Price was going to get Lindsay into City Hall, the two men would have to maneuver around Nelson Rockefeller, the state's top Republican officeholder and the party's main fund-raiser. Tensions between Lindsay and the governor were inevitable. Rockefeller had the national political stature and aristocratic wealth that Lindsay lacked, while Lindsay possessed the youth and charm that Rockefeller envied. Rockefeller represented the old politics of pragmatism and wheeling-dealing compromise; Lindsay represented the new politics of idealism and a television-friendly persona.

The first crack in the Lindsay-Rockefeller relationship occurred during a 1963 campaign for an at-large City Council seat from Manhattan. Congressman Lindsay supported his former campaign treasurer, Richard Lewisohn, while Rockefeller got the Manhattan Republican boss, Vincent Albano, to back Richard Aldrich, Rockefeller's cousin. With Albano's backing, Aldrich was supported by the county committee. Lewisohn dropped out of the race, but another Republican, John Lamula, challenged Aldrich in the Republican primary. Lamula narrowly lost by less than 500 votes, and Aldrich easily won the general election in November. Lindsay was outraged. For a man who spent much of his time railing against political cronyism and whose main rationale for being a Republican was the issue of bossism, this incident of Republican bossism was an especially bitter pill. Rockefeller, trying to restore his reputation and power after the bad publicity surrounding his divorce and subsequent remarriage, resented Lindsay's refusal to accommodate his wishes. Dorothy Schiff, the publisher of the *New York Post*, believed that "John hated him [Rockefeller]. I remember him telling me at that time that Rockefeller buys everything from women to delegates and he certainly felt that Nelson was always trying to keep him down."[20]

At the same time, Senator Jacob Javits was making noises about running for mayor. The state's top Republican vote-getter and a former congressman from predominantly Jewish Washington Heights, Javits set a March 1 deadline as necessary to launch an aggressive campaign and build an effective organization. As the magical March 1 deadline approached, Javits announced he would not run. Javits told a meeting of top Republican officials in early March that he had desperately wanted to run for mayor twelve years earlier, but was denied the nomination. In 1965, though, Gracie Mansion looked less inviting to a sitting senator. "Since when do you groom a Senator for Mayor of New York?" Javits told the group. One day later, Lindsay announced that he, too, had chosen not to seek the mayoralty. Not realizing the behind-the-scenes machinations of Bob Price, Lindsay diplomatically took himself out of contention by citing his responsibilities in Congress.[21]

Some have said that Rockefeller had no desire to see either of his two rivals gain a foothold as mayor of New York. Instead, he hoped that John Gilhooley, an able but little-known Brooklyn Republican, would receive the nomination. Other potential candidates included Congressman Seymour Halpern and State Senator John Marchi. Whatever the reasons, Republicans still did not have a candidate. With Mayor Wagner withering before their eyes, Republican hopes dangled on the thin threads of men named Gilhooley, Marchi, and Halpern.[22]

Finishing his third term, Wagner was increasingly seen as weak and ineffective. In the spring of 1965, insider polls showed him running neck and neck with Lindsay. According to the political scientist Martin Shefter, Wagner's repudiation of the Democratic clubhouses in 1961 tied him closer to organizations that supported greater government spending, like the Liberal Party, civil service unions, and civic associations like the United Parents Association, while at the same time loosening his ties to homeowners and small businessmen who favored lower taxes. Thus, during Wagner's third term spending rose twice as rapidly as it had during his first two terms, the sales tax increased from 3 to 4 percent in 1963, and the base on the city's commercial rent tax was raised.[23]

Meanwhile, Lindsay was having trouble sleeping at nights, as the guilt from abandoning his duty to run weighed heavily on his mind. August Heckscher—who later became Lindsay's second parks commissioner—noted that Lindsay was a man "impelled from within—by a dominant, rather cheerless compulsion—to act according to what he thought was right." Lindsay admitted that his decision to drop out of the race made him "very depressed." Still, Price continued to prime Lindsay for a run at City Hall: "Look, some people are lying awake nights because they are afraid they might have to run for Mayor. You're worrying because you're not running."[24]

A turning point occurred on Saturday, May 8, when Price and Lindsay walked for two hours through the Upper East Side of Manhattan, with Lindsay commenting on everything from overflowing trash cans to gaping potholes to black smoke billowing from an incinerator. Price told him: "You're the only guy who can command enough respect to clean it up." The idea of urban decay was brought home to Lindsay with a bracing immediacy on that walk. As Lindsay became increasingly agitated at what he saw, Price could tell that Lindsay was ready to run. The following day Lindsay and his family returned to Washington. On Sunday afternoon, Lindsay and his brother George went with their children to the zoo, where, while watching the bears, John announced to his brother: "I'm going to run."[25]

When Price and Lindsay spoke on Monday night, Price could sense the hesitation returning. Despite Lindsay's not having made a final decision, Price went ahead on Tuesday morning and began putting in place the final pieces in his carefully crafted scheme. Price met for lunch with Rockefeller's aides George Hinman and Bill Pfeiffer at the Algonquin Hotel. He told them Lindsay would announce for mayor in the coming days and he wanted Rockefeller to give the campaign $500,000. Later in the afternoon, Rockefeller called Price and agreed to the money but wanted Lindsay to ask for the money in person. The governor would be in Albany that evening and would send a state plane to pick up Lindsay and Price.[26]

The next piece of the puzzle involved the *New York Times*. Price, who had many friends at the paper and often bragged he could get on the front page anytime he wanted, phoned reporter Thomas Ronan to tell him Lindsay was set to run. He would give Ronan the exclusive story under certain conditions. First, Ronan could not call anyone else to confirm the story, including Lindsay. Second, Ronan would have to wait until Price phoned him at 8 P.M. before going with the story. Last, and most important, Price demanded not only that the scoop be a page-one story but also that it be the lead story with a three-column headline. Price even tried to dictate the headline to Ronan. Later that afternoon, Abe Rosenthal, a good friend of Price's, told him that no one dictated terms to the *Times*. In that case, Price said, he would give the scoop to the *Tribune*. After much gnashing of teeth, Rosenthal agreed to run the story.[27]

Meanwhile, Price called Lindsay in Washington, telling him to come up to New York that night. The congressman, worried he might miss a vote, told Price, "I'm not running for mayor." Price said he knew that after a moment of introspection, Lindsay would agree to fly to New York. Late that afternoon Lindsay flew to New York, where Price met him at the airport. Over coffee, with the governor's plane waiting, Price told him of their mission to Albany and of Price's plans to have Lindsay run for mayor. Lindsay insisted that he still was not interested in running.[28]

To add to the air of intrigue, Price signed two phony names to the airplane's log, and then he and Lindsay were off to Albany, where they met with Rockefeller. Price explained why Lindsay should run for mayor, and the governor set to work convincing Lindsay. The governor promised to guarantee $500,000 for Lindsay's campaign and granted him the independence in choosing running mates that Lindsay coveted. "I could tell from Lindsay's attitude," recalled Price, "that in another fifteen minutes he would be ready." Price then called Ronan to give him the go-ahead. Lindsay was now the Republican candidate for mayor of New York City.[29]

Later that night Lindsay returned to the city. Instead of accompanying his wife to a Broadway opening, Lindsay spent the night in discussions with Price. Rosenthal had the bulldog edition of the *Times* delivered to Price's office with the Ronan story. Lindsay was "absolutely shocked." Toward midnight, Lindsay caught up with his wife and friends at Sardi's. When they returned to their hotel, he told Mary that he was going to run.

On Wednesday morning New Yorkers read the lead story in the *Times,* whose headline was "Lindsay, in Shift, Considers Race Against Wagner." Price received his front-page lead story, but with only a two-column headline. No one was quoted in the article besides Price, who said Lindsay "was deeply troubled about the condition of the city and believes it is his responsibility to offer the people a viable alternative to what they now have at City Hall." Lindsay, Ronan wrote, "could not be reached for comment." While New Yorkers were reading about the man who might be their next mayor over their morning coffee, Lindsay and Price had a breakfast meeting with Jock Whitney and Walter Thayer of the *Herald Tribune*. Despite being angry that Price had given the exclusive story to the rival *Times*, Whitney and Thayer assured Lindsay that enough money could be raised for the campaign.[30]

Republicans saw this as a once-in-a-generation chance to win City Hall, and liberal reformers were looking for their elusive white knight. Lindsay's candidacy was one of the most exciting political events in New York politics in recent years. The timing of Price's Machiavellian scheming was perfect. No other Republicans challenged Lindsay for the nomination.[31]

On Thursday morning, Price planned visits for Lindsay to all five boroughs; the candidate was to read his declaration of candidacy, written by Price, at each stop. Lindsay's long odyssey to City Hall began at 11:30 A.M. at the Concourse Plaza Hotel in the Bronx and ended late in the afternoon at the Hotel Roosevelt in Manhattan. At each stop Lindsay reiterated his belief that "conscience and duty" compelled him to run for mayor. Whereas other men entered politics for fame or personal gain, Lindsay personified what Richard Hofstadter had earlier termed the "indigenous Yankee-Protestant" political tradition that "argued that political life ought to be run, to a greater degree than it was, in accordance with general principles and abstract laws apart from . . . personal needs, and expressed a common feeling that government should be in good part an effort to moralize the lives of individuals."[32]

In his declaration speech, Lindsay argued that under the "tired management" of the Democratic Party, New York City had become "a place that is no longer for people or for living. In these long years of one-party rule we have witnessed the decline and fall of New York City. We have seen its strength diminish, its pre-eminent place in the world of cities lost and its people beset with hopelessness and despair." Lindsay went beyond the idea of a "city in crisis" and declared that New Yorkers were witnessing "the decline and fall" of their city. He listed the city's failures in pessimistic, almost apocalyptic, terms. The city's air was polluted, its hospitals neglected, its housing expensive, its schools run down, its parks dirty and dangerous, "crime, brutality and narcotics" were "rampant," its culture was in decline, and its middle-class was fleeing for the suburbs. Throughout the campaign, Lindsay would rarely veer from his theme that New York was a city in danger, driven there by twenty years of Democratic rule. In addition, Lindsay ominously warned that individual rights had become so neglected that there was "despair and revolt among many of our people." He reiterated his belief that his candidacy was meant to signal a new approach to cities by Republicans, an approach he felt was absolutely necessary for the rebirth of the national party.[33]

Lindsay's announcement landed him on the covers of *Life*, *Look*, and *Newsweek*. *Life* wrote of the Republican candidate, "With youthful verve and the long-legged grace of a heron, John Vliet Lindsay . . . strode into the race for Mayor of New York and Republicans all over the country broke into ear-to-ear smiles." The *New York Times* headlined its story "A Man Who Can Be Mayor," while the *Herald Tribune*, rehashing its argument about Democratic culpability for the "city in crisis," took the opportunity of Lindsay's candidacy to lash out at "one-party rule insensitive to its failings, arrogant in its power, contemptuous of challenge. A one-party rule that clings to patronage and pelf while the city's spirit crumbles." In words that would later haunt Lindsay, the editorial praised him as the "choice to break the city's own cycle of despair in which ever-mounting budgets are offered not to bring rebirth and renewal, but simply to keep abreast of ever-mounting crises—crises which the spiral of borrowing and taxing, taxing and borrowing itself exacerbate."[34]

THE DEMOCRATS

Despite the good press, this was not to be a political coronation for Lindsay. Wagner remained a formidable opponent. When asked whether he could beat Lindsay, Wagner confidently replied, "Sure I can beat him. Who ever heard of a Republican winning in New York City?" Nevertheless, Wagner's twelve years as mayor had taken a physical and emotional toll. The death of his wife, Susan, in March 1964 from lung cancer hit Wagner hard and increased his concern for his two sons, Duncan, eighteen, and Robert Jr., twenty-one. There was much debate as to whether Wagner would run for a fourth term. In fact, so sure was Bob Price that Wagner would not run that he bet Lindsay a hundred dollars that Wagner would not run. Sensing Wagner's vulnerability, some Democrats were already looking for a primary fight if Wagner stayed in. I. D. Robbins, an independent Democrat and housing reformer, was the first to threaten a challenge, but he said he would drop out if Lindsay or Javits ran on a fusion ticket. The reform Democrat William Fitts Ryan, a congressman from Manhattan's West Side and a frequent Lindsay ally in Congress, also considered a challenge. On June 3, Clifton C. Carter of the Democratic National Committee wrote to President Johnson that the Brooklyn Congressman Abe Multer had come to his office hoping Johnson would encourage Wagner to withdraw. Carter predicted that Wagner would withdraw and expressed hope that Abe Beame would be the Democratic nominee, since "he is very popular, a good Johnson man, and the strongest anti–Bobby Kennedy man of the lot." Carter hoped a Beame win "would be the main bulwark to prevent turning the state over to Bobby."[35]

Wagner kept his decision under wraps. Only his longtime press secretary, Debs Myers, and his executive assistant, Julius C. C. Edelstein, knew of his decision. When Myers announced shortly before noon on June 10 that Wagner would take no questions after his press conference, reporters took this as an ominous sign. A few minutes after noon, Wagner said in no uncertain terms, stopping numerous times to dry his eyes, that "my decision is to end my service as Mayor on Jan. 1, 1966. I shall not seek or agree to re-election." He wanted to spend more time with his sons and keep a promise he had given his dying wife that this would be his last term. There was also talk of remarriage, to Deputy Mayor Edward Cavanaugh's sister, and Wagner did not want to start a new marriage while grappling with the problems of New York City. His decision was "final and irrevocable."[36]

Wagner left a fractured Democratic Party in the wake of his decision. Assemblyman Stanley Steingut, who ran the Brooklyn machine, and former Congressman Charlie Buckley, who ran the Bronx machine, both remained angry at Wagner for his repudiation of the Democratic bosses in 1961. On the other side were reform Democrats disillusioned with the direction the city had taken. Wagner's support was limited to the Manhattan machine led by J. Raymond Jones and Assemblyman Moses Weinstein's Queens clubhouse, as well as the Liberal Party. These fissures revealed more than just personal rivalries; they were symptomatic of larger changes in American liberalism and its approach to urban problems.

Wagner was a bridge between what the political scientist James Q. Wilson had called "cosmopolitan" amateur politicians and "local" professional politicians. The growing strength of the Democratic reform movement made Wagner's position untenable. Columnists Rowland Evans and Robert Novak called Wagner the "loneliest politician" because his repudiation of the Democratic machine had alienated "regular" Democrats, yet his uninspired leadership had turned off "reform" Democrats. This time, as Evans and Novak pointed out, Wagner did not have Herbert Lehman or Eleanor Roosevelt, the king and queen of New York reform politics, around to help. Both had died during Wagner's third term.[37]

The chasm between "regular" and "reform" Democrats was as wide as the distance separating the worlds of the white, working-class, home-owner in Queens and the Ivy League reform lawyer living in Greenwich Village or the Upper West Side. Though vastly outnumbered (in 1965 there were only fifty reform clubs, with approximately 25,000 members), reformers were better educated and more articulate than their parochial counterparts and, more important, had the media behind them. Only the *Daily News* represented the voice of working-class New Yorkers.[38]

By the early 1960s, Wagner found his type of New Deal liberalism insufficient to deal with two components of the Democratic coalition: upper-middle-class reformers and blacks. The difference between Wagner's liberalism and the new liberalism was made clear in the controversy over the Lower Manhattan Expressway. The exressway was the brainchild of Robert Moses, who from the 1920s to the 1960s oversaw the transformation of New York City and Long Island by means of a web of highways, bridges, parks, and housing projects. Many of his projects gave pride of place to the automobile.

Moses planned an elevated highway across Broome Street that would bring traffic from the Holland Tunnel to the Williamsburg and Manhattan Bridges. The areas that were to be sacrificed to make way for the expressway included Little Italy and the neighborhood now known as SoHo. The road would, Moses claimed, have eased traffic and further "modernized" the city.[39] The highway, a classic Moses project, was in many ways typical of traditional New Deal public works projects. Unions supported it because of jobs, and the expressway had Wagner's support. By the 1950s, however, disillusionment with Moses and his projects was growing. During the 1950s, Moses had angered upper-middle-class New Yorkers with his high-handedness in paving over a playground in Central Park for a parking lot and opposing Joseph Papp's free Shakespeare productions in Central Park. Moses' urban renewal plans, once heralded for cleaning up slums, were now criticized for corruption and their negative impact upon the city's blacks and Puerto Ricans.

By the mid-sixties, a new sensibility had arisen in the city, owing in part to the publication, in 1961, of Jane Jacobs's book, *The Life and Death of Great American Cities*. Jacobs argued that cities and neighborhoods were organic creatures that needed to be nourished, not demolished. In proposing the expressway, Moses ran into a storm of criticism from those who opposed his emphasis on automobiles, favored small-scale neighborhoods, and supported the fledgling historic preservation movement.[40]

Another factor in the changing political complexion of the city, the civil rights movement, gave to racial issues a heretofore unknown prominence. Inspired by protests against Jim Crow in the South, New York's black leaders pressured the city to integrate schools and investigate police brutality. The underside of these initiatives was race riots. In the summer of 1964, New York received an advanced warning of growing racial unrest—"the fire this time"—when a riot exploded in Harlem after a white policeman shot a black youth. Though Wagner had always been sympathetic to blacks and Puerto Ricans, the aggressive style of the civil rights movement clashed with Wagner's personality. The civil rights movement posited a form of black exceptionalism that put the problems of blacks in a special category. The Irish, Germans, Italians, and Jews never demanded that their children attend the same schools as more well-to-do "Americans," nor did they try to force their way into restrictive trade unions. Not only did the demands of blacks create resentment among whites, but traditional politicians like Wagner simply did not know how to handle such demands. Wagner knew how to build schools and deal with the teachers' union, but he was at a loss as to how to integrate the city's schools.

As a result of Wagner's confusion, critics viciously attacked him. His Eisenhower-era mix of New Deal liberalism, moderation, and plodding respectability now seemed unfashionable. The *Herald Tribune* columnist Dick Schaap summed up the indictment of Wagner as "nothing more than a neighborhood politician. . . . His vision ends at the wall of a political clubhouse. . . . He is the mayor of New York City and he belongs in Newark." Jimmy Breslin thought of Wagner as a "dumpy, narrow man." Murray Kempton called Wagner "a parochial man," saying "to find his like we must go back to the little margraves of the German principalities of the 18th century." Jack Newfield and Paul Du Brul thought that "Wagner's fatal weaknesses were passivity and procrastination. He didn't like conflict. He thought chicken soup and schmoozing could make the problems go away. The motto he learned from his father . . . was 'When in doubt, don't.'" When it became a slur to be called a neighborhood politician, Wagner knew it was time to bow out.[41]

Democrats now scrambled to decide who would receive a nomination that in past years had been an automatic ticket to Gracie Mansion. The Democratic race quickly became a four-man contest among City Council President Paul Screvane, Comptroller Abe Beame, Congressman William Fitts Ryan, and the lawyer Paul O'Dwyer. All lacked charisma and failed to energize the public. The race was essentially between Screvane and Beame, with O'Dwyer and Ryan representing the liberal reform elements of the party, a distinctly minority faction in 1965. O'Dwyer was the younger brother of the disgraced former mayor, Bill O'Dwyer, who had left office in 1950 amid accusations of ties to organized crime and later surfaced in Mexico. A radical lawyer born in Ireland, O'Dwyer was known for defending union miners and Southern blacks.

Ryan, a mercurial politician from Manhattan's West Side, was beloved by reform Democrats but never caught fire outside the tight circle of reform clubs. During a summer water shortage, Ryan managed to arrange a photo-op at a supposed water leak in the northwestern section of Central Park, where he stood in a gushing stream of water with his pants rolled up to his knees. It got him some good publicity, but it was not enough to compensate for both his lack of recognition beyond the West Side and his less-than-engaging personality. He did manage to win the support of the Committee for Democratic Voters (CDV), the voice of the city's reform movement, which had been founded by Eleanor Roosevelt and Herbert Lehman. But prominent reformers such as Thomas Finletter, Francis W. H. Adams, and Mrs. Herbert Lehman backed Screvane, as did many other reformers who had been close to Wagner. Two Bronx reform Democratic Congressmen—James Scheuer and Jonathan Bingham—also backed Screvane. In the end, each local reform club voted independently, and roughly half voted to back Screvane.

Screvane was the early favorite and displayed the confidence of a front-runner. A former sanitation man who had worked his way up the Democratic hierarchy, Screvane was, by association with Wagner, the de facto head of the moderate reform movement that Wagner had created in 1961. He was widely seen as Wagner's handpicked successor, having been chosen in 1961 as his running mate, for the post of City Council president. Beame, who also had been Wagner's running mate in 1961, for comptroller, had a more uneasy relationship with the mayor. Closely allied with the Bronx party boss, Charlie Buckley (no relation to William F.), and Stanley Steingut, the party boss of Beame's home borough of Brooklyn, Beame was seen as the candidate of the party clubhouses.

Beame, a Brooklyn Jew, chose his running mates to balance the ticket by ethnicity, by religion, and by borough. He chose Frank O'Connor, an Irish Catholic from Queens, for City Council president and Mario Procaccino, an Italian Catholic from the Bronx, for comptroller. Screvane's picks were more unorthodox. He used the same guidelines as Beame, but in addition tried to pick people who had little association with the unpopular Wagner and would offer youth and vigor to match Lindsay. For comptroller the Queens native, himself half-Irish and half-Italian, chose Orin Lehman, forty, a handsome, crippled war hero and grandnephew of the former governor. For City Council president Screvane chose Daniel Patrick Moynihan, a thirty-eight-year-old Harvard professor working in Lyndon Johnson's Department of Labor. Moynihan, an Irish Catholic who grew up in Manhattan's Hell's Kitchen, on the West Side in the forties and fifties, helped balance the ticket, but his status as an intellectual and his poor speaking style hampered his effectiveness. (Both Ryan and O'Dwyer, the two most liberal candidates, included black Democrats on their tickets.)

Screvane, though running ahead of Beame for much of the primary, ran a bad campaign. He lost the endorsements of two groups that had been key to Wagner's political success: the Liberal Party and the Central Labor Council, the city's most powerful labor organization. Although the putative candidate of Wagnerian reform, Screvane was the most conservative of the four candidates. His equivocation on integrating the city's unions and his attacks on the Mobilization for Youth poverty program for allegedly harboring Communists and subversives damaged his reputation among liberal Democrats. Throughout the campaign, Beame, the diminutive accountant, constantly attacked the still-unpopular Wagner, calling Screvane a "rubber stamp" for Wagner's policies and portraying himself as a paragon of fiscal responsibility. Beame's primary campaign's slogan, a direct slap at Mayor Wagner's indecision, which was legendary, was the rather uninspiring "Vote for decision at City Hall."[42]

A TORY FOR MAYOR?

This was not to be a traditional campaign. On June 24, William F. Buckley Jr., the thirty-nine-year-old founder and editor of the conservative *National Review*, announced that he would run for mayor as the candidate of the four-year-old Conservative Party. If Wagner's difficulties showed the cracks within New Deal liberalism, Buckley's entry in the race was a harbinger of future trends.

The seeds of a new American conservatism could be found in two books published within a decade of each other. The European émigré Friedrich Hayek's *The Road to Serfdom*, published in 1944, made the argument for economic conservatism by defending individual liberty and capitalism. Published in 1953, Russell Kirk's *The Conservative Mind* laid the foundation for a social conservatism rooted in tradition, natural law, and religion. Yet the actual birth of postwar American conservatism should be credited to Buckley's 1955 founding of the *National Review* magazine. Buckley, whose book *God and Man at Yale* (1951) roiled the liberal establishment with its denunciation of his alma mater for its growing secularism and affinity to big government, was joined at his new magazine by assorted conservative writers as well as ex-liberals, ex-Trotskyites, and ex-Communists. Dedicated to the principles of anticommunism, free-market economics, and a traditionalism rooted in Roman Catholicism, *National Review* brought together the conservative forces that had been left in disarray by the Great Depression and created an intellectual framework for attacks upon liberalism. It also gave respectability to conservatism, an ideology that had been seriously tainted by European fascism. In response, a grassroots political conservatism began to grow with the creation of such groups as the Young Americans for Freedom (1960) and the New York State Conservative Party (1961).[43]

No man better represented this phenomenon than Buckley. An Irish Catholic whose wealth was derived from his family's oil business, Buckley lived in Stamford, Connecticut, and kept an apartment in Manhattan. He spoke in the fast-disappearing, clipped accent of East Coast WASPs. A champion debater at Yale, Buckley laced his speech with obscure words, enjoyed verbal jousting, and relished his adroitness with the English language (as well as Latin, French, and Spanish). Though almost as tall as Lindsay and exactly four years younger (they shared the same birthday, November 24), Buckley did not attract the kind of glamorous comparisons as Lindsay. As one commentator wrote, the conservative was "all Tory hauteur laced with wit." While the voice imparted the seriousness of an Oxford don, the body implied a mischievous impishness. When he spoke, his body contorted, his face puckered, his mouth twisted, and his eyes would roll, then widen and gleam with delight at one of his own well-placed barbs against an unsuspecting foe. Though many dismissed Buckley as a mere entertainer, he saw himself as a messenger of ideas. Buckley told his advisers that he wanted his campaign for the mayoralty "to be a campaign of ideas. After all, we're here to really articulate ideas, and I don't want any of these bumper stickers, balloons, and straw hats. We don't need that kind of stuff. We'll just do it on the ideas." Buckley was on a mission he had begun fourteen years earlier: to make conservatism a respectable and powerful alternative to American liberalism.[44]

Shortly before the formal announcement of his candidacy, Buckley wrote a piece entitled "Mayor, Anyone?" Agreeing with Lindsay and others that New York was a city in crisis, Buckley argued that New York and other cities were increasingly becoming "unpleasant and costly. It is unpleasant to have to pay a high cost for unpleasantness." Buckley then put forth a ten-point platform for a potential mayoral campaign: legalize drugs and gambling; open up the taxi business to all noncriminals with cars; require welfare recipients to perform public service work for the city; encourage open-shop laws regarding unions; form enterprise zones for black and Puerto Rican businessmen in depressed areas; enforce tougher juvenile crime laws; grant communities more power in policing their own streets; and end school busing. Buckley later claimed that the title of the piece had been foisted on him by his sister Priscilla, an editor at *National Review*, and that he felt "no reader in his right mind would be likely to infer from the streamer that Buckley was actually announcing that he would run for mayor and that this was his trial balloon." But Buckley has also been quoted as saying that he "reached that decision [to run for mayor] in forty-five minutes after" a speech he made two months earlier, in April 1965, to nearly 6,000 Catholic policemen (one quarter of the police force) at the New York Police Department's Holy Name Society Communion breakfast after Mass at St. Patrick's Cathedral.[45]

Given Buckley's reputation as a wordsmith and a controversialist, it is no surprise that one of the major factors in his run for mayor was a speech. With Mayor Wagner and Police Commissioner Michael Murphy in attendance, Buckley attempted to link rising crime rates with the larger issues of the decline in traditional values and authority. In the shadow of recent Supreme Court decisions like *Mapp v. Ohio* (1961), which restricted police powers, Buckley decried the atmosphere in which "the doctrine that a man is innocent until proved guilty seems to have been stretched to mean that the apprehending officials are guilty unless proved innocent," and where "it is considered [in New York City] far less extraordinary that a criminal should break a law, than that a criminal should be apprehended for doing so." In this world turned upside down, Buckley saw a society "in which order and values are disintegrating . . . [and] the wrath of the unruly falls with special focus on the symbols of authority, of continuity, of tradition." Buckley observed that this was an age "infatuated with revolution and ideology." Not only were the police the prime targets of those "principal agents of revolution," Buckley told his audience of Catholic policemen, but so was the Catholic Church, with its "unyielding devotion to eternal truths which resist the plastic manipulations of the willful revolutionaries." Attacks upon the police were therefore linked with attacks upon the Church; the enemies of one were the enemies of the other. When a policeman looked at the protester shouting at him from across a barricade, Buckley implied, he was also looking at an enemy of the Catholic Church.[46]

What got Buckley into trouble were remarks he made about the murder of a white Detroit housewife, Viola Liuzzo, who was in Alabama doing civil rights work, and about a clash between police and civil rights protesters in Selma, Alabama. His remarks about Liuzzo were designed to tweak the press by asking why the murder "occupied the front page from one end to another, if newspapers are concerned with the unusual, the unexpected? Didn't the killing merely confirm precisely what everyone has been saying about the South?" His remarks about the Selma police were in keeping with the overall thesis of the speech: again criticizing the media, Buckley argued that though viewers saw ample pictures of police beating protesters with clubs, they saw nothing of the confrontation that preceded the melee, as taunting protesters defied police orders. Buckley was being cute, especially with his remarks about Liuzzo, but he hit upon what was fast becoming the third rail of American politics—race.

Though his audience of Catholic policemen warmly received Buckley's words, the New York press did not. An April 5, 1965, *Herald Tribune* story by Fred Ferretti was headlined "6,000 N.Y. Police Applaud a Defense of Selma Cops." The *Post* and *Times* followed suit and were joined by a chorus of protests from civil rights groups and liberals. New York State Supreme Court Justice Samuel Hofstadter sent a telegram to Police Commissioner Murphy complaining that "5600 members of the force cheered an attack on national civil rights leaders that would have done credit to the most rabid race-baiters." After publicly condemning the speech, former Brooklyn Dodger Jackie Robinson, a Rockefeller Republican, wrote Buckley that he was not surprised by his "upholding the gestapo-like troops of little Governor Wallace . . . considering the kind of philosophy that you have constantly projected. It's my belief that this philosophy poses a distinct threat to our democracy." Robinson believed the threat to be so dangerous that he demanded an investigation of John Birch Society members in the police department. Mayor Wagner distanced himself from the speech, but did not specifically condemn it.[47]

It was no accident that the speech was delivered before a Catholic police group. Catholics had been some of the staunchest supporters of the New Deal, yet their innate conservatism was pulling them away from more liberal members of the coalition. Catholics, members of a hierarchical church, were more comfortable with authority than Protestants and Jews.

Buckley's speech was early evidence of the existence of a "silent majority," more than four years before the term was used by President Richard Nixon. Buckley told the assembled policemen that although "the voices of the one seem sometimes so very much noisier than the voices of the other, that other world, the world of sensible men and women, looks on you with pride and gratitude. Sustained by the implicit gratitude of the people, you are also sustained no doubt during this holy season by the knowledge of the silence with which the author of all values walked during his own days on earth."

Buckley also linked the travails of the victims of the "noisy minority" to those of Jesus, who suffered from the slings of official, putatively enlightened opinion. The aristocratic and loquacious Buckley was an unlikely spokesman for the "silent majority" of working- and middle-class Americans. In seeking to awaken the feelings of these "sensible men and women," Buckley made liberals uneasy.[48]

Early in the campaign, most commentators felt Buckley would take Republican votes from Lindsay. It was commonly thought that Buckley had entered the race as a personal vendetta against Lindsay for his heretical liberal Republicanism and his abandonment of Goldwater the previous year. Buckley denied the charge, claiming he and his magazine were hostile to all liberal Republicans, not just Lindsay, and that *National Review* had published only one negative article about the New York congressman. Buckley suggested he would be less critical of Lindsay if the congressman decided to become a Democrat. To bolster the claim that his feelings for Lindsay were not personal, Buckley pointed out that his older brother Jim was a close friend of David Lindsay's from their days at Yale, had been an usher at his wedding, and was godfather to one of his children.

Buckley saw his race as a battle for the soul of the Republican Party rather than as the expression of a personal vendetta. He wanted to make clear that Lindsay's brand of Republicanism was "no more representative of Republican thought than the Democratic Party in Mississippi is representative of the Democratic Party nationally." Despite his protests, Buckley's personal attacks on Lindsay throughout the campaign revealed deeper feelings. Conservative Party cofounder and Buckley adviser Kieran O'Doherty thought Buckley possessed "a special animus toward John Lindsay." Buckley biographer John Judis wrote, "Lindsay . . . in Buckley's mind, had enjoyed political success as much on the basis of his social connections and his WASP good looks as on the basis of his intelligence and political acumen. Buckley wanted not only to cut short Lindsay's rise to the presidency, but to expose what he believed to be his lack of depth and intelligence."[49]

Buckley called Lindsay's ten-point proposal for the economic rejuvenation of New York City "the most conspicuous effrontery on human intelligence I have ever . . . seen" and "sheer and utter rhetorical hokum." In the heat of the campaign, Lindsay criticized Buckley's book, *God and Man at Yale*, as "badly written." When informed of the comment, Buckley replied, "I ask Mr. Lindsay: 'How can you tell?' " When Lindsay questioned Buckley's running for New York office while residing in Connecticut, Buckley retorted, "I don't know why Mr. Lindsay is so hostile to Connecticut. Perhaps because he went there to be educated and, for manifest reasons, is displeased with the results." When asked what issue he scored hardest against Lindsay, Buckley replied, "Mr. Lindsay's pretentiousness."[50]

After gaining the approval of the Conservative Party chairman, J. Daniel Mahoney, Buckley made his formal announcement on June 24. Mixing wit, sarcasm, and earnestness, Buckley announced that despite being a Republican, he would be the Conservative Party nominee for mayor "because the Republican designation is not, in New York, available nowadays to anyone in the mainstream of Republican opinion." After excoriating Lindsay for "stressing his acceptability to the leftwardmost party in New York, the Liberal Party," Buckley then moved on to his next target: Mayor Wagner. Agreeing with Lindsay and other critics about New York's plight, Buckley argued that "after twelve years of his attentions, New York boils with frustration, injustice, and demoralization." Lindsay could not have said it better.[51]

Buckley pinpointed the root cause of New York's decline in the desire of politicians to "satisfy major voting blocks [*sic*] in their collective capacities." What good was it, Buckley asked rhetorically, if an electrician made fifteen dollars an hour but could not afford an apartment because his rent reflected the cost of paying an electrician fifteen dollars per hour? Buckley placed "no single objective ahead of the necessity to control" New York's rising crime rate. In addition, Buckley took pointed jabs at black leaders like Adam Clayton Powell Jr. and James Baldwin, arguing that "we cannot help the Negro by adjourning our standards as to what is, and what is not, the proper behavior for human beings."

Lindsay's assistant press secretary, Oliver Pilat, saw this as an "opaque highbrow appeal . . . to certain lowbrow prejudice," but in fact it is hard to believe Buckley was using "code words" to gain votes. Winning was not really the goal of his campaign. When asked how many votes he expected to receive, Buckley irreverently responded, "Conservatively speaking, one." The only positive comment on his entry into the race came from the *Daily News*, which proclaimed itself "delighted to see Bill Buckley jump into the fight, and thereby stir the local 'liberals' of all categories to slavering, slobbering rage. They've been asking for this sort of challenge from a fearless conservative for a long time, and we're overjoyed to see them get it at last."[52]

Buckley moved quickly to fill out his ticket. Instead of adding known political figures from various backgrounds to balance it, Buckley chose two middle-aged, middle-class white Irish Catholics with no political experience: Rosemary Gunning from Queens for City Council president and Hugh Markey, a Staten Island accountant and president of the Staten Island Zoo, for comptroller. Mrs. Gunning was well known as the executive secretary of the Parents and Taxpayers Association (PAT), a group created to defend the concept of neighborhood schools and fight school busing. (She was elected in 1968 as a Republican-Conservative to the state assembly.) The all–Irish-Catholic ticket was taboo in modern New York City politics—but Buckley argued that he did not even know Mrs. Gunning's religion until he read it in the newspaper.[53]

To Buckley, who was carrying on Goldwater's national campaign from the previous year, the word "conservative" meant more than reactionary stand-pattism. It now defined an increasingly distinct political ideology. Buckley's campaign was based on four political tenets. First, he argued that law and order had to be restored. "The problem in New York," stated a Buckley campaign brochure, "is *too much crime*, not too much police brutality." Second, Buckley wanted to reduce taxes and government spending in order to restore fiscal responsibility. Third, he wanted to reform welfare. Lastly, Buckley called for an end to school busing and a return to neighborhood schools. "The duty of our public schools is to educate. Our schools should not be turned into laboratories for social experiments." These themes, though specific to New York, summarize much of the domestic ideology of modern conservatism.[54]

In addition to these more sober themes, Buckley included one campaign position that was uncharacteristically nonideological. To help ease Manhattan's traffic congestion, Buckley recommended the construction of a bikeway above Second Avenue from 125th Street to First Street, connected to crosstown spurs. Not only would it ease traffic, but it would also stimulate New Yorkers to healthful exercise. Many people mocked "Buckley's Bikeway," adding to the belief that his campaign was merely a dilettante's fancy. But the idea, strange as it seemed coming from a conservative, was oddly practical and ahead of its time in predicting the fitness boom and the need for alternatives to automobile-clogged streets. Despite this appealing quirkiness, Buckley still scared liberals. The *Post*'s James Wechsler called the Buckley campaign an example of "right-wing primitivism."[55]

Buckley's presence allowed Lindsay to use the sledgehammers of both anti-bossism and ideological liberalism. The former appealed to traditional reform constituents who wanted clean government and fiscal responsibility—the city's business elite and middle-class homeowners. The latter allowed Lindsay to shore up his support among liberal reformers, blacks, and

Jews—all traditional Democratic voters. To Wechsler, "Lindsay's candidacy was essentially a test of the city's instincts; it was a roll call of decency and dignity." In the face of Buckley's challenge, Lindsay presented himself as a man who would protect New Yorkers from a dangerous pseudo-Nazi right-wing movement.[56]

What Buckley signaled by his choice of running mates was that he would not make appeals to religious or ethnic identity in order to win votes. He said he knew nothing "harder in politics than to escape the coils of racial and religious opportunism." He chastised Lindsay for pandering to racial and ethnic factions, which Buckley thought the "equivalent of plopping an Indian warchief's headdress on his head, puffing a peace pipe, and saying something on the order of, Me-um like-um Navajo people." At his first press conference, Buckley laid out the rules: "I will not go to Irish centers and go dancing. I will not go to Jewish centers and eat blintzes, nor will I go to Italian centers and pretend to speak Italian." Buckley's attitude toward ethnic politics, noted John Judis, "was the same as his attitude toward his own ethnicity: He was not Irish, but American." Buckley's ambivalence vis-à-vis the obvious fault lines of New York's ethnic politics gave his campaign a surreal feel. At the press conference he called to announce his running mates, Buckley was asked what he would do if elected. "Demand a recount," he declared. This comment, one of the most widely quoted of all his campaign pronouncements, gave the impression that Buckley was not a serious candidate. Unfair though this impression may have been, it was one that Buckley could never quite shake.[57]

"HE IS FRESH AND EVERYONE ELSE IS TIRED"

Though mayoral campaigns usually did not begin in earnest until after the September Democratic primary, Lindsay began campaigning almost from the time of his May announcement. There was plenty of work to do, mostly in three areas: fund-raising, building an independent Lindsay organization, and what Bob Price called "retail campaigning." It is estimated that the Lindsay campaign eventually raised close to $2 million at a time when there were few rules concerning campaign donations. Contributors included the city's business and social elite, people like John Loeb, Walter Thayer, Mrs. Winthrop Aldrich, Mrs. Vincent Astor, William Paley, Paul Warburg, Mrs. August Belmont, Bennett Cerf, Harold Vanderbilt, DeWitt Wallace, Henry Ford II, Mr. and Mrs. Nicholas Biddle, General Lucius Clay, and Roger Blough, the former head of U.S. Steel. Nelson Rockefeller's $500,000 donation led to charges that the governor was bankrolling Lindsay. Through a campaign spokesman, Lindsay made clear that he didn't want Rockefeller on the campaign trail, he didn't want the governor making stump speeches on his behalf, and he didn't want any money from him.[58]

In later years, Lindsay tried to explain his disavowal of Rockefeller's aid: "It was not in their interests or in my interest to have that widely broadcast and become the dominant theme of the campaign." Lindsay bitterly complained: "Maybe Nelson figured that if he was responsible for that much money, he owned you. Money is power, and people are afraid of it." One former Rockefeller aide noted that the Governor had a way of "consuming" people around him, and Lindsay wanted to keep the meddling Rockefeller at arm's length. Price believes Lindsay did not want anything to do with the governor during the campaign "because Rockefeller didn't listen to him." Because the two liberal Republicans disagreed on so little, Price said, "most of the fights were ego fights," petty conflicts between two proud, stubborn politicians.

Price also wanted to keep Rockefeller out of the race, but for different reasons. One obvious way the Lindsay campaign could stress its nonpartisan nature would be to distance itself from the Republican governor. Also, Lindsay's people wanted to localize the campaign and feared that if they brought out big Republican guns like Rockefeller, the Democrats would retaliate with members of the Kennedy clan. In 1965, Rockefeller's popularity was in the tank. His 1964 primary loss to Goldwater, his divorce and remarriage, and his imposition of a state sales tax had all tarnished his image. His entire family and nearly every one of his aides pushed him not to run for reelection in 1966.[59]

For his part, Rockefeller called Price a number of times and "was very hurt" by the disavowal. He had not expected that kind of rebuff from Lindsay after making such a generous financial contribution. "Well, not all investments work out," Rockefeller recalled in a 1975 interview. "I didn't do it [the $500,000 campaign contribution] as a personal investment. I did it because I thought he was the best person to be mayor of the city of New York on the Republican side who had a chance of getting elected. Well that didn't get us off to the best start." Hugh Morrow, a Rockefeller aide on loan to the Lindsay campaign, put the matter more bluntly: "That $500,000 was one of the worst investments in the history of American politics as far as Nelson Rockefeller was concerned." As one Rockefeller biographer noted, Lindsay's rejection of the governor "was a new experience for Nelson Rockefeller; he had expected gratitude, or at least deference, from Lindsay. But the younger man's outright denial of his patron was insufferable." Rockefeller was so angry that Lindsay had publicly denied his generous support that he arranged for Emmet John Hughes, a confidant and *Newsweek* columnist, to publicize the governor's side of the story. When Oliver Pilat asked Lindsay about Hughes's contention that Rockefeller had lent Lindsay $500,000, Lindsay responded, "Hogwash, hogwash."[60]

Price could have chosen to fashion a campaign around a barrage of television advertising that would showcase the attractive, articulate candidate, but he didn't do this. Because the existing Republican organization was weak—with the exception of Vincent Albano's Manhattan Republicans—and tended to be at best ambivalent about Lindsay, something else needed to be created. Price chose to marshal the campaign's resources toward old-fashioned "retail" campaigning—based on grassroots neighborhood organizing—at least for the first half of the campaign. The campaign focused less on television advertising, direct mail, or polling, and concentrated on building a storefront organization throughout the city to replace the old political machine. Price set up 122 Lindsay storefronts throughout the city, manned by 25,000 volunteers. The strategy received much criticism, but Price convinced Lindsay he knew the city well enough to pull off this block-by-block campaign. The historian Chris McNickle estimated that the Lindsay campaign spent only about 20 percent, or $200,000, of its $2 million budget on television and radio advertising. Price himself believed that the campaign spent about $300,000 on television. [61]

The strategy also called for introducing Lindsay to as many New Yorkers as possible. It was important to convince voters that Republicans—at least this Republican—did not have horns and a tail. The summer campaign was not focused on issues, but on getting Lindsay in front of the people and in the papers as much as possible. Crowds at the beach clubs of Brooklyn and the Bronx were ready-made. There was Liza Minnelli singing on stage with Lindsay; Sammy Davis Jr. campaigning with Lindsay at Coney Island; Lindsay walking the streets of Brooklyn's black ghettos, surrounded by adoring black children; Lindsay in his bathing suit, showing off his lean, athletic body while diving into a pool in the Rockaways. He pressed the flesh in Jewish neighborhoods in the Bronx and spoke to lukewarm crowds of Irish and Italians in Staten Island and Queens. These walking tours showed the candidate at his best: relaxed, warm, funny, and caring. Though a proper, even prudish, man in public, Lindsay was known for having a flirtatious side in private. In working-class Bushwick, Brooklyn, Lindsay spotted two beautiful young women leaning out of a third-floor window, one with a man and the other alone. Lindsay kept looking up at the women, smiling, then looked at his watch and yelled, "I'll be right up!" Even when thousands of New Yorkers fled the summer heat, they could not escape John V. Lindsay. In the last weekend of July, he was trawling for votes in the resort towns of the Catskills in upstate New York, the summer vacation retreat for thousands of Jewish New Yorkers. In August, he was on the beaches of Nassau County with Phyllis Diller; early September found Lindsay stumping in the Pennsylvania Poconos, another Jewish retreat.[62]

Lindsay seemed to be everywhere. His campaign possessed a spirit of idealism, whimsy, and innocence that has rarely been seen in New York politics. JOHN LINDSAY IS SUPERCALIFRAGILISTICEXPIALIDOCIOUS, declared a billboard in Midtown Manhattan's Bryant Park. Posters appeared all over the city showing a smiling, jacketless Lindsay confidently striding down a slightly dreary New York street. His white shirt, with pen in breast pocket, was appropriately wrinkled for such a man on the move. Behind him were smiling black children, a sign for Danto's Stetson Hats, and a man in a suit in the distant background walking resolutely ahead. Above Lindsay's head was the unofficial motto of the campaign, taken from a Murray Kempton column: "He is fresh and everyone else is tired." The campaign attracted journalists from, among other places, Italy, Peru, West Germany, England, and Denmark, who seemed to find in Lindsay a successor to John Kennedy. Lindsay was big, but was he big enough to win in a Democratic town?

While his charisma was drawing international attention, Lindsay's positions on the issues began to draw the attention of American liberals. A July article by Yale Law School professor Alexander M. Bickel in *The New Republic* signaled the potential substantive importance of Lindsay's candidacy. Bickel hoped a Lindsay victory would not only resuscitate the national Republican Party (along sufficiently progressive lines, of course) but also provide a bully pulpit from which to vent a sense of moral outrage over the crisis of the city. Bickel hoped Lindsay would provide the leadership on race relations that Wagner had not by integrating the city's schools and "build[ing] attractive housing to draw the middle class into ghettos . . . and low-income housing outside the ghetto." Similarly, Lindsay found praise from James Wechsler, the liberal editorial-page editor of the *Post*. Wechsler felt Lindsay's liberalism was symbolized by two fountain pens given to the congressman by President Johnson—one for supporting the 1964 Civil Rights Act and the other for supporting the 1965 legislation that created Medicare. Wechsler contrasted this to Abe Beame, "whose voice to the best of my knowledge and recollection was never gallantly raised in local conflicts such as the school integration crisis." While traditional reform themes continued to dominate Lindsay's campaign, the growing influence of liberal ideology on the issues of Vietnam, poverty, and race was also evident.[63]

In a speech before a group of Manhattan lawyers one week after announcing for mayor, John Lindsay proposed to revise the Civilian Complaint Review Board, whose purpose was to deal with the public's complaints concerning police actions but whose membership had consisted solely of three police officers. His proposal would have added four civilians to the board, to be named by the mayor, and would have required that one of the three policemen be a patrolman rather than a higher-ranking police official. Critics felt the board was too favorable toward the police, making it difficult for citizens to register complaints. The result, according to Lindsay, was that New York was "faced with a situation in which too many New Yorkers who have no wish to thwart the law have come to view the policeman as an enemy rather than a friend." The issue seemed to be a noncontroversial good-government measure to improve the quality of law enforcement and ease tensions between police and citizens. What Lindsay could not have realized was how, with political lines sharply drawn and tensions running high, the battle over the board would quickly subsume his first year in office.

Fairly or unfairly, this issue would define for many New Yorkers Lindsay's feelings toward crime and the police.

Taking the argument further, Lindsay connected New York's rising crime rate to this uneasy relationship between minorities and the police: "I fear that a part of the failure to deal successfully with crime in New York is a result of the unfortunate breakdown in the relationships between the police and a substantial part of the people of our city." Thus, Lindsay blamed crime, in part, on the unfair treatment received by the city's minority population from police, whereas Buckley connected rising crime to a breakdown in authority, as he declared in his speech at the police department's Holy Name Society Communion breakfast. Had Lindsay known the outcome of this battle, he would not have been so sanguine about the idea that this reform would "reestablish the feeling of good will in our city between those who govern and those who are governed. I say that we can clear the air and relieve the tensions which are keeping us from the important business of living in this greatest of all cities."[64]

On the issue of Vietnam, Lindsay added his name to the list of Vietnam War opponents in April 1965, nearly three years before the Tet Offensive and only one year after Congress had passed the Gulf of Tonkin Resolution, which had given President Lyndon Johnson war-making powers and which Lindsay had voted for. In a commencement speech at Oakland University in Michigan, Congressman Lindsay declared Vietnam to be "probably the most unwanted war in this country's history." The speech showcased Lindsay's unease with the American war effort while still stopping short of a firm antiwar position (which was rare in 1965).[65]

In contrast to his antiwar reputation, which would flourish during the late 1960s, Lindsay did not originally plan to make the Oakland speech a bold leap into the tiny ranks of war opponents. Lindsay accepted the invitation to speak at the Oakland commencement not because he wanted a platform for his antiwar views, but because it would be his first honorary college degree. The original topic of his speech was to be "The Programmed Society," a standard early 1960s speech about the role of the individual in mass society. With Lindsay on vacation in the Bahamas, his speechwriter James Carberry, who had been hired three months earlier, was left to pen the speech. Instead of writing about the programmed society, Carberry took it upon himself to draft, without the congressman's knowledge, an antiwar speech for him. Carberry's original text for the speech contained blunt talk about Vietnam: "The time has come to think the unthinkable about Vietnam. The first of these heresies is that reunification of North and South Vietnam may be an essential element of a permanent settlement of that country's civil war." Another passage spoke of the possibility of Communist leadership of the newly unified Vietnam: "If the people of Vietnam, in free, open and honest elections, give control of their government to the Communists, I think they have every right to do so." Carberry also attacked Vietnam's President Diem as well as the domino theory, thus calling into question the basic rationale of pursuing the conflict in Vietnam. He sprang the new speech on his boss in a telephone call to the Bahamas. To Carberry's relief, Lindsay did not kill it. He suggested Carberry send the speech to Bob Price for editing. The politically savvy Price cut out attacks on the domino theory and President Diem, as well as a passage that specifically called America's involvement in Vietnam a mistake.

Carberry met John and Mary Lindsay in Detroit the night before the speech, and the two men ironed out a final moderate version. Speaking in front of the Oakland graduates and their parents, Lindsay supported "the recent acceleration of our military efforts, including the air strikes against North Viet Nam, to the extent the bombings show we will not quit Viet Nam" and declared that "the Communists must come to terms." Yet he also argued that "we cannot solve the problem by unlimited military escalation." He feared such "an expansion of the war conceivably could lead to another episode of terror to which we have assigned the cumbersome euphemism, 'nuclear confrontation.'" Lindsay talked about the need for an "honorable peace" and felt that the goal of U.S. policy should be the creation of a unified Vietnam.[66]

The conservative Midwestern crowd's response to the speech was tepid. "They seemed attentive, but they weren't visibly reacting," recalled Carberry. Lindsay felt uncomfortable by the silence and grew angry at Carberry for drawing him into such treacherous political waters. Lindsay thought the speech was a political disaster. On the ride to the airport after the speech, Lindsay told Carberry: "That speech was probably a mistake. A big mistake." Carberry, in a panic, prepared to resign. Lindsay's attitude toward his speech took a turn for the worse during a discussion with their driver, who politely took issue with Lindsay's antiwar remarks, arguing for the need to stop Communist aggression. According to Carberry, a chastened Lindsay spent most of the two-hour trip to the Detroit airport talking about the Communist threat with his driver. Carberry remembers that "Lindsay was far from cocky. He was, instead, convinced the speech had wrecked his future in politics." But Carberry managed to keep his job.

Lindsay generally steered clear of the war issue for the next two years. When asked his position on Vietnam at a Queens luncheonette during the summer of 1965, Lindsay simply responded, "Negotiate" and "Get out if we can." When thousands of New Yorkers marched down Fifth Avenue on the Saturday before the 1965 city election to support the nation's war effort in Vietnam, Lindsay did not attend. The only candidate present was William F. Buckley. If Lindsay was growing more ambivalent about the war, Buckley exhibited no such qualms. He had earlier made news by criticizing antiwar protesters for their "epicene resentments," calling them "young slobs" and "self-conscious boulevardiers of protest." Buckley wondered how these protesters would have reacted if "a platoon of American soldiers who have seen the gore in South Vietnam had parachuted down into their mincing ranks."[67]

In many ways, Lindsay's ambivalence to the war mirrored the attitudes of his Silk Stocking constituency. The results of a 1965 questionnaire showed that only 5.6 percent of district residents wanted to withdraw from Vietnam. Thirty-two percent wanted to negotiate an end to the war, and an equal number wanted to either continue the present level of military and economic assistance or intensify the military effort. Thus, in 1965 even the relatively liberal and cosmopolitan constituents of the Silk Stocking district were evenly split between continuing the conflict and negotiating an end to it. Only a handful of residents wanted to pull out. Lindsay, as congressman and candidate, mirrored these views. Halfway into his first term as mayor, however, the early equivocations on Vietnam would disappear and Lindsay would emerge as a prominent antiwar voice.[68]

FUSION

Lindsay set about building an operation modeled on Mayor Fiorello La Guardia's three successful "fusion" campaigns for mayor. He pledged to "reestablish in New York City a nonpartisan government—a fusion of diverse political interests for the single purpose of achieving good government. Fusion government had been adopted four times previously in New York City, and it succeeded, in the main, every time." First, he put as much distance between himself and the Republican Party as possible. Campaign literature rarely mentioned party affiliation, instead referring to Lindsay as the "fusion candidate for mayor." When called "the Republican candidate" on the campaign trail, he corrected the offender and replied, "Not Republican, *fusion*, remember that." A Lindsay campaign handbook reminded campaign workers "that the underlying principle of John Lindsay's campaign is fusion—a political movement uniting citizens regardless of party affiliation to elect the best candidate for Mayor of New York. Do not become involved with other candidates or local contests." He named La Guardia's widow and Senator Jacob Javits co-chairmen of the Citizens Committee for Lindsay. Lindsay expressed little interest in having former President Eisenhower stump for him, upsetting his old boss, who let it be known through General Lucius Clay that he thought Lindsay's Civilian Complaint Review Board plan was a mistake.[69]

There was cooperation between the Lindsay campaign and the Democratic reform movement in Bronx County. During the summer of 1965, Lindsay volunteers worked on petition drives for Bronx Democratic reform candidates who were challenging machine-backed candidates. Two such candidates were Robert Abrams, running for a state assembly seat in the Pelham Parkway section, and Harrison Goldin, running for a state senate seat from Highbridge. The young, inexperienced Lindsay campaign workers learned the ropes of New York politics in preparation for the general election (there was no Republican primary for Lindsay), and the Lindsay camp won the loyalty and support of reform Democrats like Abrams and Goldin in November. Hence, Republican reform and Democratic reform were united in 1965 against the common enemy: the Democratic machine.[70]

Martin Shefter has noted the similarities between New York reform as embodied in 1965 by John Lindsay and previous reform movements. First, the cries of reform were initiated by "young professionals who wanted to displace machine politicians as the key actors in municipal government." Second, reform was backed by a business community unhappy with the traditional Democratic fiscal policies. Third, reformers were concerned with the status of new city residents—in 1965, mostly blacks and Puerto Ricans. Last, reformers were allied with "key figures in the national government who sought to alter the policies of the municipal government." During the 1960s, these national figures were Great Society liberals. There was one key difference, though, between previous reform movements and the 1965 coalition. Whereas previous generations of reformers were mostly united in their concern with reducing municipal spending and cutting city taxes, there was tension within Lindsay's reform coalition between those favoring traditional fiscal conservatism and those favoring greater government spending to reduce inequality, improve city services, and ameliorate the situation of black and Puerto Rican newcomers.[71]

Helping create Lindsay's fusion ticket was the Liberal Party. Alex Rose and David Dubinsky, the leaders of the New York Liberals, were strong backers of Mayor Wagner, and his withdrawal left them looking for a new candidate. Though the number of votes the Liberal Party produced each election day was small, these votes were an important swing element that could be easily moved behind a candidate to provide a margin of victory in a tight race. The party also could bestow the imprimatur of liberalism and good government, which was worth more than the two hundred thousand votes it controlled. All of this was due to the creative genius of Rose, the president of the United Hatters, Cap, and Millinery International Union, who used the leverage of the Liberal Party to gain patronage for Liberals just like any clubhouse Democratic organization.[72]

After Wagner dropped out of the race, Price met with Rose at the old Hotel Astor, on Broadway between Forty-fourth and Forty-fifth (demolished in 1969). The young political operative looked upon his elder with uncharacteristic awe and respect. The Liberal Party leader agreed to endorse Lindsay under the condition that Liberals would receive one-third of all city jobs and judgeships, a chunk of money to use during the campaign, and the right to name one of Lindsay's running mates. Price agreed. (Liberals did get many appointments to the Lindsay administration, but nothing approaching the one-third agreed upon.) Later, Lindsay would name Timothy Costello, a professor at New York University and member of the Liberal Party, as his running mate for City Council president.

Rose warned Price that before he could bestow the endorsement upon Lindsay, the candidate would have to appear before the party's executive committee to explain his stand on the issues. Beame would also speak. Price asked Rose to give him the questions that would be asked. Rose did so, along with the answers that the Liberals wanted to hear. In the days leading up to the appearance, Price used Rose's questions and answers to prep Lindsay, never telling the candidate what they were. At the Liberal Party meeting Lindsay performed superbly. But he left stunned, realizing that the questions Price had grilled him on were the very same questions he had been asked at the meeting. When he returned to the campaign office, Lindsay asked Price where he got the questions. Price told him they came, along with the answers, directly from Rose. Lindsay was mildly upset, his Protestant conscience troubled. Wasn't that fraudulent and unfair to Beame, he asked his campaign manager?[73]

Now a Democrat was needed for the Lindsay ticket—preferably a Jewish Democrat. A number of Democrats, mostly nonpoliticians, were mentioned. But Price says his first and only choice for the slot was Milton Mollen, a Brooklyn Democrat who was head of Wagner's Housing and Redevelopment Board at the time of the announcement. He believed Mollen was the campaign's most realistic chance to find a Democrat willing to defy his party. Mollen was an awkward choice. Not only had Lindsay been bashing the Wagner administration, but Charles Moerdler, president of the New York Young Republicans and soon-to-be Lindsay's first commissioner of buildings, had written a report in early 1965 specifically condemning Mollen's housing policies. Lindsay was so impressed by the report he read it into the *Congressional Record*, calling the report a "devastating documentary." But Price had decided upon Mollen.[74]

In a meeting before Mollen's announcement as Lindsay's running mate, Moerdler confronted Mollen and repeated his attacks upon the Wagner administration's housing policies. Mollen told the Lindsay camp he was just following Wagner's instructions, which he felt obliged to carry out. He had no problems with Moerdler's criticisms and felt them justified. He said he was more than willing to run against his own record. An angry and betrayed Paul Screvane lashed out at Mollen, who reportedly had attended Screvane campaign meetings and, according to Screvane, had lobbied for a position on Screvane's ticket, a charge Mollen denied. I. D. Robbins called Mollen "the least effectual person in the Wagner administration," and said he "wouldn't hire Mollen to build a privy." Price is reported to have explained, half jokingly, the choice of Mollen: "We already have the good government people. Now we are looking for the bad government people." This time, though, political expediency would rule the day. Lindsay now had a well-balanced ticket: a Republican WASP from Manhattan, a Jewish Democrat from

Brooklyn, and an Irish Catholic Liberal (with an Italian-sounding surname) from Staten Island.[75]

THE CAMPAIGN BEGINS

The lackluster Democratic primary ended on September 14 with Beame coming from behind to defeat Screvane by almost 60,000 votes. Procaccino and O'Connor were also victorious. So convinced had the Lindsay team been that Screvane would beat Beame that a bet was made between the Lindsay and Beame camps on the outcome of the election. After the primary, the Beame campaign received their money in a paper bag, a doubly sweet victory and, at least for this election season, their last. Beame possessed the natural advantage of running as a Democrat, but lacked Lindsay's charisma and Buckley's wit. Much as Lindsay was running away from the Republican label, Beame needed to steer clear of the Democratic machine. In addition, Beame needed to implore his fellow Democrats to "repel the threatened invasion of City Hall by the party of Goldwater and Nixon." Beame tried to convince the Village Independent Democrats, a reform-minded local Democratic club, that "no matter how you slice it or how he hides it, John Lindsay is the candidate of the Republican Party, the candidate of Nelson Rockefeller."[76]

Beame also needed help from Washington to push the idea that only a Democratic mayor could work with President Johnson. One campaign pamphlet proclaimed in its headline: "The Beame Team Has the Know How To Do More For New York." William Connell, an aide to Vice President Hubert Humphrey, reported to Humphrey on a Beame campaign meeting he attended in late September. Although the Beame team was upbeat and felt it could win, it wanted a Johnson endorsement, as well as Humphrey's help in campaigning for Beame, especially among Jewish and reform voters. Humphrey had already sent a congratulatory telegram to Beame on primary night. Connell assured the Beame people that Humphrey would meet with them at the annual Al Smith dinner and attend a late October Beame fundraiser. Most important for Democrats, Connell noted, was that "there is an excellent chance of beating Lindsay, and to knock off Lindsay now is to foreclose his effective candidacy in 1968 or 1972. We *have* to do everything possible to beat him."

Despite the assurances, Johnson and Humphrey were ambivalent about Beame. Connell argued that since Beame had released the contents of Humphrey's congratulatory message, he had little choice but help Beame. Most ominously for Beame, Connell wrote: "A Vice Presidential commitment to go up for Beame will take the pressure off the President to do so until late in the campaign, when he can decide whether or not he wants to go in." It was apparent that Johnson was considering not endorsing his party's nominee for the mayoralty of the nation's largest city. If he should fail to do so, it would knock out one of the legs of the chair of Beame's campaign strategy: If a New York Democrat could not even get the support of a Democratic President, what kind of Democrat was he? A presidential nonendorsement would, in effect, give New York Democrats a free pass to pull the lever for Lindsay.[77]

Beame's strategy was much like Muhammed Ali's rope-a-dope: sit on the ropes, take the punishment of his opponents, jab at Lindsay by reminding voters of his Ivy League Republicanism, and rely on traditional Democratic allegiances to carry him to Gracie Mansion. He was running, he told New Yorkers, because "I owe this city a debt. . . . The city has given me everything I have and I want to pay it back." If Lindsay was running on a bold platform that would change the city's future, Beame was running on his résumé and on the city's traditional Democratic heritage. As for Lindsay, his strategy was to retain his "city in crisis" attacks and push hard against Beame's association with the Democratic bosses. Lindsay would try to yoke Beame to the increasingly unpopular Wagner administration and capitalize on Comptroller Beame's support of Wagner's policies. Beame voted with Wagner in all but four votes on the Board of Estimate, the city's main governing board, leading a Lindsay campaign flyer to charge, "The odds are 15,312 to 4 that Beame will be just another Wagner. . . . Naturally he likes it as it is. He's satisfied. Are you? The truth is that Abe Beame is 99 and 44/100 percent pure Wagner—with the most insidious political machine since Boss Tweed thrown in to boot."[78]

It would be a classic reform campaign, run against a man who, Lindsay aides felt stood for "bossism, for the old-guard clubhouse machinery, for everything we oppose." Beame's image as a nondescript political professional from Brooklyn did have one advantage. According to a Lindsay adviser, "Beame is so small and earnest. How are we ever going to incite people to rise up against their friendly neighborhood bookkeeper?"[79]

By the time Beame became the Democratic nominee in September, Lindsay's campaign had already begun to lose steam. First, Lindsay weathered the accidental death in mid-July of his older sister, Mrs. Cooper Schieffelin, who was found late at night floating face down in the pool at her family's estate on Nassau County's Gold Coast. Second, the summer heat seemed to sap the interest level of voters. Lastly, Lindsay was in danger of being overexposed. As the journalists Peter Maas and Nick Thimmesch wrote after the election: "New Yorkers will only watch a show so long and then they look at something else." Lindsay campaign aide John Deardourff detailed the campaign's malaise in an early October memo. He estimated that, on the basis of volunteer telephone surveying, Lindsay was behind by between eight and ten points and blamed Lindsay's "muddled image" for dulling the early excitement of his campaign. The candidate and his campaign seemed to lack a "sharp focus." Deardourff dated this slippage to Lindsay's selection of Mollen as a running mate, which turned off many liberals. In addition, Lindsay's moralistic cries and righteous indignation began to sound tired, even to those predisposed to believe such claims. As one reformer remarked: "How can I come out publicly for a man who says the slums of New York are as bad as the slums of Calcutta?" The Village Independent Democrats (VID), the reform club that had defeated Carmine DeSapio, voted in October not to endorse a candidate for mayor. Despite the fact that most VID members would vote for Lindsay, the *Village Voice* reported "a marked falling off of enthusiasm for the Republican Congressman since he announced last May he would run."[80]

With seven weeks left in the campaign, Beame was the uneasy frontrunner, Lindsay was stalled in second place, and Buckley was an amusing sideshow. Then, on September 17, the Newspaper Guild called a strike that shut down New York's papers (except the *New York Post*) for twenty-three days. (The *Herald Tribune* resumed publication after ten days.) Meanwhile, the print-media-starved candidates relied on two television debates and one radio debate during the strike to fuel interest in their candidacies. Though handsome and photogenic, Lindsay came across a little stiff during the television debates. Buckley, stinging Lindsay with verbal jabs, stole the show. Voters who previously knew Buckley only from the printed page could see the wit and jocularity in the flesh. Theodore White called Buckley a "star" on television, whose style "would have made him Oscar Wilde's favorite candidate for anything." Beame performed like the clubhouse politician he was: solid, not slick, comfortable with the issues, but somewhat plodding. The debates transformed Buckley into a serious contender who, at the very least, could steal enough votes to throw the race one way or another.[81]

For now, it looked as if Buckley's victory by subtraction would victimize the Republican Lindsay. The debates solidified the feeling that Lindsay was losing ground. The news from the first polls reinforced the Lindsay fade; the *Herald Tribune*'s first poll on October 7 put Beame ahead of Lindsay, 45.7 percent to 35.6 percent, with Buckley getting 10.2 percent. Price was not concerned with the malaise lingering over the Lindsay campaign: "Let me tell you about the so-called sag," he told a reporter. "A campaign is like a book. You can't read one chapter and say it's poor. You have to read the whole book." Price was ready for the next chapter.[82]

All summer long, the Lindsay campaign had been plagued by Buckley supporters who heckled the candidate on his walking tours of the outer boroughs. Oliver Pilat accompanied Lindsay during his neighborhood jaunts, and the pages of his diary are filled with his observations of the hecklers. Violence seemed to bubble just under the surface of these trips to white ethnic neighborhoods.

On a June trip to Queens, Pilat reported that Irish-American teenagers followed Lindsay around chanting "Fake," "Traitor," and "Communist," and carrying signs saying SUPPORT YOUR LOCAL POLICE, and DOWN WITH SO-CALLED REVIEW BOARDS. To Pilat, these youths were "poorly dressed, ignorant, tough, and loud." He approvingly quoted a British reporter who called them "lumpenproletariat." Pilat reports that John's twin brother, David, "with a murderous look," rushed at one of these teens, a small boy who had been calling the candidate a Communist. Pilat held back David Lindsay, but admits that he later shouldered the kid out of Lindsay's path: "If a cop had not been watching, I might have ridden that kid right into the gutter." These right-wing protests tested the tolerance of liberals who traditionally defended dissent and free speech.[83]

These conservative protests continued into the fall campaign. In heavily Irish Bay Ridge, Brooklyn, Lindsay was greeted with repeated chants of "Lefty, Lindsay." Pilat often complained that the police assigned to protect Lindsay were sympathetic to the hecklers. Sid Davidoff, twenty-six, was the Lindsay campaign's advance man and the head of Lindsay's Raiders, a group of muscular young men—many of them, like Davidoff himself, former college wrestlers—who protected Lindsay on his neighborhood walks. After a young Jewish man told Pilat the protesters sounded like Nazis to him, Pilat suggested to Davidoff that he give the Raiders "some exercise." Davidoff demurred, but promised that after Lindsay left, he and some of his men would note who the troublemakers were and "take direct action."[84]

Part of the problem was that many of the police were pro-Buckley and not very cooperative with the Lindsay campaign. Davidoff remembers seeing policemen wearing orange BUCKLEY FOR MAYOR buttons, and some even joined in booing Lindsay. In this atmosphere, Davidoff believed "we had to be our own enforcers." Mike Long, now head of the New York State Conservative Party, remembers squaring off against Davidoff at a local Republican club in the Cypress Hill section of Brooklyn. Long and his friends had come to heckle Lindsay. Davidoff saw the group as potential trouble and headed their way. The two men faced each other down for minutes, narrowly avoiding a fist fight. Davidoff also attacked a teenager named George Marlin (who would later become the Conservative Party's candidate for mayor in 1993 and head of the Port Authority), while Marlin was handing out "Buckley for Mayor" literature in Flushing, Queens.[85]

In an August stop in Brooklyn, Lindsay was again heckled in ugly tones. Lindsay found the heckling reminiscent "of some of the worst moments of history. It ought to alert New Yorkers that the city is beset with extremism of a dangerous kind." One week later, after a block party in Coney Island, a heckler ripped Lindsay's shirt with the sharp end of his Buckley placard, slightly scratching the candidate's chest. The assault earned the protester a sharp slap in the face from Mary Lindsay. Lindsay's speechwriter Jim Carberry remembers that after one appearance in Brooklyn, "An Irish-looking kid, apple-cheeks and pale skin and blond hair and a little beefy" approached Lindsay wanting to shake the candidate's hand. When Lindsay went to shake the young man's hand, the candidate quickly pulled his hand away. "I thought for a minute he [Lindsay] was going to hit him," Carberry said. Then he noticed that the kid, who was wearing a Buckley button, had something other than a friendly handshake in mind. Hidden in the palm of his hand was a thumbtack. The months of heckling were obviously getting to Lindsay. After an appearance in the German-Irish neighborhood of Ridgewood, Queens, Lindsay's car was mobbed by Buckley supporters shouting "Bum" and "Communist." In response, a weary Lindsay shouted through the closed window of his car, "Fairies, Fairies!"[86]

Lindsay had been ignoring Buckley as much as possible, but his success in the debates was now causing voters to pay attention. Lindsay would have to turn Buckley into Barry Goldwater, a dangerous threat to the city who incited, however tacitly, his extremist supporters toward bigotry and hate. The Liberal Party's Rose and Dubinsky had been urging such an approach for much of the campaign, but Price and Lindsay balked until they saw the early poll results. One top Lindsay aide said, "More people are becoming aware of Buckley than I ever would have dreamt in a serious society." Lindsay would, in the words of his running mate Timothy Costello, rip "the sneering clown's mask from Buckley" and reveal for all goodhearted New Yorkers "his negative, divisive preachings as the threat they really are to peace on earth, to the progress in the nation, to the uplifting of our city."[87]

Though the strategy was counterintuitive on its surface—why go after the third-place candidate and ignore your real challenger?—it had few drawbacks. It would reduce Buckley's vote, which was edging toward 20 percent in some polls, animate the lethargic Lindsay campaign, energize his liberal supporters, and scare Jewish voters who might be leaning to Beame. The implicit message was that if Lindsay was the modern candidate, then Beame and his clubhouse friends were premodern, and Buckley, with his discussion of "immanatizing the eschaton," was downright medieval. This new strategy recast Lindsay as the sole liberal in the race, bravely battling the forces of Buckley and Buckley (Charlie, the Bronx boss, and Bill) who wanted to send New York back to the days of corruption and reaction. The white knight would slay the twin devils of the clubhouse bosses and right-wing extremism.[88]

The first attempt to put this strategy into play backfired. In early September, Price leaked a story to Woody Klein, a *New York World-Telegram* reporter, that "William F. Buckley . . . and some of his colleagues had been responsible for smashing windows of several Lindsay storefronts in Brooklyn and Queens." When Klein asked how he knew it was true, Price responded with characteristic bluntness: "Because I'm telling you."[89]

Without independent confirmation, Klein went with the story on the basis of the word of two Lindsay aides. "Hate Tactics Hit Lindsay" blared the next day's banner headline. In the story, an unidentified Lindsay aide claimed the campaign was being victimized by "vicious right-wing hate tactics." Klein's source had told him that "windows in volunteer storefronts have been smashed, telephone lines have been slashed, mail has been opened and destroyed, and several aides have received threatening letters." Deeper in the story, though, the evidence gets weaker when Klein lists the actual instances of "hate" tactics: Lindsay's being heckled at campaign stops; Buckley stickers being plastered on Lindsay storefront windows; Lindsay storefronts picketed by men chanting "Fusion is confusion" and "Lindsay loves Communists"; and a man entering a Brooklyn storefront yelling about Lindsay and Communists who disrupted the office for an hour. Buckley denied responsibility for any of these incidents.

The following day's *Times* reported that Lindsay had not even known about these events until the previous day and he refused to blame Buckley, saying, "I cannot ascribe these actions to any one person or party." Klein came to the conclusion that Price had leaked the story without Lindsay's approval. The most interesting part of the story is that no one from the Lindsay campaign ever named which storefronts had their windows broken, nor did anyone register any such complaints with the New York Police Department. It is likely that Lindsay's Raiders, under the direction of Sid Davidoff, broke some of the windows at their own campaign storefronts, then blamed it on the Conservatives. According to Davidoff, "Half of it [the accusations against the Conservatives] was true. Half of if wasn't. We did to them as much as they did to us." The issue of right-wing extremism was dropped for a month, but then it returned with a fury.[90]

The next attack on Buckley began after an October appearance by Lindsay before a meeting of the Parents and Taxpayers Association (PAT) at Richmond Hill High School in Queens—the heart of Buckley country. A constant drumbeat of heckling nearly drowned out Lindsay's voice. His argument for a change in the makeup of the Civilian Complaint Review Board further incited the crowd, who constantly shouted "Judas" in reference to Lindsay's abandonment of Goldwater and his disavowal of his Republican heritage. At the press conference he held the next day, Lindsay called the previous night's heckling "a doctrine of hate." Lindsay said the crowd at Richmond Hills "reminded him of some of the worst moments of history." He called his Conservative opponent "a candidate of the ultra Right" and linked these outbursts with Nazism, warning that New York "is beset with radical rightism and extremism of the most dangerous kind." To leave no doubt how the Lindsay campaign felt about Buckley, the office of Lindsay's Raiders at campaign headquarters was decorated with a cartoon of Buckley wearing a Nazi armband.[91]

By linking Buckley with fascism and reaction, Lindsay appealed to the historic fears of Jewish and black New Yorkers. "In the streets," Lindsay proclaimed, "the Buckley campaign becomes a racist campaign." He did not believe Buckley himself was a racist, but, Lindsay said, "the city is a powder keg and Buckley is doing his best to light the fuse." Lindsay continued the barrage by claiming, "If the Buckley point of view, which is negative and backward, were ever to achieve ascendancy, it would literally mean that the streets would be totally unsafe instead of fifty percent unsafe, the way they are now.

It would mean bloodshed in the end because that's what it would come down to." Clearly, Lindsay was warning that if Buckley ever became mayor, the city would be at war.[92]

In a WINS radio interview the day before the election, Jackie Robinson echoed this line of argument in even more incendiary language:

> If they [Buckley and his running mates] get a substantial number of the votes here in this city, it could only mean that we have a lot more bigots than we figured . . . and we have already decided, with the talk of the Klan coming into New York, that we've got to get ready and prepare ourselves for the ultimate. . . . So I say very frankly to you that if Buckley and the other people who are supporting him garner a substantial number of votes here, you can look for problems in this city. . . . I think Negroes have to protect themselves and I am calling upon the Negroes, just after this election, let's get together and let's get prepared.

When Buckley complained about Robinson's remarks, Robinson lost his composure and told reporters, "He's a liar and a bigot and that's just what he is." Robinson claimed he was not promoting violence, but rather "what we're advocating is preparedness." In a letter to Bruce Felknor, executive director of the nonpartisan Fair Campaign Practices Committee, the Buckley campaign complained that at a Lindsay rally in Brooklyn, Lindsay pointed to two Buckley hecklers and yelled, "That's Buckley's racists and bigots!" causing the crowd to press in on the two men, yelling "Bigots! Bigots!" A policeman prevented a fight between the two men and four black youths from the Lindsay entourage. The Lindsay campaign responded with its own letter to Felknor five days later, complaining that Buckley "is carrying the banner of ultra-reactionary, radical right elements in the campaign."[93]

Meanwhile, Lindsay's associates were doing their best to darken the political waters. Senator Javits was the only high-ranking Republican Lindsay allowed to stump for him because he could help with the Jewish vote. On October 14, Javits told a campaign audience that Buckley "wants to turn back the clock of social progress and return us to the dark ages of our society." Before Jewish audiences the senator said, "Mr. Buckley's sole purpose in this campaign is to politically assassinate John Lindsay. . . . If we let this kind of campaign prevail, then I fear for freedom in New York City." Speaking to a reporter, Javits reiterated the view that Buckley "wants to assassinate us [liberal Republicans]." Coming less than two years after the assassination of John Kennedy, such rhetoric not only was in bad taste but also poisoned the air of political civility. Javits later accused Buckley of wanting to send welfare recipients to "concentration camps." This accusation stemmed from Buckley's idea of exploring the feasibility of "relocating chronic welfare cases outside the city limits," as well as quarantining drug addicts. Lindsay, too, chimed in with references to "concentration camps." Such attacks finally got to Buckley, who exploded at a final radio debate the Thursday prior to the election. When Buckley accused Lindsay of scaring Jewish voters, Lindsay was stunned and replied: "Mr. Buckley's statement . . . that I am appealing to Jewish voters is an offensive and irresponsible comment and I'll ask him not to make it again." Of course, his campaign had been targeting the Jewish vote for most of the campaign and the rhetoric used was anything but subtle. Exasperated, Buckley replied with rare anger that Lindsay was "trying to do to the Jewish voters what the Ku Klux Klan has been trying to do to the white people in the South, keep them scared."[94]

One of Lindsay's running mates went so far as to criticize Buckley as a bad Catholic. Timothy Costello, the pipe-smoking professor and fusion candidate for City Council resident, was a liberal Catholic. He called Buckley "a threat to the city, the nation, and the Church." He intoned to a mostly Catholic audience at Fordham University, "When Mr. Buckley attacks the War on Poverty, when he proposes we restrict our poor, he is in direct conflict with the teachings of our church and the history of its work in this city." He also censured Buckley for his criticisms of Pope John's encyclicals *Pacem in Terris* and *Mater et Magistra*. Angry over what he saw as Buckley's cavalier approach to race and religion, Costello said he refused "to accept the possibility that we, the largest Catholic Community, the greatest city on earth, will fall prey to doctrines of ignorance, fear, hatred, and intolerance." Although the *Times* reported that Costello had said a vote for Buckley was an anti-Catholic vote, Costello never made such a statement directly. Lindsay said he would not take issue with his running mate's remarks, since he himself was not Catholic and was not as familiar with Catholic doctrine as Costello. Buckley responded by saying that to call him anti-Catholic was as convincing as calling Abe Beame an anti-Semite. With remarkable grace, Buckley added, "If I am a bad Catholic, I shall be punished by Someone I fear far more than the New York Catholic voter."[95]

The race descended into predictable foolishness on all sides. Lindsay said Beame could not wait for Herbert Lehman and Eleanor Roosevelt to die so that he could "double cross" reform Democrats. In response, Franklin Roosevelt Jr., a Beame supporter, hyperventilated that Lindsay's comment was "one of the most despicable acts of any candidate in my memory." Lindsay responded by calling Roosevelt a "hatchet man," and Lindsay allies recalled FDR Jr.'s smearing of Hubert Humphrey in the 1960 primary on Kennedy's behalf by wondering out loud where Humphrey had spent World War II. Buckley accused Lindsay of being soft on Communism because of his attempts to abolish the House Un-American Activities Committee; he also stated that he and Lindsay, along with two other Yale students, had heckled Communists at a 1948 rally while Lindsay was in law school and Buckley an undergraduate. Lindsay called the charge an "illusion" and claimed he never met or saw Buckley at Yale.[96]

Though certainly the victim of a smear campaign, Buckley himself made some blunders that turned away some of the support he might have received. Buckley was determined not to run a traditional campaign. Instead, he often spoke off the cuff, saying things that appeared insensitive or outrageous when seen in print or taken out of context by his all-too-eager opponents. He spoke as the intellectual provocateur he was by profession, not the political candidate he transformed himself into by whim. During a July speech to a group of prominent black New Yorkers, Buckley said, "You suffer disadvantages that the white man did not suffer. The Jew with his crooked nose, the Italian with his accent, the Irishman with his drunkenness or whatever—they had a difficult time. But it was nothing like the great disadvantage you have suffered." Buckley meant no offense, but he did not understand the circumspection required of politicians, especially when it came to ethnic and racial matters.

In the same speech Buckley also attacked James Baldwin for saying that blacks who threw garbage out of their windows in Harlem were engaging in a form of social protest. Buckley asked rhetorically: "Why should people throw garbage out their windows—in order themselves to wallow in it? You don't wallow in it. I don't wallow in it. But why excuse the fact [that some people do]?" The use of the words "wallow" and "garbage" while discussing blacks set off alarm bells. In another instance, Buckley condemned the Lindsay and Beame campaigns' infatuation with thinking in terms of voting by ethnic, racial, and religious blocs. "I beg you to say," Buckley mockingly challenged Lindsay, "I, John Lindsay, forty-three, white, Protestant, of sound mind and body, do believe in the principles of the neighborhood school. . . ." While hardly inflammatory words, Buckley was accused of injecting religion into the race. (This was a few days before Costello's remarks about Buckley's Catholicism.)[97]

If Buckley's use of language inadvertently frightened liberal voters, his campaign tactics turned away some voters predisposed to his conservative ideology. Buckley's background, bearing, and speech put him worlds apart from the working- and middle-class supporters his campaign attracted. His decision not to march in the Pulaski Day parade, the annual Polish American parade held on Fifth Avenue, was unwise campaigning. Though the decision not to participate had been made by Buckley's aide Neal Freeman without Buckley's knowledge, his boss did not protest. Freeman, in a letter to organizers, declined their invitation to march in the parade on the grounds that Buckley had "pledged himself to make no specifically ethnic or nationalist appeals. . . . [The policy] is to treat the voters of New York as responsible adult-individuals and not as members of monolithic voting blocs." What sounded to Buckley and his advisers like high-minded consistency came off to others as stuffy—as Buckley later admitted. Not only did Buckley eschew ethnic campaigning, but also, according to a campaign aide, "Every time he went to Queens, he thought he was taking off for Istanbul or something and he fought it." Buckley mostly stayed clear of rallies and street campaigning, even refusing the request of Conservative Party official who wanted Buckley and his family to ride in a motorcade in Brooklyn, for fear that he would look hypocritical in the face of his criticisms of Lindsay's walking tours. Moral consistency, combined with a tinge of Manhattan snobbishness, made for bad political judgment.[98]

Lindsay seemed to be conceding the white ethnic vote. Price had long targeted middle-class liberal Jewish voters as the key voting bloc, along with as many blacks as Lindsay could pick off. A campaign memo to Charles Moerdler and Robert Price noted: "The Irish as a group are basically politically conservative and are opposed to Lindsay's liberal image." They opposed Lindsay's stand on school busing, HUAC, and welfare. Most important, the issue of the Civilian Complaint Review Board was killing Lindsay among Irish Americans, who had long been associated with the police department.[99]

One incident reveals the mind-set of the Lindsay campaign toward white ethnics. Late in the campaign, Walter Swift, a local rank-and-file Democrat from Inwood, came forward to accuse Elliot Saron, the manager of Lindsay's Inwood storefront, of trying to persuade Swift to solicit votes for Buckley from the Inwood Irish and distribute Buckley literature in the neighborhood in the hope of drawing away votes from Beame. Swift taped his conversations with Saron and released them to the press. Swift claimed that Werner Kramarsky, Milton Mollen's campaign manager, was behind the idea. Kramarsky denied the charge. (After the election, Kramarsky became one of Lindsay's mayoral assistants.)[100]

The Buckley campaign quickly pounced on the Swift tape to highlight what it felt were the underhanded tactics of the Lindsay campaign. What was revealing about this matter was not only the strategy to draw conservative Democrats away from Beame to Buckley, but also the attitudes toward these voters. Saron characterized the Inwood Irish as "from the shanties" and told Swift that "because they're sufficiently unsophisticated—because, you know, they've got such blinded mentality—you could pull this off. What I would say—you know, get in there and act like an idiot for approximately three weeks." After the release of the tape, James Farley, chairman of the Beame campaign and the former national chairman of the Democratic National Committee, said he could not see how anyone "of Irish or Italian extraction" could vote for Lindsay.[101]

In addition to playing off white ethnics against Beame and Buckley and appealing to the fears of Jewish and black New Yorkers, the Lindsay campaign also hit one hot button issue that affected all New Yorkers: crime. Internal Lindsay campaign polls found that public safety was the most important issue for white voters, no matter their class or ethnicity. During the campaign, Lindsay reminisced about wandering around Central Park at all hours without worry as a child in Manhattan during the 1920s and 1930s, arguing that such freedom was impossible in 1965. The perception of a dangerous city was very much based on reality. From 1955 to 1965, murders in New York more than doubled, from 306 to 681 per year. The number of robberies and car thefts nearly tripled, while assaults and thefts doubled. The murder rate was twice as high as when Wagner took office twelve years earlier, despite the addition of almost 7,000 policemen, a 35 percent increase in law enforcement personnel.[102]

One murder during the heat of the campaign highlighted the growing dangers and incivility of New York living. Twenty-eight-year-old Arthur Collins was riding the IRT's Lexington line with his wife Trudy and infant daughter when a drunk wandered through his subway car molesting people and causing a disturbance. At the 125th Street stop, Collins ejected the man forcibly from the car. The man ran back onto the train and plunged a knife into Collins's heart, killing him almost instantly. Echoing a growing disgust with crime and the declining quality of life in New York City, Trudy Collins's stepfather told a newspaper, "This place is a jungle. It stinks. You know what I think Trudy's going to do? Pack up and get out of this jungle. I'd like to do it myself." In response to the murder, Lindsay called for victims of violent crimes to be financially compensated by the city, arguing that Collins's widow "lost her husband through 25 years of neglect in New York City."[103]

The *Herald Tribune*, in the final days of the campaign, ran a five-day series on the front page about the growing fear of crime, called "The Lonely Crimes." Written by Jimmy Breslin and Dick Schaap, the stories put a human face on the city's brutal crime statistics: "Women carry tear-gas pens in their pocketbooks. Cab drivers rest iron bars on the front seat next to them. Store owners keep billy clubs next to the cash register. And people enter the parks and the subways and the side streets of New York, the most important city in the world, only in fear. The fear is justified. The weapons are justified."

Schaap told of one Herbert Peters, who had used his life savings to buy a small grocery store on Eighty-eighth and Second in Manhattan, only to be held up one night: "Peters practically shakes as he talks, he is so terrified. He's terrified because, in 1965, in New York City, he decided to go into business for himself on a main avenue on the East Side of Manhattan." A man named Brand was robbed and beaten in Riverside Park in the summer twilight. Morris Berkowitz, sixty-one, was stabbed and beaten one Saturday by black thugs, one of whom yelled, "Kill him, he's white." Berkowitz lived and worked in the transitional neighborhood of the Brownsville section of Brooklyn, where he owned a small umbrella and luggage store on Sutter Avenue. It was a neighborhood that had once been working-class Jewish but was now poor and black.[104]

Lindsay pinpointed crime as the city's most serious problem, noting that "the double padlock has become the symbol of New York City." He told an elderly Manhattan Jewish group that, if elected mayor, he would "spare no money and no effort—I WILL SPARE NOTHING—to insure the safety of the streets, your homes, hallways." The Lindsay campaign's position paper on crime declared:

> No problem facing New York City and no issue in this campaign is more important than the problem of rising crime and the safety of our cities. . . . Every day New York City is a more dangerous place to live than the day before. . . . The fear which wracks our citizens today is the fear to walk the streets and ride the subways . . . and enjoy the parks. It is a fear that has made thousands and thousands of our citizens prisoners in their own city. It is a fear that more than any other factor has staggered the city's spirit and morale. . . . We must provide a 24-hour police presence for every single block of New York City.

Despite the rhetoric, Lindsay's "Operation Safe City" was a pale list of campaign promises. Apart from promising to add 2,500 more policemen, the list focused on minor bureaucratic changes such as improving police communications, "a war on paper work," the use of civilians to do clerical work in the police department, and improving police stations.[105]

The Liberal Party's slogan for the Lindsay campaign, which appeared in pamphlets and advertisements in the city's subways, was "Breathe Easier; Sleep Better; Feel Safer; With the Lindsay Team." A Lindsay campaign flyer declared:

> New York is a city afraid. We're afraid to walk our streets, afraid to play in our parks, afraid to ride in our subways, and even afraid behind the locked doors of our own homes. In our city there is a murder every 14 hours, a reported rape every six hours; a reported assault every 12 minutes; a reported theft every three minutes. In ten years, our city's crime rate has jumped 33 percent. In the past year alone, major crime skyrocketed almost 15 percent. This increasing lawlessness, and the terror it creates, cannot be tolerated.

Lindsay campaigned in Kew Gardens, Queens, on the spot where Kitty Genovese, a nurse, had been murdered a year and a half earlier. Genovese was stabbed to death one night while dozens of her neighbors heard, but ignored her cries for help. Her murder became a symbol of rising crime and the increasing indifference of citizens to the plight of their neighbors. At Kew Gardens, Lindsay mourned, "Something has gone out of the heart and soul of New York City." One Lindsay campaign television ad showed a picture of dark and desolate Central Park, with a voice-over claiming that "fear has entered the bloodstream of the city." The ad implied that the high crime rate was yet another legacy of twelve years of tired Democratic rule.[106]

The previous year, Buckley's *National Review* had argued in an editorial that in reference to rising crime, especially black on white, "What is happening, or is about to happen—let us face it—is race war." As angry as Lindsay was over the increasingly dangerous New York streets, he was careful not to scapegoat blacks and Puerto Ricans. To a voter who said the parks were no longer safe because of "newcomers," Lindsay responded, "That is not true. Crime is committed by every race and group and is not limited to any one. . . . And so, my good sir, if you feel yourself threatened, that is true. But not so threatened as those in the isolated sections, the ghettos. So that is our problem. The guilt is universal." Breslin and Schaap's *Herald Tribune* series was a muted portrayal of young blacks and Puerto Ricans preying mostly on elderly whites living in transitional neighborhoods. Breslin and Schaap tried to put this disturbing fact in context by condemning the racial caste system of the South and blaming it for New York's rising crime rates: "But every time the judge and jury [in the South] gets up from the grass and goes into the court and lets a white man go because he shot a colored man, every time they make a mockery of justice in sleepy Hayneville [Alabama], we pay for it here in New York, where colored people seethe in their tenements and Puerto Ricans load up on junk, or wine, and then go out to steal for money."[107]

Another example of the fault lines in thinking about crime occurred at a non-campaign-related event at the 28th Annual Judicial Conference of the Third Judicial Circuit of the United States. With Chief Justice Earl Warren in attendance, former New York Police Chief Michael J. Murphy unleashed a blistering attack on the Warren Court for "unduly hampering" police. Policemen, Murphy argued, "are forced to fight by Marquis of Queensbury [*sic*] rules while the criminals are permitted to gouge and bite." More significant than Murphy's comments, however, was the response they elicited from Professor Yale Kamisar of Michigan University Law School. The audience "roared with laughter" as Kamisar "made a bitingly humorous reply to Mr. Murphy," calling his remarks "simplistic, narrow-minded, and politically expedient." Kamisar charged that cries of "coddling criminals" and "crime crisis" were "an old, old story," heard at various times in our nation's history, and there was no need to give in to "police hysteria" and compromise our constitutional liberties. Kamisar's cavalier attitude toward crime ignored both the statistics showing increasing crime as well as the perception among New Yorkers that their streets were less safe. This exchange revealed the bitter split between elite opinion and the concerns of average men and women. For Murphy, his opponents were not just wrong, but were dangerous elitists in judicial robes and ivory towers; for Kamisar, his opponents were not just wrong, but bigoted and stupid.[108]

Such attitudes were on display in the portrayal of Buckley and his supporters by some in the New York media. Jimmy Breslin called Buckley "the elegant cracker," thereby linking Jim Crow defenders in the South with

Northern conservatives. The *Post* columnist James Wechsler wrote that Buckley "addressed his appeal to the city's McCarthyite residue and to the practitioners of refined racism. . . . His ethnic appeal is pure white." The *Times*, in its most scathing editorial of the campaign, accused Buckley of "pandering to some of the more brutish instincts in the community, though his appeals to racism and bigotry have been artfully masked." Walter Lippmann wrote: "There is no real precedent in American politics for the kind of wrecking operation that Buckley is conducting." In his 1968 book, *Lindsay's Campaign: A Behind the Scenes Diary*, Oliver Pilat, the journalist-turned-press-secretary, described how elite media opinion meshed with that of the Lindsay campaign in its denunciation of conservative ideas and Buckley as their representative. Pilat declared that an "ultra rightist" hates liberals, "he opposes minority groups and labor unions, he relegates women and artists to subordinate roles in society. He whittles away constantly at the bourgeois press. He is a super-patriot and a conservative in religion, he favors unrestrained police activity at home and imperialism abroad, he creates a domestic atmosphere of impending change. Quite a few of these criteria apply to Buckley." It seemed almost impossible for most liberals to describe Buckley and his followers without using such words as "hate," "bigot," "racism," "backlash," and "dangerous."[109]

ENDORSEMENTS

Lindsay received the lion's share of newspaper endorsements, including those of the *Times, Post, Herald Tribune, New York World-Telegram and Sun, Village Voice,* and *Jewish Daily Forward.* The Lindsay endorsements began the day after the Democratic primary, when the *Post,* disheartened by the victory of the machine-backed Beame, came out for Lindsay. The *Post's* publisher, Dorothy Schiff, was the granddaughter of the Jewish philanthropist Jacob Schiff. Though the elder Schiff's politics, like those of many other German Jews, were Republican, Dorothy Schiff became a liberal Democrat. The paper's support of Lindsay signaled to "those who care about humane, progressive, creative government" that it was acceptable to vote Republican, especially for a Republican who offered "the prospect of fresh, independent liberal leadership for the city."

In supporting Lindsay, the *Times* argued that he would bring exciting changes to a dreary city. A Lindsay administration, argued the *Times* editors, "would be an exciting adventure in willingness to try the new and to accomplish great things through dedication, spirit, and decisive action." At a luncheon meeting with the editorial staff of the *Times* a few days prior to the election, Buckley was told by one editor, "Do you realize that as a practical matter, your candidacy . . . is likely to result in a grave setback to the fortunes of New York City by depriving the city of a Lindsay administration?" (The *Times* was so enamored of Lindsay in 1965 that Abe Rosenthal, by then the deputy managing editor, and Arthur Gelb, the metropolitan desk editor, upon hearing the news of Lindsay's victory, reportedly hugged each other and yelled, "We've won!")[110]

The *Herald Tribune* said, "New York demands rebirth in government, and this freshness can come only by [a] Lindsay victory." The *New York World–Telegram and Sun* argued, "Where Beame symbolized a shabby yesterday, John Lindsay symbolizes a brighter tomorrow." The *Daily News, Amsterdam News,* and *New York Journal–American* supported Beame, as did the three papers owned by S. I. Newhouse: the *Staten Island Advocate*, the *Long Island Press*, and the *Long Island Star-Journal*. The closest Buckley received to an endorsement was from the *Daily News,* which, though endorsing Beame, hoped "Buckley will get a heavy vote as a lesson and a warning to Republicans all over the United States." With blacks still indebted to Johnson for the previous year's Civil Rights Act, the *Amsterdam News,* an important black newspaper, endorsed Beame as a member of Johnson's Democratic Great Society team.[111]

Lindsay seemed to enjoy the support of most of the city's "better classes." As the journalist Noel Parmentel noted in an *Esquire* article, "Everybody is for Lindsay. All the Right people and most of the Wrong ones. Walter Lippmann and Sammy Davis . . . Dick Nixon and The Village Voice . . . Inez Robb and Norman Mailer . . . Wall Street and Madison Avenue . . . Cherry Grove and the Maidstone Club . . . the Rat Pack and the Council on Foreign Relations." Liberal New Yorkers were especially enthralled with the young reformer. Murray Kempton wrote that Lindsay "represents our last chance for civility." Similarly, Mary Perot Nichols said that Lindsay "offers us the only chance for a renaissance in city living." The socialist Michael Harrington spoke for many liberal New Yorkers when he said that "as a democratic radical who sees in the civil rights–labor–liberal wing of the Democratic Party the starting point for serious social change, I want to serve notice on that party that every time they give me an impossible candidate like Beame, I am voting for someone else." Walter Lippmann stated, "If the best interests of the City of New York were apparent to the voters, there would be no question but that John Lindsay would win the mayoralty in a landslide." Norman Mailer, in his inimitable and sometimes incoherent way, also endorsed Lindsay.[112]

By October, Lindsay geared his campaign toward liberal New Yorkers. A flyer with a picture of a standing Lindsay at a debate surrounded by his two seated opponents asked: "Will the real liberal please stand up?" It continued by stating the only reason the "reactionary forces of conservatism are determined to destroy John Lindsay's candidacy for Mayor of New York" was that Lindsay was the only candidate carrying the liberal banner. Also assisting Lindsay was his appearance at a Wall Street rally in the last week of the campaign where he was viciously booed by Buckley supporters. For a Republi-

At a June 1965 press conference, Mayor Robert F. Wagner (center) tearfully announces that he will not seek reelection. Lindsay later pinned much of the blame for the decline of the city on the shoulders of Wagner and his Democratic administration. (AP/Wide World Photos)

Lindsay "dives" into the 1965 mayoral campaign. A young and attractive candidate, Lindsay was a perfect subject for such photo opportunities. (Katrina Thomas)

Lindsay sings along with Liza Minnelli at a 1965 campaign rally in Coney Island, Brooklyn. Lindsay's son, John Jr., is seen at the far left of the photo. (Katrina Thomas)

The conservative journalist William F. Buckley entered the 1965 mayoral campaign in part because of Lindsay's lack of support for Barry Goldwater in 1964. Buckley's attacks on Lindsay from the right helped strengthen Lindsay's stand with liberal New Yorkers. Although Buckley finished third, he foreshadowed the increasing rightward shift in American politics. (Bettmann/Corbis)

Mike Quill, leader of the Transport Workers Union, waves to supporters before heading to prison for his role in the January 1966 transit strike. Quill would be dead of a heart attack by the end of the month. (New York Daily News)

Deputy Mayor Robert Price (right) served as John Lindsay's political alter ego and 1965 campaign manager. Less than a year into office, though, the two men decided to part ways. (New York Daily News)

New York's glamour couple, John and Mary Lindsay, enjoy a night on the town. Some resented Lindsay's patrician style, but others credited him with bringing style and grace to city government. (Library of Congress)

Lindsay and Governor Nelson Rockefeller overlook a diorama of Manhattan. The relationship between the two liberal Republicans would quickly disintegrate over questions of how to run the city and who would be the state's top Republican. (New York Daily News)

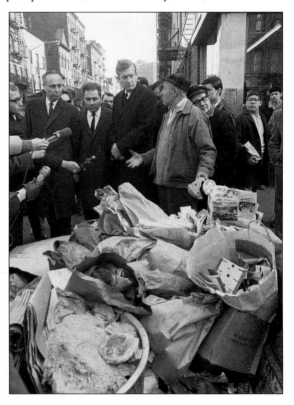

John Lindsay winds his way through mounds of garbage stacked on the sidewalks of Manhattan's Lower East Side in February 1968, at the height of the sanitation workers' strike. (Bettman/Corbis)

Governor Otto Kerner of Illinois, chairman of the President's Advisory Commission on Civil Disorders, joins Vice Chairman John Lindsay for an October 1967 press conference. The Kerner Commission, guided strongly by Mayor Lindsay, blamed white racism for the conditions of the black ghettos. (Library of Congress)

Albert Shanker, head of the United Federation of Teachers, addresses a rally of teachers to protest the dismissal of 12 union teachers from the Ocean Hill–Brownsville school district. Shanker's shrewd handling of the controversy angered Mayor Lindsay but solidified Shanker's position as one of the most prominent union leaders in the city. (United Federation of Teachers Archives; UFT Photo Collection; Robert F. Wagner Labor Archives, NYU)

Reverend Herbert Oliver (left) and Rhody McCoy (right) were two leaders of the controversial Ocean Hill–Brownsville school district in Brooklyn. This experiment with community control of schools ran into vehement opposition from teachers' union and was soon abandoned. (New York Daily News)

New York City police break through student demonstrators on the campus of Columbia University in April 1968. (Bettman/Corbis)

No single event tarnished Lindsay's image more than the city's poor response to the February 1969 snowstorm. Two days after the storm, a dejected Lindsay walks the snow-clogged streets of Queens. (NYT Pictures)

Lindsay (center) shakes hands with Republican John Marchi (right) and Democrat Mario Procaccino (left), his two opponents during the 1969 mayoral campaign. (New York Daily News)

Jerry Grote (left) and Rod Gaspar (right) of the New York Mets spray Lindsay with champagne after the "Miracle Mets" World Series victory in October 1969. Pundits said that this photo of Lindsay, whose improbable reelection campaign had a similarly miraculous outcome, helped humanize him in the minds of voters. (New York Daily News)

Thousands of hardhat construction workers, many carrying anti-Lindsay signs, march near City Hall on May 15, 1970, in support of President Nixon and the Vietnam War. (AP/Wide World Photos)

John Lindsay at City Hall, July 1972. Nearly seven years as mayor had taken its toll on Lindsay, as had his failed bid for the Democratic presidential nomination earlier that year. (New York Daily News)

In November 1997, John Lindsay towers over two of his mayoral successors, David Dinkins (left) and Abe Beame (center). (New York Daily News)

can mayoral candidate in New York trying to appeal to working-class voters, there could be no better gift than to be booed on Wall Street.[113]

If the endorsements of Mailer, Kempton, Lippmann, and Harrington were not enough to convince liberal New Yorkers to abandon the Democratic Party temporarily, there was one more endorsement that would soothe their concerns. Edward Koch made a big splash in 1963 when he defeated Carmine DeSapio, the boss of Tammany Hall, for the position of male district leader in Greenwich Village. In a rematch, Koch again defeated DeSapio in a September 1965 election. With these victories, Koch, a liberal lawyer and reform Democrat, gained a reputation as a giant killer. In consultation with his friend Henry Stern, a Liberal Party leader, Koch decided on the Sunday before the election to come out for Lindsay and again buck the city's Democratic clubhouse. William Fitts Ryan had already announced that he would vote for Beame, but was not endorsing him, a signal to his reform Democratic supporters that a vote for Lindsay was acceptable. In anticipation of his momentous decision, Koch did not sleep Sunday night. The next morning, he called Carol Greitzer, the female district leader and a fellow reformer, and Marty Berger, the president of the Village Independent Democrats, and both agreed to endorse Lindsay publicly. At eleven o'clock, Koch, Greitzer, and Berger announced they were backing Lindsay. Koch told the reporters assembled in his tiny, cluttered Wall Street office there were three reasons for switching party allegiances in this election: bossism, the lack of imaginative leadership among Democrats, and the future of the Democratic Party. Lindsay called Koch later in the day to thank him personally and told the press that because of their battles with DeSapio and his clubhouse, these reformers "have been a force for good in New York and for reform."

Bob Price believed that Koch's endorsement made Lindsay mayor, but it was an uncomfortable decision for Koch. The Greenwich Village politician was extremely nervous and worried about the danger his endorsement might cause his political career. That Monday, Koch was invited to appear with Lindsay on television. When he arrived, Koch felt immediately uncomfortable. "I looked around the room at all of the Republican faces and reminded myself why I was a Democrat," Koch remembered. "These are not my kind of people, I was thinking. These are richies. I don't like them politically or socially. They don't like me or what I represent. We have nothing in common." Koch told Price of his discomfort and bowed out of the televised announcement, but his endorsement gave Lindsay authenticity among liberal Democrats who might normally be queasy about Republicans. So disturbed were Democratic officials that after the election they put Koch on trial for party disloyalty. By this time, though, the Democratic machine was so weakened by reform attacks that they could no longer enforce party discipline, and Koch went unpunished for his act of betrayal.[114]

On October 18, Beame received the endorsement of Mayor Wagner, who had backed Screvane in the primary. In addition to the endorsement, Wagner also took the opportunity to lash out at the "calumny" heaped on his administration, calling the attacks "unjustified slurs." On the same day Beame received another, less welcome, endorsement. Sitting in Congressman Adam Clayton Powell Jr.'s Abyssinian Baptist Church in Harlem, Beame received the preacher-politician's endorsement. "It is time for New York to prove we can elect a Jew as mayor," Powell intoned from the pulpit. In some ways, Powell's announcement was in keeping with the religious and ethnic overtones of the campaign. Far from swelling Jewish pride, though, Powell's remarks offended Jews, who took pride in their political independence and served to remind voters of Beame's association with the Democratic machine and the unscrupulous Powell.[115]

One endorsement would have trumped all the others: President Lyndon Johnson's. If Beame was running on the belief that only a Democratic could be elected mayor of this Democratic city and work with a Democratic President, it would help to have a strong statement of support from that President. When Vice President Humphrey came to New York for a fund-raising dinner on October 26, there was talk he would bring an endorsement from Johnson, who was recovering from a gallstone operation. Although rumors had buzzed around the Beame campaign about an imminent presidential endorsement, Humphrey limited his remarks to his own warm feeling about the Beame ticket and the sentiment that the President "sends his warm regards, hearty greetings and good fellowship." Some suggested that Johnson did not want to become involved in local politics and did not want to embarrass himself by endorsing a losing candidate. Some even went so far as to assume, from his nonendorsement, that Johnson was really supporting Lindsay. They speculated that Johnson was angered by the Beame camp's inflation of the need for a presidential endorsement, which had put Johnson in a bind. Beame claimed he never sought the presidential endorsement, thinking it meaningless in a local campaign, and that it was his campaign staff who wanted it.[116]

After Humphrey's nonendorsement, President Johnson told Beame, through an intermediary, that he wanted to speak with him. Beame called Johnson at the hospital where he was recovering from surgery and the two spoke for almost twenty minutes. The President relayed to Beame his disappointment over Humphrey's lack of an endorsement and said he would take care of the misunderstanding. Putting an end to three days of rumors about his intentions, Johnson finally released an endorsement through his press secretary, Bill Moyers, that "the President is strongly and enthusiastically behind him [Beame]. . . . Mr. Beame knows that if the President voted in New York he would cast his vote for Mr. Beame and his ticket." The night before the election, Humphrey issued another statement declaring his and the President's strong support for the Beame ticket.[117]

If Lindsay trod the city's streets energetically and Buckley shunned such displays as a matter of principle, Beame stumped uneasily. Senator Robert Kennedy, hoping to consolidate his power in New York with a Democratic victory, campaigned for Beame. Kennedy had backed Screvane in the primary, but quickly joined the Beame camp and tried to take over the campaign. Kennedy complained that he was not being used in black neighborhoods like Harlem and Bedford-Stuyvesant, where Lindsay had already become a familiar face. Instead, Kennedy was used in predominantly white working-class neighborhoods. At one stop in an Irish Catholic enclave in the Bronx, Kennedy succumbed to more of the bizarre religious scare tactics that seemed to infect the entire campaign. In front of a Catholic church, Kennedy made a subtle reference to Lindsay's WASP background before a group of Catholic children and their parents: "If the Republicans get in, who knows what they'll do to All Saints' Day." Kennedy and the rest of the Beame team tried repeatedly to get the candidate to show some righteous anger, a trait Lindsay had mastered. Beame felt Kennedy was a great asset, but admitted there was one drawback. After Kennedy introduced Beame to a crowd, the Senator would move to the side of the platform and allow Beame to speak. Unfortunately, sometimes the crowd would move over to the more charismatic Kennedy, leaving the staid Beame with less than the full attention of his audience.[118]

Stumping for Beame was not a job that Kennedy performed willingly. Jack Newfield followed Kennedy on the final weekend of the campaign and saw that the senator "was not displaying much enthusiasm" in his appearances for Beame. The reason, according to Newfield: "Kennedy personally felt that Beame was an embarrassing, losing candidate, who did not have any grasp of the larger issues." One campaign adviser told Beame to "be like Truman," the small-town haberdasher who was transformed into a fiery populist on the stump. Kennedy's brother-in-law and political crony, Steve Smith, argued violently with Beame's team. In the words of Beame's campaign manager, Edward N. Costikyan, "The real problem was that Bobby Kennedy wanted to remake Abe Beame into a Kennedy-type of candidate." But it was too late to try to change the sixty-year-old candidate. In the final television debate before election day, Beame tried to enliven his attacks upon Lindsay, repeatedly accusing the congressman of lying. "I dare him [Lindsay] to let the people see his face on television when I ask him to explain his vicious lies," Beame warned before the debate. "I will hold him up to the electorate as a liar unfit for public office." In retrospect, Beame felt this last-minute change in his mild-mannered character hurt him. "I could visualize the little old ladies and the other people listening in saying, how could I call this knight in shining armor, this handsome young man, a liar."[119]

In the final days of the campaign, with the Beame campaign showing signs of weakness, Lindsay turned his attention to the black vote. He was aided by his strong civil rights record in Congress and the support of prominent blacks such as Sammy Davis Jr., Lionel Hampton, Ossie Davis, Ruby Dee, Dick Gregory, Jackie Robinson, Sugar Ray Robinson, James Farmer of CORE, Bill Booth of the state NAACP, and Rose Morgan, the former Mrs. Joe Louis and a prominent Harlem businesswoman. Lindsay displayed a palpable empathy for blacks. Speaking in October at a Liberal Party dinner, Lindsay said, "The better-off must finally learn that there are no islands anymore; that their security can be protected and preserved only if those less fortunate are rescued from the long night of misery and deprivation. . . . As long as inequity remains a dominant fact of life for millions, New York will be a powder keg of unrest." It was clear that Lindsay was speaking directly to the problems of black New Yorkers. He argued that "the challenge to municipal leadership [is] to enlist the city's minorities as part of the team, to make them 'insiders' with a share of the American Dream instead of isolated, resentful 'outsiders.' " In a June speech to the United Council of Harlem Organizations, Lindsay promised black New Yorkers a "ten-point program to help relieve the summer tensions and frustrations in the slums and neighborhoods of our city," including more summer jobs, keeping schools open for summer remedial tutoring, 100 additional play streets, an expanded human relations program for the police department, an independent Civilian Complaint Review Board dominated by citizens, not police, and an executive assistant on civil rights whose sole responsibility would be to keep in touch with "the moods, tensions and stress of the slum neighborhoods of our city."[120]

An October press release from the Lindsay campaign stated: "Race relations may be the most important issue in New York's progress or decay in the next ten years." It went on to delineate an ambitious program to improve the situation of black New Yorkers: expand Head Start, appoint qualified blacks to the administration, end "de facto" segregation, demand equal treatment at city hospitals, "make business work actively to train and hire Negroes on a mass scale," "launch massive job development and slum rebuilding programs together," and "induce all unions to strive for equal rights in their own ranks." A "Dear Resident of Harlem" letter from the Lindsay campaign asked Harlem blacks to "rebel with us against the do-nothing attitude at City Hall." He also offered some decidedly less adventurous but more practical promises for Harlem residents: buses on Seventh Avenue every ten minutes, an end to poor housing, regular street cleaning, and a Harlem branch of City Hall. But Lindsay's concern for blacks was developing in an atmosphere when many whites were growing ambivalent about the civil rights movement. A 1964 *Times* poll showed that 54 percent of whites felt the civil rights movement should slow down.[121]

Price planned a heavy blitz in minority neighborhoods in the waning days of the campaign to counteract Johnson's last-minute endorsement of Beame. Lindsay spent fourteen hours that final Monday trekking through Harlem and the Bronx, telling crowds, "I'll be here always." Then, well past midnight, Price and Lindsay decided to have Lindsay go on the air and field questions at the black radio station WWRL. Between 2 and 3 A.M., mere hours before the polls were to open, Lindsay fielded phone calls from the city's black residents.[122]

A VICTORY FOR REFORM

When the votes were finally tallied, Lindsay finished with 1,149,106 votes (43.3 percent); Beame 1,046,699 votes (39.5 percent); and Buckley 341,226 (12.9 percent). Over 2.6 million New Yorkers cast their ballots in the November 1965 election, a turnout of 80.8 percent of registered voters, the third largest turnout in the city's history up to that point. This was high in comparison to later mayoral elections.[123]

Though victorious, the Lindsay campaign was an anachronism. Though it was a victory for Lindsay and for Price's strategy of retail campaigning, many believed that the charismatic and attractive candidate's talents had been wasted and that a modern television campaign would have won Lindsay a bigger victory. David Garth, brought in by Price to run the small television side of the campaign, believes that the 1965 campaign would have been stronger had there been more emphasis on television. Richard Aurelio, who ran Lindsay's 1969 reelection campaign, chose not to follow Price's strategy. "I always felt that Lindsay in his first campaign should have won by a bigger margin," said Aurelio, "because I thought that he had much more going for him." The Lindsay team did run some television advertisements, but they were unsophisticated and usually featured a tense Lindsay reading his indictment against Democratic rule, often biting off his scathing words in a fury at the crisis that had befallen the city. His words were coupled with shots of a decaying city: air pollution, a rundown school, slum housing.[124]

One quarter of Lindsay's vote total (293,194) came from the Liberal Party line on the ballot, representing more than double his margin of victory. In eight state assembly districts, Lindsay pulled more than one third of his vote on the Liberal Party line, mostly in middle-class Jewish areas like the Upper West Side, Coney Island, and Midwood. In one heavily Jewish area—Flushing, Queens—Lindsay's total Liberal tally surpassed his Republican total. Lindsay carried Manhattan, Queens, and Staten Island, while Beame won his home borough of Brooklyn and Charlie Buckley's Bronx. Lindsay won thirty-nine of the city's sixty-five assembly districts, and Beame won the remaining twenty-six. Beame won every black and Puerto Rican district, but by smaller margins than one would expect for a Democrat. Beame voters were concentrated in predominantly working-class Jewish neighborhoods, where the Democratic clubhouses still had strength.

Lindsay received 40 percent of the black vote. In addition, Lindsay won a respectable 25 percent of the Puerto Rican vote. He took approximately 40 percent of the traditionally Democratic Jewish vote, eroding Beame's core voting bloc. Although Beame carried working-class Jewish areas like East Flatbush, Williamsburg, Crown Heights, and Midwood in Brooklyn, Manhattan's Lower East Side, and the Grand Concourse area of the Bronx, he lost wealthier Jewish areas such as Riverdale in the Bronx, Forest Hills and Rego Park in Queens, and Flatbush, Brooklyn.

The keys to Lindsay's victory were his strong showings in his Manhattan congressional district, in Republican-leaning Queens and Staten Island, in middle- and upper-middle-class Jewish neighborhoods, plus whatever black and Puerto Rican votes he could steal from Beame. The importance of the latter groups was indicated by the neighborhoods Lindsay chose to visit the day after his victory. Ignoring his Manhattan district and white Catholic areas in the outer boroughs, Lindsay traveled to Harlem, the black Brooklyn ghetto of Bedford-Stuyvesant, and the middle-class, Jewish Rego Park neighborhood in Queens to celebrate the victory of the first Republican mayor in twenty years.

Buckley, though he won no assembly district outright, managed to finish second in four districts, edging out Beame in the Republican districts of northern Staten Island, Bayside and Ridgewood in Queens, and Bay Ridge in Brooklyn. Buckley's top twelve assembly districts comprised all of Staten Island, northeastern Bronx, the Bay Ridge section of Brooklyn, and the Ridgewood, Richmond Hill, and Sunnyside sections of Queens. Buckley's poorest showings were in districts with large numbers of blacks and Puerto Ricans, like the South Bronx, Harlem, and central Brooklyn.

When compared to Barry Goldwater, who had taken more than 800,000 votes in New York City the previous year, Buckley's total looks paltry. One must remember, though, that Goldwater had the advantage of running on the Republican line rather than as a third-party candidate. In the 1961 mayoral race, Lawrence Gerosa, running as a third-party, pro-taxpayer candidate, had polled 321,996 votes, slightly less than Buckley. In the following year's gubernatorial race, the Conservative Party candidate, Paul Adams, an obscure upstate college professor, received only 237,119 votes in New York City, nearly one third fewer than Buckley.

Many observers felt that Buckley hurt Beame more than he hurt John Lindsay. This was based on two factors: (1) Buckley presented a convenient target for Lindsay with which to revive his sagging campaign and strengthen his liberal credentials among reformers, blacks, and Jews; and (2) Buckley did well among conservative, white, ethnic Democrats who would normally vote for Beame.

The first point is no doubt true, but the second is harder to prove. After the election, Buckley heatedly denied the charge of having drawn voters away from Beame: "It was not I who wrote Mr. Beame's speeches; not I who posed, beaming, alongside Adam Clayton Powell Jr.; not I who attempted to demonstrate to the voters that John Lindsay was a conservative Republican; not I who accused conservative-minded New Yorkers of desiring to construct concentration camps. It was taxing enough to run my own campaign, without having to run Mr. Beame's." In a postelection memo to Buckley, his advisers Dan Mahoney and Bill Rusher argued that Buckley had taken evenly from both Lindsay and Beame. The memo discussed internal Lindsay polls showing Buckley taking his first 75,000 votes from Lindsay, but two from Beame for every one from Lindsay thereafter, for roughly an even split. Buckley, however, still claimed that most of his vote was Republican. Twelve of the fifteen most Republican assembly districts in the city were the strongest Buckley districts. The three Republican districts not showing strong Buckley numbers were in Lindsay's Silk Stocking congressional district. The twelve strong Buckley districts were in the white Catholic outer boroughs. Thus, Beame supporters were correct to conclude that Buckley's strong showing among the Irish Democrats of Inwood and Sunnyside and other white Democrats in northeastern Bronx had drained strength from their candidate.

Yet something else had happened. The Irish, Germans, and Italians were not just Democrats switching over to vote for Buckley. Many switched permanently to the Republican Party. It is impossible to tell how many Buckley voters would have switched to Beame in a two-way race, but it is certain that all of Buckley's top twelve assembly districts were won by Lindsay. These districts' voters proved receptive to the Republican message, either Buckley's conservative type or Lindsay's more liberal variety.[125]

Political analyst Kevin Phillips showed that eleven of the city's white Catholic districts had already been voting for Republican candidates like Nelson Rockefeller in 1954, Dwight Eisenhower in 1956, and Richard Nixon in 1960. Outer borough neighborhoods such as Bay Ridge, Bensonhurst, Staten Island, Ridgewood, Elmhurst, Maspeth, Sunnyside, Cambria Heights, Bayside, Douglaston, Throgs Neck, and Parkchester gave between eighty and forty percent of their votes to these Republicans. In keeping with this tradition, these Republicans stayed with Lindsay for the most part. Lindsay polled well in these traditionally Republican districts, winning them all by a plurality. Pollster Oliver Quayle noted after the election that Lindsay did "surprisingly well among Catholics generally," especially Irish and Italian. New York's Italians had long been attracted to the Republican Party for many reasons: Fiorello La Guardia's (nominal) Republican identity, Franklin Roosevelt's slur against Italians when he described Mussolini's invasion of Ethiopia as a "stab in the back," and the native conservatism of Italian-Americans.[126]

A Louis Harris poll found Lindsay kept three-quarters of his Republican base. He won roughly the same percentage as Goldwater did in 1964 among WASPs (61 percent) and Italians (40 percent), yet his showing among the

Irish and German was significantly lower, due to Buckley's strength among these two groups. Lindsay won 50 percent of the German vote (as opposed to Goldwater's 64 percent) and 40 percent of the Irish (opposed to Goldwater's 55 percent). This was a strong showing for Lindsay, gaining the support of forty to fifty percent of Irish, German, and Italian voters. Lindsay, of course, did much better among Jews, blacks, and Puerto Ricans than Goldwater. Overall, Lindsay did well among New York's white ethnics voters. In his study of Canarsie, Brooklyn, sociologist Jonathan Rieder estimated that Lindsay won a plurality of 40 percent in Canarsie's Italian districts. The Irish, Italians, and Germans of the city were attracted to Lindsay, like most other New Yorkers, by his good looks, charm, and vigor, as well as his reform themes which appealed to middle-class homeowners.[127]

The events of 1965 bore many earmarks of traditional New York reform: a splintered Democratic opposition, a "fusion" campaign supported by the city's economic elite, a Democratic Party embarrassed by scandal (the "city in crisis" served as a substitute for muckraking-generated scandals), and charges of "bossism." Lindsay spoke the impassioned language of urban reform that New York voters had been hearing for nearly eighty years. There was a widespread sense that Lindsay was the embodiment of civic virtue, a man who would save the city from the corrupt Democratic machine. In an October 1965 appearance on *Meet the Press*, Lindsay called his campaign "a crusade to bring decency and good government to New York City." John Kennedy's observation "Sometimes party loyalty demands too much" became a hallmark of Lindsay's appeal to Democrats. Echoing La Guardia, he reminded voters that there was no Republican or Democratic way to pick up the garbage. A typical Lindsay stump speech exhorted the crowd, "If you are willing to ride a wave of reform you'll vote for the Lindsay team and start all over again. If you'll give me a chance, I can help this city to grow. . . . If New York is ungovernable, we're all through. I say to New Yorkers, rise up. Let's go, New Yorkers. We shall overcome our troubles. Let's go to work, let's go; let us build a new city. . . . If you are willing to join a revolution, a new movement in New York City to break open the existing establishment, then come with me." As Nelson Rockefeller noted, "Voters react to you intuitively. And that's the important thing John has going for him—they can *feel* his independence."[128]

Along with this exaltation of the dashing and glamorous John Lindsay was the denigration of the machine-backed Abe Beame. F. Scott Fitzgerald captured this upper-class snobbishness toward urban politicians a half century earlier in his novel *This Side of Paradise*. Fitzgerald's alter ego, Amory Blaine, asks, "Why is it that the pick of the young Englishmen from Oxford and Cambridge go into politics and in the U.S.A. we leave it to the muckers?—raised in the ward, educated in the assembly and sent to Congress, fat-paunched bundles of corruption, devoid of 'both ideas and ideals' as the debaters used to say."

Short, bland, and uninspiring, speaking with the accent of his Brooklyn youth, Beame had to deal with an increasingly image-conscious electorate and a press that consistently drove home the point that Beame was ordinary. The Yale-educated Buckley himself once said of Beame that he constantly stressed his New York City education, "which fact should be obvious." During the campaign a voter asked Buckley, "Could you imagine Mrs. Beame greeting the Queen of England at Kennedy Airport?" Some middle- and upper-middle-class Jews felt shame toward Beame, along the lines of "we can do better than Beame."[129]

Though some criticism of Beame's clubhouse connections was legitimate, a segment of New York's liberal electorate, so egalitarian in the abstract, could not see this product of lower-middle-class Brooklyn representing their city. Analyzing Beame's critics, the *Journal–American* columnist William White summed up the arguments of Beame's critics: "He has no 'style.' He is 'dull'! He is short and lacking in glamour. He is—though this point is only carefully used—not 'aristocratic' to a curious group of Democratic snobs which is forever screeching against 'discrimination' when practiced by others." When some liberals looked at Abe Beame, Democratic candidate for mayor of New York City, either they did not see themselves, or they saw what they were trying so desperately to escape. Beame's time would come, but only after the bitter disillusionment with New York's Camelot had set in.[130]

In contrast to Beame, Lindsay appeared wealthy, attractive, and charming. True to his Republican reformism, Lindsay promised a can-do, pro-business attitude at City Hall. "The essential element for New York City," he argued, "is a climate that will foster economic growth." Evoking the theme of a moral crusade to clean up the corruption of New York City, Lindsay once asked a reporter rhetorically, "How the devil can you ever make a city like this honest?" In a similar tone of exasperation, Lindsay asked Oliver Pilat, "What can you do about a city as crooked as New York?" Lindsay entitled an October article he wrote for the *Saturday Evening Post* "Can New York Be Saved?" It was clear that the answers to these questions, in Lindsay's mind, were contingent upon his election as mayor.[131]

Lindsay's victory put him on the cover of both *Time* and *Newsweek*. If Lindsay could revive New York's fortunes, *Newsweek* argued, "his claim on the GOP future would be nearly indisputable." The *Times* hailed Lindsay's victory with the conviction that "the thorough research and thoughtfulness that went into the writing of position papers during his campaign will stand him in good stead now." In the wake of the Goldwater debacle, some saw Lindsay's victory as heralding a new progressive Republicanism. *Business Week* predicted "that the future of Republicanism lies with the moderates, the so-called liberal wing." The conservative *Wall Street Journal* applauded Buckley's strong showing, but also hailed Lindsay's victory, while interpreting it differently from the liberal press, as a "revolt against bad government" and a signal of New York's growing sentiment against the "liberal shibboleth of unlimited government." Barry Goldwater, still smarting from Lindsay's betrayal in 1964, was not about to concede anything. "Lindsay feels that everything that can be done to win an election should be done," complained Goldwater, "even if it means completely forgetting Republican principles."[132]

WRITING OF LA GUARDIA'S 1933 VICTORY, the historian Arthur Mann argued that the "Little Flower's" supporters "came from voters of every sort and condition, but in largest proportion from the middle and wealthy classes. This fits with what scholars have recently discovered and professional politicians have known for a long time—that both suburbs and silk-stocking districts generate the most power for anti-boss movements." And so it was with John Lindsay. The core of Lindsay's support came from traditional reform voters. Lindsay's strong showing among well-off Jews can be explained by their attraction to his position as the only "liberal" in the race, but also to their position as upper-middle-class reformers (those living in Manhattan especially) and middle-class homeowners (those living in outer-borough middle-class neighborhoods like Riverdale or Flatbush or Rego Park). Lindsay's coalition comprised a remarkable mixture of diverse groups: Silk Stocking Manhattan Republicans, the city's business elite, middle- and lower-middle-class white Catholic homeowners in the outer boroughs, liberal Manhattan reformers, middle-class Jews in the outer boroughs, and a small but significant number of blacks and Puerto Ricans. Such a diverse coalition was bound to fracture under the pressures of governing, as had all previous reform coalitions—but none had done so as dramatically or as furiously as would Lindsay's.[133]

For a moment on the night of November 2, 1965, a man could believe that the mayoralty of New York City might lead to the White House; a city could believe that a handsome mayor's righteous moralism would revive the spirit of Camelot and raise the fortunes of a city in decline; and a nation could still put its faith in liberalism to maintain its values, affluence, national security, and civil order. Within four years, all of these beliefs would become untenable.

FIGHTING THE
"POWER BROKERS"

One of John Lindsay's handicaps is that he was
the greatest mayor the city ever had before he
took office.

—Robert F. Wagner, June 1967[1]

John Lindsay was often compared to John Kennedy. On the surface, the similarities were striking. Both men were young, good-looking, athletic, and idealistic. They had attractive families with young children and intelligent brothers who served as advisers. They were both World War II naval officers who cultivated a patrician style. Both tapped an optimistic spirit within the American people and goaded the country toward a better tomorrow. Both married strong-willed women from privileged backgrounds—in fact, Mary Lindsay and Jacqueline Kennedy were both products of Miss Porter's School in Farmington, Connecticut, and Vassar College.

Yet the similarities ended at the surface. Lindsay was annoyed by the constant comparisons to Kennedy. He once defined a crucial difference between himself and Boston's lace-curtain Irish aristocrats: "I'm not plotting and planning to the top like the Kennedys do." The journalist Noel Parmentel noted that "no two politicians have ever been more unalike than John Fitzgerald Kennedy and John Vliet Lindsay. For one thing John Lindsay is a better person than was Kennedy. More honest, more honorable." Lindsay, as would soon become apparent, did not have the stomach for the political intrigue and hardball that were Kennedy family hallmarks. "Jack Kennedy was not in John Lindsay's class," Parmentel observed. "John Lindsay is not in Jack Kennedy's league."[2]

Lindsay's Protestant pangs of conscience would have amused the Catholic Kennedys, who felt at ease in a world of personal and political realpolitik. In contrast to the high-flying Kennedys, Lindsay was "one of the most bourgeois people alive," a "Scarsdale Galahad," wrote Parmentel, who "could easily pass muster as a scoutmaster in Peoria, a Lutheran . . . layman in Wichita, a vice-chairman of the civic-affairs committee of the Toledo Lions Club, a 14th degree Mason (York Rite) in Sioux Falls." Inevitably, Lindsay's squeaky-clean image, so admirable in the abstract when couched in the airy language of a campaign, would become tarnished when exposed to the harsh oxidizing force of New York politics.[3]

Lindsay rushed head-first into his mayoralty. According to the political scientist Martin Shefter, postwar New York reformers aimed at three institutions: the regular Democratic organization; Robert Moses' public-works empire; and the municipal bureaucracy. The first two years of Lindsay's Republican administration can be seen as an extension of this reform mission. Having vanquished the Democratic clubhouse in the person of Abe Beame to gain the mayoralty in the 1965 election, Lindsay next went after other centers of power within the city. He wanted to stop Moses and his pro-automobile agenda; wrest power away from the police department's "Irish Mafia" and teach the police to treat the city's residents, especially its minorities, more humanely; and devolve power away from the centralized, public-school bureaucracy and back to local communities.[4]

Following the "city in crisis" theme, Lindsay wrote after his inauguration: "Our cities exact too much from those who live in them. They are not only increasingly expensive places in which to live or work; more and more, the price of city living is being paid by a sacrifice of fundamental personal freedoms." He promised an honest, efficient, fiscally responsible, socially progressive government where "the public interest must prevail over special interests, the good of the community over the desires of any group."[5]

When Lindsay took office, he seemed to follow Theodore Roosevelt's 1894 advice to urban reformers: "The first [rule] is the gospel of morality; the next is the gospel of efficiency." Lindsay's first term embodied both themes. His moralism consisted of a strong belief in civil rights and in putting the public interest ahead of selfish private interests. He excoriated those who profited from human misery, warning that anyone used to business as usual would be sorely disappointed by his administration.[6]

Often, however, Lindsay rubbed many people raw with his moralistic style. Early in his administration he acquired an array of nicknames—Mr. Clean, Captain Marvel, Sir Galahad, Prince Valiant, and the White Knight—none of which was meant to be flattering. The journalist Barbara Carter noted that the new mayor had "more than a touch of arrogance, for the city's leading WASP is on occasion waspish. He 'demands' this, he 'will not tolerate' that. 'Pay attention to me,' he raps out sharply, as if he were the teacher of an unruly class."[7]

His inaugural address previewed Lindsay's moralistic side. Speaking at City Hall Plaza on a dreary but unseasonably balmy sixty-one-degree New Year's Day, Lindsay said he would "go forth with a selfless perspective" against the "enemies" of the city—"greed, ignorance, bureaucracy, prejudice and defeatism—in high places and low." The journalist Steven Weisman, in a 1972 article entitled "Why Lindsay Failed," observed, "Lindsay's congressional career had taught him little of the need for subtle bureaucratic maneuvering, for understanding an opponent's self-interest, or for the great patience required in a sprawling government." He would soon find that although it might be easy to paint negligent owners of slum buildings or striking municipal workers as "enemies" of the city, in fact most city issues involved reasonable and decent, if sometimes flawed, people with different priorities and beliefs.[8]

Lindsay moved away from the traditional reform goal of the professionalization of city government. For earlier reformers, the best government was one where politicians were constrained from meddling in city agencies, where municipal employees' allegiances were not to any party or politician, but to their department. Civil service reform and seniority rules were designed to create a professionalized bureaucracy. Lindsay, though, was convinced that the city workforce had become ossified. In his first two and a half years he increased the number of municipal jobs exempt from civil service requirements from 1,500 to 12,800. In his attempts to exercise control over the Transit Authority and Triborough Bridge Authority, the Board of Education, and the police department, Lindsay proved willing to ignore traditional reform goals of separating politics from government.[9]

Not only was Lindsay's first year full of the usual missteps and embarrassments that would be expected from any new administration, especially a reform administration staffed with many nonprofessionals with little municipal government experience, it was also marked by arrogance. Lindsay, elected with only 43 percent of the vote, lacked a strong party organization to support him. Being a WASP, he had no ethnic base to rely on. He faced an overwhelmingly Democratic City Council, as well as the politically ambitious Democrats Frank O'Connor and Mario Procaccino in the positions of City Council president and comptroller. Even where Lindsay had Republican support, it proved unhelpful. Staten Island Borough President Robert T. Connor had priorities very different from Lindsay's. Governor Nelson Rockefeller was angered by Lindsay's ingratitude for his help during the election and jealous of his potential strength within the party. Republican state legislators, hailing mostly from upstate New York, had a political philosophy closer to the small-town conservatism of the Midwest than the Silk Stocking liberalism of Manhattan and were hostile to New York City and its free-spending fiscal policies. Politically, John Lindsay was very much alone.

In his 1970 book, *Lindsay's Promise: The Dream That Failed,* Woody Klein observed, "Being Mayor of New York did not seem to come easily or naturally to John Lindsay." Instead of building a governing coalition, Lindsay told his former Yale classmate Bob Sweet, he was "gonna burn up all of my credit cards" and not worry about the political impact of his decisions. If Wagner was unwilling to face tough problems, Lindsay was drawn to them like a moth to a flame.[10]

In the first half of 1966, Lindsay challenged the unions, Robert Moses, and the state legislature. The results were mixed, but he did show New Yorkers he planned to conduct city business in a new way.

THE 1966 TRANSIT STRIKE

At five o'clock on the morning of New Year's Day, 1966, the Transport Workers' Union (TWU) shut down the subways and buses, depriving Lindsay of a political honeymoon. (Ferries, some private bus lines, and commuter trains were unaffected by the strike.) Three hours later, a Seventh Avenue IRT train that entered the 241st Street terminal in the Bronx was the last passenger train to ride the rails for the next twelve days. For New York, more than for any other city in the country, mass transit is the oxygen that keeps city life breathing. The city's first ever transit strike would choke the city, especially the island of Manhattan, whose 22.6 square miles was home to approximately 1.6 million people and the workplace for almost twice that number.

The strike spawned a number of jokes. Sammy Davis Jr. congratulated Lindsay for eliminating crime in the subways on his first day in office. Another joke told of a drunken man who, after stumbling into the subway after a night of New Year's reveling and finding the subways closed, said, "My God, Wagner's gone to Mexico and taken the subways with him." The point of the joke was that Mayor Wagner had left for Mexico with his new bride, Barbara Cavanaugh, and his two sons while still technically mayor, on the afternoon of December 31, leaving the transit crisis in Lindsay's lap. When asked at the airport about his early departure, Wagner replied, "This is Lindsay's show now." Wagner also missed the inauguration. Before he left for Mexico, Wagner told the city, "Perfection in the conduct of government has thus far been achieved only in Heaven. I expect that will continue to be the case in the future. . . . The troubled years will not be over with the end of 1965. My judgment is that the present phase will extend well into the next four years and perhaps beyond." Years later, in tones of barely concealed contempt, Wagner claimed to have warned Lindsay to pay close attention to the transit crisis. "Well," Wagner said, "he thought he had a lot of these young fellows around him, that reform and good things in New York would start on January first, when he took over."[11]

Wagner's animosity for Lindsay ran deep. In a television interview just after the election, Lindsay told reporters that Gracie Mansion was "in quite bad condition at the moment . . . it needs a lot of cleaning up." Wagner took

Lindsay's remarks as a personal insult. Everyone knew that Wagner's first wife had died in 1964 and he was unable to keep up Gracie Mansion without the help of a spouse. Wagner had recently remarried and moved out of Gracie Mansion to a nearby apartment. Coming on the heels of a campaign in which Lindsay heaped abuse on the lame-duck mayor, Lindsay's remarks verged on insensitivity toward Wagner's private sorrows. Nor did it help when Lindsay's remarks landed on the front page of the *Times*. Louis Craco, a Lindsay transition aide, claimed that Lindsay did not mean offense. The interview was taped in the early-morning hours after the November 1965 blackout and Lindsay was working on only a few hours of sleep. Whether intentional or not, when Craco called Wagner's office the day after the interview aired to discuss negotiations with the TWU, he was told by a Wagner aide, "Wagner's going to Mexico. You fuckers can deal with Quill yourself."[12]

TWU President Michael Quill, born in Ireland to a family of staunch Irish Republican patriots, brought a feisty temperament to the job of organizing the heavily Irish-American transit workers. The union's fierce independence was due to the fact that it was created when the transit system was mostly in private hands. Not until 1940 did New York City purchase the privately owned Interborough Rapid Transit Company (IRT) and the Brooklyn-Manhattan Transit Company (BMT) and integrate them with the city-owned Independent line (IND) to create a unified subway system.

The TWU, founded in 1934, was one of the radical unions that came together to form the Congress of Industrial Organizations (CIO) in 1935. For its first fifteen years its leadership was dominated by Communists; "Red Mike," as Quill was called by his foes, was a member of the Communist Party of the United States (CPUSA) who followed the Soviet line and defended the Hitler-Stalin Pact in 1939. "I would rather be called a Red by a rat, then be called a rat by a Red," he declared. He was also elected for one term to the City Council on the left-wing American Labor Party ticket in the 1930s. Quill quit the CPUSA after the Party opposed the 1948 subway fare increase (on the grounds that it would add a financial burden for workers who rode the subway to their jobs) that the TWU thought necessary to support wage increases. In fact, "Red Mike" Quill spent much of his career balancing his radicalism with the more conservative Catholicism of his union members, and after his break with the CPUSA, Quill purged his former Communist allies from the union, thereby consolidating his power.[13]

Quill's name has become permanently associated with the 1966 transit strike, but it was arguably Mayor Wagner who made it a possibility when he signed Executive Order 49 into law on March 31, 1958. The act gave municipal unions the right of collective bargaining. Alex Rose, the vice chairman and effective head of the Liberal Party, president of the United Hatters, Cap and Millinery International Union, and a Wagner adviser, had urged Wagner to sign the bill, which became known as the "Little Wagner

Act" (a reference to federal labor legislation introduced by his father, Senator Robert F. Wagner, in 1935). Toward the end of his life, though, Rose came to regret doing so because "the city is not an employer in the traditional sense. Profits do not exist. Workers are not extracting a share of the profits but rather a share of taxes. Unlike bargaining in the private sector, municipal collective bargaining is part of the political rather than the adversary process."[14]

The labor expert Raymond Horton argues that collective bargaining for public sector unions was "a truly progressive stance," but he says Wagner's real goal in signing the bill was not to pass progressive legislation but "to enhance *his* control over the personnel system." Using collective bargaining, Wagner gained greater power to deal with unions and grant them favors in return for vital political support. Whatever Wagner's true motives were, collective bargaining ultimately paved the way for greater militancy in later years. Between 1960 and 1965 there was only one major strike—the 1965 welfare workers strike—and six that were mostly "brief and inconsequential." The post–1965 labor situation was decidedly more stormy.[15]

Regarding the transit workers, Quill and Wagner seemed to develop a workable modus operandi following passage of the 1958 law. Every two years, Quill would propose an outrageous increase in wages and benefits and threaten a Christmas or New Year's strike if his demands were not met. (A second transit union—the 2,000-member Amalgamated Transit Union—would join the TWU in negotiations.) Then, following a predictable script, Quill would sit down with Mayor Wagner in private and iron out an agreement. When the TWU was created, most workers were eking out an economically marginal existence. By the 1960s, transit workers were better off economically, allowing some to move into their own homes in Queens, Staten Island, or the suburbs. By 1965, hourly wages for transit workers ranged from $3.46 for motormen and mechanics to $2.74 for change-booth clerks. But the $6,299 average yearly pay for transit workers in 1965 was still below the salary the United States Bureau of Labor Statistics deemed "modest" for a family of four in New York City. Furthermore, bus and subway mechanics received less money than other city workers in comparable occupations. Quill, though, received $29,185 a year in salaries and expenses, enough to afford a thirty-seventh-floor apartment in a luxury building off Central Park West.[16]

By the mid-sixties there were two new factors that affected Quill's traditional bargaining tactics. First, the membership of the TWU was becoming less Irish and more black and Puerto Rican, and conflict within the union was slowly building. This moved Quill toward a more contentious and demanding negotiating stance. According to the historian Mark Maier, Quill needed to prove that the TWU "was not in cahoots with the Transit Authority. That charge was especially credible to black and Hispanic workers who resented representation by a predominantly white leadership." Most minorities worked as sweepers and token clerks. The hourly pay differential between these unskilled workers and their skilled counterparts was nearly one dollar per hour. Quill was sympathetic to minorities and the unskilled and he was being pressured to close this wage gap. Meanwhile, Quill was squeezed by skilled workers who saw their counterparts in the police, fire, and sanitation departments, as well as those working for private-sector commuter railroads, earning more money. If unskilled workers thought the wage gap was too large, skilled workers thought it was too small. At one point the motormen discussed forming a breakaway union for skilled transit workers.[17]

In the face of this growing militancy and division within his union, Quill needed a big payday for every faction. Quill's November 1965 proposal included a four-day, thirty-two-hour work week, a 30 percent pay increase, half-pay pensions after twenty-five years' service, regardless of age, and six weeks of vacation a year after only one year of service. Transit Authority Chairman Joseph O'Grady was "flabbergasted" at the demands, which he estimated would cost between $250 and $680 million for two years. "There isn't enough gold in Fort Knox to pay this bill," O'Grady said.

The second change for Quill and the transit union was John Lindsay's election. A top transit union official reportedly said while watching the 1965 election returns, "Now we have to have a strike. This guy is going to be tough, and we need a big settlement this year. I don't see how we can get it without striking." Whereas Wagner had a close relationship with labor and possessed an intuitive feel for negotiations, Lindsay had neither. Wagner made a point to have union officials over to Gracie Mansion for drinks, invite them and their wives to formal dinners and parties, and do favors for their families. This way, when it came time for negotiations, the mayor and the union leaders spoke as friends rather than antagonists. Depending on one's point of view, Wagner used the relationship to convince union leaders to take less money or the union leaders used their coziness with the mayor to win fat settlements.[18]

Lindsay spurned the old system of bargaining. Part of his attitude toward unions was philosophical. Previous labor negotiations, he felt, were based on friendships between Wagner and labor leaders like Quill and Harry Van Arsdale. Lindsay gave the impression that this form of compromise and negotiation was more than a little distasteful. He refused to become a deal maker, believing that just such an accommodating attitude toward municipal unions was partly to blame for New York's troubles. The mayor-elect was also concerned that any deal with the TWU be fair to black and Puerto Rican workers. Lindsay believed if he gave the Irish leadership a lump-sum settlement to divide as they wished, the mostly white skilled workers would gain at the expense of unskilled minority workers.[19]

Raymond Horton calls Lindsay's early troubles with municipal unions a "clash of life-styles." The social world of municipal unions was foreign to

Lindsay, who felt awkward around labor leaders. In turn, union leaders resented the change in attitude from the Wagner days. "Whether by choice, dint of personality, or accident," writes Horton, "the city's municipal union chiefs felt snubbed by Mayor Lindsay." One TWU official, Ellis Van Riper, talked about Lindsay's "I am God" attitude. Edward Herlihy, later to become a top Lindsay labor aide, noted, "Lindsay looked down on blue collar workers, and Mike Quill picked up on this right away." Horton writes, "If any commonality of opinion emerged from interviews with numerous union leaders and officials it was anger with Mayor Lindsay." One union official recalled the mood of his colleagues upon Lindsay's election: "There wasn't a union leader in town who didn't want to get even with Lindsay." The new mayor's tough attitude toward labor worried even the leaders of the city's private-sector unions, like Pete Brennan of the Buildings Trade Council.[20]

There was a hint of naiveté in Lindsay's stand on unions. Lindsay wanted to act as the neutral arbiter of the city's public interest. He would substitute the more formal collective bargaining for the more informal horse-trading of traditional labor negotiations and balance union demands with the city's ability to meet those demands. Bob Price believed Lindsay did not understand "the mechanics of how important unions are to the life of the city." Lindsay's advisers had, he said, an "MBA way of settling strikes which might work in Bridgeport but doesn't work in a union town" like New York. To make matters worse, A. H. Raskin, the *Times*'s labor expert and a member of the editorial board, was seen as dictating to the mayor-elect a get-tough policy with the municipal unions. Veteran labor negotiator Theodore Kheel complained that the *Times* had become "a party to the negotiations." In December, the *Times* ran eight editorials on the transit negotiations, all of them advocating a firm stand against the TWU. "If, once again, Mr. Quill can club the city into an inordinately high settlement," went a typical *Times* editorial, "every other Civil Service union will get the message that even with the change in administrations, coercion is still the way to get things from City Hall. No conclusion could be more destructive of orderly government or municipal solvency."[21]

Quill saw the WASP, good-government mayor as the perfect foil to shore up his leadership of the TWU. Jimmy Breslin wrote, "John Lindsay looked at Quill and he saw the past. And Mike Quill looked at John Lindsay and he saw the Church of England." Though the union leader was a genial, warm man in private, in public he could be brusque and sharp-tongued. He thumbed his nose at authority. Throughout negotiations during November and December, Quill repeatedly and purposely mispronounced the mayor-elect's name as "Lindsley." He berated Lindsay at private meetings and in public press conferences. He was unmerciful.[22]

Shortly after the election, Quill had threatened to take the TWU out on strike when the current contract ran out on January 1, 1966. Lindsay proposed ten names as possible mediators for the strike, none of whom had intimate knowledge of New York's labor problems. Quill rejected all ten names. One person left off the list was Ted Kheel, whom Lindsay associated with Wagner-era dealmaking. Kheel was one of the city's chief labor mediators. He was close to Wagner and was trusted by most unions, making Lindsay doubly suspicious. Quill kept demanding that at least one member of the negotiating committee should be intimate with transit issues. This was seen as a not-so-veiled reference to Kheel. According to the journalist Thomas Brooks, "The word from Lindsay's quarter was: 'No deals, no Kheel.' "[23]

The tensions between Wagner and Lindsay continued. Both men wanted to choose their own members of the mediation panel. To prod the politicians into action, Quill moved up the tentative strike date to December 15, two weeks before the end of the TWU's biennial contract. (Quill later moved the deadline back to January 1.) In the face of the strike threat, Lindsay and Wagner agreed to a compromise three-man mediation panel. Two of the picks, Nathan Feinsinger and Sylvester Garrett, were Lindsay appointees. Mayor Wagner appointed the third man: Ted Kheel. Neither Feinsinger, who was named chairman of the panel, nor Garrett was from New York. Both men, whom Kheel respected, had acted as labor arbitrators for companies such as General Motors and U.S. Steel.

Meanwhile, the Johnson administration was keeping close tabs on the strike. Gardner Ackley, the chairman of the President's Council of Economic Advisers, wrote to Johnson about the impeding transit strike. His main concern was that Quill's demands were way over the President's anti-inflationary guidelines for labor deals. "Quill's demands, as usual, are exorbitant," wrote Ackley.[24]

For most of December, negotiations went slowly, if they went at all. Lindsay was, according to Kheel, "literally under instructions from the *New York Times* not to meet with Quill." Despite this, behind-the-scenes intrigue was already beginning. Contrary to Kheel's claims, Lindsay secretly met with Quill a number of times in December at the Williams Club. Lindsay claimed that Quill told him flat out, "There's going to be a strike. There is nothing you can do about it. . . . There will be a strike and I say it will be ten days and then it will be over." Bob Price (who was soon to be Lindsay's first deputy mayor), met with Quill in secret five times during December in the offices of Quill's doctor, the heart specialist Hyman Zuckerman. The crusty union leader seemed to warm to Price, but he made it clear that he wanted an increase from $3.46 to $4 dollars per hour for motormen, with a similar 15.5 percent increase for all other TWU workers. For his own survival, Quill needed the union to strike not only to shore up his own support within the union, but also to teach the anti-union mayor-elect a lesson about who really ran the city.[25]

Lindsay's first direct public involvement in the negotiations occurred on December 27, when he met with the union representatives, the Transit Authority, and the three-man mediation panel. Kheel found Lindsay "very stiff" in his first public encounter with Quill. After the meeting Lindsay entered his limousine in a somber mood and, after a long pause, told Woody Klein, "This is going to be a bitch." As the New Year's Day deadline loomed, Lindsay again met with union officials and the Transit Authority at midday on Friday, December 31. When Lindsay complained that the union was waiting until the last minute, Quill bellowed at Lindsay, "Mr. Mayor, we are tired of taking *bubkes* from a *schmuck* like you. Why don't you grow up and stop being a juvenile." He referred to the next mayor of New York as "a boy in knee pants." Quill had acquired the Yiddish slurs, another weapon in his arsenal, from his Jewish wife. (Reportedly, Price had to translate Quill's insults for Lindsay.) After an hour, Quill left the meeting.

With the transit strike imminent, Lindsay was officially sworn in at a private ceremony at City Hall at 6:04 P.M. on December 31. The public ceremony would take place the next day, according to city tradition. Later that night, the new mayor returned to the bargaining table in the basement of the Americana Hotel. The Transit Authority had just made a $25 million offer to the transit workers—a 3.2 percent wage increase. It was promptly received with "derisive laughter" from the union. Quill denounced the offer as "peanuts." He then gave a vicious, vituperative denunciation of the mayor designed to make Lindsay walk out. "You are nothing but a juvenile, a lightweight, and a pipsqueak," a red-faced Quill screamed at Lindsay in his harsh, Irish brogue. "You have to grow up. You don't know anything about the working class. You don't know anything about labor unions."

Lindsay refused to take Quill's bait. If the union leader's speech symbolized his bullying, theatrical, anti-authority style, the mayor's response was typical of his own views of propriety and public-mindedness. It was a few minutes past midnight and he was now speaking with the full authority of the mayoralty. "I don't mind your words about me personally," Lindsay replied. "But I will not have you address the office of the mayor that way. It is an affront to the people of the City of New York." Lindsay, using the authority of his position as spokesman for 8 million New Yorkers, then went on to demand that Quill look beyond the interests of his 33,000 members. "I call upon you and all of your members not to walk out on your city," declared Lindsay in his first test as mayor of New York. "I am inheriting a bankrupt city with a multitude of problems. I therefore call upon you in the public interest to respect the city in which you live and all of its eight million inhabitants. . . . We have an obligation to stretch ourselves." Lindsay spoke to Quill as if the union head had been a faithful reader of the *Herald Tribune*'s "City in Crisis" series. Quill looked at Lindsay and thought he was crazy: "We do not agree with you that the city is bankrupt. We do not think that the city is as bad as you say it is. I would urge you to stop campaigning. The election is over, Mr. Lindsley."[26]

The press reaction to the strike was uniformly critical. The pro-Lindsay *Herald Tribune* editorialized:

> The trouble is that Mike Quill has been pampered by City Hall for many years. Having been indulged, he and his union think their routine has become a permanent affair. What they don't seem to understand, however, is that there will be a new mayor in charge. Under John Lindsay the facts of city life will be different. Mr. Quill may well find his bluff called. For the old absurdity and arrogance has worn thin. If this is a fact, Mr. Lindsay will know how to deal with it.

To the *Post*, Quill appeared "hell-bent" on a strike that would hurt thousands of working-class New Yorkers who relied on mass transit. The *Times* hoped Lindsay would show that "the city will not capitulate to such tyranny by granting wage increases and other concessions beyond those justified by economic reality." The *Times* wanted the Condon-Wadlin Act enforced; the act stated that "civil service employees have no legal right to strike."[27]

Condon-Wadlin was passed by the state legislature in 1947 after labor problems erupted in Buffalo and Rochester. The act forbade state and local government employees from striking. It mandated serious penalties for municipal union members that walked off their jobs, including automatic termination. If striking workers were rehired, they would not be entitled to any wage increases for three years and would serve a five-year probationary period without tenure. The act was designed to prevent strikes, but its penalties were so harsh they were unenforceable. Still, the Transit Authority sought to enforce the measure against the TWU. As the strike loomed on New Year's Eve, State Supreme Court Judge George Tilzer issued an injunction against the TWU that Quill promptly tore up.

Lindsay's first day as mayor was hectic. After the late-night meeting with Quill and the Transit Authority, Lindsay and his aides went to City Hall to survey their new offices. They managed to get some sleep in the early-morning hours on cots and couches in City Hall before beginning their first full day, including the formal inauguration. After having breakfast with his family at the Roosevelt Hotel, the Mayor held a press conference. Terming the TWU's action "an illegal action," Lindsay pressed for enforcement of the injunction against the union. Lindsay urged that no one drive into Manhattan on Monday unless he was engaged in "providing food, fuel, or medical services," his presence was "essential" to his business, or he would suffer "unusual and severe economic hardship." In addition, Lindsay declared that city schools would be closed on Monday. As Quill had privately predicted to Lindsay, the strike was on.[28]

Only one quarter of the 3.2 million people who normally entered Manhattan on a weekday could get to their destination on Monday. For New

Yorkers worried about the response of their employers if they did not come to work, Lindsay reassured them during a Sunday news conference, "Don't worry about that. I'm asking all employers right now to make full provision for employees who do not come to work." He told New Yorkers, "Employees should not fear that they will be prejudiced if they don't come to work." After all, if every employee tried to make it into Manhattan by automobile, the streets would be so clogged that nobody could get to work anyway.[29]

In a symbolic gesture, Lindsay walked to work Sunday morning, covering the three-and-a-half-mile, seventy-block trip from the Roosevelt Hotel to City Hall with his long strides in a brisk fifty minutes. The next day, Lindsay would again eschew his official car and walk to work. New Yorkers had gone into the voting booths two months earlier with an image of an energetic candidate, and, as the reporters who could not keep up with Lindsay could attest, the mayor was out to prove that image a reality.

Quill remained his usual vociferous self. Under the threat of incarceration, he said he was prepared to "rot in jail." He urged New Yorkers to defy Lindsay's plea not to drive into Manhattan. On the first workday of the strike, traffic was below normal. Commuter railroads, though, were jammed, and both Grand Central Terminal and Penn Station were forced to shut their doors during the evening rush hour to prevent overcrowding. By Tuesday, there was massive traffic congestion. Men and women could no longer afford to sacrifice their salaries to keep the streets open, and employers could not afford to pay employees who stayed home. Commuters waiting to get back home to Westchester and Connecticut by train were faced with serpentine lines stretching outside Grand Central Terminal along Forty-second Street and around to Vanderbilt Avenue. In front of Penn Station, homebound commuters packed the entire block of Thirty-third Street between Eighth and Ninth Avenues. Cabs were scarce and picked up multiple fares. Car pools were common, with cars often picking up hitchhiking commuters along the way. Washington Square Park in Greenwich Village was used as a parking lot.

The city's editorial pages kept up the barrage against Quill and his union. The *Journal–American* called the strike a "sabotage of organized society." The *Herald Tribune* called Quill a "pompous bore" whose strike was "against the people, not against the Transit Authority." The *Post*'s James Wechsler wrote that Quill "chose to declare war against the wrong man at the wrong time for the wrong reasons." The *Times* saw Quill's behavior as indicative of "his concept that the people of New York are the enemy he is determined to blackjack into surrender. He represents 'the last hurrah' of a cynical Old Guard type of unionism that has long been outdated."[30]

On Tuesday, Quill and eight other union leaders were jailed for contempt of court. Two hours after entering jail, Quill suffered a heart attack that put him in the hospital. When the mediation panel's Chairman

Feinsinger heard the news, he felt that it "was the beginning of a Greek tragedy." In Washington there was unease at the White House. Johnson's aide Joseph Califano warned the President that New York Democrats were starting to grumble about his lack of involvement in the strike, especially in light of his administration's recent pressure on the steel industry to roll back price increases.[31]

On Wednesday, Labor Secretary W. Willard Wirtz wrote to the President after spending most of the previous day in consultation on the strike situation. He told Johnson the situation was "shot full of politics and personalities." Besides the public conflict between Lindsay and Quill, there was a "serious division" among the three-man mediation panel as well as political splits among the three-man Transit Authority. Kheel, according to Wirtz, was "bitter about Lindsay." Wirtz also believed that Feinsinger, who suffered from Parkinson's disease and other ailments, had "lost control" of the mediation panel. In addition, Wirtz wrote that Bob Price was "trying to by-pass everyone else and make a private settlement with Quill." Feinsinger had told Wirtz it would take $50 million to settle the strike, and Ted Kheel had told him it would take $55 to $60 million, Wirtz reported to the President. The strike, Wirtz had been told, would last two to five more days. Wirtz, in discussion with the AFL-CIO's George Meany and the Liberal Party leader, David Dubinsky, wanted to propose a new six-man panel, including Dubinsky and New York's Central Labor Council leader, Harry Van Arsdale, to mediate the strike; they proposed that Quill agree to return to work for thirty days so a settlement could be reached. (The panel never became a reality.) Above all, Wirtz warned the President to stay away from the situation since any settlement would be above his anti-inflationary guidelines.[32]

In a memo the next day, Wirtz recounted a telephone conversation he had had with Lindsay on Wednesday, in which the Mayor said he was prepared to go as high as $48 or $50 million to settle the strike, which he considered within the President's guidelines. "He says he is convinced that this amount can be justified on the basis of real inequities between the transit workers and other N.Y. City employees. He says that the $50 million is his 'absolute and final limit.' " Thus, even before the settlement and only five days into the strike, Lindsay seemed willing to grant the TWU a large settlement.[33]

With no end in sight, Thursday morning brought what Traffic Commissioner Henry Barnes called "the longest rush hour in the city's history," from 4:45 A.M. to sometime after 11 A.M. City businesses were losing money with each day of the strike, but the writer Nora Ephron brought some humor to the situation by pointing out the havoc the strike was playing on New York's dating scene: "With no subways running, budding romances have been nipped simply because she lives on the East Side and he lives on the West." On the other hand, Ephron noted that men were instructing cabbies to pick up the first blonde they saw and New Yorkers were making dates with strangers courtesy of car pools.[34]

While New Yorkers tried to cope with the effects of the transit strike, Quill was moved to the prison ward at Bellevue Hospital in order to recover from his heart attack. Negotiations stalled. On Thursday, Secretary Wirtz met Lindsay, Price, and the mediators at City Hall. Price wanted to send Ted Kheel to Bellevue to talk to Quill. But Kheel believed Price had more authority to talk to Quill. Price was beginning to feel that he was in "troubled waters" with the transit negotiations, but he went to visit Quill anyway. Quill, in an oxygen tank with his doctor nearby, could only speak for ten seconds without the oxygen. When the doctor pulled back the oxygen tank, Quill held up his four fingers as a way of telling Price the strike stops when he gets four dollars for the motormen. With that, Price wished Quill well and left.[35]

Keeping Quill's associates in jail made them martyrs in the union's eyes, which they realized was a tactical advantage. When Harry Van Arsdale and George Meany presented a proposal to free Quill from jail, TWU official Douglas MacMahon told the men, "Why don't you guys mind your own business?"[36]

Lindsay summoned the union, the mediation board, and the Transit Authority to City Hall on Sunday. MacMahon took over negotiations for the TWU. According to MacMahon, bargaining "didn't start until we went to City Hall. There we began to get some give and take." Bargaining continued throughout Sunday night and into Monday morning. A $50 million settlement was taking shape—twice the Transit Authority's original offer. When Lindsay went to sleep on a couch in the City Hall gym at 3 A.M., Price continued the negotiations. While Lindsay was sleeping, Price threw on the table a $500-a-year supplementary pension benefit that the union had long wanted, but which the Transit Authority had long fought. Both the union and Transit Authority members were surprised by Price's move. One union negotiator said, "That $500 benefit alone is going to cause Lindsay a lot of trouble when he comes to bargain with other city employees." Later, John Gilhooley, a member of the Transit Authority, complained bitterly about Price's concession:

> They tried to get this benefit from us for years. We said ridiculous. You'd break the bank. We said no, no, no. But then these wise guys got into the negotiations. . . . Mastermind Price left us out entirely and during the course of the evening gave away the store. Price gave it away. And when they came out of the room one of the labor guys came over to me and said, Geez, you know what happened? We got the five-hundred-dollar pensions. . . . When we raised it, Price said, What's wrong with that? . . . Price's exact words were: I'm for pensions. After that, it was on the table and it couldn't be taken off. It was that kind of naiveté and stupidity that contributed to the whole bungle. . . . This naive jerk walked in and tried to settle it. Once in he increased the total cost of the package by fifty-four percent.

Years later, when Price was told of Gilhooley's comments, he declared, "I can't believe that, but if I did it, I did it. If they say I did it. I'm amazed that I had such authority. I was not experienced. Where was the mayor?" In retrospect, Price calls the pension throw-in a "budget buster" and "the wrong thing to do," but he felt at the time it was necessary to end the strike.[37]

Price was already beginning to consolidate his power within the administration, to the growing chagrin of Lindsay. Price reportedly told Governor Rockefeller during the strike, "Lindsay's attention span is only two or three minutes, so you had better deal with me." Harvey Rothenberg, the Mayor's appointments secretary, writes that when he told Lindsay about this remark, "I knew I hit a raw nerve when I noticed the telltale movement of Lindsay's jaw muscles." The Lindsay-Price collaboration, so successful up to this point, would quickly unravel under the pressures of governing the city.[38]

Meanwhile, the union was still not satisfied and ended talks early Monday morning. Perhaps the TWU smelled blood and thought it could exact further concessions. Or maybe it wanted to prolong Lindsay's agony. Besides, a union rally at City Hall was scheduled for Monday afternoon. Why ruin a solidarity demonstration with an early settlement? The demonstration went off as planned, and was a rousing affair attended by 10,000 to 15,000 people. Lindsay was burned in effigy. With Quill still in the hospital, MacMahon addressed the crowd, telling them, "I've never met such amateurs in all my life. I tell you it was a sad day when Bob Wagner left this town. This guy [Lindsay] doesn't know what the hell he is doing." Lindsay's press secretary, Woody Klein, reported that he had never seen Lindsay as angry as he was when he heard about the rally and MacMahon's remarks.[39]

Lindsay's response to the rally was his famous "power brokers" speech, which he gave a few hours later. Lindsay said the strike had been brought on by "a small group of men who would not listen to reason." He recommended three alternatives if the strike was not settled soon: that the panel make recommendations on all terms of the settlement; that a fact-finding commission be appointed; and that arbitration be considered. The most memorable part of Lindsay's speech, though, came at the end. Claiming the strike was a test of whether New York City could be "intimidated" by its municipal unions, Lindsay said he "would not allow the power brokers in our city or any special interests to dictate to the city the terms under which it will exist in New York. I will not yield to unreason because it holds a gun at the head of reason." When later pressed to define the "power brokers," Lindsay only vaguely spoke of "that group of special interests in New York City who for long years have sought to control the engines of government in our city through all of the political systems and other avenues of tentacle control around the machinery of government." The *Times* called the speech an "inspiring blend of courage, reason and resolution." In one broad swipe against the TWU, other municipal unions, the Wagner administration, and the city bureaucracy, Lindsay articulated his theme of reform government. When a

Times reporter asked Lindsay's press secretary, Woody Klein, to identify the "power brokers," he answered, "They know who they are. The mayor doesn't have to say any more than he wants to."[40]

Meanwhile, the strike was slowly grinding down New Yorkers. As A. M. Rosenthal wrote after the strike: "The transit strike wasn't at all amusing, and one benefit is that it will be a long time before advertising men and politicians again will embarrass real New York lovers by calling it a fun city. The strike didn't make New Yorkers kinder, better, more honest or meaner—only wearier." That Monday morning the rush hour had begun at 4:30 A.M. and a record number of cars and trucks entered Manhattan.[41] Frustrated at the negotiations, Lindsay asked the mediation panel to make recommendations for a settlement. Kheel informed Lindsay that the mediation panel would not make recommendations or serve as fact finders or arbitrators; its task was simply to mediate discussion between the parties. After this refusal, Lindsay demanded they make recommendations. To this Kheel responded that if the mayor asked, the panel would inform him what they felt a fair settlement would be. Throughout Wednesday, the mediation panel ironed out a twelve-page report and submitted it to Lindsay by late afternoon. By this time, Kheel had quietly taken over the chairmanship of the panel. Under the pressure of negotiations, an already ill Feinsinger became even sicker. When Feinsinger began suffering from nosebleeds, his doctor unsuccessfully urged him to quit. Instead Feinsinger ceded control to Kheel. Thus, the man Lindsay had spurned only a month earlier was now in charge of negotiations.[42]

In its report, the mediation panel emphasized "that we do not report our view as arbitrators, or fact finders, but solely as mediators giving you our thought concerning a basis for resolution of the remaining differences between the parties." It reiterated the belief that "a complete agreement could no doubt ultimately be achieved through collective bargaining, and in an ordinary dispute the bargaining should be permitted to run its full course." But of course, as the mediators admitted, "this was no ordinary dispute." The panel stated that its recommendations were based on what the parties had already agreed to during negotiations.[43]

The strike was finally settled in the early-morning hours of Thursday, January 13, having lasted only three days longer than Quill had earlier predicted to Lindsay. Both the city and the union agreed roughly to the mediation panel's recommendations, despite the panel's protestations that they were not making recommendations. The agreement basically followed what Quill had been demanding in private since December: that the motormen's fifty-four-cent raise to four dollars per hour would be used as a base wage, which translated into roughly a 15 percent raise for all transit workers. The increase would be "backloaded" to ease the financial burden to the city: the first 4 percent raise would be retroactive to January 1, the next 4 percent would kick in on January 1, 1967, and the final 7 percent would come on July 1, 1967. A total of $3 million dollars would be spent over two years to improve working conditions in the subways. There was also the $500 supplementary pension bonus agreed to earlier by Price.

The first city bus hit the road sometime after six o'clock on Thursday morning, January 13. Because of technical problems, it took the subways a little longer to get up and running, but by Thursday evening's rush hour most subways were back on the tracks. With the strike officially over, a judge released Quill from the prison ward at Bellevue Hospital and released the other eight TWU officials from jail. Despite the high settlement, Lindsay reassured the city that he would work to save the fifteen-cent fare. Governor Rockefeller promised the city $100 million to help keep the fare down. But considering that the Transit Authority was already operating with a deficit before the huge settlement, the days of the fifteen-cent transit fare were numbered.

The actual cost of the settlement was the subject of much debate. The Mayor, with an interest in keeping the settlement figure low so as not to appear to have caved in to the union, gave the figure at $52 million over two years, almost twice the deal the TWU had received in 1963. The Transit Authority's Joe O'Grady estimated the cost at $70 million. Kheel stuck to the $52 million estimate. As expected, the union stuck with the higher figure. Additionally, Lindsay announced that the thirteen-day strike had cost New York as much as $500 million. The Commerce and Industry Association of New York estimated the losses at $800 million. The city government estimated that the strike cost it $6 million each working day from lost sales taxes, business taxes, and real estate taxes and from money spent in overtime for city workers.[44]

The Condon-Wadlin Act proved useless. Not only could municipal unions strike against the taxpayers who paid their salaries and paralyze the city, they could also get large settlements as a reward. A harsh law existed on the books, but few politicians wanted to enforce it fully. To enforce Condon-Wadlin would have meant literally breaking the transit union. It was an idea too ugly for most people to contemplate.

In public, Lindsay played the role of a forceful leader, rallying his flock to overcome the debilitating effects of the strike. New Yorkers did not seem to blame him for the strike. One poll claimed that 75 percent of New Yorkers approved of the Mayor's actions during the disruption.[45]

Ted Kheel has said that the solution to any labor impasse is always present at the beginning. This was certainly the case with the 1966 transit strike. The final agreement was not all that different from what the union had requested in December. So why the delay? Lindsay, adhering to a strict ethical code, could not sit down and hammer out an agreement, while the union was all too happy to make the impetuous Mayor suffer. In retrospect, Price believed it would have been easier to settle the strike in December by agreeing to Quill's demand for four dollars per hour for motormen, roughly what was agreed to after the twelve-day strike. But, Price says, "Lindsay thought it was immoral." And there was another reason. As he explained to Lindsay in December, Quill wanted a strike and Quill was going to have one, no matter what. The transit strike reinforced the belief that an illegal strike by a municipal union could be financially remunerative, with only token costs to the union. In the eight years following the 1966 settlement, the average annual wage increase for TWU workers would be 9 percent.[46]

President Johnson was particularly unimpressed with Lindsay's performance. Since Labor Secretary Wirtz and Gardner Ackley, the chairman of the President's Council of Economic Advisers, had advised the President to stay out of strike negotiations, Johnson never once denounced the union during its strike. The day the city's buses and subways returned to action, Johnson came out with this statement: "I do not believe that any settlement that violates the guideposts to this extent is in the national interest." An angry Lindsay responded that "perhaps the President is not as familiar with all the facts in the case." For political cover, Lindsay leaked an informal report that the panel had written on the settlement. In his analysis, Feinsinger claimed that "all the money items involved in the proposed agreement are clearly within the confines of the guidelines." Feinsinger felt that the President's guidelines included some flexibility in handling issues of inequality in basic wage scales. He pointed to the pay differential between transit mechanics and mechanics at other city departments as one example of this inequity that the settlement was meant to rectify.[47]

In response to Lindsay's comment calling into question the President's knowledge of the facts of the settlement, Secretary Wirtz fired off a blunt telegram to Lindsay on the night of Friday, January 14: "Your recollection and your arithmetic are wrong." Wirtz reminded Lindsay that he, Wirtz, had on numerous occasions during the strike impressed upon the Mayor the necessity of reaching a settlement within the President's guideposts and that Lindsay had agreed. "This settlement may have been necessary to release the city from unconscionable bondage," Wirtz concluded, "but it was unquestionably far outside the stabilization policies."[48]

Johnson's statement no doubt had political implications. He was eager to knock down a prominent young Republican whose recent upset election had rocketed him into the national spotlight. But the President was also very concerned about the economics, and not just the politics, of the settlement. On Saturday, January 15, after Wirtz's telegram, Ackley summarized Lindsay's and Feinsinger's poststrike statements. "There can be no question that the settlement was far above guideposts," wrote Ackley. He estimated that, using the $52 million figure, the settlement worked out to a 4.6 percent yearly wage increase, above the President's guidepost ceiling. Of Feinsinger's analysis Ackley wrote: "It suggests he has never looked at an official statement of the guideposts." Contrary to Feinsinger's claim, Ackley wrote that "there is no guidepost exception for 'inequities.'" The only exceptions were for workers at the bottom of the wage scale. Ackley argued that unions could always find someone who got paid more than their workers and correcting such "inequities" would be futile and costly. Besides, noted Ackley, "New York's transit workers are the highest paid in the country."[49]

After these recriminations dampened the enthusiasm for the labor deal, one of the mediation panel's members spoke anonymously to the *World-Telegram*. "This was a nightmare of incredible mistakes and fumbles by all the parties involved," the man told the paper. He painted a picture of the chaos that enveloped the whole process, with pressure being put on Quill to strike and Transit Authority officials feeling pushed out by the Lindsay team. "The people around Lindsay were too undisciplined; none of them knew what the other was doing at the negotiations," the mediator said. Each of the three mediators vigorously denied leaking the story. Woody Klein found the story slightly distorted but still "very nearly accurate." The TWU's Douglas MacMahon seconded the mediator's observations. "I got the impression for days," MacMahon said after the strike, "that Lindsay was not serious. He seemed to be up on Cloud Nine about what it would take to settle this."[50]

Quill held a press conference after being released from the hospital. His harshest words were reserved for President Johnson, who, he said, "played cheap politics with the lives and fortunes of the people of this city." Ironically, he had only kind words for Mayor Lindsay, perhaps in recognition of the good deal the TWU had received. "Mayor Lindsay did everything he could once he realized the seriousness of the situation," Quill said. "I called him a pipsqueak and an amateur in the heat of battle and under war conditions, and I will have to hold those kind of words for now." The repentant Quill also kept up the charade about Price's visit to the hospital. According to Quill, Price "never offered me a deal. He did not talk money to me.... [E]verything he said was above board." Two days later, the sixty-year-old Quill was dead of heart failure.[51]

TAKING ON THE POWER BROKERS

Lindsay soon took on another power broker: Robert Moses. No other man shaped the face of New York City and its surroundings more than Moses. Many of the city's parks, highways, bridges, urban renewal projects, and public housing bear Moses' mark. From the numerous positions he held from the 1920s to the 1960s, Moses helped build the highway system that surrounds and slices the city. He was responsible for the Cross Bronx Expressway, the Major Deegan Expressway, the Van Wyck Expressway, the Bruckner Expressway, the Harlem River Drive, the Henry Hudson Parkway, the Brooklyn-Queens Expressway, the Belt Parkway, and the Gowanus Expressway. Moses built bridges to connect those expressways: the Triborough Bridge, the Verrazano Narrows Bridge, the Henry Hudson Bridge, the Whitestone Bridge, and the Marine Parkway Bridge. All of this construction helped funnel traffic and people into and out of the city. Moses was instrumental in the growth of the suburbs of Long Island, building the Northern State and Southern State Parkways, and he also was responsible for the creation of Jones Beach and numerous other parks and beaches on the Island. He built the Hutchinson River, Sprain Brook, and Saw Mill River Parkways, which wind their way through scenic Westchester County. He built parks, swimming pools, and public housing; refurbished the Central Park Zoo; built Shea Stadium, Lincoln Center, and the New York Coliseum; planned the World's Fair of 1964–65; and oversaw the city's slum clearance efforts. He accomplished all of this while never holding elective office.

By the late 1950s, Moses ran into opposition on many fronts. His attempt to pave over a playground in Central Park created an uproar among angry mothers; he opposed Joseph Papp's free Shakespeare in Central Park; he angered Bronx citizens by his construction of the Cross Bronx Expressway. The business dealings in the city's Title I housing program managed by Moses also came under increased scrutiny. Worst of all, Moses' philosophy ran counter to the developing anti-automobile sentiment. Many felt that Moses, who himself never learned to drive, had designed a metropolitan area for the benefit of drivers and had slighted mass transit. Moses' proposal in the early 1960s for the Lower Manhattan Expressway, which was to cut across Manhattan from the Holland Tunnel to the Williamsburg Bridge, was seen as one more indignity.[52]

At the height of his power, during the mid–1940s, Moses held eleven different government posts simultaneously, including city parks commissioner, chairman of the Triborough Bridge and Tunnel Authority (TBTA), city construction coordinator, and member of the city's planning commission. By 1966, Moses's only positions were the city's arterial highway coordinator and, most important, chairman of the TBTA. From this position, Moses controlled the money collected from the tolls at New York's bridges and tunnels, which funded his building schemes. The TBTA's yearly surplus was in contrast to the yearly deficits of the Transit Authority. The Lindsay administration was pro–mass transit and anti-automobile and believed subway riders deserved as much of a subsidy as automobile drivers. Lindsay had opposed Moses' Lower Manhattan Expressway while in Congress, but it was left to Deputy Mayor Price to clarify the administration's philosophy when he said, "Cities are for people, not for automobiles." (Lindsay later waffled on the roadway and finally canceled the project during his 1969 reelection campaign, when he badly needed the votes of Manhattan reformers who opposed the road.)[53]

Not surprisingly, the mayor was fervently anti-Moses. Lindsay actively criticized Moses, as did the man he appointed to head the Parks Department, Thomas P. F. Hoving. Price remembers that "Lindsay never really liked Moses." According to Lindsay's Transportation Commissioner, Arthur

Palmer, Lindsay's attitude was "For Christ's sake, throw the old bastard out on his ear!" The Lindsay campaign's position paper on parks, written by Hoving, was a frontal attack on the Moses legacy. The campaign's position paper on transportation policy indirectly attacked the Moses empire by arguing that funds for bridges and roads were plentiful, while the city's mass transit system was starved for funds. If Lindsay were elected, Moses would have to share the proceeds from the bridge and tunnel tolls with mass transit. In response to criticism from Lindsay, Moses responded after the election, "If you elect a matinee-idol mayor, you're going to get a musical-comedy administration."[54]

One incident in the early months of the Lindsay administration highlights the mutual dislike between Moses and Lindsay. The mayor, Moses, and Price were dining together at the "21" Club in Midtown Manhattan. Moses got angry at something Lindsay said, got up from the table, and began yelling at his two dinner companions. More than any other restaurant in the city, the "21" Club is the place where movers and shakers dine, drink, and socialize. Drawing attention to the young Mayor, Moses gave Lindsay his comeuppance in front the "power brokers" he so fervently castigated from City Hall. With characteristic histrionics, Moses screamed that he could never understand how Lindsay got elected and that Lindsay would ruin the city. "He was a great actor," Price remembers. When he had sufficiently embarrassed Lindsay, Moses stormed out of the restaurant, leaving the mayor of New York sheepishly staring at his silverware. When Price and Lindsay left a short time later, they realized that both of their city cars and Lindsay's police guard were nowhere to be found. Apparently, when Moses left "21" he told the drivers and the police guard they were no long needed and could go home for the night.

The mayor and Price were left standing on East Fifty-second Street late in the evening with no way to get back uptown to Gracie Mansion. People on the street recognized the mayor and started asking for autographs. They could not hail a cab, partly because there were so few cabs crossing Fifty-second Street, but mostly because it would have been humiliating for the mayor to be seen hailing a cab late at night. They finally decided to take the uptown IRT subway at Fifty-first Street. Lindsay and Price got off at Ninety-sixth Street, one stop beyond their normal stop, figuring fewer people would see them. They then walked ten blocks to Gracie Mansion, pretending to be on a late-night, impromptu walking tour of the Upper East Side. From Gracie Mansion, Price rode to his nearby apartment in a city car. When Price arrived home, a still irate Lindsay called him and promised, "I am going to kill that son of a bitch." The next day, Price got back at Moses by having the old power broker's car sent up to a Harlem fire station for repairs.[55]

In February 1966, amid this atmosphere of mutual hatred, Lindsay offered his plan to reorganize the city transit system by placing the Transit Authority and the TBTA under the control of a new superagency, the City Transportation Administration. In his campaign, Lindsay had promised to solve the financial problems facing mass transit by bringing all the city's transportation policy under one roof: "The key in approaching the entire financing problem is the same as for solving the planning and operational problems: coordination and unification." The main thrust of the plan was to use the TBTA's surplus to subsidize the deficit-ridden Transit Authority, giving more money to mass transit. It would also curb Moses' power. The TBTA board was made up of three commissioners. It would be years before Lindsay could name the two members that would give him a majority. Lindsay's transportation task force recommended waiting Moses out. They advised Lindsay to make the TBTA part of Lindsay's new transportation superagency. Lindsay also had to make sure that Moses could not spend any of the surplus; this way the TBTA would be forced to use its surplus to pay off its bonds, incurred mostly in the building of the Verrazano Narrows Bridge in 1964. When the bonds were retired, the agency could be merged into the superagency under the city's control.

But Lindsay, prodded by Transportation Commissioner Arthur Palmer, went ahead with plans to close up Moses' shop immediately. Palmer made things worse by saying publicly that the reorganization was meant to convert the TBTA surplus immediately for the city's use, rather than the "wait-them-out" strategy proposed by Lindsay's task force. Palmer, a middle-aged banker, had no experience in government or transportation. One member of Lindsay's transportation task force said, "Palmer never knew what was going on to begin with." He was "as stupid as they come." Because of Palmer's gung-ho approach, Moses was able to paint the transit reorganization battle as a raid on TBTA funds. He issued a memo, backed by the two other members of the TBTA, calling the mayor's reorganization plan "poorly advised." Such a merger, Moses advised, would hurt the TBTA's bondholders and be unfair to car users who pay tolls. Worst of all, Moses warned, the plan was illegal. Moses was not about to relinquish his power to a young upstart like Lindsay. What had Lindsay built? Lindsay could help kill Moses's Lower Manhattan Expressway, but Moses was not about to let the mayor drive him out of the TBTA.

The *Times* supported Lindsay's move, but worried that the new Transportation Administration would be completely under the control of the mayor. Under his original proposal, the mayor would have appointed the head of the new Transportation Administration as well as the members of a newly constituted Transit and Triborough Authority and had a veto over transit policy. This would have given Lindsay virtually complete control over all transportation within the city limits. The *Times* editorialized, "We are confident that the present mayor could be trusted to use this power wisely; but there will be other mayors in City Hall."[56]

Before any transit plan could be implemented, the state legislature needed to approve it. When Lindsay went to Rockefeller in February to offer his proposal, the governor was noncommittal. The members of Lindsay's transportation task force saw this for what it was: the end of the transportation reorganization. Without Rockefeller's support the proposal was dead in the water. But Lindsay's aides still believed they could win in Albany without Rockefeller's support. Lindsay's legislative aide in Albany, Richard Rosen, explained to reporters the administration's strategy in handling the state legislature: "The way you handle legislators is with power." Unfortunately, the mayor and his aides had not adequately measured the balance of power in Albany. Rosen was a young aide with little Albany experience. Though Lindsay and other liberals held Moses in contempt and figured him washed up, Moses still had powerful friends and was able to fend off Lindsay's challenge. Had Rockefeller been behind Lindsay's proposal, the weakened Moses might have been defeated. But the governor had other plans. And they certainly did not include giving more power to John Lindsay.

Assembly Speaker Anthony Travia, a Brooklyn Democrat, and Senate Majority Leader Earl Brydges, a Niagara Falls Republican, also felt only contempt for Lindsay. According to Moses' biographer Robert Caro, they saw Lindsay as "an intellectual lightweight who combined a truly astonishing ignorance of how things got done in Albany with an arrogance that led him to lecture them privately and publicly on how to do their jobs." Even more detrimental to the transportation reorganization bill's chances was that the mayor had nothing to offer the legislative leaders in return for their support. Rockefeller, who already had a good working relationship with the Albany leadership, could offer legislators money in the form of increased education aid or roads for their districts. In this respect, the mayor of New York was at a distinct disadvantage.

Palmer met with Moses three times, never at Palmer's office and always on Moses' turf. Though Palmer was supposed to tell Moses he was being forced out, these meetings turned into lectures by Moses on the nature of political power in New York City. Palmer only half understood it at the time, but Moses was signaling to Lindsay that there was no way he would relinquish control of the TBTA. Palmer thought he could take on Moses himself, but, as Price has said, "That's like me feeling I could hit in fifty-one straight games at Yankee Stadium." Lindsay wanted to fire Moses directly, but Palmer advised him that he did not have the power to do so.[57]

The dramatic highlight of the Moses-Lindsay battle occurred on March 10, 1966, at a public hearing in Albany. Rosen said that Travia had told him the hearing would be "a friendly little thing, casual." All he wanted was the mayor and another person testifying. On the other side, Travia told him, would be a few opponents. What Lindsay and Rosen did not realize was that an avalanche of political opponents had been lined up by Moses to speak against the reorganization bill. According to one member of the task force, Rosen had failed to contact proponents of the transportation reorganization. Where Lindsay had gone to Albany with only two aides, an array of "power brokers" was scheduled to speak against the bill, something Lindsay and his men found out only shortly before the start of the hearing. Former New York Governor Thomas E. Dewey, former Mayor Wagner, union leaders, bankers, bond attorneys, and a spokesman for David Rockefeller's Chase Manhattan all spoke in opposition to Lindsay's plan. "There was enough muscle against that thing," said a state senator, "to have beaten *anything*." Lindsay had been set up. When Lindsay spoke, Moses could barely conceal his laughter. The normally poised mayor "stared down with almost painfully obvious nervousness at the full battery of microphones before which he had been lured." Moses still had plenty of friends and supporters like unions and bankers who benefited from the TBTA's public works projects and the bonds it issued. Mayor Wagner criticized his successor's plan. The Transit Authority member John Gilhooley, a Republican and Rockefeller ally, called the plan a "political power grab." When the two days of hearings ended, Travia said the legislature could not act on Lindsay's bill anyway until it received a home-rule message from the City Council. For all intents and purposes, the bill was dead.[58]

But Lindsay did not give up. After the state legislature passed the buck to the City Council, Lindsay accused state legislative leaders of "irresponsibility." When the City Council held hearings on the bill in late May, Lindsay warned that if members did not support his reorganization plan, "their rejection will be viewed as the result of a cynical bargain with the upstate leadership working in collaboration with the special interests that lobby against any changes."[59]

Moses further twisted the knife in the mayor. If Lindsay wanted the TBTA's surplus for the city's mass transit, Moses would foil him by spending it. In July 1966, Moses announced that he had committed the TBTA's $40 million surplus toward road and bridge repairs. In response to the further indignity, Lindsay did something he should have done months earlier. At the end of a public celebration of the thirtieth anniversary of the opening of the Triborough Bridge, Moses received a message from the mayor's office. He was being dismissed as the city's arterial highway coordinator, which left the power broker with control only over the TBTA.[60]

Ultimately, the whole battle over Lindsay's transportation reorganization bill was an exercise in futility. Lindsay was not the only person who coveted the vast TBTA surplus. Rockefeller had his own transit plan and neither Moses nor Lindsay were part of it. Rockefeller respected Moses. They were both stubborn, pragmatic political types who would steamroll over anyone who stood in the way of their ambitions. If Moses stood in the way of Rockefeller's plans, he would have to be moved. In 1962, Nelson's brother Laurence wanted to become the state parks commissioner, a post held by Moses. Whatever respect or admiration Nelson had for Moses would not stop him from giving his brother what he wanted. Moses was told to resign and Laurence Rockefeller became the state parks commissioner.[61]

Nelson Rockefeller continually sought to increase the power and reach of state government, and transportation reorganization was an idea handed to him on a silver platter. Comprehensive transportation reorganization on a regional, not city, level had been in the works since the beginning of the Rockefeller administration in 1958. By the early 1960s, New York Central, which operated the Westchester County and Connecticut commuter railroads, and the Pennsylvania Railroad, which ran the Long Island Railroad, both wanted out of the commuter rail business. Throughout his life Rockefeller thought big—and the idea of transportation was very big: it would bring significant gains in state government authority as well as revenues from the gold mine that was the TBTA. In 1965, Rockefeller's aide William Ronan created the Metropolitan Commuter Transportation Authority (MCTA), which folded the commuter railroads into a state authority. By early 1966 Ronan was already working on plans for a larger transit authority that would have responsibility for commuter railroads, the city's subway system, and Moses' Triborough Bridge and Tunnel Authority. Through duplicity, savvy, patience, and sheer force of will, Rockefeller eventually maneuvered Moses out of power. On March 1, 1968, the Metropolitan Transportation Authority (MTA) was born. For the first time in over forty years, Moses held no public posts.[62]

The MTA was Nelson Rockefeller's baby. Though the city was granted a seat on the MTA board and Moses was given a symbolic seat, New York City had lost control over its transit system. Rockefeller had extended the power of New York State into transportation, creating a vast and powerful public authority with power over the commuter railroads, the city transit system, and the Triborough Bridge and Tunnel Authority. In some ways this was a blessing in disguise. Though the city lost the surplus revenue from the TBTA that Lindsay had sought to tap, it was relieved of responsibility for its subways and buses, including negotiating with the TWU. It could also disclaim responsibility for subsequent rises in the transit fare.[63]

That Rockefeller was at work creating the MTA was no state secret, so it is hard to imagine why the Lindsay administration formulated its own reorganization plan. It seemed to be consciously picking a fight with Rockefeller. Roswell Perkins, one of the men involved in devising Lindsay's transportation reorganization plan, was formerly Rockefeller's counsel and had worked closely with Ronan. If anyone should have known about the depths of Rockefeller and Ronan's plan, it was Perkins. Only in 1966 could Lindsay—still fresh from his election victory and imbued with a sense of self-righteousness and invulnerability—think he could outrace Rockefeller to the millions of dollars in Triborough money that awaited the victor.

The battle between state and city government, between Rockefeller and Lindsay, would become a central theme during the late 1960s and early 1970s. This was a battle over money, power, and prestige. Ultimately, though, it was a fight over who would govern New York City: the idealistic reform mayor or the cagey, pragmatic governor.

THE FIGHT FOR A CITY INCOME TAX

Lindsay's battles with the transit union and Robert Moses exposed his political weakness and naiveté, but he managed to score some success with his plan for a city income tax. Fiscal problems inherited from Robert Wagner necessitated more revenue. If Lindsay wanted to get a city income tax, he would have to get the approval of the state legislature, a task that would require political skills that had not been in evidence during the battle with Moses.

In late December, Lindsay's budget study group predicted a $412 million deficit for the 1965–66 fiscal year and an estimated deficit of nearly $600 million for 1966–67. In his first fireside chat, Mayor Lindsay addressed himself to the city's financial situation and set forth a group of measures to cut costs and generate revenues. He proposed a hiring freeze; a 10 percent cut in city agencies; opening an office in Washington to press for more federal funds; a request for almost $600 million in aid from Albany; the unification of the city's transportation agencies; a possible increase in the city's real estate tax limit from 2.5 to 3 percent; a consolidation of city departments into ten superagencies; and, finally, tax reform. He spoke of creating a tax system of "greater fairness and greater revenues." Current city taxes, Lindsay argued, were "arbitrary and discriminating. They do not produce the revenue this government needs to do justice to New York." It was obvious Lindsay was talking about some kind of new tax that would raise more money, but according to an aide, the mayor refused to mention raising taxes because he did not want to "frighten anyone." Lindsay would not be satisfied with merely balancing the budget by paring government services. During the Great Society, needs had to be met. For that taxes were needed.[64]

In his campaign, Lindsay opposed the transit fare increase, calling maintenance of the old fare "essential." Candidate Lindsay had also come out against the creation of a city income tax, saying it "would not be good for the city and it would terrify middle-income groups. New York City would then be a city for the very rich and the very poor." He promised he would balance the budget without a city income tax because such a tax "would drive business and people out of New York." He also promised to achieve fiscal stability by "squeez[ing] an awful lot of fat out of the present budget. . . . I believe that between $300 and $400 million a year can be saved simply by consolidating agencies and supplying good management." These promises sufficed for the campaign, where he was rarely pressed by reporters to clarify his positions, but they would not hold up in the real world of city government. New York's fiscal situation would force the institution of a city income tax and the raising of the fifteen-cent subway fare.

During the campaign, Abe Beame told Ed Costikyan, his campaign manager, that if he were asked his stance on a city income tax, he would have to say that he favored it.[65] As comptroller in the last Wagner administration, Beame had also been the lone political voice warning about Wagner's use of selling bonds to cover current expenses. Usually bonds were issued only for capital expenses: bridges, roads, or schools. Wagner, facing a budget shortfall, used money raised by the sale of bonds to pay the day-to-day operating costs of city government. His motto was: "A bad loan is better than a good tax." The "capitalization of expenses" was seen as a dangerous accounting procedure. Nevertheless, Wagner was able to sell bonds worth $255 million dollars on the assumption that the bonds would be redeemed by the revenue raised by increasing the city's real estate tax. Meanwhile, the money from the bond would help close the present gap in the city's operating expenses. This type of "revenue anticipation note" was risky because sometimes the tax never got implemented—as happened in this case. Wagner resorted to other budget gimmicks in his third term, such as advancing the collection dates for taxes due on July 1, 1965, to June 30, 1965. This moved revenues due the first day of fiscal year 1965–66 back to the last day of the previous fiscal year, helping balance the 1964–65 budget, but taking away $45 million dollars from fiscal year 1965–66.

Lindsay did not make things fiscally easier with his own budget. Although Lindsay promised a fiscally conservative administration during his campaign, his first budget of $4.6 billion was the largest in the country next to the federal budget, larger than the budgets for all fifty states, including New York State. The city budget had increased fivefold in the twenty years since World War II, doubling since the mid-fifties. Spending was outrunning revenues. Lindsay's budget was a 16 percent increase over the last Wagner budget. Speaking before the City Council, Lindsay said, "The budget is large, but the needs of the people of New York are great. The budget is frugal, because the demand for economy in our government is compelling." The biggest increase was in welfare spending; the Welfare Department received over $650 million to care for the nearly 600,000 New Yorkers who were indigent, $129 million more than the previous year's budget. Leading city Democrats such as City Council President O'Connor, Comptroller Procaccino, and City Council Majority Leader David Ross argued that the budget was not in keeping with the fiscal belt-tightening Lindsay had promised in his campaign.[66]

Lindsay also came up with the idea of "Urbanaid," in which the federal government and the state would increase funding to the city for a series of ambitious social programs. In August 1966, Lindsay trekked to Washington to testify before a Senate subcommittee run by the Connecticut Democrat Abraham Ribicoff on the "crisis of the cities." In grandiose language, Lindsay argued that the historical comparison to the city's problems went back some 3,000 years to the Old Testament and the ten plagues which were visited upon the Egyptians." What was required, Lindsay argued, was $50 billion from the federal government over the next decade in order to transform the city into "a thoroughly livable and exciting place in which to live." The journalist Jack Newfield wrote that the subcommittee's members reacted to Lindsay "as if he were Allen Ginsberg requesting the legalization of LSD." The staunchest opposition to Lindsay's plan came from Newfield's idol, Senator Robert Kennedy, who called the proposal "totally unrealistic" and repeatedly sparred with the mayor. The two wrangled over the exact federal contribution to the city's coffers.[67]

Things were no easier for Lindsay back home. When the City Council questioned Lindsay's budget, the mayor responded, "You gentlemen will have to tell me how many policemen to cut, how many firemen, how many hospital workers, how many teachers." Later in the hearing, he told councilmen how city departments were complaining to him that the budget was too stingy. "This budget has been cut to the bone," declared the mayor. The truth was that Lindsay was not as beholden to middle-class, taxpaying homeowners as were previous reformers. More important, in Lindsay's mind, was the support of Alex Rose's Liberal Party. When he was seeking the Liberals' nomination the previous summer, Lindsay had promised Rose and other Liberals that he was more concerned with "meeting human needs" than in balancing the budget.

Lindsay spoke to the city about his budget on the evening of March 3, 1966, at the CBS studios on West Fifty-seventh Street. In his "characteristically intense" manner, the mayor began by bluntly stating, "Our city is facing a financial crisis." Saying money was needed for basic services, Lindsay laid out his $520 million tax package. It had four elements. First, a new business tax would replace the old gross receipts tax. Second, a personal income tax would be levied against all New York City residents and against income earned in the city by nonresidents (called by some a "commuter tax"). The personal income tax would be graduated from 1 to 5 percent. This was exactly half of the New York State tax, and would add an extra $14 per year to the tax bill of a family earning $5,000; $107.50 for a family earning $10,000; and $271.50 for a family making $15,000. Third, there would be an increase in the city's water tax. Finally, Lindsay proposed a 50 percent increase in the stock-transfer tax. "New York City is faced with a choice between financial disaster and financial health," Lindsay ended his appeal. "There is no question as to which we must do. We must face reality."[68]

The old gross receipts tax had two major flaws. First, because of an exemption Mayor La Guardia had granted during the 1930s, the tax did not even touch the city's most profitable industry: banks. Second, because the old tax was levied on the total gross income of a business instead of the net income, those hit hardest by the proposed tax were high-volume businesses with a low profit margin. Two mainstays of the city economy fit exactly this profile: the garment and printing industries.

Technically, New York City does not have the ability to raise its own taxes, since it possesses only limited "home rule." Nearly one third of the city's expense budget came from state and federal aid. Thus city leaders must become supplicants to the legislature in Albany in order to govern the city. Nineteen sixty-six being an election year, the reception of Lindsay's plan in Albany was cool. Still, Lindsay forged onward, arguing, "If I am frustrated, it is the people who will be the loser." Lindsay received little support from his fellow Republicans in Albany. Senate Majority Leader Earl Brydges and Assembly Minority Leader Perry Duryea both called for action by the City Council before they would take any steps, something along the lines of a simple vote by the Council in favor of the proposal, enough to provide political cover for uneasy state lawmakers. Suburban legislators of both parties vowed to oppose the "commuter tax" on their constituents. A week later, Governor Rockefeller made his first comments on the tax plan, saying he too would withhold his endorsement until the City Council had acted.[69]

Lindsay responded to their concerns with a characteristic appeal to public-mindedness. "Let the objectors think about the city a little bit as they turn their backs on it every day at five o'clock," declared the mayor in words tinged with bitterness and condescension. After such reconsideration, Lindsay hoped these workers who fueled the city's economic machine would be willing to make "a reasonable contribution" to the city's coffers. Albany Republicans began clamoring for a linkage between an increase in taxes and an increase in the transit fare, something Lindsay had not included in his original tax plan. Senate Minority Leader Joseph Zaretzki, a Democrat from Washington Heights, also questioned the plan. Calling the tax a "heavy burden," Zaretzki noted that Lindsay's tax plan would average out to a payment of almost $100 by every city resident. "That's a fine antipoverty program," Zaretzki bitterly remarked. Lindsay sarcastically responded to Albany's equivocation: "I am glad to see that the legislators are all working with individual and collective courage for which I congratulate them."[70]

Senator Jacob Javits, a liberal Republican with an eye toward the 1968 national ticket, withheld his support for Lindsay's plan until further study. Wagner, in an interview, said he did not see a need for a city income tax. Comptroller Mario Procaccino proposed a 1 percent stock-transfer tax, more punitive than Lindsay's stock tax, that would have raised enough revenue to replace the income tax. In response to Wall Street's cries, Procaccino said, "That's all right. Wall Street didn't elect me." Placing himself as the defender of the working class who would be hit by new income taxes, Procaccino asked, "Why must we always milk the public good and never touch the sacred cow?"—the sacred cow of Wall Street.

Lindsay did not do much better with members of the City Council. Though the reform Democrat Ted Weiss praised the mayor's plan, some members were alienated by Lindsay's attitude. The Brooklyn Democratic councilman George Swetnick said the mayor "talked to us like schoolchildren in short pants." Most councilmen took a wait-and-see attitude to the plan, unwilling to give the benefit of the doubt to a man to whom they felt no personal warmth. Politically, Lindsay was still very much alone.

As opposition to the tax continued to build, Lindsay grew testy. In fiery, angry remarks at the annual dinner of the Citizens Budget Commission, a nonpartisan fiscal watchdog group, the mayor warned that if the state legislature did not pass his tax plan, he would "take to the streets to remind the voters in the fall that Albany—all of Albany—is responsible." Lindsay went on to say he was "determined that no matter how bloody and how costly the battle," he would succeed because the future of American cities and America itself was at stake. "The battle for greatness is being fought on the side streets and gutters and alleys of the great cities," said the mayor. It was vintage Lindsay: the certainty of the correctness of his position; the unwillingness to compromise; the moralizing against his enemies; and the belief that America's fate was tied to that of its cities.

Naturally, Lindsay's remarks angered both city and suburban lawmakers. Assembly Speaker Anthony Travia, a Brooklyn Democrat, warned Lindsay "to start acting like a mayor." Senator Zaretzki offered to show Lindsay around his Washington Heights district and introduce him to the voters, quipping that Lindsay would "be the greatest campaign manager I've ever had." Furthermore, suburban legislators detested the commuter tax, and Lindsay's threat to campaign against them would have only added to their popularity. One Nassau County Republican senator said, "If he took to the streets to campaign against me in Nassau because I voted against the commuter tax, that would be a plus for me." In raising taxes, Lindsay was on shaky political ground and with his threats he further alienated those whose votes he needed.[71]

Lindsay's comments to suburban lawmakers highlighted the controversy over the commuter tax, which was necessary not just to raise revenue, but also to counter the effect the new income tax would have on the city's residents. If the city raised taxes on its citizens alone, it might lead to a further exodus of the middle and upper-middle class to the suburbs to avoid the consequences of the tax. This was why commuters and residents were to be taxed at the same rate in Lindsay's original plan. The mayor had to eliminate the incentive for residents to flee the high taxes and growing disorder of the city for the greener and cheaper pastures of suburbia. But the way he expressed this concept was alienating: Lindsay warned that "the non-residents who use the spokes of that system should recognize the dangerous irony in exploiting the hub." Thus, suburban residents who came to work in the city were seen as "exploiters" of the city. Lindsay wrote about the relationship between city and suburb in 1967: "More sensible and constructive relationships must be achieved, also, between the central cities of America and the communities surrounding them. 'Surrounding' may be too flat a word; some mayors would replace it with 'draining' or 'choking.' My own view is that envy, selfishness and hostility in our metropolitan areas vitiated the creation of a better liaison between the core city and its satellites."

Lindsay saw suburbs as an impediment to urban rejuvenation. One can argue about the extent of the suburbanites' "use" of city resources; commuters paid the same transit fares as city residents, paid for their commuter railroads, and paid hefty tolls on the city's bridges and tunnels that subsidized the building and care of the city's infrastructure.[72]

Meanwhile, a major element of Lindsay's reform coalition—the city's business community—also balked at the tax plan. The president of the New York Stock Exchange called Lindsay's plan "bad medicine" and threatened to move the exchange out of the city. The head of the American Stock Exchange also criticized the proposed stock-transfer tax, although he did not threaten to take the exchange out of the city. A month after the announcement of the tax plan, two major business groups, the Commerce and Industry Association and the Economic Development Council of New York, came out against the tax plan. The former group said Lindsay's tax plan would lead to "economic chaos" and "drive many firms and tax-paying residents away from the city." The latter group, consisting of twenty-six leading corporate executives from such companies as General Foods, Macy's, Con Edison, Chase Manhattan Bank, Brooklyn Union and Gas, New York Life Insurance, and New York Telephone Company, suggested replacing Lindsay's plan with a 2 percent flat income tax, a smaller business tax, and a twenty-five-cent transit fare. Lindsay answered in a predictably angry tone. "It's about time these elements [banking and insurance companies] begin to give greater support to the city and its needs," the mayor said, "Up to now they have made no contribution—not so far. None. Zero."[73]

As June approached, the tax plan stalled in Albany. The mayor was stuck between Democrats with little motive for helping a Republican mayor and Republicans with no desire to raise taxes and help a party maverick. Lindsay again went on the offensive, saying he hoped legislators would not be "guilty of political cowardice" and gut his proposals. Reaction to the use of the word "cowardice" was swift. Senate Majority Leader Brydges said, "Mayor Lindsay could scarcely have more effectively scuttled our efforts to reach agreement on a tax program for New York City than he did by his unwarranted, ill-advised, intemperate and insulting name calling directed at all the members of the Legislature." Assembly Minority Leader Duryea said that Lindsay had "completely destroyed" the climate in Albany and that his fellow legislators felt the mayor had "insulted them." As Duryea said, "It's awfully difficult to call a man a coward and then the next day ask him to do something for you."[74]

Meanwhile, Bob Price was conducting behind-the-scenes talks with legislators in Albany to cut back on the tax proposal. It was assumed that when Bob Price spoke, it was on behalf of the mayor. Legislative leaders in Albany and City Council President David Ross supported a scaled-back, compromise tax bill. The mayor publicly moved toward a compromise, something unthinkable two months earlier. He said he could live with a commuter tax half of the rate for city residents, but later backtracked and said he was still behind the idea of taxing commuters at the same rate as city residents. Reportedly, the Liberal Party's Alex Rose had talked Lindsay into sticking with the full commuter tax. In turn, Price became angry that Lindsay had reneged on a deal Price negotiated. Many people have traced Price's resignation later in the year to the controversy over the tax bill.

In addition, Governor Rockefeller blasted Lindsay for being "misinformed and totally irresponsible" by saying that massive budget cuts would be required if a compromise tax package were enacted. Rockefeller was facing a tough reelection campaign that fall and was already under fire for imposing a 2 percent state sales tax the previous year. In order to be reelected, Rockefeller needed the support of suburban voters who would be hit by a commuter tax. In search of neutral ground, the governor tried to put himself forward as an "honest broker" in negotiations between the mayor and the state legislature. Lindsay was angered by Rockefeller's public stand of neutrality, believing it masked his private machinations against the tax plan.

Personal feuding and election-year worries dragged on the process. By the middle of June, more than three months after Lindsay had made his tax proposal, a breakthrough in negotiations appeared. The mayor, governor, and legislative leaders spent three painful days of negotiations at the governor's mansion. The negotiations were so tense, according to one participant, that Lindsay "could have walked if someone coughed at the wrong time." Ultimately, all sides agreed upon a compromise tax package estimated at $253 million, less than half of what Lindsay originally asked. Commenting on the deal at an Albany press conference, the *Times* reporter Sydney Schanberg said that Lindsay looked "like someone who had just been rescued from sharks." The mayor stated, "The essence of compromise is that you have to give more than you want to, and nobody is totally happy with the result." For a man to whom "compromise" was not a positive word, the deal was not satisfying. Though the tax plan was less ambitious than the original, Lindsay could still claim success. For the first time, New York City had a city income tax and a commuter tax. Lindsay also won the replacement of the city's gross receipts tax with a more general business income tax. But Lindsay did not get as big a tax as he had wanted. Lindsay's original income tax plan would have brought in $385 million a year; the compromise plan would earn the city only $150 million. Where Lindsay's plan would have taxed city residents and commuters at the same rate, in the new plan the personal income of city residents was taxed at .4 to 2.00 percent, and that of commuters was taxed at a flat rate of roughly .25 percent.[75]

The other loss for the city was an increase in the transit fare. The subway fare had remained at a nickel from the inception of the subway system in

1904 until 1948. When Mayor John Hylan ran for reelection in 1921, he called the nickel fare a "property right" for middle- and working-class New Yorkers. After his victory, retaining the nickel fare became the rallying cry for mayoral candidates and the fare was made virtually untouchable. Unfortunately, the costs of running the subway system gradually outpaced the nickel fare. In 1948, the fare was raised to a dime and five years later it was increased to fifteen cents, where it remained until 1966. Upstate legislators were unsympathetic to the cries of city dwellers for retaining the fare. These lawmakers felt the city was already receiving a subsidy for mass transit. Part of the tax compromise was that the fare would increase to twenty cents, which would be the third increase in sixteen years. The transit system had been losing riders, and the Transit Authority was running a deficit with a fifteen-cent fare. (By 1972, New Yorkers would be paying thirty-five cents to ride the city's subways and buses.)[76]

Finally, on June 30, the Republican-controlled state senate approved the compromise bill by a vote of 37 to 27. Nineteen Republicans and eighteen Democrats voted for the bill and seventeen Republicans and ten Democrats voted against it. Three of the five city Republican senators and eighteen of the twenty-five city Democratic Senators supported the bill. (Only three senate Democrats were from outside New York City: two from Buffalo and one from Albany. None hailed from the suburbs of New York City.) No Republican from suburban New York voted for the bill because of the commuter tax. The following day, the Democratic-controlled assembly approved the tax measure on two votes: 94 to 63 in favor of the city income tax and 99 to 57 in favor of the commuter tax. The assembly's ten city Republicans were split evenly on both bills, while the city's Democrats supported the city income tax 42 to 19 and the commuter tax 59 to 1. Again, no suburban New York Republican voted for the commuter tax, and two voted for the residents' tax. Six of the eight suburban Democrats voted against the commuter tax. Immediately following the vote, the City Council approved the tax package.

Later, when the mayor was looking back on his relationship with the legislature during the battle over the tax plan, he had second thoughts on his aggressive stance. "It probably *was* a tactical error for me to say I'd go into the constituency of each guy who didn't go along with us on taxes and campaign against him. It doesn't work to *say* that. . . . And my charge of legislative cowardice did inflame some of them." According to Price, Lindsay "didn't know how to get people to vote." Yet Lindsay believed his aggressiveness helped galvanize support in the city. "It got a lot of people behind us," Lindsay noted, "the non-white community especially, supported us all the way."[77]

Indeed, the city's fiscal problems were dire. In July 1966, Standard & Poor found that New York was the "leading example" of urban blight, which would lead to "staggering fiscal problems." In response, it lowered the city's bond rating. According to the Standard & Poor report, New York faced "a steadily mounting burden of expense for welfare and other services that promises to outpace the growth of revenue sources over the foreseeable future." Thus began the city's uneasy relationship with a financial community grown wary of fiscal priorities that favored "meeting human needs" and ignored fiscal reality and the long-term health of the city.[78]

REFORMING CITY GOVERNMENT

Lindsay made reform sound easy during the campaign, convincing New Yorkers that all that was needed to turn around the problems of the city was a strong will and an administration that "cared." The transit strike, the tax battle, and the transit reorganization fiasco emphasized the intractable nature of governing New York. Undaunted by the challenge of governing the nation's largest and most chaotic city, however, Lindsay continued with the major theme of reform government: changing the structure of city government and making it more responsive to the city's residents.

Early in Lindsay's first term, the *Herald Tribune* columnist Dick Schaap dubbed New York "Fun City," a phrase that embodied the hopes of New Yorkers for a more livable city. Lindsay expressed the feeling of excitement about the possibilities of urban living. "These will be adventurous years in American cities," Lindsay wrote, "for in their span we shall do much to decide whether major cities will rise proudly at the center or disintegrate at the core of our intensely populated and still expanding urban complexes. The outcome will be crucially important, for the issue in the struggle to achieve livable cities is not only the nature of our increasingly urban society, but the nature of our future civilization." Despite the trouble surrounding him, Lindsay tried to remain upbeat about the future. If the problems of big cities were hopeless, Lindsay said in an April 1967 interview, "then the country is gone! People are determined to live in the cities."[79]

In his inaugural address, the new mayor had promised that he and his men would be visible throughout the city. "We will visit the slums and the waterfront. We will go into the schools, hospitals, and prisons," Lindsay proclaimed. The mayoral assistant Robert Blum remembers an angry Lindsay complaining at a cabinet meeting that he saw too many commissioners driving home on the East River Drive. He told them he never wanted to see them using that route again. Instead, they were to drive home through the city's neighborhoods. By taking local roads, they would get to know the city and be seen by city residents. Just as Lindsay had walked the city's streets relentlessly to connect with voters during the campaign, he continued his high visibility as mayor, thus signaling to all that his administration cared enough about the city and its residents to walk among them. Visibility equaled concern. When a fire broke out on Flatbush Avenue in Brooklyn in January, the mayor showed up dressed in formal evening wear. Lindsay was riffing off his reform predecessor, Mayor Fiorello La Guardia, who regularly showed up at the scene of fires.[80]

The idea of action was central to the Lindsay administration. "We've got to get *moving!*" the mayor would implore. He wanted "doers" who could shake up the sleepy bureaucracy and make things happen for the city. During La Guardia's tenure, the bureaucracy was staffed by legions of capable men, many of them civil engineers, who had graduated from City College, St. John's, or Fordham University. These Jewish, Italian, and Irish New Yorkers who were graduates of local colleges were often shut out of good jobs in the private sector because of prejudice against their backgrounds, especially during the lean years of the Depression. Civil service was their best chance to get ahead. In the postwar years, as prejudice lessened and the private sector expanded, opportunities outside government beckoned, and the city bureaucracy began to lose many of its most talented men to the private sector. Now the city bureaucracy attracted less-qualified applicants, and it began to stagnate. By the time Lindsay took office, the thought of a bright, effective city bureaucracy was just a memory. To test how city bureaucrats treated citizens, Lindsay would sometimes call up city departments personally to make an inquiry. The frustrations were apparent from the beginning. "Sometimes I feel I'm pushing my shoulder against a mountain," Lindsay said. "My feet are churning away and the mountain won't budge."[81]

New Haven became Lindsay's model for reforming city government. In the 1950s and early 1960s, this small Connecticut city was well known as a laboratory for urban renewal under Mayor Richard Lee, and so it was no surprise that Lindsay looked to New Haven for the modern urbanists who would remake Gotham. Lindsay asked Mitchell Sviridoff, the former president of the Connecticut AFL-CIO and head of New Haven's antipoverty agency, to study New York City's social services programs. Sviridoff was also a believer in the reorganization of city departments and envisioned a human resources superagency that would bring together the Welfare Department, the Youth Board, antipoverty programs, and manpower training programs under one administrative roof. The Sviridoff Report found that "throughout the broad field of human resources, a vast array of separate programs is operating in the city—with little or no coordination, sometimes working at cross-purposes, and often puzzling and frustrating the people whom they are designed to serve. . . . The problem is to pull all these services together in terms of a set of clear overall objectives." In the wake of the report's publication, Lindsay created the Human Resources Administration and appointed Sviridoff to head it. The new agency symbolized Lindsay's ambitious attempt to reformulate city government and make the city into a laboratory for Great Society social policy. Lindsay also asked Ed Logue, who was in charge of urban redevelopment in New Haven, to study the possible consolidation of the city's housing and development agencies. Although the Lindsay administration did create a scaled-down version of Logue's proposed Housing Administration, Logue never received a high-ranking job in the Lindsay administration. The Lindsay administration feared that if the ambitious Logue received that much control and power, he might become another Robert Moses.[82]

A traditional goal of urban reform has been to make city government more efficient. During his campaign, Lindsay promised he would trim $300 to $400 million in fat from the budget by consolidating city agencies into a more efficient system. After the election, Lindsay appointed a task force headed by Louis Craco, a young Republican lawyer, to examine the issue.

In its introduction, the December 1966 Craco Report argued that if New York hoped to save itself from its present crisis, it would have to utilize modern management techniques: "New York City, confronted by municipal problems of enormous magnitude, beset by pressures of incredible intricacy, simply does not possess administrative machinery adequate to the task of conducting its business effectively. This fact poses the challenge to fashion a governmental instrument supple enough to be readily responsive to the policy decisions of the City's elected leaders and efficient enough to deliver municipal services to its people when and where needed, without waste of money or time."

One problem the report pinpointed was the "piecemeal expansion" of city government in the years after the Second World War. Past mayors had responded to each new problem by creating a new city agency. The Craco Report listed twenty-nine such agencies created since 1944, including the Division of Veterans Affairs, the Youth Board, the Department of Traffic, the Community Mental Health Board, the Department of Relocation, the Department of Public Events, and the Council Against Poverty. "The bureaucratic maze though which the policy must wend its way in the process of being implemented results in delay, confusion, and, in many cases, a failure to execute the policy at all," the report stated. It gave one example of this confusion: the paving of city streets. Three city agencies were in charge of street paving. The Department of Public Works had responsibility for streets over bridges; the Department of Parks had authority for parkways and roads through city parks; and the Department of Highways had jurisdiction over everything else. A ten-mile stretch of Cross Bay Boulevard and Shorefront Parkway in Queens was maintained by three city departments, as well as the Triborough Bridge and Tunnel Authority. This was the kind of overlapping jurisdiction and bureaucratic confusion the Lindsay administration hoped to eliminate.[83]

The Craco Report presented a reorganization plan that called for condensing more than fifty city agencies and departments into ten new "superagencies": Financial Management, Health Services, Housing and Development, Human Resources, Recreation and Cultural Affairs, Transportation, Economic Development, General Services, Environmental Protection, and Corrections. The reorganization plan came under heavy fire from incumbent commissioners whose powers were threatened by the reorganization. One of these was Traffic Commissioner Henry Barnes, a Wagner holdover whose successes included making Madison and Fifth Avenues one way and installing "walk/don't walk" lights at intersections. Under the reorganization plan, Barnes's department would fall under the jurisdiction of the Transportation Administration.

The Craco plan was one of the first urban reorganization plans in the country to include an environmental agency—four years before the first Earth Day in 1970. Craco wanted to integrate the collection of garbage with the disposal of garbage, and thus he put the Sanitation Department under the control of the new Environmental Protection Administration.

Lindsay touted the reorganization plan as a budget saver. Yet when administration officials hounded Craco about how much money the plan would actually save, his response was "Not much if at all."[84]

The City Council eventually passed the reorganization reform, but some complained that it added another layer of bureaucracy on top of municipal government and removed the mayor one step further from some areas of city government. Sviridoff later said he believed that a good deputy mayor could have accomplished as much as any superagency: "The notion that you could create an administrative agency that could effectively coordinate programs that had important relations with each other" was "a mistake in assumption." Lindsay's Democratic successors, Abe Beame and Ed Koch, scaled back the superagencies, although some, such as the Human Resources Administration, still exist today.[85]

Another of Lindsay's government reforms was the idea of neighborhood city halls, which would bring government closer to the people. Writing in the *Saturday Review*, Lindsay suggested that the nation's mayors "might explore the establishment of neighborhood offices throughout their cities to give residents a line into City Hall when they want answers or action on such perennial problems as better street lights, smoke abatement, vandalism, landlord-tenant disputes, and enforcement of dog leash laws." Democrats such as City Council President David Ross feared that these neighborhood city halls would recruit candidates to run against Democrats. Price hoped to use these neighborhood offices to build a political organization loyal to Lindsay and independent of both the Democratic machine and Republican Party, but Bob Blum, who was in charge of creating the organizations, was less interested in political machinations than in good government reforms. Blum used London's neighborhood government system as his model. Former Mayor Wagner assailed the plan as "silly," and Carol Greitzer, a reform

Democratic District leader in Greenwich Village who had supported Lindsay in 1965, disparaged the idea as "nothing more than municipal service stations for minor repairs like broken street lights, rats, missing traffic signs, etc." The City Council refused to appropriate money for the project. By the end of 1967, Lindsay managed to start six neighborhood city halls using private donations. Most of the six were in poor, minority areas: Washington Heights, in Upper Manhattan; Flushing-Corona and Flushing-Hillcrest in Queens; Brownsville, in the Bronx; East New York, in Brooklyn; and Fordham–East Tremont, in the Bronx.[86]

Another example of Lindsay's urban reform was his decision to hire outside consultants to help streamline city government. Between 1965 and 1969, city expenditures on contracts for outside consultants rose from $8 million to $70 million. The Lindsay administration hired McKinsey and Co. to introduce a program of systems analysis for government operations. In February 1967, Budget Director Fred Hayes asked the Ford Foundation for $4.5 million over five years to fund an urban systems analysis from the Rand Corporation. The Ford Foundation's Louis Winnick expressed his apprehensions about the funding to his boss, McGeorge Bundy, the foundation's president. "We're holding out for City Council participation to help it from becoming a mayor's plaything. [This] is what's wrong with Lindsay's proposal. He's really asking for a $4 or $5 million personal kitty for consultants that would spare him the unpleasantness of going through the City Council and Board of Estimate who have not been impressed with the services of RAND-type guys in the past."

Instead, the Ford Foundation gave the Lindsay administration $900,000 over three years to fund the Rand studies. The Lindsay administration had already paid Rand $3 million dollars from the city's coffers for the establishment of the New York City-Rand Corporation. With the Ford money, Lindsay ordered four studies by Rand: of the New York Police Department, the Fire Department, the city's health services, and the Housing Administration. The Lindsay administration ran into trouble in the second term when word leaked that the Rand study on housing would recommend scrapping rent-control laws. In February 1970, ten city councilmen sued the Lindsay administration for access to the report. Having control over the city's finances, Comptroller Abe Beame stopped payment on all money for outside consultants, thereby quashing Lindsay's personal think tank. The following year, a New York court ruled that the Board of Estimate had to approve all city contracts over $2,500, foreclosing the possibility of hiring outside consultants independently, which Lindsay had hoped would be an end run around the City Council, Board of Estimate, and city bureaucracy.[87]

Reform also emanated from Lindsay's most active commissioners. One of those was the Parks Department chief, Thomas P. F. Hoving, the thirty-five-year-old former curator of the Metropolitan Museum's Cloisters and the son of the president of Tiffany's. A tall, dashing patrician with an art history background and a touch of eccentricity, Hoving worked to rebuild the city's park system. "We want to generate a hell of a lot of interest," Hoving declared. Like Lindsay, he had a reformer's zeal, a taste for the new and modern, a disdain for his predecessors, and a keen public-relations sense. He proclaimed, "The old rinky-dink, hand-me-down stereotype of park is out, OUT!" He wanted to democratize the use of city parks and take the "No" out of park signs. He sought to clean out the corruption that had set in among the old guard in the department.[88]

Hoving was a whirl of activity. His most famous innovations were "Hoving Happenings." At one of these "happenings," on a Sunday afternoon in May, Hoving opened Central Park to adults and children alike to paint away on a 105-foot canvas with paint provided by the city. Though producing little of artistic merit, these events became a symbol of the possibilities of Fun City. Hoving also held a kite party in Central Park, though kites had been banned there for sixty years. He organized a huge game of capture-the-flag for children. The sight of two handsome young patricians, Lindsay and Hoving, skating together at the opening of Lasker Rink in Central Park was a sure photo-op. There was another public relations coup on the Lower East Side: a mound of dirt brought into Tompkins Square Park to fill in tree pits had become a favorite play site for local children. When filling began and the mound shrank, the community protested. Hoving proclaimed that the mound of dirt would remain, and "Hoving Hill" was born.

Hoving also did his part to aid in the Lindsay administration's effort to keep the city cool during the summer of 1966. "We definitely did bread and circuses," recalls Hoving. Much of the Parks Department activity that summer was, in his words, "pre-explosive preventive maintenance." Hoving promoted the idea of vest-pocket parks—small playgrounds tucked into empty spaces in the city's slums. According to Hoving, these parks were designed to "keep their [ghetto kids'] fucking minds off getting drugs and shooting each other." Hoving's most enduring legacy was his decision to close Central Park to automobile traffic on Sundays in the summer. It was soon expanded to weekends throughout the year.[89]

Another crusading Lindsay official was Buildings Commissioner Charles Moerdler. The thirty-year-old commissioner found corruption deeply ingrained among his department's building inspectors. He tried to improve the training of building inspectors and also to weed out excessive red tape, not only to improve efficiency but also to remove the oxygen on which corrupt inspectors lived: complicated regulations. He declared war against landlords who neglected their buildings and forced their tenants to live in squalor.[90]

Despite some genuine reforms, Lindsay's first year in office was often dominated by symbolism and public relations. Moerdler ordered new uniforms for building inspectors without pockets. The reason: inspectors would no longer be able to "pocket" bribes. Lindsay implemented the Night Owl Watch Service, saying, "There's a lot of lonely people in this city, and this way they feel someone is watching over them at night." Under this plan, one member of the administration—the "night mayor"—would spend the night in City Hall sleeping on a cot. He would be available for any emergencies and could keep track of what was happening in the city after hours. The plan ran into skepticism from Lindsay's own staff. Lindsay official Timothy Costello said after his experience as night mayor, "I don't think it will last myself."[91]

Television was growing in importance to politicians, and Lindsay, blessed with a handsome face and commanding presence, sought to take advantage of this fact. The journalists Jack Newfield and Paul Du Brul felt that "Lindsay was always preoccupied with the appearance rather than the reality of things. . . . [He] often asked his aides, when making a decision, how will this be played in the *Times?* How will it look on the six o'clock news? The image of things dominated Lindsay's mind to a fault." When the mayor gave a televised fireside chat in the Blue Room of City Hall to discuss the city's fiscal problems, law books were carted in to be placed on specially made bookshelves to give the impression of a homey private study. In November 1967, Lindsay began a weekly half-hour television show, *With Mayor Lindsay,* broadcast on Sunday night. Already a fixture on Sunday morning local and national talk shows and an occasional guest on Johnny Carson's *Tonight* show, Lindsay hoped to increase his visibility and connect to voters.[92]

If the new mayor tried to project an image of energy, action, and good government, he also betrayed a certain peevishness and thin skin. One observer noted that from the beginning Lindsay projected a belief in the "magisterial conception of his own office, a sense that this authority and superior perspective permitted him to monopolize the political process, and that because he was the mayor, everyone else had to defer to his point of view." John and Mary Lindsay did not like constituents calling them by their first names, an informality among strangers that, they felt, was a breach of basic etiquette. Lindsay felt that citizens and the press disrespected his position. "The office of the mayor needs a lot more dignity than it's had in the past," Lindsay told Nat Hentoff. Lindsay complained about the way he was treated by citizens at Board of Estimate hearings, where "people come in and are literally rude to the mayor. It's unbelievable. That kind of behavior wouldn't be tolerated anywhere else in the legislative or the executive branches of government."[93]

One incident that symbolized the mayor's problems with the press and his growing peevishness was the "I am the mayor" incident, in March 1966. Lindsay was returning from a trip to Washington, D.C., when reporters accosted him at the airport wanting answers about a recent controversy concerning City Hall interference with the police department. When Lindsay entered his car, a reporter stuck a microphone in the window and said, "Lindsay, you'd better answer our questions—or we'll get you." An angry Lindsay responded, "I don't have to talk to you—I am the mayor and you have an obligation to treat me with respect." Woody Klein describes Lindsay's response to the reporter not as arrogant, but more "perplexed" and "disturbed" at the rough treatment. The following the day, the *Daily News* ran the story about the incident under the headline "Mayor Back, Angry, Silent." Despite the fact that it was a normal response to a rude threat, the phrase "I am the mayor" would be thrown back at Lindsay over the years as evidence of his arrogance. [94]

The press had been attracted to the handsome young candidate during the election, but the relationship quickly changed once Lindsay became mayor. In his first week in office, Lindsay ordered Press Secretary Woody Klein to stop reporters from wandering around City Hall. He wanted them restricted to Room 9, the press briefing room. "The mayor is entitled to some privacy," Lindsay told Klein. When Klein, a former reporter, tried to suggest to the mayor that this might not go over very well, Lindsay replied, "They're just a bunch of God damn animals. Why the hell should I have to put up with all of their shenanigans, anyway? I'm the mayor and if I want them out of my office, out they go." This set up a ministorm that, though it did not completely destroy Lindsay's favorable press, certainly led the press to probe more deeply into his administration and to cease giving him the benefit of the doubt. In addition, Lindsay's selection of Woody Klein as press secretary exacerbated the tensions between him and the press during his first year. Klein, a former investigative reporter, was feisty and aggressive and had a big ego. These traits made for a tenacious reporter, but they made for a terrible press secretary.[95]

Lindsay frequently complained about the press's coverage of petty issues at the expense of more substantive issues. An example of Lindsay's treatment in the press was the minifuss over the hiring of an official City Hall photographer whose salary was to be paid from antipoverty funds. The *Times* made the matter a front-page story, noting that the photographer, a Bryn Mawr graduate and friend of the Lindsays named Katrina Thomas, was listed in the Social Register. Petty though it may have been, it was the type of story that an administration keen on good public relations should have foreseen and headed off. Lindsay, a man who castigated the patronage of the Democratic Party, seemed to be engaging in much of the same. The use of antipoverty money only added to the surreal nature of the story.[96]

But there were more serious concerns. An unfortunate scandal in Lindsay's first term tarred Lindsay's image as a good-government reformer. In December 1967, controversy surrounded Lindsay's friend James Marcus, commissioner of the Department of Water Supply, Gas and Electricity. Though Marcus had no experience in politics, he was able to work his way into Lindsay's political circle and became one of the mayor's young assistants. He brought to city government charm, personality, business experience, and, most important, the right social connections. Marcus was married to the daughter of John Davis Lodge, the former governor of Connecticut. Marcus's wife was also a close friend of Mary Lindsay's, and John Lindsay was godfather to Marcus's son. On the basis of these social credentials, Lindsay put his trust in Jim Marcus. Unfortunately, nobody ever checked on his background or business experience.

After Marcus served as a campaign volunteer and a dollar-a-year mayoral assistant, Lindsay tapped him for water commissioner. When Lindsay later announced his reorganization of city departments, he named Marcus head of the new Environmental Protection Administration. When Sanitation Commissioner Samuel Kearing, another young Lindsay aide, was passed over for the job he resigned from the administration. Then, on December 12, 1967, Marcus abruptly resigned, acknowledging that Manhattan District Attorney Frank Hogan was investigating one of Marcus's business deals in Philadelphia. Lindsay said Marcus's "performance in office has been excellent and our friendship through government service and before has been close."

A week later, the FBI arrested Marcus and five other men, including Antonio (Tony Ducks) Corallo, a member of the Luchese crime family. Marcus was, according to one writer, "a charming failure." Despite appearances, Marcus was broke. He had lost money on the shady business deals that Hogan was investigating and owed money to Corallo, a Mafia loan shark. Graft seemed like an easy way to pay back Corallo, and Marcus was accused of having arranged a kickback on an $835,000 city contract to clean up the Jerome Park Reservoir in the Bronx.

To get money for the Jerome Park Reservoir project, Marcus had to convince Lindsay that the project was an "emergency" situation in need of immediate city money. This was the kind of publicity Lindsay craved. Where previous administrations had let the reservoir decay through neglect and indifference, Lindsay would cut the red tape and take action. Lindsay toured the reservoir with Marcus before awarding the contract. Because it was an emergency, the contract did not have to go through competitive bidding, and thus Marcus was able, with the unwitting complicity of the administration and the Board of Estimate, to award the contractor Henry Fried the contract. Fried kicked back $40,000 to Corallo, who used part of it to cover what Marcus owed him. Lindsay came back five months later for a photo-op in the newly scrubbed and spiffy park, a shining example of the benefits of reform government.[97]

This was the highest case of official corruption since Deputy Fire Commissioner James Moran had been convicted of conspiracy and extortion during the administration of Bill O'Dwyer in the late 1940s. As the journalist Warren Moscow observed, "Marcus could not have happened in a Tammany administration in which a man of loose morals might have been appointed, but not without full knowledge of his weaknesses. No one in the Lindsay administration looked behind the Marcus facade or checked into his bogus business references. It was just assumed that he was what he said he was." Lindsay felt personally wounded by the Marcus affair. He told a cabinet meeting, "This unfortunate human being has got himself and the city into a fine fix." If the charges against Marcus were true, Lindsay said, then Marcus lied to him and other city officials. "I consider this a betrayal of a personal and public trust." An anonymous friend of the mayor said, "No one will ever know what this did to John. He's a man of simple and high principles. The thought that John Davis Lodge's son-in-law might be a thief could never penetrate that WASP mind—never."[98]

In the long run, the Marcus scandal did not tarnish the Lindsay administration. Lindsay himself was above reproach on the issue of honesty and integrity. Stanley Isaacs, a leading liberal Republican and former city councilman, said of Lindsay, "I just cannot conceive of his ever doing anything wrong in matters of conscience and morality. It's just impossible."[99]

But other images of Lindsay were forming in the mind of the public. Every year, the New York press corps puts on the Inner Circle Production, in which they spoof the city's politicians. The cover of the 1966 program pictured Lindsay as a combination Don Quixote–White Knight on a horse accompanied by Bob Price as his Sancho Panza. The Lindsay character in the production, played by the *Daily News* reporter Edward O'Neill, sang a song to the tune of "Supercalifragilisticexpialidocious" from the musical *Mary Poppins*.

> *I ran for public office on a platform quite loquacious*
> *I promised everything on earth in manner very gracious*
> *The public loved my smiling face and figure most curvaceous*
> *But no one really challenged all my arguments fallacious.*
> *But now I'm in, I'm just the neatest guy you've ever seen.*
> *I've swept and dusted everything for I am 'Mr. Clean'* . . .
> *I started out as mayor with an attitude ferocious.*
> *In politics it seemed to me that I am quite precocious.*
> *They called me what I used to like, but now it seems atrocious*
> *Supercalifragilisticexpialidocious.*

Lindsay proved that though he might be too high-minded and moralistic as mayor he was no prude or wallflower after hours by stealing the show at Inner Circle with his response to the reporters, a song-and-dance routine performed with the actress Florence Henderson and choreographed by his Broadway friends.[100]

Despite the occasional fun Lindsay might have, Woody Klein noticed that the mayor was quickly becoming impatient. The pace of change was too slow for his tastes. Contrasting himself with his successor, Robert Wagner said, "I guess I happen to have patience and John hasn't." Instead of seeing this slow pace as being a natural function of democracy, especially in the byzantine world of urban politics, Lindsay saw the roadblocks as maliciously inspired. Who but the ignorant, selfish, or spiteful would oppose his reasonable, if sometimes drastic, proposals? This impatience was often interpreted by the press and public as arrogance. Paul Screvane, the former Democratic City Council President, noted, "There's a lack of humility in the administration from the top down." It was not the first time that Lindsay was so criticized, nor would it be the last.[101]

OF RIOTS,
RACIAL TENSIONS, AND
THE YOUTH REBELLION

Lindsay is always pregnant with trouble.
—Richard Nixon, 1969[1]

New Yorkers are a street people whose lives are dominated by the daily human interactions on the city's sidewalks. Streets and sidewalks are inherently egalitarian; people who would not interact otherwise—rich and poor, white and black—constantly bump into each other. According to Jane Jacobs, public peace in the city "is not kept primarily by the police, necessary as police are. It is kept primarily by an intricate, almost unconscious, network of voluntary controls and standards among the people themselves, and enforced by the people themselves."

With increasing racial tension and the growing activism of antibourgeois radicals, this system of social control had begun to fray during the late 1960s. Lindsay became the focal point for much of these social changes. As a candidate, John Lindsay saw the necessity of taking to the streets to make contact with voters. As mayor, he saw the importance of his presence in the streets in easing tensions and conveying a sense that city government cared about everyone. The liberal political scientist Andrew Hacker later noted, "John Lindsay's presence in Gracie Mansion awakened the consciousness of people who might otherwise have stayed with the mood and mentality of earlier eras. During this eight-year period whole classes of individuals became more assertive than they had ever been in the past." The many ambiguities of the Lindsay administration were reflected in the streets as nowhere else.[2]

119

TENSIONS IN EAST NEW YORK

Just when it looked as if Lindsay's public-relations strategy would crash in the face of increasing press scrutiny and politically unpopular stands like raising taxes and the subway fare, he was given the opportunity to shine. When violence erupted during July 1966 in the East New York section of Brooklyn between gangs of white, black, and Puerto Rican youths, Lindsay tested his idea that a vigorous, hands-on mayor could both keep the city calm and show his concern for the city's minorities. If the spirit of the civil rights movement were to continue in the urban North, mayors would have to earn the goodwill of the black community. Attaining this goodwill was the only way to keep the streets peaceful. Yet, the sociologist Jonathan Rieder has written, "In retrospect, one can see that the encounter of a Yankee mayor and his liberal Jewish emissaries with young Italian toughs [in East New York] presaged the emerging cultural war between patrician conscience and plebeian rancor." Even Lindsay's apparent successes seemed to add to the turmoil and ill feelings engulfing the city.[3]

East New York, located in east-central Brooklyn, was a working-class neighborhood on the edge of collapse in 1966. Until the late 1950s the area was working- and middle-class white, mostly Jewish and Italian. To the west was the black ghetto of Brownsville, a formerly working-class Jewish neighborhood known in the 1930s as the home of Murder, Inc.; it was also the neighborhood where literary critic Alfred Kazin grew up. The 1939 *WPA Guide to New York City* called East New York "less congested than neighboring Brownsville, but otherwise indistinguishable from it in appearance and social composition." That social composition included "Italians, Jews, Germans, and Russians who moved in from Brownsville, Bushwick, and other near-by crowded localities." By the late 1960s, the Jewish population in Brownsville, over 175,000 strong in the 1930s, had shrunk to less than 5,000 mostly elderly residents. The last Brownsville synagogue closed in 1972. The fate of Brownsville would soon befall East New York.[4]

The elevated BMT subway ran down Van Sinderen Avenue, which divided Brownsville from East New York and also functioned as a de facto racial line, for few blacks lived east of the subway line, in East New York. By the early 1960s, however, blacks began settling there, and the racial line moved seven blocks east, to Pennsylvania Avenue, as whites fled and more blacks and Puerto Ricans moved into the vacant tenements. Most of the remaining whites in East New York lived south of New Lots Avenue. As described by Lindsay's assistant Barry Gottehrer, East New York quickly became "an abandoned neighborhood, with one of the highest rates of infant mortality, drug abuse, abandoned buildings and welfare, and the lowest employment in the city. Many poor people . . . were finally dumped here, as were the 'problem families' who had been evicted from public housing."[5]

White East New Yorkers, according to a contemporary account by the journalist Nora Sayre, lived in an anarchic community with little neighborhood organization. Family-oriented Italians were especially adamant about defending their homes. The Irish, according to Sayre, had authoritarian families and their drinking was "lavish." East New York Jews were less successful than other Jews who had moved to better neighborhoods or the suburbs. Because of this, Sayre noted, "Bitterness at their own professional failures, plus the strain of aborted ambitions, has resulted in many nervous breakdowns. This particular Jewish group is known for its poor mental health." Lindsay's aide Robert Blum found the white section of East New York "just as much a wasteland as the almost completely Negro and Puerto Rican western part of East New York." During the 1960s, this neighborhood seemed ripe for violence.[6]

When tensions initially threatened to explode into violence in July 1966, the Lindsay administration was puzzled. Despite its Democratic leanings, East New York benefited from the infusion of energy and concern that Lindsay showed for poor neighborhoods. In early 1966 his administration had pinpointed East New York as a potential problem, and, according to Gottehrer, the neighborhood "received a blitz of services, the removal of automobiles that, stripped of wheels and engines, littered the blocks like giant dead bugs. Plans had been made to rejuvenate parks and playgrounds; building inspectors had descended in droves to check for violations." But the fix was only short term. Soon, "the alleys were once again filled with trash, the building inspectors had moved on, leaving the violations uncorrected, and plans for local parks had been stalled in red tape and bureaucratic confusion." Gottehrer later admitted that the experiment in "massive" short-term aid had failed. Blum found in East New York "no social programs of a lasting nature aimed at lessening" racial tensions. He wrote the mayor, "The situation cries out for a long range program of intensive community organization, designed to accommodate both elements to the accelerating changes in the social and racial character of the neighborhood."[7]

What occurred in East New York in July 1966 was not a riot in the traditional sense. Instead, low-level gang warfare between blacks, whites, and Puerto Ricans threatened to explode into a much larger racial disturbance and spread to other neighborhoods. Lindsay's first summer as mayor was also the first anniversary of the Watts riot in Los Angeles, and the nation anxiously waited to see how its cities would cope. While trouble was brewing in East New York, race riots broke out in Chicago and Cleveland. Lindsay was desperate to avoid any such catastrophe in New York and began impromptu walking tours of the city's slums during the summer, explaining, "I think it's important for the people in the ghettos to see their mayor. They've got to feel somebody is interested in them. You can tell from the double-takes how much the visits are appreciated." According to Gottehrer, "Lindsay wanted to be where the action and the people and the problems were." Children followed alongside him and people greeted him with shouts of recognition from their windows. While other big city mayors walked through poor neighborhoods only after riots, Lindsay came before the troubles and without a large police entourage.[8]

His sandy-blond head bobbing above the crowd, Lindsay walked the Puerto Rican neighborhood of East Harlem on the night of July 18, weaving his way among the sidewalk congo-drum players. The next day he went to the Flatlands, in Brooklyn, directly south of Brownsville and East New York, where a group led by the Reverend Milton Galamison was protesting the administration's plan for an industrial park in that area (Galamison and his supporters instead wanted a school built on the property). As soon as Lindsay emerged from his car, the crowd recognized him and he was hoisted up on two men's shoulders. The sight of Lindsay pacified the angry crowd. This image of Lindsay, held aloft among a sea of black faces, became etched in public memory. Such walks, according to Gottehrer, were "the trademark of the mayor who cared and who wasn't afraid." Lindsay credited the relative quiet of New York's ghettos during his tenure with the fact that he and his aides "gave a damn and cared. And we were out there all the time."[9]

But tensions in East New York flared up on Thursday, July 14, 1966, when a group of whites terrorized William Hanks, a black grocery store owner at Livonia Avenue and Hendrix Street. The violence continued on July 18, when a woman was shot in the hip by an unknown assailant. Members of the police department and several Lindsay aides went to investigate the problems and keep the neighborhood calm. According to Lindsay's aide Jay Kriegel, the tensions in East New York were "an education for all of us . . . a recognition of how removed City Hall was from way out there in the streets." The mayoral aides were on alien turf in eastern Brooklyn. Accustomed to Manhattan's numbered streets and avenues, they were lost among East New York's unfamiliar street names and patterns.[10]

The problems in East New York centered on a triangle of land at a cement traffic island where New Lots and Livonia Avenues meet Ashford Avenue, at the last stop on the IRT's No. 3 line, New Lots Avenue.

Throughout most of the previous year, white, black, and Puerto Rican youths had been squaring off at the station. Blacks lived north of the tracks, Puerto Ricans lived in the western edge of the neighborhood, and whites lived south of the triangle. White youths saw themselves as protecting their turf from an encroaching minority presence. The 1960 census shows that at that time, the three census tracts surrounding the subway station had white populations of 88, 97, and 96 percent. The areas with the largest black presence in 1960 were north of New Lots Avenue, though even these were still majority white in 1960. The white population was heavily Jewish and Italian, and a smaller number of both Jews and Catholics traced their ancestry to Poland. Jews tended to congregate west and south of the subway stop, whereas Italians dominated east of the station. The neighborhood was almost uniformly working class.

Some white youths formed an organization called SPONGE—"the Society for the Prevention of Niggers Getting Everything." (The newspapers, to avoid racial insensitivity, substituted the word "Negroes" when they wrote about SPONGE.) The club's membership was mainly Italian-American youths and numbered less than one hundred. Its name had long been an inside joke among neighborhood whites and played off their belief that blacks were "sponging" off the government at their expense. The group made headlines in 1965 when it battled members of CORE (Congress of Racial Equality) who were protesting the lack of opportunities for blacks at the World's Fair. SPONGE's leader, James (Sandy) McMenemon, was a twenty-four-year-old Wall Street clerk. When a SPONGE member was asked why an Irish-American was speaking on behalf of the predominantly Italian group, his response showed how racial solidarity cut across ethnic and religious lines: "Because Irish, Jewish, and Polish guys are on our side, that's why." Blacks and Puerto Ricans complained that they were constantly harassed near the subway by white youths shouting "Go back to Africa, Niggers!" They claimed white youths would drive through black neighborhoods threatening and intimidating blacks. Whites complained about increasing crime. One told Lindsay, "The niggers give our women a rough time. They ruin the neighborhood. They bring in dope, they bring trouble."[11]

On July 20, Blum warned the mayor about the situation in East New York, arguing that the "situation is not temporary, and the tension will get much worse in the coming months." Those tensions erupted into a mini-riot on the night of Thursday, July 21. That day, the mayor had decided to visit East New York. The mayor went into the neighborhood blind, without knowing the local players, accompanied only by his aides. (In future visits to this neighborhood and to the city's slums, Lindsay would be accompanied by community leaders friendly to the mayor.) Because of this, Blum, one of the few Lindsay aides with knowledge of Brooklyn, believed Lindsay's visit was a bad idea. The young Manhattan lawyer had served as one of three Brooklyn coordinators on Lindsay's 1965 campaign, spending many hours setting up campaign storefronts and gathering volunteers. Running into Lindsay as he was about to leave for East New York, Blum tried to convince him to postpone his visit until they knew more about the situation. According to Blum, an angry Lindsay ignored him and "stomped" off to a waiting car.[12]

The mayor's visit created a situation where people were milling about the streets in an agitated state. At 5 P.M., shortly after Lindsay left East New York following a meeting with whites at Frank's Restaurant, an eleven-year-old black child named Eric Dean was killed by a sniper. Lindsay quickly returned to East New York and visited the dead boy's mother. In the early evening, pickets from SPONGE took their places on the cement triangle by the subway, chanting "Two, four, six, eight, We don't want to integrate," while police barricades separated them from black counterprotesters. Later that night blacks looted East New York. Barry Gottehrer remembers the night's events "were total chaos. The mayor should never have been out there."[13]

Meanwhile, rumors multiplied concerning Eric Dean's death. A group calling itself United Black People passed out leaflets that charged, "White pickets protest integration in New Lots section of Brooklyn 75th Pct., Eric Dean, 11 years old, was shot on his way home by white racist gangs or police, unknown . . . tonight find out the facts, killer-at-large, Eric Dean shot on way home by white gang—whitey has done it again—innocent Eric Dean was shot down by white racist cops or gangs—whitey wanted for murder, justice now."[14]

Later that night, a three-year-old black child named Russell Givens was critically wounded by a sniper in East New York. Nearly a thousand policemen were called into the neighborhood. Tire jacks, bottles, Molotov cocktails, and bricks rained down from rooftops at the police, ten of whom received minor injuries. Despite such provocation, Police Commissioner Howard Leary ordered his policemen "to keep their billies on their belts and their guns in their holsters" unless their lives were threatened.[15]

Human Rights Commissioner William Booth addressed a group of 100 black youths to persuade them to go home. When one asked why blacks could not walk down the white area of New Lots Avenue, Booth replied, "I'm an American and you're American and we can go anywhere we want to." Upon hearing this, the mob ran for New Lots Avenue shouting that they were looking for "whitey." Booth later blamed the riot on whites for trying to drive blacks out of the neighborhood: "They wouldn't let Negroes pass a white line for years. . . . They would wait at subway stations as Negroes came out and would either steer them away or beat them up."[16]

Whereas blacks looked upon Lindsay's presence positively, whites booed and jeered the mayor when he walked through the Italian section of East New York. "Go back to Africa, Lindsay, and take your niggers with you," shouted one anonymous voice. Charles Koslow, who owned a kosher butcher shop that had been looted during Thursday night's actions, cursed Lindsay: "I got him in hell—and I never cursed anyone before." Nor was the violence solely black versus white. Along Alabama Avenue, constant violence erupted throughout the weekend between blacks and Puerto Ricans, forcing some families to move out of their homes.[17]

On Friday night, police beefed up patrols in East New York, Harlem, and the South Bronx. The city remained relatively quiet. Lindsay, who had hardly known where East New York was before July, now urged New Yorkers to "cooperate in removing the tensions and keeping conversations and dialogue going, particularly among the races." He wanted to find out about problems before riots began, not after. He invited fifty young people from East New York—white, black, and Puerto Rican—to come to City Hall and meet with him on Saturday morning. They talked for three hours about the problems in their neighborhood. When Barry Gottehrer later looked back at the meeting, he had second thoughts: "Would I have done it [called the meeting] two years later? Not a chance. Did I agree to it? Yes. [But] no one was in control. . . . We didn't even know if these guys were leaders." Bob Price was against the meeting, seeing the potential political disaster in inviting to City Hall neighborhood toughs of different races. Lindsay overruled Price. The mayor and his aides, in office less than a year, were flying through the crisis by the seat of their pants.[18]

Later Lindsay said, "I do not think City Hall has ever witnessed that kind of meeting—the language and the exchanges were brutal. But it represented for these youths the first sign of any kind of communication with each other." Shouting dominated the meeting and a fist fight almost broke out between two youths. Gottehrer called it "among the best theater I have ever seen in my life." By the end of the meeting, Lindsay had achieved a measure of calm as the participants discussed their fears and their problems. The mayor was able to get a photo of the leaders of the black and white groups reluctantly shaking hands. After the meeting, Lindsay told reporters the cause of the disturbances was "a history of neglect by all of the forces that should be at work to build a great city." He promised that "the answer is going to be a really massive rebuilding of this great city."[19]

Concerned about opening up lines of communication in these neighborhoods, Lindsay aides relied on some unorthodox methods. The most famous was the use of Albert Gallo, a mobster with influence in Brooklyn's Italian-American neighborhoods. Lindsay's Youth Board director, Frank Arricale, got in touch with Rabbi Samuel Schrage, a well-respected Brooklyn community leader. Rabbi Schrage, who knew the Gallo brothers, suggested to Arricale that the Mafia might be the best way to keep the Italian kids in East New York in line. So Arricale and Schrage paid a visit to Gallo at his mother's candy store on President Street in Brooklyn. They told him they wanted his help in easing tensions in East New York. Gallo asked, "What will I get for this?" Rabbi Schrage said he would pray for Gallo. Arricale replied by likening the Gallos to the Rockefellers: "The Rockefellers started out as a bunch of robber barons, but by doing good works their name is blessed. Maybe the Gallos could do the same thing." Gallo, smiling at Schrage, replied with the Jewish saying "From your lips to God's ear." Worried that the police might think he was in the neighborhood stirring up trouble, Gallo asked for, and received, a letter on the city's Youth Board stationery signed by Arricale stating that Gallo was chairman of the Emergency Citizens Committee for Harmony in East New York and was "helping to reduce tension and promote understanding."[20]

Gallo called meetings throughout the neighborhood with the local Italian community and warned that bloodshed was to be avoided. Gottehrer assumed Gallo was interested in keeping the peace because riots would have been bad for business: gambling, narcotics, prostitution. Stories, perhaps apocryphal, circulated about Gallo. One had an Italian American youth telling Gallo, "We don't want anything to do with those niggers." Gallo slapped the youth and replied, "Don't you ever use that word again, you Goddamned wop!" Another story had Gallo throwing a young Italian up against the wall and knocking him unconscious after he called blacks "niggers." True or not, the news gave Gallo great publicity and turned him into a minor folk hero.

Not everyone was pleased about the apparent cozy relationship between the Lindsay administration and gangsters. Brooklyn District Attorney Aaron Koota called a grand jury to look into the matter. Koota told reporters, "There is no real proof that the Gallos did a damn thing." Gottehrer, who was not involved with the Gallo meeting, agrees: "To this day I don't even know if he did anything." The grand jury found no grounds for further action, but released a statement saying it "deplored" the conduct of the Youth Board in enlisting the Gallos' aid "and cloaking them with indicia of official authority." The action, the grand jury continued, was "inimical to proper law enforcement and damaging to the prestige of duly constituted authority." In addition, Italian-American organizations were angry at Arricale for reinforcing the stereotype of Italians as all having Mafia connections.[21]

Even though there was one death and scores of injuries, the events in East New York could not be considered a major riot. But even while the Lindsay administration enjoyed an apparent "victory," trouble was brewing. Policemen had to ignore not only verbal threats but bricks and other objects hurled from rooftops. They were under orders not to go after the perpetrators, so as to avoid any incident that would lead to a full-blown riot. The police did not take kindly to this policy. Nor could they have been pleased about the use of gangsters like the Gallos as "peacemakers." In their eyes, it was a world upside down, with policemen seen as suspicious and criminals seen as heroes.

The Lindsay administration's riot-control policy called for flooding an area of disturbance with massive numbers of police who would form a perimeter around the rioters, allowing looting within a small area, but preventing it from spreading to the rest of the city. Thus contained, the riot would die out. According to Barry Gottehrer, "The idea was to get as many cops as possible out to an area and form a perimeter. Whatever was happening, Leary would let it happen for the first evening. When the crowds started to thin out, the perimeter would be moved in, and ultimately— whether it took one night or two or three—the police would regain the neighborhood." Leary feared that allowing police to apprehend rioters would spur greater violence. As Sanford Garelik, Leary's deputy, put it, "We'd lose a skirmish to avoid losing the war. If there were a handful of cops on the scene and a couple of hundred kids broke out in looting, we didn't want to go in shooting and then have things get really out of hand. I'd trade glass for lives any day. We'd try to establish a perimeter, keep things from spreading until more men got there and we could control by sheer weight."

Police were also under orders not to use police sirens and lights, believing that such actions would further incite the mob. Gottehrer declared, "It's better to have a few broken windows than to have this place burned down." Unfortunately, this approach meant that some inner-city stores might have to be sacrificed, and left businesses like Charles Koslow's butcher shop vulnerable. The dangers of operating a business in the inner city increased as store owners realized they could not rely on the city for protection.[22]

In 1970, an American Jewish Committee report described the decline of East New York from a stable working-class neighborhood to a minority ghetto. Jews had made up sixty percent of the neighborhood's residents in 1957. But by the late 1960s Jews "appear to have flown" out of East New York. The report observed: "As one drives around the neighborhood, one has the impression that this is a blighted area, barren, empty and deserted, a kind of urban Appalachia." The AJC report found that of forty-one synagogues in East New York in 1959, only four remained in 1970. Jewish shopkeepers, fearful of vandalism and crime, followed their customers out of the neighborhood. By 1970, some middle-class Jews remained in the single-family houses and middle-income housing projects south of Linden Boulevard.[23]

White Jewish residents described their neighborhood to the AJC investigator: "Teenage youths are seen at 9:00 P.M. going up a street of two-family homes, ringing doorbells until they find one in which nobody is at home. They break a pane in the door and walk in. . . . A local bakery, possibly the last Jewish bakery in East New York, was robbed and broken into six times in a two month period." In 1966, there were seven crimes reported for every 100 residents. One out of every seven youths in the neighborhood between the ages of seven and twenty was arrested during 1965. In 1968, there were 408 fires in vacant buildings. In 1970, nearly 40 percent of East New York residents were either on or eligible for welfare. Over half of the population was under eighteen years old, and 45 percent of the young people lived in female-headed households, meaning that East New York was dominated by youths lacking male supervision. [24]

Lindsay may have been able to prevent a riot, but he could not stem white flight and the subsequent neighborhood deterioration. In 1960, East New York was 85 percent white. Seven years later, it was 80 percent black and Puerto Rican. By 1970, only two neighborhood census tracts had a majority white population. By 1980, East New York was almost completely black and Puerto Rican, with only a few elderly whites remaining. The three census tracts surrounding the New Lots Avenue subway station that had been overwhelmingly white in 1960 were over 90 percent black and Puerto Rican by 1980.

In 1971, a policeman who had grown up in East New York and moved out in 1967 said of the neighborhood, "This place makes Bedford-Stuyvesant look beautiful. In ten years it was completely destroyed." His old house had become abandoned and was decaying and cinder-blocked, with garbage piling up in the yard. One journalist described the area in 1971:

The vacant houses in East New York, many in the Model Cities tract, are now burned out, vandalized, shattered, filled with old shoes, smashed furniture, forgotten dogs and a sour effluvium of neglect and despair. Professional "strippers" often brazenly drive up in trucks in broad daylight and remove the copper, brass and lead plumbing, the sinks and radiators for sale to scrap-metal dealers. Windows and doors are sealed with tin or cinderblocks or left open and broken. . . . The sidewalks and streets are littered with garbage, wind-whipped newspapers and rotting mattresses. A smashed telephone booth lies on its side in the middle of the sidewalk, the phone coin box ripped out. Broken glass is always being crunched underfoot.

What had just a decade earlier been a stable, working-class community was now a bombed-out slum. Parts of New York City suffered such "quiet riots" of self-destruction and destabilization, which worked as effectively to destroy a city as the fires of Watts or Newark.[25]

Assigning the blame for this situation was complicated. Poor blacks began moving to East New York in the 1950s and 1960s. Poor migrants from Puerto Rico soon followed. East New York whites, understandably fearful of the effect of poor welfare families on their stable neighborhood, sold their homes. White-owned businesses, fed up with petty thievery, break-ins, and violent robberies, closed up shop and left the neighborhood. The practice of blockbusting was rampant: real-estate agents played on people's fears to persuade them to sell quickly, usually at a loss. Landlords got as much rent as they could and let their buildings become rundown. Many building owners simply abandoned their now-valueless buildings rather than put up with the hassle of running a building in a slum. Many renters soon withheld rent because of poor conditions, speeding the deterioration. Banks were less likely to grant mortgages in areas like East New York, correctly seeing the area as a dangerous and unwise investment. As the neighborhood declined, new residents took less interest and care in their surroundings. Wanton destruction, vandalism, crime, and littering were pervasive. New York City had always seen its share of poverty. But this kind of destruction was entirely new. From the South Bronx to Harlem to Central Brooklyn, parts of New York began to resemble the bombed-out cities of postwar Germany.

The Jewish and Italian residents of East New York saw their neighborhood changing rapidly before their eyes and they did not like what they saw. One Jewish man said he had been "shocked" by the lifestyle of the new Puerto Rican residents. "My family began to feel unsettled by the men hanging around during the day, and the crime and the drugs," he remembered. His neighborhood had been quiet on High Holidays, but with the increasing numbers of Puerto Rican immigrants, "suddenly there was noise and gangs and bodegas. We no longer felt comfortable sleeping outside on mattresses on the fire escape on hot summer nights." A former Italian resident of East New York was even blunter: "The neighborhood was totally destroyed as soon as the blacks moved in. Buildings started burning down, and we had more crime. My sister and two of my little cousins went trick or treating one night, and about six or seven niggers ripped them off." So what did East New York's Jews and Italians do? They left.[26]

KEEPING THE CITY COOL

Lindsay had jumped into his first summer blindly, improvising as he went along. There was little coordination between city agencies to head off disturbances, and the Police Department was isolated from other city agencies and the Mayor's office, yet it was increasingly called on to handle ghetto disturbances. By the summer of 1967, Lindsay was better prepared. Lindsay established the Summer Task Force, which was under the direction of Barry Gottehrer, to monitor potentially troublesome neighborhoods and aid these communities. The project's goal was "to establish a continuing dialogue between the city administration and neighborhood leaders." The former *Herald Tribune* reporter slowly evolved into the "mayor's man" in the city's ghettos, dealing with community leaders, and spent many a night drinking with black activists in places like the Glamour Inn at Seventh Avenue and 127th Street in Harlem. The journalist Nicholas Pileggi described Gottehrer as a "short, unpretentious young man in a sports shirt and slouch" with "straight black hair combed back, deep, sad, dark eyes, a strong nose angled down[;] the whole contour of this face projects such uncontentious melancholy that many of his battles . . . are de-escalated with a wan smile and a handshake." Gottehrer seemed an unlikely choice for such an assignment, but his low-key manner and unthreatening appearance allowed him to operate in areas that might have proved troublesome for other whites.[27]

In 1967, the Summer Task Force identified thirteen potential trouble spots: Central Harlem and East Harlem in Manhattan; the Rockaways, Corona, and South Jamaica in Queens; the South Bronx and Fordham-East Tremont in the Bronx; and Bedford-Stuyvesant, Brownsville, East New York, Bushwick, Williamsburg, and Coney Island in Brooklyn. A Lindsay staffer was assigned to each neighborhood to serve as task force coordinator, targeting influential community leaders who could help ease tensions should trouble arise. Of the Summer Task Force Gottehrer wrote that it "provided the Mayor with a direct and immediate link to the most troubled and deprived neighborhoods of our city and it likewise provided the neighborhoods with a direct line to City Hall. In effect, the Summer Task Force could become an effective 'eyes and ears' of the Mayor and a 'political rabbi' for the community. The neighborhood now had a friend at City Hall accessible and concerned at all times."

Task Force leaders would help coordinate city services at a local level, whether the problem be fixing potholes, building a park, or getting money for summer jobs. Most important, the Task Force head, with direct access to the mayor, would hold the entities in the bureaucracy accountable for their actions, whether it be the Sanitation Department, Traffic Department, or Police Department. In addition, the task forces would gather information from the Police Department and other sources in these areas that could help them handle potentially violent situations.

In addition, a Citizens Summer Committee was formed in 1967, headed by Tom Hoving, now back at the Metropolitan Museum, and Andrew Heiskell, chairman of the board of Time Inc. Working with the mayor's Commission on Youth, the Citizens Summer Committee raised $650,000 from corporate sponsors such as Union Carbide, Chemical Bank, Chase Manhattan, Mobil Oil, and Metropolitan Life to provide summer programs for inner-city youths. The programs funded included Operation Bookmobile in Bedford-Stuyvesant and Bushwick areas of Brooklyn; the Harlem Cultural Festival; Operation Puerto Rican Repertory Theater; Operation Jobs, which provided 5,000 summer jobs; Operation Sports Rescue, with members of the New York Knicks; Operation Plane Ride, which took inner-city children on their first plane ride; and Operation Beat the Heat, which offered 2,000 weekend bus trips for children to beaches, airports, and state parks. In September 1967, Lindsay announced that the Summer Task Force would become the Urban Action Task Force and operate year-round, overseeing smaller task forces that operated out of individual neighborhoods.[28]

As head of the Urban Action Task Force, Gottehrer grew extremely close to the Five Percenters, a group of black militants led by Clarence 13X Smith, better known as Allah. Smith was born in Virginia in 1928 and served in the U.S. Army in the Korean War. He later moved to New York and joined the Nation of Islam at Malcolm X's Temple No. 7 in Harlem. By 1963, Smith had left the Nation of Islam, changed his name to Allah, and formed the Five Percenters. The origin of this name was Allah's belief that 10 percent of humans were devils, who kept 85 percent of the world oppressed. A righteous 5 percent was destined to lead the oppressed out of their slavery. In 1964, the Five Percenters came under suspicion for the murder of a Jewish shopkeeper and his wife in Harlem. In the summer of 1965, Allah warned, "If we don't get some of the poverty money to build our own Mosque we're going to kill all light skinned babies, bomb the houses of Negro policemen, and riot." Later that year he was arrested for unlawful assembly and disorderly conduct at a Harlem rally, Allah was admitted to Matteawan State Hospital for the criminally insane, where he was diagnosed as a paranoid schizophrenic with delusions of grandeur. He was released in 1967. From the time of his arrest, Allah was kept under surveillance by the FBI as a potentially dangerous subversive with signs of emotional instability. The FBI estimated that there were no more than two hundred active Five Percenters, many of whom were involved in shaking down Harlem businesses.

In the summer of 1967, Gottehrer helped the Five Percenters open a storefront academy on the corner of 126th Street and Adam Clayton Powell Boulevard. (Now called the Allah School in Mecca, the academy still exists at the same location. Posted in the storefront window is a faded autographed photo of John Lindsay, whom Allah called "the greatest mayor ever.") On June 13, 1969, Allah was gunned down on a Harlem street.[29]

The purpose of the Urban Action Task Force was riot prevention. Barry Gottehrer decided to bypass middle-class blacks and concentrate on militant groups like the Five Percenters and the Harlem Mau Maus. Gottehrer felt that during a riot he could count on the Allahs of Harlem to help cool the situation, while more respectable blacks would not be around. Lindsay's critics charged the administration with trying to "buy off" potential rioters, like the Five Percenters, with city money. The Lindsay administration also created the Special Neighborhood Improvement Program (SNIP). Budgeted for $8 million in 1968, SNIP worked quietly behind the scenes to funnel money into the city's ghettos to keep the peace during the tense summer.[30]

Despite these efforts, Gottehrer remained pessimistic about the Urban Action Task Force's chance to make concrete and long-lasting improvements: "This business about the Task Force mysteriously stopping riots is pure bunk. All the Task Force does . . . is make us a little more aware of what the people in the city need. Most of the time we can't provide them with more than a sympathetic ear. We can't solve the real problem of a city by cutting red tape. We're really a Band-Aid operation, a holding action until more substantive programs arrive."

Though Gottehrer tended to downplay the importance of the task forces, others were more positive. Lindsay's aide Ted Mastroianni, who was in charge of the Lower East Side task force, believed that they "made a difference because people knew that there was hope. I don't think we made a substantive difference by cleaning up people's housing or getting better sanitation. But I think they felt that there was someone out there who cared for them. Sometimes that is more important than actually getting a change." The question was, how long could this "hope" last while conditions continued to deteriorate?[31]

One sign that the summer of 1967 might prove more chaotic than the last was the June arrest of sixteen members of the radical Revolutionary Action Movement on charges of plotting to kill the moderate civil rights activists Roy Wilkins and Whitney Young. The suspects, also charged with advocating criminal anarchy and conspiracy to commit arson, were found in possession of over thirty weapons, including one machine gun, three carbines, a dozen rifles, a machete, 1,000 rounds of ammunition, police riot helmets, walkie-talkies, and 275 pounds of heroin. One of the ringleaders was Herman Ferguson, an assistant principal at P.S. 40 in Queens.[32]

THE EAST HARLEM RIOT OF 1967

As the summer of 1967 approached, Lindsay hoped to further his reputation as a riot stopper. Although New York never suffered the devastating riots of other big cities, there was trouble in East Harlem. But was it a riot? Historian Paul Gilje defines a riot broadly "as any group of twelve or more people attempting to assert their will immediately through the use of force outside the normal bounds of law." (He excludes organized crime, actions by American Indians, and slave revolts.) Lindsay would have probably restricted the use of the term to disturbances that included large numbers of deaths and major destruction of property, such as occurred during the 1863 New York City draft riots or the 1965 Watts riot. Though the 1967 disturbances in East Harlem were not in the category of these riots, the neighborhood saw a large assembly of individuals exerting their will through violence outside of the traditional structure of law: a riot by most people's definition.[33]

In the summer of 1967, major riots exploded in Boston, Cincinnati, Buffalo, Atlanta, Cleveland, Newark, Detroit, and numerous small cities around the nation. In the week starting July 23, the week of the Detroit conflagration, East Harlem exploded as well. Sandwiched between the remnants of Italian Harlem, east of Third Avenue, and black Harlem, west of Fifth Avenue, was the Puerto Rican enclave called Spanish Harlem. The disturbance began with a shooting of a civilian by an off-duty policeman. Two white officers dressed in civilian clothes, Anthony Cinquemani and Thomas Ryan, were driving home at the end of their shifts when they passed the corner of East 111th Street and Third Avenue shortly after midnight on Sunday, July 23. They spotted twenty-seven-year-old Renaldo Rodriquez standing over another man whom Rodriquez had just slashed with a knife in an argument over a craps game. The two officers stopped their car to break up the fight. When they confronted Rodriquez, he turned on the police and threatened them with his knife. According to neighborhood youths who witnessed the incident, Rodriquez then chased Patrolman Cinquemani. "The cop backed up, then turned around and ran and stopped and backed up again," one witness told reporters. Then Cinquemani shot Rodriquez three times, killing him.

Rumors spread through El Barrio, the local name for the Puerto Rican neighborhood, that the policemen had shot Rodriquez while trying to muscle in on a craps game, that Rodriquez was shot point-blank, and that Rodriquez did not even have a knife. A small crowd quickly gathered at the scene of the killing, and some people started breaking windows and looting along Third Avenue. The New York Police Department's Tactical Patrol Force (TPF) was called in at 3:30 A.M. One policeman is reported to have yelled to the crowd, "Go home. You didn't lose anything. You just lost another spic." This comment further angered residents. The TPF used billy clubs to clear the area, creating more ill will.

Mayor Lindsay got to the scene sometime after 4 A.M. and began talking to the rioters. One of them, an eighteen-year-old father of two, told the mayor, "If they [the police] want war, we'll give them war. We may go down but we'll take some of them with us." Lindsay set up a meeting with community representatives at Gracie Mansion for later in the morning. The mini-riot died out around 6 A.M.; a handful of policemen and rioters had been injured. Lindsay was careful to minimize the night's violence, calling it "a demonstration, not a riot."

Tensions ran high all day Sunday. Sometime before 10 P.M., teenagers rolled garbage cans into the middle of Third Avenue at 111th Street and set their contents on fire. Protesters threw bottles at passing cars. A police car pulled up and a policeman cleared the street, as bottles crashed all around. Later, a crowd moved north along Third Avenue, heading for the police station at 126th Street. With rioters linked arm in arm, the crowd looked somewhat like a parade. Along the way, protesters smashed store windows at furniture stores and a linoleum store. According to journalist Pete Hamill, who witnessed the riot, "Every window that was not barricaded seemed to go in and some of the kids reached through grates and caved in the glass with soda bottles." Barry Gottehrer and Sid Davidoff drove up to East Harlem Sunday night. Gottehrer described the atmosphere: "I was soon aware that we were moving through a kind of no man's land illuminated by half a dozen fires set in trash baskets and piles of debris."

Gottehrer and Davidoff later spotted NYPD Commissioner Leary's car parked on a sidestreet off Third Avenue. Inside they found Leary asleep in the backseat. As fires burned in the streets and bottles occasionally crashed down, Leary explained that with his policemen already positioned, there was little for him to do but wait. "I might as well catch a nap," he told them.[34]

The police adopted a hands-off policy and allowed the mob to roam from 111th Street to 125th Street. A 250-man force stationed at 126th Street was prepared to defend the station house. Chief Charles McCarthy of the TPF claimed Commissioner Leary ordered the police to hold back as a concession to community leaders, but as the mob approached 126th Street, the police attacked, swinging their clubs. The mob scattered briefly, but continued to skirmish with the police all night. Rioters looted the A&P supermarket at 110th and Third, using garbage cans to smash the windows. Rioters stole soda bottles that became the weapons of choice for the evening. Much of the rioters' violence was directed against the police, especially the TPF, who were viewed as insensitive outsiders. Over a thousand policemen flooded the area, and their anger grew as the crowd threw more bottles and bricks. Snipers fired at the police from rooftops at 111th and Lexington, and the police shot back at the rioters at times. More stores were looted, including a clothing store and a Key Foods supermarket. A liquor store on 110th and Lexington was looted after rioters tore off the protective steel grating and broke the windows. Rioters looted an estimated twenty-five stores in the area around

Third Avenue from 105th to 125th. The riot ended just as the sun began to rise.[35]

Monday night marked the third straight night of what the *Times* called an "anti-police demonstration" in East Harlem. This night's disturbance was set off by another misunderstanding. Rumors spread that Lindsay would visit the neighborhood at 10 P.M. When there was no sight of Lindsay, some community leaders warned Human Rights Commissioner William Booth that Lindsay better show up "or else." A group of one thousand rioters then attacked a Gulf gas station at 109th Street that they mistakenly thought was a shelter for the police. A kid with a bullhorn shouted to the crowd, "Where is Lindsay? It's the same old bullshit! He promised and he broke the promise." Lindsay consulted with Commissioner Leary, who warned him the rioters were too drunk for an appearance to make any difference, and he decided against visiting the area. Hamill noted that the kids were "seething, ready to be unleashed and some people were trying very hard to unleash them." A kid with a bullhorn then yelled, "The only way we gonna get any respect is to break this place into little pieces. Let's go." The mob smashed windows and tried to set fire to gas tanks. Low-level warfare went on the whole night, with bottles being thrown at police, snipers firing from rooftops, and continued looting.

One mob set upon a news reporter and his camera crew, pelting them with bottles as they fled. The mob then turned over their car, setting it on fire, and pelted the firemen responding to the fire with bottles. Now that a riot had begun, Lindsay changed his mind and visited East Harlem. He stayed in the area until almost 4:00 A.M., joined by prominent Puerto Ricans such as the boxer Jose Torres and Bronx Borough President Herman Badillo. Later, some estimated the crowd at two thousand, but Lindsay hoped to downplay the disorders by claiming there were only two hundred rioters. Again, Lindsay claimed that despite the looting, the snipers, and the bottle throwing, what had passed in East Harlem was not a riot but a "disturbance," caused "by years and years and years of neglect, poverty, and decay."[36]

This time, the riots turned fatal. A woman who had long been active in fighting against neighborhood drug dealers, Emma Haddock, was killed by a gunshot while watching the riot from the window of her apartment at 150 East 103rd Street. Her daughter was shot in the leg. The second victim was a twenty-two-year-old man shot to death in the middle of 112th Street. Throughout Monday night, the *Times* reported, "Mobs overturned automobiles and set them afire, looted stores, pulled fire alarms, and pelted firemen and policemen with bricks and bottles."

Rioting also spread to the Puerto Rican ghetto of Mott Haven in the South Bronx, where seven policemen were wounded; one needed fifty stitches in his arm from a knife slashing and one was grazed by a bullet. During the riots, Ted Mastroianni, Police Inspector Eldridge Waithe, and a police sergeant traveled crosstown to black Harlem to see if the troubles had spread. Along the way, a sniper fired on their car. The three men got out of the car and crouched by the curb. A panicked Mastroianni turned to Waithe, one of the highest-ranking black officers on the force, and asked him what they should do. Waithe jokingly replied, "What do you mean *we*, white man?" The sniper continued firing and the men were trapped for nearly ten minutes until a police backup arrived.[37]

After a third night of assault from the bottles, bricks, and sniper fire, the police had become more agitated and more tempted to use violence. Hamill noted that "there was little doubt that some cops had really gone to work on people without specific provocation. [Police Inspector Sanford] Garelik and the police brass had tried almost desperately to keep the men under control. . . . "

This was, according to Hamill, "a fight between the police and the people of East Harlem." Neighborhood residents drew a chalk line across Third Avenue between 110th and 111th Streets that expressed the feelings fueling the riots: PUERTO RICAN BORDER. DO NOT CROSS, FLATFOOT. This statement captured the hatred for the police and the growing separatism and nationalism in the Puerto Rican community, no doubt influenced by the growing Black Power movement. East Harlem community leaders distributed a letter throughout the neighborhood summarizing their view of the cause of the riots: "Since Saturday July 22, the residents of East Harlem have been subjected to unnecessary physical violence. It is disgraceful that New York's finest is New York's obscenest. The language used by police assigned to the area was in itself a crime We don't care what their personal prejudices are, but when on duty we demand respect. It is important that they realize that we are dealing with HUMAN BEINGS and as such must be treated with dignity. They must give respect in order to receive it."[38]

On Tuesday, Mother Nature intervened and rain dampened any enthusiasm for more violence, although one man was killed in the South Bronx. That day, Lindsay walked through the slums of Central Harlem, South Bronx and Corona, Queens, as well as East Harlem, repeating his claim that the looting and rioting was minimal. Again, he sought to pin the blame on a small group of two hundred youths, many of whom had "had too much beer." Local businessmen like Max Goodman, the owner of Jay's Men Shop on Third Avenue since 1928, complained that the police were too lenient on rioters, letting them destroy property, smash windows, and loot stores.

BROOKLYN ERUPTS

By Wednesday, order had returned to Spanish Harlem, but the virus of disorder had spread to other communities. A pack of two hundred youths left Central Park after a concert by Smokey Robinson and the Miracles and ran down Fifth Avenue. Around Forty-sixth Street they smashed the windows of three stores and looted two haberdasheries. One store, Blye Men's Shop, claimed it lost $15,000 of merchandise. Another gang broke off from the main group and ran toward Columbus Circle where they attacked a young white couple near the subway station. They beat the two, stripped the wife, and robbed the husband. Seventeen teenagers, mostly from the Bronx and Upper Manhattan, were arrested for the Midtown looting. Some were students and some were employed, including a gas station attendant, a mail clerk, a bookkeeper, and a cashier. Most embarrassing for the Lindsay administration was that four of those arrested were employees of city poverty agencies.

In Brooklyn, on Friday, July 27, black militants took the opportunity of a city in crisis to create more havoc. Sonny Carson, the head of the Brooklyn chapter of CORE spoke to a group of student government interns who had moved to Bedford-Stuyvesant that summer to study ghetto conditions. Gottehrer said Carson was near the top of the NYPD's list of the fourteen worst people in New York. Sid Davidoff called Carson a "dangerous" man. When Carson and another member of CORE got up to speak, they began a racist tirade, ordering the student summer volunteers to

> get the hell out of Bedford-Stuyvesant. We don't want any white people in the community; it is our turf; whites are evil, all whites. All whites are racists; all whites including everybody in this room have killed our grandfathers. You're all racists; the CIA killed Malcolm X; you are all responsible; every white person is responsible for Malcolm X's murder and the CIA's actions; slavery in the South was all backed by your grandfathers. You all backed black slavery, and you get the hell out of the community; whites are no good; get out, we don't need you, we don't want you. This community is going to be burned down, and you're going to be burned with it if you don't get the hell out.

That night, a police sergeant saw Carson going throughout the neighborhood making speeches and inciting residents to riot.[39]

In the early morning hours of Sunday, July 29, someone threw a bottle through the window of a furniture store on Nostrand Avenue. Sonny Carson later recalled: "It was not only a riot . . . it quickly became an insurrection, as thousands of young Brothers began to assemble on the avenue. Shortly before nightfall rocks were being thrown at the honky firemen who had come to put out small rubbish fires that were being lit; windows were now being broken and stores liberated. . . . All through the night Brothers and Sisters marched through the streets, yelling and burning and confronting the police." Carson denied that he was urging people to burn down the neighborhood. The usual pattern of rioting ensued: window smashing, looting, and burning garbage cans. Police had to be restrained by their superiors, as rioting continued until daybreak. One observer's analysis of the situation was that

> the cops are not doing anything aggressive. . . . And yet the white cops on the beat hate the guts of young blacks. But they're afraid because

they have no backing on top. From Lindsay, to Leary, to Garelik, to Sealy, the Irish Mafia has been hamstrung in the police department of New York City. And that is why there were no full-scale riots this summer or last in New York City. The cops don't feel free to take action because the liberal brass on top won't tolerate it; and they're going to butcher any local cop; they're going to tear him apart if he does hit or shoot. They don't want that shooting.[40]

Shops on Nostrand Avenue between Fulton Street and Atlantic Avenue had their windows broken and merchandise stolen. Lindsay, as had become his custom, met with community leaders and with members of CORE at their Nostrand Avenue headquarters on Sunday. During the meeting, Carson, an expert at intimidation, angrily castigated Lindsay, "often waving a finger within inches of the Mayor's face." He told Lindsay that if he would get the white cops out of the neighborhood, tensions would decrease. Another CORE member said, "This was only a skirmish, and only that, because some brothers and sisters wanted to keep the community from burning."[41]

One final small riot broke out in the first week of September in Brownsville when a black policeman killed a fourteen-year old black youth, who, with three accomplices, was trying to mug a seventy-three-year-old Jewish man. Again, Sonny Carson placed himself in the center of the disturbance. He called Barry Gottehrer after the boy was killed and warned, "Some white cop has shot a kid in Brownsville, and if the kid dies, Brooklyn's going to burn." This false rumor that the policeman was white further incited residents. For three straight nights Brownsville suffered disorders along Ralph Avenue from Bergen Street to Eastern Parkway. Robert Blum remembers walking the streets of Brownsville with Barry Gottehrer during one night of rioting. The two white mayoral assistants walked up and down Ralph Avenue unmolested, the mob somehow understanding that they were neither cops nor reporters. Blum remembers seeing young blacks firebombing buildings. Police and firemen were pelted with bricks, stones, Molotov cocktails, and bottles. Firemen refused to answer calls in the neighborhood during the riots and only resumed their duties after being promised that every fire truck would have a police escort. Only when Blum and Gottehrer got near the police were they in danger of being hit by flying objects. A bottle thrown from a rooftop hit Blum directly in the head.[42]

This time the mayor met with Carson and others in the local police precinct, the "worst possible place in the world to meet with a group of militants," according to Gottehrer. He saw the hatred in the eyes of the policemen who watched their mayor enter the precinct house to meet with Carson. The CORE leader was more interested in publicity than in working to keep the neighborhood cool. He was also interested in money. In a June 1967 letter to Mayor Lindsay, Carson had written that it would be "a real cool summer," just as long as the city kept funneling money to CORE. Carson had promised that the meeting would be private, but instead he turned it into a full-blown press conference where CORE members loudly denounced police brutality. Then a Carson associate went up to a white *Daily News* photographer and smashed his camera to the floor for no apparent reason. It was another show of intimidation in the racial circus of Sonny Carson and the Brooklyn CORE. When Gottehrer returned to his car after the meeting, he found that two of his tires had been slashed, the windshield was smashed out of its frame, and someone had stomped on the hood.[43]

The president of the Uniformed Firefighters' Association, Gerald J. Ryan, complained that retirements among firemen had increased fourfold during the summer of 1967 and he blamed this on the increasing number of physical attacks on them. During the summer of 1967, firemen were shot at nine times and were the targets of bricks, bottles, and stones thrown at their trucks on seventy separate occasions. Ryan believed that even more incidents went unreported. Some inner-city fire companies constructed shields of chicken wire over their trucks to protect firemen from projectiles. "New York City firemen are, increasingly, the targets of attacks by unthinking and malicious individuals—youngsters and adults alike," said Ryan. "Our men are very unhappy at being the brunt of these attacks." The firemen's union spent $15,000 on an advertising campaign designed to combat the angry faces, epithets, and flying objects they encountered in the slums. "You wouldn't fight a friend," read the slogan. "So, don't fight the fireman—he's your friend. Welcome him to your neighborhood."[44]

In the summer of 1968, the *Times* reported that firemen, especially those in inner-city neighborhoods, were arming themselves with blackjacks to protect themselves from attacks. Firemen from Engine Company 46 in the Bronx were attacked thirteen times over a three-month period that year. One disgusted Bronx fireman, believing that false alarms were often set to lure firemen onto the streets so they could be attacked, complained, "We're not here for their protection. We're here for their entertainment. It's a toy with them." Another fireman summed up the confusion many of the working-class white firemen felt about the attacks: "But we can't appreciate why anyone would want to hurt us. It's bewildering. They're rebelling against the establishment. What establishment? . . . We're part of the establishment all of a sudden?"[45]

In this time of increased hostility toward firemen, the city needed them more than ever. Fires in slum areas increased, as did the number of false alarms. Fire alarms increased almost fourfold between 1965 and 1969 from 68,000 to 240,000. There were nearly 72,000 false alarms in 1969, compared to 18,000 in 1950. By 1974 the number of false alarms had reached nearly 160,000 per year. "False alarms are a form of vandalism," wrote Andrew Hacker in 1975, "yet another symptom of a capriciousness pervading the city." The harassment of firemen continued throughout Lindsay's tenure. In May 1969, Press Secretary Tom Morgan wrote the mayor after a weekend of disturbances in Harlem that the "harassment of fireman is increasing. The youth took particular delight in pelting Fire Department officials merely watching firemen work." Daniel Patrick Moynihan, in his controversial "Benign Neglect" memo of 1970, called slum fires "a 'leading indicator' of social pathology for a neighborhood. They come first. Crime, and the rest, follows." In 1970, firemen in two Bronx engine companies and one ladder company responded to between 8,386 and 9,111 fires—almost twenty-three alarms per day for each company. In 1971, Barry Gottehrer complained that the attacks on firemen were increasing with each passing year. Despite these problems, a Bronx fireman complained that the police and city officials refused to consider the frivolous pulling of fire alarms a serious criminal offense. Even worse was that arson "was officially ignored," said one firefighter. "They got the fire reports downtown every day, they knew the runs and workers and all the suspicious fires. Every fire in a vacant building had to be arson."[46]

Was Lindsay's riot-control strategy a success? Lindsay's later assessment that New York's problems did not resemble the devastation and death found in Detroit or Newark was correct. The administration handled the situation with sensitivity, coordinating police response and soothing community feelings. There was never any need to call the National Guard. Still, on three separate occasions during the summer of 1967, certain areas of the city were in anarchy. The police did not protect store owners' property. The police and firemen were targets not only of verbal taunts but also of bricks, bottles, and fire bombs. But Lindsay refused to call such disturbances riots. Ted Mastroianni noted, "We had some major problems. We always called them disturbances. Molotov cocktails were always designated as unidentified objects . . . and the press would go along with it." Coincidentally, in late July, just as the East Harlem riots were heating up, Lindsay was named vice chairman of the National Advisory Commission on Civil Disorders (called the Kerner Commission, for its head, Illinois Governor Otto Kerner). According to Gottehrer, Lindsay "took pains to emphasize" to him that as one of the most liberal members of the panel, if his ideas were going to carry any weight there had to be no riots in the city's streets. So Lindsay defined away any rioting.[47]

The 1968 report of the Kerner Commission divided the 1967 riots in American cities into three categories: major disorders, serious disorders, and minor disorders. The July riots in East Harlem and Brooklyn and the Labor Day riot in Brooklyn were defined as serious disorders: "isolated looting, some fires, and some rock throwing; violence lasting between one and two days; only one sizable crowd or many small groups; and use of state police though generally not National Guard or federal forces." Only eight of the over two hundred riots that occurred in 1967, including the massive rioting in Newark and Detroit, were defined as major disorders. Twenty-five people were killed and 725 people were injured in Newark; 43 were killed and 324 people were injured in Detroit. The next most serious riot was in Milwaukee, where 4 people were killed. Though the New York riots were not as massive as what occurred in Detroit and Newark, they were more serious than the Kerner Report's definition implied. Three people died and 45 were injured in July and 1 person died and 58 were injured in September. These numbers, though much less tragic than Detroit's or Newark's, are similar to the numbers in the city's previous three twentieth-century riots.[48]

On his walks through the mean streets of New York, Lindsay sought to convey the message that his administration cared about minorities that had previously been neglected by city government. In August, three weeks after the riots in East Harlem, Lindsay returned to referee an exhibition boxing match between the world lightweight champion, Carlos Ortiz, and his sparring partner. A temporary ring was set up on 112th Street off Third Avenue. The crowd greeted the mayor with chants of "Viva Lindsay." Jack Newfield wrote, "The message is that he cares, the medium is his presence. It doesn't matter that the only change flowing from his visits is that a few vacant lots are cleaned up the next day. It is enough that he comes to bring visibility to invisible people." Jay Kriegel noted, "No mayor before and no mayor since or ever will walk . . . as many times along 125th Street" as John Lindsay did.[49]

Blum summed up Lindsay's emphasis on race: "John has an absolute and total belief in the Bill of Rights and in civil rights. And there was never any doubt on any issue with John where the effect was that black or Hispanic people in this city might be degraded in any fashion. . . . The city could only survive if the blacks and Hispanics in New York had the same sense of propriety and proprietorship of this city that the Irish had obtained in the late 1800s and the Jews had obtained and the Italians had attained." Speaking before the 44th Annual Congress of Cities in the week of the riots in East Harlem and Bedford-Stuyvesant, Lindsay talked about urban violence. He contended that most slum dwellers "want to *see* something. They want visible, palpable evidence that their city cares about the conditions under which they live and is working to change them." Their goal was "to share in the material and intellectual rewards that others now enjoy in a free society." Lindsay argued that Americans needed to commit themselves "to a permanent investment in the attainment of ordinary justice before those to whom even common decency is denied." Only in recent years had the government begun to address urban issues and then only in a timid manner, he charged.

Despite his unprecedented visibility, the mayor's reception was not always favorable. On a July 1967 walking tour along 135th Street in Harlem, an estimated five hundred black protesters heckled Lindsay. In addition to booing and chanting, some in the crowd taunted, "Get that cracker. Get that cracker." A month later, Lindsay attended the opening of a sidewalk café at Frank's Restaurant on 125th Street. A much smaller group of black nationalists shouted: "We don't want Paris in Harlem, we want Africa." Others said, "Let's start the Harlem riot right here." Lindsay's speechwriter Jim Carberry remembers seeing, during one walking tour, a young black child dancing backward in front of Lindsay, pointing to invisible snipers on the rooftops and saying, "Hey, Mayor, just keep looking up." An even younger boy later asked Lindsay as he was getting into his car, "Hey, Mayor, you bulletproof?" Carberry was shocked, not only at the threat of violence, but at the young age of the kids issuing the threats. In 1969 Roy Innis, head of Manhattan CORE, looked back on Lindsay's ghetto walks and said he "found the sight of Lindsay's tall, blond head parading around Harlem rather distasteful. I am convinced that he viewed himself as some kind of Great White Father or Lawrence of Arabia."[50]

In the past, the urban poor could rely on local political clubhouses to even out the rough edges of poverty. Political machines served as an extension of city government, a human face in an often inhumane world. By the 1960s, however, political machines in America were on their last legs. For the previous ten years in New York they had been on the losing end of a battle with reformers who were trying to eliminate "boss" influence. Lindsay's 1965 victory over Beame represented a repudiation of the Democratic clubhouse. On the one hand, reformers were bashing the machine as corrupt and undemocratic; on the other hand, they were bemoaning the lack of care in poor neighborhoods. In its place, Lindsay and others tried to create a network of federal and local poverty programs that would fund "community leaders" who would, in essence, serve as de facto "bosses" providing services and jobs to neighborhood residents. The results of this change looked less than promising.[51]

HIPPIES IN THE 'HOOD

Racial disturbances were not the only problems facing John Lindsay's New York. A growing rebellion of white youths was taking hold, especially in Greenwich Village and the East Village. Protests against the Vietnam War, growing in strength and vehemence, strained the city's social fabric.

Ground zero for the hippie rebellion in New York was MacDougal Street in Greenwich Village. The Village's reputation as a bohemian haven dates back to the early part of the twentieth century. But by the 1960s, this culture was back in full swing. Young people from all over the country were attracted by the ability to explore unconventional lifestyles, as well as the Village's numerous coffee houses and folk music clubs. Drug use was common. Washington Square Park became a hangout for wayward youths. According to Woody Klein, Lindsay's former press secretary and a Village resident,

> The previous summer—1966—had been noisy, crime-ridden, and crowded in the Village. Now it was the spring of 1967 and the atmosphere was growing worse. Dope addicts freely wandered through the streets, the Bowery bum population had moved over to our section

of the Village, and on weekends young mobs shouted and screamed throughout the nights, set off firecrackers, revved up their motorcycles and even attacked and robbed several local residents. . . . My wife and I don't enjoy going out here at night because of these crowds. And I certainly wouldn't go through here on a Saturday night."

But the police were under orders not to arrest disorderly young people on the streets of Greenwich Village. Angry at the Lindsay administration's hands-off attitude, Klein began writing about the "mess on MacDougal" in a column for a free weekly, *The Villager*.[52]

Residents formed the MacDougal Area Neighborhood Association (MANA) to fight against these trends. Alongside the youth culture lived many middle-class professionals and working-class Italians who had been in the neighborhood for decades. After the murder of a young marine in the Village, MANA's cries became more heated. MANA seemed to unite reformers and regulars, as Carol Greitzer and City Councilman Ed Koch marched alongside Italians Americans who supported the Democratic boss, Carmine DeSapio. Emanuel Popolizio, the head of MANA, complained that Lindsay had done nothing to clean up the area. Two priests from the Church of Our Lady of Pompeii on Bleecker Street called the area a "jungle" and "Sodom and Gomorah."[53]

The Lindsay administration proved unable to handle the competing interests of hippies and residents. The inability to enforce the law reinforced the perception of the mayor as unsympathetic to the white working and middle class. These men and women could not fathom the social changes and behavior they saw around them and could not understand the accommodating attitude their city government seemed to be taking. This reinforced the growing belief that New York City was more concerned about tolerating various lifestyles than in making the city a haven for middle-class values. If it could not do the latter, how could it hope to keep the middle-class from fleeing to the suburbs?

A few blocks east of MacDougal Street was the East Village, whose heart was Tompkins Square Park, as Washington Square Park was the heart of Greenwich Village. Abbie Hoffman, who moved there in 1966, said that in his neighborhood, "it's like everyone is on a never-ending TRIP." The East Village, though, remained somewhat rougher and seedier than its neighbor to the west. Whereas Greenwich Village had quaint streets lined with attractive brownstones, the East Village was filled with older, rundown tenements and the blocks grew dreary heading east toward the Puerto Rican ghetto in so-called Alphabet City—the Lower East Side's Avenues A, B, C, and D.[54]

Tompkins Square Park was divided. Older Ukrainians spent sunny days sitting in one corner of the park; Puerto Ricans and blacks each had their own corner; and white hippies had the fourth corner. The four corners of the park were as far apart as the four corners of the earth. Barry Gottehrer admitted that little could be done with the competing ethnic groups and community activists in the East Village. The best they could hope for was a truce, because "close contact inspired arguments, competition and gang wars rather than brotherly love." On the Tuesday afternoon after Memorial Day in 1967, the park erupted. The Parks Department had issued a permit to a group of hippies to use the bandshell in the park, but others were sitting on the grassy areas of the park playing bongo drums and chanting Hare Krishna mantras. Some of the older Ukrainians complained about the noise to a Parks Department official, who then filed a complaint with the police. When two cops went to the park to tell the kids to keep quiet and stay off the grass, the hippies laughed at them.[55]

The reaction toward the policemen's order was indicative of the anti-authority attitude of the hippies. As the hippies thumbed their noses at the police, the police were sure to respond in kind, enforcing the respect for authority they felt was due them. More hippies joined the protest, which now numbered two hundred, and refused to leave the grass. Dozens of cops arrived as reinforcements. To the hippies' cries of "fascists," the police forcibly removed them, using their nightsticks freely. Meanwhile, nearly two thousand spectators lined the park to watch the spectacle. Two protesters and seven policeman were hurt.[56]

Captain Joseph Fink, the commander in the East Village's Ninth Precinct, had good relations with the different groups, but was off duty that day. If he had been on duty, the clash might not have occurred. Fink was the type of policeman whom Lindsay had hoped would "humanize" the department: a Jewish cop who grew up on the Lower East Side and was tolerant of the hippies. However, most cops were not so obliging. The *Village Voice's* Joe Flaherty recounts a conversation between two policemen overheard at the Ninth Precinct building. "Fuck these people, they don't wash or pay taxes and they think they can shit up the park for normal people," one cop said of the hippies. Flaherty, a junior-league Jimmy Breslin for the hip set at the *Village Voice*, wrote that Fink's dilemma was "to penetrate such thick skulls." The immediate response to the Tompkins Square Park disturbance from the Lindsay administration was from Wilbert Tatum, director of community relations at the Buildings Department and night mayor for the day. Tatum blamed the incident on an "uninformed employee of the Parks Department," and on the "deployment of a great number of policemen."[57]

The following day, Parks Commissioner August Heckscher (Hoving had left the position in December 1966) declared the contested grassy section "troubadour area," and took away the KEEP OFF THE GRASS signs. Yet problems still continued in the park. The following Thursday, a group of Puerto Ricans became angered by a folk-rock band performing at the bandstand in the park and attacked the group. A few days later, a white employee of the *Daily News* was slashed after he tripped over a group of Puerto Ricans in the park. After the knife wielder was arrested, some in the neighborhood agitated to free the man. The *Voice's* Don McNeill blamed the attack on the victim, who did not understand the "mores" of the neighborhood, "the first one being that you never insult a Puerto Rican."

When a group of hippies and Puerto Ricans, calling themselves "Serenos" ("peacekeepers" or "nightwatchmen" in Spanish), later met with Lindsay in City Hall, their presence incited another disturbance. A group of six hundred landlords was at City Hall to protest the city's rent-control laws. Seeing the "Serenos" leave City Hall and angry that their pleas were being ignored, the landlords stormed the building. Windows and glass panes on the front door of City Hall were smashed. "Lindsay sees the hippies," shouted the landlords' leader, Vito Battista, "but he won't see the taxpayers." Lindsay called the landlord protest "irresponsible and crude" and ordered police to arrest any lawbreaker. Tensions throughout the city were high, with seemingly every neighborhood nursing a private grievance.[58]

CENTRAL PARK

The focal point for many of the social changes in the city was its parks. Nowhere was this clearer than in the jewel of the city's parks system, Manhattan's Central Park. Parks Commissioner Thomas Hoving wanted to be seen as an innovator in the design and use of parks. By closing the park to automobile traffic on Sundays, being photographed riding his own bike in the park, and creating what were known as "Hoving Happenings," he succeeded in generally boosting the park as a recreational resource for all New Yorkers and in enticing more and more New Yorkers into the park.

Opening up access created conflicts over the vision of the park, however. It caused strain on the upkeep of the park's grass, shrubs, and plants. It also caused political strain as the park became a center for antiwar protests and countercultural activity such as love-ins, drug taking, loud music, and engaging in other uncivil behavior. Though a patrician Republican, Hoving was sympathetic to the counterculture. Robert Moses called Hoving a "recreational leftist." Hoving did appoint Henry Hope Reed, a park traditionalist, to the unsalaried position of curator of Central Park. In October 1966, Reed sent Hoving a memo calling "Hoving Happenings" "grotesque travesties" and a desecration of the park. In response, Hoving wrote the word "Crap!" on top of the memo.[59]

After Hoving left his position, in December 1966, Reed publicly blasted his former boss's policies. He objected to the "commercial invasion" of a Barbra Streisand concert sponsored by Rheingold Beer, as well as new buildings like Lasker Rink and the stage built for the Shakespeare in the Park performances. Reed felt these creations were blights upon the park's natural beauty. Lindsay and Hoving did successfully block the construction of a café on Central Park South that had been proposed by Huntington Hartford, heir to the A&P supermarket chain fortune.

Throughout the park's history there had been conflicting visions of its role: Moses saw a "recreational park" of ballparks and playgrounds; Reed had an Olmstedian vision of the park as a naturalistic refuge from city life; and Hoving had a "vision of happenings, protests, and liberalization." It soon became clear which vision would win out. When Hoving left the Parks Department in December 1966, August Heckscher, another patrician New Yorker and former head of the Twentieth Century Fund, replaced him as parks commissioner. "To put tidiness as the first or only consideration, and to be blind to the big things that were happening," Heckscher later wrote, "seemed a betrayal of the city's best hope."[60]

Heckscher, whose grandfather, the philanthropist August Heckscher, had been responsible for the construction of many ballparks and playgrounds in the park, viewed the young rebels with a mixture of awe and delight: "These dissidents and incendiary spokesmen were in many cases the best members of the community. For all their faults, they had the breath of life in them." Heckscher tried to execute the Lindsay administration's policy that "parks ought to be the safety valve for all this protest, that they ought to be the area where these great dramas were acted out." Heckscher's exuberance for these changes was palpable:

> People in great numbers and of all varieties came out into the parks and squares and streets, and there they professed the values they lived by, exhibited the latest fads and fashions, paraded, demonstrated, acted out their emotions, walked, bicycled, made love, just sat. It was quite a spectacle. It was a source of alarm for politicians who raised the slogan of "Law and Order" to the level of Holy Writ, for bureaucrats charged with keeping the grass green, and for some people scared by the abundance of life.

Heckscher believed "it was a glorious thing that New York should show in the public sphere this outburst of, and the expression of, all the passions of the social order." The center of gravity for the counterculture in the park was the Bethesda Fountain. One guidebook has noted that during this era, "With scant discouragement from permissive city governments, crowds of young people gathered there to smoke marijuana, play guitars, have an occasional bit of sex and generally 'let it all hang out.' "[61]

Given a choice between the young rebels and the middle-class New Yorkers who felt threatened by their actions, Heckscher's choice was clear. His attitude toward middle-class New Yorkers and their vision of the city and its parks was one of condescension. Speaking of the concerns of residents of Little Neck, Queens, an affluent, suburban enclave near the Nassau County border, Heckscher commented, "In less obvious and dramatic ways these good middle-class citizens existed, or tried to exist, apart from the stress of the modern city." Andrew Hacker echoed Heckscher's criticism of those who wanted a haven for simple middle-class values and basic services from their city. "If a citizen's priority goes to clean sidewalks, safe streets, and polite salesclerks," wrote Hacker in 1975, "he should move to a place that is content to be safe, clean, polite—and not much more." New York was a place of energy and imagination; the city could boast of "the most flamboyant street gangs, the most brazen graffiti, and the most sophisticated pimps of any large city." Heckscher's priorities seem to imply that the only "authentic" urban existence was one of chaos, danger, and unruliness; the search for stability, comfort, and tranquillity was somehow not compatible with the image of the "Fun City."[62]

The historians Roy Rosenzweig and Elizabeth Blackmar noted the irony in this policy of opening up the park: "Part of the point of the 'love-ins' and 'be-ins' and 'fat-ins' that filled the park was to challenge playfully the conventions of 'appropriate' public behavior. . . . A park originally designed to exemplify the city's official culture now opened its gates to powerful alternative and oppositional 'countercultures.' " Some New Yorkers saw the parks as a green refuge for relaxation, an affirmation of the glory of the city. Others wanted to turn the park "into a headquarters of political or cultural revolution."

These two goals could not co-exist, yet the Lindsay administration and its parks commissioners remained blissfully unaware of the strains their policy was causing. Conservative New Yorkers criticized Lindsay for giving, in the words of Bronx Republican Congressman Paul Fino, "the city's punks, vietniks and banana-sniffers, flag burning rights in Central Park." In addition, Central Park is bordered on three sides by the some of the most expensive residential real estate in the United States. Such behavior, so close to these homes, made some uncomfortable. One elderly woman berated Heckscher after a festival in the park: "Commissioner, how could you ever do such a thing—encouraging all these *ruffians* to come into the park!"[63]

There was a price to be paid for opening up the park. Roger Starr described Central Park after one "Hoving happening" as resembling "the washrooms on a commuter railroad car." In a 1971 *Times* op-ed, essayist Marya Mannes described the state of Central Park: "In the last few years, vast areas of trodden earth have spread like mange across the hills and hollows of listless grass. The edges of lakes and ponds are garlands of scum and bottles and wrappers and paper cups. Litter overflows the baskets near the foodstands, lies under benches, catches on twigs. Broken glass glints in the rocks where mica once glittered." Mannes described the area around Bethesda Fountain as "a combination of decadence and barbarism; cut-rate Fellini Satyricon." The mayoral assistant Edward Skloot wrote Lindsay in 1972: "The sum of several years of publicity and special events has been a massive influx of people—often exceeding 100,000 persons on a summer Saturday and Sunday." More seriously, though, these visitors did not seem to be content to just stroll or make use of recreational facilities. They vandalized, brutalized, and littered in a way that showed little respect for public space. Central Park came to symbolize the increasing shabbiness and deterioration of the city at large. Skloot wrote: "Beside the question of numbers, people have also become much rougher with the Park. What can't be plucked or stolen is often mauled and destroyed. This includes most private planting of flowers and shrubs. It also includes tree branches and whole bushes."[64]

Such complaints did little to move Heckscher, who recalled that a sociologist at the Twentieth Century Fund had told him that "vandalism . . . was simply a way in which certain elements of my constituency used the parks. It was a form of recreation. Some people liked to sit on the benches; others like to tear them up. As commissioner, I would have to accommodate myself to both types." Though Heckscher found such a view "disconcerting," there was, he said, "an element of truth in it." Vandalism and graffiti, therefore, were merely how citizens registered their unhappiness with city parks. "We were not, perhaps, giving park users what they wanted," argued Heckscher. To him, such vandalism was quite rational. "Some of what went for malicious destruction could be seen as an attempt on their part to rectify an error in design or conception: the failure, for example, to put a gate in a place where (from their point of view) it was obviously needed," he wrote. "Again: it is the nature of young people to build up, and then to destroy and to build anew."[65]

In 1966 and 1967, Central Park was home to a number of antiwar rallies. The first, in March 1966, was led by the pacifist A. J. Muste. It was, in the words of Rosenzweig and Blackmar, the second "oppositional political event" in Central Park's history. (The first was a 1914 women's suffrage rally.) The next big protest occurred on April 15, 1967, when over 100,000 people, led by Martin Luther King and Benjamin Spock, marched from Central Park to the United Nations to protest the war in Vietnam, chanting "Hey, hey, LBJ, how many kids did you kill today?" At the park, young people burned their draft cards. The Committee to Aid the National Liberation Front built a forty-foot-high tower out of cardboard tubing from which they hung Vietcong flags. An American flag was taken from a flagstaff in the park and burned. Two weeks later, Heckscher had a change of heart and announced that no longer would Central Park be used as a staging area for political demonstrations. Heckscher was angered by the "totally unjustified" act of burning the American flag and complained that damage to trees, shrubs, and grass cost the city $4,500. The following day, Lindsay said that applications for use of the park for demonstrations would be judged on their "practical merits."[66]

In addition to antiwar protests, New York was the site of a large pro-war demonstration on May 13, 1967. An estimated 70,000 people marched down Fifth Avenue for a "Support our boys in Vietnam" parade. In a boisterously patriotic display, veterans, carpenters, Teamsters, longshoremen, off-duty policemen, priests, nuns, and many average citizens marched down

Fifth Avenue waving Old Glory and singing "God Bless America." At the reviewing stand were Lieutenant Governor Malcolm Wilson, Frank O'Connor, Attorney General Louis Lefkowitz, and Senate Majority Leader Earl Brydges. Mayor Lindsay did not attend. Pro-war marchers, angry at Lindsay's snub, yelled, "Where's the mayor?" as they marched past the reviewing stand.[67]

The parade did not go without incident. A group of Teamsters attacked a young man with long hair and sandals walking on the sidewalk and not participating in the march. East Village radicals, led by James Fouratt and a Day-Glo–caped Abbie Hoffman, formed what they called the Flower Brigade and demanded to march in the parade; they hoped this publicity stunt would incite a violent reaction from the pro-war crowd. They succeeded and were forcibly turned away by pro-war marchers at Park Avenue and Ninety-third Street. Fouratt called the attack "more frightening and scary than I had ever expected it to be." Hoffman described the incident in his own unique way: "Zonk, fists, red paint, kicks, beer cans, spitting—the whole American Welcome Wagon treatment."[68]

The tensions and violence were predictable, indicating the deep schism the war was creating. Many Americans felt threatened by antiwar protesters and hippies, some of whom did not merely protest the war but actively supported the North Vietnamese. Even those who were genuine pacifists were seen as failing to lend support to their fellow Americans fighting and dying thousands of miles away. That this caused bad feeling is no surprise. Furthermore, the counterculture was deliberately antibourgeois—that was its raison d'etre and that's why it was called the counterculture. Their dress, manners, and speech were all designed to anger and provoke mainstream middle-class Americans.

LINDSAY AND THE COUNTERCULTURE

The disruptions in the city's streets and parks was evidence of the growing countercultural movement in the nation. To more and more of Americans these cultural changes were bewildering, as well as infuriating. The sociologist Jonathan Rieder wrote: "Braless women, antiwar veterans, communal living, wife-swapping, flagrant homosexuality, the unruly, androgynous hair of the hippies, the American flag customized with peace decals—all these things were bizarre signs, as if a mocking deity had tampered with the primal order of things."[69]

Lindsay paid close attention to these changes and commented on them publicly. It is instructive to note the different approach Lindsay and his former boss, Dwight D. Eisenhower, took to these social changes. Where Eisenhower looked aghast at the youths, Lindsay tried to understand them and saw positive things coming out of their actions. Generational differences certainly were a factor in their different responses, but not the only one. In fact, the private Lindsay in many respects shared the same traditional values and biases as men of Eisenhower's generation. Instead, the differences in the two men's views regarding the antiwar protests and the youth counterculture stem from a difference in political ideology.[70]

Eisenhower, in an interview commemorating his seventy-fifth birthday in 1965, criticized the "sloppy" behavior and appearance of some American youths of the time: "I believe that in things like this we are going too far away from the old virtues and rules of life, rules that have been thousands of years in the making and now they are being flouted. There are certain values we should keep, values like decency in our conduct and dealings with others, pride in ourselves, self-reliance, dedication to our country, respect for law and order.

"All this long hair," the General complained, "this lack of decorum—and look at the way they dress. I've always thought that sloppy dress was indicative of sloppy thinking." The women were just as bad, said Eisenhower, "hair stringing down over their faces so they look like baboons. Disgusting." The moral decay he saw reminded the former president "of the dying days of the Roman Empire." What he saw at Berkeley made him think America was in the midst of "some kind of deterioration that ought to be fought tooth and nail." What really angered Eisenhower was that so many youths seemed "so loath these days to respond to words like patriotism." Eisenhower criticized the antiwar demonstrations because they divided the American people and threatened the nation's freedoms. "Maximum liberty," the general argued, can only occur within an "orderly society."[71]

In 1967, Eisenhower chastised the American public for the decline in respect for law enforcement, the growing rebellion on American campuses, and for tolerating urban riots. "I think that we, as a people, should be deeply ashamed of all this," the ex-president wrote in *Reader's Digest*. America seemed "to be plunging into an era of lawlessness, which in the end can lead only to anarchy. And anarchy is a destroyer of nations. I repeat: We ought to be ashamed!" Eisenhower went on to call urban riots "the most shameful outcropping of lawlessness" and felt this was "a situation unacceptable in a civilized nation." While expressing sympathy for the man down on his luck, Eisenhower wrote that "the fact that society has treated him badly does not give him the right to smash a store window and take what he wants, or to attack our police with animal ferocity."[72]

Lindsay had a different reaction to these same changes. He told students at Manhattan's Hunter College in December 1967, "The most profound movement in America in the Sixties is the entirely refreshing attitude of doubt that young people express toward their elders." At Princeton University, Lindsay drew a comparison between rebellious college students and the "thousands of idle youths" in America's slums. Both groups, seemingly so different, were linked in Lindsay's eyes by their alienation from modern society: "Both suffer the malady of powerlessness—powerlessness in the face of huge institutions which routinely cause fundamental dislocations in the lives of people they affect each day." Whereas Eisenhower saw only long hair, disrespect, and a lack of patriotism in the student radicals, Lindsay told his college audience, "Yours is a generation which seems more and more to believe in the battle for change in American life." Lindsay hoped to harness this energy into reforming the city.[73]

Lindsay's thinking bore a strong resemblance to the 1962 "Port Huron Statement," the founding document of the radical Students for a Democratic Society (SDS). Though there is no evidence that Lindsay had ever read the document, the idea of participatory democracy and the sense of alienation expressed in the document seem to have filtered down to Lindsay. The Port Huron Statement, with its talk of man's "loneliness, estrangement, isolation" from his fellow man, was an early portrait of the alienation of a segment of American youth. It spoke of "the actual structural separation of people from power, from relevant knowledge, from pinnacles of decision-making. . . . [where] major social institutions create the circumstances in which the isolated citizen will try hopelessly to understand his world and himself." Compare this with Lindsay's plea for a more responsive city government: "City Hall must extend itself to the residents of the city, whose only personal contact with their government often takes the form of a policeman, a housing inspector, or an ambulance driver. The widespread estrangement—often a pronounced alienation—that characterizes the relationship between a city government and its citizens can be bridged by granting people a strong, direct voice in the affairs of their city."[74]

Though Lindsay may often have sounded like the student radicals during the early and mid-sixties, his idealism was rooted in the much older tradition of urban reform politics. The student movement, drawing from a different intellectual well, would shortly take on a life of its own in both its political radicalism and in its members' personal behavior. These changes would make the words of the Port Huron Statement seem quaint a mere five years later and put the straight-laced Lindsay in an awkward position regarding his erstwhile allies.

Regarding the Vietnam War, Lindsay was fairly quiet during his first two years. He had tentatively made his mark as a critic of the war in his April 1965 Oakland University speech and continued in that vein in a January 1966 interview when he called Vietnam the "most unwanted war" in American history. He reiterated his opposition to the bombing of North Vietnam and called for "solid diplomacy" to end the war, but also admitted that "you can't pack your bags up and sneak out. We're committed too deeply." By mid-1967, Lindsay said of Vietnam, "I just think there should be a greater effort to make peace, and less emphasis on escalation."[75]

But the mayor soon began criticizing the war in terms that would become a running theme in his political repertoire. "What it comes down to is, which is the more important in the long run—funds for Southeast Asia or for Brownsville?" Lindsay asked in 1968, answering, "I'm for Brownsville." While Lindsay had shown little enthusiasm for America's presence in Southeast Asia, he had previously failed to articulate a clear antiwar message. As antiwar protests grew, though, Lindsay's position moved from vague comments critical of the war to a vocal and energetic antiwar stand.[76]

ANTIWAR PROTESTS AT WHITEHALL

One incident further placed the Lindsay administration on one side of the growing culture war: the involvement of the mayoral aides Sid Davidoff and Barry Gottehrer in a week-long protest demonstration in December 1967, called "Stop the Draft Week," at the military induction center on Whitehall Street in Lower Manhattan. Whitehall was made famous in the 1967 song "Alice's Restaurant," in which the song's composer, Arlo Guthrie, sang about being "injected, inspected, detected, infested, neglected, and selected" by the draft board. During the week-long protest thousands of protesters threatened to disrupt the city and tie up traffic. Before the protests began, Lindsay and Gottehrer met with Dr. Benjamin Spock and David McReynolds of the War Resisters League to discuss the protests. The protesters, the mayor, and the police worked out the logistics of the protest, right down to the place where protesters would be arrested. Gottehrer and Davidoff were to be the mayor's liaisons at the protest.[77]

Monday's protest was quiet. In the early-morning hours of Tuesday, December 5, police arrested 264 antiwar protesters who tried to barricade the induction center. Among those arrested were the poet Allen Ginsberg, Dr. Spock, and the historian Conor Cruise O'Brien. Things went smoothly. Though the military inductions continued, the antiwar protesters were able to make their statement. The police contained the protesters and peacefully arrested the demonstrators.

Wednesday's protest was less orderly. The protesters sought more controversy than the timid events of the previous two days had generated. Many wandered up to City Hall and then to the United Nations. Chief Inspector Sanford Garelik ordered an estimated 4,000 to 5,000 policemen, including plainclothesmen and undercover cops dressed as hippies, to supervise the 2,000 protesters. The policy of flooding a demonstration with massive numbers of policemen allowed them to contain the protesters. The journalist Sally Kempton, who took part in Wednesday's demonstration, described it as a "police triumph." Kempton wrote that the protests quickly evolved into a struggle to outsmart the police, "to elude them long enough to reach a destination and make a stand." On Thursday, in what Gottehrer called "an on-the-spot decision," the protesters were allowed to hold a rally at the United Nations. He was angered when police arrested protesters at the UN for protesting without a permit, and Sid Davidoff worked to get those arrested out of jail.[78]

By Friday the protest had degenerated into chaos, despite the fact that there were fewer than 2,000 protesters instead of the 10,000 predicted. These protesters were younger and much less sympathetic to symbolic displays of civil disobedience. They were disenchanted with traditional sit-ins and demoralized by the police. They wanted action. After five days of protests, Gottehrer noticed that "the police were restive and angry, and were less and less concerned with the niceties of civil liberties." Gottehrer and Davidoff negotiated with the protest leaders to settle on a route from Whitehall up Broadway to Union Square, at Fourteenth Street. The protesters did not have a permit to assemble at Union Square, but the mayoral aides said that would be overlooked. They helped usher the crowd up Broadway toward Fourteenth Street. Little did the two aides realize that their actions during this march would soon catapult them out of relative obscurity and onto the front pages of the city's newspapers.

As the protesters approached Union Square, a large group split off eastward toward a building housing military offices. This was not what Davidoff and Gottehrer had agreed to, but by now they had lost control of the crowd. The police moved in and tried to restore order, cornering a few hundred protesters against the building wall. It is unclear what caused the police to move against the trapped protesters—the obscene taunts from the crowd, a thrown object, an inadvertent push, or just the sight of their long hair and sloppy dress. Kempton claims the police action began when a policeman told a protester standing on a trash can to get off. The protester responded, "Fuck you." However it began, twenty to thirty policemen formed a flying wedge and charged the crowd with clubs flying. One hundred and forty protesters were arrested. Gottehrer was frustrated by his inability to control the protesters and felt the police overreacted.[79]

The following week, leaders of the Patrolmen's Benevolent Association (PBA), including John Cassese, PBA president, called for the resignations of Davidoff and Gottehrer, charging they had hindered police during the protests. Neither Davidoff nor Gottehrer had any official capacity at the demonstration; Davidoff was deputy buildings commissioner and Gottehrer was chairman of the mayor's Urban Action Task Force. Lindsay argued that his aides were observing the protest on his behalf. Cassese claimed they "were trying to intimidate the policemen" and that Lindsay was "doing his best to demoralize the department." The PBA even criticized Davidoff and Gottehrer for their clothes. Instead of wearing suits and ties as would befit their official positions, they were dressed in turtlenecks and khakis, no different in the eyes of the police than the demonstrators. (Davidoff was offended by the suggestion that he dressed like a hippie. His style, he told a reporter, was "mod.")

There was even criticism within the Lindsay administration. Traffic Commissioner Henry Barnes, a Wagner holdover, said he wished "these people [Gottehrer and Davidoff] would be as concerned about traffic problems as they were about whether the marchers got where they wanted to go." Barnes called the week-long protests "the most horrible, ridiculous, outrageous thing I've ever seen." With great melodrama, City Council President Frank O'Connor also called for the resignation of the two aides: "Not even in the worst days of political rule in New York has there been such a bold, brazen effort to politically interfere with the police department." Gottehrer later wrote that he and Davidoff "were two available bodies to flesh out the charges of City Hall interference and tools in a philosophical battle between the mayor and the police union over civilian control of the police."[80]

The mayor gave Gottehrer and Davidoff, who were quickly becoming Lindsay's Rosencrantz and Guildenstern, the opportunity to clear the air. On Tuesday morning, the two aides called a press conference in Gottehrer's cramped, cluttered office in the Tweed Courthouse. (His office was intentionally kept away from City Hall because of the types of people—hippies, black militants, radicals—with whom he routinely dealt.) Gottehrer was convinced that if they did not use the opportunity of the press conference to clear themselves of charges of wrongdoing, they would be fired. Davidoff worried that City Hall might disavow them and hide them away for the remainder of Lindsay's term. Though Davidoff claimed Gottehrer was "a nervous wreck," the two men answered questions in a direct and open manner, securing their position in the administration and blunting accusations from the PBA. The incident made Gottehrer and Davidoff public figures, with all of the burdens this status carries. In the eyes of some, they were defenders of antiwar protesters and meddlers in police business. For the remainder of the Lindsay administration, every policeman knew the names Gottehrer and Davidoff. Everyone from policemen to black militants to political operatives to the man on the street knew that when these two obscure aides spoke, they spoke for Lindsay.[81]

The mayoral aides tried to act as "neutral arbiters" of the surrounding turmoil, functioning, Gottehrer said, "as liaison between the police and demonstrators. There are people in this city who won't talk to policemen—people in Harlem bars and peace offices downtown." Sid Davidoff explained, in response to a negative letter from a New York resident, that he was "there in an official capacity as an observer trying to curtail any animosity generated by each side." Had this been a week-long pro-war demonstration that sought to shut down the *Village Voice* for its antiwar articles, would Lindsay and his aides have taken the same stance, and let the protest continue? Probably not. By staying in close contact with protest leaders, Gottehrer and Davidoff gave an official stamp of approval to the protesters' actions.[82]

Though the criticism of Gottehrer and Davidoff soon abated, the ill will between the Lindsay administration and the police continued. Lindsay would never be known as a "law and order" mayor. He would never gain the trust of the naturally suspicious NYPD. Gottehrer remembered that after the December 1967 brouhaha, "the average cop thought we [Gottehrer and

Davidoff] were bad, bad people. Everything that ever happened to them, they would blame it on those two guys in City Hall." Lindsay might have survived these problems in normal times, but as crime increased dramatically and New Yorkers took sides in the battle between their mayor and the men in blue, there was little doubt on whose side the majority of New Yorkers would come down.[83]

5

THE CIVILIAN COMPLAINT
REVIEW BOARD

To comprehend the minicontroversy over Sid Davidoff and Barry Gottehrer's involvement in the December 1967 Whitehall Street antiwar demonstration, one has to understand the uneasy relationship between Lindsay and the police department. This unease was born of a struggle that began in the 1950s, when some New Yorkers began crusading for a Civilian Complaint Review Board to monitor charges of police brutality. The issue remained on the back burner, however, until Lindsay took office in 1966.

The New York Police Department (NYPD) is a unique structure, what one journalist called the city's "subtlest and most complex" bureaucracy. The department is a quasi-military organization that achieved a measure of independence from City Hall after the early 1950s. With their own unwritten code of conduct, policemen inhabit a world where violence is an accepted method of dealing with an untidy, dangerous society. Ethnically, the police department has traditionally been Catholic and Irish. In 1965, the top brass was almost exclusively Irish, and the rank and file consisted mainly of Irish and Italians. The department developed into a relatively secure civil-service career for the city's lower-middle-class white Catholics. Blacks, WASPs, Jews, and Puerto Ricans were a distinct minority on the force. A typical policeman's ideological outlook was conservative and traditional. Many patrolmen and officers lived in white ethnic neighborhoods in Queens and Brooklyn, a world away from high-toned Manhattan or the slums of Harlem or central Brooklyn. Some policemen had moved to Staten Island and others to the suburbs.[1]

Lindsay's choice of his twenty-six-year-old aide, Jay Kriegel, a recent Harvard Law School graduate with no law-enforcement experience, as his point man on police matters exemplified the mayor's growing problem with the police department. Kriegel had met Lindsay in early 1965 while working for the House Judiciary Committee, during his final year in law school, as a volunteer expert on voting-rights laws. He joined Lindsay's mayoral campaign as a volunteer, and worked his way into the mayor's confidence. Kriegel personified Lindsay's "kiddie corps" of young, Ivy League aides who worshiped the mayor and shared his impatience with the city's "power brokers." Barry Gottehrer called Kriegel "extremely bright, at times overbearing, ambitious like nearly everyone else close to the mayor." Woody Klein found Kriegel "a brash young man who was not at all personable, but was nevertheless extraordinarily bright and quick." Because Kriegel spent so much time with the mayor, Mary Lindsay used to say, "Jay doesn't need an apartment. He lives in my husband's ear."[2]

Lindsay would soon find himself at odds with the New York Police Department, and with a sizable number of New Yorkers, over the issue of a civilian-dominated Review Board to monitor police behavior. The controversy would define Lindsay's administration and have a serious effect on law enforcement issues for the rest of his tenure as mayor.

ON THE ROAD TO CIVILIAN REVIEW

The issue of reforming the city's police department predated Lindsay's tenure. The Civilian Complaint Review Board controversy began in October 1950. In that year eighteen civil liberties, community welfare, ethnic, and religious groups that made up the Permanent Coordination Committee on Police and Minority Groups met to consider the problem of police "misconduct in their relations with the public generally and police misconduct in their relations with Puerto Ricans and Negroes specifically."[3]

These charges led to the creation of the "first" Civilian Complaint Review Board, staffed with only police representatives. The board was reorganized and strengthened in 1954, when newly elected Mayor Robert Wagner appointed Francis W. H. Adams police commissioner. The "second" Civilian Complaint Review Board came into being in 1955 in response to Adams's work. Though still without civilian members, it was more receptive to civil liberties issues and community concerns than the earlier board, and for the next nine years the issue of police brutality was muted.

The issue reemerged in April 1964, when City Councilman Theodore Weiss, a reform Democrat from the West Side of Manhattan, introduced a bill for a Civilian Complaint Review Board consisting of nine civilians appointed by the mayor. The reappearance of this issue was directly related to the civil-rights movement. With the Jim Crow system in the South crumbling in the face of sit-ins, protest marches, voter-registration drives, and school integration battles, Northern liberals began to look in their own backyards. The issue of police treatment of minorities, as well as open-housing laws and busing of schoolchildren, became the backbone of the Northern civil rights movement.

The Weiss bill had virtually no support in the City Council. Police Commissioner Michael Murphy (who had been appointed by Wagner in 1961) called the new charges of police brutality "maliciously inspired" and "hate rousing of the lowest type . . . aimed at destroying respect for law and order and are in effect, calculated mass libel of the police." In response, some blacks began calling the commissioner "Bull" Murphy, after the Alabama sheriff Bull Connor. In 1964, Malcolm X called Murphy "a dangerous man" because "almost all his public statements give the policeman courage to incite to violence." A shocked and angry Murphy proudly answered, "My name is Michael Murphy. I am fifty years old. I am a native New Yorker, born in the Elmhurst section of Queens. I still live there. I have no nickname." The irony is that for the previous decade, under Adams and Murphy, the police department had been governed by men considered "liberal" in police circles, men attuned to modern sensibilities and without a trace of racial bias.[4]

The City Council allowed the Weiss bill to die. In the summer of 1964, though, a race riot in Harlem erupted in response to the shooting death of a black youth by a white off-duty policeman. Though it became harder to sweep the issue of police brutality under the rug, Mayor Wagner handled the issue as he had many others—through delay and procrastination, hoping the cries for reform would soon pass.

The actual incidence of police brutality has never been easy to measure. The political scientists Stephen David and Paul Peterson have noted:

> There is little solid evidence that black suspicion of the police is due to discriminatory behavior by white policemen against blacks in particular. It is true that policemen make racial slurs when referring to blacks behind their backs and, sometimes, to their faces. But if police call blacks "niggers" and "coons," that seems little different than their references to Italians as "wops" and to people of Polish descent as "Polacks." Street language is not invariably polite; it hardly seems the root of the problems. More significantly, it is difficult to find conclusive evidence in modern departments that policemen treat blacks in a discriminatory fashion.

According to the National Advisory Commission on Civil Disorders, also known as the Kerner Commission (after its chairman, Governor Otto Kerner of Illinois), 20 to 25 percent of young adult blacks said police had either used insulting language to them or searched them without good reason. The numbers for young adult whites were 5 to 15 percent. Considering the subjective quality of definitions of insulting language and frisking without good reason, police brutality was not endemic and not solely directed against blacks. The numbers cited by the Kerner Commission for those who had been physically abused by police was even lower. Eight percent of young adult blacks had been roughed up, compared to 2 percent of their white counterparts. A 1964 *Times* poll found that 12 percent of Harlem residents believed there was "a lot" of police brutality; 31 percent believed there was "a little"; 20 percent felt there was "none at all"; and 34 were "not sure." Only 9 percent had ever witnessed such an act. A Louis Harris poll found that although 52 percent of blacks believed in widespread police brutality, only 13 percent had been victims or had witnessed an incident.[5]

The main problem in inner-city ghettos was not too much law enforcement, but too little. Contrary to conventional wisdom, police in black neighborhoods were less interested in brutally enforcing middle-class morality than in avoiding the messy tangle of crime and pathology. As the Kerner Report noted, "Police maintain a much less rigorous standard of law enforcement in the ghetto, tolerating there illegal activities . . . that they would not tolerate elsewhere." There were many reasons for this attitude: an indifference to black victims, payoffs made to overlook illegal gambling and prostitution, and the desire of white cops to avoid dangerous, racially charged situations. The Kerner Report quoted studies of black residents in Harlem and Los Angeles in which inadequate police protection ranked higher than police brutality as the major reason for the lack of respect of black for police.[6]

The City Council's City Affairs Committee voted 4 to 1 against the Weiss bill, with Weiss the sole yea vote, and it finally released its majority report on the issue of a Civilian Complaint Review Board in May 1965. The report concluded: "The Civilian Complaint Review Board currently with the Police Department of New York City has performed ably, and well, without any fault or cause for blame." The report examined complaints to the NYPD's Civilian Complaint Review Board from 1959 through 1964 and found an average of 183 complaints per year, mostly for use of undue force. Less than 7 percent of these complaints were ordered to trial. One quarter of the cases that went to trial were subsequently dropped. Over those six years, forty-seven policemen ultimately faced punishment: six were dismissed, four resigned, three retired, and thirty-four were fined or disciplined.[7]

The numbers do not really tell much, though. Opponents of a Civilian Complaint Review Board could argue the statistics showed police brutality was not much of an issue. The board's proponents could argue the numbers showed police officers were being shielded by the present Civilian Complaint Review Board and that the high rate of dismissal of civilian complaints showed that they were not taken seriously.

Murphy, who had a good relationship with civil libertarians, reportedly told one of them that if the pressure subsided, he would appoint civilians to the Review Board. But in 1965, including civilians on the board would have given the impression that Murphy was caving in to outside pressure, and he would have lost the respect of his men. Murphy resigned in May 1965, reportedly fed up with the accusations leveled against him and his department.

Vincent Broderick, from within the department, was hired to fill out Murphy's term. Meanwhile, the issue of a Civilian Complaint Review Board was kept alive, for the candidate John Lindsay promised to create a "mixed" Review Board with both police and civilian members.[8]

LINDSAY VERSUS THE POLICE

When Lindsay became mayor, an immediate question was what to do with Commissioner Broderick when his term expired on February 21, 1966. Broderick was tall, lean, and distinguished-looking. His education, in contrast to that of the typical traditional New York Irish policeman, resembled Lindsay's: Andover, Princeton, and Harvard Law School. He was, in the words of the liberal journalist Jack Newfield, "a man of uncommon decency," a thoughtful public servant, and a police "liberal" along the lines of his predecessors Francis Adams and Michael Murphy. Jay Kriegel remembers Broderick as a "a very decent man who was actually trying to be a reform commissioner." The problem was that if Lindsay was to institute his plans for a Civilian Complaint Review Board, he would need a police commissioner sympathetic to that goal. Although Broderick stated publicly that he would not oppose such a board nor resign his post if it were created, this was not enough for Lindsay. He wanted a commissioner fully behind the proposal.[9]

Further complicating matters were accusations that Deputy Mayor Bob Price was interfering with the operations of the police department. Price possessed the biggest personality in the administration, at times overshadowing his boss, and he quickly become a lightening rod for criticism of the administration. His brash style was not effective in governing a city. Questions were raised about Price's use of police cars to get coffee and food and to chauffeur him home.

Price began a whispering campaign that Broderick was a goner. When Woody Klein confronted Price about a leaked story in mid-December 1965 about Broderick's imminent demise, Price responded, "I don't have to tell you what I do. I don't have to tell Lindsay either. I know what's best for him—I know what is better for him than he does."[10]

The first major conflict between the administration and the police department was the attempt by Price to stop Broderick from filling vacancies for six detective positions. This move gave the impression that those vacancies would be filled by political friends of the mayor. Price claims that he put a hold on the vacancies because the New York Civil Liberties Union told the Lindsay administration that the department's detectives were too "homogeneous": male Irish Catholics who lived in Queens. Price says that patronage was not an issue because he did not know anyone to put into the detective's slots. He just wanted time to study how to make the detective force more diverse. Broderick refused to accommodate Price, claiming it would set a precedent of political meddling, and the administration backed off.[11]

Soon after Lindsay was elected, he appointed the former federal judge Lawrence E. Walsh (later the special prosecutor during the Iran-Contra affair) head of a Law Enforcement Task Force, which was to examine the operation of the New York Police Department. Written by Kriegel, the Walsh Report brimmed with reform rhetoric. Modernization was its catchword. Its theme was that the department was deficient in nearly every aspect: "Our study has revealed so many practices and procedures that are either outmoded, inefficient, or undesirable that we have no reservations as to the need for a thoroughgoing reevaluation of the Department's operations." Therefore, the panel felt, the police "must be subjected to an unrestricted and unstinting review of long-standing traditions, attitudes, and practices."

The report chastised the department for having uniformed officers performing clerical functions, for swamping officers with paperwork, for an inefficient communication system, and for unfair hiring and promotion practices. The report called community relations "essential to all law enforcement and therefore an integral part of all police work." It endorsed Commissioner Broderick's idea of precinct community councils and argued that a Civilian Complaint Review Board was the only way to regain public confidence. The report attacked the powerful "Irish mafia" that ran the department by questioning the objectivity of the standards used for selection of detectives and wondered whether civil-service qualifications for policemen "disproportionately discriminate against any single group."[12]

As promised, Lindsay would leave no stone unturned in the push for a more efficient, modern, and progressive government. Left twisting in the wind by the administration, Broderick came out forcefully against the board as conceived by Lindsay. In a late January interview, the commissioner said having civilians on the board would lead to a climate where police would be less willing to act. With only two weeks left in his term, Broderick sent a seven-page letter to Mayor Lindsay, which he released to the press even before it reached the mayor. A scathing reply to the Walsh Report, it was written by a man unencumbered with the desire to placate his boss. Broderick attacked the Law Enforcement Task Force report for dredging up the "bromides of the past" and for being "unwilling or unable to separate valid criticism and suggestions from undocumented folklore." He was angered that the Task Force did not include a single member of the department (although a former deputy commissioner, Leonard Reisner, was on the panel and supported the report). Broderick called "manifestly wrong" the assertion that there was "a lack of strong public support for the police in the performance of their duties." Instead, he asserted, "Never, in the history of the City, has public confidence in the Police Department been so high, or public support for the police been more vigorous."[13]

In his letter, Broderick agreed with Lindsay that the plight of the poor and minorities were of desperate concern. But he felt the problems of discrimination, unemployment, poor housing, and education would not be solved by a Civilian Complaint Review Board. Instead, Broderick asked Lindsay rhetorically: "Is it not time, Mr. Mayor, for responsible leaders such as yourself, to renounce this cruel hoax, this bromide, this palliative of an independent civilian review board? Is it not time for us to stand up and say that we intend to deal with substance and not with shadow? . . . Is it not time, Mr. Mayor, for you to say that you renounce political expediency?"

Broderick argued that a Civilian Complaint Review Board would "lower the morale of the Police Department" and "dilute the nature and the quality of the protection which they will render to the public." After releasing the letter, Broderick told reporters, "I am asking the Mayor to recognize . . . that the Police Commissioner runs this department—not the Deputy Mayor." Broderick added that his problem was not with Lindsay, but with "the group of young men working for him."[14]

For Lindsay, Broderick's letter represented yet another instance of the lack of respect he felt due him as mayor. Lindsay fumed to his aides, "This is the rudest letter I have ever received. I couldn't imagine writing a letter like this to the mayor." Flushed with anger, Lindsay was ready to fire Broderick immediately—"I ought to let this guy have it right now"—until Klein and Kriegel calmed him down. Still, Frank O'Connor, Lindsay's nemesis and a potential challenger of Rockefeller in November, defended Broderick, as did former Commissioners Adams and Murphy.[15]

Lindsay's public response to Broderick was muted. Speaking on February 13, he laid out the importance of an independent Review Board: "I, as Mayor, as chief executive, have a right and should resolve this question. And I propose to resolve it along the lines of the proposal that I made. And the more I examine it, the better I think it is."

On Tuesday, February 15, Mayor Lindsay hired Howard Leary, the police commissioner of Philadelphia, to replace Broderich as commissioner. Lindsay had been in contact with Leary since soon after the November election. Lindsay was impressed with the fact that Leary had already worked with an independent review board in Philadelphia.

The new commissioner was, of course, an Irish Catholic, although his mother was German. The fifty-four-year-old professional was only five feet, seven inches tall, one inch less than the minimum height requirement for New York City policemen. He had spent ten years in Philadelphia as a patrolman and ten more years as the department's top uniformed cop, and from there had become deputy commissioner and finally commissioner. Leary's pro-review-board stance and his handling of the 1964 Philadelphia riot won him praise from groups like the NAACP, the Urban League, CORE (Congress of Racial Equality), and the SNCC (Student Nonviolent Coordinating Committee).[16]

But Broderick refused to fade quietly. Soon after Leary's appointment, Broderick went public with the story that he had been invited in January to City Hall to meet Constantine Sidamon-Eristoff, a mayoral assistant in charge of personnel. He never got to meet Lindsay's patronage director, but the invitation gave the impression that the administration saw the police department as another city department that it could staff with its supporters. This impression was especially devastating in a reform administration that had warned of the dangers of clubhouse politics if Abe Beame were elected mayor. Later, in March, Broderick received a standing ovation at the NYPD's annual Holy Name Society Communion breakfast, the same venue where the previous year William F. Buckley delivered his controversial speech on civil rights. Commissioner Leary declined to appear, claiming he was ill.[17]

Former Commissioner Adams made public his belief that Leary faced tremendous political pressure to place certain people in positions in the police department. (Adams actually called Fiorello La Guardia the worst in dealing with the police department because the whirlwind mayor meddled with "everything.") Adams claimed the NYPD was a "military organization" run by the commissioner and if the mayor did not like it, he could always appoint another commissioner.[18]

In their classic 1960 study of New York government, *Governing New York City: Politics in the Metropolis*, Wallace Sayre and Herbert Kaufman noted that the police commissioner had very limited powers. A close-knit police bureaucracy defended the traditions of the force from radical reforms. They wrote: "The Police Commissioner—isolated from the Mayor and other elected officials, from the party leaders, and from other agencies, and confronted by an unstructured, fragmented constituency—is thus cut off from effective external alliances and thrust back upon his own limited resources in attempting to lead and direct the police bureaucracy." Policing the city, like so much else in American life during the 1960s, was becoming increasingly politicized. Leary and his successors not only would have to navigate the bureaucratic waters of the police department, but also would find themselves captive to the social and political upheavals roiling the nation. Torn between gaining the respect of their men and following the prevailing political winds, police commissioners like Leary found their already precarious position within the police bureaucracy weakened just as the rank-and-file policemen grew more confused and embittered.[19]

As Adams had predicted and Broderick had implied, Commissioner Leary quickly made two high-level appointments that revived the charge of political influence. Twenty-five-year veteran Sanford Garelik had been rumored to be in line for the position of chief inspector, the department's highest-ranking uniformed member. Although Leary claimed he chose Garelik as the most qualified for the position after careful study, the commissioner had only met him the day before he appointed him, lending credence to the rumors that Garelik was a political appointee. Leary also promoted Officer Lloyd Sealy to assistant chief inspector.[20]

Leary, Garelik, and Sealy were outsiders within the clannish department. Leary was from Philadelphia, Garelik was Jewish, and Sealy was black. Leary would prove to be a disappointing choice, remaining for many a political sphinx. Barry Gottehrer, who worked closely with Leary, said of him, "No one could ever really figure him out." Bob Sweet, who replaced Bob Price as deputy mayor in early 1967, said Leary's appointment was one "that should have been great, but wasn't."[21]

What made Garelik's appointment so controversial was his friendship with Alex Rose, the leader of the Liberal Party and a major Lindsay ally. (It was also rumored, incorrectly, that Bob Price and Garelik were cousins.) In December 1965, Senator Jacob Javits had recommended Garelik to Lindsay as a candidate for police commissioner. A decorated police veteran who had held a number of high-profile assignments before being appointed chief inspector, Garelik was chosen, according to Price, "mainly because he was a friend of the Liberal Party." Sweet called him a "creature" of Alex Rose. The new chief inspector had been an outsider among the clique of officers that had surrounded Broderick, and what was worse, neither Garelik nor Sealy had been in line for promotion. Garelik had been an assistant inspector in charge of the Central Office Bureau Squad. As he admits, this was "not a position that would be succeeding the Chief Inspector." For his part, Sealy jumped two ranks—assistant inspector and inspector—to become Garelik's deputy.[22]

The appointments of Garelik and Sealy helped the mayor among blacks and Jews, but they had the opposite reaction among the Irish. Lindsay made a point of breaking up what had come to be known as the "Irish mafia" that had run the police department since the nineteenth century. As Jimmy Breslin quipped, "If you want a rug seller, get an Arab. If you want a cop, get an Irishman." By the 1960s, the department was the last preserve for the descendants of Erin who had once been the city's dominant ethnic group. Robert Daley, who served as deputy police commissioner for public relations under Patrick Murphy in the early seventies, spoke about the importance of the NYPD among the city's Irish. "One of the nice things about the Police Department, not only for me but for all of us, was that one was continually running into men who had once been schoolmates. A lot of us from Good Shepherd [an Irish American Catholic parish in the Inwood section of Upper Manhattan] later would end up in the Police Department," wrote Daley. "The brotherhood that ran all through the Police Department was very deep, and caused by a number of things, but one of them was this, that it bound all of us up in the lives we had in this city."[23]

Lindsay's assistant Donald Shaughnessy noted that Lindsay's police reform would reap great political benefits among blacks and Puerto Ricans. Shaughnessy, whose father was a policeman, said that "the breaking up of the

Irish mafia that's been in control of that department for so long was a special delight for me." Lindsay overlooked the effect his actions would have on those Irish still remaining in the city who felt their once-substantial power giving way to more recent immigrants. As Nathan Glazer and Daniel Patrick Moynihan wrote in their 1963 study of New York, *Beyond the Melting Pot*, "The cumulative effect of this process has been to produce among a great many Irish people a powerful sense of displacement. It is summed up in a phrase they will use on hearing an Irish name or being introduced to another Irishman. 'There are still some of us left,' they say."[24]

Lindsay wanted a more liberal, humane police department. Garelik told the Shomrim Society, a fraternal order of Jewish policemen, that he had been working at "humanizing the department." Jack Newfield seconded the idea that "Lindsay has humanized the Police Department." One of the ways the department began to humanize its operations was a May 11, 1966, order from Commissioner Leary forbidding police entrapment of homosexuals.[25]

The implicit assumption was that the Irish, and the police department they ran, were in need of the "humanizing" touch of non-Irish such as Garelik or Sealy. The *Post's* James Wechsler noted (as did many other press accounts) that Garelik was fond of classical music and had an interest in sociology: "He is not an ordinary gendarme." They seemed to be making the point that Garelik's interest in elite pursuits made him a more worthy appointment than the average Irish cop. Liberal New Yorkers wanted a police force made in their image: liberal, "humanistic," and sensitive to minorities. For Wechsler, the policemen who opposed these changes were those "whose fiscal consciences are not wholly clear [a swipe at corrupt policemen], or whose Birchite allegiances render them uncomfortable in the new atmosphere or whose sinecures are threatened."[26]

Within a week of the appointments of Garelik and Sealy, Chief Inspector John Shanley, Assistant Chief Inspector William McQuade, and Chief of Detectives Philip Walsh—the three highest-ranking uniformed officers in the department—announced their resignations from the police force after being bounced from their posts. Shanley quit the department after being replaced by Garelik, who had jumped over both McQuade and Walsh. McQuade was reportedly asked to resign. "They have their plans," McQuade said, "and I guess I don't fit in." (McQuade was later invited back to the department by Leary, but declined the offer.) All three believed they were victims of political meddling. Walsh, who had lost his son in a car accident the previous week, said that after he heard Shanley had been replaced, he knew it was time to quit. "I wouldn't work two minutes for his successor [Garelik]," he said in an interview. He made it clear that Lindsay's Law Enforcement Task Force had created bad blood in the department—in Walsh's words, it was "simply mouthing platitudes." Shanley reported that when he protested his replacement by Garelik to Leary, the new commissioner responded, "That's politics. It's a rough business." Leary denied making the comment.[27]

The controversy was still raging more than three weeks after Lindsay hired Leary and a month after Broderick's letter. Broderick gave a speech at Fairleigh Dickenson University criticizing the intrusion of politics in the running of the police department. To the mayor Broderick's criticism sounded like a "vendetta" against his Civilian Complaint Review Board. Lindsay warned his critics they were "treading on dangerous ground" with their attacks. Meanwhile, former Mayor Wagner and City Council President O'Connor expressed their concern about Lindsay's relationship with the police. In a March 9 press conference, a visibly angry Mayor Lindsay attacked critics like Broderick and O'Connor, warning the latter that if "he wishes to be responsible as President of the City Council, he'll exercise some restraint on the subject." Lindsay reminded his critics that ultimately the mayor ran the police department. "It is high time those who resist all change recognize that there will be changes," expounded Lindsay on what was now becoming a standard theme of his young mayoralty.[28]

The relationship between Leary and Garelik did not prove harmonious. One observer stated that the two men "hated each other's guts." Garelik admitted that his relationship with Leary was "unusual." Leary suspected that Lindsay might eventually replace him with Garelik. The commissioner delegated much of the day-to-day running of the department to Garelik. During most of the disturbances throughout the city, it was Garelik who was on the front line, while Leary remained at police headquarters or, as during the East Harlem riot, slept in his car. Leary would often return to Philadelphia for weekends, leaving the department in Garelik's hands. When members of the Old Guard police brass asked Leary why he delegated so much authority to Garelik, he told them that someday Garelik would make a mistake—and when that happened, Garelik would be blamed, not Leary.[29]

CRIME CONTROL VERSUS CIVIL RIGHTS

In April 1966, William F. Buckley, a forceful opponent of the Civilian Complaint Review Board, published an article in the *National Review*, by J. P. McFadden that discussed the board in the context of Martin Luther King's call for civil disobedience. McFadden felt that the civil rights movement's seemingly selective idea of which laws to obey was corroding America's legal system. The Civilian Complaint Review Board, he felt, would only intensify this trend. According to McFadden, opponents of the Civilian Complaint Review Board believed there was "a serious moral crisis in America today and that part of it is demonstrated in disregard for authority: in the homes, in the schools, and more recently in the streets." McFadden continued by painting a society fraying at its seams, a theme that Barry Goldwater had played in 1964 and that was brought home by urban riots and growing disorders on college campuses. Civilian Complaint Review Board opponents "point to the skyrocketing rate of dope addiction, to soaring police figures on crimes of violence. They read—it's an everyday occurrence—of repeated acts of brutality by young hoodlums." To conservatives alarmed by the changes in society and rising crime, the Civilian Complaint Review Board seemed like the wrong answer to the wrong problem.[30]

Defenders of the board saw these social changes in a more benevolent way; they were the necessary consequences of the fight for freedoms long overdue. They saw the authority championed by conservatives at *National Review* as an excuse for keeping down blacks and women. William Booth, Lindsay's human rights commissioner, applauded Garelik's appointment and took swipes at Shanley and Walsh. "Garelik is attuned to the needs of the Negro community," Booth said, "where Shanley and Walsh were not." Garelik could "communicate with the Negroes, where Shanley and Walsh could not." Because of this, Booth saw the appointment as a step toward easing tensions in ghetto neighborhoods. Some even thought the Civilian Complaint Review Board did not go far enough. The NAACP general council warned that Leary's appointment "should not obscure the fact that Mayor Lindsay's proposed Civilian Complaint Review Board is defective and that it does not provide the independence and impartiality which is essential to the restoration of public confidence in the police." Despite this, the NAACP backed Lindsay's Civilian Complaint Review Board in its official publication, *The Crisis*.[31]

Two incidents during February and March of 1966 hurt the police and added ammunition for Civilian Complaint Review Board proponents. The first occurred in a Harlem bar in the early-morning hours of February 20, when four white policemen questioned a woman named Gertrude Williams. They ordered the thirty-two-year-old woman into a backroom and asked her to lift her skirt so they could examine her private parts. Ostensibly, the policemen were looking for transvestites. That the officers were white and Mrs. Williams was black made it worse, and gave critics of the police yet another example of racial bias. For blacks, the incident indicated a lack of respect. It gave fodder not only to the campaign to install a Civilian Complaint Review Board, but also to militants like Roy Innis, head of Manhattan CORE, who called on blacks to "escalate the war" on "vicious racist acts by police." Many of the supporters of a Civilian Complaint Review Board felt that it would make the city safer by providing an avenue to deal with such friction between police and minority communities. According to a *World Journal Tribune* editorial, the Civilian Complaint Review Board would be "an essential safety valve for the entire community. Without safety valves, overheated boilers have a tendency to blow up."[32]

The other issue was a minor flap created when Commissioner Leary, in his first press conference, told reporters he would permit members of the right-wing John Birch Society to remain on the police force as long as their membership did not interfere with their work. Although no official records were kept, best estimates put the number of Birchers in the NYPD at between 300 and 500 in a 27,000-member force. Even those estimates were probably high, since both members and opponents had reason to inflate the numbers. The following day, Lindsay asked Leary for a report on the Birch Society in the department. The sight of Lindsay, the civil libertarian, demanding lists on the political affiliation of policemen was odd.[33]

The Birchers sent the *Post*'s editorial page into a froth. While decrying any "purges" of Birch Society members in the police department, the *Post* called for Leary to condemn the Birchers. The paper called again for the implementation of the Civilian Complaint Review Board, which would not only punish brutal and racist cops but would "underline the point that there will be no departmental sanctuary for . . . political zealots in uniform." This raised the specter that some Review Board proponents, despite their professed civil libertarianism, wanted to use the board to weed out "unacceptable" political views. What really bothered the *Post* editorial writers and other liberals was "a right-wing bias that pervades too many sectors of the police."[34]

Lindsay denounced the Birch Society as "terrible, infamous, and hostile to everything I think is decent." Taking issue with Leary, he thought that being a Bircher might be inconsistent with being a police officer and that the John Birch Society could "hurt a free system." His reasoning: "They have said some things that are unbelievable about leaders of our country, including Presidents." For some reason, the Birch Society so agitated liberals like Lindsay (except for the ACLU, which defended the right of policemen to belong to the Birch Society) that they tossed out their cherished civil libertarianism. The NAACP's executive director, Roy Wilkins, echoing the campaign of 100 percent Americanism from earlier in the century, claimed that "a man cannot be a 100 percent John Birch member and a 100 percent policeman." Bowing to the critics, Leary soon changed positions and called the John Birch Society "abhorrent."[35]

A NEW BOARD

On May 17, 1966, Commissioner Leary issued General Order No. 14, creating a seven-man Civilian Complaint Review Board (CCRB): four civilians and three policemen. The Lindsay board replaced the eleven-year-old board that had been staffed exclusively by police. In early May, Lindsay appointed an eleven-man committee to screen prospective members of the new board. Though lauding the police for their conduct during the previous year's blackout and the recent transit strike, Lindsay made clear he believed the NYPD had lost the confidence of many New Yorkers. "In several areas of this city, that confidence has broken down," Lindsay argued. "A widespread cause is the suspicion that citizens who feel they have been mistreated by police officers do not receive a fair, impartial hearing of their complaints." The eleven-man search committee, chaired by Lindsay's mentor, former Attorney General Herbert Brownell, was made up of prominent liberals such as the Liberal Party's Donald Harrington; Orin Lehman, the nephew of former Governor Herbert Lehman; and Morris Abram, the president of the American Jewish Committee. The panel was racially diverse, with three blacks and one Puerto Rican.[36]

Hundreds of letters and telegrams flooded the screening panel with suggestions for individuals to serve on the board. One of the most inventive suggestions came from William F. Buckley, who in a telegram to Brownell offered his thoughts:

> Urgently recommend Vincent Broderick, Michael Murphy, Stephen Kennedy and Francis Adams for consideration of your Committee. Assuming four civilians must be added to police complaint review board, a point which neither the Conservative Party nor I concede, these four former police commissioners should be selected. They combine required experience, integrity and judgment in unique measure. Their selection would redeem Mayor Lindsay's foolhardy campaign pledge with minimum damage to law enforcement in New York City.[37]

John Cassese, the president of the Patrolmen's Benevolent Association (PBA), pledged to use every dollar in the PBA's treasury to fight Lindsay's board, promising to take the matter to court, the City Council, the state legislature, and, if necessary, to a ballot referendum on the issue in November. "I'm sick and tired of giving in to minority groups with their whims and their gripes and shouting," explained Cassese. "I don't think we need a review board at all." The city's human rights commissioner, William Booth, denounced Cassese's remarks as an "appeal to basic prejudice and bigotry." Cassese, a former patrolman born and raised in the working-class Greenpoint section of Brooklyn, was an unpolished public speaker. So, the PBA's public relations man, Norman Frank, gradually became the spokesman for the anti-review-board forces.

By 1966, the Patrolmen's Benevolent Association numbered 20,000 members and had long been one of the strongest interest groups in the city. Although technically not a union, the PBA was able to mobilize support not only for wage and workplace demands, but also for changes in law enforcement policy.[38]

After receiving little satisfaction in the courts or from elected officials, PBA volunteers began circulating petitions in early June for a referendum to repeal the Review Board. Board opponents needed 30,000 signatures to put the referendum on the November ballot. If the city council did not act on the originally submitted referendum question within sixty days of the submission, 15,000 additional names were required. By July 7, 1966, the PBA had 51,852 signatures. On the same day, the Conservative Party submitted

40,383 signatures for their own anti-review board referendum, which was worded only slightly differently from the PBA's. Meanwhile, the Guardians, a fraternal order representing 1,300 of the city's black policemen, called the board the "most important step toward wiping out the fears and the unequal treatment suffered by the members of our minority group."[39]

Aryeh Neier, the executive director of the New York Civil Liberties Union (NYCLU), predicted "a nasty campaign." Sidney Zion, covering the story for the *Times*, called the PBA's anti-review-board slogans "demagoguery" against which the NYCLU would "employ sweet reason." He wrote that a win by the PBA would "surely be interpreted as an anti-Negro, anti–Puerto Rican vote." According to Zion, community activists saw police slogans such as "Don't handcuff the police" and "We might as well close up shop" as subtle references to keeping minorities in their place. All the city newspapers supported the new board, except one: the city's largest-circulation newspaper, the *Daily News,* opposed it, warning that "the civilian section [of the board] will be infested sooner or later with cop-haters, professional liberals, representatives of pressure groups and the like."[40]

Lindsay responded to the referendum issue immediately. He believed that "highly organized, militant right-wing groups" were out to kill the board. Lindsay warned of the possibly "inflammatory" situation a referendum battle could create. He met with PBA representatives on July 12, later telling Klein that he "put it to him [Cassese] and Norman Frank. I told them that if anything happened in New York—if there was a blow-up—they would be responsible. I think they were a little floored. I hit them where it hurt." The blame for any riots, Lindsay warned subtly, would fall on the heads of the PBA and other board opponents.[41]

Four days after the signatures were deposited with the Board of Elections, Lindsay named the seven-man Civilian Complaint Review Board that would begin hearing complaints in July. It was by all accounts a very liberal board. Its chairman was Algernon Black, the senior leader of the New York Society for the Ethical Culture and a vice president of the NAACP. Among the other three civilians were a black (Walter Murray, a professor of education at Brooklyn College); a Puerto Rican (Manual Diaz Jr., the head of the Puerto Rican Community Development Project); and a white Irish Catholic (Thomas Farrell, a lawyer at the law firm of Paul, Weiss, Rifkind, Wharton, and Garrison and a member of the Catholic Interracial Council). Of the three police representatives named, one was black and the other two were Irish. Two of the three policemen were holdovers from the old board. The board's civilian director was the lawyer Harold Baer.[42]

Though some may have wanted Brownell or another *éminence grise* with a judicial or legal background put on the board to give the appearance of balance and fairness, the screening committee's early lists included no such graybeards. The committee made its recommendations to the mayor ten days after the announcement of its appointment. The screening panel forwarded eight names to Lindsay, including the four who were eventually named to the board. The most prominent name on the list was the social scientist Kenneth Clark. The other three names forwarded to the mayor were Helen Hall, the director of the Henry Street Settlement House; Ann S. Kheel, the wife of the labor mediator Theodore Kheel; and Manuel Zapata, a Puerto Rican lawyer.[43]

Cassese called the appointments "so pro-civil rights and so pro-Lindsay, I think Lindsay went out of his way to get these four." Aryeh Neier later agreed: "It looked too much like an effect for a balanced ticket and lent itself to all the force that the police could generate. It was just too much of that character." Although those who served on Lindsay's CCRB were decent, honorable individuals, they possessed little citywide influence or stature.[44]

One incident that symbolized Lindsay's problems acclimating himself to the intricacies of local politics was his 1966 visit to Francis Cardinal Spellman, archbishop of the New York Archdiocese and the most powerful Catholic in the country. To Lindsay, Spellman was another "power broker" whose past meddling in government would be unacceptable during his administration. (At Lindsay's inauguration, for the first time in at least twenty years Spellman was not seated near the mayor-elect. Nor did Lindsay ever consult with Spellman about filling city offices, as Wagner had done. Although Lindsay's behavior toward the cardinal could have been interpreted as a mild slap at the city's Catholics, it merely showed Lindsay's awkwardness when his principles collided with political reality. Spellman did not forget the snub.)

When Lindsay met Spellman for lunch to discuss the CCRB, he badly wanted the cardinal's seal of approval. He offered Spellman a position on the CCRB in exchange for the city's financial help for one of the city's Catholic hospitals. Spellman turned down the hospital deal, but said he would be happy to help Lindsay with the board. Lindsay was so ecstatic and grateful that one person present said, "He looked like he'd give the Cardinal his wife." His ecstasy was short-lived. Spellman agreed to help only under the condition that the mayor also name the Episcopal bishop of New York as cochairman. An angry Lindsay knew that Spellman was toying with him, since neither man would take on such a politically sensitive assignment. Spellman told Lindsay mischievously, "You didn't really want me to violate the ecumenical spirit of Vatican II."[45]

The battle over the independent CCRB had begun. According to Roger Starr, this battle "marked the point at which the Lindsay administration found that it had picked the strategy of social progress over the strategy of 'good government.'" The effect of such a policy was already being felt on the street. In September, a writer studying Manhattan's West Side testified before a U.S. Senate subcommittee that he found police were reducing their activity for fear of being charged with police brutality. Though Commissioner Leary denied the accusation, the *Times* ran a front-page story with quotes from officers confirming the charges. One officer, who remained anonymous, said, "The cops learn early in life that if you make a mistake the department just won't back you up." Though the charges were anecdotal, they confirmed what CCRB opponents feared: that police "noninvolvement" would affect the department's ability to combat crime. One Brooklyn precinct captain said, "Somehow, through an underground grapevine, whatever it is, there's this feeling that you'll go unprotected if you get involved—especially with a member of a minority group. Just a couple of years ago a young policeman would approach a group of Negroes hanging out on a corner and say 'Break it up.' . . . Now instead of going over the tendency is to do nothing."[46]

Barry Gottehrer noted that during the July 1966 East New York disturbances, the Lindsay administration was weakest in its "relationship with the police. . . . The police at the precinct level resented us, didn't know what we were doing in the neighborhoods, thought we were trying to strong-arm them and interfere with their work. They believed the rhetoric of the PBA's campaign against the CCRB—the picture of the policeman with his hand tied behind his back—and, because they felt themselves the real victims, forced to answer for all of the city's failures, the man on the beat began to hate the mayor and his people and what they believed he stood for."[47]

Lindsay campaigned on the promise to bring city government closer to the people, arguing for the need to reduce the alienation Americans felt concerning their government. Yet he opposed the Review Board referendum, whose purpose was to allow the people to voice their opinion on one of his major proposals. The Citizens Union, the bastion of New York reform and the group responsible for bringing voter referenda to New York years earlier, supported the principle of the PBA's right to put their referendum question on the ballot (but still supported the existence of the Review Board), much to the disappointment of liberals. Lindsay received a temporary break when City Clerk Herman Katz rejected both petitions for not dealing with real amendments to the city charter, the only basis for a referendum. Ultimately, the courts ruled that both referenda questions were legal and could be put on the November ballot. (The Conservative Party eventually took its question off the ballot so as to avoid confusion on election day.)

The exact wording of the PBA referendum question was as follows:

> Shall there be adopted a local law entitled "A Local Law to amend the New York City Charter in regard to the establishment of a procedure for handling civilian complaints against members of the police department." Inserting a new Section 440, requiring that any board established by the civilian complaint against police department members

shall consist only of full time members of the police department or at least one year prior police department service; and providing that neither the Mayor, the Police Commissioner nor any other administrator or officer of the City may authorize any person, agency, board or group to receive, investigate, hear, recommend, or require action upon such civilian complaints, and providing further, that such section shall not prevent investigation or prosecution of police department members for violations of law by a court, grand jury, district attorney, or other law enforcement agency?

Lindsay had trouble understanding why anyone would oppose such a reasonable idea as the Civilian Complaint Review Board. He considered his board a compromise between an all-civilian board and an all-police board.

Daniel Patrick Moynihan later summarized the thinking behind the idea of the CCRB: "At the risk of overgeneralizing, the Civilian Review Board was a proposal that originated in the liberal upper-middle-class white community of the city as a measure to control the behavior of less liberal, lower-middle-class white city employees toward members of the black and Puerto Rican community of varying social classes." The strongest support for the board (and opposition to the referendum) came from Manhattan elites. Many were wealthy Protestants and Jews. Liberals tended to know few policemen and were far removed from the most dangerous areas of the city, thanks either to geographical distance or the sheltered life that wealth creates. As Moynihan noted, "Persons not at all exposed to a social problem were acting in ways quite insensitive to the problems of those who were."[48]

After the November election, the CCRB's chairman, Algernon Black, admitted that a major problem with the city's liberals was that "we move too much within our own circle and fail to communicate adequately with those who use a different vocabulary and live in a different world." This led to an attitude of condescension toward white, lower-middle-class policemen. At a police graduation ceremony in March, a Lindsay official, Timothy Costello, a strong proponent of the board, told the new policemen that they should look at the board "less as something that is being imposed on you and more as something that is being given to you to help maintain your self-respect." It is doubtful that the young recruits, let alone the seasoned veterans of the force, thought they had a self-respect problem. Some supporters resorted to psychological explanations such as the Marxist political theorist Theodor Adorno's "authoritarian personality" to explain the mind of the policeman. Others saw them as hopelessly "square," unthinking, and low-brow. One journalist, Thomas Brooks, wrote, "Cops are conventional people. . . . All a cop can swing in a milieu of marijuana smokers, interracial dates, and homosexuals is the nightstick. A policeman who passed a Lower East Side art gallery filled with paintings of what appeared to be female genitalia could think of doing only one thing—step in and make an arrest."[49]

In addition to their negative attitudes toward policemen, those who supported the Civilian Complaint Review Board possessed a certain view of how society should deal with crime. Marjorie Friedlander, coordinator of the New York City Review Board Conference,[50] wrote in expression of her group's support for the mayor's Law Enforcement Task Force report: "I took particular note of the Report's avoidance of a spirit of repression and punitiveness in crime control. I warmly responded to its humanitarianism and rehabilitation orientation in law enforcement." Thus, civilian review was needed not only to curb police brutality, but also to foster a more humanitarian vision of criminals. Since crime was a product of social forces such as poverty and discrimination, "repressive" law enforcement techniques would only add more oppression to the lives of the poor and increase crime.[51]

Another problem for Lindsay was his choice of Algernon Black to head the board, a man the writer John Corry noted had "that hint of self-importance that so often accompanies the social crusader." William F. Buckley—surely exaggerating—called Black "the most spectacularly disqualified man to investigate a criminal situation in the history of the United States. A man who knows as much about crime as Quakers do about war. . . . He has always backed oddball, left-wing causes. A man who wouldn't know the difference between a blackjack and a crucifix."[52]

Some charges against the board were unfair and hyperbolic. John Cassese charged that "communism and Communists are somewhere mixed up in this fight. If we wind up with a review board, we'll have done Russia a great service—whether by design or accident." But others charged that the board was antipolice, and this seemed closer to the mark. At a postelection staff meeting, even members of the New York Civil Liberties Union (NYCLU) stated that they believed that "Al Black was the worst possible choice because he fits everyone's image of a liberal (except those who think him a hard-core Communist)."[53]

In his book, *The People and the Police*, published after the CCRB debacle, Black laid out his beliefs on the role of the police in society:

> Historically the police have almost always been a reactionary force defending the king and emperor, the nobility and the aristocracy, the institutions of property and repression. Historically they are identified with the upper classes and against the masses. Normally they would tend to defend the employer and the factory against the workers and the unions, the landlords against the tenants, and in Western culture the white people and their power and privilege against those who challenge these. As the police represent authority, they become the focus for all the resentments which Negroes hold against a system of law and property and politics which denies them equality of opportunity and a fair share of the good things of American life.

Policemen would have been chagrined to find that Black believed them to be "the instrument through which injustice is imposed and sustained. By their presence they are party to the imposition of the whole ghetto imprisonment." Black added to this notion of the police as the defenders of the indefensible by noting the "widespread police opposition to the abolition of capital punishment."[54]

To oppose the referendum, a group calling itself the Federal Associations for Impartial Review (FAIR) was established, headed by Bronx Borough President Herman Badillo; Herbert Brownell; the labor negotiator Theodore Kheel; the black labor union leader A. Philip Randolph; and Morris Abram. Both New York senators strongly opposed the referendum. Robert Kennedy agreed with Review Board supporters who saw civil rights as the real issue of the campaign: "If it [the Board] fails in the city of New York," argued New York's junior senator, "it will have a major effect throughout the country and will set back the cause of civil rights and progressive government."[55]

David Garth, who created the television ads for Lindsay's mayoral campaign, ran the FAIR campaign; its motto was "Don't be a yes man for bigotry: Vote no!" (The fact that in order to support the Civilian Complaint Review Board one had to vote no against the referendum added confusion to an already heated issue.) According to FAIR, to oppose the board was tantamount to bigotry. As one leader of FAIR said: "Before this campaign is over, people will feel ashamed to do anything but vote against this referendum." Review Board leaders would try to use shame and guilt to move the conscience of the city.

Where Review Board supporters saw the referendum as a civil rights battle, its opponents saw crime as the central issue. The PBA minced no words in its campaign and went for the jugular. One pro-referendum television advertisement proclaimed: "The addict, the criminal, the hoodlum—only the policeman stands between you and him." A newspaper advertisement pictured an empty street littered with paper, smashed storefront windows, and a cash register lying on the sidewalk. It was a picture of a Philadelphia street after its 1964 riot. Underneath the photo ran the caption "This is the aftermath of a riot in a city that *had* a civilian review board." This was a direct slap in the face for Leary, who was Philadelphia's police commissioner during the riot. Citizens were sternly warned, "Crime and violence are the terrifying realities of our time. No street is safe. No neighborhood is immune. New York's police force, probably the finest in the world, is all that stands ready to protect you and your family from the ominous threat of constant danger in the streets."[56]

A group calling itself the Independent Citizens Committee Against the Civilian Review Board placed a series of advertisements in newspapers and on billboards throughout the city. The most famous of these pictured a terrified young white woman in a raincoat standing alone in the dark outside a subway station. Below the picture was the warning "The Civilian Review Board must be stopped. Her life . . . your life . . . may depend on it." The NAACP's Roy Wilkins called the ad the "slimiest kind of racism." Lindsay said, "The only thing it didn't show was a gang of Negroes about to attack her. It was a vulgar, obscene advertisement if I've ever seen one." The ad tapped in to the deepest fears of New Yorkers concerned with rising crime, calling the referendum battle a "fight against the spread of crime in the streets." In such an environment, "Only the policeman stands between your family and the continuous threat of the hooligan, the addict, and the criminal."[57]

Even some CCRB supporters recognized what Garth admitted after the campaign: "It [the CCRB referendum] was one of the greatest hoax campaigns ever. The issues were phony." The *Times's* Sidney Zion noted that Lindsay's CCRB was a weak entity with the power only to refer cases for discipline to the police commissioner. In order to assuage the fears of voters worried about tying the hands of policemen in the wake of increasing crime, Review Board supporters were put in the position of arguing that Lindsay's board really was not all that tough. They almost seemed to be saying, "Vote for the review board. It's ineffective."[58]

While the controversy over the referendum heated up, the Civilian Complaint Review Board itself was in full swing. Its record from July through October 1966 was mixed. On average there were just over one hundred complaints per month. Almost half were brought by whites. Complaints to the Review Board increased from 106 in 1959, to 324 in 1965, and 413 in the first four months of 1966. Though it is highly unlikely that police abuses dramatically increased between 1959 and 1966, the publicity surrounding the new CCRB probably caused an increase in reports of suspected abuses.[59]

Some who backed the Review Board in public voiced private reservations. The Columbia law professor Walter Gellhorn said in private he favored a European-style ombudsman rather than a civilian board. Paul Chevigny of the New York Civil Liberties Union, who later published a book about police abuses, privately doubted whether the board would work. He felt the benefits would be purely political. Roger Baldwin, a founder of the American Civil Liberties Union, wrote in late 1964 that the ACLU should push for a "civilian board whose primary duty would be to study and promote reforms, and perhaps to hear complaints only on appeal from a police disciplinary body with the power of recommendation only."[60]

Even if some supporters were skeptical of the effects of the Civilian Complaint Review Board, they still saw the issue as pitting progressives against the forces of reaction, hatred, and bigotry. Senator Javits noted the fear of crime that many board opponents voiced, but was unmoved. "To them there are some nefarious forces that conduct crime in the streets," said Javits, "and we must blindly trust the police, no questions asked." Where CCRB opponents trusted the police, it seemed that many board supporters did not.[61]

Yet local Republicans had been using the crime issue in their campaigns since 1961—a Louis Lefkowitz for Mayor campaign song went: "Safe in the park / When you go home after dark / Lefkowitz, Fino, and Gilhooley!" Lindsay too had used the fear of crime effectively and incessantly during his mayoral campaign, but now he said very little about the issue. By 1966, Lindsay and his liberal allies accused those talking about crime of "using code words to capitalize on racial fears and hostility," as Garth put it. Zeroing in on this contradiction, Moynihan asked, "Why this pattern of exploiting fear in one election and ignoring it in the next? Guilt?"[62]

ANOTHER CAMPAIGN

FAIR's organizational structure and financial support were surprisingly weak. FAIR did not begin its campaign until after Labor Day because supporters were fearful of stirring up racial tensions during the tense summer months. A further problem for the campaign was that it was missing the man who had brilliantly organized Lindsay's 1965 mayoral campaign: Bob Price. The deputy mayor wanted nothing to do with the CCRB issue. Later he said of the CCRB that it was "a bad idea. It wouldn't pass. Lindsay had enough [on his plate] in his first year. . . . I wouldn't touch it," Price remembers. "I had no interest in it. I thought it was a stupid idea. I paid no attention to it. I didn't want to be tainted by even knowing there were meetings going on."[63]

Lindsay the moralist pushed ahead with his idea no matter the political dangers. He believed the issue was one of fairness to the city's minorities and regretted that his deputy mayor did not feel the same way. Price passed off control of the campaign to David Garth, who to this day believes that Price, who had given Garth his big break in the 1965 election, let him run the doomed CCRB campaign "to cut me down to size. . . . I don't think he gave it to me as a 'thank you.' " Money was a big problem. Price had built up fund-raising contacts throughout the city during the 1965 campaign, but now he refused to raise funds. One ACLU postmortem noted, "The City Hall apparatus was incompetent in fundraising and as a result, most of the money was raised through NYCLU's efforts." According to Gottehrer, Price "hung us out to dry." Garth's specialty was television advertising, not political organization and mobilization. But FAIR had little money with which to buy ads, so Garth's talents were largely wasted.[64]

The Lindsay team, which had just finished a grueling citywide campaign less than a year earlier, was not looking forward to heading back on the campaign trail. "The last thing you expect to do a year after you've gone through an election is to go back into another long election," said Kriegel. "People want to govern. They're tired. They're not ready for a campaign."[65]

The Review Board's biggest problem turned out to be its major supporter: John Lindsay. According to the NYCLU memo, "Lindsay was one of the crosses which had to be borne. There was a great amount of public sentiment against him." The *Daily News* reporter Edward O'Neill noted that many New Yorkers would vote against the referendum "as a protest against the Mayor's shenanigans." Javits's aide Dick Aurelio wrote to his boss that the major problem was that the FAIR campaign "was building up to a vote of confidence in Lindsay's administration, and this unnecessarily complicates the issue with other often emotional city issues." Having angered working- and middle-class voters by raising taxes and the transit fare, Lindsay was now asking for their vote on the sensitive issue of police review. Referendum supporters repeatedly referred to "Lindsay's board" in an attempt to link it with the unpopular mayor. One mayoral aide later said, "People were grumbling that he [Lindsay] was 'spending all his time in the ghetto with *them* while he's raising *our* taxes.' "66

Despite his unpopularity, Lindsay made no attempt to lessen his visibility on the issue. On Sunday morning, October 16, at Manhattan's St. George's Episcopal Church, Lindsay took to the pulpit to make the case for the CCRB. The Rev. Edward O. Miller, in introducing the mayor, called the CCRB "a working mechanism for bridging the gap between the minuscule citizen and the mammoth, depersonalized state. At least four out of seven on the Board are not part of the establishment against which you are protesting. Presumably they see problems through the eyes of fellow citizens."

Overall, Lindsay's address was a measured and articulate call for the civilian review of the police, which reflected his moral certitude on this issue. Lindsay had told Woody Klein, "I have never been so sure of anything in my life." Arguing that support for the CCRB was a "moral question," at St. George's Lindsay affirmed his position: "I have no doubt in my mind whatsoever, so convinced am I of its rightness." The mayor said he hoped the board would "receive the support of all those who care and think, who know and believe in rightness in this our city." Lindsay ended his speech with a quote from the Book of Common Prayer: "Almighty God, who hast created man in thine own image; Grant us grace fearlessly to contend against evil, and to make no peace with oppression; and that we may reverently use our freedom, help us to employ it in the maintenance of justice among men and nations, to the glory of Thy holy name; through Jesus Christ our Lord." Lindsay's choice of reading echoed his own view of politics: fighting against evil and making no peace with oppression.67

Assisting Lindsay and the FAIR campaign was labor organizer Ted Kheel. The relationship between Lindsay and Kheel had begun on shaky ground during the transit strike. Lindsay associated Kheel with the policies of the Wagner administration and the city's power brokers, but the mayor quickly realized that Kheel was indispensable to the Review Board campaign, and the original iciness between the two men soon melted. Kheel, one of five members of FAIR's citizens committee, was also the main spokesman in defense of the Review Board, and he debated opponents such as Vincent Broderick, Norman Frank, and William F. Buckley.

Kheel's debate with Buckley took place on Buckley's television show, *Firing Line*. Kheel avoided inflammatory rhetoric or antipolice arguments and focused on the wording of General Order 14. He emphasized the twelve-year existence of a police review board to hear civilian complaints. The only change in Lindsay's board was the inclusion of four civilians. "Why is being on the payroll of the police the indispensable criteria [*sic*] set up by the referendum for membership on the board?" Kheel asked. Who could argue with the inclusion of respected members of the community sitting on a police review board? Kheel told Buckley that if the PBA's referendum won, Broderick, a former police commissioner and as qualified a civilian as could be imagined, would be prohibited from sitting on the board.

Buckley conceded some of Kheel's arguments, but argued that one could not examine an issue like the Civilian Complaint Review Board in a vacuum of abstraction. One had to examine how such an order like General Order 14 was carried out, not just its wording. "The higher reality," according to Buckley, "is that there has been interspersed between them [the police] and the commissioner an alien group of exquisite political and ethnic composition exactly designed to appeal to every disparate ideological and racial segment in the community."

Kheel accused Buckley of "confounding the issue," but Buckley argued that the board would only exacerbate racial tensions: "The pressures for the civilian review board are primarily generated from a small group of representatives of the nonwhite segments of the New York City population who have been addressed by demagogues [who] have told them the New York police force is anti-Negro and anti–Puerto Rican. . . . I think the very fact that we are willing to set up such a structure as this tends to give the impression that it is and this causes a quite anticipated resentment."

Kheel countered: "Anytime the integrity of government is questioned by somebody, rightly or wrongly, it is a very good idea to reinforce the integrity of the governmental process." In this case, liberals and minorities were losing faith in the ability of the New York Police Department to enforce the law fairly. For Kheel, the authority of the police could only be strengthened by outside review. For Buckley, such oversight would only reinforce negative views of the police. Buckley made it clear he felt such criticism of the police was irrational, asking Kheel if he favored a panel to study the question of whether Eisenhower was a Communist, since the John Birch Society had leveled such criticisms of Communist influence against the former president.[68]

Unfortunately, the relatively civil tone of the *Firing Line* debate did not carry over to the rest of the fall campaign. If Review Board opponents shamelessly exploited the public's fear of crime, CCRB supporters were just as shameless in exploiting other fears. One area of controversy was the increasingly strident tone of FAIR's antireferendum rhetoric, which was reminiscent of some of the anti-Buckley rhetoric of the 1965 campaign. This was the work of David Garth, who was eager to play political hardball. One tactic was to link the PBA with the American Nazi Party, which had passed out leaflets in favor of the referendum. In September, Garth accused John Cassese of being "desperate enough to ally himself with the John Birch Society and the American Nazi Party by employing these same witch-hunting tactics." FAIR literature regularly lumped the PBA, the Conservative Party, and the American Legion together with the John Birch Society and neo-Nazi groups as Review Board opponents. A FAIR press release warned: "The campaign against the Civilian Review Board is being waged by a coalition of right-wing groups—the Conservative Party, the fascist National Renaissance Party, the John Birch Society, and the American Legion allied with the PBA against the forces of reason and civic leadership in this city." Though these extremist groups did oppose the CCRB, linking them with more mainstream opponents was an attempt to prove guilt by association.[69]

In the same vein, the American Jewish Congress produced pro–Review Board leaflets geared to a Jewish audience. On one column the leaflet listed liberal groups supporting the board, such as the Anti-Defamation League of B'nai B'rith, the American Jewish Committee, and the Citizens Union. The other column listed board opponents: "George Lincoln Rockwell and the American Nazi Party, James Madole and the National Renaissance Party, the John Birch Society, and others." Jewish voters were warned: "Don't be hoaxed by appeals to racial bigotry," and "Don't strengthen the forces of McCarthyism." How could they avoid such disasters? Simply by voting against the referendum and in favor of Lindsay's Review Board.[70]

Lindsay seemed to encourage this type of political smearing when he complained about his opponents, "All you have to do is walk through Yorkville [a German American neighborhood on Manhattan's Upper East Side] on a Saturday morning and you'll get flooded with literature of the American Renaissance Party, a neo-Nazi party." He was correct about the nastiness of material distributed by neo-Nazi groups, but he inflated their strength and lent credence to the notion that those opposed to the Review Board were allied with unsavory and immoral people.[71]

The NAACP's president, Roy Wilkins, accused the PBA of organizing "a sly and dirty campaign against New York's Negro citizens." Wilkins also wrote a letter to black religious leaders urging them to preach against the referendum from the pulpit. "The Police [sic] Benevolent Association, the Conservative Party, the John Birch Society, the American Renaissance Party and others who want to kill the Board are no friends of the Negro," wrote Wilkins. "Remember all the Negro-haters are lined up against the Board."[72]

In October the Anti-Defamation League published a report on the referendum campaign entitled "The Birch Society's Role in the Anti-Civilian Review Board Campaign." The report stated: "It is clear that forces of the

Radical Right in general, and the JBS [John Birch Society] in particular, are furnishing the foot soldiers for the forces that seek to overthrow the review board." The report accused the John Birch Society of using "various front groups in the referendum campaign, while minimizing any public involvement of the Society itself" and said that this was "consistent with its own past practices. In this way, the Society has been able to gain strength by picking up support from individuals on issues which are in no way identified with the John Birch Society."[73]

While liberals tried to paint the Civilian Complaint Review Board's opponents as Nazis, conservatives attacked its supporters as Communists. One right-wing newsletter attacked Black for his affiliation "with more than 2 dozen officially cited Communist fronts," including the American Youth Congress; National Council of American-Soviet Friendship; Citizen Victory Committee for Harry Bridges; American Friends of Spanish Democracy; the Committee for a Democratic Far Eastern Policy; and Non-Partisan Committee for the Reelection of Congressman Vito Marcantonio.[74]

In this charged environment of political name-calling, even Hubert Humphrey fell victim to the charge of bigotry. In an October speech to the International Association of Chiefs of Police, Humphrey criticized civilian review boards in general. He said that when he was the mayor of Minneapolis in the 1940s, he never saw a need for a Civilian Complaint Review Board and handled the review of police procedures himself. Referendum supporters now began counting the Democratic vice president as a CCRB opponent, much to the embarrassment of New York liberals. A few weeks later, ACLU Executive Director John de J. Pemberton Jr. wrote to Humphrey telling him that the PBA's referendum campaign had been characterized by civil rights, religious, and civic groups as "an outright appeal to racism and fear," to which he had, however unwittingly, given aid. Pemberton urged Humphrey to reconsider his position so that his statement would not be "misused to re-inforce attitudes of bigotry and racial hatred." Humphrey amended his original statement on a television interview program ("I don't have any particular antipathy, or any particular antagonism toward a civilian review board"), but his response was halfhearted and included the caveat: "I just don't want a civilian review board to be one that undermines the authority of the police."[75]

More damaging to the FAIR campaign was the position of Commissioner Leary. Though his selection had been based almost entirely on his support of the Civilian Complaint Review Board and his ability to work with one in Philadelphia, Leary walked a careful line during most of 1966. Not wanting to upset the police rank-and-file, he muted his comments in favor of the board. At an impromptu question-and-answer session in early September, Leary said, "I don't think we need it. The review board is going to prove here what it proved in Philadelphia—that brutality is not practiced to the degree that some advocates of the review board believe." Nevertheless, he also said that he supported, as he had in the past, Mayor Lindsay's efforts to change the makeup of the Review Board. In the face of such tepid support, Lindsay forced Leary to come out strongly for the board, but was unable to get his police commissioner to campaign actively against the referendum question. Leary felt that such activism would destroy his credibility among the police.[76]

As the election neared, it became clear that the forces supporting the referendum would overwhelmingly defeat the Civilian Complaint Review Board. FAIR campaign coordinator Aryeh Neier called the Civilian Complaint Review Board "a losing issue." Lindsay admitted in October that he was "not at all sure that we're going to win." In Brooklyn, Democratic campaign workers handed out anti–Review Board stickers along with literature for the Democratic candidate for governor, Frank O'Connor. A Lindsay staffer said he even saw two Liberal Party storefronts in Brooklyn and the Upper West Side of Manhattan with anti–Review Board signs in their windows.[77]

With the charges of bigotry leveled against the referendum forces apparently falling on deaf ears, supporters of the Civilian Complaint Review Board had one more case to make. Referendum opponents claimed that hidden in the referendum question was a so-called "sleeper clause" that, as the Association of the Bar of the City of New York put it, "could reduce the present powers of the Mayor, the City Council, the Commissioner of Investigation and the Commission of Human Rights to investigate civilian complaints against members of the Police Department in areas ranging from lax enforcement of traffic regulations to bribery, graft and corruption." The part of the referendum question alluded to read: "[N]either the Mayor, the police Commissioner nor any other administrator or officer of the City may authorize any person, agency, board or group to receive, investigate, hear, recommend or require action upon such civilian complaints."

CCRB supporters knew they would lose the vote if New Yorkers interpreted the salient issue as crime: New Yorkers didn't want to hamstring the police in their fight against crime. But the issue of corruption was different. Most New Yorkers were aware that corruption existed in police ranks. If the issue of civilian review of complaints against the police could be changed from a debate over crime into one where the police were depicted as trying to insulate themselves from investigations into malfeasance, enough New Yorkers would overcome their fear of crime and vote against the referendum. One FAIR leaflet played on this fear of an unaccountable police department, asking in its headline, "Do New Yorkers Want a Police State?" The mayor asked whether the city was "willing to let the Police Department of this city become a law unto itself." Lindsay also came out with a statement the weekend before the election in which he criticized the "sleeper clause" and quoted approvingly the New York Bar Association's statement that the "sleeper clause" would "virtually insulate the Police Department, alone among city agencies, from scrutiny by other official bodies." Lindsay's Corporation

Counsel, J. Lee Rankin, testified before a state senate committee that "the question remains as to whether this language is used to make the Police Department independent of all other parts of the government." Rankin's conclusion: "It certainly would appear so."[78]

Referendum supporters hotly denied this claim. Maintaining they only wanted to prevent a Civilian Complaint Review Board as established by Lindsay, they ran an advertisement signed by one former mayor, five congressmen, and three former police commissioners denying the "sleeper clause" charge. They pointed out that the referendum included, after the section in question, the following statement: "[T]his section shall not be construed to prevent investigation or prosecution of members of the Police Department for violations of law by a duly constituted court having jurisdiction, a grand jury, district attorney or other law enforcement agency." This alone would prevent what Review Board supporters feared: an unaccountable police department. In addition, Review Board opponents noted that the mayor, the NYPD's deputy commissioners, and the commissioner of investigations could continue to exercise their rights under the city charter to investigate complaints. The only thing the referendum prevented was the delegation of powers to a special Civilian Complaint Review Board whose powers lay outside of the city charter.[79]

The list of Review Board supporters read like a list of the city's traditional civic, religious, labor, civil liberties, and civil rights groups.[80] Bobby Kennedy's major concern with the FAIR campaign was that it needed to broaden itself to reach those in the city's Catholic community. According to Dick Aurelio, Kennedy thought the Review Board campaign "was taking on the aspect of a Jewish-Negro cabal against everyone else." He wanted "more prominent Catholics of the Polish, Irish, and Italo-American communities" included in the FAIR campaign. Unfortunately, Cardinal Spellman had rebuffed Lindsay's attempt to draw him into the fray, and Kennedy's relationship with Spellman was tense. Kennedy realized that many of the people lining up against the Review Board—including members of the PBA, the Conservative Party, and the American Legion—were Catholic.[81]

At issue was how New Yorkers felt about their policemen and how these policemen felt about their city. According to the Harvard law professor Jerome Skolnick, "A Goldwater type of conservatism was the dominant political and emotional persuasion of [New York] police." Another student of the NYPD noted that white policemen saw themselves as "a besieged and aggrieved group."

> They are under sharp attack by the department, the public, the press, the courts, and their black colleagues for using methods that they feel are needed to carry out the special and valuable duties for which they are responsible. They feel abandoned by a liberal, reform-minded administration and by a budget-minded but "political" or "regular" administra-

tion that they believe have both compromised their law enforcement function to satisfy the political pressures of minority groups. . . . To their eyes, police work has been devalued. . . . They now see themselves as victimized and betrayed by the society they are obligated to serve.

Political scientist James Q. Wilson noted that Lindsay symbolized to policemen "that segment of the urban middle class which has deserted the police . . . [and] represents the hypocritical liberal who wants both to maintain law and order and to win the votes of the lawless." As Jay Kriegel admitted: "The 1965 campaign in a real sense was run against the police force. Not that we thought they were racists, but that the department was old and tired and badly in need of modernization. But institutionalized racism was an important issue—the problem of brutality and the lack of minorities on the force. The cop on the street took it all as a criticism of himself."[82]

THE RESULTS: BACKLASH?

The referendum question overturning the Civilian Complaint Review Board won by almost two to one, 63 to 37 percent. Jay Kriegel admitted, "We got rolled." Only twenty-one of the city's sixty-eight assembly districts voted no on the question. Thirteen of these districts were in Manhattan, the only borough where the referendum question failed to carry a majority. The other eight districts were in predominantly black and Puerto Rican areas. The only Queens district to vote against the referendum question was in the southeast corner of the borough, an area with a large percentage of blacks.

The best analysis of the Civilian Complaint Review Board referendum was a survey of 374 Brooklyn whites conducted by the American Jewish Committee. This sample voted for the referendum question much as the rest of the city had: 64.6 percent in favor, 31.9 percent against. Catholics were most favorable to the anti–Review Board referendum: 83.1 for versus 16.2 percent against. Jewish voters also favored the referendum, but by a much closer margin: 55.1 to 40.2 percent. Those with a college degree were evenly split. The only group to oppose the referendum question and favor the Review Board were those in professional and technical careers, by 51.6 to 46.8 percent. Even those earning over $15,000 voted yes 59.3 to 39 percent. One important difference between Catholics and Jews was that 54 percent of white Catholic Brooklynites had relatives or close friends on the police force, whereas only 21 percent of white Jewish Brooklynites had such ties.[83]

The survey found white Brooklynites more scared of crime than the average American. Whereas 85 percent of Americans said they felt very safe during the day, only 65 percent of whites in Brooklyn felt safe. While 44 percent of Americans said they felt very safe alone after dark, only 27 percent of white Brooklynites agreed with that statement. Nearly half of the Brooklynites surveyed said they felt either somewhat or very unsafe after dark alone. Sixteen percent of Americans said they stayed home because it was unsafe, but 40 percent of Brooklyn respondents felt scared enough to lock themselves inside their homes. Half of Americans said they did not worry about having their homes broken into, but only one quarter of Brooklynites felt so secure. Just as economic hard times can lead to political instability, concerns for personal safety helped heat up New York politics.[84]

The survey also found that white Brooklynites were ambivalent about blacks. Though virulent racism was notably absent and most respondents "were quick to reject the most extreme stereotypes of racial prejudice . . . they [white Brooklynites] voiced substantial concern about problems they associated with blacks." Sixty-three percent agreed with the statement "The trouble with letting certain minority groups into a nice neighborhood is that they gradually give it their own atmosphere." Sixty-two percent thought that the civil rights movement was moving too fast.[85]

The defeat of the Civilian Complaint Review Board was a thorough and bitter repudiation of both Lindsay and the city's liberal establishment. The AJC study concluded: "The civilian review board referendum proved to be a rout for civil rights forces. For the first time in years, New York City's electorate rejected a liberal position on the ballot." The results showed that the city's liberal elite commanded little authority at the ballot box, especially on the issue of crime. For Lindsay, the election unalterably defined his mayoralty. Though his vocal and passionate defense of the CCRB won him the support and adulation of the city's minorities, he angered many middle- and working-class whites.[86]

Yet the battle over the CCRB took place within a larger political context that year. A dominant theme of the 1966 national elections was the so-called "white backlash." The *Amsterdam News* argued that "white backlash is not so much a backlash as a frontlash. The whites aren't hitting back at the Negroes, but moving full steam ahead against them as they always have." On the other side, the *Wall Street Journal* argued that what some called "backlash" was really an "issue of violence." While arguing that the country had been inching forward on civil rights, the *Journal* went on to say that "unhappily, the effort does not satisfy the civil-rights leaders, the disorders persist, and it is only natural that white people, in their turn, are finally expressing their own dissatisfaction. Defined in this way, backlash is not only an inevitable but a legitimate political issue. The issue is: Why should the nation have to put up with continuing violence?" Mirroring the split in the way New Yorkers saw the Civilian Complaint Review Board referendum, the *Amsterdam News* saw the white "backlash" as a negative reaction to the civil rights movement while the *Journal* argued that the issues were crime, violence, and anarchy. "Resistance to that trend, be it called backlash or whatever, is essential in a civilized society," the *Journal* concluded.[87]

William F. Buckley wrote after the 1966 election that what was being called "backlash" was "a growing resentment . . . a growing transcendence, of the disabling tendency to view all controversial questions in black and white." Though some would argue that conservatives benefited politically from such stark racial differences, Buckley pointed to the increasing tendency in the nation to turn every issue into a racial issue. Supporters of the Review Board did not merely argue that it was a good government reform or a way to curb police brutality. They saw it as a battle between white liberals and blacks versus racist whites. The ACLU, in its election postmortem, acknowledged, "We have proved that when the concept of race or civil rights attaches to a referendum, it cannot win."[88]

Partly because of the backlash issue, it looked as though 1966 might well be the year for a strong showing for Republicans, who looked forward to winning back a large numbers of seats they had lost in the devastating 1964 Goldwater debacle. In addition, Southerners registered their dissatisfaction with the 1964 Civil Rights Act. In 1966, voters gave Republicans forty-seven new seats in the House, three more seats in the Senate, and eight additional governorships. Many gains were in the South, where John Tower was reelected in Texas, Strom Thurmond won for the first time as a Republican in South Carolina, and Claude Kirk became the first Republican governor of Florida since Reconstruction. The biggest election of the year was the race for governor in California, where Ronald Reagan, running on a strong conservative platform, defeated the incumbent liberal Democrat Pat Brown.[89]

Yet most of the new Republican congressmen and governors elected in 1966 were moderate to liberal. The year of the supposed "backlash" brought victories for such liberal Republicans as Mark Hatfield in Oregon, Charles Percy in Illinois, Clifford Case in New Jersey, George Romney and Robert Griffith in Michigan, Daniel Evans in Washington, Raymond Shafer in Pennsylvania, Howard Baker in Tennessee, Ed Brooke in Massachusetts (the first black Senator since Reconstruction), and Winthrop Rockefeller in Arkansas. In Maryland, a little-known Republican from suburban Baltimore County named Spiro Agnew was elected governor. With the support of a political coalition that would come to be identified with John Lindsay, Agnew, a racial moderate, won with the support of blacks, Jews, and upper-income whites. He defeated Democrat George Mahoney, a Catholic who campaigned almost exclusively against the issue of open housing, using the theme "Your home is your castle."[90]

The nation's most prominent liberal Republican, New York Governor Nelson Rockefeller, ran for a third term in 1966. Opposing Rockefeller were Democratic City Council President Frank O'Connor, the top vote getter in the city the previous year; Franklin Roosevelt Jr., running on the Liberal ticket; and Paul Adams, the vice president and dean of Roberts Wesleyan College in Rochester, running as a Conservative. Rockefeller easily won re-election to a third term, thanks to a strong showing in the New York suburbs and Upstate. O'Connor, a strong candidate on paper, ran a poor campaign.

He started late and suffered from party infighting over his connection to the city's political machines. Roosevelt's presence in the race siphoned off liberal votes from O'Connor. The Queens Democrat outpolled Rockefeller in the city by 80,000 votes, getting almost exactly the same number of votes as Abe Beame had the previous year.[91]

The campaign caused a further rift in the relationship between mayor and governor. Rockefeller felt Lindsay was hoping for an O'Connor win, which would have given the mayor greater control over the state party and allowed him to blame a Democratic governor for the city's problems. Lindsay was a no-show at Rockefeller headquarters on election night, leading one Rockefeller aide to say, "If it had gone the other way, you can bet Lindsay would be over congratulating O'Connor right now." In light of the sniping between O'Connor and Lindsay that had gone on throughout 1966, though, Lindsay's supposed sympathy for the City Council president was no doubt exaggerated.[92]

Of the four candidates for governor, only Adams opposed the Civilian Complaint Review Board. Rockefeller tried to finesse the issue, saying he was for the Review Board, but would not campaign for it because it was a "home rule" issue. In reality, the governor was always interested in the affairs of the city. But Rockefeller and his aides were more confident of the police and more suspicious of the havoc a Civilian Complaint Review Board might wreak than was Lindsay. Hence, though the governor was publicly in favor of the board, in private he was at best neutral about the idea and did little to help FAIR's faltering campaign.[93]

Ironically, the fact that most of New York's political leadership supported the Civilian Complaint Review Board probably contributed to its political defeat. The personal squabbles between Lindsay, Javits, and Kennedy prevented them from uniting their formidable political powers behind the FAIR campaign. Likewise, Rockefeller, O'Connor, and Roosevelt all supported the board to some extent, but the gubernatorial campaign prevented them from appearing together in support of the board and forced Mayor Lindsay, a nominal Rockefeller supporter, to walk a fine line in campaigning for the board with O'Connor and Roosevelt.

THERE WERE OTHER FACTORS THAT EXACERBATED the tensions surrounding the Civilian Complaint Review Board campaign: the charges of political interference in the early months of the Lindsay administration; the drive to break up the "Irish mafia"; the push for more minorities on the force; and the restrictions put on the police during civil disturbances and riots. Lindsay wanted to exert civilian control over the police. As Lindsay noted one year later, "The Mayor has a role to play in the fixing of policy in all matters in the city. We have a policy role to fill, just as the President does with the Joint Chiefs of Staff." But the police did not accept these changes passively. At the wake for Traffic Commissioner Henry Barnes, Lindsay went to shake hands with the police guard. One cop told the mayor, "No," and turned away. According to an observer, Lindsay "was really crushed" by this response and talked about the indignity in the car ride back from the wake.[94]

The Lindsay administration continued to meddle in police matters by retaining the Rand Corporation to study the department and make recommendations for improved efficiency. Both Rand Corporation President Harry Rowen and New York City-Rand Institute President Peter Szanton called the attempted study a failure. The police department distrusted outsiders who had no law enforcement experience. The attitude of the Rand analysts only made matters worse. They possessed an aura of arrogant, aloof intellectuals and could not work with police officials. Thus the efficiency-minded mayor clashed yet again with the tradition-bound police department, further eroding their already tense relationship.[95]

Lindsay wagered much of his political capital on a largely symbolic issue. The Civilian Complaint Review Board would not have improved the lives of minorities living in slums. According to Bayard Rustin, the board was only "psychologically necessary." As one NAACP official noted, "It is not police brutality that makes people afraid to walk the streets at night."[96]

The main purpose of the CCRB was to send a signal to poor blacks and Puerto Ricans that the city cared. The political scientist Aaron Wildavsky called this type of political issue a "minus/sum" game—one where everyone is worse off than before. Its objective

> is to force a racist response from the voters who are fearful of their safety on subways and in the streets. The game begins with a publicity campaign focusing on fascist police, various atrocities, and other lurid events. The police and their friends counter with an equally illuminating defense: nothing is wrong that a little get-tough campaign would not cure. The game ends with a ballot in which white voters are asked to choose between their friendly neighborhood policeman and the specter of black violence. . . . But the game is a perfect loser: everyone's feelings are exacerbated and the conflict continues at a new height of hostility.[97]

The effort to expand the CCRB to include civilians sent other signals. One was that policemen were bigots. The other was that, contrary to Lindsay's campaign rhetoric, crime was not the most serious issue facing the city—police brutality was. New Yorkers were looking for a crimefighter who could work with the police. What they got was a mayor who saw the police as another "power broker." Branding supporters of the referendum as bigots ("Don't be a yes man for bigotry") angered people who simply feared walking the streets.

The Civilian Complaint Review Board battle produced many fissures: conservative versus liberal, white versus black, white ethnic versus liberal elite, authoritarian versus civil libertarian, law-and-order versus civil rights. It was also a labor fight between the Lindsay administration and the PBA. Lindsay's problems with Irish transit workers, Irish and Italian policemen, and Irish firemen highlighted his difficulties with working-class white ethnics. In 1968, Lindsay would be faced with a strike by the heavily Italian sanitation union, three bitter strikes by the heavily Jewish teachers' union, and increasing tension between City Hall and the NYPD. Lindsay would eventually work his way to an accommodation with most municipal unions, but the resentments among working-class whites remained.

Lindsay's support for a Civilian Complaint Review Board crippled his relations with the police. A later police commissioner, Patrick Murphy, wrote: "Lindsay proceeded to handle the N.Y.P.D. roughly and peremptorily." The mayor "resented cops" and "imposed his ideas on them." The interference by Lindsay aides in the December 1967 antiwar rally was, according to Murphy, "deeply resented by the rank and file. Whatever punishment the department deserved for entering into political action against the Mayor on the review board issue, the demeaning and contemptuous treatment it received seemed excessive."[98]

After the 1965 mayoral election, the *Herald Tribune* columnist Dick Schaap wrote: "The police of New York like William Buckley. . . . He lost only in the real world." To many like Schaap, the police did not inhabit "the real world," but a world of Goldwaterite paranoia and reaction. One year later, though, the concerns of the police and those of average New Yorkers had grown closer than many people had ever imagined.[99]

1968 AND THE RISE OF
"DISSENSUS" POLITICS

> In this murk, one theme resounded: the virtue
> of polarization.
>
> —Todd Gitlin, *The Sixties:*
> *Years of Hope, Days of Rage*[1]

The year 1968 marked the halfway point in Lindsay's first term. From the moment transit workers began their strike in the early morning hours of New Year's Day 1966, Lindsay faced a series of crises and controversies, some serious and some petty. By the end of 1967, he was no longer the "fresh" candidate of the 1965 campaign, but he had won some victories. Though the Civilian Complaint Review Board referendum was a personal and costly defeat and his transit reorganization effort failed, Lindsay could point to some solid achievements: the creation of the city's first income tax, his efforts to quell the racial crisis in East New York, the innovations of the park system during Thomas Hoving's short tenure, and the reorganization of city agencies. Lindsay admitted to the chaotic nature of his first year in office and the ineptitude that often characterized his young administration when he called 1966 his "year of tooling up."

AT THE HALFWAY MARK

When he first took office, Lindsay had been politically naive, with little knowledge of the operations of city government and few contacts with the men who had such knowledge. What Lindsay did have was a moral certitude that angered many of his constituents. The unevenness of Lindsay's first term set the tone for his entire mayoralty. One individual who worked for Lindsay in his first term said,

> Anyone around City Hall then knew that Lindsay had no control all the way down the line. He tried to do it all with his top assistants, whom he appointed, who had no followings of their own. And you just can't run a city that way. [When] Bill O'Dwyer was mayor . . . he knew the city and how it works to a "T." He knew the first name of the guy you had to call to get a pothole filled on a particular block out in Brooklyn. . . . Wagner always knew the clubhouse pol or the power broker . . . who was responsible for getting that pothole filler his job in the first place. But Lindsay—he only knew his own assistant. And his assistant—he only knew Lindsay. And nobody knew the pothole filler or how to reach him.

Lindsay's first budget director, Fred Hayes, said, "Lindsay ran for mayor knowledgeable about the problems of the city or their symptoms. . . but with no more than 'white paper' sophistication about the running of the city government."[2]

It soon became clear that Lindsay was no longer the White Knight who, by rescuing New York, would save America. In a mid-1967 poll, 51 percent of New Yorkers were unhappy with the mayor's performance. The newly anointed national political savior was, much to Lindsay's dismay, Robert Kennedy. While Lindsay tackled the thorny issues of urban government, Kennedy, from his perch in the United States Senate, floated above the muck, occasionally dropping down to offer his opinion to the cameras, fleeing just as quickly. The political reporters Rowland Evans and Robert Novak wrote in late 1966 that private polls matching Kennedy against Lindsay in a statewide race showed the Senator besting the mayor two to one.[3] While not concerning himself with specifics, Kennedy could ride the aura attached to his family name while playing vaguely on themes dear to liberals. He was running for president on an image and a promise, much as Lindsay had run for mayor in 1965. Lindsay, stuck in the morass of city politics, no longer had that privilege. His national political ambitions seemed to be, for the moment, at a standstill.

As 1968 approached, there was little proof that New York City had risen above "crisis" status. Some were still turned off by Lindsay's personality. One reform Democrat who voted for Lindsay said he was disappointed in the mayor's attitude: "I mean self-righteousness, arrogance, claims to omniscience. He comes on as if he's bearing the white man's burden. With him, it's a matter of noblesse oblige rather than facing people as people." Liberal New Yorkers, who saw Lindsay as a kindred spirit throughout his years in Congress and in his mayoral campaign, began to wonder whether their faith in the elegant Republican was not somehow misplaced. Carol Greitzer, the reform Democratic Greenwich Village female district leader who bucked her party in November 1965 to support Lindsay, voiced serious doubts about Lindsay before his first year was even over.[4]

The ambivalence of New York liberals toward Lindsay is best personified by *Village Voice* columnist Jack Newfield. After the mayor's first year in office, Newfield called Lindsay "as decent a human being as endures in the swamp of our national politics, one of the best since Stevenson: courageous, considerate, truthful, ethical, idealistic." Was Lindsay doomed to follow Stevenson into that world of decent, but ineffectual, politicians to whom liberals often attached their hopes? By May 1967, Newfield's enthusiasm had waned. He noted the mayor's "exasperating squareness, his puritan innocence, his Boy Scout pep talks. . . . He seems too repressed, too stiff, too hard to talk to, too little introspective." At the dawning of the Age of Aquarius, Lindsay's moralistic reform began to look out of date. Still, despite the mayor's weaknesses, he was "Pericles defending Athens against the barbarians at the gate" when compared to his critics. Lindsay's sensitive handling of the long, hot summer of 1967 brought a newfound appreciation for the mayor. Newfield sensed a new Lindsay toughened by his experiences in the ghetto that summer, experiences that seemed to wash away some of his Boy Scout qualities. In short, according to Newfield, Lindsay "has finally grown."[5]

A few months later, Newfield was again calling Lindsay the "Uptight White Knight." Though admitting that no Democrat could do better than Lindsay had in his first two years, Newfield saw in Lindsay the same flaws as the WASP characters who inhabited the worlds of John Updike and John Cheever: he seemed a man incapable "of making contact with his own deepest and truest feelings." The mayor was "prissy and uptight." An anonymous City Hall regular was quoted on the same subject: "The question is whether he's deeper than an oil slick."[6]

Lindsay attracted smart and competent people to City Hall. Since the New Deal, Washington, D.C., had been seen as the place to be for those interested in public policy. As the federal government gained power, working in local government became less glamorous. Lindsay tried to change this image. Under Lindsay, city government became an attractive and exciting place to work for intelligent and energetic young men and women. When the mayor spoke of his top commissioners, like Police Commissioner Howard Leary, Corporation Counsel Lee Rankin, Housing Commissioner Walter Washington, Budget Director Fred Hayes, and Welfare Commissioner Mitchell Sviridoff, he called them "modern men." They were the "urbanists" who would drag the city out from under its crisis.

Despite some of the good appointments, Newfield pinpointed a major problem for Lindsay: "his judgment of people." Of course, there was James Marcus (see Chapter 3). But there were other poor personnel choices. Lindsay's budget aide Peter Goldmark later admitted, "We had a lot of turkeys the first time around." The reformer I. D. Robbins complained, "I never thought that the appointments were great in the first place." In addition, a former Lindsay aide noted that the private side of the mayor inhibited his effectiveness with his staff and commissioners: "I don't think John has ever really been close to anyone in his life except his brothers and his wife. No one really knows what really goes on in that mind."

Then there was the Sam Kearing episode. Sam Kearing had been the commissioner of the Sanitation Department, but he left the administration on bad terms after not being named to head the new superagency that would contain the Sanitation Department. At a December 1967 testimonial dinner held for him by the Uniformed Sanitationmen's Association, Kearing challenged the effectiveness of Lindsay's reform government: "The condition of the city is not improving. Decay is everywhere. I know of no major city agency that is functioning better today than it was two years ago." In private, Kearing was reportedly telling people: "John Lindsay couldn't run a gas station, much less a city."[7]

In late 1967, Newfield observed:

> Mayor Lindsay's blowup with Sam Kearing again dramatized what may prove to be the mayor's Achille's [sic] Heel—his inability to sustain close long-term relationships with his aides. First, Lindsay broke with his political alter ego, Bob Price [who had left the administration in late 1966]. And now Kearing, one of the Administration's most effective commissioners, has been fired. City Hall insiders speak of Lindsay's rigidity of temperament as the cause of the splits. "The real trouble with John," one of his ardent former admirers said, "is that he can't have an equal relationship with someone his own age, like Kearing. He can only relate to father figures, like Herb Brownell, or else all those teeny-boppers on his staff who idolize him."[8]

The first two years of the Lindsay administration saw a high turnover in top-level personnel. The firebrand housing chief, Charles Moerdler, left. Mitchell Sviridoff resigned after a year to go and work for the Ford Foundation. Walter Washington, the housing commissioner, left New York to become the first mayor of Washington, D.C. Thomas Hoving left after the first year to take over at the Metropolitan Museum of Art.

Perhaps the biggest change in Lindsay's first year was the abrupt departure of Deputy Mayor Bob Price, who traded the world of politics for the world of finance when he left to take a job with the Dreyfus Corporation. Some of Lindsay's mistakes—the handling of the transit strike and the complaints of interference with the police department—derived from Price's wheeler-dealer style. Having been with Lindsay since 1958, Price felt he knew how to handle Lindsay. He summed up his relationship with the mayor in a way that showed its fundamental unhealthiness: "Lindsay needs people who don't need him. . . . You must not show your loyalty to him. . . . Lindsay is a guy who has to be told what to do. I know Lindsay better than he knows himself. I know what's good for him and what's bad for him. And I know that there are certain things you just don't tell Lindsay." Jack Newfield described Price as "psychologically dominating the mayor." Sid Davidoff admits that "Price was too strong a voice" in Lindsay's first year.[9]

Publicly, both Price and Lindsay claimed that Price had only agreed to be deputy mayor for a year. Price came from a working-class background and was always interested in making money to support his young family. To this day, Price is adamant that "there was no split" between him and Lindsay. Price wanted to make money, but he also "wanted to get back into the stream of the Republican Party," and thus, Price admitted, he "wanted to edge away from Lindsay," whose already legendary political independence continued to grow in City Hall. Despite their assurances to the contrary, there was a real split between the two that shattered their eight-year professional relationship. Lindsay later said, "Nobody seems to know that there was increasing disagreement between us—on how you pick people for the administration, on policy, on how you run a government. Bob tends to be a fixer. I don't mean that pejoratively. I mean he looks for ways to manipulate problems so that they'll be smoothed over for a time. That's good in the short run, but it's not the way to build a whole new structure of government."

Some observers felt that the split was caused by Lindsay's forgetting who had gotten him to City Hall in the first place, and others felt that Price was too big for his britches. Charles Moerdler believes both explanations were correct. Tom Hoving thought that "Lindsay finally got fed up with being bossed around by Price." According to Hoving, Price "thought he was Mayor and thought Lindsay was a stupid guy." Even Price admits that a December 1965 cover story in the *New York Times Magazine*, entitled "Second Man at City Hall," got on Lindsay's nerves. The cover showed Price manning the phones at his desk with Lindsay sitting next to him. The position of the two men in the photo and the title caption implied that it was Lindsay who was really the "second man at City Hall."[10]

Many believed that the split occurred in early summer during budget negotiations when Price made a deal with Governor Rockefeller that accommodated the wishes of the leaders of the state legislature but seriously compromised Lindsay's tax plan. After Price had made the agreement—he was used to making decisions for Lindsay by proxy—Lindsay refused to honor the compromise. Price then realized that he could no longer work for Lindsay, and Lindsay felt that he could no longer trust Price to uphold his policies.

By the end of 1966, Robert Sweet, a fellow Republican and friend of Lindsay's since their years at Yale, replaced Price as deputy mayor. Though Sweet portrayed himself as a patrician, he, like Lindsay, was from a humble background. According to one newspaper profile, "It was at considerable family sacrifice, and with the aid of scholarships, that the Sweets sent young Robert, an only child, to the Horace Mann School in New York and the Taft School in Watertown, Conn." Sweet was an even-tempered man without the Machiavellian streak of Bob Price. Roger Starr said of him and his influence, "The Lindsay administration's suspicion of the previous administration began to fade only after Robert Sweet . . . had become Deputy Mayor." When the *New York Times Magazine* profiled Sweet, the title of its article was telling: "Robert Sweet is the Unabashed No. 2 Man at City Hall (And delighted to be there)." Sweet brought to the job of deputy mayor a sense of calm that helped smooth over the rough edges of the reform administration. He also brought an attention to the minutiae of city government, rather than the love of pure politics that was Price's trademark.[11]

There was another important change: the easing out of Press Secretary Woody Klein at the end of 1966 in favor of Harry O'Donnell. Klein, a former reporter, was widely viewed as a disaster as press secretary because he reinforced some of Lindsay's grating tendencies. O'Donnell had been Lindsay's campaign press secretary, but he could not work with Price. When Price announced he was leaving the administration, O'Donnell agreed to return. His down-to-earth qualities, combined with Sweet's genteel manners, had a soothing effect on Lindsay. One reporter said, "Like a fine jeweler, O'Donnell has polished and refined the mayor's image to its present sparkle, and he has been a softening influence on the mayor." Lindsay was gearing up for the most turbulent period in his political career.[12]

1968 AND THE POLITICS OF PROTESTS

As a mayoral candidate, Lindsay looked ten years younger than he actually was. But by the beginning of 1968 he seemed less the White Knight of reform than a forty-six-year-old mortal man. One could begin to see the toll of being mayor written on Lindsay's face. He was still handsome and fit, but his visage grew hardened and no longer emitted that healthy patrician glow. Lindsay looked like a man burdened from the long hours on the job, the bitter political battles, and the misery he encountered in the streets. Sometimes Lindsay even had that same hangdog look Robert Wagner used to wear. With characteristic humor, Lindsay told a reporter that to be mayor of New York, "you have to be a little bit nuts. It's not in the job description, but it helps."[13]

The problems of city government looked as intractable as ever. Lindsay's opponents looked stronger than he could have imagined. Growing numbers of middle-class New Yorkers were turned off by the mayor's style and policies. Liberals, who now placed their hopes with Bobby Kennedy, began questioning Lindsay's commitment. And a cultural revolution brewed beneath the surface of society, as thousands called into question basic American values and sought to halt the massive American military machine fighting in Southeast Asia. As if Lindsay did not have enough trouble already, his next two years would prove to be more chaotic, violent, and controversial than his first two.

The late 1960s stand as a turning point in American history, an era of tumult, chaos, protests, and even revolution. Sociologist Todd Gitlin has written: "One can see the late Sixties as a long unraveling, a fresh start, a tragicomic Kulturkampf, the overdue demolition of a fraudulent consensus, a failed upheaval, an unkept promise, a valiant effort at reform camouflaged as revolution—and it was all of these. Whatever the image, the contending forces labored under a cloud of impending doom, or salvation, or both. Everything could be lost, everything could be gained." No year was more crucial to this era than 1968. It was the year of America's peak military involvement in Vietnam; of the assassinations of Martin Luther King and Robert F. Kennedy; of the election of Richard Nixon; and the protests at the Democratic Convention in Chicago. [14]

Throughout the sixties, some liberal activists had been arguing for a disruptive politics that would radically change the status quo. Charles Silberman, in his 1964 book *Crisis in Black and White*, called for "rubbing raw the sores of discontent." In 1968, Columbia professors Francis Fox Piven and Richard Cloward coined the term "dissensus politics" in a *New Republic* article, "Dissensus Politics: A Strategy for Winning Economic Rights," in which they discussed the possibilities of such a politics. As opposed to "consensus politics," dissensus politics would be used to gain benefits for minorities and the poor by driving people apart, not by uniting them in a common interest. According to Piven and Cloward, dissensus politics occurs when a group acting on behalf of a minority

> engages in actions which are designed to dislodge (or which threaten to dislodge) not only that minority, but more important, other significant constituent groups in that same alliance. Through the cadre's ability to generate defections among other groups in a coalition, its impact becomes far greater than the voting power of the minority. If the strategist of consensus looks for issues and action to bring groups together, then the strategist of dissensus looks for issues and actions which will drive groups apart.

Such politics found their fullest expression on the streets of New York. In 1968, John Lindsay would have to deal with continued labor troubles, riots, antiwar protests, and the effects of the youth counterculture. American politics and society would never be the same after 1968. And neither would John Lindsay.[15]

100,000 TONS OF GARBAGE

Labor troubles still plagued Lindsay. The year 1968 began with the threat of the biennial transit workers strike. Lindsay did not want a repeat of the fiasco that had welcomed him into office two years earlier. This time there was no talk of independent fact finders or arbitrators and no denunciations of "power brokers." Instead, Lindsay asked Ted Kheel to mediate the discussions with the TWU. After thirty-nine hours of continuous negotiations, a settlement was reached on New Year's morning. Mediators ironed out a deal worth nearly $70 million over two years. Kheel said that Lindsay "handled himself perfectly. . . . The difference between this Lindsay and the Lindsay of the 1966 transit dispute is like the difference between day and night." One unnamed union official noted that two years ago, union leaders had the feeling that the Ivy League Lindsay "looked down on us. This time he treated us as equals." In addition to 5 and 6 percent wage increases for 1968 and 1969, respectively, the deal proposed that transit workers over fifty would get half-pay pension plans after twenty years of service. Other municipal unions would surely expect this benefit—it had already been granted to policemen, firemen, and sanitationmen—in future negotiations. Victor Gotbaum, the executive director of District 37 of the American Federation of State, County, and Municipal Employees, said in reaction to the transit deal, "We're licking our chops."[16]

Lindsay managed to dodge a bullet with the TWU negotiations, but there was another strike on the horizon. The Uniform Sanitationmen's Association (USA), led by John DeLury, had been working without a contract since June 30, 1967. DeLury refused to cooperate with Lindsay's Office of Collective Bargaining, whose staff oversaw the administration of municipal labor relations. Instead, DeLury and the USA wanted to negotiate directly with the mayor and his aides. DeLury had created not only an effective municipal union but also a forceful political machine that exerted its influence at the ballot box. Edward N. Costikyan, the former leader of Tammany Hall, said of the union, "I would today rather have John DeLury's sanitationmen with me in an election than half the party headquarters in town." DeLury was powerful enough to cause Lindsay trouble.[17]

As early as January 1968, Deputy Mayor Robert Sweet warned DeLury, "The Mayor has told me to tell you that he'll go to any lengths to keep this settlement in bounds. He'll even resist a strike." The Lindsay-appointed mediators eventually struck a deal with DeLury. On Friday morning, February 2, the USA leader presented the proposal to 7,000 of his men gathered for a rally at City Hall Park. As soon as DeLury announced the deal, though, the angry sanitationmen booed and shouted him down. As the union head moved through the crowd, his men pelted him with eggs. They wanted to strike and DeLury would have to go along with them. The mediators had offered a $400 wage increase retroactive to July 1, 1967, along with double time for Sunday work and an increase in the city's contribution to worker pensions. All in all, it was a fairly generous offer, more generous than what the policemen's and firemen's unions had won the previous year. But the union wanted more. It demanded a $600 increase retroactive to July 1, 1967. This would have meant a 7 to 9 percent wage increase for the 10,000 members of the USA. When DeLury presented his $600-per-man demand, the mayor responded brusquely: "The request is impossible. We reject it." DeLury was puzzled by the mayor's unwillingness to offer a counterproposal. The strike began that day.[18]

There was more to the sanitationmen's complaints than just money. Many think of the late 1960s as a time of anger among blacks, women, and young people, but others also felt alienated. Along with the anger at working without a contract for over six months, the largely Italian-American sanitationmen were, according to Charles Morris, "angry at the city, angry at the changes in working conditions, angry at the apparent preference shown the minorities; they felt like second-class citizens ('garbagemen') and wanted to strike almost for catharsis." Raymond Horton, a student of New York's labor relations, noted that in Lindsay's first term, labor unrest grew because "municipal unions had grown so powerful—politically and organizationally—that they no longer could be contained easily by any labor relations system." According to Horton, Lindsay's new Office of Collective Bargaining "only compounded the basic problem—the emerging discrepancy in resources and influence between the major municipal unions and public officials in New York City."[19]

Lindsay was paying a price for his aloof attitude toward unions and their leaders. Though Wagner had made strong efforts to develop personal relationships with union leaders, Lindsay did not. Horton observed: "Whether by choice, dint of personality, or accident, the city's municipal union chiefs felt snubbed by Mayor Lindsay. They resented this." When Horton interviewed union leaders in 1968 and 1969, they "openly expressed strong feelings of personal dislike for the mayor."[20]

After three days, the strike turned ugly. The *Times* described the city as "a vast slum as mounds of refuse grow higher and strong winds whirl the filth through the streets." An estimated 10,000 tons of garbage accumulated each day on the city's streets. As he did during most city emergencies, Mayor Lindsay took to the streets to inspect the trash situation. His choice of sites betrayed the limited vision of his concern: the black and Puerto Rican slums of Harlem and the South Bronx, the Silk Stocking East Side of Manhattan, upper-middle-class Brooklyn Heights, and the middle-class Jewish area of Forest Hills in Queens. Two days later, Lindsay visited the Lower East Side, Bedford-Stuyvesant, and Flatbush. The Lower East Side was "the worst" the mayor had ever seen. Garbage was piled chest-high. Egg shells, coffee grounds, milk cartons, orange rinds, and empty beer cans littered the sidewalks. The union seemed unconcerned about the health hazards created by the strike. Paul O'Dwyer, a left-wing Democrat and USA's lawyer, called the threats posed by the garbage pileup "not something new. It is that the middle class of New York may have to live for a little while the way the poor people live all the time."[21]

On Monday, the fourth day of the strike, Lindsay publicly broached the subject of bringing in the National Guard to clean up the streets, citing the emergency health situation facing the city. The previous day, Bob Sweet had met with Governor Rockefeller's executive secretary, Alton Marshall, and General A. C. (Buzz) O'Hara, the chief of the New York National Guard. They had discussed plans for bringing in the National Guard and General O'Hara agreed to look into the logistics and come up with a plan.[22]

Meanwhile, the USA was found guilty of violating the state's Taylor Law, which had superseded the Condon-Wadlin Act in 1967 and which outlawed strikes by municipal unions. The union was fined and DeLury was sent to jail to serve a fifteen-day sentence. Following the lead of Mike Quill two years earlier, DeLury saw a jail sentence as a path to martyrdom and a sure way to strengthen control over his union. DeLury reportedly asked Lindsay, "John, for God's sake, can you arrange for me to go to jail alone? Don't send any of my colleagues in the union, because I have to be the martyr. Otherwise I'm ruined."[23]

On Wednesday, the sixth day of the strike, Lindsay turned up the rhetoric. The city was staring at the possibility of a huge snowstorm the next day. Lindsay gave the striking garbagemen a Thursday, 7 A.M., deadline to return to work. He lashed out at the strikers: "In a city noted for its tolerance, conditions are rapidly becoming intolerable. In a word, New York is a mess—all because of this degrading, unconscionable and unlawful strike." Lindsay gave the union three choices: round-the-clock negotiations; recommendations from the mediators that would be sent to union members to vote on secretly; or submitting the dispute to an impartial panel of fact finders. If the union rejected these proposals, Lindsay would "use the full powers of this office to protect the health and welfare of the people of this city, people who are disgusted, revolted, and possibly endangered by the uncollected filth that litters New York." Recalling the fiery reform rhetoric of the first year of his mayoralty, Lindsay promised, "I will not pay blackmail. We intend to fight lawlessness with every lawful resource we have."[24]

As Lindsay increased the heat of his rhetoric, he also began to lose control of the strike talks. He had the idea of ordering truck drivers and other workers from other city departments to pick up the garbage, but it was rejected by District Council 37's Victor Gotbaum, who said such an order would cause his municipal workers to go out on strike. On Thursday, Lindsay requested from Governor Rockefeller "whatever assistance may be available under law," adding "that means the possible use of the New York State National Guard." Morris Iushewitz, secretary of the Central Labor Council, called such an idea "union-busting of the worst sort." When Lindsay's proposals were rejected, he called a health emergency in the city, the first since

1931, when New Yorkers were warned about the dangers of a typhoid outbreak. The mayor reiterated his belief that the sanitationmen had "no moral or legal right to cripple an essential city function to achieve their own monetary ends." The governor got DeLury released from jail temporarily to discuss a possible settlement, one that Lindsay quickly rejected. The mayor did not want to grant the union anything that would be seen as a reward for its illegal behavior.

By Thursday, the seventh day of the strike, Rockefeller had gained control of strike negotiations. Although Rockefeller in private conversations led Lindsay to believe that he might call in the National Guard, he never seriously considered the idea. There were too many risks associated with the plan. And DeLury and his union, it should be noted, had been strong political supporters of Rockefeller during his 1966 reelection race. [25]

On Friday Rockefeller told New Yorkers, "I can call out the National Guard and if necessary I will call out the National Guard. But I would like to say to everybody in this city and throughout the state where many of these people live that there are very real risks as far as the stability and the structure of organized labor and the organized community life in this great city of ours are concerned." The governor warned that after the strike was settled, "having military men come in to collect garbage but also to break a strike in this city would have the most serious repercussions, be inflammatory—there could be fighting on the streets and I think we've got trouble enough in this city."[26]

After the strike was over, a reporter asked the governor if the fear of rioting stopped him from calling in the National Guard. Rockefeller responded, "Well, did you, by any chance, see Rap Brown on television. . . . He said, 'This is what we're waiting for. We want the troops. We want to overthrow the government. We want to have rioting. We want to fight the soldiers. Bring them on!' " Rockefeller was turning the tables on Lindsay, using the mayor's standard ploy to reject any plan that had the possibility of sparking a riot. Six years later at a Senate hearing, Rockefeller recalled his reasoning: "I think this could have spread to a racial war, and I could visualize these National Guardsmen, if you will forgive me saying so, who are young men from offices and architects and so forth, trying to pick up these huge garbage cans, and they would all have had hernias. And they would have been suing the state for years." Rockefeller's chief of staff, Alton Marshall, feared the National Guard might be more trouble than they were worth. Putting the mostly white, Upstate guardsmen into the inner city would have led to a situation where either the National Guard would be attacked or the itchy trigger of a National Guardsman would cause civilian deaths. Marshall also agreed with Rockefeller that the weekend warriors were probably physically incapable of the strenuous labor involved in trash removal.[27]

Another factor weighing on the governor's mind was the 1914 Ludlow Massacre, when his father, John D. Rockefeller Jr., asked the governor of

Colorado to call in the National Guard to one of his mines when striking workers threatened to take over. Seventy strikers were killed in the bloody episode. Speaking in uncharacteristically emotional tones behind closed doors, the governor's "voice trembled and his eyes showed tears" as he told USA leaders that he knew "what the National Guard means. I know personally. The National Guard was used to break a strike in which a family corporation was involved when I was a child. Men and women were killed. The consequences of military force are terrible. I cannot inflict that upon a city already wracked with problems. I will not use the National Guard." When Rockefeller finished, "the silence was harrowing," and the labor leaders left the room. When they returned five minutes later, the governor apologized for losing his composure.[28]

The most troubling consequence of calling out the National Guard would have been widespread labor strikes throughout the city. This was made quite clear when the governor called the city's major labor leaders into his office at 22 West Fifty-fifth Street on Thursday, February 8, to ask them if they could help with DeLury. According to Alton Marshall, "They stuck to a man with DeLury." Then Joseph Treretola, head of the local Teamsters, warned, "Governor, you call out the National Guard and I'll shut this town down so tight even babies won't get milk." This line effectively quashed any talk of bringing in the National Guard. "I never in my entire life ever believed anybody more than I believed him [Treretola]," remembers Marshall. "It just went up the back of my neck. . . . Jesus, they mean it." Bob Sweet remembers that the USA negotiator Jack Bigel warned him that the strike would have to be settled soon before it spread to a citywide general strike.[29]

As New Yorkers watched trash pile up outside their homes, they were also watching the battle of two titanic political egos. By this time, the relationship between Lindsay and Rockefeller had become severely strained. By 1968, a former Rockefeller aide has said, "Rockefeller had endured what he regarded as two years of government-by-dilettante in New York City. When he spoke Lindsay's name, his lips compressed, his brow furrowed, and his voice lowered to a contemptuous rasp. His manner suggested an aging suitor forced, resentfully, to compete for Lady Destiny's hand with an effete Prince Charming."

Marshall called the friction between the two liberal Republicans an "old buck, young buck syndrome." Rockefeller felt he was due some deference from the younger Lindsay. In turn, the proud Lindsay felt that he did not owe anyone deference, least of all the deal-making, compromising Rockefeller.[30]

Years of steaming about what Rockefeller perceived as Lindsay's ungratefulness reached a head by the second Friday of the strike. Rockefeller had had enough of Lindsay. That night he called his counsel, Bob Douglass, in Albany. "I'll be up Sunday night, and I want a bill ready authorizing the state [to] take over sanitation in New York City. Use the Public Health Law. Use anything. Just get it done," the governor ordered. Douglass worked night and day throughout the weekend on the bill. On Monday, after he handed the bill to Rockefeller, Douglass collapsed from exhaustion and had to be taken to the hospital.[31]

Amid the tension, the difference between the city's and the union's positions was shrinking. City and union leaders had agreed to $400 before the strike, but that had been rejected by the union rank-and-file. The first offer from the governor's five-man panel, which he created to settle the strike, was $425, which Lindsay rejected. He explained his reasons over the phone to Rockefeller: "First, it sanctions negotiations with an illegally striking union. Second, the amount is excessive. Now is the time to break these public-service unions." Deputy Mayor Sweet got on the phone to the USA's lawyer, Paul O'Dwyer, and further explained that the issue was not about money. "The mayor feels that there is a principle," Sweet told O'Dwyer. "We cannot yield to an illegal strike." To this, O'Dwyer responded, "Principle ain't gonna clean your streets." After the rejection, arbitration was decided upon, with the union calling for a $400 floor and the city calling for a $375 ceiling. The governor announced on Saturday that the state would temporarily take over the city's Sanitation Department, under the guise of a health emergency, and grant the sanitationmen a $425 increase for a one-year contract, an increase of only $25 from what the city had agreed to before the strike. This difference amounted to only a $250,000 difference for the one-year contract. On Saturday night, DeLury and his men accepted the offer from Nelson Rockefeller, a man they trusted and supported. The union agreed that a final contract would be decided upon in arbitration. With over 100,000 tons of garbage waiting for them, DeLury ordered his men back to work.[32]

The bill Douglass crafted would have expanded the governor's power under Section 1301 of the state's Public Health Law. The new law would have given the governor the right, in the case of a public health emergency, to take over the Sanitation Department and solve the emergency if the city proved unable to do so. One of the authors of the state's Taylor Law, which presumably outlawed strikes by municipal workers and was supported and signed by Rockefeller, called the governor's move the "crassest kind of political move. Why should anybody behave himself now? What the governor has said to every civil service union, in effect, is: 'If you got enough muscle, the community will knuckle under.'"[33]

Lindsay was furious. Rockefeller would take credit for ending the strike, the city would lose control of its Sanitation Department, and Rockefeller's union cronies, the dreaded "power brokers," could chalk up another victory over the people of New York. "I am shocked," said an angry Lindsay, "that Governor Rockefeller has capitulated to the union that is striking unlawfully against eight million New Yorkers. This strike was called in defiance of a state law sponsored and signed by Governor Rockefeller himself. I had hoped that the governor would join me in combating the extortionist demands of the sanitation union. I deeply regret that he has chosen not to do so." He called Rockefeller's proposed takeover of the city's Sanitation Department "a direct, and dangerous threat to the principle of home rule—not in New York City alone, but in every city of the state and possibly the nation." Furthermore, Rockefeller's plan "corrupts the fundamental rights of the people of New York City and their elected representatives. It contravenes the division of government powers that is fundamental to the processes of democratic government."

Lindsay felt Rockefeller's plan was an attack not only on the mayor, but on the political rights and liberties of the city. Not only that, but Lindsay brought up the salient point: Who would pay for this increase in the sanitationmen's wages? The state or "the city that steadfastly refused to pay them?" To force the city to pay for increased wages that it had previously refused to pay seemed to make a mockery of New York City's home rule. (Under Rockefeller's plan, the cost of paying the sanitationmen, plus administrative costs, would come out of the state's aid to the city.)[34]

Rockefeller's plan would have to be approved by the state legislature. Here Rockefeller ran into political difficulties. Democrats, supportive of unions and lenient toward strikes, would normally tend to support the governor's bill. Republican legislators, who disapproved of strikes and wanted to punish offending unions, would be least likely to support their governor. Republicans upheld their part and bucked the Republican governor, whom many saw as too liberal. Democrats, meanwhile, though sympathetic to the union, did not want to help a Republican governor. Why should they get caught in a personal battle between the Republican mayor and a Republican governor? And why should they pass legislation to improve Rockefeller's image just in time for the presidential campaign?

Amid the acrimony surrounding Rockefeller's bill, Lindsay laid out his reasons for asking for the National Guard to clean the streets of New York. In a speech in Buffalo to the State Publishers Association, Lindsay explained a discussion he had during the strike with a major labor leader who opposed his plan. Lindsay asked him if he would have agreed to call in the Guard if it were a summer riot. The leader agreed he would support it. "He was convinced that the chaos caused by an illegal strike should not be fought with the same powers that would be employed against the chaos caused by mob violence," Lindsay said. "He simply wouldn't admit that both are criminal actions." Lindsay argued that the issue was one of equal protection under the laws, especially for minorities living in slums who saw the National Guard called in when they rioted, but not when an illegal strike left mounds of garbage on their streets for over a week. "The issue," stated the mayor, "is whether the guard is available only to combat disorder in the slums caused by the people of the slums. My view is that the source of disorder is irrelevant." Lindsay sternly said that he would like to think that when the National Guard was called out thirteen times nationwide in the summer of 1967 to battle rioters it was "ordered because the rule of law was defied, not because [the law] was defied by Negroes." Lindsay continued:

> A man can cope with the discrimination on a personal level when he can see and hear and react against what is being done to him. The calculated, demeaning hypocrisy inherent in the enforcement of society's laws against that individual and the suspension of them for others is more than he should be asked to endure. The sanction of the laws must be applied reasonably and justly to all, whether they live in the poverty of The Other America or in the affluence of The Insulated American. The law is identified with neither.[35]

Above all, Lindsay's call for the National Guard was based in his strong sympathy for the needs and feelings of blacks and Puerto Ricans living in the inner city. Rockefeller publicly stated that one reason he did not want to call the National Guard was the fear of inciting a riot in the inner city. But Lindsay countered that *not* having the National Guard visible in the inner city cleaning up garbage would reinforce the feeling that government was unconcerned about poor minorities. Like almost every other issue that he faced in his term as mayor, Lindsay viewed the garbage strike as a civil rights issue. Whereas his concern for the poor and oppressed was admirable, the average middle-class white must have been asking why the mayor should not call out the National Guard for his neighborhood as well.

As the state legislature stalled, the sanitationmen were at work cleaning up the mounds of garbage left from its nine-day strike. The union was working without a contract, since DeLury had accepted his good friend Nelson Rockefeller's word on a deal. Politically, Lindsay appeared strong and principled, while Rockefeller looked weak and craven before an illegally striking union. Public opinion began turning against Rockefeller. A poll for the *Times* nearly two weeks after the end of the strike found that 59 percent of New York State residents and 61 percent of New York City residents supported Lindsay's stance in the strike. New Yorkers were evenly split on whether the National Guard should have been called to clean the streets. The *New York Times* labor commentator, A. H. Raskin, whom the USA dubbed the city's "labor commissioner," said the fallout of the strike

> was the first time in many decades that outraged public opinion had ever materially affected the outcome of a strike. . . . It also reflects a deeper sense that all society will disintegrate if no one ever takes a determined stand in support of the rule of law. That feeling stems from all the frustrations of crime in the streets, urban riots, high taxes, inflation, the war in Vietnam, poisoned air and everything else that makes it a daily torture to get out of bed.[36]

On Saturday, February 17, the city and the union submitted their differences to an arbitrator, the first time this had occurred in the city. DeLury was ambivalent about arbitration, saying he opposed it "because it is a breakdown in collective bargaining . . . but it was either that or blood in the streets." Less than two weeks later, the arbitrator, Vincent McDonnell, the chairman of the State Mediation Board, came up with a settlement. According to Bob Sweet, it was an agreement under the guise of arbitration, with the final settlement drawn up by McDonnell, Sweet, and the USA's negotiator, Jack Bigel. "It was arbitration, but nobody wanted to take a chance that the arbitration would not be agreeable," said Sweet. The union received $400 retroactive to July 1, 1967, and $425 retroactive to January 1, 1968. The union did not get the double overtime on Sundays that they had demanded. DeLury could claim that he had gotten more in this deal than he would have received under the original agreement that had been hooted down by his men two weeks earlier. Lindsay, though he had just given the union a fairly generous increase, still appeared as a tough politician willing to stand up to the unions. Raskin noted, "Suddenly, the mayor didn't look like a stiff-necked, petulant bumbler any more. The people overwhelmingly sided with him in his not-one-penny-for-tribute stand."[37]

THE KERNER COMMISSION

If Lindsay was less than empathetic toward the demands of municipal workers like the sanitationmen, his concern for the poor and for minorities was unquestioned. As a member of the House Judiciary Committee, he had an important hand in shepherding the 1964 Civil Right Acts through Congress. He actively campaigned in black neighborhoods during the 1965 campaign, and went on to win 40 percent of the black vote. Thus it came as no surprise when President Lyndon Johnson, in July 1967, named Lindsay vice chairman of the National Advisory Commission on Civil Disorders. The nation's cities had been torn by riots the previous three summers and Johnson wanted a commission to examine the underlying causes of the disorder. [38]

The official chairman of the "riot commission" was Otto Kerner, the Democratic governor of Illinois, and the commission came to be known as the Kerner Commission. From the beginning, however, Lindsay assumed virtual leadership of the panel. According to the Lindsay aide Peter Goldmark, who along with Jay Kriegel served as one of Lindsay's top aides on the commission, Kerner was "a rather low energy, sleepy character." Into this vacuum swept the energetic, dynamic Lindsay, whom Goldmark called "the moral and the effective leader" of the commission. Lindsay pushed the commission to go into the field and visit the nation's ghettos. The members spoke not only with traditional black politicians but also with black militants. With his participation on the Kerner Commission, Lindsay was able to bring his ideas about ghetto relations to a national audience.[39]

From the beginning the Kerner Commission was a headache for the Johnson administration. Johnson's adviser Joseph Califano, who served as his liaison to the Kerner Commission, wrote to the President in February 1968 to outline the limits he had set out for the commission. It was "not to call for any spending of money, clearly not to criticize the guns and butter program, clearly not to touch the war and national priorities, clearly not to criticize the administration and what the government had done but to praise the Great Society and say we should continue with it."[40]

Though Johnson had created the commission and was known to be sympathetic to the black community, he worried about the political impact of the commission's report. He also worried that Lindsay—a Republican, a potential 1968 challenger, and an increasingly vocal critic of the President's Vietnam policy—would use the commission to embarrass the President. According to Goldmark, Johnson "was tearing his hair out at the White House . . . worried that the commission would go off on its own and say something bold. . . . He worried that the stance they took . . . would make Johnson's efforts on the War on Poverty and domestic issues look inadequate and imperfect." Johnson was unhappy when the Kerner Report was finally made public in early 1968.[41]

The Kerner Report was one of the most searing critiques of American race relations to date, but it was not originally conceived as the radical document it became. The catalyst for this shift was John Lindsay. The political scientists Michael Lipsky and David Olson wrote a study of the politics of the Kerner Commission itself, in which they described how, "During the last two weeks of deliberations, John V. Lindsay, the most outspoken liberal on the panel, became increasingly concerned that the general fatigue of the commissioners and staff and the need under the pressure of deadlines to 'lock up' sections of the document was working in favor of the more conservative commission members. At its last meeting Lindsay indicated that he felt the report was losing focus." According to the journalist Andrew Kopkind, Lindsay believed the draft report was "wishy-washy." In a memo to commission members in January 1968, Lindsay wrote that the "major failing of the report is the lack of urgency. . . . This is the most serious domestic crisis we have faced in the past century. There can be no delay. We need action. . . . And we need no lesser level of response—a wartime level of resources and commitment with a full domestic strategy." He was angry that the commission voted down any mention of the Vietnam War as a contributing factor in rioting. So Lindsay decided to create a summary that would serve as an introduction to the commission's report. Kriegel and Goldmark spent a sleepless night drafting the summary to present at the commission's final meeting.[42]

Though the commission's members represented diverse ideological standpoints, they wanted to present a unanimous report. When Lindsay introduced his controversial summary statement, he knew that some members would not go along with it. Instead of insisting that he could not sign the final report unless it included this statement, Lindsay told the members, "I'm sure we want to polish this somewhat, but I am also equally sure that at heart these are the thoughts that we have all come to after all of these months together walking the streets of American cities." The effect of this strategy was to take the pressure off Lindsay as the one who would disunite the commission with his summary and to force the burden of a "dissent" upon the conservatives. As Goldmark recalls: "The whole electric energy, which we knew had been built up there . . . could have fallen on John had he said 'and I can't sign a report unless it says this.'. . . What he succeeded in doing was in drawing someone else offside." Thus, when one of the more conservative members stated his objections to the Lindsay summary, "all the other commissioners jumped on him." The Lindsay summary was then incorporated, with some minor changes, as the introduction to the report.[43]

In words that have now become part of the national dialogue, the report's summary stated: "Our nation is moving toward two societies, one black, one white—separate and unequal." It spoke in loud and clear terms placing the blame squarely on white America for the recent urban riots. It reminded its readers that "what white Americans have never fully understood—but what the Negro can never forget—is that white society is deeply implicated in the ghetto. White institutions created it, white institutions maintain it, and white society condones it." The view that seemed to be expressed in the Kerner Report was of blacks not as the agents of their own destiny, but as pawns in an oppressive game played by whites. It was a vision that reduced blacks to mere clay figures that could be molded by the dominant society, for good or bad. If America continued on its present course, the report warned, it could expect even more violence. Yet the country could make a choice to avert further damage. The commission proposed "a commitment to national action—compassionate, massive and sustained, backed by the resources of the most powerful and the richest nation on this earth."[44]

Political scientist Martha Derthick has observed of presidential commissions in general: "To be believed, it is first necessary to be heard, and to be heard it is helpful to use passionate, extreme language. The organizational need to command attention impels the use of crisis rhetoric." The report's summary certainly fit the bill. With its controversial summary, the commission became the collective voice of white America, telling its black brethren, in the words of Goldmark, "in order for you to become part of this country and its future, we will makes ourselves vulnerable." Its harsh denunciation of "white racism" was the issue the press picked up on. The first article on the Kerner Report to appear in the *New York Times* was headlined "Johnson Unit Assails Whites in Negro Riots." Yet some have suggested that a broad denunciation of white racism was not the original goal of the report. As Lipsky and Olson write, "Interviews with commission participants also suggest that the Kerner Commission did not intend to become so prominently identified with the 'white racism' theme. Furthermore, in the discussion of the violence encouraged by 'white racists,' the commission was referring to Klansmen and their spiritual kin, not the more ubiquitous practitioners of 'white racism' whom it has generally been credited with condemning."[45]

Much of the Kerner Report's heated and moralistic rhetoric can be traced to John Lindsay. His imprint can also be seen in the section "What Is to Be Done?" In describing the role of the new urban mayor, the report summarized Lindsay's goal as mayor: "As leader and mediator, he must involve all those groups—employers, news media, unions, financial institutions and others—which only together can bridge the chasm now separating the racial ghetto from the community. His goal, in effect, must be to develop a new working concept of democracy within the city." It was an adventurous role, one Lindsay felt was necessary to bring minorities into the American mainstream.[46]

The Kerner Report predicted three possible paths for the future. First, American cities could continue on their present path. Such a choice would risk "a seriously greater probability of major disorders, worse, possibly than those already experienced." If present policies continued, more blacks might rebel against the government, provoking a violent white reaction. In what could easily be the most pessimistic words ever to come out of a presidential commission, the Kerner Report warned that such a spiral of violence in the face of national indifference to ghetto conditions could possibly lead to "a kind of urban apartheid with semi-martial law in many major cities, enforced residence of Negroes in segregated areas, and a drastic reduction in personal freedom for all Americans, particularly Negroes."[47]

The second path was what the report called the "Enrichment Choice," whereby the government would invest large sums of money in lifting inner-city residents above the poverty line and creating a black middle class. The drawback to such a model would be that it would not tackle the increased segregation of blacks within big cities. The third path, the "Integration Choice," would fulfill many of the goals of the Enrichment Choice, but it would add the complete integration of the races. The goal was to "out-move" minorities from the inner cities to the suburbs, where jobs, good schools, and decent housing were plentiful. The Kerner Commission preferred the Integration Choice. It was bold, costly, and painful. The commission was aware of the difficulties such a choice would cause for the country, but argued that the alternative was worse: unless America undertook a massive redistribution of wealth to cities and a massive redistribution of minorities out of the cities, nothing short of a racial Armageddon would occur, destroying America's democracy.

Speaking before a group of students at the University of Denver in March 1968, Lindsay discussed some of the ideas from the Kerner Commission. Not only were issues like poor housing and schools causing despair in

America's slums, but slum residents, Lindsay told the students, were "no longer satisfied with the menial jobs they have been allocated, irrespective of their ability. The Negro has been washing cars, shining shoes, and mopping floors for most of this Century, and now he understandably wants something better." This attitude severely hampered any attempt to get the ever-growing number of welfare recipients off the dole and into the workforce.

Mitchell Sviridoff, the head of the Human Resources Administration (HRA), recognized the need for a "workfare" program to ease people off welfare and tried to institute such a program in the city. He did not have a problem with the poor starting at menial positions, but he was stymied by others at the agency who did. "I couldn't get my bureaucracy to go along with it," Sviridoff later complained. One of those blocking reform was Cyril Tyson, the manpower commissioner at HRA. Tyson said in 1967 that he would not place unemployed blacks as cab drivers, feeling it was the type of dead-end job to which minorities had too long been consigned. To which the Lindsay critic Roger Starr responded, "Naturally, the taxicab drivers of New York, many of whom have sent children through college and graduate school, regarded Tyson's comments as a gratuitous insult."[48]

In the years after the publication of the Kerner Report, the conditions in black urban ghettos worsened. In 1972, Lindsay tried to keep the spirit of the Kerner Report alive. He and Senator Fred Harris of Oklahoma headed the Commission on the Cities in the '70s to reexamine the situation of minorities and American cities. Needless to say, the two men were not optimistic. In the report published by the commission in 1972 they wrote that since 1968, "separation and inequality have proceeded apace." Despite the efforts of urban liberals like Lindsay, the commission stated that "everywhere we went we encountered a bitter feeling that the good things of American life were in the main accessible only to those who were willing to allow their individual and communal identities to be homogenized in the famous American melting pot." By 1972, the criticism of American ghettos and race relations was becoming a more generalized critique of the American melting pot, of the "homogenous" conformity that destroyed the separate identity of American minorities.[49]

The 1972 Lindsay-Harris report condemned "white racism" in even harsher terms than the Kerner Report, arguing that American blacks

> see that American institutions, public and private, have a myriad of procedures, practices, and attitudes that effectively exclude people with nonwhite skins and non-European ancestry from full participation, economic or political or social, in American life. They see institutional racism in a public school system that makes little or no effort to educate certain children on the ground that the system failed to educate the parents and, therefore, the children are "culturally disadvantaged," that is, ineducable. . . . They see it in employers who set hiring standards that

treat equally everybody who has credentials that certain people are almost sure not to have. They see it in policemen who arrest certain people more often than others for petty offenses and then cite arrest statistics to prove that such people are prone to crime and should be arrested often.

The responsibility for this condition, the report concluded, fell across the spectrum of so-called white institutions: "the banks, the utilities, the real estate industry, the automotive industry, local zoning boards, state highway departments, the Veteran's Administration, the Federal Housing Administration, the Congress, and so on and on." This harsh critique of American society put Lindsay light-years beyond his reform Republicanism. Lindsay remained pessimistic as late as 1993, arguing that "the same problems exist today" in the ghettos as existed twenty-five years earlier. Lindsay's reason for this lack of progress: "The white community doesn't give a damn."[50]

The historians Stephan and Abigail Thernstrom have criticized this unrelenting pessimism about race relations, which they term the Kerner Report's "misguided prophecies" and "lurid predictions." The Thernstroms argue that the Kerner Report has been used as "a mantra for critics who seek to deny or downplay the great progress that has been made on the racial front." They point to a number of trends that make the Kerner Report less relevant today than it was in 1968. First, the dire prediction of American cities dominated by poor black populations has not occurred. Today, only four major American cities—Detroit, Washington, New Orleans, and Baltimore—have predominantly black populations (St. Louis and Cleveland are close to 50 percent). Though most American cities have seen decreases in their white population, the fear of a situation developing where all-black cities are surrounded by all-white suburbs has not come to pass.

Second, the report ignored the great progress that black Americans had made. Black life expectancy increased from 53 years of age in 1940 to 63.6 years in 1960. Home ownership among blacks increased from 23 percent in 1940 to 38 percent in 1960. On the economic front, black incomes were over 150 percent higher in 1960 than they were in 1940. Between 1940 and 1970, the percentage of black men holding white-collar jobs increased from 5 percent to 22 percent. The black middle class had grown.

Third, the report never foresaw the phenomenon of black suburbanization. Between 1970 and 1995, the percentage of the black population living in suburbs doubled from 16.1 percent to 31.9 percent, and the percentage of suburbia that was black nearly doubled, from 4.8 percent to 8.1 percent. Last, the Kerner Report did not take into account the dramatic changes that would occur in the wake of the 1965 Immigration Act. The Kerner Report saw America solely in black and white, whereas the reality of the last thirty years has been an influx of Hispanics and Asians into many American cities, adding to the dynamism of the urban economy and culture. The basic battle between black and white predicted by the Kerner Commission has not occurred.[51]

Other problems with the Kerner Report also seem clear. Writing in 1996, the political scientist Gareth Davies said of the report: "Blacks and whites are consistently judged by the different standards" and the "fear of appearing racist frequently deterred its members from balanced analysis." Another critic of the report points out that the Kerner Report neglected to discuss those victimized by riots: "One weakness of the report that remains unexplained is its failure to interview any of the hundreds of storekeepers whose shops were either looted or burned. The lootee . . . was the forgotten man in the aftermath of riot."[52]

The Kerner Report is still sometimes invoked during discussions of racial issues, but in fact has since largely fallen into obscurity. (A twenty-fifth anniversary edition of the report went out-of-print soon after publication.) The tone and theme of the report is very much that of John Lindsay, from its sweeping denunciation of white racism to its good-versus-evil mentality of race relations to its picture of gloom, violence, and destruction if drastic measures were not instituted. The Kerner Report is a pessimistic document. It places very little trust in the good character of the white community and it holds out very little hope for the ability of the black community to succeed.[53]

Depending on one's point of view, the fires that burned in American cities in the wake of the assassination of Martin Luther King two months after the Kerner Report's publication were evidence either of its essential validity or of its ultimate impotence.

WALKING THE STREETS, AGAIN: THE KING RIOTS OF 1968

Much of Lindsay's first two years in office were devoted to keeping the streets of the city's ghettos cool. Lindsay staked a good portion of his national political reputation as much on his ability to prevent massive rioting and looting as on his good looks. According to his deputy press secretary, Bob Laird, Lindsay was "instinctively at home" in poor, black ghettos. The most severe test of Lindsay's ability to prevent riots presented itself in the wake of the assassination of Martin Luther King, Jr. in early April 1968.

On the night of April 4, the mayor and his wife were attending the opening of a Broadway play. Lindsay's media consultant, David Garth, called the theater with the news that King had been shot, and an NYPD detective informed the mayor of the news as the second act was just beginning. The mayor bolted from his seat and called Police Commissioner Leary and Barry Gottehrer of the Urban Task Force, who informed Lindsay that crowds were gathering in Harlem and Bedford-Stuyvesant. One witness described the brewing scene in Harlem: "People were spontaneously going bonkers. There was a lot of running and yelling and smashing of windows and throwing of rocks and stuff. The cops were taking a defensive attitude, like: 'Let them vent their steam.' "[54]

Both the mayor's aides and the police believed it was too dangerous for Lindsay to be in Harlem that night, but as Sid Davidoff said, "Lindsay didn't care. He was going." Accompanied by Garth and Press Secretary Harry O'Donnell, Mayor Lindsay headed for Harlem. He believed that "somebody just has to go up there. Somebody white just has to face that emotion and say that we're sorry." Barry Gottehrer, who arrived in Harlem before the mayor, remembered that all he could hear from the loudspeakers along 125th Street that normally blared out soul rhythms was the voice of Martin Luther King.[55]

The mayor's car arrived at 125th Street and Eighth Avenue around 10:30 P.M. When the mayor got out of the vehicle, according to Garth, "There was a mob that was so large that it went across 125th Street from storefront to storefront." As the mayor's entourage entered the crowd, Garth thought to himself, "My life is over." Lindsay described the scene on 125th Street: "I kept moving, but finally I was hemmed in from all sides. Occasionally, I could hear my name shouted, and at other times I could hear men and women weeping or moaning. . . . We edged to a clearing in the crowd, when another group of men moved close—also men I knew. The groups began arguing about which was the better route for me to take." When O'Donnell faced a swarm of angry Harlemites coming down the street toward the mayor's entourage, the beefy, white press secretary with the jowly face later told people it was at that moment he realized, to his terror, how much he resembled a Southern sheriff.[56]

Lindsay spoke to the crowd, telling them in heartfelt, impromptu words his sadness at King's death. The presence of the mayor, already a familiar and respected face on the streets of Harlem, seemed to ease the anger of the crowd. Lindsay was being protected by Harlem operators whom he had gotten to know during previous night walks. One group to which the Lindsay administration turned was Allah's Five Percenters. Barry Gottehrer had spent much time earning the trust of Allah and his men and it seemed to pay off the night of April 4. Barry Gottehrer, a natural worrier, saw Lindsay's light-colored head bobbing above the crowd and thought, "Jesus, this is just the night for someone to take a shot at him." A fight broke out between the Five Percenters and some bodyguards sent over by a Harlem labor leader. Lindsay was jostled and confused. He later told Gottehrer that he mistakenly believed one group was out to kill him and the other out to save him, but he wasn't sure who was who. Manhattan Borough President Percy Sutton, who was with the mayor, convinced Lindsay to get inside Sutton's limousine and avoid the scene.[57]

In some ways, Lindsay's reaction to the King riots represented a high point in his administration. David Garth calls Lindsay "the most courageous man I've ever seen" for walking through the angry Harlem crowd. And surely he was courageous. Tom Morgan, who became Lindsay's press secretary in 1969, wrote twenty-five years after the riots that New York "had every right to be proud of itself in the aftermath of Martin Luther King's killing, proud of its citizens, its institutions, its mayor." The *Village Voice's* Jack Newfield wrote: "in the collective American fantasy of 'High Noon' updated, tall, grim Lindsay strides down Lenox Avenue, into a subsiding storm of bricks. It is a comforting fantasy Lindsay has earned because he is the only white Mayor in America . . . to have the grudging trust of the black underclass." Jimmy Breslin wrote about Lindsay's reception in Harlem that first night: "He looked straight at the people on the streets and he told them he was sick and he was sorry about Martin Luther King. And the poor he spoke to who are so much more real that the rest of us, understood the truth of John Lindsay. And there was no riot in New York."[58]

But contrary to the plaudits heaped on Lindsay, what happened on the night of April 4 was a riot. New York did not experience the massive rioting, looting, and burning that followed King's death in Washington, Chicago, Baltimore, and countless smaller cities throughout the nation, but riots did occur. Lindsay tried to play down the damage done, saying that the city "has remained relatively peaceful. No serious disorders have taken place." Yet four days after the riots began, the *Times* concluded in a headline "Damage Here Since Slaying of Dr. King Is Near '64 Riot Level." Borough President Percy Sutton, speaking on Thursday night, agreed: "This is worse now than it was in [the Harlem riot of] 1964. We had personal attacks then but now we've got property attacks. And it's getting worse, much worse."

During the 1964 riot 465 people were arrested; 373 were arrested in 1968. In 1964, there were 600 incidents of arson and burglary; in 1968 there were 592. In 1964, 118 civilians and policemen were injured; in 1968, 77 were injured, 41 policemen and 36 civilians. Sixty intentionally set fires were reported in Harlem and central Brooklyn during the first four days of riots. The *Times* reported that "hundreds of stores had been sacked or vandalized in Harlem and dozens in Brooklyn Bedford-Stuyvesant section." The *Post* reported that looters destroyed hundreds of stores up and down Lenox Avenue and across 125th Street on Thursday night. Worse, there were numerous reports of police standing by and doing nothing while looters ran in and out of stores. The *Amsterdam News*, though it acknowledged that New York did not suffer the same fate as Washington and Chicago, did admit that the rioting left Harlem "ravaged." There were scattered reports of snipers, including one attack directed against firemen responding to a torched business at 126th Street and Lenox Avenue. Besides the property damage, two people died in the riot: a forty-one-year-old man was stabbed to death in the middle of a crowd of rioters and a sixty-one-year-old man died in his apartment when looters set fire to the business on the ground floor.[59]

The mayor ordered the Sanitation Department into Harlem early the next morning to clean up the trash left over from the previous night's looting and rioting. Two journalists, Gloria Steinem and Lloyd Weaver, speculated that Lindsay "had learned from two hot summers that slum-dwellers who wake up to neatness and order are much more likely to keep it that way." But the Lindsay administration had an additional motive. It was desperate to prove there had been no rioting in the city. By cleaning things up early, it could avoid the adverse publicity that came with pictures of trash-strewn, riot-torn streets.

Rumors abounded the day after the riot. Gottehrer estimated that during the hot summers of the late 1960s, his office would receive as many as a thousand calls on a Friday night predicting imminent violence or passing on the latest rumor. Whites feared the "Great Black Rebellion" would finally descend upon their neighborhoods. Yet except for a few incidents south of 110th Street, the rioting was mostly contained in Harlem and the black ghettos of Brooklyn. The rumors in the black neighborhoods were just as desperate as in the white. Gottehrer heard rumors circulating that white gangs were prepared to invade and burn down Harlem. Gottehrer and his staff were "busy tracking down rumors that the Harlem subways were no longer running, that black people were being shot in the streets, that a white army was moving uptown with guns."[60]

A week after the riot, a group of one hundred black and Puerto Rican small businessmen whose stores had been destroyed by looters complained that Lindsay had underestimated the damage caused by the riots and had been insensitive to their concerns. They complained about the lack of police protection caused by "an attitude of appeasement and condoning [that] seemed to perpetuate the trouble." Louis Hernandez, a member of the Bedford-Stuyvesant Puerto Rican Merchants Association, charged that "the Mayor makes it seem as if nothing is going on. But places like Brownsville look like they were bombed out and you can see the shells of small stores . . . that are no longer in business." In Brownsville, Sol Glazer, the owner of an appliance store damaged by a fire during the riot, told a reporter that the "country is going to the dogs" as he pointed to the damage surrounding his business.[61]

To some New Yorkers, the police seemed to give criminals a free ride. In 1967, New York State passed a law prohibiting police from firing their guns unless their lives were threatened or another life was threatened or they were apprehending a felon who had used or threatened to use deadly force. The legislation was in keeping with Lindsay's policy of reducing police brutality. In a March 1967 speech at the Georgetown University Law Center, Commissioner Leary explained why it was necessary to curb police power: "Permitting the police to shoot suspected criminals who are not a danger to life and limb, would, I believe, not only increase the risk of riots in sensitive communities, but also subtly increase the tolerance of—indeed glorification of—violence which is a significant problem in our society." This policy led to the charge that the Lindsay administration "handcuffed" the police. Later, former Buildings Commissioner Charles Moerdler admitted that "John Lindsay, in contrast to Rudy Giuliani, tended to handcuff the police a lot more."[62]

There were two reasons behind Lindsay's desire to minimize the riots. First, there were political considerations. If Lindsay was to achieve higher office, he would do so on the strength of his ability to prevent riots. Thus, any talk of riots—even if they were not the massive riots of Watts, Newark, Detroit, or Washington—would have tarnished Lindsay's political image. The second reason to minimize the riots stemmed from a desire not to portray slums as chaotic and dangerous areas. To engender sympathy for poor black ghettos, Lindsay wanted to avoid contributing to negative stereotypes of these neighborhoods and their residents.

Lindsay contrasted himself with Chicago's mayor, Richard Daley. Where Daley gave orders for his police to shoot to kill rioters and shoot to maim looters, Lindsay took the opportunity of the riots to portray himself as a progressive, enlightened urban leader. In response to Daley's "shoot-to-kill" proclamation, Lindsay declared, "We happen to think that protection of life, particularly innocent life, is more important than protecting property or anything else. . . . We are not going to turn disorder into chaos through the unprincipled use of armed force. In short, we are not going to shoot children in New York City." Commissioner Leary told Jimmy Breslin, "Sixty percent of the looters were under sixteen. What were we supposed to do, shoot the next Martin Luther King?"[63] According to a *Post* reporter on the scene the first night of rioting, "Even the most blatant looters got only a whack across the bottom from riot cops with nightsticks."

"They had to make a decision," wrote Breslin. "Crack down on the looters and risk a major riot, or stand back and try to clear the area and let the couches and bottles of whisky go where they were going. The police stood back. In John Lindsay's New York, lives are more important than stores." Lindsay, remarking on the sight of military troops on the streets of Washington, shook his head and said, "Troops. In a country that is supposed to be civilized." Despite Lindsay's pacifist stand, Barry Gottehrer reports that the mayor and Commissioner Leary had signed an agreement with the state and the federal government concerning the use of National Guard troops should the riots escalate.[64]

To Lindsay, the King riots were a vindication of the Kerner Commission's conclusions. "It was safe now for almost anyone to decry the split in the country and the division between the races," Lindsay told an audience of Harvard students two weeks after King's death. The mayor hoped that the "honesty" of the Kerner Report would now be shared by the rest of white

America whose world was shattered by the sight of massive rioting. "Did we really need such overwhelming proof as disruptions in 110 additional cities?" Lindsay asked his college audience. "We had hoped that the commission's report would end this debate, that the candor of the report would encourage others to adopt a new honesty in their discussions of the problems of the cities and the relationships between the races. But that honesty was not forthcoming." Lindsay admitted that he believed riots might be "something that had to come, the price we must pay for this affluence."[65]

GIVING A DAMN

His experience on the Kerner Commission and with the King riots confirmed Lindsay's commitment to trying to do something about the plight of the black community. The title of an August 1968 *Reader's Digest* interview with Lindsay summarized his view of America's ghettos: "We Can Lick the Problems of the Ghetto If We Care." Lindsay argued that American blacks were so severely damaged by slavery that their ability to succeed was seriously in doubt unless whites "cared" enough to do something about it. "No other group in our country has been so systematically and deliberately deprived, over centuries, of the education, the skills and the social structure that are needed to achieve success," wrote Lindsay. In 1968, when walking through the conservative white Brooklyn neighborhood of Bay Ridge, which Lindsay carried in 1965, residents asked the mayor why taxes that came from whites had to be spent in black neighborhoods. Lindsay responded, "We have three hundred years of neglect to pay for."[66]

Lindsay was already trying to make up for this neglect with the creation of the New York Urban Coalition in 1967, which was part of the national Urban Coalition, headed first by Time Inc. Chairman Andrew Heiskell and later by John Gardner, President Johnson's former secretary of Health, Education, and Welfare. The aim of the Urban Coalition was to improve life in the ghetto. The list of the 105 New York Urban Coalition members was top-heavy with business and legal types, union leaders, and advocates for minorities. Chosen as chairman of the local coalition was Christian Herter, a New England Brahmin (St. Paul's and Harvard), son of one of Eisenhower's Secretaries of State, and a vice president of Mobil Oil. [67]

New York's Urban Coalition focused on job training for ghetto residents, street academies for at-risk children, and aid for minority businesses. The coalition spent $4 million in 1968 and close to $6 million in 1969, all of it raised privately. One could argue that business elites, frightened by urban riots, gave money to the Urban Coalition to "buy off" the urban poor. This is what Tom Wolfe, in his novel *Bonfire of the Vanities*, termed "steam control."

The advertising firm of Young & Rubicam created the Urban Coalition's slogan. Designed to prod complacent middle-class New Yorkers, the coalition's slogan was "Give a Damn." The problems of the slums could be solved, the argument went, if only people gave a damn about what went on there. GIVE A DAMN buttons with white lettering on a black background were produced in massive quantities. The Urban Coalition created public-service newspaper ads, billboards, and bus advertisements. The ads, which could be seen throughout the city during much of 1968, were designed to shock the comfortable with the reality of slum life: "It's still the 1930s in the Ghetto," "Six out of ten nonwhite children grow up poor," "Almost half of all nonwhites have to live in substandard housing," and "White dropouts earn more than Nonwhite High School Graduates."

Television advertisements designed by Young & Rubicam further drove home the point about the plight of the ghettos. One advertisement, bearing the headline "Send Your Kid to a Ghetto for the Summer," introduced the viewer to the recreation options of the average inner-city child: open fire hydrants, or play stickball in the street or in abandoned, trash-filled lots that served as playgrounds. Why should poor black children have to play under conditions that middle-class parents would never subject their kids to? The advertisement failed to mention that generations of poor whites in the city had played stickball and opened fire hydrants to cool off in their youth. A second ad, with mild anti-Semitic overtones, portrayed an obviously Jewish landlord showing a substandard slum apartment to a black man, who unhappily agrees to take the decrepit domicile. Another ad showed famous figures—Barbra Streisand, Johnny Carson, Lloyd Bridges, Sandy Koufax, George C. Scott, Fran Tarkenton, Otto Preminger, Nelson Rockefeller—each sporting A GIVE A DAMN button. The pop group Spanky and Our Gang even performed the campaign's theme song, "Give a Damn."

The most famous television ad featured eight-year-old students from PS 197 in Harlem. The black and Puerto Rican students were asked, "What do you want to be when you grow up?" The answers from the well-scrubbed, well-dressed, well-mannered children were about the kinds of dreams shared by all children. It was designed to humanize residents of the ghetto and make the white middle class more sympathetic to their plight, seeing in these children's answers the hopes and aspirations of their own children.[68]

The potential danger of the mixture of dissensus politics and riot politics occurred in July 1968. When Congress cut back the amount of money available to ghetto youth for summer jobs, Lindsay lashed out at Washington, saying that Congress found millions of dollars more for "the acceleration of a war on the other side of the world than it did to the prevention of violence and bloodshed on the streets of our own cities." The mayor concluded by laying the blame for future riots at the steps of Capitol Hill: "If violence occurs in our cities, those in Washington who have almost ignored our pleas for Federal help will have to assume their share of responsibility."[69]

One week later, 1,500 youths, mostly black and Puerto Rican, led by twenty-nine-year-old Willie Smith, the director of the city's Neighborhood

Youth Corps, marched on City Hall. The rally got out of hand and the youths rampaged in the streets surrounding City Hall, breaking windows in the Woolworth Building, looting newsstands and food wagons, mugging a middle-aged woman, assaulting the police, and stomping on and smashing six cars parked in the City Hall lot. The cars included those owned by Republican Councilman Joseph Modugno, the wife of Lindsay's appointments secretary, Harvey Rothenberg, and a city car used by the mayoral aide Teddy Mastroianni. No doubt a combination of Smith's leadership and Lindsay's earlier warnings had set off the crowd. Smith, a city employee, told reporters after the disturbance, "Violence—that's the only thing this city understands." Signs held by the young demonstrators exemplified the riot ideology prevalent under Lindsay: "Earn or burn," "No money—no peace," "A cooler New York is up to you," and "Give us something to do this summer besides rioting."[70]

Councilman Modugno, a Lindsay critic, accused the mayor of giving "orders to the Police Department not to take any action" against those Modugno called the "punks and bums [who] are taking over the city." The mayor denied the charge, as he had in previous incidents, calling the violence "disgraceful" and worrying that the disturbance would further hinder the possibility of getting more funding. Yet Smith and the demonstrators could be seen as merely acting out their part of the riot drama as outlined by Lindsay, who reiterated that the disturbance was just another warning that if cities did not get adequate financial aid, they were in danger of becoming victims to violence and riots.

Mitchell Ginsberg, the head of the city's Human Resources Administration, wanted to suspend Smith from his Neighborhood Youth Corps job, but the mayor's aides disagreed vehemently. Nat Hentoff reported that one aide warned, "The black communities will blow up if you do that." The mayor and his aides then drove with Ginsberg to Central Park and discussed the matter for an hour and a half. Lindsay told Ginsberg, "If you stand by this decision, there may be riots and burning and killing. Again, what do you want to do?" Ginsberg held to his belief that Smith had erred and suspended him for four days.[71]

In an era of protests and radicalization, even New York City policemen became more vocal and active in pressing their complaints. A group of policemen calling themselves the Law Enforcement Group began circulating demands during the summer of 1968, including the complete abolition of the Civilian Complaint Review Board, a reimposition of stricter standards for entry into the Police Academy, a grand jury investigation of the "coddling" of criminals by the city's courts, and the use of private rooms in private hospitals for policemen injured on the job. These policemen, many of whom served in Brooklyn, were outraged over the actions of the Black Panthers, many of whom openly called for violence against police. The police group was formed in reaction to the ambush shooting of Patrolmen Thomas Dockery and Leonard Fleck in the Crown Heights section of Brooklyn in early August. In response to a fabricated call of domestic violence, the two policemen arrived on the scene and, as they got out of their car, were shot by someone hiding in the nearby bushes. Suspicion quickly centered on local Black Panthers whose headquarters were nearby.[72]

With the Law Enforcement Group threatening to usurp the power of the Patrolmen's Benevolent Association, John Cassese, the PBA's president, publicized a statement calling on all policemen to "promptly obey all lawful orders and instructions issued by a superior officer or by higher authority within the department." This tug-of-war within the NYPD caused Commissioner Leary to issue a statement reminding policemen that they must "adhere to the police of the Department and . . . follow the Department's military chain of command . . . Any member of the Department who fails to respond to the orders of a superior officer will be promptly subjected to disciplinary action."[73]

In the first week of September, a trial of three Black Panthers charged with attacking policemen in Bedford-Stuyvesant was taking place in a Brooklyn courtroom. A scuffle erupted outside the courtroom between a group of 150 off-duty police officers and a smaller group of Black Panthers and white supporters. The off-duty policemen, some wearing WALLACE FOR PRESIDENT buttons and shouting "We're white tigers," set upon the opposing demonstrators with nightsticks, fists, and kicks until they were separated by a group of on-duty policemen. A few of the attacking officers were thought to be members of the Law Enforcement Group. The leader of the Panthers, Jorge Aponte, said of the incident, "This signals open warfare. . . . The Police Department has declared war not only on blacks but also whites and against any person that disagrees with the system."[74]

ABBIE HOFFMAN AND THE "PROPHETIC MINORITY"

By 1968, the city was dealing not only with angry black youths but also with alienated white youths. The members of the counterculture added their concerns to the mix of dissensus politics and to Lindsay's troubles.

Lindsay's good looks, antiwar position, and sympathy for student rebels made him an instant hit among the young. In a February 1971 Gallup poll, Lindsay was named the most popular national politician among college students, beating Eugene McCarthy, Edmund Muskie, George McGovern, and Ted Kennedy. From the second half of 1967 to the end of 1968, the mayor spoke before university audiences across the country sixteen times. In February 1968 Lindsay told students at the University of Oregon: "There is obviously much in our capacity to dissent from, to rebel against." Lindsay saw three types of American youth. The first group, worthy of his scorn, were the "basically apathetic and malleable" youth who would "follow the path of the mass of students in each decade before, those whose dreams and values have not surpassed the bounds of personal economic and social success." The second group were those who repudiated materialism "in favor of the pursuit of a life that is flowery, melodious, colorful, and interdependent." This Lindsay found unsatisfactory because it led some into a "life dependent upon drugs," and for others "an inward retreat from the travails of society."[75]

Then there were those who followed a third course, those who were what Lindsay termed the "prophetic minority," after the title of a 1966 book by the journalist Jack Newfield. "They are the activists—or, perhaps, more precisely, the protesters," said Lindsay. "They react to the world not by turning their backs upon it, but by facing it honestly and forthrightly—as it is. . . . Those who would rebel against the conventions of our society have sound grounds, in logic and in conscience, for doing so. I should remind you, however, that the rebel who overturns society's conventions, must take on the corresponding obligation to construct new and better conventions in their place."

Lindsay chose to embrace the country's youth rebellion, though with some reservations. While encouraging the rebels, he sought to temper their enthusiasm and instill a measure of responsibility in them. The encouragement part came easy to Lindsay, but the tempering part proved more difficult.

The Lindsay administration did little to keep order in the city's public spaces. It seemed to forget about the "obligations" of which the mayor had spoken. In August 1968, the *Times* ran a devastating article entitled "Derelicts and Hippies are Making Washington Square a Nightmare Area." Monsignor James Searson, of New York University's Holy Trinity Chapel on Washington Square, complained, "We've lost pascal candles, acolyte benches, and tabernacle candles made in Spain and costing $500. They've stolen everything but the cross. We've had defecation in the confessionals and one case of attempted rape. Last April, a man dragged a girl into a confessional and tried to attack her." According to Monsignor Searson, walking through Washington Square Park was "like walking through an open ward of a mental institution." Drunks and drug addicts regularly invaded his services.

At another church in Greenwich Village, Our Lady of Pompeii on Bleecker Street, Father Guido Caverzan complained about finding people using the confessional as a urinal, of drug addicts "lying in the sanctuary screaming and crying," and of men exposing themselves to parishioners during services. Farther up Sixth Avenue, at St. Joseph's Church, Monsignor Timothy Herlihy complained that donations placed in the church's poor boxes were constantly being pilfered and that the church's steps were "the filthiest place I've ever seen in my life" with drunks and vagrants congregating there, leaving beer and food and relieving themselves on the columns or church door. Monsignor Herlihy summed up the attitude in the Village: "People feel they can do whatever they like here, that they have absolute license, and to hell with the community." The Lindsay administration, according to Herlihy, seemed to feel that "everything goes." The city's public spaces became ungovernable, leading people to consider the whole city ungovernable. The Lindsay administration seemed unconcerned and unable to deal with what came to be known as quality-of-life issues.[76]

Three years later, the journalist Clark Whelton painted an even darker picture of Greenwich Village in the *Village Voice*:

> Greenwich Village—lovely, liberal Greenwich Village of the charming streets and historic brownstones—is poised on the edge of disaster. . . . Drug freaks and high pressure panhandlers huddle on the corners along Sixth Avenue. Spoiled, arrogant teenagers from the suburbs, who use the Village as a vomitorium for all the hatred they've been forced to swallow by other people in other places, roar through Sheridan Square in daddy's Buick, looking for another after-hours club and another source of drug information when they find that the Haven is full. Addicts from Harlem take the "A" train down to the Village because heroin is cheaper on Waverly Place than on 125th Street, and the women in Washington Square are easy to intimidate with accusations of racial prejudice. Burglars, muggers, and stick-up teams have learned that any neighborhood which will tolerate all of the above has got to be ripe for the picking.

The Village had deteriorated so much in the last five years that, according to Whelton, New York and other cities were "poised on the brink of being abandoned by the people who make them work." Whelton also reported that the increase in crime and disorder was accompanied by the rumor that police were told to ease up on arrests in order to keep the area cool. Whelton discounted the rumor, attributing it to policemen still angry at Lindsay for meddling in police business. He likened this belief to the rumor of alligators in the city's sewers. Both had become "part of the official mythology of New York."[77]

One person who represented the counterculture in New York City was Abbie Hoffman. A mentally unstable thirty-one-year-old, Hoffman moved to the East Village in 1966 from Massachusetts. There he formed a loose-knit group of hippies known as the Yippies (Youth International Party), which combined the political sensibilities of Fidel Castro with the whimsy of Andy Warhol. Lindsay's aide Ted Mastroianni was head of the Lower East Side Task Force (a unit of the Urban Action Task Force) and worked together with Hoffman. Mastroianni likened Hoffman to a Charlie Chaplin figure with a "great sense of theater" whose goal was to "make fun of the system."

Hoffman modeled his troupe after a group of San Francisco hippies called the Diggers. He set up the "Free Store" in the East Village, which provided secondhand clothes and used household products for free. Unfortunately the Free Store effort soon collapsed. According to Hoffman, "One week it was assaulted by everyone. First, a group of Negroes threw a garbage can through the window. Then another one came in with a hammer. . . . Then some

Puerto Ricans came in and grabbed a girl, took her out, and raped her. The whole place is one big amphetamine trip. There's no community. No one can make it here." The underside of life in the East Village was drug abuse, motorcycle gang warfare, and violence.[78]

The Lindsay administration used the same theory on Hoffman as it used with black militants in the city's ghettos. They would try to co-opt him and get him to help them cool down the tense East Village. He and some of his compatriots were put on the city payroll. Hoffman was a "community liaison" for the Urban Action Task Force, receiving $100 weekly from the Lower East Side Youth Council (as did his compatriots Jerry Rubin and James Fourrat). Similarly, Captain Joseph Fink, the commander of the Ninth Precinct in the East Village, worked closely with Hoffman. According to Barry Gottehrer, Hoffman and Fink "had an informal agreement that Abbie could have a good deal of leeway if he didn't put Fink in the position of having to arrest him. They negotiated around the letter of the law, and Abbie would get his hippie demonstrations, his street theater, and his publicity, and Fink was spared the threat of having to arrest dozens of hippies daily on all kinds of charges. Fink wouldn't put up with smoking dope in his precinct house, but his police didn't go out of their way to find it on a hippie either."[79]

Street theater was Hoffman's stock in trade. On August 24, 1967, Hoffman and a number of Yippies went to the visitor's gallery above the trading floor of the New York Stock Exchange and threw hundreds of dollar bills onto the floor of the exchange, temporarily disrupting trading. Sometimes Hoffman would push the limits in front of Fink. When a group of blacks were arrested in Tompkins Square Park for smoking pot, Hoffman, tripping on acid, went to the stationhouse to complain to Fink. He repeatedly yelled, "Diggery is niggery" and told Fink, "If you thought I was a nigger you'd arrest me. I feel like a nigger, and you've got to do it. If a nigger can get arrested, why can't I?" Fink refused to take the bait and went back to his office with Hoffman following him. Once in Fink's office, Hoffman, in a psychedelic rage, kicked in a large trophy case filled with the precinct's medals, plaques, and awards. The trophy case was Fink's prized possession and the sight of its destruction sent the captain into a rage of his own. Finally, Fink arrested Hoffman.[80]

In another incident, Abbie Hoffman and his friends claimed to have created a special foam which, when applied to a person's skin, would make that person automatically have sex with the next person, male or female, the "foamed" person next came into contact with. Believing the Yippies were master chemists because of their drug use, some people took this news seriously. Hoffman called the press down to the East Village for a demonstration. A young couple, who were clearly part of the performance (although this was not known by the press), walked down the street when they were set upon by some Yippies and sprayed with the special foam. They immediately took their clothes off and proceeded to have sex on the sidewalk at Seventh Street and Avenue A. Later, Hoffman took his foam to the local police precinct house, where he sprayed the rough-looking on-duty sergeant. The poor sergeant began to moan and yell, panicked at the thought that the foam would automatically force him to have sex with the police lieutenant standing nearby.[81]

The foam incident was a clever, though ultimately innocent, joke. But not all of Hoffman's pranks were as harmless. In March 1968, the Yippies wanted to celebrate the Ides of March. Instead, they passed over the Ides (March 15), and chose a day a week later, March 22, to hold a "Yip-in" at Grand Central Terminal. A leaflet advertised the Yip-in as "a spring mating service celebrating the equinox, a back-scratching party, a roller skating ink, a theater . . . with you as performer and audience. Get acquainted with other Yippies, for other Yiptivities and Chicago YIP Festival this summer bring: Flowers, Beads, Music, Radios, Pillows, Eats, Love and Peace. Meet later on at Sheep Meadow to Yip Up the Sun."

Hoffman informed Ted Mastroianni about the Yip-in, but the administration was convinced the event would draw few people. What they did not know was that WBAI, a public radio station that had served as an unofficial town crier for the counterculture, was advertising the Yip-in over its airwaves. In addition to Hoffman's rag-tag band of East Village anarchists, druggies, and hipsters, hundreds of desperately emulative suburban teenagers also showed up to join the festivities at the cavernous station. Hoffman told a *Times* reporter (who quoted a "Mrs. Abby Hoffman") that if the Lindsay administration, having been forewarned, "wanted to stop us, they could have had the police shut the doors" to Grand Central.[82]

An estimated 3,000 to 6,000 people crammed the main hall of Grand Central Terminal at midnight, March 22. One observer described how "balloons floated to the blue-domed roof of the waiting room and so many young people gathered, in all kinds of hippie garb, in capes and granny skirts and velvet coats and top hats and one or two in tails, many in blue jeans, in floppy hats and bells and necklaces." The city was unprepared for such a massive gathering in the very public Grand Central. Barry Gottehrer said that by the time he and other officials "reached Grand Central most of our options were gone. Garelik was there, and a platoon of policemen were ready to see action. The longer we waited, the more people joined the party, and the more restive the police grew." Gottehrer describes Garelik and other police officials as "physically restraining" their men while Hoffman's minions were writing "Fuck you" on the walls of Grand Central and railroad officials were "bellowing in rage." Hoffman pleaded with Gottehrer for a megaphone so that he could control the crowd. Gottehrer was furious with Hoffman: "Abbie, you blew it. Why didn't you bring your own damn megaphone and clear this place an hour ago? Look at this mess. This thing is so fucked up now I don't know what we can do about it."[83]

The *Village Voice*'s Don McNeill said the Yip-in's "promotion was as heavy as the planning was weak." Barry Gottehrer wrote of "naive young people" who "had expected a big party that was presumably well planned for them; instead, Abbie had no plan or program for the people once they arrived." Grand Central became "a sea of heads" that increasingly drew angrier and angrier. At around one in the morning, firecrackers and cherry bombs exploded. What really angered the police was when one youth climbed to the top of the information booth in the center of Grand Central and unrolled a banner with the slogan "Up Against the Wall, Motherfucker." The largely apolitical protest soon turned toward political themes as shouts of "Long, hot summer" and "Burn, baby, burn" were heard. Then someone broke the hands off the clock above the information booth and spray-painted "Peace Now" on its face. Gottehrer and Garelik then decided to send in the police to clear out Grand Central.[84]

Given orders to clear the area, the police did so with nightsticks flailing. Witnesses later claimed that police gave no orders to disperse before taking action. Ted Mastroianni recounts how "a wedge of cops came and all I remember was seeing this wave of people falling in front of me and it was almost like this avalanche of people." Don McNeill was thrown against a glass door despite (or perhaps because of) his press pass. He needed five stitches in his head. In the end, fifty-seven people were arrested and twenty-three were taken to the hospital.[85]

Alan Levine, of the New York Civil Liberties Union, called the police action "the most extraordinary display of unprovoked police brutality I've ever seen outside of Mississippi." Nat Hentoff called the incident yet another case of police rioting. But the Yip-in was doomed to degenerate into anarchy from the start. As McNeill wrote, the actions of Hoffman bordered "on gross incompetence and irresponsibility." The Lindsay administration also deserves blame for neither discouraging the demonstration nor coordinating it. Thousands of kids were crammed into Grand Central at the same time hundreds of commuters were trying to catch the last trains back to the suburbs. Again New York's public spaces were held hostage for a night to the whims of a man like Abbie Hoffman, who cared little about the consequences of his actions. When things went badly, the police were called in and predictably inflicted their own punishment against the youths they so despised. Deep down, the grievances of the police were against the Lindsay administration, whose members they felt were "soft" on antiwar protesters, black militants, and hippies.[86]

Even after the Grand Central debacle, the Lindsay administration continued to fund Hoffman. In the summer of 1968, Barry Gottehrer, believing Hoffman had "credibility with young people that we needed," hired him to write a pamphlet "explaining where there were safe places to stay, what hospitals to call if they had a bad drug trip, what clinics would help if they got VD. Knowing Abbie, I figured he would also give them some information we did not think they should have." Aware of the political risk of hiring Hoffman, Gottehrer worked hard to cover the paper trail linking Hoffman to Lindsay. "I worked out an elaborate arrangement with the minister of a church in Greenwich Village," he recounted. "I agreed to pay a certain amount of money from our private funds for what we described very generally as a publication, the church subcontracted the project out to a writer and then had it printed. I paid the church and the church paid all the bills. The deal was arranged around the premise that the writer would be Abbie."

Gottehrer went over the Hoffman funding with Mary Lindsay, but discussed it with her only in hypothetical terms. He claims he went away from the meeting convinced that John Lindsay would have backed him up if the book's funding had become public. Hoffman later admitted that his book was funded by the city, saying he "made a deal that I would never tell where the money came from and it was an honest deal." With his characteristic mixture of humor and paranoia, Hoffman wrote: "Somewhere in New York in a safe deposit box are photostatic copies of all the check transactions between the City of New York, the in-between party and the printer. The Red Squad (Bureau of Special Services) knows all this and would like to use the evidence against Mayor Lindsay. If I ever get killed or convicted on serious charges in New York the photostatic copies go straight to the *Daily News*."[87]

Out of this subsidy came Hoffman's famous book *Fuck the System*. The book was a guide for young people to mooch their way through New York. It gave information on free food, clothes, money, rent, movies, as well as on drugs and sexually transmitted diseases. Hoffman's philosophy was a warped version of "Fun City." "What would happen if large numbers of people really decided to fuck the system?" he asked in the book. "What would happen if large numbers of people in the country started getting together . . . hustling free fish on Fulton Street and passing out brass washers to use in the laundromats and phones? . . . What if this movement grew and busy salesmen sweating under the collar on a hot day decided to say fuck the system and headed for welfare? What if secretaries got tired of typing memos to the boss's girlfriend in triplicate and took to panhandling in the streets?" Hoffman ended his book with this disclaimer: "If you paid money for this manual you got screwed. It's absolutely free because it's yours. Think about it." In fact, the book should have been absolutely free because it had been completely subsidized by the taxpayers of New York City.[88]

Gottehrer was anything but displeased with the book, which he called "everything I expected and more." Though he bemoaned the inclusion of information on panhandling and cheating the telephone company and Transit Authority, Gottehrer still found the book "perfect" and "hysterically funny." Years later, Hoffman went underground to escape a cocaine charge. When he resurfaced in 1980, Gottehrer wrote a letter to Manhattan District Attorney Robert Morgenthau on Hoffman's behalf, arguing for leniency. According to Gottehrer, the now-middle-aged hippie had "played an extremely constructive and positive role in helping to build bridges between city government and the radical young who flowed into New York's Lower East Side." He called Hoffman "one of the most creative public advocates I had ever met. His creativity and commitment forced our government in New York and other governments to face up to the inequities of our society. While some may have questioned his methods, Abbie Hoffman forced us to think and forced us to respond." He concluded that Hoffman "gave much of himself to make our city and our country a better place in the 1960s and I hope that this will not be overlooked in reaching your decision."[89]

VIETNAM

Though John Lindsay had voiced questions about the war as early as 1965, his opposition had mostly been muted and equivocal. By 1968 that was no longer the case.

In a March 1968 speech to students at Queens College, Lindsay received what Richard Reeves of the *Times* called "one of the most enthusiastic receptions of his political career." The *Times* chose to give the speech a front-page, four-column story, though its headline, "Mayor Urges Youths to Aid War Resistance," was misleading: Lindsay was only urging "resistance movements" within the two major political parties. But the headline summed up what both Lindsay's supporters and detractors felt about him. Many American youths, disillusioned with the war and unwilling to serve in the army, saw Lindsay as a hero. Critics saw Lindsay as weakening support for the war and American soldiers.[90]

In 1968, Lindsay began taking his antiwar message on the road. He told students at the University of Denver in March 1968 that U.S. policy in Vietnam "contravenes our ideals and heritage. . . . The [Johnson] administration apparently is willing to devastate a country in order to salvage its own pride. . . . I think it's wrong to send more American men to fight and perhaps to die in an unwanted war. I think the course we have followed toward more bloodshed, more destruction, should be abandoned." He prodded the young students toward political activism. If they wanted to end the war in Vietnam, they should volunteer for candidates who shared their position. "The resistance movement," Lindsay told the crowd, "got haircuts, shaved, put on ties, and went into politics." Lindsay attacked the more radical forms of antiwar activism, such as draft-card burning, as "negative, bizarre, and often self-indulgent methods of dissent."[91]

On Saturday April 27, 1968, Lindsay faced a dilemma. New York City was home to both an antiwar demonstration at the Sheep Meadow in Central Park and a so-called Loyalty Day parade up Fifth Avenue in support of the troops in Vietnam. Senator Jacob Javits and Comptroller Mario Procaccino both marched in the Loyalty Day parade, but the mayor dropped by only for the last ten minutes of the march. Signs welcoming Lindsay included: "Lindsay for Dogcatcher" and "Hypocrite Lindsay Go to Your Pink and Yellow Friends at Central Park." Later in the day, Lindsay spoke to a much more friendly crowd, the almost 90,000 antiwar protesters. Considering there were fewer than 3,000 marchers at the Loyalty Day parade, it was increasingly clear that there was more political weight on the side of the antiwar protesters.[92]

Later, in the summer of 1968, Lindsay took his antiwar message to the Republican Party convention, hoping to nudge his party toward a more dovish stance. In testimony before the party's committee on resolutions, Lindsay repeated his belief that the war in Vietnam "calls into severe question our right to inflict destruction on a developing country that for decades has been fighting for its own independence against both Asian and Western armies. The course we have been following in Vietnam, I submit, has not been one of a great nation." Like many, Lindsay was still unclear about what he would do about the war. He told the unsympathetic Republicans that he "never believed that the United States can, or should, withdraw unilaterally from Vietnam. Neither have I believed that constant escalation would achieve a military victory."[93]

In an open memo on Vietnam to the convention delegates, Lindsay tried to expand on his views on ending the war. He reiterated his belief that South Vietnam's fate should be decided by South Vietnam alone. A workable peace, in Lindsay's opinion, was one that assured the departure of both American and North Vietnamese troops from the South. The first step along this road was for the United States to halt the bombing of North Vietnam. Lindsay also wanted a bilateral halt to the escalation of war in the south and an end to military incursions into Laos. Lastly, Lindsay called for specific proposals for troop withdrawal in order to induce North Vietnam to join with the United States in demilitarizing South Vietnam. Of course, Lindsay's whole plan was contingent upon the belief that North Vietnam wanted to withdraw from South Vietnam, even in the wake of an American withdrawal. In 1968, Lindsay avoided the rhetoric of antiwar activists and sought to frame his critiques in the guise of rational foreign policy objectives. Soon, though, Lindsay's rhetoric would grow sharper as the antiwar movement gained in strength.

Very little traditional Cold War thinking entered into Lindsay's foreign policy statements. Rather than directly attacking the Cold War foreign policy of the postwar years, Lindsay seemed to pretend it did not exist. He complained that the United States rationalized its involvement in Vietnam by defining it as protecting a small nation from subversion, yet "the United Nations, comprising dozens of countries comparable to Vietnam, has never endorsed our intervention." Lindsay objected to the fact that American foreign policy in the Third World "clung to the status quo when every natural force was challenging the status quo. We have aligned ourselves with stability in situations where stability meant suppression. We have supported the most conservative, sometimes dictatorial regimes in countries that were seething with popular demand for progressive reform."[94]

Lindsay saw the war in Vietnam and the crisis of the cities as inexorably linked. He told a group of Harvard students in April 1968, "For the truth, I'm afraid, is that we cannot achieve either the cities or the society we would like as long as we continue the war in Vietnam. We cannot spend more than $24 billion a year in Vietnam and still rebuild our cities. We cannot speak of non-violence at home when we are displacing, maiming, and killing thousands of Asians for the professed purpose of protecting the peace in a land half way across the world."[95]

THE YEAR 1968 SAW JOHN LINDSAY carefully navigating the waters of "dissensus" among minorities, disillusioned youth, and antiwar activists. Many of these forces would converge in April 1968 on the Upper Manhattan campus of Columbia University, threatening the authority of the city's leading institution of higher learning and posing a thorny dilemma for the Lindsay administration and the police.

COLUMBIA UNIVERSITY, 1968:
A SCHOOL UNDER SIEGE

"Up against the wall, motherfucker! This is a
stick-up."

—From a poem by LeRoi Jones

The crisis at Columbia University in the spring of 1968 symbolized the
tumult and turmoil of the late sixties. Since the university is a private
institution, the student takeover at Columbia was not a direct challenge for
the Lindsay administration. John Lindsay, though sympathetic to the growing complaints of student radicals, wisely stayed out of direct involvement in
the crisis. But he couldn't stay completely uninvolved.

The original catalyst for the crisis at Columbia was the university's proposal to build a gym in Morningside Park, which as a city park was under
the jurisdiction of the Parks Department. The plan was hotly protested, and
the policies of Lindsay's Parks Department helped fan the controversy over
the proposed Columbia gym. And once the protests broke out, a number of
Lindsay's top aides were directly involved in the negotiations at Columbia
and were a presence on the campus for the entire time. The controversial behavior of the police at Columbia can only be understood within the context
of the tensions between the New York Police Department and the Lindsay
administration. The student takeover at Columbia was yet another in a long
line of crises that bewildered John Lindsay's New York—and another crack
in the armor of postwar liberalism.

PLANNING FOR A GYM

In 1897, Columbia University moved four miles uptown, from its Midtown
campus to Morningside Heights. This was before the construction of the

229

subway, so the neighborhood was relatively undeveloped and the university had the opportunity to build its own self-contained campus on land purchased from the Bloomingdale Insane Asylum. After the IRT subway line that had been built uptown beneath Broadway opened in 1904, the neighborhood developed quickly. The Columbia campus was soon surrounded by an urban neighborhood of apartment buildings that left little empty land.[1]

The southern boundary of Morningside Heights, at 110th Street, is topographically flat and of a piece with the northern stretches of the Upper West Side. On its other three sides the neighborhood sits high upon a rocky plateau (hence the name). To the east, the cliffs of Morningside Park drop off sharply some one hundred feet to the gridlike street pattern of central Harlem. Frederick Law Olmsted and Calvert Vaux designed Morningside Park, completing their work in 1887. It runs north for thirteen blocks, almost three quarters of a mile, and is roughly one block wide. The majority of the park consists of a heavily wooded, rocky slope that gives the park a wild, untamed feeling. Olmsted described the planned park in 1873: "The only surface within it not sharply inclined are two small patches lying widely apart, against the northeast and southeast corners respectively; most of the remainder being precipitous hill side, formed by the rounded face of a ledge of gneiss, difficult, unsafe, and in parts, impracticable to travel over."[2]

Safety was always a problem in Morningside Park—even in 1873, when Olmsted wrote, "Argument is hardly necessary to prove that by no appropriate treatment could a ground having the natural features of Morningside Park, be made a safe and respectable place of resort at night." In 1965 the Lindsay campaign wrote a position paper on parks, in which Morningside Park was described as "number *one* on a list of the 12 most feared parks in the US . . . [and] has rightfully been called 'a raw no-man's land between a ghetto and affluence.' " Diana Trilling wrote that in her many years of living in Morningside Heights she never knew "anyone, black or white, who has dared use the park even for a short-cut, let alone for relaxation."[3]

The beginning of any discussion of the 1968 Columbia crisis starts with the university's plan to build a gymnasium in Morningside Park. In the 1950s Columbia sought to upgrade its athletic facilities to keep up with its Ivy League competitors, and not having its own land to build on it looked to Morningside Park. In the early 1950s, the university entered into an agreement with the city to construct a seven-acre athletic field on the southern edge of the park. The university would use the fields on weekdays during the school year, and the Harlem community would use the fields on weekends and in the summer. Under the agreement, the university also undertook to organize athletic programs for Harlem children. But what the university really needed was a new gymnasium.

The deal to build a gym in Morningside Park had its inception in 1958, when university officials approached Parks Commissioner Robert Moses with a plan. Columbia chose not to demolish buildings in the neighborhood to make way for a new gym, since that would have meant displacing large numbers of residents. Instead, the university proposed that the city would lease to the university 2.1 acres of the park, on which it would build its gym. On the ground floor would be a community gym. Above this would rise the university's gym, climbing up the steep, rocky ledge of the park toward an entrance on Morningside Drive. The state legislature, the governor, the City Council, and the Board of Estimate would all have to approve the fifty-year lease. The City Council unanimously passed a home rule message asking Albany for passage of the bill, which Mayor Wagner signed. In February 1960, bills were introduced in both houses of the state legislature to authorize the leasing of the park land to Columbia. (The state Senate bill was introduced by James Watson, a black representative from the Morningside–West Harlem district.)[4]

In March, both houses of the state legislature unanimously passed the bill, and Governor Rockefeller signed it in April. In July, the city's Board of Estimate held public hearings on the gymnasium. Speaking in favor of the gym were representatives of the Adult-Youth Association, the Grant-Morningside Neighborhood Group, and the Morningside Citizens Committee. In opposition to the gym were representatives of the Fine Arts Federation, the Municipal Arts Society, the Citizens Union, St. Luke's Hospital, and the Cathedral of St. John the Divine. The Board of Estimate approved the lease and Manhattan Borough President Edward Dudley signed off on the fifty-year lease. In August 1961, Columbia's president, Grayson Kirk, and the new Parks Commissioner, Newbold Morris, signed the deal. It granted Columbia the air rights over the 2.1 acres of parkland in exchange for the upkeep of the community gym (estimated to cost Columbia between $5,000 and $10,000 per year) and $3,000 per year in rent.

Over the next few years, questions about the project were raised in a number of quarters, and soon it was surrounded by controversy. In 1966, *Columbia College Today* described the initial innocence and goodwill behind the university's decision to build the gym.

> On the surface the idea of constructing the gymnasium . . . seems remarkably lacking in controversy. . . . It is to be built on a huge rock outcropping; so almost no trees or grass will be disturbed. By using the park site instead of a city block, no residents of Morningside Heights will be displaced. Also by using the park site, Morningside Park, for decades an untended no man's land of broken bottles, crumbling, dangerous cement stairs, and unpruned trees and bushes, would be made clean, safe, and horticulturally lovely again. . . . And, the "Chinese Wall" effect of the deserted park between Morningside and Harlem will be partially eliminated and the park turned into an interracial meeting place full of activity. Perhaps best of all, the community would be given a fine indoor facility.[5]

The *New York Times* had an expressed belief that city park land should be inviolate, but in the case of the Columbia gym it made an exception, praising it in a 1961 editorial: "Morningside Park is one of the all-too-many 'danger spots' among our parks where incidents of crime and rowdyism recur. . . . The character of the entire park . . . could be helped by this gymnasium." In the same year, in her seminal work, *The Death and Life of Great American Cities,* the social and urban critic Jane Jacobs called Columbia's plan for a gym in Morningside Park a "constructive step," noting that if the university could add activities like music and shows to the park, it "could convert a dreadful neighborhood liability into an outstanding neighborhood asset."[6]

But Columbia waited too long to get started with the project. Under the terms of the lease, the university had until August 1967 to break ground on the gym, a deadline that was later extended. According to the journalist Roger Starr, the reasoning behind the delay was that the university wanted to raise money for the gym, feeling that it would be easier to get funds before the building was built than after it was completed. Starr believed that the university already had enough money in 1961 to build the gym, whose cost had been estimated then at $6 million. The delay caused an increase in costs of the building to $13 million (the university had raised only an additional $5.2 million by 1968, causing an overall economic loss on the delay). Worse, it was also a huge political blunder. In 1961, the political will was present both in the university and in the city. But there were already signs of trouble.

Some critics began taking issue with the proposed design of the gym. During the late 1950s and early 1960s, Columbia had engaged in a building boom on campus. Each new building was designed in the uninspiring, modernist architecture of the early postwar years. Such buildings stood in marked contrast to the elegant Beaux Arts style of the older McKim, Mead & White buildings. In 1959, Columbia architecture students termed the style of Ferris Booth Hall, the new student center, "bad Miami Beach decor." (The building was demolished in 1996.) In 1962, students and faculty picketed the ground-breaking for the new business school building. The gym would become just another piece of monstrous, modern architecture invading Columbia's campus. The architecture critic Ada Louise Huxtable argued that the gym was "certainly not going to be a particularly sensitive building." It was a "blockbuster," and its "huge masonry build will never blend with its rustic setting."[7]

And in 1966, Columbia encountered a vastly different political environment. First, the civil rights movement mobilized greater political action among blacks. It increased the sensitivity of the black community to both real and perceived insensitivity on the part of the white community. Motives that looked progressive and benevolent in 1961 looked more suspect by 1966. Some blacks were fearful of the encroachment of the predominantly white university into Harlem. Younger Harlem politicians, like state Senator Basil Patterson and state Assemblyman Percy Sutton, were less inclined to go along with such deals. These two men introduced legislation in Albany in 1966 to repeal the 1960 agreement by the state legislature to grant the lease to Columbia.

In many people's eyes, the gym was becoming a symbol of a more disturbing trend in American society. To critics like Huxtable, the Columbia gym revealed "the deep and bitter split and many-layered misunderstanding between a privileged urban university and an unprivileged community." Harlem leaders and radical students at Columbia began calling the planned facility "Gym Crow." The top floors of the gym were reserved for the university, while the bottom section was for the Harlem community. The university calculated that 88 percent of the building would be reserved for the university while only 12 percent was set aside for the community. There would be two separate entrances for the gym, with no interior connection between the two gyms. Harlem residents would not have access to the other 88 percent of the gym. University students would enter from Morningside Drive, above the park, while community residents would enter from Morningside Avenue, on the bottom of the park. C. Richard Hatch, the executive director of the Architect's Renewal Committee in Harlem, wrote that the entrance for "the Harlem community is approached from the lower level through a separate and unequal entrance." Two entrances, opponents argued, separate but unequal. The *New Republic's* James Ridgeway called it an "apartheid gym," and the journalist Roger Kahn called the gym "subtly racist."[8]

Another change in the political environment occurred when John Lindsay became mayor and promised a new way of doing business. Lindsay's campaign paper on the city's park system, written by Thomas Hoving, made specific mention of the Columbia gym. The Lindsay administration promised, if Lindsay was elected, to "control further encroachment" on the park. "Columbia University's plans for the erection of a gymnasium must be restudied to determine whether or not this next step in the encroachment process is valid," the paper warned. After the election, very possibly alluding to the Parks Department deal with Columbia, Lindsay told Nat Hentoff, "Tom Hoving says he feels like a new cook coming into a kitchen where there's a huge stove on which the old cook left a lot of pots simmering. Every time he picks up a cover, he feels like dropping it down again immediately—the stench is so bad. Some of the contracts that were let out—and not only in the Parks Department—are appalling!"[9]

No man was more associated with the growing opposition to the Columbia gym than Tom Hoving, whom John Lindsay named his first parks commissioner. Hoving's opposition was rooted in three basic beliefs. First, the surrounding neighborhood should always determine how to use the parkland. Second, since parkland in the city was scarce, it should not be developed. Third, public park land should never revert to private hands. "The gymnasium happens to be the only example in the entire history of the Parks Department when a significant part of public land was going for a very long period of time for a private institution, for their private usage," Hoving argued. "It's a very, very bad precedent." Hoving decided to go after the Columbia gym with a "total vengeance." He had already killed both Huntington Hartford's plans to build a café on the southern edge of Central Park and the proposed Adele Rosenthal Levy memorial in Riverside Park.[10]

The Columbia administration's attitude riled Hoving: "I was amazed, annoyed, and more than that I was angered." At a press conference early in the Lindsay administration, Hoving declared, "I think the gymnasium project is disgraceful. The public should get more than twelve percent of this particular pie." He promised that he would "try and persuade the Columbia people to change the site." Although he did not think he could stop the gym, Hoving believed if "we are going to have to live with this big ugly structure built on community land, then the community and not Columbia should get the most benefit." By April 1966, Hoving was quoted in a neighborhood newspaper as saying, "I am dead set against this gymnasium and I will fight as hard as I can to stop it."[11]

None of this endeared Hoving to Columbia's administration. Roger Starr noted that university officials "saw Mr. Hoving as a double agent—a city official sworn to uphold his government's laws and to execute its responsibilities, yet who was quoted as having said he would defeat, *by extra-legal means if necessary*, a contract entered into by that same city government." One Columbia trustee, Benjamin Buttenwieser, called Hoving the "real villain of the piece. He fanned the flames in no uncertain fashion, claiming it was a misuse of park land for a private university to put up a gymnasium." In October 1967, Columbia did agree to include an Olympic-size pool in the community gym in response to community protests and the prodding of Hoving and his successor, August Heckscher.[12]

Such a concession, though, did little to ease tensions over the gym. In the heady days of civil rights protests, the rhetoric by opponents of the gym intensified and took on heavy racial connotations. A January 1966 editorial in the *Amsterdam News* said the construction of the proposed gym would be "a slap in the face to every black man, woman, and child in Harlem." The paper sounded the theme that would ring throughout the Columbia campus two years later: the building of the gym was a "bigoted act."[13]

Yet the opinion among ordinary Harlem residents was more divided. When the college student newspaper, the *Columbia Spectator*, polled Harlem residents in November 1967 about the gym, it found that more than half had not even heard about it. Of those who had heard of it, almost half supported its construction. A poll of Harlem residents commissioned by *New York* magazine found that 48 percent of those questioned favored the construction of the gym. Twenty-six percent of respondents were opposed and 27 percent were undecided or did not know about the project. Of those supporting the gym, 58 percent believed that the gym facilities should be equally shared between the community and the university, and 34 percent supported the gym unconditionally.[14]

Whatever opinions average blacks had of the gym, black militants fanned the flames of racial tension surrounding the issue in Morningside Heights. In December 1967, H. Rap Brown, the man who coined the slogan "Burn, baby, burn," came to Columbia to speak at a rally against the gym. "If they build the first story blow it up," Brown told his audience. "If they sneak back at night and build three stories burn it down. And if they get nine stories built, it's yours. Take it over, and maybe we'll let them in on weekends." State Senator Basil Patterson, who shared the platform with H. Rap Brown, defended his appearance by saying, "I don't agree with Brown, but I would stand with anyone against that racist gym." Patterson, a supposedly "moderate" black leader, was quoted in a neighborhood newspaper mouthing the same sentiments as the radical Brown, if only in more careful language. "Columbia shall not build a gym in this park," Patterson said. "Let the first bulldozers come here and you'll know what we mean."[15]

Soon after the April 1968 student takeover, Columbia appointed an independent Fact-Finding Commission to study the disturbances. The commission's conclusions were that the gym opponents' rhetoric glossed over a few pertinent realities. First, it was unrealistic to expect Columbia to share its facilities with the community. The distinguished panel, headed by the Harvard law professor Archibald Cox, concluded: "We know of no university willing to surrender control over major facilities used by its students." Second, the division of the area of the gym between university and community use was irrelevant, since "the size of the building the University constructs for itself has little or nothing to do with the adequacy of the facilities the community receives in return for the use of the land." [16]

Third, the Cox Commission pointed out that the separate entrances for the university and the community were based on geography, not racial prejudice. Because the community gym was on the ground floor of the park, it made sense to make the entrance at the bottom of the park. Had Columbia made one entrance for the university and the community on top of Morningside Park, Harlem residents would have had to walk one long block up a steep incline on 110th Street and then another three blocks up Morningside Drive. Lastly, the community was receiving a brand-new gym completely free in what had been a dangerous, underutilized park. After the construction of the gym, almost twenty-four acres of the parkland would still be left.

The growing controversy over the gym brought up some troubling questions. Columbia had a legal deal with the city to construct their gym in Morningside Park. Roger Starr pointed out, "If contractual relationships between governments and private parties cannot be extended longer than the favor of the public, who will enter into contracts with the government? And if governments can reshape contracts retrospectively, to win public favor, why should they remain hampered by a Constitutional restriction against reshaping laws retrospectively, to make unpopular persons guilty of offenses for acts that were not illegal when committed?"[17]

The Cox Commission found that "much of the difficulty appears to be traceable to the conflict between, on the one hand, the older commercial philosophy that the acquisition of land is purely a matter of financial power in the market place and, on the other hand, the newer emphasis upon community renewal, egalitarianism, and social cooperation." Despite this, the commission's ultimate conclusion on the gym was very clear: "The Commission finds that there was no impropriety in the original project, and that the University acted in complete good faith in negotiating an agreement with the Parks Department which was considered fair to both the University and the community." The Columbia administration's maneuvers surrounding the gym were carried out in good faith," said Ada Louise Huxtable, adding, "It is not the product of a monstrous and evil deviousness ascribed to the university by its enemies. The institutional mentality is not diabolical. It is simply grossly imperceptive. It has meant well and behaved with consummate wrongheadedness." Even Commissioner Hoving testified before the commission that "his review of the Parks Department files revealed no evidence of fraud or undue influence in connection with the negotiation of the lease." [18]

Still, the Cox Commission believed that the real problem surrounding the gym "was whether there could be genuine understanding of the underlying needs and aspirations the socially conscious were seeking to express." Columbia had angered many residents of Harlem and Morningside Heights with its attitude toward the outside community. Amalia Betanzos, a member of the Riverside Democratic Club and later a Lindsay aide, said the university operated in a "very high-handed attitude" toward its neighbors. Most colleges—whether urban, rural, or suburban—have strained "town-gown" relations. But in New York City, such tensions were magnified.[19]

PRELUDE TO A TAKEOVER

At their core, concerns about the new gym were connected to the university's expanding real estate holdings in the Morningside Heights area, an action taken in response to the deterioration of the neighborhood. Jane Jacobs noted that by the early 1950s, "Morningside Heights was becoming a slum so swiftly, the surly kind of slum in which people fear to walk the streets, that the situation posed a crisis for the institutions" in the neighborhood, including Columbia, Union Theological Seminary, and the Julliard School of Music. Beginning in the 1930s, the large apartments of Morningside

Heights were divided up into smaller units. During World War II, the blocks between West 110th and 113th Streets and Amsterdam Avenue and Broadway were placed off limits to Navy midshipmen training at Columbia because of the plethora of prostitutes working out of the buildings. In 1958, the *Times* wrote in apocalyptic terms about how "the cancer of slum living has spread through all Morningside Heights, driving out the good and the decent, dragging other housing down to its level, despoiling the schools and turning side streets and parks into fearsome places." In response, an urban renewal project was undertaken to tear down the tenements in the northern part of the neighborhood and replace them with middle-class and public housing. Even this did not stem the tide, and the neighborhood deteriorated further.[20]

Columbia had the choice either to leave its Morningside campus, as it had left Midtown some sixty years earlier, or to make its stand as an urban university. It chose the latter course. (Columbia was not the only city university faced with such a choice; in 1973, New York University abandoned its uptown campus in the Bronx, designed by Stanford White, and sold it to the City University of New York.) Columbia decided to stabilize the neighborhood by buying up apartment buildings in the area and converting them for use by the university community.

During the 1960s, Columbia purchased over one hundred buildings, transforming itself into one of the largest landlords in the city. Other Morningside Heights institutions—Barnard College, Union Theological Seminary, and the Jewish Theological Seminary—also purchased neighborhood apartment buildings. Many of the apartments were single-room occupancy buildings (SRO), once-elegant buildings whose spacious apartments had been divided up during the 1930s and 1940s. By the 1960s, the residents of these SROs were often elderly and poor, but many were vagrants, welfare families, drunks, drug users, and prostitutes. By one estimate, 7,500 people, many of them black and Puerto Rican, had been forced out of their apartments on Morningside Heights in the twenty years since the end of World War II. (By 1997, only two SROs still existed in the neighborhood.)

A good example of the tensions over Columbia's expansion was the 1966 purchase of the Bryn Mawr Hotel at Amsterdam Avenue and 121st Street by a company representing Columbia and other Morningside Heights institutions. Despite its high-sounding name, the Bryn Mawr was known throughout the area as a haven for prostitutes and drug dealers. Residents of the building filed suit against the university, accusing it of driving out nonwhites. Columbia eventually won the suit, demolished the Bryn Mawr, and built a large, modern (and aesthetically unappealing) dormitory for Barnard College students.[21]

In the mid-sixties, while fighting a battle over the character of its own neighborhood, Columbia also found itself in the middle of the growing debate over the war in Vietnam. Between 1965 and 1968, Columbia witnessed at least six major demonstrations on campus on war-related issues. In May 1965, radical students disrupted a Naval Reserve Officers Training Corps awards ceremony. When university security was unable to contain the protesters, the university administration called in the New York Police Department. The protesters eventually succeeded in their aims, as the Navy permanently abandoned the ceremony by 1968. In the next three years, recruiters from the CIA, Marine Corps, and Dow Chemical were harassed and intimidated by radical students. In response to these protests, President Kirk instituted a prohibition in September 1967 on protesting indoors: "Picketing or demonstrations may not by conducted within any University building." The prohibition was weakly enforced and only served to incite further the radical students. In addition, radical students and professors complained about Columbia's involvement with the Institute for Defense Analyses (IDA), a consortium of universities designed to carry out research for the military.

These tensions were bound to explode sooner or later. The catalyst for this inevitable explosion was the Students for a Democratic Society (SDS). In the mid-sixties, the Columbia chapter of SDS was riven by internal factions between those who sought a more intellectual, abstract radicalism (they called themselves the Praxis Axis) and those who wanted to take direct and forceful actions against the university (Action Faction). In the early spring of 1968, the latter faction won control of the group. That faction's leader, Mark Rudd, then in his junior year, was known for his confrontational style. At the April 9, 1968, Martin Luther King Jr. Memorial Service at the university chapel, St. Paul's Chapel, eleven hundred people packed the church to voice their grief. A handful of SDS members, led by Rudd, were prepared to take the opportunity to protest what they saw as the university's racism. When the university's vice president, David Truman, walked to the podium to deliver a few words, Rudd walked up the aisle of the chapel and took to the podium before him. Described by the Columbia sociologist Daniel Bell as "a tall, hulking, slack-faced young man with a prognathic jaw and blue-gray eyes so translucent that his gaze seems hypnotic," the Columbia junior used the solemn memorial service to deliver his denunciation of the university. "Dr. Truman and President Kirk are committing a moral outrage against the memory of Dr. King," Rudd said. "Columbia's administration is morally corrupt, unjust, and indulges in racist policies." Rudd then proclaimed that SDS would "protest this obscenity." After finishing his remarks, Rudd walked down the aisle and out of the chapel, followed by approximately forty acolytes. Truman then began his speech. After the ceremony, the university chaplain, John Cannon, announced that any student "who feels moved by the spirit of truth, who wishes to speak his mind, is able to speak in this chapel at any time."[22]

Three days later, President Kirk gave a speech at the University of Virginia in honor of Thomas Jefferson's 225th birthday. He sought to pinpoint the root cause of the student disturbances roiling campuses like Columbia. These protests, he argued, put the country in "a more perilous condition than at any time since the convulsive conflict between the states a century ago." Kirk saw the driving force behind the student radicals as an "inchoate Nihilism whose sole objectives are destructive."[23]

Kirk's speech brought a response from Mark Rudd in the form of a public letter. The letter was deliberately provocative and insulting, using profanity and a lack of respect as a weapon to attack university authority. Rudd criticized Kirk for living "in a very tight self-created dream world," which obstructed his view of reality. Rudd forcefully articulated the goals of radical students: "If we win, we will take control of your world, your corporation, your university and attempt to mold a world in which we and other people can live as human beings. Your power is directly threatened, since we will have to destroy that power before we take over." In many ways, Rudd's letter seemed to confirm Kirk's analysis of the nihilistic nature of student radicals. Rudd finished his letter with a quote from the poet LeRoi Jones that would become the theme of the Columbia protesters: "Up against the wall, motherfucker, this is a stick-up."[24]

THE PROTEST BEGINS

At noon on Tuesday, April 23, two groups of campus activists joined together to begin one of the most famous student protests of the 1960s. SDS joined with the Students Afro-American Society (SAS), which had previously been rather nonpolitical and had had little contact with the white SDS. According to the editors of the *Columbia Spectator*, "The blacks had never held a major political rally on campus and had generally left political agitation to the whites." In the 1968, there were only approximately 80 black students enrolled at Columbia. But on that day, nearly 500 students, black and white, gathered at the Sundial, a popular campus meeting point at the center of campus. They heard speeches from Nick Freudenberg and Ted Gold, of SDS, and Cicero Wilson, the president of SAS. Freudenberg called Kirk and Truman "war criminals." Wilson was mainly concerned with the Columbia gym and the university's relations with its Harlem neighbors. "This is Harlem Heights, not Morningside Heights," he told the mostly white crowd while waving his fist in the air. "What would you do if somebody came and took your property?" Wilson asked. He warned of the dangers to Columbia if racial violence erupted: "Do you think that this white citadel of hypocrisy will be bypassed if an insurrection occurs this summer?"[25]

Radical students weren't the only ones unhappy with the state of affairs at Columbia. The week before the April 23 protest, conservative students had distributed leaflets across the campus. Across the top of the flyer was written "TIRED?" twenty-one times. The message read in part:

Tired of a two-standard University that gives virtual immunity to SDS agitators while you are subject to immediate suspension if you toss a paper airplane out of a window? Tired of an environment where you cannot listen to a guest speaker and be sure he won't be physically harassed by SDS? Of an environment where your sacred privacy of worship is allowed to degenerate into political showmanship? Must one group be allowed to dictate this University's future? On Tuesday, April 23, SDS plans another demonstration against IDA. . . . Be there; lend your presence to a more healthy balance at Columbia University. Don't be there and you might as well hang forever. Can democracy survive at Columbia University? Will Mark Rudd be our next dean? Be there on the 23rd—prepared.

As radical students began massing at the Sundial, a group of about one hundred counterdemonstrators gathered on the steps of Low Library, near the Sundial, looking down uneasily at the protest, guarding the building from the radicals.[26]

Avoiding the counterprotesters massed on the front steps of Low Library, the SDS protesters headed for a side entrance. The university, expecting trouble, had locked the door. Then, a voice in the crowd encouraged protesters to march to the site of the Columbia gym, in nearby Morningside Park. The Cox Commission termed this early protest as "entirely haphazard." In fact, Rudd, the putative leader of the demonstration, seemed to have little control over it.

At the construction site in Morningside Park, protesters scuffled with police, and one student was taken into custody. A number of students then regrouped, returned to campus, and entered Hamilton Hall, which housed classrooms and the office of Dean Henry Coleman. Shortly thereafter, Coleman entered his office. Coleman remembers: "I came into Hamilton and there was a mob inside. It was a mixed group, not just SDS. . . . I had to make a decision on whether or not to go in, and it seemed to me that it was my office, my secretarial staff was in there and my initial reaction was that I should walk in." After Coleman entered his office, Mark Rudd is reported to have said: "Now we've got the Man where we want him. He can't leave unless he gives in to some of our demands." Dean Coleman was now a hostage inside his office. One radical student inside Hamilton recalled, "To reciprocate for Fred's detention [Fred was the student arrested at the gym construction site] Dean Coleman is held hostage."[27]

President Kirk was at the Harvard Club in Manhattan when he heard about the Hamilton Hall takeover. His first instinct was to send in the police to clear the building and free Dean Coleman. However, Vice President David Truman feared there was a "dangerous mix in Hamilton with the SDS and the SAS on one side and the other students opposing them, and we don't want to throw a spark in there." When Kirk asked Truman what might happen, the esteemed political scientist responded, "A hell of a battle." Truman was worried about rumors that black protesters had guns. Faced with Truman's strong opposition to calling the police, Kirk relented. Coleman himself seemed content in his role as hostage and opposed calling the police. "I felt that this would simmer down after they had had a night of it," Coleman said afterward, "and I was perfectly prepared to sit in here for a night. That wasn't going to bother me."[28]

The radical protesters inside Hamilton put up posters of Lenin, Malcolm X, Stokely Carmichael, and Che Guevara in the lobby of the building, prompting one conservative student to remark, "It makes me sick to my stomach to see a filthy communist's picture hanging over the College Dean's office." The radicals also hung a Vietcong flag out of one of the windows in Hamilton. Conservative students, already agitated over the low-level guerrilla warfare of SDS, began massing outside as well as inside the building, uneasily mixing with their radical adversaries.[29]

Meanwhile, divisions began to appear between black and white radicals. In the early-morning hours of Wednesday, April 24, black protesters asked their white allies to leave Hamilton, which they did at 5:30 A.M. According to James Simon Kunen, one of the white protesters inside Hamilton, Mark Rudd told the group that "the blacks told us to leave Hamilton because they do not feel that we are willing to make the sacrifices they are willing to make." Rudd further noted that the black protesters "have carbines and grenades and . . . they're not leaving." In an interview after the spring disturbances, Ray Brown of SAS told an interviewer that the white students were ejected from Hamilton because they "were not prepared to dramatize the issue through a confrontation with students and faculty." Bill Sales of SAS complained that the black students had decided to barricade Hamilton Hall, but the white students wouldn't go along with this. According to Sales, the white students in Hamilton "were vacillating and voting over and over again and unable to make a clear decision on their role. If they had remained it would probably have diluted the effectiveness of the protest." Yet again, Rudd was losing control of the protests.[30]

The white radicals were imbued with a mixture of naiveté, ignorance, and revolutionary rhetoric, all tinged with the antiparental and anti-authority attitudes of middle-class white teenagers. They were, in the words of Daniel Bell, "still playing in the doll's house of revolution." Black students, on the other hand, suffered from none of this. Their goal was to stop the construction of the gym and prevent Columbia's expansion in Harlem. They were more serious and more disciplined than the white radicals. Rudd told his fellow SDSers that "the blacks have guns and are prepared to make a stand. . . . That's their fight, we have our own."[31]

Hamilton Hall was left in the hands of approximately seventy blacks, one third of them nonstudents, who proceeded to barricade themselves inside the building. Left without a building to occupy at 5:30 in the morning and embarrassed by their eviction from Hamilton for insufficient radicalism and seriousness, the white radicals started for Low Library and tried to force the door open. When that proved unsuccessful, they grabbed a wooden plank and broke the window of the glass door to gain entry. A security guard who tried to keep the students at bay was cut in the arm by the broken glass. Once inside, the students went directly for President Kirk's office, making it their headquarters. They rifled through files and made copies of the president's documents in what the Cox Commission later termed as "plainly dishonorable acts." By sunrise, Low Library was occupied by two hundred students.

Later that morning, the police stormed Low Library and entered Kirk's office, but the remaining students moved to another room in Low. The police were able to save a valuable Rembrandt painting that was hanging in Kirk's office, but they did nothing to evict the students from the buildilng or prevent other students from reentering the building later. It was one of the more puzzling actions during the whole conflict. In assessing the controversy later, the Cox Commission's only explanation for this inaction was that the university and police were more concerned with the blacks in Hamilton than with the whites in Low. Even if this is correct, it stands as one of many examples of poor planning and indecisive actions on the part of the university.

Later on Wednesday night, Low was again filled with protesters. Also on Wednesday night, architecture students took over Avery Hall and on Thursday morning graduate students invaded Fayerweather Hall. Later on Thursday, a small group of outside militants, including Tom Hayden, took over Mathematics Hall and barricaded themselves inside. By Thursday, a total of five buildings on the Columbia campus were occupied by radical students and outside agitators.

On Thursday, April 25, the *New York Times* denounced the "Hoodlumism at Columbia":

> The destructive minority of students at Columbia University, along with their not so friendly allies among community militants, have offered a degrading spectacle of hoodlum tactics—the exaltation of irresponsibility over reason. Whatever causes these students claim to be supporting have been defiled by their vandalism. Disruptive physical force, unscrupulously applied against institutions which are properly reluctant to reply by calling in the police can halt the orderly process of academic as well as governmental activities. It requires neither superior intelligence nor a college education to prove this theory of revolutionary politics.[32]

Of course, SDS and other university critics duly noted that the *Times's* publisher, Arthur Ochs Sulzberger, was also a trustee of Columbia University. The newspaper's coverage of the Columbia revolt only added to the radicals' belief in the immorality of establishment liberalism.

In opposition to this establishment liberalism, many protesters proclaimed their revolutionary goals. They genuinely believed that the overthrow of a university administration that they saw as complicit in the subjugation of blacks and the perpetuation of an immoral war was only a prelude to a larger revolution against a sick and immoral society. Tom Hayden, who helped occupy Mathematics Hall, called for "two, three, many Columbias." Writing in the aftermath of the Columbia revolt, Hayden said, "Students at Columbia discovered that barricades are only the beginning of what they call 'bringing the war home.' " Mark Rudd argued most plainly the revolutionary nature of the Columbia radicals:

> Perhaps nothing upsets our enemies more than this slogan (Up against the wall, motherfucker!). To them it seemed to show the extent to which we had broken with their norms, how far we had sunk to brutality, hatred, and obscenity. Great! . . . The truth is almost as bad: the slogan defined Grayson Kirk, David Truman, the Trustees, many of the faculty, the cops as our enemies. Liberal solutions, restructuring, partial understandings, compromise are not allowed anymore. The essence of the matter is that we are out for social and political revolution, nothing less.

Looking back on the spring protests, the Columbia SDS later proclaimed: "The Strike did not follow the lines of civil disobedience. The Strike at Columbia was an insurrection."[33]

RACIAL ANXIETY

The Columbia administration worried that a police action aimed at black students would anger the Harlem community. Three weeks earlier, New York City had seen three days of sporadic rioting in response to the assassination of Martin Luther King. On Wednesday night, the city's Human Rights Commission chairman, William Booth, State Senator Basil Patterson, Manhattan Borough President Percy Sutton, and Assemblyman Charles Rangel met with President Kirk to warn about the possible ramifications of the protests and the gym construction to the Harlem community. They also met inside Hamilton Hall with the leadership of the black radicals. Instead of trying to help diffuse the situation, Sutton and Rangel told the blacks that they supported them. Sutton told the students, "Whatever you do, we're with you." Mayoral aide Barry Gottehrer wrote later: "It was an atrocious assertion. The politicians could not back it up, and clearly misled the students. The students were encouraged to believe that the highest-ranking black officials in New York City supported their illegal takeover of a building belonging to a private university." Roy Innis, the leader of the

Harlem branch of CORE, appeared outside Hamilton Hall on Thursday morning. With some members of his group among those holding Dean Coleman, Innis said, "I'm proud of these kids. They've got the dean in what you might call *an extended dialogue*."[34]

The prospect of a black uprising sweeping over Morningside Heights frightened both faculty and administration. Between 1950 and 1960, the white population of Morningside Heights had declined from 91 to 73 percent, the Puerto Rican population had doubled, and the black population had increased sevenfold. Some black radicals stoked whites' fears of racial change in the neighborhood. At the April 23 protest, Cicero Wilson, the president of SAS, told a crowd of mostly white radicals, "Remember that in a few years when you get off at the 116th Street subway station and head for your classrooms you'll be the minority and we'll be the majority."

For many professors, Morningside Heights was not just their place of business, but the neighborhood in which they lived and raised their families. Diana Trilling frankly admitted her fear of racial change:

> Columbia, the campus itself and its immediate vicinity where many of the faculty live, has for some years been an island, a white island, constantly shrinking. This is not something that is much talked about among the faculty, but it makes itself felt in the steady migration of the faculty to the suburbs; and among those who continue to live in the University-owned apartment houses on Claremont Avenue and Riverside Drive, west of the campus, or in the Amsterdam–Morningside Drive area to the east, it plays a not inconsiderable part in curtailing the freedom of movement of the residents, especially after dark, and in the venturesomeness they can permit their children.

Many Columbia faculty members who lived in Morningside Heights believed that a police action against the blacks in Hamilton Hall would lead to racial warfare that would place their families in danger.[35]

In many ways, the response of black students was the mirror opposite of Trilling's complaints about Morningside Heights becoming a shrinking "white island." If whites feared the incursion of blacks in Morningside Heights, blacks feared the incursion of whites into their neighborhood. Bill Sales of SAS argued that the construction of the Columbia gym in Morningside Park foreshadowed similar incursions into Harlem, stating: "Columbia will, over the next decade or so, employ this same method . . . to acquire land in the surrounding community in order to expand the University's living accommodations: in other words, to turn West Harlem into a white enclave." Dan Elf, a member of Harlem CORE, told a television reporter, "I saw drawings, actual drawings of what Morningside Heights should look like ten years from now, and it didn't look like to me as if there was a black face in the crowd. . . . I think Columbia University is used as an instrument by the power structure to buy back Harlem." Sales told television host David Suskind that if the university's expansion continued, "The community might strike back in terms of burning Columbia to the ground." Sales then repeated the claim that Harlem was "part of a redevelopment plan of Columbia University which will . . . in the next decade transform that community into a white haven."[36]

"The underlying issue in the dispute raging at both Columbia University and the Schomburg Collection [the Schomburg Center for Research in Black Culture, a division of the New York Public Library in Harlem]," wrote the playwright Lofton Mitchell in a piece for the *Amsterdam News*, "is that the people of Harlem live in mortal fear of having their community taken from them. They know that an integrated Harlem will remove whatever political power, culture, and brotherhood exists here." Blacks did not want whites moving into their neighborhood, one in which blacks were fairly recent arrivals themselves. "I certainly do not want to live next door to people with whom I can only discuss the weather," wrote Mitchell about the prospect of white neighbors. In conclusion, Mitchell likened the university administration to "rattlesnakes, ready to cut us down, reminding us of the constant fear of being evicted from our Harlem."[37]

A DIVIDED UNIVERSITY

There were other problems at Columbia. In the twenty years following the end of World War II, the number of undergraduate and graduate students at Columbia more than doubled. Meanwhile, the number of teachers increased by only 50 percent but the number of administrators necessary to administer the sprawling university increased nearly tenfold. At the same time, the ratings of Columbia's individual academic departments declined dramatically. Not only were students alienated from an increasingly cold and remote university bureaucracy, but their level of instruction was perceived to be declining as well. The Cox Commission examined this issue and concluded: "In mid–1966, a national survey of graduate studies by the American Council of Education was published. It detailed a significant and widespread decline at Columbia in all areas of study—physical and natural sciences, social sciences, and the humanities—between 1957 and 1966. Where Columbia had theretofore consistently ranked among the first three universities in the country, the current ranking of individual departments dropped uniformly below fifth place and, not infrequently, below tenth."[38]

Discontent among conservative students and the faculty added to the confusion. The disruption wrought upon the university by radical students created a countermovement of conservative students. The division between conservative and radical students went beyond political differences, and served as an illustration of the cultural chasm growing in the nation. Some, but not all, of the conservative students were athletes, or "jocks." They had shorter hair and dressed in a more traditional style, sometimes in jacket and tie. They were more accepting of authority and more traditional in their social views. Conservative students called their adversaries "pukes," an expression of their revulsion at the dress and manners of the radicals. "Just looking at these dirty, bearded twerps with their sneers and their sloppy girlfriends is enough to make a guy vomit," said one "jock." The contempt was mutual. Mark Rudd called the Majority Coalition, a group of conservative students opposed to SDS, "the most isolated and pathetic people on campus."[39]

The contrast between conservative and radical students went deeper; one member of the conservative Young Americans for Freedom (YAF) summed up the differences between SDS and the conservatives with the words "We're Staten Island. They're Scarsdale." The difference between Staten Island and Scarsdale was not only one of class, but of ethnicity: Staten Island was largely white and working class, and Scarsdale was largely Jewish and professional. This contrast was reflected in the Columbia student body, and on other campuses nationally. National studies of student activists from the 1960s have shown that most conservatives were Protestants and Catholics of Northern European heritage. The SDS membership, on the other hand, was overwhelmingly Jewish. (Juan Gonzalez, now a columnist for the *Daily News*, was one of the few minority members of Columbia SDS.) The American Jewish Committee was "frankly worried about the Jewish aspect of the Columbia trouble," so much so that they interviewed a number of Jewish faculty members at Columbia to gauge the problem. "Prominent among the student rebels were Jewish students," wrote the AJC report. "Frequently references to faculty supporters of the strike included Jewish names." Despite this concern, the report concluded that, despite the involvement of Jewish students, "no one regarded the student uprising as other than a revolt of youth against the Establishment. The idea that the conflict might be Jewish-Gentile (rebels vs. administration) never occurred to the men interviewed." But the very fact that this study was deemed necessary reveals the importance of ethnic divisions among student activists.[40]

The Columbia administration and faculty showed little sympathy for the conservative students. What they most feared was that left-wing action would produce a massive and violent right-wing reaction. Columbia's Dean Herbert A. Deane was forthright in summarizing this belief:

> The most likely consequences of violent protests by the left, such as the demonstrations led by student "revolutionaries," are, therefore, a resurgence in ultra right-wing movements and an even more widespread swing towards conservatism in this country. We already see ominous signs of these developments, such as the sharp rise in former Governor Wallace's standing in the national polls. . . . Some of our young revolutionaries may tell us that they welcome a "temporary" strengthening of reaction, since the far right will eliminate or weaken

the social-democrats, liberals, and conservatives and thus sharply polarize society into two completely hostile segments, the forces of revolution and those of reaction, and that they will emerge victorious from this confrontation. Our response can only be that right-wing repression would destroy all that we value in American society.

Alexander Platt, associate dean of student affairs, was more concerned that conservative students would take matters into their own hands than that radicals had broken the law and infringed on the rights of students wanting to attend class. Walter Metzger, a history professor appalled by the conservatives, believed "these boys were in an acute sense of anger, and it seemed to me they desired to express themselves in physical forms." The "acute sense of anger" among SDS members over the gym and the war and their desire to "express themselves in physical forms" did not seem to bother Metzger.[41]

As conservative students pushed the administration in one direction, the faculty began pushing them in another. A group of liberal professors grew increasingly frustrated by the inaction of the administration and its lack of interest in the faculty's opinion. Fearing an outbreak of violence on campus, they created the Ad Hoc Faculty Group, headed by the government professor Alan Westin. The group seceded from the university's traditional faculty council and welcomed radical junior faculty and untenured professors.[42]

Members of the Ad Hoc Faculty Group hoped "that third-party intervention, free from the intransigencies of either side, could find a placable and equitable way out." Yet the creation of the Ad Hoc Group was based on faulty assumptions. First, they saw themselves as a neutral, objective force on campus that would sort out the competing interests of the different factions. In reality, however, the faculty was not objective. Many faculty members sympathized with the protesters. The second problem was that the faculty possessed no authority, either rooted in law or university rules, to make any decisions. An ad hoc group of faculty members possessed as much power to settle the protests as an ad hoc group of university janitors. Walter Metzger believed that the reason that the faculty group would ultimately fail was in its ad hoc nature. "To salvage authority, one needs authority—or at least some authorization," wrote Metzger. "To exercise power without anointment, to mediate at no one's behest, is almost to guarantee defeat."

The student radicals picked up on this lack of authority quickly. Student protester James Simon Kunen remembered Allan Westin entering Mathematics Hall to offer a deal that included a tripartite disciplinary committee made up of students, faculty, and administrators. Kunen remarked, "Professor Allen Westin, liberal, comes and offers us a tripartite committee which he has no authority to constitute and which we don't want." Mark Rudd had nothing but contempt for the Ad Hoc Faculty Group and the "basic liberal conception" of mediation. He believed the faculty did not "understand that at times we'd be impolite about this or 'intolerant' of this other side's rights. . . . They were naive in thinking that they could be in the middle and they were naive in some of the things they did. . . . In addition, they were the people we had to fight the most. They would come round to the buildings, trying to scare people saying the bust was coming, the jocks were coming, beware of the right-wing reaction, time is of the essence, all of those phrases." When the Ad Hoc Faculty Group invited Rudd to present his demands in person, Rudd angered even sympathetic faculty by calling the group's recommendations "bullshit."[43]

Lindsay's aides, including Barry Gottehrer, Jay Kriegel, and Sid Davidoff, had been monitoring the situation since the disturbances began and had had discussions with all of the groups involved, including the Ad Hoc Faculty Group. The faculty exasperated Lindsay's aides. "Stoned on good intentions, high moralism, and lack of sleep," Barry Gottehrer wrote, "they [the Ad Hoc Faculty Group] were the least coherent individuals we dealt with on Morningside Heights. . . . The faculty was idealistic to the point of inanity." He also found himself "dismayed to see professors whose work I had studied in college and whose intelligence I respected crying and hysterical" when the protests grew tense. Gottehrer called the liberal faculty "nuts" and "assholes," saying "they were literally crazy." Sid Davidoff accused the Ad Hoc Faculty Group professors of being the kind of intellectuals who would bring fascism to America. When a faculty member asked what that meant, Davidoff replied, "What are you going to do when the radical right starts taking buildings?" Dean Herbert Deane complained that the Ad Hoc Faculty Group "was not very helpful, in fact it confused things . . . twenty-five amateur negotiators. The students didn't know what was being said and who had the authority to say it. . . . That's the vice of the profession—academics are good with words. But they're not usually in a position where their words have any consequence." The Columbia history professor Peter Gay believed the faculty "put itself in the middle, as though the students and Administration were two equals confronting one another . . . I would have to say that it does seem to me that the Ad Hoc Group hardened the lines of division and stiffened resistance." The physics professor and Nobel Prize winner Polykarp Kusch found the Ad Hoc Faculty Group "difficult, noisy, irrational, not the deliberation of men of reason. . . ." The historian Richard Hofstadter soon grew weary of the Ad Hoc Faculty Group, of which he was a member:

> I disliked the atmosphere of the Ad Hoc Faculty Group, which seemed increasingly as days went on to show the following tendencies: A split between the junior and senior faculty, an increasing spirit of animosity, an increasing factionalism between right and left, and an increasing failure to get anywhere with the students. Also it seemed to me that the faculty, toward the end of the week, were beginning to forget that force was intro-

duced on the campus by the seizure of the buildings by the students, and we're thinking only of the force that might come if the police came.[44]

Some faculty members openly sided with the protesters. The radical junior professors Richard Greeman, Mike Ross, and Bob Zevin were reportedly in constant touch with protesters, telling them that the longer they held out, the more radical the faculty would become. The sociology professor Immanuel Wallerstein believed that the "revolt by young people has also been, in many ways, intellectually liberating for the entire American left. It liberated the left from the cramping fears instilled in them by the anti-Stalinism of the cold war period." Wallerstein argued in favor of amnesty for the radicals on the grounds that Columbia's "own moral position is too weak for it to allow itself to be in the position of moral accuser."[45]

Wallerstein also praised the personal liberation from authority he found among the radical students. What some saw as rudeness, sloppiness, promiscuity, and drug addiction, Wallerstein saw as "breaking the cycle of socialization by which society prevented the growth of left ideology and action among the young." Richard Goldstein, covering the Columbia revolt for the *Village Voice* (the paper termed it "the Groovy Revolution") made a similar point: "Don't underestimate the relationship between litter and liberty at Columbia. Until last Tuesday . . . the university was a clean dorm where students paid rent, kept the house rules, and took exams. Then the rebels arrived in an uneasy coalition of hip, black, and leftist militants. They wanted to make Columbia more like home, so they ransacked files, shoved furniture around, plastered walls with paint and placards."

The editor of the *Columbia Spectator*, Robert Friedman, noticed this attitude of personal liberation early in the spring of 1968.

> For as long as anyone could remember, undergraduates on their way from the student activities center in Ferris Booth Hall to their classes in Hamilton Hall had walked by way of the round-about brick paths set down by Columbia's architects at the turn of the century. But this year an ominous stripe began to appear on South Field [a grassy area in the center of campus] along the diagonal which marks the shortest route between the two buildings. Despite signs posted by the administration, students refused to use the paved paths their predecessors had followed and began to cut a new path straight across the grass. By mid-April the situation had become critical—holes were torn in the fences, hedges were forced apart and the defiant brown stripe worn across South Field seemed destined to remain.

In the words of Professor Wallerstein: "Personal liberation is necessary to free the inner psyche from the social controls instilled in it by the dominant social system."[46]

INCHING TOWARD A POLICE ACTION

With all of the chaos and divisions on campus, the administration had to figure out a politically acceptable way to clear the protesters out of the occupied buildings. The greatest fear among both members of the administration and those at City Hall was the situation of the blacks in Hamilton Hall. The history professor Orest Ranum recalled that on the Ad Hoc Faculty Group, "there was almost an hysteria among whites about what the blacks might do." President Kirk remembered that the situation of black students in Hamilton Hall "did complicate the matter of calling in the police." Kirk blamed the lack of action on the Lindsay administration, which, he argued, worried that bringing in the police to clear Hamilton "might conceivably be a spark that would set off the situation in Harlem once more" only three weeks after the King riots.

The situation was politically impossible. Kirk and Truman wanted the police to clear out Low Library on Wednesday, but leave the more sensitive situation in Hamilton alone. Vice President David Truman testified before the Cox Commission that he had been told by police that this was impossible. The police would not selectively enforce the law; either all of the buildings would be cleared out or none of the buildings would be cleared. Kirk, in an interview soon after the controversy, concurred with Truman's story of City Hall's not wanting to appear tough on whites and lenient on blacks. Assistant Chief Inspector Eldridge Waithe disputed Kirk and Truman's accounts, contending that the university, still holding out for a peaceful solution, did not want any of the buildings emptied forcibly. Waithe told the Cox Commission that someone under his command did tell administration officials about their opposition to selective enforcement of the law, but that the conversation occurred later. Whatever the reason, the protest continued and in fact escalated in the face of official inaction.[47]

The administration tried again to clear the buildings on campus in the early-morning hours of Friday April 26. At one o'clock in the morning on Friday, Truman spoke before an Ad Hoc Faculty Group meeting. According to one account, Truman stayed in the back of the room and announced to the professors that the university was ready to call in the police. "Gentlemen, I'm going to make an announcement I don't think many of you are going to like," Truman told the professors. "We are afraid the situation is one in which we are simply going to call in the police now." His words were greeted with cries of "Shame! Shame!" from the faculty. Some of the more left-wing faculty were on the verge of hysterics. Reverend William Starr, the college chaplain, shouted at Truman, "Liar, liar!" Eric Bentley, professor of drama, theatrically announced his resignation. The math professor Serge Lang, a veteran of the Berkeley student protests while a professor there, called for a vote of censure against the administration by the Ad Hoc Faculty Group.[48]

The Ad Hoc Faculty Group had decided from the outset that one of its functions would be to place members of the faculty physically between students and the police. As history professor Robert Fogelson put it, "It's time for professors to interpose their bodies between contending forces. That's dangerous but we have to take a chance." The group passed a resolution stating that "unless the crisis is settled, we will stand before the occupied buildings to prevent their forcible entry by police and others." Soon thereafter, members of the faculty, mostly leftists affiliated with the Ad Hoc Faculty Group, began forming a ring around Low Library, which served not only as a buffer between radical and conservative students, but also as a defense against a police action.[49]

A member of the Ad Hoc Faculty Group, Seymour Melman, stopped Barry Gottehrer and Sid Davidoff on campus, begging them with tears in his eyes to stop the police action. "These are our children," wept Melman, "We beg of you, don't let them use the police." Gottehrer asked Melman whether he could convince the protesters to leave the buildings in forty-five minutes if the city promised to stop the gym construction. "The man [Melman] looked aghast," recalled Gottehrer, "and my question went without an answer." Then President Kirk asked Chief Inspector Sanford Garelik what would happen to faculty members blocking the buildings in the event of a police action. Garelik told him that they would be arrested. According to one account, "Kirk paled and said that that could not be done." When a small group of plainclothesmen tried to enter Low Library, the door was blocked by two left-wing faculty members, Terence Hopkins and Richard Greeman, and Reverend Starr. Greeman was wounded in the ensuing fight—one account has Greeman suffering a bloody nose, and another has him getting a cut on the back of the head. One professor yelled during the scuffle, "This is our university. It does not belong to the police." Another professor, Sidney Morgenbesser, told Vice President Truman that the police action would "be done at the expense of faculty blood." When Truman saw a bloodied Greeman, he called off the police action.

At 3:30 A.M., more than two hours after announcing to the Ad Hoc Faculty Group his decision to call in the police, Vice President Truman spoke in front of Low Library to a thousand assembled students and faculty. "The faculty committee has persuaded the University administration to postpone the request for police action on campus while the faculty and administration continue their efforts to effect a peaceful solution to the situation," he said. As the campus takeover reached its fourth day, the administration yet again equivocated, stumbling inevitably toward an even more disastrous conclusion.[50]

By the weekend university officials faced a divided campus. Black radicals occupied one building, while white radicals of various political extremes held four others. The faculty was divided. Finally, conservative students were milling around campus, anxious and aggravated that the university seemed incapable of ending the revolt and resume classes. Meanwhile, the police were waiting in buses outside the Columbia campus for orders.

Gottehrer had nothing positive to say of the Columbia administration. "We spent most of those days trying to persuade Kirk and David Truman that they had to compromise," remembers Gottehrer. "They spent . . . most of those days trying to figure out what they could do other than compromise." Gottehrer was dismayed at the attitude of the Columbia administration "that all they had to do was bring the police on and school would open tomorrow." Lindsay's aides knew that a police bust would mean a serious disturbance for the university.

Though the Columbia administration was certainly lacking in leadership during this crisis, it is somewhat unfair to criticize them for their inability to compromise with the protesters. Mark Rudd and SDS had little desire to compromise. The radicals had nothing but contempt for the liberal notion of compromise.[51]

Though the administration was loath to take the step, a police bust was inevitable. On Saturday, William Petersen, president of the Irving Trust Company and chairman of the Columbia Board of Trustees, called John Lindsay. Petersen wanted the mayor to come up to Columbia and act as a mediator. Lindsay had avoided the Morningside campus all week, preferring to work through his young aides. Now Petersen was telling the mayor, "We want you to come up here, walk around the campus and talk to people. All we want you to do is perform miracles—you know, the way you do when you walk around the city and prevent riots." But the trustees would not give the mayor any authority to negotiate with students and the administration. Needless to say, Lindsay did not take up Petersen's offer.[52]

Lindsay, already leery of getting involved in the Columbia morass, had his intuition strengthened when he spoke with Kingman Brewster, president of Yale University and an old friend. According to Barry Gottehrer, Brewster warned Lindsay that "the very future of the American university depended on punishing the strikers. If they were to give amnesty at Columbia to students who had occupied buildings, willfully destroyed records and defied every authority, it would henceforth be impossible to run any university." David Garth has said that Brewster told Lindsay, "We have to make a stand." Thereafter, Lindsay refused to get involved in the events at Columbia. When the Ad Hoc Faculty Group voted late Sunday night to make a direct appeal to Lindsay to intervene in the dispute, Lindsay followed Brewster's advice and stayed out of the fray. The mayor had little to gain and much to lose from an active involvement in the controversy. Lindsay also learned that if the university administration filed a formal complaint against the students and requested police action, he had no power to stop the use of police on the Columbia campus.

At the same time, however, Lindsay's aides grew more concerned about the imminent police action. Although they had backed the earlier police action, they were much more wary of any use of the police now. As Professor

Immanuel Wallerstein put it, where Kriegel, Davidoff, and Gottehrer had been "hawks" early in the standoff, they were "doves five days later." Despite the sudden pacifism from City Hall, Kirk and Truman decided that after almost a week of protests, they had no choice but to call in the police. When the president and vice president finally made their decision, Davidoff told them, "This is going to be an impossible situation." But the Columbia administration continued to believe that once the police cleared the buildings, the campus would return to normal in a few days.[53]

THE POLICE BUST

The police bust began around two-thirty on the morning of Tuesday, April 30. The mayoral aide Ted Mastroianni remembers the sight of the police preparing for the bust: "I remember looking out the window and there were legions of cops and the streetlights were glistening on their helmets. It really looked like the Roman legions. It was sort of scary." The building that created the fewest problems was Hamilton Hall. The Columbia administration, the Lindsay administration, and the NYPD were all extraordinarily cautious about the possible ramifications of dealing with the black occupiers in Hamilton. Assistant Chief Inspector Waithe was in command of the police at Hamilton, and Human Rights Commission Chairman William Booth and Kenneth Clark were there as observers. During negotiations, the black protesters were offered the chance to leave the building without being arrested, but they declined. Instead, the police entered the building without incident, and the protesters vacated the building peacefully, through a tunnel underneath the building, escorted by the police.[54]

The other buildings proved more difficult. At Low Library, many protesting students resisted arrest—about half, the police estimated—by dragging their feet. The police report stated that Paul Carter, the vice provost at Columbia, who witnessed the bust, believed the operation "was carried out with a minimum of force." Mathematics Hall, containing the most radical protesters, was a different story. A police report called those occupying Mathematics "abusive." They "used vile and obscene language" directed at the police and "covered the floor with soapy water in order to make the arrest process more difficult." The police encountered more resistance from the students inside Fayerweather and Avery Halls. In Fayerweather, 278 people were arrested, half of whom had to be carried out "bodily." The police officer in charge stated that policemen were bombarded with furniture, bottles, and "other miscellaneous objects." In Avery, 53 students refused to leave peacefully and were arrested and carried out by police. According to the NYPD report, a university representative who accompanied police at Avery believed "the police could have been more gentle," and "described the process as one similar to a hazing line and complained that the police pummeled the students as they passed down the stairwell."[55]

The evening's most brutal event occurred after the buildings had been cleared. At around 5 A.M., the police, agitated and angry at the students, waited at the center of campus for orders to leave. Students, both protesters and spectators, were also milling around the campus, yelling obscenities at the blue intruders and denouncing the administration for bringing about the violence. A group of policemen suddenly broke ranks and began chasing the students across South Field. More police joined in, using their nightsticks indiscriminately against any student who crossed their path. Police chased some students into dorms. Mounted police chased other students down Broadway. The police action was most likely a reaction by frustrated policemen to student heckling. The policemen saw an opportunity to punish what they saw as a group of spoiled, ungrateful children who had been given too much latitude by society. The sight of police chasing and beating students, many of whom had not participated in the takeover, solidified the view of an out-of-control police force. Even Sandy Garelik, the police officer in charge at Columbia, believes that the South Field incident was "uncalled for." In all, the police arrested a total of 705 students in the early-morning hours of April 30.[56]

MAKING SENSE OF THE VIOLENCE

Hysteria was the dominant tone of many contemporary accounts of the police raid. For example, one doctor who treated injured students stated, "Last night I saw the naked face of fascism at Columbia University." Liberals lashed out at the administration and the police. The Columbia anthropology professor Marvin Harris, who sympathized with the radical students, described the police bust for readers of *The Nation* as an accumulation of wanton acts by the police: "Many students were thrown or dragged down stairways. Girls were pulled out by the hair; their arms were twisted; they were punched in the face. Faculty members were kicked in the groin, tossed through hedges, punched in the eye. Noses and cheekbones were broken. A diabetic student fell into a coma. One faculty member suffered a nervous collapse. Many students bled profusely from head wounds opened by handcuffs wielded as weapons."

Times reporter Steven V. Roberts, writing in the *Village Voice*, likened President Kirk to "a cracker sheriff breaking up a sit-in or a voter registration drive." Roberts portrayed the police as subhuman, sadistic monsters, "a special kind of human that enjoys smashing other humans, especially when they are defenseless." The journalist Nat Hentoff argued that the police action at Columbia was the seventh "police riot" in the city that year. Preston Wilcox, a Harlem activist, told Hentoff that during the night of the police bust at Columbia he "really got a sense of what it's like to be in a police state." Hentoff repeatedly quoted observers calling the police "animals." One reporter said, "Those goddamned plainclothesmen were fucking brutes.

They were a bunch of animals." An anonymous mayoral aide told Hentoff: "There's no question about it, some of those cops were just animals."[57]

Daniel Bell, a member of the Ad Hoc Faculty Group, expressed his opposition to the police bust in more intellectual terms. Though generally contemptuous of the student radicals, Bell argued that "the university is not the microcosm of the society; it is an academic community, with a historic exemption from full integration into the society." Because of its anomalous position, Bell argued, the university "can deal with disruptions—or its threats—not by invoking civil force but by rallying an entire community to establish rules of common procedure. Disruptive students can only be contained by a faculty and by other students, not by the police."[58]

Mayor Lindsay read a prepared statement about police behavior at a news conference on Thursday: "A great majority of the police called into the Columbia campus by President Kirk and his administration conducted themselves with great professionalism and restraint, sometimes under the most severe provocation. They are to be commended for their performance. Some police officers, however, from reports of independent persons in whom I have confidence, used excessive force."[59]

Barry Gottehrer put the police action in perspective: "The violence on the campus certainly occurred because the police hit people, but at the same time, had people not sat down in front of those buildings, there would have been little or no violence. Many of those who, arms linked, blocked doors, were non-tenured professors who felt, apparently, that as faculty members they were entitled to define law to policemen, and that surely the police would respond to their logical position."

Other responsible observers at Columbia also downplayed the violence. History professor Robert Fogelson, a member of the Ad Hoc Faculty Group and an expert on riots, found the police bust to be "basically a routine major police action. By that, I mean it had to be rough in some parts." Fogelson believed "excessive force" was used in some of the buildings, but that "there were almost no permanent injuries, partly because the policemen did not go in there with their clubs." Peter Gay said of the police action: "I know of course that the so-called 'unspeakable' violence was certainly not unspeakable. . . . After all, the hospital records suggest that there were very few serious injuries; and one would also have to add that there was a certain amount of student brutality, by which I do not mean merely taunting the cops but actually throwing things at them." The Cox Commission concluded that "although the police force may have become excessive, a share of the responsibility for the injuries they [*sic*] inflicted falls upon those students and faculty who, by resisting the police either actively or passively, made it necessary for the police to use force with the inherent risk that it might easily get out of hand." Peter Kenen, an economics professor, agreed, calling "the behavior of some members of the faculty . . . more inflammatory than that of the students."[60]

An examination of the injuries paints a clear picture: the number of serious injuries was minimal. Eighty-seven people were treated at St. Luke's Hospital and 16 were treated at Knickerbocker Hospital. Of these 103 individuals, 77 were students, 14 were policemen, 8 were faculty members, and 4 were unidentified. The Cox Commission's assessment was that "the character of injuries ranged from heavy bruises and scalp lacerations to sprains and severe fright." The most serious injuries reported were two fractures and one dislocated shoulder.[61]

Nearly two years after the incident, the NYPD's Civilian Complaint Review Board, made up of four members of the police department, issued a preliminary report on the behavior of the police during the Columbia controversy. One hundred seventy-four complaints were filed as a result of police action at Columbia, of which 106 were deemed "unsubstantiated." Thirty-eight were "conciliated by the Assistant Director of the [Civilian Complaint Review] Board," and 3 of the complaints merited a recommendation of charges. (There is no record of what these charges were or how they were resolved.) One complaint was still pending at the time of the March 1970 report. The remaining 26 complaints arose "out of notice of claim filed with the Comptroller which were filed since plaintiffs would not submit to interview."

The CCRB concluded that "obviously, illegal force was used by some students, and unnecessary force by some police officers. . . . Many students did not engage in peaceful civil disobedience. A great variety of missiles, from bottles to furniture, were hurled at police officers resulting in injuries to some of them." Despite this, "The violent reaction by some police officers to the passive acts of the students was unjustified. There was deliberate bumping on the ground of persons under arrest who were being carried to patrol wagons." The CCRB found fault with some superior officers who "did not exert the leadership expected of them, and failed to control their subordinates effectively." The board also criticized the "inadequate manpower" at the scene. The city assigned only 1,400 policemen to arrest the demonstrators. If there were over seven hundred demonstrators and four policemen were required to handle properly a limp protester, the police were deficient in manpower for their task on the night of April 30. According to the report, "The university officials grossly underestimated the number of students in the buildings."

The CCRB's biggest criticism was the inability of police and university officials to clear the campus of nondemonstrators:

> The campus should have been cleared of all persons prior to the police entering buildings. It is probable that there would have been fewer students choosing to remain in the buildings after they had seen their fellow students removed from the campus, and it would have been easier for the police to clear buildings. The presence of hundreds of students

and faculty who were nonparticipants in the demonstration contributed
to the chaotic and disorderly condition on the campus. Many of these
persons attempted to interfere with the police entering buildings for the
purpose of evicting the students. The police should have removed all
these people first, instead of trying to remove them and enter the buildings at the same time.

Another police report, written just days after the police action, stated
clearly that the "University Administration asked the Department not to
clear the campus during the operation. . . . Much of the difficulty in carrying out the operation resulted from interference from students allowed to remain on the campus at the university's request." Though Columbia's campus
can be closed to the outside world by shutting the main gates, many of the
college's dorms are within the campus gates. The police should have required
nondemonstrators to remain in their dorms. This would have prevented the
rush of the police on South Field. Faculty members should also have been
cleared away from the buildings before police attempted to retake any of the
buildings.[62]

Actually, the most serious injuries at Columbia occurred among the police: fourteen policemen received minor injuries during the action and one
officer suffered a heart attack, reportedly after being kicked in the chest by
a student. The most serious injury on the Columbia campus occurred on
May 1, the day after the police bust. The police had remained on campus to
maintain order, and Patrolman Frank Gucciardi, thirty-four, had just arrived
on campus. According to Gucciardi, "[The Columbia students] taunted us.
They threw food at us out the windows and wastepaper baskets and
books. . . . One kid up there was throwing globs of this white glue down on
us. All of our uniforms were splattered with white. Then another kid in the
mob grabbed for my coat and pulled. He ripped all the buttons off." Another
member of the taunting mob knocked Gucciardi's hat off his head. When
he bent over to pick it up, "suddenly I felt like a truck hit me." A student had
jumped from the second story of a nearby building, had landed on top of
Gucciardi, and then had run away. Gucciardi suffered a severe spinal injury,
spent twelve weeks in the hospital, and endured two surgeries and endless
back pain. The student was never caught.[63]

But what stuck in the public's imagination was the police violence
against the students. Yet the police reaction—or overreaction—has to be
seen in the context of the strife that had occurred within the police department during the first two-and-a-half years of the Lindsay administration. The police were bitter about Mayor Lindsay's plan to expand the
Civilian Complaint Review Board, about Commissioner Leary's order to
restrain police behavior during riots, and about the general public's growing disrespect for the police. Journalist Roger Kahn writes that a veteran
policeman told him off the record that the reaction of the police at

Columbia was a rebellion against Sanford Garelik and Lindsay. "Pretty much on the level of captain on down," the policeman told Kahn, "a lot of the men wanted to make Garelik look bad." Sid Davidoff also blamed the behavior of the police on Garelik. "As good a tactician as he was, I found that Sandy, when he had to clear an area, would clear it without regard to what the cost would be," argues Davidoff. Garelik believed that Commissioner Leary "had more or less set him up" by insisting that Garelik remain inside his command post and not leave to inspect the situation firsthand. Thus, Garelik had little knowledge of the size of the crowds or the people poised outside the building ready to block the police. Garelik also complained that he had been kept out of negotiations between City Hall and the Columbia administration.[64]

Another explanation for the police behavior was the behavior of the student radicals. The police had been on campus for almost a week prior to the bust, doing very little but listening to the obscenities hurled at them from the cream of the Ivy League crop. Predominantly Irish and Italian working-class policemen were faced with the angry taunts of upper-middle and middle-class youths. Garelik says that his policemen "were really provoked." President Kirk thought the police handled themselves as well as could be expected because there was "a great deal of deliberate baiting of the police." Diana Trilling painted an unpleasant picture of the attitude of the student radicals:

> The revolutionary students spat at people they disliked, including senior faculty members. An old couple crossing the campus was shouted at: "Go home and die, you old people, go home and die." A law professor, my neighbor, walking with his wife near the campus gates, was gratuitously punched in the stomach by a passing student wearing the red armband of his militancy. . . . At a tense moment on the steps of Low Library a Barnard girl-demonstrator jumped up and down in front of the faculty line . . . shouting "Shit, shit, shit, shit."[65]

A report on the Columbia incident by the NYPD's First Deputy Commissioner John F. Walsh concluded that "violence against the police was on a large scale. Objects were thrown on them, even before they entered the buildings and again while inside the building from persons above them. Police were punched, bitten, and kicked with many attempts made to kick policemen in the groin. A pattern was seen in the use of females to bite and kick the policemen."[66]

Roger Kahn described a meeting of student rebels dedicated to "rattling pigs." One Columbia radical addressed the group:

> What we are dealing with is a certain kind of Irish Catholic prudity, with a lot of sadism thrown in. We've seen these men before. They beat

up black kids and take graft, but they get off their rocks with a priest once a week. So they have this crazy sense that they're guardians of morals. They're the kind of guys who have a hard time with sex, a hard time getting hard is what I mean. So here's what we want to do. We want to shake them. . . . Well, you can always pick up your shirt. They won't know whether to jerk off or go blind. But if that's too rough, take 'em apart with words. Tell 'em their mother sucks black cocks, or takes black cocks in the ass. The important thing is you got to use these words. I know that can be tough. We aren't all completely liberated. But if we use words like sucks about their mother, these fuckin' cops will blow like a balloon. And when they blow, they'll be there naked and the whole country will see the naked face, the naked ass, of fascism.

Barry Gottehrer also noticed the cop baiting, noting that it was worse among the girls at Barnard. "A girl would yell, 'Go fuck yourself, you pig,' and the cops were very upset," remembers Gottehrer. "The longer they were there, the worse they felt. When the bust finally came, when they had their chance, some cops were very hard on the women." Don Elliott, a reform Democrat from the Morningside area and Lindsay's chairman of the City Planning Commission, recalls that during the protests "the co-eds would use enormously provocative language and would spray the cops with hair spray and do everything they could to incite them." When one policeman told a young female student to move, she refused, telling him, "Your sister sucks off your mother." At this insult, the policeman hit her.[67]

Nor were black policemen let off the hook. The day after the bust, police were stationed around campus and forced to absorb the epithets and curses from angry students. Black students yelled things at the black men in blue such as "Hi dumb Blackie. You helped beat up Black students earlier this morning didn't you. Well you've still got to go back to your ghetto community" and "Hi nigger cop. I wouldn't stand near you for nothing. You contaminate us."[68]

One New York police sergeant complained about the treatment of police in general during this time:

Have you ever seen those college kids shouting at the police? I've never seen anything like them for meanness and cheapness. The language that comes out of their mouths; you begin to wonder whether you're in a mental hospital. I mean it. Those kids go crazy when they see us. The uniform seems to trigger something in them. They become dirty, plain dirty. They use the worst language I've ever heard. They make insulting gestures to us. They talk about killing us. The girls make sexual overtures—when they're not swearing. Swearing, that's not the word for what you hear! Someone has never really taught those wise-guy kids good manners.[69]

The use of the word "pig" was commonplace among Columbia students. "It's some joke, ain't it, a rich kid calling a police officer pig," one policeman said. "These smart-ass college kids think they're so big they can get away with anything they want. I don't have to take that, particularly from smart-ass college kids." In a study of the attitudes of New York policemen during the 1960s, one policeman talked about how affluent white kids would freely disrespect the working-class police: "They will come up and tell you—and I have had it happen to me while I was standing on the corner, 'Hey, Pig Crook!' These are little white kids, apparently Jewish." The American Jewish Committee prepared a paper on the Columbia revolt, in which the authors spoke of being disturbed by "hearsay regarding antisemitic remarks made by police during the campus troubles, many of which were specifically directed against Barnard girls on the scene." The faculty members interviewed denied hearing such remarks, but also said that they would not have been surprised if such incidents did occur. They "all thought there was sufficient provocation for an 'emotional reaction' on the part of the police."[70]

The police certainly felt the class aspect of the tensions between themselves and the students. They saw the students as spoiled brats who had opportunities that they and their children could never enjoy. Columbia students were not only exempt from military service, but they were actively fighting against the war, and sometimes, as in the case of those flying the Vietcong flag from Hamilton Hall, siding with the enemy. Many policemen no doubt had military experience and had brothers, sons, and cousins fighting in Vietnam.

After the police cleared the students out of Kirk's office, the university president walked through with a policeman. Surveying the damage and vandalism, the policeman said, "You know, Mr. President, for the first time in my life I am glad that my father didn't have enough money to send me to college." Another policeman said of his experiences at Columbia: "What I saw at the college was something terrible. . . . Kids acting like bums, and showing no respect for the law. These same kids who shoulda been down on their knees thanking the Lord that He had let them go to college. I woulda been on my knees myself. . . . Everything I got in life I worked for. It gets me sore when I see these kids, who been handed everything, pissing it away, talking like bums, dressing like pigs."

Another policeman told Roger Kahn, "I thought the place [Columbia] and the people up there would be real special. Instead, it was nothing but a lot of pinkos."[71]

LINDSAY AND THE STUDENT REBELLION

It is striking how little respect Lindsay aides had for the Columbia protesters. Ted Mastroianni remembers the first time he, Kriegel, Davidoff, and

Gottehrer met Mark Rudd. "He was sitting in the corner, but he was in a squat," remembers Mastroianni. "We thought we were going to find this incredible, dynamic, wild leader." Instead, the mayoral aides found a bewildered, scared undergraduate who told Kriegel, "I think it's out of control. I don't know what I did." This first impression of Rudd "really bowled all of us over." Jay Kriegel, one of Lindsay's more liberal aides, called the members of SDS "little bastards." The Columbia protesters were "nasty, vicious, provocative, wild . . . this was not a nice crowd of people. This is not civilized debate." David Garth mockingly called the Columbia protesters the "Right on! kids from Great Neck" and admitted that if he were a policeman at Columbia, "I probably would have shot one" of the protesters. "They were really obnoxious." Don Elliott found the police behavior at Columbia "really very understandable." Labor leader Victor Gotbaum, a Lindsay ally, called the SDSers "the biggest pains in the ass. . . . The truth is, they really didn't want to work with anybody."[72]

Yet Lindsay's response to the Columbia protesters was somewhat ambivalent. The day after the police action, Lindsay released a statement saying, "Students have a right to protest, to dissent, to demonstrate." He then qualified that statement by saying "the right is basic, but not supreme," and that the Columbia rebels "clearly exceeded even the most liberal perimeters of the right to assemble and dissent." He concluded his statement by stating his wish that Columbia "will address itself more fully than it has in the past to its relationship with, and role within, the larger community." Lindsay's statement brought an attack from his nemesis, William F. Buckley. "Mr. Lindsay has a genius for bringing out the worst in liberalism," sniped the conservative commentator.[73]

At a commencement speech at the Bronx High School of Science a month later, Lindsay attacked university administrators, though not by name, as the cause of much of the campus unrest. "The student discontent," Lindsay told the teenagers, "says that [universities] have not spent enough time examining the ways they teach and researching the human and emotional needs as well as the intellectual requirements of young Americans who are growing up in a brand new world." Lindsay predicted that many of the students in the audience "will become allied with the forces of change on your campuses." The mayor defined himself as a "disciple of change" and argued that the purpose of change was to make institutions more "relevant, but not to destroy" them. Lindsay found no reason to condemn directly the actions of the student protesters.[74]

Three weeks after the initial police bust, Lindsay was still trying to find a middle ground between defending the right to dissent and attacking the chaos created by student protesters. He told students at Pittsburgh's Duquesne University that those "who would rebel against the conventions of our society have sound grounds, in logic and in conscience for doing so." Society, Lindsay implied, was badly in need not just of fixing, but of a major overhaul. But he also warned that rebels who overturn "society's conventions must take the corresponding obligation to construct new and better conventions in their place."[75]

In December 1968, Lindsay went to the Morningside Heights campus to give a speech to Columbia students. He reaffirmed his sympathy with the goals of student radicals, but complained that their extremism would create a situation that would hinder social change. "Unreasoning surrender and unreasoning upheaval both threaten to impede the urgent, authentically revolutionary work of this generation," Lindsay told the students. Throughout his speech, the mayor was heckled by a small group of SDS radicals who shouted, "Cut it out, Johnny." Despite the heckling, the *Times* reported that the vast majority of the 1,500 students in the audience strongly applauded Lindsay. His harshest words were reserved for the intolerance of the student left. How were liberal goals advanced, Lindsay wondered, "by shouting down a speaker—or calling him obscene names? . . . I think we should recognize that those techniques are nothing more than the tactics of suppression."

Still, Lindsay issued no direct condemnation of the student takeover and saw little need to chastise their behavior; in fact, he found their goals noble. "Whatever the last year has taught us," concluded Lindsay, "it has taught that your effort and your energy may not be sufficient to build a better America, but it is necessary to that effort. I do not come to promise you that all we seek will be won if you continue speaking and acting for these goals— but I do come to say that without you, we cannot win. You have seen how much is at stake. You have reminded us of the work to be done. Now help us to do it."[76]

At the heart of the Columbia revolt were the tactics used by the student protesters. What kind of tactics would the New Left use to pursue its goals? The Cox Commission linked the troubles at Columbia with a growing tolerance in the country for forceable dissent in the pursuit of political goals.

> The past decade has seen a marked change in attitudes toward the acceptability of disobedience, harassment, and physical obstruction as methods of influencing social and political action. Tactics that would have been so widely condemned 10 or 15 years ago as to be self-defeating are now accepted and approved in many quarters as moral endeavors to achieve worthy ends. This is especially true among political liberals and youth. The spreading use of such tactics and the much, much wider spirit of tolerance toward their use not only increased the likelihood of resort to physical seizure and occupation of buildings but enabled the rebels to escape unanimous condemnation and gain widespread support among students and faculty once the seizure occurred.[78]

Were these young rebels the philosophical offshoots of their liberal elders or did they have their own, independent strain of thought? In 1997, *New York Times* critic Edward Rothstein laid out the basis for the latter conclusion. "The New Left" wrote Rothstein, "was not a variant of liberalism. . . . It was a different order of politics, in which conversion was as important as reason and renunciation was as important as idealism." The older liberalism of Rothstein and others "was a product of the Enlightenment," which championed rational discourse and incremental reform. The radicalism of the 1960s, according to Rothstein, was not part of this tradition because of its irrationality, violence, and desire to "overturn the world."[79]

On the other side was M. Stanton Evans, a conservative columnist, who argued that "the new left is operating within a conceptual framework supplied by the professoriate. Its ideological position is an extension of the liberal view and not a repudiation of it." Evans noted that the response of both the New Left and liberals to such issues as Vietnam, the Cold War, civil rights, and "egalitarian economics" was similar. "The new left perceives events through the lenses provided by the ideology of liberalism." Evans believed, further, that the New Left responded to these issues "with emotions liberalism has designated as appropriate." Although not all of the liberal faculty at Columbia would have designated the Columbia takeover and the behavior of the students as "appropriate," they certainly reacted more favorably to the protesters than they would have if the university had been taken over by members of the conservative Majority Coalition.[80]

Whether the New Left and mainstream liberalism were blood brothers or just passing acquaintances, the student protests helped throw the dominant liberalism of postwar America into a tail spin. John Lindsay tried to balance himself between these two ideologies, with great consequences for his political future. The historian Allen Matusow described how the New Left's "insistent challenge threw mainstream liberals on the defensive. Confronted by the rage of their own children, mainstream liberals moved left. Those who did not—the Johnsonian liberals of the Democratic Party, the corporate liberals of new left demonology—lost their capacity to shape events." Speaking of the student revolt at Harvard in 1969, Roger Rosenblatt could easily have been describing Columbia in 1968: "Liberalism rolled over on its back like a turtle awaiting the end."[81]

AFTERMATH

During the summer of 1968, Grayson Kirk announced that he was stepping down as president of Columbia. He said his retirement had nothing to do with the student protests a few months earlier, but no one, of course, believed that. Vice President Truman, a respected scholar and the natural successor to Kirk, also left Columbia, his reputation in tatters. (He later became president of Mount Holyoke College, where he served admirably for many years.) The construction of the gym in Morningside Park was postponed and eventually canceled. According to Gottehrer, "There is no gym on their strip of park, whose shrubbery once again is cover for muggers. If anyone in the neighborhood thinks these days about Columbia's gym, they probably wish it had been built after all. The neighborhood could use it. But then, no one really talks about it any more." Not surprisingly, Columbia saw the number of applications for admission in the fall of 1969 drop by over 20 percent. It was the only Ivy League school to suffer a drop in applications.[82]

In the spring of 1969, Columbia again saw SDS on the rampage. On April 17, two hundred radicals took over Philosophy Hall but left the building voluntarily after one day. Two weeks later, radical students, some armed with clubs and chains, took over two other campus buildings. The radicals tried to evict some of the faculty from the buildings, and struck government professor James Young in the face with a club. Getting little sympathy from the campus at large, the students left the buildings in the middle of the night after warrants were signed for their arrest. The protest soon fizzled. One Columbia protester, Susan Stern, described feeling "beaten, depressed, miserable, and confused" as the radicals left the two buildings at dawn. Yet the virus of rebellion spread to other city campuses during the spring of 1969. Two hundred mostly black and Puerto Rican students at Brooklyn College invaded and vandalized the president's office and, according to the *Times*, "created general disorder there for three hours." At Queens College, a group of mostly black students roamed the campus "overturning bookcases, emptying card catalogs and smashing display cases in the main library. They also threw chairs and tables through large plate-glass windows in the faculty dining room . . . "[83]

Many of the leaders of Columbia SDS went on to form the core of the increasingly radical national SDS and its violent splinter group, the Weather Underground. Mark Rudd became one of the leaders of SDS's Days of Rage in Chicago in the fall of 1969. Rudd, though, reportedly avoided arrest and bodily harm, solidifying a reputation for cowardice he first earned at Columbia. Kirkpatrick Sale described Rudd at Chicago: "A tall, hunched figure in a coat and tie suddenly emerged from the darkness, looked around as if bewildered, stood for a moment, and walked quickly off: it was Mark Rudd, in 'straight' disguise, a general who it seems had decided not to march with his troops." At a December 1969 meeting of SDS at Flint, Michigan, Rudd gave a speech that highlighted the growing violence of the student radicals. "It's a wonderful feeling to hit a pig. It must be a really wonderful feeling to kill a pig or blow up a building." J. J. Jacobs, another leader of Columbia SDS, who became a Weatherman, was quoted as saying at Flint, "We're against everything that's 'good and decent' in honky America. We will burn and loot and destroy."[84]

Ted Gold, another Columbia conspirator, veered further into violence in the years after Columbia. Journalist Dotson Rader met with Gold at the

West End Gate, a bar near Columbia, some time after the 1968 crisis. "He told me that we have to teach people that violence is not an abstraction," Rader said. "We have to confront them with it so that they can see what they're doing. . . . You see, our lives aren't really threatened by the Vietnam war now, and the liberals can continue along their comfortable ways. I still remember Ted saying, 'We've got to turn New York into Saigon.'" A few minutes after noon on March 6, 1970, an explosion ripped apart a Greenwich Village townhouse at 18 West Eleventh Street owned by the father of Cathy Wilkerson, a member of the Weather Underground. (The townhouse was once the boyhood home of the poet James Merrill.) Three Weathermen were killed, including Ted Gold; his body was ripped to shreds when the bomb he was working on, filled with one-and-a-half-inch roofing nails, exploded.[85]

Violence also marked the career of Dave Gilbert, the fourth Columbia SDS member who joined the Weathermen. Gilbert grew up in Chesnut Hill, a wealthy Boston suburb, and his father was a vice president of Hasbro Industries. Gilbert—along with Kathy Boudin, who had escaped from the 1970 Greenwich Village explosion, and a number of black revolutionaries—took part in the October 20, 1981, robbery of $1.6 million from a Brinks truck in Nanuet, New York. Gilbert and the others were captured as they bungled the getaway, but not before they murdered two policemen and one Brinks guard and injured one policeman and one Brinks guard. In a letter to his 1968 comrades written from jail and read at the twentieth anniversary of the 1968 Columbia rebellion, Gilbert wrote: "The struggle has turned out to be much longer, more difficult, and complex than we had imagined."[86]

John Lindsay's own struggle to reform New York was also growing more difficult and complex. As the New Left challenged traditional liberalism, Lindsay was caught in the middle. This would become apparent as the battle over how to reform the New York City public schools came to a head.

8

FROM INTEGRATION TO DECENTRALIZATION TO COMMUNITY CONTROL: REFORMING THE NEW YORK CITY PUBLIC SCHOOLS

> The children of the poor—no matter what their race or ethnic origin—have never done well in the schools of New York City.
>
> —Diane Ravitch[1]

Talk of decentralizing the school system—like the Civilian Complaint Review Board issue—predated John Lindsay's tenure. Both controversies dated back to 1954. Much as it had with the Review Board, the civil rights movement provided the impetus for education reform. But it was under Lindsay's mayoralty that the forces of school reform converged. Lindsay saw education reform as a way of making the city more responsive to the long-neglected needs of New York's minorities. Lindsay also saw school reform as yet another battle against an inefficient and uncaring bureaucracy, in this case the Board of Education. The issue of school decentralization led directly to the crippling 1968 teachers' strikes and the controversy over the experimental Ocean Hill–Brownsville school district in Brooklyn.

School reform decentralization did not follow a straight line; rather, it traced a series of lines that converged in the ghetto streets of Ocean Hill–Brownsville. It began with grassroots resistance in the black community to the Board of Education's slow pace in integrating public schools. This grassroots movement was aided by left-wing activists who created the intellectual underpinnings for an attack on the school bureaucracy. Then the Ford Foundation, eager to fund experiments that would improve the lives of minorities, entered the fray. Ultimately, this coalition abandoned the idea of integration and pushed for community control of ghetto schools. If minority children were to be relegated to ghetto schools, these activists argued, their parents should at least have control over those schools. On the other hand, decentralization, supported by Lindsay and much of the city's elite, represented mostly procedural and administrative changes in the school system. Decentralization did not equal community control. Community control represented a radical change, supported by the black community and education activists, that would have transferred much of the power over education from teachers and the Board of Education to parents and local communities.

In attempting to reform the public-school system, Lindsay faced a problem common to many well-to-do New Yorkers: neither he nor his wife had ever set foot inside a public school as a child, and all four of the mayor's children attended private school. In 1966, the Lindsay's oldest daughter, following in her mother's footsteps, was attending Miss Porter's School in Farmington, Connecticut. The three youngest attended private schools in the city. (To be fair, Mayor Wagner's two sons did not attend public schools either.) This made the difficult task of reforming the city's schools even more arduous, for it lessened the moral authority of the mayor on an issue of great importance to parents.

With over 1.1 million students, 70,000 teachers, 43,000 administrators, and 900 schools, the New York school system was (and remains) the largest in the country. During the second half of the 1960s, this system would undergo tremendous turmoil. One reason school reform ultimately failed was that political leaders like Lindsay sent ambiguous signals about the extent and meaning of reform. The promise of reform was great: increased control by parents over the city's schools. Unfortunately, the legal mechanism and political will to create such change was not present. Neither Lindsay nor minority parents had enough political strength and savvy to bring about such massive changes.

THE AGE OF INTEGRATION

The issue of school reform emerged in the wake of the Supreme Court's 1954 *Brown v. Board of Education* decision. The New York City Board of Education reacted swiftly to the decision. First, it created the Commission on Integration to come up with recommendations on how best to integrate the city's schools. Second, the board issued a statement affirming the Supreme Court's opinion that "segregated racially homogeneous schools damage the personality of minority group children." The board stated fur-

ther that "public education in a racially homogeneous setting is socially unrealistic and blocks the attainment of the goals of democratic education.
Whether this segregation occurs by law or by fact . . . it is now the clearly
reiterated policy and program of the Board of Education to devise and put
into operation a plan which will prevent the further development of such
schools and would integrate the existing ones as quickly as practicable."

The late 1950s and early 1960s represented the high point of the belief in
integration, when it was thought that social problems would be minimized
if only the barriers between the races were eliminated. Yet, as the education
critic David Rogers wrote in the 1960s, despite a decade of the "most 'advanced' policy statements ever written on school desegregation . . . there has
been little implementation." The board took little substantive action on its
noble rhetoric.[2]

The year after the *Brown* decision, a Public Education Association study
found that 42 New York City elementary schools had 90 percent or more
blacks and Puerto Ricans and 9 junior high schools had 85 percent or more
blacks and Puerto Ricans. These 51 schools represented 8 percent of the
city's elementary and junior high schools. Though the segregated schools
tended to be older, less maintained, and had fewer experienced teachers, the
teacher-to-pupil ratios and per-pupil expenditures were roughly similar to
those of predominantly white schools.

Three years after *Brown*, the Board of Education created a master plan to
integrate the city's schools. The plan included busing students, transferring
teachers, zoning new integrated school districts, and building new schools in
areas bordering black and white neighborhoods to facilitate integration. The
plan's wording, though, was ambiguous enough to blunt its effect. Thus, integration plans were again stalled. The school superintendent at the time
supported the concept of neighborhood schools, and Mayor Robert Wagner
was determined to stay out of school affairs. Still, as three academic supporters of school reform noted, "The board was ahead of most of the country merely by virtue of its attempt."[3]

In 1959, new school superintendent John Theobald, a supporter of integration, ordered the transfer of a few hundred black students from overcrowded schools in Bedford-Stuyvesant to underutilized, mostly white
schools in Ridgewood and Glendale, Queens. Though this was done to relieve overcrowding and not to achieve integration, the move set off opposition among whites and helped spark the neighborhood schools movement.
The transfer idea was an isolated move. It disappointed blacks who hoped for
a more sweeping gesture to integrate the city's schools and angered whites
who feared the effect of inner-city schoolchildren on their schools. Education
critic Diane Ravitch, in *The Great School Wars: A History of the New York City
Public Schools*, noted that the fight for neighborhood schools was about the
right of communities "to control their schools and to exclude outsiders who
had not earned the privilege of residing in their neighborhoods."[4]

A year later the board proposed an open enrollment program whereby black junior high school students in overcrowded schools were allowed to transfer to underutilized schools in white neighborhoods. But only 677 students of the 20,000 eligible took advantage of the program. One reason was that many minority parents, much like white parents, wanted their children educated in their own neighborhood. Principals, superintendents, and teachers were also accused of sabotaging the effort by not informing black parents or dissuading them from making the move. These educators feared losing some of their best and most motivated students. Another integration plan introduced in 1962 paired twenty-four schools in white neighborhoods with schools in black neighborhoods from grades one through six. The plan was that during the first three years black and white students would attend school together in one neighborhood, and during the next three years they would attend school together in the other neighborhood. Unfortunately, though many pairings were proposed, only a handful were implemented and few proved successful.[5]

By the early 1960s, the city had accomplished very little to foster integration, despite the Board of Education's encouraging words. Meanwhile, changing demographics made the task of integrating city schools more difficult. During the 1950s, New York City lost over 800,000 mostly middle-class whites and gained over 700,000 mostly poor blacks and Puerto Ricans. In 1940 the city's black population was merely 6 percent. By 1968, blacks made up nearly 20 percent of the city's population. The number of schools in the city with more than 90 percent minorities grew from 8 percent in 1955 to 28 percent by 1968. By 1963, minorities represented 40 percent of the students in New York's public schools. Between 1957 and 1964, the percentage of white students in the city's public schools decreased from 68.3 percent to 54.5 percent. The white student population declined from 64.6 to 42.5 percent in the Bronx and from 72.3 to 53.6 in Brooklyn. Many whites either left the city or put their children in private schools. One estimate had 40,000 white pupils leaving the city's schools every year during this time, and a report by the state commissioner of education, James Allen, predicted that this number would rise as high as 60,000 in the coming years.[6]

Despite these changing demographics, Commissioner Allen tried to reignite the spark for integration. Commenting on all state schools in 1963, Allen said, "The racial imbalance existing in a school in which the enrollment is wholly or predominately Negro interferes with the achievement of equality of educational opportunity and must therefore be eliminated from the schools of New York State." He challenged school districts to create plans to undo the racial imbalance in their schools. He declared that any school with more than 50 percent minorities was racially unbalanced and, by definition, was failing to provide equal opportunity. Allen's statements were certainly liberal and humanitarian, but, as Ravitch pointed out, "Stating that predominance of a particular racial or ethnic group in a school makes that school inferior is, on the face of it, a libel against that group, whether they are black, Italian, Jewish, or whatever."[7]

Despite Allen's prodding, by 1964 the Board of Education had concluded that ending racial imbalance in schools was impossible. It refused to consider involuntary busing and felt that any timetable for integration, a constant demand by civil rights leaders, was unrealistic. Instead the board offered to improve the racial balance in one-fifth of the city's predominantly minority schools and improve education in all ghetto schools. This timid response led to a citywide boycott of schools on February 3, 1964, led by Reverend Milton Galamison, pastor of Siloam Presbyterian Church in Brooklyn, in which almost half of the city's children stayed away from school.[8]

Trying again to revive the issue of integration, Commissioner Allen came out in May 1964 with a report calling for the desegregation of the city's schools. The Allen Report criticized the Board of Education for its inability to handle the situation: "Nothing undertaken by the New York City Board of Education since 1954, and nothing proposed since 1963 had contributed or will contribute in any meaningful degree to desegregating the public schools of the city." The Allen Report was titled "Desegregating the Public Schools of New York City," but actually the plan it proposed did not target desegregation directly. What the Allen Report called for was a change in the structure of the city's school system from six years in elementary school, three years in junior high school, and three years in high school to a system of four–four–four. The first four years of elementary education would remain at the neighborhood level. For grades five to eight, students would travel to more integrated intermediate schools, two years earlier than under the present system, and then on to high school for grades nine to twelve. This reorganization was scheduled to be completed by 1973. New schools would have to be built, most in border areas between white and black neighborhoods.

Yet this plan, like all previous plans the past ten years, would not have achieved integration, given the existing demographics and political realities. With fewer white students in the public schools, integrating schools along the lines of Allen's proposals would have required a massive citywide redistribution of students.

Another question that cropped up was the number of black teachers in the city's public schools. By 1968 there were only three black principals in the entire school system, all female. In addition, there were fifty-five black assistant principals, four black acting principals, and forty-five black acting assistant principals. This came to less than 3 percent of all supervisory positions. Almost 8 percent of all regular city teachers in February 1966 were black.[9]

Academic performance in the city's public schools was poor. In the 1966–67 school year, one-third of the city's public school children were at least one year behind the national average in reading and math. The number of sixth-graders scoring below the state-defined minimum standards increased from 31 percent in 1965 to 45 percent in 1966, compared to 20 percent and 23 percent statewide. Only two-thirds of the city's public high school students scheduled to graduate in 1967 actually did. Only one-third received academic diplomas. In 1963, of the roughly 21,000 students receiving academic degrees, just 331 were Puerto Rican and 762 were black.[10]

Many school critics tried to portray New York City as just as segregated as the South, albeit as a result of residential patterns rather than law. Although most of the discussion centered on elementary and intermediate schools, a look at Brooklyn and Queens high schools shows that they *were* integrated, even in 1960. In that year, seven of the thirty-two high schools in these two boroughs had between 54 and 22 percent minority students. By 1964, eleven of thirty-three high schools had more than 20 percent minority students. Some of these schools, such as Brooklyn's Boys High School, Prospect Heights, Eastern District, and Thomas Jefferson, were quickly becoming overwhelmingly minority. By 1968, only three of the thirty-seven high schools in these two boroughs had fewer than 10 percent minority students. Eight schools had more than 50 percent minorities. Demographic shifts in these two outer boroughs were integrating schools, although many would quickly turn predominantly minority as white students left their rapidly changing neighborhoods and schools for private schools or the suburbs.[11]

THE EMERGENCE OF I.S. 201

Harlem's Intermediate School 201 was originally conceived, in 1958, to ease overcrowding at nearby schools. But by the time it opened for the new school year in September 1966, it had become a symbol of a new attitude among the city's black community toward integration. Minority parents had grown frustrated by the lack of progress on integration, by the ineffectiveness of the Board of Education, by the lack of initiative shown by Mayor Wagner, by the political forces arrayed in opposition to integration, and by the innumerable practical and demographic obstacles facing integration. Such frustrations caused blacks to ask whether separate always had to mean unequal.[12]

I.S. 201 is located in an area of light industry and blighted tenements called the East Harlem Triangle. On Madison Avenue between 127th and 128th Streets, it is in the shadow of the Metro North railroad tracks that funnel commuters from their homes in the suburbs to their jobs in Manhattan. Architectural historian Robert A. M. Stern noted that I.S. 201, which cost $5 million to build, was part of a transformation in the design of public schools toward "fortified strongholds, refugees against the decaying city." According to Stern, "None was more hostile in its impact" than I.S. 201.

> The school confronted its neighborhood with windowless facades consisting of two floors of brick and concrete carried on pilotis. An open ground-floor space beneath the building was intended for public use as a passageway or recreation area, but the space was so low, especially in relation to its width and length, that it was dark and dreary and proved uninviting. Inside, the lack of windows in the classrooms (there were windows in the corridors) was meant to heighten students' concentration by isolating them from their undesirable surrounding, but the design became a symbol for the status of inner-city blacks as "invisible" members of society.

The windowless school was designed to prevent noise from the trains, shut out dreary views of the surrounding neighborhood, and eliminate the problem of broken windows caused by vandals. The school was air-conditioned (although it took two years to get it to work properly). Still, according to one woman involved at I.S. 201: "Many parents in the community are unimpressed by the design of the building, and unimpressed by the fact that it cost more than five million dollars—the most expensive in the city. There are already complaints and rumors that with no windows the lighting will not be adequate, the children will all suffer from eye strain, that air conditioning all the time is unhealthy."[13]

A second problem was the school's name: the Arthur A. Schomburg School. There was some confusion as to how the school was named. The local parents association, the Harlem Parents Committee, claimed it was given responsibility for naming the school, but was slighted when the Board named the school after Schomburg before hearing the committee's suggestions. Daniel Schreiber, district superintendent of schools, claimed that the name was agreed to at a meeting of the local school board, but that those not present at the meeting later objected. Part of the complaint against the name was the belief among many that the school had been named after a German Jew. In reality, Arthur Schomburg (born Arturo Schomburg) was a recognized bibliophile and historian of black culture who was born in Puerto Rico to a black mother and white father. He moved to New York in 1891 and became active in the Harlem Renaissance. He sold his extensive collection of books, prints, paintings, pamphlets, and photographs to the New York Public Library in 1926, and it became the nucleus of the Schomburg Center for Research in Black Culture, located in Harlem. In many ways, the choice of Schomburg was perfect for a school that was to be evenly divided between black and Puerto Rican students. The temporary controversy over the name highlighted how suspicious minority parents were of the Board of Education.[14]

By far the school's biggest problem was its location. Built in the middle of a black and Puerto Rican neighborhood, far from the nearest white schoolchild, I.S. 201 was destined to be segregated. The school was built there mainly because it would cause the least displacement of people. Board of Education officials assured black leaders that integration was their goal for I.S. 201 and that white students from Queens, just over the Triborough Bridge, would be attracted to the new school's superior facilities and programs. I.S. 201 was designed to be a "magnet" school, providing quality, cutting-edge education, including smaller-than-average class size, cultural and recreation centers, and greater parental involvement. The Board of Education selected a well-respected white principal, Stanley Lisser, to run the school. Lisser, dedicated to making the school a model for inner-city education, handpicked a teaching staff for I.S. 201 that was nearly one-half black.

In an attempt to attract white students to the new school, the Board of Education sent flyers to Queens parents extending "an invitation to education for a modern world" at I.S. 201. "For successful living in a democratic, multi-cultural and multi-racial city, nation and world," the flyer read, "pupils today must be provided not only with top-flight instruction but also with opportunities for study and play with youngsters of differing backgrounds." It played up the award-winning design of the school, the air-conditioning, the high-quality, handpicked staff, small class sizes, parental and community involvement, and a progressive curriculum with "special emphasis upon the contributions of Afro-Americans and Puerto Ricans." Despite the good intentions of the board, most Queens parents were put off by the school's distance from their homes, its blighted and dangerous neighborhood, and the growing controversy over the school itself.[15]

By early 1966, it was obvious that few white children would attend I.S. 201. Instead, the school's population would be split between blacks and Puerto Ricans. This was not what black leaders thought of as "integrated." Civil rights activist Isaiah Robinson wrote to School Superintendent Bernard Donovan about the situation: "We have knowledge that your office with deliberate calculation intends to use Puerto Rican students on a 50–50 basis to give the impression that I.S. 201 is racially integrated. This tactic, sir, will attract the strongest, most militant protest from this organization and others allied with us in the struggle for real racial integration of New York City schools. This in itself will turn I.S. 201 into a battleground."

At a meeting between pro-integration white liberals and the Harlem Parents Committee, Robinson hinted, half jokingly, that since whites were not coming up to Harlem schools and black students were not being invited to downtown schools, blacks should accept their segregation and run their own schools.[16]

THE BUNDY REPORT

Throughout the fall of 1966, John Lindsay made one thing clear: He was determined to exert his influence over education policy. He criticized the Board of Education for the "clumsy aspects" of its handling of the I.S. 201 controversy. In contrast to Mayor Wagner, who ceded authority in school matters to the Board of Education and the superintendent of schools, Lindsay saw himself as a "partner" in education policy with the Board of Education, the teachers, and the communities. While he would respect the independence of the Board of Education, his goal for reforming the city included the school system. He wanted to break up the power of the Board of Education and its bureaucracy and bring more control to local groups. People were alienated from government, according to Lindsay, because power had become too centralized. Though he did not make it explicit, Lindsay gave notice that he considered the city's educational bureaucracy just another "power broker" in need of taming.

Lindsay inherited the Board of Education's handling of school integration, as well as the situation at I.S. 201. Despite these problems, the Lindsay administration was determined to push the ball forward on school reform. First, the head of the Human Resources Administration, Mitchell Sviridoff, was a believer in decentralizing the school system. "Most people don't realize that the notion of school decentralization did emanate from the Human Resources Administration," said Sviridoff. "We were of the view that the integrationist policy was never going to work." Mario Fantini, an education expert at the Ford Foundation and an early advocate for community control of schools, wrote in October 1966 that he believed "the strategy of the newly formed Human Resources Division of the Lindsay administration has been to utilize [I.S.] 201 as a lever for considering broader problems of urban education. The most central concern of the Human Resources Division is how to break up the bureaucratic educational system which to date has been relatively impervious to outside influence." According to Fantini, Sviridoff wanted to break up the centralized school system into a "sub system network" made up of a "cluster of schools responsible to a decentralized Board composed of local leadership and representatives from various agencies in the community." Fantini wrote that Sviridoff was interested in getting "universities, industrial firms, teachers' unions, parents" involved in running these decentralized schools.[17]

On another front, Lindsay's budget director, Fred Hayes, suggested to the mayor in 1966 that the city was being shortchanged in the aid it received from the state for education. Though New York City consisted of five counties, it was considered by the state as one entity for the purposes of dispensing education aid. Apportionment of state aid was based on real estate values (areas with lower values got proportionately more assistance), and the higher property values in Manhattan and Queens skewed the balance for the entire city, pushing the city over the state average and disqualifying the entire city school system for extra aid. If each borough were treated by the state as a separate county, the Bronx, Brooklyn, and Staten Island would receive more money. The total gain for the city would have been $54 million for 1966 and over $100 million the following year. Hayes proposed to get the extra funding by breaking up the school system in name only, leaving the basic school administration intact.[18]

The state legislature was not eager to allow the city this loophole. It feared other cities would try similar schemes to extract more education money from Albany's coffers. Instead, the legislature offered to give the city the extra money it sought on the condition that it actually break the school system down into five separate systems. The idea had intrigued Republican State Senator John Marchi for some time. Had it happened, Marchi's borough of Staten Island would have received more school funding. Marchi, later known as the godfather of the Staten Island secessionist movement, was also interested in gaining more autonomy for his forgotten borough.

To carry out its will, the state legislature ordered Lindsay to prepare "a comprehensive study and report and formulate a plan for the creation and development of educational policy and administrative units within the city school district of the city of New York" by December 1, 1967.[19]

Lindsay created an entity, the Mayor's Advisory Panel on Decentralization of the New York City Schools, to conduct the study and make a report. To head the panel he chose McGeorge Bundy, the president of the Ford Foundation. Journalist David Halberstam described Bundy as "aristocratic, a Brahmin, and yet not a prisoner of the Brahmin world, with a cold, lucid mind. Some of us thought of him as the best the country could offer." Lindsay also named to the panel Lloyd Garrison, president of the Board of Education (he was later replaced by Alfred Giardino, who also took over as president of the Board of Education); Francis Keppel, who had until recently served as national commissioner of education in the Johnson administration; Antonia Pantoja, president of the Puerto Rican Forum; Mitchell Sviridoff; and Benetta Washington, director of the Women's Training Center of the Job Corps and wife of the housing administrator, Walter Washington. The Ford Foundation's Mario Fantini was named staff director. Bundy, Keppel, Sviridoff, and Washington were viewed as non-New Yorkers, and so the panel was vulnerable to attacks that it was composed of outsiders with little standing in the city or knowledge of its schools. Conspicuously missing from the panel were representatives of two groups: middle-class whites and the teachers' union. According to Marilyn Gittell, "The union was asked, the union was begged, the union was coddled"; Fantini repeatedly asked Albert Shanker, the head of the United Federation of Teachers (UFT), to be a part of the panel. Journalist Martin

Mayer reported that people at the Ford Foundation circulated word that Bundy wanted to include a representative from the UFT on the panel, but Lindsay had vetoed the idea.[20]

It is surprising that no member of the panel represented parent associations from the outer boroughs such as the Parents and Taxpayers Association. These groups had been fighting for neighborhood schools in response to busing and forced integration since the early 1960s. The Bundy Panel could have been a terrific opportunity to bring together minorities and conservative whites around the idea of local control of schools. Instead, the interests of the white middle class were ignored, perhaps because of the lingering bitterness among liberals that these whites had opposed the post-*Brown* integration plans.

The Board of Education, the main body responsible for education policy, worried that Lindsay would use the decentralization controversy to reduce its power and meddle in policy. Along these lines, it especially resented the Bundy Panel. Even before the members of the panel were named, Board of Education President Lloyd Garrison (also a member of the panel) sent a telegram to the legislative leaders in Albany and Governor Nelson Rockefeller marking off the board's territory. "If there is to be any legislation concerning decentralization of the New York City public school system," Garrison wrote, "such decentralization plans should be the responsibility of the Board of Education of the City of New York. The Board of Education is the legal entity for the conduct of the city's schools and it has the experience and the information from which to make the most effective plans."[21]

The Bundy Panel released its recommendations in November 1967, summarizing its view of the school system in a letter to Lindsay accompanying the report: "We find that the school system is heavily encumbered with constraints and limitations which are the result of efforts by one group to assert a negative and self-serving power against someone else." The report began by pointing out that the "New York City school system, which once ranked at the summit of American public education, is caught in a spiral of decline." It placed the cause of this decline primarily on the shoulders of the large, complex bureaucracy that ran the system. In place of this bureaucracy the Bundy Panel recommended a "community school system, consisting of a federation of school districts and a central education agency." The number of new local school systems would be between thirty and sixty and would have control over all elementary and secondary education within its borders. The community boards would be partly elected and partly appointed. The report suggested that each district receive an allocation of funds, distributed from the central authority according to an objective formula. The community board would be allowed to hire a superintendent to run the district's schools. The Bundy Panel sought to retain tenure rights for teachers who already had tenure, but suggested that all future tenure decisions be made by the community boards. The boards would also be allowed to hire teachers and professional staff from "the widest possible sources so long as hiring is competitive and applicants meet state qualifications."[22]

Had they been instituted, these recommendations would have broken the monopoly of the teachers' union and destroyed the power of the education bureaucrats at Board of Education headquarters at 110 Livingston Street. Though it did not state so explicitly, the Bundy Report had implications for two fundamental aspects of public education in the city. First, it acknowledged that the education innovations of the previous decade had generated virtually no answers for how to educate poor minority children. Devolving power back to smaller units with greater parental and community involvement was an admission of the failure of the education establishment. Second, the Bundy Panel practically ignored the issue of integration. While most education statements of the previous decade at least paid lip service to integration, the Bundy Report seemed to admit the difficulties, if not the impossibility, of integration. This occurred despite a warning in 1966 from Mario Fantini to Bundy that "in no way should the task force be viewed as an alternative to integration, but rather as dealing with those basic problems and issues which can lead to quality education."[23]

Many observers pointed out that the Bundy Panel's recommendations sought to remake the city's schools along the lines of more successful suburban school systems. As the *Times*'s education reporter, Fred Hechinger, noted, the decentralized powers granted to the communities in the Bundy Report "seem[ed] to differ very little from those of a school board in Scarsdale, Palo Alto, or Shaker Heights. Behind the plan is this theory: If suburban school districts can let their citizens, who are elected or in a few cases appointed to the local school board, run their educational affairs, why not try the same approach in the city?" The Council of Supervisory Associations of the Public Schools of New York City (CSA), the union representing school principals and administrators, noted that this "analogy is highly inaccurate," mainly because suburban school districts possess the power to collect and distribute revenue, whereas the community districts foreseen by the Bundy Panel "are artificially created areas and in few cases have the characteristics of true communities. It is easy to envision the squabbles that will arise among them over what they consider their fair share of educational funds."[24]

The response to the Bundy Report was swift and critical. Alfred Giardino, now the Board of Education president and a member of the Panel, viewed it as a vehicle through which Lindsay could exert control over education policy. The Board of Education released a statement opposing the Bundy Report, stating: "The strong difference that the Board of Education has with the panel is with its desire to go all the distance in one fell swoop by untried methods." It also warned that personnel decisions in schools would be seriously affected if the Bundy Report was implemented.

The Council of Supervisory Associations (CSA) also opposed the Bundy plan. The CSA argued that the city's school system had "achieved demonstrably excellent results over the years and continues to achieve superior educational results in most respects." Its main problems lay in "coping effectively with the education needs of disadvantaged children." The New York Board of Rabbis called the plan "a potential breeder of local apartheid." Even Bronx Borough President Herman Badillo, a reform Democrat, came out against the Bundy Report, echoing the UFT's warnings: "I can't think of anything that would be more conducive to civil strife. The election of local neighborhood boards would create strife because in many areas candidates would be running on ethnic lines."[25]

The United Federation of Teachers, though it supported a limited form of decentralization with safeguards for teachers' rights, nevertheless criticized the report. In its policy statement, the UFT said the plan would "irreparably harm the education system. . . . The Bundy model is not decentralization; it is Balkanization." The teachers also worried about teacher tenure and security. "Under the Bundy report," warned the UFT, "charges could be brought against a tenured faculty member by a community board of laymen with no professional expertise. This proposal is anti-professional. It would encourage local vigilantes to constantly harass teachers. No teacher with professional integrity could teach in such a district."[26]

The criticism from the UFT was not inevitable. In a friendly letter to Mario Fantini in June 1967, the UFT's Sandra Feldman had offered her ideas about decentralization. She believed that the Board of Education, under any decentralization plan, should retain powers to certify teachers, enforce educational standards, and set citywide education policy. But she also acknowledged that "local boards, whether elected or otherwise democratically selected, should have a large degree of decision-making power," including hiring their own district supervisor. In addition, "individual schools should have the right to prepare their own budgets, and should have some freedom to decide what to spend money on." Feldman made clear her desire that any plan safeguard teachers' rights. Teacher certification needed to continue, and local governing boards should not have the right to interview teachers, although their appointed administrators could. Teachers, not the community, would also choose textbooks and have the right to remove disruptive students. The tone of the letter suggested that the UFT was willing to work toward implementing some form of moderate decentralization, or at least it was in the summer of 1967.[27]

The Bundy Report was merely as an advisory document, not a precise blueprint for change. Mario Fantini said on television after the report's release, "If it [the Bundy Report] just engages the interested parties in a serious dialogue about reform, I think the panel itself would be pleased." Yet David Seeley, Lindsay's education adviser to the panel, later wrote that he "was somewhat surprised to hear McGeorge Bundy say at one meeting that he felt the job of the panel was purely intellectual—to develop the best plan possible—and that it would be up to the mayor to develop the political support for the plan." It was now up to Lindsay, who had created the Bundy Panel, to draft legislation and bring it before the state legislature in Albany. Considering the lingering ill will toward the mayor in Albany over his tax plan, it would be a difficult fight.[28]

On both the public relations front and the legislative front, the Lindsay administration's push for a decentralization bill floundered. Seeley and others noted that neither the Lindsay administration nor the Bundy Panel had adequately come to terms with the political strategy necessary to implement such a plan. For this reason, Seeley believed that the Bundy proposal was "dead on arrival." Lindsay, normally outspoken in defense of his initiatives, was unusually quiet regarding decentralization. He had spent his first two years clashing with the power brokers and "burning his credit cards." On the issue of school decentralization, though he personally may have been a strong supporter of the idea, he did not show the public fight and intensity that marked his battles for a Civilian Complaint Review Board or for his tax plan. As Maurice Berube wrote: "Certainly, much was lost by the mayor's caution. Lindsay's ability to transform most political issues into moral crusades would have appreciably helped the Bundy plan's chances had he decided to make a fight of it. Rather, Lindsay only seemed to be going through the motions of supporting the Bundy plan. He made few emphatic statements urging the plan either to the press or on his weekly television program." The bill Lindsay ultimately sent to Albany watered down Bundy's recommendations somewhat, allowing the Board of Education to retain some powers.[29]

David Seeley, who lobbied legislators for Lindsay's bill, saw the plan as "dead . . . deservedly killed by the way in which it had been mishandled." An official in the state Education Department called it "an impossible bill. It was so complicated that everybody threw up their hands in horror. . . . It was almost as though someone set out to sabotage the effort." One student of the episode called Lindsay's legislation "extraordinarily cumbersome and ill-conceived. . . . It was drafted by the corporation counsel, rather than by legislative staff. Perhaps it was the rush of time, perhaps a jealous guarding of his own prerogatives, or perhaps merely inexperience. In any event the legislation confounded many of the Albany veterans." Lindsay had not built public support for the Bundy plan, nor had he built political support among Albany legislators. There would be no legislation until the spring of 1968, and that legislation far from solved the problems of decentralization.[30]

As Mitchell Sviridoff noted, the Bundy Report called for administrative decontrol of the school system, not community control. Lindsay argued that the "fundamental problem limiting classroom education in the present system lies not with the inadequacies of staffing or program but with the unresponsive structure of the administrative machinery." Thus, poor ghetto education was not the fault of teachers, as community control supporters argued, but of an "unresponsive" bureaucracy. As elite supporters of decentralization focused on bureaucratic failures, grassroots community control activists continued to damn the white power structure for miseducating their children. Their solution to this problem would entail going beyond bureaucratic decontrol. As the Bundy Panel was recommending moderate decentralization of the school system, Bundy's underling, Mario Fantini, was using Ford money to subsidize a more radical version of education reform: complete community control of ghetto school districts by minority parents.[31]

THE RISE OF THE MILITANTS

The issue of community control was driven, in large part, by radicals within the black community. Frustration with the slow pace of school integration led to a growing militancy. But there was a dark side to this: increasing violence and hostility directed at the mostly white teachers and principals. Black militancy was a strong influence on education reform in New York during the 1960s.

In December 1966, the Board of Education was temporarily taken over by black and white militants, an event that symbolized the changing tactics of the members of the school reform movement. During a hearing on the school's budget, Lillian Wagner, the president of the PTA at Junior High School (J.H.S.) 263 in Brownsville, Brooklyn, demanded to speak out of turn. When the board refused to recognize her, protesters in the audience disrupted the meeting. Board President Garrison, a descendent of the abolitionist William Lloyd Garrison, abruptly adjourned the meeting and the board members left the room. The protesters then took over the board members' chairs, declaring that the board had "abdicated." In its place, the protesters declared themselves the "People's Ad Hoc Board of Education." The members of the new "board" were familiar names among education activists. Reverend Milton Galamison, the leader of the 1964 school boycott, was the president of the new "People's Board." Other members were Babette Edwards, a veteran of the I.S. 201 controversy and member of the Harlem Parents Committee; Robert Nichol, a white Protestant minister; David Spencer, the chairman of the I.S. 201 community council; Ellen Lurie and Rosalie Stutz of the militant education reform group EQUAL; and John Powis, a white Catholic priest who was a member of the Brownsville–Ocean Hill Independent Local School Board in Brooklyn.[32]

The "People's Board of Education" released a statement that should have put the mayor and the Board of Education on notice to the actual goals of the militants: "The People's Board plan proposes that all appropriations will come directly to the local School Board, school personnel to be hired by community supervisory bodies, and program and policy for education to be worked out by each community, using the School System's Central Headquarters as a resource center." For these militants, decentralization meant complete community control of local schools. The Board of Education and the teachers' union would, for all intents and purposes, be powerless under such a regime.[33]

On Tuesday morning, when President Garrison tried to retake his seat to restart the budget hearing, Galamison refused to move, declaring Garrison "out of order." The board members, unable to take their seats, left and allowed the militants another day's stay. The response to the sit-in was muted. Garrison said that he was not angry because he understood "the tensions and difficulties that have caused the emotions given full reign here." Though Mayor Lindsay remarked that he was "not persuaded that sit-ins and shouting matches are going to improve education in the city," he did not call for the militants' removal nor issue a direct denunciation of the protesters. Nor did the mayor defend the board. He was eager to appoint his own people to the board, who would then pursue his policies. Ravitch later noted that "this highly publicized sit-in made the board look ridiculous as well as ineffectual. . . . More and more, the board had the appearance of a paper tiger, a giant apparatus incapable of asserting power." Of course, the desire of the "People's Board" was clear: "We're trying to get rid of the Board of Education," said Galamison. "There's no other solution."[34]

The embarrassment ended late Wednesday afternoon when the protesters again refused to leave. Police cleared the room and arrested twelve protesters, including Galamison. Lindsay's chairman of the city Commission on Human Rights, William Booth, went to the Board of Education headquarters after the arrests to make sure there were no "explosions," but also to show his support for "the parents in their attempt to secure action from the Board of Education."

More troubling than the apparent acceptance of the takeover was the growing intimidation of white principals and teachers in inner-city schools. In 1966 there were 213 attacks on public school teachers; the following year there were 224. In December 1966, a group of thirty protesters blockaded the office of Kate Tuchman, a white Jewish principal of P.S. 125 on the border of Morningside Heights and Harlem. Earlier, a group of militants had asked Tuchman to "waive" her right to be principal. They barricaded her in her office for nearly an hour, waiting for her answer to their "request." Two of the people involved, Babette Edwards and Robert Nichol, were both active in the I.S. 201 controversy and the People's Board of Education. Their appearance at P.S. 125 suggested that protests came not from parents at the grass roots, but from a highly motivated and vocal band of militants.[35]

The following spring, black militants in Brooklyn engaged in low-level terrorism against white principals and teachers in schools in Brownsville and Bedford-Stuyvesant. At P.S. 284, fifty predominantly Jewish teachers refused to work for a half hour after a flyer attacking teachers was distributed. Written on some of the notes were messages such as "Out of here you no good Jew bastard" and "Don't come back here in Sept. if you know what's good for you." Two days later, the principal of P.S. 284, William Emmer, asked to be transferred out of the school. He and nine teachers had been singled out by Brooklyn CORE, led by Sonny Carson, and the Brownsville Community Council for lacking "sincere interest" in the children and for abusing them. By June, thirty of the fifty teachers at P.S. 284 asked to be transferred out of the school. The previous week, Harry Levine, principal of J.H.S. 258 in Bedford-Stuyvesant, requested a transfer after Brooklyn CORE demanded he leave the school. Levine said he had been threatened. CORE asked all principals in Brooklyn's ghetto schools to create a plan to improve reading scores and hire more black teachers. The response was unsatisfactory to CORE, and Carson said his group considered all but five of the thirty-two principals in the area to be "fired." Michael Romano, president of the Elementary School Principals Association, wrote that black radicals "really don't want white principals in the schools."[36]

Superintendent Bernard Donovan and Board of Education President Alfred Giardino condemned the intimidation of teachers and principals in a joint statement. They warned that education could not occur in "an atmosphere of unrest and tension brought about by unreasonable and threatening demands. . . . This is particularly true when the pressures have overtones of racial or religious bigotry." Sonny Carson was undeterred: "If Donovan thinks we are kidding, he had better wait until September and see what happens when those teachers, those principals try to come back to our community." In early June, CORE demanded that four principals be removed from their posts for "the mistreatment and abuse of the too few black teachers in the Brooklyn public schools." In late June 1967, Carson and nineteen other CORE members forced their way into the UFT offices in Manhattan and refused to leave for twenty-one hours. They carried signs saying UFT: STAY OUT OF THE BLACK COMMUNITY. In response to the attacks on teachers and principals, the Anti-Defamation League asked the city's Commission on Human Rights to investigate "blatant and vicious anti-Semitic outbursts and racist behavior."[37]

One of the worst examples of the intimidation of school personnel occurred on January 19, 1968. Four black men entered J.H.S. 117 in the Clinton Hill section of Brooklyn asking to see the principal, John O'Connor.

The men, none of whom had children at the school, wanted to talk to O'Connor about an anonymous letter to the *Amsterdam News* that claimed that children had been locked out of school two weeks earlier on a frigid day. When O'Connor arrived, the men read the letter to him. One man called the principal "honky" and pushed him. When the acting assistant principal, George Elias, stepped in, he was pushed. Robert Goldberg, head of the social studies department, became involved. One secretary who witnessed the fight called it a "wild-Western brawl, with fists flying everywhere." O'Connor, forty-seven, and Goldberg, twenty-nine, were knocked out, while Elias, forty-five, was knocked down. A secretary fainted. Goldberg and O'Connor were brought to the hospital and stayed overnight, and O'Connor required three stitches inside his mouth. Only one of the assailants, Allie Lamont, twenty-nine, was caught. Lamont lived in Coney Island, a few miles south of Clinton Hill. The following day, Superintendent Donovan called for an emergency allocation of $1.25 million to create an armed security force throughout the city's school system.[38]

Some parent and community representatives seemed to condone the violence. Margaret Campbell, chairman of the Parents Organizations of District 13, in Bedford-Stuyvesant, said, "We don't say that anybody should beat up anybody. But we also say that nobody should have to feel that they have to beat someone. This system has made people feel like this. While we don't condone it, we're in a position where we cannot condemn it, knowing the root causes." Eulalee Ledlard, vice president of the parents association at J.H.S. 258 in Bedford-Stuyvesant and a member of the Parents Organizations of District 13, said in response to Donovan's request for a school security force, "If Superintendent Donovan is going to put guards or armed men in the schools to stand between the school and the community, we parents are all going to become Mr. Lamonts." Albert Vann, president of the African-American Teachers Association, called the attack at J.H.S. 117 "but an inkling of the increasing hostility felt by the black community as it begins to realize that it has no control over forces that directly and adversely affect its life, and the lives of its children. Daily hundreds of children are physically abused; daily thousands of children are psychologically and academically whipped." Some parents did condemn the attacks, such as the anonymous "irate parent" of two children who had graduated from J.H.S. 117 who wrote to the *Amsterdam News* to denounce the assault on O'Connor, calling him "a man of high caliber who has the interests of his students at heart." O'Connor, meanwhile, released a statement denying that any child had been locked out in the cold.[39]

In early February 1968, the UFT took out a full-page advertisement in the *Times* in the form of an open letter to the citizens of New York entitled "End Chaos in the Schools." The UFT's Al Shanker wrote: "Teachers in our public schools are becoming targets of a mounting volume of attacks by extremist groups. . . . Ugly pressure tactics are employed. School officials are hounded and harassed. Teachers are deprived of the most elementary right of due process. Threats and intimidation are the order of the day. Teachers are beaten in their classrooms by self-styled prophets of education reform. School after school has been enveloped by a climate of fear and chaos." In the face of what he felt was the Board of Education's capitulation to the demands of black militants, Shanker called for third-party arbitration in every disciplinary case against a teacher. Above all, Shanker issued a warning that would have grave consequences for the city. "The Executive Board of the UFT is recommending to our membership," Shanker wrote, "that whenever a teacher is dismissed or punished without the benefit of impartial review, we will close down the entire school district in which this action has occurred. And we will keep it closed until the injustice has been redressed."[40]

One incident pushed the controversy over I.S. 201 from an issue of decentralization to one of community control driven by Black Power sentiment: the February 1968 Malcolm X memorial held at the school. The memorial was described as lasting some four to six hours, with between 600 and 1,000 people in attendance, many from out of town. Many of those in the audience were high school students and younger children accompanied by their parents. The acting principal, Martin Frey, denied approval for the meeting, but Superintendent Donovan overruled him on the condition that no child from I.S. 201 could attend. Later Donovan claimed he was told the ceremony would be "dignified" and "educational" and that it would be held after school. Although it was a public program, reporters were barred from the assembly, except for a black reporter from the *Amsterdam News*. A policeman was also refused entrance to the auditorium, having been told it was a private meeting. The program consisted of speeches by Malcolm X's widow, Betty Shabazz, by the author James Baldwin, and an I.S. 201 aide, Herman Ferguson, as well as a play by LeRoi Jones. (Ferguson was free on bail, after being charged with owning weapons and plotting to kill the moderate civil rights leaders Roy Wilkins and Whitney Young.)

The *Amsterdam News* later reported about the program that blacks "fared much worse and endured many more stinging insults from their own black brothers than did whites who were not present but who were hollering more and very loudly. No one was spared!" Blacks were referred to as "stupid, black, niggers," "Uncle Toms," and "the white man's niggers" who frequented "white, dirty ass Jewish-owned bars." One running theme of the program, according to the *Amsterdam News*, was the need "to avenge Malcolm's death." James Baldwin, who called America the "Fourth Reich," was booed off stage after he began talking about good white liberals. The assembly was mostly dedicated to raising the self-esteem of blacks, with Afro-centric music and dance and salutes to Malcolm X.[41]

What caused the uproar was the blatant antiwhite attitudes that permeated the program. The most offensive moments came during Jones's play, performed by his Spirit House Movers and Players. One character said,

"We're not going to let the white man get us to killing each other. We're not going to eat his nasty ass pig. Wake up." He went on to call the white man "a diseased white bitch" who gave his diseases to blacks because of "the white man who ate filth." Another character said: "White people, your ass will be set on fire." Next, a twenty-minute pantomime was performed, which the *Amsterdam News* reporter described as follows:

> The silent drama opened with the white man on all fours while the black man walked proudly upright. Then the white man steals his knowledge from the black man and gradually lowers the black man until he becomes a prone, head-scratching, obeying servant. . . . Suddenly, there appears on stage a tall, black thinking brother, dressed completely in black. He forces the white man to return this stolen knowledge . . . The man in black then removes his head-scratching brother from the white man's slavery spell. Next he forces the white man back to crawling on all fours.

The play received a "deafening, sustained standing ovation."

The other offensive part of the program was a speech by Ferguson, whose talk of blacks arming themselves landed on the front page of the *Times* with the headline "Negroes Urged at I.S. 201 to Arm for 'Self-Defense.'" Besides referring to Donovan as "that honkie Irishman," Ferguson talked of the need for self-defense among blacks. He likened the war in Vietnam with the supposed attack upon the black community being planned by white officials. According to Ferguson, after destroying black America, the white man will "come in with his defoliation chemicals and spray all the watermelon patches, and remove all vestiges of us." Ferguson believed the "army is stockpiling supplies and ammunition and all the other things that are necessary for an all-out war in selected areas around the country." Ferguson spoke of the necessity of owning and using firearms: "When the deer hunting season comes in, in the fall, I certainly don't want any brother to have the unfortunate experience of developing 'buck fever' when he sees his first deer, zeros in on him, and then can't squeeze off the shot." In light of the paucity of deer in Queens, he was surely talking about human targets.[42]

Members of the I.S. 201 community council complained that the press blew the Malcolm X event out of proportion, unfairly maligning the educational aspirations of the ghetto community and reinforcing stereotypes among whites that made them less sympathetic to black demands. But at the very least, the Malcolm X memorial was a poor political move on the part of the Harlem community. Blacks who felt betrayed and ignored by the "white Establishment" expressed themselves in a way that only exacerbated tensions between the races. Had a white school held such an event and voiced antiblack feelings in the open, the reaction of the black community would certainly have matched, if not exceeded, the white community's reaction to what occurred at I.S. 201.

Despite all of this, the *Amsterdam News* reporter argued that the I.S. 201 program, "taken in sequence and context, was not an anti-white rally." The paper's editorial page called the uproar surrounding the service "lamentable," not because of the "alleged anti-white segments," but because "it gave further ammunition to those who seek to knock down Mayor Lindsay's plan to decentralize New York City's school system that is now before the Legislature." A report by the city's Commission on Human Rights called the charge of racism against the memorial service "unjustified." It found the memorial to be "solemn and dignified," although Ferguson's remarks were called "objectionable." The commission felt it was unfair to tar the memorial service with a racist feather for the unfortunate remarks of one man, whom the report said was not originally scheduled to speak. The memorial, in the words of the report, "was an example of the distinct merit of the idea of community control as it may operate in any district: the school being used as a community institution in honoring the community's own heroes."[43]

Superintendent Donovan said, "It is most unfortunate that an experiment designed to demonstrate the effectiveness of community participation should be endangered by irresponsible actions. Our schools cannot become the vehicles of political power, racism or ideological struggles." The Board of Education expressed its "shock" at the program and ordered Donovan to "establish clear control" over the East Harlem school. The ACLU defended the program on the ground that the Board of Education had no right to "concern itself with the content of what is said at any meeting by a private group on public property." (Since the program was held during the school day in a public school with students in attendance, the board did have authority over it.)

Mayor Lindsay offered his first comments on the affair the following day at a news conference in Oregon, where he was giving a political speech: "I hold no brief for the extreme position he [Mr. Jones] defines as black power. I respect him as a playwright, but I would not want to live in a city governed under his definition of black power." The mayor's education adviser, David Seeley, came down hard on the program: "I don't think that teaching racism or race-hatred of any kind ought to be permitted in a public school in New York City, whether the school system is centralized or decentralized." A few days later, the mayor, still in Oregon, gave a fuller statement of his attitude toward black militants. "The Board of Education must find a middle ground that prevents an impossible confrontation over I.S. 201," said the mayor. Lindsay refused to condemn the program for fear of driving the majority of the black community into the arms of the militants, saying, "It pays to avoid showdowns over questions that force the majority of the black community onto the side of a few militants."

At an Albany hearing four days later, Seeley pressed his attacks on the I.S. 201 memorial in the face of his boss's equivocation. "We're breeding revolutionaries in our city," Seeley told a committee headed by State Senator John Marchi. "We're goading minority groups into positions of hostility." Seeley also accused the Board of Education of being a "weak and vacillating instrument." More than a week after the memorial program, Lindsay finally said that though he understood the reasons for "a good deal of unhappiness and discontent" in East Harlem, he did not support the content of the Malcolm X memorial. "I am sure I can speak for lots of other people in condemning that kind of talk," the mayor said. "It's very bad indeed."[44]

By early 1968, the racial aspect of school decentralization and community control was unquestioned. Frustrated by poor schools and poor student performance and no doubt motivated by antiwhite and anti-Semitic animus, some blacks lashed out at the school system and its teachers. Statements coming out of I.S. 201 repeatedly used the term "genocide." David Spencer said black children were "being slaughtered through educational genocide." An October 1966 leaflet from the Parent and Community Negotiating Committee for Intermediate School 201 accused the Board of Education of seeking "to address itself to the criminally inferior education in Harlem only when a crisis erupts in the streets. . . . How can we save our children from the Board of Genocide?" In a letter to UFT President Shanker, the committee accused the union of winning the right "to retain the license to continue to miseducate and destroy Black and Puerto Rican children of New York City without being accountable to anyone."[45]

Such inflammatory language linked the poor performance of minority students to a deliberate policy by the Board of Education. Worse, it painted, in wildly conspiratorial language, a picture of a race war by whites against poor minority children. The word "genocide" was surely intended not only to invoke the horrors of the Holocaust, but also to irritate Jews, who were heavily represented in the city's school system as teachers, principals, and administrators.[46]

How seriously should one take the rantings of a small number of militants? One I.S. 201 activist, Dorothy Jones, said that "These groups, however much people outside Harlem may dislike and/or fear them, are a legitimate part of the Harlem scene." Diane Ravitch, noted the destructiveness of their rhetoric:

> The language of the militant protest groups took on an importance of its own, for words, no less than actions, have consequences. Implicit threats of violence ("whatever means necessary") and accusations of monstrousness ("educational genocide") contributed to an atmosphere in which flamboyant hyperbole replaced rational discourse. Where rational communication is impossible, so also are settlements which sat-

isfy both sides. How can anyone compromise with someone who is "destroying" his children? If politics and negotiation are scorned, the only alternatives left are total victory or total defeat.

Increasingly it looked as if total victory or total defeat would be the only options in the school battles of the late 1960s. Since total victory is rarely achieved in politics, total failure was the more likely scenario for education reform in New York.[47]

In addition to rising militancy among blacks, Lindsay also had to deal with rising militancy within the teachers' union. In 1961, the United Federation of Teachers had taken advantage of the city's liberal policy for collective bargaining for municipal unions and had won the right to represent all city teachers in contract negotiations. Since 1964, the UFT had been headed by Al Shanker, a tall, lanky, thirty-eight-year-old former math teacher. Shanker, who was born on the Lower East Side and grew up in Queens, considered himself a socialist. Ravitch noted: "Most UFT members, like Shanker, were from Jewish families which had immigrated from Eastern Europe and formed a cultural milieu where unionism, socialism, anarchism, and radicalism were avidly discussed."[48]

In September 1967, the UFT went on strike for over two weeks mostly over nonsalary issues such as how to deal with disruptive children and the expansion of the More Effective Schools (MES) program, which increased money for ghetto education. Deborah Meier, a white teacher in Harlem, wrote, "a serious deterrent to attracting teachers is the city's schools' reputation for unruly pupils and difficult classroom discipline." Al Vann of the Afro-American Teachers Association condemned the notion of the disruptive child, arguing that it was an example of cultural bias against black children who did not conform to middle-class notions of behavior. Nevertheless, the young union flexed its muscles with it first major strike, proving it could shut down the schools at will, regardless of state laws that forbade strikes by municipal unions. The 1967 strike helped solidify Shanker's position as the leader of the UFT and a major player in the city's education policy. But the strike gave minority parents ammunition for their belief that teachers really did not care about their children.[49]

THE BIRTH OF COMMUNITY CONTROL

Many saw the drive for school decentralization as threatening the older model of integration. Mario Fantini described a November 1966 meeting between Lindsay's Human Resources Administration chief, Mitchell Sviridoff, and black leaders such as Percy Sutton, Milton Galamison, and Livingston Wingate of the antipoverty program HARYOU-ACT. They warned that the Bundy Panel's recommendations should not be "presented as an alternative to school integration." These black leaders, Fantini wrote, were worried because they felt that "unless Negro groups continue to emphasize integration they will lose much of the 'lever' for change."[50]

Despite such concerns, more militant black leaders were willing to scrap integration in favor of community control of local schools. CORE's national director, Floyd McKissick, said the desire to integrate black students into white schools was akin to saying "mix Negroes with Negroes and you get stupidity. . . . Maybe a school committed to respect the individual, a school enjoying the confidence and support of the community, a school recognized to reflect its faith in the pupil and the parent can achieve excellence—even if that community is poor and black." Preston Wilcox, a professor of social work at Columbia University and a Harlem activist, had already begun questioning the assumption that segregation equaled inferiority. He summed up the indictment against the city's schools: "The present system has failed, and is failing, in its task of enabling minority group youth to seize the opportunities America holds out to its other citizens." In 1966, Wilcox wrote a paper entitled "To Be Black and to Be Successful," which became popular among community control activists. It asked the question: "Cannot J.H.S. 201 be utilized as an experimental school through the development of a strategy and a plan which places the responsibility for educational and administrative policy in the hands of the local community?"[51]

Wilcox's original plan was modest, especially when compared to later community control ideas. He called for the creation of a "school-community committee" made up of "ghetto-relevant individuals": parents, community leaders, and educational professionals. The committee would select, screen, and interview principals; hold open meetings where parents and teachers could bring complaints; "insure that the curriculum is both relevant and elevating to the lives and experience of the youth in the ghetto"; and supervise and administer after-school and weekend programs. The committee would also, oddly, "approve all news stories about the school and/or the students."[52]

As frustration and alienation mounted within the black community, liberal intellectuals began attacking the city's public school system. These critics charged that the schools were run by a closed and static bureaucracy, unwilling to reform itself and interested only in self-perpetuation. In the face of bureaucratic intractability, the quality of the city's schools was declining. The journalist Martin Mayer wrote in 1965: "The tradition of success is almost gone—in increasing numbers, teachers and principals live with the expectation of failure and weave a safety net of excuses. . . . All change is resisted because it implies a criticism of the present." Nowhere was this more evident than in the fact that by age twelve, the average black or Puerto Rican student was a full two years behind his or her white counterpart. Another critic wrote: "Five years of research on the New York schools have led me to the depressing conclusions that it is a 'sick' bureaucracy, incapable of reforming itself from within. Its structure and day-to-day operations regularly subvert the realization of its stated goals, prevent any flexible accommodations to changing client demands, and make orderly administration little more than a pleasant fantasy." Jason Epstein, writing in *The New York Review of Books*, charged that ghetto children were "largely without a functioning educational system at all, and the present school administration has shown that it is incapable of supplying them with one."[53]

At the forefront of the intellectual attack on the city's schools was Marilyn Gittell, an assistant professor of political science at Queens College. Maurice Berube, who had worked professionally with Gittell during the decentralization controversy, called her "a liberal who, when confronted by the evidence, arrived at radical conclusions." On the other side, Al Shanker referred to Gittell as "either brilliant and dishonest, or stupid as hell. Either way, you wouldn't like her." In 1963, she had written a report on the city's schools for Mayor Wagner's Temporary Commission on City Finances, which was eventually published in 1967 as the influential *Participants and Participation*. Gittell found that in education, poor minority parents had no voice in how their children were educated, and education policy was the preserve of unaccountable administrators at the byzantine Board of Education. Though her analysis was radical, Gittell's proposals were modest. She called for breaking up the school system into five borough-based districts. This would encourage greater participation at the local level among parents and begin to break the power of the school bureaucracy at the Board of Education.[54]

Gittell continued to write voluminously about the deficiencies of the school bureaucracy, and her writings brought her to the attention of community control activists. She worked as a consultant, intellectual guru, and go-between for the black communities. Gittell summarized the mood of those favoring vast reforms of the education system: "Within the ghetto, there is increasing belief that only the kind of redistribution of power that assures the ghetto community a greater role in the policy process will be acceptable. The survival of America's urban communities will depend upon their ability to respond to these pressures; somehow they must make the adjustments necessary to accommodate these demands."[55]

Equality of educational opportunity was increasingly tied to student performance. If students were not performing up to grade level, they must not be receiving the same quality education as better-performing students.

Not all intellectuals reached the same conclusions. The sociologist James Coleman undertook a study of educational opportunity for the U.S. Office of Education and wrote up his conclusions in a report, "Equality of Educational Opportunity." He suggested that student performance was determined as much by what was going on in the student's home as by what was going on at the student's school. By warning of deeper troubles facing minority children, the Coleman Report seemed to throw cold water on education reform, especially decentralization. Furthermore, if what Coleman said was true, no one could argue that the problems of minority children in the schools were due to solely a lack of funding. Nevertheless, the growing unease with New York schools was accompanied by an increase in school spending. In 1956–57, New York City spent $457 million on public schools; by 1966–67, the number had almost quadrupled, to $1.618 billion. During the same period, enrollment had increased by only one fifth. In the 1966–67 budget, the Board of Education spent over $64 million just on projects for educationally deprived children.[56]

Still, the community control message continued to take hold at I.S. 201. One parent leader, Helen Testamark, told reporters, "Either they bring white children in to integrate 201 or they let the community run the school—let us pick the principal and the teachers, let us set the educational standards and make sure they are met." When the Ad Hoc Parent Council at I.S. 201 met with Mayor Lindsay, Superintendent Donovan, and Board of Education President Lloyd Garrison, it was told that its plans for community control were against the law and impossible to enact.

Charles E. Wilson, the unit administrator for the I.S. 201 district, wrote about the struggles in the school and placed them within the civil rights struggle. "But 201 is more than a location," wrote Wilson. "At one and the same time, it is a site, the scene of apparently unending struggle, and a symbol of the dogged determination of the parents and community activists to have a voice in determining the future of their own children. Finally, 201 is a monument to the idea that resistance to oppression, in whatever form it takes, is the beginning of freedom."[57]

Ellen Lurie, a white leader of EQUAL, wrote to Preston Wilcox in January 1967, laying out the strategy for community control. "We are, after all, pushing for TOTAL DECENTRALIZATION," wrote Lurie, who acknowledged that such a goal could not be achieved "without great struggle." The decentralization that would become associated with John Lindsay and McGeorge Bundy was mainly an administrative one whose aim was to lessen the power of the city's education bureaucracy. But Lurie, Wilcox, Gittell, and others wanted something more far-reaching. Total decentralization meant, for Lurie, that "local districts are *completely* self-directing, within the regulations of the State Department of Education." The local boards that controlled these districts would have "complete power to review and appoint all staff in the district," including the hiring and firing of the superintendent. They would also have control over a lump-sum budget distributed by the Board of Education, as well as the ability to negotiate directly with the UFT over class size, job training, supervisory ratio, and the use of assistants. Only teachers' minimum salary level would be set by the Board of Education.[58]

In a defense of community control written for the *Amsterdam News* in 1968, Wilson and David Spencer (by then the president of the I.S. 201 Governing Board under the community control experiment) claimed that the "strongest argument" for community control "is found in the schools of the disadvantaged communities." Spencer and Wilson gave voice to the frustrations of ghetto parents and educators about the conditions that existed in these schools, which they called "factories of failure." Here, "irrelevant curriculum, uncertain teaching methods, pathological fear, and staff hopelessness combine with insidious self-defeating attitudes to preserve an outdated system of teacher-supervisor relationship and pupil-teacher relationship." Spencer and Wilson argued that although the Board of Education spoke of reform, it reacted "only fitfully and grudgingly to provide the most minimal kinds of adaptions."[59]

Throughout his congressional career and up to 1966, Congressman John Lindsay, was a strong supporter of integration, but nothing more—he was never willing to propose massive busing to achieve integration. When I.S. 201 parents met with Mayor Lindsay in July 1966, they found him unhelpful, despite his pro–civil rights reputation. They promised that if I.S. 201 was not integrated, they would close it down. The mayor's refusal to force the Board of Education to act immediately on their demands angered the parents. Lindsay, irritated at the intransigence of the parents, left early, and the meeting ended in a fiasco. Lindsay later wrote one of the parents, Babette Edwards, to apologize for leaving early. In his letter, he set forth his two goals for I.S. 201. First, "the school must have an outstanding creative program which offers academic opportunities of the highest quality. The program must be the expression of a viable partnership between the Board of Education and the community." Second, Lindsay called for a campaign "to encourage through every available means white parents outside the district to send their children voluntarily to I.S. 201 in September." Integration was still Lindsay's goal for I.S. 201. The only community control Lindsay offered was a "viable partnership" between the community and the Board of Education.[60]

But this approach was not acceptable to the Parent and Community Negotiating Committee for Intermediate School 201. In August 1966 the group circulated a leaflet asking "parents and friends of Central and East Harlem" to "help fight to keep Intermediate School 201 closed!!" The leaflet argued that "the Board is forcing our children to continue to be destroyed by a totally inadequate school system. I.S. 201 will be another inferior school if we allow it to open under the Board's terms." Babette Edwards wrote Mayor Lindsay: "We intend to do everything in our power to stop 201 from being used if it is not operated as an integrated school. . . . 201 has become a symbol for the Harlem community. . . . If massive demonstrations perpetuate violence in the coming days and weeks you will bear the full responsibility."

A summer session planned by the Board of Education for I.S. 201 was canceled because of the controversy. Helen Testamark, an I.S. 201 parent, warned that "blood would flow in the streets of Harlem if the school was opened." When Superintendent Donovan tried to set up a meeting with the Parent and Community Negotiating Committee, the group postponed it until September 6, moving the date closer to the opening of school to put pressure on the board. At the meeting, Donovan offered to form a community council to work with the school's staff, helping to screen personnel, but without the right to hire and fire teachers. The parents rejected this compromise.[61]

Parents grew angrier, more convinced than ever that the Board of Education was purposely and deviously thwarting the ambitions of black children. Another leaflet by the I.S. 201 community group in the late summer of 1966 shows how the idea of total community control captivated black parents. The group demanded either "integrated quality education" or "total community control." If the Board of Education did not integrate I.S. 201, "then the school must be totally controlled by residents and parents from the community who will hire staff, review textbooks and curriculum, regularly evaluate the school's academic achievement and have full responsibility for the school's program." Citing the fact that 85 percent of minority students were reading significantly below grade level, the committee asserted, "We can do no worse. The school must be run by people who care." Finally the leaflet let it be known, in bold letters, that the Harlem parents "pledge ourselves to keep 201 closed by whatever means are necessary until these demands are met!!"[62]

Dorothy Jones summed up how Harlem viewed the school controversy by the summer of 1966: "Given the problems of teacher attitudes, bureaucracy, and all of the failure to achieve proper education in other schools in the community, the only way we can see of achieving this goal [quality schools in Harlem] is for the parents and community to have a real role in the selection of staff, the determination of program, and the evaluation of the education in the school."[63]

In early September, with schools due to open on Monday, September 12, Superintendent Donovan and Board President Garrison decided not to open I.S. 201 with the rest of the city's schools. Harlem parents threatened to boycott the school if they did not gain control of its operation. The parents' demands boiled down to two issues: the establishment of a community council to control the school and the hiring of a black principal. Meanwhile, as classes began in the rest of the city, parents and community residents marched on an empty I.S. 201. One protester shouted, "We got too many teachers and principals named Ginzberg [sic] and Rosenberg in Harlem. This is a black community. We want black men in our schools."[64]

On Saturday, September 17, Donovan proposed the following: "There would be established a community education council . . . which would work with persons designated by the Superintendent and board of education jointly on the question of Intermediate School 201." The community council would be given a voice in personnel decisions and curriculum, and Donovan promised to "explore possibilities of contracting to community agencies certain aspects of the program of the school." In addition, Donovan seemed to suggest that he would replace the school's principal, Stanley Lisser, with a black or Puerto Rican. "Having in mind the state and city anti-discrimination laws, Dr. Donovan could not, of course, pledge to appoint a Negro or Puerto Rican," admitted Dorothy Jones. "It was agreed that the appointment would be of a 'mutually agreed upon person.' There was tacit acceptance of the fact that only a Negro or Puerto Rican would be a 'mutually agreed upon person.' " There was pressure on Donovan and the board to do something about Lisser. Helen Testamark stated the parents' desire in purely racial terms: "It's not really Mr. Lisser. It's just that he's white and only a Negro or Puerto Rican is acceptable to us." Harlem CORE's leader, Roy Innis, said half menacingly, "If I were Mr. Lisser, I would not come here. It might not be safe for him."[65]

Assuming that Lisser would not remain as principal, parents decided that they would not boycott the official opening of the school, set for Tuesday, September 20, at least for the time being. By Monday morning, though, Donovan had changed his mind and informed the parents that Lisser would remain as principal. By midday, Donovan reversed himself again. While eating lunch, Lisser received a call from Board of Education headquarters. Though he did not divulge the content of the call, immediately afterward he requested to be transferred out of I.S. 201. Donovan agreed to replace Lisser temporarily with a black assistant principal, Beryl Banfield. She refused the appointment, objecting "to being chosen on the basis of color, not competence." In response to Lisser's removal, virtually all the handpicked staff at I.S. 201, black and white, refused to teach. On Tuesday, September 20, the first day of classes at I.S. 201, fifty-three of the fifty-five teachers stayed home. This time, as Dorothy Jones noted, "The children were in the school and the teachers were out." Thirty-five Harlem principals wrote to Donovan protesting the treatment of Lisser. As the *Times's* education writer Fred Hechinger put it, "The Board of Education, in trying to achieve peace at Intermediate School 201, paid so much for a truce with neighborhood parents that it found itself in a new war with its own professional staff."[66]

On Tuesday, Donovan changed course again and reinstated Lisser. On Wednesday, school opened with Lisser as principal. The I.S. 201 Community Council sent a telegram to Mayor Lindsay, Donovan, and Giardino expressing its anger at the reversal: "We . . . are shocked at the irresponsibility shown by the Board of Education towards the Harlem community by breaking a public agreement between the Board and the parents. Once again the Board has shown contempt for the Harlem community by appeasing those forces who wish to deny equal education to our ghetto children. The Board of Education's action has pitted white against black and we will hold them responsible for any actions the community may take."

Though the telegram was born of great frustration with the bumblings of Donovan and the Board of Education, its disingenuousness is clear. No one was denying an equal education to the children at I.S. 201, certainly not Lisser and his teachers, who seemed to care genuinely about creating a special atmosphere at the new school. Nor was it the Board of Education who made race an issue at I.S. 201. The decision by the parents that only a black principal could serve I.S. 201 pitted blacks against whites more than any decision of the board.[67]

The I.S. 201 Parent and Community Negotiating Committee wrote to Al Shanker explaining its frustration with the process: "If a clearly established and reasonable role for parent and community involvement in the schools cannot be established, other steps will be taken to assure that teachers in ghetto schools teach. We intend to use whatever means necessary to stop teachers White or Black from coming into the ghetto to cripple out children's lives."[68]

Thirty protesters tried to block Lisser from entering the school Wednesday morning, including Stokely Carmichael, the head of the Student Nonviolent Coordinating Committee (SNCC), CORE's Floyd McKissick, and whites from EQUAL. Five people were arrested as protesters chanted, "Black teachers for black Harlem." Innis told reporters, "This was only a brief skirmish—a prelude to war." Attendance at the school approached 90 percent. The small number of protesters and the high attendance figure lend credence to the view that the protests were orchestrated by a small band of militants, many of whom did not even have children in the school. Most Harlem parents seemed more interested in having their children educated at the new school than in the abstract slogans of community control.

To some blacks, I.S. 201 symbolized the duplicity of the system and its indifference, if not malice, toward black children. One writer sympathetic to the I.S. 201 protesters noted: "The parents had, so to speak, taken a guided tour through an urban 'power structure' of 'White America.' And if vanquished, they were simply not impressed. As they saw it, white officials lied and cheated; white officials transformed immoral practices into professional virtues; white officials were often silly, frequently unintelligent and consistently wrong." Speaking at a Princeton University conference in 1969, I.S. 201's David Spencer summarized the frustrations of Harlem parents: "If you think that Harlem parents feel that the City is and has been plotting against us, you're damn right—they have been, for a long time now." Alice Kornegay, active in the Harlem community control movement, said, "I don't believe anything I am told by that Board. They are liars, all of them. . . . When you deal with that Board, the only thing you can be sure of is that you'll get screwed and messed over." Frustration at the incompetence of the board easily melted into paranoia and conspiracy theories. Donald Elliott, the mayor's liaison to the Harlem parents, found the Harlem parents "a difficult group to work with." The Ford Foundation, according to one of its reports, "had become the only link between the embittered I.S. 201 parents and community representatives and institutions outside of Harlem."[69]

Though the whole I.S. 201 episode was thrust upon the Lindsay administration unasked for, the mayor's behavior during the crisis was one of confusion and missteps. He gave conflicting statements supporting the idea of community control one day and criticizing it the next. In contrast to the comfort he felt on his walking tours of the city's ghettos, Lindsay seemed uneasy in dealing with the demands of black parents. He visited the school and met with Lisser, whom the mayor called "one of the finest" principals in the system. Lindsay also came out against parental vetoes of personnel decisions. None of this won him the support of Harlem parents. One community activist noted, "The mayor was totally insensitive to and out of touch with the needs and aspirations of the ghetto."[70]

Although the protests at I.S. 201 ended the following week, the controversy did not. Social scientist Kenneth Clark came out with a plan for community control that would have paired I.S. 201 with a local university, which would assist the community in governing the school. Frustrated with the events at I.S. 201, Clark found the Board of Education unresponsive and duplicitous and the parents suspicious and demanding. The UFT attacked the proposal and the board eventually rejected it as Clark gave up in exhaustion and frustration. Later, Shanker said that the I.S. 201 controversy was one where the "very integrity of the school system was at stake for if we had not prevailed, we would enter an era where only a Jewish principal could be appointed in a predominantly Jewish neighborhood, Italians in Italian neighborhoods, Irish in Irish neighborhoods."[71]

Stanley Lisser left I.S. 201 in the spring of 1967, before the end of the school year. By January 1968, only 20 percent of the original fifty-eight teachers at I.S. 201 remained, and all three assistant principals left in January 1968. *Times* reporter Leonard Buder visited the school in January 1968 and found it in a state of "bedlam." He saw numerous fights between pupils, chaos between classes, littered hallways, and bulletin boards stripped bare and defaced. One black teacher said of I.S. 201, "This isn't a school, this is a jungle." Another black teacher noted that the main problem in the school was discipline, adding that the children "know their parents are hostile to the school and they come here feeling that way too. They're uncontrollable."[72]

This viewpoint was shared even by those sympathetic to the I.S. 201 experiment. The Ford Foundation described the school as an "armed camp. Vandalism was rampant; children roamed through the halls. Pieces of school tiling were ripped up. . . . Seriously undermanned, several of the staff were observed standing in the hallways with yardsticks to protect themselves." Marilyn Gittell called the school "an object of hate." When the left-wing journalist Andrew Kopkind visited I.S. 201, he found much of a teacher's time was taken with trying to maintain classroom discipline. Another observer noted, after speaking with I.S. 201 teachers, that the school had become "just another Harlem school." Discipline was the main problem: "There was chaos in the halls and in the classroom." Between October 1967 and February 1968, forty students asked to transfer out of I.S. 201 because of safety concerns. Thirty of the forty students were Puerto Rican, causing some concern that the battle for community control was really a call for black control over schools, leaving East Harlem's Puerto Ricans out in the cold.[73]

THE EXPERIMENTAL DISTRICTS

In April 1967, as the Bundy Panel began its work and I.S. 201 struggled through its first year, the Board of Education attempted to appease community control activists by granting approval for three experimental school districts where limited community control could be tested. The board announced that the districts, which were planned to go into effect right away, were "to involve representatives of the community, parents, and staff more effectively in the conduct of school programs as well as in new approaches to teacher training and in curriculum development." The districts would be run by elected school boards consisting of parents and community members. In turn these boards would hire an administrator who would direct the operations of the district's schools. Despite the experimental nature, the districts' "basic functional relationships would remain the same." The districts would include I.S. 201 in East Harlem and four of its feeder schools; the eight schools of the Ocean Hill–Brownsville district in Brooklyn; and the Two Bridges district, in the shadow of the Manhattan and Brooklyn Bridges in Lower Manhattan, consisting of five schools. All three districts were predominantly minority. (Two Bridges had a diverse mix of Asians, Hispanics, blacks, and some whites.) Though the board agreed to set up these districts, they would not allocate any extra money for the experiment. To fill part of the breach, the Ford Foundation agreed to fund the three districts. Just as important as the money, Ford offered Mario Fantini as a full-time consultant.[74]

David Spencer was clear about the meaning of these experimental districts. He said at the press conference to announce the Ford Foundation grants: "The Board of Education will call it decentralization. We like to carry it further. We call it community control." Community control activists and black militants would use this opening to achieve their goals. In late 1967, the African-American Teachers Association argued for "an honest-to-goodness community controlled school system. . . . By community controlled schools, we mean the right of a community to run its school system with complete autonomy." As the Ford Foundation later noted, "It was clear that Donovan looked upon these demonstrations as the beginning of a cautious, very gradual process that would take a long time. It was also clear that

Livingston Street [the Board of Education], the communities and the Bundy group had very different perceptions of the urgency for action."[75]

A Ford Foundation officer described the type of people who made up the activists in the experimental districts. "The community groups proposing these experiments are representative of the most militant, the most alienated, the most mistrustful, the most volatile grass-roots people challenging the education system in New York City. They are certainly not 'do-gooders' and they are not compromisers. They are suspicious of any establishment ideas and associations and even raise questions about our own interest in their problems."[76]

Community control supporters later regretted the choice of districts for use in the decentralization experiment. Other observers came to understand the consequences of that poor choice. Barry Gottehrer explained: "In choosing three of the most deprived neighborhoods of the city, instead of selecting at least one middle-income area where the experiment would not pit black against white, school spokesmen indicated that they wanted to go into schools where nothing else had worked. Once this decision had been made . . . the confrontation, in retrospect, was inevitable." White community control activists also realized the mistake. The Ford Foundation's Richard Magat later admitted that "the great strategic mistake of the time . . . was not having a practically all white community group" included as an experimental district. Lindsay himself later acknowledged that "because of an initial mistake in establishing these districts solely in black and Puerto Rican neighborhoods—a mistake for which I bear my share of the responsibility—the dispute took on ugly racial and religious overtones." Fantini, Gittell, and Magat wrote: "A thrust for substantive reform, such as community control, must include some appeal to this group [middle-class whites] on the grounds of self- or common-interest. . . . On this count, the fact that none of the three demonstration districts in New York was in a predominantly white neighborhood was a major shortcoming."[77]

THE STAGE HAD BEEN SET FOR A SHOWDOWN. Minority parents were suspicious of and frustrated by the Board of Education. Thirteen years after the *Brown* decision, they saw little change in the city's schools. The teachers' union was suspicious of decentralization, seeing ample evidence that such reform would impinge on their civil service prerogatives. The pattern of intimidation of teachers and principals was established. Separatist black-nationalists, hungry for attention, were all too willing to inflame the situation. The experimental districts, created almost in passing and with few guidelines, would become the focal point for the more radical idea of the community control of schools.

By early 1968, education reform had produced chaos. The three experimental districts began groping in the dark with their newfound freedom, as

minority parents, led by militants, took the approach that the pronouncements of the Board of Education, the mayor, and the Bundy Panel had given
them free reign to institute community control of schools. No better recipe
for pandemonium and chaos could have been written. As the Ford Foundation later wrote: the "kindest thing one can say about the activities of that
summer [1967] is that no one was really sure of what he was doing."[78]

9

COMMUNITY CONTROL AND THE 1968 TEACHERS' STRIKES: THE DEBACLE AT OCEAN HILL–BROWNSVILLE

The demands of the people of Ocean Hill–Brownsville were simple: they demanded the responsibility to educate their own children.

—Rhody McCoy[1]

B y the middle of 1968, John Lindsay had reached the peak of his popularity. The mayor of New York was a respected figure on the national political scene. In the first six months of that year, Lindsay had stood up to the demands of the sanitationmen's union in the face of thousands of tons of uncollected garbage piling up on the streets. He gained stature by leading the National Advisory Commission on Civil Disorders and walking courageously through the tense streets of Harlem immediately after the death of Martin Luther King. This high profile translated into a slow and steady buzz about the possibility that Lindsay might be picked as the number-two man on the national Republican ticket that year.

But such heights can only be sustained for a short time in New York. Lindsay had been elected with only a plurality of the vote in 1965 and had done little to broaden his political support in preparation for the 1969 reelection campaign. Though no one believed that the goodwill toward Lindsay could possibly continue forever, few expected the full-blown explosion of anger and hatred that would be unleashed during the fall of 1968. By

November 1968, journalists at *Time* would write about "John Lindsay's ten plagues" and *U.S. News and World Report* likened New York to a "disaster area."[2]

In an obscure corner of Brooklyn, John Lindsay's political future was badly weakened as his plans to decentralize the city's public school system and the black community's desire to control its own schools collided head on not only with the powerful teachers' union, but with the city's latent racial and ethnic tensions. This collision resulted in the teachers' strikes of the fall of 1968. The largely Jewish teachers' union was seen as standing in the way of the black community's desire to educate its children. The teachers' strikes highlighted the ineptitude of the Lindsay administration in handling city affairs, the increasing power of municipal unions to cripple the city at will, and the growing alienation, anger, and resentment building up in the black community. The strike also marked a glaring low-light in the continuing decline of the city's public schools, a slide that more than thirty years later shows no sign of stopping.[3]

OCEAN HILL–BROWNSVILLE

If Harlem's I.S. 201, located in the first of the experimental districts, set the spark for decentralization and community control, then Brooklyn's Ocean Hill neighborhood, the site of the second experimental district, was the place where the spark ignited a flame of racial tensions that would engulf the entire city.[4] (The third experimental district, Lower Manhattan's Two Bridges, also experienced problems, but did not receive the same attention because it lacked the media-savvy figures and dramatic personalities of Ocean Hill. Educationally, it generated even less success.) One commentator described the neighborhood around Ocean Hill as

> a tiny piece of urban blight resting on a gently sloping section of glacial moraine in Brooklyn. From one side of this ancient hill spreads the vast wretchedness of Bedford-Stuyvesant, from the other, the vast wretchedness of Brownsville. The two great Negro ghettos of Brooklyn merge at Ocean Hill, but Ocean Hill has never quite belonged to either slum. It is a no-man's-land between two no-man's-lands. Its inhabitants are the overflow of hopelessness and poverty from two of the most desolate communities in the land.

Barry Gottehrer said of it: "Three out of every four families in the district received some kind of public assistance; the unemployment rate stood at 17 percent, 36 percent for young black males. Dilapidated tenements and boarded-up storefronts filled the garbage-strewn streets. Dozens of anti-poverty groups had rented stores from which they tried to dispense services, but there was little to build on—no jobs, no supermarkets, no movie theaters, no economic stability of any kind." Another writer said the area reminded him of "Berlin after the war; block after block of burned-out shells of houses, streets littered with decaying automobile hulks."[5]

According to Jimmy Breslin, this part of Brooklyn was possibly "the worst slum in the U.S." Breslin described the area in 1968: "The stores on the avenues are empty and the streets are lined with deserted apartment houses or buildings that have empty apartments on nearly every floor. At night, kids set fires to the empty buildings and apartments. Women on welfare sit up all night to watch for fires which could kill their children." The journalist Martin Mayer added to this portrait of a fraying neighborhood and its inhabitants the information that "less than a third completed high school. . . . More than half the households subsist on less than $5,000 a year; about 70 percent are Negro, about 25 percent are Puerto Rican. Though there are some blocks of pleasant, owner-occupied private houses, most people live in deteriorating houses and tenements, and much of the area's housing is simply being abandoned by its owners." This neighborhood reportedly had the highest drug addiction rate in the country. A journalist writing in *The New Republic* called Ocean Hill a "counterfeit community."

Rhody McCoy, the man who would be hired as unit administrator to run the Ocean Hill–Brownsville experimental district, called the area's residents "obscure, unnoticed—as though they did not exist." They were "the invisible residents of a demoralized, poverty-ridden inner city." The neighborhood was an area of transients; only 40 percent of the residents had lived in the area for more than five years. Only 18 percent of parents in the district had been born in the city; 51 percent had been born in the South, and 21 percent in Puerto Rico. Ocean Hill's schools performed at levels well below the citywide average. Seventy percent of sixth-graders scored below grade level on reading tests in 1966 (compared to 45 percent citywide and 26 percent statewide), and 77 percent scored below grade level in math (compared to 47 percent citywide and 25 percent statewide).[6]

(Although the school district was called Ocean Hill–Brownsville, the district's schools were in the Ocean Hill neighborhood, which is smaller than, and to the north, of the better-known neighborhood of Brownsville. Today, few people refer to Ocean Hill. The 1998 reference book *The Neighborhoods of Brooklyn* has no separate listing for Ocean Hill and includes information on the area in its chapter on Brownsville.)[7]

Empowered by the Board of Education and the Ford Foundation, and led by the white Catholic priest John Powis, a group called the Ocean Hill–Brownsville Planning Council prepared to show the city what the community control of schools would look like. On July 29, 1967, the group wrote a three-page proposal that laid out the creation of a governing board for the district. According to the preamble of the council's proposal: "Men are capable of putting an end to what they find intolerable without recourse to politics. . . . The ending of oppression and the beginning of a new day has often become a reality only after people have resorted to violent means. . . . The following plan . . . is acknowledged to be the last threads of the community's faith in the school system's purposes and abilities." Without the approval or consultation of the Board of Education, the Planning Council set in motion the first step of its plan—the election of a new Governing Board to run the experimental district. Included on the twenty-four-person board would be one parent and one teacher representative from each of the district's eight schools, two representatives of the school supervisors in the district, one delegate from a local university, and five community representatives to be chosen by the parent members of the board.[8]

The election began on August 3, 1967, and lasted three days. Sixty-one parents were nominated. The first day of voting was normal, as parents showed up to school to vote. But the second day of voting added a new, and to some observers suspicious, twist to the voting ritual. Parents who had been paid by the Planning Council to do so went door-to-door to solicit votes from those parents who had not shown up at the school to vote on the first day. Of the twenty paid canvassers, thirteen were also candidates in the election. When the election winners were announced on August 7, six of the eight parents who won places on the Governing Board had been paid canvassers. The new members of the Governing Board then met to elect the five community representatives to the board. Four of those named were part of the Planning Council that had originally hired the election canvassers.[9]

Turnout for the election was estimated at roughly one thousand people, 25 percent of those in the district eligible to vote in the election. District supporters used this figure—unusually high for school district elections—to demonstrate the depth of support for, and interest in, the experimental district. But others were suspicious. John Niemeyer, the president of the Bank Street College of Education, was head of the Board of Education's advisory committee on decentralization. When he released his report on Ocean Hill–Brownsville, it contained, oddly, no discussion of voting statistics. Bert Swanson, a researcher for the Niemeyer Report, said that Rhody McCoy refused to give him any evidence to prove that a thousand people had voted in the election. Nevertheless, the Niemeyer report concluded that though the election was "unorthodox," those observing the election "considered it one in which an honest effort was made to obtain the votes of all parents of the schools. . . . There was no evidence of coercion during the nominating process or during the election period itself."[10]

The man chosen to be chairman of the Ocean Hill–Brownsville Governing Board was an outspoken local churchman and civil rights leader, Reverend C. Herbert Oliver, the pastor of the Westminster Bethany United Presbyterian Church. A recent arrival from Birmingham, Alabama, he had quickly become dismayed at the poor quality of New York's public schools. His children had been doing well in Alabama's segregated schools, but soon began floundering in their new schools up North. Another vocal member of the Governing Board was, Father John Powis, who was widely seen as the most militant board member. A Ford Foundation report noted, "Powis seems to have a conspiratorial view of the establishment and the dangers of 'co-option.' And while he is extraordinarily well-informed on the school problems in Ocean Hill, he has a tendency to fit the facts into the framework of intense advocacy within which he thinks and operates." Gottehrer remembered a conversation he had with Powis, who told him, "Before this is over, blood will flow down Fulton Street and Nostrand Avenue, and flow throughout Brooklyn. Out of these wounds will emerge a better understanding." A parent member, Dolores Torres, was also considered a "militant." The fourth member of the board, Assemblyman Samuel Wright, presented a different problem. He saw the school district as an opportunity for patronage and sought to outmaneuver the Governing Board by utilizing his political base of seniors and middle-class blacks.[11]

Who would be chosen as the school district's unit administrator, the person who would actually run the new Ocean Hill–Brownsville district? Many assumed that person would be the principal of Junior High School 271, Jack Bloomfield. But the Ocean Hill Governing Board passed over the popular Bloomfield and instead chose Rhody McCoy. According to Father Powis, McCoy had impressed everyone on the Governing Board in his interview, recalling that he "knocked 'em dead." McCoy was destined to be a pivotal figure in the community-control struggle in the Ocean Hill–Brownsville district, in whom some saw a conciliator and others saw a militant.[12]

McCoy grew up in Washington, D.C., and attended Howard University. In 1949, he moved to New York and became a public school teacher and was assigned to a special public school for "teenagers considered too violent for regular classes." McCoy soon grew bitter about his lack of progress within the school bureaucracy. Beginning in the early 1960s, he was a regular visitor at Harlem's Mosque Number 7, where he heard the teachings of Malcolm X. McCoy would often drive out to Malcolm's Long Island home to speak to him. Following along with McCoy were two others who would become notorious figures in the city: Herman Ferguson and Sonny Carson. McCoy admitted that "when I talked to Malcolm X as well as [the black educators] Herman Ferguson and Wilton Anderson, we had the same idea."[13]

With McCoy at the helm, it was clear that the demonstration district in Ocean Hill–Brownsville would become more than what the Board of Education, Superintendent Donovan, Mayor Lindsay, and the Bundy Panel had ever bargained for. A 1968 newsletter from the Ocean Hill–Brownsville Governing Board set forth its goals, describing a kind of decentralization very different from that favored by Lindsay and Bundy. "Don't let anyone tell you that decentralization is worth a damn, unless you get the following powers," declared the newsletter. Those powers included the "right to hire and fire all principals, assistant principals and teachers who have state certification," the "total control of our money," the "right to buy our own textbooks and supplied [sic] by direct purchase," and the "money to rehabilitate and build our schools, using black and Puerto Rican contractors and neighborhood workers." This was not to be simply administrative decentralization, but rather a fully independent school board acting under no one's authority but its own.

An early warning about the potential for trouble at Ocean Hill–Brownsville was the choice of Herman Ferguson, a city schoolteacher, as principal of I.S. 55. The Governing Board hired new principals, chosen by the unit administrator, for the district's schools: four blacks, two whites, one Puerto Rican, and one Asian-American. Many of them, like Ferguson, were not on civil service lists and therefore were not in line for promotions to principal, according to the Board of Education. At the time he was hired, Ferguson was free on bail on charges of plotting to kill Roy Wilkins and Whitney Young and for keeping an arsenal of weapons at his home. Rhody McCoy explained his choice of Ferguson by calling him "the best man I could find." Parents in the district also supported McCoy's choice. Hattie Bishop and Dolores Torres, both active PTA members, defended Ferguson. Bishop believed Ferguson had "been framed because he's a black man." Torres liked the fact that Ferguson was determined to introduce schoolchildren to "much more Negro and Puerto Rican history." Father Powis thought there was "a very good possibility" that the charges against Ferguson would be thrown out and warned of riots should Ferguson's appointment be blocked. Although Powis said of Ferguson that "of all the black teachers I've met, he's the most brilliant," years later he admitted it was a "tactical mistake" to hire him.[14]

Ferguson left a paper trail filled with revolutionary sloganeering and dubious racial rhetoric. In a 1967 letter to the African-American Teachers Association newsletter, Ferguson, then working at Harlem's I.S. 201, said the black teachers group "must begin to assume its natural role as a revolutionary force in the just struggle for liberation that is now going on in the third world that encompasses black America, as well as Latin America, Asia, and Africa."[15]

In March 1968, Ferguson confirmed the fears of many already skeptical of the experimental district when he published an article in *The Guardian* entitled "A Black Survival Curriculum." In Orwellian tones, Ferguson described his ideal school for poor black children. Ferguson argued that it was "not enough" for blacks "to demand control of our schools. Once we really take this control, we must be prepared to teach our black youth how to survive in the hostile society that we do not yet control." Ferguson complained that the "Anglo Saxon based curriculum" led to the "enslavement" of black children. A new Afrocentric curriculum would help black children survive until they were able "to create a new order of things."

In Ferguson's ideal school, students would enter to find the building "adorned with pictures of great black fighters," such as Malcolm X, Marcus Garvey, and Muhammed Ali. The walls would be covered with uplifting slogans such as LEARN OR BURN and INSTRUCT OR DUCK. Students would begin the day pledging allegiance to the black, red, and green pan-African flag and reciting LeRoi Jones's poem "We Are Beautiful People." The morning program at school would be taken up with physical exercise, martial arts, and "instruction in gun weaponry, gun handling, and gun safety." Classes would be taught in Swahili and Yoruba.

Adding a totalitarian feeling to the school, "Loud speakers placed in the ceilings continuously bathe him [the black student] with the quiet sound of Malcolm X speaking, LeRoi Jones reading one of his poems, Aretha Franklin singing a soul song, and other black heroes speaking to him and filling him with a constant pride in his blackness." The afternoon lesson would include traditional studies, heavily laden with black history. Math classes would deal with "the logic of the numbers" as well as practical matters such as "wind velocity, muzzle velocity, and other mathematical considerations involved in firing, repairing, and making weapons." Home economics courses would stress first aid and how to "survive off the surrounding environment if all food and fuel supply lines into the black community are cut off." Shop courses would include instruction in assembling electronic equipment and gunsmithing. All of this could be dismissed as the quasi-fascistic dreaming of a crank, except that it was written by a man deemed by Rhody McCoy and the Ocean Hill–Brownsville Governing Board as worthy of becoming a principal.[16]

The Board of Education balked at naming Ferguson principal. Superintendent of Schools Bernard Donovan asked McCoy to withdraw Ferguson's name. McCoy and Oliver at first refused the request. Oliver believed that "no one had the right to judge or determine the guilt or innocence of the candidate," especially since he felt minorities too often were accused, tried, and sentenced before a trial, regardless of their actual guilt or innocence. McCoy wrote later that Ferguson's opponents failed "to understand the whole culture of black people, where black people have been convicted before they even get to the courtroom, and under different sets of standards. The history books are full of them. The double standard is law." Eventually, though, the Ocean Hill–Brownsville Governing Board relented and Ferguson's nomination was withdrawn.[17]

Meanwhile, J.H.S. 271 quickly became a focal point for black militancy in the Ocean Hill–Brownsville district. This was apparent in the school disturbances after the assassination of Martin Luther King in April 1968. According to one student, Karriema Jordan, after the King assassination, "We just threw chairs around, wrote on the walls: 'Avenge King! Kill Whitey!' It was almost a riot." Chaos reigned in the school as students ran through the halls and teachers locked themselves in their classrooms. Leslie Campbell, a teacher who had recently arrived at the school, was called upon to speak at a school assembly to calm things. William Harris, the principal of J.H.S. 271, told white teachers they might not want to attend, but some went anyway. Campbell's speech was inflammatory. "Brothers and sisters," Campbell told the eighth- and ninth-graders, "you have to stop fighting among yourselves. You have your money and finally get enough for a leather jacket, and your brother steals it. You've got to get your minds together. If you steal, steal from those who have it—stop fighting among yourselves." Campbell also told the students, "When the enemy taps you on the shoulder, send him to the cemetery. You know who your enemy is." Campbell's speech did anything but calm the children. Students continued to rampage through the school. Three teachers were hurt, including one white woman who was punched, had her hair torn, and her clothes ripped for removing a sign on the bulletin board that read MARTIN LUTHER KING WAS KILLED BY A VICIOUS WHITE MAN—PREPARE YOURSELVES. [18]

The district's first year, from the fall of 1967 to the spring of 1968, "was a disaster," in the words of Father Powis. Jack Bloomfield, who had been passed over for the job of district unit administrator, remained as the J.H.S. 271 principal until February 1968. White teachers were becoming increasingly uncomfortable with the increasingly racial focus of community control. One teacher wrote Bloomfield in October 1967, that "the hate and hostility either implied or openly expressed . . . make conditions intolerable for me and for others and actually prevent us from doing our work as it should be done." But members of the Ocean Hill–Brownsville Governing Board saw the teachers as "obstructionist." According to Father Powis, the staff at J.H.S. 271 were "miserable teachers. . . . They didn't even take any classes that year. They were guidance counselors. They used to sit in that office, kid around, smoke, drink coffee all day long." When Powis and Oliver went to meet the teachers on the first day of school in the fall of 1967, Oliver recalled: "They were extremely hostile. We could barely speak to them." In many ways, it was a chicken-or-egg situation. Were these dedicated and able teachers, as Bloomfield suggested, who became soured by the Ocean Hill Board's actions, or were the teachers merely time-punchers interested only in their union prerogatives, with little concern for minority children?[19]

Tensions increased between district officials and teachers. The Governing Board, in essence, planned to secede from the city's school system. And it became unhappy at what it saw as a lack of support from city officials for this community control experiment: "Our only reason for forming a Governing Board was 'to govern' our schools, yet it became obvious to us that every power group would do everything possible to prevent us from really ever controlling the education of our children." Mayor Lindsay and the Ford Foundation were also suspect in the eyes of the Ocean Hill Board. "The Ford Foundation has played a weird role in this entire experiment," said the

March 1968 Ocean Hill–Brownsville school district newsletter. It castigated the Ford Foundation for not giving the district more money. As for Lindsay, "it seems amazing to the members of the Governing Board that the mayor who is so preoccupied with preventing riots, doesn't come out and support an educational program that might go a long way to prevent riots or threats of riots in the future." As it looked doubtful that the city and Board of Education officials would support this radical power play, the Governing Board, according to McCoy, planned to "make decisions to force issues and to give us command of the right to make education meaningful for our children." In setting up these experimental districts, the Board of Education never clearly delineated the boundaries of power and authority. Under McCoy's leadership, the Ocean Hill–Brownsville district would force a controversy it believed would ultimately lead to the community's complete control of the school district.[20]

"TRANSFERRED" OR "FIRED"?

The confrontation at Ocean Hill–Brownsville began in May 1968 when the Governing Board dismissed thirteen teachers and six administrators. Though it was a matter of some dispute whether the teachers had been "fired" or "transferred," it was not in dispute that these educators received telegrams on May 8 telling them their services were no longer needed in the district. The letters, signed by Reverend Oliver and McCoy, read as follows:

> The Governing Board of the Ocean Hill–Brownsville Demonstration School District has voted to end your employment in the school of this District. This action was taken on the recommendation of the Personnel Committee. This termination of employment is to take effect immediately.
>
> In the event you wish to question this action, the Governing Board will receive you on Friday, May 10, 1968, at 6:00 PM, at Intermediate School 55, 2021 Bergen Street, Brooklyn, New York.
>
> You will report Friday morning to Personnel, 110 Livingston Street, Brooklyn, for reassignment.

McCoy explained the ouster by highlighting not just the teachers' incompetence but also their negative opinions of community control: "Among our reasons for asking for their transfer from our schools are their political views that affect their teaching performances, their inability to work with people in this community and their inability to communicate with children and their parents in this community. We don't have to file any charges against them because we're only demanding their transfer, not firing." Two days later, McCoy sent the ousted teachers another letter notifying them that the Governing Board "has relieved you of your teaching assignment until such time as the situation involving your termination has been resolved." Reverend Oliver voted against transferring the teachers, but when outvoted had agreed to implement the Governing Board's wishes.[21]

A bureaucrat at 110 Livingston was a faceless figure, but the teacher was known to all parents and thus was the nearest and clearest symbol of the failings of the public schools. The black community saw itself victimized by an insensitive education bureaucracy and indifferent, even racist, white teachers. Dolores Torres, a parent member of the Governing Board, felt that many white teachers in the new district "were undermining what we were trying to do. . . . All we did was dismiss these teachers. We reassigned them to 110 Livingston Street." Yet Father Powis had told at least two people that the board was going to "fire" teachers. Speaking thirty years later, Powis said of the event, "We asked them to leave or you want to call it fire. Whatever you want to call it." Though the number of ousted educators was nineteen, Torres warned that "there are many more, but we thought we would start slowly." Marilyn Gittell, the head of the Institute for Community Studies at Queens College, called the teacher ouster "an attempt to establish local discretion and to define district power over school resources (in this instance, jobs)—both poorly defined at the time the board was set up. The action or inaction of the local board and its administration was based on their desire to establish independence from the central Board and to challenge the power of the professionals in the UFT and CSA [Council of Supervisory Associations, the union of principals and administrators]." Maurice Berube was more forthright. In his view, the Governing Board felt "betrayed by Bundy and the Ford Foundation" and it "finally attempted to forcibly seize control of its schools."[22]

Two weeks before McCoy ordered the teachers out of the district, a fire occurred at P.S. 178. The Governing Board sent a telegram to Al Shanker complaining about the behavior of teachers during the fire: "The unconcern of the teachers in P.S. 178 in seeing that their classes arrived home safely during an emergency is typical. The parents are damn sick and tired and will put up with these teachers no longer. They will get the hell out or be put out of the community by the parents who are willing to use force if necessary." Foreshadowing the controversy that would soon occur, Shanker replied to the Governing Board that "teachers' rights will be protected. If you have valid complaints which can be substantiated, then you will use proper procedures rather than those suggested in your telegram. Use of the procedure which you support would be taken as evidence that your case is weak."[23]

The debate was soon raging over what exactly happened to the teachers and whether the Governing Board was within its rights to take the action it took. The UFT said the teachers had been "fired." Governing Board supporters spoke of the teachers being "transferred." If one reads the first letter carefully, the board chose to "end the employment" of the teachers in the district, calling it a "termination of employment." But the teachers were not fired from the city school system. Nor were they transferred to another school. The Governing Board simply moved the teachers from their schools in the district to Board of Education headquarters. The move was in keeping with the Governing Board's belief that it was independent of the Board of Education and had the right to hire and fire personnel. Therefore, although the teachers were "fired" from the Ocean Hill–Brownsville district, according to the way the Governing Board construed its authority, they were still technically employed by the Board of Education.

After the removal of the teachers, Al Shanker quickly accused the Ocean Hill–Brownsville Board of "vigilante activity" and complained that the teachers had been removed without due process. The claim of due process would become a rallying cry for the teachers' union. To opponents of the union, though, the due process issue was "nothing but a smokescreen behind which the effort to discredit and destroy community control could go on."[24]

It was unclear what powers the new Governing Board had over personnel. The UFT thought the Governing Board was bound by civil service rules protecting teachers' rights. Alfred Giardino, president of the Board of Education, called the move "an illegal procedure that our board will not tolerate." But Clara Marshall, the chairman of the Governing Board's personnel committee, said that the Governing Board "considered these laws written to protect the monied white power structure of this city." When eleven of the teachers and all six administrators returned to their schools in the district the following day, Rhody McCoy filed insubordination charges against them. McCoy also wrote to Superintendent Donovan requesting "a hearing be held as expeditiously as possible as a result of the charges that I am now making." McCoy instructed the eleven teachers "not to return to the school." He believed that final authority in his district rested in his office. The teachers believed they were protected by civil service rules and ultimately were responsible to the Board of Education and the superintendent of schools.[25]

The Board of Education bylaws made clear that the authority for teacher transfers rested with the superintendent of schools: "Transfer of members of the teaching and supporting staff from one school to another shall be made by the Superintendent of Schools, who shall report immediately such transfers to the Board of Education for its consideration and action." Superintendent Donovan reacted to the events a few days later by laying out what he felt were the appropriate procedures for teacher transfers: in order for a teacher to be dismissed, school officials would have to give the teacher an unsatisfactory rating for "professional performance" or charge that teacher with "actions detrimental to the students." In either case, the teacher would then be allowed a hearing on these charges. In plain language, Donovan reiterated: "A district superintendent or a unit administrator has the right to reassign a supervisor or teacher within the district for the good and welfare of the schools. He also has the right to summon a supervisor or teacher to his office for appropriate consultation. He does not have the right to dismiss, transfer to another district or retain the person in the district office for an indefinite length of time." According to the Board of Education rules—by which the Ocean Hill Board was still technically bound, despite its experimental status—the May 1968 actions of Rhody McCoy and the Governing Board overstepped their authority and violated the rights of the teachers.[26]

Later that May, 350 teachers in the district walked out to protest the Governing Board's ouster of the nineteen teachers and administrators. Superintendent Donovan closed three of the district's schools for two days to help ease tensions. Lindsay called the teachers' ouster "beyond the law," but also urged "greater understanding" of the "deep community frustrations that have led to the present situation." Lindsay complained of the failure of the Board of Education and the superintendent of schools "to define the powers and the duties of the local boards." The mayor was dismayed that no clear lines of authority had been drawn for such an important experiment. Rose Shapiro, an opponent of decentralization who had recently become Board of Education president (Giardino had resigned), admonished Lindsay in a public letter, claiming that clear rules had been drawn in December when the board granted the districts experimental status. "The sad fact," wrote Shapiro, "is that the Governing Board of the district was unwilling to act within the guidelines required by law. They were more concerned with the exercise of powers that our board could not grant." The *Times* called the experimental districts a "twilight-zone operation" that "encourages a contest of pressures by rival interests without a legal or professional framework," but urged everyone involved to let McCoy "exert his leadership and carry out his experimental mission." Adding to the confusion, the state legislature began considering proposals to institute a decentralization plan for the city as recommended by the Bundy Panel. In the face of an impotent mayor, a dawdling state legislature, and an inept Board of Education and superintendent, the experimental districts were left to define education reform on their own terms. Nothing good could come from the arrangement.[27]

A fact sheet sent to Ocean Hill residents a week after the ouster of the educators invited parents to "cooperate with our revolution to determine our own future and the future of our children!!!!!!" Though unsigned, it was clearly written by persons connected with the Ocean Hill–Brownsville Governing Board and accused teachers and assistant principals of sabotaging the experiment. The community wanted local control, which it defined as the ability to "choose our own principals, assistant principals, teachers; control our money and the construction and renovation of our school buildings." Mayor Lindsay and State Education Commissioner James Allen, both strong supporters of decentralization, were attacked as "part of the same white power structure as Shanker and Donovan!" Regarding the educators' ouster, the Governing Board stated in the fact sheet: "We were told that we had to write up charges and submit them for a hearing to Donovan and Shanker. No one understands—but they really do—that the games are over.

Decentralization means that *we* decide who will teach our children—NO DONOVAN, NO SHANKER, NO LINDSAY, NO 500 COPS—WE DECIDE!!!!!!" The fact sheet went on to say that the teachers "will not teach here—ever again. And we will not play the man's game of referring charges to Donovan or Shanker. This community will educate its own children, using its own teachers." The note ended with a bitter attack on Lindsay and a veiled threat against the police: "The man can keep his damn buildings and Lindsay better keep his own ass away from here. We will deal with his white and *negro* police—those in uniform and especially those out of uniform." McCoy stood firm, which reinforced the view that the teachers had indeed been fired. "Not one of these teachers will be allowed to teach anywhere in this city," McCoy warned. "The black community will see to that."[28]

The labor negotiator Ted Kheel attempted to mediate the dispute, but these attempts soon collapsed. Now, the issue was brought to former Judge Francis E. Rivers, a special counsel to the Board of Education. Rivers, who was black, would act as a trial examiner and present nonbinding recommendations to the superintendent of schools. The cases of ten of the teachers went before Judge Rivers. (All six of the administrators had agreed to be transferred and efforts to locate another teacher proved futile.) Four of these teachers were charged with insubordination and the other six were eventually charged with the mistreatment of children, lateness, and the inability to control students. Ultimately, though, Rivers found the cases against the teachers unconvincing. Rivers dismissed the charges using nearly identical language in each case. The evidence against the teachers failed "to sustain the burden of showing that he did not perform as a teacher with the average competence of a teacher under similar circumstances."[29]

Rivers's decision was nonbinding and purely advisory. Still, the union used the decision to demand that all the teachers be reinstated. The Ocean Hill–Brownsville Governing Board countered that it was not bound by the Rivers decision. Reverend Oliver stated: "A retired judge made a retired decision." Barry Gottehrer thought the hearings were "a shamble." Though the mayoral aide was "now looking on Ocean Hill with a more skeptical eye," he believed at least three of the teachers should in fact have been transferred, "but the case against them was so badly prepared." Journalist Martin Mayer wrote, "Even the union was a little embarrassed at the unfairness of the decision" and quoted an unnamed UFT official as saying, "I could have won cases against at least three of the ten. The problem is that McCoy and his people don't know how to present evidence."[30]

If the Rivers decision failed to solve the issue, so did the action of the state legislature. Prodded by the events in Brooklyn, legislators finally produced a bill on school decentralization in 1968, but both sides were disappointed by it. The legislation, in essence, postponed any decentralization action for another year. It asked the Board of Education to draw up a permanent decentralization plan to be submitted to the mayor, the state legislature, and the New York Board of Regents (an advisory body that oversees all educational issues in the state) by year's end. In the meantime, it ordered the Board of Education to create a temporary decentralization plan to delegate some authority to school districts. In the near term, the most important aspect of the new law was the enlargement of the Board of Education by four members. (Lindsay also appointed a fifth new member to replace the departing president, Alfred Giardino.) Lindsay was expected to choose people who were strong supporters of decentralization. And he did.

The biggest name Lindsay chose was Milton Galamison, the pastor of the Siloam Presbyterian Church in Brooklyn and a longtime school critic. Reverend Galamison had organized the 1964 boycott of the city's schools and was the leader of the 1966 "People's Board of Education." On one hand, the choice of Galamison was a welcome recognition of the legitimacy of black concerns. On the other hand, Galamison's appointment looked like a validation of militant tactics. He and his supporters on the "People's Board of Education" had declared the Board of Education invalid and illegally disrupted its business. That he was now a member of that very same Board surely grated on longtime board members. Rose Shapiro criticized Reverend Galamison for "a consistent campaign of sabotage and vilification of the board."[31]

The other appointments also mirrored Lindsay's values. They included Ernest Minott, a postal worker and chairman of the United Parents Association; Hector Vasquez, a Puerto Rican activist; Salim Lewis, an investment banker involved in Jewish philanthropy; and William Haddad, a former journalist who had worked in the Peace Corps and the Office of Economic Opportunity. Minott was the only new appointee with children in public schools, the others having sent their children to private schools. (Haddad made front-page headlines by admitting he would never send his children to the city's public schools under present conditions.) Galamison, Minott, and Vasquez were the first black and Puerto Rican members in the board's history. The Lindsay appointees were still in the minority on the side of supporting decentralization, but not for long.

Late in the summer, two antidecentralization members of the Board of Education, Clarence Senior and Thomas Burke, resigned. Lindsay replaced them with Walter Straley, vice president of AT&T, and Ana Alvarez Conigliaro, a Puerto Rican social worker. In the fall, Lindsay named John Doar to the board to replace the ailing Salim Lewis. As assistant attorney general for civil rights in the Johnson administration, Doar, a Midwesterner, had achieved national prominence by prosecuting the three men charged with murdering Viola Liuzzo, a white civil rights worker in Alabama. He had come to New York earlier in the year to head up the Bedford-Stuyvesant Restoration Corporation. The addition of these three appointees, all supporters of decentralization, gave the mayor a clear majority on the board to push for decentralization.

Despite the changes, the board's makeup in the fall of 1968 remained heavily skewed toward minorities (three members) and the white elite (seven members), out of a total membership of thirteen. The Board's two Jews—its president, Rose Shapiro, and Morris Iushewitz, the secretary of the Central Labor Council—were decentralization opponents. There were only two non-Hispanic white Catholic board members, Doar and John Lotz, since both Burke and Giardino had recently resigned. There were no Irish or Italian members and neither Doar nor Lotz had any strong ties to the city's Catholic community. In essence, 40 percent of the city was without representation on the Board of Education.

With pro-decentralization supporters on the board nearing a majority and the state legislature putting the onus upon the board to complete a decentralization plan, Lindsay made a plea for drastic decentralization. He called on the board to grant to the three demonstration districts, including Ocean Hill–Brownsville, the powers they wished for, including control over finances, personnel, and curriculum. In addition, the mayor wanted the board to move quickly to create other decentralized districts with similar powers. According to Lindsay, it was "time to deliver." The mayor also downplayed the role of black militants, saying they accounted for just 1 percent of the population and claiming that the rest of black parents only wanted "high quality education for their children." Yet while discounting the significance of black militants in the whole picture, Lindsay kept using the fear of black militants and riots to push for reform: "The danger is that resistance to decentralization will drive the 99 percent onto the side of the 1 percent." To oppose decentralization, Lindsay warned, was to create more black radicals and, implicitly, more violence.[32]

Though he did not address the issue of racial separatism directly, Lindsay said decentralization would give blacks "the sense of community that the Jews and Irish and Italians got in this city" in previous years. Of course, these other immigrant groups had never asked the city for control over their schools. And when immigrant children swamped the city's schools, their teachers rarely shared the same background and were often hostile to them. The Irish bumped into native-born Protestants, and the Jews and Italians bumped into the Irish who controlled the schools. Thus, the situation of black children, contrary to the views of Lindsay and others, was not that unusual in the history of the city.

RETURNING FOR A NEW SEMESTER

The main issue for the Ocean Hill–Brownsville Governing Board during the summer of 1968 was the fate of the ousted teachers and the nearly 350 union teachers who had walked out in sympathy with them in May. McCoy remained firm, saying the teachers "have been playing games with the community and the community is tired of games. We want them out." Shanker was equally adamant that the Ocean Hill–Brownsville Governing Board respect Judge Rivers's decision. "I have no other choice but to recommend a complete shutdown unless there is compliance," Shanker warned.

Of the 350 union teachers who had been out on strike from Ocean Hill–Brownsville schools since May, only about half sought to return to their schools in September. Meanwhile, the district considered all of these teachers fired and went about hiring their own teaching staff for the fall. For Reverend Oliver, the hiring of these new teachers was significant. "This was community control now. We weren't asking Donovan what to do and what should we do. We simply made our motion and took our action," Oliver recalled. As far as the union was concerned, all teachers had the right to return to their original teaching posts, but the superintendent had taken no stand on the issue. The union became increasingly disillusioned with Donovan and the Board of Education and concerned that teachers' rights would not be secured.

In August 1968, the UFT paper, *United Action,* criticized Superintendent Donovan over his indecision regarding the fate of the union teachers: "Dr. Donovan threatened, time and again, to bring McCoy up on charges of insubordination if he did not follow his order calling for due process, but McCoy continued to refuse." The UFT blamed Lindsay and McGeorge Bundy as well: "Whenever Donovan attempted to enforce his orders, he received a call from City Hall or the Ford Foundation warning that his 'interference' would cause a riot in the area for which he must accept full responsibility. After a few such calls, Donovan stopped issuing orders."[33]

Shanker threatened a citywide teachers' strike on the first day of school— Monday, September 9—if the union teachers were not reinstated at Ocean Hill–Brownsville. The night before school was scheduled to open, Lindsay proclaimed there would be no strike. Shanker, whose relationship with Lindsay was already tense, angrily denied that the strike was off. The mayor's press secretary, Harry O'Donnell, clarified Lindsay's words, saying that "he meant there was no reason for the illegal strike called by the union." Lindsay believed that he had reached an agreement with McCoy and the Ocean Hill–Brownsville Governing Board to take back the teachers. According to the mayor's statement on Sunday night, the Board of Education "will direct any teacher who wishes to return to the Ocean Hill–Brownsville school district to do so. . . . The local board does not agree to the return of the teachers, but will not seek to prevent their return." McCoy said the teachers "will be brought back against our wishes and will be reassigned." More ominously, he said he could not vouch for the teachers' safety once they were back at Ocean Hill–Brownsville. McCoy said: "We weren't going to fight the teachers coming back, but we would have the right to determine what the teachers would do." The problem was that the Governing Board had already hired its own teachers for the school year, so there would be no room for union teachers. This was not good enough for Shanker. He wanted all of the teachers back at their old jobs. The implied threats of violence only made things worse.[34]

Shanker made good his threat to call a citywide teachers' strike. The UFT teachers hit the picket line on Monday, effectively shutting down the entire city school system. On the first day of the strike, 93 percent of teachers stayed home, and only 4.3 percent of the more than one million students attended classes. The Council of Supervisory Associations joined the UFT on the picket line.

Shanker presented his five conditions for settlement. First, the 10 ousted teachers and 200 (out of the original 350) teachers who walked out in May had to be taken back. (The remaining 150 union teachers chose to transfer out of the district.) Second, under any decentralization plan there had to be an agency shop, whereby any teacher hired by a decentralized district would be represented by the union and would be forced to pay union dues, whether a member or not. Third, local school boards could not override "understandings" already made between the UFT and the Board of Education affecting class size, sabbaticals, leaves of absence, and lunch privileges. Fourth, any "discharge of professionals" had to come under impartial review. Last, only properly licensed personnel could be employed in city schools to supervise and instruct children.

On Monday and Tuesday, the schools in Ocean Hill–Brownsville, staffed by nonunion teachers, functioned as normal while the rest of the city's schools remained closed. By Tuesday night, the UFT and the Board of Education reached a settlement. The Board voted in favor of the agreement—only Reverend Galamison and Hector Vasquez voted against it—though the union did not get the agency shop. The two-day strike was over, but if the settlement was to succeed, Ocean Hill–Brownsville had to agree to accept back all of the union teachers. What few realized was that the Ocean Hill–Brownsville Governing Board was not a party to the settlement.

So began over two months of wrangling and power struggles. The Ocean Hill–Brownsville Governing Board, Mayor Lindsay, the Board of Education, State Commissioner Allen, and Superintendent Donovan all supported some version of decentralization or community control. But the Board of Education was weak and divided; the mayor had little real control over the city's schools, aside from his bully pulpit; Donovan was a bureaucrat who strove for consensus, not conflict. Only the Ocean Hill–Brownsville Governing Board firmly supported community control, but it lacked the political power and authority to implement its vision. The UFT was alone in opposing plans for decentralization, but only the UFT had the political strength and savvy to force an outcome.

When the UFT teachers returned to their schools in Ocean Hill–Brownsville on Wednesday, they found the way blocked by residents and parents. The epicenter again was at J.H.S. 271. There, CORE's Brooklyn director, Sonny Carson, and a dozen others prevented Fred Nauman, one of the ten ousted teachers, from entering the school. One of the protesters told the teachers, "We don't want you here." Carson himself gave vent to anti-white feelings that many in the union had suspected lingered within the community: "If it was up to me they wouldn't be letting them in simply because they were white. . . . I don't think any white person is interested in giving black children an education. . . . By whatever means necessary they are going to be kept out." Lloyd Sealy, the assistant chief inspector of the New York Police Department and the highest-ranking black officer on the force, appeared with three other black policemen and the school principal, William Harris, and ushered the teachers inside.[35]

One incident that day gave life to the union's worst fears. All union teachers from the district were told to report to the auditorium at I.S. 55 for a meeting with McCoy. At the auditorium, the teachers encountered a crowd of fifty to a hundred people who hooted and cursed at the teachers and called them "faggots and honkies." One of the teachers described the scene:

> The president of the PTA at 137 and some others walked back and forth by us pointing to various people and saying, "you, you're going to get it . . . You pigs . . . We'll never let you back. We'll get you. . . ." One man got up and went to the microphone where he informed us that if we reported to work we would be carried out in pine wood boxes. Bullets were then thrown at us. . . . One man with a violin case walked back and forth by us and acted as if he had a gun in it and made believe he was shooting us. He polked [*sic*] it at us and went "rat-atata-tat-tat."

Several teachers believed McCoy orchestrated the whole scene. "A community liaison person with the Governing Board kept giving signals to the people walking up and down," said one UFT teacher. "[McCoy] looked up at the lights at one point and then they started going on and off." When the auditorium went dark, voices shouted, "It's dark now. We can see you; you can't see us. We're going to get you now." According to a *Post* story, among the teachers exiting the auditorium, "many of the women could be seen crying as they left the building. Some men teachers, their voices trembling, said they feared for their lives and sought protection from clusters of police in the neighborhood." As the teachers filed out of the auditorium, someone threw a bullet at one of them. Another teacher described leaving the auditorium as an anti-union activist shoved and threatened teachers: "A pregnant teacher was punched in the stomach. A woman who said she was a member of the Governing Board waved the sheet with the teachers' names and addresses and chanted 'You better never come back. We have your names and we know where you live. If you come back, we know where to find you and we'll bury you.' "[36]

Returning from I.S. 55, Fred Nauman and the other UFT teachers found the entrance to J.H.S. 271 blocked again, this time by thirty or forty people. The protesters chanted at the teachers, "Go home, we don't want you." As the police cleared the way for the teachers, scuffles broke out between police and protesters. The teachers made it into the school, where they stayed for one hour and then left for home. A total of 104 UFT teachers had returned to the district schools that Wednesday.

Reverend Oliver made clear that the Governing Board had never agreed to the decision to readmit the teachers. He told reporters in no uncertain terms: "The Board of Education and the union have totally disregarded the community. We have not prevented the return of the teachers, but we cannot say that we'll prevent the community from not [sic] letting them in." When asked what role the teachers would have in the school, Reverend Oliver responded, "Their role is to get out of the community." The ten ousted Ocean Hill–Brownsville teachers became nine when twenty-eight-year-old Burton Landsman, a two-year veteran of P.S. 137, requested a transfer.

On Thursday, Shanker made his most strident accusation to date, flatly declaring that McCoy and the Ocean Hill–Brownsville Governing Board were "racists." Just reinstating the teachers would not be enough: "The teachers will not return until the Governing Board is out of power," Shanker declared. "There's no action the Governing Board can take now which will make the teachers go back with this board in power." Mayor Lindsay spent the day talking with members of the Governing Board, but it was unclear what he accomplished. Reverend Oliver read a prepared statement to the mayor: "Since the legal machinery of this sick society are [sic] forcing these teachers on us under threat of closing our schools and dissolving this district, the Board of Education should return to our district any of the teachers who wish to return. Our original decision remains as before. We refuse to sell out. If the Board of Education and the Superintendent of Schools forces them to return to a community who does not want them, so be it." Lindsay remained conciliatory toward the Governing Board, but admitted that Oliver's statement "does not give the necessary assurance in light of the events of the last few days."[37]

Unfortunately, this was not an ordinary labor dispute between employer and employee. Many in the black community felt that they had long received the short end of the stick when it came to integration and education. For many blacks the answer was community control or nothing. The UFT leaders, on the other hand, felt community control would destroy the fundamental fabric of the union, one they had worked so hard to build over the previous decade. The racial and anti-Semitic undertones teachers felt, as well as the threats of violence, only stiffened their resolve.

THE SECOND STRIKE

With tensions increasing, on Friday, September 13, the UFT teachers walked out of the city's schools for the second time in a week. The strike quickly became a racial issue, with a predominantly white union facing off against black and Puerto Rican parents. When Shanker was asked if he was worried that the strike would cause a riot, he replied, "I'm sick of being afraid of doing the right thing because people are raising the fear of civil disorders." In private meetings at City Hall and Gracie Mansion, Lindsay warned the UFT leader of the possibility that such strikes and attacks on the Ocean Hill–Brownsville district would cause angry minorities to riot. Shanker accused Lindsay of injecting race into the controversy. "The mayor has categorized every strike as a strike against the poor and the blacks and Puerto Ricans," complained the UFT head. "To have the mayor constantly telling the people of the ghetto that these people [the unions] are against you, that they are striking against you and your children, well, he is inciting polarization and racial hatred."[38]

Years later, Shanker still spoke with bitterness about Lindsay's theory of riots. He said decentralization occurred "because there was a threat: 'If you don't give power to people in the communities, the city is going to burn down.' I wish I had a nickel for every time I heard that from the lips of John Lindsay." Shanker acknowledged that for too many years whites had rejected the demands of the black community. But by the 1960s, this situation was reversed, he claimed: "The response of a type of white liberal who somehow has come to feel that because of a hundred or two hundred years of constant rejection, and saying no strictly on the basis of race, [is to say that] the way to overcome the evil of this negativism is constantly to say yes." When a reporter asked him whether he was suggesting that the Ford Foundation and the Lindsay administration were subsidizing "anarchy in this city," Shanker replied, "I think there is no question about it." He warned the Ford Foundation's Mario Fantini that he, Shanker, would make "another Civilian Review Board" out of the school crisis.[39]

As the second strike reached its second week, both sides hardened their positions. Shanker, to the rousing applause of delegates from the Central Labor Council, demanded that "Lindsay quit knuckling under to the vigilantes of Ocean Hill Brownsville." On the other side, McCoy said it would be "one cold day in hell before" teachers who had "so flagrantly disregarded their commitment to the children of Ocean Hill–Brownsville" were allowed back in the district. At a Manhattan rally hosted by the Council Against Poverty, a local antipoverty program, community control supporters spoke out against the union and the strike. Rhody McCoy told the crowd he would keep the UFT teachers out "by whatever means." Reverend Milton Galamison told the crowd, "You being minorities, almost always are being subjected to what somebody else says is law and order—not what you say is law and order." Joining McCoy and Reverend Galamison at the podium was Herman Ferguson.[40]

Those involved at the grassroots of the school controversy were fighting for community control of schools, not decentralization of the system. "Give total community control to present elected Governing Boards. . . . We will totally control our eight schools—regardless of Lindsay, Donovan, Shanker, Ford Foundation, or the white and Negro Power structure," read a flyer from the Ocean Hill–Brownsville Governing Board. "We have all our own teachers for our eight schools. Shanker and Donovan better keep the others out," the Governing Board warned. It demanded the resignation of the members of the Board of Education and the right to choose its own curriculum "regardless of 'Board of Education rules and standards' which have crippled our children for years." Unhappy that the "Board of Education's Decentralization plan gives no control of money, personnel, construction or curriculum—it gives no power period," the Governing Board warned: "Give up control or we will take it!"[41]

Milton Galamison, soon after being named by Lindsay to the Board of Education, said in an interview, "Decentralization can mean anything. . . . But when we add to the word decentralization, community control, then it becomes meaningful, then it becomes viable, then it becomes something that would be acceptable to the community." Rhody McCoy was firmly in favor of radical community control: "The basic issue has to do with total community control over the schools." A leaflet distributed by Schools & Community Organized for Partnership in Education (SCOPE), an activist group funded by the Ford Foundation and run by Reverend Galamison out of his Brooklyn church, made clear the centrality of community control. "Stop Saying 'Decentralization.' Start Saying: COMMUNITY CONTROL," read the flyer. For SCOPE, total community control meant "control of all money spent on and in the community's schools," "control of hiring and firing," "control of textbooks," and "control of negotiations with the teachers union."[42]

After Mayor Lindsay reentered strike talks, the UFT agreed to a settlement on Sunday, September 29. The mayor had been criticized for not doing enough to end the strike. Now he took charge. Negotiations occurred between the Board of Education and the UFT, with the Ocean Hill–Brownsville Governing Board left out. The UFT won most of its demands, including the right for all disputed teachers to return to Ocean Hill–Brownsville schools and the posting of neutral observers in the district to prevent harassment of returning teachers. Shanker, no friend of the mayor's, praised Lindsay before the union delegates. "He helped us get practically what was in our program. . . . He did a good job in the last few days," Shanker said. But these words only heightened the frustrations of the Ocean Hill–Brownsville Governing Board, who saw the political momentum shifting away from them. They were now powerless to effect any settlement. The

Governing Board would remain and the experimental district would continue, but community control was now becoming a toothless slogan.

The second strike had lasted seventeen days. The schools had been shut for eleven school days (thirteen including the first strike). Lindsay was generally sympathetic to the plight of the Ocean Hill–Brownsville district, but empty schools did not help anyone. Angry parents scrambling to make sure their children were occupied during the day while their schools were closed became a political liability for the mayor. In addition, the racial tensions drawn out during the strikes made possible two outcomes Lindsay wanted desperately to avoid: black rioting and white backlash.

Not having the support of the Ocean Hill–Brownsville Governing Board meant that it was highly unlikely that schools would open peacefully on Monday, September 30. To add to the insult of not being included in negotiations and being forced to take back unwanted teachers, the parents and leaders of Ocean Hill–Brownsville felt besieged by outside observers, media, and above all else, a massive police presence around their schools. Some 3,000 police were sent to Ocean Hill–Brownsville, leading to charges of an "occupation."

On September 30, the first Monday of school in over two weeks, eighty-three of the controversial teachers reported to the Ocean Hill–Brownsville district. Of the original nineteen teachers and administrators ousted in May, only five had returned. Reverend Oliver extended a less-than-enthusiastic welcome to the teachers, saying they had "no business coming back. They have no right coming back into the community over the best wishes of our people. Too many of our young people have had their futures blighted by teachers like this, and we're tired of it." The returning UFT teachers at Ocean Hill–Brownsville found themselves having to share their classrooms with the replacement teachers hired that summer by the Governing Board. This was not a situation that could last. The UFT teachers looked down at the replacement teachers as "scabs" and radicals. The replacement teachers had no respect for the striking teachers whom they felt had no concern for the students. If the Board of Education was going to fulfill its agreement with the union and avoid another strike, it would have no other choice but to force these UFT teachers back upon the Ocean Hill–Brownsville schools.

Reverend Oliver continued to voice defiance, saying the Governing Board could not abide by the agreement reached by the union and the Board of Education: "We have no intention of returning to the old days of educational genocide perpetrated by the Board of Education and the United Federation of Teachers." That Monday, John Doar visited J.H.S. 271. In the hallway, the teacher Al Vann (also president of the African-American Teachers Association) pulled Doar into a mop closet for a private talk. The two men had been friendly through Doar's work as head of the Bedford-Stuyvesant Restoration Corporation, yet the black militant warned the Midwestern lawyer to "get out of the way or we'll run right over you." Doar remembers bedlam in the halls, with students running around without supervision.[43]

Tensions increased on Tuesday, October 1. At J.H.S. 271, Vann led a handful of replacement teachers and students out of school in protest at the presence of the union teachers. In response to the ensuing chaos, the principal, William Harris, closed J.H.S. 271. Black protesters at I.S. 55 pelted policemen with bottles, eggs, rocks, steel objects, and fragments of the wooden barricades. Nine people were arrested that day and ten policemen injured. Lindsay began to lose patience with the Ocean Hill–Brownsville situation. He declared on Tuesday that the situation had "deteriorated substantially" and sternly warned that "no further disturbances of this sort will be tolerated." Superintendent Donovan threatened to fire any principal who did not admit the union teachers. Thankfully, schools throughout the city were closed on Wednesday, October 2, for Yom Kippur.

On that day, Shanker sent a telegram to Board of Education President Rose Shapiro saying that he considered the strike agreement to have already been "violated." Among his reasons were Reverend Oliver's refusal to accept UFT teachers; McCoy's statements that union teachers were not welcome; the Ocean Hill–Brownsville principals' attitude toward the returning teachers; outsiders wandering around the schools; and the fact that returning UFT teachers were put into "team-teaching relationships with teachers who hold extremist views and who refuse to teach with them." Shanker warned that unless the UFT teachers could resume their normal duties at Ocean Hill–Brownsville, "we will have no choice but to take complete and appropriate action."[44]

At the end of that week, teachers were still in school, but Shanker continued to threaten a third strike if the safety of his members was not assured. Finally, on Sunday, October 6, the Board of Education suspended the Ocean Hill–Brownsville Governing Board for thirty days for refusing to obey an order to accept back the UFT teachers. Reverend Oliver vowed to continue the fight, asking, "Since we are an elected board, how can we be suspended?" The Board of Education put Superintendent Donovan temporarily in charge of the Ocean Hill–Brownsville district and declared, for the benefit of the entire city, that the Ocean Hill–Brownsville district, despite its experimental status, was part of the city's public school system and therefore it ultimately had to answer to the superintendent and the Board of Education.

The following day, Rhody McCoy, the district's unit administrator, declared that he would still not reinstate the teachers in question. In response, Superintendent Donovan dismissed McCoy from his job as district unit administrator, saying: "Mr. McCoy has indicated to me clearly that he intends to obey the directions of the suspended Ocean Hill–Brownsville board and not those of the Board Education or the Superintendent of Schools." Seven of the eight principals in the district were also transferred out of the district for refusing to obey orders to reinstate the teachers.

Lindsay strongly supported Donovan's decision; he was gradually moving away from support for the Ocean Hill–Brownsville district and toward a more general defense of decentralization. The action was taken, according to Lindsay, because McCoy and the principals "have refused to adhere to the law." He damned the "illegal conduct" on both sides. Lindsay warned that though he still supported decentralization, there was no "magic formula which will erase the difficulties raised by community responsibility." He promised to take the "long road" toward decentralization, asking the Board of Education to spell out the rules for these experimental districts and to increase community participation in ways that did not violate teachers' rights. He asked teachers to recognize the right of communities to participate in the schools. He asked community spokesmen "to understand that it is simply not acceptable to turn grievances against our schools into racial and religious epithets." The question was: Had the situation deteriorated so fast as to make the "long road" to decentralization impossible to reach?[45]

A THIRD STRIKE

The teachers' union now seemed to be gaining the upper hand. It had been able to get the Ocean Hill–Brownsville Governing Board, McCoy, and the principals removed. It had managed to pull the mayor, normally hesitant to oppose black demands, into at least a neutral position. It was only a matter of time before the Ocean Hill–Brownsville community struck back.

On Wednesday, October 9, tensions came to a head at J.H.S. 271 as union teachers clashed with the replacement teachers. Sixteen UFT teachers inside the school left early, calling the situation inside "intolerable." Donovan ordered the school closed. Outside the school, one hundred to two hundred protesters clashed with police. McCoy and the principals, who had been removed from their jobs in the district, refused to report for reassignment. Students and teachers loyal to the Governing Board tried to enter J.H.S. 271, but were refused admittance. The city's Human Rights Commissioner, William Booth, visited the district to register his support for McCoy and the others, adding that he hoped the courts would "undo what was wrongfully done by the Board of Education" in suspending the board, McCoy, and the principals. Hoping to quell the violence, Donovan backed down somewhat and reinstated the seven principals and reopened J.H.S. 271.

In a letter to union members, Shanker traced the union's frustration to the threats and intimidation at J.H.S. 271 on October 9. He complained that Donovan and the Board of Education, faced with charges that union teachers were not being treated properly in Ocean Hill–Brownsville, kept delaying action. Schools where teachers "are forced to crawl instead of walk cannot function for children," Shanker warned. He made it clear that if the union struck for a third time, the demands for returning would be drastic: "We would seek the return of Ocean Hill–Brownsville to the City of New York and the removal, with due process, of personnel on all levels who participated in violence against teachers. We would seek the end of a self-proclaimed separate school system which flouts justice and due process in the name of 'experimentation' while operating on public funds."[46]

In retaliation for Donovan's decision to reinstate the principals and reopen J.H.S. 271, the UFT voted to strike for the third time in just over a month. The third strike began on October 14 and would continue well into November. Now it was time for Lindsay to attack the union. On his Sunday night television show, an angry mayor lashed out at the union. "You have the brute power," he said. "You do not have the moral right to make the children and parents of New York the victims of your own short-sightedness. You do not have the right to take a single school in a single district and use it to cripple this city." Lindsay knew that the union, of all the players involved in the decentralization controversy, held the most power: the power to keep one million children out of school. This greatly offended Lindsay's sensibilities. To him, the union was a "power broker" that was using its power not to help and assist those less powerful, but to further its own selfish interests.

Anticipating a negative response to the third strike from the public, the union published a full-page ad in the *Times* on the second day of the strike headlined "We Would Rather Teach Than Picket. But We Have No Choice." The crux of the controversy was the "dignity of teaching and the integrity of the classroom." The ad asked: "Should life in the classroom be guided by people who are responsibly concerned with education—or should educational policy and practice be dictated by an assortment of miscellaneous 'militants' like those now performing at school doors and in school corridors." The union portrayed the Ocean Hill–Brownsville district as being under the control of a small group of militants who threatened violence to force out the unwanted teachers and who would turn J.H.S. 271 "into a shambles." Fred Nauman, one of the ten disputed teachers, was quoted in the ad as saying of the school: "Avowed racists are teaching impressionable children. These children are being indoctrinated into a program of hatred of the police and all constitutional authority. . . . Until they received notoriety, bulletin boards contained shameful anti-white propaganda." Another UFT ad, which ran the next day, targeted Lindsay, unleashing a damning attack on the mayor. "Mayor Lindsay, When Will you Begin to Act like a Mayor in Our School Crisis?" blared the headline. Citing reports of violence against union teachers and threats at J.H.S. 271, the UFT told Lindsay "the ugly facts are before you" and asked that the mayor "put an end to vigilantism. . . . Time and again you have *seemed* to come to grips with the problem. You issued directives. You gave assurances. You made pledges. But they ended up as so many words. No action. The record of vacillation, indecision, permissiveness, and backtracking is so bizarre that the people of New York, including the parents of Ocean Hill–Brownsville, are rubbing their eyes in astonishment." The ad's tone was personal, reflecting the palpable dislike between the patrician Lindsay and the abrasive Shanker.

A third full-page ad in the *Times* at the end of the month took aim at "vigilantism" in the city's schools, not just in Brooklyn, but also on the Lower East Side and in the Bronx and upper Manhattan. "There's no room for extremism in our school," declared the UFT ad. Another full-page UFT ad showed a picture of over forty of the eighty-three disputed teachers from Ocean Hill–Brownsville. The caption of the photo was an attempt to humanize their struggle: "Meet some of the 'unwanted' teachers."[47]

If due process was the battle cry of the first two strikes, the issue of violence and threats against teachers was the driving issue of the third strike. The union cited a secret Board of Education report on the problems at J.H.S. 271 during the October 9 disturbances. Most of the charges were mild, including the report that Barry Gottehrer overheard students in the auditorium chanting "We will die for Rhody McCoy." Other charges included the tearing up of union teachers' time cards; the attempt by teachers Al Vann and Les Campbell to reopen the school after it had been ordered closed; and the harassment of Evelyn Farrar, the acting principal of the school, assigned by the Board of Education to replace Harris, who had been threatened by a group of adults and was in a "state of emotional upset." The report also told of a more serious incident in the teachers' room, in which union teachers were surrounded by nonstriking teachers who shouted, "We don't want you in this school," "White racist pigs," and "Whose going to protect you when the Police leave?" One replacement teacher, holding a stick, shouted at the UFT teachers, "If I throw this stick, I will hit an insect." In another incident, two nonstriking teachers told a union teacher: "You are going to die and they are going to put you 6 feet under." Reverend Galamison denounced the report as not "worth the paper on which it is written."[48]

On October 14 Superintendent Donovan wrote a four-page memo to members of the Board of Education about the UFT complaints. Donovan found that since the end of the second strike, "the Board of Education has carried out its commitment to return the UFT teachers to their schools and to teaching assignments although in some cases the UFT teachers are not entirely satisfied with these assignments." Donovan said that his observers had reported to him that seven of the eight schools in the district "appeared to be operating reasonably well." The situation at the eighth school, J.H.S. 271, was much tougher. Donovan told of the difficulty in assigning UFT teachers to classes and the "continual harassment and intimidation" of the union teachers. Confirming UFT complaints, Donovan wrote: "Reports from the observers indicate to me the building up of an intense racial antagonism not only among the staff members but among the pupils of the school. Bulletin boards, auditorium activities, and pictures indicated a racist approach not suitable for public schools." Because the atmosphere at J.H.S. 271 was "so hostile and inimical to effective instruction," Donovan recommended shutting the school down, transferring its teachers and students, and reopening it as a high school.[49]

Just as the third strike began, John Doar was elected president of the Board of Education, replacing the pro-union Rose Shapiro (she remained on the board), and Reverend Milton Galamison was elected vice president. Doar was an odd choice for the job. Born and raised in a small Wisconsin town, Doar moved to Washington to work in the Eisenhower Justice Department during the administration's final year. He continued in the Kennedy Justice Department and worked through the Johnson years. He had moved to New York early in 1968 to head the Bedford-Stuyvesant Restoration Corporation, which had been supported by Senator Robert Kennedy. Doar was in the Lindsay mold: a Princeton-educated, patrician-appearing (although, like Lindsay, not financially secure) liberal Republican concerned with civil rights. According to Barry Gottehrer, Lindsay liked Doar because he had "a sheen of gentility." Jimmy Breslin said of the appointment: "Mrs. Rose Shapiro . . . is a woman who belongs in a knitting shop. John Doar is different. He was in the business of human rights seven and ten years ago in the South, when anybody was eligible to get hurt and people put a lead pipe or a gun where their temper was." The problem was that Doar was new to New York. After being elected to head the Board of Education in the country's largest city, Doar freely admitted: "I don't know enough about decentralization." Thirty years later, Doar admitted that it was "madness to appoint me. And madness for me to accept. I didn't know where the buttons were. . . . Nobody was ever more unqualified to take such a job."[50]

Meanwhile, the black community rallied behind the embattled Ocean Hill–Brownsville district. The *Amsterdam News* spoke for many blacks when it pleaded with Rhody McCoy to "stick to your guns." Calling Shanker and his union "the villain in this tragedy," the paper asked, "Who owns the schools, the teachers or the people?"

Lindsay held a series of fruitless meetings with Shanker. The frustrated mayor had already bent over backward to accommodate the union, suggesting that a panel be created to hear charges against McCoy and that any school where the safety of teachers was threatened could be closed. Now Lindsay lashed out at Shanker: "Every demand of the teachers for the protection of their rights and safety has now been met. The only issue now blocking settlement of the teachers strike is whether the UFT leadership can dictate reprisals against individuals as the price of a settlement—reprisals without the due process the UFT says it is fighting for."[51]

Lindsay was thrown into an awkward role. He desperately sympathized with the demands of minorities. Yet he was faced with a teachers' strike that kept over one million children out of school for much of the fall. Lindsay felt that he had a moral obligation to end the strike. Rhody McCoy recalled that Lindsay told him in two separate meetings "that he knew this community was going about its business in a responsible way, that they were morally right and legally right. He said he knew these things, 'But,' he said, 'you have to understand. I have a strike on my hands and I've got to settle it.' " And by the beginning of November, the only way to end the strike was to give the union most of what it wanted. The city did not have much of a choice.[52]

The Board of Education was now badly divided on how to proceed. Doar and the other pro-decentralization members defied Lindsay and opposed suspending the Ocean Hill–Brownsville Governing Board and principals without due process. Rose Shapiro made clear her continued opposition to the decentralization and community control. She later said, "I did not believe that decentralization had anything to do with the education of the child; I thought it was a political ploy." She also said she believed the UFT, on the whole, was justified in striking. She called Lindsay's appointees to the Board "impossible people." Reverend Milton Galamison believed that the Board "had no clout" during the negotiations over the third strike. He accused Shapiro and Morris Iushewitz, the secretary of the Central Labor Council, of being pro-UFT and Walter Straley of being anti–Ocean Hill–Brownsville. Straley, a Lindsay appointee, turned on Milton Galamison during one heated meeting and said, "That's the trouble with you people. If you hadn't started making trouble a few years ago, with your sit-ins and demonstrations, we wouldn't be having all this trouble now." Despite the majority of the members' support for decentralization, Galamison complained that some members of the board were "so thoroughly captured by the UFT" that they could not deal with the crisis. Other members, according to Galamison, "labored with the handicaps of inherent white prejudice."[53]

The Board of Education directed the city's schools to remain open during the strike. Donovan agreed to this, but only if it could be done "without danger to the welfare and safety of children." To Reverend Milton Galamison, Donovan's directive was meaningless because local school superintendents, many of whom were sympathetic to the strike, would continue to use their powers to keep their schools closed.[54]

The charges of violence and intimidation were crucial to the UFT's case for the third strike, and the union made efforts to categorize these incidents. One UFT report on the picketing at P.S. 29 in the Bronx featured testimony from striking teachers who told of being threatened and harassed. Two striking teachers reported having anti-Semitic slurs hurled at them by pickets made up of community members. An anti-union protester called the teachers "Christ killers." This protester reportedly said to the teachers that, "Hitler did not finish the job," and that they "should all go back to Israel." Other protesters pushed a striking female teacher, yelling, "Just you try to get back in. You'll be soap and lampshades." The report claimed that some anti-

UFT protesters were female parent aides and paraprofessionals at the school. The UFT made audiotapes of the anti-union protesters' comments, some of which included the heavy use of the word "pigs" and references to "lampshades," "Christ killers," and "gas chambers."[55]

Others had a different perspective on the protests. Human Rights Commissioner William Booth toured six city schools with two other members of the commission and wrote up his impressions in a memo to Mayor Lindsay, dated October 29. At a high school in Queens, Booth's appearance visibly angered the teachers, who shouted epithets of "anti-Semite, black racist, and black Nazi" at Booth. When Booth left the school, the teachers, many of whom were Jewish, greeted him with Nazi salutes and shouts of "Heil Hitler." Booth reported that conditions in many other schools seemed fine, with a large number of students attending school and enough teachers to run them. At the two high schools he visited, however, Booth claimed white and black students were called names by their striking teachers, including "black bastards" and "hippies."

Contrary to the image of chaos that the UFT portrayed, Booth found conditions at J.H.S. 271 "excellent." A tour of the school revealed "classes in normal operation. The halls were clear and the administrative staff was working quietly in an atmosphere which had no air of tension about it. We saw no 'community people' wandering through the halls or in evidence in any way."[56]

In an attempt to combat the charge of anti-Semitism against the district's leaders, the nonunion teachers in Ocean Hill–Brownsville joined the war of full-page *Times* ads. Signed by nearly 400 teachers from the district's eight schools, the ad noted that 70 percent of the newly hired teachers were white and more than half of the white teachers (nearly 40 percent of the overall number) were Jewish. In response to Shanker's charges of black racism and anti-Semitism, the teachers wrote: "We, the undersigned teachers, are living proof that such charges are false on all counts."

Fred Ferretti, a journalist sympathetic to the experimental district, said that McCoy had originally wanted black teachers for his district. He tried to recruit teachers from Southern black colleges, but could not find enough quality teachers at the time. "The pool right now we can draw from is mostly white, a consequence of the system," said McCoy. Most of the non-UFT teachers he brought into the district were young whites.[57] Among the teachers were a University of Wisconsin doctoral student in Afro-American history, a white organizer for the Mississippi Freedom Democratic Party, a former Peace Corps volunteer, and an organizer for the left-wing Peace and Freedom Party. Many were graduates of Ivy League colleges and some had advanced degrees. Many of the young men were seeking to avoid the military draft by teaching. One of these young white teachers, sporting an ELDRIDGE CLEAVER FOR PRESIDENT button, said of his coworkers, "Thirty percent will need draft deferments in order to continue teaching, 25 percent have never taught before, all are licensed by the central board, and nearly all are 'committed' to social changes." The 1969 Ford Foundation report "And Then There Were the Children" said this group of teachers avoided "traditional classroom procedures and approaches, preferring 'unstructured' class-rooms." Replacement teacher Liz Fusco, who had previously taught in the Mississippi Freedom schools and who ultimately taught in the district for three years, said of her job at Ocean Hill–Brownsville's P.S. 178: "I went solely for the politics of it. . . . My being there was a commitment." Fusco admitted that the nonunion teachers "had no idea of how *gradually* to move from authoritarianism to liberatory education. We *played* anarchy and we got it."[58]

In the middle of November, one month into the third strike, the Ocean Hill–Brownsville Governing Board received another blow. A state appeals court ruled 3–2 that the hiring of principals by the Governing Board was illegal. Members of the Governing Board reacted defiantly to the decision: Father Powis said he had "never seen a racist as flagrant" as the judge and called the trial a "farce." Calling the trial "a perfect example of white America today," Father Powis said the Governing Board had been " 'responsible' for just too long. Maybe it's time to become 'irresponsible.' " Diane Ravitch noted that "from the beginning of the project, [the Governing Board] viewed every obstacle as an instance of racism. Whenever anything went wrong, whenever a request was denied, whenever they had to compromise for less than they demanded, they detected racism." A majority on the court declared that the Board of Education could not, "without legislative authority," delegate "to a lay Governing Board the power to determine the professional and educational qualifications for the schools in this community without regard to existing eligible lists and without regard to Civil Service examinations." The dissenting judges were left to argue that in "urgent" times the rules could be bent because the principals "had to have an intimate knowledge of the community and its cultural strengths and aspirations." McCoy's response to the decision was to say that, "the decision won't affect us in any way as far as I know."[59]

Reverend Milton Galamison, writing after the strikes, made the case for the right of the Ocean Hill–Brownsville district to stand outside of the rule of law. According to Galamison, what the Governing Board "is saying to America, in essence, is that the black community will no longer function within the rules of a system that has forfeited its right to exist." This was a startling statement coming from the vice president of the Board of Education, but it placed the issue of community control in the context of civil disobedience. Father Powis voiced similar thoughts: "You have to realize that as far as—at least as far as the black and Puerto Rican community goes, they are no longer going to permit, regardless of what your rules or your contract says—they're not going to permit assistant principals or teachers to destroy something which they have great faith in and which this year under new assistant principals and teachers is working beautifully." An aide of Al

Shanker's, Jules Kolodny, strongly refuted Powis's statement: "What we have here is a flaunting [*sic*] of all authority down the line." The Ocean Hill–Brownsville Governing Board believed itself above the law. Then again, so did the UFT, which was violating the Taylor Law against strikes by municipal unions.[60]

Assessments of Lindsay's ability to grasp the situation varied. One decentralization supporter noted that Lindsay and McGeorge Bundy, both upper-class WASPs, "advocated their school decentralization plan out of the mistaken idea that the forces of decency in the city and state would prevail." The *Post*'s James Wechsler wrote that Lindsay's flaw was "a deep-seated idealism . . . that cynics will dismiss as incorrigible innocence." The mayor believed New York could be turned into "a truly model city of tolerance, reasonableness, and compassion." Lindsay was still passionate about decentralization, telling Nat Hentoff that "many established groups, and many whites deep down, don't want to see that kind of change and don't want to see that kind of gain on the part of the disadvantaged people. They resent it very deeply although they'd be the first to complain if you had violence— violence brought about over the absence or impossibility of any change at all." At the beginning of the third strike, Jimmy Breslin saw Lindsay caught in the middle: "But with John Lindsay, always, when it comes to Brownsville or his career, he knows which way to go."

In July 1968 Lindsay had interviewed the black social scientist Kenneth Clark on his weekly television show, and the two men had commiserated about the problems of implementing school reform. Lindsay blamed "a storm of protest" by the city's white middle class for blocking school reform. Clark agreed, taking the argument one step further by claiming he suspected that middle-class whites "want to fasten on the backs of Negro and Puerto Rican children criminally inferior schools and do not want to develop any formula or technique whereby these schools can be improved." On the other side of the spectrum, the *Daily News* complained that "Mr. Lindsay has shilly-shallied and double talked, tacked and yawed, bowed to minority and special groups from the start of this decentralization dispute, rather than using the large powers he has in such situations."[61]

Despite Lindsay's charges against the white middle class's resistance to change, he did appear willing, at least in the short term, to sacrifice the demands of Ocean Hill–Brownsville. To end the strike, Lindsay was willing to close J.H.S. 271, press action against any person threatening a teacher, support Superintendent Donovan's authority over the Ocean Hill–Brownsville Governing Board, and allow all ousted union teachers back to the district in full teaching roles. Shanker, demanding the firing of the entire Ocean Hill–Brownsville Board, rejected Lindsay's offer. Shanker also began to wonder whether the union could trust the Board of Education, a majority of whom had publicly opposed the mayor's proposed plan to end the strike and supported community control.[62]

On Sunday, November 17, after a twenty-seven-hour negotiating session at Gracie Mansion, a settlement was reached by Lindsay, Shanker, and State Commissioner of Education James Allen, who was the driving force behind the agreement. It called for the removal of the Ocean Hill–Brownsville principals not chosen from civil service lists; the appointment of a state trustee, Associate Commissioner of Education Herbert Johnson, to oversee the district; the creation of a three-man state panel to monitor the treatment of teachers throughout the school system; the addition of ten extra days of school (including time during Christmas and Easter vacations) and the addition of forty-five extra minutes per day for fourteen weeks to make up for time lost during the strikes; and the retention of Rhody McCoy as unit administrator if he agreed to abide by the terms of the settlement. The Governing Board would remain suspended.

The union leadership agreed to these conditions, and the rank-and-file approved the agreement overwhelmingly, despite some dissension and lingering anger. On the other side, Father Powis called the settlement a "total capitulation to the demands of the union," while Reverend Oliver said the agreement "may be the beginning of the end of Ocean Hill–Brownsville." On Tuesday, November 19, the strike was over and teachers returned to their schools for the first time since October 11.[63]

THE AFTERMATH OF THE TEACHERS' STRIKES

Absent from the strike negotiations were two of the major participants in the crisis: the Ocean Hill–Brownsville Governing Board and the Board of Education. Later, John Doar said that City Hall had bypassed the Board of Education because of what he characterized as its "intransigence" when it came to dealing with the controversy. Doar says that Deputy Mayor Robert Sweet "pounded" him many times during the third strike, "in a nice way," to soften his position. But Doar, Galamison, and the others had no intention of changing their position. Therefore, City Hall and Commissioner Allen simply ignored the Board of Education. In his book, Barry Gottehrer criticized Doar's actions during the strike, saying Doar's "first loyalty was to his constituency [poor blacks] rather than to the mayor or the city. . . . When the inevitable moment for pragmatic decisions arrived . . . John Doar chose to remain a purist, going down with community control supporters rather than compromise and preserve at least a viable decentralization experiment."[64]

But the actors in the drama that felt the most bitterness toward the strike settlement were members of the Ocean Hill–Brownsville Governing Board. They were forced to accept a settlement that, if enforced, would end the community control experiment. "There were times when I thought Mayor Lindsay, if he could, would have gladly put every resident of Ocean Hill in a gunny sack and dropped them in the East River," Galamison wrote bitterly after the final settlement. Lindsay, he felt, was sometimes strong, "but he often panicked." Years later, Reverend Oliver was still angry about the actions of Lindsay and his aides. "Lindsay was trying his best to do what he thought was best for the city, but at our expense," remembered Oliver. "It just didn't seem that he had our interests at heart. . . . We felt we did not have Lindsay's ear."[65]

Preston Wilcox, one of the intellectual godfathers of community control, wrote an open letter entitled "The Human Response to the Attempted RAPE of Ocean Hill–Brownsville." Wilcox condemned the final strike settlement as "an attempt to rape Black people of the opportunity to control their own destinies." The idea of the black community being "raped" by the union was common. It reinforced the idea that the white establishment was demasculinizing the black community by destroying the experimental districts. Earlier that fall, Reverend Oliver used the same language: "I hate very much to see the mayor and the Board of Education hold down this community while the union rapes it."[66]

Despite the apparent defeat of the Ocean Hill–Brownsville experiment, Wilcox continued to push for community control: "The Black community is struggling to gain the *natural* right to *control* the education of its own children. It has a right to determine *who* educates its children; no one has to *give* them this right." Wilcox called the Board of Education the "Board of Miseducation" and accused the UFT of having little interest in educating minorities. He wrote that John Doar "has proven to be more liberal Down South than Up South," and Mayor Lindsay "has come across like Bwana Lindsay, patronizing and ineffective." Lindsay's final deal, according to Wilcox, "had all the characteristics of a Mississippi judgment." In response to the strike settlement, Wilcox moved further toward the principle of separatism, demanding that Milton Galamison resign from the Board of Education; that all black members of the Urban Coalition resign; that all black teachers resign from the UFT; that communities in New York City desiring community control of schools form a "Joint Board of Human Education" and refuse to cooperate with the existing Board of Education; and that "black families should refuse on a collective basis to comply with any of the decisions emanating from the South African–type strike settlement."[67]

Mario Fantini, Marilyn Gittell, and Richard Magat—the white educators and Ford Foundation officials behind the education experiment—noted that within the black community, the "mood of isolation and embattlement increased during the struggle. Instead of intensifying efforts to win over public opinion, community leaders tended more and more to picture an establishment arrayed against the community-control concept and the demonstration districts." David Spencer, the chairman of Harlem's I.S. 201 Governing Board, wrote an open letter after the strike settlement. Spencer accused Lindsay of having "destroyed" the community control experiment. "He has delivered a death sentence to hundreds of Black and Puerto Rican children who for the first time in their lives began to have some hope for a bright future," wrote Spencer. He went on to condemn "the police state tactics" used to enforce the law in Ocean Hill–Brownsville, arguing that "Mayor Lindsay's 'education under law' is the same kind of racist epithet as George Wallace's 'law and order.' "[68]

There was more to the controversy than just education policy. Just a few years later, Rhody McCoy wrote in his Ph.D. dissertation that "Ocean Hill–Brownsville was the manifestation of one element within the white community's attempt to placate the black movement at the expense of another segment of the white community." After all, John Lindsay was the man who coined the phrase the "power brokers" and made no secret of the fact that he considered bureaucrats and unions in the same category as the powerful men in finance, law, and real estate. Marilyn Gittell and Maurice Berube voiced similar concerns: "Presently, the poor and the middle-class school professionals are competing for power. The struggle will continue until the poor achieve a guarantee of their participatory role." Gittell and Berube saw community control of schools as entailing "the redistribution of power, much of it from white liberals to the black poor."[69]

Three days after the schools reopened, a controversy erupted at J.H.S. 271. A state observer stationed there reported that Fred Nauman and Cliff Rosenthal, two of the original disputed teachers, "were treated unmercifully by students. Back-talk, lack of co-operation, and insubordination were received by these teachers from students, almost as if the students had been put up to it." Nauman was accused of grabbing the arm and hurting the thumb of a four-foot-nine seventh-grader named Darrell Stewart. "The classes that day were extremely difficult, quite hostile, particularly to UFT teachers," remembered Nauman. Stewart was "one of the most hostile" students and had threatened to punch Nauman in the mouth when the teacher took attendance. Nauman saw the youth with a clenched fist and feared the student would strike him. The teacher knocked the boy's fist down, and the boy ran to the back of the room and threw a chair at the teacher. The boy claimed that Nauman assaulted him because he accused the teacher of causing the principal and four black teachers to be suspended. Shanker believed that community control supporters had framed Nauman. Herbert Johnson, the state trustee at Ocean Hill–Brownsville, waffled on whether or not to transfer Nauman.[70]

In response to the lack of action, approximately forty protesters prevented eight UFT teachers from entering J.H.S. 271. Though the blockade ended later in the day, few students remained for classes. Union teachers found that no children had reported to their classes. When a state observer asked demonstrators not to assemble on the steps of the school, one protester urged another, "Don't listen to him, honey. You see the color of his skin, don't you? This is our school, not his." Fred Nauman entered the school with a five-man police guard because there had been threats on his life. On the following Monday, McCoy sent Nauman a letter relieving him of his duties pending the assault charge, but the order was countermanded by Johnson and Nauman returned to his class, where the disorder was so bad that he could do nothing more than take attendance.[71]

Reverend Oliver and Al Vann were both arrested on trespassing charges for entering J.H.S. 271 on Tuesday, November 26. Vann, one of the suspended teachers, had resumed his duties at the school in clear violation of the strike settlement. Both men claimed they were needed to restore discipline to the school. The following day, Oliver again entered the school with a group of twenty to thirty ministers and citizens. Once inside, the group berated Johnson. Student misbehavior toward union teachers continued, leading sixteen union teachers at J.H.S. 271 to ask for transfers out of the district. In addition, Federal Judge Anthony Travia dismissed a suit brought by the Ocean Hill–Brownsville Governing Board challenging its suspension, ruling that the local board was nothing more than "an unofficial body of citizen advisers" and had "no authority to countermand any orders of the Board of Education on any subject."

Meanwhile, Leslie Campbell and Sonny Carson formed the Citywide Student Strike Committee, an organization that would incite violence and vandalism throughout the city. At a rally at Dag Hammarskjold Plaza at the United Nations on November 29, Campbell told 1,500 assembled students to "fight for what you want." On Monday, December 2, black students took to the streets. Prodded by Campbell and other militants, hundreds of bottle- and rock-throwing youths attacked police in the streets of Ocean Hill–Brownsville. Hundreds of black youths stormed schools throughout the city and created havoc in the streets and on the subways. Disorders were reported in schools in four of the five boroughs. Violence and vandalism continued for the whole week.[72]

Also on December 2, Reverend Oliver again entered J.H.S. 271 illegally with forty to fifty adults who roamed the halls at will. According to a state observer at the school, the PTA president Elaine Rooke was one of the group. She entered a union teacher's class, "swore at him as being a poor teacher and told him to get out of the room." Rooke later struck two other union teachers. One union teacher noted that "throughout the entire afternoon the situation in the corridors, and particularly the lobby, was one of confusion, disorderliness, and anarchy."

Johnson, who had already rebuffed the suspended Governing Board, forcefully imposed his authority on the district. He was met with threats and confrontation from the Governing Board's supporters, one of whom threatened his life. One story had him locked in a closet by community control supporters (a report Johnson denied). Another had a protester drawing either a knife or letter opener and attacking Johnson. Others said protesters, including Mrs. Rooke, yelled at Johnson after she had been hit by a police-man: "One more mistake, you bastard, and you're dead." Another person joined in: "Why wait for another mistake." Amid the chaos, Johnson decided to close J.H.S. 271. It remained closed for the entire week.[73]

On December 2, at a meeting attended by Johnson, James Allen, Al Shanker, Kenneth Clark, and others, the UFT leader complained that the agreement ending the strike was being "violated on a daily basis." He com-plained that because union teachers were not being protected, only eight UFT teachers were left in J.H.S. 271. A weary Johnson replied, "I am per-suaded that *I* can't carry out this trusteeship." Johnson also admitted that he couldn't keep outsiders from entering the school "except, of course, by force." Later that day, Commissioner Allen announced that Johnson was "pretty well worn out" from two weeks in the district and had decided to resign.[74]

Johnson's replacement, William Firman, an assistant commissioner of ed-ucation from Upstate New York, fared no better. Firman decided to take a hard line against the Ocean Hill–Brownsville Governing Board. On De-cember 9, with J.H.S. 271 still closed, Firman declared that if McCoy wished to be reinstated, he would have to submit a plan for J.H.S. 271 by the following day. This would have to include a plan to keep unauthorized per-sons out of the school and keep order in the classroom. Instead, McCoy ig-nored Firman and attempted on December 10 to personally reopen J.H.S. 271. McCoy was arrested. Firman sent McCoy a telegram on December 11 charging him with insubordination and ordering his immediate reassign-ment. McCoy simply ignored Firman's directive. That same day Firman re-leased a statement reporting that his "efforts to achieve a calm and viable educational atmosphere in Ocean Hill–Brownsville have met with only min-imal success to date." Firman said, "To say that I am disappointed with Mr. McCoy's unwillingness to work with me in this endeavor is a gross under-statement. . . . I must now reluctantly conclude that Mr. McCoy is unwill-ing to work under my direction." Because of Firman's hard-line attitude, Milton Galamison accused him of having a "colonialist attitude with a pa-ternalistic approach. He has been rigid beyond description and not taken stock of the kind of fluid, revolutionary situation in which he finds him-self . . ." Kenneth Clark thought Firman had "outlived his usefulness." He accused the state overseer of speaking in an "imperious tone" and of seeing himself "as a plantation overseer and as a white boss that must contain the restless natives." Having grown increasingly frustrated and ineffective, Fir-man was replaced by Wilbur Nordos on December 16. Firman needed a twenty-four-hour state police guard at his home because of threats against his life and that of his family.[75]

Nordos's approach differed from that of his predecessors. Though he rec-ognized that the Governing Board's idea of community control went "be-yond what is reasonable under present laws and regulations," he was more sympathetic to the Ocean Hill–Brownsville experiment and its leaders than his predecessors. Acknowledging in a memo to Commissioner Allen that the Ocean Hill–Brownsville supporters spoke "with a frankness that is somewhat disturbing in its disregard of more conventional, polite ways of dealing with public officials," Nordos nevertheless felt that "allowances must also be made for their supersensitivity." Nordos was all too willing to see the Governing Board as it saw itself: as a victim. "They refuse to accept a position of being to blame for the strike: they regard themselves as more sinned against than sinning," wrote Nordos. "They are all too ready to see the whole establishment as engaged, not always with deliberate intent but with the same effects, in conspiracy to prove that they cannot manage their own affairs, let alone undertake innovations." He recommended that McCoy and the Governing Board be reinstated "without further delay."[76]

To Lindsay, the bitterness of the school strike betrayed the real New York. "New York is supposed to be so liberal a city, even a cauldron of radicalism," the mayor complained. "The school battle showed us who we actually were." And you can bet that Lindsay did not like the revelation. To him and many other liberal New Yorkers, the forces of decency had not prevailed. "The parents were beginning to demand a place at the table," said the mayor. "That's what decentralization was all about. They didn't want to sit at the head of the table or even at the side. They wanted a place at the table, even below the salt." Despite the chaos, Lindsay believed "we'll have a better city" after going through the fire of the school strikes because "everyone is more mature for it."[77]

After the strike, Shanker continued to hammer at Lindsay, criticizing the mayor for creating a "deliberate strategy to build up racial animosities and particularly to arouse the ghettos." Shanker accused Lindsay's rhetoric of coming "very close to inciting racial war in the city." He did strike a more conciliatory approach, though, when he noted that Lindsay often tried to act as a moderating influence regarding the Board of Education. Lindsay, according to Shanker, was torn between his role as an advocate of decentralization and his role as mediator in a labor controversy. "You can't really play both roles," noted Shanker.[78]

Lindsay's shift from decentralization proponent to labor mediator during the school strike angered his former allies. Three teachers' strikes in one fall had caused the mayor and his aides to lose their initial enthusiasm for the experiment. Lewis Feldstein, Lindsay's chief aide on school decentralization, quickly became disillusioned. "I had a clear sense that it wasn't worth it," remembers Feldstein. "We should have caved much earlier. We didn't gain squat by this. This was not a win-win, it was a lose-lose-lose-lose. Everything from the future of those districts to the likelihood that you could make change in the citywide school system to Lindsay's personal standing and ability to govern the city."[79]

Ticknor Litchfield, a state observer at J.H.S. 271 during the fall of 1968 and a school administrator in Ramapo, New York, was sympathetic to Ocean

Hill–Brownsville and its demand for community control. But after spending a month in the middle of this confusion, Litchfield came away believing that the Ocean Hill–Brownsville Board "indulged in many more excesses than one could reasonably expect or permit from a newly formed organization, even on a philosophical basis. I feel that many of the difficulties and controversies which have ensued were unnecessary, and unfortunately most seem to have been a result of the estrangement that a black, ghetto community feels toward what it considers to be the white 'establishment.' " Litchfield put much of the blame for the tensions after the third strike on Reverend Oliver. "No matter what concessions were made by Johnson, they were simply not enough in the eyes of Reverend Oliver and his group," wrote Litchfield. "He was satisfied with nothing less than complete, total community control, right now." A Ford Foundation report later described Reverend Oliver as "a person who does not share the extremely militant persuasion of some of the Ocean Hill figures, yet will support militancy when it appears politically advisable and popular."[80]

RHODY McCOY AND RACIAL SEPARATISM

Black militancy and racial separatism played key roles in the controversy over Ocean Hill–Brownsville. Al Vann and Leslie Campbell, teachers in the district and leaders of the African-American Teachers Association, saw black values as being different from white values. In 1970, Campbell wrote that traditional "white" schools "encourage the individualist instincts . . . [and] perpetuate the idea that any knowledge worthwhile must come from a book, to set the so-called 'educated' apart from the community." Vann condemned schools for fostering "the concept of individual achievement and success at the expense of fellow human beings."

Those who attempted to judge the mood and attitude of Ocean Hill–Brownsville focused their attention on Unit Administrator Rhody McCoy. His supporters painted him as a thoughtful, moderate man, balancing competing interests with the help of his calming pipe. One observer described McCoy as a "mild mannered" man who wanted "nothing more than for the black man to take his rightful place in American society." This image may have been one of conciliation, but the reality was far different.[81]

As early as January 1968, five months before the controversial May ouster of teachers in Ocean Hill–Brownsville, McCoy used fiery rhetoric at an address at Harvard. "As history has so frequently recorded," McCoy told the crowd, "the end of oppression has often become a reality only after people have resorted to violent means." Writing in the *Amsterdam News* in 1971, McCoy voiced similar theories. He believed that "the movement for community control has provided one more vehicle for the oppression of the black and third-world communities of New York City: what were the tentative beginnings of a revolution have been perverted into just one more excuse for fascism." Martin Mayer noted: "Behind the impassive professionalism McCoy is deeply hostile to much of American society."[82]

The best window into the mind of the man who led the Ocean Hill–Brownsville district is the dissertation he wrote in 1971 for a Ph.D. in education from the University of Massachusetts, Amherst. Though some might argue that the paper was the product of a man embittered by the nasty fight and eventual defeat of the Ocean Hill–Brownsville experiment, the words reveal feelings that must have been held deep inside him for much of his adult life. It was not a conventional dissertation and it is clear that the university gave McCoy some leeway with the project. From November 1970 until March 1971, McCoy held five seminars attended by key players in the Ocean Hill–Brownsville controversy, including Kenneth Clark, Milton Galamison, Herbert Oliver, Bernard Donovan, Marilyn Gittell, Mario Fantini, and Fred Ferretti. All but Donovan could be considered strong supporters of school decentralization. Al Shanker was invited, but refused to attend. The two-volume dissertation is merely a transcript of the seminars with McCoy's summary of the discussions and his own comments added at the end.[83]

In his thesis, McCoy argued that a mysterious conspiracy doomed the Ocean Hill–Brownsville experiment to failure: "There exists a pre-determined script, established by racist, capitalist America, which makes the education of black, poor white, and Third World children in this country impossible. . . ; not only are there no options, but . . . there is no imaginable reform to the school system operating under the constraints of the socialization necessary for capitalism that would educate all children."

In his dissertation, McCoy said he was "completely convinced that the establishment of white America does not intend to have the minorities educated—they can't afford it—and they're taking every step they possibly can to see to it that they are not." McCoy's solution was simple: "A violent revolution is necessary in order to have America's public institutions serve all of its people." McCoy further explained his theory of violent revolution: "The only power of the poor in America is the power to destroy; the power of violent and suicidal assault upon the white man. Since Watts the threat of murder has held a certain political advantage. But given the failure of black people to, as yet, mount a truly revolutionary army, such violence only leads to the ruthless repression of the people; hopefully such repression will ultimately turn the tables, moving in such forces as to create a true army which will liberate blacks, whites and Third World people." In 1989, McCoy said if he could start again, he "would work endlessly, tirelessly, to destroy the system, to tear it down brick by brick."[84]

The historian Jerald Podair saw the Ocean Hill–Brownsville controversy as a clash between "white" values and "black" values. On the one hand, people like McCoy and the African-American Teachers Association called for a "black value system" based on "collective work and responsibility, cooperative economics, and unity." On the other hand, the UFT defended middle-class values, teaching children, in the words of Al Shanker, "to *make it* within our society."[85]

OCEAN HILL–BROWNSVILLE AS A LABOR PROBLEM

Labor relations was a notorious Achilles heel for Mayor Lindsay. The *New York Times* labor expert, A. H. Raskin, noted at the end of 1968: "Many—and probably most—of the top leaders in local labor are genuinely convinced that Lindsay despises them and that his aim is to 'bust' unions in the municipal service." Michael Harrington, author of *The Other America*, wrote: "John Lindsay has not once given the slightest hint that he has any sympathy for, or understanding of, unionism. He has botched every negotiation he has handled, in part because he is so obviously contemptuous of organized workers. He is capable of a charismatic relationship to the underorganized ghetto, but not of any on-going participation in collective bargaining."

A public school teacher expressed his belief that "Lindsay was ineffectual in dealing with this matter because . . . his real sensibilities were not affected by what was happening to the UFT teachers. In a subtle way he approved of what was happening or, at the least, he inwardly felt that the harassment was 'justifiable when you consider all the circumstances.' " The teacher accused Lindsay, John Doar, and liberal intellectuals of being unable to "deal open-mindedly with a teacher group in our present society who represent, in the main, a lower-middle-class ethos." Lew Feldstein, the mayor's point man on school decentralization, admitted the administration was "relatively inatten-tive" to the UFT. "They weren't the people we hung around with," said Feld-stein.[86]

John Doar, Lindsay's choice as president of the Board of Education, ob-served in early 1968: "It is our position that a basic conflict exists between labor-union concepts and civil-rights concepts. Something has to give." In a battle between the demands of blacks and the demands of the union, the Lindsay administration would find itself leaning toward the former. Lewis Feldstein noticed the fervor of his boss's stand on education reform while listening to John and Mary Lindsay passionately arguing for community control one night at Gracie Mansion during the school strikes. According to Feldstein, the mayor's stand on the issue "wasn't a matter of politics, it was whether right could prevail."[87]

In the eyes of those in City Hall, Al Shanker was on the wrong side of this moral battle. Barry Gottehrer called Shanker "a terrible, terrible person," one who turned "the New York City school system and the Lindsay administra-tion into his own nuclear testing ground." Robert Sweet found the UFT head "quite an abrasive fellow" who "made a point of being an ideologue." Shanker was the only man Mary Lindsay ever banned from the living quar-ters at Gracie Mansion. Gottehrer regretted that the administration "didn't have the luxury of locking him [Shanker] out of our offices." Lindsay's aide Peter Goldmark said the mayor "sensed in Shanker and the union a total absence of effective concern for the larger issues. . . . They offered no bridges to the other side and they held a lot of the cards. That's not good enough for John Lindsay. He wants more from people." Shanker and the union failed Lindsay's test of selflessness and concern for the public interest. To the mayor, they were simply "power brokers" looking to maximize their own power by harming the larger social good. Lindsay's police guard Pat Vecchio remembers Lindsay's referring to the union leader as "an evil man." To make matters worse, Shanker offended Lindsay during negotiations at City Hall by putting his feet up on the mayor's desk and revealing his sagging socks. This, said Marilyn Gittell, "violated Lindsay's sense of decorum."[88]

A politically active Socialist in his youth, Shanker was an ardent anti-Communist in the George Meany tradition. One UFT official, George Altomare, called Shanker "the closest to someone where ideology was important in the formal sense." He was heavily involved in the battles of the 1950s and early 1960s that successfully wrested power away from the Communist-influenced Teacher's Union. Ironically, in light of the events of 1968 in New York City, Shanker proudly marched for civil rights in Selma, Alabama, in 1965.[89]

In his later years, Shanker became more conservative. He became head of the national American Federation of Teachers. In a 1997 interview, Shanker described himself as a believer "in traditional discipline and that history should not be distorted for current purposes. . . . In certain ways I could be viewed as a progressive educator and in other ways as a traditionalist."

Al Shanker became a figure of derision for many on the left. In Woody Allen's 1973 movie *Sleeper*, liberal audiences in New York got a laugh at the expense of the UFT leader. In the movie, the Allen character wakes up after being frozen for two hundred years to find the planet had been destroyed and subsequently rebuilt. The reason for the destruction, he is told, is that "over a hundred years ago a man named Albert Shanker got hold of a nuclear warhead." By the 1990s, the left still had not forgiven Shanker. Columbia professor Manning Marable called him a "racist social democrat," and the historian Paul Buhle wrote an intemperate article on the occasion of Shanker's death in 1997 entitled "Albert Shanker: No Flowers."[90]

AN IDEOLOGICAL CIVIL WAR

These ill feelings toward Al Shanker arose because the Ocean Hill–Brownsville controversy drove a wedge between liberal intellectuals sympathetic to traditional trade unionism and those sympathetic to Black Power. On one side, Maurice Berube and Marilyn Gittell complained that instead of "recognizing the community control movement as part of the same fight for respect, dignity, and democratic rights as the civil rights struggle in the South was in the early 1960s, many northern liberals condemn school activists as extremists."[91]

On the other side, Isaiah Terman, director of communications for the American Jewish Committee, noted that the "style of American liberal thinking has changed. While in former years one could rely on liberal and left-wing journals to rally behind labor causes, or to practice a certain amount of restraint in regard to ethnic name-calling," by 1969 this was no longer true. Jews especially felt angry at what they saw as the betrayal by liberals and the transfer of their loyalties to blacks. "The Jew as a member of a minority group and the union member trying to improve his condition evoke no feelings of protectiveness or defense [from liberals]," Terman wrote. "In the romantic mood of the Left, they [academics and journalists] see everything as either black or white; and the white is all bad."[92]

As befitted the world of New York intellectuals, the Ocean Hill–Brownsville controversy was fought out as much with pen and paper as on the picket line. The *Times* ran an advertisement in support of the UFT, placed by the Ad Hoc Committee to Defend the Right to Teach. The cochairmen of the group were Michael Harrington and Tom Kahn of the League for Industrial Democracy. These pro-union "Democratic Socialists" claimed that "decentralization is not the issue. . . . The real issue is job security. . . . The destruction of the UFT would mean placing teachers at the mercy of local groups throughout the city. It would mean the liquidation of the most effective organized force for improved quality education."[93]

Maurice Berube, a representative of the New Left, chastised the pro-union Old Left for having little rage "against social injustice; little compassion for the alienated, the oppressed, the mad, the sick, the old and the castoffs of middle class America. . . . In the end, the 'democratic socialist' glorifies the American way." Berube looked down at his liberal counterparts who were defending the union: "Who supports the UFT? A few prominent social democrats and liberals like Michael Harrington, Jewish groups who are rightly anxious over black anti-Semitism, others who are plainly anxious about blacks, and that anti-Semitic, anti-black white constituency (many Catholics) who support PAT [Parents and Taxpayers Group]. Quite a coalition. Certainly the larger segment would most probably support local control in the white South, but not the urban black North."[94]

Some on the left took an apocalyptic view of the school controversy. The editor of *The New York Review of Books*, Jason Epstein, likened ghetto residents to Vietnamese peasants: "In the ghettos of New York as a decade ago in the Mekong Delta, an angry and insurgent population feels that it has exhausted its last political options and is now ready for violence, even if violence means suicide." Epstein envisioned a radical new urban order to forestall this possible violence, going well beyond the community control of schools: "Perhaps, one day, it might be possible to turn other city institutions over to black leadership—the ghetto police precincts, for example, or the public utilities or the enormously powerful Transit Authority, even the bridges and tunnels and the housing and redevelopment agencies." For Epstein, the alternatives were clear: either "capitulation" by whites of these major city agencies to blacks or else a race war with whites forced into a campaign of "genocide" to put down the rebellious black community.[95]

Meanwhile, liberal journalists heaped abuse on Shanker. Jimmy Breslin accused Shanker of being "an accent away from George Wallace" and called the UFT leader the "worst public person I have seen in my time in the City of New York." The radical journalist I. F. Stone gave further voice to what many on the left thought of the situation: "The plain truth is that Lindsay is in trouble because he suddenly finds himself the mayor of a Southern town. The Mason-Dixon line has moved north, and the Old Confederacy has expanded to the outer reaches of the Bronx." Murray Kempton called Shanker a "goon" and a "law-breaker" and charged that the union was trying to "make certain that no other community body raises its head to suggest that a teacher or a supervisor do an honest day's work again." He accused Shanker of having "indulged the most protracted violation of the ethics of controversy in the memory of my life in this city." Sol Stern, writing in *Ramparts*, wrote that because of the school strikes, "white middle-class New York teachers may quietly vote for George Wallace."[96]

The pain of this split in left-wing ranks over community control took its toll on Michael Harrington. A few years after the school strikes, he wrote, "I think we were right to support the union in that battle but it is nonsense to label all who oppose it as strikebreakers and scabs. It involved complicated black and educational issues and decent people took the wrong side for the best of reasons." In his 1988 autobiography, Harrington admitted to having his political and moral allegiances pulled in all directions during the strikes. "I supported the union," wrote Harrington, "yet I was all but torn in two by my profound sympathies with those on the other side." He called the leaders of the experimental districts "morally right, legally wrong, and very ill advised by theorists from outside their community."[97]

In addition to the split in the intellectual community, the school strikes further divided upper-class New Yorkers from the rest of the city. In March 1967, a group calling themselves the Citizens Committee for Decentralization of the Public Schools was formed. The executive committee of the group, headed by Robert Sarnoff, the president of RCA and a trustee of the Whitney Museum, read like a "who's who" of elite New York, including Thomas Watson Jr., chairman of IBM; James Linen, president of Time Inc.; and James B. Conant, former president of Harvard University. In the fall of 1968, the Urban Coalition came out with its own full-page ad in the *Times* proclaiming: "If you give a damn about our children, we see only one answer. Community control of the schools." Harrington called the ad "the most obscene act of Machiavellianism on the part of white corporate wealth in recent years." To Harrington and other union supporters, the city's elite seemed to be buying racial peace at the expense of the rights of unionized workers, in this case the teachers. According to historian Jerald Podair, "New York's corporate leaders viewed community control as a hedge on their economic investments, a down payment on social stability. It also had the advantage of costing them little."[98]

McGEORGE BUNDY AND THE FORD FOUNDATION

Epitomizing elite opinion in New York was the Ford Foundation, headed by McGeorge Bundy. The foundation gave over $900,000 to fund the community control experiments in 1967 and 1968. Much of the money was channeled through the Institute for Community Studies, whose executive director was Marilyn Gittell. The breakdown of the money was $275,000 to Ocean Hill–Brownsville; $75,000 to I.S. 201 in East Harlem; $50,000 to the Two Bridges district; $229,000 for administration; and $275,000 for other projects. In addition, Milton Galamison's Siloam Presbyterian Church received a Ford Foundation grant of $160,000 in March 1968 for "programs to inform and assist communities to establish close relationships with NYC schools." Despite this financial support, the Ocean Hill–Brownsville Governing Board soon grew disillusioned with the Ford Foundation. Since the beginning of 1968, they had been asking for nearly $200,000 more in Ford Foundation grant money, mostly to hire two parents for each classroom to act as paraprofessionals. They never received the extra money.

At the time, Diane Ravitch criticized the Ford Foundation for "playing God in the ghetto." Jewish groups harped on the Ford Foundation's role in funding what they considered black anti-Semitism. They asked whether it was a mere coincidence that the Ford Foundation was founded by Henry Ford, as if the anti-Semitism of the foundation's long-dead benefactor was influencing McGeorge Bundy and Mario Fantini. Bundy felt the need to respond publicly to Shanker's charges. "Mr. Shanker is wrong—absolutely wrong—in his charges and innuendoes that the Foundation is somehow influencing the course of the strike," Bundy replied. Fantini dismissed the idea that the foundation was controlling the experimental districts it had helped create, fund, and manage. "The planning money was given to the communities with 'no strings attached,'" Fantini asserted.[99]

Smarting from the negative publicity that it was funding black militants and anti-Semitism, the Ford Foundation began backing away from controversial projects. It was unwilling to continue funding Galamison's project. "I feel cheated," wrote Galamison, "when an agency like the Ford Foundation with three and a half billion dollars is intimidated by Shanker, chickens out, and leaves the struggle to me."

The Ford Foundation also conducted its own in-house report—"And Then There Were the Children"—which took a critical look at the foundation's role in the school decentralization controversy. In the spring of 1969,

McGeorge Bundy was publicly talking of a rapprochement between the union teachers, the schools, and the parents: "The teachers are going to be here, the schools and the parents. The obvious need is to find some path for reconciliation." In the wake of the Ocean Hill–Brownsville disaster, the master labor negotiator Theodore Kheel arranged a private dinner for McGeorge Bundy, Al Shanker, and Mitchell Sviridoff (formerly commissioner of the HRA but now the vice president of the Ford Foundation). Bundy and the Ford Foundation would try to mend fences with Shanker and the UFT. Kheel says that Bundy "apologized" to Shanker during the dinner, but Sviridoff was less convinced: "There was an acknowledgment that mistakes were made. Maybe not a surrender, not an apology." Not much came of the meeting, as Shanker did not agree to forgive and forget, but it was significant that Bundy felt the need to make amends for the Ford Foundation's monetary and moral support of the demonstration districts.[100]

An aide to Bundy said his boss came "from the top of the power pyramid, where power is not shared at all, and is trying to create a system where power is shared, and all of this is the antithesis of his elitist background." But the school crisis really wasn't the "antithesis" of Bundy's elitist background: It was right in keeping with it. The power that Bundy sought to share was not his power. Had the decentralization plan been fully implemented, it would not have lessened Bundy's power or influence. It might actually have enhanced it. The problems of school decentralization and community control were far removed from the clubs, private schools, and other wealthy enclaves of Bundy and other elite New Yorkers. Bundy and Lindsay were reducing the power of others—teachers, education bureaucrats—in order to buy racial peace for themselves.[101]

EVALUATING OCEAN HILL–BROWNSVILLE

Despite the traumas of the teachers' strikes, many on the left believed that the Ocean Hill–Brownsville experiment was an educational success. In late 1968, a rash of reports appeared that extolled the virtues of the district. I. F. Stone wrote that his visit to Ocean Hill–Brownsville was "therapeutic." Whereas the UFT and the Board of Education were fighting with all their might to make the experiment fail, Stone wrote of the Ocean Hill–Brownsville educators: "I have never met a more devoted group of people. . . . Their focus is on the child." Dwight Macdonald was "impressed by the friendly, serious, relaxed atmosphere" in the Ocean Hill–Brownsville schools during a visit. Finding few instances of rowdiness, Macdonald admitted that "discipline . . . was rarely apparent," though he euphemistically termed the atmosphere there "a mildly disorderly hum of cooperative effort." Literary critic Alfred Kazin extolled the education experiment he witnessed at P.S. 178 and I.S. 55, claiming that "the flame [of learning] burns hotter than ever. . . . The intentness all over the place audibly vibrated in my ear." *Time* wrote about the new nonunion Ocean Hill–Brownsville teachers as "teachers who give a damn." Another community control supporter, Melvin Urofsky, argued in 1970 that "the local board and McCoy did not do a bad job running the Ocean Hill–Brownsville schools; given enough time, they might have proven their ability conclusively. The colonial argument that 'those people' cannot run their own affairs is becoming increasingly apparent for what it is, a racist justification for defending the status quo." Another visitor, Annette Rubenstein, wrote about the girls' bathrooms in the district's schools: "Again, perhaps no one familiar with our junior high schools can realize how extraordinary it was to find bathrooms relatively clean with few graffiti, floors unlittered, and no smoking parties in session." In contrast to the images coming out of Ocean Hill–Brownsville about antiwhite and anti-Semitic black militants, these visitors painted a picture of earnest and intent learning.[102]

Those involved with the experimental districts made the case for their preliminary success. The *New York Times Magazine* published a long article from a young, white nonunion teacher at J.H.S. 271 named Charles Isaacs who spoke glowingly about the community control experiment. Isaacs dismissed the charges of racism and anti-Semitism, citing the fact that 70 percent of the replacement teachers were white—in fact, 40 percent of the new teachers were Jewish. Fantini and Gittell echoed this idea and contended that "standards of measurement for success or failure are becoming subjective because of the political struggle enveloping the district." For those involved in the districts, however, "deviations from established procedures were viewed . . . as a source of new ideas and an opportunity for self-renewal of the subsystem."[103]

Joseph Featherstone, an editor at *The New Republic* who visited the district numerous times, wrote with some ambivalence of the experiment in the fall of 1969. Featherstone described the replacement teachers as "untrained . . . college graduates and graduate students who came this fall because of social conscience or the draft, or a desire to try their hand at teaching." He observed few classes in the district "where chaos reign[ed]. In some schools there aren't any [such classes]. They exist though." In contrast to the gushing Kazin, Macdonald, and Stone, Featherstone was unsure about the ultimate success of the decentralization experiment. But he did believe that the Ocean Hill–Brownsville schools and Harlem's I.S. 201 were doing "impressive things" and there seemed to be "more energy and more talent there than in any other two districts in the city."[104]

The community control supporter Maurice Berube wrote in 1994 that he believed the controversy was an "important chapter in the history of the civil rights movement." Community control "gave African Americans a new image. Blacks would determine their own fate, direct their own civil rights movement, and rediscover their own usable past." Berube also believed "the experiment proved to be educationally successful." As for the education benefits, Berube wrote: "The boards launched innumerable innovative programs such as the first bilingual program in the North. Students experienced heightened feelings of fate control and performed at higher academic levels than students affiliated with similar boards in other economically deprived areas. Finally, the members of these boards developed educational and political expertise." A 1972 study by Marilyn Gittell and Berube supposedly "proved" the success of the community control experiment. Citing no evidence, the study nevertheless asserted that "educational achievement was not reduced and was selectively improved" at Ocean Hill–Brownsville and I.S. 201 and that the districts "seemed well on the way to making a significant impact on their students." Yet they were forced to admit that "due to the time factor, we are left without a satisfactory evaluation of educational achievement." In the end, these "successes" were rather limited and less than concrete.[105]

One of the complaints about ghetto schools was that black children's reading ability was many grade levels behind that of their white counterparts. Therefore, one important measurement of the experimental district would be how much student reading scores increased. In late 1968, Fred Ferretti declared that McCoy had "wrought, in slightly over a year, deep organic change" in his district. Ferretti repeated McCoy's claim that the district "has succeeded in raising the reading levels of many children in the district in a remarkably short time." Assemblyman Jerome Kretchmer, a staunch defender of community control, quoted McCoy as predicting that by "February 1, 1970, every youngster in that school system will be classified as a reader." McCoy released a progress report to parents in 1970 in which he claimed that between 55 and 76 percent of the students in the district schools had made progress in reading.[106]

But the truth is that the Ocean Hill–Brownsville district refused to give its students standardized reading tests, the only district in the city to do so. Only after the demise of the experimental district did the educational failure of the Ocean Hill–Brownsville district come to light. In 1971, students citywide, including those in the eight Ocean Hill–Brownsville schools formerly in the experimental district, were given reading tests. The results were disheartening. The highest scores were in an elementary school where 24.5 percent of the students were reading at grade level. The lowest scores were at J.H.S. 271, ground zero for much of the protests and controversy. At that school, only 5.5 percent of students were reading at or above grade level. All eight district schools registered lower reading scores in 1971 than in tests taken in 1967, before the experiment began. Diane Ravitch concluded: "There is no evidence that anything was accomplished by the Ocean Hill–Brownsville Demonstration District, in terms of teaching children to read." In addition, the district schools suffered from high absentee rates among students. After the strikes, absentee levels hovered somewhere around 25 to 30 percent. A state observer who spent one month at J.H.S. 271 in the fall of 1968 wrote: "I must say that I saw no evidence of anything exceptional as far as educational program was concerned . . . In 271, the qualifications of most of the teachers were rather questionable. There was little doubt that very few of them had any sort of professional training as teachers."[107]

To supporters of community control, though, these numbers meant nothing. To Nat Hentoff, the district's struggle for political survival meant "there was limited time and energy left for 'education reform.' " A teacher in one of the demonstration districts told Fantini, Gittell, and Magat:

> Our experiment will be evaluated in terms of the established conventional criteria: reading scores, discipline, standardized achievement, tests, etc., some of which measure what they are intended to measure, for *middle-class children*. We have a problem when these criteria fail to measure the extent to which a child has been educated, when they simply test rote memorization, stifling of initiative and training in sitting through standardized examinations. Unleashed creativity or a critical outlook, for example, would probably lower a child's scores on these exams, rather than raise them. If the conventional criteria measure the wrong things, their effect is harmful to our students, yet they will determine to a great extent whether or not we will ever be free to develop our own yardsticks. In effect, we must miseducate the children before we will be allowed to educate them.

To those invested in community control, it appeared that everything about the experiment was set up for failure.[108]

For all intents and purposes, the end of the Ocean Hill–Brownsville experiment, as well as the I.S. 201 and Two Bridges districts, came on April 30, 1969. Acting on the recommendations presented in the Bundy Panel's original 1967 report—namely, to create between thirty and sixty city school districts—the New York State Legislature passed the Decentralization Act, whereby the city's school system was to be broken up into thirty-two districts consisting of at least 20,000 students each. The three experimental districts would be folded into larger districts, thereby ending whatever authority and independence they had exercised in the previous two years. The bill called for the replacement of the pro-decentralization Board of Education with a new board of seven members. Five members, one from each borough, would be elected to serve on the board (they would later be appointed by each borough president), and the mayor would appoint the other two members. The Board would hire a schools chancellor, who would report to it. Each of the thirty-two districts would have a community board and would hold elections for members who would serve up to two terms with no salary. The community boards had the right to hire and fire district superintendents, select textbooks from a list approved by the chancellor, contract for repairs and maintenance up to $250,000, and submit budgets to the chancellor, who held the right to amend the budget. Local boards had little say over teacher assignments and transfers, though. That power remained firmly protected within the purview of the Board of Education and the chancellor. Clearing up any confusion that had existed at Ocean Hill–Brownsville, these new districts were not independent districts, but merely administrative subdivisions of the Board of Education, which held final authority over the education provided in every public school in the city.

The 1969 legislation was widely seen as a victory for the UFT, whose goals—the abolishment of Lindsay's pro-decentralization Board of Education, the destruction of the three experimental districts, and the end of community control—were all achieved by the bill. As Joseph Featherstone wrote: "The first thing to understand is the magnitude of the rout of forces advocating community control." The bill was largely written and passed by the state's Republican legislators. Its few opponents were liberal and minority legislators from the city who believed the legislation was too weak regarding community control, and conservative Republican legislators from the city who believed the bill gave the districts too much power. Ultimately, as one historian observed, "The Decentralization Act was a misnomer: the new law was designed to ensure that the balance of power did not tip too far towards the various districts of the city." Harlem State Senator Basil Patterson said disappointedly, the 1969 law was "decentralization, but not community control." Community control of schools, teachers, principals, curriculum, and budget was now a distant memory.[109]

Lindsay had begun the drive toward the administrative decentralization of schools with his appointment of the Bundy Panel in 1966. But the final decentralization legislation was created without any input from City Hall. A combination of the Lindsay administration's incompetence, its inability to shepherd legislation through Albany, the mishandling of the school strikes, and the legislators' growing animus against the upstart mayor meant that Lindsay had little control over the final outcome. When the dust settled, the mayor no longer possessed control over choosing a chancellor. His powers declined from appointing the entire Board of Education to naming only two out of seven members. Over thirty years later, the result is that the mayor of New York is a mere bystander over the operations of schools in his city. The city has had thirteen chancellors since 1970, whose average tenure has been just over two years. The local community school boards are widely viewed as corrupt or incompetent, with turnout for board elections hovering in the single digits.

In Ocean Hill–Brownsville, Assemblyman Sam Wright, a member of the Governing Board, used the new legislation that his colleagues in Albany had crafted to take control of the new board. Wright wanted to get rid of McCoy and the rest of the board and use the newly drawn district, expanded from the original eight schools to twenty-four, as a patronage mill. When elections for the new district's board were held in 1970, the old Governing

Board boycotted the election, which ended up helping Wright's allies get elected. McCoy, Oliver, Powis, and the others had lost power. Wright proceeded to clear out many administrators and principals loyal to McCoy. The Ocean Hill–Brownsville experimental district had lasted only three years.

For Lindsay, the fallout from the strike was massive. *Time*, a bastion of liberal Republicanism and Lindsay boosterism, was forced to admit that "for all its dynamism and glamour, New York City, day by day, little by little, was sliding toward chaos." One popular anti-Lindsay sign during the controversy was JOHN LINDSAY, MASTER OF THE BUNGLE; HE TURNED NEW YORK INTO A JUNGLE. Martin Mayer summed up the indictment of Lindsay: "Caught in a tangle of public image, self image, naiveté and past misjudgments, he found himself playing host to a great civic disaster which acted itself out before him while he agonized over his surprising inability to control—or even to influence—the course of events."[110]

While Lindsay, Bundy, and Donovan spoke about "decentralization," black activists and radical whites turned the momentum for education reform into a political cause for the total control of local schools by the community. The mayor and school officials never recognized this dissonance. Even before the teachers' strikes, the July 1968 Niemeyer Report pinpointed the failure of the experimental districts:

> The central cause of the difficulty is the fact that from the inception of the Demonstration Projects the Board of Education and the Superintendent have had one set of purposes and expectations, while the groups seeking and wielding local power have had a different and incompatible set. The Board of Education wanted planned experiments, yet the local groups had no interest in serving experimental ends. . . . The Board did not make clear from the outset which powers could be delegated within the legal limits placed upon it, nor did the Board assume the degree of leadership necessary to cause the projects to succeed.

In its report on the aftermath of the demonstration districts, the Ford Foundation found that the "essence of the New York City school crisis was the all-around failure of leadership. The Board of Education moved too cautiously and hesitantly . . . And the machinery of 110 Livingston Street either vacillated or opted for business as usual. The mayor did not assume the active role that his earlier statements had led the communities to expect. This is evident from the minimal mention he receives in this report. In this vacuum, strong leadership was exercised consistently from only one source—Albert Shanker and the UFT." The New York Civil Liberties Union came to a similar conclusion: "Vacuums created by the absence of clearly defined lines of authority are usually filled by individual discretion, arbitrary action and administrative abuse. Only chaos can then result, as it has in Ocean Hill–Brownsville. The burden of blame for that chaos must fall on the Board of Education for leaving lines of authority undrawn and governing power undefined."[111]

The Board of Education, Superintendent Donovan, Mayor Lindsay, and the Ford Foundation created an unworkable situation with few clear guidelines that could only lead to chaos. But the Ocean Hill–Brownsville Governing Board, Rhody McCoy, and his staff and teachers are also to blame. State observer Ticknor Litchfield noted that he would have found it "difficult and uncomfortable to work as an administrator in such a school district" as Ocean Hill–Brownsville. Chaos and poor management marked the administration of the district. McCoy and his Governing Board had no desire to work under any kind of restraints. They recognized no authority other than their own. Some were drunk on power; others were drunk on conspiracy theories and racial militancy. If Lindsay, Donovan, and the Board of Education were weak, vacillating, and adrift, then the UFT and community control activists were the only players who acted with a clear sense of mission, however misguided each side may have been. In the end, though, it was only the UFT that had the political skill and savvy to impose its will upon the city.[112]

WHEN THE DUST SETTLED after the three teachers' strikes that crippled the city during the fall of 1968, the shortcomings of the Lindsay administration were clearly in view. Labor issues stymied the patrician mayor. Union members continued to be skeptical of him. Lindsay's tendency to rely on elite outside consultants, like the Ford Foundation, backfired. Finally, a deep crisis appeared in the city's schools. The public school population became increasingly minority, dashing the dreams of integration. Minority children were falling further behind. Teachers and principals grew demoralized. Crime, lack of discipline, and racial tensions increased among students. Middle-class parents continued to lose faith in public schools and in doing so, lost faith in the city.

Barry Gottehrer summed up the feeling of disillusionment and despair caused by the strikes: "It was the beginning of the end of a period when many of us truly believed that all people, even poor and powerless people, could have a good life and control over their own destinies. We were on our own way down from a great high but none of us fully realized that John Lindsay . . . was finished politically in our city and that we would all begin to change, becoming tougher, more political, more cynical, more pragmatic, less caring, less idealistic."[113]

BLACKS AND JEWS:
OLD ALLIES, NEW TENSIONS

> To begin with, anti-Jewish feeling is endemic
> among Negroes . . . because the Negroes keep
> bumping into the Jews in front and ahead of
> them.
>
> —**Nathan Glazer and Daniel Patrick Moynihan,**
> *Beyond the Melting Pot* [1]

The ultimate legacy of events in the Ocean Hill–Brownsville experimental district was a lingering distrust between two historically
sensitive minority groups who had previously been allies: blacks and Jews.
Lindsay himself stood accused of the grave sin of anti-Semitism. Many
years later, Lindsay recalled the most troublesome part of his mayoralty
was the accusation that he was "anti-Semitic, when I was not." In 1968,
Lindsay had the chance to escape the city's ethnic tensions by moving to
the U.S. Senate, but chose to remain in City Hall. With blacks and Jews,
two pillars of his liberal coalition, seemingly at odds, Lindsay faced the
task of repairing his political coalition for the 1969 reelection campaign
and garnering enough support to push ahead with liberal urban policies in
the second term.[2]

BLACK ANTI-SEMITISM

In the last forty years, the issue of black anti-Semitism has led to much
study—and controversy. A 1964 national study found that 47 percent of
blacks and 35 percent of whites were considered to be highly anti-Semitic.

A 1981 survey found 20 percent of whites and 40 percent of blacks to be anti-Semitic. A study published in 1992 by the Anti-Defamation League categorized 37 percent of blacks and 17 percent of whites as most anti-Semitic; 14 percent of blacks and 42 percent of whites were considered to be not anti-Semitic.[3]

Many New York Jews had long been aware of this antagonism from blacks—a 1970 study found that 38 percent of New York Jews agreed with the statement that blacks were anti-Semitic, and 41 percent disagreed—but their feelings on the matter varied according to their degree of religiosity and where they lived. Fifty percent of Orthodox Jews agreed with the statement that blacks were anti-Semitic, whereas only 40 percent of reform Jews agreed. On the other hand, 70 percent of nonreligious Jews did not believe in the existence of black anti-Semitism. Furthermore, in Brooklyn, nearly half the Jews believed blacks harbored anti-Semitic thoughts, whereas only one quarter of Manhattan Jews did.[4]

Pollsters Louis Harris and Bert Swanson wrote in 1970: "It is perfectly clear that by mid–1969 in New York City, much of the city's traditionally accepted feeling for blacks as underdogs had eroded and even disappeared." More Jews (45 percent) felt that blacks wanted to tear down white society than did white Catholics (34 percent), Puerto Ricans (31 percent), and white Protestants (25 percent). Twenty-two percent of Jews wanted a separate society for blacks. Some 58 percent of Jews favored racial integration, compared to 68 percent of white Protestants, 49 percent of white Catholics, and 77 percent of blacks. Within New York's Jewish community, a religious, generational, and socio-economic split was apparent. A November 1969 Harris poll found that most religious Jews felt blacks were not justified in their demands, but 60 percent of nonaffiliated Jews thought black demands were justified. Jewish college graduates agreed with black demands by 44 to 17 percent, and Jews between the ages of 21 and 34 agreed 45 to 19 percent.[5]

The issue of black anti-Semitism did not miraculously spring up in the late sixties. Blacks, most of whom were Christians who had migrated from the South, imbibed negative stereotypes of Jews in part from the atmosphere of fundamentalist Christianity. Such attitudes were carried to Northern cities, where contact between Jews and blacks increased. In 1942, the *Amsterdam News* noted: "There never has been such general anti-Semitic sentiment in Harlem as exists now." In 1946, sociologist Kenneth Clark explained the distrust between black and Jew as arising from the insecurity both groups felt within white Christian society. Some Jews felt they could "bond" with white Christians through Negrophobia; some blacks felt they could "bond" with whites by adopting fashionable anti-Semitic beliefs. Clark wrote: "We should also understand that the problem of Jewish-Negro relations probably has no important significance in itself, but serves rather to indicate the extent to which the pathologies of the dominant society infect all groups and individuals within that society." In Clark's view, the problems of Jewish racism and black anti-Semitism were caused by the sickness of the dominant white society whose own hatreds were infecting black and Jewish communities.[6]

In 1948, James Baldwin, then twenty-four, wrote of how he remembered "meeting no Negro in the years of my growing up, in my family and out of it, who would really even trust a Jew, and a few who did not, indeed, exhibit for them the blackest contempt. . . . But just as a society must have a scapegoat, so hatred must have a symbol. Georgia has its Negro and Harlem has the Jew." Almost twenty years later, Baldwin was putting the black-Jewish tensions of his Harlem youth in even starker words.

> When we were growing up in Harlem our demoralizing series of landlords were Jewish, and we hated them. We hated them because they were terrible landlords and did not take care of the building. . . . We knew that the landlord treated us this way only because we were colored, and he knew that we could not move out.
>
> The grocer was a Jew, and being in debt to him was very much like being in debt to the company store. The butcher was a Jew, and yes, we certainly paid more for bad cuts of meat than other New York citizens, and we very often carried insults home, along with the meat. We bought our clothes from a Jew and, sometimes, our secondhand shoes, and the pawnbroker was a Jew—perhaps we hated him most of all. The merchants along 125th Street were Jewish—at least many of them were.

Baldwin concluded that "the most ironical thing about Negro anti-Semitism is that the Negro is really condemning the Jew for having become an American white man." Nathan Glazer and Daniel Patrick Moynihan argued in *Beyond the Melting Pot* that in New York City black-Jewish tensions occurred because blacks often encountered Jews as shopkeepers, landlords, and employers. One of the most tense employer-employee relationships was that of Jewish women and their black female domestics. Landlord-tenant tensions have long been endemic in New York City and this has added to the friction between blacks (tenants) and Jews (landlords) so much so that the term "Jewish landlord" became a synonymous term among many New York blacks for all white landlords, Gentile or Jew.[7]

Tensions between blacks and Jews, though not a new phenomenon, came to a head in John Lindsay's New York. In December 1968, Haskell Lazere, director of the New York Chapter of the American Jewish Committee, summarized the feelings of many New York Jews: "New York City today has serious racial and religious tensions. In many instances these tensions approach hostility. They are evident not only from the public actions of some, but from the mail we have received which evinces deep concern over the rise of anti-Semitism." *Time* magazine found the problem of black-Jewish relations so serious that it merited a cover story in January 1969.[8]

The aftereffects of the Ocean Hill-Brownsville school controversy and the teachers' strikes were still being felt during the winter of 1968–69. On December 26, 1968, Leslie Campbell, a teacher at Ocean Hill-Brownsville, was the guest on Julius Lester's radio show, "The Great Proletarian Cultural Revolution," on the New York public radio station WBAI. Before the show, Campbell showed Lester some poems written by a fourteen-year-old girl in one of his classes named Sia Berhan. Lester, a noted black writer and activist, told Campbell that he wanted him to read it over the airwaves. "I think it's important for people to know the kinds of feelings being aroused in at least one black child because of what's happening in Ocean Hill-Brownsville," Lester told Campbell. On that night's program, Campbell read the poem, which was entitled "Dedicated to Albert Shanker."

> *Hey, Jew boy, with that yarmulke on your head*
> *You pale faced Jew boy—I wish you were dead*
> *I can see you Jew boy—no you can't hide*
> *I'm sick of your stuff*
> *Every time I turn 'round—you pushin' my head into the ground*
> *I'm sick of hearing about your suffering in Germany*
> *I'm sick about your escape from tyranny*
> *I'm sick of seeing in everything I do*
> *About the murder of 6 million Jews*
> *Hitler's reign lasted for only fifteen years*
> *For that period of time you shed crocodile tears*
> *My suffering lasted for over 400 years, Jew boy*
> *And the white man only let me play with his toys*
> *Jew boy, you took my religion and adopted it for you*
> *But you know that black people were the original Hebrews*
> *When the U.N. made Israel a free independent State*
> *Little four and five-year-old boys threw hand-grenades*
> *They hated the black Arabs with all their might*
> *And you, Jew boy, said it was all right*
> *Then you came to America, land of the free*
> *And took over the school system to perpetuate white supremacy*
> *Guess you know, Jew boy, there's only one reason you made it*
> *You had a clean white face, colorless, and faded*
> *I hated you Jew boy, because your hangup was the Torah*
> *And my only hangup was my color.*

Lester defended his decision to air the poem: "I wanted you [Campbell] to read it because she expresses . . . how she feels. . . . An ugly poem, yes, but not one half as ugly as what happened in school strikes, not one one-hundredth as bad as what some teachers said to some of those black children. . . . I had it read over the air because I felt that what she said was valid for a lot of black people." Compounding the outrage provoked by Campbell's reading of the poem, a month later Lester invited three students from Ocean Hill-Brownsville onto his show. One of them, Tyrone Woods, said, "Hitler didn't make enough lampshades out of them [Jews]."[9]

Lester found himself on the defensive after the incident. Yet in defending himself for airing such remarks, he inadvertently deepened the impression that anti-Semitism, or at least gross insensitivity toward Jews, was prevalent among blacks. He replied to his critics on his program on January 30, one week after the Woods incident. Lester claimed that "anti-Semitism is not a relevant one [concept] for the black community." He told his listeners: "In Germany the Jews were the minority surrounded by a majority which carried out heinous crimes against them. In America, it is we who are the Jews. . . . And the greatest irony of all is that it is the Jews who are in the position of being Germans." As for Woods's remark, Lester let it be known that it "is not one I would have made. It's not my style." Lester believed Woods "was speaking symbolically, not literally."[10]

Those associated with the poem and its airing on the radio saw little reason to rethink their actions. Berhan defended her poem by claiming that the reason for picking the title was because "I had found out, doing reading and listening to some of those people that came to the school, that the original Semites were black. That the Falashas in Africa, East Africa, were the original Semites. I felt that instead of saying that we in the black community were anti-Semitic, I felt that the UFT, Albert Shanker, were anti-Semitic." Many years later, Campbell, who had changed his name to Jitu Weusi, was still defending his actions: "I don't regret having read it. I think the response [to the poem] is raw." (Campbell was not blindly insensitive to Jews, though. As a child, he attended Camp Kinderland, a camp for Jewish "red diaper" children, and learned Yiddish from his father's left-wing friends.)[11]

At the same time, another incident was muddying the waters between blacks and Jews. In January 1969, a new exhibit opened at the Metropolitan Museum of Art entitled "Harlem on My Mind." It was part of an attempt by the museum's director, Thomas Hoving, to make the museum "relevant" and cutting-edge. Hoving wrote in his memoirs: "I looked upon 'Harlem on My Mind' as a turning point. It was going to justify my view of the museum as a moral, social, and educational force. Through 'Harlem,' the museum would pay its true cultural dues. It would chronicle the creativity of the downtrodden blacks and, at the same time, encourage them to come to the museum."[12]

The exhibit brought hundreds of thousands of visitors to the museum over its three-month run, making it the most successful Metropolitan Museum exhibit up until that time. It was a multimedia extravaganza, something groundbreaking in 1969, incorporating photographs, jazz music, newspaper articles, and wall texts. The *New York Times* critic Michael Kimmelman wrote over a quarter century later: "The show was a Molotov cocktail of then-radical exhibition techniques and reckless social politics." The exhibition's curator, Allon Schoener, had made his mark with a similar exhibit at the Jewish Museum detailing Jewish life in the old Lower East Side. But with "Harlem on My Mind," the white curator was dealing with more controversial material. Nearly twenty-five-years later, Schoener recalled the idealism and naiveté that underlay the exhibition: "I honestly believed that I could identify with the American black culture I was depicting. For a very short period in my life, I believed that I could see things from a black perspective and believed that I was tuned in to values that were important to blacks."[13]

Although Schoener had hired a few black assistants, some in the black community criticized the show as the creation of a white Jewish male with no special knowledge or experience with black culture. These critics saw the show as patronizing, a form of voyeurism and slumming by the "white" museum. Hoving noted that though Schoener was a "genius," he was "also protective of 'his' show and reluctant to allow outsiders to participate." Hoving recalls that a group of black "community experts" acting as advisers to the show's curators "proved to be spoilers almost from the first meetings." One of the experts reportedly told Schoener: "If you're another downtown Jew who's here to rip us off, good-bye." On the other hand, some blacks welcomed the show as a sympathetic treatment of African-American life and as a symbol of sensitivity by one of the nation's most prestigious museums. Milton Galamison, for instance, called the exhibit "culturally rich, proud, instructive, intensely pro-black."[14]

As black anti-Semitism became a serious issue in the city, Jewish New Yorkers also criticized the show. Jewish pickets formed outside the museum. What set off the complaint of black anti-Semitism was the introductory essay to the exhibition's catalogue. The essay was written by a high school student named Candace Van Ellison, who had met Schoener while working for a local anti-poverty program. When Van Ellison found out Schoener was doing the Harlem show, she gave him a school paper she had written that she thought might be relevant. Schoener chose Van Ellison's essay as an authentic voice of the black ghetto to introduce the catalogue. Though only two paragraphs in the whole introduction dealt with the relationship between blacks and Jews, two sentences in particular incensed Jewish groups: "Thus, our contempt for the Jew makes us feel more completely American in sharing a national prejudice. . . . Behind every hurdle that the Afro-American has yet to jump stands the Jew who has already cleared it."[15]

After the controversy began, it was revealed that Van Ellison had taken much of her original essay from Nathan Glazer and Daniel Patrick Moynihan's *Beyond the Melting Pot*, replete with footnotes citing the sociologists. The offending sentence in Van Ellison's essay was similar to a line in Glazer and Moynihan's book, which read in the original: "Perhaps for many Negroes, subconsciously, a bit of anti-Jewish feeling helps make them feel more completely American, a part of the majority group." Schoener took out Van Ellison's quotation marks around the excerpt and the footnotes and edited the piece to make it seem more of a personal essay than a term paper. When Hoving found out what Schoener had done, the prickly patrician exploded: "I almost killed him. I almost picked him up and shook him in my office." In his defense, Schoener told Hoving he "didn't want the thing [Van Ellison's essay] to sound like just a high school essay."[16]

Hoving thought the statements about Jews were political dynamite and wanted Schoener to tone down the essay. Schoener refused, telling Hoving, "These are truths. You may not like them, but they are truths. . . . Would you leave out some nasty fact—a horrible truth—about some painting in an exhibition? 'Harlem' *has* to have truth." Hoving relented and ran the essay. Despite Hoving's private anger with Schoener over the catalogue, his seeming public indifference fueled the fires of Jewish concerns. In a televised response to a reporter's question about the Van Ellison essay, Hoving said: "Her statements are true. So be it." As Hoving recalled later: "From the moment I uttered that monumentally stupid statement, I was lost."[17]

Nothing symbolized the liberal New Yorker's tortured thinking on race more than Hoving's own preface to the catalogue. As he admitted in his memoirs: "My true attitude was summed up in a trendy and defensive one-page foreword for the catalogue." In it, he spoke about growing up on Park Avenue as the wealthy son of the head of Tiffany's: "For behind the vague misty thoughts concerning other people that came through members of my family down to me, Negroes—colored people—constituted an unspoken menace, the tribe that must not be allowed to come down the Avenue. My mother went to Harlem from time to time. To the clubs, carrying the delightful sense of slumming and far-off danger, a titillation of the perilous possibility that never came to pass."

Hoving went on to talk of his family's black servants: a "wonderful maid of sunny disposition and a thin, sour chauffeur who drove me to school in moody silence." But Hoving later admitted that he had "embellished the truth" in his preface, especially regarding the maid and chauffeur. Even without the fabrication, Hoving's attitude was a bitter stereotype of guilty white liberals who feared blacks from their secure Park Avenue apartments, but were attracted to the underside of Harlem life.[18]

The Lindsay administration, which had taken a beating from the Jewish community over the Ocean Hill-Brownsville controversy, was eager to see the brushfire over the exhibition catalogue extinguished quickly. In contrast to his reaction to the school strike, Lindsay promptly and firmly came out with a statement condemning the catalogue. He claimed that the catalogue's introduction "contains remarks which can only be described as racist." The words about black-Jewish relations, according to the mayor, were "a slander on both the black and white community, as well as an insult to the Jewish community." He also denounced the catalogue for anti-Irish and anti–Puerto Rican sentiments and called upon Hoving and the museum's trustees to withdraw the catalogue for sale until the allegedly offensive remarks were expunged from the text. A mayoral aide called Hoving to pressure him to withdraw the catalogue and stem the tide of bad publicity. The aide told Hoving, "My advice is to act now. Do what the mayor wants or you're in deep shit!" When an exasperated Hoving asked whether Lindsay was "now into book burning and censorship," the mayoral aide admitted this was a political issue for the mayor—who was seeking reelection in November—not a moral one.[19]

The tense atmosphere of New York City in the winter of 1969 mandated that the catalogue be withdrawn. Arthur Houghton, chairman of the museum's board of directors, called Hoving at home and told him that the catalogue would have to be withdrawn. According to Hoving, Houghton told him, "We feel that unless we withdraw it, the museum will suffer financially to a degree that we might never recover. Think of the consequences of no city money. . . . I think the museum's current state of affairs is not . . . conducive for the raising of funds—the Jewish community being some of our more valiant monetary supporters." It was clear that if the museum continued to sell the catalogue, the Jewish community would punish it by ceasing to donate money. As the controversy was heating up, museum employees discovered that ten of its paintings, including Rembrandt's *Christ with a Pilgrim's Staff*, had been defaced in what many felt was a protest against the "Harlem on My Mind" exhibit. The damage—small *h*'s had been carved into the paintings—was not serious and the paintings were quickly repaired. But there was speculation as to what the *h*'s meant, some wondering whether the letter *h* stood for "Harlem," or "Hoving," and whether the vandals were black protesters of the show or Jewish protesters of the catalogue. Either way, the museum found itself in the midst of a controversy that threatened to dry up its funding sources and put its treasures at risk.[20]

Hoving apologized to "all persons who have been offended." But his relationship with John Lindsay would never be the same. Though once the shining star of the Lindsay administration and a friend of the patrician mayor's, Hoving today still remains bitter about the incident. He claims that Lindsay "totally stabbed me. . . . I don't think we spoke for years. . . . I couldn't deal with him ever again seriously."[21]

DEBATING ANTI-SEMITISM

In late 1968, Mayor Lindsay appointed a Special Committee on Racial and Religious Prejudice to evaluate the state of relations between blacks and whites. In large part Lindsay's move was an attempt to deflect criticism of his handling of the Ocean Hill–Brownsville controversy. The committee, headed by the retired state judge Bernard Botein, released an eleven-page report in January 1969. The Botein Report began by stating what many people had already come to believe about the city under John Lindsay: "An appalling amount of racial prejudice—black and white—in New York City surfaced in and about the school controversy. Over and over again we found evidence of vicious anti-white attitudes on the part of some black people, and vicious anti-black attitudes on the part of some white people." The report continually tried to balance the amount of bigotry found among blacks and whites. Yet it also acknowledged differences, stating that "the anti-white prejudice has a dangerous component of anti-Semitism." The report noted: "The countless incidents, leaflets, epithets, and the like in the school controversy reveal a bigotry from Black extremists that is open, undisguised, nearly physical in its intensity—and far more obvious and identifiable than that emanating from whites." (An earlier draft had the word "abusive" in the place of "obvious.") White racism differed from the more overt black bigotry in that it "tended to be expressed in more sophisticated and subtle fashion, often communicated privately and seldom reported."

In its attempt at moral equivalence, the Botein Report noted that both forms of prejudice were "equally evil, corrosive, damaging, and deplorable." Yet the vast majority of material submitted to the Botein Committee concerned itself with antiwhite and anti-Semitic feelings in the black community. Though not every charge of black racism was correct and examples of white racism certainly existed, the evidence collected by the Botein Committee pointed almost exclusively to its conclusion of black bigotry. The evidence in hand clearly did not support the charge about covert white racism—a charge that by its definition was nearly impossible to prove.[22]

The Botein Committee took no stand on the Ocean Hill-Brownsville school strike. Nor did it name specific perpetrators of bigotry—white or black.

> In this controversy, some persons have distorted the issues by the injection of bigotry. These shrill voices have espoused racism, anti-Semitism, and intimidation. Hatemongers have engendered an atmosphere of fear. It is time for concerned citizens—blacks and whites—who have been too silent, to speak up for the vast majority of citizens committed to an orderly process of change in a dynamic democratic society. Their failure to do so early, clearly, and sufficiently, we found, was in itself a contributing factor to the exacerbation of hostilities; the persistent allegations of "racism" by each side against the other—ill-defined and unspecified—themselves became harmful epithets.

Its conclusions were strong enough to satisfy most of the mayor's critics who felt he was soft on antiwhite bigotry, but vague enough not to anger blacks, who were already disappointed at the difficulties encountered by the Ocean Hill–Brownsville district.[23]

In that same month, the Anti-Defamation League released a stronger report on the same topic, entitled "Anti-Semitism in the New York City School Controversy." Its opening sentence was "The use of anti-Semitism—raw, undisguised—has distorted the fundamental character of the controversy surrounding the public schools of New York City. The anti-Semitism has gone unchecked by public authorities for two and a half years, reaching a peak during the school strike of September-November 1968 and in the post-strike period. It is still going on."

The ADL Report focused mainly on alleged incidents of anti-Semitism surrounding school decentralization, the school strike, and Jewish teachers and principals. It laid the blame at the feet of "black extremists" and denounced the "the failure of city and state public officials to condemn it swiftly and strongly enough."[24]

The ADL Report received harsh criticism in some quarters. Leonard J. Fein, associate director of the Harvard-MIT Joint Center for Urban Studies and chairman of the American Jewish Committee's Commission on Community Interrelations, critiqued the ADL report in a private letter.

> It fails to distinguish between gutter anti-Semitism—epithets and obscenities from the mouths of a mob . . . and the statements of public men; . . . it neglects entirely the counter-provocations which, though they can never justify anti-Semitism, at least help to explain it. As a result, it does not contribute to either understanding or constructive action; it merely inflames.

The *New York Post* columnist Murray Kempton lashed out against the ADL Report, calling it a "work whose standards for proof are so flimsy and whose concept of research is so incoherent as to be shocking to anyone who expected much from the ADL in such matters." What really galled Kempton was that "there is nowhere any suggestion that a quarrel which has been debased by hatred of Jews has also been debased by hatred of Negroes. Everyone knows it." Dore Schary, the national chairman of the Anti-Defamation League, responded to Kempton's charges by pointing out that the ADL had often spoken out in past years against white racism. In emphasizing white racism, Kempton ignored the fact that no Jewish spokesman was ever caught speaking of blacks in pejorative tones or ridiculing blacks because of skin color or religion. Kempton's article led Schary to ask rhetorically: "If members of the Ku Klux Klan were attacking Jews or blacks and given the same platforms on radio, television and in the press as are black extremists, I wonder whether the threshold of tolerance would be as high and the criticism against ADL by Mr. Kempton as hasty and harsh."[25]

Others took a more balanced approach to the problem. Sociologist Nathan Glazer did not deny the cases of black anti-Semitism prevalent in New York, but he noted that "so far as I can recall . . . not one [anti-Semitic view] has come from an elected representative of the black community." Glazer saw attacks on Jews as part of a larger symptom of antiwhite feelings that were "daily becoming more open and more extreme in the ghetto." The *Times* education reporter, Fred Hechinger, took a neutral stand on black anti-Semitism. Though the existence of "anti-Semitism among some Negro separatists should not be minimized," Hechinger wrote, "there is also strong indication that more of the growing anti-Semitism in the all-Negro areas is of the angry, largely economically motivated kind." These manifestations of prejudice, according to Hechinger, were symptomatic of the ignorance and frustrations that characterized the residents of poor black ghettos. In a similar vein, the Urban League's Whitney Young Jr. argued that "Jews who are caught in such conflict [Jewish shopkeeper versus black patron] aren't singled out because they are Jews but because they are whites whose presence in some ghetto institutions is resented." Young argued that black anti-Semitism was really a manifestation of overall antiwhite feelings and resentment, especially in the wake of the Black Power movement. "It [black hostility against Jewish store owners] is the natural desire of a people to replace whites who don't live in the community and who take profits out of the ghetto."[26]

Others were skeptical of the charges of black anti-Semitism. "If there was resentment of the Jewish community," says Marilyn Gittell (then the director of the Institute for Community Studies at Queens College), "it was minimal and it certainly was not extreme anti-Semitism." She qualified her observation by admitting, "Maybe there were a couple of people one might label as anti-Semitic." She also admitted that in the aftermath of Ocean Hill–Brownsville, anti-Semitism "got much worse as the issue was inflamed and fueled." Reverend C. Herbert Oliver, a key player in the Ocean Hill–Brownsville fracas, denied the charge of anti-Semitism and stated that black people in America "know nothing about European anti-Semitism but what we learn from white people." Nearly three decades later, the NYCLU's director, Ira Glasser, said, "I have always blamed Shanker for whipping up the anti-Semitism issue. I think the union manufactured much of it. It caused a rupture between blacks and Jews that hasn't healed and I think it's unforgivable." Shanker, however, defended his stance, saying, "The question wasn't so much how widespread is anti-Semitism. The real question was that in the past, if somebody were to make a remark calling somebody a kike or a nigger or a spic or something else, everybody else who was respectable would stand up and would denounce it." Shanker's greatest complaint was that much of New York's "respectable" types did not forcefully denounce antiwhite racism or black anti-Semitism.[27]

Even some Jewish leaders and other UFT members also voiced misgivings about the charge of black anti-Semitism. In October 1968, Rabbi Marc Tannenbaum, director for interreligious affairs at the American Jewish Committee, said he believed "the rank and file of the Jewish community has become emotional over the question of anti-Semitism." Eugenia Kemble, the assistant editor of the *United Teacher*, the UFT's official paper, wrote in the March 12, 1969, edition: "One thing people seem to agree on at PS 144 in Ocean Hill–Brownsville is that black anti-Semitism is not a part of the thinking of the school's staff or its students' parents." Harriet Goldstein, UFT chapter chairman at the school, said she did not "believe there was anti-Semitism, but I do think there was anti-teacher and anti-white feeling." Even Fred Nauman, one of the UFT teachers who had been dismissed by the Ocean Hill–Brownsville Governing Board, said he believed that black anti-Semitism played no role in the events in that school district.[28]

The strongest refutations of the charge of black anti-Semitism came from the white left. *The New Republic*'s Joseph Featherstone argued that since a large number of Jewish teachers crossed the picket line to work in the Ocean Hill–Brownsville district, "whatever the rights and wrongs of the dispute—and there are legitimate grievances on both sides—anti-Semitism is not the issue at Ocean Hill." Featherstone implicated the UFT in much of the controversy, writing that there was "mounting bitterness among blacks that the UFT has won by what they see as trickery. For its part, the UFT keeps the fire going: every anti-Jewish remark by every black sidewalk Savonarola is cited as further evidence of the consequence of the Ocean Hill experiment." Much as Young had argued, Featherstone believed the situation between Jews and blacks in New York was mirrored in the conflict between blacks and Irish in Boston and blacks and Italians in Newark, all manifestations of the rise in black nationalism.[29]

Journalist Fred Ferretti, a defender of the Ocean Hill–Brownsville experiment, wrote that anti-Semitism was merely a false charge drummed up by Al Shanker to destroy community control. Ferretti admitted that antiwhite feelings and anti-Semitism both existed in black communities. "What is debatable," argues Ferretti, "is its depth." According to him, "During that time [fall 1968] opponents of the educational experiment needed something to demonstrate that it couldn't work, something to obscure the educational nature of the experiment. Black anti-Semitism became that 'something.'" John Leo, writing in the liberal Catholic magazine *Commonweal*, agreed with Ferretti. He blamed Shanker for manipulating "the issue to bolster the sagging fortunes of his school strike, turning a limited labor-management question into a city-wide ethnic quarrel by playing on the fears of New York Jews." Calling the cries of black anti-Semitism a "frenzy," Leo quoted a friend as saying he never thought he would see "New York Jews running around in circles like a bunch of *Brooklyn Tablet* Catholics." (The *Tablet* was a conservative Catholic counterpart to *Commonweal*.)[30]

The denial of the existence of black anti-Semitism sometimes relied on bizarre logic. *Village Voice* columnist Nat Hentoff called the evidence of black anti-Semitism "isolated and flimsy." The real villain, according to Hentoff, was white racism. Using an intriguing metaphor, Hentoff called American whites "goyim," while suggesting that blacks were the symbolic Jews of America. Implying that a percentage of whites wanted to annihilate black Americans in much the same manner as German Nazis did European Jews, Hentoff asked, "Which among us are the Germans?" I. F. Stone advised that Jews, "as the more forward and privileged group owe the underprivileged a duty of patience, charity, and compassion. It will not hurt us to swallow a few insults from overwrought blacks." Stone's condescending remarks betrayed a central liberal racial dilemma: whites (here Stone talks about Jews) were the more "forward" and enlightened group and must therefore pity and humor supposedly less advanced blacks.[31]

If outbursts of hatred by blacks caused some Jews to overreact, the Jewish counterattack led some liberal Jews toward even stranger conspiracy theories. Rabbi Jay Kaufman, vice president of B'nai B'rith, called black anti-Semitism "a carefully introduced transplant." Kaufman admitted that Jews were sometimes overly sensitive on the issue of anti-Semitism: "A few drops of anti-Semitic venom go far in stirring Jewish reaction." Rather than fearing black anti-Semitism, Kaufman believed that the real menace was that such outbursts would "strengthen the white anti-Semitic and native fascist stratum in American life, enabling it to deal ruthlessly with both Negroes and Jews."[32]

Rabbi Alan Miller of the Society for the Advancement of Judaism in New York City called anti-Semitism—black and white—a Christian phenomenon. Miller engaged in a bit of anti-Christian bigotry by writing that "any culture which teaches the unabridged New Testament to children at an impressionable age and which includes the St. Matthew's Passion in its musical repertory is going to have anti-Semitism on its covert if not overt agenda." In 1969, Miller could still believe that "the possibility that I and my wife and my children may one day perish in an American Auschwitz is there." Miller felt that the cries against black anti-Semitism were merely being used by some Jews "as part of a deliberate policy to unite New York Jews against the legitimate aspirations of black and Puerto Rican parents and children in a school system which has abysmally failed them." Finally, Miller likened the attacks on Jews by blacks to Aristotle being kicked by a mule. Just as Aristotle ignored the mule, so should Jews ignore the arrows slung at them by blacks. After all, wrote Miller, Jews were often well educated and the black man was "largely educated in the gutter created for him by white society."[33]

The most extreme denunciation of the charge of black anti-Semitism came from the journalists Walter Karp and H. R. Shapiro. "This is the story of a political lie," they wrote, "a New York political lie that clangs through the city like a false alarm in the night. It breeds hatred between two of the largest ethnic groups in the city—as it was meant to do. It allows the powerful to step on the powerless—as it was meant to do." Karp and Shapiro saw the charge of anti-Semitism as part of a careful strategy orchestrated by the UFT "to raise Jewish people en masse against black men." Karp and Shapiro, like other critics, saw the charge of black anti-Semitism as resting on the threats of a few isolated black militants and the UFT's wide circulation of these rants.[34]

One fallout from the discussion of black anti-Semitism was the creation of the Jewish Defense League (JDL) in 1968. The guiding force behind the JDL was Meir Kahane, a thirty-six-year-old Orthodox rabbi from Laurelton, Queens, a neighborhood that was slowly undergoing conversion from a Jewish neighborhood to a middle- and working-class black neighborhood. The JDL, whose slogans included "Never again" and "Every Jew a .22," chose as its symbol a fist inside the Star of David. The JDL was born in an era of identity politics. Kahane claimed that he "understood the breakdown of the concept of the 'melting pot' and the growth of ethnic separation in the wake of Black Power. I knew that Italians, Poles, Irish and other white ethnics who made up the majority of America were resentful and would start looking inward and demanding rights for themselves." Kahane and others felt that too many liberal and secular Jews had moved away from Judaism and were more interested in black civil rights. As wealthier Jews moved to the suburbs, they often forgot about their poorer cousins still left in the city—landlords, merchants, senior citizens, Hasidim—who were victimized by crime and disorder. As Kahane wrote, "Great Neck is content while Crown Heights shudders—that is the reality of Jewish decline. Miami luxuriates while Brooklyn agonizes; that is the heart of decay."[35]

The decline of lower-middle-class Jewish neighborhoods in Queens, Brooklyn, and the Bronx heightened the unease among many Jews and provided the JDL with its main base of support. Kahane summarized this angst: "Jewish neighborhoods in inner city after inner city died. Areas where tens of thousands of Jews had lived, worked, built lives and careers, synagogues and schools, and which had come to mean warmth, familiarity, and roots, suddenly became places of horror and nightmare. Streets once free and safe at all hours of the night became dangerous during the day. Houses whose doors were never locked became fortresses of fear. And the exodus began and became a flood of panic."

Kahane wanted to defy the stereotype of the weak Jew. One of the more infamous JDL advertisements was headlined "Is This Any Way for Nice Jewish Boys to Behave?" The photo showed six young Jewish men wearing sunglasses and striking a tough pose outside a synagogue. The JDL defended the behavior of these "nice Jewish boys" by answering his question:

> Maybe there are times when there is no other way to get across to the extremist that the Jew is not quite the patsy some think he is. Maybe there is only one way to get across a clear response to people who threaten seizure of synagogues and extortion of money. Maybe nice Jewish boys do not always get through to people who threaten to carry teachers out in pine boxes and to burn down merchants' stores. Maybe some people and organizations are too nice. Maybe in times of crisis, Jewish boys should not be that nice. Maybe—just maybe—nice people build their own road to Auschwitz.

A quarter of a century after the Holocaust, the notion of survival was of paramount importance to the Jewish community. Kahane's group no doubt had an appeal to many Jews, even if most of them never joined the organization.[36]

The first JDL demonstration took place at New York University (NYU) in August 1968 to protest the appointment of John Hatchett as director of NYU's Martin Luther King, Jr., Afro-American Student Center. Hatchett was seen as unacceptable primarily for an article he had written for the African-American Teachers Association newsletter entitled "The Phenomenon of the Anti-Black Jews and the Black Anglo-Saxon: A Study in Educational Perfidy." Kahane and twelve others picketed the university, chanting, "No Nazis at NYU/Jewish rights are precious too." Twelve members of the JDL were arrested in January 1969 for trespassing and assault outside the studios of WBAI after Sia Berhan's anti-Semitic poem was read on Lester's show. In the following years, the JDL would increase its picketing of suspected anti-Semites and beef up its protection of inner-city Jews. JDL members hassled and heckled John Lindsay during the 1969 campaign. In the early 1970s, the JDL harassed Arab and Russian diplomats in New York City and occasionally went further, setting off bombs in terrorist actions.[37]

In defense of some of the JDL's tactics, Kahane said, "We knew there were a lot of people watching us on television, and we wanted to get an idea across about the Jewish boy who suffers daily in Crown Heights or Williamsburg, or Queens or in the Bronx, because he wears the yarmulke, who gets beaten up because he's an easy mark." The JDL's unofficial motto was "Jewish blood is not cheap."

LINDSAY AND THE JEWISH QUESTION

Throughout all of this turmoil, Lindsay's relationship with Jews was marked by a clear unease. Lindsay had gotten off to a mixed start with Jews. One move that won points with the Jewish community was the cancellation of a city dinner for King Faisal of Saudi Arabia that had been scheduled for June 1966. In addition to canceling the dinner, Lindsay ordered that no city official greet the king when he arrived at La Guardia Airport. Prior to his visit, King Faisal had stated, "Unfortunately, Jews support Israel and we consider those who provide assistance to our enemies as our own enemies." Mayor Lindsay realized that he could not go through with the dinner for fear of angering New York's Jewish community. In retrospect, mayoral aide Harvey Rothenberg believed that the administration "acted hastily" in the Faisal matter and wrote that Lindsay felt the same also. "In this case," wrote Rothenberg, "international diplomacy came into direct conflict with local politics, and I'm not sure we handled it as astutely as we should have."[38]

Despite such maneuvers, and despite the fact that many of his aides and commissioners were Jewish, Lindsay often found himself in conflict with the Jewish community. Early in his term, he tried to reinstate alternate-side-of-the-street parking regulations—which are in effect on workdays but not on the weekend and holidays—on Jewish High Holidays. Lindsay wanted to avoid catering to "interest groups" and making special exceptions in the law for them. When this plan raised a stir, Lindsay quickly abandoned it. Another incident that displayed the potential clash between the Lindsay administration and New York's Jewish community centered on the Brooklyn neighborhood of Sea Gate, a predominantly Jewish gated community on the peninsula west of Coney Island. In an October 1967 memo, the mayoral aide Robert Blum, head of the Coney Island Urban Action Task Force, argued for the necessity of tearing down the wall separating Sea Gate from the poor black ghetto of Coney Island, saying: "Sea Gate constitutes a ghetto in reverse: A Jewish community with a wall to keep the Christians out." The Sea Gate Homeowners Group got hold of the memo and gave it to Alex Rose. The heavily Jewish Sea Gate community was a Liberal Party bastion. The effort to integrate Sea Gate were quashed. Blum believes that Rose went directly to Lindsay and warned him to drop the issue.[39]

Another controversy surrounded the city's Commission on Human Rights. In February 1967, Rabbi Julius Neumann, a Wagner appointee to the commission, resigned from his post to protest the leadership of William Booth. "It is the function of the commission to ease tension, not to create it," said Neumann, "to build better understanding instead of whipping up animosity among people." Neumann accused Booth, who was black, of only taking an interest in complaints by blacks and ignoring black anti-Semitism. Neumann said that he believed the commission should "serve people of all creeds, races, colors," and that "this conviction does not seem to be reflected by the present human rights leadership."[40]

Other Jewish leaders had similar complaints. David Schulte, of the Anti-Defamation League, said of Booth, "The Jewish community definitely feels he was less sensitive to their problems than to the problems of other minority groups." Gerald Benjamin, in his history of the Commission on Human Rights, chronicled complaints against Booth by leaders of Jewish groups. One person complained that "the commission must be 80 or 90 percent black by now, and it is only concerned with Negro and to some extent Puerto Rican problems. It is only responsive to pressure from these groups." Another said the "last time I was there I did not see a white face." A third believed "Booth made a conscious decision to limit his constituency to blacks. He had political ambitions." Booth tried to explain himself to Benjamin: "I've spoken up in these cases [of anti-Semitism] and 85 percent of my constituency is Negro. They want me to go further. The commission is not an anti-defamation league." Booth later wrote of his tenure as human rights commissioner: "It is, has been, and will continue to be my belief that the Human Rights Commission's primary obligation is to enforce the laws providing penalties for racial discrimination. If by enforcement, if by full use of all powers, if by education of the public to the existence of the commission and its laws, troubled waters are stirred, then so be it."[41]

In response to complaints about Booth's inaction on the charges of black anti-Semitism during the school strike, Lindsay did not extend William Booth's tenure as chairman. In February 1969, in a move related to election-year concerns, Lindsay replaced Booth with Simeon Golar, a member of the city's Housing Authority and also black. Golar was a member of the Liberal Party and an ally of Alex Rose, and therefore seen as much more sympathetic to Jewish complaints.[42]

Some Jews, furious at Lindsay's inability to deal with the school strike and his unwillingness to criticize black militants, accused him of anti-Semitism. Growing up, Lindsay had little contact with Jews. Especially foreign to Lindsay were religious, Orthodox, non-Manhattan Jews. According to Bob Sweet, who was Lindsay's deputy mayor at the time of the school strike, there was not "much in his [Lindsay's] history that would lend him any expertise or relationship" in this area. "This was not something he came to either instinctively or by training," says Sweet. The mayor's major concern was the plight of blacks. "In that conflict between blacks and Jews, intuitively John was more of a civil rightser," recalled Sweet. The mayoral aide Werner Kramarsky remembers that during the school strike, Lindsay told him, "I don't understand why people call me an anti-Semite. Practically everybody around me is Jewish." The blunt Kramarsky told his boss that he could not help but be anti-Semitic "because it is not your culture." This was not what Lindsay wanted to hear and he "hit the roof."[43]

George Altomare, a close Shanker aide, was at Gracie Mansion for negotiations to end the 1967 teachers' strike. When the agreement then on the table fell through, Altomare heard Lindsay say, "It's about time I got rid of the white middle-class Jewish establishment that has run New York for so long." Jews would have taken this as prima facie evidence of religious animus, but Lindsay had nothing personal against Jews, only with their relation to urban reform. Still, the ugly charge of anti-Semitism stuck to Lindsay among a good number of New York Jews, as unfair as the charge might have been.[44]

The racial and religious tensions brought on by the teachers' strikes were made painfully clear to the mayor during an October 1968 visit to a Jewish center in Midwood, Brooklyn. The angry crowd, including many UFT members who felt Lindsay was doing little to protect teachers, booed and jeered the mayor. According to one report, the mayor "stood with facial muscles twitching, one white-knuckled hand gripping the podium" and said, "Our city will not survive if teachers are illegally transferred any more than it will if this gentleman here [Shanker] leads the teachers in an illegal strike. I say to you that there have been acts of vigilantism by both groups." Harvey Rothenberg accompanied Lindsay to the event. Amid the booing, the mayor turned to Rothenberg and asked, "Must I wear this yarmulke when they're profaning the temple?" When an ashamed Rabbi Harry Halpern, a member of Lindsay's Commission on Human Rights, asked the crowd if their behavior was "an exemplification of the Jewish faith," the crowd responded, "Yes, yes." When Lindsay left the center, a crowd estimated at 5,000 was waiting outside the center. As the mayor's car drove away, protesters threw trash at it, kicked its doors, and pounded on its hood. Rothenberg remembers that upon "entering my car, I was spat on, and people began to rock our car. Angry faces filled my windshield. I couldn't believe the scene." Lindsay "was really taken aback" by the aggressive reception in Midwood and angrily returned to Gracie Mansion.[45]

The Jewish community's fury against Lindsay over his support for school decentralization caused some problems for the mayor's Jewish aides. Lewis Feldstein, Lindsay's chief aide for the school decentralization issue, had to deal with an angry call from his mother asking how he could support the Ocean Hill–Brownsville experiment. Barry Gottehrer recalls going to a family wedding in the fall of 1968 and having relatives constantly asking him, "How can you work for that anti-Semite Lindsay? What kind of person are you? You should be ashamed!" Around the same time, Gottehrer made a speech at a Queens synagogue whose rabbi had supported Lindsay in 1965. After Gottehrer finished his speech, which he hoped would calm Jewish fears, the rabbi began to speak. "He ripped me apart, and Lindsay, and decentralization," remembers Gottehrer. When Gottehrer pulled out the *Times* ad placed by the nonstriking Ocean Hill–Brownsville teachers to rebut the charges of anti-Semitism, a man in the back of the room answered him. "There are Jews—and there are Jews," he told Gottehrer. "Those people in Ocean Hill–Brownsville aren't Jews. . . . And neither are you." The audience wildly cheered the man, and Gottehrer never spoke before another Jewish audience.[46]

One incident that highlighted Lindsay's problems with New York Jews came just after the incident in Midwood. The *Long Island Press*, a small newspaper with a predominantly Jewish readership, published a column entitled "Lindsay Told Jews: 'Control Shanker.' " The article described a tense and bitter September 1968 meeting between Lindsay and Jewish religious and lay leaders, including representatives of the AJC, ADL, the New York Board of Rabbis, and the Jewish Labor Committee, where Lindsay reportedly asked Jewish leaders to try to "control" Shanker. In response, one rabbi asked the mayor if he had asked Cardinal Spellman to control Mike Quill during the transit strike. The article further claimed that Lindsay told the Jewish leaders that "New York Jews were destroying his administration" and that "You Jews have made me use up all my Negro credit cards."[47]

The response from the mayor's office came from Harvey Rothenberg, the mayor's appointments secretary and an Orthodox Jew, who had originally set up the meeting. In a letter to the newspaper, Rothenberg wrote that the piece was "just short of being totally false" and that it "contained the most sweeping collection of mis-statements and mis-representations that could be assembled in one news story." First, the article got the date wrong for the meeting; it took place on September 16, not September 30. Rothenberg denied that Lindsay ever said Jews were destroying his administration. In response to the claim that the mayor asked his guests to "control" Shanker, Rothenberg responded: "The mayor was asked by the group what could be done to help. His reply was that both sides in the dispute had assumed 'extreme' positions; that he believed this group could contribute greatly to citywide and community brotherhood if they could exert a moderating influence." As for the remark about "Negro credit cards," Rothenberg claims that in response to the group's pleas to control black militants, Lindsay said "he was using all the influence he had in the black community and in so doing was using up his credit cards in order to bring about a peaceful solution." Rothenberg concluded by saying he had known Lindsay for twenty years and was "ashamed that even one person would give any credence whatsoever to such a Joe McCarthy-type smear attack."[48]

The *Long Island Press* article was based on hearsay and contained few reliable quotes. Others who attended the meeting, however, confirmed that there was evidence there of deep tensions between the Jewish community and John Lindsay. The AJC's Haskell Lazere was at the meeting in question and took notes. There is nothing in his notes about "credit cards" or Spellman and Quill or about Jews trying to destroy the Lindsay administration. But according to Lazere, Lindsay "alluded to Shanker negatively almost throughout his presentation and there was no doubt of his hostility to the Teachers Union. Implicit in his presentation was a desire on his part that we speak out or use whatever influence we had on Al Shanker and the Teachers Union." When one visitor questioned the mayor about the legal authority of the Ocean Hill–Brownsville Governing Board, Lindsay dismissively responded that the question "showed ignorance of the facts." Lazere described a snappish and irritable mayor who cut off some of his questioners. Lazere "was stunned by the impatience and hostility that the mayor showed. . . . His entire attitude was one of great hostility, total estrangement and great intolerance as though if we didn't support him totally, he didn't want to do any business with us." He felt the meeting was a waste of time and "exacerbated rather than eased the situation with the mayor's office." Lazere dolefully concluded, "I can say that it is the first time in my professional career that I felt a public official put me totally on the other side of working for the welfare of the community—the enemy."[49]

Other meetings with Jewish leaders in the summer and fall of 1968 were similarly tense. At an August 1968 meeting, Lindsay balked at the idea of issuing a statement explicitly condemning anti-Semitism at Ocean Hill–Brownsville. When one member of the group charged Lindsay with rewarding "trouble makers" like Rhody McCoy and Milton Galamison, the AJC's Ted Ellenoff reported, "The mayor became rather cold at this point." In a November 1968 letter to Lindsay's aide Jay Kriegel, the AJC's Barbara Chartock, wrote about a meeting between the mayor and Jewish leaders regarding black-Jewish relations. According to Chartock, many at the meeting felt Lindsay was "insensitive to Jewish interests" and uninterested in the plight of looting victims, many of them Jewish businessmen, in the wake of the assassination of Martin Luther King. Chartock also quoted the AJC's Will Maslow as saying that Lindsay "is unsophisticated in his dealings with [the] Jewish community for not realizing that they do not like to be addressed as 'you Jews.' "[50]

Lewis Feldstein, the Lindsay administration's point man on school decentralization, did not believe that his boss was an anti-Semite. Instead, Feldstein thought that part of Lindsay's problem was that he "just didn't understand the threat that Jews felt." But Feldstein also believed that Lindsay's problems went deeper. In his desire to aid minorities and the poor, the mayor ignored the needs of middle-class whites—including Jews.

> He was so focused on what he saw as the much greater source of oppression and injustice on the black and Hispanic side that he just didn't catch the other side. I think all of us, including Jewish aides like myself, didn't either. It was easier for us to see in the Sixties the feeling that what was happening to blacks and Hispanics wasn't fair than it was to realize that compensating for that could be equally unfair or risky to whites. We felt secure and we didn't feel threatened.

During the late 1960s, many New York Jews felt threatened. And they believed that their mayor had little regard for their concerns.[51]

In a taste of what would await Lindsay during the fall 1969 campaign, the *Village Voice's* Jack Newfield reported on a visit by the mayor to the Forest Hills Jewish Center during the winter of 1969. When Lindsay told the crowd that he was glad to see that elements of the black community were denouncing black anti-Semitism, shouts of "Liar!" came from the audience. Newfield wrote: "At that moment John Lindsay's handsome face turned tense and petulant, his erect body sagged into a question mark, and he was finished." Newfield, unsympathetic to the anti-Lindsay members of the crowd, wished that the mayor had stood up to them and spoken about white anti-Semitism and white racism. Instead, "he took it all sulking, his face flushed with agony, his leg tapping nervously, his voice growing weaker with each answer. . . . Lindsay's spirit was broken."[52]

By 1969, John Lindsay faced an election year in which Jewish votes would quite possibly determine whether he returned to Gracie Mansion for another term. That the Ocean Hill–Brownsville controversy drove a wedge between blacks and Jews, both strong Lindsay constituents, did not help his political fortunes. Nor did it help that a sizable number of Jewish New Yorkers felt that Lindsay took the side of blacks at the expense of Jews. If Lindsay was to win another term as mayor of New York and not be swallowed by the rising tide of anger and cynicism, he would quickly have to mend fences with the Jewish community. The election of 1969 would quickly evolve, in large part, into a campaign by Lindsay for the hearts and minds of Jewish New York.

ESCAPE FROM NEW YORK?
JOHN LINDSAY'S
POLITICAL DILEMMAS

Before being sidetracked by the Ocean Hill-Brownsville fiasco and the teacher's strikes, John Lindsay was busy building his national political stature. As the attractive and dynamic mayor of the nation's largest city, Lindsay was already a national star. His was the face of urban America, pleading with his fellow citizens not to forget the nation's great but decaying cities in their rush to suburbia. But as the ethnic and racial tensions of 1968 proved, the road from City Hall to higher office would be a rocky one. Not only did Lindsay have his hands full with Jewish complaints about black anti-Semitism and black demands for the community control of the school system, but tensions between the mayor and Governor Nelson Rockefeller were mounting. This would have serious consequences for Lindsay's political future. In addition, the mayor was growing disenchanted with the increasingly conservative direction of the Republican Party.

ROCKEFELLER VERSUS LINDSAY

By the middle of 1968 the tensions between Lindsay and Rockefeller had ruptured into guerrilla warfare. Though both were patrician liberal Republicans, the two men differed in their approach to public policy. Rockefeller was much more pragmatic than the ideological and moralistic Lindsay. In contrast to Lindsay, with his constant troubles with the city's municipal unions, Rockefeller got along well with the unions because he was willing to cut deals and create jobs on the large public works projects throughout the state. Lindsay was more sensitive to community concerns about the chaos and disruption that these plans often caused. Lindsay called Rockefeller "the last colonialist" because the governor did not "believe in local participation, in the common sense of ordinary people. He thinks he knows what's best for everyone. So he walks right in and builds things, big things. He's a colonialist."[1]

Rockefeller's aides used to say that the governor would rather be mayor of New York than the chief executive of the state. Though Rockefeller was technically a resident of Westchester County and worked in Albany, he considered himself a resident of New York City. Rockefeller was most energized by city affairs, an interest that was liable to put him on a collision course with the energetic and opinionated mayor. Those tensions were on display in 1967, when Rockefeller proposed that the buildings on Sixty-third and Sixty-fourth Streets between Broadway and Central Park West be razed to make way for a landscaped mall connecting the park with Lincoln Center. Among the buildings the mall would displace were the headquarters of the Ethical Culture Society, whose members had been strong supporters of John Lindsay. The mayor refused to comply with Rockefeller. At a meeting at Rockefeller's Fifth Avenue apartment, Lindsay repeated his refusal, sending Rockefeller into a paroxysm of anger. When the governor went to his window, overlooking Central Park toward Lincoln Center, Lindsay and his aides suspected that Rockefeller had proposed this project in order to have a direct view of Lincoln Center from his apartment. [2]

Other public works projects set the mayor and governor at odds. Lindsay and Rockefeller clashed over the building of Battery Park City and the development of Roosevelt Island. To the dismay of the Lindsay people, Rockefeller hired Ed Logue to head the state's Urban Development Corporation (UDC). Logue had been rejected for a job in the Lindsay administration, for Lindsay feared that Logue would turn into another Robert Moses. Now Logue had the power at UDC to impose his will over New York City, as well as the entire state.

At times Rockefeller made sure to put his younger colleague in his place. At a gathering at the governor's Fifth Avenue apartment, Rockefeller showed Lindsay his impressive collection of modern American art. Rockefeller knew that despite his cosmopolitan image, Lindsay was a bit of a philistine when it came to any culture higher than Broadway theater. The governor asked the dumbfounded mayor his opinion of an abstract painting. Journalist Richard Reeves recounted what happened: "As a small group of Whitneys and such gathered, Lindsay nodded and mumbled, bullets of sweat popping on his forehead, not willing to admit that the Lindsays of West End Avenue had never found the time to become knowing collectors of modern art." According to Steven Berger, who worked for Rockefeller in the early 1970s on the Scott Commission investigating the Lindsay administration, "Rockefeller saw himself as a far more serious and substantive person than Lindsay."[3]

This tension between Lindsay and Rockefeller became very apparent after the killing of Robert Kennedy on June 4, 1968. Kennedy's term ran until 1970, and it was up to Governor Rockefeller to name a replacement for New York's junior senator. The story that quickly emerged about the cautious dance between the two liberal Republican titans was that Rockefeller wanted Lindsay to ask for the Senate seat and Lindsay wanted Rockefeller to offer him the seat. In late June, the *Times* ran a front-page article headlined "Lindsay Must Ask for Kennedy Seat," in which the governor expressed concern about taking Lindsay out of City Hall and delivering the city back into the hands of the Democrats. Still, Rockefeller said, "If the mayor wants the spot, of course, he deserves prime consideration." Rockefeller was reluctant to offer Lindsay the job publicly because he was afraid that Lindsay would make a very public refusal, declaring his intention of staying in the city. This would have embarrassed Rockefeller and made his next pick for senator seem like the second choice. On the other side, Lindsay was leery that Rockefeller might be setting a trap to embarrass him by making him ask for the seat publicly and then just as publicly denying his request. Deputy Mayor Robert Sweet now says, "There was the concern on the one hand on Lindsay's part that if he asked for the job, then Rockefeller wouldn't give him the job and he'd look stupid. On Rockefeller's part, there was the fear that if he asked Lindsay for the job and Lindsay turned it down *he'd* look stupid." It turns out that Lindsay and Rockefeller were probably both right.[4]

Some people do not believe Rockefeller ever got over his dislike for Lindsay enough to offer him the Senate seat. Al Marshall, Rockefeller's chief of staff, is one who believes Rockefeller never intended to offer the job to Lindsay. Lindsay aide Peter Goldmark is another. Goldmark has said, "Rockefeller was so distrustful and so uncomfortable with John Lindsay that he didn't want to offer him the seat." Goldmark believes that Lindsay himself was never quite sure of Rockefeller's intentions at the time. "I have heard Lindsay go both ways on this in conversation," says Goldmark.[5]

The uncertainty in the Rockefeller camp regarding the Senate seat was matched by indecision at City Hall. A vigorous debate ensued within Lindsay's inner circle about whether the mayor should pursue the Senate seat. One group felt that he needed to stay in New York to carry out his urban crusade. Jay Kriegel was "violently against" Lindsay's going to the Senate. "Being mayor of New York was more important than having a clear shot at the presidency," Kriegel believed. Deputy Mayor Robert Sweet and Budget Director Fred Hayes were both in favor of Lindsay's staying in City Hall. Hayes sent Lindsay a three-page memo outlining his belief that Lindsay should stay in New York, arguing that the conventional wisdom behind opting for the Senate seat was "safety from the disasters of race and money that hang always over the head of the mayor of New York." But even though being Mayor was tough, Hayes wrote, "so far you *have* pulled it off." Hayes acknowledged that some of Lindsay's success was merely "a result of style and personality," and the question that remained was whether the Lindsay administration could "move from an accomplishment that is still heavily a matter of style to deeper structural changes in the government of the City, with the hope, ultimately, of a visible and tangible impact upon the quality of urban life." Hayes believed the answer to that question was that the administration was "at or close to the take-off point." Thus, Hayes concluded that Lindsay should stay in City Hall and fulfill his original pledge to reform city government and solve the "urban crisis."[6]

Another voice arguing against running for the Senate was Mary Lindsay's. The day after Kennedy's funeral, Lindsay asked to see his aide Robert Blum at Gracie Mansion. When he arrived, Blum found a casually dressed John and Mary Lindsay. Lindsay told Blum that though he hadn't asked for the Senate seat, he had heard that Rockefeller felt he had to offer it to him. Blum told his boss that he should remain mayor. At this Mary Lindsay said, "Doesn't that make it unanimous? Can you imagine moving back to that town when you're living here in New York?" Some have suggested that Mary Lindsay was worried about the strain on her marriage if Lindsay became a senator in Washington, D.C., and his family remained in New York. She had little desire to leave New York, nor did she want to return to the situation of her husband commuting to Washington from New York as he had done early in his congressional career.[7]

Others in the administration felt that Lindsay should jump at the chance to get the Senate seat. Sweet remembers a plane flight to Chicago with Lindsay and press secretary Harry O'Donnell soon after RFK's death, where the three debated the possibility of Lindsay's taking the Senate seat. Sweet argued in favor of staying in New York, while O'Donnell thought that a Senate seat would best position Lindsay for a shot at the presidency. O'Donnell had long believed that the key to Lindsay's political future lay in getting out of City Hall as soon as possible. According to deputy press secretary Robert Laird, O'Donnell believed that if Lindsay "had to kiss Nelson's ass in Macy's window to get the Senate seat, he should have." Lindsay's old mentor Herbert Brownell also supported Lindsay's moving out of City Hall. In January 1968, before the Senate seat ever became an issue, O'Donnell and Brownell had a long lunch. In a letter to a friend about his lunch with Brownell, O'Donnell said, "We were in agreement on so much concerning JVL—get out fast and move on to something else, if possible." David Garth, Sid Davidoff, and the speechwriter Jim Carberry were also in favor of Lindsay's moving to the Senate, the latter agreeing with O'Donnell that Lindsay "should have kissed [Rockefeller's] ass to get" the Senate seat. The mayor's counsel, Mike Dontzin, a staunch Liberal Party member, also wanted Lindsay to take the seat. Alex Rose wanted Lindsay to remain at City Hall and became angry with Dontzin for advising the mayor otherwise. Though many aides had idealistic reasons for persuading Lindsay to stay in the city, it is certainly a fact that a smaller Senate staff meant that many City Hall aides and commissioners would have been looking for other work had Lindsay become senator.[8]

Whether Rockefeller ever intended to offer the job to Lindsay, it became increasingly clear that Lindsay did not want the Senate seat. Harvey Rothenberg said that Lindsay's "wish was to have Nelson Rockefeller offer the post, and then he would publicly reject the offer." In 1967 Lindsay had been very blunt about his political future. He ruled out running for any office beyond City Hall. He even ruled out accepting the Republican vice presidential nomination if offered. "I am firmly convinced that to be a good mayor of New York City, you ought to commit yourself to that job and forget about other offices," the mayor said. As he pondered the Senate appointment, Lindsay told Nat Hentoff, "Nelson doesn't realize that if he did offer it to me and I turned it down, that wouldn't hurt him or the man who does eventually accept the appointment. . . . Sure, I'd turn it down. I've told Nelson that in power, complexity, and responsibility, my job dwarfs even his and that he ought to keep that in mind." Sweet believes Lindsay made up his mind not to go for the Senate seat on the flight to Chicago. "John decided he didn't want it," according to Sweet. "I know he decided he didn't want it." Lindsay told Robert Blum that running for Senate would be a "cop-out on the city." Immediately after his 1969 reelection, Lindsay admitted that though the decision not to go after the seat "wasn't easy," the idea of leaving the city "struck me as an abandonment of the city, and especially of the people I had talked into joining the fight for the city at a time of great stress."[9]

So Lindsay never asked for the appointment to the Senate and Rockefeller never offered the job to Lindsay. The governor did not fill the seat until September, when he nominated an obscure upstate Congressman, Charles Goodell, to replace Bobby Kennedy in the United States Senate.

Years after he left City Hall, with his political career dead and his reputation as mayor in tatters, Lindsay would look back on his refusal to pursue the Senate seat in 1968 as a major tactical error. In 1978 Lindsay told a reporter, "Maybe I should have gotten out when I had the chance—when I could have had Bobby Kennedy's seat after he was killed. The only reason I didn't was that I felt I had an obligation to all the superb people I'd uprooted and brought into government." In 1982, Lindsay wrote to O'Donnell, the most vocal proponent of his taking the Senate seat, "Please note I backed you up on the advice you gave me in 1968. You were right then, right now, always were and always will be." Had he gone to the Senate, Lindsay might have had a clearer shot at becoming president or vice president. He could have used the Senate as a pulpit for his views on cities, race relations, and foreign affairs. He could have had seats on the Judiciary and Foreign Relations Committees and become an instant statesman. Then again, Lindsay would have had a tough reelection battle in 1970. James Buckley, brother of the mayor's bête noire, William F. Buckley, ran on the Conservative ticket that year and defeated the liberal Republican Goodell in a three-way race.[10]

PRESIDENTIAL POLITICS

While playing politics with Rockefeller over Robert Kennedy's Senate seat, Lindsay and his aides were also maneuvering through the landmines

of national Republican politics. Officially, Lindsay deferred to the leader
of the state party and supported Nelson Rockefeller's presidential bid. John
Lindsay's brother George was heavily involved in the Rockefeller campaign. When a group of liberal Republicans gathered at Rockefeller's Fifth
Avenue apartment in March 1968 to decide whether Rockefeller should
run, Lindsay was there. Ten days after this meeting, though, Rockefeller
announced he would not run for president. Later that spring, Rockefeller
changed his mind and announced that he was challenging Richard Nixon
for the Republican nomination. It was to be Rockefeller's final attempt at
the prize he so longed for, but it was a poorly planned and executed attempt.

Lindsay's public support for Rockefeller did not stop him and his aides
from secretly positioning the mayor for higher office. In fact, Lindsay's behavior at the Republican convention at Miami Beach further increased the
tensions between the mayor and the governor, reinforcing the belief among
Rockefeller and his aides that Lindsay just could not be trusted. In April
1968, Robert Sweet dispatched Robert Blum to give a speech in Coral
Gables, Florida, and instructed him to travel to Miami Beach to scout out
space for a Lindsay storefront at the convention. (Blum reported back that
Miami Beach was not New York City. Everyone drove, hence campaign
storefronts were impractical.) Lindsay was at the height of his popularity,
having stared down the striking sanitationmen and walked the streets of
Harlem during the King riots. Lindsay's aides hoped to position him as an
alternative to Nixon and Rockefeller in case of a possible deadlock. They
would showcase Lindsay as a fresh voice for cities and begin building the national reputation and support within the party that he would need to be
elected to higher office. One mayoral assistant said, "We've been showing
the mayor off. If there should happen to be a convention deadlock—well,
they will at least have *seen* John Lindsay."[11]

Blum visited Miami four times before the convention to prepare the Lindsay convention headquarters. He rented rooms in the Hotel Americana and
set up a conference room for the Lindsay team's war room. A list of state delegations was drawn up and the names divvied up among the members of
Lindsay team; they would canvas support for Lindsay's nomination as either
president or vice president. Blum says, "I was in charge of our secret office at
which I presided over a short-wave radio transmitter linked to nine walkie-
talkies on the floor, three TV sets, and seven telephone lines to the floor of
the Americana and to the world outside."[12]

This exercise was mostly futile. Sid Davidoff noted, "We were all a little
bit naive." It should have been obvious that Nixon would easily wrap up the
nomination, and that Nixon would never pick Lindsay as a running mate, no
matter how much he talked about the idea in public. Nixon had only been
throwing out names to gauge the reaction among party members. Lindsay
was being pressured to consider a vice presidential offer by Herbert Brownell

and Walter Thayer, both of them Nixon men who believed Lindsay needed to show his loyalty to the Republican Party. In July, the *Times* ran a front-page story headlined "Aides Hint Lindsay Is Open to a Place on Nixon Ticket."[13]

Lindsay spoke with Jimmy Breslin about his ambivalence about running as Nixon's running mate. On the one hand, Lindsay felt he owed it to liberal Republican candidates to be on the Nixon ticket: "Well, a lot of friends of mine from the Wednesday club [a group of liberal House Republicans] have been coming to me. They say they can't win unless I'm on the ticket with Nixon. What am I going to do? I know these guys. Know their families. They have their life savings up into campaigns. They'll lose everything. I can't say no to them. If I do anything, I'll be doing it for them." On the other hand, Lindsay made it clear that he felt Nixon would never pick him. "I'd want to speak out on the cities. . . . I'm making that plain. So don't worry. Nothing is going to happen." As late as the Wednesday of the convention, Lindsay's Republican advisers were still keeping the door open for a possible Nixon-Lindsay ticket. But at a meeting that night between Nixon and Republican leaders, Lindsay received a big thumbs-down from an important segment of Nixon's coalition, Southern Republicans who were uncomfortable with Lindsay's urban credentials and civil-rights record. While liberals like Brownell pushed for Lindsay, both Barry Goldwater and Strom Thurmond emphatically rejected Lindsay.[14]

By the time the convention began, Lindsay himself had lost interest in the vice presidency. Nixon obviously had the convention sewn up and the mayor was less than taken with the Californian. Rothenberg recalls that Lindsay's liberal aides wanted him to have nothing to do with the Nixon campaign. Meeting inside a canvas cabana on the beach outside the Hotel Americana, Lindsay enlisted the aid of the journalist Theodore White to send a secret note to the Nixon people.

> Fearful of being mousetrapped by Congressional pressure to accept second place, he [Lindsay] had sent, through an intermediary friend, a message of awesome sternness to Mr. Nixon. If the Party compelled him to run, if a Party duty were made of it—then he would. But he wanted Mr. Nixon to know that if he were so chosen, he would as Vice President, feel himself free to speak out on issues, either on foreign affairs or urban affairs, whenever he disagreed with the President and make his opposition known.

In other words, Lindsay was not interested in trimming his sails for a chance to be on the ticket. As Lindsay told White, "If I were Nixon . . . I wouldn't dream of accepting my offer."[15]

The Lindsay team prepared a long memo for the Miami convention detailing the issues they wanted to highlight. First and foremost was the situation of cities: "The crisis of America's cities will be the major domestic concern of the next administration." Another memo argued:

> The mayor should act as a liberal touchstone of the Republican convention. He should be the crusading gadfly who keeps the candidates and the party honest, candid, and progressive. He should embody the impulses and biases of the new uncommitted "new politics" constituency. Although Rockefeller is attempting to do this, the mayor can do it better. His efforts will not be tarnished by the atmosphere of opportunism and ambition which hangs over Rockefeller's search for a winning coalition. Nor will it be greeted with the unanimous skepticism that followed Nixon's call for a new Republican coalition. The mayor has the credibility and the history of commitment which no major Republican figure possesses. This will be the role thrust upon him by the press and this will be the role the nation expects him to play.

Some Lindsay aides suggested that he put forward certain themes at the convention, some suggestions being "National Priorities and the Commission on Civil Disorders"; "The Urban Crisis: The Poor and the Middle Class"; "The New Republicanism"; "A New Equality"; and "Black Self-Determination." Lindsay would push for the creation of a left-of-center Republican Party: "Each candidate is having trouble carrying out the idea that the Republican Party should be the home for the vigorous and uncommitted of the middle and left of middle. The mayor can make the pitch without fear of public skepticism." The polarization of American society was a clear theme for Lindsay, one that created an opportunity for the Republican Party to choose its future path: "To this should be added a discussion of the importance of George Wallace on the right and the large, independent voting block on the left, i.e. McCarthy, RFK, blacks, youth. Which group will we, the Republicans, attract in November?"[16]

Lindsay's first official function at the convention took place Monday night, August 5, when he introduced Washington Governor Daniel Evans, the convention's keynote speaker. Lindsay, who received a warm reception from the crowd, spoke of themes that were definitely not standard Republican fare. He spoke of the cities, calling the urban situation "seething with the gravest domestic crisis since the Civil War." He made a plea for the rights of black Americans who were victims "not just of fear, but of that persistent injustice which denies their decency." Finally, he attacked the war in Vietnam, saying it ranked "among the most disastrous foreign policy blunders in our history." Despite the warm reception Lindsay received, it became clear there was a tremendous divergence between the crowd of Republicans gathered in Miami to cheer on Richard Nixon and the men surrounding Lindsay. Sitting uncomfortably in the convention hall, Lindsay's political operative Sid Davidoff told Jimmy Breslin, "I wish we were back in New York on the streets. The streets are better than this." The only problem is that no street in New York led to the White House, even indirectly.[17]

Nixon, as expected, did not choose Lindsay as his running mate, passing him over for the little-known governor of Maryland, Spiro Agnew. Though Agnew had originally run as a liberal Republican in 1966, he later strengthened his reputation among conservatives with his tough stand against the riots following the death of Martin Luther King. In a bow to Lindsay and his urban constituency, Agnew, whose home was Baltimore County, was introduced as an "urban" politician. What was not mentioned was that Agnew's home in Baltimore County surrounded but did not include the city of Baltimore. In 1968 it was a suburban and semirural area far removed from the problems plaguing its urban neighbor.

Nixon asked Lindsay to give the seconding speech for Agnew. In return for the speech, which would give a liberal imprimatur to the Nixon ticket, Nixon promised that if elected he would allow the city to buy the dormant Brooklyn Navy Yards from the General Services Administration for a low price. There was a debate among the Lindsay team on whether to accept the invitation. Some of Lindsay's younger, Democratic aides urged him to reject the offer and mount an insurgent campaign for the vice presidential nomination. Prominent liberal Republicans like Rhode Island Governor John Chafee and Massachusetts Senator Edward Brooke beseeched Lindsay to lead the fight against Agnew. But Lindsay's Republican mentor, Herbert Brownell, advised him to accept the offer. Ultimately, Lindsay decided to second Agnew's nomination and reject the insurgency run. Blum later wrote that with this decision Lindsay "garnered credit with Nixon, made himself look regular to the party, avoided having to share a philosophical faith designed by Nixon, and had an opportunity to speak to 20,000 conventioneers and 60 million viewers again and to pressure Nixon and Agnew all over again."[18]

Maryland Congressman Rogers Morton, a Nixon ally, was slated to nominate Agnew. The delegations of Nevada and Rhode Island also notified the convention of a desire to speak and to nominate a vice presidential candidate. Nevada, led by state chairman George Abbott, was rumored to be nominating George Romney, while Chafee and the Rhode Island delegation still had Lindsay in their sights. Lindsay meanwhile was nowhere to be found. He remained off the convention floor the entire evening, getting ready to second Agnew's nomination. The question for Lindsay's supporters was simple: How could they draft their man to challenge Agnew after he had seconded his nomination?

As promised, Lindsay went ahead with his seconding speech. He bounded to the platform to rousing cheers and scattered boos. Liberal forces chanted "We want John," while more conservative delegates sat glumly and motionless in their chairs. To Jim Carberry, who wrote the speech, the key was to have Lindsay "convey to the people in the convention hall that you were being a good soldier and that you were standing up there endorsing a guy you really didn't really believe in," but "you were doing it because you wanted to put yourself back in the good graces of the party." In his less-than-inspiring seconding speech, Lindsay only mentioned Agnew's name three times, preferring instead to push his theme of the urban crisis. The mayor told the Miami delegates that the Republican platform pledged the party "to a vigorous effort to transform our cities into centers of opportunity and progress." Senator Jacob Javits looked on glumly as Lindsay nominated a vice presidential candidate almost handpicked by the conservative Strom Thurmond. Further deepening the gloom of the liberal camp, conservative Texas Senator John Tower followed Lindsay to the podium. With Lindsay lining up behind Tower and Agnew, the liberals looked defeated.[19]

As the convention worked its way toward nominating Nixon and Agnew, a revolt broke out on the floor. Led by Chafee and Brooke, Republican liberals distressed by the Agnew choice sought to nominate a more acceptable alternative. The area around the New York delegation became a hotbed of activity. Though Nixon had wanted a smooth final night of the convention so that his acceptance speech would hit prime time, Oregon Governor Tom McCall was talking about the possibility of asking for a recess in the convention so that other vice presidential candidates could be nominated. Congressman Albert Quie spoke of the Minnesota delegation's desire for a more liberal alternative acceptable to big cities, minorities, and youth. Congressman Silvio Conte agitated for Lindsay among the Massachusetts delegation, while Pennsylvania's Governor Raymond Shafer also made clear his state's preference for a more liberal candidate.

After his speech, Lindsay, surrounded by his most trusted aides, returned to a make-up trailer. Liberals such as Chafee, Brooke, Washington Governor Dan Evans, and New York Congressman Charles Goodell made their way to Lindsay's trailer to entreat the mayor to accept their nomination to challenge Agnew. Pennsylvania's Shafer offered his state's eighty-four votes to Lindsay if the mayor would accept the challenge. Lindsay also received support, in addition to Rhode Island and Pennsylvania, from the delegations of Massachusetts, Minnesota, Connecticut, half of New York and Delaware, as well as some votes from Nevada. These entreaties were met with stony silence from Lindsay. Pulled in one direction by his younger liberal aides and in the other by Republican stalwarts like Brownell, Lindsay had not yet made up his mind.

Lindsay and his aides left the makeup trailer and visited Robert Blum at his communication headquarters. As Blum received reports from the Lindsay people on the convention floor, Brownell took a head count of delegates who wanted the go-ahead from Lindsay to put up his name in the hopper for the vice presidential nomination. Brownell, Nixon's man in the room and highly skeptical of challenging Nixon's chosen running mate, claimed he could not count enough votes. With or without Lindsay, though, there would be a challenge to Agnew. Nevada's George Abbott made his way to the podium to nominate a liberal Republican challenger to Agnew, not knowing whose name he would be announcing. In his trailer, Lindsay did not say a word, the color in his face changing constantly in response to the mounting pressure. Finally, he agreed to play the loyal soldier and refused to go along with the liberal challenge. Meanwhile, George Romney was, according to Blum "stupidly anxious to be an insurgent if JVL would not." When Lindsay declined to challenge Agnew, whose nomination he had just seconded an hour earlier, Abbott, already on the convention platform, was given Romney's name.[20]

Nixon was not happy about the rebellion of liberal Republicans. This was one reason Brownell had steered Lindsay away from the challenge. He felt that Nixon himself would go on the floor of the convention to oppose the liberal insurgent. He knew Nixon would use all of his force to quash the rebellion. According to historian Stephen Ambrose, Nixon asked John Mitchell for advice on how to do it. "I'm not going to stand for this kind of revolt," Nixon told Mitchell. "If the sore losers get away with something like this now, they'll do the same damn thing during my Presidency." Mitchell went to work keeping the delegates away from Romney's camp, holding the Michigan governor to only 186 votes, less than half of what Brownell had counted for Lindsay during his nonchallenge. Ultimately, Lindsay did receive 10 votes in the count, from the Pennsylvania delegation.[21]

Lindsay's behavior at Miami Beach did not sit well with some New York pundits. The *New York Times*'s Richard Reeves, a veteran Lindsay watcher, argued that Lindsay's political posturing for the sake of his future viability in the Republican Party was not what had originally endeared him to New Yorkers. Lindsay had sacrificed some of his prized political independence in Miami, especially by seconding Agnew. Said Reeves, "John V. Lindsay in Miami Beach did not seem quite the same as John V. Lindsay in New York City." At a break in the convention, Blum and David Lindsay were cooling themselves on a strip of beach outside the Hotel Americana with Jimmy Breslin. Both Blum and David Lindsay approved of John Lindsay's seconding Agnew, but Breslin argued against it: "You can't sleep with a fuckin' whore without risking diseases," Breslin told his companions. "I'm telling you this Agnew is a bad guy. A class act like Lindsay can't involve himself in seconding him." In Breslin's eyes, the decision to second Agnew made Lindsay "just an ordinary politician." Breslin believed that "the thing that allowed John Lindsay to get up and second Spiro Agnew for the office of Vice-President is the thing that is the matter with the country."[22]

In the end, Lindsay managed to maneuver around the conflicting demands of national Republican politics. He had kept his own political independence, which was necessary both to survive in New York City and to satisfy his own intensely moralistic vision of politics. Though he endorsed Nixon for president, Lindsay stayed away from him during the campaign.

Advised by Brownell and O'Donnell, Lindsay portrayed himself as a loyal Republican, albeit a dissenter on some important issues. He also raised his visibility for the possibility of a national race in 1972 if Nixon lost or in 1976 if Nixon won. Despite the cries from Reeves and Breslin, Lindsay did not seriously harm himself in New York by seconding Agnew's nomination.

What became more serious than any disillusionment liberals felt with Lindsay was the increasing incompatibility between Lindsay and the national Republican Party. Lindsay's focus on civil rights, cities, the youth movement, and the Vietnam War went against the increasing conservatism of the Republican Party. Some in the Lindsay administration openly worked for Democratic candidates for president while their boss supported Richard Nixon. Some of Lindsay's liberal aides were clearly hostile to Republicans, making the fleeting thought of a Nixon-Lindsay ticket seem farcical, and Lindsay did not work hard to garner votes for the Republican candidate from New York City's voters.[23]

It is doubtful that John Lindsay's full support would have helped Nixon much, for he won only 34 percent of the vote citywide in the three-way race, 886,822 votes in total. This was an improvement over Barry Goldwater's showing in New York City four years earlier, when he garnered only 27 percent, or 802,283 votes. Hubert Humphrey defeated Nixon in four out of five boroughs—only the reliably Republican Staten Island suported Nixon. Manhattan voted for Humphrey by almost three to one; the Bronx and Brooklyn by two to one. Humphrey even took the more conservative borough of Queens by more than 100,000 votes.

What complicated the election somewhat was the presence of George Wallace. An October 1968 article in *New York* magazine asked in its headline, "Red Neck New York: Is This Wallace Country?" Although many New Yorkers were turning away from liberalism and John Lindsay, they did not turn in Wallace's direction. The southern segregationist's appeal held little resonance in polyglot New York, even though he showed surprising strength in midwestern cities. Wallace won only 4.7 percent of the vote in the city and 5.2 percent statewide. His best showing was in the thirtieth assembly district in Queens, where he won 9.7 percent; it was an area that had been strongly resistant to school busing and was the birthplace of the Parents and Taxpayers Association (PAT). The top ten Wallace districts correlated highly with areas that had voted heavily against the Civilian Complaint Board in the 1966 referendum by four to one or greater.[24]

Also in 1968, Senator Jacob Javits coasted to reelection against the Democratic nominee Paul O'Dwyer. Running on both the Republican and Liberal Party lines, Javits won almost 300,000 more votes in the city than Nixon. Just like the presidential race, the Senate race featured a third-party candidate, James Buckley, the brother of William F. Buckley, who was running on the Conservative ticket. Buckley did not pull away enough votes to harm Javits, but he won more than one million votes statewide, or 17 percent. In New York City, Buckley won 472,123 votes, one-third more than his brother received in 1965.

Buckley's totals in the city were almost four times greater than Wallace's. There was a budding reaction in the city against liberalism, but it was not indiscriminate. Buckley carried one district, the thirtieth in Queens, and came in second in ten others. He won almost one quarter of the vote in Queens. Most conservative New Yorkers carefully pulled the lever for Buckley in his Senate race and then switched to either Nixon or Humphrey, not Wallace, for president. Buckley's success in 1968 would embolden him for another Senate race in 1970 against Republican Charles Goodell, the man Rockefeller had handpicked to replace Robert Kennedy. After two more years of chaos, racial tensions, and polarization, Buckley would win a Senate seat on the Conservative ticket.

John Lindsay entered 1969 unsure of whether to run for reelection for mayor. His first three years in office had been frustrating and bitter, allowing him precious little time for his family. Yet Lindsay was also proud of the changes he had made and of the sense of hope and excitement he had created. Having won by a plurality in 1965 and not having worked at broadening his coalition, though, Lindsay would face an uphill battle if he chose to run again. The America of 1969 was fundamentally different from that of 1965. John Lindsay had changed as well.

CONFRONTING THE WHITE ETHNICS: THE 1969 CAMPAIGN

> To be mayor of New York requires an ability to reconcile the competing visions that the city's ethnic groups hold of the metropolis.
>
> —Chris McNickle, *To Be Mayor*
> *of New York: Ethnic Politics in the City* [1]

The social disruptions that shook the United States between 1965 and 1969 were felt profoundly in New York City. In 1965 Lindsay had run against the tired Wagner administration. Running for reelection in 1969, Lindsay faced the same problems as Wagner, except he had no one to blame. In fact, the problems had gotten worse. The city had grown surlier, more dangerous, more divided. Lindsay's liberal experiment in New York City, like other liberal experiments in the second half of the twentieth century, showed that expectations of how much government could improve the lives of its citizens far outstripped the reality. The mayoral campaign of 1969 was a test of how much these social changes and urban decay would affect the career of John Lindsay.

WHICH SIDE ARE YOU ON?

The late 1960s was an era of grievances, of antiwar protesters, feminists, blacks, and restless middle-class youth. Nineteen sixty-nine also became the year of another aggrieved group: "Middle Americans." *Newsweek* published an extensive report on the "white majority" entitled "The Troubled American." *Time* named "Middle Americans" 1969's Man and Woman of the Year.

"The Middle Americans," wrote *Time*, "cherish, apprehensively, a system of values that they see assaulted and mocked everywhere . . ." Above all, Middle Americans were angry at what they felt were attempts to "tear down" America. They saw attacks upon the country they loved and the values they cherished. They were angry about antiwar protests, while at the same time being confused about the war. They were angry at black militants and the denunciations of racism that seemed directed against them. They feared the spread of drugs and pornography and opposed loose morals and slack manners. They wanted to "take the handcuffs" off police and enforce "law and order." They despised welfare loafers, for Middle Americans themselves often worked at menial jobs. They worried about inflation and high taxes. Worst of all, as *Time* magazine noted, they "felt ignored while angry minorities dominated the headlines and the Government's domestic action. If not ignored, they have been treated with condescension."[2]

In northern cities, "Middle Americans" tended to be blue-collar white ethnics. Journalist Samuel Freedman has described these Americans as the men and women "who wrested citizenship from a nativist nation, rose from privation into the middle class, and swung the pendulum of ideology from left to right." Journalist Peter Schrag argued that there was "hardly a language to describe" the white ethnic "or even a set of social statistics. Just names." It was a group that was on the receiving end of more socially accepted stereotypes than any other group, like "racist-bigot-redneck-ethnic-Irish-Italian-Pole-Hunkie-Yahoo." Whereas these working-class stiffs were once American heroes, by the late 1960s they represented the embodiment of reaction and illiberal thought. Marx predicted the alienation of the working class, but he never could have guessed it would turn out like this.[3]

New York City's Middle Americans were its outer borough white ethnics, men and women descended from German, Irish, Italian, Polish, Greek, and Jewish immigrants who were either civil servants (teachers, firemen, policemen), union members (welders, electricians, carpenters), or members of the petit bourgeoisie (clerks, accountants, small businessmen). Their culture was middlebrow, traditional, and patriotic. Jimmy Breslin described the fissure between Manhattan and the outer boroughs: "New York is not these reedy, bland, leavened, pasteurized, homogenized scarecrows running into Bonwit's. It is a real person wearing a sundress, the body a little dumpy from having children, the face a little too lined. . . . New York is not a cocktail party upstairs at Sardi's. It is a shot of Fleischmann's with a Rheingold on tap for a chaser in Neal's on Fordham Road in the Bronx. And it is not Plaza Suite. It is a motel on Woodhaven Boulevard in Queens." Some of these people had voted for Lindsay, some had voted for Beame, and some had voted for Buckley. But by 1969, none of them were happy. One man especially fueled their anger: John Lindsay.[4]

Lindsay's world was not the American Legion in Brooklyn or the civic association in the Bronx. Lindsay came from another class, a higher class, a "better" class. Writing to Jay Kriegel in 1990, Marvin Schick, who served as Lindsay's liaison to the Jewish community, condemned the administration's "failure to connect with ordinary people or really care about the feelings of others." This became apparent with Lindsay's inability to understand white, middle- and working-class homeowners living outside Manhattan. Secure enough not to rely on the city's social welfare system but poor enough not to be able to indulge in the leisure style or political reforms of the upper class, these men and women possessed what appeared to Lindsay and his liberal supporters to be parochial concerns: lower taxes, more police protection, better city services, and protection of their neighborhoods.[5]

According to the former Lindsay budget aide Peter Goldmark, the Lindsay administration overlooked something very basic: "We all failed to come to grips with what a neighborhood is. We never realized that crime is something that happens to, and in, a community." A former mayoral assistant, Nancy Seifer, spent a year trying to build bridges between City Hall and white ethnic communities, but grew frustrated at the indifference in City Hall. "There was a whole world out there that nobody at City Hall knew anything about," said Seifer. "The guys around Lindsay didn't know what a neighborhood was. If you didn't live on Central Park West, you were some kind of lesser being."[6]

And New York's white ethnics knew it. In 1967, a group of New York Italian Americans formed the American-Italian Anti-Defamation League. One of its first targets was the underrepresentation of Italians in the Lindsay administration. A Lindsay aide who attended a community meeting in the heavily Italian Belmont section of the Bronx reported back to City Hall that the community felt ignored by the mayor, who was "very unpopular in the community." Bronx Republican State Senator John D. Calandra, in a 1968 legislative report to his constituents, documented the growing anger in the city's white ethnic communities.

> The North Bronx area has suddenly and without any prior notice had its garbage collection reduced from 3 weekly pickups to 2 pickups per week. Why the decline in service by City Hall, which had a record $6 billion approved for it by our "rubber stamp," so-called City Council? Rumor has it that men and equipment have been diverted to the South Bronx. The North Bronx pays most of the taxes yet the South Bronx, which pays hardly any, gets all the services and facilities from our Mayor and City Departments. If more money is needed for our Sanitation Dept., then I suggest that our funloving Mayor "find it" the same way he found $7 million for the Youth Corps after that disgraceful, illegal, and wanton riot at City Hall. I think it's about time we in the North Bronx start thinking as to what action we must take to obtain what we need and want.[7]

The city's cabdrivers were especially disdainful of Lindsay. Journalist Jack Newfield noted, "What it all comes down to in the here and now is that Lindsay gets cheered in Harlem and Berkeley and cursed by taxi drivers and cops." One cabbie summed up the indictment against Lindsay: "I can't stomach Lindsay. He's alienated just about every man in every union in this city. . . . If you're colored, you're all right with him. If you're white, you got to obey the law." If a reporter ever needed a quick anti-Lindsay quote, all he needed was to ask his cabdriver.[8]

Jonathan Rieder, a sociologist, did a study of Canarsie, Brooklyn, in the 1970s, in which he concluded that "for a variety of reasons, liberals did not sympathize with the suffering of people like those who live in Canarsie: white discontent was morally less compelling than black plight. . . . Instead, left-liberalism hardened into an orthodoxy of the privileged classes. Was it surprising that many Brooklyn Jews and Italians looked elsewhere for champions?" Lindsay made little attempt to reach out to white ethnics and seemed to have little understanding of their backgrounds. When an interviewer asked the mayor whether there were any comparisons between the situation of black Americans and those of turn-of-the-century European immigrants, Lindsay curtly replied, "There is really no comparison."[9]

Lindsay was not blind to the animus he generated. He later acknowledged that "a broad segment of the electorate felt a special ill will toward me. Indeed, it seemed I had managed to unite a wide variety of New Yorkers in a common cause: my retirement." Responding to his unpopularity among white ethnics after his first year in office, Lindsay said, "I understand how they feel and I don't resent it. But this had to be the year of the poor in New York." In this statement, Lindsay confirmed the fear of many: that Great Society liberalism was chiefly concerned with the needs and wants of the poor. Everyone else existed on some level of privilege and therefore did not need the attention of elected officials.[10]

No one captured the growing alienation and anger of New York's white ethnics better than the journalist Pete Hamill. His April 1969 *New York* magazine article, "The Revolt of the White Lower Middle Class," was written from the perspective of someone who had sprung from the lower-middle-class streets of Brooklyn, who could walk into bars and union halls and talk to their denizens with ease and without condescension. Coming at the issue from neither the left nor the right, he could chastise whites for racism and businessmen for selfishness, condemn the destructiveness of black militants, the snobbishness of liberal intellectuals, and the lunacy of white hippies all in the same paragraph. Hamill saw a strong role for government, supported the "little guy" no matter his race, and was patriotic despite hating the war in Vietnam.[11]

Hamill was not exactly anti-Lindsay, but he did not embrace him. "Lindsay doesn't really care much about Brooklyn, nor about the white working class," wrote Hamill, "and the white working class of Brooklyn was perceptive enough to understand that." Hamill could understand that as well. "The white working class will probably never relate to John Lindsay and his St. Paul's moralizing," wrote Hamill. "They would tolerate him, I suspect, if the machine he runs would only function. But unfortunately, in his hands, it has functioned only sporadically."[12]

Hamill pointed out that the now-derided working class was once praised as the backbone of the nation. By 1969, he lamented, these men and women "can no longer make it in New York." On one side, those with incomes between $5,000 and $10,000 were squeezed by creeping inflation, higher taxes, and crumbling schools that made private-school tuition more a necessity than a luxury. On the other hand, their sensibilities were offended by the sight of a million people on welfare, by riots in the streets, by affluent college students wreaking havoc in schools, and by street crime. More and more they asked themselves, as one ironworker put it to Hamill, "What the hell does Lindsay care about me? He don't care whether my kid has shoes, whether my boy gets a new suit for Easter, whether I got any money in the bank. None of them politicians gives a good goddam. All they worry about is the niggers."

Hamill warned that white ethnics "see a terrible unfairness in their lives and an increasing lack of personal control over what happens to them." Increasingly, these white ethnics blamed this unfairness—along with the decay of the city—on blacks. The result, according to Hamill, was "a growing talk of revolt" among these working-class whites. More people bought guns and formed self-defense clubs. If such trends continued, Hamill warned, a race war could be imminent. If a revolution was going to happen, it had as good a chance of coming from the white lower middle class as from white radicals or black militants. "All over New York City tonight, in places like Inwood, South Brooklyn, Corona, East Flatbush and Bay Ridge, men are standing around saloons talking darkly about possible remedies," Hamill wrote. "Their grievances are real and deep; their remedies could blow this city apart."

The sympathy for civil rights among these whites seemed to diminish as their proximity to blacks increased. Enlightened views on race were easy to hold for whites who lived in the comfortable suburbs or in the doorman buildings of Manhattan. Jonathan Rieder noted that for whites in Canarsie, Brooklyn, "physical closeness to blacks widened the moral and social chasm between them."[13]

In 1966, Harvard psychiatrist Robert Coles identified "a certain snobbish and faddish 'interest' in Negroes from people who would not think of concerning themselves with those many white families who share with Negroes slums, poor schools, uncertain employment." A 1969 article, "Respectable Bigotry," written by a Yale graduate student, Michael Lerner (later editor of *Tikkun*), described this attitude toward white ethnics. "An extraordinary amount of bigotry on the part of elite, liberal students goes unexamined at

Yale and elsewhere," wrote Lerner. "Directed at the lower middle class, it feeds on the unexamined biases of class perspective, the personality predilections of elite radicals and academic disciplines that support their views." The bigotry of the lower middle class against its social inferiors was bitterly denounced, but the bigotry of the upper middle class was not. Lerner noted that "radicals gloat over the faulty syntax of the lower middle class with the same predictability that they patronize the ghetto language as 'authentic.'" The police and the lower middle class had to practice restraint, while the lack of restraint among hippies, radicals, and inner-city blacks was tolerated, if not encouraged. Why, asked Lerner, do liberals "patronize one authenticity and mock another"? His answer: a simple class bigotry that had become respectable and mainstream by the late 1960s, even among the "better classes" who marched against the Vietnam War and for civil rights and who patted themselves on their collective backs for their tolerance and broad-mindedness.[14]

Ironically, some black spokesmen shared this scorn toward white ethnics. The Urban League's executive director, Whitney M. Young Jr., said, "You're more likely to find prejudice among lower- and middle-class whites who've just made it—who are a generation away from WPA and welfare. I call them the affluent peasants—people with middle-class incomes but not undergirded by civilized views—by aesthetic, cultural, and educational experiences." To Young, these uncivilized "affluent peasants" needed to be cleansed of both their racial prejudice and their lower-class vulgarisms. Young also complained about what he called the "sluggish majority" of simplistic whites. "The challenge is to educate the white man and show him that it's in their own self-interest that the problems of the ghetto be resolved," said Young. [15]

The white ethnic alienation had begun well before 1969, with what social commentators called a racial "backlash" against civil rights. In September 1964, the New York Times ran a poll of New Yorkers' views on race and found that 54 percent felt the civil rights movement was moving too fast. Yet this was not what some might label a "racist" backlash. Sixty-one percent still planned to vote for Lyndon B. Johnson in 1964, compared to only 18 percent for Barry Goldwater. Civil rights leaders Martin Luther King and Roy Wilkins received high favorable ratings, though respondents viewed both Malcolm X and Adam Clayton Powell Jr. much more negatively. Belying the notion some people held of a strictly segregated city, 42 percent of whites lived in neighborhoods with black residents, and 57 percent had attended school with blacks. Sixty-six percent of whites supported the clause in the 1964 Civil Rights Act preventing discrimination in employment. Forty percent did not mind living near a number of black families, and 57 percent did not mind living near one or two black families. What most worried whites was being the only white family left in the neighborhood, as well as the school board's plan to "pair" black and white schools. Both issues were opposed by 80 percent of whites.[16]

Norman Mailer was another bellwether of the changing attitude toward blacks. There was a marked change in his views of blacks between 1957 and 1968. In an infamous 1957 article, "The White Negro," Mailer glorified what he described as the dysfunctional black community:

> Knowing in the cells of his existence that life was war, nothing but war, the Negro (all exceptions admitted) could rarely afford the sophisticated inhibitions of civilization, and so he kept for his survival the art of the primitive, he lived in the enormous present, he subsisted for his Saturday night kicks, relinquishing the pleasures of the mind for the more obligatory pleasures of the body, and in his music he gave voice to the character and quality of his existence, to his rage and the infinite variations of joy, lust, language, growl, cramp, pinch, scream, and despair of his orgasm.

Eleven years later, reporting from the Republican convention at Miami Beach, Mailer realized that "he was getting tired of Negroes and their rights." Waiting at a press conference for Ralph Abernathy, who was forty minutes late, Mailer gave vent that he "was weary to the bone of listening to Black cries of Black superiority in sex, Black superiority in beauty, Black superiority in war . . . heartily sick of listening to the tyranny of soul music, so bored with Negroes triumphantly late for appointments, so depressed with Black inhumanity to Black in Biafra, so weary of being sounded in the subway by Black eyes, so despairing of the smell of booze and pot and used-up hop in blood-shot eyes of Negroes bombed at noon."

Some would argue that the Mailer of 1957 and the Mailer of 1968 were really not that far apart. Both obsessed on the worst aspects of black America, inflating both the power and the pathology of blacks.

A growing disillusionment with the civil rights movement had set in among many whites. Pollster Louis Harris wrote, "It is perfectly clear that by mid–1969 in New York City, much of the city's traditionally accepted feeling for blacks as underdogs had eroded and even disappeared."[17]

A SNOW JOB

The anti-Lindsay sentiment that had built up in the city was crystallized during the great snowstorm of February 1969. So traumatic was the storm and so devastating was the sight of unplowed streets that more than thirty years later mayors throughout the Northeast still make getting all city streets plowed promptly after a snowfall one of their highest priorities to avoid the fiasco that befell John Lindsay.

On Sunday, February 9, 1969, fifteen inches of snow—the most since the blizzard of 1961—caught the city unprepared. The previous night, the National Weather Service had predicted merely "snow beginning early morning hours, becoming mixed with, and changing to, rain after daybreak Sunday . . . rain ending Sunday afternoon." As the storm kept piling snow on the city throughout Sunday, the National Weather Service kept adding to its snowfall estimate. The city could not handle the snow that piled up on the streets of the five boroughs. Merrill Eisenbud, the city's Environmental Protection Administrator who oversaw the Sanitation Department, was in Upstate New York and was unreachable for most of Sunday, causing the city to lose a day of snow removal. The city then found that nearly 40 percent of its snow removal equipment was unusable owing to poor maintenance. For three days, the city was in a state of near paralysis. Five outer borough parkways were closed for three days. Forty-two people were killed during the storm, half of them in Queens, and 288 were injured. The city had to wait until Wednesday for its schools to reopen, most of its streets to become passable, and its commuter rails, airports, and subways to become operational.[18]

Most embarrassing to the city was the fact that streets in Queens were still not passable by Wednesday. Lindsay received a telegram from the United Nations Undersecretary General Ralph Bunche, a Queens resident, who complained that in his seventeen years in his Kew Gardens home he had "never experienced such neglect in snow removal as now." Bunche complained that he had not seen a snow plow since Sunday: "There are no buses, no taxis, no milk, newspaper or other deliveries, and there have been no trash or garbage collection since last Friday." Bunche concluded: "As far as getting to the United Nations is concerned, I may as well be in the Alps. This is a shameful performance by the great City of New York, which should certainly condone no second-class borough."[19]

As he had when crisis struck the city's ghettos, Lindsay decided to walk the streets of an agitated Queens. This time, his presence only made things worse. Lindsay's limo got as far as Rego Park, where the mayor switched to a four-wheel-drive truck, but even that could not pass through the snow-clogged Queens streets. Stopping in Kew Garden Hills, Lindsay was greeted by a shower of boos. One woman screamed at the mayor, "You should be ashamed of yourself. It's disgusting." Having to stop again, at Fresh Meadows, Lindsay's reception was no better. One woman shrieked at Lindsay as he approached her, "Get away, you bum." The snowstorm exacerbated the conflict between the Lindsay administration and the outer boroughs. Remarks made by Parks Commissioner August Heckscher, when he wrote about the crisis years later, epitomized the attitude that had infuriated so many snowbound Queens residents: "Perhaps in that semi-suburban borough people thought they were entitled to escape natural hazards . . ."[20]

Besides a general unpreparedness for the snowstorm, there were other reasons for the poor response. The mayoral aide Robert Blum believed that the only preventable part of the snowstorm meltdown was the inability to clear the city's parkways. Because of Lindsay's departmental reorganization, it was unclear which city department was responsible for clearing the city's parkways, ensuring that they would remain covered with snow. Others criticized the Lindsay administration's hesitancy in spending the money necessary to clean the streets adequately because of worry about going over the $5 million budgeted for the year to deal with snow emergencies. During the 1961 blizzard, the Wagner administration spared no expense in clearing the streets, spending a mind-boggling $21 million in its effort and putting almost twice as many men and equipment on the street as Lindsay had. Worse yet, rumors quickly spread that sanitationmen had deliberately lifted their plows in Queens or ignored the area entirely to get back at the mayor for his behavior during the previous year's strike. Of the sabotage rumors, Sid Davidoff said, "There's no doubt about it."[21]

Perhaps the most troublesome aspect of the snowstorm episode was one that was never reported in the press. The debacle occasioned renewed charges that Lindsay did not care about the outer boroughs. John Lindsay felt he was being blamed for the weather. And he wasn't happy about it. During his walk through Fresh Meadows, Queens, when he had been greeted with a shower of boos, one woman came up to him and called him a "wonderful man." This lifted the mayor's spirits and he said to the woman, "And you're a wonderful woman, not like those fat Jewish broads up there," as he pointed to his female tormentors in a nearby building. Reporters from the Associated Press and WNEW Radio had the mayor's comment on tape, but never ran it. The *New York Times* also knew about the story, but refused to run it. John Corry, a former *New York Times* reporter, added, "Arthur Gelb [the *Times* metropolitan editor] could be tough, but he was never malicious. You don't kick a man when he's down."[22]

In February 1969, John Lindsay was indeed a man flat on his back. Had the press used this story, John Lindsay's political career would have been over. Although Al Shanker's charge of anti-Semitism could be dismissed as political and labor posturing, this statement would have given Lindsay's critics ammunition for their belief that the mayor did not have the best interests of the Jewish community at heart. In a campaign where John Lindsay would entrust his political future to the good feelings of the Jewish community, publicizing this incident would have driven away most of Lindsay's Jewish support.

TO RUN AGAIN OR NOT TO RUN

John Lindsay had turned down the chance to become senator in 1968 because he felt that by going to Washington he would be abandoning the city in its time of greatest need. By early 1969, however, it was not entirely clear that he would even run for reelection. In February 1969, Lindsay met for lunch with Richard Aurelio, a former aide to Senator Jacob Javits, at the legendary German restaurant Luchow's on Fourteenth Street. "I was looking for advice of someone from the outside on whether to run for reelection," said Lindsay. Aurelio told the mayor that "there was something historic about the [1969] campaign" and he felt Lindsay should run for reelection "because the tradition of liberalism in the city was in jeopardy." Aurelio told Lindsay he had done the right thing during the school crisis and that "he was right on the tone and direction of the city."[23]

Lindsay said that he was not sure a majority of New Yorkers would agree with Aurelio's assessment. Besides, Mary Lindsay, who had been against her husband seeking the Senate seat, was also against another term. Lindsay told Aurelio his wife was "very much against me running—she's especially bitter about the Jews . . . feels they have let me down." But Lindsay himself was less upset. "I don't feel the same way. . . . I'm detached from it all," he told Aurelio. Like most political wives, Mary Lindsay was protective of her husband. The *New York Post* columnist James Wechsler wrote that Mary Lindsay had "been waging a long, quiet battle to persuade him [her husband] to renounce the mayoralty." She was tired of the critics who blamed her husband "for every inconvenience that hits the city—by chronic complainers and people so shortsighted they only see the politics of it. All they do is object to what he has done. I don't hear them offering anything constructive."[24]

Lindsay told Aurelio that if he were to run for reelection, he wanted Aurelio to run the campaign. Like Bob Price before him, Aurelio came from humble origins. He was born and raised in a Democratic household in Providence, Rhode Island; his father, a policeman. He cut a striking figure in politics. Tall, dark, and stocky, he was "likened to a riverboat gambler with three aces up his sleeve." Aurelio's clothes were neither Ivy League proper nor modishly hip. With his bushy mustache and sideburns and his pink and purple shirts, wide ties and lapels, he was his own man. Aurelio began his professional career as a newsman in Rhode Island before moving to Long Island's *Newsday*. In the early 1960s he moved to Washington to work as an aide to Jacob Javits. Though he eventually became a Republican, his heart was never with the party. After leaving Javits's office, Aurelio took a high-paying job in a public-relations firm. But he quickly grew bored and was eager to get back into politics. When Lindsay made up his mind to run for reelection, he asked Aurelio to become his campaign manager.[25]

Having run in 1965 as the candidate who promised to solve the urban crisis, Lindsay decided that he could not abandon the city. On March 18, three months before the Republican primary, John Lindsay publicly announced that he would run for a second term as mayor of New York. At a news conference at City Hall, he made his announcement surrounded by a united front of Republican heavyweights, including Governor Rockefeller, Senator Jacob Javits, Senator Charles Goodell, Attorney General Louis Lefkowitz, and former Governor Thomas E. Dewey. In his announcement speech, Lindsay said that he "believed that the tide of physical and spiritual decay has been turned." He was running because there was "too much at stake to abandon the effort my administration has begun." Foreshadowing the dose of humility that would be forced upon him by his advisers, Lindsay added, "I won't pretend my administration has been without error or disappoint-ment." Using language he had used during his first mayoral campaign, he di-rectly attacked his Republican critics, lashing out against the "reactionary elements that seek to destroy the progressive traditions of Republicanism in New York." But in explaining his purpose in running for a second term, Lindsay again set the bar for success unrealistically high. "I believe we can end bigotry and discrimination," Lindsay told New Yorkers. "I believe we can bring safety to our neighborhoods and harmony to our city. I believe we can end the disgrace of deprivation and poverty. I believe all of us can live together in mutual respect."[26]

Aurelio's first task was to repair the mayor's tattered reputation. Just a year earlier Lindsay had been riding high. But the Ocean Hill–Brownsville school crisis and the accompanying teachers' strikes had wiped out any goodwill that Lindsay had accumulated. So did the snowstorm. These events reinforced the idea that New York City was chaotic and ungovernable. The Lindsay who once graced national magazine covers as a golden boy reformer now appeared on the November 1968 cover of *Time* under the headline "New York: The Breakdown of the City." Lindsay later wrote: "The last six months of 1968 had been the worst of my public life. . . . More fundamen-tally, the tensions between racial and religious groups in New York were breaking to the surface in an angry series of verbal and emotional con-frontations." Surveying the pre-primary scene, Aurelio noted that there "were pockets of liberals who were favorable to him [Lindsay], but it clearly looked like an incredibly uphill struggle." Columnists Rowland Evans and Robert Novak reported in their March 1969 column that polls showed that "Mayor Lindsay would be defeated for reelection today by any faintly visible Democratic candidate for one basic reason: this city's white voters believe he has catered to the black man."[27]

Feelings toward the mayor and the city began to split along very clear lines. On one side were people like the members of the Citizens Committee to Re-Elect John Lindsay who believed that "New York City is a tough place to change. John Lindsay has begun the job." The committee, which was led by establishment figures such as Christian Herter, Nicholas Biddle, Bennett Cerf, and John Loeb as well as entertainers like Joel Grey, James Earl Jones, Harold Prince, and Richard Rodgers, placed a full-page advertisement in the *New York Times* listing Lindsay's accomplishments. "We think we in New

York City are lucky to have a Mayor who knows as much about the dreadful problems of the cities as John Lindsay does," declared the committee in its advertisement.[28]

On the other side was an equally strong belief that the city had changed under John Lindsay and the change had not been for the better. Journalist Nora Sayre, in an article called "Breakdown of a Metropolis," acknowledged that "it has always been New York's nature to seem on the shore of collapse." Writers from Charles Dickens to Henry James to John Steinbeck have noted the chaotic, violent, alien nature of life in New York City. But, said Sayre, by 1969 the city's "erosions are even harsher than they were a few years ago, and . . . daily life has become fiercer." Sayre concluded: "It's become sadly apparent that New York has sagged under Lindsay and his staff." In March 1969, *Fortune* called Lindsay's New York "a nightmare for urban management." The magazine credited the mayor with a "dash and sense of mission," but worried that "style alone cannot conquer the forces of decay and disorder that threaten the city."[29]

To the conservative commentator and Lindsay nemesis William F. Buckley, Lindsay was simply "the incarnation of abstract liberalism" whose "results have been chaos." Murray Kempton complained that "under Lindsay, the air is fouler, the streets dirtier, the bicycle thieves more vigilant, the labor contracts more abandoned in their disregard for the public good, the Board of Education more dedicated to the manufacture of illiteracy than any of these elements ever were under Wagner." Jimmy Breslin described the urban scene on a drive through Brooklyn: "Block after block of hot, filthy houses and sidewalks lined with garbage cans that never seem to be collected and have been kicked over by dogs and kids. And, on so many streets, a stripped, smashed car, sitting there as a reminder of everything that is brutal and barren about city life." In 1987, political scientist Marshall Berman wrote that "nothing prepared us for the burning down and virtual destruction of many of these neighborhoods . . . those of us who lived through the 1960s and 1970s in New York often felt like soldiers in that Great War: under fire for years, assaulted from more directions than we could keep track of, pinned down in positions from which we couldn't seem to move."[30]

In January 1969, Daniel Patrick Moynihan warned President-elect Nixon of the dangers of the "urban crisis," which seemed to be affecting New York more than any other city. Summarizing a recent conference in New York, Moynihan told Nixon that churches, families, and local communities were the social intermediaries that made it possible to have a weak state. Increasingly, "It would appear these subsystems are breaking down in the immense city of New York," warned Moynihan. "If this should continue, democracy breaks down." Moynihan and other neo-conservatives saw the "urban crisis" as more of a "moral and cultural crisis than a material one." Admitting to being slightly apocalyptic in his description of New York, Moynihan warned Nixon that the "social fabric of New York City is coming to pieces. It isn't just 'strained' and it isn't just 'frayed'; but like a sheet of rotten canvas, it is beginning to rip, and it won't be too long until even a moderate force will be capable of leaving it in shreds and tatters."[31]

THE REPUBLICAN FIELD

Lindsay's goals after announcing his reelection plans were to solidify his Republican base with an eye on the June 17 primary, and put together another "fusion" campaign with an eye toward the November general election.

Fiorello La Guardia's widow was on hand at City Hall for Lindsay's reelection announcement to remind voters about the fusion theme (La Guardia had run on a Fusion Party ticket). Rounding out his ticket, Lindsay named Sanford Garelik, chief inspector of the Police Department, as his candidate for City Council president and Fiorvante Perrotta, the city's finance administrator, as his candidate for comptroller. Both men met Lindsay's needs for ethnic, religious, and political balance. Garelik was a Jewish Democrat closely allied with Alex Rose and the Liberal Party. Perrotta, an Italian-American Catholic Republican, would help Lindsay among the largest ethnic group in the city's Republican Party.

The Republican primary would prove difficult. With Lindsay looking weak within the party, conservatives Vito Battista, a Brooklyn assemblyman, and John Marchi, a state senator from Staten Island, announced their candidacies. Battista claimed that the mayoral campaign boiled down to three issues: "anarchy in the schools, terror in the streets, and runaway welfare." During the Wagner administration, Battista said, "People were afraid to leave their homes at night. Now, after four years of Lindsay, the people are afraid to leave their homes in the daytime." Battista's presence in the race was a blessing to Lindsay, since it promised to split the conservative vote that otherwise would go to Marchi. One month before the primary, though, Battista dropped out of the race and joined the Marchi ticket as the candidate for comptroller. In addition to Marchi and Battista, Brooklyn Assemblyman Robert Kelly rounded out the ticket as the candidate for City Council president. Would Republicans deny renomination to a sitting mayor in a city where a Republican mayor comes along once in a generation? Would they trade the charismatic idealism of Lindsay for the quiet reserve of John Marchi?[32]

Writing to Aurelio, Lindsay aide Barry Gottehrer admitted that he was "troubled" by his "lack of knowledge or feeling about the nature of the registered Republicans in New York City." Internal polls showed that nearly 70 percent of registered Republicans in the city opposed Lindsay. Panicked, the Lindsay campaign sought a crash course in New York City Republicanism. Lindsay volunteers pored over lists of the city's 600,000 registered Republicans to come up with an ethnic breakdown. They found that roughly 30 to 40 percent of the party was Italian, and roughly 15 percent was Irish and the same percentage German. Less than 5 percent of registered Republicans were Jewish. More bad news for the youth-oriented Lindsay was that nearly half of city Republicans were over fifty-five years old. Lindsay's only consolation was that nearly one quarter of New York Republicans were white Protestants. As one Lindsay aide said, "We're running scared. We also know now that the Republican Party is literally dying in New York City."[33]

Lindsay's longtime antagonist Nelson Rockefeller, though present at the March 18 announcement ceremony at City Hall, was generally unsupportive of Lindsay's reelection bid. Speaking at Gracie Mansion in May, the governor said that though he "personally" favored Lindsay in the June primary, he would not actively support him. In addition, Rockefeller made clear he would support John Marchi in November if Marchi won the primary, even if Lindsay ran as a third-party candidate. Some blamed the governor for assisting Marchi behind the scenes. Others felt that Rockefeller's sin was one of omission, not commission. In addition, Rockefeller's lieutenant governor, Malcolm Wilson, did not like Lindsay. Wilson, who was more conservative than Rockefeller, felt that Lindsay's brand of liberal politics did not belong in the Republican Party and he sent his allies, especially in the Bronx, to help Marchi. Lindsay managed to win the support of three of the five Republican county organizations (Manhattan, Brooklyn, and Queens); Marchi received the support of Staten Island's organization as well as that of the Bronx.

In the battle for his party's nomination, Lindsay was forced to travel through the Bronx, Queens, and Brooklyn looking for Irish and Italian Republican voters, the very groups that had grown deeply disenchanted with him during his first term. Lindsay visited Republican clubs and community groups in these neighborhoods throughout the spring. Booing and catcalls became an expected part of any Lindsay visit. August Heckscher saw the effect this treatment had on the mayor, calling it "worse than receiving a physical blow." Lindsay would steel himself up for the anger, his facing hardening and his eyes growing distant. According to Heckscher, this took its toll on Lindsay's personality: "You knew at what cost of natural warmth and sensibility this protective coating was put on." Deputy Press Secretary Robert Laird noticed that during the 1969 primary, "You could see Lindsay's body stiffening when he got out of the car" to go to events in places like Bay Ridge, Brooklyn. By 1969, the Republican mayor could no longer feel comfortable in the most Republican district in the city.[34]

Lindsay unwisely let slip his unease with Bay Ridge in remarks before the State Republican Committee less than two weeks before the primary. Making fun of Nelson Rockefeller's recent troubled trip to South America, Lindsay said, "I know that everyone in this audience is deeply sympathetic toward the man who in recent weeks was shunned, vilified, and shamefully treated during a goodwill mission to what proved to be very hostile turf—and believe me, that's the last time I'm going to visit Bay Ridge." Robert Blum noted that the remark had, not surprisingly, generated an angry reaction and warned that "it is unwise and hurtful for the mayor or his spokesman to make derogatory comments, even in jest, about any named neighborhood."[35]

It would have been tempting for Lindsay to give up on winning the Republican primary and instead concentrate on building a new coalition for the November general election. This is exactly what Aurelio wanted to do. By forsaking the primary, Aurelio felt the campaign could save money that would be better spent in the general election. But when Aurelio brought the idea up in a meeting with Lindsay's contributors at Jock Whitney's Manhattan townhouse, the big money men said no. These men were the financial backbone of Northeastern liberal Republicanism and were willing to spend lots of money on the primary. Although 1969 looked like a difficult year, they had already invested too much money in fighting Goldwaterite conservatism to just give up.[36]

THE DEMOCRATIC FIELD

A weakened Republican mayor in an overwhelmingly Democratic city presented Democrats with a rare opportunity. As many as twelve Democrats considered running for the nomination in the June 17 primary. Democrats worried openly that a large primary field would divide the party and lead to Lindsay's reelection. Eventually, New York Democrats would get the chance to choose from among five candidates.

In February, Comptroller Mario Procaccino announced his candidacy. Procaccino said he was running because he did not "believe in a Fun City. I believe in a safe city. My first priority will be safety in our streets and security in our homes." Of Lindsay he said, "Great promise. Great theatrical performance. Great flop." The Bronx politician portrayed himself as a representative of the common man, one of the celebrated Middle Americans. At the end of his announcement speech, Procaccino cried as he recalled his rags-to-riches story, from being born the son of a shoemaker in a small Italian town to becoming a candidate for mayor of New York City. Early polls had Procaccino leading the other possible Democratic candidates.[37]

A Fordham Law School graduate, Procaccino was discovered by Mayor La Guardia in 1944 when he gave a speech in Italian at a war-bond rally. Impressed with Procaccino's passion on the stump, La Guardia appointed him assistant corporation counsel. Procaccino worked his way up the city bureaucracy, eventually becoming a civil court judge. Running for comptroller on the Beame ticket in 1965, Procaccino outdrew Lindsay by nearly 30,000 votes. In contrast to the Lindsay administration's implied softness on civil disturbances, Procaccino promised his audience "one standard for everybody. There'll be no double standards." According to the journalist Nicholas Pileggi, Mario Procaccino was the candidate of the "stoop-sitting voters," a man "ethnic in the extreme . . . unabashedly patriotic, a firm believer in 'the Guy upstairs' and a heavy-handed, unsophisticated, painfully sincere man." Jimmy Breslin described the candidate as "short, waddling, crying, sweating Mario, his mustache from Arthur Avenue, his suit from the garment center, his language from all the years of all the neighborhoods of New York." When Procaccino talked about crime in the city, Breslin wrote, "He says this not with Protestant coolness, but with the Ellis Island heartbeat which had so much to do with the making of New York."[38]

Though Procaccino had an obvious emotional appeal for Democratic voters, especially in the outer boroughs, he was at a distinct disadvantage among liberal, cosmopolitan voters. The *New York Post* saw Procaccino as "short and square with a thick mustache and pin-stripe suits," and he looked "like the caricature of the Italian ward heeler, so much so that many who demand a degree of dignity in a public figure find it hard to take him seriously." To his enemies, like the *Post* editorial writers, Procaccino was the "frenetic voice of the reactionary Democratic bloc." Procaccino was also the master of the malaprop, who once introduced his running mate, Francis X. Smith, as a man who "grows on you like cancer." He could also stumble upon a pithy phrase, like when he claimed of his critics that "those who fear Mario will smear Mario." When Procaccino entered the race, the other conservative Democrats—the PBA's Norman Frank and Congressman John Murphy of Staten Island—dropped out of the race and threw their support to him.[39]

The Democrat who made the most news was former Mayor Robert Wagner. Having watched as Lindsay placed the blame for the all of the city's ills upon his shoulders, Wagner had the most personal reason for running. He did not like John Lindsay. And he did not like being blamed for the city's problems. On April 11, after weeks of rumors, Wagner officially entered the race. His entry soon drove out two Democratic candidates: Congressman Hugh Carey and former City Council President Paul Screvane. For his running mates, the Manhattanite Wagner chose the Brooklyn Irish Catholic Carey for City Council president and State Senator Seymour Thaler of Queens, a Jew, for comptroller.[40]

Wagner announced his candidacy at a news conference at the Biltmore Hotel. He flayed Lindsay indirectly for crime, increasing racial tensions, and a decline in city services: "I see it [New York] divided with people fighting people. I see people are afraid because of the safety in the streets. I see a city that's sort of falling apart and all of the services of the city seem to be falling apart." Wagner constantly jabbed at his successor, arguing that "Mayor Lindsay has made a tough time tougher. Four years ago, he said that the city was in crisis. If we were in crisis then, there is no polite way to say what we're in now. . . . We are sliding toward the Cold City, the Heartless City, the Unlivable City." Bridling at the thought of a Republican laying claim to the liberal tradition that his father helped create, Wagner reminded New Yorkers that "John Vliet Lindsay did not invent progressivism." The fifty-nine-year-old ex-mayor, with mock humility, admitted, "I am still not a movie star. But then, New York is not a movie."[41]

Throughout the primary campaign, Wagner ran as though his opponent were John Lindsay, not the other Democratic candidates. When the candidates were asked to name major problems facing the city, Wagner's reply was the shortest: "John V. Lindsay." He railed against the quality of Lindsay's appointments, the effectiveness of the superagencies, the size of the budget, and the increase in racial tensions. Wagner also lashed out against rising crime rates. One television ad depicted Wagner on a dark, rain-slicked Brooklyn street. "I wouldn't let Barbara [his wife] walk down the street alone," he told viewers. "Whatever happened to the cop on the street?" The ad ended by telling voters that if "you go to vote late, don't go alone." The Lindsay team would having nothing of Wagner's criticisms, having already compiled information about the state of the city's schools, hospitals, and Sanitation Department under Wagner. Richard Aurelio countered that the "city is in much better shape. Business is booming. New industries have moved in—the movie industry is here solely on John's initiative, and the Stock Exchange is pinned down. The Police, Fire, Hospital, and Park Departments are in much better shape."[42]

Wagner's entry also briefly threw into doubt who would get the Liberal Party's endorsement. Although Wagner was close to Alex Rose and had run on the Liberal line in 1957 and 1961, Lindsay had successfully won over the party in 1965. But in 1969, Aurelio admitted that "there was a period there where it was really nip and tuck as to whether the Liberal Party was going to endorse Lindsay or Wagner." The Liberals began their convention just days after Wagner's announcement. They had to make a decision. With the Republican nomination uncertain, Lindsay needed the Liberal line. When it became clear that Rose would stick with Lindsay, and thereby bring along the rest of the party, Wagner sent a message stating that he had never asked the Liberals to place him on their ticket. To cries from dissenters that Rose had stacked the convention, the Liberal Party endorsed Lindsay on April 16 by a vote of 276 to 36. The vote locked up the Liberal Party line for Lindsay in November.[43]

The other three Democratic candidates were Bronx Borough President Herman Badillo, Bronx Congressman James Scheuer, and the writer Norman Mailer. Badillo and Scheuer were fighting over liberal Democratic voters, and Mailer was a true wildcard of the Democratic field. If William F. Buckley carried the standard for writer-intellectuals in his 1965 campaign, Mailer followed such noble dreams four years later. The seeds of the campaign were planted in a late-March meeting at Mailer's Brooklyn Heights apartment. The assorted journalists and celebrities at the party, led by Jack Newfield and Noel Parmental, urged Mailer to run for mayor. Mailer formally announced his candidacy on May 1, and was joined by journalist Jimmy Breslin, running for City Council president. (Breslin did not take naturally to playing second fiddle to Mailer. As far as Breslin could see, Mailer's Harvard degree was the only reason he was heading the ticket. "On ability," Breslin thought to himself, "I should be mayor.") The group had wanted Gloria Steinem to run for comptroller, but she declined. According to Mailer, New York was "the greatest city in the world and it is getting ready to die a hideous death." Mailer promised to turn that around and make New York "famous around the world again for the charm, ferocity, elegance, strength, calm, and racy character of our separate neighborhoods."[44]

Mailer's two major campaign issues were decentralization of all city services to the neighborhood level ("Power to the neighborhoods") and making New York City the fifty-first state. In addition, Mailer said his campaign's theme would be "No more bullshit!" The answer to the urban crisis, according to Mailer, was community control. His plan would have prevented a catastrophe like Ocean Hill–Brownsville by granting control over city services to all neighborhoods, not just poor ones. According to Mailer:

> In the new city-state, every opportunity would be offered to neighborhoods to vote to become townships, villages, hamlets, sub-boroughs, tracts, or small cities at which legal point they would be funded directly by the fifty-first state. Many of these neighborhoods would manage their own municipal services . . . or like very small towns, they could, if they wished, combine services with other neighborhoods. Each neighborhood would thus begin to outline the style of its local government by the choice of its services.

This idea of "all power to the neighborhoods" could be taken to absurd extremes, and Mailer encouraged such thinking, proclaiming: "We are running on one profound notion. Free Huey Newton, end fluoridation. We're running on another profound notion—compulsory free love in those neighborhoods which vote for it along with compulsory church attendance on Sunday for those neighborhoods who vote for that."[45]

Mailer, who had recently won the Pulitzer Prize for his book *Armies of the Night*, considered himself to be a "left-conservative . . . running on a left-right coalition against precisely what I call the liberal-totalitarian mentality. I don't mean the liberals put people in concentration camps, for they certainly don't. But they do think that anyone who does not subscribe to their ideas is seriously deranged. . . . I believe the center is dominant in our lives so that nobody has any power over his own life any longer, and that's why I'm calling for this coalition of left and right." He argued that conservatives had been correct in "one terribly important matter: that a man has to have control over his own life."[46]

Some liberals were not buying the Mailer candidacy. Most prominent among the critics was the *New York Post* columnist James Wechsler, who complained about the lack of seriousness and the recklessness of Mailer's campaign. Wechsler was primarily concerned that Mailer would take liberal votes from the paper's favorite: Herman Badillo. Wechsler also lashed out at Jimmy Breslin as an outer borough yahoo who "exhibited a vaudevillian tendency to impersonate what is vulgarly called the common man." He reminded his readers of Breslin's early support for the Vietnam War and his willingness to attack "West Side intellectuals" on behalf of the Johnson administration.[47]

Ironically, with Mailer attacking liberalism and speaking of a "left-right coalition," it was the white ethnic Breslin who carried the banner of liberalism during the campaign. During the primary, Breslin argued that "unless we give the ghettos a chance to work out their own problems, we're going to have a situation where you'll see shotguns on Park Avenue." Speaking at the John Jay College of Criminal Justice in May 1969, Breslin complained about white policemen in black neighborhoods, calling their presence "an expression of enormous ignorance." If the present conditions continued, Breslin argued, blacks "just won't respect this law, and they're not going to respect the people who are instruments of it." Breslin also felt sympathy for college protesters. "A $25 gun knocked out Bobby Kennedy. A bunch of old labor leaders beat McCarthy. There were four hundred fifty boys killed in Vietnam last week. The question is, why is there so little campus strife?"[48]

Although Breslin, according to Jack Newfield, "comes to us from the abused class that produces our cops, taxi drivers, and *Daily News* readers," he still needed to prove to liberals like Wechsler and the *Partisan Review* and *Commentary* literary crowd that he was not a right-wing Neanderthal: "Some people are probably still surprised that he doesn't walk around with a shotgun shooting at Puerto Ricans." Clay Felker, editor of *New York* magazine, talked about the troubles he encountered from liberals for publishing Breslin's articles. "For years I listened to the liberal intellectuals give me a hard time about Breslin," Felker said. "He may have begun as a conservative Queens Catholic. But he has been changed by going to Vietnam, seeing the ghettos . . . becoming a friend of Bobby Kennedy's. If you're in the middle of that . . . you grow." Of course "growing" meant leaving behind Breslin's "conservative Queens Catholic" background.[49]

Breslin's Irish friends never forgave him for "growing." One Sunday afternoon, Breslin received an unfriendly reception at an Irish hurling game in the Bronx's Gaelic Park. He was welcomed with shouts of "Scum," "Will you look at the fat bum," and "Somebody knock his brains out, if the poor bastard has any." Breslin was not allowed into the box for political celebrities. Breslin wrote, "They are my people and they are waiting for me. They are waiting to beat the hell out of me." When he left the park, Breslin found one of his tires slashed.[50]

Meanwhile, Mailer fought to banish the doubts about the seriousness of his campaign. When Mailer spoke on Johnny Carson's *Tonight Show* about the possibility of running, James Wechsler noted how Mailer talked "with deadly solemnity, nay, even sobriety." Mailer's seriousness, though, descended into a certain pompousness. While Buckley could leaven his grandiose nature by poking fun at himself and always poking fun at Lindsay, Mailer seemed to believe that his election could truly save the city. Mailer wrote of how a "tentative confidence would reign in the eye of New York that here literary men, used to dealing with the proportions of worlds hitherto created only in the mind, might now have a sensitive nose for the balances and the battles, the tugs, the pushing, the heaves of that city whose declaration of new birth was implicit in the extraordinary fact that *him*, Mailer! and *him*, Breslin! had been voted in."[51]

If Mailer was trying hard to prove the seriousness of his campaign, his own notorious excesses and lack of control still managed to come through. Just a few days after announcing his candidacy, Mailer spoke at the Greenwich Village jazz club, the Village Vanguard. Obviously drunk, the author delivered a rambling speech laced with profanity. When interrupted, he cursed his audience by calling them "a bunch of spoiled pigs." When a friendly voice asked Mailer to talk about his plans for making the city the fifty-first state, Mailer responded, "Shut up. You're not my friend if you interrupt me when I'm talking 'cause it just breaks into the mood in my mind. So fuck you, boo." Later in the speech, Mailer mockingly called the *Post* the "greatest Jewish paper in New York" and criticized it for not taking his campaign seriously. He then launched into a tirade about Jews: "Very few people understand Jews, but I do, 'cause I'm one of them. Fuck you. Let me talk. The Jews are an incredible people at their best. At their worst they are swine. . . . All people are awful at their worst. Some are worse than others. But the Jews are sensational at their best, which is rare enough, given Miami and a fur coat. No, don't laugh, because you don't know what you are laughing at." After Mailer's speech, Breslin called Jack Newfield at two in the morning and half jokingly asked, "How do you get off a ticket? I didn't know I was running with Ezra Pound."[52]

THE PRIMARIES

The whimsy and exuberance of Lindsay's 1965 campaign was decidedly missing in 1969. "All the right people" had supported Lindsay in 1965 because he was *the* candidate, the one with the movie star looks and grand promises that everyone in their heart of hearts wanted to believe. In 1969, they supported Lindsay simply because they had no other choice.

John Marchi ran a generally inept and lifeless campaign. He had little money for advertisements and staff. He often missed scheduled campaign stops. He announced his campaign kickoff from the steps of the State Capitol in Albany, not New York, reinforcing the idea that he was too much the introspective legislator. One observer noted Marchi's style at a campaign dinner, where the candidate carried himself "with a loser's walk—his shoulders slump forward and his hands are clasped in front of him, almost like a priest's. When someone speaks to him, he nods gently, a little like a Chinese servant might. His dark eyes usually avoid strangers, searching instead for someone he knows." In the gregarious world of politics, Marchi stood out for his shyness. One friend called him "a loner—almost a mystic." The *Village Voice* even called him the "nicest hawk in town." He was also dubbed the "Perry Como of politics" for his nice-guy blandness. In an informal poll of Bronx Italian-American Republicans, a group that should have been overwhelmingly in favor of Marchi, Rowland Evans and Robert Novak found Marchi running ahead of the mayor by only 2 to 1. More damaging, many Italian-American Republicans were energized not by Marchi, but by the Democrat Mario Procaccino.[53]

Washington was certainly paying attention to the New York primary. Conservative Republicans Barry Goldwater and John Tower had both strongly urged Nixon in private not to support Lindsay in the primary. In April, Moynihan wrote to the President that Lindsay was "in awful trouble." Although he told Nixon that he realized that Lindsay was not "a special friend of yours in a political sense," he was the Republican mayor of the largest city in the country and if he lost it "might be painful" for Nixon. Moynihan suggested giving the Lindsay administration $50 million as a preprimary gift to bolster his candidacy. In response, Nixon's aide Ken Cole asked several staffers for their opinion of a Lindsay endorsement. Some suggested supporting Lindsay as "a Republican symbol of major value to the Party in the big city areas." But John Ehrlichman and Peter Flanigan, who believed that the President should stay neutral in the primary, won the argument. Still, Lindsay tried to pull the administration into the primary campaign. He repeatedly called cabinet members to ask them to make grants available to the city in time for the primary.[54]

On Tuesday, June 17, 1969, nearly one million of the city's 3.3 million registered voters went to the polls to vote in the Republican and Democratic primaries. The Lindsay campaign predicted that it could reasonably expect to receive no more than 100,000 votes of the 600,000 registered Republicans in the city. They would have to hold Marchi to under 100,000 votes. Roughly one third of the city's Republicans came to the polls, and a similar proportion of Democrats. Contrary to earlier fears, Lindsay was not swamped by an angry Republican electorate, receiving 107,000 votes, proving his campaign's prediction correct. John Marchi received 113,000 votes, and defeated the mayor for the Republican nomination. Marchi won four of the five boroughs, while Lindsay won in Manhattan, by nearly 4 to 1. Both of Lindsay's running mates, Fiorvante Perrotta and Sanford Garelik, defeated the Marchi slate.

On the Democratic side, the race came down to the two most conservative candidates: Procaccino versus Wagner. Procaccino finished first, with 255,000 votes; Wagner came in a close second with 224,000 votes. Badillo, running as a strong liberal, came in third, with 217,000 votes. Norman Mailer managed to pull in only 41,000 votes, while James Scheuer received 39,000. Thus, the plain-talking Italian neighborhood politician who had made crime in the streets his number one campaign issue would represent New York's Democratic Party in November. Procaccino had won only 33 percent of the vote and was now the head of the ticket of a very divided Democratic Party. In addition to repudiating the city's liberals, Procaccino's victory ended the political career of Robert Wagner, who made a strong showing but ultimately could not convince voters that he was capable of bringing the city back from the brink of destruction. Many no doubt were still convinced that he had helped put the city there in the first place.[55]

The primary vote in both the Democratic and Republican Parties demonstrated the ethnic and racial divisions that were then tearing the city apart. Pollster Louis Harris noted that "at the heart of the Lindsay and Badillo vote were the young people and affluent voters, along with blacks and Puerto Ricans. The heart of the Marchi-Procaccino vote was the older voters, less well-educated." Lindsay won every assembly district in Manhattan, winning nearly 78 percent of the vote in his home borough. Of the fourteen other districts won by Lindsay, all but one were predominantly black or Puerto Rican, the exception being the Jewish Kew Gardens area of Queens. Marchi even defeated Lindsay in middle-class Jewish neighborhoods like Riverdale in the Bronx, Forest Hills and Rego Park in Queens, and Flatbush and Midwood in Brooklyn.[56]

In the Democratic primary, Procaccino, as expected, won 67 percent of the Italian vote. He won pluralities in four of five city boroughs and thirty-one of the city's sixty-eight assembly districts, twelve of them heavily Italian districts like Bensonhurst, Brooklyn, South Ozone Park and Howard Beach, Queens, and his home turf of East Bronx. But Procaccino also won some heavily Jewish areas like Riverdale in the Bronx and Flatbush, Midwood, Borough Park, and Sheepshead Bay in Brooklyn. Postelection surveys had Procaccino winning 27 percent of the Jewish vote. Badillo's strong showing (he won twenty-six districts) was based on his winning all but two Manhattan districts, plus every black and Puerto Rican district in the city. Badillo won 53 percent of the black vote and 88 percent of the Puerto Rican vote. Surprisingly, Badillo also won roughly 22 percent of the Jewish vote, most of those coming from liberal reform voters in Manhattan. Wagner won roughly 37 percent of the Jewish vote and most of the eleven districts he won were in heavily Jewish neighborhoods. But his margin of victory in these areas was small. The fissure of the Jewish vote was now readily apparent, as liberal (Badillo), moderate (Wagner), and conservative (Procaccino) Democrats all found that their message had resonance among different sectors of the Jewish community.[57]

One factor especially irritating to liberals was the margin of Badillo's loss. Many liberals blamed Mailer for taking votes away from Badillo and allowing Procaccino to win. "So for practical purposes," Badillo said in 1988, "he [Mailer] is responsible for the election, because if I had gotten these 41,000 votes, I would have won. And I would have been mayor." After the primary, James Wechsler, a Badillo supporter, voiced the same frustration with Mailer. "On the morning after [the primary], one man who must have felt peculiarly foolish and frustrated was Norman Mailer," wrote Wechsler. "Surely nearly all of the 41,136 votes Mailer polled would have gone to Herman Badillo if he had pulled out; they would have been sufficient to carry the night for the Bronx insurgent." Mailer admitted after the primary vote that had he known Badillo would do so well, he "might have hesitated about running."[58]

As for Lindsay, he had not expected to win. Dick Aurelio and Alex Rose both told him privately that he would not pull off a primary victory. Still, the loss angered the proud mayor. "My own defeat at the polls was the first one I had ever taken in public life," wrote Lindsay later, "and it stung." Deputy Mayor Robert Sweet put it more bluntly, saying the mayor "was just genuinely hurt by the primary. Pissed." So angry was Lindsay after his defeat that, according to Peter Goldmark, he had "lost faith in everybody."[59]

Though calm on the outside, Lindsay was boiling on the inside and it caused him to utter words he would later regret. At a press conference the day after the primary, the mayor told reporters that "the forces of reaction and fear have captured both major parties. These parties have been captured by the very forces of hatred, fear, and negativism." His two opponents, he said, had appealed to "built-in bigotry" and hopefully the city would soon come to its senses and "reject this kind of ugliness . . . and they will reject this horrendous appeal to the most base instincts that human beings sometimes have." Lindsay then warned other Republicans not to "join forces with the ultra right." Both Marchi and Procaccino denied that they were out of the political mainstream. Procaccino described himself as a "moderate and progressive Democrat."[60]

Although Marchi and Procaccino rejected Lindsay's descriptions, others agreed with Lindsay. The *Post* said that the Marchi and Procaccino victories "corroborate the view that reaction is the order of the day and liberalism is in disorganized retreat." The *Times* called Marchi's win a victory for "the most reactionary forces" in the Republican Party, while Procaccino's victory was "a disgrace to the Democratic party and its liberal traditions." The *Times* accused the Procaccino campaign of having "an unmistakably racist overtone." The mayor received a telegram from his friend and fellow liberal Republican, Washington's Governor Daniel Evans, who "was deeply distressed to see results of last night's mayoralty primary in New York. It's obvious that the forces of reaction and hate are with us and that it's going to take some wise heads and some real courage to stand against these forces."[61]

Lindsay gave the distinct impression that he was calling New York voters bigots because they did not vote for him. Later, he called his comments a "mistake" and realized the implication of his remarks was that "New Yorkers who had chosen the primary winners were somehow racists and bigots, a statement neither politically smart nor in any way true on the merits." Yet the statement was in keeping with the way Lindsay ran both his 1965 campaign and the 1966 campaign for the Civilian Complaint Review Board. Even as he warned New Yorkers to stay away from candidates who preached fear, Lindsay would not shy away from using fear and stereotypes to damage his opponents in the general election.[62]

William F. Buckley denied that the primary vote was evidence of a "racial backlash," arguing that there "was not a hint of racism" in the campaign of the Republican Marchi. Rather, Marchi's appeal lay in his understanding that "first things come first and the very first thing in America today, whether in the dark streets of the ghetto areas or in the sunny quadrangles, is—order. Stability." In its postelection analysis, the *Post* agreed. A survey by the paper's reporters concluded: "Middle-income voters from all groups seemed to feel that the Lindsay Administration had threatened their stability—with its policies on police, schools, garbage collection, snow removal, taxation."[63]

Nixon called his aide, H. R. Haldeman, late on the night of the New York primary to tell him to wire congratulations to Lindsay. Haldeman then checked to see if Lindsay had actually won the primary. When he found that Lindsay had lost, Haldeman called Nixon back with the news. Nixon "was amazed," wrote Haldeman, "and, I think, pleased." Two days after the primary, President Nixon endorsed John Marchi, but said he would avoid campaigning. "The American people in our cities, in our small towns and in this country are fed up to here with violence and lawlessness," the president said. "And they want candidates who will take a strong stand against it." Moynihan summed up his appraisal of Lindsay's defeat in a memo to Nixon: "Voter disappointment in and rejection of a man like Lindsay" occurred not because of the mayor's programs to help the poor and racial minorities, "but because these programs have overpromised so much and delivered so little. They *have* been badly designed. They *have* been poorly administered. They *have* had more than their share of fraud and corruption." Finally, Moynihan concluded, "the truth of the matter is that Lindsay as mayor has turned in at most an indifferent performance." Regarding the fall campaign, Nixon wrote to John Ehrlichman in September: "Be sure we are *hands off in this race* as far as support for him [Lindsay] is concerned." Nixon put out an order that would, in the words of his aide Alexander Butterfield, "put an immediate freeze on the various kinds of silly ventures we've been asked to undertake in Mayor Lindsay's behalf."[64]

Vice President Spiro Agnew said he would not follow New York's Republican Senators Jacob Javits and Charles Goodell in supporting Lindsay over Marchi, saying he felt the senators were not "representative of the party in New York State." An angry Lindsay called Agnew after the primary to protest Agnew's statement of nonsupport. The mayor had, after all, seconded Agnew's nomination in Miami the previous summer, a move Jimmy Breslin called "a spit at all of us in New York." Agnew, though, felt no strong loyalty to Lindsay because of the tepidness of Lindsay's seconding speech. Rockefeller chose to follow Nixon and Agnew and not support Lindsay. In his statement, the governor never mentioned Marchi by name, repeated his claim that Lindsay had been his personal choice for mayor, and said he would not actively campaign in the mayoral race. For Rockefeller it was a tough choice. As jealous of, and irritated by, Lindsay as he was, the forces represented by Marchi were as hostile to the governor as they were to Lindsay. In addition, Kentucky Congressman Rogers Morton, the Republican national chairman, threw his support to Marchi, as did New York Republican Chairman Charles Lanigan. Despite these developments, Lindsay publicly stated that he had no desire to leave the Republican Party. "I've been an enrolled Republican all my life," the mayor said, "and I intend to stay a Republican."[65]

The Lindsay campaign was surprised at Procaccino's win, believing that its Democratic opponent in November would be Robert Wagner. "I had a team working on a strategy to move very fast after the primary to challenge Wagner," remembers Aurelio. Wagner did not seem to worry Lindsay and Aurelio. Their strategy would have been a repeat of the 1965 campaign. "We had ads already drafted . . . bringing back all the bad memories of the Wagner years," said Aurelio. "We had a montage of headlines during the Wagner years all set up." Just as in 1965, Aurelio wanted "to picture Lindsay as the new force."[66]

Many Democrats too were surprised at Procaccino's victory. Democrats were in disarray and some expressed disgust with the nominee. Robert Wagner, in his postelection comments, called Procaccino an "awful choice." Though he believed that Lindsay's mayoralty had been "awful," Wagner said, "imagine it under Procaccino!" Prominent liberals talked of entering the race in November as independents. Manhattan reform Councilman Robert Low, Manhattan Congressman William Fitts Ryan, Badillo, and labor mediator Theodore Kheel were all considered possible candidates. When the final votes were counted in the Democratic race for comptroller, Hugh Carey, who was originally called the winner, lost the race to the incumbent, Francis X. Smith, Procaccino's running mate. Carey, a longtime Kennedy ally, refused a recount because he did not want to run on the Procaccino ticket. Facing a dilemma on whom he should support now that Wagner was out of the race, Carey said the 1969 election would be "a real Hobson's choice—an incompetent liberal Republican, an inexperienced Conservative Republican, and an unimaginative Conservative Democrat." One week after the primary, Carey announced he was running for mayor as an independent candidate, but he soon dropped his plans. The liberal journalist Jack Newfield, who had been one of those who had prodded Norman Mailer to run for mayor (and later had a falling out with the candidate), called the primary election a "night for cops and cabbies to crow." With no liberal in the race, Newfield looked to Lindsay. If Lindsay did not win reelection, Newfield warned, "people will start shooting each other in the street in this city"—as if they weren't already.[67]

The conservative Nixon aide Patrick Buchanan was gleeful at Lindsay's defeat. In a memo to Nixon, Buchanan called Marchi's victory "a permanent blow to the Dewey-Rockefeller, Eastern Liberal Establishment coalition." Lindsay's loss meant the weakening of any critique of the President from the Republican left. With Lindsay's defeat, Buchanan believed that the party would "witness the unveiling of the true John V. Lindsay," since he was no longer inhibited by even a partial need to placate his Republican constituents. Buchanan correctly predicted that "Lindsay's advisers and the mayor himself are now *unleashed* to go where their predilections would lead them—and that is to the left, to attempt to assume leadership within New York of the anti-ABM [antiballistic missile deployment], anti-Vietnam, McCarthy-Kennedy-Lindsay, Ripon Republican and DSG Democratic forces in New York—and if the mayor can pull it off in November—to assume their leadership in the country." In light of this, Nixon's decision to support Marchi in the general election was the right one according to Buchanan. The *National Review* echoed Buchanan's sentiments about Lindsay's defeat, saying there was "no place for him in the national Republican Party of the 1970s. . . . Whatever happens in November, Lindsay has been consigned to the Republican equivalent of Elba."[68]

If Lindsay was angry at his rejection by fellow Republicans, there was a silver lining in the defeat. After the November election, when a reporter asked Aurelio how the Lindsay team had managed to win the election, the campaign chief responded, "First we had to lose the Republican primary." Freed from the need to cater to conservative Republican voters, the mayor could pursue a more liberal course. "The only way we were going to win it," says Aurelio, "was to remain true to our principles." That would happen by running as a third-party candidate, not beholden to either major party. Though left to run without the Republican line, Lindsay remained on the November ballot on the Liberal Party line. In addition, in August Lindsay formed a new "urban party"—the Independent Party of New York City—which would only exist for the November election and have only one candidate: John V. Lindsay.

DEMOCRATIC DEFECTIONS

Immediately after the primary, Aurelio, with the help of Ronnie Eldridge, a reform Democrat from Manhattan's West Side, began to coordinate the endorsement of Lindsay by liberal Democrats. "We went on a rampage," says Aurelio. "We saw an opportunity to orchestrate a scenario that exploited the divisions in the Democratic Party before they had an opportunity to unify." They spread out the deliberate steady stream of endorsements to make it appear as if there was a slow leakage of support away from Procaccino. The Procaccino campaign did not possess the political acumen to stem the tide.

In August, the New Democratic Coalition, a club that had been formed by former aides to Robert Kennedy and Eugene McCarthy, endorsed Lindsay. The Lindsay campaign's biggest fear was that Herman Badillo would run as an independent and attract liberal Democrats who were beginning to gravitate toward Lindsay for want of a better alternative. By the end of July, however, Badillo threw his support to Lindsay, calling Procaccino "a very dangerous man." Lindsay also received the support of four Manhattan reform Democrats: Assemblyman Albert Blumenthal, State Senator Manfred Ohrenstein, Assemblyman Andrew Stein, and City Council candidate Carter Burden. By the middle of August, twenty-one Democratic clubs had endorsed Lindsay.[69]

More endorsements soon followed. Brooklyn Congresswoman Shirley Chisolm endorsed Lindsay. "It was impossible for me to support Procaccino," the black Congresswoman later wrote. "His background, his statements, and his speeches gave black voters every reason to suspect that he was hostile to them. He seemed cut from the same cloth as the Republican nominee, a reactionary in the strict sense of the word." In mid-October, Lindsay won the backing of former Supreme Court Justice Arthur Goldberg, a leading reform Democrat and prominent voice in New York's Jewish community.[70]

Early polls had Procaccino leading both Lindsay and Marchi. Despite the party-crossing endorsements for Lindsay, many prominent Democrats still supported Procaccino. Staten Island Congressman John Murphy and Brooklyn Congressman Emmanuel Celler backed the comptroller, and the PBA head, John Cassese, quit his job to work for him. In the late summer, former City Council President Paul Screvane, former Postmaster General and Democratic National Committee Chairman James Farley, former Comptroller Lawrence Gerosa, Bronx State Senator Abraham Bernstein, Staten Island Attorney General John Braisted, and Harlem Assemblymen Hulan Jack and Mark Southall all endorsed Procaccino. Harry Van Arsdale, the head of the Central Labor Council, also endorsed him. Screvane called Lindsay "the most inept Mayor in my memory," and Farley called him "one of the worst Mayors the city ever had." As the fall began, Democratic State Chairman John Burns moved into Procaccino headquarters to coordinate the campaign's efforts to build Democratic support.[71]

Some Democrats were quick not to jump on the Lindsay bandwagon. Jimmy Breslin agreed with Pete Hamill's idea that New York liberals should make Lindsay declare himself a Democrat before they threw their support to him. Breslin wrote: "He needs us a lot more than he ever thought he would when he was in Miami last summer. . . . If Lindsay wants us so bad, let him come over and put in with us." One prominent Democrat, Manhattan Congressman Ed Koch, said he could not support the mayor, despite the fact that Koch's political club, the Village Independent Democrats, had earlier voted to endorse Lindsay. Koch called Lindsay's first term "pretty disastrous." This did not mean he would endorse or vote for either Marchi or Procaccino. In fact, Koch admitted he would "probably vote for Lindsay."[72]

The roots of Koch's disillusionment ran deep. After the 1965 election, Lindsay called Koch to thank him for his endorsement: "Ed, I'll never forget what you did." When a position on the City Council opened in 1966, Koch ran for it against the Republican Woodward Kingman. Koch had hoped, in return for his endorsement of Lindsay in 1965, that the mayor would back him for the Council or at least stay neutral in the race. Lindsay didn't and backed Kingman. But Koch defeated Kingman anyway.[73]

In 1968, Koch decided to run for Lindsay's old Silk Stocking congressional seat. His opponent was another liberal Republican WASP, Whitney North Seymour. When Koch found out that Lindsay was endorsing Seymour, he went to City Hall to talk to the mayor. When Lindsay admitted that he was supporting Seymour, Koch pulled out the front page of the *Daily News* from the day before the 1965 election, which featured Koch's endorsement of Lindsay. "Maybe you don't remember this," Koch told Lindsay, "but a lot of people do." Koch later called the incident "the end of any civility between me and John Lindsay." Koch went on to victory and Lindsay earned an enemy for the rest of his career. Years later, Mary Lindsay speculated on Koch's intense dislike for her husband: "Why is there antipathy between Koch and John? Jealousy. John's attractive and sexy; he's neither."[74]

THE "PERRY COMO OF POLITICS"

While Lindsay and Procaccino were battling over Democratic support, the Republican, John Marchi, who was running on both the Republican and Conservative Party lines, was generally agreed to be running in third place. His campaign had relatively little money and was poorly run. Marchi's campaign was built around the "forgotten New Yorker," a small-scale spinoff of Nixon's "silent majority" rhetoric. He wanted to appeal to the "decent, law-abiding citizen who recognizes his responsibility to his neighbors, his fellow citizens, and his community. Yet because he isn't part of a special interest or pressure group, he has been ignored and forgotten by the professional politicians and playboy politicians at City Hall."

The *New York Times* described a Marchi walking tour as a "cerebral experience" as the candidate expressed himself "polysyllabically and abstrusely in involved sentences his audience cannot always follow easily." He refused to pander to voters' wishes if he felt they would make bad policy. When his opponents vowed to protect the 20-cent transit fare and oppose increases in

Blue Cross medical insurance premiums, Marchi said the fare would have to be increased and that if people wanted good medical care, they would have to pay for it. According to Pete Hamill, Marchi "does not accuse voters of bad faith if they disagree with his political ideas. He so far hasn't pandered; he has spoken intelligently about most issues. . . . His temperament is cool, reasoned, even somewhat withdrawn." Marchi gave the impression that he did not *really* want to be mayor. "I can't say that the burning ambition of my life has been to become mayor," he once acknowledged. Despite his good manners on the campaign trail, Marchi occasionally showed flashes of wit and anger. He accused Lindsay of having "delusions of adequacy" and once called Jacob Javits, a fellow Republican, a "pompous, posturing ass."[75]

A Lindsay campaign memo described Marchi as "calm and quiet to the point of being dull. He never loses his temper and the only thing to get a rise out of him is to impugn his integrity as he feels that his ethics are above reproach. He is politically naive and assumes that everyone is motivated by the best of intentions. His strong European background has left him with old-world views on such matters as family and religion." The memo concluded that Marchi "has no guts for a fight." The Lindsay campaign even sent someone to Italy to research Marchi's family's background and search for any Mafia ties. (They found none.)[76]

Marchi's campaign had many problems: his lackluster style, the widespread belief that a vote for Marchi (instead of Procaccino) was a vote for Lindsay; the fact that his presence on the Conservative line scared off many Jewish voters; and that he was splitting the Italian vote with Procaccino. Though both men were Italian Americans, they could not have been more different. Marchi, born and raised in Staten Island, was the son of an Italian immigrant from the Tuscan town of Lucca in northern Italy. His father was a sculptor who made movie sets in Hollywood before moving to Staten Island and starting a company that manufactured wax fruit. Marchi was a composed and scholarly man whose style contrasted with that of the earthy and voluble Italian peasants from the Mezzogiorno, the area of Italy south of Rome. Many Italians thought Marchi (pronounced "Markey") was Irish, not Italian. Marchi was fluent in standard Italian, but that did him little good when he was campaigning in New York's Italian neighborhoods, where most Italian speakers spoke a dialect that bore little resemblance to standard Italian. In some ways, Marchi was as foreign to most ethnic New Yorkers as Lindsay. He was a northern Italian among New York's heavily southern Italian population and lived in the bucolic Ward Hill section of Staten Island, miles away from the mean streets of Brooklyn or the Bronx. In addition, Marchi attacked the Mafia hard during the campaign, calling on Lindsay to renounce the support of Anthony Scotto—the leader of the 9,000-man Brooklyn dockworkers' Local 1814 and the vice president of the International Longshoremen's Association, who was suspected of having ties to the Carlo Gambino crime family— and backing an investigation of the Mafia's effects on crime in New York. This aggressive stance toward the Mafia further alienated Italian Americans who were already sensitive to any links between their ethnicity and organized crime.

RUNNING ON THE RECORD

During the 1965 campaign, Lindsay had spent the entire summer walking the city, showing his handsome face to star-struck New Yorkers, towering over them with both his soaring promises and his six-foot-three frame. But 1969 was different. He still occasionally went on walking tours of city neighborhoods and traveled to the Jewish resorts of the Catskills, but the visits were fewer and they lacked the verve and excitement of the earlier campaign. One middle-aged woman at a Queens swimming pool was asked what she thought of the mayor. "He's gorgeous," she replied. But when asked whether she would vote for him, she said no. Others would vote for him again, but without the illusion that he would cure the ills of the city. For those who planned to stick with Lindsay, he was merely a good and decent man who meant well: the lesser of three evils. The boos and jeers seemed louder than four years earlier. It hurt Lindsay, as it would any man. Pete Hamill described the mayor before a Brooklyn synagogue: "The eyes were holding back, wary at last, the eyes of a man afraid of being hurt." Some in the campaign began to complain about Lindsay's halfhearted campaigning. "He has this Ted Williams complex," one aide said. "A thousand people cheer him and he only hears the two guys booing—then he gets uptight and blows the whole thing."[77]

To convince voters to reelect him on a third-party ticket, Lindsay tried to run on his first-term record. Shortly after Lindsay's primary defeat, Peter Goldmark outlined what he believed the campaign strategy should be. Lindsay had run the city "O.K." and learned from his mistakes. While he might not draw the line on crime as far as some people might like, he was firm on crime. Goldmark believed voters would buy this; other aides were less optimistic. In response to the mayor's question about how the city's crime rate compared with that of other large cities, Jay Kriegel wrote that New York's "competitive position is *not* very good." Of the ten largest American cities, New York had the fourth-highest crime rate per capita and the sixth-highest increase in crime for the first three months of 1969. "Consequently," Kriegel advised Lindsay, "we should avoid any discussion of our crime rate compared to that of other cities."[78]

To emphasize Lindsay's successes as mayor, the campaign released a six-page list of accomplishments. Aurelio grandly called it "the most impressive record of a first-term mayor in the City's history." Though crime had dramatically increased in Lindsay's four years, the mayor extolled his "fourth platoon" system, which had added an extra platoon of patrolmen during high-crime hours. During his first term, Lindsay added 5,500 officers to the force and moved more police from behind the desk to the streets. Under Lindsay, New York became the first city to install a 911 system. Walkie-talkies, a computer dispatch system, and motor scooters were also part of Lindsay's plan. Still, such improvements had had little effect on the crime rate.

In some areas Lindsay deserved credit: air-conditioning the subways, balancing four budgets, reducing sulfur dioxide pollution, bringing movie production back to the city, reorganizing city agencies, building forty-four mini-pools and over forty vest-pocket recreation areas, creating the Urban Action Task Forces, gaining more state and federal aid to the city, and implementing the Program Planning Budget System.

Some projects, though, had never gotten off the ground, such as the building of twelve new subway lines or the reopening of the Brooklyn Navy Yard. Other claims, like the licensing of home repairmen under the heading "Protecting the Tax Dollar" and the public education campaign on "the ten simple steps they [New Yorkers] should take to prevent burglaries," were downright silly. Some accomplishments were more ambiguous, like the claim that city expenditures for education increased 60 percent and that city teachers were now the highest paid in the country. Little was said about the quality of education and no mention was made of decentralization or community control. In housing, Lindsay's accomplishments were rightly downplayed. In the 1965 campaign, Lindsay had promised to add 160,000 new apartments in his first term. But by one estimate, fewer than 9,000 new units of public-financed housing were built between 1965 and 1970, and some of those were units that had been in the pipeline from the Wagner administration. Despite a low vacancy rate and a good economy, the construction of privately financed housing declined from ninety-three buildings with 13,000 units in 1963 to five buildings with 1,154 units in 1968. In addition, between 1965 and 1968, the city lost between 50,000 and 100,000 apartments to abandonment and decay and continued to lose an estimated 20,000 units per year after that. Most of these units were in the poverty-ridden stretches of Harlem, the South Bronx, and central Brooklyn.[79]

In 1969, most New Yorkers probably would not buy Lindsay's claims to having made great changes in city government. They could see dirty streets and read about increasing crime. Poor people knew their neighborhoods were getting worse, despite new programs and increased sensitivity. Thus, the Lindsay campaign wisely moved away from touting its accomplishments and instead focused on a more politically realistic campaign theme. New York was a tough city to govern, Lindsay argued, and the late sixties were a tough time to be mayor. Despite the strain, tensions, and limited resources, Lindsay had done the best that he could in holding the city together and articulating a progressive and humanitarian direction for the city. He may have made mistakes, but so would any other politician given the same circumstances. It may not have been a grand platform to run on, but it was Lindsay's best shot.

MEA CULPA, MEA CULPA

The major criticism of the mayor was that he was arrogant and aloof and that he did not care about the vast swath of New York east of the East River and north of the Harlem River. In 1965, people had voted for him because he was tall, good-looking, patrician, and seemingly so much better than they were. In 1965, many New Yorkers felt it would be an honor to be represented by John Lindsay. By 1969, as Jimmy Breslin noted, short and squat New Yorkers had had enough of tall.

Coming off mistakes like the failure to clean up after the snowstorm, the Ocean Hill-Brownsville debacle, and the rejection by voters of the Civilian Complaint Review Board, Lindsay would, said Aurelio, have to "show a humility and willingness to acknowledge that he might have made some mistakes in the process. . . . The arrogance had to come down."[80]

Aurelio hired the advertising firm Young & Rubicam to create the mayor's ad campaign. As in 1965, money would not be a problem for the campaign, given Lindsay's strong support among the city's financial elite. But Aurelio did not share Bob Price's faith in retail campaigning and citywide storefronts. Instead, the 1969 campaign would be a thoroughly modern one, utilizing polling and marketing techniques to identify likely voters and their opinions. Most important, it would aggressively use television ads to showcase the attractive candidate. Young & Rubicam's Tony Isadore, who had created the Urban Coalition's "Give a Damn" campaign, was in charge of media. The campaign's theme would be "It's the second-toughest job in America."

Lindsay's ample campaign funds allowed him to go on the airwaves often. Some of the ads touted Lindsay's accomplishments, such as the commuter tax, reduced air pollution, and the plan for a fourth police platoon to battle crime. Others were designed to show Lindsay as a regular guy who cared about the outer boroughs. One of these featured the legendary baseball announcer Red Barber and members of the old Brooklyn Dodgers telling voters how Lindsay cared about Brooklyn and how he was trying to reopen the Brooklyn Navy Yard. Another featured Jimmy Breslin inside a Queens apartment talking about how Lindsay supported the tenant over the landlord. Another reinforced Lindsay's opposition to the Vietnam War. It featured a young man getting on a bus, obviously heading for basic training. As the bus heads off down the street, fading to a point on the horizon, Lindsay says in a voice-over, "New Yorkers send three billion dollars every year into the war and another six billion into the war machine. That's more than the entire city budget. And you and I have to tell them to stop. Because we are not only sending them our money, we're sending them our sons." The most controversial ad showed shots of Newark, New Jersey, burned out after the 1967 riots. Reinforcing in voters' minds the idea of Lindsay's role as a riot stopper, the ad told New Yorkers to take a trip across the Hudson River to see what New York had avoided with Lindsay as its mayor.

The most well known Lindsay ad was the "I made mistakes" one. In his 1969 book *The City,* Lindsay said he believed the ad "let New Yorkers know that their grievances *had* been heard, that their discontents were understood. The simple willingness to say 'that was a mistake' had a kind of cleansing effect on much of the bitterness that had surfaced during the last years; it was kind of a signal that politicians were not beyond the reach of the people." The ad featured a relaxed Lindsay standing on the porch of Gracie Mansion, dressed in shirt sleeves with the top button open. The mayor looked earnestly into the camera and told voters:

> I guessed wrong on the weather before the city's biggest snowfall last winter. And that was a mistake. But I put six thousand more cops on the streets. And that was no mistake.
>
> The school strike went on too long and we all made some mistakes. But I brought 225,000 more jobs to this town. And that was no mistake. And I fought for three years to put a fourth police platoon on the streets. And that was no mistake. And I reduced the deadliest gas in the air by fifty percent. And I forced the landlords to roll back unfair rents. And we did not have a Detroit, a Watts, or Newark. And those were no mistakes.
>
> The things that go wrong are what make this the second-toughest job in America. But the things that go right are those things that make me want it.

Lindsay was not a completely willing subject for this experiment in humility. David Garth had to beg Lindsay to put some feeling into his reading of the ad. "Garth was groveling all over the steps of Gracie Mansion. Lindsay couldn't believe it," one observer said.[81]

Contrary to what many people thought, Lindsay never said "I made a mistake." Instead he said "that was a mistake," regarding his handling of the February snowstorm, and "we all made some mistakes," regarding the schools strikes. The ad was a clever sleight of hand. It gave people the impression that Lindsay had apologized, but allowed the proud mayor to avoid actually saying he had made a mistake. In fact, the word "mistake" appeared six times in the ad, but four of those times the word was uttered in relation to a Lindsay accomplishment ("and that was no mistake"). Even if some things did go wrong, Lindsay reminded voters, being mayor of New York City was "the second-toughest job in America."

BRINGING THE WAR BACK HOME

John Lindsay had gone on record with his views against the Vietnam War as early as 1965, but his comments then lacked fervency. Gradually, though, the mayor made more speeches critical of the war, especially before college audiences. By the summer of 1969, trailing Procaccino and desperate to attract liberal Democrats, Lindsay decided to "make Vietnam and the distorted national priorities a campaign issue." In June he spoke at an anti-ABM rally at Madison Square Garden, telling the audience that he came as a "witness" to speak "of a city which has felt the full, crippling impact of military force; a city that suffers each day destruction from our armed might. That city is not Berlin. It is not Hiroshima. It is not Hanoi. That city is New York." At an emotional speech on the Lower East Side in September, the mayor called the Vietnam conflict "a war that we should never have fought." Throughout the speech, Lindsay raised his voice, waved his finger in the air, and forcefully thumped the lectern several times to emphasize his anger at the war. Speaking to students at Queens College, Lindsay called the war "the most deadly folly in the history of our foreign policy." Behind the war, said the mayor, "lies one stark, inescapable fact: that New York City—you and I—have become prisoners of war—prisoners of the war in Vietnam." Lindsay tied the war to the urban crisis by arguing that $9 billion of tax money the city sent to Washington went to pay for the war—$3 billion in direct costs and $6 billion to pay for the military apparatus in general. Regardless of the exaggeration in Lindsay's numbers, it was clear that he had found a voice on the campaign trail. Lindsay had brought the war back home.[82]

Lindsay brought the flamboyant antiwar activist Bella Abzug into the campaign. A left-wing Democrat, Abzug formed the Taxpayers Campaign for Urban Priorities, which sought to boost Lindsay among opponents of the war. "Bella was truly a bull in the china shop," remembers Sid Davidoff, who handled Abzug during the campaign. "When Bella calls you, as you're picking up the phone she's already yelling at you. She hasn't identified herself. You don't know what the issue is, but you're hearing her voice on the other end yelling at you." Abzug helped hone the theme that dollars spent to fight the war in Southeast Asia were dollars diverted from much-needed programs in American cities. She also helped make Lindsay credible to left-wing Democrats, a group that, while sympathetic to the mayor on many issues, was reflexively wary because of his Republican affiliation and connections with the city's business elite.[83]

Lindsay tied his campaign even more strongly to the antiwar movement with his participation in the October 15, 1969, Moratorium against the Vietnam War, when numerous antiwar demonstrations were planned throughout the nation. In the city, the mayor marked the day by attending services at St. James' Episcopal Church on Madison Avenue and speaking to crowds throughout the day at New York University, Columbia University, Fordham University, City Hall Plaza, Brooklyn Borough Hall, and a union rally in the Garment District. Standing in front of 500 people outside City Hall, Lindsay flashed the peace sign and told the crowd: "We mark October 15 as a day of mourning for those who have died, a day of inquiry into the roots of the war and the path to peace, a day of hope that the work of death and destruction can be turned to the work of subsistence and a day of conscience." Speaking to an antiwar crowd in Greenwich Village later in the day, Lindsay called the Moratorium "the highest form of patriotism. It is an attempt to turn this nation away from a dangerous, self-defeating cause. . . . Those that charge this is unpatriotic do not know the history of their own nation and they do not understand that our greatness comes from the right to speak out." The mayor criticized the South Vietnamese government as "committed only to its own power and profit." But he leveled no criticism toward either the North Vietnamese government or the Viet Cong. Nor did he mention his own vote as a congressman for the Gulf of Tonkin Resolution, which had set the war in motion.

The mayor marked the occasion by decking out City Hall in black and purple mourning bunting. He also ordered that flags on all municipal buildings be lowered to half-staff. Lindsay later claimed this was meant "to be a measure of respect for those—particularly the families of those who had been killed—who still supported the struggle out of this kind of emotional tie," but the move was inevitably interpreted as a political act against the war. Lindsay later admitted that lowering the flags "produced great hostility among police and firemen in particular." As the City Hall flag was lowered to half-staff, Queens Democratic Councilman Matt Troy climbed to the roof to raise the flag back to full-staff. Shortly thereafter, the flag was lowered again. Despite the reaction, Lindsay felt "it was essential to make some kind of gesture to remind New Yorkers of what the war had done to all of us."

The PBA urged all precinct houses to ignore Lindsay's order and most did. The flag at Police Headquarters in Little Italy was at full-staff until a civilian employee lowered it to half-staff. Minutes later it was restored to full-staff, where it remained for the rest of the day. The leader of the Uniformed Firefighters' Association said that no one had the "right to order us to participate in this voluntary day of national disgrace," and most firehouses also ignored the mayor's order. Some flags in city parks also remained at full-staff. At Game 4 of the World Series at Shea Stadium,

Baseball Commissioner Bowie Kuhn first ordered that the stadium flag fly at half-staff, but then reversed himself. Over two hundred wounded Vietnam veterans from a nearby hospital were guests of the Mets and told reporters they would have physically resisted, wheelchairs and all, any effort to fly the flag at half-staff. The United States Merchant Marine Academy band refused to play the national anthem until the flag was raised.[84]

Lindsay's opponents did not share his enthusiasm for the Moratorium or antiwar protests. John Marchi, a Nixon supporter, denounced Lindsay's use of the war as a campaign issue, accusing the mayor of "plant[ing] a dagger in the back of American servicemen." Regarding the war's influence on the city's problems, Marchi reminded New Yorkers that Fiorello La Guardia had been mayor during "this country's most costly war." Despite this, "La Guardia had the garbage collected. La Guardia had the snow removed; La Guardia worked twelve months a year to see to it that the city functioned, and functioned well." Earlier in the campaign, Marchi had stated his position on the Vietnam War: "You could almost say that I believe in my country, right or wrong." Instead of complete withdrawal, the Republican candidate supported the "de-Americanization of the Vietnam war." On the democratic side, Procaccino repeatedly called the war a "mistake," but denounced Lindsay for turning "the Moratorium into a vulgar display of his own political ambitions."[85]

Lindsay never played up his own experience as a World War II veteran, something that might have eased the bitter feelings caused by his antiwar views. While Lindsay's Vietnam stand may have gained him some short-term support in the November election, it only added to the tensions and divisions in the city.

SEARCHING FOR JEWISH VOTES

Early on, Aurelio decided that the key to the mayor's reelection was the Jewish vote. Though many Jews felt that Lindsay had gone overboard in aiding blacks, Aurelio decided that the "whole thesis of our campaign was to try to appeal to the Jewish consciousness in terms of the minorities. . . . We had to bring back some of the Jews who were not angry at Blacks." Aurelio, an Italian American from Rhode Island, had first been attracted to New York City by the contributions of Jews who helped build New York's progressive politics and cosmopolitan culture. "I always thought it was so great because the Jewish middle class in this city was so sophisticated and so intelligent," said Aurelio. "I still believe New York is the most sophisticated city there is. I don't believe it will succumb to these emotional forces. The Jewish community is susceptible to intelligent argument."[86]

But the Lindsay campaign first had to address some concerns. In the fall of 1969, Lindsay received two letters from the Jewish community of Coney

Island describing the plight of lower-middle-class Jews who lived in a neighborhood with growing numbers of blacks and Puerto Ricans. Rabbi Philip Lefkowitz of the Thirty-first Street Talmud Torah complained that many Jews feared walking to the religious school. Despite attempts by the Jewish community to reach out to the black community with programs for children, it continued to endure attacks on elderly Jews in the neighborhood, anti-Semitic remarks, and the stoning of parents and children on their way to school. Samuel Schamsky, president of Young Israel of Coney Island, noted three recent attacks on the local synagogue. He wrote the mayor: "If under your administration you are unable to provide this needed protection to the Jewish community, we will be obligated for our survival to utilize the help and assistance of the JDL, and other such worthy organizations."[87]

Rabbi Meir Kahane's Jewish Defense League presented a special problem for the Lindsay campaign. Lindsay encountered heckling from JDL members during his appearances in Jewish neighborhoods. Aurelio recalled that Lindsay believed Kahane "was an evil man—a man who was a little crazy." Aurelio had breakfast with Kahane on election day, after which they strolled down Fifth Avenue. Aurelio came to the conclusion that if Lindsay won re-election, there was "no way I was ever going to ever get a reconciliation with him [Kahane]. . . . He was showing every sign of being unstable and unbalanced and hostile beyond reason." Another problem was with the *Jewish Press*, which constantly ran virulently anti-Lindsay editorials written by Kahane. In an effort to quiet the paper, the Lindsay campaign invited its publisher, Sholom Klass, to Gracie Mansion. When the mayor asked Klass for his paper's support, the publisher said many Jews believed the mayor was an anti-Semite. At this, Lindsay stormed out of the meeting. Just as it seemed the meeting would end in a failure, Klass agreed to fire Kahane from the paper if the city provided them with a new building. So a deal was struck: the city leased to the newspaper an old Brooklyn Transit Authority substation for one dollar a year and Klass fired Kahane. [88]

In the summer of 1969, Marvin Berger, the associate publisher of the *New York Law Journal*, wrote to Deputy Mayor Robert Sweet and summarized the mayor's problems within the Jewish community: "The feeling is prevalent that the mayor pays relatively little attention to the middle and lower middle class—largely small homeowners and tenants who can't afford to move to the suburbs but whose way of life is threatened by the real or imagined demands and conditions imposed by the minorities." To win back Jewish voters, Berger suggested that Lindsay appeal "to the decent instincts of the people, asking them not to succumb to racist appeals, reminding them of their unique tradition of helping the poor, the stranger, the helpless—in keeping with the teachings of the prophets, who reminded Jews of their Biblical heritage of social justice."[89]

A big step toward solidifying Lindsay's standing in New York's Jewish community was the fall 1969 visit of Israeli Prime Minister Golda Meir. Her appearance fell during the Jewish holiday of Sukkoth (the Festival of Tabernacles), a Jewish harvest festival that commemorates the flight from ancient Egypt. Lindsay and his aides took a diplomatic appearance and adroitly turned it into a not-so-subtle Lindsay-for-Mayor event. A dinner was set up in Meir's honor at the Brooklyn Museum. An Orthodox rabbi convinced Davidoff that the city's Orthodox community would not attend the dinner if it were held indoors during the holiday. What needed to be built was a *sukkah*, a tentlike structure under which religious Jews would eat during the holiday. Davidoff called Lindsay at Gracie Mansion and told him he would come by later that night to discuss something. At Gracie Mansion, Davidoff explained the holiday to the Lindsays and convinced them that building a *sukkah* was necessary. He knew that Mary Lindsay would be the most difficult to convince. "This is a state dinner," Davidoff said. "You just don't throw a ham sandwich down. You have to really plan this thing." But both John and Mary went along with the idea. The event would appeal to all Jews, from the most secular to the most orthodox. To build the *sukkah*, Davidoff had the help of the Lubavitcher and Satmar communities, ultrareligious groups that normally did not speak to each other. Yeshiva students from across the city decorated the structure.

Twelve hundred guests, including John Marchi and Mario Procaccino, attended the dinner. Some accused the mayor of playing politics with the holiday celebration. Davidoff noted years later, "One thing in the campaign that turned the tide was Golda Meir." By agreeing to attend such an event, the prime minister "clearly was saying that it was in the Israeli interest to have John Lindsay as Mayor." The comedian Victor Borge, a guest at the dinner, joked, "Mrs. Meir and Mr. Mayor, you both have something in common. You're both running for reelection and you're both dependent on the Jewish vote. Particularly you, Mr. Mayor." Lindsay, in his toast to Meir, said that everyone in the room had one message: "We stand with Israel." In a city where the proverbial three *I*'s (Israel, Italy, and Ireland) rule politics, Lindsay hoped that one out of three would be enough to guarantee his reelection.[90]

PROCACCINO VERSUS THE BEAUTIFUL PEOPLE

Another aspect of the Lindsay campaign's strategy was to make Mario Procaccino look bad. "We want him to make a fool of himself," was how Lindsay aides described this strategy. Sid Davidoff later admitted, "We played him [Procaccino] as really a bad guy. That's life. He's a caricature of himself." Rarely has a candidate so badly hurt his own chances. The Lindsay people played up the fact that Procaccino had a permit to carry a gun, insinuating dark motives to this fact. When Democratic Councilman J.

Raymond Jones, the "Harlem Fox" who had run Tammany Hall earlier in the decade, endorsed Lindsay for mayor, he condemned the Procaccino campaign as "antiblack" and called the candidate a "coward" for not freeing himself from its supposed racist appeals. The accusations of racism, and especially the "coward" charge, enraged Procaccino. Rather than take the advice of his aides and ignore the attacks, he took them personally. Six days after the Jones comments, Procaccino held a news conference to counter the charges of racism. Standing with approximately thirty campaign aides and three black supporters, including Assemblymen Hulan Jack and Mark Southall, Procaccino demanded that his accusers—Lindsay, Jones, and Senator Charles Goodell—name the racists on his staff. Brimming with anger, Procaccino pointed to his assembled aides and asked, "Which one of these is the racist? Which one is the bigot?" If Lindsay did not prove his accusations of racism within twenty-four hours, Procaccino warned, he would ask the State Division of Human Rights to investigate Lindsay's "vicious, inflammatory and dangerous accusations." Procaccino was losing his cool. A Lindsay aide said that Procaccino was "in over his head and he's proving it. We just never dreamed he would begin over-reacting . . . this early in the campaign."[91]

One journalist believed that Procaccino's weakness had to do with "his virtual isolation until recently in an Italian-American milieu and the recollection of real and imagined slights of earlier days." Yet despite losing the war in the media, Procaccino still excelled in the old-style politics. Whenever he campaigned, he was greeted with an emotionalism equal to his own. Preceding the candidate's arrival, sound trucks boomed, "Mario, son of a shoemaker. He came up the hard way, just like you and me." Procaccino told a crowd of cabdrivers, a natural constituency, that the "day is coming when the working people will run this city again."[92]

Procaccino's popular appeal showed that Lindsay's problems were caused not so much by a racial backlash as by class and ethnic friction. One Brooklyn resident complained of the lack of respect shown toward to blue-collar whites: "The liberals and the press look down on hard hats like me, but we've invested everything we have in this house and neighborhood. . . . The rich liberals, they look down on my little piece of the American dream, my little backyard with the barbecue here." Bob Laird noted how the campaign came to realize too late that "every single picture of John Lindsay in black tie at a Broadway opening or the opera . . . was just another nail in his political coffin in those communities. They weren't going to the opera. They weren't going to Broadway openings. They weren't hobnobbing with Hollywood stars. And we were just rubbing it in their face. Lindsay was just being himself." Procaccino lashed out at Lindsay as "a swinger in the city." The term "swinger" elicited thoughts not only of the upper-class socialite but also carried the connotation of the sexual libertine. Procaccino also took to calling the mayor "the actor."[93]

Perhaps the greatest contribution Procaccino made to American political history was to coin the term "limousine liberal." As William Safire defines the term, a limousine liberal is "one who takes up hunger as a cause but has never felt a pang; who will talk at length about the public school system but sends his children to private schools." Procaccino also spoke of the "Manhattan arrangement," which encapsulated the belief held by many that liberal well-to-do Manhattanites were making decisions that affected outer-borough whites. One Procaccino campaign memo urged the candidate to discuss "the dangerous precedent of putting together the discontented, the young, the poor which will be squeezing the middle class." Another campaign memo lashed out at the city's papers for supporting Lindsay and suggested that Procaccino attack the papers' owners, "rich super-assimilated people who live on Fifth Avenue and maintain some choice mansions outside the city and have no feeling for the small middle class shopkeeper, home owner, etc. They preach the politics of confrontation and condone violent upheaval in society because they are not touched by it and are protected by their courtiers, doormen, and private police guards."[94]

It only reinforced the idea that Lindsay was one of the "Beautiful People" when his campaign held a star-studded fund-raising gala in October called "Who's That With John Lindsay?" A separate *Times* ad in support of Lindsay read like a who's who of the worlds of acting (Alan Arkin, Eli Wallach), music (Diahann Carroll, Judy Collins, Richard Rodgers, Frank Sinatra), arts and letters (George Plimpton, I. M. Pei, John Kenneth Galbraith, Arthur Schlesinger), and sports (Rocky Graziano, Willis Reed, and the Mets' Ron Swoboda and Ed Kranepool).[95]

Time magazine asked each campaign for a list of prominent supporters. Lindsay's list included people like Leonard Bernstein, Dustin Hoffman, Bill Blass, Bennett Cerf, and Gloria Steinem. Even John Marchi had a few celebrity supporters, including John Wayne and Lionel Hampton. By contrast, Procaccino's list was filled with New York clubhouse politicians and old-style labor leaders. The only celebrity the Procaccino campaign could claim was the singer Alan Dale. With his pencil-thin mustache, pink shirts, malaprops, and emotional delivery, Procaccino would never be taken for one of the Beautiful People. [96]

The Lindsay campaign had to convince New Yorkers that "all the right people" were with Lindsay while all the wrong people were with Marchi and Procaccino. This had always been a major source of Lindsay's appeal. In fact, the same thing that angered some less affluent New Yorkers who saw their "swinging" mayor in black tie and mixing with Manhattan's social elite was exactly what appealed to others who wished they could lead such a life. If they couldn't, at least their mayor could.[97]

Procaccino's sense of insecurity slowly emerged as the campaign rumbled through the fall. The candidate carried around a transcript of his law school grades to show reporters. When reporters asked the law-and-order candidate about the Mafia, he responded, "I don't know any Mafias. I never have and I never will. Don't talk about the Mafia to me because I think it's insulting. . . . There's always a connection to trying to put some Italian name with a Mafia." When criticized for crying at his campaign announcement in the spring, he responded that great men throughout history, like Moses, Jesus, and Joe Namath, had cried in public. When speaking before a black audience, he tried to connect with the audience by saying "My heart is as black as yours." Procaccino padded his résumé, claiming he had graduated with honors from City College (he did not); that he was the editor of the *Fordham Law Review* (he was one of twenty-one members of the editorial board); that he was on the faculty at City College and Fordham (he taught a noncredit evening course for real estate brokers); and that he was president of Verrazano College (a college that did not exist, but was the dream of some Italian-American businessmen).[98]

The race that had been his to lose was slowly falling out of his reach. With his campaign floundering, Procaccino believed he had found an issue that would swing the momentum back his way. At a mid-October television debate, Procaccino accused Lindsay of putting young men with criminal records on the city payroll. If true, such an accusation would put specifics to the accusation that Lindsay was trying to buy racial peace in the city's ghettos. Procaccino's charge was based on an internal police department memo that named seven young men who operated the Malcolm X Cultural Center in Corona, Queens, where they worked "with hard core youths of the area in an attempt to make them useful citizens." Six of the men received $100 a week, and the director received $150 a week. The memo charged that the money, as well as the rent for the storefront, came from a city program and was administered by mayoral aides Barry Gottehrer and Sid Davidoff. One of the youths, Fred Fernandez, was a member of the Revolutionary Action Movement and had been arrested in 1967 on charges of planning to assassinate moderate civil rights leaders.[99]

The Corona center was one of fourteen "satellite storefronts" throughout the city affiliated with the city's Youth Services Agency, a division of the Human Resources Administration. The program also received private funding from the Urban Coalition and local businesses. During the summer of 1967, Parks Department funds paid the salaries of Fernandez and an associate. In the summer of 1968, the New York Times Foundation contributed $25,000 to the Urban Coalition for funding these programs. In the fiscal year 1968–69, the Youth Services Agency spent $1.2 million on these storefronts. In June 1969, when the storefront centers were brought permanently under HRA, the Malcolm X Center was not included. The reason, according to Gottehrer, was because of "the personnel on the payroll." Gottehrer denied that the mayor's office had anything to do with the Malcolm X Center: "All checks for the salaries and rent for this program have come from the Youth Board Research Institute and are signed by somebody at the Youth Services Agency," wrote Gottehrer. Still, the city had been, in some manner, funding the Malcolm X Center and the other satellite programs.[100]

At first, Lindsay denied the charge. Then he accused Procaccino of making a "Joe McCarthyite shotgun smear." Snake-bit, Procaccino could not get traction out of this issue. Moderate-to-liberal Democrats were turned off by his attacks. Procaccino, lacking the proper finesse to make such accusations stick, merely came off as a bully to the voters he most needed to reassure.[101]

As evidenced by his mishandling of this issue, Procaccino ran a poor campaign. The columnists Rowland Evans and Robert Novak called it "the most inept Democratic mayoralty campaign in modern history." The *Times*'s Richard Reeves wrote that the Procaccino campaign "must rank with the worst in American political history." Part of the problem was that the campaign was a one-man effort. Procaccino, according to the *Post*, "writes or rewrites all his speeches, oversees and frequently does his own scheduling, distributes campaign literature." Though the comptroller was not quite the dunce he was often portrayed as, he was not up to the double duty of being both candidate and campaign manager. He was a decent, but parochial, man. Guided only by his instincts and the traditions of the Bronx Democratic machine, Procaccino stumbled. Though he tried to broaden the campaign to other issues, the candidate inevitably returned to crime. He ran a campaign heavy on raw emotionalism, one-note denunciations of crime, garbled syntax and malaprops, inflated credentials, and a superinflated ego (he regularly referred to himself in the third person), all of which convinced many New Yorkers that Procaccino did not have the stature to represent their city. Abe Beame, running for comptroller, avoided Procaccino during the campaign.[102]

Procaccino ran a campaign right out of the old-time political machines' book. But this was the era of the "New Politics" of image, style, and television savvy. Procaccino could not best Lindsay in this arena. Compounding Procaccino's difficulties was the fact that as reform Democrats were gaining strength, the political bosses were losing much of theirs. Failing to recognize these changes, Procaccino made his biggest error when he refused to go after reform Democrats in those critical days after the June primary. Procaccino's adviser Victor Campione later admitted, "We come from the school that expects all party members to support the primary winner. You don't reach out to them." Unfortunately for Procaccino, that school of politics was as real as Verrazano College.[103]

Despite his weak campaign, Procaccino was also a victim of subtle and not-so-subtle prejudice. When he was elected comptroller in 1965, young, liberal Lindsay aides said with smirks, "What's a Mario Procaccino?" This attitude carried into the campaign. For many New York liberals, Mario Procaccino—from his name to his career in city government right down to his pencil-thin mustache—was the epitome of the ethnic politician. At times, Procaccino was singled out for being Italian American. At a Lindsay fundraiser, Woody Allen told his audience of New York's better classes that Mario Procaccino was probably sitting at home "in his undershirt, drinking beer, and watching Lawrence Welk on television." Such attitudes even infected Ivy League academia. Michael Lerner recalled that shortly after Procaccino announced his mayoral candidacy, a prominent Yale professor said at a dinner party, "If Italians aren't actually an inferior race, they do the best imitation of one I've seen." Everyone at the dinner table laughed. "He could not have said that about black people, if the subject had been Rap Brown," said Lerner. During the campaign, anti-Italian jokes made their way through elite circles. "Do you know that Mario is so confident he's going to be elected mayor," went one joke, "that he's bought a giant pink flamingo for the front lawn of City Hall!" Another joke had Procaccino replacing the rugs at Gracie Mansion with linoleum if elected mayor. Milton Himmelfarb, the editor of *Commentary*, though convinced most of the attacks on Procaccino were based on class differences rather than ethnic bias, wrote after the election, "Italians, especially, must wonder where contempt for class leaves off and prejudice against Italians begins. People who would not dream of telling Negro jokes regale each other with Italian jokes. . . . If I were Italian I might imagine that the humorous liberals are not conspicuously partial to Italians."[104]

ENDORSING LINDSAY

As the Procaccino collapse became more pronounced, the Lindsay endorsements continued. The nonpartisan Citizens Union endorsed the mayor, although it acknowledged that his first term had "not been an unqualified success." Lindsay also received the endorsement of the Transport Workers Union, and even the United Sanitationmen's Association, headed by John DeLury, backed Lindsay. When asked how the union could support Lindsay after the 1968 strike, which had led to his spending two weeks in jail, DeLury responded that though the strike "was a shameful episode in John Lindsay's life . . . we all make mistakes and he has worked hard to remove that blight from his record. He has more than evened the score." After the double embarrassments of the February snowstorm and the primary defeat, Lindsay learned that sanitation had become a surrogate issue for people angry with the mayor and the condition of the city. Soon after the snowstorm fiasco, the mayor had assigned a young budget aide, Steve Isenberg, to be his liaison with the Sanitation Department. "People were saying: If you can't manage this, what can you manage?" remembered Isenberg. So he set out to repair the relationship with DeLury. As the election approached, Lindsay furthered the courtship by promising to hire one thousand additional sanitationmen and give union members more overtime.[105]

Organized labor backed Lindsay thanks in large part to Victor Gotbaum, a liberal union leader who was executive director of District Council 37 of the American Federation of State, County and Municipal Employees. A Chicago native, Gotbaum was an outsider among the city's labor leaders. This made him a kindred spirit with the outsider reform mayor and impervious to the anti-Lindsay feelings of labor leaders like Harry Van Arsdale. Gotbaum brought along the union leader Anthony Scotto, whose involvement in the Lindsay campaign was controversial because Senator John McClellan, chairman of the Senate Subcommittee on Organized Crime, had linked Scotto to the Gambino crime family.[106]

Thus in his second mayoral campaign Lindsay managed to get the labor support he had lacked in 1965, even though, as the labor expert Raymond Horton noted, "Union leaders and high-ranking union officials interviewed in 1968 and 1969 openly expressed strong feelings of personal dislike for the mayor." Horton speculated that both Lindsay and the unions "perceived the utility of a short-run marriage of convenience and then cemented that relationship with public money freely distributed in collective bargaining." In return, these municipal unions kept the city free from damaging strikes. The Transport Workers Union, Uniformed Sanitationmen's Association, and District Council 37 all received generous deals from the city over the next two years. In 1969, the transit workers received an 18 percent wage increase over two years, as well as an extra week of vacation and an agreement that the Transit Authority would pay the entire cost of their pensions. In the same year, the clerical workers represented by District Council 37 received a $6,000 minimum salary and were offered the twenty-year retirement option with pension at age forty-five. (The state legislature later rejected the retirement plan for District Council 37.)[107]

Most interesting was the behavior of the United Federation of Teachers. Al Shanker, a vocal Lindsay opponent, announced his union's neutrality in the 1969 mayoral race. Much of the reason was the union's June 1969 contract, which it was estimated would cost the city between $260 and $400 million over three years. The contract granted a pay raise of 39 percent for teachers at the bottom of the pay scale and 22 percent for those with more experience and credentials. Teachers also received the much-coveted deal that would allow them to retire with a pension at age forty-five, after twenty years of service. When Shanker reported back to his delegates the specifics of the deal he said, "Some of you wondered why it was necessary to stay out so long last fall when there seemed to be no salary or other economic issue involved. Now you know." The motivation for Lindsay's largesse was his need to neutralize the opposition of the mostly Jewish teachers' union if he were to have any hope of smoothing over the bad feelings between himself and the Jewish community and win reelection. But Shanker also needed to make nice with Lindsay. The union leader had badly damaged his liberal image during the strike. Shanker toned down his rhetoric, especially regarding race, and was remarkably subdued in his comments regarding racial tensions, attacks on teachers, and student violence in public schools. He reached out to (some would say co-opted) predominantly black paraprofessionals working in city schools and convinced them to join the UFT. Cutting Lindsay some slack would help Shanker appear magnanimous.[108]

The *Times* endorsed Lindsay in not one, but two editorials, two days apart. Under the heading "Why Vote for Lindsay?" the paper praised Lindsay for improving the city's fiscal position and for preventing major riots. It also lauded his efforts to reach out to the black and Puerto Rican communities. Despite its praise for the mayor, the paper was not blind to the condition of the city in 1969: "Crime is rampant, race relations tense; transportation is archaic, housing inadequate; education is faulty, welfare burdensome; the streets are dirty, the air polluted; prices are high, and so are taxes." Still, Lindsay was an activist mayor who assumed "the burden of national leadership in the fundamental struggle of the cities to make themselves heard and felt in the halls of Congress." Therefore, "the prospects for New York City, and for urban American, would improve with his success," the *Times* said in its second editorial, headlined "Mayor Lindsay, Activist."

The *Post*, too, supported Lindsay: "In proving that he cares [about minorities and the poor], [Lindsay] has been faithful to New York's worthiest liberal traditions." The *Post* saw Lindsay's reelection as the city's "last great chance to vindicate its heritage as a city in which men of good will prevail over prejudice, reason vanquishes mindless violence, and the rule of law derives enduring strength from a sense of justice." Endorsement also came from the *Amsterdam News,* which told black New Yorkers that Lindsay was "an honest, independent man" who "embodies the true spirit of New York City, a city composed of many ethnic groups of varied colors, races and religions." The *Village Voice* endorsed Lindsay as the least of three evils, calling Marchi "unbelievable" and Procaccino "inconceivable." Another reason to vote for Lindsay, in addition to his urban activism, the paper said, was that his vocal antiwar stand made the election a referendum on Vietnam. In the same issue Michael Harrington wrote an article in support of Lindsay titled "More Pros Than Cons." Though complaining of Lindsay's Republican affiliation, his poor relations with labor, and his responsibility for "at least some of the working-class backlash sentiment in this city," Harrington believed a vote for Lindsay was still crucial to avoid backsliding toward reaction. The mayor also received endorsements from the *Long Island Press,* the *Staten Island Advocate, El Tiempo,* and WCBS-TV.[109]

The *Daily News* endorsed John Marchi. It called the state senator a "quiet, unassuming, unpretentious public servant" who refused "to make wild promises," who would cut city spending, who believed "earnestly in law and order with justice," and who would heal "the racial, social, ideological and other divisions which have developed here in the Lindsay years." As for the other candidates, the paper wrote that although Procaccino might make a popular mayor, he was an organization Democrat who would bring back Tammany-style patronage to City Hall. Lindsay, though he had "shown energy and idealism," was too liberal for the *News*, which blamed the mayor for having "greatly increased City Hall spending, largely hamstrung the police, helped split the city's 8 million people into hostile factions, and put too many weirdos into important city jobs."[110]

Procaccino did not receive a single major media endorsement.

Lindsay had managed to turn the anger of the white ethnics to his advantage, not by appealing to their frustrations but instead by playing up his enemies. John Lindsay of the Silk Stocking district could not claim a background or history of privation or persecution, but John Lindsay of Gracie Mansion could. With every cry of "Lindsay, you bum" or "Lindsay, go back to Bedford-Stuyvesant," the mayor became a victim. He was now seen as a noble and decent man cursed by bad luck and set upon by vicious enemies. The underdog story found an especially receptive audience in New York's Jewish community. As one *Village Voice* writer pointed out, "the tale of sorrows of Lindsay the mistake maker begins to sound like a story of persecution. . . . Everyone likes to feel sorry for a schlemiel, and somehow with one simple commercial Lindsay has managed to become a fellow suffering Jew." Even if the streets had grown dirty and dangerous, welfare spending and taxes had increased, and labor strikes and racial tensions had become commonplace, Lindsay was *their* mayor. He meant well. He looked good. He had class. Besides, being mayor was the second-toughest job in the country.[111]

The Lindsay camp never seriously attempted to win over outer-borough voters. One campaign research paper examined the complaints of what it called the "White Lower and Middle Income Class", which accounted for an estimated 25 and 50 percent of the electorate. The paper's author wrote that this group

> believes in the traditional values: God, country, hard work, a reasonable degree of sexual restraint. They are strongly patriotic and hold a great admiration for the military. They are slightly suspicious of all "intellectuals" and downright hostile to the intellectual elite that lives in the suburbs and has combined with the "poor" (meaning Black) inner-city resident in what they see as a conspiracy to improve the quality of life for the poor at their expense. They are strong on law and order and want the "handcuffs off the police" . . .

What these voters wanted, the paper suggested, was a politician who would be "strong on law and order (justice be damned); condemn the pornography of Times Square and advocate a limited degree of censorship to protect our children; condemn the bar on school prayers; send in the police (clubs swinging!) to control school disorders; cut welfare to get rid of the chislers. [*sic*]" The memo argued that following such a course would appeal to the "fears and prejudices" of these voters: "John Lindsay obviously cannot—and would not—take such stands on these issues."[112]

If Pete Hamill's article on lower-middle-class whites had set the tone for the early part of the campaign, Jimmy Breslin, in a private letter to Lindsay, captured the mood of the final month. Breslin, a child of lower-middle-class Irish Catholic Queens, wrote of the bars and workers of New York, but with little of Hamill's empathy. Breslin's letter to Lindsay betrayed his lack of feeling for, and dislike of, those workers whose lives he used to further his career. Breslin wrote that wherever he went in the city—the "docks in Brooklyn," the "bus stop in Laurelton," and the "candy store on Flatbush Avenue"— he heard the same two things: that "Lindsay gave the town away to the coloreds" and that "Lindsay has the cops handcuffed so they can't do a thing when one of these coloreds commits a crime." Though violent crime had been rising steadily for over a decade, Breslin dismissed such concerns. "I think the mere presence of a black face has the city in turmoil," Breslin wrote Lindsay.[113]

The mayoral campaign, according to Breslin, had "come down to just one word: black." When whites in Queens talked about the February snowstorm, they did not "really mean snow; snow is white and you're really thinking about black." Breslin thought that "all white people seem to have an unconscious reflex against black people." This obsession with race and denunciation of white ethnics as racists was in sharp contrast with Hamill's more nuanced view. Writing about the white flight from the neighborhoods of Brooklyn, Hamill allowed that "there was racial fear involved, of course, but it would be too easy to explain it all away that way. It was race plus despair plus insecurity about money plus desires for the betterment of one's children plus—the most important plus—the loss of a feeling of community."[114]

Breslin suggested that Lindsay attack these feelings head-on, ignoring the fact that much of Lindsay's problem was that he had been accusing white New Yorkers of racism for four years. New Yorkers, in Breslin's view, were "comforted with one notion: be against blacks. Hate them and fear them. You never will be alone. . . . Say black in any form: snow or garbage or City College. No one will disagree." Breslin urged Lindsay "to go right at people. So freak them, freak them all, let's challenge everybody in this city." Breslin wanted to arrange for Lindsay to speak before a group of five hundred longshoremen at the Brooklyn docks. He wanted Lindsay to ask the crowd what exactly he had given to blacks and thereby expose the crowd's racism. Lindsay wisely never took up Breslin's request.

By late fall, even Hamill, the man who skillfully and sympathetically gave voice to the anger and the hopes of the white ethnics, backed Lindsay. Hamill said that what made New York great was "class," and John Lindsay had the class to be the city's mayor. Marchi, with his condemnations of the Moratorium, spoke too much in "the tone of the *Daily News* editorials, not of a responsible man." Procaccino, on the other hand, came across as a "nasty, rude, arrogant man. . . . His emotions were vulgar and slippery." Hamill wrote that "New York forgives everything except mediocrity" and Procaccino was a man whose "emotions and ideas are mediocre." John Lindsay, in short, "has class in the best sense of that much-abused word. . . . I just can't believe that a city of champions can be run by the likes of Mario Procaccino. We've got too much class for that."[115]

A (SMALL) VICTORY FOR LIBERALISM

Better than any newspaper or union endorsement, Lindsay had the 1969 "Miracle Mets." There is no better example of Lindsay's good fortune than the World Series victory of the New York Mets. Though not much of a baseball fan (tennis was more Lindsay's sport), the mayor attended Game 5 of the World Series at Shea Stadium to watch the Mets win their first World Championship. The victory of the "Miracle Mets," who had finished last or second-to-last in each one of their first seven hapless seasons, made New Yorkers feel good about their city. Combined with the tickertape parade up Broadway in August for the *Apollo 11* astronauts, the city finally had something to cheer about in a season of anger and alienation. After the World Series victory, Lindsay made his way into the Mets clubhouse, where various players proceeded to douse him with champagne. These photos became front-page news and helped turn the stiff WASP into a regular guy, celebrating the Mets' victory with the rest of the city. "We spent the whole campaign trying to cut Lindsay down to size, humble him," said Aurelio of the clubhouse dousing. "We never could have planned anything that effective." Political scientist James Q. Wilson has noted how successful sports teams have often had a softening effect on urban politics. The divisive 1967 Boston mayoral race was muted after the Red Sox won the American League Pennant and went to the World Series. Similarly, the World Champion 1968 Detroit Tigers unified the riot-torn city that year. If the Mets, the doormats of the National League, could win the World Series, why couldn't Lindsay win reelection? Speaking at the annual Al Smith Dinner, Lindsay introduced himself as "John 'Mets' Lindsay. Now New York needs just one more miracle."[116]

The Lindsay miracle seemed to be happening. The *Daily News* straw polls at the end of October had Lindsay at 44 percent, Procaccino at 33 percent, and Marchi at 20 percent. The final poll put Lindsay at 48 percent, Procaccino at 28 percent, and Marchi at 22 percent. Though most people thought that Lindsay was leading, no one thought he was twenty points ahead of Procaccino. Procaccino promptly sued the paper over its poll, which had been conducted by Lou Harris, a pollster closely affiliated with Lindsay and Alex Rose. The *Daily News* poll seriously hurt Procaccino. Procaccino's campaign press secretary, Martin Steadman, wrote after the campaign that "the poll had shut off Procaccino's contributions. All but the most dedicated of his workers . . . stopped working. Democrat regulars who had been waiting to see which way they would have to go to protect their skins, decided that they had nothing to fear from Mario and went instead for John Lindsay. Worse than that, the reporters and commentators began to describe Procaccino's campaign as a shambles and his candidacy as a joke." In his concession speech on election night, Procaccino bitterly complained that he "was the subject of the greatest smear campaign in the twentieth century." One month after the campaign, a defeated Procaccino was still fuming. "I didn't lose the election," Procaccino said on WCBS-TV's *Newsmaker* show. "It was stolen from me . . ." Procaccino said that Lindsay "wasn't elected. He backed into the job. He didn't win." Procaccino said the election "was taken away from me" by "the Manhattan arrangement that we spoke of, and the limousine liberals." Lindsay agreed that the poll hurt Procaccino, but added, somewhat unconvincingly, that the poll also hurt his candidacy. He claimed that his own polling showed he had lost between 150,000 and 400,000 votes "because the *News* poll had convinced reluctant Lindsay voters to stay home."[117]

Despite the intensity of the campaign, turnout was only 2.4 million, down 200,000 from the 1965 campaign. Lindsay finished with 1,012,633 votes (41.1 percent); Procaccino, 831,772 votes (33.8 percent); and Marchi, 542,411 votes (22.1 percent). Meanwhile, Abe Beame easily won election as comptroller and Sanford Garelik defeated incumbent City Council President Francis X. Smith. In his acceptance speech, Lindsay called his victory "a commitment by the city as a whole toward progressive government." *The Nation* called Lindsay's victory "by far the most significant nationally." Running without the benefit of the two major party lines, Lindsay received 130,000 fewer votes than in 1965 and, for the second time, was elected with less than a majority of votes. The mayor won thirty-five of the city's sixty-eight assembly districts. As usual, Lindsay's strength lay in Manhattan, where he won all but one assembly district and defeated both Procaccino and Marchi combined by 2 to 1. Lindsay also squeaked to victory in Queens, where he beat Procaccino by fewer than 4,000 votes. Lindsay won an estimated 85 percent of the black vote, 65 percent of the Puerto Rican vote, and

45 percent of the Jewish vote, carrying every black and Puerto Rican district in the city, plus key middle-class Jewish districts like Riverdale in the Bronx, Washington Heights in Manhattan, Flatbush and Midwood in Brooklyn, and Forest Hills and Rego Park in Queens. Surprisingly, Lindsay also won roughly 25 percent of the white Catholic vote, despite running against two Catholic opponents.[118]

Procaccino won twenty-five assembly districts. He carried his home borough of the Bronx as well as Brooklyn. Not surprisingly, Procaccino won roughly 60 percent of the Italian vote. He also took 45 percent of the Jewish vote, a respectable showing, but not enough to beat Lindsay. Procaccino's strengths were in the heavily Italian northern and eastern sections of the Bronx and in the working-class Italian and Jewish neighborhoods of southern Brooklyn. In Queens, he was strong in every district except the middle-class Jewish Forest Hills.[119]

Marchi won eight assembly districts, including his home borough of Staten Island. He won only about one quarter of the Italian vote, but nearly two thirds of the dwindling Irish vote. (The Irish, long the dominant political power in the city, by 1969 made up only 8 percent of the electorate.) Marchi received just 10 percent of the Jewish vote. Besides Republican Staten Island, Marchi won the city's other traditionally Republican-Conservative neighborhoods like Bay Ridge, Brooklyn, Cambria Heights, Douglaston–Little Neck, Elmhurst, Maspeth, Ridgewood, and Ozone Park, Queens.

During Lindsay's first term, the city's electorate became more polarized. A growing segment of the city became more conservative while its liberal mayor became more liberal. This movement was made apparent by Arthur Klebanoff, a White House pollster who traced the changes in Lindsay's coalition between 1965 and 1969. He compared William F. Buckley's strongest districts in the 1965 campaign with those same districts' voting patterns in 1969. Although Lindsay carried most Buckley districts in 1965, he won only 25 percent of the vote in these areas in 1969. In 1965, Beame had easily carried the predominantly minority districts where Buckley did poorly. In 1969, Lindsay won 65 percent of the vote there, but fewer minorities voted than conservative white voters. By one estimate, blacks made up 20 percent of the city's population but only 15 percent of voters, and Puerto Ricans were 10 percent of the population and only 6 percent of voters. Though Lindsay's share of the black and Puerto Rican vote was significant, these voting blocs alone could not have reelected him.[120]

Undoubtedly, the Jewish vote was key to Lindsay's victory. The 45 percent of the Jewish vote he received, though the same as Procaccino, was a major victory, especially considering the widespread unhappiness over the school strikes and the snowstorm. Aurelio, with the help of pollster Lou Harris, knew from the beginning that the crucial Jewish vote was badly fractured.

There were upwardly mobile liberal Manhattan Jews and conservative Orthodox Jews from Brooklyn. There were upper-middle-class Jews in Riverdale and Forest Hills, who may have been liberal but shared many of the same concerns as suburbanites. There were lower-middle-class Jews in the Bronx and Brooklyn who saw urban decay firsthand, who had already fled neighborhoods like Brownsville or the South Bronx. As Milton Himmelfarb wrote, "Less prosperous Jews do not think they are defecting from liberalism. They think they are being made to pay the bill for the limousine liberals' kind of liberalism." What saved Lindsay from a mass exodus of Jewish voters, according to *Commentary's* Himmelfarb, was the Jewish tradition of "being attracted to the *edel* (cultivated) Gentile and repelled by the *prost* (common) one." No politician was more *edel* than John Lindsay and none more *prost* than Mario Procaccino.[121]

The cost of putting together this Lindsay victory was staggering. In an era before campaign financing laws, the Lindsay campaign spent more than $3 million, outspending Marchi and Procaccino combined by a ratio of nearly four to one. (This figure translates into nearly $13 million in current dollars.) Lindsay benefited by having as his finance director the chairman of Goldman Sachs, Gustave Levy, who could tap Wall Street money that would never go to Marchi or Procaccino. Oddly, no one accused the patrician mayor of buying the election.

A TALL, YOUNG, HANDSOME REFORM FUSION CANDIDATE is elected mayor with the support of the city's elite by running against the Democratic machine. Once in office, he promises efficiency and modernization in city government and hires outside experts who write studies about city agencies. He hires professionals, rather than political types, to run city departments. One critic calls his aides "scientific highbrows . . . [who] got up early in the morning and counted 166 superfluous jobs in the Department of Bridges, and abolished them and made 166 enemies, and put it into a report quite unintelligible to nine out of ten citizens, and went home and called it a grand day's political work." The mayor has problems because many New Yorkers feel he is arrogant and little concerned with their problems. Another critic writes that the mayor "saw economy, efficiency, and social reforms as ends in themselves rather than as means leading to the end of human comfort, welfare, and betterment. Many of those who worked with him suffered from . . . fatal class limitations and lack of sympathetic understanding of popular feelings and needs." The mayor creates a controversy with his education reform plan and attacks teachers when they oppose his reforms. "There is not any group in New York City that is treated better than the school teachers," the mayor complains, "and it seems to me that it ill becomes the teaching staff to try to wreck an experiment that means so much in the future lives and future development of children." Running for reelection, the fusion mayor does not win the Republican nomination and is forced to run without a major party ticket in a badly splintered, multicandidate campaign. The mayor takes a strong stand on America's involvement in a foreign war, a stand that causes him to lose support among the city's white ethnics.[122]

But this mayor is not John Lindsay, it is John Purroy Mitchel, reform mayor of New York from 1913 to 1917. The similarities in their two stories show the promises and pitfalls of reform government in New York City. Separated by more than a half century, the two men ran into many of the same problems in trying to tame the monster of city government and to appeal to New York's diverse ethnic groups. Still, there were differences between the two men. Mitchel, the grandson of the Irish patriot John Mitchel, was an Irish Catholic, although his attacks on Tammany and his alliance with the city's elite and reformers alienated his fellow Irish Catholics. Mitchel was also a Democrat who ran on a fusion line in 1913 and again in 1917 when he was denied the Republican nomination. Regarding the First World War, Mitchel was an unabashed supporter of American military involvement and a proponent of 100 percent Americanism, angering New York's German and Irish communities. By contrast, Lindsay's vigorous anti–Vietnam War stand angered New York's ethnic community, who supported the war, or at least had little sympathy for the antiwar movement.

Where Lindsay was reelected, Mitchel was defeated soundly for reelection in 1917 in a four-way race. The Tammany-backed Democrat John F. Hylan defeated Mitchel two to one, with Mitchel barely finished second, ahead of Morris Hilquist, the Socialist Party candidate. What saved Lindsay from a similar defeat was his move away from a traditional reform coalition toward a new coalition based on the liberal politics of the 1960s. Though both men lost the votes of the Irish, German, and Italians while retaining the loyalty of New York's elite, Lindsay tapped voting blocs that did not exist in Mitchel's time. Poor blacks and Puerto Ricans were attracted to Lindsay, as were liberal whites who opposed the Vietnam War, supported antipoverty programs, and were sympathetic to the complaints of the youth counterculture. Many of these Lindsay supporters were young people. Lindsay's victory was a victory of the "new politics" of television, voter canvassing, and polling over the "old politics" of sound trucks, political clubs, and the distribution of combs with the candidate's name on them. By 1969, the "old politics" not only seemed quaint, it was "uncool." Such recognition by Lindsay and his aides allowed him to avoid the fate that befell John Purroy Mitchel in 1917.

Though the question of whether Lindsay would serve another term as mayor was now answered, more questions appeared. Would Lindsay remain a Republican? Was there still room for a liberal Republican in the national party? Would Lindsay create a new coalition of liberal Democrats, Silk Stocking Republicans, and minorities to help govern the city? Would the newfound humility he had shown during the campaign carry over into the second term? Could the mayor win the support of blue-collar whites, or at least soften their anger? Could he improve city services, reduce racial tension, and avoid mishaps like the school crisis in his second term? Finally, having won with only 41 percent of the vote and possessing little status in either party, did John Lindsay have a future beyond City Hall?

CHARTING A SECOND TERM AFLOAT
AN EVER-TURBULENT SEA

"It's the second-toughest job in America."
—1969 Lindsay Campaign Slogan

Having won reelection without the support of either major political party, John Lindsay was freer than he had been in his first term. He no longer had to play to an increasingly conservative Republican audience in both the city and the nation. Yet at the same time, if he was to have a political future beyond City Hall and repair the bad feelings that had bubbled to the surface during the 1969 campaign, he would have to rebuild his political support from the remains of his original reform coalition.

Lindsay soon found that the tensions and social changes of the late 1960s would continue into the seventies. In many ways, the administrative and political blunders of the first term were absent from Lindsay's second term. But the same social changes and civil disturbances continued to rock the city. In the end, Lindsay could not repair the ill feelings he had engendered during his first term. He could not fulfill most of his promises. And he could not restore the lost idealism that had propelled him into office in 1965.

LIBERALS PUSHED LINDSAY FOR A MORE PROGRESSIVE second term. In an open letter in the pages of *The Nation*, the political scientist Theodore Lowi urged Lindsay to declare the city ungovernable and move toward a "free-wheeling, supra-bureaucratic and supra-corporate approach" to urban problems. Lowi accused the suburbs of being "parasites upon the city," and argued that Lindsay should fight for a metropolitan-area government, a

443

longtime dream of liberals that if realized would enable the city to tap in to the wealth of the suburbs to subsidize solutions to urban social problems. Liberals like Lowi still had grand designs that were almost impossible politically for Lindsay to accomplish.[1]

Yet in his second inaugural address, Lindsay struck a much less grandiose tone than four years earlier. In contrast with the attacks upon the city's "enemies" and the promises to cure an ailing city, John Lindsay now told New Yorkers: "It is best not to plan on promises and dreams." Such an approach did not mean surrendering to the city's ills, but rather coming to "an understanding that we are all human, we are all fallible." Gone were the soaring rhetoric and unquenchable moralism. Humility, not hubris, was the hallmark of the second inaugural address. There were no more attacks on "power brokers." The reform politician of 1965 had long since made his peace with "selfish" interests.[2]

The experience of the 1969 campaign seemed to impress upon Lindsay the importance of neighborhoods. In an interview at the end of December 1969, Lindsay said that one lesson he learned in his first term was that New York was a "city that's very sensitive about its representative nature—it's a highly ethnic city." It was the kind of lesson that every clubhouse politician knew in his bones and every kid growing up on the streets of the Bronx or Brooklyn could tell you immediately. But the 1969 campaign gave the Silk Stocking candidate a refresher course in ethnic politics, reminding him of the true "diversity" of the city that lay beyond Manhattan.[3]

Lindsay spent a portion of his inaugural address discussing the importance of New York's neighborhoods. "For together," Lindsay said, "these communities set the quality of life for us as a city." In his first term, in both rhetoric and action, Lindsay had paid little attention to white middle-class communities. Now he warned that if "the Bay Ridge homeowner is uncertain of his neighborhood's future, if the Harlem mother does not know if her child is learning at school, if the Forest Hills family fears to walk the streets at night, if the Morrisania office worker cannot travel home in comfort or even decency, then this city is not working for its citizens." For his second term, Lindsay offered neighborhoods "the responsibility of charting the course of their communities."

Along with his newfound interest in the city's neighborhoods, Lindsay reached out to the forgotten middle class. "For a middle class resident of New York, talking to the government is an exercise in futility, as it is in most instances for any individual dealing with any enormous bureaucracy. There is no sense that anyone is listening, no sense that anyone in power has even a measure of the problem, much less a program for changing these conditions."

For this reason, the mayor declared that 1970 would be "the year in which we move the government out into the neighborhoods. We want greater community participation in government, more responsibility for running their own affairs. Things will last a lot longer because if you build something yourself, you don't break the windows."[4]

To counter his alleged Manhattan-centric vision of the city, Lindsay released a more comprehensive plan for neighborhood government in 1970. Responding to New Yorkers' cries of alienation from their government, Lindsay called for the sixty-two existing community planning boards to be merged with the already existing Urban Action Task Forces. Each of these new community boards would include a minimum of twenty-four people, all of whom would be appointed by the mayor, the borough presidents, the City Council, and the community school boards. The boards would combine the powers of the planning boards and the Urban Action Task Forces, with the goal of making government more accountable and bringing government a little closer to the nearly 8 million residents of New York. Lindsay's earlier plan for little City Halls had failed to win passage in the City Council for fear on the part of Democrats that the mayor would turn them into political clubhouses. Now Lindsay promised that these new entities would focus on improving city services, avoid politics, and include the input of councilmen and borough presidents. Critics like Alan Hevesi, a Queens College political science professor, correctly noted that none of Lindsay's plans for neighborhood government actually took power away from existing city departments or agencies. All requests by the community boards would have to first go through the mayor.[5]

While Lindsay was making overtures to white ethnic communities and pressing on with his desire to bring government to the local level, he was also slowly making a move toward switching to the Democratic Party. After his reelection, Lindsay promised changes in his second term. He began shedding some of his staunch Republican aides. Before the 1969 campaign, the more liberal Tom Morgan replaced Harry O'Donnell as press secretary. After the end of the year, Deputy Mayor Robert Sweet was somewhat unceremoniously replaced with Richard Aurelio, the man who ran the mayor's successful reelection campaign. Aurelio possessed the sharp elbows necessary for success at City Hall, a trait that the mild-mannered Sweet lacked. Looking forward to Lindsay's second term, Aurelio said, "This is a great test for liberals. This administration will be far different than the first." Though Deputy Mayor Aurelio was a Republican, he was much more liberal and much less of a party man than Robert Sweet.

Early in his second term, Lindsay named prominent Democrats to high-level positions in his administration. Manhattan reform Assemblyman Jerome Kretchmer became head of the Environmental Protection Administration. Bronx reform Assemblyman Benjamin Altman was named head of the Rent and Housing Maintenance Commission. Howard Samuels, the first Democrat to support Lindsay in 1969, was named to head the new Off-Track Betting Corporation after losing the Democratic nomination for governor in 1970. Robert Morganthau, a former U.S. attorney and Democratic gubernatorial nominee, was named deputy mayor. Richard Brown, a former aide to Assembly Minority Leader Stanley Steingut, became the mayor's Albany representative. Ronnie Eldridge, who had joined the campaign to rally liberal Democrats to Lindsay's cause, joined the administration as a mayoral assistant. Eldridge's presence at City Hall was important because she served as a liaison to liberal Democrats and other previously marginalized groups such as homosexuals, feminists, and the Young Lords, a group of young Puerto Rican radicals.[6]

Meanwhile, the pace of social change quickened. In June 1969, eight policemen raided the Stonewall Inn off Sheridan Square in Greenwich Village for selling liquor without a license. Stonewall was a gay bar frequented by drag queens and run by the Mafia, which ran many of the city's gay bars. As police ushered the patrons out of the bar, drag queens paraded by the growing crowd outside. Some were arrested for disorderly conduct. Trouble started when the paddy wagon arrived and one drag queen refused to stay in the wagon. The crowd started yelling "Pigs!" and "Police brutality!" and objects began to fly at the small number of policemen, who soon barricaded themselves inside the empty bar. The crowd threw bricks at the bar and battered down the door. Someone poured lighter fluid into the bar and started a small fire with the police inside. The police had their guns aimed at the door and were ready to fire if any of the crowd stormed the building. Reinforcements arrived, including the Tactical Patrol Force, and police eventually subdued the crowd.

More trouble between police and gays occurred outside the bar the following night. A week after the riot, the *Daily News* ran an article about the controversy headlined "Homo Nest Raided, Queen Bees Are Stinging Mad," concluding that the police and the city had not "heard the last from the Girls of Christopher Street."[7] All three mayoral candidates managed to miss the importance of this event. Stonewall, as it turned out, would become the birthplace of the modern gay rights movement.

If the gay rights movement was just in its infancy, the women's movement was in full bloom. Feminists scored a victory in the summer of 1970 when, following a court order, Mayor Lindsay signed a bill prohibiting discrimination in public places on the grounds of sex. It was not that Lindsay was a supporter of feminism. Some critics attacked him for frequenting exclusive males-only clubs like the Yale Club and the New York Athletic Club. He held traditional views of women, and very few of his aides or commissioners were women. One member of his administration recalled Lindsay as "an old-fashioned guy" who was reluctant to place women in high office for fear they would "make their judgements on the basis of emotion." But by 1970, Lindsay was beholden to liberal Democrats like Councilwoman Carol Greitzer, who had written the city's antidiscrimination bill.[8]

The legislation was specifically aimed at McSorley's Old Ale House on Seventh Street in the East Village, a sawdust-strewn New York landmark.

For nearly a century, this working-class bar had banned women. Joseph Mitchell described McSorley's in 1940 as a "drowsy place" with a "motley" clientele including "mechanics from the many garages in the neighborhood, salesmen from the restaurant-supply houses on Cooper Square, truck-drivers from Wanamaker's, interns from Bellevue, students from Cooper Union, and clerks from the row of secondhand bookshops just north of Astor Place." But the main group at the bar were the "crusty old men, pre-dominantly Irish, who have been drinking there since they were youths and now have a proprietary feeling about the place." When the bill passed, Mc-Sorley's was forced to admit female patrons for the first time.[9]

As Lindsay's second term began, it had become quite clear that a great change in the city's racial composition had taken place. Between 1950 and 1968, the city saw a net decrease of 1,353,000 whites and an increase of 1,446,000 minorities. In the 1960s alone, the total number of whites who migrated out of the city reached nearly one million. Since there were over 300,000 additional white births in the city, the white population declined by 617,127 in the 1960s. The city saw an in-migration of 435,840 minorities during this decade, and there were over 250,000 additional minority births; thus, the actual number of minorities living in the city increased by 702,903 during the 1960s.[10]

Amid these changes, racial issues continued to roil the city. On the evening of January 14, 1970, ninety guests gathered at the conductor Leonard Bernstein's Park Avenue duplex for a fundraiser/meeting/cocktail party for the Black Panthers, twenty-one of whose members were scheduled to be tried on charges of criminal conspiracy, including a plot to bomb a number of deparment stores and parks in the city. Among the guests were the film director Otto Preminger, Harry Belafonte, Barbara Walters, and the composer Burton Lane. The wife of Parks Commissioner August Heckscher attended and donated $100 to the Panthers, saying that "the one thing we must always support is justice." The *New York Times* covered the meeting the next day on its society page, carefully pointing out the social contrast be-tween the Panthers and their newfound friends. A *Times* editorial was harsher, calling the "emergence of the Black Panthers as the romanticized darlings of the politico-cultural jet set" an affront to black Americans. In the editorial's view, the Bernstein party represented "the sort of elegant slum-ming" that degraded "patrons and patronized alike. . . . Black Panthers on a Park Avenue pedestal create one more distortion of the Negro image." Newspapers throughout the nation picked up the story. Tom Wolfe immor-talized the event in an article for *New York* magazine entitled "Radical Chic."[11]

Stung by the criticism and attention, Bernstein fought back. In a letter to the editor the following week, Bernstein claimed that what had occurred was not a party, but a meeting to discuss the trial of the Black Panthers. Por-traying himself as solely interested in civil liberties, the conductor wrote that he was concerned not with the outcome of the trial, but with the defendants' ability to receive a fair trial. "The ability of the defendants to prepare a proper defense will depend on the help given prior to the trial, and this help must not be denied because of lack of funds," said Bernstein. Two weeks later, Bernstein released another statement disavowing his support for the Panthers. "It is reasonably clear," Bernstein wrote, "that they are advocating violence against their fellow citizens, the downfall of Israel, the support of Al Fatah, and other similarly dangerous and ill-conceived pursuits. To all of these concepts, I am vigorously opposed, and will fight against them as hard as I can." But, Bernstein continued, "if we deny these Black Panthers their democratic rights because their philosophy is unacceptable to us, then we are denying our own democracy." This explanation did little to convince people that Bernstein was not guilty of poor judgment or sympathy with the Panthers. Would Bernstein throw a party and fundraiser to defend the civil liberties of Nazis or the Klan? Wolfe's "radical chic" entered the national vocabulary, and Bernstein's party came to symbolize the extremes to which whites would go to expiate their feelings of racial guilt.[12]

HARDHATS

But radical chic did not extend to the city's blue-collar workers. By 1970, protests against the Vietnam War fueled the anger of white ethnics and led to the series of disturbances that have come to be known as the hardhat riots. On the afternoon of Friday, May 8, 1970, or "Bloody Friday," hundreds of hard-hat construction workers from nearby building projects in downtown Manhattan descended upon the corner of Wall and Broad Streets, in front of the New York Stock Exchange, and battled antiwar protesters who had gathered to mark the deaths of four students at Kent State University four days earlier and protest the invasion of Cambodia.[13]

The first skirmish occurred two days earlier, when a group of antiwar protesters marching up Broadway found themselves bombarded by bottles, cans, and clumps of asphalt showered on them by construction workers from a nearby building. Farther down Broadway, a group of construction workers attacked a small demonstration at Battery Park in retaliation for the tearing down of the American flag from the construction site.

But the real action took place on Friday morning when five hundred antiwar demonstrators massed at Wall and Broad Streets, where George Washington was inaugurated president in 1789. They had hoped to shut down the Stock Exchange, but their efforts failed. By noon, their numbers had reached nearly a thousand. City Hall had been warned that the hardhats were preparing to attack the demonstrators. Some people argued that union shop stewards and the builders themselves were organizing the workers. Others noted that a few men dressed in suits seemed to be egging the hardhats on and giving them direction. One of these men was Ralph Clifford, who edited a small, right-wing newsletter. No one, though, denied that the feelings of the hardhats were their own.[14]

By noon, a mob of American flag-wielding hardhats had reached the corner of Wall and Broad Streets. There, only a thin line of police separated them from the antiwar protesters on the steps of Federal Hall (then the subtreasury building). More hardhats joined the crowd, some coming from the construction site of the World Trade Center a few blocks away. They surged through the police line and ran up the steps of Federal Hall. Once in control of the steps, the hardhats planted their flags around the statue of George Washington. Joe Kelly, a construction worker, described charging up the steps: "When we first went up on the steps and the flags went up there, the whole group started singing 'God Bless America' and it damn near put a lump in your throat. It was really something. I could never say I was sorry I was there. You just had a very proud feeling. If I live to be a hundred, I don't think I'll ever see anything quite like that again."

Wall Streets clerks, stockbrokers, bankers, and secretaries, all on their lunch-hour break, gathered to watch the disturbance, many of them cheering on the hardhats and some entering the fray. Fights broke out between hardhats, many of them carrying pipes and wrenches, and antiwar demonstrators. One conservatively dressed, middle-aged man with a history of mental illness managed to make his way through the hardhats to the top of the steps. There he thumbed his nose at the hardhats, shouted obscenities, and spat on the flag (some observers claimed he tried to chew the flag while others thought he blew his nose on it). A hardhat promptly clocked the man in the face. Meanwhile, the construction workers pushed the antiwar protesters completely off the steps and fights soon broke out among the crowd. By 12:40, a crowd of nearly 10,000 people had gathered in the area.[15]

As the hardhats moved through the streets, they attacked members of the antiwar crowd. Anyone caught flashing a peace sign or wearing his hair too long was liable to be attacked. Trinity Church, at Broadway and Wall Street, used its pews as an emergency medical center for the wounded. Over seventy people were injured that day, although none of the injuries were serious. Most were bruises, cuts, broken noses and busted teeth. The hardhats tried to storm the church, but only managed to tear down the Red Cross flag that had been erected.[16]

An hour after the battle on Wall Street, hundreds of hardhats marched eight blocks up Broadway to City Hall, chanting "U.S.A., all the way." As angry as they were toward antiwar protesters and rebellious college students, these hardhats seemed especially peeved at Mayor Lindsay. Many were upset with Lindsay's remarks after his April speech at the University of Pennsylvania, where the mayor seemed to call draft dodgers "truly heroic." Further angering the crowd, Lindsay had decided to fly the City Hall flag at half-staff to memorialize the four dead protesters at Kent State. According to Deputy Mayor Richard Aurelio, Lindsay had been reluctant to lower the flag but was prodded to action by his young, liberal staffers, many of whom felt very strongly about the Kent State killings. Sid Davidoff and other Lindsay staffers had been in Ohio to help Seth Taft, a liberal Republican, in his Senate race against Howard Metzenbaum. When Taft refused to issue a statement about the deaths, Davidoff recalls, "We pulled our whole team out of there."[17]

Soon, some four hundred hardhats stood outside City Hall chanting, "Raise the flag, raise the flag, raise the flag." The doors at City Hall were quickly locked and barricaded. (Lindsay was at Gracie Mansion.) Somehow, a uniformed mailman got to the top of City Hall and raised the flag to full-staff, to the raucous cheers of the hardhats below. Looking out at the assembled mob, Davidoff recalled, "We got thousands of hard hats singing, cops with their hats off and over their hearts singing, and this guy up there puts the flag up. They are cheering like mad. I mean, it's a scene out of *The Battle of Algiers* or *Z*. I went crazy." An angry Davidoff then grabbed one of his "strong-arm guys" and headed for the roof. Once there, he recalls, "I put the flag at half-mast and I give a V sign to those guys down there. . . . I went nuts."[18]

With the flag back at half-staff, it was the hardhats' turn to go nuts. They tried to storm City Hall, surging past the small police guard in front of the building. Inside City Hall, panic set in as police feared they could not hold off the angry crowd. According to a police report, "Fearing for the safety of the Hall itself and its occupants and being fully aware of the emotional response capability of the flag, Asst. Chief Inspector [Frederick] Kowsky . . . demanded that they [Lindsay's staff] immediately return the American flag to full staff so as to defuse the crowd . . . After some further discussion and hesitation, the City Hall group reluctantly agreed to move the American flag to full staff but insisted on keeping the New York City flag at its half way position." Kowsky was good friends with Davidoff, yet when the mayoral aide got down from the roof, the policeman grabbed his friend by the collar and threatened to arrest him if he moved. Two policemen went back to the roof to restore the New York City flag to full staff. Inside City Hall, an angry Aurelio lashed out at Davidoff for exacerbating the situation, then added, "Goddamn it, though, I wish I did it."[19]

With the flag at full-staff, the mob of construction workers appeared pacified. The hundreds of construction workers massed outside City Hall and in the adjoining park took off their hardhats and began singing "The Star-Spangled Banner." Aurelio, in charge at City Hall in Lindsay's absence, then "saw construction workers go up to seven or eight cops and demand that they take off their riot helmets while they sang the national anthem, and they did. It was an inexcusable police performance." The hardhats shouted, "Get your helmets off," and five to seven of the fifteen policemen complied "as a respectful gesture to the National Anthem," according to the police report. Barry Gottehrer and other mayoral aides complained that this behavior reinforced the belief that the police were sympathetic to the hardhats.[20]

But the calm proved only temporary. Across the street from City Hall, at a Pace University building, students hung an antiwar banner from the roof, reigniting the hardhats' anger. The students also "rained building debris down upon the heads of those construction workers," according to a police report. Other students were milling about the front of the building. Soon, dozens of hardhats charged the students, beating some of them and smashing the windows of the building. Others managed to make their way to the roof of the Pace University building and remove the banner. By 3:00 P.M., the violence had subsided and the hardhats marched back down Broadway, disappeared into the crowd, and returned to their jobs. Seventy-two people were injured, although only twenty-nine were medically treated. According to the police report, "The others merely complained of being pushed, shoved, or the like, and required no medical attention." Seven policemen were also injured. Despite the number of fights and injuries, only six people were arrested.

Reaction to the violence was quick. The *Times* saw the events as an example of the "ease with which right-wing vigilantism finds in left-wing extremism an excuse for pushing aside constituted authority and enforcing its own brutal form of injustice." The *Post* called the hardhats and their allies "cold-blooded bullies" and "hard-hat rightist brutalitarians." Pete Hamill, who had written so sympathetically about the city's white ethnics just one year earlier, could not conceal his contempt for the actions of the hardhats. "This is the work of cowards," wrote Hamill, "of men who have so forgotten what they once were or where they came from that they can act like animals and call it patriotism." To Hamill, a vocal critic of the Vietnam War, these men were "the sour children of right-wing frustration." *The Nation* saw "a pattern that contains the classic elements of Hitlerian street tactics."

No one was angrier about the police inaction than John Lindsay, who charged that New Yorkers had "witnessed a breakdown of the police as the barrier between them and wanton violence." In a statement to the press, Lindsay said: "In downtown Manhattan yesterday, peaceful protesters were interrupted by marauding bands of construction workers, who forcibly broke up legal demonstrations, beat up students and wantonly destroyed property. The violence yesterday was appalling. . . . Yesterday's violence clearly threatened the right of dissent, peaceful protest, and free assembly in our city." Lindsay ordered a full investigation of the police behavior during the disturbances. [21]

But the events of "Bloody Friday" were only the beginning. As one journalist noted, "It was the wild start of two weeks of almost daily noon-hour, flag-waving, bellicose, damn-Lindsay . . . and praise-Nixon countermarchers through downtown New York." Wearing their trademark hardhats and carrying large and small American flags, thousands of construction workers and their sympathizers continued to roam the streets of Lower Manhattan on their lunch hour. They carried signs with patriotic messages like AMERICA: LOVE IT OR LEAVE IT and GOD BLESS AMERICA. Along with the patriotic themes, the signs also expressed a fury toward Mayor Lindsay. A *Times* reporter noted that "the marchers carried signs calling the mayor a rat, a Commy rat, a faggot, a leftist, an idiot, a neurotic, an anarchist, and a traitor." Some marchers carried a coffin with the sign HERE LIES THE CITY OF NEW YORK, KILLED BY COMMISSAR LINDSAY.[22]

The left saw the hardhats as proto-fascists, but the anger these men felt was genuine. One office clerk who lost his son in Vietnam expressed anger at Lindsay. "When he stands up and says men who refuse to serve in the armed forces are heroic," the man told a reporter, "then I presume by the same category that my son that was killed in Vietnam is a coward, the way he thinks." While some were truly aggrieved, others were just plain angry. "I am an American and America wasn't made to have these pansy-assed creeps running around wild," said a thirty-five-year-old construction worker from Long Island. "I don't mind people demonstrating, but when these brats rip, spit on and chew up the flag, what are we supposed to do, stand around and kiss them?" Another man said, "A lot of good men died for that flag. We're not going to let a lot of long-haired kids and fast-talking politicians who make big money take it away from us."[23]

On May 20, less than two weeks after "Bloody Friday," union workers and hardhats organized an official rally in support of President Nixon, the military, and the war in Vietnam. In one of the largest pro-war demonstrations of the time, an estimated crowd of 100,000 marched from City Hall down Broadway. This time there was no violence, but the crowd again made Lindsay the target of its ire. An effigy of Lindsay was hung from a lamppost and set on fire, while marchers carried signs such as BURY THE RED MAYOR and LINDSAY DROPS THE FLAG MORE TIMES THAN A WHORE DROPS HER PANTS. Other signs showed support for the Nixon administration: GOD BLESS THE ESTABLISHMENT and WE SUPPORT NIXON AND AGNEW. The following day, 20,000 antiwar marchers rallied at City Hall. The mayor praised both marches as "peaceful and orderly," although one thousand antiwar protesters later marched northward and disrupted traffic, until they reached Bryant Park at Forty-second Street, where they were forcibly dispersed by police.[24]

President Nixon quickly took advantage of the hardhat riots. Seeking the support of conservative unions for the war in Vietnam, Nixon hailed the hardhats and invited Peter Brennan, head of the New York Building and Construction Trades Council, and twenty-two other union leaders to come to the White House on May 26. He thanked them for the show of support. In turn, Brennan presented the President with his own hard hat. Regarding his alliance with the Republican President, Brennan told reporters, "We're supporting the President and the country not because he's for labor, because he isn't, but because he's our President, and we're hoping that he's right." On Labor Day, 1970, Nixon invited seventy of the nation's top labor leaders and their wives to a dinner at the White House. The guests included Peter Brennan, longshoremen's union head Thomas Gleason, and Teamsters head Frank Fitzsimmons. In November 1972, President Nixon appointed Brennan secretary of labor.[25]

Nixon's support for the hardhats helped him shore up support for the war. It was also a way to embarrass Lindsay, whom the President increasingly saw as a political enemy. In June, Nixon said, "Let's only hit Lindsay and hit him hard. As [the commentators Rowland] Evans and [Robert] Novak point out, Lindsay is one of the 'militant anti-Nixon' big city Mayors." In addition, the hardhat demonstration presented a good opportunity for Nixon to speak up for "Middle Americans" and their values. Writing to his aides, Nixon expressed the need to "get with the mood of the country which is fed up with liberals."

> We'd better shape up and quit trimming the *wrong* way. It is very late— but we still have time to move away from the line of our well-intentioned liberals on our staff. . . . I can't emphasize too strongly that our Administration team—including W.H. staff had been affected too much by the unreal atmosphere of the D.C. press, social and intellectual set. Perhaps Cambodia and Kent State led to an overreaction by our own people to prove that we were pro student. . . . We must get turned around on this before it is too late. Emphasize—Anti-crime, anti-demonstrations, anti-drugs, anti-obscenity.[26]

The polarization of America was deepening. Nixon saw it clearly and chose sides. Lindsay, too, saw the polarization. Though he often spoke longingly of a "rational center" that would serve as a counterweight to the extremism of both the right and left, increasingly Lindsay's sympathies lay with the protesters of the left.

CITY SCHOOLS AFTER OCEAN HILL–BROWNSVILLE

The 1969 decentralization bill passed by the New York State Legislature killed the Ocean Hill–Brownsville district and the dreams of community control. The controversy also left the city's schools another legacy: increasing violence and disorder in the classroom. Though it is difficult to quantify school violence, it seemed to take on new proportions in the aftermath of the Ocean Hill-Brownsville dispute. Much of that violence had racial connotations. A two-month survey of city high schools by *New York*

Times reporters "indicated that racial misunderstanding appears in some schools not just as a fever that flares up now and then, but as a malignant growth." In January 1969, the High School Principals Association of New York City released a report stating: "Disorders and fears of new and frightening dimensions stalk the corridors of many of our schools. Yet in the face of these obviously clear and present dangers, our Board of Education has virtually abdicated its responsibilities for the safe and orderly conduct of our schools."

Writing about the violence in the schools in 1970, the *Times* observed, "Delinquent adolescents, masquerading as Robin Hoods in order to escape punishment, are in reality engaged in the lowest form of intimidation, shakedowns, extortion and violent assault. They avoid being treated as youthful criminals by spreading rumors of racist persecution and by denouncing legitimate arrests as police brutality." Lindsay's chief of staff, Steven Isenberg, discussed the problem with fellow Lindsay staffers in October 1972: "More consuming and clearly continuing are the incidents of crime in and around the schools. Of matters which touch people and communities nothing may go beyond violence which affects children and the parents' view that now schools not only do a lousy job of teaching, but are not even safe for teachers and students." Queens Councilman Matt Troy wrote to Lindsay in October 1973 that his daughter had recently been assaulted at her school and that he had personally intervened in three racial clashes in schools in his Queens Village district. He wrote Lindsay: "John, as a parent, and as a public official, it scare hell [*sic*] out of me to see what is going on in City Schools." [27]

The ill feelings created by the teachers' strikes immediately spilled into the classroom as the teachers returned to work in the fall of 1968. Richard Piro, a drama teacher at J.H.S. 275 in Brownsville, wrote of the problems in his school after the strike. White students—mostly Jewish—made up only 5 percent of the student body. To protect these students, teachers were forced to keep them segregated in special rooms. They ate lunch in a classroom rather than run the risk of eating in the crowded, explosive cafeteria. Everyday life in the school became a chore.

> The physical condition of the building was deplorable. Stairwells were permanently marred by great splashes of paint on the walls. Litter spilled down the stairs in surrealistic patterns dimly illuminated by broken light fixtures. . . . Char marks in corners indicated where fires had been set. The odor of human defecation and urine hung over the corridors. Hall clocks leered through broken, twisted faces. Sometime we inhaled chemical Mace sprayed by hostile students. Such incidents occurred so frequently as to be unworthy of lunchroom conversation. Several times a week brilliantly colored smoke bombs were thrown into

classrooms. . . . Teachers began reporting senseless violent confrontations with students.[28]

A teacher at Springfield Gardens High School in Queens remembered that after the 1968 strikes had ended, "There was very little learning going on. . . . The teachers were always protecting the white kids. . . . After '68 the kids wouldn't show respect for the teachers. Here was this teacher who didn't let them into school and who really didn't care about them [or] understand them. . . . There was no way you could . . . discuss the issue because there was such hate." One white replacement teacher, Liz Fusco, continued to work at her Ocean Hill–Brownsville school for three years. But then, one day, she confronted a child who had punched one of her students. Later, while teaching her class, the boy's mother entered the classroom and slapped the teacher in the face in front of her students. Feeling "defeated," "abandoned," and "powerless," Fusco left to teach in a small New England town.[29]

In December 1968, an incident in a Bedford-Stuyvesant school was eerily reminiscent of earlier incidents against school principals. Julius Nislow, the principal of the predominantly black and Puerto Rican P.S. 93, had been the victim of threats and intimidation from Sonny Carson and Brooklyn CORE for some time. When the school strike ended, a group of parents tried to block the principal from entering the school. One protester carried a sign saying NISLOW IS NOT WELCOME. NISLOW SAYS IF THEY'RE BLACK, KEEP THEM BACK. The breaking point came in early December when Nislow, who was sixty-three, received an anonymous letter threatening his family: "You have been watch [*sic*] and you have been followed . . . You have 3 children, a daughter who is a nurce [*sic*] . . . a son who is a dentist. A daughter finishing at college. Has she ever been 'RAPE'[*sic*]. The police are no great problem to us. They can only protect you and your family for a part of the time." Despite the letter, the school's parents association showed no sympathy for the principal, instead accusing him of "disrupting the school." Though condemning the letter, the association released a statement charging Nislow "with 10 years of negligence, 10 years of incompetence, 10 years of failing to educate the children of this community, 10 years of showing contempt for the community." The day after receiving the letter, Nislow asked for a transfer. Harassment and threats against school personnel were part of the reason 1,832 teachers and principals resigned from the New York City schools in 1968, five times the normal number.[30]

The tensions created by the teachers' strikes and the thwarted demands for community control only exacerbated the already potent racial troubles in the city's schools. No school suffered more turbulence during this time than Franklin Lane High School, which was located right on the Queens-Brooklyn border in what was then an all-white, conservative German-Irish-Italian neighborhood. In the 1960s, Lane had undergone a rapid change in its racial mix. In 1958, white students made up 76 percent of the school population. By 1965, the school was racially split 50–50. By 1969, whites made up only 31 percent of the student body. Many of the black children were bused in from Bedford-Stuyvesant, East New York, and Ocean Hill-Brownsville. In fact, Franklin Lane received most of the students from Ocean Hill's I.S. 55 and J.H.S. 271, the scenes of most of the tensions during the 1968 teachers' strikes. To make matters worse, Lane was also a UFT stronghold, where the union's vice president, George Altomare, taught. Built for 4,000 students, Franklin Lane had 5,600 students enrolled in 1969—though the issue of overcrowding was a problem only on paper, since attendance at Lane was never more than 60 percent.[31]

Fights between black and white students were common in the school, and the school administration was unable to keep control. As one *Village Voice* journalist wrote of Franklin Lane: "Every day there is a riot on the subway or a fight in the bathroom or an arrest in the halls or a brawl in the cafeteria or a suspension of more black students. . . . Lane is a time bomb, and everyone—blacks, whites, teachers, Board of Ed—admits it could explode any day. Yet no one has marshaled the power or imagination or trust to head off disaster."

The school's neighbors resented the influx of black students into their neighborhood and formed the Cypress Hill–Woodhaven Improvement Association to protest student disorders. (The group was headed by Michael Long, who later became the powerful head of the New York State Conservative Party.) The worst incident at Franklin Lane occurred on January 20, 1969, when a teacher, Frank Siracusa, ran down the stairs to see who had thrown a rock through his window. In the stairwell he was confronted by three black youths who sprayed him with lighter fluid, kicked and punched him, and then set him on fire. After the attack the school was shut down for several days. When the school reopened, fifty New York City policemen were stationed inside the school to maintain order, but their presence only exacerbated tensions. A few months after the incident, black students replaced an American flag in a classroom with the pan-African flag. When school officials took the flag down, a few hundred black students ran through the halls protesting the decision.[32]

The disorders in the schools troubled Lindsay. He knew they had the potential to become an explosive issue in his reelection campaign. "I want to assure every parent that we'll take whatever measures are necessary to guarantee the safety of students in our school system," said the mayor. "We simply will not tolerate any kind of disruption or violence that frightens or threatens those who are trying to get on with the business of education." He named a thirteen-member commission to come up with measures to stop student violence, but neither Lindsay's words nor the commission could stem the tide.

Throughout 1969 and into the early 1970s, school disorders became commonplace. In March 1969, two hundred black students rampaged through Eastern District High School in Brooklyn, smashing glass partitions and destroying furniture. The school had to be closed. A few days later, the school was closed again when ten fires were set throughout the school. Throughout the spring of 1969, more disorders and student riots erupted at Morris High School in the Bronx and Samuel Tilden, Bushwick, and Erasmus Hall High Schools in Brooklyn. George Washington High School in Manhattan's Washington Heights area was a frequent scene of racial battles between black and Dominican students.

OPEN ADMISSIONS AT CITY UNIVERSITY

By the spring of 1969, disorders had penetrated the city's higher-education system in the spring of 1969. For decades, the city's tuition-free public colleges and community colleges had been a haven for bright, ambitious working-class students. The City University of New York (CUNY) comprised nine four-year colleges, five community colleges, three professional colleges, and a graduate school. By the late 1960s, blacks and Puerto Ricans made up roughly 10 percent of the student body at the four-year colleges. In 1969, minority students blockaded and shut down City College in Manhattan, demanding greater representation in the student body. The protests spread to Brooklyn College and Queens College, which was closed temporarily after forty black students vandalized the campus. Writing twenty-five years later, the journalist James Traub said of the events at City College:

> There were marches and fires and fistfights, and an irrevocable taking of sides. It was a single moment that defined, in a burst of harsh light, the crisis that liberalism itself was undergoing. The racial challenge could not be either repudiated or accommodated without sacrificing cherished beliefs. Liberalism—the self-confident faith fueled by the engines of assimilation and progress—could not survive this shock.

University officials had been planning to institute an open admissions policy in the future. Now, the protests pushed them and Mayor Lindsay to implement the policy years ahead of schedule. In 1970, all city high school graduates would be eligible for admission into the CUNY system, their choice of schools dependent on their grades.[33]

The policy of open admissions had three effects on the CUNY system. First, the number of freshmen entering the system jumped from 20,000 in 1969 to 35,000 in 1970. (Since the system had already been expecting 26,000 students in 1970, this meant that the number of open-admissions students was estimated at 9,000.) CUNY did not have adequate time to prepare for the sudden increase in new students, which taxed resources throughout the system. Since tuition remained free, the additional students meant that the university system's $310 million budget, paid mostly by the city, had to be increased. Writing a decade later, Charles Morris, a former Lindsay budget aide, concluded: "City tax spending on higher education was the fastest-growing area in the city budget, jumping from $35 million in 1966 to $200 million in 1973. It was much more than the city could afford." Second, over half of the incoming freshmen were found to need some form of remedial help in math and reading. It was long known that the city's public high schools were not succeeding in educating their students. Now that burden shifted to the city's public colleges, and it was unclear whether they would be any more successful than public schools.

The last effect of the open admissions policy was on the racial balance in the CUNY system. The percentage of black and Hispanic students jumped from 10 percent in 1969 to 28 percent in 1970. By 1972, 40 percent of students were black and Hispanic. Between 1969 and 1975, the white population in the CUNY system dropped from 143,250 to 142,500, while the black and Puerto Rican enrollment nearly quadrupled, from 25,188 to 98,829. At City College, the proportion went from 13.3 percent black and Puerto Rican in 1969 to 36 percent in 1971. The number of white Catholics in the system did increase, but their proportion of the total CUNY population decreased. The losers under open admissions were Jews, who had long been the backbone of the City University system. In 1970, Jewish students made up 23 percent of the City University student body; in 1971 they made up 16 percent. At City College, Jews accounted for half of the student population (876 students) in 1969. By 1971, their numbers were roughly the same (836 students), but they accounted for only about one quarter of the student body.[34]

Thirty years later, the policy of open admissions at the City University is still controversial. Supporters say that it provides educational opportunities for poor, immigrant, and minority students. Former Lindsay aide Peter Goldmark agrees, calling the experiment in open admissions at CUNY a "tremendous success" that has proved to be a "ladder of upward mobility" for poor and minority students. Others take issue with this rosy interpretation. Mayor Rudolph Giuliani appointed an Advisory Task Force on the City University of New York, headed by a former president of Yale University, Benno Schmidt. In the group's 1999 report to the mayor, it called the system "adrift":

> Its graduation rates are low, and students who do graduate take a long time to earn their degrees. . . . Academic standards are loose and confused, and CUNY lacks the basic information necessary to make sound judgements about the quality and effectiveness of its programs. CUNY's

full-time faculty is shrinking, aging, and losing ground. . . . There is a profound lack of leadership, so profound that even though the university is inundated by public school graduates who lack basic academic skills, it has not made a strong effort to get the schools to raise their standards.

Schmidt noted that the SAT scores of incoming students in the CUNY system were low. Consequently, the City University "conducts remedial education on a huge scale." More than thirty years later, one of Lindsay's leading accomplishments is still causing deep controversy and debate.[35]

INTEGRATING CANARSIE SCHOOLS

The Ocean Hill–Brownsville controversy featured the community control of schools and the rejection of racial integration. The next major battle over a Brooklyn school would find the roles reversed. The Board of Education, the black community, and the city's liberal elite wanted to bus minority children into a predominantly white community, in opposition to the wishes of the local school board. The issues of school integration, school disorders, and community control came to a head in 1972 in the Brooklyn neighborhood of Canarsie.

In the first half of the century, Canarsie, tucked into the southeast corner of Brooklyn, hard against Jamaica Bay, was a vast, sparsely populated swampland over which hung a perpetual odor from the fires at nearby garbage dumps. It was the butt of many vaudeville jokes. By the 1960s, though, Canarsie had become a neighborhood of one- and two-family homes populated mainly by Italians and Jews, many of whom had recently fled nearby areas such as East Flatbush, Brownsville, and East New York. Canarsie's mostly working-class residents were determined to protect their neighborhood, their homes, and their way of life. Jonathan Rieder, a sociologist who wrote a study of the people of Canarsie, described them as follows:

> To keep their illusion of refuge the residents sealed out alien races, suspicious people, disturbing forces. They made their community into a fortress, a fenced land. . . . Most blocks were entirely white. Nonetheless, Canarsians felt vulnerable to encroachment from the black communities that form an arc stretching from East Flatbush to the northwest, through Brownsville due north, to East New York in the northeast. Barriers of nature—Jamaica Bay to the south, Paerdegat Basin on the western flank, and Fresh Creek on the eastern flank—protect Canarsie, but those same boundaries limit the residents' options of flight and expansion.[36]

"Who are the Canarsie people?" asked one resident. "They came from places that expired. They're not rich. They bought a home in a sanctuary, and they're afraid they are going to lose it. . . . They want to protect their turf." Canarsie residents were not going to not move again.

After passage of the 1969 school decentralization law, Canarsie schools became part of the newly created District 18, along with neighboring East Flatbush. Students from the Tilden Houses, a low-income public housing project in Brownsville, had been bused to East Flatbush's J.H.S. 271 (Meyer Levin Junior High). But as the school's minority population approached fifty percent, busing in more black children made little sense. In the fall of 1972, white and black parents at Meyer Levin refused to accept any more children from the Tilden Houses at their school, both groups fearing the potential for racial "tipping." ("Tipping" occurred when the racial makeup in a school or neighborhood reached a level that encouraged "white flight.")

Schools Chancellor Harvey Scribner decided to send thirty-two black and Puerto Rican children from the Tilden Houses to J.H.S. 211 (John Wilson Junior High) in Canarsie. In response, furious white Canarsie parents staged a four-day sit-in that closed down the school. Chancellor Scribner ended the sit-in by agreeing to move the thirty-two children to another Canarsie school, J.H.S. 68 (Irving Bildersee Junior High). This move angered blacks and liberals, who felt that Scribner had caved in to white reaction. The parents of the Brownsville students feared for their children's safety at the nearly all-white J.H.S. 68, many incorrectly believing that the school was under Mafia protection. (In reality, J.H.S. 68 was nearly two thirds Jewish.)

The day after Scribner's edict, the black parents unsuccessfully tried to enroll their children at East Flatbush's J.H.S. 271 (Meyer Levin Junior High). The Board of Education, supported by State Education Commissioner Ewald Nyquist, promptly reversed Scribner's decision and ordered the thirty-two children back to J.H.S. 211. In response, the Canarsie parents organized a two-week boycott of all local public schools, in which nearly 90 percent of the district's 97,000 students stayed home. Meanwhile, groups of parents, numbering as many as 1,500, protested the arrival of the Brownsville students at J.H.S. 211. Bands of white and black toughs roamed Canarsie streets armed with pipes and chains looking for a fight. At the end of two weeks, the boycott ended as students started to return to school. Chancellor Scribner agreed to devise a new zoning plan for the district that would more fairly equalize integration among the district's schools.[37]

On the surface, the sight of white parents trying to keep minority children out of school was an eerie and disturbing image. Such incidents brought to mind the battles over integration in the South. Jack Newfield termed the crisis "Little Rock in New York," and the *Village Voice* called it "Bunkerism in Canarsie." The reality, though, was more complex. Only about 5 percent of Canarsie was black, but J.H.S. 211 was an integrated school with a breakdown of 70 percent white and 30 percent black. Another Canarsie school, J.H.S. 285, was evenly split between blacks and whites. Moreover, the 1,600 students at J.H.S. 211 meant the school was overcrowded. Whites insisted that their protest was not racist, but motivated by fears of overcrowding and racial tipping. After all, Canarsie parents never protested the 30 percent black student population already at John Wilson Junior High. Instead, Canarsie residents, wrote Pete Hamill, "are not afraid of black people or Puerto Ricans *per se*. They are afraid of what happens when racial balance is tipped in a school."[38]

No one was quite sure where the tipping point was, but most outer-borough whites were quite sure that it existed. Canarsie parents had only to look at East Flatbush's J.H.S. 232 (Winthrop). In 1962 the school was 99 percent white in a neighborhood that was similarly all-white, when black students from Bedford-Stuyvesant began attending the school under the city's Open Enrollment plan for minority students. By 1963, 10 percent of the school was black; the following year the portion increased to 32 percent. In 1966, nearly one half of Winthrop students were black, and the following year the black-to-white ratio was 58 to 42 percent. By 1972, at the time of the Canarsie controversy, the school was 99 percent black and the neighborhood was 80 percent black. Canarsie parents, though willing to send their children to John Wilson Junior High with 30 percent black students, feared that more black students, even the thirty-two from the Tilden Houses, would begin the push toward an all-black school. As the number of black students increased, white parents feared increasing racial tensions in the school, growing disorder, and a decline in the quality of education. With the freedom to move to the suburbs, middle-class parents would not long tolerate such a situation. And in John Lindsay's New York, as one journalist noted, the white middle class was "an endangered species. If integrated schools are ever to exist here, it is the middle class which will provide the white kids."[39]

The ultimate irony is that for integration to succeed, the white middle class needed reasons to keep its children in public schools. More school busing and the toleration of disorder in the classroom only drove the white middle class away, creating schools that were increasingly segregated.

PRISON RIOTS

No area of the city was exempt from civil disturbances. Not the universities. Not the public schools. Not the streets. Not the parks. And not the prisons. In the summer and fall of 1970, four city prisons lost control of their inmates, putting Lindsay's reputation as a riot stopper to the test.

In the early-morning hours of August 10, 1970, more than two hundred inmates at the Manhattan House of Detention for Men, also known as the

Tombs, overpowered their guards at breakfast and took control of one floor of the Centre Street facility. The inmates held five guards hostage and released a list of grievances. They complained about the length of their detentions before trial (most inmates at the Tombs were awaiting trial or sentencing). They complained about the bad food, the "molded bread . . . rotten potatoes, always half-cooked; powdered eggs with the consistency of overcooked tapioca; not enough desserts." They complained about the poor quality of legal aid lawyers. They complained about the brutality of the guards toward black and Puerto Rican inmates. They complained about how their family members were insulted and propositioned by prison officials. For eight hours, the inmates controlled the ninth floor of the Tombs, meeting occasionally with Lindsay administration officials. The inmates finally agreed to release their hostages after they were allowed to publicize their grievances and were promised no retributions.[40]

The Tombs was a time bomb. Originally designed to hold 932 inmates, the prison in the summer of 1970 was home to 1,992 men. Cells constructed for one man now held two or three. The Catholic chaplain described the imposing Tombs building as "the only dungeon above ground that I know of." The day after the first prison riot, a larger one erupted at the Tombs. The first day's disturbances had been contained to one floor, but the following day's riot spread to four of the building's fifteen floors as over 800 prisoners held 3 guards hostage for nearly seven hours. When prison officials again agreed to investigate the prisoners' complaints, the inmates released the hostages unharmed. But for the previous seven hours, the rioting prisoners took out their anger against the jail, as they "set fire to bedding and furniture, smashed three-inch-thick glass windows and bombarded the streets below with pieces of furniture and broken metal pipes." It took nine days for prison officials to gain control of the jail, when eighty corrections officers stormed the fourth floor of the prison and subdued about 180 inmates. "The situation seemed to be getting worse," said George McGrath, the commissioner of the Department of Correction. "Normally after a riot it cools down after a few days—this did not."

The Lindsay administration blamed Governor Rockefeller for the problems with the jails, criticizing the state for slow-moving courts and for not transferring prisoners from the crowded city jails to less-crowded state jails. Commissioner McGrath promised the inmates, the city, and the mayor that he would investigate the problems. By October, six weeks after the Tombs riots, little progress had taken place on the prison front and the city found itself faced with a domino effect of riots in four city prisons. The first riot occurred on October 1 at the Queens House of Detention in Long Island City. Built for 196 prisoners, it housed 335 at the time of the riot, in a building Barry Gottehrer described "as depressing as the set for an old James Cagney movie." Seven guards were taken as hostages. Leaders of the riot included some of the celebrated 21 Black Panthers awaiting trial for criminal conspiracy. The prisoners made their usual list of demands and grievances and met with celebrities and officials like Muhammed Ali, Georgia State Senator Julian Bond, the attorney William Kunstler, and Congressman Adam Clayton Powell. The Lindsay administration also formed a committee to meet with the prisoners. The committee included Bronx Borough President Herman Badillo, Congresswoman Shirley Chisolm, and the Black Muslim leader Louis Farrakhan. At the news conference, two guards were released as 5 inmate leaders spoke to cameras. Three inmates wore towels wrapped around their heads like Arab headdresses. In an effort to ease the situation in Long Island City, the Lindsay administration agreed to allow three state judges hear bail-review cases for 47 inmates. The judges reduced the bail of 4 inmates and paroled 9 men on the spot. At this gesture, the inmates released 2 more hostages.

The following day, October 2, rioting spread to the Tombs and a new prison facility in Kew Gardens, Queens. At the Tombs, over 200 inmates controlled one floor where they held 18 hostages, while in Kew Gardens 900 inmates overran the entire prison facility, although they took no hostages. All told over 1,400 inmates held 23 hostages in three prisons that day. The following day a fourth city jail, the Brooklyn House of Detention, experienced a full-scale riot as 1,500 inmates took control of the prison, smashing furniture and windows, setting small fires, and taking three guards hostage.

The Lindsay administration decided to send in corrections officers to retake the Brooklyn prison. Barry Gottehrer remembers seeing the haze of tear gas in the prison and then seeing a stream of blue uniforms exiting the prisons. It was the prison guards. "Most of them had fastened their gas masks incorrectly," Gottehrer wrote, "many had never even tried one on before. The gas seeped inside the masks. They choked and fled in such a panic that they left the doors unguarded. Had the inmates recognized their advantage, some at least might have been able to escape in the confusion." Members of the administration were amazed at the ineptitude of the prison guards and their lack of equipment. Meanwhile, a predominantly Puerto Rican crowd of 3,000 gathered outside the prison, throwing bottles at police from surrounding rooftops. By late in the afternoon of October 3, guards had stormed the Brooklyn prison, freed the three hostages, and returned the prison to a semblance of order. The following morning, corrections officers took control of the Kew Gardens prison. In restoring order there, Gottehrer described how two hundred inmates were injured as the guards "ripped up their own building more vehemently than any gang of rampaging prisoners."

This left two other prisons still in rebellion. At the Tombs, Lindsay gave the prisoners an ultimatum. They were told to tune their radios to WINS and WNYC at 9:30 P.M. At this time, Lindsay told them to give up the hostages and return to their cells. In exchange, Lindsay promised to meet personally with the prisoners to hear their grievances. He sympathized with their complaints, he said, but he told them that "this city cannot tolerate violence and disorder." The mayor gave the inmates thirty minutes to comply. If they did not, he warned, "other courses of action must be taken." A few hundred members of the NYPD's Tactical Patrol Force waited outside the prison for their orders. In reality, Barry Gottehrer noted, there was no detailed plan for a storming of the Tombs. After seeing what little planning there was, Gottehrer called the mayor and told him, "We can't go in. It would be a massacre." As the prison warden cajoled and bullied the inmate leaders, the ultimatum was extended. At 11:30 P.M., the inmates released their hostages. Soon thereafter, Lindsay entered the prison as promised. "I'm here to keep the commitment I made," he told the inmates as he went on to spend three hours in discussion with them.

The last holdout was the Queens House of Detention in Long Island City, where more than three hundred inmates still held three hostages. At five o'clock on Monday morning, following the strategy used at the Tombs, Lindsay aired the same ultimatum over the radio. At first, the Queens inmates voted not to surrender and to fight. Two events changed their minds. A Correction Department official gave an impassioned speech in Spanish asking the Puerto Rican inmates to surrender. Then, Assistant Chief Inspector Frederick Kowsky turned floodlights on the police massed outside the prison, a reminder of what awaited the prisoners if they did not give up. After the inmates surrendered, Commissioner McGrath ordered that they be brought down into the prison courtyard so that their cells could be searched for weapons. Waiting for the prisoners were dozens of angry prison guards armed with baseball bats, sticks, and lead pipes, ready to exact their retribution for the rebellion. As the prisoners were forced to walk past these guards into the courtyard, Lindsay's aides and McGrath were unable to protect them. "The yard echoed with screams and shouting and the thud of clubs," wrote Gottehrer. Fearing such punishment, thirty-nine inmates, mostly Black Panthers, refused to come down to the yard. In the end, Sid Davidoff came up with the idea of bringing in a fire truck with a cherry picker to pick up the remaining inmates from the top of the building and bring them to a waiting bus, thereby avoiding the vengeful guards.

At the end of his mayoralty, Lindsay recalled, "I'd say that the most difficult moment I ever had as mayor was the Tombs riot and the simultaneous one at the Queens branch of the city detention. . . . Every second was one where any decision made or any decision not made could have meant that there would be blood all over the floor." Jay Kriegel called it the "roughest single situation I've seen in five years. It was worse than the riots, worse than the garbage strikes, worse than anything." Lindsay's staff was, as always, eager to turn the prison riots into another example of Lindsay's keeping a lid on a chaotic and alienated city, with his mixture of honesty, courage, and hands-on governance. His press secretary, Tom Morgan, even called the prison rebellions Lindsay's Cuban Missile Crisis. But Gottehrer, who was now becoming burned out from his job, sensed that the prison riots reflected deeper problems with the administration. "Although the mayor personally had shown courage, good judgment, and common sense during an extremely difficult situation," wrote Gottehrer, "he had as mayor much to answer for, because in the end it is the mayor who is responsible for his agencies and their commissioners."[41]

The prison riots showed that McGrath, a former Massachusetts correction commissioner with a progressive reputation, did not have a handle on his department. "He was now finding out," wrote Gottehrer, "apparently for the first time, that many of his men were ill trained and ill equipped." By the end of the crisis, McGrath "looked like a man alternately deranged and out on his feet."

The soothing and progressive rhetoric from Lindsay and McGrath was intended to calm everyone down, but the truth was that both men had ignored repeated warnings throughout 1969—the year before the riots—about the dangers caused by overcrowding in the city's prisons. A 1969 state report had stated that the conditions in the Tombs were "conducive to mental, moral, and physical deterioration, and thus a further threat to the public welfare and safety." Republican State Senator John Dunne, chairman of the State Senate Committee on Crime and Correction, had met with Lindsay and McGrath at City Hall in December 1969 to discuss the issue. Dunne offered state assistance with the problem if the city could quickly find short-term detention centers for prisoners. Dunne wrote another report after the prison riots, in which he noted: "After the State rendered assistance, Commissioner McGrath failed to make any serious effort, as he had promised to do, to alleviate the wretched conditions in his facilities by seeking alternate facilities." To Dunne and his committee, the poor response of the Lindsay administration to prison overcrowding was "indicative of an apparent haphazard administration of the Department of Correction." The Dunne Report noted that key positions in the Department of Correction were vacant, key department personnel were not available during the prison riots and could not be reached, morale in the department was low, and McGrath appeared "to lack knowledge about his own institutions." Though Lindsay had handled the prison riots well, the very existence of riots highlighted the poor administration of Lindsay's Correction Department. Liberals like the *Village Voice*'s Nat Hentoff and Mary Breasted criticized the mayor for his inaction in confronting prison problems. Though many New Yorkers saw Lindsay as weak on law and order issues, Hentoff criticized Lindsay from the left for not dealing with prison brutality and for ignoring police abuses at Columbia University in 1968 and during the 1970 hardhat riot.[42]

THE KNAPP COMMISSION AND POLICE CORRUPTION

Lindsay's relationship with the police department was never strong. He entered office promising to reform the department, thereby angering many policemen. He fought for an unpopular Civilian Complaint Review Board to investigate complaints against police. He limited police action during civil disturbances. What Lindsay got in return was an antagonistic police force that resented his meddling in police affairs and a public that saw the city's streets become more dangerous.

Historically, New York City has witnessed investigations into police corruption on a fairly regular twenty-year cycle. Such investigations occurred in 1875, 1894, 1913, 1930, and 1949. By 1970, the city seemed poised for another such investigation. (Another investigation—undertaken by the Mollen Commission—took place in 1993.) In the late 1960s, the Lindsay administration was presented with evidence of police corruption. It would have seemed natural for the reform mayor to root out the corruption. He had nothing to gain from protecting the police. Yet just the opposite happened. Having been beaten badly over the issue of the CCRB and fearing that any investigation into corruption would completely sever whatever goodwill remained with the police, Lindsay and his aides chose to ignore the charges of corruption. An all-out war against corruption might have made it impossible to keep the city cool. Rather than antagonize the police any further, Lindsay chose to sweep the charges under the rug.

The charges of corruption came from two policemen who could not have been more different. David Durk was a young Jewish cop from the Upper West Side, serving on a predominantly Catholic police force, a graduate of Amherst College, serving alongside men who were mostly high-school graduates. He entered the NYPD as an idealist. Where others channeled their idealism into antiwar protests, social work, or the Peace Corps, Durk became a policeman. He spoke at college campuses throughout the nation trying to convince college students they could have a big impact on the world by wearing a badge and pounding a beat. The other policeman raising charges against the NYPD was Frank Serpico, a product of working-class, Italian-American Brooklyn. Where Durk was clean-cut and fresh-faced and lived with his wife and children on the Upper West Side, Serpico was shaggy and slovenly. He lived among the bohemians and youths of Greenwich Village.

What both men had in common was a revulsion toward the kind of corruption—petty and major—they encountered on the police force. Serpico saw how policemen regularly expected and received free meals and noted the resentment it created among restaurant owners. "It was a small thing, perhaps, but in retrospect Serpico would see it as another indication of the growing estrangement between the police and much of the public," wrote Peter Maas in his book *Serpico*, "a breakdown of respect—a feeling that too many cops were taking whatever they could, not caring what anyone thought, whether or not it denigrated them, so that even the café owner, ostensibly a booster of policemen, was in fact treating them with disdain." "Cooping," the practice of finding a secluded spot on one's beat to catch a few winks, was common practice. What was more serious, though, were the payoffs policemen received from gamblers and drug dealers. Serpico witnessed how policemen regularly received a "pad," which was their share of payoffs from criminals in need of protection.[43]

Durk decided to take action. He had met Jay Kriegel in the summer of 1965, during Lindsay's first mayoral campaign, while on patrol in Central Park. Kriegel was Lindsay's point man on police matters during the campaign and would shortly become his liaison to the NYPD. Like Kriegel, Durk was a man in tune with the Lindsay plan—a young, idealistic college graduate who wanted to change the system. Like Durk, Kriegel was a graduate of Amherst College. The two became friends. The following summer, Durk offered to bring other policemen, most likely Frank Serpico, to brief Lindsay in private about police corruption. Durk told Serpico that Kriegel really cared about police corruption and would allow him and other unhappy cops to meet Lindsay and begin to reform the department. Durk and Serpico met with Kriegel in the spring of 1967. "My God, this is unbelievable," was Kriegel's response to Serpico's accusations. Though Kriegel at first seemed to favor the idea of getting the policemen a meeting with Lindsay, a few days later Kriegel told Durk the deal was off. Durk later testified that several weeks after their meeting, Kriegel finally told him that any investigation into police corruption would have to wait until after the summer because Lindsay did not want to "upset the cops." Durk believed this to mean that with potential trouble in the ghetto, the mayor's office would not want to antagonize the police. Kriegel later denied having made such a statement to Durk. He claimed he told Durk not to speak of the proposed meeting because it was "never planned, never contemplated."[44]

Durk continued to meet occasionally with Kriegel, trying to push the issue of police corruption. By the spring of 1968, Durk realized that his dealings with Kriegel and the mayor's office were going nowhere. The Lindsay administration had other concerns. Durk was angry. "That fuck Jay," Durk said after realizing the mayor's office would not act on his charges, "he's not going to do a fucking thing either." According to Durk, "Jay fucked us. He decided that if he started a real investigation into police corruption it would disrupt the department, and that might lead to riots. Lindsay's political image depended on [having] no riots in the ghettoes. . . . They told us they would investigate after the long, hot summer of 1968. Then they told us they would investigate as soon as Lindsay was re-elected in 1969." The question became: Did Kriegel ever tell Lindsay about the charges of corruption told to him by Durk and Serpico? When Serpico asked Kriegel this question, the mayoral aide responded: "Not directly. We talked about the problem. He [Lindsay] had the same problem I did."[45]

Three months before his first meeting with Kriegel in 1967, Serpico had met with NYPD Inspector Cornelius Behan, who later relayed Serpico's charges to the department's number two man, First Deputy Police Commissioner John Walsh. In October 1967, the NYPD itself began investigating Serpico's charges of police corruption among plainclothes police in the Bronx. Eight Bronx policemen were indicted for perjury (four were found guilty) and others were brought up on departmental charges. Still, the department did not initiate any department-wide investigation, preferring to take the "rotten-egg" view of corruption: its occurrence was isolated. Serpico and Durk became frustrated at what they saw as the relative inaction of the police department. This was part of their complaint to Kriegel.

Meanwhile, Durk had taken his story elsewhere in city government. During the 1967 Memorial Day weekend, Durk and Serpico met with the city's investigations commissioner, Arnold Fraiman. Technically, Durk worked for Fraiman as a police detective assigned to the department. The 1967 meeting was the first and only time Durk brought up the corruption accusations with his boss. Clearly Fraiman resented Durk. And he did not have a high opinion of Serpico either, whom he found a "psycho" and a "very strange guy." Fraiman refused Serpico's request to set up a surveillance truck to nab crooked Bronx cops; Serpico rejected Fraiman's request that he wear a wire. That put an end to the Investigations Department's involvement in police corruption.[46]

One reason for the mishandling of the police corruption issue was the difficult personalities of the men involved. According to James Lardner, a journalist sympathetic to Durk, many people did not like Durk, not just because of his whistle-blowing, but because of his manners. According to Robert Daley, the deputy police commissioner for press affairs under Commissioner Patrick V. Murphy, Commissioner Murphy "never failed to point out that . . . the district attorney and federal attorneys were all sick and tired of the endless phone calls from Durk, of the pressure from Durk to launch and complete this or that incredibly complicated investigation at once." Years later, Fraiman was very reluctant to talk about Durk. He believed that the former policeman was "not a very truthful guy." Through the years, Durk has maintained a reputation as an eccentric, whose career has been stymied by his difficult personality.[47]

On the other side, Kriegel was the epitome of Lindsay's brash young aides. Bright, ambitious, and arrogant, he was always at Lindsay's side. His manners, too, put many people off. One Lindsay aide said, "Talking to Jay Kriegel is like putting your finger in an electric light socket." Barry Gottehrer called him "one of the most unsophisticated bright people in government." Frank Serpico was difficult, too, in his own way. He was stubborn and moody. His dress and lifestyle did not endear him to his fellow cops and made him suspect in the eyes of the authorities. Bronx District Attorney Burton Roberts said of Serpico, "Frank Serpico was not the overwhelming hero he has been made out to be. I suppose it was good that he came forward. No one else was coming forward. But everything he did, you had to pull teeth."

Angry at the indifference of the police department and the Lindsay administration, Durk and Serpico told their tales of corruption to David Burnham, a reporter for the New York *Times,* in early 1970. In the middle of April, Burnham saw Lindsay's press secretary, Tom Morgan, at a cocktail party. Deciding it was time to push the story forward, Burnham told Morgan, "Tom, you know I'm working on this big piece about corruption—police corruption. It's very exciting, and I know how pleased you and Mayor Lindsay will be when it comes out." Burnham knew that his words would make it back to City Hall.[48]

With the knowledge that the *Times* story was in the works and due to appear in late April, Lindsay decided to beat the paper to the punch. On Thursday, April 23, the mayor announced the creation of a five-man panel to review the procedures for investigating police corruption. The panel, headed by Corporation Counsel J. Lee Rankin, included then Police Commissioner Leary, then Investigations Commissioner Robert Ruskin, Manhattan District Attorney Frank Hogan, and Bronx District Attorney Burton Roberts. Lindsay's move only made the *Times's* metropolitan desk editor, Arthur Gelb, more determined to publish the story. Gelb had his best reporters working through the night to put together Burnham's story. The next day, Gelb sent the City Hall reporter Martin Tolchin to read the article to Lindsay and the top police brass. The charges upset Lindsay. On Saturday, April 25, the first installment of the Burnham series appeared on the front page. Lindsay called Gelb and Abe Rosenthal to Gracie Mansion. According to the *Times* reporter John Corry, "Lindsay was angry and aggrieved . . . Abe [Rosenthal] and Arthur were firm." Lardner recounts that "Lindsay subjected them [Gelb and Rosenthal] to a harangue about taking the word of a couple of disgruntled cops." The corruption story marked the start of the *Times's* souring on John Lindsay. The romantic crush was over.[49]

Burnham's series ran for three days. It began with the curt accusation that "narcotics dealers, gamblers, and businessmen make illicit payments of millions of dollars a year to the policemen of New York." Much of the police corruption occurred among plainclothes policemen who were assigned to gambling, prostitution, and drug dealing. The story detailed how numbers runners in the city's reported $1.5 billion gambling business paid off policemen. In the Bronx, a policeman received a "pad" of between $800 and $1,000 a month in payoffs from gamblers. Burnham quoted one anonymous plainclothes officer (clearly Serpico) as saying that a policeman on the take was "only limited by his own initiative. Like you can go out and make your own scores. I heard one guy openly boasting that he made $60,000 in the past two years."

Kriegel had no comment on the series. Fraiman, by 1970 a State Supreme Court justice, denied that he had discontinued his office's investigation of police corruption. He said the information Serpico had provided him was "extremely general in nature" and it would have been illegal to have bugged the police surveillance truck as Serpico suggested.[50]

After publication of the *Times* series, Lindsay formed a new investigation unit to look into police corruption charges. This replaced the Rankin panel. It was clear that Rankin's panel, including Commissioner Leary, would not be independent enough to carry out the kind of investigation that the furor surrounding the *Times* series necessitated. The head of the new panel was the patrician Wall Street lawyer Whitman Knapp. The other panel members were attorney Arnold Bauman (he was later replaced by law professor John Sprizzo), Cyrus Vance, Joseph Monserrat, president of the Board of Education, and Franklin Thomas, president of the Bedford-Stuyvesant Restoration Corporation.

Lindsay found opposition to the creation of the Knapp Commission from an unlikely source: City Council President Sanford Garelik. When Lindsay hired Leary as police commissioner in 1966, the mayor teamed him with Garelik as chief inspector. Unfortunately, neither man lived up to expectations. The Lindsay administration found that Garelik was much more conservative than they had believed, despite his closeness to the Liberal Party leader, Alex Rose. One member of the Lindsay administration called Garelik "oafish" and not very competent. Still, Lindsay chose Garelik as his running mate for City Council president in 1969, partly because of Alex Rose and partly because Garelik was a law-and-order Jewish policeman. After Garelik was elected, however, he quickly turned into a Lindsay antagonist. John Caulfield, who served as a spy for President Nixon in New York, met with Garelik three times in 1970. "Presently, relations between Lindsay and Garelik are extremely poor," Caulfield wrote to John Ehrlichman in October 1970. According to Caulfield, Garelik was "a most insecure and unpredictable person" who voiced "*unusual* conservative opinions on many subjects bringing change in political personality." Despite this, according to Caulfield, Garelik was "surrounded by New York labor hacks of Jewish and minority group representation." Soon after being sworn in, Garelik began attacking his former running mate. Despite Garelik's opposition to the Knapp Commission, the Board of Estimate eventually passed a bill funding the commission.[51]

As the Knapp Commission began its investigation, the Lindsay administration decided that it was time for Police Commissioner Leary to leave. Though they had hailed him in 1966 as a reform police leader, Lindsay and his aides soon grew disillusioned with Leary. Lindsay later called Leary a "terrible administrator." He had been brought in from Philadelphia as an outsider who would benefit from not having any ties to the current department. But in 1970, Leary remained an outsider. His enigmatic personality alienated many in the Lindsay administration, and he never earned the loyalty of his men. Above all, Leary showed little desire to take on the established practices of the NYPD. He was so worried about the appearance of political meddling in the department that he would enter City Hall through a backdoor when he went there for meetings with Lindsay.

Lindsay and his aides had been angry at the police reaction to the hardhat riot in May and disappointed in the weak police report delivered thereafter. It was then that the mayor began to consider replacing Leary. The publication of the charges of police corruption and the naming of the Knapp Commission sealed Leary's fate. It became obvious that Leary was not interested in investigating corruption. In his response to the *Times* series, Leary called the paper's sources "prostitutes, narcotics addicts and gamblers and disgruntled policemen." Leary viewed the accusations of corruption as "McCarthyism all over." Later, Leary placed much of the blame for corruption on the "hypocrisy of society," whose moral codes deemed prostitution, gambling, and doing business on Sunday as immoral, but whose members regularly violated those codes. Leary believed that the Knapp Commission would smear the entire NYPD and complained to Lindsay throughout the summer about the investigation.[52]

In September, Leary resigned and was replaced by Patrick Murphy. The new Commissioner seemed like a stereotypical tough cop: he had been the police commissioner of Detroit and the top cop in Syracuse and Washington, D.C. The father of eight children, Murphy was an Irish Catholic who had patrolled the tough streets of Red Hook, Brooklyn. He was the former head of the city's Police Academy and was known to most city policemen. But there was more to Murphy than the big-city cop. He was widely regarded as a liberal-minded policeman. He was also something of an intellectual, having worked briefly at the Urban Institute, a Washington think tank. He was short and slight of stature, with a soft voice that spoke the language of academia and think-tanks more than the language of the streets. One journalist noted that Murphy "looks like anything but a policeman. A banker, a successful Wall Street lawyer, a department head at a university, perhaps. But not a policeman. His clothes are too well-tailored; his voice seldom rises above the intimate conversation level; his features are almost too delicate." Robert Daley, who had served as Murphy's press man, noted, "For one who had chosen always to stand in a violent arena, his life had been surprisingly devoid of violence. Trained as a bomber pilot in the Navy during World War II, he had never bombed anyone. As a cop on the beat in New York, he preferred always to use his soft, calm voice rather than his nightstick." One police detective described Murphy as a "man who nearly always had the dour look of someone who had just sucked a lemon. . . . And he often talked and acted more like a professor than a cop."

In spite of his stint at the Police Academy, Murphy was not a popular a choice among rank-and-file cops. Still, Lindsay now had a man who not only represented his views on law enforcement but also would be vigilant on the issue of corruption.[53]

Whitman Knapp thought that Murphy's appointment in September would be the end of his brief investigation. New blood was now running the department and Murphy seemed eager to root out corruption. "When he came back to New York, Murphy should have asked the mayor to disband the Knapp Commission at once," Knapp later said. "He should have said, 'You want me to reorganize and revitalize the force. I can't do this work with the Knapp Commission hanging over my head. Get rid of it.'. . . That's what I would have done in his place. But Murphy didn't do anything, and I was surprised." So Knapp moved ahead with his investigation.[54]

Few people had confidence that the Knapp Commission would uncover anything. Its budget was small and there was a time limit on its subpoena power. This did not stop Knapp from publicly criticizing Lindsay, saying that the mayor "cannot escape responsibility for a situation that develops in a department as important as the Police Department." As for Leary, the former Police Commissioner, Knapp accused him of failing "to exercise leadership in the field of corruption." As the Knapp Commission began its work, Commissioner Murphy began his own efforts to reform the department. Eight police captains were relieved of their command responsibilities. Murphy promoted his own team of reformers, many of them over more senior officers, to man the department's higher posts. The PBA president, Edward Kiernan, accused Murphy of "the systematic destruction of the finest police department in the world." With both the Knapp Commission and Murphy cracking down on police malfeasance, Kiernan said that a policeman "has to keep one eye out for assassins, the other out for departmental spies waiting to catch him in technical violations."[55]

Murphy won few friends in an already wary department. Arguably, he was not interested in earning the goodwill of his men, but rather in weeding out corruption. On the other hand, Murphy's problem, according to Robert Daley, was that he "was not and never had been a cop's cop." Patrolmen derisively referred to their boss as "Little Tin God" and "Little Boy Scout." To Daley, Murphy seemed "a kind of Thomas Aquinas of the police departments of our times. Murphy was as cool and detached as a philosopher. He would have been happier in a medieval cloister dealing ideas off the deck at the rate of one card a day, formulating an entire system to send down through the police forces of the ages." Some reports noted that policemen began turning down free cups of coffee. With such pressures on police to avoid the appearance of impropriety, one newly promoted sergeant said of Murphy: "The men hate him. But right now a cop would lock up his partner—with all the pressure that's on him."[56]

One of the most embarrassing incidents for the NYPD and the Commission was when Knapp Commission investigators found Chief of Detectives Albert Seedman's name on a list of policemen who had accepted free meals at city hotels. Chief Seedman, his wife, and another couple had received one free dinner at the New York Hilton worth $83. The papers got hold of the story and Murphy was forced to suspend the respected and colorful Seedman. The ensuing uproar at Seedman's punishment and the growing realization that the department was becoming paralyzed by the anticorruption investigation led Murphy to reinstate Seedman. In another incident, Garelik, the NYPD's former chief inspector, admitted that when he was on the force he regularly accepted gifts from businessmen.

When hearings began in October 1971, the Knapp Commission was able to bring three present and former policemen to testify about widespread corruption on the force, including their own crimes. Investigators had caught each taking bribes. The commission's short-handed investigating unit, led by its hard-charging and ambitious chief counsel, Michael Armstrong, had been following policemen and tracking down leads on corruption. The investigators got lucky when they found Teddy Ratner, an expert in bugging devices. Ratner managed to bug the phone of Xaviera Hollander, the "Happy Hooker," whose house of prostitution on Manhattan's East Side had made her famous. Hollander was paying off a policeman named William Phillips, and Ratner taped incriminating conversations between the two. Ratner turned the tapes over to the Knapp Commission, and the Knapp Commission had its first witness. According to Robert Daley, Phillips "by his own admission, was the crookedest crooked cop then living, perhaps the crookedest cop of all time anywhere. He knew names, dates, places, and the amounts of payoffs. He threw back the covers on the dirty bed." According the Knapp Commission Report, "Phillips' entire career had been one of virtually unrelieved corruption. He had, in his own words, been a 'super thief.' " At the same time, Phillips was also considered a very good, effective, and aggressive policeman.[57]

Phillips proved to be the central witness called before the Knapp Commission. His testimony resulted in the indictments of seventeen policemen and fourteen civilians, most of whom were organized crime members. In its first public hearing in October 1971, Phillips told the commission that every plainclothes policeman he knew participated in payoffs and graft. Phillips's testimony began a week of revelations about police corruption. Not only did cops take money from gamblers and construction sites, they also paid off desk sergeants at the precinct house. Phillips told the Commission that plainclothes police received a "pad" of anywhere from $400 to $1,500 a month depending on what area of the city they worked. Phillips also told of a drug bust in East Harlem where $137,000 was confiscated. The three arresting officers split $80,000 of the money. Despite these sensational charges, much of the bribery described was of a petty nature. Free meals from neighborhood eateries were common, as were Christmas tips of money and whiskey.[58]

Patrolman Edward Droge testified after Phillips. An investigator had heard Droge on tape accepting money from an arrested drug dealer in exchange for letting the dealer go. Droge told numerous stories of corruption, some petty and some not. He admitted taking money from gamblers in Brooklyn. He told how policemen often helped themselves to free goods, such as hot dogs, from local factories. He described how owners of check-cashing stores and supermarkets would pay police to escort them to the bank to make a deposit or guard their stores when they opened for the day. One tow-truck driver later testified to the common practice of having to pay police after towing cars from accidents.

The third policeman to testify was Waverly Logan. Logan had earlier been dismissed from the department for taking a hundred-dollar bribe from a suspect in return for letting him go. Logan belonged to a special police squad, the Preventative Enforcement Patrol (PEP), and testified that all but two of the squad's twenty patrolmen took bribes from drug dealers and gamblers. The Lindsay administration had created PEP as an all-minority squad specially recruited to patrol minority neighborhoods. The units had already caused controversy because many of the minority policemen were high-school dropouts and some even had minor police records.[59]

In response to the testimony, Commissioner Murphy suspended Phillips and Droge. This angered Knapp, who, according to Daley, had probably promised the men something in exchange for testifying. After Knapp threatened to denounce Murphy and Lindsay publicly, Murphy restored the men to their positions. Shortly thereafter, Phillips was arrested for the murder of a pimp and a prostitute from whom he was extorting money. His first trial ended in a hung jury, but Phillips was finally convicted of murder in December 1974 and sentenced to twenty-five years to life.

Under prodding from Lindsay critics such as Queens Councilman Matthew Troy, the Knapp Commission agreed to open a second set of hearings in December focusing on how the Lindsay administration had responded to charges of police corruption. Durk and Serpico would testify, along with Jay Kriegel, Howard Leary, and Arnold Fraiman.

Leary returned to the stand to talk about the corruption charges. His testimony before the Knapp Commission reinforced the belief of many in the Lindsay administration that Leary had been a poor commissioner. The former commissioner testified that he wished he had been informed of Serpico's complaints about corruption and that former First Deputy Commissioner John Walsh had told him about the corruption accusations, "but not in any great depths. It wasn't my practice to indulge deeply in those sort of things because I . . . believed in the competency and integrity of Mr. Walsh." At another point in his testimony, Leary responded that whatever Walsh or the other officers reported to him about corruption, "I accepted." Either Leary was covering up his knowledge of the corruption charges and his lack of action or he was truly disengaged from what was happening in his department. Either way, he appeared less than competent.[60]

Kriegel's testimony was a more serious matter. His position in the Lindsay administration and his friendship with Durk put Kriegel directly in the middle of the controversy. The crux of the matter was whether or not Kriegel ever told Lindsay about Durk and Serpico's charges and how they were unhappy with the response they received from the police department. If Kriegel had shared all he knew with Lindsay, the mayor would have been neglectful in not following up on the charges. In closed-door testimony before the commission in July 1971, Kriegel admitted to telling Lindsay that Durk and Kriegel were "not satisfied" with the department's investigation. But in his public testimony in December, Kriegel changed his story, saying that he "made recommendations to the mayor on the general problem of corruption" but did not bring up Durk and Serpico's specific complaints about how their charges were being handled.

According to his public testimony, Kriegel said he told the mayor that he had met with a police friend (Durk) and another policeman (Serpico) who told him about corruption within the department. The two had suggested that Kriegel pull a group of policemen together to meet with Lindsay and describe their experience with police corruption. According to Kriegel, "The mayor wanted to know what the conditions were, and I said that they were adamant that this had to be done secretly. . . . The mayor thought that was an unreasonable way to tie his hand should any information that was real come up at that point in time." According to this version of Kriegel's story, Serpico and Durk's need for secrecy prevented the mayor's office from acting on the charges. Kriegel "was handcuffed from doing anything about it." Kriegel made no mention of Lindsay's telling him to lay off the investigation because of the fear of riots and the damage they would do to his re-election campaign. Charges of perjury against Kriegel were briefly considered, but soon dropped.[61]

Knapp had allowed Lindsay to avoid testifying in public. The mayor held a press conference after Kriegel's testimony, denying that Kriegel had ever told him of Durk and Serpico's complaints. Instead, Lindsay said that he had told Kriegel he "could not under any circumstances as Mayor accept those ground rules [of secrecy]. . . . It would have undermined [Commissioner Leary] totally." In addition to sullying the reputation of the NYPD, the Knapp Commission was now making the Lindsay administration look bad. After all, the mayor had been elected on his promise to clean up the city from such corruption. In his best Agnew-esque rhetoric, Lindsay had lashed out at those who criticized his reaction to police corruption by calling them "petty piranhas of the political marketplace."[62]

The Knapp Commission recommended that Governor Rockefeller appoint a special deputy attorney general to wage a "war on corruption." This special investigator would spend two years investigating and prosecuting "all crimes involving corruption in the criminal process." He would investigate not only the police, but prosecutors and the court system. The city's five district attorneys protested this idea, since it would supersede their authority. It also implicated them in covering up police corruption. Nevertheless, Rockefeller followed the commission's suggestion and appointed a little-known Long Island lawyer, Maurice Nadjari, as the state's special prosecutor to investigate corruption in the city's criminal justice system. Nadjari not only investigated corruption but also took aim at the Lindsay administration, attempting to uncover illegalities in, for instance, Lindsay's 1972 presidential run.

The Knapp Commission hearings were something of a made-for-television spectacle. Many policemen felt tarred by the corruption brush and accused the commission of McCarthyite methods. Even the New York Civil Liberties Union questioned the constitutionality of the hearings. Whitman Knapp defended his commission by saying that it "became apparent that nothing would happen unless the public had its nose pushed in it." When asked whether he was concerned about the effect the hearings were having on the image of innocent cops, Knapp responded, "That's too bad."[63]

The Knapp Commission dug up a significant amount of police corruption and highlighted the type of police behavior that eroded the public's support for law enforcement. In his opening statement at the commission's first hearing, in October 1971, Whitman Knapp made clear his view of corruption. "The main thrust of our findings—and the point we wish to bring home to the public—is that the problem of police corruption cannot be solved merely by focusing on individual acts of wrongdoing," said Knapp. "It arises out of an endemic condition which must be attacked on all fronts." The Knapp Commission Report was equally blunt: "We found corruption to be widespread." Yet it should be made clear that most of the serious corruption that Knapp found was in the plainclothes division, numbering around four hundred officers. Talk of $1,000-a-month "pads" pertained almost entirely to plainclothes police. Uniformed patrolmen, as Knapp noted, received smaller payments from construction sites, bars, grocery stores, and other businesses. The question of corruption among the uniformed rank-and-file, according to Knapp, was "equally serious if less dramatic."[64]

The Knapp Commission condemned all forms of corruption, from accepting a bottle of whiskey at Christmas to fixing arrests to shaking down drug dealers. In fact, according to Knapp, it was the former group of policemen who were most to blame for corruption because they created a climate in the department that tolerated all forms of corruption: "Of course, not all policeman are corrupt. If we are to exclude such petty infractions as free meals, an appreciable number do not engage in any corrupt activities. Yet, with extremely rare exceptions even those who themselves engage in no corrupt activities are involved in corruption in the sense that they take no steps to prevent what they know or suspect to be going on about them."

Knapp found that corrupt policemen were divided into "meat eaters," like William Phillips, who took every opportunity to use their power to line their pockets, and "grass eaters," who freely accepted the gifts and payoffs without seeking them out. Opinions differed as to whether the "meat eaters" or the "grass eaters" were the bigger problem. According to the Knapp Report, "Grass eaters are the heart of the problem. Their great numbers tend to make corruption 'respectable.' They also encourage the code of silence that brands anyone who exposes corruption as a traitor." The Knapp Commission felt that the most brazenly corrupt officers like Phillips were not really the problem. Consequently, when Commissioner Murphy suspended Phillips, Knapp complained. Singling out and investigating these offenders, or "rotten apples," was, according to Knapp, "a basic obstacle to meaningful reform. To begin with, it reinforced and gave respectability to the code of silence." On the other side, Assistant Chief Inspector Sydney Cooper, a noted departmental corruption fighter, saw "meat eaters" as the real problem. If the department went after them, Cooper argued, "we'll scare off the grass eaters and the birds won't even be tempted."[65]

Certainly Knapp was correct that corruption weakened the public's faith in the police. But the commission's refusal to distinguish between a free meal or taking a ten-dollar bribe to overlook a speeding ticket and taking a monthly bribe in the form of a "pad" from gamblers caused more problems in the police department and further weakened morale. As shocking as the accusations of $1,000 monthly "pads" for policemen to ignore illegal gambling were to the public, such corruption stemmed from a deeper issue. Policemen knew that despite its illegality, people would gamble, using numbers runners and bookies. It was an established practice and was, in many ways, a victimless crime. In addition, policemen knew that gambling arrests were futile and that few gamblers received any punishment worse than a small fine. The Knapp Commission studied 108 gambling arrests and found that only 50 had resulted in a conviction. Not one of these 50 received jail time. The Policy Sciences Center examined 356 gambling arrests in Brooklyn and found 198 dismissals, 63 acquittals, and 95 convictions. Only 6 of those convicted received jail sentences, and the longest of these was one year. The other sentences averaged seventeen days. In light of these numbers, most police saw gambling money as "clean graft," as opposed to money taken from prostitutes or drug dealers. Though these facts do not excuse taking payoffs, they should have worked to mitigate the public's outrage against policemen who saw little desire on the part of the courts and the public to crack down on illegal gambling.[66]

The issue of police corruption showed that Lindsay was not fully in control of the police department. The Knapp Commission Report, though it did not criticize Lindsay directly, condemned the city's official inaction: "Al-

though Walsh, Kriegel, and Fraiman all acknowledged the extreme seriousness of the charges [of Durk and Serpico] and the unique opportunity provided by the fact that a police officer was making them, none of them took
any action," the commission concluded. "No serious investigation was undertaken until some months later when Serpico went to his division commander." At the time of the Knapp Commission Report, the NYPD was
investigating 310 cases of corruption involving 627 policemen. Twenty-six
policemen had been indicted up to that point, 34 policemen had been suspended, and 57 faced departmental charges.[67]

While the public was bombarded with stories about the corruption of its
police officers, crime and disorder continued to increase on the city's streets.
Unfortunately, the main focus of police work during this time was to stay out
of trouble. A "clean" police department was a greater priority than one that reduced crime. Rank-and-file policemen had little incentive to enforce the law
actively. Both the accusation of police brutality and the danger of being viewed
as corrupt kept police from being as active in high-crime areas as they needed
to be. Increasingly, the motto of New York City policemen was: "Don't get involved." The NYPD retreated to a reactive stance, becoming unwilling and
unable to do anything about the growing number of murders, robberies, rapes,
and assaults plaguing the city. By the early 1970s, the police were not just the
targets of anticorruption investigators and reform politicians; they increasingly
had to deal with street violence that appeared directed at them.

KILLINGS OF POLICEMEN

During the early 1970s, the incidence of attacks upon policemen increased
at an alarming rate. Some people, like Sanford Garelik, the City Council
president and former chief inspector, blamed the attacks on a criminal conspiracy of white, black, and Puerto Rican radicals funded in part by Cuba
and China. Mayor Lindsay denied the idea of a conspiracy, and most people
agreed with him. Yet whatever the reason, during Lindsay's second term policemen faced the threat of more physical attacks, in addition to terrorist
bombings and continued riots in the black ghettos of Brooklyn.[68]

In the fall of 1969, antiwar radicals led by a man named Sam Melville set
off explosions at the offices of major corporations. The targets included the
RCA Building at Rockefeller Center, the General Motors Building on Fifth
Avenue, Chase Manhattan Bank and Marine Midland Bank Building in
lower Manhattan, and Macy's department store on Thirty-fourth Street. In
October 1969 a bomb permanently shut down the Armed Forces Induction
Center at Whitehall Street. Police were also targeted for bomb attacks. In
June 1970, a bomb with the force of fifteen sticks of dynamite exploded at
Police Headquarters, injuring seven people. In September 1970, the Queens
home of First Deputy Police Commissioner John Walsh was firebombed in

the middle of the night. No one was injured and only the garage door was damaged. A red and black flag with an image of a clenched fist was found outside the house. The bombing occurred as members of the "Panther 21" were going on trial in New York for conspiracy. Earlier in the year, the house of State Supreme Court Justice John Murtagh, in the Inwood section of Manhattan, had been bombed. Again no one was injured and the house sustained only minor damage. Painted on the sidewalk in front of the house were the slogans FREE THE PANTHER 21 and VIETCONG HAVE WON. Though no pattern or conspiracy was ever uncovered surrounding these bombings, they seemed to be associated with both antiwar radicals and black militants.

By the early seventies, violent attacks on New York City policemen seemed commonplace. As Commissioner Murphy later stated, "Literally dozens of police officers had been shot, and many of them were narcotics undercover officers. Indeed, for some time in the early 1970s it was practically open season on police officers." Assaults against police had been steadily increasing since 1950. In that year there were 137 assaults. By 1966, there were assaults against 544 policemen. In just the first eight months of 1969, there were 591 attacks. In the first eight months of 1970, there were 985, with 34 policemen shot, 44 cut or stabbed, 96 bit, 217 punched, and 154 kicked. The worst years were 1970 and 1971. In 1970, 45 policemen were shot or wounded, and 10 policemen died on duty, 8 of them killed by assailants. In 1971, 13 policemen died, 10 of them killed by assailants. This figure of 10 murdered officers in one year was the highest since 1930. During Lindsay's two terms, 69 policemen died in the line of duty. (This includes those who died from nonviolent causes or accidents.) This is compared to 56 police deaths during Ed Koch's three terms and 48 police deaths during Robert Wagner's three terms.[69]

A police detective named Sonny Grosso later wrote of this time: "Cops were being lured into ambushes and gunned down by waiting execution squads. And no matter how fast times had changed, no matter what politics and radical rhetoric had done to affect the relationships between a cop and the people he was paid to serve, cop killing was against all the rules, was the one unforgivable transgression." Chief of Detectives Albert Seedman remembers a young patrolman at this time telling him, "I'm carrying my police special plus two non-reg weapons and I'm still scared shitless to walk on my beat. For my wife and my two kids, I've got to be scared. . . . And the worst of it is that up there [pointing to the general direction of headquarters] they don't give a good goddam as long as everything looks clean."[70]

The frequency of the shootings and their circumstances led many police to believe they were targets of a conspiracy by black militants. But a closer look shows that the issue of police killings was more complex. Of the ten policemen killed in 1970, five were white and five were black. All of the killers who were identified were black. Two policemen were killed off-duty in bar disputes. Another was killed by his brother-in-law. Only two of the murders appeared to be linked to black militants. Yet the killings shook an already fragile city. In late May 1971, more violence broke out. Within a span of forty-eight hours, four policemen were shot, two of them killed.[71]

On the evening of May 19, Patrolmen Thomas Curry and Nicholas Binetti were sitting in their police car on Riverside Drive. Their job on this quiet, leafy street was to provide protection for the man prosecuting the "Panther 21" trial, Manhattan District Attorney Frank Hogan, who lived at Riverside Drive and 112th Street. In the wake of the firebombing of Judge Murtagh's house, Hogan had received death threats and was granted police protection. While on duty, Curry and Binetti noticed a car traveling south on the northbound lane of Riverside Drive. The two policemen followed the car and pulled it over a few blocks away. As the two cars stopped next to each other, the passenger of the car pulled out a machine gun and fired at the policemen and then drove away. Curry and Binetti were seriously wounded, but both men survived the attack.

Two nights later, two policemen responded to a call at a housing project at 159th Street and Harlem River Drive in Upper Manhattan, the site of the old Polo Grounds. Patrolmen Waverly Jones and Joseph Piagentini were ambushed and shot from behind. Piagentini was shot eight times and Jones was shot twice. Jones was black and his partner was white. Both men were pronounced dead on arrival at a nearby hospital. That same day, the license plate of the car sought by police in the shooting of Curry and Binetti was sent to the office of the *New York Times*. Accompanying the plate was a note that read:

> Here are the license plates sort [*sic*] after by the fascist state pig police. We send them in order to exhibit the potential power of oppressed peoples to acquire revolutionary justice. The armed goons of this racist government will again meet the guns of oppressed Third World Peoples as long as they occupy our community and murder our brothers and sisters in the name of American law and order; just as the fascist Marines and Army occupy Vietnam in the name of democracy and murder Vietnamese people in the name of American imperialism are confronted with the guns of the Vietnamese Liberation Army, the domestic armed forces of racism and oppression will be confronted with the guns of the Black Liberation Army, who will mete out in the tradition of Malcolm and all true Revolutionaries real justice. We are revolutionary justice. All Power to the people.

Police ran tests on the plate and the newspaper in which it had been wrapped, and found the fingerprints of Richard Moore, one of the defendants in the "Panther 21" trial who had jumped bail. Less than two weeks earlier, the *Times* had published an op-ed by Moore defending his decision to jump bail from the "Fascist Farce of a Trial Presided over by the evil likes of John Murtagh." Two weeks later, Moore and three other men were arrested in an attempted holdup of a Bronx social club. Moore and a young Black Panther named Eddie Josephs were believed to be the two men responsible for the Curry and Binetti shooting. A short time later, a nineteen-year-old with ties to the Black Panthers named Tony Bottom was captured in San Francisco and charged in the murders of Jones and Piagentini.[72]

Another vicious police murder occurred in January 1972. Two rookie policemen, Gregory Foster and Rocco Laurie, were gunned down on the snowy evening of January 27 at the corner of Eleventh Street and Avenue B on the fringes of Manhattan's East Village. Foster, who was black, and Laurie, who was white, were both Marine combat veterans of Vietnam. They had met in boot camp, served together in Vietnam, and requested that they work together as partners on the streets of the Ninth Precinct. The murders of Foster and Laurie were particularly gruesome. Both men had been ambushed and shot from behind while investigating a double-parked car. A total of fourteen bullets were emptied into the two officers, many while the two men lay on the ground. Patrolman Foster had his eyes shot out. Witnesses reported that one of the killers jumped up and down while firing his gun in the air in a type of celebration dance. Another attacker reportedly said, "Shoot 'em in the balls!"[73]

The corner where the two policemen were murdered was a well-known drug-dealing location. This killing took place at the height of the anticorruption battles brought on by the Knapp Commission and Commissioner Murphy. Suspicion of police, especially where drugs were involved, was on the minds of many New Yorkers. Unfortunately, it was also on the minds of some of Murphy's staff. Albert Seedman remembered that one of Commissioner Murphy's top men "wondered aloud whether Foster and Laurie might have met their own end owing to some kind of drug hanky-panky. That possibility always had to be looked into, obviously. But should it be a commander's first consideration at the hour when one of his young men lay dead and the other dying? Instead of support there was a void of fear."[74]

Lindsay was anxious to play down any thought that police were being targeted by black militants. Instead, he chose to take the opportunity to argue for gun control. "It's time something was done about guns," said the mayor after the shooting of Jones and Piagentini. "Our city has the most effective gun law in the nation, but what good is it if people can easily buy guns in other states?" When Foster and Laurie were killed, Lindsay was on the campaign trail in Florida. By then a presidential candidate, he took the occasion to denounce the United States as "the most violent nation on the earth today."[75]

Almost as troubling as the indifference and suspicion of top police brass and the refusal of Mayor Lindsay to see the problem as anything more than a gun control issue was the response by the *Amsterdam News*, the city's leading black newspaper. In response to the murders of Foster and Laurie, the paper ran a story with the banner headline "Why Kill Black Cops?" which said in part: "Black residents of Brooklyn and Harlem are reacting negatively to the second assassination within ten months of a Black police officer on the streets of Manhattan. . . . While some of the scores of persons interviewed on the street were willing to accept the idea of assassinations with regard to white police, reporters encountered total rejection of the assassination of Black police."

The paper described an "attitude on the parts of many in this community of opposition, fear, suspicion, hostility—and in some instances, downright hatred for the Whites and Blacks who wear blue." The lack of sympathy for police, the editorial continued, was due to a "history of seeing White policemen as an occupying force in our Black communities, and having witnessed untold numbers of incidents where excessive force, unfair arrests, and brutal treatment was accorded blacks who had brushes with the law." Therefore, "It would be insane as Blacks to ignore the lessons of history and completely turn their sympathies to the totality of the New York Police force."[76]

Policemen, angry about both the increasing danger of policing the streets and the accusations of corruption tainting the department, undertook a six-day wildcat strike in January 1971. An estimated 85 percent of the force refused to show up for work. Luckily for the city, the work stoppage occurred in the dead of winter and the city remained relatively calm in the face of little police protection. Officially the strike was billed as a dispute over parity in pay between patrolmen and sergeants, including two years of back pay in salary increases. But police were striking over more than just pay. The wildcat strike was an expression of frustration by New York's police against a mayor they did not like and against the humiliation and anger they felt at the social changes around them. They were angry at being called pigs, at the wholesale assumption of corruption on the force, at the leniency of the court system, and at the attitude of liberals who assumed that policemen were guilty until proven innocent. The policemen finally won, and it cost the city $83 million in back pay and hundreds of millions more when the adjustment was factored into pension plans and future settlements. During this time, the city had also begun reducing the police force. Between 1970 and 1972, the NYPD lost 6,000 officers, mostly because, as the labor expert Raymond Horton noted, "labor costs for police simply rose so high that reductions in manpower were dictated by the sorry state of city finances."[77]

The police and the Lindsay administration were also having problems with riots in the Brownsville section of Brooklyn. This area had seen small-scale riots in 1967 and 1968. It had also witnessed the quiet destruction, more devastating than any riot, of housing abandonment and arson. Isolated from the city's traditional black leadership in Harlem, Brownsville was becoming an ever-worsening pocket of poverty in the increasingly black central Brooklyn. Four out of every five families in Brownsville were on welfare. Unemployment, infant mortality, venereal disease, and juvenile delinquency were all two to four times the city's average. The population went from 170,000, mostly white, in 1940 to 100,000, 85 percent black and Puerto Rican, in 1970. One Brownsville resident, returning to his old neighborhood in 1971 after six years in jail, was shocked at the decline of the neighborhood. "Although Brownsville was a slum area when I was growing up in it," wrote John Mack, "many sections reached middle-class standards." But by 1971, the "total area was a disaster. Nothing could be worse than what I saw—everywhere are abandoned buildings and long stretches of empty space where block after block of buildings had been razed to the ground. . . . The streets are literally covered with glass . . . and coupled with the dogshit and glass and paper and garbage that cover the sidewalk, everywhere you look there are abandoned cars, stripped and junked." When John Lindsay led a tour of the neighborhood for other mayors in April 1971, Mayor Kevin White of Boston said Brownsville "may be the most tangible sign of the collapse of our civilization."[78]

On two successive nights in June 1970, small bands of youths set fires in vacant buildings and looted stores in Brownsville. The rioting began when some in the neighborhood, angry at the buildup of garbage on the sidewalks, dumped garbage in the middle of Sutter Avenue and set the heap on fire. One journalist reported: "Before the violence subsided, uncollected garbage from adjacent blocks had been strewn along the streets and also set on fire. Sutter Avenue, like most of Brownsville, looked like it had been visited by war or riot long before the incident. The neighborhood, long rated the worst poverty area in the city . . . is now beset with rubble-strewn lots, abandoned and burned-out buildings and empty storefronts."

Two local butcher shops and a Key Food supermarket were looted and burned. Policemen watched as residents ran from the supermarket along the garbage-strewn sidewalk, carrying looted merchandise.[79]

The following year an even more severe riot broke out in Brownsville. In response to planned cuts in the state's social services budget, a group of black leaders and community activists calling themselves the Black Coalition began a series of protests to mobilize opposition to the cuts. Rallies were held on May 5, 1971, at the New York Stock Exchange and the United Nations. That afternoon, a crowd of residents and youths began congregating on Pitkin Avenue, Brownsville's commercial district. The Black Coalition had ordered over one hundred stores along Pitkin Avenue to close for the day, which they had done. Maurice Reid, a Black Coalition coordinator, explained the demand: "The idea was to make some merchants starve as long as our people have got to starve." A riot began around 2 P.M., when the car of an off-duty policeman was blocked by the growing crowd. When the officer tried to disperse the crowd and clear the street, he was jumped by a member of the crowd. One witness claimed that the officer had pulled his gun and pointed it at one of the protesters. After that, tensions rose and groups of rioters roamed the neighborhood setting fires and looting the closed stores. Between 5 P.M. and midnight, more than one hundred fires were reported in Brownsville, twenty of them considered serious. Bands of black and Puerto Rican youths threw bottles and rocks and barricaded streets with abandoned cars and piles of trash. By midnight the riot was under control, and bands of police were stationed on every corner along Pitkin Avenue.[80]

The riots petered out the following day, although bands of youths unsuccessfully tried to restart the riots on Thursday and Friday. Rain helped dampen the urge to riot. The final tally: fifty burned-out buildings, eighteen policemen injured, thirteen firemen injured, twenty civilians injured, fifteen stores looted, and forty-two people arrested. One policeman had been shot in the shoulder. No one was killed. In response to the riot, the president of the Uniformed Firefighters Association, Michael Maye, told the city he was "serving notice on the city administration that firefighters will either be provided with adequate police protection in times of civil disturbances or they will remain in their quarters." He wanted a "more manly" response to rioters and lawbreakers by the city. Lindsay never denounced the rioters, only saying that "violence is no answer to any issue. . . . It only serves to deepen the community's own wounds and to exhaust the energies that should be channeled into lawful and effective forms of protest." He also said he understood "the frustration and bitterness felt in this community" about "the cruel nature of recent cuts in the state budget."[81]

MURDER AT THE HARLEM MOSQUE

The attacks upon the police, Lindsay's stormy relationship with the department, and the difficulties of achieving the mayor's desired racial peace came to a head on Friday, April 14, 1972, when two policemen assigned to the Twenty-eighth Precinct in Harlem, Patrolmen Philip Cardillo and Vito Navarra, responded to a "10–13" call, meaning a fellow officer was down. The address given by the caller was 102 East 116th Street. The officers did not know that the yellow and brown building at this address was the Nation of Islam Mosque No. 7, the New York headquarters of the Black Muslims where Malcolm X used to preach. They also did not know that they were responding to a false call.

Cardillo and Navarra entered the mosque, not realizing they were in a house of worship. The distress call specified the second floor, so Navarra went upstairs, where he was confronted by fifteen to twenty men and forced back down the stairs. Meanwhile, more patrol cars arrived at the scene. One of these cops, Victor Padilla, was hit as soon as he entered the mosque and his gun was taken from him. In the small entranceway of the mosque, more than twenty people crowded together as the Muslims pummeled the policemen. As Navarra tried to head for the door, he "was punched, kicked, and stomped . . . he heard the thud of blows as Muslims and cops swung fists and billy clubs at each other, the high-ceilinged hallway resounding with screaming and cursing." The Muslims managed to force most of the police outside the mosque and then they locked the door. Remaining inside were Cardillo, Padilla, and Ivan Negron, Padilla's partner. During the struggle, Negron heard shots fired. He saw Cardillo, shot, lying on the floor and a man with a gun near the fallen policeman. Negron grabbed his gun and fired in the direction of the man with the gun. According to a ballistics report, Cardillo was shot at point-blank range with the gun pressed against his jacket. (Patrolman Cardillo would soon die from his gunshot wounds.)[82]

Police finally managed to break down the door to the mosque. Some fired in the direction of the Muslim assailants. At the sound of the shots, the Muslims fled downstairs to the basement, where seventeen were forced to remain. One of them, Lewis 17X Dupree, was identified by police witnesses as the man standing over Cardillo. But soon Louis Farrakhan, a light-skinned former calypso singer who was the leader of the mosque, arrived on the scene, as did Congressman Charles Rangel. Both men convinced the police commanders to release the prisoners. They used the threat of a riot as a bludgeon against a scared police command. "Go! Go!" Farrakhan and Rangel allegedly told Chief of Detectives Albert Seedman. "If you stay, there is nothing we can do to protect you. You'll be overrun. There'll be rioting. People may be killed." Seedman was finally ordered by his superiors to release the prisoners already in custody. Farrakhan promised Seedman that the suspects would show up at the precinct house later that afternoon. No one ever showed up, although Dupree and another Muslim were later indicted for assault during the melee.

Almost immediately, top police officials who had arrived at the mosque began to cover up the incident, preventing an investigation into who fired the shots that killed Cardillo. James Harmon, a former assistant district attorney in Manhattan who later unsuccessfully prosecuted one of the Muslims charged with Cardillo's murder, looked back at what happened and said, "Orders were given that day that should not have been followed." Just as police were beginning to restore order at the mosque, collect evidence, interview witnesses, and hold suspects for further questioning, high-ranking police department officials ordered the police out of the mosque. According to police detective Sonny Grosso, who was at the mosque and later wrote a book about the incident, the police photographer "realized that just as he had been forbidden to take photos at the end of the hallway, superior officers had stopped the ballistics men from entering the mosque to search for evidence.

It was absolutely without precedent that a ballistics detective be barred from the crime scene."[83]

One of the police officials who deliberately hampered the investigation was Benjamin Ward, the deputy commissioner for community affairs. (Ward would later, under Mayor Ed Koch, become the city's first black police commissioner.) One of the detectives at the scene, Randy Jurgensen, remembered Ward ordering white cops away from the scene and allowing black cops to remain. Incredulously, Ward told the press that, despite one seriously wounded policeman, the "Muslims exercised great restraint when the incident happened."[84]

As the investigation inside the mosque grew complicated, tensions increased on the street outside. A mob overturned an undercover police car and set it on fire and threw a white newswoman to the ground and trampled her. The crowd shouted at the police, "I hope you die, you pigs. I hope you drop dead." Bottles and bricks rained down on the police from nearby rooftops. Boys ran through the crowd spraying white reporters with lighter fluid and touching an unlit match to their clothes. Detective Jurgensen was hit in the head by a brick and had to be dragged away from the crowd.[85]

Cardillo had been taken to St. Luke's Hospital, where he remained in critical condition. Lindsay and Murphy paid their respects outside the policeman's room. The NYPD's deputy commissioner for public affairs, Robert Daley, met up with the two at the hospital. Murphy said that Daley's "eyes were bulging, he was shouting in a high-pitched, almost soprano voice." When Daley termed the events at the mosque a riot, Lindsay lashed out at him. "Riot? What do you mean riot? There can't be any riot. There won't be any riot. It never came close to being a riot. How can you say such a thing?" According to Murphy, the mayor "kept bearing down on the deputy commissioner [Daley] like a prosecutor in utterly contemptuous cross-examination of a defense witness." When Daley continued to insist that a riot had occurred, Lindsay angrily asked him how many people were involved. "Well, there are at least twelve hundred people in the streets," Daley said. The mayor responded: "What's a thousand people, twelve hundred people? You can't have a riot with a thousand people or twelve hundred people."[86]

For Lindsay and Murphy, the problem at the mosque was not that a policeman was mortally wounded. The problem was that, according to Murphy, the police commanders in Harlem had previously worked out a secret agreement with Muslim ministers: "This detailed agreement provided that mosques be accorded treatment as 'sensitive locations' by police officers. Part of the agreed treatment was that police officers would not rush into a mosque with guns. Like scores of other 'sensitive locations' as we called them, a mosque was a special situation." It is not clear, though, whether Cardillo, Navarra, and other Harlem cops were aware of this "secret agreement." And no one bothered to find out the origins of the "10–13" call that started the fiasco.[87]

When Robert Daley wanted to send out a press release explaining the department's view of what happened at the mosque, Ben Ward complained, citing the need to keep Harlem from exploding. In addition, according to Daley, "Ward said he agreed with what all of Harlem was saying at the time: that the cops had no legal right to enter that mosque. 10–13 or no 10–13. That mosque was a place of worship. Cops never would have entered a synagogue or St. Patrick's Cathedral in the same manner." Commissioner Murphy took Ward's side. Daley thought this strategy was a mistake. "Secrecy here had made the police appear guilty, when in fact they were not," wrote Daley. "Secrecy had allowed the Muslims to fill the void with accusations of racism. Secrecy had made Farrakhan into a personage of stature, and now we would have to deal with him in the future; you could count on it. Secrecy had hardened the black community against us once again; and it had accentuated the distrust of the white community. It had earned us the contempt of everybody." If the department stayed silent, Daley believed, New Yorkers "are going to start to think that we did something wrong or that Cardillo did something wrong."[88]

The police department finally decided to draft a press release on Monday afternoon, three days after the shooting. This decision was further proof that the murder of Cardillo would be swept under the rug and that the police department hierarchy blamed Cardillo and his fellow officers for overreacting. Attending the meeting to hammer out a press release were Acting Police Commissioner William Smith, Deputy Commissioner for Public Affairs Daley, Deputy Commissioner for Community Affairs Ward, Chief of Detectives Seedman and two chief inspectors. When Daley wanted to clarify that the Black Muslims were the "assailants" in the press release, Ward protested. When Daley wanted to make clear that Cardillo was not accidentally shot by another policeman, Ward protested: "How do you know he wasn't?" When Chief of Detectives Seedman told Ward that powder burns proved that Cardillo had been shot at close range and that this should go into the report, Ward changed "proved" to "indicated." A weak statement was finally drafted after three hours of haggling, but was not released to the press until Tuesday.[89]

Predictably, the Black Muslims used the mosque incident to their advantage. Led by Farrakhan, they demanded an apology from the mayor. Farrakhan accused Cardillo and Navarra of "charging into our temple like criminals and they were treated like criminals." Portraying the Muslims as "peaceful people," Farrakhan claimed that his men were only acting in self-defense. Never once did Farrakhan utter a word of sympathy for Patrolman Cardillo, who lay dying in the hospital. Farrakhan also used the episode as an opportunity to make a set of demands of the city. They included an apology from Lindsay and Murphy for the mosque incident; the dropping of charges against the Muslims arrested at the mosque; and the removal of all white policemen in Harlem and their replacement by an all-black force.

Henry Nelson, the president of the National Council of Police Societies, an organization of black policemen, and Howard Sheffey, the president of the Guardians, a group of black New York policemen, issued their own statement on the mosque incident: "We strongly deplore the actions of those members of the New York City Police Department who invaded the sanctity of Mohammed's Temple." The *Amsterdam News* termed the mosque incident an "invasion." Arguing that this incident proved the need for an all-black police force in Harlem, the paper wrote in a front-page editorial: "Perhaps it is time to admit that the snap judgments of white police officers infected through and through by the inherent racism in this society, should no longer be given free reign in our community."[90]

The mayor's office wanted to distance itself from the incident. Robert Daley was forced to tell the press that it was unclear whether Cardillo was shot by people in the mosque or by fellow policemen trying to rescue him. "I cannot comment further because what I say would sound like an attempt at justification of police action and the situation is too inflammatory in Harlem right now." To many policemen, it appeared that their superiors and Lindsay blamed Cardillo and the other policemen for what happened. In an effort to appease Farrakhan, the Lindsay administration turned its back on justice and dishonored its police officers. Feeling that the department was blaming its own men for the mosque incident, the commanding officer of the Twenty-eighth Precinct in Harlem, John Haugh, resigned in protest.

Commissioner Murphy seemed to be blaming his policemen for violating the secret agreement with the Muslims. "He [Farrakhan] didn't have to be brilliant to know that he had us over the barrel," Murphy later wrote. Two days after the incident, Murphy said on a television news program that "depending on what the facts reveal, I certainly am not above making an apology." The best that Murphy could come up with for a defense of his men was a statement that he had "no question about the motives and dedication of the police officers who went in there believing that their mission was to rescue an officer in trouble," although he might have done some things differently. When he later met with Farrakhan, the police commissioner "looked Louis Farrakhan straight in the eye and admitted to the blunder . . . that the officers in forcing their way into his mosque with guns drawn had violated that pact." Lost in this apology was Patrolman Cardillo. In fact, in a book Murphy wrote five years later, he never once mentioned Cardillo's name in his discussion of the mosque incident.[91]

When Patrolman Cardillo's funeral was held a few days later, neither John Lindsay nor Patrick Murphy attended. This broke the unwritten tradition that mayors and police commissioners pay their respects at the funeral of officers fallen in the line of duty. "I don't think they dared come," Cardillo's wife said later. "I think they were too ashamed, they knew what they did and couldn't face it." Their absence cast a cloud over the actions of Patrolman Cardillo and the other policemen, giving the impression that somehow they had done something wrong. Instead of attending the funeral Lindsay was skiing in Utah. Pat Vecchio, Lindsay's police security man, remembers that the mayor wanted to postpone the trip after hearing that Cardillo had died, but that aides convinced him that it would be better if he left town. One can only speculate that the aides wanted to distance Lindsay from the entire mosque incident. Attending in the mayor's place were his wife Mary and Chief of Staff Edward Hamilton.[92]

No matter how large a contract Lindsay would give the PBA, it could not paper over the vast social and cultural chasm between the patrician mayor and the blue-collar police force. And there was a similar distance between NYPD commissioners and the patrolmen. Robert Daley told Chief of Detectives Seedman, "There's just no support for the patrolmen. Smith, Codd, Cawly, Ward, Murphy—none of them like patrolmen." Seedman agreed. Philip Cardillo deserved better. Twenty-five years after her husband was murdered, Claudia Cardillo remained understandably bitter. "I'm still furious," she said. "Nobody took the blame for it and basically, everyone said everyone else did it, everyone else screwed up." Mrs. Cardillo later sued the city and won a settlement for more than $1 million.[93]

Though Lindsay gave policemen more money and built more precinct houses, he never fully earned the respect of the rank-and-file. Commissioner Murphy noted that part of the reason was that "Lindsay feared cops, did not trust them . . . he was uneasy around cops, worried." The effects of these numerous police killings took their toll on Lindsay, who would personally call the widow or parents of each fallen policeman. Under ordinary circumstances, this would be an emotionally draining task. But as more policemen were murdered, many relatives of the dead policemen began to blame Lindsay personally. The anger was especially acute if the police officer was white and his killer black. "Instead of receiving his call gracefully," Pat Vecchio remembers, "they would rant and fulminate against the mayor because they [the dead policemen] had been shot in minority neighborhoods. They blamed him for the deaths. He'd come off the phone white-faced and you could see the anguish." Lindsay himself noted that bearing the brunt of this anger had taken its toll on him. "You haven't seen a dead cop in a hospital and his widow looking at me as if I had pulled the trigger," said the mayor.[94]

But Lindsay's private sympathy never translated into public action. During the Harlem mosque incident, Lindsay and his aides sacrificed justice for the sake of keeping Harlem calm. Sid Davidoff admitted, "Our decision [during the mosque incident] . . . was to walk away. . . . If it [evidence] had been collected, what would you do with it? If you walk in there and make the arrests, [what] would the risks of what could result of a lingering investigation and trial do in an area that was already a tinderbox? My suspicion is that there was as much intentional botching as there was botching. It was not something that anyone wanted done. Just try to get past it and make sure that it didn't happen again."

The Lindsay administration and the top brass in the police department intentionally refused to investigate Cardillo's murder because of fear that it would lead to riots. According to Murphy, Lindsay, rather than being angry at the cold-blooded murder of a policeman, "felt that the chickens had come home to roost. He saw the Police Department undoing years of hard work in black relations with just one dumb move." The only problem is that racial tensions and violence in Harlem and the city as a whole had gotten worse during Lindsay's tenure well before the mosque incident. All of Lindsay's "hard work" in reality only seemed to set blacks and whites further apart.[95]

One police detective who had been present at the mosque, Sonny Grosso, expressed the bitterness that many policemen felt toward Commissioner Murphy over the mosque incident.

> What Murphy was making people believe was that he—as distinguished from his men—was the only source of complex understanding. The cops were a bunch of mugs. Send them into battle. Just make sure they got pointed toward the target. But explain to them what the stakes were and you were talking above their heads. . . . And to be sold down the river by talk that made them appear to be insensitive pricks, by talk that made it even harder for them to confront the problem of violent urban crime sapped them of their dignity. It made them feel worthless and ineffectual. Worse still, the talk from downtown would make tomorrow's job a tougher one, a more dangerous one.

To Grosso, the behavior of the Lindsay administration and Murphy's office surrounding the Harlem mosque "was a political sellout, an expediency designed to keep things politically cool. It was also a betrayal of the men who risked their lives under Murphy's command, who risked their lives for the sake of all the citizens of the city, not only the black ones." Chief of Detectives Seedman told Grosso in private that the mosque incident was "a cowardly assault against police officers, but nobody's gonna have the stomach to say it." Vito Navarra, Cardillo's partner, said, "I got beat up today and I saw other cops get beat up and my partner was shot and maybe he's going to die. And suddenly I'm beginning to realize that the New York Police Department ain't on my side."[96]

Nearly five years later, Lewis 17X Dupree went on trial for the murder of Philip Cardillo, and a jury found Dupree not guilty. The case against Dupree was botched by the decision to pull policemen out of the mosque, release all suspects, and cease collecting evidence. The murder of Philip Cardillo marked a low point in the administration of John Lindsay.

HISTORY HAS A WAY OF REPEATING ITSELF. Less than two weeks after Rudolph Giuliani was sworn in as mayor in 1994, a "10-13" distress call came from Harlem. Again, the address was 102 East 116th Street. Thankfully, this time no policeman was killed at the mosque, but a miniriot erupted and eight officers were hurt. Black Muslims and instigators like Reverend Al Sharpton and C. Vernon Mason attempted to use the incident to discredit the Giuliani administration. Giuliani and the police department refused to buckle and apologize. When asked about the police entering the mosque on the false report, Giuliani responded, "They acted correctly and properly and I support them." Contrary to the Lindsay approach, the new mayor used the 1994 mosque incident to isolate two of the most divisive public figures in the city: Sharpton and Mason. He and Police Commissioner William Bratton refused to meet with either man.[97]

POLITICAL DISASTER:
SWITCHING PARTIES, FOREST HILLS,
AND RUNNING FOR PRESIDENT

> The fact is that a reformer can't last in politics.
> He can make a show for a while, but he always
> comes down like a rocket. . . . He hasn't been
> brought up in the difficult business of politics
> and he makes a mess of it every time.
>
> —George Washington Plunkitt,
> Tammany Hall politician[1]

A t the start of 1970, the tone of the second Lindsay administration was noticeably different from that of the first. Richard Aurelio was Deputy Mayor, and this meant that much of the focus of Lindsay's second term would be political, not administrative. Aurelio was a political animal, much as Bob Price had been. The mundane and often tedious world of city government held little appeal for him. Lindsay no longer spoke in the words a reform politician. Gone were the condemnations of the city's "power brokers." Gone were the sermons on public duty and obligations. With Aurelio in charge, the Lindsay administration eased into more traditional wheeling and dealing. Lindsay created his own political "machine," in the form of the John V. Lindsay Associations, one in each borough. These organizations served as patronage pumps as well as handy sources of votes and bodies for political events. In four of the five boroughs, the leader of the Lindsay Associations was on the city payroll.

The new emphasis on politics and the disappearance of Lindsay's reform rhetoric disappointed some of the mayor's early supporters. But the shift did little to change Lindsay's political fortunes. When Lindsay switched parties and ran for president as a Democrat, he sealed his political fate.

SWITCHING PARTIES

John Lindsay had been moving away from the Republican Party since 1964, when he repudiated Barry Goldwater and basically ran for reelection to Congress as an independent. With each passing year, Lindsay and his party grew further and further apart. One of the big questions of Lindsay's second term was what to do about party affiliation. Although Lindsay, who had been reelected only on the Liberal Party line, denied he was considering changing parties, by 1970 he was a man disillusioned with his country and uneasy with the party in which he had been active since his days with Youth for Eisenhower. His speeches had grown darker and more pessimistic. Lindsay told the Bar Association of New York in the spring of 1970: "Something is very wrong in America. . . . Growing numbers of our citizens are convinced that the American dream is a cruel illusion or a hypocritical nightmare." By 1970, he saw great reason for the decline in faith in American society and government. The poor, black militants, white radicals, and "the politically unorthodox," according to Lindsay, "were angry." And they should be." He mentioned nothing of others dissatisfied with liberalism and the counterculture, except to say that their anger was manifesting itself, according to the mayor, in a "turning toward repression, toward repudiation of our rights and liberties."[2]

Lindsay delivered the commencement address at Williams College in June, telling his audience in the rural Berkshires about the problems of New York. The city was "a place where too many people live apart," he said. "Too many people have learned to fear each other. Too often, strident voices drown out sensible debate. And, on several harrowing occasions, division has turned the streets of our cities into battlefields." Lindsay saw the angry extremes of the reactionary and the revolutionary pulling the nation apart. Contrasted with these two extremes, Lindsay saw "the center based on reason and truth," of which he was obviously a part. He rued the fact that the ideology of the center was "not easy to articulate because it is complex and even paradoxical." Lindsay was speaking for the liberal Republicanism of his youth and the Cold War liberal Democratic philosophy of men like Robert McNamara. But this "vital center," as the historian Arthur Schlesinger Jr. called it, no longer existed. By the late sixties, thanks to the Vietnam War and the challenge from the student left, this kind of politics had lost all claims to moral superiority and leadership. As the center collapsed, these "rational" men had to choose sides. It was clear that though Lindsay condemned the violence of the left, his heart lay with its objectives and beliefs. At Williams, he condemned "the effect of verbal violence—incivility and the polysyllabic sneer—against lawyers and businessmen, students and television networks, and all citizens who feel compelled to dissent." Referring to the hardhat riot and the deaths at Kent State, Lindsay accused those who supported the war and opposed student protests of creating "an atmosphere of intimidation which all too easily breeds physical violence."[3]

Lindsay's most influential speech of this time was the Charter Day address at the University of California, Berkeley, in April 1970. The Charter Day speaker customarily receives an honorary degree from the university. Governor Ronald Reagan and the university regents, however, voted to deny Lindsay his degree. This action turned Lindsay into a hero to liberals and solidified his bona fides with the students. Before the speech, Lindsay held a secret meeting with Tom Hayden, a prominent antiwar activist and a former leader of Students for a Democratic Society (SDS). Hayden met Lindsay at a hotel to tell him that opposing the Vietnam War was the most important issue in the country. Hayden asked Lindsay to consider running for president as an antiwar candidate and urged him to continue speaking out against the war. That Lindsay would meet in private with Hayden, a participant in the 1968 takeover of Columbia University, lessened the impact of even his relatively mild criticism of the excesses of student radicals and showed how far Lindsay had moved to the left by 1970.[4]

The *New York Times* called the Berkeley speech a "strange speech for a politician—self-doubting, pessimistic, deeply critical of established institutions." The mayor began by acknowledging the low esteem with which many students held establishment politicians, noting that "when a politician speaks, an intelligent man raises his guard." Campus speeches given by politicians traditionally tend to extol public service and reinforce faith in government, but Lindsay's speech did not. "An honest man who looks behind him at the years we have been through cannot offer a reassuring message of faith in processes or institutions or slogans," Lindsay told the crowd. "Because the decade that ended a few months ago brought with it a devastating end to easy assumptions and certainties." Coming off the bruising reelection campaign, Lindsay knowingly spoke of a nation exposed to "doubt and threat. We cling to our faith in our own efficiency, but we begin to see breakdowns everywhere, and a national magazine discusses 'why nothing seems to work anymore.'" There was anger in the country, claimed Lindsay, at "large, powerful, often immovable forces." Lindsay said he shared that anger, "because these institutions do not work." Lindsay, the administrator of a city of 8 million people, might have wanted to discuss why things didn't seem to work in his city, or at least offer ways that his administration had tried to make things work. Instead, Lindsay's speech was evidence of the growing malaise of the left. Lindsay firmly believed that the nation was inching toward the repression of dissent, since, as he said, "there are men—now in power in this country—who do not respect dissent, who cannot cope with turmoil, and who believe that the people of America are ready to support repression as long as it is done with a quiet voice and a business suit." This was a not-so-subtle dig at President Nixon. Lindsay's aide Steven Isenberg, a Berkeley alum who had organized the trip, believed it was a "very, very important speech because it was a speech against repression. It was an attack on Agnew, a direct attack on Agnew and Nixon."[5]

Though some students heckled Lindsay, he also received many cheers and applause. Journalist Jack Newfield, who had grown disillusioned with the mayor, accompanied Lindsay to Berkeley. Lindsay's reception among the notoriously unruly students of Berkeley led Newfield to consider that "maybe we [New Yorkers] take Lindsay too much for granted, that perhaps we are so familiar with him that we can't see the mystery anymore, that we know his blunders too well . . . and we forget the fierce fascination Lindsay holds for the young and black outside of New York, who see him only as a dim silhouette on the horizon." Lindsay was vastly more respected and adored outside of the city than he was at home. This dissonance only added to the enigmatic nature of Lindsay's personality. "I do not really comprehend the alchemy of Lindsay's charisma, except for his remarkable looks and bearing," wrote Newfield. "His speech at Berkeley was not very specific or emotional. It was pessimistic and tentative."[6]

By 1970 John Lindsay was a Republican in name only. Since his defeat in the 1969 Republican primary, there had been talk that he might switch parties. His first political test in his second term would be the 1970 midterm election, when Nelson Rockefeller would be up for reelection. Lindsay had earlier endorsed his fellow liberal Republicans Charles Goodell for senator and Louis Lefkowitz for attorney general. At the local level, however, he appeared to be paying off reform Democrats for their support in 1969. In one announcement he endorsed twenty-nine candidates for Congress and the state senate and assembly, and of them twenty-five were Democrats, two were Liberals, and two were Republicans.[7]

Still, the most important endorsement was that for governor. In 1969, Rockefeller had supported John Marchi, the Republican mayoral candidate, over Lindsay. Would Lindsay seek revenge in 1970? Running against Rockefeller was former Supreme Court Justice Arthur Goldberg. Despite his standing in New York's Jewish community and among reform Democrats, Goldberg was an unimpressive man and candidate. Whatever complaints New Yorkers had with Rockefeller, it soon became clear that they would not turn control of the state over to Goldberg.

Despite realizing that Rockefeller would easily win reelection to a fourth term, Lindsay endorsed Goldberg late in the race. Deputy Mayor Richard Aurelio argued that Lindsay had to back Goldberg, since he was a friend of Alex Rose and Lindsay felt he owed Rose for the Liberal Party's support in 1969. If Lindsay backed Rockefeller, he would have no future in the Democratic Party. To keep his options open for a possible party switch, Lindsay had to endorse Goldberg. Most of the friends whose counsel he sought advised

Lindsay to stay neutral, but many of the "young turks" in City Hall argued in favor of a Goldberg endorsement, feeling that the Republicans had moved too far to the right and that Rockefeller had acquiesced in this.[8]

Lindsay not only endorsed Goldberg, he did so in unequivocal tones. He said Goldberg and his running mate, Harlem Assemblyman Basil Paterson, "expressed the strongest commitment to the battle for urban progress." Lindsay saw the mundane gubernatorial election in grand epochal terms, arguing that although some had counseled him to stay neutral, "silence when fundamental principles are at stake is unacceptable. History warns us against silence. If concerned men fail to fight for their convictions, they lose the battle for the future." Lindsay condemned those "who seek political gain by attacks that polarize," as well as those who "condone this politics of division by their silence." Despite the endorsement, Lindsay still claimed, "I am a Republican and I intend to remain a Republican." But few believed these words. With each move Lindsay made, he was increasingly freeing himself of his old Republican bonds.[9]

There was a fear that Rockefeller, if reelected, would punish Lindsay and the city. Rockefeller's initial reaction to the endorsement was to mock Lindsay's contention that he was putting principle over party as "absurd." The following day, Rockefeller held a press conference where he was accompanied by nineteen former Lindsay aides to show their support for Rockefeller and blunt Lindsay's contrary endorsement. The most prominent person in attendance was former Deputy Mayor Robert Sweet, who told reporters, "We didn't get everything we wanted from Albany, but I know we got some imaginative programs. Without Governor Rockefeller's support, the city would not have survived." Sweet had always worked well with the governor's staff, was always considered more of a Republican party man than many others around Lindsay, and was still somewhat angry with Lindsay over the way he had been ousted from City Hall and replaced by Aurelio. Others at the press conference included Lindsay first-termers like former Buildings Commissioner Charles Moerdler, former Finance Administrator Roy Goodman, and Lindsay's 1969 running mate Fioravante Perrotta. The press conference showed how far removed Lindsay was from his first years in office. Those attending the event and supporting the governor were Republicans who had originally supported Lindsay. They were the first wave of administration staffers, the "lawyers in suits," as someone once called them, who had been eased out in favor of Democrats as the administration shifted its strategy and outlook.[10]

Lindsay's charge that Rockefeller was uninterested in the city was unfair. On the contrary, he was probably too interested in city affairs. Partly because of numerous family land holdings in the city, the governor had been intimately involved in city affairs since he first took office and left a mighty, though controversial imprint. Lincoln Center, the World Trade Center, and Roosevelt Island were all Rockefeller projects. In addition,

Rockefeller Center, the Museum of Modern Art, and the Morningside Heights area were part of the family empire. The governor did not want the city to fail. Rockefeller rebutted Lindsay's charge of neglect by pointing out that state aid to the city had increased while Lindsay was mayor. "Don't ask me what they are doing with the money," an angry Rockefeller said, "but they are getting it."

The schism between Lindsay and Rockefeller was based less on politics or policy than on a personality clash between two proud, ambitious politicians. Rockefeller would condescendingly call Lindsay "Johnny," while Lindsay would mock the governor for his constant absence from the state. Peter Goldmark remembers being in Lindsay's office once when Rockefeller called. Lindsay taunted Rockefeller: "Hello Nelson. Where are you calling from now, Nelson? Are you calling from Amsterdam? Are you in Venezuela? Are you in the airplane?" Sometimes he reached for other taunts. When someone asked Lindsay, "Who should he speak with to find out what Rockefeller was really like?" the mayor replied, "Why not see his first wife?" Meanwhile, the governor saw himself as the top man in the state and Lindsay, a onetime protégé, as a mere upstart. After all, the New York Republican Party was widely seen as a wholly owned subsidiary of the Rockefeller empire. Despite Lindsay's defection, Rockefeller easily defeated Goldberg, winning 52.5 percent of the total vote in the three-way race (Paul Adams of the Conservative Party also ran, winning about 7 percent). Goldberg only received 40.5 percent of the vote. In the city, Goldberg outpolled Rockefeller by only 27,000 votes out of over 2 million cast.[11]

Rockefeller was now free to attack Lindsay, but he did not want to hurt the city with his efforts. Instead, he would go after Lindsay's management of the city. In his 1972 State of the State address, Rockefeller lashed out at the mayor. He suggested that city residents had a better chance of being heard during the days of the political machines than under Lindsay. The governor described John Lindsay's New York as "a place where housing can't be found, streets are unsafe, corruption undermines public trust, traffic is unbearable, garbage isn't picked up often enough and, worst of all, no one can ever seem to get anything changed for the better because as things now stand, there is not actual control over the functioning of city government." Lindsay angrily responded by calling Rockefeller a "tool of the White House." The mayor also attacked Rockefeller's record, citing the September 1971 Attica prison riot, when forty-three people—inmates and guards held as hostages—were killed by state troopers sent in by Governor Rockefeller to end the prison takeover.

Rockefeller used his power to harass the mayor. Rockefeller had appointed Maurice Nadjari as a special deputy attorney general to investigate corruption in the city's criminal justice system. Though Rockefeller used the findings of the Knapp Commission to justify hiring Nadjari, whose authority superseded that of the five city district attorneys, his real target was John

Lindsay. Nadjari would spend the next year investigating real and imagined corruption not only in the criminal justice system but also in the Lindsay administration. (In 1973, after Lindsay announced that he would not run for a third mayoral term, the two antagonists again went at each other. Rockefeller noted that under Lindsay, the city was "experiencing rampant crime, deterioration of city services, and loss of jobs." Lindsay replied by accusing Rockefeller of harassing his administration and of a "personal vendetta against me."[12])

Having broken with Rockefeller, Lindsay next attacked President Nixon. The mayor held Nixon personally responsible for the tenor of the 1970 midterm campaigns, arguing that some politicians "seek not merely to defeat their opponents but literally to eliminate them from our public life." By polarizing the debate, Lindsay argued, Nixon and others "try to convince the electorate that the only defense against the lunatic left is the mindless right." Lindsay's criticism of Rockefeller was unfair, and so was the attack on Nixon. Lindsay himself had contributed to the polarization in his mayoral elections, condemning his opponents for hatred and bigotry and raising the heat of his campaign rhetoric to win over nervous liberals.[13]

Lindsay pondered his political future at a time when his popularity was lower than it had been since the Ocean Hill–Brownsville debacle. In late 1970, a *New York Times* poll showed that 60 percent of New Yorkers gave the mayor an unfavorable rating, compared to 38 percent who rated him favorably. Yet Lindsay polled well among youths (54 percent) and minorities (66 percent) statewide. Despite Lindsay's sagging popularity in the five boroughs, the same poll showed one of the paradoxes of Lindsay's political career: the farther away from New York City one traveled, the more popular the mayor was. When a reporter asked Congressman Ed Koch during the 1972 presidential race why Lindsay was loved everywhere but New York City, Koch replied, "Well, to know him is not to love him." In Upstate New York, 48 percent saw the mayor of New York in a favorable light, compared to 26 percent unfavorable.[14]

Lindsay also found that the Republican Party, even in New York, was becoming more conservative. Barry Goldwater and Ronald Reagan, not Tom Dewey and Nelson Rockefeller, were the new idols of younger New York Republicans. The New York Teenage Republicans symbolized this new right-wing conservatism. At a 1970 meeting, these young Republicans performed a skit to the tune of "Ol' Man River" that satirized Lindsay:

> *Young John Lindsay*
> *He must know somethin'*
> *But he don't do nothin'*
> *He don't cut taxes*

He don't tow garbage
And all his speeches
Are empty verbage

These were no longer the young prep school and Ivy League types with whom Lindsay had associated as president of the New York Young Republicans during the 1950s. It was a new breed of hard-edged, conservative young Republicans who had been seared by the events of the 1960s. And Lindsay was even less at home with them than he was with Nixon and Rockefeller.[15]

Having turned his back on both of these national figures, the only question was when, not whether, Lindsay would change parties. By February 1971, the *New York Times* reported that all of Lindsay's City Hall staff had urged him to become a Democrat and run for president. Rumors swirled that Lindsay's conversion speech was already written. Amid the rumors, the mayor's old liberal Republican friends made one last attempt to convince him to stay in the party. Thirteen members of the Ripon Society of New York sent Lindsay a letter urging him to stay in the party and fight for liberal Republican principles. Signers included the men who had financially subsidized Lindsay's career—John Hay Whitney, David Rockefeller, Walter Thayer, and Gustave Levy of Goldman Sachs—as well as Robert Sweet and Charles Moerdler. But by the summer of 1971, Lindsay was not listening to his old friends anymore.[16]

On Monday, August 9, Lindsay called Richard Aurelio from Utah, where he was vacationing, to inform him that he was ready to switch parties. Two days later, on August 11, 1971, John Lindsay officially switched his party enrollment to the Democratic Party. In doing so, he said he recognized "the failure of 20 years in progressive Republican politics." The Republicans, said the mayor, "have finally abandoned the fight for a government that will respond to the needs of most of our people and of those most in need." The mayor said his decision reaffirmed his "commitment to the needs of this great and vital city and all American cities—men without jobs, families without hope, indecent housing, blighted neighborhoods, crowded hospitals, crime, poverty, polarization. These are real. And again and again I have seen them on our streets."[17]

In his announcement speech, Lindsay was tough on his old party, but somewhat ambivalent about his new home. Barely hiding his contempt for the Nixon administration, Lindsay condemned "the Government's retreat from the Bill of Rights. Washington has tapped telephones without court order; spied on our citizens with military agents; arrested thousands of people, protesters and bystanders alike, without legal authority; given minimum enforcement to the rights of minorities and even tried to censor what we see on television and read in our newspapers." Still, Lindsay had no illusions about the Democratic Party. "I will work as a Democrat without abandoning my personal independence," he said. "The party, too, is far from perfect."

Immediate reactions to Lindsay's announcement were mixed. Candidates for the Democratic presidential nomination in 1972 were cautious. Hubert Humphrey and Edmund Muskie used Lindsay's switch to attack the Nixon administration, while George McGovern reminded voters that Lindsay had seconded the nomination of Spiro Agnew in 1968. Some Democrats quickly jumped on the Lindsay bandwagon. New York State Democratic Party Chairman John Burns, who had come to the city personally in 1969 to help run Mario Procaccino's mayoral campaign against Lindsay, called the mayor "the most powerful Democrat in the state." But Democratic leaders in Queens and the Bronx were leery of the new Democrat. In Brooklyn, the Democratic boss, Meade Esposito, who had slowly become allied with Lindsay since the 1969 campaign, was supportive of the switch but worried about the Lindsay Associations cutting into the power of his clubhouse. Lindsay, the old reform politician, was now dealing with the very same bosses he had castigated in his 1965 campaign.

Others close to Lindsay also switched their party registrations, including his wife, Mary, Richard Aurelio, and Sid Davidoff. Others close to Lindsay—Tom Morgan, Jay Kriegel, Steven Isenberg, Ronnie Eldridge—were already Democrats. A few top Lindsay people, such as Corporation Counsel Lee Rankin and Transportation Commissioner Constantine Sidamon-Eristoff, chose to remain Republicans. The switch made official something that had long been unofficially acknowledged: the gradual loosening of the administration's ties to the Republican Party and concomitant softening of its reform rhetoric. The presidential campaign speeded changes at City Hall. Three months after Lindsay's decision, Aurelio and other aides left City Hall to work on Lindsay's unannounced presidential campaign, to be replaced by a new team of aides, mostly Democrats. Budget Director Edward Hamilton, just thirty-two, replaced Aurelio as deputy mayor, marking a move away from Aurelio's political stewardship to a more administratively focused City Hall. Assisting Hamilton in running City Hall were Democrats Richard Brown and Eleanor Holmes Norton and Liberal Party member Edward Morrison. Hamilton would run the city while Lindsay was running for president.

After coming out of the political closet, Lindsay seemed more at ease:

> Changing parties has been a fresh breeze in my life. They [Democrats] really talk my language. I've talked to Democrats from the suburbs who understand things like welfare reform and commuter taxes . . . I feel much freer about my own beliefs and I wonder a little bit about what I was doing all those years. . . . When I look back on my years in Con-

gress, it seems utterly ridiculous. Twenty liberal Republicans were constantly made uncomfortable, ostracized every time they voted for things like federal assistance to transportation.

But as comfortable as Lindsay generally felt after his switch, there were still uncomfortable moments. First, Lindsay turned his back on the men who had mentored his career since the early 1950s, like Herbert Brownell and Bethuel Webster. The liberal Republican wing of the party, as small as it may have become by 1971, was like a fraternal club, and these men thought of Lindsay as a son. They never said so publicly, but Brownell and Webster clearly were hurt. More ominously for Lindsay's political career, the mayor cut himself off from the men who had funded his political career since 1958. Gustave Levy said publicly that he was backing Nixon in 1972. Lindsay would have to look for new sources of campaign funding in the future.[18]

William F. Buckley could not resist a dig at his old enemy, saying that Lindsay's decision was "six years overdue. I suggested it to him in 1965." Asked why it took the mayor so long to follow this advice, Buckley responded, "It probably takes him a long time to think."[19]

Now that Lindsay had become a Democrat, the more important question was how would he be received in his new party. On that, the jury was still out. By the early 1970s, Mary Perot Nichols, a Greenwich Village activist and *Village Voice* reporter, had become so disillusioned with Lindsay that she wrote an article entitled "Bob Wagner: Where Are You Now That We Need You?" The perpetually dissatisfied Bella Abzug also had tough words for the man she had supported in 1969: Abzug, whose voice, Norman Mailer said, "could have boiled the fat off a taxicab driver's neck," wrote:

> I'm glad Lindsay's a Democrat now, but my feelings aren't clarified about whether I think he should run for President. . . . But I don't think the man has shown enough activism to justify his running for President. . . . It's true John Lindsay is a great liberal. He feels. But he has yet to prove he's an activist. And he also gets very uptight when you disagree with him. That must be his social background and temperament, which he would do well to get rid of. I don't know though, I suppose he's only got what he's got. I can't expect him to act like a Russian Jew.

What Abzug wanted was to "organize a new political coalition of the women, the minorities, the workers and the unemployed which is going to turn this country upside down and inside out."[20]

As Lindsay switched parties, one prominent Democratic constituency grew more disillusioned with the mayor. Some black New Yorkers complained that Lindsay had not done enough for their community. Though Lindsay was still respected in minority communities for his commitment to civil rights and his walks through ghetto neighborhoods during tense summers past, there was the sense that life in these areas had not actually improved during the Lindsay years. In January 1970, CORE's director, Floyd McKissick, had written Lindsay an open letter in the *Amsterdam News,* arguing that black New Yorkers deserved major representation in the second Lindsay administration in gratitude for their support. "What about a quid pro quo for the black people of Harlem?" McKissick asked. It soon become apparent that such a "quid pro quo" would never materialize, no matter Lindsay's good intentions. When the city's human rights commissioner, Eleanor Holmes Norton, a black woman, became a mayoral aide, there was talk of replacing her with a white woman. Holmes complained to Jay Kriegel that such a move would be "very disturbing" and "symptomatic of why we are in such serious trouble in the minority community. . . . The fact is that this year we have lost ground significantly in the black and Puerto Rican communities (and seeing whites take over the Human Rights Commission, of all agencies, would have been the last straw.)"[21]

In August 1971, the *Amsterdam News* devoted four pages appraising the mayoralty of John Lindsay in the wake of his switch to the Democratic Party. Congresswoman Shirley Chisolm and Housing Authority Chairman Simeon Golar praised Lindsay for his sympathy toward minorities, as well as for his support of the Civilian Complaint Review Board and open enrollment at CUNY.

The paper gave Lindsay guarded praise, but it also published articles expressing disillusionment with his policies. The paper's editorial board chairman, H. Carl McCall, a former Lindsay official, wrote: "The real issue is not that we feel better under Lindsay, but whether we are doing any better. And, obviously, we are not." He admitted that Lindsay had reached out to the black community, but because of this the black community "allowed ourselves to be romanced by John Lindsay. We have allowed ourselves to be awestruck with his image to the point of accepting, without question, his policies." The condition of the city's black neighborhoods, wrote McCall, "is far worse today than when he took office six years ago and when he was re-elected two years ago."

Beulah Sanders, chairwoman of the National Welfare Rights Organization, accused Lindsay of trying to "fool the Blacks and Puerto Ricans into voting for him again." Sanders wrote that Lindsay could not expect support from minority communities because, although he had promised them much, "during his first term things got worse for the poor and underprivileged. . . . Our fair city appears to be falling apart under the mayor's own eyes with him seemingly unconcerned." Bryant Rollins, a member of the paper's editorial board, also believed that the city was worse off after six years of Lindsay. To see the decline, wrote Rollins, "one need only glance at the street corners in Harlem; the vacant garbage-strewn lots and shells of buildings in Brownsville; the men and boys unemployed in doorways in Bedford-

Stuyvesant; the corridors of scores of public schools in all parts of the city."
Echoing other critics, Rollins said Lindsay's "greatest error was to promise
us so much." Despite the promises, "Black communities in New York City
are far worse off now than they were six years ago." Rollins also criticized
Lindsay for lacking deep contacts in the black community, for his "elitist
approach using top-name consultant firms and looking to the Ivy League
and Madison Avenue for solutions rather than to the people of the city,"
and for failing to deliver to minority communities "the goods and services
needed to improve the physical conditions in our communities." Certainly
a reservoir of good will would always exist in minority communities for
John Lindsay, but these feelings were based more on Lindsay's gestures and
rhetoric than on actual accomplishments. The newspaper's editorial concluded "that the jury is still out on the success or failure of Mr. Lindsay's
performance in office."[22]

Such ambivalence toward Lindsay was not found only among liberals and
minorities. Regular Democrat Ed Costikyan, who had run Abe Beame's
1965 campaign, wrote an op-ed for the *Times* in March 1971 asking, "Why
Not John Lindsay?" Costikyan, a former leader of Tammany Hall who had
sought to reform the clubhouse, was generally agreed to be a thoughtful and
serious person. Costikyan predicted that Democrats would not want Lindsay in their party, noting that Lindsay's "coronation" as the top state Democrat "would be the death knell of what is left of the party." Costikyan scored
Lindsay for his handling of city affairs, asking rhetorically: "Can any responsible Democratic leader seriously suggest that this record of inattention
and unconcern should be duplicated on a national scale by putting Lindsay
into the White House?"[23]

Amid such concerns, the newly minted Democrat set his eyes on the
White House. But one local issue, a housing controversy in Forest Hills,
Queens, erupted just as Lindsay turned his attention toward national politics. The situation highlighted the contradictions inherent in Lindsay's liberal policies and reopened the wounds of black-Jewish hostility. Democrat
or Republican, Lindsay still had the ability to inflame the passions of New
Yorkers.

SCATTER-SITE HOUSING IN FOREST HILLS

Lindsay spent much of the second term attempting to stay away from the
bruising and costly battles of the first. He hoped to present himself to the
nation as an urban peacemaker who kept New York cool while other cities
burned. But in 1971 the city was once again thrown into a fury. The cause
of the crisis was the Lindsay administration's attempt to build three
twenty-four-story high-rise apartment buildings to house 840 low-income families in the middle-class Jewish neighborhood of Forest Hills,
Queens.

The origins of the housing controversy date back to 1966. When the reformer John Lindsay was elected mayor, he promised an overhaul of city government and increased sensitivity toward minorities and the poor. In addition to reorganizing city agencies, reforming the police department, decentralizing schools, and opening up city parks, Lindsay also promised to focus on housing. During his campaign, candidate Lindsay had grandly promised to build 160,000 new apartments in his first term. Part of that number would include low-income projects placed in middle-class neighborhoods. After his election in 1965 Lindsay appointed a Housing and Urban Renewal Task Force, headed by a lawyer, Charles Abrams, and including the urban planner Ed Logue, architect I. M. Pei, and a housing reformer, I. D. Robbins. Their report, released in January 1966, called for a housing policy that would create greater racial and economic diversity in the city: "It has become as essential to prevent segregation as to ban it and when an existing housing project in a neighborhood is threatened with segregation, it becomes the duty of a public agency to prevent it by positive policy, even where the public agency concerned must become conscious of color to do so."

The report stated that housing should "encourage and reinforce integration when it already exists." It also emphasized that public housing "should be primarily devoted to providing buildings, not 'self-contained' projects. The buildings should be inserted as part of existing neighborhoods, not massively superimposed upon them." The Lindsay administration took the strong message of housing integration and proposed what came to be termed as "scatter-site" housing projects. Rather than just build new public housing in old ghettos and perpetuate segregation and poverty, the city would force middle-income communities to accept low-income housing in the name of integration and social justice.[24]

Large housing projects would be politically impossible anyway, so instead, the city would build numerous smaller projects "scattered" throughout city neighborhoods in all five boroughs. Eugenia Flatow, a city housing official, explained that the Lindsay administration was trying "to give people a chance to escape not just from slum buildings, but from the slum environment in the hope of giving families a different kind of environment and also of raising their level of expectations." Roger Starr, a housing expert, explained, "advocates of scatter-site housing seem to believe that sprinkling low-income families in relatively expensive neighborhoods will make a significant contribution to the advancement of the poor (and particularly the non-white poor) in American cities."[25]

As with most of the battles during Lindsay's first term, there was an element of righteous zeal and moralistic fervor to the scatter-site housing controversy. The policy was, as city Planning Commissioner Don Elliott noted, a "moral imperative" for the Lindsay administration. When these projects provoked strong opposition from middle-income residents of neighborhoods, one anonymous Lindsay official said, "I feel sorry for the homeowner in Queens who has to accept a public housing project, I really do. But I feel a lot sorrier for the Negro in Bedford-Stuyvesant who wants to get out of there." This was a moral imperative, after all, and neighborhood opposition was easily derided as selfishness at best and racism at worst. Writing about his scatter-site plan in 1968, the mayor predicted the fury. "This is a technique aimed at breaking up the ghetto by scattering small, un-obtrusive public-housing units throughout middle-class areas of the city. They wouldn't bring radical change to the neighborhood. Yet what an up-roar this proposal has raised in the white neighborhoods!" But the uproar would do little to sway the mayor from implementing his plan, at least until 1971.[26]

Problems plagued the scatter-site concept from the start. Later, Mario Cuomo wrote a report on the events in Forest Hills: "Before 1966 when this City attempted to implement the scatter-site approach, there had been relatively little in-depth study and analysis of the program's potential effectiveness. The program was largely an enthusiastic experiment in social planning. Its goals were noble but its efficacy largely unproven." Roger Starr explained that though racial and economic integration did exist in some New York communities, the results were less than conclusive. Starr described Manhattan's Upper West Side, with its mix of luxury apartments on Central Park West and West End Avenue, quaint brownstones on sidestreets, and poor tenements along Columbus Avenue. Such diversity produced a neighborhood of various income-levels, races, and religions all living within a few blocks of each other, coming together along the commercial strip of Broadway. "No matter how entertaining, then, one may find the spectacle of Broadway," Starr concluded, "it remains difficult to point to one concrete social result of the intermingling of diverse income groups, one sign of effective social action, which would not otherwise have taken place."[27]

Despite such questions and criticisms of his policy, Lindsay went ahead with plans to put up thirteen scatter-site projects throughout the city, total-ing approximately 7,500 units. (By 1972, one of these projects had been built, two were under construction, one was pending construction, and the rest were dormant.) One of the sites chosen was in Corona, Queens, a tight-knit blue-collar Italian-American community. Jack Newfield called Corona "one of the few authentic communities left in this unheavenly city." Com-munity residents rallied against the plan, fearful of their stable neighborhood being flooded by the poor. They were joined by residents of nearby Lefrak City. In 1965, the developer Sam Lefrak had built a complex of high-rise towers to house over 20,000 people just a few blocks from Corona. Pressure from Lefrak and the Corona community forced a change in the plan. The public-housing project would be moved a few blocks away to an eight-and-a-half acre site on the edge of the middle-class Jewish community of Forest

Hills, while the old Corona site would be used to build a new school, necessitated by the overcrowding in Forest Hills schools and an influx of new students living in Lefrak City.[28]

The housing project planned in Corona would have been set on four-and-a-half acres, but the school and its athletic grounds needed more land. So the city planned to condemn sixty-nine Corona homes to gain more space. Now Corona residents were unhappy about the destruction of their neighborhood for a school, and Forest Hills residents were unhappy about the public-housing project. Corona residents decided to fight the city over the sixty-nine homes and they hired a little-known lawyer, Mario Cuomo, to represent them. For years, Cuomo kept the city at bay, preventing it from demolishing the houses by tying up the matter in court appeals and bureaucratic wrangling. The Lindsay administration, though a strong proponent of local control and decentralization, showed little interest in the concerns of Corona. The residents of Corona were a proud people, who had devoted their lives to their modest homes and their community. Many of the condemned houses had been built by their owners.[29]

Even without Lindsay's help, Corona became a cause célèbre. Jimmy Breslin took up the community's cause and pushed his journalist friends to write about the residents whose homes were condemned. Breslin also began pressuring his friends in City Hall to do something about Corona. Brooklyn Assemblyman Vito Battista, the self-appointed spokesman for white ethnics, adopted the Corona cause and used his version of street theater to gain media attention. After the 1969 mayoral election, Cuomo began working with Deputy Mayor Richard Aurelio on a compromise. When alternate sites proved unworkable, Cuomo suggested a plan that would cut down the size of the athletic fields and allow most of the houses to remain. Those that couldn't be left where they were would be moved to a nearby empty lot. The plan was announced in December 1970. By this time, the actual number of homes involved in the controversy had dwindled to fifty-nine: Thirty-one houses would remain, and twenty-eight would be moved. But instead of solving the problem, the compromise further inflamed the already suspicious and aggrieved Corona residents. Some supported the compromise, while others, led by Battista, accused Cuomo and others of selling out Corona. Battista was able to frustrate the compromise legislation in Albany. Meanwhile, the backbiting and hatred tore apart the community. Breslin, who supported the compromise, regretted ever getting involved. "It's a rat nest," Breslin said in 1971. "I used up all my credits in City Hall trying to help those bastards instead of myself. Now I owe favors." Meanwhile, as one journalist wrote, by 1971 Corona was "very near death. After four years of uncertainty over what will become of their homes, people begin to give up. The hatred and the polarization have all but destroyed Corona as a community of people. As a neighborhood of houses, Corona is fast decaying. The former owners have neglected repairs because the city owns the houses. The city itself made only minimal repairs to keep the houses habitable." Eventually, in 1972, a new compromise was worked out that called for the relocation of only four houses. Legislation reflecting the compromise was passed in Albany and Governor Rockefeller signed it into law in June 1972. Despite the compromise, the bitterness of the nearly seven-year battle did not completely fade; Corona was never the same.[30]

As the Corona compromise was being worked out, construction of the Forest Hills housing project began. The neighborhood already had a mix of luxury high-rise buildings and single-family homes. The plan called for the construction of three twenty-four-story buildings for low-income residents on a site near the Long Island Expressway that had been vacant for years. As construction began in November 1971, residents mobilized against the project by forming the Forest Hills Residents Association, led by Jerry Birbach. Protesters, many of them elderly residents, picketed the site carrying signs saying LINDSAY IS TRYING TO DESTROY QUEENS. NOW QUEENS WILL DESTROY LINDSAY. At one nighttime rally, protesters threw rocks and torches at construction trailers. The mayor called the rally "deplorable" and said the "disturbance puts this city to the test of whether we have the power of our convictions; whether we shall obey the law or whether we shall defy it; whether, finally, we will guide ourselves by rationality and truth, or whether we shall permit ourselves to be misled by misunderstanding and fear."[31]

At first glance, Forest Hills did not seem like the kind of community that would oppose a low-income housing project. Forest Hills had voted for Lindsay in both 1965 and 1969. What some people did not realize was that many of the liberal, middle-class Forest Hills Jews had moved to the neighborhood from poor areas of Brooklyn and the Bronx, often fleeing in the face of the deterioration of their old neighborhoods. "There will be a huge exodus [from Forest Hills]," exclaimed one housewife. "I improved myself to move to a neighborhood like this. For what?" Forest Hills showed that middle-class whites could expropriate the language and tactics of civil disobedience. The anger of the community was real and it was raw. As one writer said, "Most residents of this predominantly Jewish middle-class area are deeply, almost desperately, opposed to the 24-story low-income housing project . . . The intensity of their anger and fear has proved intimidating." Protesters held signs saying DOWN WITH ADOLF LINDSAY AND HIS PROJECT and SAVE FOREST HILLS, SAVE MIDDLE-CLASS AMERICA and FOREST HILLS DOESN'T WANT "WELFARE TOWERS" ON 108TH STREET.[32]

In addition to concerns about the impact of the project on transportation, schools, and neighborhood services, the scatter-site controversy hit a raw nerve at the nexus of race, class, and neighborhood deterioration. The critics of the housing project possessed a set of values far removed from the notions of integration and social justice put forth by the Lindsay administration. Many Forest Hills residents were the children or grandchildren of immigrants and had grown up in poor New York neighborhoods. Jerry Birbach, the spokesman for the Forest Hills Residents Association, epitomized the social background of Forest Hills. He grew up poor in Manhattan's Lower East Side, later moved to Williamsburg, Brooklyn, went to City College at night for his degree, and built up a real estate business in Manhattan. The middle-class residents of Forest Hills believed that they had earned the right to live in their neighborhood by years of hard work and sacrifice. Now they believed that the city was giving the poor a place in their neighborhood without making them work for it. Not only did they feel that this kind of scatter-site project violated the rules of society by which middle-class people lived, but they also felt that the presence of this housing project would significantly lower the quality of life in their neighborhood. For most Forest Hills residents, the housing project meant an increase in crime, tension, and disorder. The director of the American Jewish Committee's Legal Division, Samuel Rabinove, expressed his fears about Forest Hills bluntly in a private letter:

> Forest Hills residents survey the wreckage of the other NYC neighborhoods where Jews used to live in relative peace—Brownsville, Crown Heights, Williamsburg, East New York, Hunts Point, and now Far Rockaway. They see 80-year-old women thrown to the sidewalk by youths who steal their pocketbooks, armed robbery and burglary virtually epidemic, children beaten up and subjected to extortion in schools, which are no longer scholastic achievement–oriented, all kinds of property vandalized and destroyed. . . . They are not willing to sacrifice their own children on the altar of black revenge. Can anyone blame them?

Jews who had moved away from those other neighborhoods felt they were keeping themselves just one step in front of social decay, and to them the Lindsay administration kept narrowing that gap.[33]

Lindsay administration officials and scatter-site supporters may have castigated these concerns as those of bigots, but the sociologist Nathan Glazer admitted that the "chances of such a project bringing to the neighborhood in a very short time some 500 to 600 adolescents and young men and women are all too high. That they will be a burden to the neighborhood is probable too. Many of them will extort money from children at school, beat them if they don't provide any, break windows of the neighborhood stores, rob from them, attack the elderly for money and sport. These are simple facts which the black and white people of Forest Hills are quite aware of."

In the *Village Voice*, journalist Clark Whelton articulated Forest Hills' case against scatter-site housing for the poor. "The people who live there aren't better off because the area is nicer," wrote Whelton. "They're better off because they *made* the area nicer. Unless new residents contribute the same kinds of middle-class discipline and values to the neighborhood, it will become something else." Considering all of this, Glazer concluded, "What seems quite unfair is that in their fight for a hard-won security, they [Forest Hills residents] should be labeled racists."[34]

Supporters of the project had different concerns. Some pointed to the ugliness of the attitudes of some of the housing opponents and their implicit demonization of the black poor. Others, like journalist Nat Hentoff, argued that 2,000 poor people in a neighborhood of 150,000 would have little effect on the middle-class character of Forest Hills. Others believed that people's fears of low-income housing were based on racist stereotypes. Bronx Congressman Herman Badillo argued that not only was the Forest Hills controversy "a racial one, but a distorted one in which fears are being allowed to multiply and spread without proper rebuttal." Mario Cuomo pointed out the general theme of the project's supporters. "All of the proponents argue from almost purely moral and theoretical grounds," wrote Cuomo. "The argument for, as presented by most of these people, is constructed of noble and appealing generalizations on the visceral and the surface equities. The plight of the black, the rest of the community's moral obligation, the tradition to aid the downtrodden—that's how the case is being made." Playing down the disruption the housing project would cause, City Planning Commissioner Don Elliott reassured Forest Hills that the "project is not designed to attract newcomers, but to allow hundreds of the poor and elderly to enjoy the advantage of living in Forest Hills. . . . But the project will certainly improve the lives of 840 poor and elderly families, without hurting anyone now living in Forest Hills."[35]

Supporters and opponents both agreed that the Lindsay administration was not handling the Forest Hills situation well. Paul Cowan, a supporter of the project, wrote in the *Village Voice* that the "Lindsay administration has been insensitive, short-sighted, and in its own way quite bigoted." Cowan recalled hearing a Housing Authority official calling Forest Hills residents "crackers." Commissioner Elliott later admitted that the city was never "able to get the consent of the communities" which were to accept these housing projects. Cuomo, although sympathetic to the idea of low-income housing, laid out some questions that needed to be answered:

> Is it provable that this will be good for the downtrodden? What effects will it have in terms of economic integration? Will its size result in insularizing this group and effectively creating an independent separate community, thereby defeating the objective of integration? And what effect will it have on the neighboring community? If apartments in neighboring buildings begin to show increasing vacancies, won't that result in landlords filling the space with welfare, thereby eventually spreading the welfare and low-income community throughout? Logically progressed, mightn't this result in the welfare city that some accused Lindsay of wanting years ago? And would that be good?

These were questions no one in the Lindsay administration wanted to ask, let alone answer.[36]

Many believed the Lindsay administration chose the Jewish Forest Hills neighborhood because liberal Jews would not complain about the project. As one Forest Hills rabbi said: "Lindsay assumed it was a place where he could safely deposit his housing project. After all, Jews are not given to violence: they wouldn't burn black homes." But Lindsay underestimated the anger in the Jewish community. The Queens Jewish Community Council declared, "Mayor Lindsay has shown he is not interested in the Jewish population of his constituency." Haskell Lazere, director of the New York chapter of the American Jewish Committee, felt that "whether consciously or not, the mayor has been guilty of pitting group against group in our city." Lazere and the AJC's president, Edward Moldover, wrote to Lindsay in a confidential telegram in February 1972: "We are particularly shocked that a meeting is reportedly being arranged under your auspices of Blacks and Jews to discuss the project. . . . Such a meeting will inevitably result in still more public polarization between Jews and Blacks further heightening emotions and tensions in our city, which are already severely strained."[37]

Some politcians also opposed the housing project. The newly elected Conservative Senator James Buckley, prodded the federal Department of Housing and Urban Development to kill the project. Benjamin Rosenthal, a Liberal Queens Democratic congressman, also opposed the plan. Another opponent was a little-known Manhattan congressman named Ed Koch. Though Forest Hills was not part of his district, the liberal Koch threw himself into the battle against the project. (Koch's justification for his involvement was that he was a member of the House Banking Committee, which has jurisdiction over public housing.) It was also a way for Koch to tweak the nose of his former ally, John Lindsay. "I felt that the people in Forest Hills were being pushed around in an unfair way by the Lindsay administration," Koch wrote over a decade later. "They were being made the goat." Koch traveled to the site to attend a protest rally in 1971, telling protesters: "I firmly believed that we should not destroy our middle-class communities, black or white, for any reason." Looking back on the controversy in 1996, Koch said, "I believed that three twenty-four-story buildings with 4,500 people on welfare inserted into a middle-class area would destroy the area."

Taking on such a controversial issue and placing himself on what appeared to be the "anti–civil rights side" was out of character for the Greenwich Village reformer. But it was a boon to his political career. He later acknowledged that his opposition to the Forest Hills project "did more to distinguish me among New Yorkers than anything I ever did on the House floor." It moderated Koch's reputation as a Greenwich Village liberal, created the image of Koch as a "liberal with sanity," and started him on his eventual path toward City Hall. After Forest Hills, Koch said he "no longer felt comfortable in the reform movement." He called Forest Hills his "Rubicon" because it "set me on my own independent path. It allowed me to persuade people that I was not some crazy reformer from Greenwich Village." His position, though, angered many of his former allies on the left. "I think Koch is trying to exploit people's understandable fears to further his own ambition to be mayor," wrote Jack Newfield. "I feel like grabbing him [Koch] and saying, 'Wake up, Ed, and be a mensch.'"[38]

As opposition mounted to the project, something had to be done. In November 1971, the city's Board of Estimate voted against a 559-unit low-income scatter-site project in the white middle-class Lindenwood section of Queens, near John F. Kennedy Airport. In addition, the New York State Legislature passed a bill that would have required any plans for public housing be resubmitted to the local governing body if work had not proceeded past the foundation stage after five years. The legislation was specifically written with Forest Hills in mind. Since the Board of Estimate made clear that it would rescind its support for the project if it came to another vote, the legislation would have prevented construction of the project. But Governor Rockefeller vetoed the bill, which he saw as poor legislation. Although passage of the bill would have embarrassed Lindsay, Rockefeller was not about to sanction such a bad bill just to stick it to his political rival.[39]

A few days after Rockefeller's veto in May 1972, Richard Aurelio, though he no longer worked in an official capacity at City Hall, asked Mario Cuomo to mediate the dispute in Forest Hills, much as he had done in Corona. The next day, Cuomo met with Aurelio, Deputy Mayor Ed Hamilton, Jay Kriegel, and other aides. When Housing Authority Chairman Simeon Golar entered the meeting, according to Cuomo, "it wasn't difficult to read his displeasure and it was understandable. He had been out front on this issue for months taking the flack for his hard stand." Cuomo spent the following two months meeting with all parties involved in order to come up with a compromise.[40]

When Cuomo released his report two months later, he offered a significant compromise. "Even prescinding from the attitude of the Forest Hills community," Cuomo concluded, "it seems to me that objectively viewed the project as proposed is simply too large, both in terms of its physical size and in the number of low-income units it will add to the community." Cuomo echoed the fears of the project's critics when he wrote that numerous experts in law enforcement "state flatly that from a security point of view these three twenty-four story towers are at best undesirable." Instead of three twenty-four-story towers, Cuomo's plan cut the size of the project to three twelve-story towers with a total of 432 apartments. Of these, 40 percent would be set aside for senior citizens. If a change was not made, Cuomo believed that the hostility toward the project existed "in large enough numbers of people so that it might eventually lead to large scale departures" from Forest Hills.[41]

Cuomo was in a difficult position. As a white Italian American, he had to show sufficient independence from the Lindsay administration to gain the respect of whites opposed to the project while, as a Democrat, still showing sympathy to the concerns of blacks. Cuomo found opposition to low-income housing projects among the black middle class. Residents of Baisley Park, Queens, a stable black middle-class neighborhood, opposed a low-income project as vociferously as those in Forest Hills. Talking with middle-class blacks in Hollis, Queens, Cuomo found that they "unhesitatingly said that they would not want the project in *their* neighborhood." A black barber told Cuomo he did not want to live in a project or near one because "the low-income and welfare elements are destructive and troublesome."[42]

Cuomo displayed a remarkable ability to come down on both sides of an issue. On the question of how a low-income project would affect the community, he believed that "the perfidious generalization that all low-income, or for that matter welfare, people are vandals and criminals would be universally rejected by reasonable men. On the other hand, to deny that poverty and social problems are related would be to deny the testimony of history and our own experience in the City." Cuomo was torn between the desire to appear tolerant and open-minded and the realities of the situation. "It seems clear to me that the influx of welfare families will bring with it a threat of increased crime," Cuomo wrote in his diary of the events. "That had been checked out in several sources and is a matter of almost common experience." He also spoke with Queens Congressman Joe Addabbo, who told him that the Rochdale housing project in his district "was a mess with a serious crime problem."[43]

The compromise left everyone unhappy. When Cuomo presented his report draft to Lindsay and his aides, he wrote in his diary that they were "all unhappy, I think, but none attempted to push me." Lindsay, who had previously insisted that the Forest Hills site would "absolutely not" be altered, accepted Cuomo's proposal. He came to "this decision reluctantly, but with a view that the extreme polarization caused by this project overrides the merits of the original design of the project." A group of liberal organizations released a statement, which Cuomo called "primitively absolutist," that condemned the mayor and referred to the compromise as "kissing the feet of the Forest Hills racist." On the other side, Jerry Birbach also opposed the compromise, calling it "just another low-income project" and condemning the mayor as "totally unresponsive, pompous, and arrogant." Birbach told Cuomo that unless the project was changed further, he would "burn down this town, rather than let the project tenants destroy it." Birbach's group wanted no project at all on the site.[44]

The three twelve-story buildings were eventually completed in Forest Hills, but only after it had undergone another big change. What really transformed the Forest Hills project was not just the Cuomo compromise, but the plan to make the housing project a co-op. This proposal was strongly urged by Queens Borough President Donald Manes, who saw it as an opportunity to improve the quality of potential tenants. (The idea of a co-op also appeared in an addendum to the Cuomo Report, in a letter from Paul Sandman, president of the Forest Hills Neighbors.) Residents were required to pay for "shares" in the co-op, although they were forbidden from selling them to anyone but the New York City Housing Authority. In addition, residents were required to pay a maintenance fee, and income limits for residents were slightly higher than for regular city public housing. All of this combined to develop a sense of pride among residents in their homes, despite the fact that, as one journalist wrote, the co-ops "are cookie-cutter dull and their cinder-block hallways have as antiseptic a feel as any vandal-resistant 'project.'"

Today, the compromise solution appears to be successful. Contrary to the prediction of critics, the area has not become rife with crime or drugs. A *New York Times* reporter, visiting the project in 1995, concluded that "the opponents' fears of crime and other social ills proved unwarranted. Today, the quiet atmosphere at the project belies its fiery beginnings, although some residents say the quality of life has worsened." An estimated 1,000 residents fled the neighborhood after the project opened in 1975. (Jewish immigrants from Russia and Israel bought many of the vacated homes, thereby retaining the neighborhood's religious character.) Nevertheless, Forest Hills remains to this day a middle-class enclave, relatively unaffected by the housing project.

Even Jerry Birbach, when interviewed in 1984, believed that the Forest Hills co-op was a success. Birbach, who moved from Forest Hills soon after the controversy to a suburb farther out on Long Island, suggested that much of the success of the project came from the opposition. "If it wasn't for the furor of the community," Birbach said, "that co-op wouldn't exist—a 'project' would have gone through." The worst nightmare of Forest Hills residents never came to pass, largely because the city did not build a low-income project. The racial breakdown for the project in 1976 was 63.9 percent white, 13.8 percent black, 7.9 percent Hispanic, and 14.4 percent other. In addition, nearly 31 percent of co-op residents were over the age of sixty-two. What had been created was a predominantly white co-op for the working poor and elderly. That would change in the future, however. After 1992, the city admitted to racially discriminatory practices in placing tenants in its low-income projects. Since then, one resident noted, "Everybody we get is mostly Afro-Americans and Hispanics." By 1995 the racial breakdown had changed somewhat: 52.9 percent white; 19.6 percent black; 10.2 percent Hispanic; 17.3 percent other. [45]

Whatever success could be claimed for the Forest Hills project, it had little to do with the original scatter-site plan. After all of the fury surrounding the scatter-site plan, city Planning Commissioner Don Elliott,

Lindsay's point man on the issue, admitted that if he were to do it over again, he "would do it differently." Instead of trying to put high-rise, low-income projects in middle-class neighborhoods, Elliott would emphasize the rehabilitation of existing housing. Most people now agree that housing the poor in high-rise buildings, whether in ghettos or middle-class neighborhoods, is counterproductive. If John Lindsay had been that prescient in the 1960s, he would have been spared some of the anger that he faced as he ran for president.[46]

RUNNING FOR PRESIDENT

John Lindsay, as he liked to point out, was not plotting his way to the top like the Kennedys. Though he was not without ambitions, Lindsay had a history of being led to decisions by those around him. Ultimately, Lindsay himself made the final decision on running for President, but his young aides with visions of offices in the West Wing also did their best to maneuver their boss toward such a decision. As Nicholas Pileggi wrote in 1971: "His staff is running for him, and that is the way he has always preferred to have his mind made up. . . . Today, the men who surround Lindsay are playing a familiar game, subtly nudging their reluctant candidate, slowly wearing him down, not with daily head-on debates, but with the steady drip of data upon his ample conscience." Peter Goldmark, a former Lindsay aide who had just become the Secretary of Human Services in Massachusetts, sent a letter to his former boss and his wife urging him to run for office. "I think you are emotionally spent in running the city," wrote Goldmark in July 1971. "I think you have little more to offer the city and much more to offer the country."[47]

Changing parties could be seen as a logical move for a man who increasingly felt alienated from his old party. But the run for president never made any sense. Running for president in the Democratic primary four months after switching parties was suicide. Even though Lindsay had always been politically independent and had never been a partisan Republican, such a move did little to win the trust of voters. When Lindsay told one of his staunchest supporters, labor leader Victor Gotbaum, about his decision to run for president, Gotbaum was underwhelmed. "Are you asking me or are you telling me," Gotbaum asked. "I'm telling you," Lindsay replied. To this Gotbaum responded, "John, you're going to be a fucking disaster." Gotbaum had a point. Lindsay had very little in the way of a political base in the Democratic Party. Furthermore, Gotbaum was unhappy that he had not been consulted on the move earlier, and so Lindsay had just alienated his strongest labor ally.[48]

Having turned fifty a month earlier, John Lindsay announced three days before Christmas in 1971 that he was running for president. He told voters it was time "that the people had a chance to send somebody to Washington to be the president, someone who has at least lived where the people's problems are instead of waiting for the tight, closed and unchanging political community of Washington to send somebody out to the country." The Lindsay strategy was to run against the "inside-the-Beltway" candidates: Senators Hubert Humphrey, George McGovern, Edmund Muskie, and Henry (Scoop) Jackson, as well as the President, Richard Nixon. Of the national capital Lindsay said, "For the truth about Washington is that it is a capital closed to the ordinary citizen, but open to bankrupt corporate giants, foreign dictators, and to those wealthy enough to buy privileged protection with campaign cash. For this is a government willing to travel to Peking and Moscow, but not to Harlem or Watts or Appalachia, or to the unemployed in Cape Kennedy—to the places where Americans wait for help." Richard Aurelio, now running Lindsay's improbable campaign, described the presidential run at a December cabinet meeting as "audacious and daring."[49]

Lindsay portrayed himself as a man who had faced down the problems of the city, even if he had not exactly solved them. He would run as a strong antiwar candidate with appeals to minorities and idealistic youth. Lindsay would skip the New Hampshire primary and focus on Arizona, Florida, Wisconsin, Massachusetts, Indiana, and California. Still handsome and charismatic, Lindsay would be the media candidate, the candidate of the "new politics." As one Lindsay aide noted: "Television is where Lindsay is by far the best of the field. He's got more sex appeal. We work to get maximum media attention. . . . We like to show off our candidate in situations like that where his youth and energy and athletic prowess come across."[50]

Lindsay ran in 1972 as the most left-wing candidate, a notch to the left of McGovern. Besides talking about the problems of American cities, Lindsay hammered away at the Vietnam War, especially when speaking before student groups. In January he told students at Northern Arizona University that U.S. involvement in Vietnam had "been an unmitigated disaster—for the Vietnamese, for our standing in the world, and for our national unity at home." Lindsay called for the immediate and total withdrawal of American troops from Vietnam. The following month he told students at UCLA that he had "found no one—young or old—who thinks that immoral war in Indochina should go on another day." When Lindsay spoke of the war on the campaign trail, his voice could barely conceal his anger. At a Florida news conference, Lindsay, modishly dressed in a blue shirt and a wide multicolored tie, emotionally declared, "My people have suffered because of that war. I can't tell you what agony these cities have been through." His face was tense with anger. He raised his fist up and slammed it down on the word "suffered."[51]

The patrician politician whose career had been funded by the Whitneys, Loebs, Paleys, Warburgs, Rockefellers, Vanderbilts, and Astors suddenly became an antibusiness politician, mouthing rhetoric about how "excessive corporate power is the root problem of the economy." He called for a Corporate Freedom of Information Act; a Federal Consumer Protection Agency; a halt to the "alarming concentration" of energy resources; divestiture of large agribusiness holdings; "Fair Share Income" for senior citizens; and a national investigation into the extent of corporate power in the United States.[52]

Lindsay's left-wing politics were most apparent in his work as co-chair of the "Commission on the Cities in the '70s." The commission released a report in which it contended that "nothing less than fundamental reforms in the U.S. economic and political structure are needed to redress a money-and-power imbalance as grave as the one that now exists." The group's proposals included "a guaranteed job at higher than poverty level for every person able to work"; a guaranteed higher-than-poverty-level income for every person unable to work"; a comprehensive national health insurance system; "a warm, sanitary, and spacious home for every American family"; and a strong anti-inflationary policy. Also, government would steer American industry into two large public works projects that would help American cities: building "decent housing for every American" and building "decent mass transportation for every American city."[53]

Breaking new ground, Lindsay defended women's rights, a bow to the growing feminist movement. Lindsay strongly supported abortion rights, the Equal Rights Amendment, and free universal childcare. Lindsay's new language of the Left relied heavily on the language of victimization, which was not in keeping with Lindsay's stoic WASP upbringing. As he told a Miami crowd: "Today women who have been victims of a social system that discounted their true worth must realize that they are not the only victims in America. We are all victims of that war in Vietnam. We are all victims of the Vietnam economy. We are all victimized by higher prices and products that aren't what they are advertised to be, that don't clean or taste or work the way they're supposed to . . . We are all victimized by crime."[54]

Despite the quixotic nature of Lindsay's decision to run for president, the campaign began on a strong note. Aurelio's strategy was to "surprise everyone in an early nonprimary state so they'll take [Lindsay's] candidacy seriously." The state they chose was Arizona. In the January 1972 primary in Arizona, Lindsay came in second to Muskie with 23.6 percent of the delegates, and ahead of George McGovern. Lindsay picked up only six delegates for the Miami convention, but he showed strength in the Phoenix area and among young voters, blacks, and Hispanics. The media campaign, run by David Garth, spent little money, but plastered the state with billboards reading LINDSAY—ARIZONA LIKES A FIGHTER—VOTE JANUARY 29.

The state into which the Lindsay campaign poured its greatest effort was Florida, which was holding its primary on March 14. Aurelio later wrote, "The advice I gave him was . . . Concentrate everything in Florida, where Muskie will fall apart, and you will finish second or third, with enough momentum to do well in Wisconsin, Massachusetts and Indiana; then stage a toe-to-toe climactic battle with Humphrey in California, and go on to the Miami convention with enough delegates to be a major force in determining the ticket, even if you are not on it."

Florida would seem a strange place for an urban mayor to make his stand. Though it did have a major city—Miami—with a large Jewish population, as well as pockets of blacks throughout the state, for the most part Florida in 1972 was a conservative state.[55]

Small problems dogged Lindsay during the run-up to the Florida primary. The campaign got off to a bad start when Sid Davidoff, who was helping Aurelio run the campaign, showed up at his Miami hotel with his huge dog. The sight of this huge dog walking through the lobby of the fancy hotel angered the staff and guests. Davidoff was thrown out of the hotel, the story made the newspapers, and it looked as though arrogant New Yorkers were trying to run roughshod over Florida. In addition, Davidoff's advance people, imported from New York, turned off many Floridians. They were tough, streetwise characters whom the journalist Theodore White described as "Manhattan city people; and New York City Hall under John Lindsay had turned over its political operations to some of the most parochial pavement politicians of the times." The Forest Hills crisis haunted Lindsay, especially among the Jewish residents of Miami. To be sure, many Floridians were former New Yorkers, but they had not necessarily been happy New Yorkers. Many had become disillusioned with the city and had left it behind for permanent sunshine and palm trees. These ex–New Yorkers left behind friends and relatives in the city who would commiserate via long-distance phone calls about how dangerous the city was, how dirty the streets were, how intolerable John Lindsay's New York had become.[56]

Perhaps the most famous event of the Florida primary occurred when a former New York bonding agent, Bob Blaike, who had been a Democratic district leader in the Morningside Heights area before moving to Florida, hired a plane to fly a banner over the beaches of Miami while Lindsay was campaigning. In a message aimed directly at Miami's Jews, the banner read: LINDSAY SPELLS TSOURIS—*tsouris* being the Yiddish word for "trouble."

The Lindsay campaign in Florida was snake-bit, although one could argue that it was bedeviled less by bad luck than by poor planning. According to Aurelio, Lindsay was disappointed with his Florida campaign: "I think he felt that a lot of people sabotaged him." Congresswoman Shirley Chisolm, the first black woman to run for president, had promised Lindsay that she would not run in Florida, thereby leaving the black vote to the mayor. For some reason she later went back on her word and decided to run in Florida. The Lindsay campaign also believed it was sandbagged by Miami Mayor David Kennedy, who had earlier agreed to support Lindsay, but soon after switched to Humphrey. The Lindsay people also erred in their belief that George Wallace would stay out of Florida. To make matters worse, a school-busing referendum also appeared on the primary ballot, bringing out busing opponents who would never vote for the liberal Lindsay.[57]

Media events were scheduled almost daily to show off the campaign's most prized possession: John Lindsay. Television ads also featured Carroll

O'Connor, then starring as Archie Bunker in the comedy series *All in the Family*. O'Connor told Floridians to "vote your hopes, not your fears," and then stuck a cigar in his mouth and became Bunker, adding "ya know what I mean, stick with me as part of the Lindsay contiguency [*sic*]." It was unclear what constituency this ad was geared to, since it was unlikely liberals would listen to the political advice of America's favorite bigot, nor would conservatives be fooled into voting for the liberal Lindsay. Another ad was more direct. Charles Evers, the mayor of Fayette, Mississippi, and brother of the slain civil rights worker Medger Evers, told voters in a commercial, "John Lindsay has proven over the years he's for all the people, the blacks, the whites, the Puerto Ricans, and all of those who need to be cared for."

Lindsay's charisma was obvious. Large crowds of people often came to hear this exotic and handsome politician. Politically, though, Lindsay proved not ready for primetime. He regularly attacked Wallace and tried to turn the primary into a race between himself and the Alabama governor. He challenged Wallace to a debate, which Wallace turned down, but refused to debate the liberal George McGovern. He went out of his way to take stands that would alienate large groups of Florida voters, but felt uncomfortable arguing on behalf of more mundane middle-class issues. His stands in favor of gun control and busing were not simply political positions, but extended arguments about morality and good government. Speaking before the Florida legislature, Lindsay spoke of busing as "a moral issue, for when we debate busing now we are debating what this country stands for; we are debating our loyalty to the deepest and most abiding faith of the American people; and yes, we are debating whether we mean to provide justice and equality to our black brothers. . . . I am for busing because if the choice is between inconvenience and the repudiation of the Constitution, I stand with the Constitution." (In his first term, Lindsay had opposed busing New York schoolchildren as a way to achieve integration, angering the black community and setting the stage for the community control movement.) He castigated Senators Humphrey, Jackson, and Muskie for their positions on busing. According to Theodore White, Lindsay "had distilled an indignation of conscience and a ferocity of expression which overwhelmed good judgment. Compared to John Lindsay, even George McGovern was a man of compromise."[58]

At a speech in Orlando, the mayor spoke passionately to a crowd of middle-class whites about life in the big city in 1972, about drug abuse, crime, slums, and welfare, telling them that what divided America was "fear, the legacy of race and poverty, the refusal of big government to make big institutions be accountable to the public for what they do." The crowd was unmoved by Lindsay's rhetoric. Most, noted White, had "fled here from the North to escape just the scene that John Lindsay was describing. If there was any fight in them it was to defend the sun and the quiet to which they had come to doze and dream far from the sirens in the night. And here was

Lindsay with his furious eloquence, bringing to these green lawns and tranquil places, the nightmares of the shrill nights they had fled."[59]

The Lindsay campaign expected a strong showing in Florida, but it was sorely disappointed on March 14. Lindsay received a mere 7 percent of the vote, finishing a weak fifth. George Wallace won with 42 percent, followed by Humphrey, Jackson, and Muskie. As he had in Arizona, though, Lindsay edged out McGovern. Lindsay's poor showing doomed his already dubious candidacy. Many Democrats, already skeptical of the new convert, were eager to portray Lindsay a failure.

The Wisconsin primary was next on the itinerary, and Lindsay would not let the Florida debacle stop him from campaigning there. Sid Davidoff remembers that after the Florida primary the mayor told his demoralized aides, "If Mary has to drive the car and I have to hold the microphone, we're going to Wisconsin. We're going with you or without you." Though they knew that John had been defeated, the Lindsays believed they owed it to their supporters in Wisconsin not to abandon the campaign.[60]

Most people knew that Lindsay's campaign was through. The Brooklyn Democratic boss, Meade Esposito, dealt the final blow in his typically pithy style. Two weeks after Lindsay's Florida defeat, the veteran political boss said, "I think the handwriting is on the wall; Little Sheba better come home." The Brooklyn boss not only verbalized what most political observers believed—that Lindsay's presidential hopes were finished—but by calling Lindsay "Little Sheba" he also cut the patrician politician down to size by announcing that the little boy's game of presidential politics was over.[61]

That Esposito, one of the last old-style political bosses in the city, was a Lindsay ally in 1972 speaks poorly to Lindsay's political progress. Having run as an independent reform politician in 1965, excoriating the "power broker" and the "bossism" of the Democratic Party, Lindsay now found himself making nice with those very same bosses. In exchange for backing Lindsay, patronage flowed to Esposito's clubhouse. Lindsay had also warmed up to the Bronx Democratic boss, Patrick Cunningham, calling him a "tough, sophisticated, skilled and quiet fighter in the ranks of political change. We shall be needing this kind of leadership to pull the party together." Bronx Borough President Robert Abrams, a reform Democrat, said that in light of Lindsay's relationship with Cunningham, he regretted endorsing Lindsay for mayor in 1969. It is no wonder that New York liberals, long Lindsay's champions, had grown disillusioned with the mayor.[62]

After the Florida defeat and Esposito's comment, the Wisconsin primary was anticlimactic. On April 5, Lindsay finished sixth with just 7 percent of the vote. With this defeat, Lindsay bowed out of the race, saying that the "returns are clear and they mean that I cannot honestly continue as a candidate and therefore I am withdrawing." It was time to return to New York and repair his political reputation.

It is unclear exactly what John Lindsay sought to accomplish with his presidential run. Nearly everyone thought that it was a fool's mission. Ronnie Eldridge, one of the presidential campaign's top aides, said of the race, "I always thought they [Lindsay and Aurelio] knew something that I didn't know." It turned out that they didn't. At the height of the campaign, David Garth had been so frustrated with the campaign that he wanted no part of it, joking that he would pay $10,000 just to get out of his commitment. Theodore White wrote of Lindsay's presidential campaign, "It may be said that rarely has so eloquent a spokesman for so profoundly important a cause presided over so blundering a political campaign."[63]

Eight years later, Lindsay summed up his failed campaign: "I was trying to reach the country with a message about the cities, and no one wanted to hear. . . . They were just deaf to it. I didn't feel personally rejected; they just weren't interested in my message." Lindsay's campaign for president, then, was an attempt to highlight the importance of urban issues as well as raise the mayor's profile in his new party. Lindsay was not playing to win. "To my knowledge, either privately or publicly, he never even entertained the thought of winning the nomination," said Aurelio. "He just knew that that was not realistic. And above everything else, John Lindsay is not a dreamer—he is very realistic when it comes to things of that sort." Writing to Barry Gottehrer three years after the campaign, Sid Davidoff voiced similar sentiments. "I never really convinced myself that Lindsay would be president in 1972, but I did believe that he could be a focal point—or counterpoint—to move our national leaders and institutions closer to understanding what you and I learned years before by being in the streets," Davidoff wrote.[64]

Lindsay not only lost badly, but he also failed to raise his profile in the Democratic Party and draw attention to the urban crisis. According to Aurelio, the hardest thing on Lindsay was that the Democratic Party never made cities a high priority in 1972. The television reporter Ralph Penza noted that at the Miami Convention, Lindsay "maintained a very low profile. He sat in the front row there . . . but he did very little in the way of actual political involvement." Not a single major speech at the 1972 Democratic Convention dealt with the substantive problems of cities. "We didn't lose in the Florida primary," Lindsay told Aurelio as they watched the convention, "we lost tonight." Aurelio added, "I think that really did depress him, and he was very depressed at that moment."[65]

John Lindsay had pinned his national political hopes on the importance of cities. If the vast majority of Americans lived in cities, then the problems of New York City must be the problems of the rest of the country. And Lindsay, as spokesman for urban America, would be well positioned to bring his message of urban renaissance to this receptive audience of newly urbanized Americans. During the presidential campaign, Lindsay argued in a

Harper's Bazaar article that "one cannot, finally, escape from the common reality of all our cities because we have become a nation of cities. . . . I believe most Americans recognize this. We see ourselves as an urban people whether we reside in the inner core or the outer suburb, the small city or the metropolis."[66]

But Lindsay's statistics were wrong. Although Americans were leaving "rural" areas, they were not moving to large cities. According to the Census Bureau's definition at the time, any area with a population greater than 2,500 inhabitants was defined as "urban." But towns with populations of 2,500 or 10,000 hardly fit anyone's vision of a "city." From 1920 to 1960, the percentage of the population living in cities over 500,000 remained relatively constant while the percentage of the population residing in cities of less than 50,000 increased by 50 percent. The demographic growth was really at the level of small cities and suburbs rather than large, central cities. In 1960, 58.3 percent of Americans lived in rural areas or cities with populations of under 50,000, whereas only 15.9 percent lived in cities of over 500,000. The nation's largest cities—those of more than one million— were home to only 9.8 percent of the nation's population. Thirty years later, the trend away from large cities continued. In 1990, 64.4 percent of Americans lived in rural areas or cities with populations of less than 50,000 inhabitants, whereas only 12.1 percent lived in cities of over 500,000. The nation's largest cities, those of more than one million, were home to only 8.1 percent of the nation's population. The United States was not an urban nation, but rather one of suburbs and small towns.[67]

When Lindsay left Wisconsin, his presidential dreams in tatters, he returned to a city that was continuing to deteriorate. He had been absent from the city and on the national campaign trail since December, leaving the operations of city government in the hands of Deputy Mayor Edward Hamilton. Still, the city was limping. In 1972, Gail Sheehy noted that Lindsay seemed to attend to "a city that is losing faith in its own survival." The journalist Josh Greenfield asked Lindsay on the campaign trail about "the evidence of the eyes. Anyone coming into New York is instantly aware that the city is still on a downhill decline." In an appearance on *Meet the Press* in February 1972, Lindsay was asked, "Could you look the people of New York City in the eye right now and tell them the city is in grand shape and is in better shape than when you became mayor?" Knowing that the real answer was no, the mayor responded, "I can look them in the eye and say we have confronted every single problem that is there head-on and we haven't shoved anything under the rug."[68]

There was something more at stake for Lindsay in the presidential race than the role of cities. When the dust had settled after the national conventions in the summer of 1972, the journalist Richard Armstrong summarized what had happened in *The New York Times Magazine:* "What the mayor truly lost out on the road was not just a couple of primaries, but rather an irreplaceable mystique, the quality that in 1965 led fathers on Brooklyn street corners and in Catskill resorts to hold up their small children for a glimpse at the man who was going to be President someday." The Lindsay mystique, so powerful in 1965, had steadily been chipped away in the nation's second-toughest job.[69]

In 1972, Lindsay grasped for a prize that was beyond his reach. He returned to the city a beaten man. His aides, who had dreamed of the White House, were deflated. So was New York City. No one talked about Fun City anymore.

ASSESSING THE LINDSAY YEARS

During the late 1960s and early 1970s, many New Yorkers felt their city was spiraling into hopelessness and decay. In nearly every complaint, people mentioned the danger in the streets and the doubling of the welfare rolls. In addition, though Lindsay had been elected on a platform of fiscal restraint, he substantially increased spending, imperiling the city's fiscal health. Yet most New Yorkers could see few tangible results for all of this spending. As hard as Lindsay tried to reform city government, he could not get a handle on its most pressing problems.

"LAW AND ORDER"

No issue better exemplified the urban crisis than crime. The political scientist Marshall Berman, who grew up in the Bronx, remembered the 1960s as the "years when violence, and violent death, became everyday facts of city life. . . . So many ordinary, decent people like ourselves, who had worked all their lives to stay clean, suddenly found themselves entangled—as victims, witnesses, or survivors—in ferocious crimes. There was nowhere you could get away from it. We all learned (often without noticing that we were learning) to be very alert in public places, to respond to subliminal signs." A city where people are scared to walk the streets or even leave their homes is not a healthy community. One cannot have a successful urban community, with diverse populations mingling in a high-density area, when citizens are suspicious of each other and lack confidence in law enforcement. John Lindsay's New York saw a devastating rise in crime. This phenomenon tore at the city's social fabric, adding further suspicions between the races, and weakening the authority of political leaders like Lindsay.[1]

The rise in crime did predate Lindsay's tenure. Between 1955 and 1965, murders increased 123 percent; robberies 25 percent; assaults 88 percent; and burglaries 31 percent. Lindsay campaigned for mayor in 1965 specifically to make the city safer. "I WILL SPARE NOTHING—to insure the safety of the streets, your homes, hallways," Lindsay promised voters. To Lindsay the candidate, rising crime was yet another ill effect of years of Democratic rule.

Unfortunately, John Lindsay's tenure as mayor saw only higher and higher rates of crime. Of course, New York was not unique in experiencing this phenomenon. During the 1960s and early 1970s, nearly all large American cities witnessed escalating crime rates. Political scientist James Q. Wilson noted that during the 1960s "crime soared. It did not just increase a little; it rose at a faster rate and to higher levels than at any time since the 1930s and, in some categories, to higher levels than any experienced in this century."[2]

Contrary to the common belief that New York City is the most dangerous city in the nation, the city's per capita crime rate has always been considerably lower than that of most large American cities. In 1965, before Lindsay took office, New York's per capita murder rate was 8.0 per 100,000 residents, putting it behind Boston, Philadelphia, Chicago, Los Angeles, Detroit, Washington, and St. Louis. Similar trends can be found in the other crime categories.

Though New York's per capita crime rate was low in comparison to that of other big cities, New York saw a higher rate of increase during the Lindsay years than most other big cities did. Between 1966 and 1973, New York's murder rate climbed 137 percent—an increase second only to Detroit among the nation's twenty largest cities. New York's rate of increase and rank among these cities in car thefts was 84 percent, rank fifth; robberies—209 percent, rank seventh; assaults—64 percent, rank seventh; and rapes—112 percent, rank eleventh. Only in burglaries and theft (which actually declined slightly in New York between 1966 and 1973) did New York compare favorably to most of the other nineteen cities.[3]

But for New Yorkers it was little consolation to hear that they were relatively safer than residents of Detroit, Dallas, or St. Louis. They were concerned about the reality of the streets in front of their homes and the safety of their subways and parks. The increase in crime was startling and disturbing; it was something that every New Yorker could feel. The city began accepting high rates of crime as the price of urban living, but at a deep cost to its collective psyche and self-esteem.

In 1969, *New York Times* reporter David Burnham wrote of the toll that crime was taking on the city.

> The fear is visible: It can be seen in clusters of stores that close early because the streets are sinister and customers no longer stroll after supper for newspapers and pints of ice cream. It can be seen in the faces of women opening elevator doors, in the hurried step of the man walking home late at night from the subway. The fear manifests itself in elaborate gates and locks, in the growing number of key rings, in the forma-

tion of tenants' squads to patrol corridors, in shop buzzers pressed to admit only recognizable customers. And finally it becomes habit.

These images of the city contrasted with the life of a previous generation in New York—and not for the better. *New York Times* reporter Murray Schumach wrote in 1968 that

> there is little doubt that the slums of the nineteen twenties and thirties, for all their poverty and congestion, were much safer for the public than they are today. Middle-aged New Yorkers can recall that before World War II they used to walk without fear on the city streets in any section at night. Those who grew up in such slums as Brownsville or Harlem remember that during the day they left doors open for ventilation and at night they often slept on roofs, fire escapes, parks or beaches. After concerts in Lewisohn Stadium, couples strolled down dimly lighted Riverside Drive without concern about muggers. Transit policemen were not needed on subway trains late at night and ice cream parlors did not worry about staying open until midnight to get the business of crowds leaving the last neighborhood movies.

Even adjusting for the usual rosiness of nostalgia, the city had clearly changed. In the sixties, much of New York's crime was senseless violence and thievery, which the police pleaded powerless to stop.[4]

The issue of crime also took on racial connotations. As the journalist Jim Sleeper wrote many years later, "Violent crime is only the most obvious source of many whites' growing conviction that a disproportionate number of blacks are unwilling or unable to join the larger society to share in a common endeavor." A study of the 543 murders that were solved in the city during 1966 found that blacks committed 332 (61 percent) of those murders. Whites accounted for 20 percent and Puerto Ricans 12 percent. (The others murders involved mixed groups of whites, blacks, and Puerto Ricans.) Regarding interracial murders, black-on-white murders accounted for 8 percent, while white-on-black accounted for only 1 percent.[5]

Crime in New York had its biggest effect on minority neighborhoods. For stores in the Harlem business districts along 116th and 145th Streets, crime and theft became a cost of doing business. In 1966, the owner of an appliance store on 145th Street, who had lost $3,000 worth of merchandise during a break-in, called the strip "the worst block of all New York. You'll find hardly a business on this street that hasn't been robbed recently. Harlem is a jungle." Black and white businesses on 116th Street reported similar stories. One refrigeration and gas maintenance company had a total of fourteen burglaries in two years; a nearby glass and mirror factory had six. A men's clothing store reported three burglaries in its first month of operation. Police reports noted that thirty-four of the forty-seven businesses along 116th

Street between Seventh and Eighth Avenues had been burglarized during the first nine months of 1968.[6]

In 1967, an *Amsterdam News* editorial stated: "We can't get rid of crime by ignoring or compromising with it. And we can't use slingshots or statistics to fight animals bent on killing." The paper called for "restoring the legitimate, unbiased use of firearms by our police, the return of the right of a man to defend his home against robbers." At the end of 1968, the New York NAACP called for an end to "the reign of criminal terror in Harlem." Their report on crime demanded that in Harlem, "the attitude toward crime and criminals must change," and noted that there were "people known to cheer when some offender rushes from a store." The report called for greater police protection in Harlem, harsher criminal penalties for murderers and drug dealers, and "vigorous" enforcement of the city's anti-vagrancy laws. The report reminded New Yorkers who the true villains were: "It is not police brutality that makes people afraid to walk the streets at night."[7]

Crime also affected the northern Manhattan neighborhood of Inwood. Long a working-class Irish enclave, Inwood and nearby Washington Heights saw an influx of immigrants from the Dominican Republic during the 1960s. In response, many of the Irish moved to suburbs like those in Rockland County, New York, and Bergen County, New Jersey. Those who remained, though, felt their lives increasingly constrained by fear. According to one study of the changing face of Inwood, by the late 1960s

> robberies, muggings, and rapes struck a much wider range of people, especially the elderly. And burglaries made people feel vulnerable even in their own homes. It was not just the reality of crime that hurt. It was also the perception of crime and the raw fear that seeped into every corner of daily life. . . . At its best, life on a block in northern Manhattan once made many Irish feel like part of one big happy family. Now they felt more like vulnerable individuals—alone, isolated, and fearful of the sound of footsteps behind them on a dark street. Fear of crime combined with a rush of changes that signaled the end of life as the Inwood Irish had recently known it.

The many Irish bars in the neighborhood experienced a rash of holdups, and many customers felt that the streets were just too dangerous for late-night bar hopping. Crime and racial conflict became hopelessly interwoven.[8]

Similar developments were occurring in the Bronx. The neighborhoods of Mott Haven, Morrisania, and Hunts Point had dissolved into the amorphous "South Bronx," a graffiti-splattered area filled with burned-out buildings, chronic drug abuse, Puerto Rican gangs, and roving bands of wild dogs. According to Dr. Harold Wise of the Martin Luther King, Jr., Health Center in the South Bronx, by 1973 the area had become a "necropolis—a city of death. There's a total breakdown of services, looting is rampant, fires are everywhere." Forty percent of residents were on welfare and 30 percent of employable individuals were unemployed. As the social decay crept northward, so did the boundaries of the South Bronx. Along the Grand Concourse area, elderly residents felt threatened by muggers and businessmen began to experience more break-ins. One eighty-year-old woman was held up three times in four years. A local dry cleaner had been robbed six times in six months during 1969. Other businesses had similar stories. In the Grand Concourse police precinct, overall crime had risen 69 percent in 1968. According to one report, "Bands of rowdy youths waylay children and make off with their bicycles. Pocketbook snatchings are so common that women try to outwit criminals by hiding their purses in shopping bags. In the evenings, muggers hide in the lobby alcoves of apartment buildings or under stairways."

The journalist Jill Jonnes documented the white Jewish flight from the South Bronx:

> The Jews moved because what they saw in these new families scared them: the symptoms of poverty and social disintegration that they had struggled so hard to escape from on the Lower East Side and to avoid in their own lives on Charlotte Street. . . . They saw men standing around the streets drinking and gambling. They saw families with too many children crammed into too small a space. They encountered housewives who didn't understand the neighborhood codes about garbage disposal. They saw sons and daughters growing up too much on the streets without supervision. They saw casual attitudes toward sex, procreation and marriage. They saw men without steady, decent jobs.

Fear gripped residents as they fled the city streets and park benches for the security of their multilocked fortress apartments.[9]

In a 1968 letter to Brooklyn Congressman Emmanuel Celler, one constituent wrote, "Thousands of people of Jewish faith have stood by helplessly to see their businesses destroyed, their lives in constant peril as politicians blithely court the Negro vote and ignore those who elected them to office. Why is it your sworn duty to protect robbers, muggers, and rapists?" In 1967, Jay Kriegel received a letter from the Rabbi Eugene Sack, of Park Slope, Brooklyn:

> My fervent good wishes in your efforts to bring a little law and order to the city. Last week the neighborhood grocer's delivery boy was beaten and stabbed and severely wounded by a gang of young hoodlums whose color I will not mention. We have installed extra locks in our house. Also, we are considering bars for the windows. The neighbors are gathering to hire extra private police and shortly, I will begin to consider that great American privilege of carrying firearms for personal protection and the protection of my family.

In relaying the letter to Lindsay, Kriegel called the rabbi "one of the calmest, most liberal men I know." He also worried that if the letter was "indicative of sentiment in that area, we have an even worse problem than I thought." Edward Bates, owner of Bates Pontiac Corp. on the Grand Concourse in the Bronx, wrote to the mayor about the effect that robberies and thefts were having on his inner-city business. "Frankly, in all our years in business, we have never been faced with a dilemma as seemingly unsolvable as the thefts and burglaries to which we are continuously exposed," wrote Bates. "Our neighborhood is overrun with hoodlums and prowlers. In the last 3 weeks, 35 batteries were physically removed from new cars. Tires and accessories have been stolen and brand new cars damaged during the thefts." Earlier, two of Bates's workers were held up in broad daylight while going to the bank.[10]

Another disturbing trend was the increase in attacks upon houses of worship. In the fall of 1969, eleven synagogues were desecrated, causing a political problem for Lindsay among the Jewish voters he was so assiduously courting for reelection. The spate of attacks was indicative not only of greater lawlessness and disorder in the city, but of a general lack of respect toward symbols of authority. Attacks against synagogues, yeshivas, and Jewish centers heightened the fears of New York's already jittery Jewish community. The spokesman for the National Society of Hebrew Day Schools warned Lindsay in a telegram that a "rash of fires and vandalism" created a climate of fear so that "learning has been effectively throttled."

In December 1968 alone, there were 90 crimes at houses of worship in the city. In 1969, there were 1,039 such attacks. Of those attacks, 633 were burglaries, 50 were arson, and 356 were vandalism and criminal mischief. Fifty-four percent of the December 1968 attacks and 37 percent of the 1969 attacks were against Jewish targets. A majority of criminal mischief (vandalism and desecration) occurred at synagogues, whereas most of the burglaries took place at Christian churches. In 1969, the arsons were roughly split between Jewish and Christian targets.

These attacks did not follow any discernible pattern. Of the 112 people arrested for desecrating religious buildings, 86 were under the age of twenty. The racial breakdown of those arrested also showed no distinct pattern. Seventy-one of those arrested were white and 41 were black. Whites accounted for each of the eleven arson arrests and nineteen of the twenty-five criminal mischief arrests. The racial breakdown of those arrested for robbery was nearly fifty-fifty. Though it was clear that no one group had specifically targeted another group in the rash of attacks on religious institutions, such attacks were yet another piece of evidence of the growing hostility, dangers, and incivility of life in New York City.[11]

Crime stories soon began to dominate the pages of the city's newspapers. The *New York Times* would regularly place reports of shocking violence and brutal muggings on its front page. When a Harlem sniper shot and killed a Penn Central brakeman while he was standing in the train doorway at the

125th Street station in 1969, the story became page one news. By 1972, the number of front-page crimes stories had markedly increased. It was almost as if the *Times* was deliberately trying to punish Lindsay for his daring to run for president while the city deteriorated. In February 1972, the elderly labor leader David Dubinsky was mugged and robbed of ninety dollars on his way to buy milk in Greenwich Village three days before his eightieth birthday. That story became front-page news. When a blind female newspaper vendor in Morningside Heights was robbed five times in one year, it too became front-page news.[12]

Other crimes shocked the city during 1972. Across the street from the blind woman's newspaper stand on Amsterdam Avenue and 122nd Street, Wolfgang Friedmann, a professor of international law at Columbia University, was stabbed to death in broad daylight. One day later, a sixty-year-old doctor was assaulted, robbed, and stabbed on 125th Street while walking to the nearby train station. A week later, the director of the New York Academy of Trial Lawyers was beaten and robbed at five in the afternoon at 109th Street and Fifth Avenue. These crimes took their toll on the city. The sociologist Amitai Etzioni wrote: "Many people I know are no longer just worried about being mugged, they are semi-hysterical and quite desperate."[13]

To the public, Lindsay's response to the increase in crime seemed equivocal. The wife of a city worker living in Canarsie, Brooklyn, summed up the popular critique of the mayor: "Lindsay was soft on the criminals and hard on the police." But Lindsay still tried to exude the aura of a crimefighter. In 1968, Deputy Mayor Robert Sweet told the press that Lindsay took the problem of "safety in the streets and turned it around." One way Lindsay had attacked crime was by giving the New York Police Department "ten times as many walkie-talkies." Lindsay's other anticrime measures included a new communications system, the installation of a "911" system, and the creation of a "fourth platoon" of police officers to patrol the streets during the high-crime times of 6 P.M. to 2 A.M. Lindsay also added 4,000 policemen.[14]

None of these measures, however, changed the city's basic approach to the crime problem. Lindsay was skeptical that stronger police enforcement could bring down the crime rate. Delivering the commencement address at Vassar College in 1968, Lindsay said, "Peace cannot be imposed on our cities by force of arms, nor can people be converted at the point of a gun. . . . A shotgun aimed at a black teenager will no sooner achieve stability than a gasoline-filled bottle in the hand of that teenager will erase poverty." Earlier that year, in a speech before the Urban Coalition's Eastern Regional Conference, Lindsay blamed the fear of crime for increasing racial polarization. Though the fear was "legitimate," Lindsay said that people "are rapidly losing sight of the distinction between the problem of urban street crime and the complex dilemma of civil disorders. They are different problems requiring different responses. The mounting crime rate cannot be attributed to one segment of the community and used to justify repressive actions against it. We cannot turn our ghettoes into armed camps and condone the wanton use of force. This will not ensure the safety of our citizens as they daily walk our cities' streets. But it would heighten tensions and increase the possibility of wide-spread social disruption." Lindsay feared that any attempt to reduce crime would aggravate minorities and lead to large-scale riots. More crime, he seemed to be saying, was the price to be paid in order to avoid riots.[15]

To Lindsay, the calls for "law and order" were clearly more dangerous than rising crime. "What is dividing Americans so badly from one another is the diagnosis and remedy too many of us seem ready to apply," wrote Lindsay in 1968. To heed the calls of "law and order" would present Americans with two stark choices: "to choose between the random terror of the criminal and the official terror of the state." In breathlessly hyperbolic words, Lindsay described the consequences of the latter scenario: "We might then have to concede, openly and candidly, that the Great Experiment in self-government died, the victim of violence, before its 200th birthday."[16]

Lindsay was swept away by analogies between the Prague Spring and the possibilities of repression at home, seeing a kind of moral equivalence between Communist soldiers and American policemen: "Look to Prague and you will find your bayoneted soldier every five feet. You will see the blood of young men—with long hair and strange clothes—who were killed by tanks which crushed their nonviolent protest against Communist tyranny. If we abandon our tradition of justice and civil order, they will be *our* tanks and *our* children."[17]

Liberals like Lindsay saw "law and order" as code words for racism and oppression. Violence and robbery happened because of "root causes" like poverty and racial discrimination. James Vorenberg, a professor at Harvard Law School and a former director of President Lyndon Johnson's Crime Commission, said in 1969, "To a considerable degree, law enforcement cannot deal with criminal behavior. The most important way in which any mayor could be held responsible for crime is the extent to which he failed to fight for job-training programs, better schools, and decent housing. . . . With the possible exception of how we treat first offenders, I have become convinced that improvements or changes in the police, the courts or correctional agencies are holding actions at best."[18]

In the 1960s, some people actually denied that crime was becoming a serious problem. James Q. Wilson noted that crime was only mentioned in passing in the 1968 Democratic Party platform and little was said of the issue at the convention. "The incumbent attorney general, Ramsey Clark, was quoted as saying that he did not think we were having a crime wave at all," wrote Wilson. In a book published two years later, Clark urged Americans to turn their attention away from street crime to the "far more corrosive" effects of white-collar crime. The political scientist Andrew Hacker in 1975 explained the logic behind this appeal: "In all probability, muggers take much less from individuals than do corporate, syndicate, and white-collar criminals. Many executives swindle more on their taxes and expense accounts than the average addict steals in a year. Unfortunately concentrating on street crime provides yet another opportunity for picking on the poor."

Hacker admitted that the city was becoming less safe in 1975, but he also firmly believed that "the upsurge in crime expresses a new sense of freedom on the part of classes which were once kept sternly in their place. Earlier generations maintained tight control over large segments of the population, particularly the poor. One consequence of relaxing these controls is an increase in crime." According to Hacker, "The city should count itself fortunate that so small a part of its population has taken to theft. That so many individuals remain honest while being treated so stingily by society should be a source of both amazement and confidence." Lloyd Ohlin, a Harvard Law School professor and a member of President Johnson's Crime Commission, believed that crime statistics were "almost worthless" and that the media "exacerbated the fear of crime in the public."[19]

One reason for the increase in crime and other disorders was a change in the nature of policing in New York. A policeman's goal was no longer to enforce order on the streets or prevent crime; it was to stay out of trouble and avoid the appearance of corruption. The police had to prevent any misunderstanding or incident that might lead to a riot. William Bratton, who became New York's Police Commissioner in 1994, has written: "The only way you can control a police department from headquarters is if your aim is to prevent police from doing anything, rather than to have them function effectively—and for many years that was precisely the aim of the NYPD. The organization didn't want high performance; it wanted to stay out of trouble, to avoid corruption scandals and conflicts in the community." David Durk, a former policeman, called this the "Kitty Genovese phenomenon among cops." (He was referring to the notorious 1964 Genovese case, in which witnesses who didn't want to get involved stood by and did nothing while a young woman was beaten to death.) Durk believed that "since Knapp, the real problem with the police department has been massive malingering, and it's totally justified, given the disciplinary policies of the department. If a cop makes an off-duty arrest, the first question he gets asked is 'Were you drinking?' and the second question is 'What did you get involved for?'" Durk's biographer, James Lardner, called it the "deep, dark open secret of the police world . . . that many cops did not care because they weren't convinced that anybody who counted wanted them to."[20]

Another cause of increasing disorder was the move from a proactive police department that kept order on the streets by showing a strong street presence to a reactive department that patrolled neighborhoods by car instead of on foot. Criminologist George Kelling has called this "stranger policing." Ironically, Lindsay's greatest accomplishments in law enforcement—the "911" system and an improved police communications systems—only made the department more reactive. The goals of the modern police department were better response time and faster arrest clearance rates. The police therefore became a more distant presence in a neighborhood, responding only after crimes had been committed. If the police could arrest more people, gather more evidence, solve more crimes, the city would be a safer place. Yet the idea of order maintenance as a device to combat crime was ignored. Combined with the fear that too much police involvement could cause riots or opportunities for corruption, this policy opened the way for more crime and disorder.[21]

"QUALITY OF LIFE" ISSUES

Meanwhile, soaring crime rates were changing the look of the city. Following the 1964 riots, Harlem businesses began putting up folding iron gates to protect their businesses. But these proved ineffective against thieves and looters, especially after the 1968 King riots. So more durable steel roll-up barriers, which covered the entire storefront, began appearing. They made their first appearance along the business districts of Harlem, before spreading to other parts of the city. Today they are still a visible presence on New York streets.[22]

The city was also becoming a canvas for graffiti. This was something more serious than "Kilroy was here" or obscene writing on bathroom walls. According to Lindsay's Budget Bureau, by March 1973, 63 percent of all subway cars, 46 percent of all city buses, and 50 percent of all public housing were "heavily graffitied." The yearly cost to taxpayers for cleaning up the vandalism was $10 million and rising.[23]

In the early 1970s, New Yorkers slowly noticed graffiti creeping into their daily lives on their subway and bus rides. Most of the early graffiti writers came from Washington Heights and were Hispanic or black teenagers. They mostly used black Magic Markers, later graduating to spray-paint. Soon, though, graffiti evolved from simple black markings to colorful spray painted montages expanding out in dizzying spirals across the city's buildings and subways. Kids would sneak into subway yards at night and vandalize entire subway cars, inside and out. Many subway windows were completely covered with graffiti, making it difficult for riders to tell which stop they were at. Graffiti moved from the subways to the buses, to public housing projects, to the city's parks and monuments. Large splotches of colorful graffiti soon spread to the side of buildings and to the steel gates pulled down over storefronts at night. It was everywhere. In 1980, the *Times* noted that "the spread of graffiti in recent years beyond New York's subways to its monuments and landmark buildings and the parks has no real equivalent elsewhere."[24]

Unlike his reaction to the crime problem, Lindsay attacked graffiti publicly and vigorously. The sight of graffiti disgusted him. At a ribbon-cutting ceremony for a new pool in Brooklyn, Lindsay was angry that the pool had already been marked up by graffiti before it opened. Upon returning to City Hall, the mayor burst into Chief of Staff Steven Isenberg's office and, "with four-letter-word fervor," ordered him to do something about the problem. According to

Isenberg, Lindsay "was just livid" at the vandalism he had witnessed and publicly called graffiti writers "insecure cowards." Lindsay believed graffiti was "profoundly depressing—it truly hurt people's moods. The life would go out of everybody when they saw the [subway] cars defaced." He asked the City Council to impose fines and jail sentences for anyone caught spraying graffiti and called for stricter laws regarding the sale of aerosol paint cans.[25]

The problem was that the mayor did not control the city's subways. This was now the purview of the Metropolitan Transportation Authority, created by Governor Rockefeller in 1968 and now under the leadership of William Ronan, a Rockefeller ally. The slow response to graffiti was due in part to the tensions between Lindsay and the MTA. The mayor took to blaming Ronan for the graffiti and for ignoring the mayor's suggestions for cracking down on vandals. In addition, lax judges and courts routinely let vandals off when they were arrested. The mayor's own parks commissioner, August Heckscher, took his boss to task over his crackdown. "Politicians unaware of its [graffiti's] classic origins sought stringent laws to combat the menace, and the mayor used every occasion to flay its perpetrators," wrote Heckscher. Critics like Lindsay, wrote Heckscher, believed that "if this was art, it was debased and bore about the same relation to graphics as street violence to ritual and drama. If it was a way of affirming identity, it was a pathetic indication of what the great city was doing to human values."[26]

In contrast to Lindsay's view, graffiti soon became a chic new art form for many New Yorkers. In a *Times* op-ed in 1973, Mitzi Cunliffe, a lecturer in design at the school of architecture at London's Thames Polytechnic, wrote that graffiti "trumpets the indestructible survival of the individual in an inhuman environment. . . . The Graffitists cock a snook at private property in this most thing-centered temple of a thing-centered civilization." In 1973, *New York* magazine created the "Taki Awards" which it bestowed upon the best subway graffiti art of the year. The award was named for one of the first recognized graffiti artists in the city, identified by his tag "Taki 183." According to the magazine, the award was a "recognition of this grand graffiti conquest of the subways." The award for "Station Saturation" went to the Broadway and 103rd Street station, where graffiti nearly covered the entire tile wall of the station. Artists like Claes Oldenburg praised graffiti, while *New York* magazine enlightened its upscale readers as to the differences between "Bronx," "Manhattan," "Brooklyn," and "Combo" styles of graffiti. Richard Goldstein wrote that the most significant thing about graffiti was that it brought "together a whole generation of lower-class kids in an experience which is affirmative and delinquent at the same time." Andrew Hacker wrote, "New York can boast the most flamboyant street gangs, the most brazen graffiti, and the most sophisticated pimps of any large city." Even recently, historian Joshua Freeman described the explosion of graffiti as a refusal by predominantly poor minority youths "to accept the social invisibility to which they had been relegated."[27]

Perhaps the most famous defense of graffiti came from the pen of Norman Mailer, who wrote an essay in 1974 entitled "The Faith of Graffiti." To Mailer graffiti was romantic, exhilarating, dangerous, and noble. He called it "the expression of tropical peoples living in a monotonous iron-gray and dull brown brick environment," which "erupted biologically as though to save the sensuous flesh of their inheritance from a macadamization of the psyche." As he had in "The White Negro," Mailer flirted with the idea of the "noble savage": "Graffiti is the expression of a ghetto which is near to the plague, for civilization is now inimical to the ghetto. Too huge are the obstacles to any natural development of a civilized man. In the ghetto it is almost impossible to find some quiet location for your identity. No, in the environment of the slum, the courage to display yourself is your only capital, and crime is the productive process which converts such capital to the modern powers of the world, ego and money."

Though he had promised neighborhood autonomy in his 1969 mayoral campaign, Mailer now seemed oblivious to complaints that graffiti writers were vandalizing neighborhoods. Instead, Mailer saw graffiti writers as "famous in the world of wall and graffiti as Giotto may have been when his name first circulated through the circuits of those workshops which led from Masaccio through Piero della Francesca to Botticelli, Michelangelo, Leonardo and Raphael. Whew!" To Mailer, the idea of making convicted graffiti writers clean up subway cars was akin to "condemning Cézanne to wipe out the works of Van Gogh."[28]

While some members of the city's better classes extolled the virtues of graffiti, others saw graffiti as a visible signal that the city had become a more dangerous place. And the city could do nothing about it. In response, many people simply stopped riding the subways. To those who defended graffiti writers, mayoral aide Steve Isenberg retorted: "The thing I'd really like to ask all those intellectual phonies is how they would react if some guy decided to write a novel with his Flair pen along the length of the Kennedy Arts Center. I have a suspicion they wouldn't think it was such a marvelous creative expression or some admirable drive towards immortality." Isenberg called graffiti "ugly, mindless, epidemic, and occasionally racist and obscene. The most important notion to be discredited probably is that graffiti vandalism and defacement of property can be cloaked with the justification or excuse that it is an acceptable form or pop art." Writing in 1979, Nathan Glazer argued that graffiti contributed "to a prevailing sense of the incapacity of government, the uncontrollability of youthful criminal behavior, and a resultant uneasiness and fear."

> The subway rider—whose blank demeanor, expressing an effort simply to pass through and survive what may be the shabbiest, noisiest, and generally most unpleasant mass-transportation experience in the developed world, has often been remarked upon—now has to suffer the knowledge that his subway car has recently seen the passage through it

of the graffiti "artists". . . . He is assaulted continuously, not only by the evidence that every subway car has been vandalized, but by the inescapable knowledge that the environment he must endure for an hour or more a day is uncontrolled and uncontrollable, and that anyone can invade it to do whatever damage and mischief the mind suggests.

Nor were graffiti writers simply harmless pranksters reaffirming their culture. A 1974 NYPD study found that 40 percent of fifteen-year-olds arrested for writing graffiti were arrested again for more serious crimes within the next three years.[29]

Yet another change in the face of the city during the Lindsay years was the condition of Times Square. Though long known as a seedy section of town where illicit heterosexual and homosexual relations flourished, during the late 1960s the area's reputation for sleaze and sex solidified—for such behavior was no longer kept hidden. A 1971 *Times* survey of Times Square sex businesses found that the "commercialism of sex in mid-Manhattan has increased enormously" since 1968. Police Commissioner Patrick Murphy noted: "There is no question about the fact that prostitution has been growing steadily, especially in Midtown, despite the thousands of arrests." He called the boom in porn and sex shops "shocking." Prostitutes openly plied their wares on the streets wearing provocative clothing that left little to the imagination. Pimps controlled the streets. Violence and drug dealing became commonplace. Live sex shows, porn theaters, and "massage parlors" operated in the open. The architectural historian Ada Louise Huxtable wrote, "By the 1960s, this was an area in deep trouble; social, cultural, and commercial changes had advanced far beyond the city's control." The decline of the Times Square area affected Broadway theaters, as patrons were often accosted and harassed on their way to the theater.[30]

At first Lindsay ignored the problems in Times Square. "I don't think that it's gotten worse," said the mayor. "I remember, back in 1958, when I was a Congressman and this area was part of my district, I used to get the same kind of complaints except for the harassment." But Lindsay began hearing from his friends who worked in the theater district about the problems. Failure to deal with Times Square, they warned, could threaten the future of Broadway. Thus prodded, Lindsay created the Times Square Law Enforcement Coordination Committee in 1972. By the end of 1973, the committee reported that police had made 1,895 arrests for prostitution and had closed down 176 massage parlors and nine hotels. In addition, 529 people had been arrested for promoting obscenity at bookstores, peepshows, and movies.[31]

Rising crime rates, graffiti, and other urban disorders gave rise to concern over "quality of life" issues. Fresh from his humiliating defeat in the presidential primary, Lindsay hoped that by tackling the problems of graffiti and Times Square, he might improve his image as a good administrator. Unfortunately, he arrived too late to have any real impact. Graffiti and the sleaze of Times Square continued unabated through the 1970s and into the 1980s. And when Union Carbide pulled out of New York in 1977, a company official explained the decision in noneconomic terms: "It is an image we have to contend with. And it isn't just crime and high living costs. It's the city's changing ethnic mix, which makes some people uncomfortable, and the graffiti on the subways, the dirt on the streets, and a lot of other things."[32]

The most famous postulation of the "quality of life" theory was James Q. Wilson and George Kelling's 1982 *Atlantic Monthly* article "Broken Windows." Wilson and Kelling argued that before the 1960s, the main goal of urban police was to maintain order on the streets. They did this by walking a beat, checking on businesses, rustling away drunks and vagrants, talking with pedestrians, and keeping an eye on suspicious characters. When political and judicial restraints were placed on the police—such as instituting civilian review boards and overturning antivagrancy laws—they pulled back traditional methods of keeping order. What happened next was often a steady spiral of decay and crime.

> A stable neighborhood of families who care for their homes, mind each other's children, and confidently frown on unwanted intruders can change, in a few years or even a few months, to an inhospitable and frightening jungle. A piece of property is abandoned, weeds grow up, a window is smashed. Adults stop scolding rowdy children; the children, emboldened, become more rowdy. Families move out, unattached adults move in. Teenagers gather in front of the corner store. The merchant asks them to move; they refuse. Fights occur. Litter accumulates. People start drinking in front of the grocery; in time, an inebriate slumps to the sidewalk and is allowed to sleep it off. Pedestrians are approached by panhandlers. . . . If the neighborhood cannot keep a bothersome panhandler from annoying passerby [*sic*], the thief may reason, it is even less likely to call the police to identify a potential mugger or to interfere if the mugging actually takes place.

Wilson and Kelling concluded that if "victimless" disorders—like graffiti, pornography, prostitution, public drunkenness, and loitering by rowdy youths—were tolerated, more serious crimes would soon follow.[33]

The steady accumulation of disorder and the consequent decrease in police power and authority led to a situation where many New Yorkers felt that the streets no longer belonged to them. Lindsay, the purveyor of "Fun City," civil libertarian, and critic of the police department, received much of the blame. Not only was Lindsay unable to reverse the crime wave, but he failed to rally citizens behind the issue of a safer city. New Yorkers were looking for answers from behind their locked doors and barred windows. Lindsay gave them no hope.

For too many individuals, the city became a fearsome and dangerous place governed by individuals unable and unwilling to do anything about it. John Lindsay did not fix the first broken window.

WELFARE

After crime, welfare was the second most volatile issue during the Lindsay years. Like the rise in crime, the dramatic rise in welfare rolls began during Robert Wagner's tenure as mayor, but reached its startling heights during the Lindsay administration. As with crime, New York was not unique in seeing increased welfare dependency. This was a national trend, but for a variety of reasons New York became most associated with the welfare crisis. And also as with crime, Lindsay proved unable to make a dent in the welfare explosion. This failure harmed his ability to govern New York and crippled his national political ambitions.

The growth in the number of people on welfare in New York was striking: from 328,000 welfare recipients, or about 4 percent of the population in 1960 to 531,000 recipients, nearly double the 1960 figure and 8 percent of the population in 1965. By 1972, nearly 1.25 million New Yorkers—16 percent of the city's population—received public assistance. New York City saw the most rapid growth rates in its welfare rolls, about 16.4 percent per year, between 1965 and 1970. But the national annual growth rate of 15.8 percent was not far behind. What made New York stand out, though, was the sheer magnitude of the numbers. The idea of having over one million welfare recipients was a psychological barrier that many people could not comprehend. Historian Fred Siegel has pointed out that New York City's welfare population was larger than the population of fifteen states. One in ten welfare recipients in the nation lived in New York City. In addition, welfare, like many other urban issues of the time, took on a racial dimension. In 1970, 13 percent of women receiving Aid to Families with Dependent Children (AFDC) in New York were white, 40 percent were Puerto Rican, and 47 percent were black.[34]

The costs of welfare predictably soared. During Lindsay's first term, spending on welfare rose from $400 million to $1 billion. Expenditures on welfare grew 52 percent in 1968 alone. If one adds the cost of Medicaid, for which all welfare recipients were eligible, the amount reached over $2 billion. By 1970, total public assistance for the poor accounted for roughly 28 percent of the city budget.[35]

This welfare explosion worried many Americans. It challenged traditional notions of work and public assistance. Lindsay articulately summed up these concerns in a 1969 memo to President Nixon: "Welfare is unpopular with all segments of society and, in its neglect of the working poor, increases polarization between the minority-group poor and the working class. Welfare has been unable to achieve its objectives of providing both minimally adequate living standards and incentives to self-support. It is un-economical from a cost-effective point of view and is often demeaning and destructive to people."

In 1972, Pete Hamill was even more stark in his criticism of welfare and its effect on the city. "Should programs that started long ago as temporary 're-lief' become permanent and self-enlarging? And what was the responsibility of the welfare recipients themselves? What must New Yorkers ask them to give back to the city in return for welfare?" Furthermore, this huge increase occurred during the strong economy of the 1960s, leading many to wonder where new welfare recipients were coming from. In New York City during this time, unemployment declined from 6 percent to around 3 percent.[36]

The dramatic rise in welfare rolls coincided with the growth of the radical welfare rights movement. The architects of this movement were Richard A. Cloward and Frances Fox Piven, two professors of social work at Columbia University. Cloward and Piven argued that nationally 8 million Americans were eligible for welfare but did not receive benefits. Cloward and Piven called for "a massive drive to recruit the poor *onto* the welfare rolls." The result would mean "fiscal disruption for local and state governments." Such a collapse, Cloward and Piven argued, would produce a powerful impetus toward major economic reform: namely, the institution of a guaranteed annual income that would end poverty.[37]

The writings of Cloward and Piven had a strong influence on welfare policy. In the mid–1960s, the National Welfare Rights Organization (NWRO) was formed, headed by George Wiley. Nearly half of the organization's members were in New York City. The NWRO used the politics of confrontation—protests and sit-ins at welfare offices—to increase welfare benefits and expand the number of welfare recipients. Beulah Sanders, the second vice president of the NWRO and chair of the New York City-Wide Coordinating Committee of Welfare Rights Groups, explained the group's philosophy at a 1967 U.S. Senate Finance Committee hearing:

> I do not believe that we should be forced to work. I do not believe that we should be forced to take training if it is not meaningful. If you are going to give us something that we can hope for and advance in, possibilities to go on to higher salaries, then I would agree to do it. This is why we have had the disturbance in New York City and across the country. We, the welfare recipients, have tried to keep down the disturbance among our people, but the unrest is steadily growing.

In the spring of 1968, the NWRO began an intensive campaign of demonstrations at welfare offices across the city. Activists claimed that in five weeks of protests, they won $3 million for welfare clients through additional benefits and special grants, such as money for spring clothing, school graduation expenses, telephones, and summer camp expenses.[38]

There was a debate over the impact that welfare rights organizations were having on rising welfare rolls. Two social historians, Larry Jackson and William Johnson, argued that such activities "had a major influence on the level of [welfare] applications in 1968. . . . Welfare rights organizations encouraged applicants, first by the information and publicity resulting from their demonstrations, and second by their influence on the grant level which, in turn, encouraged applications." On the other hand, Daniel Patrick Moynihan, writing in 1969 (he was then an adviser to Nixon on urban affairs) argued that the welfare rights movement had little effect on rising welfare applications, since "a comparison of neighborhoods where organizing efforts did take place and those where it did not fails to show any significant difference." Still, welfare rights activists helped take away the stigma from receiving public assistance. To a growing number of activists, welfare was a right. Welfare recipients—or clients, as they came to be called—had the right to demand higher benefits and owed society nothing in return. But such protests also caused greater resentments by taxpayers against the welfare system and its "clients." Frank Arricale, a former Lindsay aide, later noted: "They [NWRO] believed that out of chaos will come a new organization. Out of chaos comes more chaos; they didn't know that!" Charles Morris, a Lindsay budget aide, later wrote: "The violence of the [welfare rights] movement was frightening. The driving energy behind the campaign for civil equality was transmuting into incendiary destruction."[39]

The welfare rights movement showed its influence on the Lindsay administration with the appointment of Mitchell Ginsberg as welfare commissioner. (Ginsberg later succeeded Mitchell Sviridoff as head of the Human Resources Administration.) Ginsberg, a colleague of Cloward and Piven's at the Columbia School of Social Work, immediately began liberalizing welfare rules. His first step was to outlaw "midnight raids" on female welfare recipients to check whether they were living with a man, which would make them ineligible for AFDC. He pushed case workers to find people who were eligible for welfare but were not on the rolls. His office worked with welfare-rights activists to monitor welfare centers. He also liberalized eligibility requirements by getting rid of the interview, investigation, and home-visit process for new applicants and replacing it with a simple system of self-declaration of need by the client. The rate of rejection for welfare cases dropped from 40 percent in 1965 to 23 percent in 1968. The *Daily News* dubbed the welfare commissioner "Come-and-Get-It" Ginsberg. Years later Sviridoff admitted that the "so-called innovative things we did in welfare in those early days, I personally, retrospectively do not consider those successful." According to Sviridoff, the Lindsay administration had been "responsive to the pressures of the welfare rights movement. I consider all of that a mistake." For Sviridoff, easing welfare eligibility requirements "contributed to the negative impact of welfare" on the city.[40]

Welfare benefits became not only easier to receive but also more generous. Some studies showed that increases in welfare benefits had actually begun to outstrip increases in wages. Between 1962 and 1967, welfare grant levels in New York City rose by 45 percent. This occurred while average weekly earnings in New York State rose by 30 percent. After examining New York City's welfare crisis, David Gordon, an economist, concluded "that the largest source of the increase in welfare stemmed from the increase in real grant levels." With the stigma of welfare lifted and benefit levels increased, welfare seemed a good option for unskilled and semi-skilled New Yorkers at the lower end of the income scale. According to Jackson and Johnson, "welfare applicants appear to have been economically rational."[41]

The increase in the number of people receiving welfare was a shock to the values of many New Yorkers. As more people joined the welfare rolls and a larger percentage of the city budget went for social services, the agency that administered welfare, public assistance, and other poverty programs—the Human Resources Administration (HRA)—came under increased scrutiny. A series of investigations uncovered widespread corruption and mismanagement at HRA, which further weakened the public's confidence in city government. Investigations conducted in 1968 by the Manhattan DA's office, the city's Department of Investigations, and the U.S. Department of Labor found substantial fraud at HRA. Most damaging was proof that a group of city workers had embezzled between $400,000 and $1 million from the Neighborhood Youth Corps, a division of HRA, which handled summer job programs for inner-city youths. In the summer of 1967 the program received $13.1 million in federal funds and $5.5 million in city funds. The audit revealed that corrupt bureaucrats had made out checks in the names of fictitious people and cashed them at two check-cashing stores. One out of every five checks from the Corps was fraudulent. Another 1968 report warned of serious mismanagement in HRA's Community Development Agency. In May 1968, Josephine Nieves, the acting northeast regional director of the federal Office of Economic Opportunity (OEO) warned Commissioner Ginsberg: "I must share my very deep concern about the fiscal problems that HRA-CDA have been experiencing in an overall sense, as well as in its day-to-day operations." The HRA was one of the famed superagencies created by the Lindsay administration.[42]

The extent of corruption and mismanagement at HRA became public when the *New York Times* published a lengthy exposé in January 1969. The paper reported that more than 100 investigators from the DA's office, the city's Investigations Department, and federal agencies had looked into HRA's problems. Charles Morris summarized the findings:

> No-show jobs and patronage were rife. Program funds were hopelessly commingled; procedures to pay monies through the city comptroller were regularly circumvented; and millions of dollars were held in private

checking accounts to pay for wages, overtime, and expenses without making the required deductions and with no offsetting entries on the city's books. Accounts were unbalanced for months at a time, and payments were made to work-program recipients without any effort to determine if they were actually on the job.

This mismanagement led to outright thievery. The *Times* exposed numerous cases of embezzlement and theft. In one case, four HRA checks—totaling more than one million dollars—made their way into a Swiss bank account. Another case involved four young HRA aides who called themselves the "Durham Mob." The four, who originally hailed from Durham, North Carolina, stole at least $1.75 million in HRA funds by producing counterfeit checks made out to nonexistent individuals. The group's activities were uncovered when a policeman discovered over 100 Youth Corps checks in a briefcase in the back of an illegally parked car.

The controversy over welfare abuse deeply concerned Richard Nixon, who hadn't even been sworn in as President when the *Times* report was published. "This New York welfare mess is probably typical of a problem which exists all over the country," Nixon wrote his senior staffers. "I want a thorough investigation made, with all the resources that we have at our disposal, so that we can set the stage for what we have to do later in cutting some of the purely political programs." Anger over welfare abuses quickly became a national issue. Nixon noted that the American public was "outraged and, in my view, they should be."[43]

Secretary of Labor Willard Wirtz said in January 1969 that even though problems existed in antipoverty programs in other cities, they were "nothing like New York." An OEO audit called the administration of city manpower programs a "monstrosity." A July 1969 City Council study of the Human Resources Administration found that "the HRA super-agency's effectiveness has been compromised by chaotic accounting and record-keeping procedures in HRA fiscal which are conducive to loss and misappropriation."

Lindsay's views on welfare were less clear than Nixon's. Lindsay believed that the HRA system was "pretty good" and he backed Ginsberg, calling the former professor "a very tight-reined, a very tough administrator." Ginsberg defended himself by noting that the "overwhelming proportion of funds . . . have been expended for their designated purpose."[44] Lindsay remained skeptical about "workfare" programs. When he testified before the Senate Finance Committee hearing, Connecticut Senator Abraham Ribicoff called New York "one of the filthiest cities anywhere" and suggested putting welfare recipients to work cleaning the streets. Lindsay was shocked at the suggestion: "The use of welfare mothers with brooms and spikes in the middle of Fifth Avenue brings us back to the dark ages." The mayor thought that Ribicoff's suggestion was "rather extraordinary in view of modern thought." Instead, Lindsay became a leading proponent of a national income-maintenance program. In 1969, he warned New Yorkers, in the moralistic tones that had been the hallmark of his first term, that the key to victory in the war against poverty was not to "succumb to that laziness of spirit or failure of imagination."[45]

Yet the welfare crisis took its toll on Lindsay. The city's million-plus welfare recipients hung like an albatross around the mayor's neck, especially as he hoped to run for higher office. As Charles Morris noted, Lindsay grew "disenchanted" with welfare during his second term. Late in his second term, his hopes for changes in welfare "concentrated almost solely on ideas to transfer a greater share of the costs to the state and federal government," wrote Morris. By 1971, Lindsay's growing skepticism toward the welfare system as it then existed was apparent. When Jule Sugarman, who had replaced Ginsberg as head of the HRA, requested a 7.2 percent cost of living increase in welfare benefits to offset inflation in 1971, Budget Director Edward Hamilton wrote Lindsay that he "could see no case against this adjustment on the merits," although it would be costly. "To deny it is to impose a cut in the real income of the poorest people in the city," wrote Hamilton. Responding to the request a few days later, Lindsay told Deputy Mayor Richard Aurelio, "I think it would be a mistake for the City to take any position that indicates approval of a cost of living income in welfare benefits." By late 1971, the Lindsay administration began to implement some administrative reforms in the area of social welfare. Not until June 1972 did John Lindsay finally declare his goal of "zero caseload growth" in welfare. Soon after, the city's welfare caseload reached a plateau.[46]

As with the crime issue, it is hard to disentangle Lindsay's share of the blame for the welfare crisis. In Lindsay's defense, it must be acknowledged that the welfare rolls had been rising under Mayor Wagner. And Lindsay was not the only politician in the 1960s who supported the idea of liberalizing welfare rules and benefits. After finding that cities across the country had seen increases in welfare rates similar to New York's, Charles Morris concluded: "Welfare in New York City . . . was not very much different from welfare anywhere else."[47]

John Lindsay's New York was not unique in the matter of welfare. This does not help explain what caused the sea change in welfare policy during the 1960s. Even Morris agreed that "to the extent that Lindsay and Ginsberg were national spokesmen for the most liberalized attitudes, they bear a share of the responsibility for the rise in the caseload." These attitudes, which made it easier for people to get on the welfare rolls, combined with the poor administration on the part of HRA, meant that in the end, a high percentage of welfare recipients in the city were in fact technically ineligible and should not have received welfare. In 1972, the New York State Department of Social Services found that nearly 14 percent of the city's welfare recipients were ineligible for benefits, but still remained on the rolls. (City officials continued to maintain that the actual figure was closer to 3 percent.) This cost the city about $100 million a year.[48]

An additional failure of Lindsay's welfare policy was his inability to recognize the problem of illegitimate births. Critics like Daniel Patrick Moynihan began to notice that as welfare dependency increased, so did the number of children born out-of-wedlock. These children, most of whom grew up in female-headed households, were more likely to be poor and to end up on public assistance. In 1972, more than half of all individuals on welfare—nearly 640,000—were children. In a memo to President Nixon, Moynihan noted that 43 percent of all live births in central Harlem in 1963 were illegitimate. Four years later, the number had risen to 56 percent. Whether welfare caused greater family instability or family break-ups led to greater welfare dependence, there is little doubt that the issue of illegitimacy has been one of the most serious issues of the last forty years, with disastrous implications for inner-city families and neighborhoods. Of this significant demographic change, John Lindsay said nothing. In fact, just after Lindsay's election in 1965, Moynihan briefed Lindsay and his poverty task force about the growing seriousness of the issue of illegitimacy and family breakdown. "I must report," Moynihan told President Nixon in 1969, "that [Lindsay] and the rest of the group dismissed the idea [of the problem of illegitimacy] as ridiculous." The Lindsay team believed that "the 400,000 plus number of welfare recipients on the rolls was simply a mark of the incompetence of the Wagner administration." The legacy of increased welfare dependency was the subsequent increase in illegitimacy. By the 1990s, the percentage of births that were out-of-wedlock reached as high as 80 percent in some areas of the city.[49]

Another legacy of the Lindsay years regarding welfare that cannot be overemphasized was the change in the attitudes regarding welfare and work. Welfare became a right, divorced from the values of work. Liberal politicians and intellectuals looked down upon ideas of self-sufficiency, responsibility, and strong families. It was impossible and even immoral, they argued, to make poor people live by these middle-class values. Lindsay fully supported this change in attitude. He did not stand outside the conventional wisdom of the times. He did not suggest possible alternatives to the issue of welfare dependency. He did not create the welfare mess, but he acquiesced to it and accepted most of its assumptions and values.

Weakened public confidence in the efficacy of government programs, wasted taxpayer dollars, the rise of the "welfare cheat," increasing rates of illegitimacy and family instability, and the seemingly intractable nature of poverty despite the best efforts of welfare rights activists and social service bureaucrats—this is the legacy of welfare, not just in New York, but in the entire nation.

It was not until the welfare reforms of the 1990s that national attitudes toward work and welfare began shifting toward more traditional core values. This change led to shrinking welfare rolls, even in New York City.

THE SCOTT COMMISSION

In addition to the difficulties that the Lindsay administration encountered in dealing with the issues of crime and welfare, it also faced the often intractable problems of the administration of city government and the management of the city's fiscal and budgetary responsibilities.

Arguments over the management of city finances widened the already large rift between Mayor Lindsay and Governor Rockefeller. During the tense 1971 budget battle, Rockefeller showed little willingness to offer more state aid, while Lindsay threatened gloom and doom if the city's needs were not met. A compromise was finally reached, but not before each man lashed out at the other in public. The governor blamed Lindsay for "declining city services due to inept and extravagant administration of city government." Speaking of the Rockefeller administration, Lindsay said that he could not recall "any leadership of this great State so opposed to progressive change, so ready to punish the poor . . . and so determined to extract the last pound of flesh from its opponents."[50]

Rockefeller, still smarting from a collection of slights from Lindsay over the years, decided to exact political revenge. Angry at being portrayed as a miser for not providing the city more financial aid, Rockefeller struck back in the summer of 1971 by forming the Temporary State Commission to Make a Study of the Governmental Operation of the City of New York, headed by Stuart Scott, a former president of the New York State Bar. The Scott Commission, as it was known, also included Democratic Congresswoman Shirley Chisolm, General Lucius Clay, Herman Kahn of the Hudson Institute, and the industrialist Robert Milano. The hard-charging Stephen Berger, who was active in reform Democratic circles, was named the commission's executive director.

Berger began to organize a series of task forces to investigate the operations of city government and also to carry out direct research into various projects. Scott held public meetings on the matter. The Lindsay administration denounced the Scott Commission as a political hatchet job and refused to comply with its authority to call witnesses and gather evidence. A court battle ensued over the commission's jurisdiction. In a 1972 letter to Scott, Deputy Mayor Edward Hamilton complained that Berger's actions "confirm a wide-spread impression among New Yorkers that the Scott Commission will pursue nothing more than an empty and vindictive political attack on the mayor and the city."[51]

Stephen Berger later admitted that the accusations that the Scott Commission was a politically motivated vendetta against Lindsay were "partly true." But the Commission also stemmed from Rockefeller's real concerns about the direction of the city. The governor was concerned about the city's ever-increasing budget and the seemingly poor management of city government. And Berger was not a hack. He had a real interest in city government and later went on to run the state's Emergency Financial Control Board and the Port Authority of the City of New York. The other members of the commission were respected figures and the members of the individual task forces were highly regarded academics.[52]

In April 1973, the Scott Commission published its findings in a series of reports. They included studies of city pensions, the Housing and Development Administration, the Health and Hospitals Corporation, the Mitchell-Lama housing program, urban renewal in Brownsville, the city's social services system, the city's economic base and fiscal capacities, and the possibilities of restructuring and decentralizing city government. Taken as a whole, the reports were a harsh indictment of the Lindsay administration. "Despite the extensive and expansive response of the City government to the 1960s," the report concluded in its final report that "a widespread feeling of disenchantment, almost anomie, pervades the citizens of New York."

A running theme throughout the reports was that Lindsay's reorganization of city government into "superagencies" was not working: "The superagency concept, which is difficult to fault in principle, has been far from the administrative panacea it originally appeared to be." As Stephen Berger put it years later in more colorful language, the Lindsay reorganization was a "fucking nightmare." The Scott Commission's task force on housing, headed by Frank Macchiarola (who later became schools chancellor), concluded: "Notwithstanding the best of intentions, the Housing and Development Administration (HDA) has been found severely wanting." The Scott Commission task force on health care concluded that the creation of the Health and Hospitals Corporation "had little direct effect on the well-known shortcomings of the municipal health care system. The people of New York City are not being materially better served by the Health and Hospitals Corporation than by its predecessor agencies."[53]

Though few can argue with the idea of simplifying city government, the actual implementation of Lindsay's reforms left something to be desired. Some agencies, like the Environmental Protection Administration, worked well. But others did not. "Governmental reorganization into superagencies, which theoretically appeared to be a major administrative breakthrough, did not result in improved service delivery, better management and efficiency, but instead fostered waste and inefficiency," the Scott Commission concluded. Nor, by 1973, did New Yorkers feel their city government was any more responsive or accountable to their needs. Charles Morris, a veteran of the Lindsay administration, reluctantly concluded in his 1980 book, *The Cost of Good Intentions*, that the Lindsay administration had fallen short of the mark: "The final question is not whether the successes outweighed the failures, but whether, making reasonable allowance for the times and the trends, the Lindsay administration fell short of what they might reasonably have accomplished. My own judgement is that they did, and by substantial margins."[54]

Unsurprisingly, Stephen Berger took a hard line against the Lindsay administration. In a 1999 interview he said, "Lindsay sort of epitomized the public management style which said that whatever we do, because we are right, is OK. Even if we bankrupt ourselves on the way, it doesn't matter because we are doing the right thing."[55]

THE FISCAL HEALTH OF NEW YORK CITY

John Lindsay took office in 1966 promising a reform administration that would reverse the reckless fiscal policies of the Wagner years. He would trim excess spending and waste from the budget, reduce the city's reliance on debt, and introduce measures to improve the efficiency of city services.

Lindsay's first three budgets were fairly successful attempts at responsible fiscal policy. Part of this was due to the booming economy of the 1960s. Unemployment was only 3.1 percent in the city in 1968. Tax revenues streamed into the city's coffers, thanks in large part to the new city income tax Lindsay created in 1966. From 1966 to 1969, the city added 183,000 jobs. Lindsay balanced the city's budget during these years, but he did not do it by cutting spending. There was a staggering increase of nearly 50 percent in spending during that time, escalating the drive toward more spending that had begun under Wagner (which candidate Lindsay had criticized in 1965). In fact, the annual percentage increase in spending in each of Lindsay's first three years was higher than in any year during the Wagner administration.

Lindsay's spending during his first term was also financed by a marked increase in aid from the state and federal governments, which increased from 26.5 percent in fiscal year 1962 to 37.7 percent in 1966 to 48.6 percent in 1973–74. (This figure topped 50 percent during the fiscal crisis of the mid–1970s.) Lindsay deserves credit for cajoling more money for the city, especially from the state. This trend is also traceable to the growing role of the federal government during President Johnson's Great Society. Federal aid was 4.5 percent of the city's total revenue in 1961 but had increased to 21.6 percent by 1973. Also, this trend shows that Governor Nelson Rockefeller, contrary to Lindsay's accusations, was actually quite generous to the city, as state aid to the city increased nearly fivefold between 1961 and 1973.[56]

In his book *Political Crisis/Fiscal Crisis: The Collapse and Revival of New York City*, political scientist Martin Shefter concluded: "During his first three years in office, Mayor Lindsay pretty much kept his promise to put the city's finances back in order." But there was trouble on the horizon. As Budget Director Fred Hayes lamented in 1969, "We're going broke on $6.6 billion a year." The vice president of the city's Chamber of Commerce noted in

1968 that "city spending is growing faster than the growth of local taxpaying ability. The city's population is virtually static, and the local rate of economic growth is insufficient to meet the rapidly rising costs of local government." Lindsay's finance administrator, Roy Goodman, warned as early as 1968, that unless "New Yorkers can be spared successive local tax increases, Fun City will become Run City as middle-class New Yorkers dash to the nearest exit."[57]

As spending continued to rise, the Lindsay administration began to look at some novel approaches to increase revenues. The mayor banded together with five other New York State mayors to lobby Albany for increased funds. Lindsay proposed what he called "Urbanaid" in 1969 to replace the per capita grant system of aid to cities and towns with a new system of revenue sharing. Under Lindsay's plan, more than 27.5 percent of the receipts from the state's income tax would be set aside for distribution to cities and towns. Of course, New York City would be the big winner under Urbanaid, receiving roughly 70 percent of the state revenues set aside under the plan. The idea of Urbanaid revealed Lindsay's tendency to look for solutions for the city's problems beyond the city's borders.

Urbanaid had three problems. First, since this money would be more than the money currently allocated under the per capita grant system, the increased aid would have to come from somewhere—namely, higher income taxes on all state residents. Lindsay's proposal: "The full Urbanaid package could probably be financed with relatively modest additions to the State tax program." Second, the division of Urbanaid money among cities would be calculated on the basis of the amount of spending by cities and towns financed from local tax revenue. Under this plan, cities and towns would have an incentive to increase such spending in order to get a larger share of the Urbanaid revenues. Finally, the project was ultimately doomed by the appearance that this was a money grab by New York City for more money from the rest of the state. Urbanaid never went beyond the proposal stage.

Meanwhile, the national economy went into a recession by 1969. The city's unemployment rate rose to 4.8 percent in 1970 and 6.7 percent in 1971. Tax revenues slowed. For the first time in six years, the city's unemployment rate was higher than the national rate. Inflation continued to take its toll on the average New Yorker's wallet and on the city's budget. But whereas the nation bounced back from the recession in the early 1970s, the city did not. After gaining 183,000 jobs in Lindsay's first term, the city's economy took a nosedive in 1969, losing 257,000 jobs between 1969 and 1973. By 1977, it had hemorrhaged another 338,000 jobs. Thus, between 1969 and 1977 the city lost 16 percent of its jobs. While per capita personal income in constant dollars grew in the nation by 6.5 percent between 1970 and 1975, New Yorkers saw a net decrease of 1.4 percent in their income. As

Joshua Freeman put it: "Whereas most of the country quickly recovered from the 1969 recession, New York continued to slide."[58]

The manufacturing segment of the New York economy continued its freefall. The number of manufacturing jobs had dropped from a high of nearly 1.1 million in 1947 to 864,000 when Lindsay took office to 653,000 in 1973. It would continue to fall in the 1980s, dipping below 500,000. The construction industry lost 35,000 jobs between 1969 and 1977; the garment industry, 17,000. The city's white-collar financial, insurance, and real estate sector (FIRE) grew by more than 15 percent during Lindsay's first term, but contracted by nearly 50,000 jobs between 1969 and 1977. Such changes had a devastating effect not only on employment opportunities for New Yorkers but also on the city's budget. As Charles Morris noted, "The wholesale job loss after 1969 was in the most tax-productive sectors of the city's economy and was nothing short of a financial disaster."[59]

One area of employment that did not see shrinkage was government. During Lindsay's tenure, the city bureaucracy grew by 90,000 workers. Another area of slight job growth—of 4,000 new jobs between 1969 and 1977—was in the low-paying service sector. This was part of a larger economic trend as industry began seeking cheaper labor in other parts of the country and the world. In 1946, 41 percent of the city labor force worked in blue-collar jobs as craftsmen, laborers, and foremen. By 1970, that number was only 29 percent. By 1970, city, state, and federal governments employed more people in New York than the docks, banks, and garment industry combined.[60]

New York City was also undergoing rapid demographic changes. Since the end of World War II, the city had been absorbing hundreds of thousands of poor and unskilled workers, just at a time when the manufacturing industry—one of the few areas of the economy that employs unskilled labor at decent wages—was declining in the city and in the rest of the country. A study of mobility in the New York metropolitan area between 1965 and 1970 by Andrew Hacker showed that the city was losing its draw as a magnet for workers. Some 283,000 individuals moved into the city during this time, but 343,000 left it for the suburbs and another 147,000 moved to the New York City suburbs from elsewhere in the nation. Those moving to the city tended to be young (67 percent were under twenty-nine years of age) and well-educated (54 percent had some college education). In contrast, those fleeing New York for the suburbs tended to be older and less-educated (66 percent had no college training) and were predominantly in blue-collar or service jobs.[61]

As the national and local economy softened, the city continued to spend money, although at a slower rate than in Lindsay's first term. In Lindsay's eight years as mayor, city spending increased 133 percent. In constant dollars, the increase was more than 61 percent over eight years. Between 1961 and 1975—under Wagner, Lindsay, and Beame—city spending increased by nearly 360 percent, or nearly 150 percent in constant dollars. Martin Shefter calculated that overall spending increased not only in absolute terms but also as a percentage of the city's total personal income. That figure rose steadily from 6.8 percent to 9.5 percent during Wagner's three terms (1952–65). Under Lindsay's eight years, it shot up even higher, from 9.5 percent to 15.4 percent.[62]

Spending increases were not consistent across the board, but were concentrated in certain areas of the city budget. By fiscal year 1973–74, the city was spending $4 billion in just three areas: welfare, hospitals, and higher education. Growth in these areas of city government—often called redistributive because they cause money to flow from richer to poorer segments of the population—grew faster than more traditional areas of the city budget, such as sanitation, fire, police, infrastructure, and transportation. What made this situation especially burdensome in New York City was that the city was funding some areas of government—such as the City University system and city hospitals—for which other cities did not provide. It was as if the city was being punished for its generosity.

Another big chunk of city spending went to the wages and pensions of city workers. According to Shefter, the cost for each city employee (wages, pensions, fringe benefits) nearly tripled between 1961 and 1975. The 1973 Scott Commission report on city pensions found that the retirement costs of city workers had risen from $261 million in 1961 to $806 million in 1973. The study predicted that if present trends continued, the cost to the city for pensions of retired city workers would reach anywhere from $1.1 billion to $2 billion by 1980. Despite such staggering numbers, Charles Morris believed that after analyzing the labor costs of other cities and "despite Lindsay's apparent ineptitude in dealing with the unions, overall changes in employee compensation appear to be not much different [in New York City] from those found anywhere else." Nevertheless, such high labor costs did little to ease the city's fiscal burden.[63]

Increased spending caused the city to run major deficits. Tax revenues could not cover the difference, nor would the already generous state government add much more to the city's coffers. So the city turned to debt financing. Martin Shefter noted that during Lindsay's second term budget deficits began to be "papered over with various accounting gimmicks." The city "financed these deficits by selling short-term notes and long-term bonds, and when its notes fell due they were redeemed by selling additional bonds." Throughout his first term, Lindsay had carefully kept the city's debt at manageable levels. But by June 30, 1974, the city's short-term outstanding debt was $3.4 billion. As Charles Morris pointed out, this heavy reliance on debt financing was, with some exceptions, unique among American cities during this time. The financial community had willingly played the debt game with the city, making huge profits off the sale of these bonds. But by the mid–1970s, a continuing weak economy and growing jitters in the financial community would cause this house of cards to collapse.[64]

WHO WAS RESPONSIBLE for the economic collapse of the city? Everyone and no one. Changes in the city's population, deindustrialization of the American economy, and large-scale changes in the international economy had dramatic effects on New York's economy. Federal mandates like Medicaid and state mandates burdened the city with increased basic costs. Governor Rockefeller deserves his share of the blame as well, as do Robert Wagner, who started the vast increase in city spending, and Abe Beame, who acquiesced in it as comptroller and, later, as mayor. Budget gimmicks were the sole preserve of no one politician. The city's banks also deserve blame for not anticipating the effects of economic changes, for not demanding greater fiscal austerity, and for feeding the city's debt machine.

John Lindsay must also accept his share of the blame. Unlike previous reform mayors, John Lindsay did little to stem wasteful government spending or lighten the tax burden for the city's workers and homeowners. His concern for the poor and expansion of social services led to larger and larger outlays. Such spending was acceptable during the good economic times of Lindsay's first term, but he failed to understand the ramifications of the economic changes of the early 1970s, and his consequent failure to alter the city's spending habits proved disastrous. Writing in 1973, the Scott Commission concluded that "the City can no longer command the resources required to perform the staggering tasks of income redistribution and service provision to which it has committed itself; but its leaders have not yet adjusted either their attitudes or their spending decisions to this situation." The city could no longer afford its promise of a large and generous city government. Nor did the vast billions seem to solve many social problems or even adequately handle basic city functions like education, garbage collection, and road repairs.[65]

Lindsay's reliance on higher personal, business, and user taxes gave the city the highest tax burden of any city in the nation. In 1972, New Yorkers paid 8.9 percent of their total income in city taxes, 50 percent higher than the twenty next largest cities. Little thought went into the effects these taxes had on New Yorkers, especially middle-income residents and businesses. By the 1970s, New York was no longer an attractive place to do business. Fortune 500 companies fled to the suburbs, while small entrepreneurs were burdened by high taxes and regulations. As a consequence, the city no longer produced the well-paying jobs that turned immigrants and the poor into middle-class taxpayers.[66]

By the early seventies, New Yorkers had become inured to high crime rates, welfare dependency, poor city services, and chronic budget deficits as the price of urban living. In the eyes of many, the city suffered during the Lindsay years. And so did American liberalism.

16

"GOOD-BYE TO ALL THAT"

> "[Being mayor is] like being a bitch in heat. You
> stand still and you get screwed, you start
> running and you get bit in the ass."
>
> —John Lindsay, *The Edge* (novel, 1976)[1]

John Lindsay's political career effectively ended on Wednesday, March 7, 1973, when he shocked few people by announcing that he would not seek a third term as mayor of New York City. His poor showing in the 1972 Democratic presidential primary had taken the wind out of his career. With the March announcement, his lame-duck status became official.

Some have speculated that Lindsay would have had a difficult time winning the Liberal Party nomination for a third straight election. Though Lindsay believed he could have received the Liberals' support, Alex Rose reportedly told him that "some of your best friends, including myself, feel you'd be better off not to run again" and advised him to set his sights on higher office at a later time. One former ally, labor leader Victor Gotbaum, said in an interview that Lindsay would have "a terribly difficult uphill climb" if he ran for reelection. "I'd rather he didn't," Gotbaum concluded. Not surprisingly, disillusionment had set in. The pollster Lou Harris, who joined the Lindsay team as a consultant at the recommendation of Rose, noted, "The one thing [Lindsay] had was a certain fundamental integrity on the issues. When he lost that, he had nothing. When I learned he had taken money from city contractors [to fund his presidential campaign], I told him he had sold his soul for a pittance." In order to make his way in his new party, Lindsay had to make peace with the Democratic machine. Richard Reeves wrote in *New York* magazine, "After seven years of Lindsay, it's hard to remember what his campaigns were about. The mayor in 1972 is in the Bronx calling Democratic leader Patrick Cunningham a great man, and Abraham (Bunny) Lindenbaum, 'a power broker' of the Wagner years, is back at City Hall talking real-estate deals. How can anyone tell that Beame or Procaccino didn't win?" Reeves, who as a *New York Times* reporter had covered Lindsay for two terms, asked: "What do you say about a Mayor who failed?"[2]

The *New York Times* paid less and less attention to the mayor after his presidential run. Part of this had to do with the fact that many reporters lost respect for Lindsay. This was a far cry from the era when the *Times* editor A. M. Rosenthal had mingled socially with the mayor, and Lindsay aides dictated editorials to John Oakes, the *Times* editorial page editor. The ownership and editorial staff of the paper had once been Lindsay's biggest cheerleaders. By the early 1970s, that had changed. In 1972, Nicholas Pileggi wrote, "It is no exaggeration to say that a mood of bitter disenchantment with the mayor pervades the paper's third-floor newsroom. . . . Suspicion and distrust of Lindsay abound." David Burnham, the reporter who broke the Serpico story, said of Lindsay, "I personally think he's kind of fraudulent." Murray Schumach thought Lindsay deserved to be compared to the huckster Jimmy Walker, rather than the respected La Guardia. The *Times* reporter Steven R. Weisman summarized the Lindsay years:

> The mayor has never been able to stop the city's downward spiral. Services have continued to decline, division has deepened among races and economic classes, and there have been unending crises. . . . Outlays for welfare and antipoverty programs increased, but the problems they sought to attack mounted even faster. New taxes were imposed one after another—a bank tax, an income tax, a commuter tax, a stock transfer tax, higher real-estate taxes—but the quality of life in New York City has never seemed more bleak, its government never more sluggish, wasteful, and finally even helpless.

The *Times* urban affairs reporter David Shipler accused Lindsay of exaggerating his accomplishments. Lindsay received little praise from New York liberals, wrote Shipler, because he "traveled a road to the right of his rhetoric." Shipler criticized Lindsay for the conditions in the city's jails, for wasting Model Cities grant money, for placing welfare families in crumbling hotels, for failing to take action against police corruption, and for emphasizing law enforcement over the rehabilitation of criminals.[3]

If Lindsay had chosen to run for a third term, it would have proved even more difficult than the 1969 race. By March 1973, four Democratic candidates were ready to challenge him: Bronx Assemblyman Albert Blumenthal, who received the reform New Democratic Coalition endorsement; Congressman Herman Badillo; Congressman Mario Biaggi; and Comptroller Abe Beame. Even former allies like City Council President Sanford Garelik and former Environmental Protection Administrator Jerry Kretchmer were contemplating running. As if to prove that the political stars were not aligned in his favor, Lindsay's retirement announcement shared space in the papers with the indictment of Norman Levy, who had been tax commissioner in his administration (and head of the Brooklyn John V. Lindsay Association), in a ticket-fixing scheme.

It was time for Lindsay to bow out gracefully. A 1972 Gallup poll showed that six out of ten New Yorkers thought the city worked poorly under Lindsay. Another poll showed that 45 percent of New Yorkers thought their neighborhoods had gotten worse under Lindsay. Less than one in six thought their neighborhoods had improved. The previous eight years had also been a time of ideological change throughout the country. Lindsay had grown more liberal while the public had grown more conservative. In January 1974, the *Times* reported that more New Yorkers considered themselves conservative (33 percent) than either moderate (31 percent) or liberal/radical (27 percent).[4]

By 1973, John Lindsay was tired and he was no longer fresh. One journalist noted that while still dashing and handsome, Lindsay had "changed during his eight years in office. He looks paler and older than his 51 years. His hair is silvered, the lines in his lean cheeks are deeper and under the classic chin there is a hint of slackness." Lindsay's former aide Jeff Greenfield noted in a *New York Times Magazine* piece that by March 1973, "Lindsay's hair is longer, grayer, thinner; his face handsomer, decades older, creases cutting deep into his patrician profile, furrows latticing his brow." The cover of the issue that ran Greenfield's piece was a close-up photo of Lindsay with each heavy line on his face attributed to a major crisis during his eight years as mayor. Despite this, Lindsay said being mayor of New York was the "best eight years of my life. I don't expect it ever to be that good again." And in many ways it wasn't.[5]

Lindsay made his decision quickly, telling his wife late Monday night and then calling his children. He broke the news to his closest aides the following evening. On Wednesday, he told the assembled press, in a speech lasting less than five minutes, that "eight years is too short a time, but it is long enough for one man." Lindsay felt that his administration's greatest accomplishment was that it was "determined that this city would hold together in the face of social stresses that tore many cities apart. And it held." His administration, he said, was "willing to meet with any group, walk down any street, and face every problem and dilemma with a strong sense of responsibility and accountability." In conclusion, the mayor promised that he would "continue to fight for progressive, independent government for New York" and "give my voice and my strength" to the fight "for rational urban priorities." That night, Lindsay's inner circle threw a party for the mayor at "21." Lindsay's security guard Pat Vecchio remembered that the party "was probably the time I saw him the most down in all those years, more so than any primary defeat or strike." At the beginning of the event, Vecchio noticed that "Lindsay was really out of it. He was chagrined. He was down." By the end of the evening's festivities, though, Lindsay's mood had lightened. Maybe it was the lifting of the burden of governing the nation's largest and most chaotic city.[6]

Reaction to the mayor's announcement was muted. The praise was faint. Few of his enemies gloated, though Queens Democratic Councilman Matthew Troy said, "He'll be a power to reckon with, at least until his looks start fading." The *Daily News*, never a fan of the mayor, said that Lindsay "made what future generations may deem his greatest contribution to the welfare of New York City yesterday when he announced he would not seek a third term." While he was a "gracious, witty, charming, personable and thoroughly honest" man, the paper wrote, Lindsay "ran a loose ship and the results of that slackness show in mounting budgets, soaring taxes, a bloated payroll and a woeful decline in services." The *Times* summarized the conventional wisdom when it agreed that "the time has come for him to conclude his service as Mayor of New York." While praising Lindsay for keeping the city calm during turbulent times and for "bringing the plight of the cities to the attention of the nation," the paper complained that Lindsay and his administration "lost their hold on the imagination of the average citizen. There have been indications of laxity and maladministration." In addition, the paper noted a "severe loss in the confidence of his political constituency" as the mayor's popularity "in recent months hit what must be for him an all-time low."[7]

The *Post* acknowledged that there had been "flaws and failures of administration" and that Lindsay "placed excessive trust in some aides who proved unworthy of it." Still, the paper credited him "with deep dedication, a tenacious refusal to panic under fire, and a consistent effort to stimulate the best instincts of his fellow citizens." For James Wechsler it was lonely being a Lindsay defender in 1973, even among the salons of liberal Manhattan. Though Lindsay "did not achieve many miracles," Wechsler wrote, "far too often he was condemned for the wrong reasons." *The Nation* believed that despite the uneasiness with Lindsay in 1973, future generations of New Yorkers would look back fondly on his administration: "One looks back, for example, on Mayor Wagner and Mayor O'Dwyer with affection, and back still further to La Guardia with hopeless longing. So it has been and will be with Mayor Lindsay. . . . New Yorkers will surely not look back in anger at the Lindsay years."[8]

The *Village Voice*, which had supported Lindsay as far back as his congressional days, was also ambivalent. Under the heading "John Lindsay: Goodbye to All That," the writer Clark Whelton concluded: "John Lindsay spoke for parts of the city and the city came apart. . . . He meant well. It's just that John Lindsay is a creature of air. . . . He could walk on air. The people he tried to lead couldn't. When John Lindsay sinks into obscurity, he will sink up." Another *Voice* writer, Alan Weitz, wrote about how a man of great promise had been destroyed by the turmoil that he left behind: "One wanted to forget that though there had been no large riots, it would be folly to say the city had 'held.' One wanted to forget that the deliverance of services was often inadequate. That industry and businesses have been leaving the city. That most communities feel shut out from City Hall. That there was corruption. And one wanted to forgive. But it couldn't be done. The city is in turmoil and it is useless to deny it."[9]

By 1973, few of Lindsay's original advisers remained. Jay Kriegel was the only original "young turk" left standing. In eight years, Lindsay had gone through four deputy mayors, four police commissioners, three press secretaries, and three budget directors. Barry Gottehrer was gone. So were Richard Aurelio and Sid Davidoff, both of whom turned their attention away from politics and toward the restaurant business. Corruption had tarnished the mayor's good-government image. Not only had Tax Commissioner Levy been indicted, but in 1973 the head of the Youth Services Agency, Ted Gross, was convicted and sentenced to three years in jail for receiving over $40,000 in bribes. An audit found over $300,000 of improper spending at the agency. Gross was the second high-ranking Lindsay official to be sentenced to jail for corruption. Questions were also raised about Lindsay administration deals concerning Yankee Stadium and the Hunts Point Terminal Market. Finally, like a symbolic coda on the Lindsay era, in December 1973 a section of the elevated West Side Highway collapsed. The city was literally falling apart.[10]

When Lindsay left office at the end of 1973, the *Post* praised him "for the courage and grace he displayed under fire in countless situations" as well as for giving "law and order a human, rational dimension." Former Parks Commissioner August Heckscher praised his former boss in vague terms for never appearing discouraged, for leaving "with his essential qualities intact." According to Heckscher, Lindsay "held to undeviating standards ... showed an unfailing constancy of outlook and purpose," and "emulated the best quality of the New Yorkers he has served." Victor Gotbaum said, "He was elegant where the rest of us had a piece of vulgarity in us." Maybe Lindsay was, as Jimmy Breslin had written in 1969, too tall to be mayor of New York. Lindsay himself noted years later, "The thing that hurts me most is being a six-foot-four WASP, particularly in this part of the world."[11]

As Lindsay's mayoralty drew to a close, the *Daily News* asked a number of prominent New Yorkers to grade Lindsay's performance. Predictably, Sid Davidoff and Richard Aurelio gave their former boss high marks. "I'd say he was a fighter, one who deeply believed in confronting problems rather than papering them over. ... He's a far better administrator than he has been given credit for," Aurelio answered. "What the hell," Davidoff said, "I'd give him a 9.9 [out of 10] as a mayor." But others were disappointed. Gotbaum said, "I'd rate him between 6 and 7, but I'd be disappointed, because I had hoped for an 8 or 9." Kenneth Clark rated Lindsay a 5 or a 6, and the journalist Richard Reeves gave him a six, "which means, I guess, that I think he barely passed or failed very well—probably the latter."[12]

In the years since Lindsay has left office, conventional wisdom has held that the charismatic John Lindsay was a terrific politician, but a lousy day-to-day administrator of city government. For instance, Nat Leventhal, Lindsay's rent control administrator and later deputy mayor under Ed Koch, believed Lindsay "was not interested in being a good manager or good administrator. He didn't see the job of mayor as being the day-to-day head of the government."[13]

Other former Lindsay aides, though, have disagreed with the conventional wisdom, arguing that in reality Lindsay was a solid administrator but a lousy politician. "Between 1972 and 1973, I think Lindsay hit a full stride and maturity in terms of managerial capabilities," said Steve Isenberg, his chief of staff during those years. Jeff Greenfield wrote that "Lindsay's greatest triumphs were substantive and managerial; his greatest failures were political." He called Lindsay's biggest failure his inability to "persuade average middle-class New Yorkers that he really cared about them." Peter Goldmark also thought Lindsay went unappreciated as an administrator, but he agreed with Greenfield about Lindsay's political acumen. "A great politician," Goldmark stated, "would have understood why all of this was so difficult for the middle calss in Queens and Brooklyn, particularly for the Jewish middle class, and that their apprehensions and fears were legitimate. John Lindsay knew they were there, but in his stomach, he didn't understand them."[14]

Though Lindsay's faults as a politician were obvious, his strengths as an administrator were less clear. After his presidential campaign, Lindsay focused his attention on city administration. He wanted to prove that he was a good administrator, not the charming dilettante portrayed by critics. At the end of his mayoralty, Lindsay told a reporter that what made him happiest "is the most mundane of all and that is just straight management and administration. It's the hours and hours spent on the production line." In October 1972, Isenberg reiterated the new focus of the Lindsay administration on "quality of life" issues. "We need a persistent, visible approach, defined by the mayor, which touches all fronts: drugs, schools, street crime, organized crime, and courts," wrote Isenberg. "The City's physical appearance is a constant worry for JVL and one which is a prime indicator for him on the tone of the city and how responsive the bureaucracy is to his pressure and direction." But in many ways it was too late. It is true that the real passion of the Lindsay administration, like most previous reform governments, was to rationalize and economize city government. Government reorganization, "superagencies," reforms of the budget process, and the use of outside consultants to examine the city bureaucracy were hallmarks of the administration. But Lindsay's reforms did nothing to lower the crime rate or even stabilize it. They did not improve the quality of education in the public schools or streamline welfare. They did nothing to keep city spending in check or reduce the need for short-term borrowing. Former Police Commissioner Patrick Murphy noted that Lindsay's problem was not mediocrity "but dense ambiguity. He had managed to attract to his governing team a glittering array of talent from the business, foundation, and academic worlds, but somehow the city still seemed to drift, like a space station that had lost its orbit." If Lindsay was a successful adminis-trator, why were so many people convinced that the city was still in de-cline? Were New Yorkers blinded by petty resentments of their patrician mayor? Or were their perceptions based in reality?[15]

One area where the perceptions and reality of New York City were inter-woven was in the films of the era. Certainly movies in no way present a pho-tographic or journalistic description of reality, but they are nevertheless instructive in deciphering the image of New York in the nation's mind. With the creation in 1966 of the Mayor's Office of Film, Theater, and Broadcast-ing, Lindsay—himself a frustrated actor and show-business buff—encour-aged the film industry to use the city's streets to shoot its movies, and indeed three hundred and sixty-six movies were filmed in New York City during Lindsay's administration. Ironically, though, quite a few of these portrayals of John Lindsay's New York were the opposite of his vision for the city. In many of these movies, the *New York Times* film critic Vincent Canby wrote, "New York City has become a metaphor for what looks like the last days of American civilization. . . . It's run by fools. Its citizens are at the mercy of its criminals. . . . The air is foul. The traffic is impossible. Services are dimin-ishing and the morale is such that ordering a cup of coffee in a diner can turn into a request for a fat lip."[16]

This had not always been the case. *Marty* (1955), *The Sweet Smell of Suc-cess* (1957), *Breakfast at Tiffany's* (1961), *The Man in the Gray Flannel Suit* (1956), *The Apartment* (1960), *The Seven-Year Itch* (1955), *Butterfield 8* (1960), and *How to Marry a Millionaire* (1953) showed a city safe for lonely butchers, sleazy gossip columnists, prostitutes, and adulterers. New York may have been a tough city full of temptations, sin, and malevolence, but at least it functioned. Humor could also be found in its lonely streets, sterile of-fices, and high-rise apartments. In *Barefoot in the Park*, a 1967 adaptation of a play by Neil Simon, Robert Redford and Jane Fonda played newlyweds liv-ing in their cramped Greenwich Village apartment. Though the movie is filled with the frustrations and chaos of New York living, it has an innocence and madcap humor that would have been unrecognizable a few years later.

By the late 1960s, Washington Square Park was no longer a place for young newlyweds to walk barefoot.

The tone of New York movies changed by the late 1960s and early 1970s. It became darker. Filmed on location, these movies featured the city—dirty and dangerous—as the leading actor. No mere amusing backdrop, the city was a near-immovable obstacle to the happiness of men and women determined to live there. *Midnight Cowboy* (1969) and *Taxi Driver* (1976) portrayed the seediness and alienation of urban life, a city of pimps, prostitutes, hustlers, and the just plain down-and-out. As Pauline Kael wrote of Martin Scorcese's *Taxi Driver*, "The city never lets you off the hook. There's no grace, no compassion." Scorcese's New York was a "voluptuous enemy" which gave off "the stench of Hell."

Crime—a seedy kind of crime—became the center of many New York movies of the time. *The French Connection* (1971), *Panic in Needle Park* (1971), *Across 110th Street*, (1972), *The Taking of Pelham One Two Three* (1974), *Law and Disorder* (1974), and *Dog Day Afternoon* (1975) are just a few examples. The classic New York crime movie is *Death Wish* (1974), in which the mild-mannered architect Charles Bronson turns into a vigilante when his wife is murdered. One film critic said *Death Wish* "is given over to characters who voice every bigotry about New York that runs rampant in the rest of the world. . . . One is hardly likely to forget this film's blasphemous dislike of New York." No doubt many of these movies exaggerated New York's problems, but the image of an increasingly dangerous and chaotic city was real enough.

Another set of movies had little to do with crime, but instead dealt with the city's ability to drive people to insanity and wreak havoc on middle-class life. In *The Prisoner of Second Avenue* (1975), Jack Lemmon enters into a warlike existence with the city, driven to insanity by every inconvenience and inhumanity the city throws at him. *Network* (1976) is as much about the pent-up hatreds and alienation of New York life as about the hollowness of television news. *Desperate Characters* (1971) focuses on an upper-middle-class couple in Brooklyn Heights trying to live amid the desperation and decay that surrounds them. Vincent Canby wrote of the movie's main characters, "They are childless, middle-class city dwellers, coming apart in a world whose problems have grown beyond the liberal's capacity to comprehend, much less solve. . . . The subways they ride are inhabited by two kinds of people, those who talk to themselves and those who pretend not to notice. The streets are boobytrapped with garbage and dog excrement and drunks who might be stiffs." Still another movie, *Joe* (1970), features Peter Boyle as a frustrated working-class stiff so angered by the social changes and decay he sees that he too turns violently antisocial. With these portrayals, the image of New York City as a place of danger, decay, and division became solidified in the nation's mind.

As HAS OCCURRED AFTER EVERY REFORM MAYORALTY in New York, Lindsay was succeeded by a regular Democrat, Abe Beame, the man whom he had defeated in 1965. In a four-way Democratic primary Beame defeated Herman Badillo (who came in second), Mario Biaggi, and Albert Blumenthal but did not win a majority of the vote. Under the new post-Procaccino election rules, a runoff election was held in which Beame handily defeated Badillo. In the fragmented November general election, turnout was down by over 700,000 votes from 1969. Beame won over 56 percent of the vote in November. The Republican candidate, John Marchi, came in second with 16 percent of the vote. Blumenthal, running with the Liberal Party endorsement, won 15 percent; and Biaggi, running as a Conservative, won 11 percent. The political excitement of the Lindsay years was over. It was finally Beame's time to govern.

As Beame took the reins at City Hall, Lindsay settled into life as a private citizen. There was talk that he might challenge Senator Jacob Javits in 1974 or Senator James Buckley in 1976, though neither race ever materialized. He spent much of his first year out of office living abroad on what he termed a "sabbatical" in Europe. Returning to New York, the Lindsays settled into a large duplex apartment on Manhattan's Upper West Side. Mary volunteered at the nearby Museum of Natural History. John became a full partner at his old law firm, Webster, Sheffield, Fleischmann, Hitchcock & Chrystie, representing American companies abroad, especially in Iran. He made more money than he had ever made before, an important fact considering he was not originally wealthy. The ex-mayor spent nearly half of his time in the seventies as an on-air personality at ABC-TV doing interviews for *A.M. America*, and as a substitute host for the show's successor, *Good Morning America*. With this job, Lindsay could stay in the limelight and indulge his interest in entertainment without, as one journalist wrote, "exposing himself to the lacerating fire he seems so readily to attract." He had a small role as a United States senator in Otto Preminger's *Rosebud*. (Reportedly, Lindsay turned down the role of the politician Robert De Niro's character sets out to assassinate in Scorcese's *Taxi Driver*.)[17]

He also published a novel in 1976 titled *The Edge*, which received less-than-glowing reviews. Christopher Lehmann-Haupt wrote in *New York Times*: "Everything is wrong with *The Edge*. . . . There is nothing about politics in the story that a high-school freshman couldn't have imagined." The novel features Mike Stuart, a good-government, pro-civil-liberties congressman, who bears a strong resemblance to John Lindsay. The book is set in a nation beset by chaos, riots, unemployment, and crime. Martial law is imposed and the army patrols the streets. Congressman Stuart opposes the "Special Powers" bill, whereby martial law is imposed, and helps rally opposition while uncovering a potential coup by military leaders associated with the quasi-fascistic Leadership Party. The voice of John Lindsay is everywhere in the novel, from Stuart's principled opposition to the bill, reminiscent of Lindsay's battles while in Congress, to a black congressman's thoughts on the Leadership Party—"They wear American flag pins on their lapels as if they had an exclusive on the flag. I tell you I can't take them"—to the character Mayor James Carr, who complains, "I was the biggest law-and-order man in town—that's why I've always got re-elected—but we're sure beginning to pay a helluva price for it." Stuart walks the streets during the riots, like another well-known politician, and listens sympathetically as rioters explain, "No one's paying any attention to us, so we have to do this." Opponents mob Stuart, much as they did Lindsay, screaming "Go home, Stuart," "Drop Dead, Stuart," and "Hey, Stuart, ya fag you." The only interesting way to read the book, suggested Lehmann-Haupt, was to assume that Congressman Stuart was really Lindsay. But to do so would suggest "not only that Mr. Lindsay is a poor novelist but that he is an incompetent politician as well. And this makes the reader feel twice foolish—once for having read Mr. Lindsay and once for having voted for him in his political days." To Lehmann-Haupt, "it is preferable to pretend that *The Edge* simply never happened."[18]

The novel, though, is useful in mining Lindsay's political thoughts. If the right believed that the country was descending into an orgy of violence and permissiveness, the left believed that the nation was heading toward a fascist reaction. In his 1970 speech at Berkeley, Lindsay had argued that the war on crime would lead politicians to "erase the Bill of Rights." *The Edge* exhibits these liberal fantasies, with right-wing superpatriots seeking to overthrow the Constitution in order to quell disturbances. Stuart, like Lindsay, sympathizes with the rioters, who take action not because they are criminals, but because no one is listening to them. Lindsay's novel not only betrays his limited literary abilities, but also shows the outmoded nature of his political vision. Congressman Stuart is the white knight who tries to save the country with his principled devotion to both the Constitution and the disenfranchised. No doubt John Lindsay saw himself in the same light. So did his wife. As one family friend said in 1975, Mary "seems more and more convinced that he is the only politician who will pull this country out of the mess we're in."

Meanwhile, by the fall of 1974 it was becoming clear that New York's finances were in a mess. Short-term debt had reached $5.3 billion. New York City accounted for over 40 percent of the short-term tax-exempt borrowing in the nation. With an estimated $1.7 billion budget deficit, the city ran out of money in April 1975. Banks that had previously been more than happy to sell the city bonds in anticipation of future revenues at generous interest rates now refused to lend the city any more money. They feared that the city was near default and they might have to swallow the costs of the defaulted notes. In 1975, Governor Hugh Carey established the Municipal Assistance

Corporation (MAC) to restructure the city's debt. MAC demanded that the city cut spending and revise its accounting practices. Although left-wing critics see the fiscal crisis and the creation of the MAC as an attempt by banking elites to take control of the city, the reality of the city's financial distress was undeniable. It would take years for the city to dig itself out of this mess, which it did partly by means of spending cuts and the investment of municipal unions' pension funds in MAC bonds. Though the fiscal crisis culminated during Beame's watch, many people looked back at John Lindsay and his fiscal policies as the precipitators of the crisis.[19]

Lindsay made clear that he had little respect for his successor. "He was not trained to be a leader," sniffed Lindsay. "He was trained to be an accountant." He asserted that he, unlike Beame, would not have allowed the fiscal crisis to occur: "As long as I live, I will insist I wouldn't have let it happen. We would have acted quick! Decisively! That was our way, to confront problems head on, to do anything that had to be done. And I mean anything— massive layoffs, cuts in services, anything!" Unable to handle the city's finances, Beame effectively lost control of the city to the Municipal Assistance Corporation. The fiscal crisis ended the brief allure of the accountant-politician.

In the 1977 Democratic primary, Beame finished third in a field of six. Ed Koch won but did not receive a majority, so there was a runoff between Koch and the second-place finisher, Mario Cuomo. With polls showing that 20 percent of city Democrats blamed John Lindsay for the fiscal crisis—ahead of the banks, the unions, and Abe Beame—both candidates attacked Lindsay. Cuomo, whose political career had begun when Lindsay chose him to mediate the Forest Hills housing controversy, ran an ad that morphed Koch's face into Lindsay's. Koch's campaign theme, written by the former Lindsayite David Garth, was "After eight years of charisma and four years of clubhouse, why not try competence?" After Koch was elected Mayor, Lindsay warned that if the new mayor made him a scapegoat for the city's problems, "I'll go public, and very hard. . . . I guarantee you you'll see some fire." But Koch was still angry at Lindsay. Later Koch bragged that during his years as mayor, he "tortured him [Lindsay] at every opportunity. He deserved it."[20]

In January 1978, the *New York Times Magazine* called Lindsay "An Exile in his Own City." Norman Mailer called him the "most maligned man in New York." Lindsay called the attacks leveled by Beame, Koch, and Cuomo "enormously frustrating" and "*obscene*." A sense of bitterness crept into Lindsay's stoic persona, although he was careful to shield such thoughts from the outside world. David Garth observed, "He believes unequivocally in biting the bullet, stiff upper lip, and all the rest of it." That Beame and Koch, men he believed were his inferiors, blamed him for the city's ills must have tortured Lindsay. "In a way, he's a rather sad figure," one friend said of Lindsay. "He can't accept the fact that life is just unfair sometimes, and that he's had to take the fall for what happened to the city. He's obsessed by that, plagued by the feeling that he's been scapegoated." Richard Aurelio remembered that "every time there's another attack," Lindsay called him. Aurelio got the impression that the criticism hurt the former mayor "very, very deeply." Lindsay's former corporation counsel, Norman Redlich, came to Lindsay's defense on the op-ed page of the *Times*. "I ask only that the people of this city call a halt to the shameful and inaccurate heaping of blame on a Mayor who deserves far better from a city he labored so hard to preserve," wrote Redlich.[21]

Lindsay told a reporter in 1980 that he would "take the blame where it's due and I'll share the responsibility for what happened," but he could not resist adding that "the quality of life was better when I left office than it is now, and who woke up the nation to the urban crisis. I did. Fiscal reforms were begun while I was in office. I wish they could have been completed." He complained that his speech to a group of Canadian urbanists in Toronto went unmentioned in the New York press, despite the fact that whenever Lindsay traveled in the United States or abroad, "I'm always amazed by how interested people are in finding out what's in my head." Comparing New York in 1980 to the city during his tenure as mayor, Lindsay said, "The quality of life was better ten years ago than it is now. You cannot ride the subways without fear today, and you could ten years ago. They're snatching necklaces from the necks of women and snatching pocketbooks in the open and they didn't ten years ago. We are severely polarized now. We were not then." The dreamy pull of nostalgia made Lindsay forget the crime and divisions that characterized the city in the 1960s and early 1970s.[22]

Lindsay seemed to believe that American life in the late 1970s resembled his book *The Edge*. What the country needed was a courageous young politician like Congressman Stuart ... or John Lindsay. Surveying the national scene, Lindsay complained, "We're certainly getting more and more mediocrity." Mary Lindsay, always her husband's strongest advocate, said, "A lot of people would like to see John Lindsay back in government. He's desperately needed. . . . There's just no leadership in this country." With his reputation in tatters, there was little Lindsay could do about the issues for which he cared. "There are times I feel very frustrated," said Lindsay in 1978, "because I can't do anything about it." Republicans wanted nothing to do with the liberal turncoat, and Democrats held him at arm's length. President Jimmy Carter showed little interest in bringing the former urban boy wonder into his administration.

Still, Lindsay was a political animal and could not resist one final foray into electoral politics. According to Steven Isenberg, Lindsay "wanted back in. He was a public man and for him to be off stage was too painful. He wanted another shot at it." So against the advice of Isenberg and most of his former aides, John Lindsay entered the Democratic primary for U.S. Senate in 1980. If he won, he would face his old Republican ally, Jacob Javits, then seventy-six and suffering from the early stages of Lou Gehrig's disease. Lindsay's opponents were Bess Myerson, Liz Holtzman, and Queens District Attorney John Santucci. Ironically, Lindsay was the favored candidate not of city voters, but of Upstate voters attracted by his celebrity status. The man who ran for president in 1972 to put the problems of cities on the national agenda said very little about cities during his 1980 Senate race. Instead, Lindsay ran as a moderate liberal, supporting a balanced budget and opposing the MX missile program. Missing was the soaring rhetoric of his first term as mayor.[23]

One of Lindsay's campaign aides, Amalia Betanzos, admitted that the senate run "was a badly run campaign." Lindsay directed his own campaign, relying only on a few advisers. Money was tight. "The Beautiful People," wrote journalist Joe Klein, "apparently have moved on to other charities." Lindsay's campaign was largely issueless. Lindsay seemed to be running for personal redemption from the slings and arrows he had received in the wake of the fiscal crisis. Speaking of the 1980 Senate campaign, one former aide (who wished to remain anonymous) noted, "He wants vindication. He became very bitter after he left office and Beame and Koch blamed him for everything that had gone wrong with the city." As if to prove that victory was not in the cards, Lindsay broke his collarbone on Father's Day while riding his bicycle. A dog chased Lindsay and upset the bike, and the former mayor fell over the handlebars. "This was definitely not the break we were looking for in the campaign," joked an ailing Lindsay.

Most troubling, though, was that there was no rallying around the former mayor. Not only were the large campaign contributors missing, but so were the "young turks" who had begun their careers in his administration. Betanzos complained that "some of the people who had been very much involved in the Lindsay administration . . . whom Lindsay made . . . didn't participate actively in that campaign. . . . Everybody was doing other things." To add insult to injury, two of the other Democratic candidates—Myerson and Holtzman—had gotten their start in politics in the Lindsay administration, the former as commissioner of consumer affairs and the latter as a mayoral assistant. (When Myerson was in the Lindsay administration, it was rumored that she and the mayor were having an affair. When asked who started the rumor, Lindsay replied, "I did." Another wag said the rumor was natural since Lindsay and the former Miss America were the two best-looking people in the city.) Other former Lindsay associates worked for other candidates. David Garth, the media guru who worked on the 1965 and 1969 campaigns, was on Myerson's staff, and Werner Kramarsky, a former aide, was an adviser to Holtzman. Only Betanzos and Steven Isenberg remained with Lindsay. Jay Kriegel explained his absence from the Senate campaign: "I'm trying to build a business here and enjoy my middle age. I think most of the others who were with John in the old days feel the same—we wish him well, but the old days are gone and we are in a different period in our lives." Betanzos believed that Lindsay "was hurt by the fact that many former aides didn't flock to his campaign."[24]

One poll showed Lindsay with a greater unfavorable (44 percent) than favorable rating (37 percent). Still, he held out hope for a miracle. He presented himself as a seasoned, rational politician, standing between Holtzman and Myerson. He was, Klein noted, "somewhere above the fray." He made women swoon again, even if he had aged. But Lindsay's support was noticeably shallow. John Corry said that Lindsay's campaign committee was "made up almost exclusively of prominent members of the American Society of Composers, Authors and Publishers and Actor's Equity, stray celebrities, and lawyers who graduated from Yale." While Myerson had the backing of Ed Koch and Pat Moynihan, and Holtzman had Ed Costikyan and the New Democratic Coalition, Lindsay had Leonard Bernstein and Cy Coleman.

When the primary rolled around in September, the miracle never arrived. Lindsay came in a weak third with 16 percent of the vote. Liz Holtzman won a surprise victory with 41 percent of the vote, easily defeating Bess Myerson, who finished second. Lindsay finished fourth in the conservative boroughs of Staten Island and Queens and third in the other three boroughs. Most surprising was his weak showing in Manhattan, where he received only 20 percent of the vote. On the East Side and in Midtown, the heart of Lindsay's old silk stocking district, the former mayor pulled less than 15 percent. His strongest showings were in black and Puerto Rican districts like Harlem, Springfield Gardens, the South Bronx, East New York, Bedford-Stuyvesant, Brownsville, Bushwick, and Ocean Hill, areas of the city's greatest hopelessness and despair. The primary loss "knocked the wind out" of Lindsay, said Betanzos. "He was hurt by it." More telling was the defeat of Jacob Javits in the Republican primary by the little-known Long Island conservative Alfonse D'Amato. It was clear that Lindsay was not truly at home in the Democratic Party, and it was equally clear that liberal Republicanism was dead.

After the Senate campaign, Lindsay remained at Webster, Sheffield. Some of his former aides now worked in the Koch administration, including Deputy Mayors Nathan Leventhal and Stanley Brezenoff, and Parks Commissioner Gordon Davis. David Garth was now a top adviser to Koch. These men worked out a "nonaggression pact" between Lindsay and Koch which tempered the backbiting, at least temporarily. But Lindsay still privately criticized Koch for polarizing the city, and Koch could not resist tweaking the former mayor. Lindsay continued to believe that he had been unfairly scapegoated for the city's problems but that he would soon receive the respect due to him for what he had accomplished was mayor. "There's a great sense of nostalgia out there," Lindsay said. "I continue to run into people from all walks of life who say that was the time the city was exciting and together and somehow cities were being noticed for the first time."[25]

Lindsay occasionally gave his opinion on contemporary politics. He thought the Carter administration "were just plain bumblers" but found the Reagan administration more troublesome. Lindsay believed Reagan "is a cowboy and there is nothing but arms as a policy." In 1985, the former mayor gave the Herbert H. Lehman Memorial Lecture at Lehman College in New York. Entitled "Bipartisan Hopes in an Age of Polarization," Lindsay's speech was mostly directed at the policies of the Reagan administration, although he mentioned the President's name only three times. "The tone coming from the top is clear," Lindsay said. "If you're not with us, you're against us and America." The man who had once longed for a position on the House Foreign Affairs Committee condemned Reagan's foreign policy, saying that a policy "based primarily on military superiority is not worthy of this country. . . . We've been the major military power on earth for seven decades. Yet America once represented not an arsenal, but a bastion of freedom." He criticized the MX missile, the deployment of Pershing missiles in Western Europe, the Strategic Defense Initiative, and aid to the contras, while warning of the power of "more farsighted, assertive trading partners like Japan." But Lindsay's main concerns still centered on domestic policy. In 1990 he continued to argue for more spending on cities: "With money, there's hope. Without money, there's no hope. You've got millions and millions of dollars for armaments, guns, and munitions, but nothing for the cities. And most of the minorities—white and non-white—are in the cities. . . . And the federal government just washes its hands of the whole thing. They run off to Saudi Arabia, they run off to see Gorbachev, and they don't know where they are going."

Lindsay, the man who decades earlier had worked with Hungarian refugees fleeing Soviet tanks, now seemed to be turning toward isolationism.[26]

In a 1995 letter to the *Times*, Lindsay criticized welfare reform and argued that an "increase in the minimum wage, more spending on preventative health care, education and job training and, when necessary, substance abuse programs to rehabilitate addicted parents and make them employable are cost-effective, humane commitments to the nation's future." Lindsay wanted the federal government to assume the costs of such programs. Echoing some of the themes of his 1969 campaign, he criticized the government for "maintaining a gigantic global military establishment long after our only significant antagonist has collapsed." Lindsay pleaded: "It's time to spend public resources on the right things and stop spilling vast portions of the wealth to no good purpose." But Lindsay had become a man without a party. In the 1980s and 1990s, people who blamed Lindsay for the fiscal crisis were not about to listen to his views on contemporary politics.[27]

Beginning in the late 1980s, Lindsay's former aides began meeting at occasional "alumni reunions." The invitations for the first, in 1987, said: "Remember those good old days in New York City, when we were young, beautiful, invincible, and we all really cared?" Over four hundred people, including the Lindsays, showed up for this first reunion. Former Press Secretary Tom Morgan characterized the attendees as "the unrepentant and the unindicted, and the unappreciated." Though most were no longer the idealists of twenty years earlier, they still defended their boss and his vision. Nat Leventhal lamented the lack of idealism in the city when he noted that "if John Lindsay ran for Mayor today, he'd be laughed out of town. People don't want vision and crusades; they want their garbage picked up and the homeless off their doorsteps." Other New Yorkers were less charitable. Henry Stern, who worked in the Lindsay Parks Department and was Parks Commissioner under both Ed Koch and Rudy Giuliani, called Lindsay "a patrician, radical dope." Ed Koch noted dryly that "Lindsay is not held in high regard these days, except by the coterie that worked for him."[28]

LINDSAY THE MAN REMAINS something of an enigma. Jack Newfield said of him, "If there is any quibble with Lindsay it is in the murky terrain of personality and psyche." Partly owing to an ingrained WASP reserve and a refusal to wear his emotions on his sleeves, Lindsay's character was difficult to read. Barry Gottehrer called Lindsay "a reserved man, not at all open in his personal relationships." The journalist Nora Sayre found Lindsay to be "rather like an old-fashioned debutante, radiant in public, but sulky in private—especially in interview. He had little to say, and was irritated by questions that had anything to do with black New Yorkers."[29]

"Whether at City Hall or away, he reveals very little of himself to even his closest aides," wrote Nicholas Pileggi. "Somehow, despite the published litany of his political position, despite the urbane and witty performance on late-night talk shows and his daily coverage in the press, the man is still missing." One of Lindsay's former speechwriters, Jeff Greenfield, noted that there "was with Lindsay always a sense of distance; [distance] from those who worked with him, but also from those he governed." Former Deputy Mayor Bob Price, Lindsay's closest confidant during his early days in politics, said in 1991:

> If you think John is vague now, you should have seen him twenty years ago. I was always afraid he was going to walk in front of a truck. He's just a remote guy. He used to drive me nuts whenever we traveled together. He just never cared and he was forever missing planes, buses, trains. He missed everything. It never bothered him. . . . John has al-

ways had that certain self-confidence that must come from being taller than everyone else in the room. It's that WASP confidence that somehow the world will fit in around you. He just would not move his ass for anyone or anything. It would never occur to John, for instance, to return a phone call, or answer mail, or call up a guy for a drink or get anywhere on time.

Lindsay had few close friends his own age and felt comfortable only among his family, the older Republican lawyers who mentored him at the start of his career, and the young aides who worshipped him as mayor and saw him as the key to their futures.[30]

Lindsay fancied himself something of an intellectual. Throughout his political career, he wrote articles and reviewed books on urban affairs, civil liberties, and foreign policy. He published two books on his experience in New York. Yet, the charge of being an intellectual lightweight followed him his whole career—perhaps his good looks invited the criticism. But there was some merit in the accusation. First, Lindsay entered office with little knowledge of the operations of city government. Second, the "politcian as intellectual" is a feat that few individuals have ever managed to pull off. Politics lends itself to instant judgements and simplistic slogans. And Lindsay's writings never seemed to rise above that formula.

As distant and enigmatic as Lindsay may have been, he also embodied many positive attributes. He was an honest man who entered politics purely for public service, though no doubt he was also, at times, impelled by the siren song of political ambition. He cultivated smart aides and used them well. He brought a sense of idealism and style to city government. He showed little Machiavellianism toward his fellow human beings. He displayed a sense of generosity to those around him that was rare for a politician. He had an often randy sense of humor, usually displayed in private.

Today, there is a lack of consensus as to whether Lindsay was, on the whole, a successful mayor. Many of Lindsay's former aides believe that their former boss has received a bad rap. There is surely no way, they argue, that John Lindsay, who represented such high moral values and cared so deeply, could be responsible for the deteriorating condition of the city. Lindsay partisans put forth three major defenses of Lindsay's performance as mayor. First, Lindsay brought an excitement and a sense of purpose, at least early in his tenure, to a city badly in need of both. According to Pat Vecchio, Lindsay's former bodyguard, the mayor brought "style and class to New York City." Second, says former Lindsay press aide, Robert Laird, one of Lindsay's biggest achievements "was the way he guided New York through what may have been the most convulsive period of social change in the twentieth century (maybe ever)." In this environment, Lindsay displayed a unique courage in walking dangerous ghetto streets to calm the city. Lindsay himself contended that one of his most important contributions as mayor was to "have given leadership to a city that did not burn down."[31]

Third, Lindsay's defenders cite his record of accomplishment. As mayor, Lindsay made his mark on the city in ways big and small, good and bad. The city's income and commuter taxes are both Lindsay contributions. He reorganized city departments into superagencies. Though many of these agencies have since devolved to their status before Lindsay's reorganization, the Human Resources Administration and Health and Hospitals Corporation still exist. Off-Track Betting and the Department of Consumer Affairs were also the creations of the Lindsay administration. He passed a rent stabilization law in 1969 that regulated the rents of most postwar apartments. Air pollution was reduced and the subways became air-conditioned under Lindsay's watch. He also presided over the construction of Roosevelt Island and Battery Park City. Though Lindsay's attempt to turn Madison Avenue into a car-free pedestrian mall failed, he did manage to close Central Park to cars during weekends. Open admissions in the City University system was another major Lindsay administration achievement. Lindsay also fought for and won increased state and federal funding for the city. And he brought minorities into the city's mainstream.[32]

But for each defense, there is also a countercharge. Lindsay did indeed bring glamour and a sense of flair to the city, but there was also an arrogance to Lindsay and his administration. Spurred on by brash young aides, Lindsay ran roughshod over the city during his first term. The mayor also exuded a certainty of belief and moral righteousness that was unseemly. He accused opponents of bigotry or lack of public-spiritedness. And Lindsay's vision of the city excluded many of those who lived outside Manhattan—namely middle- and lower-middle-class Catholics and Jews.

Second, though New York did not experience the devastating riots that Los Angeles, Washington, Newark, and Detroit suffered, its streets were anything but calm. And even without major rioting, New York still suffered the fate of "quiet riots." During Lindsay's tenure, many formerly stable working-class neighborhoods collapsed under the collective weight of arson, negligence, vandalism, and indifference. Whole areas of the city became hollowed-out places of hopelessness and despair.

During one of the most tumultuous eras in American history, Lindsay was a deeply polarizing figure. He was a divider, not a uniter. Under his administration, racial and ethnic divisions only worsened. The flight of businesses and the middle-class to the suburbs continued unabated.

Third, Lindsay's record of accomplishments is a mixed bag. It is true that John Lindsay did not cause the urban crisis, but one must not discount the fact that it worsened and deepened during his watch. The city taxes Lindsay instituted increased the tax burden on the average New Yorker and encouraged the continued flight of businesses and the middle class from the city.

Lindsay's new superagencies were supposed to be models of bureaucratic efficiency, yet they resulted in little actual improvement in city services. Crime increased dramatically and disastrously, while police powers were curbed. Graffiti began to blight to city's buildings and subways, while Times Square sank even further into squalor. Nearly 200,000 units of housing were abandoned during Lindsay's tenure. Lindsay's rent-stabilization bill, though benefiting some tenants with government-controlled rents, strengthened rent control in the city and continued to stifle the private housing market. Today's public school system, with its thirty-two separate school boards, is a weak and sad reminder of the doomed battle for community control and decentralization. Meanwhile, education in the city's public schools had gotten worse. Welfare rolls also increased dramatically during Lindsay's term, as they did throughout the nation. City spending increased, despite the promises of fiscal responsibility. Short-term debt piled up to pay for this spending. Lindsay—along with Wagner, Beame, and Rockefeller—helped drive the city into fiscal insolvency.

Two of the most important public works projects of the Lindsay era—Roosevelt Island and Battery Park City—were actually state projects conceived by Nelson Rockefeller. Considering the visually uninspiring designs of both projects and the fact that the city's fiscal crisis prolonged their ultimate completion, it is curious that Lindsay defenders would want to take credit for them. Above all, people began to lose confidence in the city. Lindsay with all of his talent and energy, could not halt the city's downward slide.

But maybe no man could have. His defenders argue that the problems Lindsay faced were the same ones faced by big-city mayors across the country. But this is a weak defense of the Lindsay record. John Lindsay was supposed to be a different kind of mayor. Different from Robert Wagner. Different from Chicago's Richard Daley. The reason for the urban crisis, Lindsay told New Yorkers during his 1965 campaign, was a lack of leadership, idealism, and concern, all of which Lindsay possessed. He promised to lead New York out of the morass created by previous administrations. But he could not. And when things became difficult and the condition of the city deteriorated, Lindsay's supporters fell back on the idea that at least he had *tried*. The greatest criticism of John Lindsay is that he failed to live up to the promise of his early years and meet his own standards for reforming the city. He knew little more than anyone else about how to save America's cities and he did his share to make matters worse. In the end, John Lindsay was like other big-city mayors.

Despite this, no one denies that perhaps Lindsay's greatest accomplishment—and the one of which the former mayor was most proud—was his ability to attract smart and energetic people to work in city government. Sid Davidoff recalls: "John had such star quality. He didn't have to beat himself on the chest. He could let other people shine. He got his smiles knowing that so many people who worked with him went on to great success." Many of these former aides see their experience in the Lindsay administration as the highlight of their careers. The political idealism of the administration paralleled the idealism of their youth. Speaking of the Lindsay team's concern for the poor, Lindsay's budget aide David Grossman once told the young aides, "You guys believe you have to catch every sparrow that falls." Others took a less sanguine view. Stephen Berger, former director of the Scott Commission, called the Lindsay people "smartass, East Side, know-it-all kids excessively impressed with their own knowledge."[33]

This they may have been, but in the years since Lindsay left office his former aides have made their own mark on the world. Sid Davidoff is a powerful lobbyist in New York Democratic politics; Barry Gottehrer is a Washington lobbyist; Peter Goldmark was the head of the Port Authority and then the director of the Rockefeller Foundation, and is now the publisher of the *International Herald Tribune;* Nat Leventhal was the executive director of Lincoln Center, a position that Gordon Davis now holds; Steven Isenberg was publisher of *Newsday* and is now acting president of Adelphi University; Robert Sweet is a respected federal judge; Jeff Greenfield is a correspondent for CNN; Richard Brown is Queens district attorney; Bob Price owns a successful cellular phone company; Richard Aurelio is the former head of Time-Warner Cable; Norman Redlich was the dean of the New York University Law School; Roy Goodman is a New York state senator; Leon Panetta served in Congress and as Bill Clinton's chief of staff. Lindsay's former police bodyguard, Pat Vecchio, has served for many years as the supervisor of Smithtown, Long Island. Many prominent female politicians also got their start in the Lindsay administration: Councilwoman Ronnie Eldridge, former Congresswoman Liz Holtzman, Congresswoman Eleanor Holmes Norton, Bess Myerson, and the New York Historical Society head Betsy Gotbaum. In addition, many well-known people worked in their younger years as low-level Lindsay staffers, including *Brill's Content* editor Steve Brill, former National Security Adviser Sandy Berger, Lesley Stahl of CBS, and Dreamworks' Jeffrey Katzenberg (whose nickname at City Hall was "Squirt").

City politics have also changed since the Lindsay years. The old machine/reform dialectic that defined city politics for nearly one hundred years had disappeared. In 1993, Rudolph Giuliani, a reform Republican running on a "fusion" ticket, challenged a sitting Democratic mayor who had begun his career in the Manhattan political machine. Most liberals, the descendants of the old Democratic reformers, backed the Democrat, David Dinkins. Bob Price, Lindsay's 1965 campaign manager, endorsed Dinkins, while Edward Costikyan, who led Tammany Hall from 1962 to 1964 and served as Abe Beame's 1965 campaign manager, endorsed Rudolph Giuliani. John Lindsay supported Dinkins, saying that the Harlem Democrat best represented his former coalition. That was true. Dinkins found his constituency in Lindsay's old top-down alliance of liberal, upper-middle-class whites and minorities, whereas Giuliani combined the anti-Lindsay coalition of white ethnics and outer-borough homeowners with support from Manhattan's business elite. By the 1990s, the politics of conservative versus liberal had replaced the politics of reform versus machine.[34]

The longest-lasting consequence of the Lindsay years on the city's political landscape has been the rise of the white ethnic sensibility. Most successful city politicians in the ensuing three decades have represented this constituency. Former Governor Hugh Carey once represented the Irish and Italian areas of Brooklyn in Congress. Former Governor Mario Cuomo began as an obscure Italian-American lawyer from Queens. Senator Daniel Patrick Moynihan grew up in a poor Irish family in Manhattan's Hell's Kitchen. Former Mayor Ed Koch, the self-described "liberal with sanity," grew up in a working-class Jewish family in the Bronx and Newark, New Jersey, and learned how to deal with Italian Americans as a councilman from Greenwich Village. Mayor Rudolph Giuliani is the son of an Italian American tavern owner from Brooklyn. Even liberal Senator Charles Schumer comes from the heart of middle-class Jewish Brooklyn that has long been ambivalent about liberalism. The era of the patrician WASP politician in New York has passed.[35]

EPILOGUE

In November 1991 Lindsay turned seventy. As one journalist wrote, "like the city itself, John Lindsay remains a powerful presence, yet he is crumbling." The handsome, tall, athletic politician—whose image was that of an active man diving into swimming pools, wading through adoring crowds, riding a bike, playing tennis, and power-walking to City Hall during the transit strike—was physically deteriorating. In his later years, Lindsay suffered from Parkinson's disease, had heart surgery, and suffered two strokes.[1]

After his law firm—Webster, Sheffield—dissolved, Lindsay went to work for another firm—Mudge, Rose, Guthrie, Alexander & Ferdon—which went bankrupt in 1995. Medical bills ate into Lindsay's savings. Money, never as abundant in the Lindsay family as his patrician ease may have suggested, became a problem. In 1996, Mayor Giuliani named Lindsay to unpaid positions as president of the city's Sister Cities Program and special counsel for the city's Commission for United Nations, Consular Groups, and International Business. With these appointments, the former mayor would receive health benefits and could be on the city payroll for the additional two years he needed to be eligible for a city pension. For most of the 1990s, John and Mary Lindsay split their time between a house in Old Lyme, Connecticut, and a one-bedroom apartment on Manhattan's Upper East Side.[2]

It is Thanksgiving week, 1997, at the Lindsays' Manhattan apartment. The John and Mary Lindsay who answer their apartment door do not look like the glamorous and stylish couple of Sardi's and Broadway but, rather, like a typical Middle American elderly couple. Lindsay's dashing good looks have faded and the strokes have seriously affected his speech. The seventy-six-year-old former mayor has trouble getting around, but his handshake is firm and he is in good spirits. The skin on his face is taut, pale, and lined, his hair gray and thinning. But the old warmth is still there. And his eyes. They are bright, shining blue eyes. If the rest of his body is deteriorating, his eyes are lively reminders of the vigor and energy of his old self.[3]

John Lindsay sits for an interview, his words coming out only with great difficulty. Throughout most of the interview, Mary sits nearby paying bills. Occasionally, she interrupts her husband to clarify a point he is making. One journalist described Mary Lindsay as "independent, strong-willed, as disarmingly blunt as her husband is circumspect." She is still her husband's staunchest defender, and, as that journalist noted, beneath her "good cheer is a touch of steel." The years of accusations, insults, and blame—the usual side effects of a political life—seem to have obviously taken their toll on the protective Mary Lindsay. Given the harsh criticisms directed at him over the years and the fact that his once-promising political career had ended prematurely, one could excuse some bitterness on the part of John Lindsay. To add to his woes, his body gave out long before it should have. But the former mayor seems surprisingly at peace.

By the 1990s, John Lindsay had become a man out of time. The dashing candidate of 1965 was a distant memory. While Ed Koch remained in the spotlight, writing newspaper columns and books and doing television commercials, Lindsay remained a sadly neglected figure. While Koch has lived out his twilight years in material comfort and has enjoyed a celebrity status, Lindsay lived a life constricted by lingering doubts about his mayoralty and failing health.

It seems a cruel twist of fate that as Lindsay's health deteriorated, the city surrounding him was rejuvenated. Today New Yorkers are more optimistic about their city and tourists flock there. As the essayist Phillip Lopate wrote in 1999, "For whatever reason, the city feels more livable than it did twenty-five years ago; it has managed to outlive its own death." Crime is down, the parks look better, the streets are cleaner, and the welfare rolls have shrunk. Rudy Giuliani made the city appear governable, although perhaps not perfectible. Though Giuliani has never criticized Lindsay directly, he clearly governed as the "un-Lindsay." Lindsay surely could not help but see that the city had been revitalized under a man very much his opposite in background, style, and politics.[4]

In the 1990s, other cities also experienced a similar revitalization. People stopped abandoning urban centers, for they had come to see city life as a viable and exciting option. But this was accomplished under the leadership of reform mayors—such as Stephen Goldsmith in Indianapolis, John Norquist in Milwaukee, Michael White in Cleveland, Dennis Archer in Detroit, and Richard Daley in Chicago—who were the antithesis of John Lindsay: pro-business, fiscally conservative, pro-police, and pro—welfare reform. They were less interested in expanding the size and scope of city government than in making cities work within their means. Whether the improved fortunes of cities are the direct results of their good work or the fortuitous effect of a strong economy, it is hard to deny that these mayors have brought a degree of stability and renewed faith to their cities.[5]

The ultimate verdict on John Lindsay's mayoralty is that he did little to stem the "urban crisis." Just as it was Murray Kempton who defined Lindsay's early political career with the statement "He is fresh and everyone else is tired," so it was he who captured the mood toward Lindsay in later years. Looking back from the vantage point of 1991, the dean of liberal journalists called the former mayor "a splendid flop. . . . Failures can have their splendors," he wrote, "and above and beyond all the variously unsuccessful Mayoralties that have been New York's ration for the last 40 years, John Vliet Lindsay's is the only shining failure."[6]

Lindsay tied his political fortune to the health of the nation's cities. But the continued crisis in American cities undermined the claim of liberals like Lindsay to govern the nation. John Lindsay failed because he could not make the city work; liberalism sputtered because of the tragic failure of men like Lindsay.

In late 1999, John and Mary Lindsay moved to an assisted-living community in Hilton Head, South Carolina, where the ailing former mayor could receive better care. He spent his last year hundreds of miles away from the city he loved and governed.

He died late in the evening of Tuesday, December 19, 2000. His family said that complications from pneumonia and Parkinson's disease were the cause of his death. The former mayor's passing temporarily resurrected Lindsay's ghost from the recesses of the city's collective memory. For a brief time, it was the mid-1960s all over again and old battle lines were redrawn. Former aides remembered Lindsay's walks through tense ghetto streets, the idealism he inspired, and his leading role as national spokesman for urban America. Other voices reminded the public of the dark side of the Lindsay years and the toll taken on the city's fiscal health and social fabric. Everyone remembered his charm, charisma, and sense of style.

But as the memorials end, the brave, charismatic, but ultimately flawed mayor recedes into the past, his cries of reform just a faint echo of a distant era in American politics when John Lindsay was as fresh and attractive as his ideas.

NOTES

The following abbreviations and shortened forms are used in the notes.

ARCHIVES AND COLLECTIONS

ACLU Papers: American Civil Liberties Union Papers, Mudd Library, Princeton University

AJC Archives: American Jewish Committee Archive, New York City

Brownell Papers: Herbert Brownell Papers, Dwight D. Eisenhower Presidential Library, Abilene, Kansas

Buckley Papers: William F. Buckley Jr. Papers, Yale University

Columbiana Collection: Columbiana Archives, Columbia University

CUOHA: Columbia University Oral History Archives, Butler Library, Columbia University

Ford Foundation Archives: Ford Foundation Archives, Ford Foundation Headquarters, New York City

Galamison Papers: Milton Galamison Papers, Schomburg Center for Research in Black Culture, New York Public Library

Javits Papers: Jacob Javits Papers, State University of New York at Stony Brook

JVL Papers, Yale: John V. Lindsay Papers, Yale University.

JVL Papers, NYCMA: John V. Lindsay Papers, New York City Municipal Archives

La Guardia and Wagner Archives: La Guardia and Wagner Archives, La Guardia Community College, New York City

LBJ Library: Lyndon B. Johnson Library, University of Texas, Austin

Milbank Memorial Library: Milbank Memorial Library, Teachers College, Columbia University

NYCMA: Municipal Archives of New York City

NAACP Papers: NAACP Papers, Library of Congress, Washington, D.C.

Nixon Presidential Materials: Richard M. Nixon Presidential Materials, College Park, Maryland

NYS Archives: New York State Archives, Albany, New York

O'Donnell Papers: Harry O'Donnell Papers, American Heritage Center, University of Wyoming, Laramie, Wyoming

UFT Papers: UFT Papers, Robert F. Wagner Labor Archives, New York University

WHCF, LBJ Library: White House Central File, Lyndon B. Johnson Library, University of Texas, Austin

PERIODICALS

AN = Amsterdam News

DN = Daily News

NY = New York magazine

NYHT = New York Herald Tribune

NYP = New York Post

NYT = New York Times

NYTM = New York Times Magazine

VV = Village Voice

WSJ = Wall Street Journal

INTRODUCTION

1. One indicator of the crisis of American cities is the drastic decline in population that most Northern cities suffered for much of the postwar era. From 1950 to 1990, Baltimore lost 23 percent of its population, Boston 28 percent, Chicago 23 percent, Cleveland 45 percent, Detroit 44 percent, Minneapolis 29 percent, Newark 37 percent, Philadelphia 23 percent, Pittsburgh 45 percent, St. Louis 54 percent,

and Washington, D.C., 24 percent (Bureau of the Census, U.S. Department of Commerce, 1950, 1990).

2. Nora Sayre, a writer and journalist who wrote about Lindsay and New York City in the late 1960s for the *New Statesman*, told the author that when she recently updated her collection of essays, *Sixties Going On Seventies*, she dropped the essays on Lindsay because she felt he had become a forgotten figure.

3. John V. Lindsay, *The City* (New York: W. W. Norton, 1969), p. 20. Harry Stein, "An Exile in His Own City," *NYTM*, 8 January 1978. John Corry, *My Times: Adventures in the News Trade* (New York: G. P. Putnam's Sons, 1993), p. 102.

4. Woody Klein, *Lindsay's Promise: The Dream That Failed* (London: Macmillan, 1970). Mary Perot Nichols, "Is There a Chance for New York City?" *VV*, 28 October 1965. Ibid., "Where Are You Now That We Need You?" *VV*, 1 April 1971.

5. Nat Hentoff, *A Political Life: The Education of John V. Lindsay* (New York: Alfred A. Knopf, 1969). It is interesting to note that in his recent memoir, *Speaking Freely: A Memoir* (New York: Alfred A. Knopf, 1997), Nat Hentoff never mentions John Lindsay's name. Ibid., "John V. Compromise," *VV*, 31 August 1972. Jack Newfield and Paul Du Brul, *The Abuse of Power: The Permanent Government and the Fall of New York* (New York: Viking Press, 1977), p. 150.

6. Stein, "An Exile in His Own City."

7. Melvin G. Holli, *The American Mayor: The Best and the Worst Big City Leaders* (University Park, Pa.: Pennsylvania State University Press, 1999). *NYT*, 15 January 2000. *DN*, 24 May 2000. Paul Peter Jesep, "Mayor John Lindsay of NYC: A Revisionist View," *The APIC Keynoter*, Winter 1999. Abe Beame ranked fourteenth worst, Ed Koch ranked fifteenth worst, and John Purroy Mitchel ranked seventeenth worst. Robert Wagner was ranked the seventeenth best mayor. Though these rankings reflect a measure of subjectivity, they show the overall low regard in which Lindsay and his successors are held.

8. Charles Dickens, *American Notes for General Circulation* (London: Chapman & Hall, 1842). Henry James, *The American Scene: Henry James: Collected Travel Writings, Great Britain and America* (New York: Library of America, 1993). E. B. White, *Here Is New York* (New York: Harper Brothers, 1949), pp. 24–25. John Steinbeck, "Autobiography: Making of a New Yorker," *NYT*, 1 February 1953. Richard Whalen, *A City Destroying Itself: An Angry View of New York* (New York: William Morrow, 1965), p. 18. Tom Wolfe, "Oh Rotten Gotham—Sliding Down into the Behavioral Sink," *World–Journal Tribune*, 9 October 1966. *U.S. News and World Report*, 24 January 1966. For a view of the seamy underbelly of New York City in the late-nineteenth and early-twentieth centuries, see Luc Sante, *Low Life: Lures and Snares of Old New York* (New York: Vintage Books, 1991). In a similar vein is Caleb Carr's novel set at the turn of the last century, *The Alienist* (New York: Random House, 1994).

9. On the 1977 blackout, see Robert Curvin and Bruce Porter, *Burning! Looting! New York City, July 13, 1977* (New York: Gardner Press, 1979), and New York City Department of Planning, "Blackout Commercial Damage Survey, New York: Preliminary Findings," 1977.

10. Ford Foundation, "R and D & NYC = C: Assessment of a Grant to the New York City-Rand Corporation," November 1971, p. 1, Folder 001989, Ford Foundation. Roger Starr, "The Decline and Decline of New York," *NYTM*, 21 November 1971. Robert A. M. Stern, Thomas Mellins, and David Fishman, *New York 1960: Architecture and Urbanism Between the Second World War and the Bicentennial* (New York: Monacelli Press, 1995), p. 1212. Andrew Hacker, *The New Yorkers: A Profile of an American Metropolis* (New York: Twentieth Century Fund, 1975), pp. 1–2. For attempts to make sense of urban decay, see Wesley G. Skogan, *Disorder and Decline: Crime and the Spiral of Decay in American Neighborhoods* (New York: Free Press, 1990), and Catherine E. Ross and John Mirowsky, "Disorder and Decay: The Concept and Measurement of Perceived Neighborhood Disorder," *Urban Affairs Review* 34, no. 3 (January 1999).

11. Saul Bellow, *Mr. Sammler's Planet* (New York: Penguin Books, 1969), pp. 9, 304.

12. Philip Roth, *Portnoy's Complaint* (New York: Random House, 1967).

13. Nora Sayre, *Sixties Going On Seventies* (London: Constable, 1974), p. 426.

14. Aaron Wildavsky, "Recipe for Violence," *NY*, 20 May 1968. Sayre, *Sixties Going On Seventies*, p. 222. Jeff Greenfield, "Reading John Lindsay's Face," *NYTM*, 29 July 1973.

15. Bob Price, Lindsay's campaign manager and first deputy mayor, said, "I always said that he [Lindsay] would have been a good chairman of the Senate Foreign Relations Committee and a very bad governor of the state of New York" (interview of Bob Price by author, 21 March 1997).

CHAPTER 1

1. The following account of Lindsay's early years was based on Daniel E. Button, *Lindsay: A Man for Tomorrow* (New York: Random House, 1965), pp. 11–24; Nick Thimmesch, *The Condition of Republicanism* (New York: W. W. Norton, 1968), pp. 196–204; Casper Citron, *John V. Lindsay and the Silk Stocking Story* (New York: Fleet Publishing, 1965); and Jerry Talmer, "Battle for City Hall: The Story of John Lindsay," *NYP*, 25 October 1965.

2. John Lindsay was always uneasy about the term WASP and jokingly referred to himself as an ASP—after all, he once asked, how many Anglo-Saxon Protestants were not white? When asked about the power of New York's WASPs, Lindsay said, "They're an endangered species. . . . You realize you can't call any other ethnic group by its pejorative name, but you can say 'Wasp.' As if they didn't bleed" (Lindsay quoted in Nelson W. Aldrich Jr., *Old Money: The Mythology of America's Upper Class* [New York: Alfred A. Knopf, 1988], p. 281).

3. Thimmesch, *The Condition of Republicanism*, p. 195. Lindsay made the list called "The Prep Pantheon" in the *Official Preppie Handbook* (New York: Workman Publishing, 1980), edited by Lisa Birnbach: "Imparted to the Big Apple the well-known Preppy habit of spending somebody else's money. Wore khakis on walking tour of Harlem" (p. 198).

4. Nicholas Pileggi, "Inside Lindsay's Head," *NY*, 4 January 1971; interview of Pat Vecchio by author, 13 October 1999; and interview of Steven Isenberg by author, 1 September 1999.

5. John V. Lindsay, *Journey into Politics: Some Informal Observations* (New York: Dodd, Mead, 1967), p. 3.

6. Gloria Steinem, "She Will Not Vegetate in Gracie Mansion," *NYTM*, 9 January 1966.

7. Button, *Lindsay: A Man for Tomorrow*, p. 17.

8. Lindsay's first public political pronouncement as president of the Young Republicans sounded the traditional, if bland, call for good government: "I urge another crusade to select an outstanding Republican candidate for Mayor in 1953 to be supported by all parties and groups fighting for good city government" (Citron, *John V. Lindsay and the Silk Stocking Story*, pp. 7–8).

9. Roger Starr, "John V. Lindsay: A Political Portrait," *Commentary*, February 1970.

10. For background on the Silk Stocking District, see Citron, *John V. Lindsay and the Silk Stocking Story*. While representing the district in the New York State Assembly, Roosevelt railed against the stereotypical Silk Stocking reformers, "the refined gentlemen who shook their heads over political corruption and discussed it in drawing rooms, but were wholly unable to grapple with real men in real life." For the history of the nickname, see William Safire, *Safire's New Political Dictionary: The Definitive Guide to the New Language of Politics* (New York: Random House, 1993), pp. 709–710.

11. Coudert quoted in Citron, *John V. Lindsay and the Silk Stocking Story*, p. 57. *NYTM*, 6 February 1966.

12. Tom Wolfe, *Radical Chic and Mau-Mauing the Flak Catchers* (New York: Farrar Straus and Giroux, 1970). Michael Barone, Grant Ujifusa, and Douglas Matthews, *The Almanac of American Politics, 1974* (Boston: Gambit, 1973), p. 690. Michael Barone and Grant Ujifusa, *The Almanac of American Politics, 1986* (Washington: National Journal, 1985), pp. 936–939. In one of the many ironies of New York City politics, Congressman Ed Koch, who represented the district from 1969 until 1977, personified the liberal cultural revolution of the 1960s, whereas Mayor Ed Koch personified the neo-conservative counterrevolution of the 1970s and 1980s.

13. Button, *Lindsay: A Man for Tomorrow*, p. 57.

14. Robert Blum, "Remembrances of Robert Blum," document in author's possession.

15. Nat Hentoff, *A Political Life: The Education of John V. Lindsay* (New York: Alfred A. Knopf, 1969), p. 40.

16. Ibid., p. 39.

17. Between 1947 and 1997, only three New York City congressmen have served on the House Armed Services Committee: James Heffernan (1947–1949), Gary Clemente (1949–1953), and Lester Holtzman (1955–1957). Clemente and Holtzman represented Queens and Heffernan represented Brooklyn. All three were Democrats. As can be seen by their short service on the committee, none gained enough seniority or power there to have much impact. In the forty years since 1957 no city congressmen have served on the committee. In the postwar years, the House Armed Services

Committee has been the preserve of Southern congressmen of both parties. Bella Abzug, upon her election to Congress in 1970, made getting a seat on the Armed Services Committee one of her first priorities, with the goal of reducing military spending. She failed to win a seat on the committee. The liberal Brooklyn congresswoman Elizabeth Holtzman once bragged that in her four terms in Congress during the 1970s she never once voted for a defense authorization or appropriation bill. See Bella S. Abzug, *Bella! Ms. Abzug Goes to Washington* (New York: Saturday Review Press, 1972), pp. 14–17, and John Corry, "The All-Star Race," *NYTM*, 22 June 1980.

18. Button, *Lindsay: A Man for Tomorrow*, pp. 79–80, 85.

19. Hentoff, *A Political Life*, pp. 30, 49.

20. John V. Lindsay, "Religious Aspects in the Life and Times of Oliver Cromwell," Senior Thesis, Yale University, 1943, p. 83, Group 592, Series VII, Box 1, Folder 1, JVL Papers, Yale. Hentoff, *A Political Life*, p. 54. Arthur Mann, *Yankee Reformers in the Urban Age* (Cambridge, Mass.: Harvard University Press/Belknap Press, 1954), p. 242. Edward C. Banfield, *The Unheavenly City Revisited* (Boston: Little, Brown, 1970), pp. 274–275.

21. Ibid., p. 34.

22. Citron, *John V. Lindsay and the Silk Stocking Story*, p. 110.

23. Lyndon Johnson, State of the Union Address, *NYT*, 5 January 1965. John Lindsay, quoted in *Look*, 6 April 1965.

24. Letter from John V. Lindsay to Charles Percy, Chairman of the Republican Platform Committee, 15 July 1960, Group 592, Series IX, Box 21, Folder 2, JVL Papers, Yale.

25. Another incongruity in Lindsay's civil rights record was the fact that his home, Stuyvesant Town, had strict clauses preventing blacks from residing there.

26. The ragged northern boundaries of the Seventeenth District had the look of intentional gerrymandering. Until 1960 the district's boundary line went up the East River to Eighty-ninth Street, west on Eighty-ninth to Third Avenue, north to Ninety-first Street, west one block to Lexington Avenue, north to Ninety-sixth Street, one block west to Park Avenue, north to Ninety-seventh Street, one block west to Madison Avenue, north to Ninety-eighth Street, one block west to Fifth Avenue, and up Fifth Avenue to 110th Street. The 1960 redistricting added the area east of Third Avenue from Fifty-ninth to Eighty-ninth. The reason this boundary zigzags to the northwest is that the farther east one goes on Manhattan's Upper East Side, the farther south Harlem extends. Fifth Avenue is still predominantly white until 110th Street, which is the northern boundary of Central Park. North of 110th Street is considered part of Harlem and is black, Puerto Rican, and Democratic (Citron, *John V. Lindsay and the Silk Stocking Story*, p. 95). Edward Costikyan, as the leader of what was left of Tammany Hall, in the early 1960s brought a lawsuit challenging the shape of the Seventeenth Congressional District. He lost the case, but found out that Adam Clayton Powell Jr., the Harlem congressman from the neighboring district, was partly responsible for the makeup of the Silk Stocking District. Powell wanted to

load as many black Democrats into his district as possible, so as to make it impossible for anyone to challenge him. According to Costikyan, Powell told him the Manhattan district lines were drawn in Harlem's Red Rooster Restaurant by Powell and a Republican functionary. Such an accommodation was beneficial to both the Republicans and Powell (letter from Edward N. Costikyan to author, 10 March 1998).

27. Button, *Lindsay: A Man for Tomorrow*, p. 40. Button, an upstate journalist, ran successfully for Congress in 1966 from the Albany area as a Lindsay Republican. Running on an antiwar and antimachine platform, he defeated an entrenched incumbent from Albany's Democratic machine. Button served two terms in Congress. Citron, *John V. Lindsay and the Silk Stocking Story*, p. 110.

28. Transcript of WCBS-TV's *New York Forum*, 11 June 1961, p. 2, Series IX, Box 21, Folder 7, JVL Papers, Yale.

29. Lindsay, *Journey into Politics*, pp. 115–116. Fred Siegel, *The Future Once Happened Here: New York, D.C., and L.A., and the Fate of America's Big Cities* (New York: Free Press, 1997).

30. Barry M. Goldwater, with Jack Cassidy, *Goldwater* (New York: Doubleday, 1988), pp. 116–117. On Barry Goldwater, see also Mary C. Brennan, *Turning Right in the Sixties: The Conservative Capture of the GOP* (Chapel Hill: University of North Carolina Press, 1995); Lee Edwards, *Goldwater: The Man Who Made a Revolution* (Washington, D.C.: Regnery Publishing, 1995); and Robert Alan Goldberg, *Barry Goldwater* (New Haven: Yale University Press, 1995). See also Statement of Rep. John V. Lindsay (NY) before the Republican Platform Committee, San Francisco, 9 July 1964, Series X, Box 26, Folder 27, JVL Papers, Yale.

31. Ibid.

32. Edwards, *Goldwater: The Man Who Made a Revolution*, pp. 236, 262.

33. John Lindsay, Speech before the American Society of Magazine Editors, 15 September 1964, Series X, Box 26, Folder 27, JVL Papers, Yale.

34. *NYHT*, 5 November 1964. Transcript of John Lindsay's appearance on *Meet the Press*, 8 November 1964, Series IX, Box 23, Folder 17, JVL Papers, Yale. Barry Goldwater, *Conscience of a Conservative* (Shepardsville, Ky.: Victor Publishing, 1960), p. 73.

35. *NYT*, 17 July 1964.

36. Ibid., 4 August 1964.

37. Robert G. Smith, "Destiny's Tot," *National Review*, 6 October 1964. In a long letter to Goldwater on 21 December 1964, George Romney made clear his reasons for not endorsing him for president. It was clear that Romney's main concerns were the Arizonan's position on civil rights and the issue of "extremism." Romney wrote that Goldwater's "campaign never deviated from the Southern-rural-white orientation" (*NYT*, 29 November 1966).

38. *New York Journal–American*, 8 November 1964. *Business Week*, 7 November 1964. *WSJ*, 5 November 1964. *NYP*, 24 November 1964. Ibid., 8 November 1964. *NYHT*, 8 November 1964. John V. Lindsay, "The New GOP," *The Atlantic*, January 1965.

CHAPTER 2

1. George F. Will, "Looking Back to 1965," *The Public Interest,* Fall 1995.

2. The following account of election night 1965 was based on Peter Maas and Nick Thimmesch, "The Fight for City Hall: Anatomy of a Victory," *New York Herald Tribune Magazine,* 2 January 1966; "Elected," *The New Yorker,* 13 November 1965; and interview of Bob Price by author, 20 January 1997.

3. Jack Newfield, *Bread and Roses Too* (New York: E. P. Dutton, 1971), p. 172.

4. Michael Kramer and Sam Roberts, *I Never Wanted to Be Vice-President of Anything! An Investigative Biography of Nelson Rockefeller* (New York: Basic Books, 1976), p. 293. Interview of Bob Price by author, 21 March 1997.

5. Oliver Pilat, *Lindsay's Campaign: A Behind the Scenes Diary* (Boston: Beacon Press, 1968), pp. 8–9. The Lindsay quote is from *The Lindsay Years,* a videotape produced by the Lindsay Reunion Committee, 1990. *NYT,* 23 December 1973.

6. Remarks by Rep. John V. Lindsay (R-NY) Before the Executives' Club of Chicago, 22 January 1965, Group 592, Series IX, Box 23, Folder 24, JVL Papers, Yale. In a February 1968 speech to the Multnomah County (Oregon) Republican Central Committee's Lincoln Day dinner, Lindsay made a finer distinction, telling his audience that 70 percent of voters were now living in metropolitan areas. See Group 592, Series VII, Box 136, Folder 124, JVL Papers, Yale.

7. Remarks by Rep. John V. Lindsay (R-NY) Before the Executives' Club of Chicago, 22 January 1965.

8. Emanuel Tobier, "Economic Development Strategy for the City," in Lyle C. Fitch and Annmarie Hauck Walsh, eds., *Agenda for a City: Issues Confronting New York* (Beverly Hills, Calif.: Sage Publications, 1970), p. 32. Richard Whalen, *A City Destroying Itself* (New York: William Morrow, 1965), p. 18.

9. "A Tough Day in New York," *Look,* 2 November 1965. *NYHT,* 25 January 1965. Barry Gottehrer, *New York City in Crisis* (New York: David McKay, 1965), pp. v–vi.

10. Richard Kluger, *The Paper: The Life and Death of the New York Herald Tribune* (New York: Alfred A. Knopf, 1986), pp. 699–703. According to Kluger, during the 1965 campaign, "The paper practiced something close to advocacy journalism . . . in forwarding Lindsay's candidacy." As the returns came into the *Herald Tribune's* newsroom on election night, the paper's publisher, Walter Thayer, reportedly declared, "Well, we did it!"

11. Interview of Barry Gottehrer by author, 29 February 1997. Nicholas Pileggi, "Rules of the Power Game," *NY,* 23 December 1968.

12. Gottehrer interview. Kluger, *The Paper,* p. 701.

13. *NYHT,* 26 January 1965. Ibid., 25 January 1965.

14. Ibid., 27 January 1965.

15. Jerry Talmer, "Battle for City Hall: John Lindsay on the Campaign Trail," *NYP,* 29 October 1965. Woody Klein, *Lindsay's Promise: The Dream that Failed* (London: MacMillan, 1970), p. 25. Harvey Rothenberg, *Reminiscing* (Harvey Rothenberg, n.p., n.d.), p. 19. Lindsay's campaign press secretary, Harry O'Donnell, believed that during the campaign Price had either bugged his office or tapped his

phone. Memo from Harry O'Donnell to John Lindsay, 7 November 1965, Box 5, HOD Memos to Mayor Lindsay Folder, Harry O'Donnell Papers.

16. 20 January 1997 Price interview.

17. Interview of Charles Moerdler by author, 26 June 1997.

18. Price interview.

19. Ibid. James M. Perry, "The New Politics: Selling Lindsay Retail," *NY*, 29 April 1968. Interview with Robert Blum by author, 1 April 1997.

20. Kramer and Roberts, *I Never Wanted to Be Vice-President of Anything!* p. 290.

21. *NYT*, 2 March 1965.

22. Maas and Thimmesch, "The Fight for City Hall," p. 6.

23. Martin Shefter, *Political Crisis/Fiscal Crisis: The Collapse and Revival of New York City* (New York: Basic Books, 1987), pp. 60–61.

24. *NYT*, 15 May 1965. August Heckscher, *Alive in the City: Memoir of an Ex-Commissioner* (New York: Charles Scribner's Sons, 1974), p. 126.

25. Maas and Thimmesch, "The Fight for City Hall."

26. Price interview.

27. Rosenthal's chumminess with Price did not sit well with everyone in the *Times* newsroom. See John Corry, *My Times: Adventures in the News Trade* (New York: G. P. Putnam's Sons, 1993), p. 113.

28. Price interview.

29. Ibid.

30. *NYT*, 12 May 1965.

31. Maas and Thimmesch, "The Fight for City Hall," p. 7.

32. Richard Hofstadter, *The Age of Reform: From Bryan to F.D.R.* (New York: Vintage Books, 1955), p. 9.

33. Transcript of speech, "Lindsay Declares Candidacy for Mayor," 13 May 1965, Series IX, Box 23, Folder 22, JVL Papers, Yale.

34. *Life*, 28 May 1965. *NYHT*, 14 May 1965.

35. Memo, Clifton C. Carter to the President, 3 June 1965, Ex PL/ST32, Box 56, WHCF, LBJ Library.

36. *NYT*, 11 June 1965.

37. James Q. Wilson, *The Amateur Democrat: Club Politics in Three Cities* (Chicago: University of Chicago Press, 1962), pp. 10–11.

38. For an examination of the connection between urban reform and the urban machine, see John D. Buenker, *Urban Liberalism and Progressive Reform* (New York: W. W. Norton, 1973), and J. Joseph Huthmacher, *Senator Robert F. Wagner and the Rise of Urban Liberalism* (New York: Atheneum, 1968).

39. Robert Caro, *The Power Broker: Robert Moses and the Fall of New York* (New York: Vintage Books, 1975). The expressway was eventually shelved after Lindsay became mayor.

40. See Jane Jacobs, *The Life and Death of Great American Cities* (New York: Random House, 1961).

41. Schaap quoted in Charles R. Morris, *The Cost of Good Intentions: New York City and the Liberal Experiment, 1960–1975* (New York: W. W. Norton, 1980), p.

22. Murray Kempton, "Can Lindsay Make It? He's the GOP's Best Chance for a Comeback," *The New Republic*, 5 June 1965. Jack Newfield and Paul Du Brul, *The Abuse of Power: The Permanent Government and the Fall of New York* (New York: Viking Press, 1977), p. 142.

42. Interview with Edward N. Costikyan by author, 13 November 1996.

43. The best discussion of postwar intellectual conservatism can be found in George H. Nash, *The Conservative Intellectual Movement in America Since 1945* (New York: Basic Books, 1976). The best discussion of the rise of American political conservatism is in Jerome L. Himmelstein, *To the Right: The Transformation of American Conservatism* (Berkeley: University of California Press, 1990).

44. John B. Judis, *William F. Buckley, Jr.: Patron Saint of the Conservatives* (New York: Touchstone, 1990), p. 239.

45. William F. Buckley Jr., "Mayor Anyone?" *National Review*, 15 June 1965, p. 498. Ibid., *The Unmaking of a Mayor* (New York: Viking Press, 1966), p. 93. Judis, *William F. Buckley, Jr.*, p. 237. The Holy Name Society Communion breakfast was not an unusual setting for controversy. Twelve years before Buckley's speech, Cardinal Spellman invited Senator Joseph McCarthy to speak before the assembled policemen, and afterward the cardinal defended McCarthy's actions in his own remarks to the society's members. See John Cooney, *The American Pope: The Life and Times of Francis Cardinal Spellman* (New York: Times Books, 1984), pp. 218–219.

46. "Remarks to the New York Police Department Holy Name Society, April 4, 1965," reprinted in Buckley, *Unmaking of a Mayor*, pp. 311–314.

47. *NYHT*, 5 April 1965. John Leo analyzed the *Herald Tribune* article for the *National Catholic Reporter* (12 May 1965) and found it "a wretched story." Of the twenty-six direct quotes from Buckley's speech Ferretti used, Leo counted nineteen that were inaccurately quoted. Ferretti had used a dubious journalistic practice of stringing together partial quotes to prove his not too subtle point that Buckley was defending the racist Alabama police to the applause of one quarter of the city's police force. Buckley filed a libel suit against the *Herald Tribune*, which later, after much wrangling, agreed to reprint Leo's article along with a publisher's apology. *NYP*, 6 April 1965. Buckley, *Unmaking of a Mayor*, p. 19.

48. On the term "silent majority," see William Safire, *Safire's New Political Dictionary: The Definitive Guide to the New Language of Politics* (New York: Random House, 1993), p. 708. President Nixon gave his "silent majority" speech in a televised address to the nation on 3 November 1969, in Washington: "If a vocal minority, however fervent its cause, prevails over reason and the will of the majority, the Nation has no future as a free society. . . . And so tonight—to you, the great silent majority of my fellow Americans—I ask for your support." It was Spiro Agnew, however, who had first used the term, in a 9 May 1969 speech: "It is time for America's silent majority to stand up for its rights, and let us remember the American majority includes every minority. America's silent majority is bewildered by irrational protests." Buckley captured the majoritarian sentiment of modern American conservatism in his oft-repeated comment, "I would rather be governed by the first two thousand people in the Boston telephone directory than the faculty of Harvard University."

49. Maas and Thimmesch, "The Fight for City Hall." Judis, *William F. Buckley, Jr.*, p. 237.

50. Memo from William F. Buckley Jr. to Neal Freeman, Jim Buckley, Marvin Liebman, Dan Mahoney, and Kieran O'Doherty, August 19, 1965, Group 576, Box 297, Folder 46, Buckley Papers. Pilat, *Lindsay's Campaign*, pp. 283–284. Press Release, 25 October 1965, Box 310, Folder 148. *New York World–Telegram and Sun*, 28 October 1965.

51. For an account of Buckley's entrance into the 1965 mayoral campaign, see J. Daniel Mahoney, *Actions Speak Louder* (New Rochelle, N.Y.: Arlington House, 1968), pp. 265–270. Barry Goldwater signed off on an endorsement of Buckley, to wit: "Today, in New York, there is only one candidate for Mayor who is running on Republican principles, and who is proud to identify himself with those principles. In my opinion, Bill Buckley is the only true Republican running for Mayor of New York, and I urge all good Republicans to vote for him in November." Buckley never used the endorsement because he feared that if he garnered less than the 800,000 votes Goldwater received in the city in 1964, it would be looked upon as a further weakening of the conservative movement. See Buckley, *The Unmaking of a Mayor*, pp. 277–278.

52. Pilat, *Lindsay's Campaign*, p. 95. *DN*, 26 June 1965. "Statement by William F. Buckley Jr., Announcing His Candidacy for Mayor of New York, June 24, 1965," *National Review*, 13 July 1965.

53. Conservative Party Chairman J. Daniel Mahoney admitted to the Irish dominance of the party, writing that it "cast a green glow over" the Conservatives. As for the all-Irish Buckley ticket, Mahoney wrote that the "whole point of our campaign was to talk some sense on the issues which had been ritualized out of all contact with reality in New York City politics. It would hardly accord with that approach to break up our ticket in the name of ethnic balance—the hoariest of the rituals of Gotham politics" (Mahoney, *Actions Speak Louder*, p. 283).

54. "Buckley for Mayor" pamphlet, Local History Collection, Box 030016, Folder 16, Local Residents Series, Maxwell K. Nelson Sub-Series, La Guardia and Wagner Archives.

55. Buckley, *Unmaking of a Mayor*, pp. 222–223.

56. *NYP*, 3 November 1965.

57. Buckley, *Unmaking of a Mayor*, pp. 120–121, 130. Judis, *William F. Buckley, Jr.*, p. 250.

58. *NYP*, 16 May 1965. Although Rockefeller's $500,000 was referred to as a "loan" in the press, it is pretty clear that this was a straight campaign donation.

59. Lindsay quoted in Kramer and Roberts, *I Never Wanted to Be Vice-President of Anything!* p. 293. Price interview. Interview of Bob Douglass by author, 22 April 1997. Interview of Ed Kresky by author, 16 April 1997.

60. Rockefeller and Morrow quoted in Kramer and Roberts, *I Never Wanted to Be Vice-President of Anything!* p. 294. Joseph E. Persico, *The Imperial Rockefeller: A Biography of Nelson A. Rockefeller* (New York: Simon & Schuster, 1982), p. 216. Price interview. Emmet John Hughes, "An Untold Tale," *Newsweek*, 12 July 1965. Maas

and Thimmesch, "The Fight for City Hall." Pilat, *Lindsay's Campaign*, p. 116. Lindsay softened his attitude toward Rockefeller somewhat in an 11 July 1965 appearance on *Meet the Press* (as reported in the *NYT*, 12 July 1965). The candidate said he would definitely support Rockefeller if he chose to run for reelection as governor in 1966. When asked about Rockefeller's financial assistance, which he had previously denied receiving, Lindsay said, "They've promised to raise a substantial amount." Lindsay claimed that no specific dollar amount was agreed to, saying, "Apparently from news reports . . . they are prepared to. I hope they are—he and his friends."

61. Chris McNickle, *To Be Mayor of New York: Ethnic Politics in the City* (New York: Columbia University Press, 1993), p. 209. *NYT*, 26 January 1966. For an excellent discussion of the technical aspects of the Lindsay campaign, see Elisabeth Griffith, "John Lindsay: Candidate and Campaign, 1965— An Analysis of the New Politics" (Senior Thesis, Wellesley College, 1966), pp. 72–80.

62. Nat Hentoff, "Profiles—The Mayor: I," *The New Yorker*, 7 October 1967.

63. Alexander M. Bickel, "Liberals and John Lindsay," *The New Republic*, 3 July 1965. James Wechsler, "Man vs. Myths," *NYP*, 16 September 1965.

64. Pilat, *Lindsay's Campaign*. Statement of John V. Lindsay (R-NY) Before the New York County Lawyers Association, 20 May 1965: Establishment of Joint Police-Civilian Review Board, Box 26, Folder 25, JVL Papers, Yale.

65. The following discussion of the background of Lindsay's Oakland speech comes from James R. Carberry, "Getting Out Front on Vietnam or How the Homeliest Girl in Michigan Saved My Job," unpublished manuscript, in author's possession.

66. John V. Lindsay, "North vs. South, East vs. West—A Call for New Directions in Vietnam," Oakland University Commencement Address, Rochester, Michigan, June 1965, and "Congressman John V. Lindsay's Position on Viet Nam," both in Box 23, Folder 22, JVL Papers, Yale.

67. Pilat, *Lindsay's Campaign*, p. 93. *NYT*, 22 October 1965. Buckley for Mayor Press Release, 21 October 1965, Box 310, Folder 148, Buckley Papers. *New York World–Telegram and Sun*, 18 October 1965. Clifton de Berry, the Socialist Workers Party candidate for mayor in 1965, argued that the war was a local issue that took money away from urgent local public needs such as housing, education, air pollution, and unemployment. See *NYHT*, 24 October 1965. Lindsay, the urban reformer, was relatively quiet on this issue in 1965. Four years later, though, he would run for reelection using the exact same arguments as de Berry.

68. Results of Rep. John V. Lindsay's 1965 Legislative Questionnaire, Group 592, Series IX, Box 23, Folder 21, JVL Papers, Yale.

69. John V. Lindsay, *Journey into Politics: Some Informal Observations* (New York: Dodd, Mead, 1967), p. 139. Pilat, *Lindsay's Campaign*, p. 103. Lindsay Election District Handbook, Official Manual, Committee to Elect John Lindsay Mayor of the City of New York, 1965, JVL Papers, Yale. In his successful 1993 mayoral campaign, Rudolph Giuliani ran a similar "fusion" campaign in the mold of La Guardia's, downplaying his Republican affiliation and choosing two Democrats as running

mates; one of them was Herman Badillo, who had been elected Bronx borough president in 1965 as a reform Democrat. For a discussion of the role of fusion and reform movements in New York City politics, see Shefter, *Political Crisis/Fiscal Crisis*, pp. 21–29, and Kenneth Finegold, *Experts and Politicians: Reform Challenges to Machine Politics in New York, Cleveland, and Chicago* (Princeton: Princeton University Press, 1995).

70. Moerdler interview.

71. Shefter, *Political Crisis/Fiscal Crisis*, pp. 21–29, 41–42.

72. Interview of Meade Esposito by Chris McNickle, 16 October 1988.

73. Price interview.

74. Mollen would go on to some minor fame as the head of the Mollen Commission, which investigated police corruption in the early 1990s.

75. Price, who has remained friendly with Mollen, denies ever saying this about the candidate. Price quoted in Pilat, *Lindsay's Campaign*, p. 138. Moerdler interview.

76. Costikyan interview. Mary Perot Nichols, "Do They Love Him Now as They Did in May?" *VV*, 14 October 1965.

77. Memorandum to the Vice President from William Connell, 24 September 1965, Ex PL/ST32, Box 56, WHCF, LBJ Library.

78. Pilat, *Lindsay's Campaign*, p. 241. Lindsay campaign flyer in Mayoralty Campaign File, Box 110715, Campaign Literature Folder, Office of the Mayor JVL Papers, NYCMA.

79. David Murray, "How the Campaign Shapes Up," *NYP*, 16 September 1965. *NYT*, 11 September 1965.

80. Maas and Thimmesch, "The Fight for City Hall." Memorandum from John Deardourff to John V. Lindsay, Robert Price, George Lindsay, and Harry O'Donnell, 2 October 1965, in Griffith, "John Lindsay: Candidate and Campaign," Appendix 3. Nichols, "Do They Love Him Now As They Did in May?"

81. Theodore White quoted in Judis, *William F. Buckley, Jr.*, p. 249.

82. Richard Armstrong, "Second Man at City Hall," *NY*, 26 December 1965.

83. Pilat, *Lindsay's Campaign*, pp. 96–97.

84. Ibid., p. 99.

85. Interview of Sid Davidoff by author, 9 April 1997. In some ways, Lindsay's Raiders were the direct descendants of La Guardia's Ghibboni, a group of young Italian street toughs headed by Vito Marcantonio, who protected La Guardia and battled Tammany Hall toughs during the "Little Flower's" campaigns. See Thomas Kessner, *Fiorello La Guardia and the Making of Modern New York* (New York: Penguin Books, 1989), p. 140.

86. Pilat, *Lindsay's Campaign*, pp. 184, 268. Interview of Jim Carberry by author, 20 May 1997.

87. *NYP*, 15 October 1965.

88. In an interview with the *Herald Tribune*, Buckley discussed the anti-utopian ideas of the contemporary philosopher Eric Vogelin, who was popular among conservatives, in relation to New York politics: "There is a modern fallacy that government can save New York. Vogelin points out that the principal heresy of the age is

the attempt to take eschaton [the religious concept of man's final state] and secularize it. Attempts to immunize it have failed" (*NYHT*, 3 October 1965).

89. Klein was working on the side for the Lindsay campaign and helping draft position papers and working on speeches. In return, Charles Moerdler and Bob Price would feed him tips. Klein became Lindsay's first press secretary at City Hall, and later wrote a book about the Lindsay mayoralty.

90. Klein, *Lindsay's Promise*, pp. 10–14. *New York World–Telegram and Sun*, 9 September 1965. *NYT*, 10 September 1965. Davidoff interview.

91. *NYP*, 15 October 1965.

92. Pilat, *Lindsay's Campaign*, p. 289. *NYHT*, 16 October 1965. Transcript of the *Martha Dean Show*, October 7, 1965, Box 309, Folder 145, Buckley Papers.

93. Transcript of WINS Radio News Conference, 31 October 1965, quoted in Buckley, *Unmaking of a Mayor*, pp. 149–150. Arnold Rampersad, *Jackie Robinson: A Biography* (New York: Alfred A. Knopf, 1997), p. 405. Pilat, *Lindsay's Campaign*, p. 303. Letter to Bruce Felknor, Executive Director of Fair Campaign Practices Committee, 20 October 1965, Box 310, Folder 148, Buckley Papers. Lindsay Campaign Press Release, 25 October 1965, Container 103, New York State Liberal Party Papers, New York Public Library.

94. Pilat, *Lindsay's Campaign*, p. 302. Jerry Talmer, "Battle For City Hall: John Lindsay—The Rows with His Own Party," *NYP*, 28 October 1965. Buckley, *Unmaking of a Mayor*, p. 158. Near the end of the campaign, a befuddled Beame, trying to shore up the Jewish vote that was slipping away from him, tried to one-up Lindsay in political smearing. Beame, calling Buckley the "clown prince of politics," stated that behind Buckley's "warped humor and twisted wit are sinister and evil philosophies." While appealing to man's basest instincts, Buckley "campaigned on a program of fear and prejudice, of hatred of neighbor for neighbor." Buckley's program, according to Beame, was "alien and repugnant to the American way of life" (*NYT*, 30 October 1965). Beame's heart was not really in these last-minute attacks, though, as evidenced by the fact that in a whispered aside during one of their last debates, Beame tried to apologize to Buckley for using the term "concentration camp" (Buckley, *Unmaking of a Mayor*, p. 165).

95. *NYP*, 21 October 1965. *NYT*, 16 October 1965. Buckley, *Unmaking of a Mayor*, pp. 132–135. Lindsay was not unique among New York's reform politicians in helping fan the city's racial and ethnic flames in order to get elected. Of La Guardia, Robert Moses had written, "In exploiting racial and religious prejudices La Guardia could run circles around the bosses he despised and derided. When it came to raking the ashes of Old World hates, warming ancient grudges, waving the bloody shirt, tuning the ear to ancestral voices, he could easily outdemagogue the demagogues" (Moses, *La Guardia: A Salute and a Memoir* [New York: Simon & Schuster, 1957], p. 37).

96. Given that Jim Buckley and David Lindsay were good friends and that Bill and John overlapped for two years at Yale, there is no reason to doubt Buckley's story. Admitting to such an incident would have proved embarrassing for Lindsay.

97. Buckley, *Unmaking of a Mayor*, pp. 145–148.

98. Ibid., pp. 250–252. Judis, *William F. Buckley, Jr.,* p. 250.

99. "Irish New Yorkers and Lindsay," Memo from John Parker to Charles Moerdler and Robert Price, Series VI, Box 93, Folder 101, JVL Papers, Yale.

100. Interview with Werner Kramarsky by author, 23 April 1997.

101. *NYT,* 25 October 1965. A transcript of Saron's remarks is reprinted in Buckley, *Unmaking of a Mayor,* pp. 122–129. Farley is quoted in *NYT,* 28 October 1965.

102. *New York World–Telegram and Sun,* 27 October 1965. Crime statistics from Kenneth Jackson, ed., *The Encyclopedia of New York City* (New Haven: Yale University Press, 1995), p. 298.

103. *NYHT,* 11 October 1965. *NYT,* 12 October 1965. In the previous year's presidential election, Lindsay's Republican bête noire, Barry Goldwater, had made "crime in the streets" a major campaign issue, but to no avail. See Robert Alan Goldberg, *Barry Goldwater* (New Haven: Yale University Press, 1995), pp. 218, 229.

104. Jimmy Breslin and Dick Schaap, "The Lonely Crimes," *NYHT,* 25–29 October 1965. Jimmy Breslin had a similar experience in 1991 while he was covering the Crown Heights race riot. While reporting on the riot, Breslin was dragged from a taxi and beaten by a crowd of blacks shouting antiwhite slurs.

105. Talmer, "Battle for City Hall." Lindsay Campaign White Paper on Crime and Safety, Series VI, Box 91, Folder 76, JVL Papers, Yale.

106. Liberal Party advertisement is quoted in Daniel P. Moynihan's Foreword to David W. Abbott, Louis H. Gold, and Edward T. Rogowsky, *Police, Politics, and Race: The New York City Referendum on Civilian Review* (Cambridge, MA: American Jewish Committee and MIT, 1969), p. 3. Lindsay campaign flyer, in Mayoralty Campaign File, Box 110715, Campaign Literature Folder, JVL Papers, NYCMA. *NYT,* 13 October 1965.

107. *National Review,* 16 June 1964, p. 479. Breslin and Schaap, *NYHT,* 29 October 1965.

108. *NYT,* 10 September 1965. Yale Kamisar, "When the Cops Were Not 'Handcuffed,' " *NY,* 7 November 1965. Edward C. Banfield, *The Unheavenly City Revisited* (Boston: Little, Brown, 1970), pp. 74–75.

109. *NYHT,* 21 October 1965. *NYP,* 5 October 1965. *NYHT,* 24 October 1965. *NYT,* 23 October 1965. *NYP,* 29 October 1965. Pilat, *Lindsay's Campaign,* p. 301.

110. Corry, *My Times,* pp. 100–118.

111. For endorsements, see *NYP,* 15 September 1965; *NYT,* 14 October 1965; *NYHT,* 18 October 1965; *New York World-Telegram and Sun,* 19 October 1965; *DN,* 22 October 1965; *AN,* 23 October 1965; *VV,* 28 October 1965. Following Buckley's meeting at the *Times* a reporter asked what he would do first if elected. Buckley quipped, "Hang a net outside the window of the [*Times*] editor." Later he added that he should have added the recommendation of "a commission to investigate the desirability of suspending such a net" (Buckley, *Unmaking of a Mayor* pp. 301–303).

112. Noel E. Parmentel Jr., "John V. Lindsay: Less than Meets the Eye," *Esquire,* October 1965. *New York World-Telegram and Sun,* 14 October 1965. *NYHT,* 24 October 1965. *VV,* 28 October 1965.

113. Lindsay flyer reprinted in Buckley, *Unmaking of a Mayor*.

114. Michael Harrington, "When Ed Koch Was Still a Liberal," *Dissent*, Fall 1987. Edward I. Koch with Daniel Paisner, *Citizen Koch: An Autobiography* (New York: St. Martin's Press, 1992), pp. 85–90. *NYT*, 2 November 1965. Edward I. Koch with William Rauch, *Politics* (New York: Simon & Schuster, 1985), p. 69.

115. *NYT*, 19 October 1965. Maas and Thimmesch, "The Fight for City Hall."

116. *DN*, 27 October 1965. *NYT*, 28 October 1965. Maas and Thimmesch, "The Fight for City Hall." Interview of Abraham Beame by author, 7 January 1997.

117. *NYT*, 30 October 1965. *NYHT*, 31 October 1965. Beame interview.

118. *NYHT*, 2 November 1965. Maas and Thimmesch, "The Fight for City Hall." Costikyan interview. *NYHT*, 29 October 1965. Beame interview. Jack Newfield, *Robert Kennedy: A Memoir* (New York: New American Library, 1969), p. 150.

119. Newfield reports that Kennedy was upset that many "shadowy figures with underworld connections" were seen around Beame headquarters, including Kennedy's nemesis, Roy Cohn. Beame's campaign manager, Edward Costikyan, confirms this. He says that after Beame won the primary, the campaign office was inundated with shady characters and machine hacks. "Every sharpie in town wanted to be there," Costikyan remembered. Roy Cohn even planted himself in Costikyan's office. Costikyan had to ask Mario Biaggi, a decorated ex-policeman and later a congressman, to clear out the campaign headquarters. See Newfield, *Robert Kennedy*, pp. 149–150, and Costikyan interview.

120. Pilat, *Lindsay's Campaign*, pp. 235, 284. John Lindsay, "Can New York Be Saved?" *Saturday Evening Post*, 9 October 1965. Lindsay Campaign News Release, Excerpts from Remarks by Congressman John V. Lindsay, Candidate for Mayor, at the United Council of Harlem Organizations, June 26, 1965, Series IX, Box 23, Folder 20, JVL Papers, Yale.

121. Lindsay Campaign News Release, 22 October 1965, Series VI, Box 104, Folder 251, JVL Papers, Yale. "Dear Resident of Harlem," John Lindsay for Mayor, 28 October 1965. Griffith, "John Lindsay: Candidate and Campaign," p. 104. *NYT*, 21 September 1964.

122. Pilat, *Lindsay's Campaign*, p. 329. Maas and Thimmesch, "The Fight for City Hall."

123. The remaining 4 percent of the 1965 vote (115,420) was split among Vito Battista, of the United Taxpayer Party; Clifton de Berry, of the Socialist Workers Party; and Eric Hass, of the Socialist Labor Party. The high 1965 turnout was not out of the ordinary in postwar New York. In Robert Wagner's three mayoral campaigns from 1953 to 1961, turnout was regularly between 2.2 and 2.5 million. The turnout for William O'Dwyer's 1949 reelection was higher than in 1965, as was the 1950 special election after O'Dwyer resigned. In that contest, the lackluster Vincent Impellitteri, Ferdinand Pecora, and Edward Corsi managed to draw nearly 2.7 million voters to the polls. Turnout throughout the 1970s and 1980s was low but picked up during the Dinkins-Giuliani campaigns of 1989 and 1993, which brought out 59.6 and 57.5 percent of voters, respectively.

124. Perry, "The New Politics." Interview with David Garth by author, 4 June 1997. Richard Aurelio Oral History, CUOHA.

125. Joseph Alsop, "Thank You, Mr. Buckley," *NYHT,* 8 November 1965. Statement sent to the press by William Buckley Jr. on 3 November 1965, reprinted in *National Review,* 16 November 1965. Memo to William F. Buckley, Dan Mahoney, and Bill Rusher from Neil McCaffrey, 9 December 1965, Box 293, Folder 5, Buckley Papers.

126. Kevin Phillips, *The Emerging Republican Majority* (Garden City, N.Y.: Anchor Books, 1970), p. 161.

127. *Newsweek,* 15 November 1965. Louis Harris, "New Yorkers Analyze Lindsay," *Washington Post,* 8 November 1965. Jonathan Rieder, *Canarsie: The Jews and Italians of Brooklyn Against Liberalism* (Cambridge, MA: Harvard University Press, 1985), p. 128.

128. Transcript of *Meet the Press,* 17 October 1965, Campaign Material Series, 1965, Box 070005, Folder 1, Abraham D. Beame Collection, La Guardia and Wagner Archives, La Guardia Community College. Pilat, *Lindsay's Campaign,* p. 185. Rockefeller quoted in Kramer and Roberts, *I Never Wanted to Be Vice-President of Anything!* p. 288.

129. F. Scott Fitzgerald, *This Side of Paradise* (New York: Charles Scribner and Sons, 1920), p. 165. Buckley, *Unmaking of a Mayor,* p. 284. Buckley later was ashamed of having made the comment about Beame's education. He also spoke of Mrs. Beame's "natural dignity and unmanicured grace," which he would have "proudly proffered Her Majesty."

130. *New York Journal–American,* 29 October 1965.

131. Lindsay, "Can New York Be Saved?" Ibid., "The Future of the American City," *Saturday Review,* 8 January 1966.

132. Talmer, "Battle for City Hall." Pilat, *Lindsay's Campaign,* p. 250. "A Tough Day in New York," *Look,* 2 November 1965. *Business Week,* 6 November 1965. *WSJ,* 4 November 1965. *Newsweek,* 15 November 1965.

133. Arthur Mann, *La Guardia Comes to Power, 1933* (Philadelphia: J. B. Lippincott, 1965), pp. 153–154.

CHAPTER 3

1. "New York," *The Atlantic Monthly,* June 1967.

2. Nick Thimmesch, *The Condition of Republicanism* (New York: W. W. Norton, 1968), p. 221. Noel E. Parmentel Jr., "John V. Lindsay: Less Than Meets the Eye," *Esquire,* October 1965.

3. Parmentel, "John V. Lindsay."

4. Martin Shefter, *Political Crisis/Fiscal Crisis: The Collapse and Revival of New York City* (New York: Basic Books, 1987), pp. 42–56.

5. John V. Lindsay, "The Future of the American City," *Saturday Review,* 8 January 1966. *NYT,* 2 January 1966.

6. Roosevelt quoted in Kenneth Finegold, *Experts and Politicians: Reform Challenges to Machine Politics in New York, Cleveland, and Chicago* (Princeton: Princeton University Press, 1995), p. 25.

7. Barbara Carter, *The Road to City Hall: How John V. Lindsay Became Mayor* (Englewood Cliffs, N.J.: Prentice Hall, 1967), p. 190.

8. *NYT,* 2 January 1966. Steven R. Weisman, "Why Lindsay Failed as Mayor," *The Washington Monthly,* April 1972.

9. Martin Shefter clarified Lindsay's rationale somewhat when he noted, in *Political Crisis/Fiscal Crisis: The Collapse and Revival of New York City,* that "many of these positions were in the city's antipoverty programs, and had been placed in the exempt class because their very purpose would have been defeated if they had been classified as ordinary civil service positions. Had these jobs been awarded to candidates who scored highest on competitive written examinations, there would have been no guarantee of distribution [of jobs] to the intended clientele of the antipoverty programs—namely blacks and Puerto Ricans" (p. 90).

10. Woody Klein, *Lindsay's Promise: The Dream That Failed* (London: Macmillan, 1970), p. 103. Interview of Robert Sweet by author, 22 April 1997.

11. Carter, *Road to City Hall,* p. 35. Oral History of Robert F. Wagner, p. 353, CUOHA. *NYT,* 15 November 1966.

12. Interview of Louis Craco by author, 14 May 1997.

13. For a history of the Transport Workers Union, see Joshua B. Freeman, *In Transit: The Transit Workers' Union in New York City, 1933–1966* (New York: Oxford University Press, 1989).

14. Ibid., p. 334. Ken Auletta, *The Streets Were Paved with Gold* (New York: Random House, 1975), p. 48. For the "Little Wagner Act," see Mark Maier, *City Unions: Managing Discontent in New York City* (New Brunswick, N.J.: Rutgers University Press, 1987), pp. 48–49.

15. Raymond Horton, *Municipal Labor Relations in New York City: Lessons of the Lindsay-Wagner Years* (New York: Praeger, 1973), pp. 36, 51.

16. Thomas R. Brooks, "Lindsay, Quill and the Transit Strike," *Commentary,* March 1966. *NYT,* 6 January 1966.

17. Maier, *City Unions,* pp. 41–43. Interview of Theodore Kheel by author, 9 April 1997.

18. Charles Morris, *The Cost of Good Intentions: New York City and the Liberal Experiment, 1960–1975* (New York: W. W. Norton, 1980), p. 86.

19. Interview of Bob Price by author, 21 March 1997.

20. Horton, *Municipal Labor Relations in New York City,* pp. 82–83. Michael Marmo, *More Profile Than Courage: The New York City Transit Strike of 1966* (Albany, N.Y.: State University of New York Press, 1990), p. 104. Interview of Alton Marshall by author, 27 March 1997.

21. Kheel interview. Price interview. *NYT,* 13 December 1965.

22. Carter, *Road to City Hall,* p. 163. In an otherwise uneventful January 1966 State of the State address, Nelson Rockefeller was able to move his audience of state legislators only once. When Rockefeller called the mayor of New York "Lindsley,"

the legislators roared in laughter. It was the only bit of emotion—positive or negative—that Rockefeller was able to elicit.

23. *NYT,* 4 December 1965. Brooks, "Lindsay, Quill and the Transit Strike." Marmo, *More Profile Than Courage,* p. 53. Kheel interview.

24. Memo from the chairman of the Council of Economic Advisers to the President, 8 December 1965, Gen LA 6/Transit, Box 30, WHCF, LBJ Library.

25. Kheel interview. *NYT,* 23 December 1973. Price interview. Klein, *Lindsay's Promise,* p. 41.

26. Ibid., p. 48.

27. *NYHT,* 2 December 1965. *NYP,* 2 January 1966. *NYT,* 1 January 1966.

28. "Statement by Lindsay on Transit Strike," *NYT,* 2 January 1966.

29. *NYT,* 3 January 1966.

30. *New York Journal–American*, 3 January 1966. *NYHT,* 4 January 1966. *NYP,* 3 January 1966. *NYT,* 5 January 1966.

31. "Mediator," *The New Yorker,* 22 January 1966. It was reported then, and has since become folklore, that before being sentenced to jail, Quill said belligerently, "The judge can drop dead in his black robes." The headline for the *Times* editorial that day was "The Judge Can Drop Dead!" The comment was in keeping with Quill's tone and personality, but he was not really telling the judge to drop dead. His declaration continues, ". . . and we would not call off the strike. We will defy the injunction and go to jail" (*NYT,* 5 January 1966).

32. Memo, Joseph Califano to the President, 5 January 1966, Gen LA6/Transit, Box 30, WHCF, LBJ Library. Memo, W. Willard Wirtz to the President, 5 January 1966, Gen LA6/Transit, Box 30, WHCF, LBJ Library.

33. Wirtz Memo, 6 January 1966. Oral History of Robert F. Wagner, p. 566, CUOHA.

34. Nora Ephron, "A Roadblock for Romance," *NYP,* 6 January 1966.

35. Price and Kheel interviews. The meeting between Price and Quill eventually leaked out to the press. Since Price's hospital visit went against Lindsay's desire to avoid behind-the-scenes intrigues, the administration tried to keep the meeting quiet or at least disguise the nature of the meeting. At first Price issued a "no comment" to a reporter's question about whether he had visited Quill at the hospital. Feinsinger claimed he only heard about the meeting after it occurred. Later, Price issued the following comment to the *Times*: "I deny that any deal was made or attempted or that the union reneged on any deal. Mayor Lindsay had indicated as early as December that the way to resolve this dispute was through mediation, which would set an important pattern for future city negotiations." The *Journal–American* related that Price's visit was designed to let Quill know that Lindsay had no desire to see the labor leader return to prison after his recovery. See "A Hospital Visit from Mike Quill: The Full Story," *New York Journal–American,* 22 January 1966. *NYT,* 18 January 1966.

36. James Wechsler, "Quill Turned Down Freedom," *NYP,* 12 January 1966. A. H. Raskin, "Politics Up-ends the Bargaining Table," in Sam Zagoria, ed., *Public Workers and Public Unions* (Engelwood Cliffs, N.J.: Prentice-Hall, 1972), p. 130.

37. Brooks, "Lindsay, Quill and the Transit Strike." Gilhooley and Price quoted in Auletta, *Streets Were Paved with Gold*, pp. 61–62. Price interview.

38. Harvey Rothenberg, *Reminiscing* (Harvey Rothenberg, n.p., n.d.), pp. 26–27.

39. Klein, *Lindsay's Promise*, p. 71.

40. Lindsay's speech reprinted in the *NYHT*, 11 January 1966. *NYT*, 12 January 1966. Klein, *Lindsay's Promise*, p. 319.

41. *NYT*, 13 January 1966.

42. Kheel interview.

43. *NYT*, 13 January 1966.

44. Ibid., 14 January 1966.

45. Ibid., 1 March 1966.

46. Freeman, *In Transit*, p. 335. Price interview. *NYP*, 22 December 1973. During the eleven-day transit strike in 1980, Mayor Ed Koch took a belligerent stand toward the TWU reminiscent of Lindsay's in 1966. Koch's feistiness won him the admiration of many New Yorkers fed up with the union and inconvenienced by the strike. The major difference is that Koch could afford to take a harsh public stance against the union because the city was not a party to the negotiations. The Metropolitan Transportation Authority (MTA), a state authority, was in charge of dealing with the TWU. The MTA was not created until 1968, so the 1966 negotiations fell upon the mayor and the city's Transit Authority.

47. For Feinsinger's reaction to Lindsay's use of his report, see "Mediator." Brooks, "Lindsay, Quill and the Transit Strike."

48. Wire from W. Willard Wirtz to Mayor John V. Lindsay, 14 January 1966, Gen LA6/Transit, Box 30, WHCF, LBJ Library. *NYP*, 16 January 1966.

49. Memo from Gardner Ackley to the President, 15 January 1966, Gen LA6/Transit, Box 30, WHCF, LBJ Library. *NYT*, 14 January 1966.

50. "Mediator Tells the Inside Story," *New York World-Telegram*, 17 January 1966. Richard J. Whalen, " 'This Lindsay' Takes on that City," *Fortune*, June 1966. Klein, *Lindsay's Promise*, p. 85.

51. *NYP*, 26 January 1966.

52. The classic, though extremely critical, treatment of Moses' career is Robert Caro, *The Power Broker: Robert Moses and the Fall of New York* (New York: Vintage Books, 1975). For essays critical of Moses' legacy see Marshall Berman, *All That Is Solid Melts Into Air: The Experience of Modernity* (New York: Penguin Books, 1988), pp. 290–312, and Gore Vidal, "What Robert Moses Did to New York City," *United States, Essays, 1951–1991* (New York, Random House, 1993), pp. 773–786. For a more balanced view of the Moses legacy, see Kenneth T. Jackson, "Robert Moses and the Planned Environment: A Re-Evaluation," in Joann P. Krieg, ed., *Robert Moses: Single Minded Genius* (Interlaken, N.Y.: Heart of the Lakes Publishing, 1989).

53. *NYT*, 3 January 1966. Price interview.

54. Caro, *Power Broker*, pp. 1118, 1121. "Lindsay Campaign White Paper on Parks and Recreation," 8 Oct. 1965, Series VI, Box 91, Folder 86, JVL Papers, Yale. Price interview.

55. Price interview.

56. *NYT,* 21 January 1966. *NYT,* 18 February 1966.

57. The description of Lindsay's battle with Moses in Albany is told in Caro, *Power Broker,* pp. 1117–1131. Dick Netzer, who was a member of Lindsay's transportation task force and is now a professor of public policy at New York University, took issue with Caro's description of the controversy in his review of *The Power Broker.* Netzer charged that Caro relied on the self-serving recollections of two unnamed Lindsay aides, Palmer and Rosen, who, Netzer claims, were themselves most responsible for the failure of Lindsay's bill. Still, Netzer described the whole episode as a "humiliating debacle" (Dick Netzer, "The Man and the City," review of Robert Caro, *The Power Broker, The New Republic,* 7 September 1974, and interview of Dick Netzer by author, 1 February 1997). Price interview.

58. Caro, *Power Broker,* pp. 1124–1128.

59. Ibid., pp. 1124–1125. *NYT,* 24 May 1966.

60. Caro, *Power Broker,* pp. 1123–1124. *NYT,* 12 July 1966.

61. Caro, *Power Broker,* pp. 1071–1078.

62. Interview of Ed Kresky, April 1997. Because of Ronan's power, the MTA was jokingly referred to as the "Holy Ronan Empire."

63. Caro, *Power Broker,* pp. 1132–1144.

64. *NYT,* 22 December 1965. Lindsay's fireside chat reprinted in *NYT,* 20 January 1966.

65. *NYHT,* 23 August 1965. *NYT,* 25 August 1965. Transcript of *Meet the Press,* 17 October 1965, Abraham D. Beame Collection, Campaign Material Series, 1965, Box 070005, Folder 1, NYCMA. Interview of Edward N. Costikyan by author, 13 November 1996.

66. *NYT,* 4 March 1966. Klein, *Lindsay's Promise,* p. 147.

67. *NYT,* 23 August 1966. Jack Newfield, "Lindsay: A Year Later," in Jack Newfield, *Bread and Roses Too* (New York: E. P. Dutton, 1971), p. 177.

68. *NYT,* 4 March 1966.

69. For a description of home rule, see Wallace S. Sayre and Herbert Kaufman, *Governing New York City: Politics in the Metropolis* (New York: W. W. Norton, 1965), pp. 584–586.

70. *NYT,* 5 March 1966. *NYP,* 4 March 1966.

71. *NYT,* 25 March 1966.

72. Klein, *Lindsay's Promise,* p. 148. John V. Lindsay, *Journey into Politics: Some Informal Observations* (New York: Dodd, Mead, 1967), p. 142.

73. *NYT,* 3 and 5 April 1966.

74. *NYT,* 24 May 1966.

75. Interview of Murray Drabking by author, 29 May 1997. *NYT,* 17 June 1966.

76. On the history of the nickel fare, see Clifton Hood, *722 Miles: The Building of the Subways and How They Transformed New York* (Baltimore: Johns Hopkins University Press, 1993), pp. 214–239.

77. Nat Hentoff, "Profiles: The Mayor—II," *The New Yorker,* 14 October 1967. Price interview.

78. Richard Reeves, "A *Great* Mayor, *That* Bum?" *NYTM*, 1 January 1967.

79. *NYP*, 3 January 1966. Lindsay, "The Future of the American City." Whalen, " 'This Lindsay' Takes On That City." "What's Ahead for New York City: Interview with Mayor Lindsay," *U.S. News & World Report*, 10 April 1967.

80. Interview of Robert Blum by author, 17 April 1997.

81. Nat Hentoff, "The Mayor—I," *The New Yorker*, 7 October 1967, pp. 59–60. Ibid., "The Mayor—II," p. 68. Interview of Donald Elliott by author, 30 April 1997.

82. Interview of Mitchell Sviridoff by author, 22 October 1997. Sviridoff Report quoted in "The Mayor's Task Force on Reorganization of New York City Government," December 1966, pp. 33–34.

83. "Mayor's Task Force," pp. 1–5, 12.

84. Craco interview. "Mayor's Task Force."

85. Sviridoff interview.

86. Lindsay, "The Future of the American City." Blum interview. *VV*, 18 June 1966. *NYT*, 24 June 1966. Carol Greitzer, "A Politico Looks at JVL: What Went Wrong?" *VV*, 8 September 1966.

87. Shefter, *Political Crisis/Fiscal Crisis*, p. 89. Letter from Louis Winnick to McGeorge Bundy, 17 March 1967, Ford Foundation Archives. On the role of systems analysis in Lindsay's first term, see Morris, *Cost of Good Intentions*, pp. 48–55. On the Rand Institute's involvement in the Lindsay administration, see Ford Foundation, "R and D & NYC = C: Assessment of a Grant to the New York City-Rand Corporation," November 1971, Folder 001989, Ford Foundation Archives.

88. Interview of Thomas Hoving by author, 21 May 1997. Bernard Weinraub, "A Happening Called Hoving," *NYTM*, 10 July 1966.

89. Robert A. M. Stern, Thomas Mellins, and David Fishman, *New York 1960: Architecture and Urbanism Between the Second World War and the Bicentennial* (New York: Monacelli Press, 1995), pp. 773–781. Hoving interview.

90. Interview of Charles Moerdler by author, 26 June 1997.

91. Lindsay quoted in Hentoff, "The Mayor—I," p. 60. Costello quoted in *NYT*, 28 February 1966. Klein, *Lindsay's Promise*, p. 115.

92. Jack Newfield and Paul Du Brul, *The Abuse of Power: The Permanent Government and the Fall of New York* (New York: Viking Press, 1977), p. 137.

93. Weisman, "Why Lindsay Failed as Mayor." Hentoff, "The Mayor—I."

94. Klein, *Lindsay's Promise*, p. 129. *DN*, 3 March 1966.

95. Klein, *Lindsay's Promise*, pp. 62, 105. Interview of Bob Laird by author, 7 May 1997.

96. *NYT*, 21 January 1966.

97. Warren Moscow, *The Last of the Big-time Bosses: The Life and Times of Carmine De Sapio and the Rise and Fall of Tammany Hall* (New York: Stein & Day, 1971), pp. 201–204. Walter Goodman, *A Percentage of the Take* (New York: Farrar Straus and Giroux, 1971). *NYT*, 19 December 1967.

98. August Heckscher, *Alive in the City: Memoir of an Ex-Commissioner* (New York: Charles Scribner's Sons, 1974), p. 103. *NYT*, 20 December 1967. Richard Reeves, "The Impossible Takes a Little Longer," *NYTM*, 28 January 1968.

99. Nat Hentoff, *A Political Life: The Education of John V. Lindsay* (New York: Alfred A. Knopf, 1969), p. 29. Former Lindsay aides have also commented on the fact that Lindsay always reached for the check when dining with aides and subordinates, a rare trait in politics. It is also a more amazing fact considering that Lindsay was not terribly wealthy. The security man Pat Vecchio, who spent eight years with the mayor, remembers that Lindsay would reach for the check "all of the time." Lindsay's standard routine was to take out his credit card and say, "I have to use it or they will cancel it." He once gave Vecchio a three-year-old Pontiac station wagon. Interview of James Carberry by author, 20 May 1997. Drabkin interview. Interview of Pat Vecchio by author, 13 October 1999.

100. Program of the Inner Circle Production, 5 March 1966.

101. Ruth Cowan, "The New York City Civilian Review Board Referendum of November 1966: A Case Study of Mass Politics" (Ph.D. diss., New York University, 1970), p. 434. *NYT,* 7 April 1966.

CHAPTER 4

1. *NY,* 7 April 1969.

2. Jane Jacobs, *The Death and Life of Great American Cities* (New York: Vintage Books, 1992), pp. 31–32 (original edition, New York: Random House, 1961). Andrew Hacker, *The New Yorkers: A Profile of an American Metropolis* (New York: Twentieth Century Fund, 1975), p. 16.

3. Jonathan Rieder, *Canarsie: The Jews and Italians of Brooklyn Against Liberalism* (Cambridge, MA: Harvard University Press, 1985), p. 24.

4. Alfred Kazin, *A Walker in the City* (New York: Harcourt, Brace & World, 1951). *The WPA Guide to New York City* (New York: New Press, 1992), p. 500. For the situation in Brownsville, see Gerald Sorin, *The Nurturing Neighborhood: The Brownsville Boys Club and Jewish Community in Urban America, 1940–1990* (New York: New York University, 1990), pp. 154–188, and Joseph B. Judge, "Brownsville: A Neighborhood in Trouble," *Dissent* (September–October 1966). Judge called Brownsville in the 1960s "a community of unrelieved poverty, dirt, decay, drunkenness, and despair."

5. Barry Gottehrer, *The Mayor's Man* (Garden City, N.Y.: Doubleday, 1975), pp. 4–5.

6. Nora Sayre, "A Riot Averted," in *Sixties Going On Seventies* (London: Constable, 1974), pp. 298–299. Memo from Robert M. Blum to John V. Lindsay, 20 July 1966, in author's possession.

7. Gottehrer, *The Mayor's Man,* pp. 4–5. Blum memo.

8. *NYT,* 19 July 1966.

9. Gottehrer, *The Mayor's Man,* p. 11. Lindsay quoted in Adam Isidore, director, *Give a Damn Again,* 1995, in author's possession.

10. Interview of Jay Kriegel by author, 4 February 1997. Before the tensions in East New York became evident, many in the Lindsay administration were not sure

where the neighborhood was. One joke sums up the difference between the Wagner and Lindsay administrations: "If a letter carrier in Brooklyn awakened with sore feet, Bob Wagner's arches hurt and Lindsay wondered where Brooklyn is" (Roger Starr, *The Rise and Fall of New York* [New York: Basic Books, 1985], p. 23).

11. *NYT,* 24 July 1966. Gottehrer, *The Mayor's Man,* pp. 6, 13. Gottehrer found the white youths "loud and rowdy." They "talked as rough as they looked." When they protested, their "faces were contorted with hatred."

12. Blum memo. Interview of Robert Blum by author, 22 May 1997.

13. Interview of Barry Gottehrer by author, 29 February 1997. Blum interview.

14. Telephone message from Brooklyn Homicide, reprinted leaflet verbatim, 23 March 1966, Police Department (2), Box 68, Folder 855, Departmental Correspondence, Office of the Mayor, JVL Papers, NYCMA. Dean's funeral cost over $1,100, more than the $450 that welfare allowed for funerals. Mrs. Dean, a single mother on welfare, could not afford the burial. Lindsay and William Booth, Human Resources Administration commissioner, had promised that the funeral expenses would be taken care of, but they could find no city funds to cover the cost. Instead, the mayor and some of his aides chipped in the money to bury the young boy. The police later arrested seventeen-year-old Ernest Gallashaw, a black teenager from the neighborhood, for the murder of Eric Dean. Gallashaw was later acquitted by a jury after the prosecutor's main witness, a thirteen-year-old boy, recanted his testimony. Gallashaw was arrested again in January 1968 for renting machine guns to a group of bank robbers.

15. Woody Klein, *Lindsay's Promise: The Dream that Failed* (London: Macmillan, 1970), p. 208.

16. *NYT,* 22 July 1966.

17. John V. Lindsay, *The City* (New York: W. W. Norton, Inc., 1969), p. 96. *NYP,* 22 July 1966. *NYT,* 24 July 1966.

18. *NYT,* 23 July 1966. Gottehrer interview.

19. Lindsay, *The City,* p. 99. *NYT,* 24 July 1966.

20. Interview of Frank Arricale by author, 12 June 1997. Rabbi Schrage achieved notoriety in 1964 when he and other Brooklyn Jews formed a radio-car patrol called the Maccabees to patrol their neighborhoods after there was an increase in crimes against Jews by blacks. Some called the Maccabees a vigilante group and others saw them a sad necessity in urban America in the 1960s. See "Maccabees and the Mau Mau," *National Review,* 16 June 1964, p. 479. Fred Shapiro and James Sullivan, *Race Riots: New York, 1964* (New York: Crowell, 1964), pp. 125–126.

21. There were three Gallo brothers: Albert, Larry, and Joey. Albert was the main figure involved in the East New York situation. Gottehrer claims, incorrectly, that Joey Gallo was the main figure. "Crazy Joe" Gallo, who was said to have kept a pet lion, received eternal notoriety in 1972 when he was gunned down in a mob hit while eating a late-night meal at Umberto's Clam Bar in Little Italy. On the use of the Gallo brothers in East New York, see Gottehrer, *The Mayor's Man,* pp. 26–27; Sayre, "A Riot Averted," pp. 300–303; *NYTM,* 23 October 1966; and Gottehrer interview.

22. James Lardner, *Crusader: The Hell-Raising Career of Detective David Durk* (New York: Random House, 1996), p. 83. Gottehrer, *The Mayor's Man*, p. 70. Garelik quoted in Charles R. Morris, *The Cost of Good Intentions: New York City and the Liberal Experiment, 1960–1975* (New York: W. W. Norton, 1980), p. 77. Nicholas Alex, who interviewed numerous policemen in his examination of the attitudes of white New York City police in the sixties and seventies, found that the restraints put upon police during civil disturbances was a major bone of contention. "Policemen resent being advised by their officers to 'let it lie' or to 'play it cool' when a city area is under great tensions" (Nicholas Alex, *New York Cops Talk Back: A Study of a Beleaguered Minority* [New York: John Wiley, 1976], p. 72). See also Nicholas Pileggi, "Barry Gottehrer's Job is to Cool It," *NYTM*, 22 September 1968.

23. Selma Ehrenfeld, "The East New York Experiment: Working with Jews in a Polarized Community," National Project on Ethnic America, American Jewish Committee," unpublished manuscript, August 1970, AJC Archives.

24. Ibid., pp. 2–3.

25. Richard Rogin, "This Place Makes Bedford-Stuyvesant Look Beautiful," *NYTM*, 28 March 1971. See also Daniel Yergin, "Ballad of a Changing Neighborhood," *NY*, 19 August 1968.

26. Rieder, *Canarsie*, pp. 22, 24. By the 1980s and 1990s, East New York had the reputation for being one of the most dangerous and violent neighborhood in the city.

27. Pileggi, "Barry Gottehrer's Job Is to Cool It." Gottehrer, *The Mayor's Man*, pp. 92–95. *AN*, June 1965.

28. Barry Gottehrer, "Summer in Our City: New York City, 1967 and 1968," report, NYS Archives. *DN*, 4 March 1968. *NYP*, 27 April 1968. Gottehrer interview.

29. For a history of the Five Percenters, see Yusef Nuruddin, "The Five Percenters: A Teenage Nation of Gods and Earths," in Yvonne Yazbeck Haddad and Jane Idleman Smith, eds., *Muslim Communities in North America* (Albany: State University of New York Press, 1994). "The Bomb: The Greatest Story Never Told," 1987, downloaded from the web site http://sunsite.unc.edu/nge/thebomb.html. FBI Files, Subject: Clarence 13X Smith, File Number 100-444363. *AN*, 5 June 1965. Gottehrer, *The Mayor's Man*, p. 92, 101.

30. Memo from Sanford Garelik, Chief Inspector, New York Police Department, to All Commands, 26 May 1967, Robert W. Sweet, Deputy Mayor, Correspondence, Law Enforcement, 1966–1969, Box 5037, JVL Papers, NYCMA. Blum interview. Gottehrer, *The Mayor's Man*, pp. 107–108.

31. Pileggi, "Barry Gottehrer's Job Is to Cool It." Interview of Ted Mastroianni by author, 12 December 1997.

32. *NYT*, 22 June 1967. Marlene Nadle, "The Bomb That Ticks in the Black Ghetto," *VV*, 6 July 1967. For the classic discussion of Black Power, see Stokely Carmichael and Charles Hamilton, *Black Power: The Politics of Liberation in America* (New York: Vintage Books, 1967). For critiques of Black Power, see Christopher Lasch, "The Trouble with Black Power," *New York Review of Books*, 29 February 1968, and Randall Kennedy, "Reflections on Black Power," in Stephen Macedo, ed., *Reassessing the Sixties* (New York: W. W. Norton, 1997).

33. Paul A. Gilje, *Rioting in America* (Bloomington: Indiana University Press, 1996), p. 6.

34. During another crisis, Leary was found waiting out the trouble in a movie theater. Gottehrer, *The Mayor's Man*, p. 72. Interview with Sid Davidoff, 9 April 1997.

35. Pete Hamill, "El Barrio: Hot Night," *NYP*, 24 July 1967. *NYT*, 24 July 1967. On the TPF, see Nicholas Pileggi, "'Gestapo' or 'Elite'? The Tactical Patrol Force," *NYTM*, 21 July 1968. Anger at the Tactical Patrol Force was not limited to minority communities. Italian Americans in the Belmont section of the Bronx complained that the TPF was an invading force in their neighborhood, bossing around residents during tense times. These residents also felt that the TPF went easy on blacks and Puerto Ricans but were tough on neighborhood whites. These complaints occurred the same week as the East Harlem riot. Memo from Martin Shulman to Jay Kriegel, 25 July 1967, Robert W. Sweet (Deputy Mayor) Files, Correspondence, Law Enforcement, 1965–1969, Police Department Folder, JVL Papers, NYCMA.

36. Pete Hamill, "El Barrio: The Line," *NYP*, 25 July 1967.

37. Mastroianni interview.

38. *NYT*, 25 July 1967.

39. Henry Etzkowitz and Gerald M. Schaflander, *Ghetto Crisis: Riots or Reconciliation?* (Boston: Little, Brown, 1969), pp. 146–153, 163. Gottehrer, *The Mayor's Man*, p. 76. Davidoff interview. In the mid–1970s, Carson and his associates were tried on murder and kidnapping charges. Carson was acquitted of murder but served seventeen months in prison on the kidnapping charge. See Tamar Jacoby, "Sonny Carson and the Politics of Protest," *City Journal*, Summer 1991. Carson would achieve a measure of infamy during the 1989 mayoral campaign when it came to light that the Dinkins campaign had paid him $9,500 for a supposed "get-out-the-vote" effort. When confronted with the charge of anti-Semitism, Carson replied, "I'm anti-white. Don't just limit me to a little group of people" (*NYT*, 20 October 1989).

40. Mwlina Imiri Abubadika (Sonny Carson), *The Education of Sonny Carson* (New York: W. W. Norton, 1972), pp. 149–150.

41. *NYT*, 30 July 1967.

42. *NYT*, 6 and 7 September 1967. Blum interview.

43. Gottehrer, *The Mayor's Man*, p. 76. Carson's letter to Lindsay quoted in Jerald E. Podair, "Like Strangers: Blacks, Whites, and New York City's Ocean Hill–Brownsville Crisis, 1945–1980" (Ph.D. diss., Princeton University, 1997), p. 69.

44. *NYT*, 9 August 1967. Ibid., 14 August 1967.

45. *NYT*, 15 July 1968.

46. Hacker, *The New Yorkers*, p. 3. Memo from Thomas Morgan to John V. Lindsay, 13 May 1969, Group 592, Series XII, Box 227, Folder 41, JVL Papers, Yale. Moynihan memo reprinted in the *WSJ*, 9 March 1970. Dennis Smith, *Report from Engine Company 82* (New York: McCall Books, 1972), pp. 11, 15. Letter from Barry Gottehrer to Major Owens, Commissioner of Community Development Agency, 2 June 1971, Executive Assistant to the Mayor (Carl P. Irish) Files, c. 1969–1973, Box 110504, JVL Papers, NYCMA. Ford Foundation, "R and D &

NYC = C: Assessment of a Grant to the New York City-Rand Corporation," November 1971, Folder 001989, p. 1, Ford Foundation Archives. Jill Jonnes, *We're Still Here: The Rise, Fall, and Resurrection of the South Bronx* (Boston: Atlantic Monthly Press, 1986), pp. 232–233.

47. Mastroianni interview. *NYT,* 6 September 1967. For a discussion of the politics of riots in the 1960s, see Kenneth O'Reilly, "The FBI and the Politics of the Riots, 1964–1968," *Journal of American History,* June 1988.

48. Kerner Commission, *Report of the National Advisory Commission on Civil Disorders* (Kerner Report) (New York: Bantam Books, 1968), pp. 113, 158–163. Three people were killed in New York's 1935 riot, 6 people were killed in the 1943 riot, and 1 person was killed and 118 injured in the 1964 riot. On the Harlem riot of 1943, see Dominic J. Capeci, *The Harlem Riot of 1943* (Philadelphia: Temple University Press, 1977). On the Harlem riot of 1964, see Shapiro and Sullivan, *Race Riots, 1964.*

49. Interview of Robert Blum by author, 1 April 1997. Jack Newfield, "John Lindsay Emerges from Summer and Smoke," *VV,* 7 September 1967. Nat Hentoff, "The Mayor: Your City as Much as Mine," *The New Yorker,* 3 May 1969. Kriegel interview.

50. Interview of Jim Carberry by author, May 1997. *NYT,* 8 July 1967. *NYT,* 13 August 1967. *AN,* 19 August 1967. *Manhattan Tribune,* 15 February 1969.

51. John Lindsay, "Violence in the Cities: A Better Place to Live," address to the 44th Annual Congress of Cities, 31 July 1967, reprinted in *Vital Speeches of the Day,* 1 September 1967.

52. Klein, *Lindsay's Promise,* p. 276. For a view of the darker side of the counterculture, see J. Anthony Lukas's Pulitzer Prize–winning article, "The Two Worlds of Linda Fitzpatrick," *NYT,* 16 October 1967. Fitzpatrick was the eighteen-year-old daughter of a well-to-do Greenwich, Connecticut, family who was found murdered with a friend in the boiler room of an East Village building in early October 1967. Lukas recounts her life of drugs, panhandling, and numerous men, contrasting it with her parents' (willful) ignorance of her new life.

53. Leticia Kent, "Marching on MacDougal: Immovable vs. Irresistible," *VV,* 13 April 1967. Klein, *Lindsay's Promise,* pp. 141–142, 276–277. Part of Ed Koch's political success as mayor in the late 1970s and 1980s can be traced to the skills he learned representing Greenwich Village in the 1960s as district leader, councilman, and congressman. Koch was then known as a staunch liberal, but as his activity in MANA suggests he learned the need to balance the interests of his liberal constituents with those of more conservative working-class voters. It is difficult to picture Lindsay marching down MacDougal Street with members of MANA.

54. Marty Jezer, *Abbie Hoffman: American Rebel* (New Brunswick, N.J.: Rutgers University Press, 1992), p. 71. For a history of the East Village see Janet Abu-Lughod, ed., *From Urban Village to East Village: The Battle for New York's Lower East Side* (Cambridge, Mass.: Blackwell, 1994).

55. Gottehrer, *The Mayor's Man,* pp. 137–139. Don McNeill, "The Youthquake and the Shook-Up Park," *VV,* 8 June 1967.

56. *NYT,* 31 May 1967. A judge later threw out the charges against those arrested. For the next twenty-five years, Tompkins Square Park would remain one of the most contested areas in the city. In the summer of 1988, a curfew was instituted in the park. As gentrification moved in from the west, the East Village became home to more white middle-class professionals, whose values clashed with those of the white punks and squatters who lived in the neighborhood. In August 1988, a clash broke out between police, many on horseback, and an organized group in the park shouting "Die yuppie scum," "Gentrification is class war," and "It's our fuckin' park." Tensions over the curfew continued for the next three years and ended with the closing of the park in June 1991 for over a year. See Janet Abu-Lughod, "The Battle for Tompkins Square Park," in Abu-Lughod, *From Urban Village to East Village,* pp. 233–266.

57. Joe Flaherty, "The Precinct's the Same Only the Script's Changed," *VV,* 8 June 1967. On Captain Joseph Fink, see Saul Braun, "The Cop as Social Scientist," *NYTM,* 24 August 1969.

58. *NYT,* 3 June 1967.

59. Roy Rosenzweig and Elizabeth Blackmar, *The Park and the People: A History of Central Park* (Ithaca: Cornell University Press, 1992), p. 493. *NYT,* 27 June 1967.

60. Ibid., p. 492. August Heckscher, *Alive in the City: Memoir of an Ex-Commissioner* (New York: Charles Scribner's Sons, 1974), p. 6.

61. Heckscher, *Alive in the City,* pp. 3, 80. Oral History of August Heckscher, p. 10, CUOHA. *Barnes and Noble Complete Illustrated Map and Guidebook to Central Park* (New York: Silver Lining Books, 1999), p. 42.

62. Heckscher, *Alive in the City,* p. 92. Hacker, *The New Yorkers,* pp. 143–144.

63. Rosenzweig and Blackmar, *The Park and the People,* pp. 489, 493–98.

64. Roger Starr, "John V. Lindsay: A Political Portrait," *Commentary,* February 1970, p. 38. Marya Mannes, "Up in Central Park—Ugh!" *NYT,* 22 April 1971. Memo to John V. Lindsay from Edward Skloot, 10 May 1972, Group 592, Series XIII, Box 239, Folder 6, JVL Papers, Yale.

65. Heckscher, *Alive in the City,* p. 230.

66. *NYT,* 16 April 1967. Ibid., 1 and 2 May 1967.

67. Ibid., 14 May 1967. Joe Flaherty, "The Hawks in May: A Day to Remember," *VV,* 18 May 1967.

68. Jezer, *Abbie Hoffman,* pp. 104–105.

69. Rieder, *Canarsie,* p. 132.

70. For a good explanation of the counterculture, see Theodore Roszak, *The Making of a Counterculture* (Berkeley: University of California Press, 1995).

71. *NYHT,* 14 October 1965.

72. Dwight D. Eisenhower, "We Should Be Ashamed," *Reader's Digest,* August 1967.

73. Lindsay's Hunter College speech quoted in *DN,* 12 December 1967. Address by John V. Lindsay, Mayor of New York City, Before the American Whig-Cliosophic Society, Princeton University, Princeton, New Jersey, "The Changing

Challenges of Our Cities," 30 November 1966, Group 592, Box 65, Folder 246, JVL Papers, Yale.

74. James Miller, *Democracy Is in the Streets: From Port Huron to the Siege of Chicago* (New York: Simon & Schuster, 1987), 329–374. John V. Lindsay, "The Future of the American City," *Saturday Review*, 8 January 1966. In speeches, Lindsay often referred to Jack Newfield's sympathetic book on the budding youth rebellion, *The Prophetic Minority* (New York: New American Library, 1966).

75. *NYT*, 30 January 1966. *National Review*, 13 December 1966. Jack Newfield, "A Political Comer: Yes; A Brooding Hamlet: No," *VV*, 25 May 1967.

76. Nat Hentoff, *A Political Life: The Education of John V. Lindsay* (New York: Alfred A. Knopf, 1969), p. 139.

77. For descriptions of the "Stop the Draft Week" protests, see Gottehrer, *The Mayor's Man*, pp. 111–130.

78. Sally Kempton, "A Week of Confrontation: The Rough Side of New York," *VV*, 14 December 1967.

79. Gottehrer, *The Mayor's Man*, p. 121. Kempton, "A Week of Confrontation."

80. *DN*, 11 December 1967. *NYT*, 14 December 1967. Gottehrer, *The Mayor's Man*, p. 128.

81. Kenneth Pitchford, "The Lower East Side: Longhairs are Dangerous," *VV*, 28 November 1968, p. 63. Gottehrer, *The Mayor's Man*, p. 129–130. Gottehrer interview. Davidoff interview.

82. Davidoff letter, Series XIV, Box 247, Folder 117, JVL Papers, Yale.

83. Gottehrer interview.

CHAPTER 5

1. Steven R. Weisman, "Why Lindsay Failed as Mayor," *The Washington Monthly*, April 1972, p. 52.

2. Barry Gottehrer, *The Mayor's Man* (Garden City, N.Y.: Doubleday, 1975), p. 8. Woody Klein, *Lindsay's Promise: The Dream that Failed* (London: Macmillan, 1970), p. 223.

3. Ruth Cowan, "The New York City Civilian Review Board Referendum of November 1966: A Case Study of Mass Politics" (Ph.D. diss., New York University, 1970), p. 36.

4. Cowan, "The New York City Civilian Review Board Referendum of November 1966," p. 126. *VV*, 4 June 1964. Francis W. H. Adams was one of the city's leading reform Democrats. He had helped Eleanor Roosevelt and Herbert Lehman organize the Committee for Democratic Values (CDV), to battle against the Democratic clubhouses during the 1950s.

5. Stephen M. David and Paul E. Peterson, *Urban Politics and Public Policy: The City in Crisis* (New York: Praeger, 1973), p. 245. Kerner Commission figures reprinted in James Q. Wilson, *Thinking About Crime*, 2nd ed. (New York: Basic Books, 1983), p. 93. *NYT*, 27 July 1964. Louis Harris and Bert E. Swanson, *Black-Jewish*

Relations in New York City (New York: Praeger, 1970), p. 83. On the issue of police brutality, see Albert J. Reiss, "How Much 'Police Brutality' is There?" *TRANS-action* (July–August 1967). For a good discussion of the use of force by New York City policemen, see Craig Horowitz, "Show of Force," *NY,* 22 September 1997.

6. Kerner Commission, *Report of the National Advisory Commission on Civil Disorders* (Kerner Report) (New York: Bantam Books, 1968), pp. 307–308.

7. "Majority Report of a Special Subcommittee to Study the Feasibility of Creating an Independent Civilian Complaint Review Board to Investigate and Make Recommendations Concerning Allegations of Police Brutality," City Affairs Committee, New York City Council, 18 May 1965, Group 592, Series XVI, Box 366, Folder 493, JVL Papers, Yale.

8. Cowan, "The New York City Civilian Review Board Referendum of November 1966," p. 129.

9. Interview of Jay Kriegel by author, 4 February 1997. Broderick was a man of impeccable liberal credentials. When the liberal reform congressman James Scheuer ran for mayor in the 1969 Democratic primary, Broderick was Scheuer's running mate for comptroller. Harlem Assemblyman Charles Rangel was the slate's candidate for City Council president. Broderick served on the board of directors of the Metropolitan Applied Research Center, headed by the sociologist Kenneth Clark. In 1968, Broderick was a supporter of Robert Kennedy's presidential campaign, and signed an advertisement in the *New York Times* (8 May 1968) that included a reprint of an Arthur Schlesinger article in support of Kennedy. (Other signers of the ad included Lauren Bacall, Herman Badillo, Truman Capote, David Dinkins, Reverend Milton Galamison, Norman Mailer, Franklin Delano Roosevelt Jr., and Livingston Wingate of HARYOU-ACT.)

10. Klein, *Lindsay's Promise,* p. 23.

11. Interview of Bob Price by author, 27 March 1997.

12. "Report to Mayor-Elect John V. Lindsay by the Law Enforcement Task Force," 31 December 1965, Robert W. Sweet (Deputy Mayor) Files, Correspondence, Law Enforcement, 1965–1969, Box 110609, Office of the Mayor, JVL Papers, NYCMA.

13. Press Release, 7 February 1966, Police Department (3), Box 68, Folder 856, Departmental Correspondence, JVL Papers, NYCMA.

14. Vincent Broderick Letter to John Lindsay, 8 February 1966, "Police 1966–7," Box 85, Subject Files, JVL Papers, NYCMA. Klein, *Lindsay's Promise,* p. 111.

15. Ibid., p. 110.

16. *New York Journal–American,* 16 February 1966.

17. Cowan, "The New York City Civilian Review Board Referendum of November 1966," pp. 242–243.

18. *NYT,* 29 January 1966.

19. Wallace S. Sayre and Herbert Kaufman, *Governing New York City: Politics in the Metropolis* (New York: W. W. Norton, 1965), pp. 285–292.

20. Cowan "The New York City Civilian Review Board Referendum of November 1966," p. 323.

21. *NYT,* 3 April 1967. Interview of Robert Sweet by author, 22 April 1997.

22. Price interview. Sweet interview. Interview of Sanford Garelik by author, 14 April 1997.

23. Robert Daley, *Target Blue: An Insider's View of the NYPD* (New York: Delacorte Press, 1973), p. 414.

24. Nat Hentoff, *A Political Life: The Education of John V. Lindsay* (New York: Alfred A. Knopf, 1969), p. 123. Nathan Glazer and Daniel Patrick Moynihan, *Beyond the Melting Pot: The Negroes, Puerto Ricans, Jews, Italians, and Irish of New York City,* 2nd ed., (Cambridge: MIT Press, 1970), p. 262. For a good study of a neighborhood that slowly lost its Irish character in the postwar years, see Robert W. Snyder, "The Neighborhood Changed: The Irish of Washington Heights and Inwood Since 1945," in Ronald H. Bayor and Timothy J. Meagher, eds., *The New York Irish* (Baltimore: Johns Hopkins University Press, 1996). The contrast between Boston and New York is striking. Boston, which never received the diversity of immigrants as did New York, still retains a strong Irish ethnicity. In contrast, one can walk the streets of New York today and, with the exception of the occasional Irish bar and the annual St. Patrick's Day parade, never realize the extent of the earlier Irish dominance in New York. New immigrants from Ireland are settling in the old neighborhoods in the Bronx and Queens, but they are merely a drop in the varied stew of immigrants that have settled in the city in the last twenty years. In 1990, less than 10 percent of New Yorkers claimed Irish heritage. Almost half of these were only of partial Irish descent. A good example of the dwindling influence of the Irish in New York City is that three of the four Democratic candidates for mayor in 1997 boycotted the St. Patrick's Day Parade that year to protest the decision by the Ancient Order of Hibernians not to allow a homosexual group to march. Such a decision would have spelled political death decades before.

25. *NYT,* 31 October 1966. Jack Newfield, "John Vliet Lindsay: Uptight White Knight," *VV,* 4 January 1968.

26. *NYT,* 31 October 1966. *NYP,* 3 March 1966.

27. In 1996, Rudolph Giuliani, widely seen as a pro-police mayor, appointed the first Jewish police commissioner, Howard Safir. Unlike the appointment of Garelik thirty years earlier, Safir's appointment created no outcry. In fact, the new commissioner's religion was barely mentioned.

28. The outcry notwithstanding, it was not unusual for a new police commissioner to replace the men in surrounding positions. It was also little noticed that two of the three veteran officers named by Garelik as replacements for the retiring officers were Irish (the other was German-American). *NYT,* 10 March 1966. *NYP,* 9 March 1966. Excerpts of Broderick's speech at Fairleigh Dickinson were published in the *National Review,* 5 April 1966, and the *NYP,* 2 March 1966.

29. Garelik interview. Bernard Weinraub, "Not Exactly a Jimmy Cagney Cop," *NYTM,* 30 October 1966.

30. J. P. McFadden, "Who Will Protect the Police?" *National Review,* 5 April 1966.

31. *NYT,* 5 March 1966. NAACP Press Release, 19 February 1966, Group IV, Box A27, Government: New York City Civilian Review Board Folder, NAACP Papers.

32. *NYHT,* 3 March 1966. *World–Journal Tribune,* 13 October 1966.

33. A similar controversy took hold in the NYPD in 1940 when it was discovered that hundreds of policemen, mostly Irish Catholics, belonged to the anti-Semitic Christian Front. See Gerald Astor, *The New York Cops: An Informal History* (New York: Charles Scribner's Sons, 1971), pp. 216–217.

34. *NYP,* 25 February 1966.

35. *NYT,* 25 February 1966.

36. Press Release, "Mayor John V. Lindsay's Television Report on the Civilian Review Board," 2 May 1966, Group IV, Box A52, John V. Lindsay Folder, NAACP Papers.

37. Telegram from William F. Buckley to Herbert Brownell, 9 May 1966, Box 231, New York City Mayor's Civilian Review Board (4) Folder, Brownell Papers. Brownell's response to Buckley was "Could you please let me know whether the persons you have recommended have consented that their names be considered and are willing to serve if selected" (Letter from Herbert Brownell to William F. Buckley, 9 May 1966, Box 231, New York City Mayor's Civilian Review Board [4] Folder, Brownell Papers).

38. *NYT,* 19 May 1966.

39. Press Release, 15 March 1966, Police Department (4), Box 68, Folder 857, Departmental Correspondence, JVL Papers, NYCMA.

40. Sidney Zion, "Civilian Review Board: Now a 'Nasty Campaign,' " *NYT,* 3 July 1966. *DN,* 5 July 1966.

41. *NYT,* 9 July 1966. Klein, *Lindsay's Promise,* p. 202.

42. Baer would achieve a measure of notoriety in 1996 when, as a federal judge, he threw out evidence in a drug case because of a supposedly illegal search by police. In Washington Heights, a neighborhood in Upper Manhattan that had become a center for the city's drug trade, police observed four men putting packages into a car with out-of-state license plates. When the men saw the police, they ran. The policemen stopped and searched the car and found seventy-five pounds of cocaine and four pounds of heroin in the trunk of the driver's car. The case caused a stir not only because Judge Baer threw out the case against an obvious drug dealer, but because of a biting critique of the police contained in his decision. Judge Baer wrote: "Even before the prosecution and the public hearing and final report of the Mollen Commission, residents in this neighborhood tended to regard police officers as corrupt, abusive, and violent. After the attendant publicity surrounding the above events, had the men not run when the cops began to stare at them, it would have been unusual" (*NYT,* Letters to the Editor, 26 January 1996). The Republican presidential candidate, Bob Dole, denounced Baer, a Democratic appointee to the bench, for his decision.

43. Letter from Herbert Brownell to John V. Lindsay, 27 May 1966, Box 231, New York City Mayor's Civilian Review Board (3) Folder, Brownell Papers.

44. *NYT,* 12 July 1966. Cowan, "The New York City Civilian Review Board Referendum of November 1966," pp. 268–269.

45. For the Cardinal Spellman episode, see John Cooney, *The American Pope: The Life and Times of Francis Cardinal Spellman* (New York: Times Books, 1984), pp. 302–304.

46. Roger Starr, "John V. Lindsay: A Political Portrait," *Commentary,* February 1970. *NYT,* 3 September 1966.

47. Gottehrer, *The Mayor's Man,* p. 51.

48. Daniel P. Moynihan, Foreword to David W. Abbott, Louis H. Gold, and Edward T. Rogowsky, *Police, Politics, and Race: The New York City Referendum on Civilian Review* (Cambridge, MA: American Jewish Committee and MIT, 1969), p. 2. The best defense of the review board is Theodore Kheel, "Facts and Myths About the Police Review Board," *New York World–Journal Tribune,* 23 October 1966.

49. Cowan, "The New York City Civilian Review Board Referendum of November 1966," p. 408. *NYT,* 11 March 1966. Jerome Skolnick, "Why Cops Behave the Way They Do," *New York World–Journal Tribune,* 23 October 1966. For a psychological critique of the police, see Arthur Niederhoffer, *Behind the Shield: The Police in Urban Society* (Garden City, N.Y.: Doubleday, 1967). For a recent antipolice polemic, see David K. Shipler, "Living Under Suspicion," *NYT,* 7 February 1997: "Of the country's institutions, police departments are probably the furthest behind in addressing racism in their ranks," Shipler wrote. To rectify this, Shipler argues that police departments must "retrain officers and screen applicants for subtle bigotry."

50. Members of the Conference included the NYCLU's Aryeh Neier, Michael Harrington, Thomas Brooks, and two future civilian appointees to the review board, Manuel Diaz and Thomas Farrell.

51. Letter from Marjorie M. Friedlander, Coordinator of New York City Review Board Conference, to Mayor John V. Lindsay, 7 March 1966, Police Department (4), Box 68, Folder 857, Departmental Correspondence, JVL Papers, NYCMA.

52. John Corry, "The Man of That Board," *NYTM,* 6 November 1966. Buckley quoted in "Civilian Review Board: Yes or No," *Firing Line,* Program 32, Taped 7 October 1966, Buckley Papers.

53. Cassese quoted in *NYT,* 20 September 1966. Notes on NYCLU Staff Meeting, 14 November 1966, Box 1082, Folder 19, ACLU Papers.

54. Algernon D. Black, *The People and the Police* (Westport, Conn.: Greenwood Press, 1968), pp. 25, 26, 36.

55. *NYT,* 13 October 1966.

56. Independent Citizens Committee Against Civilian Review Boards, advertisement, *NYT,* 3 November 1966.

57. Independent Citizens Committee Against Civilian Review Boards, advertisement, *DN,* 26 September 1966. Roy Wilkins, "A Sly Campaign Against Negroes," *AN,* 15 October 1966. *VV,* 20 October 1966.

58. Cowan, "The New York City Civilian Review Board Referendum of November 1966," p. 427. *NYT,* 11 September 1966.

59. Civilian Complaint Review Board statistics, Series XVI, Box 366, Folder 494, JVL Papers, Yale. Press Release from Vincent Broderick, Police Commissioner, 8 February 1966, Robert W. Sweet (Deputy Mayor), Files, Correspondence, Law Enforcement, 1965–1969, Police Department Folder, JVL Papers NYCMA.

60. Gellhorn quoted in Box 1082, Folder 19, ACLU Papers. Paul Chevigny, *Police Power: Political Abuses in New York City* (New York: Pantheon Books, 1969).

61. *WSJ,* 12 October 1966.

62. Cowan, "The New York City Civilian Review Board Referendum of November 1966," p. 349. Moynihan, Foreword to *Police, Politics, and Race,* p. 3. Lefkowitz campaign song quoted in Richard Armstrong, "Robert Sweet Is the Unabashed No. 2 Man at City Hall," *NYTM,* 29 September 1968.

63. Cowan, "The New York City Civilian Review Board Referendum of November 1966," pp. 311–312. Price interview.

64. Price interview. Notes on NYCLU Staff Meeting, 14 November 1966, Box 1082, Folder 19, ACLU Papers. Interview of Barry Gottehrer by author, 29 February 1997. Interview of David Garth by author, 4 June 1997.

65. Kriegel interview.

66. Notes on NYCLU Staff Meeting. *DN,* 24 October 1966. Memo from Dick Aurelio to Jacob Javits, undated, Series 5, Subseries 2, Box 11, "1966 Campaign—Civilian Review" Folder, Javits Papers. Stephanie Harrington, "Why We Lost the Review Board," *Dissent,* January-February 1967.

67. Klein, *Lindsay's Promise,* p. 245. "The Police Department's Civilian Complaint Review Board, Addresses presented at a Special Civic Service on Sunday morning, 16 October 1966, by John V. Lindsay and Edward O. Miller," St. George's Episcopal Church, Box 1082, Folder 19, ACLU Papers.

68. Kheel and Buckley quotes from "Civilian Review Board: Yes or No," *Firing Line,* Program 32, Taped 7 October 1966, Buckley Papers.

69. Undated Press Release from FAIR (Federated Association for Impartial Review), Series XVI, Box 374, Folder 594, JVL Papers, Yale. Yet another irony of New York politics is that David Garth, who was so adamant about throwing around the charge of bigotry and racism during the 1960s while working for FAIR and John Lindsay, later in his career became closely associated with both Ed Koch and Rudolph Giuliani, who themselves were accused by their opponents of bigotry for their hard line against crime.

70. American Jewish Congress leaflet, undated, Series 5, Subseries 2, Box 11, "1966 Campaign—Civilian Review" Folder, Javits Papers.

71. *NYT,* 20 September 1966. *NYT,* 26 October 1966.

72. *AN,* 15 October 1966. Letter from Roy Wilkins, 27 October 1966, Group IV, Box A27, Government: New York City Civilian Review Board Folder, NAACP Papers.

73. Cowan, "The New York City Civilian Review Board Referendum of November 1966," pp. 345–346. ADL Report, October 1966, Series XVI, Box 374, Folder 594, JVL Papers, Yale.

74. Right-wing attack on Algernon Black, 13 July 1966, Newsletter on file, Series XVI, Box 374, Folder 594, JVL Papers, Yale.

75. *NYT,* 9 September 1966. Letter to Hubert Humphrey from John de J. Pemberton Jr., Executive Director, American Civil Liberties Union, 24 October 1966, Box 1082, Folder 19, ACLU Papers.

76. *NYT,* 23 October 1966. *DN,* 9 September 1966. Cowan, "The New York City Civilian Review Board Referendum of November 1966," p. 325.

77. Neier quoted in Cowan, "The New York City Civilian Review Board Referendum of November 1966," p. 354. Lindsay quoted in Klein, *Lindsay's Promise,* p. 245. Harrington, "Why We Lost the Review Board."

78. Statement by Mayor John V. Lindsay on the "sleeper clause," and "Statement of J. Lee Rankin, Corporation Counsel, before the Senate Committee on City of New York of the Senate of the New York Legislature, 19 October 1966, 5 November 1966, Box 230, New York City's Mayor's Civilian Review Board (1) Folder, Brownell Papers.

79. *NYT,* 29 October 1966. "Sleeper clause" advertisements, *NYT,* 7 November 1966. Evidence that the "sleeper clause" was in reality a nonissue is the fact that six years later the Knapp Commission that was investigating police corruption was not hampered by the provisions in the referendum.

80. Among these groups supporting the review board were the American Jewish Committee, Anti-Defamation League, Americans for Democratic Action, American Veterans Committee, Citizens Union, Catholic Interracial Council, Congress of Racial Equality, Drug and Hospital Employees Union—Union 1199, International Ladies' Garment Workers Union, Liberal Party of New York State, NAACP, New York Civil Liberties Union, Presbytery of Greater New York, Unitarian-Universalist Council of New York City, United Federation of Teachers, Urban League, Young Democratic Club, Young Republican Club, Youth Against Poverty, and the Women's City Club.

81. Memo from Dick Aurelio to Jacob Javits, undated, Series 5, Subseries 2, Box 11, "1966 Campaign—Civilian Review" Folder, Javits Papers. Most of the politicians opposed to the CCRB were white ethnics, including Congressmen Paul Fino, John Murphy, James Delaney, and Hugh Carey, former Mayor Vincent Impelliteri, and Comptroller Mario Procaccino. Opposition to the CCRB was not universally Catholic, though. Norman Frank, of the Patrolmen's Benevolent Association, was Jewish, as was the radio broadcaster Barry Gray, who came out against the board despite having backed Lindsay the year before. Congressman Seymour Halpern, a liberal Republican from Queens and Lindsay ally, also opposed the board.

82. Skolnick, "Why Cops Behave the Way They Do." Nicholas Alex, *New York Cops Talk Back: A Study of a Beleaguered Minority* (New York: John Wiley, 1976), p. 204. James Q. Wilson, "Enforcing the Law in a Divided Community," *New York*

World–Journal Tribune, 23 October 1966. Kriegel quoted in Charles R. Morris, *The Cost of Good Intentions: New York City and the Liberal Experiment, 1960–1975* (New York: W. W. Norton, 1980), p. 92.

83. David Abbott, Louis Gold, and Edmund Rogowsky, "Police: The Civilian Review Board Controversy," in Jewel Bellush and Stephen M. David, eds., *Race and Politics in New York City: Five Studies in Policy-Making* (New York: Praeger, 1971), pp. 73, 84.

84. Abbott, Gold, and Rogowsky, "Police: The Civilian Review Board Controversy," p. 79.

85. Ibid., p. 87.

86. For a postelection discussion of the CCRB referendum campaign from a liberal perspective, see Harrington, "Why We Lost the Review Board"; James J. Graham, "Backlash in Brooklyn," *Commonweal*, 9 December 1966, p. 288, and George D. Younger, "The Defeat of New York's Civilian Review Board," *Christianity and Crisis*, 12 December 1966. Younger likened the review board defeat to the victories of Adolf Hitler in Germany and Hendrik Verwoerd in South Africa.

87. *AN*, 15 October 1966. *WSJ*, 6 October 1966. William Safire claims that the first use of "backlash" as "civil-rights recoil" was in a 16 June 1963, Rowland Evans and Robert Novak column. Evans and Novak wrote that the defeat of President Kennedy's depressed area bill was not "the first backlash of civil rights turmoil." See William Safire, *Safire's New Political Dictionary: The Definitive Guide to the New Language of Politics* (New York: Random House, 1993), p. 34. Novak credits the economist Eliot Janeway with using the term in his newsletter in the summer of 1963. Janeway, an economic consultant, New Deal Democrat, and friend of Lyndon Johnson's, worried that the effects of automation, combined with a possible recession and a tight job market, might turn whites against blacks and endanger the traditional Democratic coalition. See Eric Goldman, *The Tragedy of Lyndon Johnson* (New York: Alfred A. Knopf, 1969), pp. 173–174.

88. *National Review Bulletin*, 22 November 1966. Notes on ACLU Staff Meeting, 14 November 1966, Box 1082, Folder 19, ACLU Archives.

89. On the 1966 Reagan-Brown campaign, see Matthew Dallek, *The Right Moment: Ronald Reagan's First Victory and the Decisive Turning Point in American Politics* (New York: Free Press, 2000).

90. Lucy Dawidowicz, "The 1966 Elections: A Political Patchwork," report, American Jewish Committee, New York, 1967. Though Agnew was generally considered a racial moderate, he later hardened his stance on civil rights after the 1967 riots in Baltimore. Agnew became especially displeased with a group of local black leaders he met with following the riot. Agnew accused his guests of being "beguiled by the rationalizations of unity . . . intimidated by veiled threats . . . stung by insinuations that you were Mr. Charlie's boy, by epithets like 'Uncle Tom.'" See Jules Witcover, *The Resurrection of Richard Nixon* (New York: G. P. Putnam's Sons, 1970), p. 350. Thomas Byrne Edsall with Mary D. Edsall, *Chain Reaction: The Impact of Race, Rights, and Taxes on American Politics* (New York: W. W. Norton, 1992), p. 85.

During Agnew's 1966 campaign, Bob Price sent a number of Lindsay people, led by Sid Davidoff, to Maryland to assist their fellow liberal Republican.

91. O'Connor, who had been a vocal critic of the Lindsay administration and supporter of Broderick earlier in the year, remained silent on the police issue during the campaign. Already under suspicion by the city liberals who felt he was too close to the Democratic clubhouses, O'Connor felt he would further alienate liberal Democrats if he opposed the board. Regarding his political philosophy, O'Connor told a reporter, "I've had to become a liberal. My parents were Irish immigrants—lovely people—but too busy making a living and taking care of the family to be concerned with these things. So many of the ideas I held as a young man I've discarded. . . . I can only repeat that I wasn't born a liberal. I've had to fight my background to become one." Freed from election-year pieties, O'Connor spoke out the following year against attacks upon the police. In a speech at the Emerald Society, an organization for Irish policemen, O'Connor said it was "about time that we concentrated on the important problems of the Police Department, and not on hearsay, rumor and group insult" (*NYTM,* 16 January 1966, and *NYT,* 20 April 1967).

92. Richard Reeves, "A *Great* Mayor, *That* Bum?" *NYTM,* 1 January 1967.

93. Interview of Alton Marshall, 27 March 1997.

94. Lindsay quoted in *NYT,* 13 December 1967. Hentoff, *A Political Life: The Education of John V. Lindsay,* p. 238.

95. See "R and D + NYC = C: Assessment of a Grant to the New York City–Rand Institute," November 1971, pp. 95–97, Folder 001989, Ford Foundation Archives.

96. Moynihan, Foreword to *Police, Politics, and Race,* p. 4.

97. Aaron Wildavsky, "The Empty-Head Blues: Black Rebellion and White Reaction," *The Public Interest,* Spring 1968.

98. Patrick V. Murphy and Thomas Plate, *Commissioner: A View from the Top of American Law Enforcement* (New York: Simon & Schuster, 1977), p. 143. For a discussion of the Civilian Complaint Review Board controversy, see Tamar Jacoby, "The Uncivil History of the Civilian Review Board," *City Journal,* Winter 1993.

99. *NYHT,* 3 November 1965.

CHAPTER 6

1. Todd Gitlin, *The Sixties: Years of Hope, Days of Rage* (Toronto: Bantam Books, 1987), p. 289.

2. Josh Greenfield, "Heeeeeere's John!—The Media Candidate," *Life,* 25 February 1972. Frederick O'R. Hayes, "Change and Innovation in City Government," in *Urban Affairs Annual Review* (Los Angeles: Sage Publications, 1974), p. 135.

3. "New York," *Atlantic Monthly,* June 1967. *New York World–Journal Tribune,* 23 October 1966. In what became a popular form of political temperature taking, New York cab drivers were often asked to comment on the mayor. After Lindsay's first year, journalist Richard Reeves noted that the common response to Mayor Lindsay

from most New York hacks was "That bum." Complaints about the tax hike and the transit fare increase were coupled with the cry that would become louder in future years: "And you tell me what he's done for white people!" Lindsay himself addressed this last concern of the city's middle- and working-class whites: "I understand how they feel and I don't resent it. But this had to be the year of the poor in New York" (Richard Reeves, "A *Great* Mayor, *That* Bum?" *NYTM*, 1 January 1967).

4. Nat Hentoff, "Profiles: The Mayor—I," *The New Yorker*, 7 October 1967. Carol Greitzer expressed the growing disillusionment with Lindsay among the city's liberals: "There is no aura of being open-minded, ready to be moved by the merits of a particular argument. And when people desperately and despairingly quote from one of his own previously held positions, his jaw muscles tighten. Perhaps worst of all, he simply makes no comment, offers no 'yes but' explanations. There is literally no discourse. People are puzzled that he has failed to bring to bear his tremendous prestige, his presence, his personality—to push for the thing he valiantly and gallantly championed as a minority Congressman" (Carol Greitzer, "A Politico Looks at JVL: What Went Wrong?" *VV*, 8 September 1966).

5. Jack Newfield, "Lindsay: A Year Later," in Jack Newfield, *Bread and Roses Too* (New York: E. P. Dutton, 1971), pp. 176-177. Ibid., "A Political Comer: Yes; A Brooding Hamlet: No," *VV*, 25 May 1967. Ibid., "John Lindsay Emerges from Summer and Smoke," *VV*, 7 September 1967.

6. Ibid., "John Vliet Lindsay: Uptight White Knight," *VV*, 4 January 1968. Richard Reeves, "The Impossible Takes a Little Longer," *NYTM*, 28 January 1968.

7. Jeff Greenfield, "Reading John Lindsay's Face," *NYTM*, 23 July 1973. I. D. Robbins Oral History, p. 246, CUOHA. *NYT*, 19 December 1967. Reeves, "The Impossible Takes a Little Longer."

8. Reeves, "The Impossible Takes a Little Longer." *VV*, 23 November 1967.

9. Woody Klein, *Lindsay's Promise: The Dream That Failed* (London: Macmillan, 1970), pp. 284, 217. Interview with Sid Davidoff, 9 April 1997.

10. Interview of Bob Price by author, 21 March 1997. Nat Hentoff, *A Political Life: The Education of John V. Lindsay* (New York: Alfred A. Knopf, 1969), p. 194. Interview of Charles Moerdler by author, 26 June 1997. Interview of Thomas Hoving by author, 21 May 1997. Richard Armstrong, "Second Man at City Hall," *NYTM*, 26 December 1965.

11. Richard Armstrong, "Robert Sweet Is the Unabashed No. 2 Man at City Hall," *NYTM*, 29 September 1968. Roger Starr, "John V. Lindsay: A Political Portrait," *Commentary*, February 1970.

12. Martin Arnold, "The Lindsay Inner Circle," *NYTM*, 15 October 1967. Klein, *Lindsay's Promise*, p. 266. After Klein published his book in 1970, he wrote Lindsay a letter explaining himself. Lindsay, who was very hurt by what he felt was Klein's betrayal, replied with a two-word letter: "What book?"

13. Lindsay quoted in "The Lindsay Years," videotape produced by the Lindsay Reunion Committee, 1990.

14. Todd Gitlin, *The Sixties: Years of Hope, Days of Rage* (Toronto: Bantam Books, 1987), pp. 286-287. For other discussions of the late 1960s see Maurice Isserman and

Michael Kazin, *America Divided: The Civil War of the 1960s* (New York: Oxford University Press, 1999); David Farber *The Age of Great Dreams* (New York: Hill & Wang, 1994); Paul Berman, *A Tale of Two Utopias: The Political Journey of the Generation of 1968* (New York: W. W. Norton, 1996); Stephen Macedo, ed., *Reassessing the Sixties* (New York: W. W. Norton, 1997); Jules Witcover, *The Year the Dream Died: Revisiting 1968 in America* (New York: Warner Books, 1997); Terry H. Anderson, *The Movement and the Sixties* (New York: Oxford University Press, 1995); and David Caute, *The Year of the Barricades: A Journey Through 1968* (New York: Harper & Row, 1988).

15. Charles E. Silberman, *Crisis in Black and White* (New York: Random House, 1964), p. 331. Frances Fox Piven and Richard A. Cloward, "Dissensus Politics: A Strategy for Winning Economic Rights," *The New Republic*, 20 April 1968.

16. *NYT*, 2 January 1968. *U.S. News & World Report*, 12 February 1968. The TWU's generous retirement deal has been credited with the early retirement of 7,000 skilled transit workers in the two years following the new contract. This includes, according to the labor historian Joshua Freeman, "nearly all those who remained from the generation that had organized and nurtured the TWU." More important, these retirements of skilled workers have been blamed for the numerous maintenance and safety mishaps suffered by the city's transit system in the 1970s. See Joshua B. Freeman, *In Transit: The Transit Workers Union in New York City, 1933-1966* (New York: Oxford University Press, 1989), p. 335; and Brian J. Cudahy, *Under the Sidewalks of New York: The Story of the Greatest Subway System in the World* (New York: Fordham University Press, 1995), p. 147.

17. Interview of Edward N. Costikyan by author, 13 November 1996.

18. Sweet quoted in Roger Kahn, "On the Brink of Chaos," *Saturday Evening Post*, 27 July 1968.

19. Raymond Horton, *Municipal Labor Relations in New York City: Lessons of the Lindsay-Wagner Years* (New York: Praeger, 1973), p. 72. For a good description of the sanitation strike, see Charles R. Morris, *The Cost of Good Intentions: New York City and the Liberal Experiment* (New York: W. W. Norton, 1980), pp. 103-106.

20. Horton, *Municipal Labor Relations in New York City*, pp. 82-83.

21. *NYT*, 3 and 5 February 1968.

22. Kahn, "On the Brink of Chaos."

23. DeLury quoted in Michael Kramer and Sam Roberts, *I Never Wanted to Be Vice-President of Anything! An Investigative Biography of Nelson Rockefeller* (New York: Basic Books, 1976), p. 298. On the Taylor Law, see William B. Gould, "The New York Taylor Law: A Preliminary Assessment," *Labor Law Journal*, June 1967.

24. "Mayor's Statement on the Strike," *NYT*, 8 February 1968.

25. Letter from Harry O'Donnell to Roger Kahn, 3 March 1968, Box 5, O'Donnell Papers.

26. *NYT*, 10 and 11 February 1968.

27. Kramer and Roberts, *I Never Wanted to Be Vice-President of Anything!* p. 297. Interview of Alton Marshall by author, 27 March 1997.

28. For Rockefeller and the National Guard, see "Nine Days that Shook New York City," Uniformed Sanitationmen's Association Record, undated.

29. Marshall interview. Interview of Bob Sweet by author, 21 October 1997.

30. Joseph E. Persico, *The Imperial Rockefeller: A Biography of Nelson A. Rockefeller* (New York: Simon & Schuster, 1982), p. 216.

31. Persico, *The Imperial Rockefeller,* p. 217. Marshall interview. Interview of Bob Douglass by author, 22 April 1997.

32. Kahn, "On the Brink of Chaos."

33. A. H. Raskin, "How to Avoid Strikes by Garbagemen, Nurses, Teachers, Subway Men, Welfare Workers, etc.," *NYTM,* 25 February 1968.

34. *NYT,* 11 and 12 February 1968.

35. Ibid., 14 February 1966.

36. Ibid., 23 February 1968. Raskin, "How to Avoid Strikes."

37. A. H. Raskin, "Politics Up-ends the Bargaining Table," in Sam Zagoria, ed., *Public Workers and Public Unions* (Englewood Cliffs, N.J.: Prentice Hall, 1972), p. 134. "Nine Days that Shook New York City." Sweet interview.

38. The eleven members of the Kerner Commission were Governor Otto Kerner (D-Illinois), Mayor John Lindsay, Senator Fred Harris (D-Oklahoma), Senator Edward Brooke (R-Massachusetts), Congressman James Corman (D-California), Congressman William McCulloch (R-Ohio), I. W. Abel (president, United Steelworkers of America), Charles Thornton (CEO, Litton Industries), Roy Wilkins (executive director, NAACP), Katherine Graham Peden (former commissioner of commerce, Kentucky), and Herbert Jenkins (chief of police, Atlanta). Kerner, Lindsay, Harris, Brooke, Wilkins, and Jenkins were the commission's "liberal" members. Corman, McCulloch, Abel, Peden, and Thornton were its "conservative" members.

39. Interview of Peter Goldmark by author, 13 June 1997. Interview of Jay Kriegel by author, 4 February 1997.

40. Memo, Joseph Califano to the President, 28 February 1968, FG 690, Box # 387, WHCF, LBJ Library.

41. Goldmark interview.

42. Michael Lipsky and David Olson, *Commission Politics: The Processing of Racial Crisis in America* (New Brunswick, N.J.: Transaction Books, 1977), pp. 132-133. Goldmark interview. Bill Barnhart and Gene Schlickman, *Kerner: The Conflict of Intangible Rights* (Urbana: University of Illinois Press, 1999), p. 213. Andrew Kopkind, "White on Black: The Riot Commission and the Rhetoric of Reform," in Anthony Platt, ed., *The Politics of Riot Commissions, 1917-1990* (New York: Collier Books, 1971), p. 389.

43. Goldmark interview. Kopkind, "White on Black: The Riot Commission and the Rhetoric of Reform," p. 390.

44. National Advisory Commission on Civil Disorders, *Report of the National Advisory Commission on Civil Disorders* (Kerner Report), pp. 1-2.

45. Goldmark interview. Derthick quoted in Gareth Davies, *From Opportunity to Entitlement: The Transformation and Decline of Great Society Liberalism* (Lawrence, Kans.: University of Kansas Press, 1996), p. 204. *NYT,* 25 February 1968. Lipsky and Olson, *Commission Politics,* p. 134.

46. Ibid., p. 299.

47. Ibid., pp. 395-408.

48. Address by John V. Lindsay, Mayor of the City of New York, at the Opportunities Unlimited Program, Student Union Lounge, University of Denver, Denver, Colorado, Saturday, 30 March 1968, in author's possession. Interview of Mitchell Sviridoff by author, 22 October 1997. Starr, "John V. Lindsay: A Political Portrait."

49. Senator Fred R. Harris and Mayor John V. Lindsay, cochairmen, Commission on the Cities in the '70s, *The State of the Cities: Report of the Commission on the Cities in the '70s* (New York: Praeger, 1972), pp. 6, 11.

50. Ibid., pp. 16-17. Lindsay quoted in "Give a Damn Again," in author's possession.

51. Stephan Thernstrom and Abigail Thernstrom, *America in Black and White: One Nation, Indivisible* (New York: Simon & Schuster, 1997), pp. 81-82, 204-213. For a more pessimistic view of present-day race relations, see Douglas Massey and Nancy Denton, *American Apartheid: Segregation and the Making of the Underclass* (Cambridge, Mass.: Harvard University Press, 1993).

52. Davies, *From Opportunity to Entitlement,* pp. 203-204. Max Geltman, *The Confrontation: Black Power, Anti-Semitism, and the Myth of Integration* (Englewood Cliffs, N.J.: Prentice Hall, 1970), p. 42. On the effects of urban riots on small businesses, see Jonathan J. Bean, " 'Burn, Baby, Burn': Small Business in the Urban Riots of the 1960s," *The Independent Review,* Fall 2000.

53. For a defense of the conclusions of the Kerner Report, see Andrew Hacker, *Two Nations: Black and White, Separate, Hostile, Unequal* (New York: Charles Scribner's Sons, 1992).

54. John V. Lindsay, *The City* (New York: W. W. Norton, 1969), p. 103. The most comprehensive article on the King riots in New York is Gloria Steinem and Lloyd Weaver, "Special Report: The City on the Eve of Destruction," *NY,* 22 April 1968.

55. "Voice of New York," *NY,* 11 April 1988.

56. Lindsay, *The City,* p. 104. Thomas B. Morgan, "The King Assassination," *NY,* 19 April 1993. Interview of David Garth by author, 4 June 1997. Interview of Bob Laird by author, 7 May 1997.

57. Steinem and Weaver, "Special Report." Barry Gottehrer, *The Mayor's Man* (Garden City, N.Y.: Doubleday, 1975), p. 211.

58. Garth interview. Morgan, "The King Assassination." Jack Newfield, "Man of La Gotham: A Walker in the City," *VV,* 25 April 1968. Jimmy Breslin, "Mayor of All the People," *NYP,* 8 April 1968.

59. *AN,* 13 April 1968. *NYT,* 8 April 1968. *NYP,* 5 April 1968. One business destroyed in the riot was a Harlem store owned by Barry Schwartz, who had also just gone into the clothing business a few weeks before the April 1968 riot with his friend Calvin Klein. Schwartz remembers that when he and Klein surveyed the ransacked store, there was very little left. They filled a few shopping bags with what remained and Schwartz "went out on the sidewalk, took the keys, threw them into the store, went downtown," where the two men built a fashion business. But the problems for white store owners in Harlem did not begin in

1968. In 1964, Schwartz's father was stabbed to death in the store. *NYT,* 21 April 1999.

60. Gottehrer quoted in *Life,* 24 May 1968. Steinem and Weaver, "Special Report." Gottehrer, *The Mayor's Man,* p. 214.

61. *NYT,* 16 April 1968. Ibid., 10 April 1968.

62. Paul Chevigny, *Police Power: Police Abuses in New York City* (New York; Pantheon Books, 1969), p. 238. Interview of Charles Moerdler by author, 26 June 1997. Lindsay also appointed some notoriously lenient judges. The most famous example was Criminal Court Judge Bruce M. Wright, nicknamed "Let-em-Loose Bruce" because he released on $500 bail a suspect in the shooting of a policeman.

63. *NYT,* 17 April 1968. Breslin, "Mayor of All the People." *NYP,* 5 April 1968.

64. Breslin, "Mayor of All the People." Gottehrer, *The Mayor's Man,* p. 213.

65. Address by John V. Lindsay, Mayor of the City of New York Before the Members of the Harvard Republican Club and the Harvard Student Body, 20 April 1968, Group 592, Box 76, Folder 619, JVL Papers, Yale. *Life,* 25 May 1968.

66. John V. Lindsay, "We Can Lick the Problems of the Ghetto If We Care," *Reader's Digest,* August 1968. Larry L. King, "Lindsay of New York," *Harper's Magazine,* August 1968.

67. *NYT,* 11 October 1967. Two members of the Urban Coalition, Father John Powis and David Spencer, were already involved in the school decentralization controversy.

68. In his 1995 documentary "Give a Damn Again," Adam Isidore, the son of the man who created the original "What do you want to be when you grow up?" ad, set out to track down the children. He hoped to renew interest in the problems of the slums. Though he failed to spark much excitement for another Great Society, the film remains a very useful document. Belying the gloom of Lindsay and others, many of the children in the ad made out reasonably well. There were the usual stories of jail, drugs, and single-parent families, but there were also men and women with happy marriages and children and relatively successful careers. Their childhood in Harlem in the 1960s did not consign all of them to the bottom of the economic and social ladder forever.

69. *NYT,* 3 July 1968.

70. Ibid., 11 July 1968.

71. Hentoff, *A Political Life,* p. 241. Smith was not the only black militant kept on the city payroll. Robert Collier was a Parks Department recreation director in the Tompkins Square area. Prior to his city work, Collier served time for smuggling dynamite for the purpose of blowing up the Statue of Liberty, the Washington Monument, and the Liberty Bell. He served over two years in prison. Parks Commissioner August Heckscher released a statement saying that Collier had "paid his debt to society." The Department of Personnel said Collier could not be employed because he did not have a college degree and his salary eventually had to be paid with private funds. Unfortunately, Collier continued to get into trouble with the law. He was tried and acquitted in 1971 for conspiring to blow up public places and was arrested in 1973 for selling grenades to an undercover police officer. Barry

Gottehrer called Collier "alternatively one of our most successful community organizers and one of our biggest worries" August Heckscher, *Alive in the City: Memoir of an Ex-Commissioner* New York: Charles Scribner's Sons, 1974, pp. 82-85. Gottehrer, *The Mayor's Man*, p. 148.

72. *NYT*, 3 and 8 August 1968. Ibid., 13 September 1968. Albert A. Seedman and Peter Hellman, *Chief!* (New York: Arthur Fields Books, 1974).

73. *NYT*, 16 August 1968.

74. *NYP*, 5 September 1968.

75. *Newsweek*, 1 March 1971. Address by John V. Lindsay at University of Oregon, 22 February 1968, Group 592, Series VII, Box 136, Folder 124, JVL Papers, Yale. The colleges Lindsay spoke at were: Harvard University, University of Oregon (twice), Columbia University, University of Illinois, University of Wisconsin, Duquesne University (Pittsburgh), University of Denver, Queens College, Vassar College, Syracuse University, University of California at Berkeley, University of Southern California, Occidental College, Notre Dame, and Oregon State.

76. *NYT*, 9 August 1968.

77. Clark Whelton, "To Save the Village (1)," *VV*, 11 March 1971. Ibid., "To Save the Village (2)," *VV*, 18 March 1971.

78. Marty Jezer, *Abbie Hoffman: American Rebel* (New Brunswick, N.J.: Rutgers University Press, 1992), p. 89.

79. Gottehrer, *The Mayor's Man*, p. 134.

80. Jonah Raskin, *For the Hell of It: The Life and Times of Abbie Hoffman* (Berkeley: University of California Press, 1996), p. 116. Gottehrer, *The Mayor's Man*, p. 143. Jezer, *Abbie Hoffman*, p. 92. Interview of Ted Mastroianni by author, 12 December 1997.

81. Ibid.

82. Jezer, *Abbie Hoffman*, p. 130. *NYT*, 24 March 1968.

83. Jezer, *Abbie Hoffman*, p. 133. Gottehrer, *The Mayor's Man*, p. 135.

84. Raskin, *For the Hell of It*, pp. 134-135.

85. Don McNeill, "The Grand Central Riot: Yippies Meet the Man," *VV*, 28 March 1968. Gottehrer, *The Mayor's Man*, p. 136. Mastroianni interview.

86. McNeill, "The Grand Central Riot: Yippies Meet the Man." Nat Hentoff, "Keeping the Cops from Rioting," *VV*, 4 April 1968.

87. Gottehrer, *The Mayor's Man*, p. 144. Interview of Barry Gottehrer by author, 7 July 1997. Hoffman, *Revolution for the Hell of It*, p. 229.

88. Hoffman, *Revolution for the Hell of It*, p. 219.

89. Gottehrer, *The Mayor's Man*, pp. 144-145. Letter from Barry Gottehrer to Robert Morgenthau, 18 September 1980, in author's possession.

90. *NYT*, 15 March 1968. Ibid., 20 March 1968.

91. Address by John V. Lindsay, Mayor of the City of New York, at the Opportunities Unlimited Program, Student Union Lounge, University of Denver, Denver, Colorado, Saturday, 30 March 1968, in author's possession.

92. *NYT*, 24 April 1968.

93. Text of Testimony by John V. Lindsay, Mayor of New York City and Delegate from New York State before the Committee on Resolutions of the 1968 Republican National Convention, 31 July 1968, Group 592, Box 362, Folder 423, JVL Papers, Yale.

94. "Memo to: Convention Delegates; From: Mayor John V. Lindsay, New York; Subject: Vietnam," *Look*, 20 August 1968.

95. Address by John V. Lindsay, Mayor of the City of New York Before the Members of the Harvard Republican Club and the Harvard Student Body, 20 April 1968, Group 592, Box 76, Folder 619, JVL Papers, Yale.

CHAPTER 7

1. For an excellent discussion of the development of Morningside Heights, see Andrew S. Dolkart, *Morningside Heights: A History of Its Architecture and Development* (New York: Columbia University Press, 1998).

2. Letter from Frederick Law Olmsted to Salem H. Wales, 11 October 1873, in Frederick Law Olmsted, *The Papers of Frederick Law Olmsted*, Vol. 4, *The Years of Olmsted, Vaux & Company, 1865–1874* (Baltimore: Johns Hopkins University Press, 1992), p. 651.

3. Olmsted letter in ibid., p. 655. "Lindsay Campaign White Paper on Parks and Recreation," 8 October 1965, Series VI, Box 91, Folder 86, JVL Papers, Yale. Diana Trilling, "On the Steps of Low Library: Liberalism and the Revolution of the Young," *Commentary*, November 1968.

4. For a description of the early years of planning for the gym, see Cox Commission, *Crisis at Columbia: Report of the Fact-Finding Commission Appointed to Investigate the Disturbances at Columbia University in April and May 1968* (New York: Vintage Books, 1968), pp. 76–78. Roger Starr, "The Case of the Columbia Gym," in Daniel Bell and Irving Kristol, eds., *Confrontation: The Student Rebellion and the Universities* (New York: Basic Books, 1968), pp. 116–118.

5. "Morningside's Late, Late Show," *Columbia College Today*, Fall 1966.

6. *NYT*, 3 August 1961. Jane Jacobs, *The Death and Life of Great American Cities* (New York: Vintage Books, 1992), pp. 109–110 (original edition, New York: Random House, 1961).

7. Marta Gutman and Richard Plunz, "Anatomy of Insurrection," in Richard Oliver, ed., *The Making of an Architect: 1881–1981* (New York: Rizzoli International, 1981). Dolkart, *Morningside Heights*, p. 326. Ada Louise Huxtable, "How Not to Build a Symbol," *NYT*, 24 March 1968. See also Ada Louise Huxtable, "Expansion at Columbia: A Restricted Vision and Bureaucracy Seen as Obstacles to Its Development," *NYT*, 5 November 1966; Allan Temko, "A Brilliant Plan Gone Awry?" *Columbia College Today*, Fall 1962; and Fred Hechinger, "Columbia Scored on Architecture," *NYT*, 5 December 1962.

8. Huxtable, "How Not to Build a Symbol." C. Richard Hatch, "Pleonexia on the Acropolis," *Architectural Forum*, July–August 1967. James Ridgeway, "Colum-

bia's Real Estate Ventures," *The New Republic,* 18 May 1968. Roger Kahn, *Battle for Morningside Heights: Why Students Rebel* (New York: William Morrow, 1970), p. 18.

9. "Lindsay Campaign White Paper on Parks and Recreation," 8 October 1965, Series VI, Box 91, Folder 86, JVL Papers, Yale. Nat Hentoff, *A Political Life: The Education of John V. Lindsay* (New York: Alfred A. Knopf, 1969), pp. 87–88.

10. Cox Commission, *Crisis at Columbia,* pp. 78–79. Interview of Thomas Hoving by author, 21 May 1997. Hoving quoted in Proceedings of the Fact Finding Commission (Cox Commission), p. 3570, Box 4, Folder 21, CUOHA.

11. *NYT,* 24 July 1968. Kahn, *The Battle for Morningside Heights,* p. 94. Starr, "The Case of the Columbia Gym."

12. Hoving interview. Starr, "The Case of the Columbia Gym." Benjamin Buttenwieser Oral History, p. 523, CUOHA. There is an interesting irony to Hoving's complaints about the encroachment of private institutions into public parks. In 1967, after leaving the Lindsay administration to become director of the Metropolitan Museum of Art, Hoving undertook an ambitious plan to expand the museum farther into Central Park. The extension was to include the new wing for the Temple of Dendur. Hoving, who understood the controversial nature of such an encroachment on the city's parks, justified his effort by saying, "Anything we build will be, in some manner, a sympathetic extension of the park." This was a far cry from Hoving's attacks on Columbia's planned gym. See Robert A. M. Stern, Thomas Mellins, and David Fishman, *New York 1960: Architecture and Urbanism Between the Second World War and the Bicentennial* (New York: Monacelli Press, 1995), p. 790.

13. *AN,* 29 January 1966.

14. *Columbia Spectator* poll quoted in Daniel Bell, "Columbia and the New Left," in Bell and Kristol, *Confrontation,* p. 70. George Nash and Cynthia Epstein, "Harlem Views Columbia University," *NY,* July 8, 1968.

15. Jerry Avorn et al., *Up Against the Ivy Wall: A History of the Columbia Crisis* (New York: Atheneum, 1969), p. 20; Kahn, *Battle for Morningside Heights,* p. 96; and Starr "The Case of the Columbia Gym."

16. Cox Commission, *Crisis at Columbia,* p. 85.

17. Starr, "The Case of the Columbia Gym." Huxtable, "How Not to Build a Symbol."

18. Cox Commission, *Crisis at Columbia,* pp. 40, 84.

19. Interview of Amalia Betanzos by author, 27 May 1997.

20. Jacobs, *Death and Life of Great American Cities,* p. 6. *NYT,* 9 June 1958. Dolkart, *Morningside Heights,* pp. 325–334.

21. On Columbia's real estate expansion, see Hatch, "Pleonexia on the Acropolis"; Stern, Mellins, and Fishman, *New York 1960,* pp. 736–740, 745–751; Dolkart, *Morningside Heights,* pp. 326–336; and Ridgeway, "Columbia's Real Estate Ventures."

22. Cox Commission, *Crisis at Columbia,* pp. 73–74. Kahn, *Battle for Morningside Heights,* p. 108. Bell, "Columbia and the New Left," pp. 70–71.

23. Grayson Kirk, "The Umpirage of Reason," in Immanuel Wallerstein and Paul Starr, eds., *The University Crisis Reader: The Liberal University Under Attack* (New York: Random House, 1971), pp. 424–427.

24. Mark Rudd, "Reply to Uncle Grayson," in Wallerstein and Starr, *The University Crisis Reader,* pp. 428–429.

25. Avorn et al., *Up Against the Ivy Wall,* pp. 38–39.

26. Ibid., pp. 40–41. Cox Commission, *Crisis at Columbia,* pp. 99–102.

27. Avorn et al., *Up Against the Ivy Wall,* p. 49. Simon James, "The Diary of a Revolutionist," *NY,* 27 May 1968. Simon James was the pseudonym used by James Simon Kunen, a Columbia SDS member, whose recollections of the Columbia revolt were published as *The Strawberry Statement: Notes of a College Revolutionary* (New York: Avon Books, 1970). The book was eventually turned into a movie of the same name, though it bears little resemblance to the events that occurred at Columbia.

28. Avorn et al., *Up Against the Ivy Wall,* pp. 54–56. Grayson Kirk Oral History, CUOHA.

29. Avorn et al., *Up Against the Ivy Wall,* p. 57.

30. Kunen, *The Strawberry Statement,* p. 31. Sales and Brown quoted in Stephen Donadio, "Columbia: Seven Interviews," *Partisan Review,* Summer 1968.

31. Bell, "Columbia and the New Left," pp. 77–78. Avorn et al., *Up Against the Ivy Wall,* pp. 61, 65. Kahn, *Battle for Morningside Heights,* p. 150.

32. *NYT,* 25 April 1968.

33. Tom Hayden, "Two, Three, Many Columbias," *Ramparts,* 15 June 1968. Mark Rudd, "We Want Revolution," *Saturday Evening Post,* 21 September 1968. Paul Rockwell, "The Columbia Statement," 12 September 1968, reprinted in Wallerstein and Starr, *The University Crisis Reader,* p. 28.

34. Barry Gottehrer, *The Mayor's Man* (Garden City, N.Y.: Double-day & Company, Inc., 1975), p. 162. Kahn, *Battle for Morningside Heights,* p. 150. For a view of the situation of black radicals at Columbia, see Stephen Donadio, "Black Power at Columbia," *Commentary,* September 1968.

35. Trilling, "On the Steps of Low Library." David Rothman Oral History, p. 50, CUOHA. Numbers on the racial breakdown of Morningside Heights are from Kahn, *The Battle for Morningside Heights,* p. 84.

36. Donadio, "Columbia: Seven Interviews." Transcript of Elf interview in Folder G.4, Radio and TV Reports, Columbiana archives. Sales quoted in transcript of David Suskind Show, WNEW-TV, 12 May 1968, Folder G.3, Columbiana Archives.

37. Lofton Mitchell, "The Fear of Losing Harlem Behind the Rage and Anger," *AN,* 4 May 1968. A cartoon in that same issue of the *Amsterdam News* showed a black man with the word HARLEM written across his chest being strangled by the tassels from a mortarboard labeled COLUMBIA UNIVERSITY GYM. One of the arms pulling on the tassel strangling the man was labeled MAYOR LINDSAY.

38. Figures on Columbia are quoted in Dankwart A. Rustow, "Days of Crisis," *The New Leader,* 20 May 1968. Cox Commission, *Crisis at Columbia,* pp. 43–44.

39. "Six Weeks that Shook Morningside." Rudd, "Symbols of the Revolution," p. 292. Some of the conservative counterprotesters at Columbia were New York Governor George Pataki, then a law student, and William Barr, who served as attorney general under George Bush.

40. *The American Enterprise,* May–June 1997, p. 39, "Faculty Thoughts on the Jewish Role in the Student Disorders at Columbia University," November 1968, Columbia University 1968 Folder, AJC Archives. For a history of the Young Americans for Freedom, see John A. Andrew, *The Other Side of the Sixties: Young Americans for Freedom and the Rise of Conservative Politics* (New Brunswick, N.J.: Rutgers University Press, 1997), and Gregory L. Schneider, *Cadres for Conservatism: Young Americans for Freedom and the Rise of the Contemporary Right* (New York: New York University Press, 1999). On the role of Jewish students in the New Left, see Nathan Glazer, "The Jewish Role in Student Activism," *Fortune,* January 1969, and ibid., "The New Left and the Jews," *The Jewish Journal of Sociology,* December 1969.

41. Herbert A. Deane, "Reflections on Student Radicalism," in Avorn et al., *Up Against the Ivy Wall,* p. 290. Alexander Platt Oral History, CUOHA. Walter Metzger Oral History, CUOHA.

42. Kahn, *Battle for Morningside Heights,* p. 167. Bell, "Columbia and the New Left," p. 83. The members of the steering committee of the Ad Hoc Faculty Group included Alan Westin (government), Alex Dallin (government), Dankwart Rustow (government), Immanuel Wallerstein (sociology), Terence Hopkins (sociology), Alan Silver (sociology), Daniel Bell (sociology), James Shenton (history), David Rothman (history), Robert Fogelson (history), Walter Metzger (history), Robert Cumming (philosophy), Sidney Morgenbesser (philosophy), Robert Belknap (Russian literature), and Seymour Melman (industrial engineering).

43. Walter Metzger, "Authority at Columbia," in Wallerstein and Starr, *The University Crisis Reader,* pp. 335–336. Kunen, *The Strawberry Statement,* p. 36. Mark Rudd, "Events and Issues of the Columbia Revolt," in Gary R. Weaver and James H. Weaver, eds., *The University and Revolution* (Englewood Cliffs, N.J.: Prentice Hall, 1969), p. 136.

44. Gottehrer, *Mayor's Man,* pp. 165–166, 177. Interview of Barry Gottehrer by author, 7 July 1997. Avorn et al., *Up Against the Ivy Wall,* p. 109. Kunen, *The Strawberry Statement,* p. 134. Donadio, "Columbia: Seven Interviews." Polykarp Kusch Oral History, CUOHA. Richard Hofstadter Oral History, CUOHA.

45. Avorn et al., *Up Against the Ivy Wall,* p. 161. Immanuel Wallerstein, "Radical Intellectuals in a Liberal Society," in Wallerstein and Starr, *University Crisis Reader,* pp. 471–477. Grayson Kirk Oral History, CUOHA. Donadio, "Columbia: Seven Interviews."

46. Wallerstein, "Radical Intellectuals in a Liberal Society," pp. 471–477. Richard Goldstein, "The Groovy Revolution: Fold, Spindle, Mutilate," *VV,* 2 May 1968. Friedman quoted in Avorn et al., *Up Against the Ivy Wall,* p. 24.

47. Orest Ranum Oral History, CUOHA. Grayson Kirk Oral History, CUOHA. Cox Commission, *Crisis at Columbia,* pp. 160–161.

48. Avorn et al., *Up Against the Ivy Wall,* pp. 107–108. Marvin Harris Oral History, CUOHA. Terrence Hopkins Oral History, CUOHA.

49. Kahn, *Battle for Morningside Heights,* pp. 168–169.

50. Avorn et al., *Up Against the Ivy Wall,* pp. 109–110, 114–115. Gottehrer, *The Mayor's Man,* p. 166. *NYT,* 26 April 1968.

51. Gottehrer interview.

52. Gottehrer, *The Mayor's Man,* p. 168.

53. Ibid., p. 169. Interview of David Garth by author, 4 June 1997. Avorn et al., *Up Against the Ivy Wall,* p. 180. Immanuel Wallerstein Oral History, CUOHA.

54. Interview of Ted Mastroianni by author, 12 December 1997.

55. Cox Commission, *Crisis at Columbia,* pp. 162–167. Report from First Deputy Commissioner John F. Walsh, to Police Commissioner Howard Leary, 4 May 1968, Series 592, Box 137, Folder 140, JVL Papers, Yale.

56. Avorn et al., *Up Against the Ivy Wall,* pp. 194–198. Arrest totals from Proceedings of the Fact Finding Commission (Cox Commission), Box 5, Arrests Folder, Columbiana Archives.

57. Avorn et al., *Up Against the Ivy Wall,* p. 205. Marvin Harris, "Big Bust on Morningside Heights," *The Nation,* 10 June 1968. Steven V. Roberts, "The University that Refused to Learn," *VV,* 9 May 1968. Nat Hentoff, "Columbia's Gift to the Mayor," *VV,* 9 May 1968.

58. Bell, "Columbia and the New Left," pp. 101–107.

59. *NYT,* 3 May 1968.

60. Gottehrer, *The Mayor's Man,* pp. 177–178. Robert Fogelson Oral History, CUOHA. Donadio, "Columbia: Seven Interviews." Cox Commission, *Crisis at Columbia,* p. 166. Peter Kenen Oral History, CUOHA.

61. Injury totals from Proceedings of the Fact Finding Commission (Cox Commission), Box 5, Arrests Folder, Columbiana Archives. Cox Commission, *Crisis at Columbia,* p. 142.

62. Report of the Civilian Complaint Review Board, 29 March 1970, Group 592, Box 366, Folder 496, JVL Papers, Yale. Report from First Deputy Commissioner John F. Walsh to Police Commissioner Howard Leary, 4 May 1968.

63. *Baltimore Sun,* 10 July 1968. *NYT,* 27 December 1968.

64. Kahn, *Battle for Morningside Heights,* p. 206. Robert Fogelson Oral History, CUOHA. Interview of Sid Davidoff by author, 9 April 1997. Interview of Sanford Garelik by author, 14 April 1997. Gottehrer, *The Mayor's Man,* p. 176.

65. Garelik interview. Grayson Kirk Oral History, CUOHA. Trilling, "On the Steps of Low Library: Liberalism and the Revolution of the Young."

66. Report from First Deputy Commissioner John F. Walsh to Police Commissioner Howard Leary, 4 May 1968.

67. Kahn, *Battle for Morningside Heights,* pp. 195–196, 205. Gottehrer, *The Mayor's Man,* p. 177. Interview of Donald Elliott by author, 20 April 1997.

68. *AN,* 4 May 1968.

69. Robert Coles and Jon Erikson, *The Middle Americans: Proud and Uncertain* (Boston: Little, Brown, 1971), pp. 50–59.

70. Nicholas Alex, *New York Cops Talk Back: A Study of a Beleaguered Minority* (New York: John Wiley, 1976), p. 120. "Faculty Thoughts on the Jewish Role in the Student Disorders at Columbia University," November 1968, Columbia University 1968 Folder, AJC Archives.

71. Grayson Kirk Oral History, CUOHA. Kahn, *Battle for Morningside Heights,* p. 204.

72. Mastroianni interview. Interview of Jay Kriegel by author, 4 February 1997. Garth interview. Elliott interview. "Voice of New York," *NY,* 11 April 1988.

73. Statement by Mayor John V. Lindsay, Tuesday, 30 April 1968, Group 592, Box 137, Folder 140, JVL Papers, Yale. Buckley quote from transcript of *Twin Circle Forum,* WOR-TV, 12 May 1968, Folder G.3, Columbiana Archives.

74. *NYT,* 22 June 1968.

75. Ibid., 22 May 1968.

76. Ibid., 13 December 1968. "Address by The Honorable John V. Lindsay, Mayor of the City of New York Before the Student Body of Columbia University, Dodge Hall, McMillan Theater, Thursday, 12 December 1968," Folder A.6.1, Columbiana Archives.

77. *NYT,* 18 February 1969. *DN,* 12 December 1967.

78. Cox Commission, *Crisis at Columbia,* p. 25.

79. Edward Rothstein, "Rude Awakenings from '60s Dreams," *NYT,* 1 May 1997.

80. M. Stanton Evans, "Nihilism, a Product of the Liberal System," in Wallerstein and Starr, *The University Crisis Reader,* pp. 430–435.

81. Allen J. Matusow, *The Unraveling of America: A History of Liberalism in the 1960s* (New York: Harper & Row, 1984), p. 344. Roger Rosenblatt, *Coming Apart: A Memoir of the Harvard Wars of 1969* (Boston: Little, Brown, 1997), p. 216. For a critical and caustic view of the 1969 disturbances by a former Cornell professor, see Walter Berns, "The Assault on the Universities: Then and Now," in Stephen Macedo, ed., *Reassessing the Sixties: Debating the Political and Cultural Legacy* (New York: W. W. Norton, 1997). For a history of the 1969 Cornell student revolt, see Donald Alexander Downs, *Cornell '69: Liberalism and the Crisis of the American University* (Ithaca, N.Y.: Cornell University Press, 1999).

82. Gottehrer, *The Mayor's Man,* p. 180. *NYT,* 9 February 1969.

83. *NYT,* 18 April 1969. Ibid., 1 May 1969. Ibid., 2 May 1969. Susan Stern, *With the Weathermen: The Personal Journal of a Revolutionary Woman* (Garden City, N.Y.: Doubleday, 1975), p. 50.

84. Todd Gitlin, *The Sixties: Years of Hope, Days of Rage* (New York: Bantam Books, 1987), p. 400. Kirkpatrick Sale, *SDS* (New York: Vintage Books, 1973), pp. 608–609. On the Weathermen, see "Weathermen," *Esquire,* August 1970; Harold Jacobs, ed., *Weatherman* (New York: Ramparts Press, 1970); and Stern, *With the Weathermen.*

85. J. Kirk Sale, "Ted Gold: Education for Violence," *The Nation,* 13 April 1970.

86. On Dave Gilbert and the "Brinks Robbery," see John Castellucci, *The Big Dance: The Untold Story of Kathy Boudin and the Terrorist Family that Committed the Brinks Robbery Murders* (New York: Dodd, Mead, 1986).

Chapter 8

1. Diane Ravitch, "The Autopsy Proves the Corpse is Dead," *VV,* 16 March 1972.

2. Ibid., *The Great School Wars: A History of the New York City Public Schools,* 2nd ed. (New York: Basic Books, 1988), p. 252–253. David Rogers, "Obstacles to School Desegregation in New York City: A Benchmark Case," in Marilyn Gittell and Alan G. Hevesi, eds., *The Politics of Urban Education* (New York: Praeger, 1969), p. 123. For a background on the Board of Education's post-*Brown* integration policy, see Marilyn Gittell, *Participants and Participation: A Study of School Policy in New York City* (New York: Praeger, 1967), pp. 40–45; and Bert E. Swanson, *The Struggle for Equality: School Integration Controversy in New York City* (New York: Hobbs, Dorman, 1966).

3. Marilyn Gittell, "Professionalism and Public Participation in Educational Policy-Making: New York City, A Case Study," in Gittell and Hevesi, *The Politics of Urban Education,* p. 159. Mario Fantini, Marilyn Gittell, and Richard Magat, *Community Control and the Urban School* (New York: Praeger, 1970), p. 6.

4. Ravitch, *Great School Wars,* p. 259.

5. For an example of the failure of pairing schools, see "Integration Misfire: White Pupils Desert Voluntarily Paired Brooklyn School," *WSJ,* 21 October 1966. The article describes two schools in Brooklyn Heights: P.S. 8, a predominately white school, and P.S. 7, a predominately black and Puerto Rican school. The white parents—affluent, professional, and liberal—initially welcomed pairing. In 1964, the first year of the experiment, 358 of the 923 children in P.S. 7–8 were white. But many white parents quickly became disillusioned, not because of racism, but because of the declining quality of education in the paired schools. The following year, many parents, even those who had vocally supported the pairing plan, pulled their children out of the experiment. By 1965, the number of white students in P.S. 7–8 had dropped to 251.

6. David Rogers, *110 Livingston Street: Politics and Bureaucracy in the New York City Schools* (New York: Random House, 1968), p. 15. Gittell, *Participants and Participation,* p. 68. Martin Mayer, "Close to Midnight for the New York Schools," *NYTM,* 2 May 1965. The percentage of white students enrolled in public schools be-

tween 1958 and 1966 remained relatively stable in Staten Island, southern Brooklyn, Manhattan (except for the Lower East Side, where the percentage of white students fell from 45 to 22 percent), and Queens (except for southeastern Queens, where white students declined from 75 to 46 percent). The biggest changes in racial balance between 1958 and 1966 occurred in the schools of the Bronx and central Brooklyn. In District 7 (South Bronx), the percentage of white students fell from 23 to 7 percent; in District 9 (Kingsbridge–Morris Park), 62 to 35 percent; in District 12 (central Bronx) 43 to 10 percent. In Brooklyn the numbers were similar: in District 17 (Brownsville), 53 to 17 percent; in District 19 (northeast Brooklyn) 69 to 24 percent; in District 15 (Sunset Park), 61 to 40 percent; in District 14 (Williamsburg–Greenpoint), 35 to 14 percent. See Mayor's Advisory Panel on Decentralization of the New York City Schools (Bundy Panel), "Reconnection for Learning: A Community School System for New York City" (Bundy Report), November 1967, in Gittell and Hevesi, *Politics of Urban Education,* pp. 261–276.

7. Ravitch, *Great School Wars,* p. 268.

8. On the 1964 boycott, see Estelle Fuchs, *Pickets at the Gate* (New York: Free Press, 1966), and Clarence Taylor, *Knocking at our Own Door: Milton A. Galamison and the Struggle to Integrate New York City Schools* (New York: Columbia University Press, 1997), pp. 116–175.

9. Memo from Theodore H. Lang, Deputy Superintendent of Schools, to Bernard Donovan, 18 July 1968, Tables 1, 2, Files of the Mayor's Advisory Panel on Decentralization of the New York City Schools, Box 14568, Research and Ethnic Folder, Ford Foundation Archives.

10. Melvin Zimet, *Decentralization and School Effectiveness: A Case Study of the 1969 Decentralization Law in New York City* (New York: Teachers College Press, 1973), p. 2.

11. Racial percentages in Brooklyn and Queens high schools in Harold Saltzman, *Race War in High School: The Ten Year Destruction of Franklin K. Lane High School in Brooklyn* (New Rochelle, N.Y.: Arlington House, 1972), pp. 222–223.

12. For discussions of the I.S. 201 controversy, see Carolyn Woods Eisenberg, "The Parents Movement at I.S. 201: From Integration to Black Power, 1958–1966," (Ph.D. diss., Columbia University, 1971); Ravitch, *Great School Wars,* pp. 292–311; Andrew Kopkind, "Down the Down Staircase: Parents, Teachers, and Public Authorities," *The New Republic,* 22 October 1966; Jeremy Larner, "I.S. 201: Disaster in the Schools," *Dissent,* January–February 1967; and Thomas K. Minter, "Intermediate School 201, Manhattan: Center of Controversy" (Harvard University, 2 June 1967).

13. Robert A. M. Stern, Thomas Mellins, and David Fishman, *New York 1960: Architecture and Urbanism Between the Second World War and the Bicentennial* (New York: Monacelli Press, 1995), p. 883. Eliot Willensky and Norval White, *AIA Guide to New York City,* 3rd ed. (New York: Harcourt Brace Jovanovich, 1988), p. 444. Dorothy S. Jones, "The Issues at I.S. 201: A View from the Parent's Committee," *Integrated Education,* October–November 1966.

14. Ravitch, *Great School Wars,* p. 295. Eisenberg, "The Parents Movement at I.S. 201," pp. 65–66.

15. A copy of the I.S. 201 flyer is found in Minter, "Intermediate School 201, Manhattan," Appendix 1.

16. Minter, "Intermediate School 201, Manhattan." Robinson's letter to Donovan quoted in Eisenberg, "The Parents Movement at I.S. 201," p. 84.

17. Interview of Mitchell Sviridoff by author, 22 October 1997. Memo from Mario D. Fantini to McGeorge Bundy and Champion Ward, 11 October 1966, Files of Mayor's Advisory Panel on the Decentralization of the New York City Schools, Box 14566, I.S. 201 Folder, Ford Foundation Archives. Memo from Mario D. Fantini to McGeorge Bundy, 28 November 1966, Files of the Office of the President, McGeorge Bundy, Series II, Subject Files, Box 13, Folder 164, Ford Foundation Archives.

18. Gittell, *Participants and Participation,* pp. 61–67.

19. David Alan Bresnick, "Legislating New York City School Decentralization" (Ph.D. diss., Columbia University, 1972), p. 46.

20. David Halberstam, "The Very Expensive Education of McGeorge Bundy," *Harper's Magazine,* July 1969. Martin Mayer, *The Teachers Strike: New York, 1968* (New York: Harper & Row, 1969), p. 105. Interview of Marilyn Gittell by author, 4 November 1997.

21. Garrison telegram quoted in Bresnick, "Legislating New York City School Decentralization," p. 47.

22. Mayor's Advisory Panel on Decentralization of the New York City Schools, "Reconnection for Learning."

23. Joseph Featherstone, "Community Control of Our Schools," *The New Republic,* 13 January 1968. Memo from Mario D. Fantini to McGeorge Bundy, 28 November 1966.

24. *NYT,* 9 November 1967. Council of Supervisory Associations of the Public Schools of New York City, "Response to the Lindsay-Bundy Proposals," Interim Report No. 2, January 1968, in Gittell and Hevesi, *The Politics of Urban Education,* pp. 277–287 (see p. 278).

25. *NYT,* 9 and 10 November 1967. Council of Supervisory Associations of the Public Schools of New York City, "Response to the Lindsay-Bundy Proposals." Ravitch, *Great School Wars,* p. 335. Bresnick, "Legislating New York City School Decentralization," pp. 47–48.

26. Excerpts from UFT Statement, 28 November 1967, in Maurice Berube and Marilyn Gittell, eds., *Confrontation at Ocean Hill–Brownsville: The New York School Strikes of 1968* (New York: Praeger, 1969), pp. 219–221.

27. Letter from Sandra Feldman to Mario Fantini, 12 June 1967, Files of the Mayor's Advisory Panel on the Decentralization of the New York City Schools, Box 14567, UFT Folder, Ford Foundation Archives.

28. *NYT,* 13 November 1967. David Seeley, "Decentralization of the New York City Schools" (Ed.D. diss., Harvard University, Graduate School of Education, 1970), p. 16. Interview of David Seeley by author, 22 January 1998.

29. Maurice Berube, "Scarsdale, Yes—Harlem, No," *Commonweal,* 21 June 1968.

30. Seeley, "Decentralization of the New York City Schools," p. 24. Bresnick, "Legislating New York City School Decentralization," pp. 57–58. Letter from John V. Lindsay to Nelson Rockefeller, Members of the State Legislature, Members of the Board of Regents, 2 January 1968.

31. Sviridoff interview. Letter from John V. Lindsay to Nelson Rockefeller et al., 2 January 1968.

32. On the "People's Board of Education," see Taylor, *Knocking at our Own Door,* pp. 182–184.

33. People's Board of Education, Press Release, 28 February 1967, Office of the Mayor (John V. Lindsay), Assistant to the Mayor (Barry Gottehrer), 1970–1971, JVL Papers NYCMA.

34. Ravitch, *Great School Wars,* p. 308. *NYT,* 21 December 1966.

35. *NYT,* 8 December 1966. Barbara Carter, *Pickets, Parents, and Power: The Story Behind the New York City Teachers' Strike* (New York: Citation Press, 1971), p. 119.

36. *NYT,* 18 and 20 May 1967.

37. Ibid., 22 May 1967. Ibid., 8 June 1967. Mwlina Imiri Abubadika (Sonny Carson), *The Education of Sonny Carson* (New York: W. W. Norton, 1972). See also Ravitch, *Great School Wars,* p. 317.

38. *NYT,* 20 January 1968. *AN,* 27 January 1968.

39. *NYT,* 24 January 1968. Letter from Albert Vann and anonymous parent in *AN,* 3 February 1968.

40. *NYT,* 6 February 1968.

41. *NYT,* 22 February 1968. *AN,* 2 March 1968.

42. "Transcript of Tape—I.S. 201—Herman Ferguson," in author's possession.

43. *AN,* 2 March 1968. New York City Commission on Human Rights, "Report on Three Demonstration Projects in the City Schools," February-March 1968, pp. 10–11.

44. *NYT,* 25 February 1968.

45. Ravitch, *Great School Wars,* p. 307. David J. Ayers, "The Effects of Ethnicity, Class and Occupation Affiliation Upon Political Style: A Theoretical and Historical Analysis of the Sociological Influence Shaping Competing Positions in the Controversy Over the Movement for Community Control for Public Schools in New York City, 1966–1969" (Ph.D. diss., Sociology Department, New York University, 1996), p. 201. Eisenberg, "The Parents Movement at I.S. 201," pp. 156, 273.

46. The author has seen, as late as 1996, flyers for local school board candidates in Brooklyn that discuss the "genocide" of minority students in public schools.

47. Jones, "The Issues at I.S. 201: A View from the Parents' Committee," p. 25. Ravitch, *Great School Wars,* pp. 306–307.

48. Ibid., p. 318.

49. Meier, "The New York Teachers' Strike." Jerald E. Podair, " 'White' Values, 'Black' Values: The Ocean Hill–Brownsville Controversy and New York City Culture, 1965–1975," *Radical History Review,* Spring 1994, p. 46.

50. Memo from Mario D. Fantini to McGeorge Bundy, 28 November 1966.

51. McKissick quoted in Robert C. Maynard, "Black Nationalism and Community Schools," in Henry Levin, ed., *Community Control of Schools* (Washington: Brookings Institution, 1970), p. 102. Preston Wilcox, "One View and a Proposal," *Urban Review,* July 1966. Interview of Preston Wilcox by author, 23 December 1997. Wilcox was influenced by Leonard Covello, the respected principal of Benjamin Franklin High School in the then-heavily Italian neighborhood of East Harlem. In the 1940s, Covello attempted to create a "Community Centered School" that would make the public school more responsive and relevant to the Italian American community. Covello's plan, unlike plans for community control put forward by Wilcox and others, was not a racially or ethnically "separatist" program.

52. Preston Wilcox, "To Be Black and to Be Successful," 21 February 1966, in author's possession.

53. Rogers, *110 Livingston Street.* Mayer, "Close to Midnight for the New York Schools." David Rogers, "The New York City School System: A Classic Case of Bureaucratic Pathology," in Annette T. Rubenstein, ed., *Schools Against Children: The Case for Community Control* (New York: Monthly Review Press, 1970), pp. 129–130. Jason Epstein, "The Politics of School Decentralization," *The New York Review of Books,* 6 June 1967.

54. Maurice Berube, *American School Reform: Progressive, Equity, and Excellence Movements, 1883–1993* (Westport, Conn.: Praeger, 1994), p. 83. Ford Foundation, "And Then There Were the Children: An Assessment of Efforts to Test Decentralization in New York City's Public School System," p. 34, May 1969, Folder 002149, Ford Foundation Archives. Gittell, *Participants and Participation.* Gittell interview.

55. Ibid., "Education: The Decentralization—Community Control Controversy," in Jewel Bellush and Stephen M. David, eds., *Race and Politics in New York City: Five Studies in Policy-Making* (New York: Praeger, 1971), p. 135.

56. *City Almanac,* February 1967, Section 2. For an overview of the Coleman Report, see James S. Coleman, "Equal Schools or Equal Students?" *The Public Interest,* Summer 1966, and Christopher Jencks, "A Reappraisal of the Most Controversial Educational Document of Our Time," *NYTM,* 10 August 1969. According to Coleman, "Per pupil expenditures, books in the library, and a host of other facility and curricular measures show virtually no relation to achievement if the 'social' environment of the school—the educational backgrounds of other students and teachers—is held constant. . . . The sources of inequality of educational opportunity appears to lie first in the home itself and the cultural influence immediately surrounding the home."

57. Charles E. Wilson, "201—First Steps Toward Community Control," in Rubenstein, ed., *Schools Against Children,* p. 212.

58. Memo from Ellen Lurie to Preston Wilcox, 16 January 1967, Box 14, Folder 100, Galamison Papers.

59. Spencer and Wilson, "The Case for Community Control—In Harlem." *AN,* 18 and 25 May 1968.

60. Letter from John V. Lindsay to E. Babette Edwards, 27 July 1966, Files of the Mayor's Advisory Panel on Decentralization of the New York City Schools, Box 14566, I.S. 201 Folder, Ford Foundation Archives.

61. Edwards letter quoted in Eisenberg, "The Parents Movement at I.S. 201," p. 150. Minter, "Intermediate School 201, Manhattan," Appendix 2, p. 8.

62. Ibid., Appendix 3.

63. Jones, "The Issues at I.S. 201," p. 20.

64. Martin Mayer, "Frustration Is the Word for Ocean Hill," *NYTM*, 19 May 1968, p. 59. *NYT*, 13 September 1966. The *Times*'s education reporter, Fred Hechinger, found the "street agitation" surrounding I.S. 201 to be "flagrantly anti-white and anti-Semitic." Andrew Kopkind, who sympathized with the Harlem parents, noted that the pickets at I.S. 201 had taken an increasingly "tougher tone" and had been joined by local black militants dressed in African robes. Carolyn Eisenberg minimized the more unsavory aspects of the I.S. 201 controversy, saying it "demonstrated scant awareness on the part of blacks of the relevance of the Jewish issue to the conflict. Jews themselves appear to have been more sensitive to it. It is primarily because of this latter fact that the matter bears discussion." Babette Edwards believed most I.S. 201 parents did not even know that Lisser was Jewish. See Eisenberg, "The Parents Movement at I.S. 201," pp. 207, 303.

65. Jones, "The Issues at I.S. 201," p. 22. *NYP*, 21 September 1966. It was clear that Lisser's main liability was his race. Because of the high percentage of Jewish principals and teachers in Harlem (and the whole city school system), there were also anti-Semitic undertones. Harlem parents claimed to have seven pages of complaints against Lisser, but refused to take action on the charges. Andrew Kopkind repeated the smear: "Lisser was not a well-loved figure in Harlem (he had had problems of a similar kind at other schools)." But another observer, Jeremy Larner, noted that the "complaints were compiled by a black nationalist teacher who first clashed with Lisser when the teacher insisted on the right to administer corporal punishment." Larner could not find one serious complaint against Lisser, finding him "a thoughtful, worried man devoted to the welfare of his pupils and staff." These two interpretations were indicative of the splits on the left. Kopkind was a New Left radical who sympathized with militant blacks more than with middle-class principals and teachers. Larner, writing for Irving Howe's Old Left journal, *Dissent*, sympathized with the teachers' union and the teachers and principals. See Kopkind, "Down the Down Staircase," p. 13, and Larner, "I.S. 201: Disaster in the Schools," pp. 30–31. See also Stanley Plastrik, "Making the Teachers America's Scapegoat," *Dissent*, January–February 1968.

66. *NYT*, 21 September 1966. Eisenberg, "The Parents Movement at I.S. 201," p. 241. Jones, "The Issues at I.S. 201," p. 22.

67. Eisenberg, "The Parents Movement at I.S. 201," pp. 250–251.

68. Ravitch, *Great School Wars*, p. 306.

69. Eisenberg, "The Parents Movement at I.S. 201," p. 321. Spencer quoted in Ford Foundation, "And Then There Were the Children." Kornegay quoted in

Daniel H. Perlstein, "The New York City School Crisis: Teacher Politics, Racial Politics and the Decline of Liberalism" (Ph.D. diss., Stanford University, 1994), p. 275. Interview of Donald Elliott by author, 30 April 1997. Richard Magat, "The Ford Foundation's New Currency: Advancing Social Change on the Quiet and on the Cheap," 17 April 1967, Folder 010718, Ford Foundation Archives.

70. Eisenberg, "The Parents Movement at I.S. 201, 1958–1966," p. 264.

71. Ibid., p. 272.

72. *NYT,* 1 February 1968.

73. Ford Foundation, "And Then There Were the Children," p. 149. Kopkind, "Down the Down Staircase," p. 14. Eisenberg, "The Parents Movement at I.S. 201," p. 327. *NYT,* 8 February 1968. Sociologist Christopher Jencks argued in 1969 that discipline was the best criterion of success in inner-city schools, not academic achievement. "From this perspective," wrote Jencks, "the best index of a school's success or failure may not be reading scores but the number of rocks thrown through its windows in an average month" (Jencks, "A Reappraisal")

74. Ford Foundation, "And Then There Were the Children," p. 14. On the Two Bridges district, see Adele Spier, "Two Bridges Model School District: A Profile," Institute for Community Studies, Queens College, February 1969, and Ford Foundation, "And Then There Were the Children," pp. 67–121.

75. *NYT,* 7 July 1967. "A.T.A. on Bundy Report," *African-American Teachers Association Forum,* November–December 1967. David Spencer and Charles Wilson, "The Case for Community Control—In Harlem," *AN,* 1 June 1968. Ford Foundation, "And Then There Were the Children," p. 15.

76. Ibid., p. 123.

77. Barry Gottehrer, *The Mayor's Man* (New York: Doubleday, 1975), p. 185. Richard Magat Oral History, p. 78, Ford Foundation Archives. John V. Lindsay, *The City* (New York: W. W. Norton, 1969), p. 22. Fantini, Gittell, and Magat, *Community Control and the Urban School,* p. 236.

78. Ford Foundation, "And Then There Were the Children," p. 20.

CHAPTER 9

1. Rhody A. McCoy, "Educational Issues Swamped by Politics," *AN,* 11 December 1971.

2. *Time,* 1 November 1968. *U.S. News and World Report,* 4 November 1968.

3. One of the best discussions of the Ocean Hill–Brownsville crisis is Jerald E. Podair, "Like Strangers: Blacks, Whites, and New York City's Ocean Hill–Brownsville Crisis, 1945–1980" (Ph.D. diss., Princeton University, 1997). For an overview of the effect of the Ocean Hill–Brownsville controversy on the city, see Fred Siegel, *The Future Once Happened Here: New York, D.C., L.A., and the Fate of America's Big Cities* (New York: Free Press, 1997), pp. 32–45, and Tamar Jacoby, *Someone Else's House: America's Unfinished Struggle for Integration* (New York: Free Press, 1998), pp. 158–226.

4. Although the school district was called "Ocean Hill–Brownsville," most of the schools were in the smaller Ocean Hill neighborhood, rather than the larger Brownsville area.

5. Richard Karp, "School Decentralization in New York," *Interplay Magazine,* August-September 1968. Barry Gottehrer, *The Mayor's Man* (New York: Doubleday, 1975), pp. 186–187. Sol Stern, " 'Scab' Teachers," *Ramparts,* 17 November 1968. Marvin Hoffman, "Conflict in a Counterfeit Community," *The New Republic,* 9 November 1968.

6. Martin Mayer, *The Teachers Strike: New York, 1968* (New York: Harper & Row, 1969), p. 18. Jimmy Breslin, "The View from Brownsville," *NYP,* 16 October 1968. Rhody McCoy, "The Year of the Dragon," in Maurice R. Berube and Marilyn Gittell, eds., *Confrontation at Ocean Hill–Brownsville: The New York School Strikes of 1968* (New York: Praeger, 1969), p. 52. John Niemeyer, "Final Report of the Advisory Committee on Decentralization" (Niemeyer Report), July 1968, Chapter 4, p. 3. Ford Foundation, "And Then There Were the Children: An Assessment of Efforts to Test Decentralization in New York City's Public School System," p. 260, May 1969, Folder 002149, Ford Foundation Archives.

7. Citizens Committee for New York, *The Neighborhoods of Brooklyn* (New Haven, CT: Yale University Press, 1998), pp. 40–43.

8. Mayer, *The Teachers Strike,* p. 26. Diane Ravitch, *The Great School Wars: A History of the New York City Public Schools* (New York: Basic Books, 1974), pp. 322–323.

9. Niemeyer, "Final Report of the Advisory Committee on Decentralization," Chapter 3, p. 14.

10. Naomi Levine, *Ocean Hill–Brownsville: Schools in Crisis, A Case History* (New York: Popular Library, 1969), p. 38. Marilyn Gittell with Maurice Berube, Frances Gottfried, Marcia Guttentag, and Adele Spier, *Local Control in Education: Three Demonstration School Districts in New York City* (New York: Frederick A. Praeger, 1972), p. 10.

11. Interview of Herbert Oliver by author, 24 February 1968. Interview of John Powis by author, 3 December 1997. Ford Foundation, "And Then There Were the Children," p. 176.

12. Barbara Carter, *Pickets, Parents, and Power: The Story Behind the New York City Teachers' Strike* (New York: Citation Press, 1971), pp. 47–48. Jack Bloomfield, "The Untold Story of Ocean Hill," Box 1, Folder 2, Teachers Action Caucus Papers, UFT Papers. Powis interview.

13. On McCoy's early career, see Jonathan Kaufman, *Broken Alliance: The Turbulent Times Between Blacks and Jews in America* (New York: Simon & Schuster, 1995), pp. 129–134. Harry Hampton and Steve Fayer, *Voices of Freedom: An Oral History of the Civil Rights Movement from the 1950s through the 1980s* (New York: Bantam Books, 1991), p. 492.

14. *NYT,* 3 September 1967. Carter, *Pickets, Parents, and Power,* p. 39. Powis interview. On Ferguson's role in the I.S. 201 experiment, see Niemeyer, "Final Report of the Advisory Committee on Decentralization," Chapter 3, pp. 8–9.

15. Herman Ferguson, letter to the editor, *African-American Teachers Association Forum*, November–December 1967.

16. Ibid., "A Black Survival Curriculum," *The Guardian*, 9 March 1968. Ferguson was convicted and fled to Guyana, where he remained until 1989, when he returned to the United States and turned himself in.

17. Ravitch, *The Great School Wars*, p. 326. Melvin Urofsky, ed., *Why Teachers Strike: Teachers' Rights and Community Control* (Garden City, N.Y.: Anchor Books, 1970), pp. 138–139.

18. Hampton and Fayer, *Voices of Freedom*, p. 485. Steven Mufson, "A Dream Deferred: Ocean Hill–Brownsville Remembers," *VV*, 6 June 1989. Fred Nauman Oral History NS09–053, UFT Papers. On Leslie Campbell, see Jim Sleeper, *The Closest of Strangers: Liberalism and the Politics of Race in New York* (New York: W. W. Norton, 1990), pp. 69, 246. The African-American Teachers Association, led by Al Vann and Leslie Campbell, was a focal point for racialist thought in the city. It should surprise no one that the organization received much of its funding from the federal government and from the New York Urban Coalition. When the money was eventually cut off, in the early 1970s, the organization folded. See Podair, "Like Strangers," p. 303.

19. Bloomfield, "Untold Story of Ocean Hill." Powis interview. Oliver interview.

20. "Ocean Hill–Brownsville Demonstration School District Newsletter," March 1968, Box 8, Folder 12, Board of Education Papers, Milbank Memorial Library. Rhody McCoy, "The Formation of a Community-Controlled School District," in Henry Levin, ed., *Community Control of Schools* (Washington, D.C.: Brookings Institution, 1970), p. 187. Powis interview.

21. Letters in Box 5, Folder 134, Albert Shanker Subject Files. UF7 Papers. *AN*, 25 May 1968.

22. Hampton and Fayer, *Voices of Freedom*, pp. 494–495. *Eyes on the Prize II: Power! 1967–1968* (video), vol. 3. Ford Foundation, "And Then There Were the Children," p. 41. Marilyn Gittell, "Education: The Decentralization–Community Control Controversy," in Jewel Bellush and Stephen M. David, eds., *Race and Politics in New York City: Five Studies in Policy-Making* (New York: Praeger, 1971), pp. 154–155. Maurice Berube, "Scarsdale, Yes—Harlem, No," *Commonweal*, 21 June 1968. Powis interview.

23. Telegram from the Governing Board of the Ocean Hill–Brownsville School Project to Albert Shanker, 25 April 1968, and Telegram from Albert Shanker to the Governing Board of the Ocean Hill–Brownsville School Project, 26 April 1968, both in Folder 4, Box 1, Albert Shanker Subject Files UF7 Papers.

24. *NYT*, 10 and 11 May 1968. "The Burden of Blame: A Report on the Ocean Hill–Brownsville School Controversy," New York Civil Liberties Union, 9 October 1968, Box 22, Folder 21, Series 378f, Isaiah Robinson Papers, Milbank Memorial Library.

25. Letter from Rhody McCoy to Bernard Donovan, 10 May 1968, in Box 5, Folder 134, Albert Shanker Subject Files, Wagner Labor Archives, NYU.

26. Press Release from Superintendent of Schools, Bernard Donovan, 13 May 1968, United Parents Association Papers, Series 11.1, Box 2, Folder 17, Milbank Memorial Library.

27. *NYT,* 15 and 17 May 1968.

28. "Fact Sheet: To the People of Our Community," May 1968, Board of Education Papers, Box 8, Folder 13, Milbank Memorial Library. *NYT,* 16 May 1968.

29. *NYT,* 6 September 1968. "Administrative Hearing into Complaints of Rhody A. McCoy, Unit Administrator of Ocean Hill–Brownsville, Requesting Transfer of Teachers: Report and Recommendations of Francis E. Rivers, Esq., Special Trial Examiner, 26 August 1968," in Berube and Gittell, *Confrontation at Ocean Hill–Brownsville,* pp. 83–101; also in Box 2, Folder 68, Albert Shanker Subject Files, UF7 Papers.

30. Ford Foundation, "And Then There Were the Children," p. 44. Ferretti, "Who's to Blame in the School Strike." Gottehrer, *The Mayor's Man,* pp. 197–198. Mayer, *The Teachers Strike,* p. 63. Shanker later corrected himself, saying, "I said something that, from the point of view of consequences, is akin to that, but it's really not against any of those teachers. What I did say was this. When we agreed to submit to arbitration, we knew that the way arbitrators work is they usually slice things in half. . . . What happened was the governing board turned down Kheel, as a result of which, instead of getting an arbitrator, we got a judge" (Urofsky, *Why Teachers Strike,* p. 171).

31. *NYT,* 30 August 1968. On Milton Galamison, see Clarence Taylor, *Knocking at Our Own Door: Milton A. Galamison and the Struggle to Integrate New York City Schools* (New York: Columbia University Press, 1997).

32. *NYT,* 24 July 1968.

33. United Action, August 1968, Vol. 2, No. 1, Folder 46, Box 2, Albert Shanker Subject Files, UF7 Papers. Mayer, *The Teachers Strike,* p. 52. Oliver interview.

34. Mayer, *The Teachers Strike,* pp. 65–66. *NYT,* 9 September 1968.

35. *Eyes on the Prize II.* For an analysis of Sonny Carson's history of race baiting, see Tamar Jacoby, "Sonny Carson and the Politics of Protest," *City Journal,* Summer 1991.

36. *NYP,* 11 and 12 September 1968. Mayer, *The Teachers Strike,* p. 70. Notarized letter from Arlene Rachansky, 20 September 1968, Box 1, Folder 8, and Affidavit of Thomas Scalise, both in Box 3, Folder 90, Albert Shanker Subject Files, UF7 Papers.

37. Mayer, *The Teachers Strike,* pp. 64–65. *NYP,* 12 September 1968. *NYT,* 13 September 1968.

38. *NYP,* 13 September 1968. *WSJ,* 20 December 1968.

39. *NYT,* 20 December 1996. Urofsky, *Why Teachers Strike,* pp. 185–187. Transcript of Searchlight Program, WNBC-TV, 15 September 1968, p. 8, Box 14568, Decentralization Project Folder, Ford Foundation Archives. Ford Foundation, "And Then There Were the Children," p. 50. For Al Shanker's explanation of the strikes

and decentralization, see Albert Shanker, "The Real Meaning of the New York City Teachers' Strike," *Phi Delta Kappan,* April 1969.

40. *NYT,* 26 September 1968.

41. "Ocean Hill Speaks and Acts," 1968, Box 8, Folder 12, Board of Education Papers, Milbank Memorial Library.

42. "Man in Office," WNBC-TV, 21 July 1968, Box 13, Folder 92, Milton Galamison Papers, Schomburg Center. *Eyes on the Prize II.* SCOPE leaflet in Box 8, Folder 3, Board of Education Papers, Milbank Memorial Library.

43. Interview of John Doar by author, 13 February 1998.

44. *NYT,* 5 October 1968. Gottehrer, *The Mayor's Man,* p. 148.

45. *NYT,* 9 October 1968.

46. "Dear Colleague" letter from Albert Shanker, undated, Box 2, Folder 47, Albert Shanker Subject Files, UF7 Papers.

47. *NYT,* 15, 16, 23, and 31 October 1968.

48. "Incidents at PS [*sic*] 271, 9 October 1968," Nathan Brown Files, Board of Education Papers, B.1, Box 11, Folder 1, Milbank Memorial Library. *NYP,* 15 October 1968. *NYT,* 15 October 1968. Milton Galamison, "The Ghosts of McCarthy," p. 9, unpublished, Box 13, Folder 81, Galamison Papers.

49. Memo from Bernard E. Donovan to Members of the Board of Education, 14 October 1968, Box 14, Folder 97, Galamison Papers.

50. *NYP,* 26 October 1968. Doar interview. Jimmy Breslin, "Running Other People's Lives," in Peter Manso, ed., *Running Against the Machine: The Mailer-Breslin Campaign* (New York: Doubleday, 1969), p. 18.

51. *AN,* 19 October 1968. Naomi Levine, *Ocean Hill–Brownsville: Schools in Crisis, A Case History* (New York: Popular Library, 1969), p. 70. *NYT,* 13 November 1968.

52. Urofsky, *Why Teachers Strike,* p. 142.

53. Doar interview. Gottehrer, *The Mayor's Man,* p. 194. Milton Galamison, "View from the Eleventh Floor," p. 47, unpublished manuscript, Box 13, Folder 80, Galamison Papers. Rose Shapiro Oral History, NS09–43, UFT Archives, Wagner Labor Archives, NYU.

54. Galamison, "View from the Eleventh Floor," pp. 51–54.

55. "Report on Picketing, P.S. 29 Bx, Week of October 21, 1968," Box 5, Folder 136, Albert Shanker Subject Files, UF7 Papers.

56. Memo from William H. Booth to John V. Lindsay, 29 October 1968, Box 346, Folder 205, JVL Papers, Yale, and "Report on Three Demonstration Projects in the City Schools," New York Commission on Human Rights, February-March 1968, JVL Papers, NYCMA.

57. Ferretti, "Who's to Blame in the School Strike."

58. Charles S. Isaacs, "A JHS 271 Teacher Tells It Like He Sees It," *NYTM,* 24 November 1968. Ford Foundation, "And Then There Were the Children," p. 209. Daniel H. Perlstein, "The New York City School Crisis: Teacher Politics, Racial Politics and the Decline of Liberalism" (Ph.D. diss., Stanford University, 1994), pp.

130, 142. Carter, *Pickets, Parents, and Power,* p. 100. For a description of the situation in city schools during the school strike from an anti-union teacher at the Bronx High School of Science, see Robert Rossner, *The Year Without an Autumn: Portrait of a School in Crisis* (New York: Richard W. Baron, 1969).

59. *NYT,* 16 November 1968. Ravitch, *The Great School Wars,* pp. 343, 369. In January 1969, the New York State Court of Appeals, the state's highest court, overruled the lower courts and allowed the principals to return to their jobs.

60. Galamison, "View from the Eleventh Floor." "The New York City School Crisis," WCBS-TV, 29 September 1968 (transcript), Box 4, Folder 122, Albert Shanker Subject Files, UF7 Papers.

61. Maurice R. Berube, " 'Democratic Socialists' and the Schools," *New Politics,* Summer 1969, p. 61. Nat Hentoff, *A Political Life: The Education of John V. Lindsay* (New York: Alfred A. Knopf, 1969), p. 327. Breslin, "The View from Brownsville." Podair, "Like Strangers," pp. 68–69. James Wechsler, "A Man Alone," *NYP,* 22 October 1968. *DN,* 14 November 1968.

62. *NYT,* 22 October 1968.

63. Ibid., 18 November 1968.

64. Doar interview. Gottehrer, *The Mayor's Man,* p. 193.

65. Galamison, "View from the Eleventh Floor," p. 48. Oliver interview.

66. Open letter from Preston Wilcox, Chairman of the National Association of Afro-American Educators, undated, in author's possession. United Bronx Parents flyer, 25 September 1968, Box 4, Folder 122, Albert Shanker Subject Files, UF7 Papers.

67. Open letter from Preston Wilcox.

68. Mario Fantini, Marilyn Gittell, and Richard Magat, *Community Control and the Urban School* (New York: Frederick A. Praeger, 1970), p. 237. "Dear Friend," Letter from David Spencer, undated, Box 5, Folder 135, Albert Shanker Subject Files, UF7 Papers.

69. Rhody A. McCoy, Jr., "Analysis of Critical Issues and Incidents in the New York City School Crisis, 1967–1970 and their Implications for Urban Education in the 1970s," 2 vols., vol. 1, pp. 111–112 (Ph.D. diss., University of Massachusetts, 1971). Berube and Gittell, *Confrontation at Ocean Hill–Brownsville,* pp. 4–5, 8.

70. *NYT,* 26 and 27 November 1968. Ticknor B. Litchfield, "Experience in Ocean Hill–Brownsville: October–December 1968," p. 28, Box 6, Ocean Hill–Brownsville Folder, State Education Department, Commissioner's Office, Administrative Assistant's Subject File, NYS Archives.

71. Ibid., p. 30.

72. *NYP,* 2 December 1968. *NYT,* 3 December 1968.

73. Litchfield, "Experience in Ocean Hill–Brownsville," pp. 35–36. Oliver interview.

74. Notes on 2 December 1968, meeting, written by David Seeley, in author's possession. *NYT,* 3 December 1968.

75. Memo from William Firman to Rhody McCoy, 9 December 1968; telegram from William Firman to Rhody McCoy, 11 December 1968; statement of William Firman, 11 December 1968, all in Box 6, Ocean Hill–Brownsville Folder, State Education Department, Commissioner's Office, Administrative Assistant's Subject File, NYS Archives. Carter, *Pickets, Parents, and Power*, p. 138. Ravitch, *Great School Wars*, p. 377.

76. Memo from Wilbur Nordos to James Allen, 24 January 1969. *NYT*, 12 December 1968.

77. Hentoff, *A Political Life*, p. 327. *NYP*, 22 November 1968.

78. *NYP*, 26 November 1968.

79. Interview of Lewis Feldstein by author, 6 November 1997.

80. Litchfield, "Experience in Ocean Hill–Brownsville," pp. 42–43. Ford Foundation, "And Then There Were the Children," p. 175.

81. Urofsky, *Why Teachers Strike*, p. 111. Though his name has become synonymous with community control and Ocean Hill–Brownsville, Rhody McCoy actually lived in the suburb of Roosevelt, Long Island, miles from the ghettos of central Brooklyn. Al Shanker also lived outside the city, in semirural Putnam County, over an hour north of the city. Thus, two of the main protagonists in the controversy that paralyzed the city's schools and polarized its citizens did not even live within the city limits.

82. Rhody McCoy, "The Year of the Dragon," in Berube and Gittell, *Confrontation at Ocean Hill–Brownsville*, p. 53. Martin Mayer, "Frustration Is the Word at Ocean Hill," *NYTM*, 19 May 1968. Rhody McCoy, "Education Issues Swamped by Politics," *AN*, 11 December 1971. See also Hampton and Fayer, *Voices of Freedom*, pp. 495–496.

83. McCoy, "Analysis of Critical Issues and Incidents." Urofsky, *Why Teachers Strike*, p. 172.

84. McCoy, "Analysis of Critical Issues and Incidents," vol. 1, pp. xi-xii, and vol. 2, p. 131. Mufson, "A Dream Deferred."

85. Jerald E. Podair, " 'White' Values, 'Black' Values: The Ocean Hill–Brownsville Controversy and New York City Culture, 1965–1975," *Radical History Review*, Spring 1994, p. 49. Ibid., "Like Strangers: Blacks, Whites, and New York City's Ocean Hill–Brownsville Crisis, 1945–1980," p. 236.

86. A. H. Raskin, "Why New York Is 'Strike City,' " *NYTM*, 22 December 1968. Michael Harrington, "The Freedom to Teach: Beyond the Panaceas," *VV*, 3 October 1968. Patrick Harnett, "Why Teachers Strike: A Lesson for Liberals," *VV*, 31 October 1968. Feldstein interview.

87. Raskin, "Why New York Is 'Strike City.' " Charles Morris, *The Cost of Good Intentions: New York City and the Liberal Experiment, 1960–1975* (New York: W. W. Norton, 1980), p. 115.

88. Interview of Barry Gottehrer by author, 7 July 1997. Gottehrer, *The Mayor's Man*, pp. 184, 205. Interview of Robert Sweet by author, 22 April 1997. Interview of Peter Goldmark by author, 13 June 1997. Interview of Werner Kramarsky by author, 23 April 1997. Feldstein interview. Interview of Marilyn Git-

tell by author, 4 November 1997. Interview of Pat Vecchio by author, 13 October 1999.

89. Charles Morris has suggested that Shanker was heavily involved in many of the purges of Communist teachers in New York and that he was also responsible for the controversial pro–Vietnam War stance the union took in 1967. See Charles R. Morris, *American Catholic: The Saints and Sinners Who Built America's Most Powerful Church* (New York: Times Books, 1997), pp. 247–248.

90. *NYT,* 24 February 1997. Manning Marable, *Race, Reform, and Rebellion: The Second Reconstruction in Black America,* 1945–1980 (Jackson: University Press of Mississippi, 1991), p. 118. Paul Buhle, "Albert Shanker: No Flowers," *New Politics,* Summer 1997.

91. Berube and Gittell, *Confrontation at Ocean Hill–Brownsville,* p. 8. Maurice R. Berube, " 'Democratic Socialists' and the Schools," *New Politics,* Summer 1969.

92. Memo from Isaiah Terman, "The Left-of-Center Press and Ocean Hill–Brownsville," 10 April 1969, New York City School Decentralization 1969 Folder, AJC Archives.

93. *NYT,* 20 September 1968. Among the advertisement's signers were Columbia sociology professor Daniel Bell, journalist Thomas Brooks, economist Robert Heilbroner, *Dissent* editor Irving Howe, economist Leon Keyserling, Dwight Macdonald (although he later denounced it), theologian Reinhold Niebuhr, Harvard political scientist Martin Peretz, *Partisan Review* editor William Phillips, and historian Arthur Schlesinger, Jr.

94. Berube, " 'Democratic Socialists' and the Schools." Berube and Gittell, *Confrontation at Ocean Hill–Brownsville,* p. 147.

95. Jason Epstein, "The Politics of School Decentralization," *The New York Review of Books,* 6 June 1967. Maurice R. Berube, "The Unschooling of New York's Children," *Commonweal,* 25 October 1968.

96. Jimmy Breslin, "The View from Brownsville," *NYP,* 16 October 1968. Jimmy Breslin, "Albert Shanker's Game," *NYP,* 31 October 1968. *I. F. Stone's Weekly,* 4 November 1968. Murray Kempton, "Time to Tell Off Shanker," *NYP,* 26 September 1968. Ibid., "Sidney Hook and Company," *NYP,* 14 November 1968. Stern, " 'Scab' Teachers."

97. Letter from Michael Harrington to "Carl and Everyone Else," 6 September 1971, Box 1, Folder 6, Democratic Socialists of America Papers, Wagner Labor Archives, NYU. Michael Harrington, *The Long Distance Runner: An Autobiography* (New York: Henry Holt, 1988), p. 77. See also Maurice Isserman, *The Other American: The Life of Michael Harrington* (New York: PublicAffairs, 2000), pp. 282–283.

98. Ravitch, *Great School Wars,* p. 337. David Seeley, "Decentralization of the New York City Schools" (Ed.D. diss., Harvard University, 1970), p. 25. Michael Harrington, "An Open Letter to Men of Good Will (with an aside to Dwight Macdonald)," *The New York Review of Books,* 2 January 1969. Podair, "Like Strangers." *NYT,* 1 November 1968, Urban Coalition advertisement. The list of

signers of the ad included Preston Robert Tisch, Gustave Levy, Bernard Lasker, Andrew Heiskell, Schuyler Chapin, Jerry Orbach, Francis Plimpton, Thomas Hoving, Lewis Rudin, Edgar Bronfman, John Hay Whitney, Walter Thayer, Rod Steiger, Eli Wallach, Arthur Houghton, Whitney North Seymour, David Susskind, John McCloy, Paul Newman, Sidney Lumet, Hal Prince, Richard Rodgers, David Rockefeller, Christian Herter, Lauren Bacall, Alan Arkin, Leonard Bernstein, Bennett Cerf, Alan King, McGeorge Bundy, Bethuel Webster, and Norman Lear.

99. Diane Ravitch, "Foundations: Playing God in the Ghetto," *The Center Forum,* 15 May 1969. Statement by McGeorge Bundy, President of the Ford Foundation, 13 November 1968, in author's possession. Urofsky, *Why Teachers Strike,* p. 104. Ford Foundation, "And Then There Were the Children," pp. 60, 189.

100. Ibid. Richard Armstrong, "McGeorge Bundy Confronts the Teachers," *NYTM,* 20 April 1969. Interview of Mitchell Sviridoff by author, 22 October 1997. Interview of Theodore Kheel by author, 15 July 1997. *NYT,* 27 October 1968. Galamison, "Ghosts of McCarthy," pp. 15–16.

101. David Halberstam, "The Very Expensive Education of McGeorge Bundy," *Harper's Magazine,* July 1969.

102. *I. F. Stone's Weekly,* 4 November 1968. Macdonald, "An Open Letter to Michael Harrington." Alfred Kazin, "The Holy Flame of Learning," *NYT,* 9 November 1968. "Teachers Who Give a Damn," p. 50. *NYT,* 21 October 1968. Urofsky, *Why Teachers Strike,* p. 27. Annette T. Rubenstein, "Visiting Ocean Hill–Brownsville in November 1968 and May 1969," in Rubenstein, ed., *Schools Against Children: The Case for Community Control* (New York: Monthly Review Press, 1970), p. 229. *WSJ,* 10 April 1969.

103. *NYT,* 23 October 1968. Charles S. Isaacs, "A JHS 271 Teacher Tells It Like He Sees It." Mario Fantini and Marilyn Gittell, "The Ocean Hill–Brownsville Experiment," *Phi Delta Kappan,* April 1969.

104. Joseph Featherstone, "Ocean Hill Is Alive, and, Well . . . ," *New Republic,* 19 April 1969. See also "What Else Is New at Ocean Hill?," *Newsday,* 23 November 1968.

105. Maurice Berube, *American School Reform: Progressive, Equity, and Excellence Movements, 1883–1993* (Westport, Conn.: Praeger, 1994), pp. 85, 88–89. Gittell et al., *Local Control in Education,* pp. 112, 137.

106. Fred Ferretti, "Who's to Blame in the School Strike," *NY,* 18 November 1968. Diane Ravitch, "Community Control Revisited," *The United Teacher,* 20 February 1972.

107. Ravitch, "Community Control Revisited." Ibid., *Great School Wars,* p. 391. Ibid., "The Autopsy Proves the Corpse Is Dead," *VV,* 16 March 1972. Litchfield, "Experience in Ocean Hill–Brownsville," p. 45.

108. Nat Hentoff, "Mugging a Corpse," *VV,* 2 March 1972. Fantini, Gittell, and Magat, *Community Control and the Urban School,* p. 193.

109. On the 1969 school decentralization bill, see "A Summary of the 1969 School Decentralization Law for New York City," The Office of Education Affairs, 1969;

Richard K. Scher, "Decentralization and the New York State Legislature," *Urban Review*, September 1969; Joseph Featherstone, "Choking Off Community Schools," *The New Republic*, 19 July 1969; *NYT*, 1 May 1969; and Derek Edgell, *The Movement for Community Control of New York City's Schools, 1966–1970* (Lewiston, N.Y.: Edwin Mellen Press, 1998), pp. 354–355.

110. "John Lindsay's Ten Plagues," *Time*, 1 November 1968. Mayer, *The Teachers Strike*, p. 12.

111. Feldstein interview. Ford Foundation, "And Then There Were the Children," p. 254. Niemeyer, "Final Report of the Advisory Committee on Decentralization" Chapter 1, pp. 8, 10. "The Burden of Blame." "NYCLU Reply to the Ad Hoc Committee for Justice in the Schools," in Berube and Gittell, *Confrontation at Ocean Hill–Brownsville*, p. 161.

112. Litchfield, "Experience in Ocean Hill–Brownsville," p. 45.

113. Gottehrer, *The Mayor's Man*, p. 202.

CHAPTER 10

1. Nathan Glazer and Daniel P. Moynihan, *Beyond the Melting Pot: The Negroes, Puerto Ricans, Jews, Italians, and Irish of New York City*, 2nd ed. (Cambridge, Mass.: MIT Press, 1970), p. 71.

2. Lisa Anderson, "The Lindsay Era," *Chicago Tribune*, 10 September 1990. Recent books on the sometimes tortured relationship between blacks and Jews include Jonathan Kaufman, *Broken Alliance: The Turbulent Times Between Blacks and Jews in America* (New York: Simon & Schuster, 1995); Cornell West and Michael Lerner, *Jews and Blacks: Let the Healing Begin* (New York: G. P. Putnam's Sons, 1995); Murray Friedman, *What Went Wrong: The Creation and Collapse of the Black-Jewish Alliance* (New York: Free Press, 1995); and Paul Berman, ed., *Blacks and Jews: Alliances and Arguments* (New York: Delacorte Press, 1994).

3. *NYT*, 23 October 1968. Leonard Dinnerstein, *Antisemitism in America* (New York: Oxford University Press, 1994), p. 209. Anti-Defamation League, "Highlights from an Anti-Defamation League Survey on Anti-Semitism and Prejudice in America," 16 November 1992.

4. Louis Harris and Bert E. Swanson, *Black-Jewish Relations in New York City* (New York: Praeger, 1970), p. 105. One scholar who argued against the existence of black anti-Semitism was the sociologist Gary Marx, who found no support for the contention "that anti-Semitism is more widespread among Negroes than among whites, any more than it could be shown that [Negroes] single out Jews for special enmity" (Gary Marx, *Protest and Prejudice: A Study of Belief in the Black Community* [New York: Harper & Row, 1967], p. 147). For a critique of Marx's argument, see Lucy Davidowicz, "Can Anti-Semitism Be Measured?" *Commentary*, July 1970.

5. Harris and Swanson, *Black-Jewish Relations in New York City*, pp. 43, 54, 106. Poll by Louis Harris and Associates, November 1969, New York City School Decentralization 1969 Folder, New York City Chapter, AJC Archives.

6. Kenneth Clark, "Candor About Negro-Jewish Relations," *Commentary*, February 1946. For a general discussion of the history of black anti-Semitism in America see Dinnerstein, *Antisemitism in America*, pp. 197–227.

7. James Baldwin, "The Harlem Ghetto: Winter 1948," *Commentary*, February 1948. Ibid., "Negroes are Anti-Semitic Because They're Anti-White," *NYTM*, April 1967. Glazer and Moynihan, *Beyond the Melting Pot*, pp. 71–72. In an essay entitled "My Jewish Problem and Theirs" (playing off the title of Norman Podhoretz's famous 1963 article "My Negro Problem—and Ours"), Harold Cruse recounts the tensions between blacks and Jews in the Communist Party in 1940s New York. See Harold Cruse, "My Jewish Problem and Theirs," in Nat Hentoff, ed., *Black Anti-Semitism and Jewish Racism* (New York: Richard W. Baron, 1969), pp. 143–188

8. "The Black and the Jew: A Falling Out of Allies," *Time*, 31 January 1969. Letter from Haskell L. Lazere, Director, American Jewish Committee, New York Chapter, to Hon. Bernard Botein, Chairman, Special Committee on Religious and Racial Prejudice, 10 December 1968, Anti-Semitism, 1962–1968 Folder, AJC Archives.

9. Julius Lester, *Lovesong: Becoming a Jew* (New York: Henry Holt, 1988), pp. 47–65. Poem quoted in Fred Ferretti, "New York's Black Anti-Semitism Scare," *Columbia Journalism Review*, Fall 1969. Another irony is that today Lester has become a practicing Jew.

10. Julius Lester, "A Response," in Hentoff, *Black Anti-Semitism and Jewish Racism*. For a defense of WBAI, see Nat Hentoff, "The Siege of WBAI," *VV*, 6 February 1969.

11. Harry Hampton and Steve Fayer, *Voices of Freedom: An Oral History of the Civil Rights Movement from the 1950s Through the 1980s* (New York: Bantam Books, 1991), pp. 506–507.

12. Thomas Hoving, *Making the Mummies Dance: Inside the Metropolitan Museum of Art* (New York: Simon & Schuster, 1993), pp. 164–165. Interview of Thomas Hoving by author, 21 May 1997.

13. For a description of the controversy surrounding the "Harlem on My Mind" show, see Michael Kimmelman, "Culture and Race: Still on America's Mind," *NYT*, 19 November 1995.

14. Hoving, *Making the Mummies Dance*, pp. 166–167. Milton Galamison, "Color Me Black," unpublished, Box 12, Folder 74, Galamison Papers.

15. Allon Schoener, ed., *Harlem on My Mind: Cultural Capital of Black America, 1900–1968*, catalogue of exhibition "Harlem on My Mind" (New York: Random House, 1968)

16. Hoving, *Making the Mummies Dance*, pp. 176–177. Glazer and Moynihan, *Beyond the Melting Pot*, p. 77. Hoving interview.

17. Hoving, *Making the Mummies Dance*, pp. 168–170.

18. Thomas Hoving, Preface to Schoener, *Harlem on My Mind*. Ibid., *Making the Mummies Dance*, pp. 167–168.

19. *NYT,* 17 January 1969. Hoving, *Making the Mummies Dance,* p. 171.

20. Hoving, *Making the Mummies Dance,* p. 175. *NYT,* 17 January 1969.

21. Hoving interview.

22. The appendices to the Botein Report, containing examples of bigotry submitted to the committee, can be found in Office of the Mayor, Assistant to the Mayor, Barry Gottehrer, 1970–1971, Office of the Mayor, JVL Papers, NYCMA.

23. Excerpts from the Report of the Special Committee on Racial and Religious Prejudice (Botein Report), 16 January 1969, Group 592, Box 346, Folder 204, JVL Papers, Yale, and Maurice R. Berube and Marilyn Gittell, eds., *Confrontation at Ocean Hill–Brownsville: The New York School Strikes of 1968* (New York: Praeger, 1969), pp. 174–176. *NYT,* 17 January 1969.

24. Botein Committee, "Anti-Semitism in the New York City School Controversy," A Preliminary Report of the Anti-Defamation League of B'nai B'rith, January 1969, Group 592, Box 346, Folder 206, JVL Papers, Yale. *NYT,* 23 January 1969.

25. Fein letter quoted in Ferretti, "New York's Black Anti-Semitism Scare," p. 26. Murray Kempton, "The ADL Report," *NYP,* 24 January 1969. Letter from Dore Schary, *NYP,* 28 January 1969.

26. Nathan Glazer, "Blacks, Jews and the Intellectuals," *Commentary,* April 1969. Fred Hechinger, "Racism and Anti-Semitism in the School Crisis," *NYT,* 16 September 1968. Whitney M. Young Jr., "The Myth of Black Anti-Semitism," *AN,* 28 September 1968. See also Herbert J. Gans, "Negro-Jewish Conflict in New York City: A Sociological Evaluation," *Midstream,* March 1969.

27. Hampton and Fayer, *Voices of Freedom,* p. 505. Interview of Marilyn Gittell by author, 4 November 1997. Oliver quoted in Melvin Urofsky, ed., *Why Teachers Strike: Teachers' Rights and Community Control* (Garden City, N.Y.: Anchor Books, 1970), p. 229. *NYT,* 22 December 1996.

28. Transcript of the Rabbi Marc Tannenbaum on "The World of Religion," CBS Radio, 24 October 1968, NYC School Decentralization (Ocean Hill) Tannenbaum Episode Folder, AJC Archives. Kemble quoted in Ferretti, "New York's Black Anti-Semitism Scare," pp. 23–24. Goldstein quoted in Eugenia Kemble, "Ocean Hill–Brownsville," *United Teacher,* 20 December 1967. Fred Nauman Oral History, NS09–053, UFT Papers.

29. Joseph Featherstone, "Inflating the Threat of Black Anti-Semitism," *The New Republic,* 8 March 1969.

30. Ferretti, "New York's Black Anti-Semitism Scare." John Leo, "Black Anti-Semitism," *Commonweal,* 14 February 1969.

31. Hentoff, *Black Anti-Semitism and Jewish Racism,* pp. xii, xvii. *I. F. Stone's Weekly,* 4 November 1968. In his recent memoir (*Speaking Freely: A Memoir,* Alfred A. Knopf, 1997), an older Hentoff is much more critical of black anti-Semitism.

32. Jay Kaufman, "Thou Shalt Surely Rebuke Thy Neighbor," in Hentoff, *Black Anti-Semitism and Jewish Racism,* pp. 43, 55.

33. Alan Miller, "Black Anti-Semitism—Jewish Racism," in Hentoff, *Black Anti-Semitism and Jewish Racism*, pp. 85, 88–89, 93.

34. Walter Karp and H. R. Shapiro, "Exploding the Myth of Black Anti-Semitism," *The Public Life*, 21 February 1969. Ferretti, "New York's Black Anti-Semitism Scare."

35. On the Jewish Defense League, see Robert I. Friedman, *The False Prophet: Rabbi Meir Kahane from FBI Informant to Knesset Member* (New York: Lawrence Hill Books, 1990); Rabbi Meir Kahane, *The Story of the Jewish Defense League* (Radnor, Pa.: Chilton Book Company, 1975); and Roy Bongartz, "Superjew," *Esquire*, August 1970. *WSJ*, 4 November 1969.

36. *NYT*, 24 June 1969.

37. John F. Hatchett, "The Phenomenon of the Anti-Black Jews and the Black Anglo-Saxon: A Study in Educational Perfidy," *African-American Teachers Association Forum*, November–December 1967.

38. Ibid., 24 June 1966. Harvey Rothenberg, *Reminiscing* (Harvey Rothenberg, n.p., n.d.), p. 79, in author's possession. Lindsay's action was not unusual. New York's mayors have often used their position to make foreign policy statements that they felt would go over well with certain segments of New York's population. Robert Wagner acted in a similar manner by refusing King Faisal's brother, Saud, any official city reception on a 1957 visit to New York. Rudolph Giuliani similarly has snubbed both the PLO's Yassar Arafat and Cuba's Fidel Castro.

39. Memo from Robert Blum to Norman Redlich, 10 October 1967, in author's possession. Interview of Robert Blum by author, 17 April 1997.

40. *NYT*, 15 February 1967.

41. Gerald Benjamin, *Race Relations and the New York City Commission on Human Rights* (Ithaca, N.Y.: Cornell University Press, 1972), pp. 203–205. William Booth, "Racism and Human Rights" in Hentoff, *Black Anti-Semitism and Jewish Racism*, pp. 117–118.

42. *NYT*, 5 February 1969.

43. Sweet interview. Interview of Werner Kramarsky by author, 23 April 1997. Interview with Morris Scherer, 6 November 1968, AJC Archives.

44. Altomare quote in Sanford Blair Oral History, NS9–008, UFT Archives.

45. *NYT*, 16 October 1968. Barry Gottehrer, *The Mayor's Man* (New York: Doubleday, 1975), p. 201. Rothenberg, *Reminiscing*, pp. 39–40. Interview of Peter Goldmark by author, 13 June 1997.

46. Interview of Lewis Feldstein by author, 6 November 1997. Gottehrer, *The Mayor's Man*, pp. 198–201. Sometime after leaving City Hall, Gottehrer converted to Christianity.

47. Martin Gershen, "Lindsay Told Jews: 'Control Shanker,'" *Long Island Press*, 17 October 1968.

48. Harvey Rothenberg, letter to the editor, *Long Island Press*, 18 October 1968. Memorandum from Harvey Rothenberg, Administrative Assistant to the Mayor,

Re: Long Island Press Article of 17 October 1968 by Martin Gershen, 22 October 1968, Box 346, Folder 205, JVL Papers, Yale.

49. Notes by Haskell Lazere, Director of New York Chapter of AJC on a 16 September 1968 meeting between John Lindsay and the leadership of New York's Jewish community, NYC School Decentralization (Ocean Hill) 68–69 Folder, AJC Archives.

50. Letter from Barbara Chartock to Jay Kriegel, 11 November 1968, Group 592, Box 56, Folder 1022, JVL Papers, Yale. Report from Ted Ellenoff, Re: Meeting at Gracie Mansion with John V. Lindsay, 12 August 1968, Mayoralty Folder 1961–1973, AJC Archives.

51. Feldstein interview.

52. Jack Newfield, "The Jewish Backlash and an Embattled Mayor," *VV*, 6 February 1969.

CHAPTER 11

1. *NY*, 9 March 1970.

2. Interview of Alton Marshall by author, 27 March 1997. Michael Kramer and Sam Roberts, *I Never Wanted to Be Vice-President of Anything! An Investigative Biography of Nelson Rockefeller* (New York: Basic Books, 1976), pp. 13–14. Interview of Donald Elliott by author, 30 April 1997.

3. Richard Reeves, "Rockefeller and Lindsay: An Old Rivalry Turns Personal and Savage Feud," *Life*, 25 June 1971. Interview of Steven Berger by author, 22 September 1999.

4. *NYT*, 30 June 1968. Interview of Robert Sweet by author, 21 October 1997.

5. Marshall interview. Interview of Peter Goldmark by author, 13 June 1997.

6. Interview of Jay Kriegel by author, 4 February 1997. Memo from Frederick O'R. Hayes to Mayor John V. Lindsay, 17 June 1968, Box 114, JVL Miscellaneous 1968 (3) Folder, Brownell Papers.

7. Blum interview. Rothenberg, *Reminiscing*, p. 65. Interview of Jim Carberry by author, 20 May 1997.

8. Sweet interview. Interview of Bob Laird by author, 7 May 1997. Letter from Harry O'Donnell to Ken DeKay, 6 January 1968, Box 2, OD Vol. 1 Folder, O'Donnell Papers. Carberry interview. Interview of Mike Dontzin by author, 4 June 1997.

9. Rothenberg, *Reminiscing*, p. 66. *NYT*, 22 May 1967. Kramer and Roberts, *I Never Wanted to Be Vice-President of Anything!* p. 302. Sweet interview. Blum interview. John V. Lindsay, *The City* (New York: W. W. Norton, 1969), p. 25.

10. Harry Stein, "An Exile in his Own City," *NYTM*, 8 January 1978. Letter from John V. Lindsay to Harry O'Donnell, 20 August 1982, Box 2, OD Vol. 1 Folder, O'Donnell Papers.

11. Marshall interview. Blum interview. Larry L. King, "Lindsay of New York," *Harper's Magazine*, August 1968, p. 40.

12. Material on the Miami Beach organization in the Robert W. Sweet Files, Political Data Box, Office of the Mayor, JVL Papers NYCMA.

13. *NYT,* 14 July 1968. Interview of Sid Davidoff by author, 2 December 1997.

14. Jimmy Breslin, "The Distortion of John Lindsay," *NY,* 26 August 1968.

15. Rothenberg, *Reminiscing,* p. 59.Theodore H. White, *The Making of the President: 1968* (New York: Atheneum, 1969), p. 251. Interview of Pat Vecchio by author, 13 October 1999. White speaks of Lindsay's sending an "intermediary friend," but Rothenberg and Vecchio identify the emissary as White himself.

16. "Undated Memo" and "Domestic Issues" memos, Robert W. Sweet Files, Political Data Box, Office of the Mayor, JVL Papers, NYCMA.

17. Lindsay's remarks in *NYT,* 6 August 1968. Davidoff quoted in Breslin, "The Distortion of John Lindsay."

18. Nicholas Pileggi, "Inside Lindsay's Head," *NY,* 4 January 1971. Robert Blum, letter to his father and stepmother, 17 August 1968, read to author.

19. Carberry interview. "Text of an Address by the Hon. John V. Lindsay Mayor of the City of New York and Delegate from New York State, Seconding the Nomination of Gov. Spiro T. Agnew of Maryland as Vice President of the United States," 9 August 1968, Box 114, JVL Memorandum 1968 (2) Folder, Brownell Papers.

20. Breslin, "The Distortion of John Lindsay." Blum, letter to father and stepmother, 17 August 1968.

21. Stephen E. Ambrose, *Nixon, Volume 2: The Triumph of a Politician, 1962–1972* (New York: Simon & Schuster, 1989), pp. 174–175.

22. Richard Reeves, "Man on a Tightrope," *NYT,* 16 August 1968. Blum interview. Breslin, "The Distortion of John Lindsay."

23. Many Lindsay aides actively and publicly worked for Eugene McCarthy in the Democratic presidential primary. Werner Kramarsky, a mayoral assistant, ran McCarthy's Indiana campaign. Deputy Mayor Timothy Costello, Frank Arricale, Lewis Feldstein, and Deputy City Administrator Philip Finkelstein all took time off to work for McCarthy. According to one Lindsay aide, "In the last week of the campaign, you couldn't find anyone in the Parks Department. They were all out ringing doorbells for McCarthy" (*NYT,* 22 June 1968).

24. Douglas Kiker, "Red Neck New York: Is This Wallace Country?" *NY,* 7 October 1968.

CHAPTER 12

1. Chris McNickle, *To Be Mayor of New York: Ethnic Politics in the City* (New York: Columbia University Press, 1993), p. 3.

2. "The Troubled American," *Newsweek,* 6 October 1969. "Man and Woman of the Year: The Middle Americans," *Time,* 5 January 1970. For a less sympathetic treatment of Middle Americans, see Elizabeth Hardwick, "Mr. America," *New York Review of Books,* 7 November 1968.

3. Peter Schrag, "The Forgotten Americans," *Harper's Magazine*, August 1969. Samuel G. Freedman, *The Inheritance: How Three Families and America Moved from Roosevelt to Reagan and Beyond* (New York: Simon & Schuster, 1996), pp. 21–22. The late 1960s and early 1970s saw the publication of a spate of books about white ethnics. See Peter Binzen, *Whitetown, U.S.A.* (New York: Random House, 1970); Robert Coles and Jon Erikson, *The Middle Americans: Proud and Uncertain* (Boston: Little Brown, 1971); Murray Friedman, *Overcoming Middle Class Rage* (Philadelphia: Westminster Press, 1971); Andrew Greeley, *Why Can't They Be Like Us?* (New York: E. P. Dutton, 1971); Louise Kapp, *The White Majority: Between Poverty and Affluence* (New York: Random House, 1970); Richard Krickus, *Pursuing the American Dream: White Ethnics and the New Populism* (Bloomington: Indiana University Press, 1976); Michael Novak, *The Rise of the Unmeltable Ethnics* (New York: Macmillan, 1971); Joseph Ryan, ed., *White Ethnics: Their Life in Working Class America* (Englewood Cliffs, N.J.: Prentice Hall, 1973); Arthur B. Shostak, *Blue-Collar Life* (New York: Random House, 1969); and Perry Weed, *The White Ethnic Movement and Ethnic Politics* (New York: Praeger, 1973).

4. Jimmy Breslin, "Is Lindsay Too Tall to Be Mayor?" *NY*, 28 July 1969. Richard Reeves, "Middle Class Revolt," *NYT*, 2 November 1968.

5. Letter from Marvin Schick to Jay Kriegel, 8 August 1990, in author's possession.

6. Memo from Robert M. Blum to John V. Lindsay, 20 December 1966, in author's possession. Jeff Greenfield, "Reading John Lindsay's Face," *NYTM*, 29 July 1973.

7. *NYT*, 4 May 1967. Memo from Martin Shulman to Jay Kriegel, 15 July 1967, Robert W. Sweet, Correspondence, Law Enforcement, 1965–1969, Police Department Folder, Office of the Mayor, JVL Papers, NYCMA. "Legislative Report from State Senator John D. Calandra," August 1968, Group 592, Series XI, Box 213, Folder 62, JVL Papers, Yale.

8. Jack Newfield, "John Vliet Lindsay: Uptight White Knight," *VV*, 4 January 1968. Nat Hentoff, *A Political Life: The Education of John V. Lindsay* (New York: Alfred A. Knopf, 1969), p. 289.

9. Jonathan Rieder, *Canarsie: The Jews and Italians of Brooklyn Against Liberalism* (Cambridge, MA: Harvard University Press, 1985), pp. 262–263.

10. John Lindsay, "We Can Lick the Problems of the Ghetto If We Care," *Reader's Digest*, August 1968. Ibid., *The City* (New York: W. W. Norton, 1969), pp. 20–21. Larry L. King, "Lindsay of New York," *Harper's Magazine*, August 1968.

11. Pete Hamill, "The Revolt of the White Lower Middle Class," *NY*, 14 April 1969. See also Gloria Steinem, "The Souls of (Lower-Middle-Class) White Folk," *NY*, 22 September 1969.

12. Pete Hamill, "What's with the Brooklyn Democrats?" *NY*, 14 July 1969. Ibid., "Looking at Lindsay: A Probable Disaster," *VV*, 27 March 1969.

13. Krickus, *Pursuing the American Dream*, p. 221. Rieder, *Canarsie: The Jews and Italians of Brooklyn Against Liberalism*, p. 66.

14. Robert Coles, "The White Northerner: Pride and Prejudice," *The Atlantic,* June 1966. Michael Lerner, "Respectable Bigotry," *American Scholar,* Autumn 1969.

15. *NYT,* 2 November 1968.

16. *NYT,* 21 September 1964.

17. Norman Mailer, "The White Negro: Superficial Reflections on the Hipster," *Dissent,* Summer 1957. Norman Mailer, *Miami and the Siege of Chicago: An Informal History of the Republican and Democratic Conventions* (New York: World Publishing, 1968), pp. 51–53. Louis Harris and Bert E. Swanson, *Black-Jewish Relations in New York City* (New York: Praeger, 1970), p. 106.

18. Charles Morris, *The Cost of Good Intentions: New York City and the Liberal Experiment, 1960–1975* (New York: W. W. Norton, 1980), p. 118. See *NYT,* 11, 12, and 13 February 1969.

19. Bunche telegram quoted in *DN,* 13 February 1969.

20. Heckscher, *Alive in the City,* p. 134.

21. Interview of Robert Blum by author, 17 April 1997. Interview of Sid Davidoff by author, 2 December 1997. Interview of Robert Laird by author, 7 May 1997. Laird, Lindsay's deputy press secretary at the time, was told by a public relations person at the Sanitation Department that the sanitationmen had lifted their plows in Queens. Steven Isenberg, the mayoral aide in charge of sanitation, wrote the mayor in mid–1969 telling him that the Sanitation Department's Ed Crosswell "makes clear that we are, in fact, the victims of a good deal of malfeasance" in the Department. Memo from Steven L. Isenberg to Mayor John V. Lindsay, 7 July 1969, in author's possession.

22. John Corry, *My Times: Adventures in the News Trade* (New York: G. P. Putnam's Sons, 1993), p. 115, and Memo from Harry O'Donnell to John V. Lindsay, 20 December 1969, Box 5, HOD Memos to Mayor Lindsay Folder, Harry O'Donnell Papers. Josh Greenfield, "In the Beginning: A Political Satire," *NY,* 22 December 1969.

23. Robert Wool, "The Stalking of the President," *Esquire,* July 1971.

24. Aurelio Diary, 8 February 1969 entry, Group 592, Series XI, Box 226, Folder 35, JVL Papers, Yale. *NYT,* 21 February 1969. Ibid., 20 March 1969. *NYP,* 14 March 1969.

25. Wool, "The Stalking of the President." Interview of Ronnie Eldridge by author, 17 August 1999. Martin Arnold, "The Aurelio Perplex: 'Are You Running with Me, Lindsay?' " *NY,* 14 June 1971.

26. *NYT,* 19 March 1969.

27. *Time,* 1 November 1968. Lindsay, *The City,* p. 22. Interview of Richard Aurelio by Chris McNickle, 17 June 1988, in author's possession. *NYP,* 12 March 1969.

28. *NYT,* 6 March 1969.

29. "A Nightmare for Urban Management," *Fortune,* March 1969. Nora Sayre, "Breakdown of a Metropolis: Is New York Ungovernable—or Just Badly Governed?" *New Statesman,* 14 February 1969.

30. William F. Buckley Jr., "Confusion in Fun City," *NYP,* 3 April 1969. Kempton quoted in John R. Coyne Jr., "Is John Lindsay Ungovernable?" *National Review,*

17 June 1969. Breslin, "Is Lindsay Too Tall to Be Mayor?" *NYT,* 8 February 1970. Marshall Berman, "Ruins and Reforms: New York Yesterday and Today," *Dissent,* Fall 1987.

31. Memo from Daniel P. Moynihan to the President Elect, 9 January 1969, January 1969 Folder, White House Central Files, H. R. Haldeman Files, Box 49, Nixon Presidential Materials.

32. Fred Ferretti, "Vito's Big Deal," *NY,* 2 June 1969.

33. Richard Aurelio Oral History, p. 57, CUOHA. Memo from Lance Liebman to Richard Aurelio, 19 March 1969, Office of the Mayor, Executive Assistant to the Mayor (Carl P. Irish, c. 1969–1973), Mayoral Election Folder, Office of the Mayor, JVL Papers, NYCMA. *NYT,* 3 April 1969. Peter Goldmark divided the city's Republicans this way: 12 percent black, Jewish, and Puerto Rican; 45 percent Italian; 15 percent WASP; and 28 percent other (Irish, German, Eastern European). Memo from Peter Goldmark to Steve Isenberg, 5 March 1969, in author's possession.

34. Heckscher, *Alive in the City,* pp. 130–131. Laird Interview.

35. *NYT,* 6 June 1969. Memo to Thomas Morgan from Robert Blum, 10 June 1969, Group 592, Series XII, Box 227, Folder 41, JVL Papers, Yale.

36. Richard Aurelio Oral History, COOHA, p. 65. Interview of Richard Aurelio by author, 29 December 1997.

37. *NYT,* 19 February 1969. Richard Reeves, "Old Gloom Fills City's Democrats," *NYT,* 21 February 1969. Jerome Wilson, "Lindsay vs. the Field," *The Nation,* 17 March 1969.

38. Nicholas Pileggi, "The More the Mario," *NY,* 14 April 1969. Breslin, "Is Lindsay Too Tall to Be Mayor?"

39. *NYP,* 7 June 1969. *NYT,* 6 June 1969.

40. *NYT,* 17 April 1969.

41. Ibid., 12 April 1969. Robert Wagner's Announcement, Office of the Mayor, Executive Assistant to the Mayor (Carl P. Irish), 1969–1973, Box 110504, Office of the Mayor (John V. Lindsay), NYCMA.

42. *NYP,* 10 June 1969.

43. Richard Aurelio Oral History, p. 84, CUOHA.

44. *NYT,* 2 May 1969. On Mailer's mayoral race, see Mary V. Dearborn, *Mailer: A Biography* (Boston: Houghton Mifflin, 1999), pp. 259–272.

45. Norman Mailer, "Why Are We in New York?," *NYTM,* 18 May 1969. Peter Manso, ed., *Running Against the Machine* (New York: Doubleday, 1969), p. 64.

46. Manso, *Running Against the Machine,* pp. 58, 45.

47. James Wechsler, "An Odd Couple," *NYP,* 25 April 1969.

48. Breslin speech at John Jay College of Criminal Justice quoted in Manso, *Running Against the Machine,* p. 40. Bill Reel, "The Bore Buster," *DN,* 1 June 1969. Jimmy Breslin, "The Political Discovery of the Year," *NY,* 3 November 1969.

49. Jack Newfield, "Jimmy Breslin: Have You Read Him Lately?" *VV,* 31 July 1969.

50. Jimmy Breslin, "And Furthermore, I Promise," in Manso, *Running Against the Machine.*

51. James Wechsler, "An Odd Couple," *NYP,* 25 April 1969. *NYT,* 17 April 1969. Mailer, "Why Are We in New York?" Manso, *Running Against the Machine,* p. 286.

52. Norman Mailer, "At the Village Gate," in Manso, *Running Against the Machine,* pp. 59–64. Breslin quoted in *NY,* 11 April 1988, p. 69.

53. Richard Reeves, "Lindsay Tries to Stay in There, While. . . ." *NYP,* 13 June 1969.

54. Memo from Bryce Harlow to Dwight Chapin, 21 May 1969, 1969–1970 Folder, White House Central File, EX LG New York City, Box 18, Nixon Presidential Materials. Memo from Ken Cole to Peter Flanigan et al., 28 April 1969, Folder PL 1–32 [1969–1970], White House Special Files, Confidential Files, Box 47, Nixon Presidential Materials. Memo from Harry Dent to President Nixon, 20 June 1969, June 1969 Folder, White House Central Files, President's Handwriting, Box 2, Nixon Presidential Materials. Memo from John Ehrlichman to John Whitaker, 16 July 1969, PL 1–32 [1969–1970] Folder, White House Special Files, Confidential Files, Box 47, Nixon Presidential Materials.

55. In reaction to Procaccino's victory, the city's Democrats instituted a rule that a candidate must win more than 50 percent of the primary vote to win the nomination. If no candidate won 50 percent, there would be a runoff between the two top vote getters.

56. *NYT,* 19 June 1969.

57. Ibid.

58. *NY,* 11 April 1988. *NYP,* 19 June 1969.

59. Lindsay, *The City,* p. 31. Interview of Robert Sweet by author, 21 October 1997. Interview of Steven Isenberg by author, 1 September 1999.

60. *NYT,* 18 June 1969.

61. *NYP,* 18 June 1969. *NYT,* 19 June 1969. Telegram from Daniel Evans to John V. Lindsay, 18 June 1969, Group 592, Series XII, Box 227, Folder 41, JVL Papers, Yale.

62. Lindsay, *The City,* p. 32.

63. *NYP,* 21 June 1969. Ibid., 6 November 1969.

64. *The Halderman Diaries,* entry for 17 June 1969. Memo from Daniel Patrick Moynihan to Richard Nixon, 19 June 1969, June 1969 Folder, Presidential Office Files, President's Handwriting, Box 2, Nixon Presidential Materials. Annotated News Summaries, 8 September 1969, September 1969 Folder, Presidential Office Files, Box 30, and Memo from Alexander Butterfield to John Ehrlichman, 1 July 1969, both Nixon Presidential Materials. Harvey Rothenberg, Lindsay's appointments secretary, claims to have received an anonymous phone call during the campaign telling him that all of the mayor's phone lines were tapped. Nixon had been using Jack Caulfield, a former New York City police detective, to report on Lindsay. Rothenberg also claims the Nixon camp tried to dig up a scandal regarding the

mayor's twin brother, David. See Harvey Rothenberg, *Reminiscing* (Harvey Rothenberg, n.p., n.d.), p. 62.

65. Memo from Dwight Chapin to H. R. Halderman, 19 June 1969, 1969–1970 Folder, White House Central File, EX LG New York City, Box 18, Nixon Presidential Materials. Breslin, "Is Lindsay Too Tall to Be Mayor?"

66. Aurelio interview (McNickle). Wagner research, 1969 campaign, Group 592, Series VI, Box 96, Folder 126, JVL Papers, Yale.

67. *NYP,* 18 June 1969. Ibid., 28 June 1969. *NYT,* 25 June 1969. Jack Newfield, "Cops and Cabbies: A Night to Crow," *VV,* 26 June 1969.

68. Memorandum to the President from Patrick J. Buchanan, 20 June 1969, June 1969 Folder, Presidential Office Files, President's Handwriting, Box 2, Nixon Presidential Materials. *National Review,* 15 July 1969.

69. *NYT,* 30 July 1969. Aurelio interview. Eldridge interview. In reality, the final count of Democratic politicians that rejected Procaccino for Lindsay was small: five of the city's seventeen Democratic congressmen; four of the city's twenty-one Democratic State Senators; ten of the city's fifty-six Democratic assemblymen; six of the city's thirty Democratic councilmen; and two of the four Democratic borough presidents.

70. Shirley Chisholm, *The Unbought and Unbossed* (Boston: Houghton Mifflin, 1970), p. 125.

71. *NYT,* 14 August 1969.

72. Breslin, "Is Lindsay Too Tall to Be Mayor?" Joe Pilati, "Koch, Lindsay Man in '65, Can't Endorse Him Now," *VV,* 28 August 1969. In the 1997 mayoral election, Koch said he could not endorse Mayor Rudolph Giuliani for a second term, because of a personal falling-out between the two men. But he admitted that he would most likely vote for Giuliani over his opponent, Ruth Messinger, whom Koch found too liberal.

73. Edward I. Koch with William Rauch, *Politics* (New York: Simon & Schuster, 1985), p. 79. Interview of Thomas Hoving by author, 21 May 1997.

74. Edward I. Koch with Daniel Paisner, *Citizen Koch: An Autobiography* (New York: St. Martin's Press, 1992), pp. 92–99. Hoving interview. Mary Lindsay quoted in Koch with Rauch, *Politics,* p. 79.

75. *NYT,* 3 September 1969. Ibid., 6 October 1969. *NYP,* 1 October 1969.

76. "Confidential Report on John Marchi," undated, Box 110504, Office of the Mayor, Executive Assistant to the Mayor (Carl P. Irish, c. 1969–1973), Office of the Mayor, JVL Papers, NYCMA. Memo from Barry Gottehrer to Richard Aurelio, undated, Group 592, Series VII, Box 160, Folder 526, JVL Papers, Yale.

77. *NYT,* 2 September 1969. Jack Newfield, "Lindsay: He's Tougher Than Anyone Else," *VV,* 4 September 1969. Pete Hamill, "The Enemy Camp," *NYP,* 8 October 1969.

78. Memo from Peter Goldmark to Richard Aurelio et al., 15 July 1969, Group 592, Series VII, Box 161, Folder 540, JVL Papers, Yale. Memo from Jay Kriegel to

John Lindsay, 16 July 1969, Group 592, Series XII, Box 227, Folder 41, JVL Papers, Yale.

79. "Lindsay Record Called Best of Any First Term Mayor," Press Release, Committee to Reelect John Lindsay, 18 September 1969, Group 592, Box 136, Folder 122, JVL Papers, Yale. Flora Sellers Davidson, "City Policy and Housing Abandonment: A Case Study of New York City, 1965–1973" (Ph.D. diss., Columbia University, 1979). George Sternlieb, "New York's Housing: A Study in *Immobilisme*," *The Public Interest*, Summer 1969. The urban planner Peter Marcuse has estimated that during the late 1960s and early 1970s, New York lost between 125,000 and 175,000 units of housing. See Herbert J. Gans, *The Urban Villagers: Group and Class in the Life of Italian-Americans*, rev. ed. (New York: Free Press, 1982), p. 388. Charles Morris estimated that nearly 200,000 housing units were abandoned between 1965 and 1974. See Morris, *The Cost of Good Intentions*, p. 143.

80. Aurelio interview (McNickle), pp. 6–7.

81. Lindsay, *The City*, p. 38. Lindsay ad from Lindsay Reunion Committee (producers), "The Lindsay Years," videotape, 1990. Robert Sam Anson, "The World According to Garth," *New Times*, 20 October 1978.

82. Lindsay, *The City*, p. 42. Address by John V. Lindsay before a Rally to Stop the ABM [Deployment], 25 June 1969, Group 592, Box 362, Folder 423, JVL Papers, Yale. Mary Breasted, "Lindsay Woos Students; Puts It to Nixon," *VV*, 25 September 1969. *NYT*, 27 September 1969.

83. Davidoff interview.

84. Lindsay, *The City*, pp. 42–43. *NYT*, 16 October 1969. *NYP*, 15 October 1969.

85. Richard Reeves, "Here Comes the Next Mayor," *NYTM*, 2 November 1969.

86. Aurelio interview (McNickle), p. 2. Robert I. Friedman, *The False Prophet: Rabbi Meir Kahane from FBI Informant to Knesset Member* (New York: Lawrence Hill Books, 1990), p. 104. Harvey Aronson, "The Man Who Manages the Mayor," *NY*, 9 June 1969. Aurelio interview.

87. Letter from Rabbi Philip Lefkowitz to Mayor John V. Lindsay, 24 September 1969, and Letter from Samuel Schamsky to Mayor John V. Lindsay, 16 October 1969, both in Subject Files (1966–1973), Box 58, Folder 1086, Office of the Mayor, JVL Papers, NYCMA.

88. *NY*, 11 April 1968, p. 68. Aurelio interview (McNickle), p. 15. Friedman, *False Prophet*, pp. 103–105.

89. Memo from Marvin Berger to Robert Sweet, 21 July 1969, Group 592, Series XI, Box 210, Folder 42, JVL Papers, Yale.

90. McNickle, *To Be Mayor of New York*, p. 233. Interview of Sid Davidoff by Chris McNickle, 14 September 1988, La Guardia and Wagner Archives. Davidoff interview. *NYP*, 1 October 1969.

91. *NYT*, 19 September 1969. Davidoff interview, p. 26. *NYT*, 17 September 1969.

92. Tom Buckley, "What is a Mario Procaccino?" *NYTM*, 10 August 1969. John R. Coyne Jr., "New Politics and Old," *National Review*, 4 November 1969. *NYT*, 6 October 1969.

93. Rieder, *Canarsie*, p. 200. Laird interview. Robert L. Bartley, "Little Guy vs. 'Limousine Liberals,'" *WSJ*, 16 September 1969.

94. William Safire, *Safire's New Political Dictionary: The Definitive Guide to the New Language of Politics* (New York: Random House, 1993), p. 413.

95. "Who's That with John Lindsay," 11 October 1969, Group 592, Series VII, Box 176, Folder 126, JVL Papers, Yale.

96. "New York: The Revolt of the Average Man," *Time*, 3 October 1969.

97. *NYT*, 3 November 1969.

98. *NYP*, 13 October 1969.

99. Memo from Commanding Officer, 17th Division, to Deputy Commissioner—Community Relations, New York Police Department, 10 March 1969, Group 592, Box 227, Folder 40, JVL Papers, Yale.

100. Memo from Barry Gottehrer to Robert Ruskin, Robert Sweet, and Jay Kriegel, 21 October 1969.

101. See *NYT*, 21 and 22 October 1969. *NY*, 12 January 1970, pp. 6–7. Other examples of criminals employed by the city in full knowledge of their backgrounds were the Neighborhood Youth Corps's Willie Smith and the Parks Department's Robert Collier.

102. *NYP*, 30 October 1969. Reeves, "Here Comes the Next Mayor."

103. *NYP*, 30 October 1969.

104. Krickus, *Pursuing the American Dream*, pp. 210–211. Lerner, "Respectable Bigotry." Milton Himmelfarb, "Jewish Class Conflict?" *Commentary*, January 1970.

105. *NYT*, 14 October 14. Isenberg interview.

106. *NYT*, 18 October 1969.

107. Raymond Horton, *Municipal Labor Relations in New York City: Lessons of the Lindsay-Wagner Years* (New York: Praeger, 1973), pp. 43, 82–83, 85–86.

108. *NYT*, 25 June 1969. David Selden, *The Teacher Rebellion* (Washington, D.C.: Howard University Press, 1985), pp. 153–154.

109. *NYT*, 17 and 19 October 1969. *NYP*, 20 October 1969. *AN*, 18 October 1969. *VV*, 30 October 1969.

110. *DN*, 22 October 1969.

111. Ron Rosenbaum, "When in Brooklyn, Play Gimpel the Fool," *VV*, 23 October 1969.

112. Carl Tinstman, "The Lindsay Campaign and the White Lower/Middle Class," September 1969, Group 592, Series VII, Box 161, Folder 532, JVL Papers, Yale.

113. Letter from Jimmy Breslin to John Lindsay, 28 September 1969, and Memo from Jeff Greenfield to Richard Aurelio et al., 3 October 1969, both in Group 592, Series XI, Box 227, Folder 40, JVL Papers, Yale. For more of Breslin on the outer boroughs, see Breslin, "The Political Discovery of the Year."

114. Pete Hamill, "Brooklyn: The Sane Alternative," *NY*, 14 July 1969.

115. Peter Hamill, "John Lindsay," *NYP*, 20 October 1969.

116. McNickle, *To Be Mayor of New York*, pp. 233–234. James Q. Wilson, "The Mayors vs. the Cities," *The Public Interest*, Summer 1969. To show how linked Lind-

say and the Mets were in 1969, a local sports magazine put on its cover a faithfully stylized re-creation of Washington's famous crossing of the Delaware, with Gil Hodges as Washington and assorted Mets players on board. Also on the boat was John Lindsay, "scanning the horizon possibly for TV cameras on shore" (*Jock-New York*, April 1970).

117. Interview of Mario Procaccino, "Newsmaker," WCBS-TV, 14 December 1969. *DN*, 3 November 1969. John V. Lindsay, "The Summer of My Discontent," *NY*, 22 December 1969.

118. *The Nation*, 17 November 1969.

119. Not so surprisingly, Procaccino moved steadily rightward after 1969. He endorsed Governor Nelson Rockefeller in his 1970 reelection race, in part because Rockefeller's Democratic opponent, Arthur Goldberg, had been a prominent pro-Lindsay Democrat in 1969. In return for his endorsement, Procaccino later became a special assistant to Rockefeller, Commissioner of Taxation and Finance, president of the State Tax Commission, and a member of the Battery Park City Authority. In addition, Procaccino endorsed the Conservative Party's candidate for Senate that year, James Buckley, against the Republican, Charles Goodell, and the Democrat, Richard Ottinger. In announcing for Buckley, Procaccino complained that the "Democratic Party has been captured by the radical left." The former comptroller said he could stand with Buckley "one hundred percent. Law and order, respect for our police and firemen, first-rate neighborhood schools for all the neighborhoods, a fair day's wage for a fair day's work, and scrupulous regard for the taxpayer."

120. Arthur M. Klebanoff, "Is There a Jewish Vote?" *Commentary*, January 1970. Memo from Art Klebanoff to Daniel P. Moynihan, 5 November 1969, 1969–1970 Folder, White House Central Files, EX LG NYC, Box 18, Nixon Presidential Materials.

121. Himmelfarb, "Jewish Class Conflict?"

122. On John Purroy Mitchel, see Edwin R. Lewinson, *John Purroy Mitchel: The Boy Mayor of New York* (New York: Astra Books, 1965); Augustus Cerillo Jr., "The Reform of Municipal Government in New York City from Seth Low to John Purroy Mitchel," *New York Historical Society Quarterly*, January 1973; Kenneth S. Chern, "The Politics of Patriotism: War, Ethnicity, and the New York Mayoral Campaign, 1917," *New York Historical Society Quarterly*, October 1979; Julian Street, "New York's Fighting Mayor: Shall Tammany Stay Out or Come Back?," *Collier's Weekly*, 25 August 1917. Mitchel died tragically less than a year after his 1917 defeat; he joined the air corps and perished in Louisiana in a training accident.

CHAPTER 13

1. *NYT*, 2 December 1969. Theodore J. Lowi, "Dear Mayor Lindsay," *The Nation*, 8 December 1969.

2. *NYT*, 1 January 1970.

3. Ibid., 25 December 1969.

4. Ibid., 8 November 1969. Ibid., 30 November 1969. Ibid., 25 December 1969. John V. Lindsay, *The City* (New York: W. W. Norton, 1969), pp. 46, 48.

5. John V. Lindsay, "A Plan for Neighborhood Government for New York City," June 1970, New York State Library, Albany, New York. Alan Hevesi, "A Critique of Lindsay's Plan," *Community* (Institute for Community Studies, Queens College), March 1971.

6. Interview of Ronnie Eldridge by author, 17 August 1999. For a brief history of the Young Lords, see Pablo Guzman, "La Vida Pura: A Lord of the Barrio," *VV*, 21 March 1995.

7. Martin Duberman, *Stonewall* (New York: E. P. Dutton, 1993). Lucian Truscott IV, "Gay Power Comes to Sheridan Square." Howard Smith, "Full Moon over the Stonewall," *VV*, 3 July 1969. *DN*, 6 July 1969.

8. Nat Hentoff, "The Mayor: Your City as Much as Mine," *The New Yorker*, 3 May 1969.

9. *NYT*, 11 August 1970. Joseph Mitchell, "The Old House at Home," in Joseph Mitchell, *Up in the Old Hotel* (New York: Vintage Books, 1993).

10. Emanuel Tobier, "Economic Development Strategy for the City," in Lyle C. Fitch and Annmarie Hauck Walsh, eds., *Agenda for a City: Issues Confronting New York* (Beverly Hills, Calif.: Sage Publications, 1970), p. 32. *NYT*, 30 December 1971, 6 March 1972.

11. *NYT*, 15 January 1970. Ibid., 16 January 1970. Ibid., 1 March 1970. Tom Wolfe, *Radical Chic and Mau-Mauing the Flak Catchers* (New York: Farrar Straus and Giroux, 1970).

12. Statement by Leonard Bernstein, 30 January 1970, Black-Jewish Relations, 1970–1974 Folder, AJC Archive.

13. On the hardhat riots, see Joshua Freeman, "Hardhats: Construction Workers, Manliness, and the 1970 Pro-War Demonstrations," *Journal of Social History*, Summer 1993; Thomas Williams, "My Hardhat Problem—And Yours," *Esquire*, October 1970; Fred J. Cook, "Hard-Hats: The Rampaging Patriots," *The Nation*, 15 June 1970; Andy Logan, "Around City Hall," *The New Yorker*, 6 June 1970; Nancy Banks, "The Hard-Hat Riot of 1970 and the Building of the New Majority" (unpublished paper, Columbia University, 1998).

14. *NYP*, 8 May 1970. Ibid., 9 May 1970. *NYT*, 9 May 1970. *WSJ*, 11 May 1970.

15. Richard Rogin, "Joe Kelly Has Reached His Boiling Point," *NYTM*, 28 June 1970.

16. One of the injured antiwar protesters, a young woman named Ruth Messinger, was the 1997 Democratic mayoral candidate.

17. Interview of Richard Aurelio by author, 29 December 1997. Interview of Sid Davidoff by author, 2 December 1997.

18. *NY*, 11 April 1988.

19. New York Police Department (NYPD), "Report Relating to the Role of the Police in Connection with Disorder Which Occurred in Lower Manhattan on 8

May 1970 as a Result of Peace Demonstration by Various Student Factions and Counter Demonstrations by Construction workers and other Sympathizers," Group 592, Series XIV, Box 256, Folder 337, JVL Papers, Yale. *NY*, 11 April 1988. Davidoff interview.

20. NYPD, "Report Relating to the Role of the Police." Martin Arnold, "The Aurelio Perplex: 'Are You Running with Me, Lindsay?' " *NY*, 14 June 1971.

21. *NYT*, 9 May 1970. Ibid., 10 May 1970. See *NYP*, 9, 12, and 13 May 1970. Cook, "Hard-Hats: The Rampaging Patriots." Statement by Mayor John V. Lindsay, 9 May 1970, Group 592, Series VIII, Box 175, Folder 124, JVL Papers, Yale.

22. *NYT*, 12 May 1970. Ibid., 12 May 1970. Ibid., 16 May 1970.

23. Rogin, "Joe Kelly Has Reached His Boiling Point."

24. *NYT*, 21 and 22 May 1970.

25. Memo from H. R. Haldeman to Charles Colson, 15 September 1970, Nixon Presidential Materials.

26. Nixon quoted in Memo from H. R. Haldeman to Dwight Chapin, 19 June 1970, 1969–1970 Folder, White House Central File, EX LG New York City, Box 18, Presidential Office Files, Box 32, News Summaries, September 1970, Nixon Presidential Materials.

27. *NYT*, 22 January 1969. Ibid., 9 February 1970. Ibid., 24 October 1970. Memo from Steven L. Isenberg to Edward Hamilton, Tom Morgan, Jay Kriegel, 26 October 1972, in author's possession. Letter from Matthew Troy, Councilman, 16th District, to Mayor John V. Lindsay, 25 October 1973, Box 13, Folder 177, Subject Files (1966–1973), Office of the Mayor, JVL Papers, NYCMA.

28. Richard Piro, *Black Fiddler* (New York: William Morrow, 1971), pp. 190–191, 234–235.

29. Daniel H. Perlstein, "The New York City School Crisis: Teacher Politics, Racial Politics and the Decline of Liberalism," (Ph.D. diss., Stanford University, 1994), pp. 91–92, 130–132.

30. *NYT*, 20 November 1968. Ibid., 5 December 1968. *NYP*, 6 December 1968. Barbara Carter, *Pickets, Parents, and Power: The Story Behind the New York City Teachers' Strike* (New York: Citation Press, 1971). Nislow letter in Box 392, Folder 22, UFT Papers.

31. On the problems at Franklin Lane High School, see "School Crisis at Franklin K. Lane and Canarsie High Schools," Box 5, Folder 146, Albert Shanker Subject Files, UF7 Papers, NYU; Harold Saltzman, *Race War in High School: The Ten Year Destruction of Franklin K. Lane High School in Brooklyn* (New Rochelle, N.Y.: Arlington House, 1972); and Jonathan Black, "Lane HS: The Time Bomb Could Explode Any Day," *VV*, 25 December 1969.

32. *NYT*, 22 January 1969. Black, "Lane HS."

33. On open admissions at City University, see James Traub, *City on a Hill: Testing the American Dream at City College* (Reading, Mass.: Addison-Wesley, 1994); Solomon Resnik and Barbara Kaplan, "Report Card on Open Admissions: Remedial Work Recommended," *NYTM*, 9 May 1971; Jack E. Rossman, Helen S. Astin,

Alexander W. Astin, and Elaine H. El-Khawas, *Open Admissions at City University of New York: An Analysis of the First Year* (Englewood Cliffs, N.J.: Prentice Hall, 1975); L. G. Heller, *The Death of the American University: With Special Reference to the Collapse of City College of New York* (New Rochelle, N.Y.: Arlington House, 1973); Martin Mayer, "Higher Education for All? The Case of Open Admissions," *Commentary*, February 1973; David E. Lavin, Richard D. Alba, and Richard A. Silberstein, *Right Versus Privilege: The Open-Admissions Experiment at the City University of New York* (New York: Free Press, 1981).

34. Charles R. Morris, *The Cost of Good Intentions: New York City and the Liberal Experiment, 1960–1975* (New York: W. W. Norton, 1980), pp. 156–157.

35. Morris, *The Cost of Good Intentions*, p. 192. Interview of Peter Goldmark by author, 13 June 1997. Press Release, Mayor's Office, "The Mayor's Advisory Task Force on the City University of New York Presents its Findings and Recommendations to Mayor Giuliani," 7 June 1999. See also Heather MacDonald, "CUNY Could Be Great Again," *City Journal*, Winter 1998.

36. Jonathan Rieder, *Canarsie: The Jews and Italians of Brooklyn Against Liberalism* (Cambridge, MA: Harvard University Press, 1985), pp. 19–20.

37. Rieder, *Canarsie*, pp. 203–232. See *NYT*, 18, 20, 24, 25, 28, and 30 October and 2 and 10 November 1972.

38. Jack Newfield, "Little Rock in New York," *VV*, 2 November 1972. Dalton James, "Out of the Family and into the Street," *VV*, 9 November 1972. Pete Hamill, "School Bus Named Desire," *NYP*, 1 November 1972.

39. Clark Whelton, "The Vanishing White Man," *VV*, 9 November 1972. *NYT*, 6 November 1972.

40. For a discussion of the prison riots, see Barry Gottehrer, *The Mayor's Man* (Garden City, N.Y.: Doubleday, 1975), pp. 261–287. *NYT*, 15 October 1970.

41. *NYT*, 23 December 1973. Gottehrer, *The Mayor's Man*, p. 284.

42. "The Tombs Disturbance: A Report," New York State Senate Committee on Crime and Correction, 5 October 1970, NYCMA. Gottehrer, *The Mayor's Man*, p. 271. Nat Hentoff, "The Mayor on Trial in the Tombs," *VV*, 27 August 1970. Mary Breasted, "Rituals of Rebellion: What Broke Down?" *VV*, 8 October 1970.

43. Peter Maas, *Serpico* (New York: Viking Press, 1973), p. 62.

44. James Lardner, *Crusader: The Hell-Raising Career of Detective David Durk* (New York: Random House, 1996), pp. 98–99. Maas, *Serpico*, pp. 178, 181. Knapp Commission, *Knapp Commission Report on Police Corruption* (New York: George Braziller, 1972), p. 200.

45. Jack Newfield and Wayne Barrett, *City for Sale: Ed Koch and the Betrayal of New York* (New York: Harper & Row, 1988), p. 158. Lardner, *Crusader*, p. 152. Maas, *Serpico*, pp. 180, 257.

46. Interview of Arnold Fraiman by author, 14 October 1999.

47. Lardner, *Crusader*, pp. 7, 91, 121. Robert Daley, *Target Blue: An Insider's View of the NYPD* (New York: Delacorte Press, 1973), p. 348. Fraiman interview.

48. Lardner, *Crusader*, p. 180.

49. *NYT,* 24 April 1970. John Corry, *My Times: Adventures in the News Trade* (New York: G. P. Putnam's Sons, 1993), pp. 117–118. Lardner, *Crusader,* pp. 183–184.

50. See *NYT,* 25, 26, and 27 April 1970.

51. Memo from John Caulfield to John Ehrlichman, 10 October 1970, John Caulfield Folder, John Ehrlichman Papers, Box 30, Nixon Presidential Materials. *NYT,* 24 July 1970.

52. Daley, *Target Blue,* p. 42. *NYT,* 29 April 1970.

53. Ibid., pp. 49–50, 55. Sonny Grosso and John Devaney, *Murder at the Harlem Mosque* (New York: Crown, 1977), p. 34. *NYT,* 1 September 1971.

54. Knapp quoted in Daley, *Target Blue,* p. 54.

55. *NYT,* 2 July 1971. Ibid., 3 September 1971.

56. Daley, *Target Blue,* pp. 56, 111, 482. *NYT,* 20 September 1971.

57. Daley, *Target Blue,* p. 298. Barbara Davidson, "The Knapp Commission Didn't Know It Couldn't Be Done," *NYTM,* 9 January 1972. Knapp Commission, *Report,* p. 51.

58. See *NYT,* 20 and 21 October 1971.

59. Daley, *Target Blue,* pp. 314, 319–320.

60. *NYT,* 15 December 1971.

61. Ibid., 21 and 22 December 1971.

62. Ibid., 23 December 1971.

63. Ibid., 30 October 1971.

64. Knapp Commission, *Report,* pp. 1–2, 277.

65. Ibid., pp. 3, 4, 7. Tom Buckley, "Murphy Among the 'Meat Eaters,' " *NYTM,* 19 December 1971.

66. Knapp Commission, *Report,* pp. 72–73.

67. Ibid., pp. 193–194, 202.

68. On the police shootings, see James Lardner and Thomas Reppetto, *NYPD: A City and Its Police* (New York: Henry Holt, 2000), pp. 271–272.

69. Patrick V. Murphy and Thomas Plate, *Commissioner: A View from the Top of American Law Enforcement* (New York: Simon & Schuster, 1977), pp. 253–254. Herbert Klein, *The Police: Damned If They Do, Damned If They Don't* (New York: Crown, 1968), p. x. *NYT,* 9 September 1970.

70. Grosso and Devaney, *Murder at the Harlem Mosque,* p. 13. Albert A. Seedman and Peter Hellman, *Chief!* (New York: Arthur Fields Books, 1974), pp. 490–491.

71. Gerald Astor, "The New York Ten," *NYTM,* 12 December 1971.

72. Seedman and Hellman, *Chief!* pp. 440–441. *NYT,* 22 May 1971. Richard Moore, "A Black Panther Speaks," *NYT,* 12 May 1971.

73. Seedman and Hellman, *Chief!* p. 487.

74. Ibid., p. 491. Clark Whelton, "The Blood on Avenue B," *VV,* 10 February 1972.

75. *NYT,* 20 May 1971. Ibid., 29 January 1972.

76. *AN,* 5 February 1972. Ibid., 12 February 1972. One year later, the tone of the paper changed completely as it shed some of its militant rhetoric. A front-

page editorial on the shootings in 1973 blamed them on "the criminal element which refused to go to work and make a decent living, but instead, chooses to make his living by stealing and robbing others of the fruits of their labor." Whereas one year earlier it had rationalized black hatred toward police, the paper now sought to reassure police that the silent majority of black Harlem supported them: "Be assured that the loud mouthed vocal minority on the corners who boo and jeer when you lock up a criminal are not representative of the hard working people watching from their apartment windows . . . Your support, your backup are the people behind those closed doors who stay off the streets because the streets have too often become the property of the hoods" (*AN*, 17 February 1973).

77. Raymond Horton, *Municipal Labor Relations in New York City: Lessons of the Lindsay-Wagner Years* (New York: Praeger, 1973), p. 110. *NYT*, 20 January 1971. On the issue of police and fireman parity pay, see Morris, *The Cost of Good Intentions*, pp. 120–124.

78. John Mack, "Return to Brownsville," *VV*, 23 December 1971. On the racial changes and increasing poverty in central Brooklyn, see Harold X. Connolly, *A Ghetto Grows in Brooklyn* (New York: New York University, 1977).

79. *NYT*, 13 June 1970.

80. *AN*, 15 May 1971. *VV*, 27 May 1971. *NYT*, 6 May 1971.

81. Ibid., 7 May 1971.

82. Daley, *Target Blue*, pp. 536–537. Grosso and Devaney, *Murder at the Harlem Mosque*, pp. 41–49.

83. Ibid., pp. 45, 56.

84. Ibid., pp. 81–82.

85. Daley, *Target Blue*, pp. 533–34. *NYT*, 15 April 1972.

86. Ibid., p. 535. Murphy and Plate, *Commissioner*, p. 180.

87. Ibid., p. 176. Grosso had been in the area searching for Twymon Myers, one of the suspected killers of Officers Piagentini and Jones. Grosso believed that the false "10–13" call was made to pull him off the stakeout.

88. Daley, *Target Blue*, pp. 539, 546. *NYP*, 13 and 15 April 1972.

89. Grosso and Devaney, *Murder at the Harlem Mosque*, pp. 90–91. Daley, *Target Blue*, pp. 549–551.

90. *NYT*, 16 April 1972. *AN*, 22 April 1972. Ibid., 29 April 1972. Farrakhan seemed to have impressed others in the Lindsay administration. Barry Gottehrer got to know him and said of the minister, "I grew to respect him very much" (Gottehrer, *The Mayor's Man*, pp. 240–241).

91. Murphy and Plate, *Commissioner*, pp. 175–176, 178. *NYT*, 17 April 1972.

92. *NYP*, 13 April 1997. Interview of Pat Vecchio by author, 13 October 1999.

93. Daley, *Target Blue*, pp. 554, 562. *NYP*, 13 April 1997.

94. Murphy and Plate, *Commissioner*, p. 179. *NYT*, 14 August 1971. Vecchio interview.

95. Murphy and Plate, *Commissioner*, p. 179. Davidoff interview.

96. Grosso and Devaney, *Murder at the Harlem Mosque*, pp. 77, 97.

97. William Bratton with Peter Knobler, *Turnaround: How America's Top Cop Reversed the Crime Epidemic* (New York: Random House, 1998), pp. xx–xxviii. See *NYT,* 11 and 13–16 January 1994. Bratton later wrote that police "discovered that the entire incident had been deliberately created by local drug dealers who had been chased away from the area around the mosque by the Muslims. In retaliation, they had made the call to provoke a confrontation between their two enemies, the Muslims and the police."

CHAPTER 14

1. William L. Riordon, *Plunkitt of Tammany Hall: A Series of Very Plain Talks on Very Practical Politics,* ed. Terrence J. McDonald (Boston: St. Martin's Press/Bedford Books, 1994), pp. 58–59.

2. John V. Lindsay, "The Rule of Law," reprinted in *Congressional Record,* 10 June 1970, p. 19114.

3. "To Choose Again," Commencement Address by Mayor John V. Lindsay, Williams College, 7 June 1970, Group 592, Box 175, Folder 124, JVL Papers, Yale.

4. Interview of Steven Isenberg by author, 16 October 1999.

5. Text of an Address by Mayor John V. Lindsay at 102nd Charter Anniversary Exercises on Berkeley Campus of University of California, 2 April 1970, Group 592, Box 172, Folder 20, JVL Papers, Yale. *NYT,* 3 April 1970. Isenberg interview.

6. Jack Newfield, "Hunger for a Hope in Reagan Land," *VV,* 9 April 1970.

7. *NYT,* 13 October 1970.

8. Interview of Richard Aurelio by author, 29 December 1997.

9. *NYT,* 20 October 1970.

10. *NYT,* 21 October 1970.

11. Richard Reeves, "Rockefeller and Lindsay: An Old Rivalry Turns Personal and Savage Feud," *Life,* 25 June 1971. Interview of Sid Davidoff by author, 2 December 1997. Interview of Peter Goldmark by author, 13 June 1997.

12. *NYT,* 19 January 1972. Ibid., 9 April 1973.

13. *NYT,* 27 October 1970.

14. Edward I. Koch with William Rauch, *Politics* (New York: Simon & Schuster, 1985), p. 79. *NYT,* 20 October 1970.

15. Samuel G. Freedman, *The Inheritance: How Three Families and America Moved from Roosevelt to Reagan and Beyond* (New York: Simon & Schuster, 1996), p. 275.

16. *NYT,* 11 August 1971.

17. Ibid., 12 August 1971.

18. Ibid., 29 August 1971.

19. *NYP,* 12 August 1971.

20. Mary Perot Nichols, "Bob Wagner: Where Are You Now That We Need You?" *VV,* 1 April 1970. Bella Abzug, *Bella! Ms. Abzug Goes to Washington* (New York: Saturday Review Press, 1972), pp. 3, 49, 179–180, 230–231.

21. Floyd McKissick, "Open Letter to Mayor Lindsay," *AN*, 24 January 1970. Memo from Eleanor Norton to Jay Kriegel, 10 December 1971, Group 592, Series XIII, Box 239, Folder 4, JVL Papers, Yale.

22. *AN*, 28 August 1971. *NYT*, 8 November 1971.

23. Edward N. Costikyan, "Why Not John Lindsay?" *NYT*, 15 March 1971. Interview of Edward Costikyan by author, 13 November 1996.

24. Mario M. Cuomo, *Forest Hills Diary: The Crisis of Low-Income Housing* (New York: Vintage Books: 1974), p. 66. "Report of Housing and Urban Renewal Task Force," 10 January 1966, NYCMA.

25. *NYT*, 4 July 1966. Roger Starr, "The Lesson of Forest Hills," *Commentary*, June 1972.

26. Interview of Don Elliott by author, 30 April 1997. *NYT*, 4 July 1966. John V. Lindsay, "We Can Lick the Problems of the Ghetto, If We Care," *Reader's Digest*, August 1968.

27. Mario Cuomo, "Report of Investigation Concerning Forest Hills Low-Income Housing Project," 25 July 1972, pp. 3–4, Box #0074A2, Folder #2, La Guardia and Wagner Archives. Starr, "The Lesson of Forest Hills."

28. Jack Newfield, "Crushing of Corona by a Plastic Glacier," *VV*, 26 November 1970. On the early history of the housing controversy in Corona and Forest Hills, see Ross Gelbspan, "Corona: Cause for a Day," *VV*, 8 July 1971, and Walter Goodman, "The Battle of Forest Hills—Who's Ahead?" *NYTM*, 20 February 1972.

29. Robert S. McElvaine, *Mario Cuomo: A Biography* (New York: Charles Scribner's Sons, 1988), pp. 172–174. Mario M. Cuomo, *Forest Hills Diary: The Crisis of Low-Income Housing* (New York: Vintage Books, 1974), pp. 11–13.

30. Ibid., pp. 17–18. Gelbspan, "Corona: Cause for a Day." *NYT*, 2 December 1970. Ibid., 3 December 1970.

31. *NYT*, 20 November 1971.

32. Paul Cowan, " 'Them' in Forest Hills," *VV*, 23 December 1971.

33. Letter from Samuel Rabinove to Albert Vorspan, 22 February 1972, Forest Hills Folder, 1971–1973, AJC Archives. In her book about the South Bronx, Jill Jonnes described the experience of Jews whose neighborhood was undergoing a rapid demographic change: "The Jews moved because what they saw in these new families scared them: the symptoms of poverty and social disintegration that they had struggled so hard to escape from on the Lower East Side and to avoid in their own lives on Charlotte Street. . . . They saw men standing around the streets drinking and gambling. They saw families with too many children crammed into too small a space. They encountered housewives who didn't understand the neighborhood codes about garbage disposal. They saw sons and daughters growing up too much on the streets without supervision. They saw casual attitudes toward sex, procreation and marriage. They saw men without steady, decent jobs. They saw a people who often didn't want to be in New York at all, who resented having to come so far for the lousy jobs they did find" (Jill Jonnes, *We're Still Here: The Rise,*

Fall, and Resurrection of the South Bronx [Boston: Atlantic Monthly Press, 1986], p. 222). For a similar reaction of Italian Americans in Carroll Gardens, Brooklyn, see Jim Sleeper, *The Closest of Strangers: Liberalism and the Politics of Race* (New York: W. W. Norton, 1990), pp. 118–119.

34. Nathan Glazer, "When the Melting Pot Doesn't Melt," *NYTM*, 2 January 1972. Clark Whelton, "Battle of Forest Hills," *VV*, 25 November 1971.

35. Nat Hentoff, "Bringing the Constitution to Forest Hills," *VV*, 30 December 1971. Herman Badillo, "The Forest Hills Affair: Beyond Stereotypes," *VV*, 2 December 1971. Cuomo, *Forest Hills Diary*, p. 62. Transcript of Donald Elliott, Guest Editorial, WCBS-TV, 29 December 1971, Forest Hills Folder, 1971–1973, AJC Archives.

36. Cowan, " 'Them' in Forest Hills." Cuomo, *Forest Hills Diary*, pp. 62–63.

37. Stephen D. Isaacs, *Jews and American Politics* (Garden City, N.Y.: Doubleday, 1974), p. 174. *NYT*, 19 November 1971. Telegram from Haskell Lazere and Edward Moldover to John V. Lindsay, 11 February 1972, Forest Hills Folder, 1971–1973, AJC Archives. Memo from Haskell Lazere to Bertram Gold, 3 February 1972, both in Forest Hills Folder, 1971–1973, AJC Archives.

38. Edward I. Koch with William Rauch, *Politics* (New York: Simon & Schuster, 1985), p. 130. Edward I. Koch with Daniel Paisner, *Citizen Koch: An Autobiography* (New York: St. Martin's Press, 1992), pp. 113–118. Jack Newfield, "My Back Pages," *VV*, 16 December 1971. Interview of Ed Koch by author, 16 September 1996.

39. *NYT*, 14 May 1972.

40. Cuomo, *Forest Hills Diary*, pp. 27–28.

41. Ibid., "Report of Investigation Concerning Forest Hills Low-Income Housing Project."

42. Ibid., *Forest Hills Diary*, pp. 37–38, 88, 91.

43. Ibid., "Report of Investigation Concerning Forest Hills Low-Income Housing Project." Ibid., *Forest Hills Diary*, pp. 57, 93.

44. Ibid., pp. 107, 116, 122. *NYT*, 20 August 1972.

45. Barry Jacobs, "Forest Hills Has Changed Its Mind," *VV*, 11 December 1984. *NYT*, 22 October 1995.

46. Elliott interview.

47. Nicholas Pileggi, "Inside Lindsay's Head," *NY*, 4 January 1971. Letter from Peter Goldmark to John and Mary Lindsay, 20 July 1971, in author's possession.

48. Interview of Victor Gotbaum by author, 21 September 1999.

49. Statement by Mayor John V. Lindsay, 28 December 1971, Group 592, Series VIII, Box 172, Folder 46, JVL Papers, Yale. Memo from Steven L. Isenberg to Richard Aurelio, 27 December 1971, in author's possession.

50. On Lindsay's presidential campaign, see Martin Arnold, "The Aurelio Perplex: 'Are You Running with Me, Lindsay?'" *NY*, 14 June 1971; Robert Wool, "The Stalking of the President," *Esquire*, July 1971; Frank Trippett, "Lindsay,

Aurelio & Co. Hit the Road," *NYTM,* 21 November 1971; Paul R. Weich, "He Looks Good, Like a Candidate Should," *The New Republic,* 15 January 1972; Gail Sheehy, "Is Lindsay Running Out on New York?" *NY,* 17 January 1972; Josh Greenfield, "Heeeeeere's John!—The Media Candidate," *Life,* 25 February 1972; and Jack Shepherd, "The Sun-Kissed Lindsay," *Saturday Review,* 11 March 1972.

51. Speech by John V. Lindsay at Northern Arizona University, 15 January 1972, Group 592, Series VIII, Box 172, Folder 18, JVL Papers, Yale. Speech by John V. Lindsay at the University of California at Los Angeles, 23 February 1972, Group 592, Series VIII, Box 172, Folder 48, both in JVL Papers, Yale. Lindsay Reunion Committee (producers), "The Lindsay Years," videotape, 1990.

52. Press Release, Lindsay '72, 25 February 1972, Group 592, Series VIII, Box 172, Folder 31, JVL Papers, Yale.

53. Senator Fred R. Harris and Mayor John V. Lindsay, Co-Chairmen, *The State of the Cities: Report of the Commission on the Cities in the '70s* (New York: Praeger, 1972), p. 107.

54. Press Release, Lindsay '72, 8 March 1972, Group 592, Series VIII, Box 172, Folder 26, JVL Papers, Yale. Statement by Mayor John V. Lindsay, 6 March 1972, Box 1, Folder 3, Office of the Mayor, JVL Papers, Subject Files (1966–1973), NYCMA.

55. Richard Aurelio, "How to Run Your Campaign (if at all)," *NYTM,* 16 September 1973.

56. Theodore H. White, *The Making of the President: 1972* (New York: Atheneum, 1973), p. 89.

57. Richard Aurelio Oral History, p. 149, CUOHA.

58. Stephanie Harrington, "Lindsay Goes Walking on the Florida Waters," *VV,* 2 March 1972. *NYT,* 23 February 1972.

59. White, *Making of the President,* pp. 90–92.

60. Davidoff interview.

61. *NYT,* 28 March 1972.

62. Richard A. Armstrong, "The Re-Education of John Lindsay," *NYTM,* 8 October 1972.

63. Interview of Ronnie Eldridge by author, 17 August 1999. Interview of David Garth by author, 4 June 1997. White, *Making of the President,* p. 89.

64. Joe Klein, "Lindsay's Comeback: The Ghost Walks," *NY,* 30 June 1980. Letter from Sid Davidoff to Barry Gottehrer, 10 March 1975, in author's possession. Richard Aurelio Oral History, p. 145.

65. Ibid., p. 150.

66. John Lindsay, "In Defense of *New York,*" *Harper's Bazaar,* February 1972.

67. Daniel J. Elazar, "Are We a Nation of Cities?" *The Public Interest,* Summer 1966. Bureau of the Census, U.S. Department of Commerce, 1960, 1990. Gallup poll cited in James Q. Wilson, "The Urban Unease: Community vs. City," *The Public Interest,* Summer 1968.

68. Sheehy, "Is Lindsay Running Out on New York?" Greenfield, "Heeeeeere's John!—The Media Candidate." Transcript of "Meet the Press," 13 February 1972, Group 592, Series VIII, Box 177, Folder 153, JVL Papers, Yale.

69. Armstrong, "The Re-Education of John Lindsay."

CHAPTER 15

1. Marshall Berman, "Ruins and Reforms: New York Yesterday and Today," *Dissent,* Fall 1987.

2. James Q. Wilson, *Thinking About Crime* (New York: Basic Books, 1979), p. 14.

3. Crime data come from Federal Bureau of Investigation, "Uniform Crime Reports," 1966, 1973. According to the 1970 census, the twenty largest American cities were New York, Chicago, Los Angeles, Philadelphia, Detroit, Houston, Baltimore, Dallas, Washington, Cleveland, Indianapolis, Milwaukee, San Francisco, San Antonio, San Diego, Boston, Memphis, St. Louis, New Orleans, and Phoenix.

4. *NYT,* 4 February 1968. Ibid., 3 June 1969. John R. Coyne Jr., "Is John Lindsay Ungovernable?" *National Review,* 17 June 1969.

5. Jim Sleeper, *The Closest of Strangers: Liberalism and the Politics of Race in New York* (New York: W. W. Norton, 1990), p. 36. *NYT,* 18 April 1967.

6. Ibid., 20 February 1966. *AN,* 16 November 1968.

7. *AN,* 30 September 1967. Ibid., 11 January 1969. *NYT,* 13 December 1968. Orde Coombs, "Fear and Trembling in Black Streets," *NY,* 20 November 1972.

8. Robert W. Snyder, "The Neighborhood Changed: The Irish of Washington Heights and Inwood Since 1945," in Ronald H. Bayor and Timothy J. Meagher, eds., *The New York Irish* (Baltimore: Johns Hopkins Press, 1996), pp. 450–451.

9. *WSJ,* 7 November 1969. Jill Jonnes, *We're Still Here: The Rise, Fall, and Resurrection of the South Bronx* (Boston: Atlantic Monthly Press, 1986), p. 222. *NYT,* 15–18 January 1973. In *The Death of an American Jewish Community: A Tragedy of Good Intentions* (New York: Free Press, 1992), Hillel Levine and Lawrence Harmon relate the racial complications of muggings among elderly Jews living in Dorchester, a Boston neighborhood undergoing a shift from Jewish to poor black. "Young black hoodlums in Dorchester had developed a bizarre marksmanship ritual in which they would razor-slash the back pants pockets of the elderly Jewish men so that their wallets would fall to the ground. The less skillful thugs inflicted flesh wounds, which proved more embarrassing than life-threatening. Each fresh assault caused Dorchester Jews to harden their hearts to the city's blacks and to the suburban Jews who supported their causes. . . . The experience of lying face down on a hospital gurney while an intern sutured one's backside was hardly conducive to progressive thinking" (p. 126).

10. Letter from Eugene Sack to Jay Kriegel, 29 March 1967, Correspondence, Law Enforcement (1965–1969), Robert W. Sweet (Deputy Mayor) Files, Correspondence, Law Enforcement, 1965–1969, JVL Papers, NYCMA. Letter from

George Kamenow to Emmanuel Cellar, 23 May 1968, Crime (1), Box 298, Papers of Emmanuel Cellar, Manuscript Division, Library of Congress. Letters from Edward Bates to John V. Lindsay, 28 March 1969, 24 September 1969, Box 15, Folder 175, Office of the Mayor, JVL Papers, Office of the Secretary, Confidential Subject Files (1966–1973), NYCMA.

11. Memo from Commanding Officer, Chief Inspector's Investigation Unit to Chief Inspector, 27 February 1969, Series XVI, Box 375, Folder 614, JVL Papers, Yale. Letter to Jay Kriegel, 21 April 1970, Office of the Mayor, JVL Papers, Office of the Secretary, Confidential Subject Files (1963–1975), Box 15, Folder 173, NYCMA. *NYT,* 28 November 1969.

12. Ibid., 16 March 1969. Ibid., 21 February 1972.

13. Ibid., 28 September 1972. Ibid., 5 November 1972. Amitai Etzioni, "Mugging Is Now the Number One Topic," *VV,* 12 October 1972.

14. Jonathan Rieder, *Canarsie: The Jews and Italians of Brooklyn Against Liberalism* (Cambridge, Mass.: Harvard University Press, 1985), p. 128. Memo to Robert W. Sweet from Jay Kriegel, 5 September 1967, Robert W. Sweet, Correspondence, Law Enforcement, 1965–1969, Crime Commission Folder, Campaign File, Box 110715, Campaign Literature Folder, Office of the Mayor, JVL Papers, NYCMA. *NYT,* 30 December 1968. Jonathan Rieder, *Canarsie: The Jews and Italians of Brooklyn Against Liberalism* (Cambridge, Mass.: Harvard University Press, 1985), p. 128.

15. Commencement Address by Mayor John V. Lindsay, Vassar College, 2 June 1968, Box 78, Folder 675, JVL Papers, Yale. "Speech to the Urban Coalition Eastern Regional Conference," 12 January 1968, Series VII, Box 136, Folder 124, JVL Papers, Yale.

16. John V. Lindsay, *The City* (New York: W. W. Norton, 1969), p. 168.

17. John V. Lindsay, "Law and Order," *Life,* 27 September 1968.

18. *NYT,* 3 June 1969. Michael Tomasky, "The Left and Crime," *Dissent,* Fall 1997.

19. Wilson, *Thinking About Crime,* p. 4. Andrew Hacker, *The New Yorkers: A Profile of an American Metropolis* (New York: Twentieth Century Fund, 1975), pp. 2, 107, 116. James Q. Wilson, "A Reader's Guide to the Crime Commission Reports," *The Public Interest,* Fall 1967. *NYT,* 4 February 1968.

20. William J. Bratton and William Andrews, "What We've Learned About Policing," *City Journal,* Spring 1999. James Lardner, *Crusader: The Hell-Raising Career of Detective David Durk* (New York: Random House, 1996), pp. 336–338.

21. William Bratton with Peter Knobler, *Turnaround: How America's Top Cop Reversed the Crime Epidemic* (New York: Random House, 1998).

22. *AN,* 30 November 1968.

23. "Cost of Graffiti to the City of New York," 21 March 1973, Bureau of the Budget, Box 46, Folder 825, Office of the Mayor, JVL Papers, Subject Files (1966–1973), NYCMA.

24. *NYT,* 21 July 1971. Caryl S. Stern and Robert W. Stock, "Graffiti: The Plague Years," *NYTM,* 19 October 1980.

25. Interview of Steven Isenberg by author, 16 October 1999. *New York Sunday News*, 6 May 1973. Craig Castleman, *Getting Up: Subway Graffiti in New York* (Cambridge, Mass.: MIT Press, 1982), pp. 135–147.

26. August Heckscher, *Alive in the City: Memoir of an Ex-Commissioner* (New York: Charles Scribner's Sons, 1974), pp. 231–232.

27. Mitzi Cunliffe, "The Writing on the Wall," *NYT*, 29 July 1973. Richard Goldstein, "This Thing Has Gotten Completely Out of Hand," *NY*, 26 March 1973. Hacker, *The New Yorkers*, p. 144. Joshua B. Freeman, *Working-Class New York: Life and Labor Since World War II* (New York: New Press, 2000), p. 283.

28. Norman Mailer and Mervyn Kurlansky, *The Faith of Graffiti* (New York: Praeger, 1974).

29. Nathan Glazer, "On Subway Graffiti in New York," *The Public Interest*, Winter 1979. *NYP*, 8 September 1973.

30. *NYT*, 11 July 1971. Ada Louise Huxtable, "Reinventing Times Square: 1990," in William R. Taylor, ed., *Inventing Times Square: Commerce and Culture at the Crossroads of the World* (New York: Russell Sage Foundation, 1991), p. 361. See also Laurence Senelick, "Private Parts in Public Places," in Alexander J. Reichl, ed., *Reconstructing Times Square: Politics and Culture in Urban Development* (Lawrence, KS: University of Kansas Press, 1999), pp. 340–342.

31. Isenberg interview.

32. Freeman, *Working-Class New York*, p. 274.

33. James Q. Wilson and George Kelling, "Broken Windows," *The Atlantic Monthly*, March 1982. Wesley G. Skogan, *Disorder and Decline: Crime and the Spiral of Decay in American Neighborhoods* (New York: Free Press, 1990). See also George L. Kelling and Catherine M. Coles, *Fixing Broken Windows: Restoring Order and Reducing Crime in our Communities* (New York: Touchstone, 1996).

34. Temporary State Commission to Make a Study of the Governmental Operation of the City of New York (Scott Commission), "Social Services in New York City," 1973. Blanche Bernstein, "Welfare in New York City," *City Almanac*, February 1970. Fred Siegel, *The Future Once Happened Here: New York, D.C., and L.A. and the Fate of America's Big Cities* (New York: Free Press, 1997), p. 49.

35. Charles Morris, *The Cost of Good Intentions: New York City and the Liberal Experiment, 1960–1975* (New York: W. W. Norton, 1980), pp. 71, 185.

36. Memo from John V. Lindsay to Richard M. Nixon, 7 May 1969, 5/1/69 to 7/31/69 Folder, White House Central Files, EX WE Files, Box 1, Nixon Presidential Materials. Pete Hamill, "Lindsay's Rome," *NY*, 19 June 1972. Bernstein, "Welfare in New York City."

37. Richard A. Cloward and Frances Fox Piven, "A Strategy to End Poverty," *The Nation*, 2 May 1966. Siegel, *The Future Once Happened Here*, pp. 52–54.

38. Larry R. Jackson and William A. Johnson, *Protest by the Poor: The Welfare Rights Movement in New York City* (Lexington, Mass.: Lexington Books, 1974), pp. xxiv-xxv, 13, 122. Siegel, *The Future Once Happened Here*.

39. Jackson and Johnson, *Protest by the Poor*, p. xxv. Memo from Daniel P. Moynihan to President Richard M. Nixon, 31 January 1969, Beginning–3/12/69 Folder,

White House Central Files, EX WE, Box 1, Nixon Presidential Materials. Arricale quoted in Sleeper, *The Closest of Strangers*, p. 94. Morris, *The Cost of Good Intentions*, p. 71.

40. Morris, *The Cost of Good Intentions*, pp. 70–71. Interview of Mitchell Sviridoff by author, 22 October 1997.

41. David M. Gordon, "Income and Welfare in New York City," *The Public Interest*, Summer 1969. Nathan Glazer, "Beyond Income Maintenance—A Note on Welfare in New York City," *The Public Interest*, Summer 1969. "Welfare in New York City." Jackson and Johnson, *Protest by the Poor*, p. xxv. See also Blanche Bernstein, *The Politics of Welfare: The New York City Experience* (Cambridge, Mass.: Abt Books, 1982).

42. *NYT*, 14 September 1968. Ibid., 5 October 1968. Letter from Josephine Nieves to Mitchell Ginsberg, 31 May 1968, WE 9, Box 32, White House Central Files, LBJ Library.

43. Memo from Richard M. Nixon to John Mitchell, Bob Finch, Bryce Harlow, Pat Moynihan, and Bob Haldeman, 15 January 1969, Memoranda, Jan. 1969 Folder, White House Special Files, Papers of H. R. Haldeman, Box 49, Nixon Presidential Materials.

44. *NYT*, 12–17 January 1969. Morris, *The Cost of Good Intentions*, pp. 117–118. Council of the City of New York, "Final Report of the In-Depth Study of the Human Resources Administration of the City of New York," 24 July 1969, p. 5, NYCMA.

45. Siegel, *The Future Once Happened Here*, p. 57. Lindsay, *The City*, pp. 143–163.

46. Morris, *The Cost of Good Intentions*, p. 71. Memo from Edward Hamilton to John V. Lindsay, 16 March 1971, Group 592, Series XIII, Box 239, Folder 2, JVL Papers, Yale. Memo from John V. Lindsay to Richard Aurelio, 22 March 1971, Group 592, Series XIII, Box 239, Folder 2, JVL Papers, Yale.

47. Morris, *The Cost of Good Intentions*, pp. 188–189.

48. Bernstein, *Politics of Welfare*, p. 25. State Study Commission for New York City, "Social Services in New York City," 1973.

49. Memo from Daniel Patrick Moynihan to President Richard M. Nixon, 31 January 1969, Beginning–3/12/69 Folder, White House Central Files, EX WE, Box 1, Nixon Presidential Materials. "Welfare in New York City."

50. *NYT*, 4 and 11 June 1971.

51. Letter from Edward Hamilton to Stuart Scott, 3 October 1972, Group 592, Series XIII, Box 240, Folder 9, JVL Papers, Yale.

52. Interview of Stephen Berger by author, 22 September 1999. Morris, *The Cost of Good Intentions*, p. 150.

53. Scott Commission, "Final Report of the Temporary State Commission to Make a Study of the Governmental Operation of the City of New York," April 1973. Ibid., "A Super Agency Evaluated: New York City's Housing and Development Administration," 1973. For a history of the Health and Hospitals Corporation, see Sandra Opdycke, *No One Was Turned Away: The Role of Public Hospitals in New York City Since 1900* (New York: Oxford University Press, 1999), pp. 147–158.

54. Berger interview.

55. David Grossman, "The Lindsay Legacy: A Partisan Appraisal," *City Almanac,* October 1973. Morris, *The Cost of Good Intentions,* p. 214. Scott Commission, "Final Report," p. 10.

56. Dick Netzer, "The Budget: Trends and Prospects," in Lyle C. Fitch and Annmarie Hauck Walsh, eds., *Agenda for a City: Issues Confronting New York* (Beverly Hills, Calif.: Sage Publications, 1970), p. 652. Scott Commission, "Final Report," p. 16. Bernard R. Gifford, "New York City and Cosmopolitan Liberalism," *Political Science Quarterly,* Winter 1978, p. 582.

57. Martin Shefter, *Political Crisis/Fiscal Crisis: The Collapse and Revival of New York City* (New York: Basic Books, 1987), p. 106. *NYT,* 1 June 1969. Ibid., 2 February 1968. *U.S. News and World Report,* 12 February 1968.

58. Freeman, *Working-Class New York,* pp. 251–252. Gifford, "New York City and Cosmopolitan Liberalism," p. 561. All statistics on employment in New York City come from U.S. Department of Labor, Bureau of Labor Statistics, *Employment, Hours and Earnings, States and Areas, 1939–1982* (Washington, D.C.: Government Printing Office), pp. 578–579, 590–592.

59. Morris, *The Cost of Good Intentions,* pp. 140–141.

60. Freeman, *Working-Class New York,* pp. 165, 201.

61. Hacker, *The New Yorkers,* p. 45. Scott Commission, "Final Report," pp. 6–8.

62. Charles Brecher and Raymond D. Horton, *Power Failure: New York City Politics and Policy since 1960* (New York: Oxford University Press, 1993), p. 20. Shefter, *Political Crisis/Fiscal Crisis,* pp. 114–124.

63. Morris, *The Cost of Good Intentions,* pp. 155–170, 185–194. Bernard Jump, "New York City Pensions," January 1973.

64. Shefter, *Political Crisis/Fiscal Crisis,* p. 106. Morris, *The Cost of Good Intentions,* p. 202.

65. Scott Commission, "Final Report," p. 15.

66. Brecher and Horton, *Power Failure,* p. 191. On the impact of taxes on New York City, see C. Lowell Harriss, "Tax Issues in New York City," *City Almanac,* February 1972.

CHAPTER 16

1. John V. Lindsay, *The Edge* (New York: W. W. Norton, 1976), p. 125.

2. Chris McNickle, *To Be Mayor of New York: Ethnic Politics in the City* (New York: Columbia University Press, 1993), pp. 239–240. Richard Reeves, "The Boss of New York and Other Powerful People," *NY,* 1 January 1973.

3. Steven R. Weisman, "Why Lindsay Failed as Mayor," *Washington Monthly,* April 1972. Nicholas Pileggi, "John Lindsay and 'The New York Times': The End of the Affair," *NY,* 20 March 1972. David Shipler, "The Two John Lindsays," *The New Republic,* 1 May 1971. John Corry, *My Times: Adventures in the News Trade* (New York: G. P. Putnam's Sons, 1993), pp. 112–118.

4. *NYT,* 15 January 1974. Jeff Greenfield, "Reading John Lindsay's Face," *NYTM,* 29 July 1973.

5. *NYP,* 7 March 1973. Greenfield, "Reading John Lindsay's Face." *NYT,* 23 December 1973.

6. *NYP,* 7 March 1973. Interview of Pat Vecchio by author, 13 October 1999.

7. *Newsweek,* 19 March 1973. *DN,* 8 March 1973. *NYT,* 8 March 1973.

8. *NYP,* 8 March 1973. *The Nation,* 26 March 1973.

9. *VV,* 15 March 1973.

10. On Yankee Stadium and the Hunts Point Market, see Jack Newfield and Paul Du Brul, *The Abuse of Power: The Permanent Government and the Fall of New York* (New York: Viking Press, 1977). Davidoff, who progressed from a campaign bodyguard on Lindsay's 1965 campaign to the mayor's top political operative, made President Nixon's so-called "Enemies List." In the memo, Nixon's aide Charles Colson called Davidoff "a first class S.O.B., wheeler dealer, and suspected bagman."

11. *NYP,* 31 December 1973. *New York Sunday News,* 16 December 1973. *NYT,* 2 January 1974. *Newsday,* 9 February 1987.

12. *DN,* 16 December 1973.

13. Interview of Nat Leventhal by author, 19 October 1999. Interview of Steven Isenberg by author, 1 September 1999.

14. Greenfield, "Reading John Lindsay's Face." Interview of Peter Goldmark by author, 13 June 1997.

15. Memo from Steven L. Isenberg to Edward Hamilton, Tom Morgan, and Jay Kriegel, 26 October 1972, in author's possession. *NYT,* 23 December 1973. Patrick V. Murphy and Thomas Plate, *Commissioner: A View from the Top of American Law Enforcement* (New York: Simon & Schuster, 1977), p. 16.

16. Vincent Canby, "New York's Woes Are Good Box Office," *NYT,* 10 November 1974. Robert A. M. Stern, Thomas Mellins, and David Fishman, *New York 1960: Architecture and Urbanism Between the Second World War and the Bicentennial* (New York: Monacelli Press, 1995), pp. 1174–1196.

17. *The New Yorker,* 8 April 1974. *NYT,* 3 May 1975. Ibid., 22 April 1977. By the late 1970s, according to Lindsay, *Good Morning America* "turned more to show biz, sex, and violence, and I wasn't interested in that, so we had a parting of the ways."

18. Lindsay, *The Edge. NYT,* 26 January 1976.

19. On the New York City fiscal crisis, see Ken Auletta, *The Streets Were Paved with Gold* (New York: Random House, 1975); Roger E. Alcaly and David Mermelstein, eds., *The Fiscal Crisis of American Cities: Essays on the Political Economy of Urban America with Special Reference to New York* (New York: Vintage Books, 1976); Martin Shefter, *Political Crisis/Fiscal Crisis: The Collapse and Revival of New York City* (New York: Basic Books, 1987); Fred Ferretti, *The Year the Big Apple Went Bust* (New York: G. P. Putnam's Sons, 1976); William K. Tabb, *The Long Default* (New York: Monthly Review Press, 1982); Charles R. Morris, *The Cost of Good Intentions: New York City and the Liberal Experiment, 1960–1975* (New York: W. W. Norton,

1980), pp. 215–240; James Ring Adams, "Why New York Went Broke," *Commentary*, May 1976.

20. Edward I. Koch with Daniel Paisner, *Citizen Koch: An Autobiography* (New York: St. Martin's Press, 1992), p. 97. Harry Stein, "An Exile in His Own City," *NYTM*, 8 January 1978.

21. Ibid. Joe Klein, "Lindsay's Comeback: The Ghost Walks," *NY*, 30 June 1980. Norman Redlich, "In Defense of Lindsay," *NYT*, 15 February 1978.

22. Stein, "An Exile in his Own City." John Corry, "The All-Star Race," *NYTM*, 22 June 1980. *NYT*, 27 August 1980.

23. Isenberg interview.

24. Klein, "Lindsay's Comeback." Corry, "The All-Star Race." Interview of Amalia Betanzos by author, 27 May 1997.

25. *NYT*, 29 August 1983. Leventhal interview.

26. John V. Lindsay, *Bipartisan Hopes in an Age of Polarization*, Herbert H. Lehman Memorial Lecture, Lehman College, City University of New York, 28 March 1985, Lehman College Publications, No. 18 (monograph). Lisa Anderson, "The Lindsay Era," *Chicago Tribune*, 9 September 1990.

27. *NYT*, 5 March 1995.

28. *NYT*, 9 November 1987. Geoffrey Stokes, "Before the Fall: The Politics of Hope, Revisited," *VV*, 24 November 1987. *Newsday*, 6 November 1987.

29. Nora Sayre, *Sixties Going On Seventies* (London: Constable, 1974), p. 209. Barry Gottehrer, *The Mayor's Man* (Garden City, N.Y.: Doubleday, 1975), pp. 309–311.

30. Nicholas Pileggi, "Inside Lindsay's Head," *NY*, 4 January 1971.

31. Letter from Robert Laird to Robert Sweet, 6 May 1997, in author's possession. *NYT*, 25 November 1973.

32. Robert W. Laird, "Lindsay's Record as Mayor Is Still a Very Hot Topic," *DN*, 24 May 2000.

33. *DN*, 21 December 2000. Isenberg interview. Interview of Stephen Berger by author, 22 September 1999.

34. Edward N. Costikyan, "Why Dave's in Trouble," *NYP*, 12 October 1993. Bob Price, "Republicans for Dinkins," *NYP*, 19 October 1993. The former Lindsay aide Sid Davidoff became a close friend and tennis partner of Dinkins's and a top city lobbyist during the Dinkins years.

35. Michael Harrington, "When Ed Koch Was Still a Liberal," *Dissent*, Fall 1987. Recounting how he learned to listen to the white ethnic sensibility, Moynihan told a story of being in Syracuse in 1959 when William Buckley came to speak. When Buckley's microphone died, a fireman from a heavily Irish neighborhood fixed it, saying "This is Tipperary Hill and we want to hear you, Bill." Moynihan said that it had occurred to him "that if a fireman from Tipperary Hill wanted to hear Bill Buckley, Maybe a Democrat like me ought to find out what he [Buckley] was like" (Douglas Kiker, "Red Neck New York: Is this Wallace Country?" *NY*, 7 October 1968).

EPILOGUE

1. Rachel Zimmerman, "Looking for Lindsay," *New York Observer*, 30 March 1992.

2. *NYT*, 3 May 1996.

3. Interview of John V. Lindsay by author, 19 November 1997.

4. Lopate quoted in Ric Burns and James Sanders, *New York: An Illustrated History* (New York: Alfred A. Knopf, 1999), p. 547. Rudy Giuliani and his aides studied Lindsay's successful 1965 campaign to learn how a Republican could become mayor of New York running as a "fusion" candidate. See Wayne Barrett, *Rudy! An Investigative Biography of Rudolph Giuliani* (New York: Basic Books, 2000), p. 441.

5. On the reform mayors of the 1990s, see Peter Beinart, "The Pride of the Cities," *The New Republic*, 30 June 1997; Fred Siegel, *The Future Once Happened Here: New York, D.C., and L.A., and the Fate of America's Big Cities* (New York: Free Press, 1997); Stephen Goldsmith, *The Twenty-first Century City: Resurrecting Urban America* (Washington, D.C.: Regnery, 1997); William D. Eggers, ed., *Revitalizing Our Cities: Perspectives from America's New Breed of Mayors* (Los Angeles: Reason Foundation, 1995); and John O. Norquist, *The Wealth of Cities: Revitalizing the Centers of American Life* (Reading, Mass.: Addison-Wesley, 1998).

6. Murray Kempton, "Lindsay: A Splendid Flop," *Newsday*, 24 April 1991.

INDEX

About the Author

Vincent J. Cannato received his Ph.D. in American History from Columbia University. An expert in New York City history, Cannato spent several years giving walking tours of the city. He has contributed to *The Wall Street Journal*, *The New Republic*, the *Weekly Standard*, and *The Washington Post*. He is an adjunct fellow at the Hudson Institute in Washington, D.C.